# CHRIST

The Experience of Jesus as Lord

# CHRIST

The Experience of Jesus as Lord

*Edward Schillebeeckx*

Translated by John Bowden

A Crossroad Book
THE SEABURY PRESS · NEW YORK

1980
The Seabury Press
815 Second Avenue
New York, N.Y. 10017

The original Dutch version of this book was published
under the title *Gerechtigheid en liefde: Genade en
bevrijding* by Uitgeverij H. Nelissen B.V., Bloemendaal,
Holland, in 1977

Printed in the United States of America

Library of Congress Cataloging in Publication Data

Schillebeeckx, Edward Cornelis Florentius Alfons,
    1914-
    Christ, the experience of Jesus as Lord

    Translation of Gerechtigheid en liefde.
    Continues the author's Jesus.
    "A Crossroad book."
    Includes bibliographical references and index.
    1. Jesus Christ—Person and offices. 2. Bible.
N.T.—Theology. 3. Grace (Theology)—Biblical
teaching. 4. Salvation—Biblical teaching. 5. Ex-
perience (Religion) I. Title.
BT202.S33313   1980        234        80-50120
ISBN 0-8164-0136-5

For Father

Hold fast to love and justice,
and wait continually for your God (*Hosea 12.6*)

This English version is dedicated by the publishers – and the translator – to Jean Cunningham, editorial assistant *par excellence*. Those theologians whose books go through her hands are the most fortunate in the world.

# Contents

# Prologue

Exposed as a foundling and brought up under Egyptian protection, cared for by Pharaoh's daughter, far away from where his people, the Hebrews, were living, 'one day Moses went out to his brothers' (Ex. 2.11a) and 'looked upon their forced labour' (Ex. 2.11b). At this first conscious meeting with his people, 'he saw an Egyptian beating a Hebrew, one of his brothers' (2.11c). Moses became angry, intervened and killed the Egyptian.

The next day, at a second meeting with his people, Moses saw 'two Hebrews struggling together' (Ex. 2.13). A passionate champion of justice, he wanted to mediate between the two men and settle the dispute. But his people, the Hebrews, rejected him (Ex. 2.14): 'Moses supposed that his brethren understood that God was giving them deliverance by his hand, but they did not understand' (Stephen's speech, Acts 7.25–28).

A little later, resting by a spring, Moses saw how some maidens, bringing their cattle to drink, were brutally driven away by shepherds who wanted their flocks to drink first. Once again Moses sprang up in holy indignation against these violent men (Ex. 2.15c–17).

These are three stories about Moses before he was called by God. A young man, who took the side of those who were at a disadvantage – without much thought, straight from the heart. And at the same time he was the leader who was not accepted by his brethren.

After these events had been forgotten, 'the people of Israel groaned under their bondage, and cried out for help, and their cry under bondage came up to God. And God heard their groaning, and God remembered his covenant with Abraham, with Isaac, and with Jacob. And God looked down graciously on the Israelites and had pity on them' (Ex. 2.23–25).

Then God called the man who had shown such solidarity with his people: Moses – of whom it was later written that he spoke with God as with a friend, 'as a man speaks with another whom he loves' (Ex. 33.11), 'face to face' (Ex. 33.11), 'mouth to mouth' (Num. 12.6–8). 'Yahweh said: "I have seen the affliction of my people in Egypt, and have heard their cry because of their taskmasters; I know their sufferings, and *I have come down to deliver my people* . . . to bring them out of that land to a good and broad land, a land flowing with milk and honey" ' (Ex. 3.7f.). 'I will send

17

you to Pharaoh that you may bring forth my people, the sons of Israel, out of Egypt' (3.10). Moses will have to tell the people: '*He is* has sent me to you' (Ex. 3.14), which means: 'I am concerned with you' (Ex. 3.16). God's name is: solidarity with the people.

Moses, a suffering servant of God, 'who bears the burden of the people' (Deut. 1.37; 4.21f.; Ex. 32.30–32), 'a prophet from among you, from your brethren' (Deut. 18.15–18) becomes the liberator of Israel. 'By faith Moses, when he had grown up, refused to be called the son of Pharaoh's daughter, choosing rather to share ill-treatment with the people of God than to enjoy the fleeting pleasure of sin. He considered abuse suffered for the Christ greater wealth than the treasures of Egypt' (Heb. 11.24–26).

'For the law was given through Moses; grace and truth came through Jesus Christ' (John 1.17).

A few righteous men could have saved the city of Sodom (Gen. 18.23–32); indeed, just one righteous man would have been enough to save Jerusalem (Jer. 5.1), and 'many' were saved thanks to the suffering prophet, the suffering, righteous servant of God (Isa. 53).

The New Testament proclaims that the one 'suffering righteous man', the one unique and eschatological 'suffering prophet', Jesus Christ, has saved the whole world. Neither the vision that turns against suffering nor the message – not even the message of Jesus – bring deliverance of themselves. Both message and vision, after all, are rejected. Even suffering does not bring salvation. The one who brings salvation is the suffering witness, the crucified one, the man who makes the supreme sacrifice for righteousness and love and precisely because of that suffers through and for others, for the sake of the God who is concerned for mankind: he brings salvation. Before one who gives up his life, in solidarity with God's own merciful identification with vulnerable, yet at the same time evil and unfathomable men, man finally bends the knee and kneels before him. 'My Lord and my God' (John 20.28).

'But there are also many other things which Jesus did; were every one of them to be written, I suppose that the world itself could not contain the books that would be written' (John 21.25). These words express the boldness with which the New Testament set about relating to the contemporary world not only the testimony to the life of Jesus Christ of Nazareth but the Tanach – the Law, the Prophets and the Writings (see p. 907 below). The account of the life of Christians in the world in which they live is a fifth gospel; it also belongs at the heart of christology.

Edward Schillebeeckx

# Introduction

Jesus, the story of a new life-style

1. It began with an encounter. Some people – Aramaic- and perhaps also Greek-speaking Jews – came into contact with Jesus of Nazareth and stayed with him. This encounter, and what took place in the life of Jesus and in connection with his death, gave their personal lives new meaning and new significance. They felt that they had been born again, that they had been understood, and this new identity found expression in a similar solidarity towards others, their fellow-men. This change in the course of their lives was the result of their encounter with Jesus, for without him they would have remained what they had been (see I Cor. 15.17). It had not come about through any initiative of their own; it had simply happened to them.

This astonishing and overwhelming encounter with the man Jesus became the starting-point for the New Testament view of salvation. To put it plainly, 'grace' has to be expressed in terms of encounter and experience; it can never be isolated from the specific encounter which brought about liberation. Furthermore, this means that any further reflection on the meaning of grace and salvation must always go back to the original 'source experiences' without which any theology of grace soon turns into mythology and ontology (in the pejorative sense).

So the story of a new quality of life, a new life-style, began with an encounter. However, interpretation begins long before the point when people ask about the significance of what they have experienced. Interpretative identification is an intrinsic element of the experiences itself; to begin with, perhaps, it is still implicit, and only later is it brought to the level of reflection. The renewal of life which Jesus had evoked from his disciples and the process which he had started off led the disciples to reflect on their experience. They began to analyse it, to consider its various aspects and give it a place in their consciousness, which was full of many other things and ideas. Familiar things became familiar in a new way, now that the followers of Jesus had a completely new focal point. On the basis of their common experience they arrived at what we might call a Christian theory of grace, the beginnings of what in Christian

19

tradition is called a 'theology of grace': soteriology, a thematic account
of the meaning of Christian redemption and Christian salvation.

These experiences were also set down in writing. Every single New
Testament writing, every gospel and every epistle, is concerned with the
salvation experienced in and through Jesus. The experiences of grace
expressed in them to the praise of God indicate one and the same fundamental event, but each writing expresses it in a different way. This
compels us to ask: what are really the formative, constitutive or constructive elements in these New Testament understandings of grace? This
question is concerned with their content as articulated in its logical
context and above all as a meaningful invitation to men in search of
happiness and fulfilment, for the world and for themselves.

However, the synoptic gospels and the Pauline and Johannine writings
(to mention the three main strands in the New Testament) arise out of
an earlier history in which grace had already been experienced and
analysed: this history extends from the Old Testament through the period
between the Testaments to the time of the early church. In the spiritual
climate in which the New Testament Christians lived and the New
Testament was written, disappointments had changed the old Jewish
dream of a just kingdom on earth under the rule of an Israelite theocracy
into the idea of a world which was both temporally and spatially on two
levels. There was the old age and the heavenly new age to come: this
new age would either descend to earth or would be the time when at least
part of the earth, the world of the righteous, would 'arise'. In both
instances, any renewal of life was seen in terms of a super-terrestrial,
heavenly mode of being. However, the concern here was less with a
'hereafter' than with a mysterious sharing and involvement of the earthly
in super-terrestrial, heavenly spheres – though we should not suppose
that these people of late antiquity were naive: it is not as though they
had no awareness of a difference between what they meant by all this
and the thinking-in-models with which they attempted to articulate the
reality to which they were referring. It is, however, the case that for them
'model' and 'reality' formed a closer unity than they do for us. Be this as
it may, here are the presuppositions which were shared in one way or
another by the Christians whose voices we hear in the New Testament.

At the same time, from the beginning the New Testament concept of
grace was directed along certain lines by the Jewish tradition, in which
disaster was experienced as a consequence of disobedience towards God's
commandments. Because of their disobedience, men were entangled in
sin and guilt. Salvation was then quite naturally experienced as the
reconciliation of the sinner with God, the possibility of access to the
kingdom of God. This is indeed a fundamental notion, though to our
present sensibilities it seems to put everything that can be included in

the experience of disaster on a somewhat narrow basis. For if man has a right to speak anywhere, it is surely at the point of defining what he himself experiences as disaster and lack of freedom (though he may well have blind spots here). Thus the experience of disaster already formulated in the Jewish tradition can develop into a new, Christian analysis, the experience of salvation in Jesus (and it is with this analysis that we are concerned in the New Testament).

Hearing and experiencing that Jesus Christ opened up a new way of salvation immediately confronted the disciples of the time with a danger, that of simply filling out the social and religious view of the world which they already had with the name 'Jesus'. For if disaster is sin, and salvation therefore reconciliation and the forgiveness of sins, then it is Jesus who by his death on the cross has expiated the guilt of sin. In that case he is the one who brings us into the kingdom of God by taking us out of death into the spiritual realm of light, God's own world. If that is the case, the chief danger, that Jesus becomes merely a symbolic point of reference for what is experienced from other sources as salvation and disaster, is very great indeed. However, we can see how the New Testament is constantly on its guard against this obvious view. Such a view does, however, keep rearing its head among the Christian communities. So while the writers of the New Testament use religious conceptions from this spiritual milieu, they distinguish them clearly from their experience of Christ.

Furthermore, philosophical and anthropological presuppositions also play a role in the New Testament history of experiences of grace with Christ. They derive from the culture of the first century which was becoming increasingly amorphous and syncretistic, not because of a lack of ideas but because of a superfluity of them. This was especially the case during the last decades of the century. In cultural terms, Palestine was not Syria, and Syria in turn was different from Asia, the Roman province of Asia Minor, which was itself culturally different from Greece and Egypt. Egypt, with its cultural record housed in the two great libraries at Alexandria, attained heights far beyond those reached by the Palestinian community at Qumran and its collection. Jewish, oriental, Hellenistic and gradually even Christian traditions began to fuse. This complex situation acted as a cultural melting-pot from which at a later stage, in the second century, a distinct religious philosophy was to emerge, based on a completely new synthesis: gnosis or gnosticism. A particularly significant influence on the New Testament was exerted by the attitude to life current in late antiquity, which, for example in its fear of demons, expressed a special dissatisfaction over this world and its society. That is evident above all when Christianity rejects this particular feeling of the time.

Anyone who is aware of all this will immediately understand why we cannot relate the New Testament theology of grace and salvation directly to our times. We begin to realize that a purely *theological* analysis of the New Testament concept of grace has a chance of providing inspiration and a sense of direction for Christians only if this theological analysis is coupled with an analysis of historical circumstances, both then and now.

Furthermore, history shows us that over the course of church history a radicalism or monism of grace has continually provoked a counter-movement. Paul gave rise to the Letter of James and above all the Pseudo-Clementines; Augustine to Pelagius, Bañez to Molina, Jansenism to the 'Jesuit doctrine of grace', Martin Luther to Thomas Münzer, the trad-itional doctrine of redemption to the modern theology of liberation. Almost every theology of grace at the same time provokes a related criticism. True, the criticism has been suppressed time and again, but it keeps recurring in a different form; at a later stage it is often rehabilitated and taken up into a new synthesis. This historical swing of the pendulum demonstrates how there is something in man (above all in the truly religious man) which struggles against excessive praise of God *at man's expense*. From this we see that a theology of grace which does not include this element immediately comes up against a profoundly human protest and loses any chance of success.

On the other hand, no meaningful Christian theology of grace can ignore the absolute initiative of God without at the same time infringing the potentialities of our human existence. Any man who does not have an egotistic attitude to life, who is aware that he constantly lives by virtue of the favour and goodwill of others, experiences in a variety of ways that there is such a thing as 'grace'. Man achieves his identity precisely in being confirmed by others (within structures and within a society which make this possible). And in this solidarity many people will sometimes be able to experience a deeper mystery of universal mercy – and as a result perhaps be able to call upon 'God' in prayer.

In this book I want to analyse the New Testament experience of grace and salvation from God in Jesus Christ as an orientation for what we might call a first attempt at a modern Christian soteriology.

2. The perspective of this book is different from that of its predecessor, *Jesus. An Experiment in Christology,* of which it is a continuation. At this point I am not concerned, as in the first volume, with those features of the 'historical Jesus' which may have led to the New Testament confession of him. Now I am immediately concerned with the New Testament elaboration of what Christians experienced in their encounter with Jesus the Lord. I might say that the first volume was a 'Jesus book', though it did not neglect the Christ; this second volume is a 'Christ book', though it does not forget Jesus of Nazareth. The consequence of this new

approach is that the method also differs from that of the earlier book. Some critics of that book have made the same mistake over it that they accuse me of making over holy scripture, in that they fail to respect the particular literary genre and type of communication presented by a specific text (in this case my book). They did not read and understand the book 'as it was', but either wanted to give it some position in the *history of ideas* or, in reaction to form criticism and redaction criticism, and their justified plea for structural analytic treatment of the text as a whole failed to see that in its particular literary genre my text was dominated by a single, all-pervasive literary intention (namely to penetrate as adequately as possible into the history of the origin of Christianity). The first book was not concerned with the New Testament *texts* as such. That is, however, the case with this second volume. Here I am no longer dealing with form, redaction and tradition criticism in order to get as close as possible to the 'historical Jesus', but am taking the texts seriously in their unity and as a whole. This means seeing them in their specific *literary* context against the background of the literature of the time, within the specific socio-cultural reality of the milieu above all of those for whom these New Testament texts were directly written, so that they could be read aloud in the liturgy.

We may regret the fact that modern exegesis of the New Testament did not first grasp this literary method of reading and understanding the texts 'as they are', only then to go on to investigate the further perspectives on the results that this approach produced which might be gained through form criticism, redaction criticism and the history of traditions. From the point of view of literary criticism, the dominant trend in modern exegesis began at the wrong end. However, we should not forget that at least the original form critics (and above all Martin Dibelius) tended to analyse texts primarily in a literary-critical way. However, their aim was historical and not primarily literary-critical: they were concerned with the historical Jesus (who was denied by many people at that time); this is true even today, though the questions are now put differently. As long as the Christian movement is seen not as the religion of a book or as a movement which was brought into being by inspiring literature, but as a movement deriving from a living person with a place in history, this historical approach also remains valid and fundamental for religion. Here the tradition of the church's account of Jesus is the presupposition for the discussion of the history of Jesus.

However, if we regard the New Testament as literature which needs to be read and understood – and this is primarily the case for interpreters and believers – then (as I already said in the first volume, pp. 90f.) form criticism and redaction criticism will not give as much of an insight into what *the text* means to say (the acceptance of a particular tradition and the omission of another is itself 'redaction', so that from a literary-critical point of view, everything in a text is 'redaction'). In that case we will not be able to *begin* by splitting the text into redaction and tradition or into a number of independent units. It has to be taken as a whole. But if Christianity does not live only from sacral literature – though this cannot be left out of Christianity and as such even represents a fragment of grace – and if, moreover, New Testament texts, in addition to a whole variety of other linguistic functions, also have a referential function by pointing to the historical event in, with and about Jesus of Nazareth, then we will not make any progress by excluding critical questions, and referring to the special logic of the 'religious language game' on the basis of the fact that these texts are *religious* texts. There is no way of denying the autonomy of this language game with its own criteria and its own logic. On the contrary, from a theological point of view it is extremely important, and if we recognize it for what it is we will avoid many theological pseudo-problems. However, such a recognition does not mean that no communication is possible between the different language games (e.g. the historical and the religious) and that one and the same man would have to live simultaneously in two completely disparate language games. In that case these would function like cages in which the same men were held prisoner, in the last resort in a state of schizophrenia: believers here and historians there.

Still, I am clear (more so than in the first volume) that even if our concern is historical – and this can be pursued only by means of particular texts – we must first use the method of literary criticism and only then use other methods to get through to the historical 'sub-stratum'. If that happens, I believe that we shall arrive at a more varied and even richer historical picture of Jesus than we discover when (as at present) we follow the reverse sequence. Furthermore, this points to what I have called the never finished study of the Jesus event. The use of particular methods also occurs as an event in a history.

However, quite apart from the question of the proper assessment of my intention in my first book about Jesus, in this second volume I am no longer concerned with the historical phenomenon of Jesus in our history, nor with the reactions to this event before the writing of the New Testament: all this is presupposed on the basis of my first book (even if it has not been 'solved' once and for all). Here we are directly concerned with the question how *New Testament Christianity* experienced and analysed salvation in and through Jesus, and with the question of the historical circumstances (then and now) through which this New Testament witness forms a normative orientation for our experience and interpretation of salvation in Jesus. That is a different set of problems and a different literary genre from those of the first book. An author who writes about

Jesus is not judged directly by already existing 'christological' criteria, but by his approach and perspective. A contemporary christology which is faithful to Jesus and the gospels, which comes to influence our questing awareness and in so doing communicates salvation, can only be built up by stages. Perhaps it will be possible to make a beginning on what is called 'christology' *after* this second volume. I would be inclined to call even this second volume a prolegomenon: not out of a certain critical scepticism (though also in fear of over-hasty totalizations), but because I am convinced by the Christian eschatological vision that any christology which is relevant to life is only possible in the form of a *pro-legomenon:* a word before the last word, a search for the right 'legomenon' or word. For in our history I know redemption only in fragments which are experienced personally and collectively; in which, however, Jesus remains the critical and productive promise of an undefinable definitive future salvation. Nowhere do I see signs of an 'objectively completed' redemption. Yet I believe that our action in helping people, healing them and bringing them political liberation, fragmentary though it may seem, has definitive value in and of itself, even when it fails. It is precisely to this that the living God will grant an even greater future. 'He gives a new face to darkness and light, to all that we do.'

Even in his Christian view of grace and redemption, the Christian will have to remain aware of his human condition. To that I want to devote this second volume, and thus at the same time fulfil a promise made in the first.

*Part One*

---

# The Authority of New Experiences and the Authority of the New Testament

At present it is clear that many believers and quite evidently a number of students of theology are reluctant to engage in theological activity which has its starting-point in scripture and tradition (a method which, moreover, presupposes the knowledge of various dead languages: Hebrew, Greek and Latin, not to mention others, if it is to produce fruitful results). They are of the opinion that a modern, living theology must begin from men's present-day experiences. They want to begin 'at the other end'.

I think that this problem, put in such a way, is a false dilemma (see below). However, this question brings up the even older suspicions of many theologians about 'experiences'. They do not seem to be aware that with such an attitude they remove the basis for any 'divine revelation'. In my view this gulf between *faith* and *experience* is one of the fundamental reasons for the present-day crisis among Christians who are faithful to the church.

Precisely so that we can gain some insight into the meaning of 'a theology of grace', redemption and salvation, I would like to present an analysis of the special authority which lies in 'experiences' and an analysis of the authority of holy scripture which is apparently opposed to it.

In this analysis I shall not be immediately concerned with experience in the more superficial sense of 'It says nothing to me', 'It means something to me', even if 'experience', the phenomenon to be analysed, does have something to do with this. Nor am I so concerned with experience in the sense of a particular state, disposition and feeling, or of qualities of experience, although these emotional aspects are essential, above all in religious experiences. In the analysis the main emphasis will be on the particular cognitive, critical and productive force of human experiences. Under this aspect, above all, revelation has everything to do with 'experience'.

29

Chapter 1

# The authority of new experiences

'Back to the rough ground' (L. Wittgenstein)

*Literature*: The concept of 'experience':[1] T. Adorno, *Negative Dialektics*, ET London 1973; id., 'Thesen über Tradition', in *Ohne Leitbild*, Frankfurt 1967, 29–41; Ian G. Barbour, *Myths, Models and Paradigms*, New York and London 1974; id., *Issues in Science and Religion*, Englewood Cliffs and London 1966; H. D. Bastian, *Verfremdung und Verkündigung*, Munich 1967; H. Berger, *Erfahrung und Gesellschaftsform*, Stuttgart 1972; P. Berger and T. Luckmann, *The Social Structure of Reality*, New York and London 1967; H. Blumenberg, *Legitimität der Neuzeit*, Frankfurt 1966; P. Engelhardt, 'Die Frage nach Gott', in *Neues Glaubensbuch*, ed. J. Feiner and L. Vischer, Freiburg im Breisgau [13]1975, 21–64, 72–100; H.-G. Gadamer, *Truth and Method*, ET London 1975, 310–25; L. B. Gilkey, *Naming the Whirlwind: The Renewal of God-Language*, Indianapolis and New York 1969; A. Hahn, *Religion und der Verlust der Sinngebung*, Frankfurt 1974; E. Heintel, *Einführung in die Sprachphilosophie*, Darmstadt 1972; A. Heuss, *Verlust der Geschichte*, Göttingen 1959; H. Holzhey, *Kants Erfahrungsbegriff*, Basel/Stuttgart 1970; M. Kaiser, *Identität und Sozialität*, Munich/Mainz 1971; F. Kambartel, *Erfahrung und Struktur. Bausteine zu einer Kritik des Empirismus und Formalismus*, Frankfurt 1968; W. Kasper, *Glaube und Geschichte*, Mainz 1970, 120–43 (in *GuL* 42, 1969, 329–49); A. Kessler, A. Schöff, C. Wild, 'Erfahrung', in *Handbuch philosophischer Grundbegriffe* 2, Munich 1973, 373–86; B. Liebrucks, 'Über das Wesen der Sprache', in *Erkenntnis und Dialektik*, The Hague 1972, 1–20; J.-B. Metz, 'Joy and Grief, Cheerfulness, Melancholy and Humour or "the Difficulty of Saying Yes" ', Editorial to *Concilium*, Vol. 5 no. 10 (ET of Vol. 10 no. 5), May 1974, 7–12; D. Mieth, 'Narrative Ethik', *FrZPhTh* 22, 1975, 297–326; id, *Dichtung, Glaube und Moral*, Mainz 1976; M. Müller, *Erfahrung und Geschichte*, Munich 1970; W. Pannenberg, 'Christianity as the Legitimacy of the Modern Age', in *Basic Questions in Theology* 3, London 1973 (US title *The Idea of God and Human Freedom*, Philadelphia 1973), 178–91; J. Pieper, *Überlieferung*, Munich 1970; M. Polanyi, *The Great Transformation*, New York 1974; H. H. Price, *Thinking and Experience*, London 1953; L. Richter, 'Erfahrung', in *RGG*[3], Tübingen 1958, 550–2; L. Reinisch (ed.), *Vom Sinn der Tradition*, Munich 1970; P. Ricoeur and E. Jüngel, 'Metaphorische Wahrheit', in *Metapher* (Sonderheft *Evangelische Theologie*), Munich 1974, 22–44, 45–70; H. Rombach,

'Erfahrung', in *Lexikon der Pädagogik*, Vol. 1, Freiburg im Breisgau [2]1970, 375–7; W. Schapp, *In Geschichten verstrickt*, Hamburg 1953; id., *Philosophie der Geschichten*, Leer 1959; R. Schaeffler, *Religion und kritisches Bewusstsein*, Freiburg/Munich 1973; E. Schlink, 'Thesen zur Methodik einer kontextuellen Theologie', *KuD* 20, 1974, 87–90; W. Schneiders, *Die wahre Aufklärung*, Munich 1974; S. Schmidt, *Bedeutung und Begriff*, Brunswick 1969; W. Stegmüller, *Hauptströmungen der Gegenwartsphilosophie*, Stuttgart [3]1965; id, *Probleme und Resultate der Wissenschaftstheorie*, Vol 2, *Theorie und Erfahrung*, Berlin 1970; M. Theunissen, *Gesellschaft und Geschichte*, Berlin 1969; J. Track, 'Erfahrung Gottes. Versuch einer Annäherung', *KuD* 22, 1976, 1–21; id., 'Religiöse Interpretation der Wirklichkeit', *KuD* 20, 1974, 106–36; S. Unseld, *Zur Aktualität Walter Benjamins*, Frankfurt 1972; B. Willms, 'Theorie, Kritik und Dialektik', in *Über T. Adorno*, Frankfurt 1968, 44–89; B. L. Whorf, *Sprache, Denken, Wirklichkeit*, Hamburg 1963; K. A. Wolff, *Versuch zu einer Wissenssoziologie*, Berlin/Neuwied 1963; J. Wössner (ed.), *Religion im Umbruch*, Stuttgart 1972; P. Zulehner, *Säkularisierung von Gesellschaft, Person und Religion*, Vienna 1973; id., *Geschichte, Ereignis und Erzählung*, Poetik und Hermeneutik 5, ed. R. Koselleck and W. Stempel, Munich 1972; *Neue Anthropologie*, ed. H.-G. Gadamer and P. Vogler, four vols, Stuttgart/Munich 1972–73.

## §1   Experience is always interpreted experience

'The distinction between discovery and invention or between fact and theory will, however, immediately prove to be exceedingly artificial.'
T. S. Kuhn, *The Structure of Scientific Revolutions*, Chicago 1962, 52.

The basic meaning of the Dutch word for experience is travelling through the country[2] and thus – through exploration – being taken up into a process of learning. Experience means learning through 'direct' contact with people and things. It is the ability to assimilate perceptions.

It is of the nature of this process of learning by experience that the new experience is always related to the knowledge that we have already gained. This gives rise to a reciprocal effect. The discoveries about reality that we have already made and put into words open up new perspectives: they direct perception in our experience to something particular; they select and demarcate, they guide our attention. In this way they become the framework within which we interpret new experiences, while at the same time this already given framework of interpretation is exposed to criticism and corrected, changed or renewed by new experiences. Experience is gained in a dialectical fashion: through an interplay between perception and thought, thought and perception. The function of experience is not to find room for constantly new material in existing patterns of thought which are taken as unalterable, and which are constantly confirmed as a result – though there are also experiences which bring confirmation. No, the connection between experience and thought is rather that the constantly unforeseen content of new experiences keeps forcing us to think again. On the one hand, thought makes experience possible, while on the other, it is experience that makes new thinking necessary. Our thinking remains empty if it does not constantly refer back to living experience.

Granted, we recognize a difference between the objective and the subjective, but we have grown away from the Cartesian dualism of subjectivity and objectivity. The experience of ourselves and the world cannot be completely analysed in terms of a difference between objective and subjective. Therefore 'to find salvation in Jesus' is not *either* a subjective experience *or* an objective fact. To experience salvation is experience *and* interpretation at the same time. In experiencing we identify what is experienced, and we do this by classifying what we experience in terms of already known models and concepts, patterns or categories. We see whether something fits or not. I see something and say, 'a chair'. Experiencing this thing, I interpret it and identify it in the process of experiencing it. For I do not interpret this thing as a chair; I *see* a chair, though this seeing is intrinsically also an interpretation. The same is true of seeing in faith. Religious faith is human life in the world, but experienced as an encounter and in this respect as a disclosure of God. This latter is not an interpretation in the sense of a theory which is subsequently presented as a retrospect on *recalled* experiences; it is the *particular way* in which religious men in fact *experience* the events of their life. Here the experience influences the interpretation and calls it forth, but at the same time the interpretation influences the experience. Man experiences actively, with his whole being and having, and contributions of object and subject can never be distinguished with complete exactitude. What we experience as objective – what comes to us – is dependent on our concepts and our terms of reference, even independently of our projects and the interests which are served as a result.

Furthermore, the content of every new experience is put into words: a new experience is also a speech event. Speech is an ingredient of experience. However, a whole tradition of experience has already been accumulated in the pre-existing language which we use to describe experience, and this also colours our experiences. For the believer, this also means that the original element of religious experience will be expressed in the structures of the prevailing tradition: experiences are communicated socially. For that very reason, experience is only competent where it takes into account the presuppositions under which it came into being.[3]

Moreover, there is the objectively existing form of society in which we live here and now, for example in the West. This form not only exists outside us but also lives within us. Thus the subject who experiences is in reality also part of existing society and not an 'abstract individual'. To a considerable degree the personal needs, expectations and possibilities of experience of any person are already prescribed by the society in which he or she lives. The world of our concrete experience is also a manipulated world. Therefore new experiences have 'authority' only when all this has been taken into account.

Consequently experience is a richly nuanced totality in which experience, thought and interpretation run together in the same way as past, present and expectations of the future. This throws us up against the question of the objectivity and subjectivity of what we call 'new experiences', and thus raises the question of their authority.

The capacity for answering, in other words the sphere of resonance within us, which makes us capable of taking up and digesting an appeal from outside – or from our innermost depths – influences the magnitude and depth of our experience. Personal involvement in no way prevents our being open to what encounters us objectively. A man with a musical ear will hear more in a symphony than someone with little feeling for music. Does that mean that he is more subjective? Or is it not rather the case that this subjective capacity is the very element that makes him open to hear all that is to be heard in this symphonic reality? In other words, our real experiences are neither purely objective nor purely subjective. On the one hand, they are not purely subjective; for we cannot simply make something out of something at our whim. At least partially, there is something which is 'given', which we cannot completely manipulate or change; in experience we have an offer of reality. On the other hand, it is not purely objective; for the experience is filled out and coloured by the reminiscences and sensibilities, concepts and longings of the person who has the experience. Thus the irreducible elements of our experiences form a totality which already contains interpretation. We experience in the act of interpreting, without being able to draw a neat distinction between the element of experience and the element of interpretation.

However, there are elements of interpretation in our experiences which find their basis and their source directly in the experience itself, as the content of a conscious and thus to some degree transparent experience, and at the same time there are elements of interpretation which are brought to us from elsewhere, at the least from outside this experience. Thus for example an experience of love has interpretative elements in the very act of experiencing, suggested by our own particular prior experience of love. The love experienced is automatically aware of what love is; it even knows more than it can express at the particular moment. This interpretative identification is an intrinsic element in the experience of love. Later, this experience of love will perhaps also be expressed in language taken from *Romeo and Juliet*, the biblical Song of Songs or Paul's hymn to love, or perhaps from phenomenological and philosophical descriptions of what love is. This further analysis is no indifferent or superfluous addition to love. Interpretation and experience exercise a mutual influence on one another; real love lives on the experience of love and on its own progressive interpretative expression of itself, which makes possible the deepening of experience and reveals this to itself from the experience. As we shall see when we analyse the New Testament, this is equally true of what believers call experiences of grace. And these in particular have a very close connection with experiences of love.

This analysis shows that there is no experience without 'theorizing'; without guesses, hypotheses and theories. Specific, private, so-called direct experiences are always communicated by general terms – in prereflective experience as well as in scientific empiricism and philosophical experience. This is also true of everything that we call 'religious experiences'. We experience reality – on all these levels – always through models of reality. Thus our experience of the daily rising of the sun is a direct experience, but it is communicated through a model of reality, just as the 'scientific experience' of Copernicus and Galileo was gained by means of a model. In pre-critical experiences the models are concealed and remain unnoticed. Hence the criticism of '*le monde vécu*' by E. Husserl or '*le langage vécu*' by M. Merleau-Ponty, because even these so-called 'direct experiences' are already full of human constructs.

It emerges from this that man is a constructive, rational being: a *projecting* existence. Nevertheless, reality remains the final criterion: it can destroy all our projects or at least weigh them down or change them. Men live by guesses and hypotheses, projects and constructs, and therefore by trial and error; their projects can constantly be blocked by the resistance or the refractoriness of reality, which will not always fit in with these rational anticipations. These projects are very different and as such are not universally valid. But where reality offers resistance to such outlines and implicitly therefore guides them in an indirect way, we come into contact with a reality which is *independent* of us, which is not thought of, made or projected by men. At this point we have a revelation of that which cannot be manipulated, a 'transcendent' power, something that comes 'from elsewhere', which asserts its validity in the face of our projects and nevertheless makes all human plans, products and considerations possible, by virtue of its critical and negative orientation. It is clear that human thought is not enough for mankind, even if this too becomes evident only through the mediation of his human thought and action. Surprising, unexpected, new ways of perceiving are opened up in and through the resistance presented by reality. In this respect real experience only becomes productive when inherited insights are given critical consideration as a result of the resistance offered by reality, when something new is experienced or when what has already been experienced is suddenly seen in a different context. On our side we have to experiment, make conjectures, and frame hypotheses, i.e. 'reflect', if reality is to reveal itself to us as that which is confirmed, corrected, shattered and constantly given new direction by what we contrive. The permanent resistance of reality to our rational inventions forces us to constantly new and untried models of thought. Truth comes near to us by the alienation and disorientation of what we have already achieved and planned. This shatters the so-called normativeness or the dogmatism of the factual, of what is 'simply given'. The hermeneutical principle for the disclosure of reality is not the self-evident, but the scandal, the stumbling block of the refractoriness of reality.[4] Reality is always a surprising revelation for thought, for which thought can only be a witness. In such experiences of what proves completely refractory to all our inventions we shall finally also discover the basis for what we rightly call revelation.

Were reality simply to confirm or 'verify' our human projects, we would never know exactly whether we were dealing with 'reality'. This confirmation can indeed illuminate something of reality, but we have no guarantees of that; a logical project directed elsewhere can equally well 'correspond' with reality. A project game within a system can be ever so coherent, yet this coherence does not say anything about its truth-value. Many scientists therefore avoid the term truth and speak only of the *validity* of scientific insights. Moreover, with some justification scientific theorists have consequently abandoned the principle of verification as a decisive method (at least as a universal principle); the case for this is all the stronger because it is pure convention which decides at what point the endless process of verification shall be called to a halt. By contrast, the 'negativity' which makes us revise earlier insights as a result of the resistance offered by reality is productive; it has a quite special positive significance as a 'revelation of reality', even though it may be dialectically negative and critical. People learn from failures – where their projects are blocked and they make a new attempt, in sensitive reverence for the resistance and thus for the orientation of reality.

This demonstrates that human experience is *finite*, that man is not lord of reality, for all his plans, though without them experiences would be impossible. Absolute knowledge is not granted to man, yet he refuses to take refuge in scepticism. Reality constantly directs our planning and reflection like a hidden magnet. It is a knowledge which cannot be completely objectivized and articulated. Precisely because of this, the negative experience of contrast is never an end in itself; in that case it would be destructive and unproductive.

By coming up against resistance, our planned search continually follows a new orientation. In offering this resistance 'the truth' stimulates and directs our ever wider searching. Thus it proves that on the one hand man is a theory-forming, rational being, and that on the other hand precisely because of this he stands under the norm of a reality which he has not planned. Men are not blank screens on which reality projects the reflective images. On the contrary, man as it were begins to develop a theory of the world but in so doing finds himself constantly opposed by the special quality, the otherness, of this reality which forces him to ever new attempts and is always ahead of him. Thus the revelation of reality in human designs and experiences never takes place through a direct appeal to 'experience'. The authority of experiences will reveal itself in a *dialectical* appeal to experience. Experience is supported and constrained by a permanent reference to the inexhaustibility of the real. It is not controlling reality, but allowing oneself to be guided by reality in all plans to control it, that opens up a way to human living. We must have something to say ourselves, and then listen to the reactions. This is the way in which men arrange their life – in everyday life, in science, in religion. In view of the negativity or the 'refractoriness' in all this, one might say that the intensity but also the authority of the experience of life culminates in 'suffering', in the suffering of disaster and failure, in the suffering of grief, in the suffering of evil, in the suffering of love. Here are the great elements of the revelation of reality in and through men's *finite experiences*.

## §2    The authority of experiences

> From this time forth I make you hear new things, hidden things which you have not known. They are created now, not long ago; before today you have never heard of them, lest you should say, 'Behold, I knew them' (Isa 48.6b–7).

The preceding analysis conceals two questions:

(*a*) How must our thought be framed to make experience possible? That means experience in which the real presents itself in such a way that it goes beyond our projects and in so doing shows its authority.

(*b*) How must we understand 'experience', which on the one hand breaks through the dogmatism of human thought and on the other hand guards this thought against scepticism and a surrender of the will for truth?[5] This is the question of a way of thinking which does not dogmatically preclude new experiences and yet of a view of human experiences in which these do not block any will to the truth in the form of a meaningless chaotic mass. From this it already emerges that the authority of experiences does not come from the experience itself or from the emotional capacity to experience fascination and thrill (as R. Otto thinks). The quality of experience is not the measure, but what is measured; the authority of (new) experiences is itself defined by the surprising nature of reality, which continually proves different from what we think. The real, with which man has to do in his experience, is a never to be repeated, surprising event.

It can hardly be denied that authoritarian institutions and conformist groups often show as it were innate mistrust of new experiences, of 'experience' *tout simple*. They instinctively feel that in experiences an authority can present itself which is a criticism of the normativeness of the factual and of any authority which would merely assert itself as contingent facticity and thus as power. That they must nevertheless acknowledge the critical and productive force – the authority – of experiences emerges from the fact that they often seek to manipulate new experiences. It is also striking that 'the powers' (in no matter what areas) only refer to experience if this is not critical and productive, but confirms what already exists. Indeed such experiences are instructive, and may not be brushed aside; but here we find only one aspect of the authority of experiences. Above all, experiences which put in question our established thinking and acting open up new perspectives. But precisely out of fear of the reflection or the change which they require, they are often manipulated: their critical force is not allowed, but they are 'integrated', and in this way their sting is taken away.

Only if we take all these circumstances into account can we speak of the authority of experiences as these stand under the presupposition of freedom and are also allowed space within the institution. The question arises whether 'the system', and that means not only the deposit of all experiences which have been had and accumulated at an earlier stage, but often also 'experiences' which have been 'manipulated', and thus ideologically transmitted, can make room for new experiences. Not in the superficial sense of adaptation to what already exists, but as an alteration of what has been acquired, perhaps a total alteration – without destroying the critical force of the recollection of earlier experiences. A new 'divergent' experience is a challenge, it subjects the prevailing models of experience to criticism. Experience is therefore never 'innocent'. For it is communicable. Anyone who has had an experience *ipso facto* becomes himself a *witness*: he has a message. He describes what has happened to him. This narration opens up a new possibility of life for others, it sets something in motion. Thus the authority of experience becomes operative in the telling. The authority of experience has a narrative structure.[6]

We term the totality of an individual's experiences 'life-experience'; this coincides with a conviction about life which is lived out in practice. In the case of a historical collective we then speak of a *tradition*, the particular tradition of experience of a community which makes history, e.g. of Christianity, Buddhism, Islam – Western or African cultures. Experience is retained in reminiscence and language: it becomes a living 'deposit', which is handed on as tradition. Experiences which are handed down – tradition – are at the same time a means of objectifying new experiences and integrating them in what has already been attained. Experience is traditional experience: experience and tradition are therefore not opposite *per se*: they make one another possible. Even new experiences are possible only within the sphere of a tradition. Our thought and experience are subject to historical and social influence. Reflection means thinking with presuppositions. This bond to a particular cultural tradition of experience is on the one hand positive: it makes understanding possible. On the other hand it is negative: it limits our understanding, is selective, and already guides new experiences in a particular direction. In its direction, this understanding is limited by the distinctiveness of one's own tradition.[7] That is why even a very old tradition of experience is always subject to the challenge of new experiences. Of course these do not have authority simply and solely because they are new. For we have no guarantee at all that the history of human experience is only progressive and not at the same time also regressive. Therefore the discerning of spirits, the *discretio spirituum*, is an essential part of what we call the authority of experiences. This capacity for distinction is the result of critically digested perceptions. As I have said, experience is interpretative and interpretation also makes experiencing possible; the authority of experience is therefore an authority *from* experiences and *for* new experiences.

If the authority of experience is an authority gained from a many-sided and yet directed process of experience – which does not, however, mean *anarchic* openness to the future, specifically without critical recollection of past experiences – and at the same time directed openness for new experiences, then the widening possibility of the integration of new experiences, which does not manipulate but reinterprets what has already been attained, is a pointer towards the power of a particular tradition of experience. Humanly speaking, this is a demonstration of plausibility, of its meaningful authenticity and its foundation in truth. In that case the credibility of the given tradition is strengthened, or it gains force. For the virtues of a particular tradition emerge more clearly from the way in which the tradition is able to accord a real place to new and above all 'divergent' experiences – dynamically remaining itself, without eclecticism or false *aggiornamento*. On the other hand, a (religious) tradition which ✗ cannot cope with new experiences and therefore negates them, avoids them or brands them *per se* as 'diabolical modern temptations' forfeits moral authority, even if this refusal is based on age-old and honourable traditions (the presuppositions of which are not, however, explored). Furthermore, in that case there is a danger that this traditional community becomes a 'holy remnant'; it asserts itself by forming ghettoes and aggressively asserting its own group identity. At that point, it is not in fact swearing by the authority of its own tradition of experience but by the letter of what was once the expression of authentic experiences in a particular historical situation. Climaxes then become points of stagnation.

All this is also true on the individual level. Anyone who has come to experience of life or a conviction about life which is lived out in practice will try to digest new experiences within his own experience of life. Sometimes this proves successful; sometimes less so. In the long run, however, one can be compelled by the resistance offered by constantly new experiences to revise some presuppositions of one's own convictions about life. Initially this usually happens by giving way or correcting one's own view of life to some degree. Only when all attempts at integration fail is one confronted with the possibility of a collapse in one's convictions about life, at least if it is a matter of remaining true to oneself. (For it is also possible to assert one's rights more and more stubbornly and aggressively against increasing evidence from experience.) This proves once again the authority of critical experiences (quite apart from the question whether they have been formulated properly or wrongly). We can, however, still ask whether an accumulation of negative experiences will in fact bring the committed believer to change his convictions about life. The Christian and even the Stoic will say: Neither death nor life nor anxiety nor tribulation, *nothing* can separate us . . . Suffering and a number of empirical proofs do not seem to be able to shift the believer from his faith that God loves him. No accumulation of empirical indications to the contrary will cause such faith to totter. This has to do with the force of non-cognitive, emotional elements in man's experiences and conviction of life. The experience of faith is capable of living with doubt. ✗ Within his own varied projects for life everyone can give good reasons for his convictions about life, despite experiences to the contrary: the history of our human experiences is not so clearly negative or positive. Above all, religious and para-religious and even atheistic convictions about life are highly resistant to falsification from negative experiences. But if anyone wants to maintain the relevance of experience for faith, then negative experience cannot be the last word. Moreover, in the last resort the emotional elements must draw their strength from the cognitive element or the evidence of experience in the conviction of faith. If the particular value of the aspect of knowledge or the evidence of experience were irrelevant, there would be no way of distinguishing illusion from reality. If existing convictions about life are not in any way connected with actual experiences, they become empty and irrelevant, even if it seems that someone only gives up the conviction when more meaningful alternatives present themselves.[8]

As will become even clearer as we proceed, to have come this far is to say that <u>experience of something new and surprising will always also be an experience of the familiar, though of a different kind from what we might have imagined</u>. We discover the familiar through alienation or negative experiences and nevertheless see it in a form that surprises us. Discovering something new is also a rediscovery. This does not do away with alienation from oneself, which in fact becomes an essential element in the real knowledge of truth; it brings the new element into view as something that is to a degree familiar and expected, even if this also goes beyond all our expectations. The new is never *radically* the 'wholly other', for the simple reason that in our experiences we ourselves are part of this reality which reveals itself to us. Reality has already revealed itself, albeit in such a way that we only recognize this revelation as something that is already familiar to us as a result of alienations from ourselves.[9]

## §3 Revelation and experience

'I bear witness to experience and appeal to experience . . . I say to one who hears me, "It is your experience. Reflect on it, and dare to acquire as experience what you cannot reflect on". . . . I have no doctrine. I am simply pointing to something. I am showing reality. I am showing something in reality which has not been seen, or has not been seen adequately' (M. Buber, *Werke* I, Munich and Heidelberg 1968, 1114).

Literature (in addition to the literature already cited at the beginning of chapter 1):

1. *The concept of 'revelation'*

T. P. van Baaren, *Voorstellingen van openbaring phaenomenologisch beschouwd*, Utrecht 1951; H. Berkhof, *Christelijk Geloof*, Nijkerk [3]1973, 43–109; H. Bouillard, 'La formation du concept de religion en Occident', in *Human-isme et foi chrétienne*, Paris 1976, 451–62; W. Bulst, *Offenbarung*, Düsseldorf 1960; R. Bultman, 'The Problem of "Natural Theology"', ET in *Faith and Understanding*, London 1969, 313–31; id. 'The Question of Natural Revelation', ET in *Essays Philosophical and Theological*, London and New York 1955, 90–118; K. Goldammer, *Religionen, Religion und christliche Offenbarung*, Stuttgart 1965; F. G. Downing, *Has Christianity a Revelation?*, London 1964; E. Heck, *Der Begriff Religio bei Thomas von Aquin*, Paderborn 1970; F. Konrad, *Das Offenbarungsverständnis in der Evangelischen Theologie*, Munich 1971; H. Kuitert, *The Necessity of Faith; or, Without Faith You're as Good as Dead*, ET Grand Rapids 1976; R. Latourelle, *Théologie de la révélation*, Bruges 1963; W. Luypen, *De erwtensoep is klaar*, Bilthoven 1970; id., *Theologische overwegingen*, Bruges 1971; id., *Theologie is antropologie*, Meppel 1974; id., 'Christelijk geloof. Een confessionele hogeschool?', in *Tussentijds*, Tilburg 1975, 205–35; J. Moltmann, 'The Revelation of God and the Question of Truth', *Hope and Planning* (ET of *Perspektiven der Theologie*), London 1971, 3–30; G. Moran, *Theology of Revelation*, London 1966; G. Scholem, 'Offenbarung und Tradition als religiöse Kategorie im Judentum', in *Über einige Grundbegriffe des Judentums*, Frankfurt 1970; F. Schupp, *Auf dem Weg zu einer kritischen Theologie*, Freiburg 1974; M. Seyboldt et al., *Die Offenbarung. Von der Schrift zum Ausgang der Scholastik* (Handbuch der Dogmengeschichte, Vols I–II), Freiburg im Breisgau 1971 (with a detailed bibliography); G. Schiwy, *Strukturalismus und Christentum*, Freiburg im Breisgau 1969; W. Veldhuis, *Geloof en ervaring*, Bilthoven 1973; H. Waldenfels, *Offenbarung*, Munich 1969.

2. *The language of faith, religious language or the language of revelation*

Ian Barbour, *Myths, Models and Paradigms*, New York and London 1974; P. Barthel, *Interprétation du langage mystique et théologie biblique*, Leiden 1967; L. Bejerholm (and G. Hornig), *Wort und Handlung*, Gütersloh 1966; K. Bendall and F. Ferré, *Exploring the Logic of Faith*, New York 1962; M. Black, *Models and Metaphors*, Ithaca 1972; W. T. Blackstone, *The Problem of Religious Language*, New York 1963; J. Bockenski, *The Logic of Religion*, New York 1965; E. Bonvini, 'Interrogations sur le langage religieux', in *Humanisme et foi chrétienne*, Paris 1976, 157–68; E. Cassirer, *Philosophie der symbolischen Formen*, three vols, Berlin 1923, 1925 and 1929; M. Clavel, *Dieu est Dieu, nom de Dieu*, Paris 1976; Mircea Eliade, *Images and Symbols*, ET London 1961; F. Ferré, *Language, Logic and God*, New York and London 1961; A. Flew(ed.), *Logic and Language*, two vols, Oxford 1951; H. Fortmann, *Als ziende de onzienlijke*, three vols, Bussum 1964, 1965 and 1968; J. Gill, *The Possibility of Religious Knowledge*, Grand Rapids 1971; G. Gusdorf, *Mythe et métaphysique*, Paris 1953; P. Helm, *The Varieties of Belief*, London 1973; R. Hepburn, *Christianity and Paradox*, London 1958; J. Hick, *Faith and Knowledge*, London [3]1967; H. Hubbeling, *Is the Christian God-Conception Philosophically Inferior?*, Assen 1963; A. Jeffner, *The Study of Religious Language*, London 1972; E. Lévinas, *Autrement qu'être ou au-delà de l'essence*, The Hague 1974; J. Macquarrie, *God-Talk*, London and New York 1967; P. Munz, *Problems of Religious Knowledge*, London 1959; W. de Pater, *Theologische Sprachlogik*, Munich 1971; id., 'Theologie en taal als communicatie', in *Tussentijds*, Tilburg 1975, 139–50; I. T. Ramsey, especially *Religious Language*, London and New York 1957; P. Ricoeur (*opera omnia*) and in this connection especially *La métaphore vive*, Paris 1975; R. Schaeffler, *Religion und kritisches Bewusstsein*, Freiburg im Breisgau – Munich 1973; R. Schreiter, *Eschatology as a Grammar of Transformation*, Oxford 1974; P. Tillich, *Symbol und Wirklichkeit*, Göttingen 1962; id., *The Dynamics of Faith*, London and New York 1957; A. Vergote, *Interprétation du langage religieux*, Paris 1974; J. Wisdom,, 'Gods', in A. Flew, *Logic and Language*, Vol. 1, Oxford 1951; id., *Paradox and Discovery*, Oxford 1965; also *New Essays in Philosophical Theology*, ed. A. Flew and A. McIntyre, London and New York 1955; S. E. Toulmin, R. W. Hepburn and A. McIntyre, *Metaphysical Beliefs*, London 1957.

## I. RELIGION IS A RELIGION OF REVELATION

The narrative character of testimonies to new experiences through which a new way of life is also opened to others is a mark of the whole of the New Testament. In all its writings it is the story of new experiences – of experiences of grace – even when *for the purposes of argument* it wants to direct experiences oriented elsewhere (often because they have been manipulated by taking for granted the spirit of the time) along the lines of the gospel. Originally the authority lies more in the experiences narrated than in the 'apologetic' argumentation.

The New Testament was made possible by a previous tradition of Christian experience and, as a testimony to collective experience of grace, the whole of the New Testament forms a tradition. In this it is above all, even for us today, a critical and productive reminiscence and an offer of a chance of experience – at least if, with the help of the concepts of earlier Christian experiences, we pay more attention to the experience formulated in it than to the ancient conceptuality in which it was formulated, despite the fact that in the form of interpreted experience these two elements formed a complete unity, even for the New Testament writers.

One of the fundamental tasks of theology is to attempt to put into words new experiences, with their criticism of earlier experiences, to reflect them and to formulate them as a question to the religious tradition, the church, and to the social and cultural circumstances in which the church finds itself. By virtue of this activity the theologian becomes vulnerable, because here he is in a special way a searcher, and because he is experimental and hypothetical in his assertions. For it is by no means clear from the start which elements in new experiences are important and which irrelevant for Christian faith. The theologian looks for the cognitive and productive force and significance of new experiences, instead of simply working on the concepts used in the New Testament and during the course of church history, in which earlier experiences were expressed.[10] On the other hand, this first attempt is not chaotic or arbitrary; for by discerning the spirits the theologian attempts to discover whether new experiences are really the present echo of the inspiration and orientation which, in the context of the recollection of the biblical mystery of Christ, present their identity anew in these experiences or prove alien to them.

At all events, from the preceding analysis of experiences in their historical context, it will have become clear that the blunt opposition between the authority of a revelation handed down in tradition and the authority of new experiences is at the least pre-critical and naive. People often say, 'Good! I accept the significance of experiences, but *alongside that* there is also the authority of revelation, the "Word of God".' Others, in contrast, confuse what we have called 'experiences' with pietistic or 'personal' experiences; each draws what is said about experiences in the direction of their pietism and along the lines of their own religious attitude, or, on grounds of anti-pietistic rationality, rejects this analysis. Wherever I have presented the essence of these notions in lectures to 'free-thinking theologians', I have found that 'experiences' are mocked. Where I have come across a group with a more pietistic attitude, my audience has been enthusiastic. I think that both categories have the point.

We must begin from the fact that 'revelation' is an element in the self-understanding of all religions. Religions and religions of revelation are quite simply synonymous. This aspect of the history of religion in no way implies the assertion that alongside such truths which are accessible to human reason there are also supra-rational truths which then become the object of religious faith.

## II. TWO LEVELS OF TRUTH?

To some degree the identification of revelation with truths which were quantitatively added to the truths discovered by natural reason, and which were then handed down by authority and had to be accepted in obedience to external authority, already began in the theology of the Middle Ages;[11] however, this theology drew a distinction between revelation and the truth of faith. In medieval theology, revelation is not the doctrine of salvation, but a statement about its origin. There the concept of revelation functions as a 'meta-language'; it says something about the non-objectifiable derivation and source of certain statements. For Thomas Aquinas, everything that the believer considers in the light of the revelation of God is *revelabile*, i.e. the object of revelation.[12]

Against the background of the Enlightenment and the deism that was flourishing at the time, the First Vatican Council, in an anti-deistic context, sanctioned the identification of revelation with additional new truths going beyond the bounds of reason.[13] As a result, what had earlier been theological meta-language was now used in the sense of language about objects. Thus the objectifying thought of the deism rejected by the First Vatican Council became a special presupposition of this council. The result was that revelation began to consist formally in a quantitative extension of the content of our knowledge, thanks to divine communication: revelation becomes a particular group of truths and statements, the object of faith, alongside a series of truths accessible to reason.[14] The Enlightenment had seen revelation as the historical, outward form of a content which was already immanently present in critical human reason, and it was the moral and religious ideal of man to discover its particular content independently of the help of the outward form of historical revelations (helpful though these might be in pedagogical terms). Revelation therefore became the development of an immanent totality of meaning which justifies itself and comes to complete fulfilment in history.[15] Salvation and redemption then become a determination which can be brought into being by the autonomous development of critical reason and human freedom. The Enlightenment repudiated a revelation which was already being presented in baroque scholasticism as a quantitative addition of new knowledge, inaccessible to reason, to those truths which could be arrived at by the light of reason. The Enlightenment protested in the name of critical reason and the beginnings of freedom against a type of divine information which alienated itself from human reason and freedom itself – against a revelation which was understood along the lines of the model of authority and subjection, in which human experience and theory have no role to play.

Against this background the official churches, and above all the Roman Catholic church, are somewhat reluctant to make any appeal to experiences (which in any case were often misunderstood as 'states of feeling' in the narrow sense of the word: purely subjective, inner intimations), above all when experience becomes the criterion for theological statements. This restraint is even more understandable since modernism seemed to explain statements of faith as pure symbols, cyphers of human experiences and primal longing. The concept of revelation began to be interpreted antithetically: not from human experience, but *ex auditu*, from hearing, based on the authority of the God who reveals himself to our

world with which he has a vertical relationship.[16] Furthermore, there was
also reason for restraint in an age in which human, narrow-minded,
enlightened reason was regarded unhistorically and in narrowly rationalistic terms as a merely controlling knowledge (though many philosophers of the Enlightenment were at the same time very modest about
rational human possibilities!). To identify experience with a controlling
knowledge, culminating in an absolute knowledge (though it was Hegel,
rather than the Enlightenment, who spoke in the latter terms), goes
against the very nature of experience.[17] As has already been said, experience becomes tradition, and tradition provokes new experiences.

It is clear from the same Vatican Council that the restraint of the
official church over experiences was not a tenet of faith. The Council saw
a source for the understanding of faith in the mediation between the
content of faith and human sense-experience.[18] Besides, over the centuries
Christian theology has been an attempt to combine faith and human
experience. However, the same history shows us that these attempts have
often led to the reduction of faith. In that case, however, we may ask
how far this is a matter of experiences which are stunted, manipulated
and interpreted one-sidedly.

Now that the deism of the Enlightenment has disappeared over the
horizon of Christian life, the church can be rather more open to human
experience. However, the result of the Dogmatic Constitutions on revelation, *Dei Verbum*, promulgated at the Second Vatican Council, is a kind
of compromise between the opposition to deism expressed at the First
Vatican Council[19] and the earlier Christian view of revelation as God's
communication of himself in salvation history as the God who is gracious
towards mankind.[20] In the Pastoral Constitution *Gaudium et Spes*, promulgated by the same Council, more room is given to human experience.
'God reveals himself by revealing man to himself.'[21] The revelation of
God is concerned with an understanding of oneself and the world, and
therefore with interpreted experience.

## III. ENCOUNTER WITH THE WORLD, THOUGHT AND LANGUAGE: EXPERIENCE AND REVELATION

I do not intend to present a 'complete' theology of revelation, with all its
implications in the life of a church. I am simply concerned to demonstrate
the basis of revelation in experience: there can be no revelation without
experience.

The problem takes the following form. On the one hand, there is no
single argument from outside the Christian faith which can justify this
faith; on the other hand, the salvation which is freely offered to us cannot

remain outside human life and experience. Of itself, this suggests that the relationship between faith and experience must be an *indirect* one, and that there can be no question of an easy, direct correlation. God reveals himself by revealing man to himself.

The very fact that revelation comes to us in human language – as in the Old and New Testaments – shows that revelation is essentially concerned with human experience. However, language is the deposit of a common *experience*. Revelation is experience expressed in the word; it is God's saving action as experienced and communicated *by men*. Furthermore, the language of faith is not a terminology which presents direct descriptions and assertions. In linguistic terms, the concept of 'revelation' is a protest against the exclusiveness of language which is directly descriptive and assertive. The concept of revelation is a meta-theoretical expression of a particular way of speaking, a language the prime concern of which is not to describe and explain, but which nevertheless is an indirect expression of reality on the basis of real experiences.[22] This must be analysed in detail.

### A. God's revelation in the form of human ideas

H. Kuitert has posed the problem very acutely: all human speech about what comes 'from above' ('it has been revealed') is uttered by human beings, i.e. from below.[23] He goes on to say that Christianity consists of projections, words and usages which have been worked out 'down here' and not 'up there'. We know God's revelations only in the form of human ideas and words about divine revelation. According to T. Baarda, 'the argument that "all language about up there comes from down here" says either too much or too little'.[24] I am not quite sure precisely what he means, but I do see the problem. The 'too little' indicates that 'talk down here' is prompted by an initiative from up there; the language of faith is a *responsive* language. 'Too much' seems more problematical. However, it must be conceded that the responsive element is also interpretative; and as such it too comes from 'down here'. But that still does not settle things. In our analysis of experience we saw that people 'have experiences' above all when their plans and reflections, their anticipations of knowledge, come up against the refractory nature of reality, which thus reveals itself indirectly. This resistance directs all our reflections. It reveals a reality which is independent of all human plans, which does not come from men, but 'from elsewhere'. That does not mean that it comes from above, but rather that something which escapes the prevailing pattern of human knowledge makes this knowledge possible, directs it and shatters particular identifications. The basis of human thought is something that has not been contrived by men. Perhaps this is in itself an indication that truth is to be found not so much in our responsive language as in that which causes us to ask questions, and in our conscious ignorance. The clear and unequivocal character of our answers contains the relative element which derives from us and which is transcended by the reality which addresses us and can never be clearly explained. Man comes up against limits in all his experiences of knowing and trying. In these boundary experiences he is no longer the prisoner of the system of his transitory planning. Consequently reason is only rational if it recognizes this boundary experience. Reality is always more than and different from what we imagine it to be. From a negative, critical point of view this is because of our experience that man cannot ground the possibilities of his own existence, his knowledge and his ability in his own planning and his own reflection. This raises the *question* whether he may not and cannot experience reality, to the degree to which it escapes human planning, as a *gift* which frees man from the impossible attempt to find his basis in himself, and makes it possible for him to think and plan endlessly, although this reality which is independent of him is for its part the basis and source of responsible human action in reason, freedom and planning.

It is by no means immediately clear that the character of this gift is *personal*, i.e. that it comes to us from the hand of a living and creative God who establishes the basis of all meaning and in so doing at the same time opens the future to mankind. However, this talk of God is primarily not something that we invent ourselves; we always find it already present historically in our human tradition as a possibility of human experience; we find it there before us as testimony to an experience, particularly in a large number of religions. As this talk of God is also the origin and basis of our culture, and even now is a significant social force, no one who wants to maintain a responsible attitude towards our world can avoid what may well prove to be a harsh confrontation with this tradition of religious language. In that case, however, we must also ask whether this religious language does not find its own context of experience in fundamental experiences of meaning which are combined with experiences of meaninglessness: of suffering as a result of evil and injustice; of suffering as a result of grief and inadequacy; of suffering as a result of love – elements which cannot be rationalized or removed, and which cannot fully be done away with through any human attempts at projection or productivity. This appearance and disappearance of meaning shows that we cannot grasp it, and that meaning comes to us from reality. We are addressed, called and summoned by it. All this has a structure which seems to compel us – however tentatively – to adopt a personal model in order to explain as fully as possible this experience of meaning, though without taking into account the limitation which inalienably divides two people, for all their intimacy.

The question is: does experience of God not have an understandable foundation precisely in the context of the experience of meaningfulness? In other words, is a perspective opened up *within the horizon of our experience* on a meaning which cannot be reduced to our history of projects, discoveries and constructs of meaning and yet reveals itself in this very history of human projects? However, that is only possible if this perspective too can be *experienced* as a perspective: as the token of a greater, final salvation to come; in other words, if in fact we have partial experiences of meaning, of salvation or 'being saved'. What makes negative experience of contrasts in reality into productive experiences is the meaning that can be found in them if we struggle with the pain of the contrast. Partial experiences of meaning and salvation are therefore had *in practice*; there is no question of a theory of salvation detached from any practice. A decision of faith which does not find any point of contact in human experience is irrational (whether or not it is called pure 'decisionism' or 'intuition'). Furthermore, in this instance it is left to man's subjective judgment to decide on the objectivity and validity of God's revelation. Even talk of a promise of total meaning ceases to be empty words or unproductive interpretation only in the experience of partial meaning and salvation. Only then can revelation be understood meaningfully as the *manifestation* of a transcendent meaning in the dimension of our historical horizon of experience and in the *responsive affirmation* of this manifestation. The offer of grace and the answer of faith are the two facets of one and the same rich reality, so that we can say with Lévinas, 'L'appel s'y entend dans la réponse.'[25] However, this cannot happen in such a way that God's action is *reduced* to this human action. For by nature it is only an indication. The transcendent lies *in* human experience and its expression in the language of faith, but as *an inner reference* to what this experience and this language of faith have called to life. Being addressed by the divine is made manifest *in* the religious answer. We cannot speak in objectifying or descriptive terms of revelation, apart from the faith of the community. This is not a denial of the objective validity of the revelation, but a denial of any objectifying and limiting 'scientific' objectivity (which is a stunted objectivity and cannot serve as model for what we may call 'objectivity'). Only in historical human experience and human practice does revelation shine out as God's action: by virtue of its transcendence this cannot be added to the efforts of historical man to create meaning. God's saving action cannot be added to human action, but it cannot be reduced to man's liberating action either. Antoine Vergote is therefore right when he declares that religious language needs models both for verticality from above and verticality from below, on the one hand to express 'transcendence' in imagery, and on the other to give 'immanence' symbolic expression.[26] What is involved is, however, a sense for the depth or the height *within* the direct encounter or the historical togetherness of human beings in the world. The gift, or God's grace, is not revealed either from above or from below, but horizontally, in the encounter of human beings with one another within our human history.

## B. Revelation, an interpretative element? Seeing as . . . or interpreting as . . .?

It is sometimes said that the element of revelation does not lie in experience but in its interpretation. In that case revelation is merely an *interpretative element*. It was said above that experience is a dialectical phenomenon, an essential interweaving of encounter with the world (above all in and through actual practice), of thought and language, in a historical 'entanglement with history'. Human existence *is* this dialectical interweaving. The encounter of many generations with man and the world makes the particular language game of a culture what it is. Experience is therefore the pre-reflective horizon which is already given, the incomplete totality of the way and means through which a group of people approach their world and through which this world presents itself to them. A tradition of experience is the ongoing historical expression of the ways and means by which people deal with the world, live in it and understand it. In other words, it is the historical horizon of the experience of particular men.

Religious language shares in this dialectical interweaving of encounter with the world, thought and language. In thought, language and experience it is the expression of a *unique* encounter with the world. In that case, religion is a particular manner of human existence, a specific form of the dialectical unity of encounter with the world, thought and language. Thus in interpretative and responsive human experiences which are put into words, revelation becomes a 'revelation' which must be formally affirmed.

We may now ask what are the relations in this dialectical unity. Is the believer's encounter with the world religious? Is his thought religious? Is his language religious? Are these religious experiences or religious interpretations of human experiences? Are the experiences themselves relevant to religion, or is it simply that universal human experiences are being interpreted in religious terms?

When the contrasts are put in this way, the dialectical unity of encounter with the world, thought and language has already been broken up. We cannot see 'the religious' isolated in one of these three elements of one and the same experience which is interpretative in its experiencing and in which language is an intrinsic ingredient of this experience. According to Langdon Gilkey, there are criteria for denoting experiences relevant to religion outside religious interpretation and language.[27] That I cannot understand. Experiences are always already interpreted – albeit implicitly – and loaded with theory. The criterion itself is already dependent on models and paradigms; this emerges from the fact that Gilkey himself identifies 'ultimate questions' *a priori* with *religious* questions. This may be true, but it will have to be demonstrated critically. However, this does define the place or context in which religious language can be understood meaningfully, while at the same time making clear why others do not want to speak in religious terms. That is why I prefer to say that for the believer this dialectical unity is itself religious in such a way that in the 'hierarchy' of these three elements the 'earlier' aspect always has a greater density than what is expressed inadequately in the 'subsequent' aspect. At the same time, though, these are not chronological elements but three elements of an *analysis* of what experience comprises. In this sense language, and here the language of faith, is really the weakest element in the totality of this dialectical unity.

If the religious element or faith is co-extensive with revelation – revelation manifests itself in the religious response – then it is equally impossible to reduce the element of revelation to an interpretation in faith. There is the offer of revelation and the human, interpretative experience of revelation. Not only does the religious man interpret in a different way from the non-believer, he lives in a different world and has different experiences. Thus for the believer the exodus through the Red Sea can in fact be taken as an expression of an *experience* and not as a secondary interpretation or a superstructure which can be detached from this context of experience.[28]

We must be more specific in asserting that revelation is an interpretative experience by connecting revelation with its correlate, religious faith. The occasion for this is an example given by Ludwig Wittgenstein: in the twilight we see a small bush as a rabbit.[29] Are we seeing something or are we seeing something as . . . or are we interpreting it as. . .? This distinction is subtle, but not insignificant. Above all, where we have experiences of totalities, we find ourselves in a kind of twilight in which different experiences – or are they interpretations? – are possible. John Wisdom's parable is well known.[30] Two people return after a long absence to the jungle where they have left their garden untended by any human hand. When they arrive, they find the garden decked with well-kept flowers among the weeds. A conversation develops between the 'believer' and the 'non-believer'. One says, 'A gardener must have been here.' After careful investigation this hypothesis has to be given up. So does the hypothesis that someone has been there while everyone was asleep.

Besides, a gardener would have pulled up the weeds. Nevertheless, the garden looks cared for. 'There is some purpose here,' says one. Some aspects point to a gardener, others (weeds: 'meaninglessness') point to his absence or perhaps to the fact that some malicious person has been at work. However, a hedge all round, bloodhounds, and finally an electric fence show no trace of a mysterious visitor. Thereupon the 'believer' says: the gardener must be invisible, inaudible, intangible, and the sceptic retorts: in that case, what remains of your original gardener? What is the difference between an invisible, inaudible gardener who slips through every trap, and an imaginary gardener? Such assertions die the death of a thousand qualifications. The final result is that one remains convinced of the existence of a 'good God', whereas the other cannot imagine him at all. These two assertions, Wisdom claims, do not reflect any difference in the facts that both men have discovered in the garden: weeds and beautiful things. At this point, Wisdom says, the 'gardener hypothesis' has ceased to be experimental; the difference between the one who denies the hypothesis and the other who accepts it is not the question that the first expects something that the other does not. To say 'there must be a good God' is not a forecast about events in this world which would be different from what would be expected by someone who did not believe in God. In other words, this assertion does not give us any *information* about how things are in reality, about 'meaning' and 'meaninglessness'. These assertions are void of information, and because they ostensibly convey information, they are pseudo-statements. A. G. N. Flew adapts the parable to fit this conclusion and in so doing makes scientific thought the criterion and paradigm of all knowledge. Wisdom, however, interprets the parable differently. He does not by any means conclude that the whole discussion ends up in a 'non-lieu', in other words, that there should be no problems and no dispute between the believer and the non-believer. The believer certainly says something about his experience (the garden). The question then is whether there is not a 'non-experimental' point of dispute between the two. One uses the name God in connection with the garden and the other does not. This difference in what they say about the gardener is connected with a difference in attitude, emotion and quality of experience. Granted, it is impossible to test such a nomenclature as an expression of an attitude, but it can affect what is experienced, the garden, and is by no means arbitrary. Thus God's love differs from human love; it is not irreconcilable with a 'tolerance of suffering'; this love seems to be reconcilable with anything. However, Flew asks Wisdom, What is left of the term 'love'? What is the difference between saying 'God loves us' and 'God hates us' when all circumstances (whether things go well with us or not) are compatible with *both* assertions? In his interpretation of the parable Flew concentrates on pointing to elements of the same, unequivocal experiences which are common to both believer and unbeliever; Wisdom, on the other hand, points to the difference in interpretation. One sees the garden, which is the object of the experience of both, as the creation of God, the other sees it as a self-sufficient reality.

The parable is taken further in the philosophy of religion. Two men are on a journey together. All the time, one sees his journey as a pilgrimage to the heavenly city; he interprets the pleasant stretches as encouragment and the hindrances as trials of his endurance. The other believes nothing of this, and sees their journey as an aimless ramble. Since he has no choice in the matter, he enjoys the good stretches and endures the bad, for better or worse. In discussion between them it is clear that the two do not differ in their experimental experiences of the good and the bad; they differ in their view of the purpose and destination of their journey. 'When they turn the last corner, it will be apparent that one of them has been in the right all the time and the other wrong.'[31] However, in essence this conception of an eschatological verification is correct. 'He will judge the living and the dead.' Above all, however, Christianity escapes a 'pure eschatologism' because it points to a particular experience with one historical event, to Jesus. The Christian makes a statement about God which relates to a this-worldly reality – Jesus of Nazareth, and only on his foundation does eschatological verification become significant. There must already be some basis for experience in the present. Without this basis, religious statements are in the meantime purely hypothetical – we can never know.

For others, who follow the example of R. M. Hare, general statements by believers and non-believers express a 'blik'.[32] Two people can agree completely over demonstrable elements in their experience, and yet in the last resort have radically different views. What the so-called progressive will see as clear historical symptoms of a relaxation of Russian policy will be regarded by the 'anti-Communist' as so many proofs of the diabolical cunning of the Soviet Union in its aim to gain sole control of the world. Facts can be experienced or interpreted in two different ways. Statements about them can hardly be nullified. According to Hare they are significant as the expression of a 'blik', that is, a 'view of' and a line of behaviour which precedes all knowledge of the world and is presupposed by it. He calls this a deeper level of meaning than that of purely descriptive statements, but they can be neither verified nor falsified.

This discussion was continued later on another level. In both cases, for the believer and the unbeliever, it seems to be concerned with a 'seeing as' (seeing the world as God's creation, as self-sufficient). The question is, Precisely what is that? Do we have to say, 'I *experience*, I see something *as*. . .' Or, 'I *interpret* what I experience or see *as*. . .'? Many of those involved in the discussion who have abandoned pure empiricism affirm that the experience itself is interpretative; the difference lies in the question whether the *identification* lies only on the level of interpretation or rather on the level of experience. According to some, to call an event, say, an experience of grace is in fact an experience of grace; for others, in contrast, it is to interpret experience of an event accessible to all men as grace. According to Ronald Hepburn,[33] theists and atheists have the same experiences, but interpret them in different ways. With many authors, empiricist presuppositions still lurk in the background; above all, the 'cognitive' aspect is identified with empirical verifiability; where this is impossible, statements are merely ways of expressing psychological dispositions.[34] John Hick[35] believes that it is more precise to say, 'I experience or I see something as (a chair, a shrub, a bush)'; Ian Barbour,[36] on the other hand, prefers to say, 'I interpret it as. . .', though he is only talking of a shift of accent.

Barbour's mistake seems to me to lie in his starting-point; in his explanation he begins from experiences which are illusions, projections (in the twilight a bush is seen as a rabbit), albeit not without a basis in experience of reality. If experience is interpretative, there can also be false interpretations. In fact we have experiences within a concept (I experience or see a chair). We are aware of the possibility of different frameworks of reference. The problem ends up by being that with conscious men there is no such thing as uninterpreted experience. The alternative forms in which Hick and Barbour pose the problem disguise the complexity of the real situation. Not only the reflective but even the pre-reflective consciousness makes identifications in the course of experiencing: both neglect the element of identification too much and call attention one-sidedly to the interpretative element in identification. Besides, Gestalt psychology[37] has demonstrated that, for example, a drawing of a configuration of cubes can be looked at differently from different directions. They are seen differently and not just interpreted differently. We see something against a background or a horizon. The element of structure or form is not added on in our thinking, it is an intrinsic element of our perception. So we see something in a different way and do not just interpret it differently. We can certainly take all the different perspectives together in theory, but we cannot see them all together at the same time. Thus the element of identification lies *in* the experience itself (one might say that we see 'the interpretation', or better, we see interpretatively). There is no neutral given in experience, for alternative interpretations influence the very way in which we experience the world.

Nature and human history are similarly 'ambivalent': they can be seen as 'figures' against different backgrounds; they can thus be experienced in different ways.[38] One particular kind of alternative vision of worldly reality is expressed in metaphorical and symbolic language. This symbolic language is the only adequate way[39] of expressing certain dimensions. Only those who regard directly descriptive language as adequate language and thus regard it as the criterion for all language will talk of '*just* symbolic' language. They forget, however, that there is no such thing as directly descriptive language and that theory and interpretation permeate all descriptive language. So the religious man also *experiences* grace; he does not just interpret it. It therefore seems to me short-sighted to say that the non-believer only trusts his experiences, whereas the believer builds castles on the same experiences. It is not a question of a contrast between experience and interpretation, but of alternative 'interpretative experiences'. Both the believer and the non-believer have interpretative experiences. Wittgenstein says that the world is not the same to a happy man as it is to an unhappy man;[40] he lives in another world. To call God good, even in suffering, is to give a definition of 'good' in which 'good' and 'God' *define each other,* thus shattering our limited concept of good. Only when we call God good do we know what a Christian means by 'good', and at the same time we arrive at a particular concept of goodness which then has a foundation in eschatology and partial experience.

The consequence of this analysis is that there is no reason for a contrast between a 'propositional' understanding of revelation (e.g. the creed) and an experiential understanding of revelation[41] through the dialectical unity consisting of encounter with the world, thought and language. If statements are to have meaning and truth, they must be rooted in human existence as experience. In fact, if religious faith is reduced to an 'amen' to propositional statements, this yes-word (which of course is also a no-word) in fact means nothing. Religious language only becomes valid in the full context of experience of this language – both linguistic and non-linguistic. The demand means that the propositional understanding of revelation cannot be excluded, but must be kept in a right relation to the experience with which this propositional language is associated. The element of 'revelation' can thus be known *in* the experiential encounter with the reality of the world, *in* the interpretation of this experience as an intrinsic element in that encounter, and *in* the religious language of faith – albeit (in the same 'logical sequence') in ever dwindling and diminishing measure, because 'controlling' knowledge and human 'plans' are increasing to the same degree. *Allowing oneself to be determined* by a surprising disclosure of reality is given *limited human expression.*

C. The immanence of transcendence: the possibility of expressing the reality of revelation

I said earlier that transcendence lies *in* human experience, but in such a way that this experiential content contains an intrinsic reference to what makes this experience possible and is not constituted by the experience itself. Can we say anything about this reality which escapes us? Does it allow itself to be expressed? I believe that this is possible and necessary in two directions: (*a*) in a 'mystical' direction and (*b*) in an ethical direction.

(*a*) Mystical thematization of the inexpressible

In so-called mystical or 'religious' thematization man seeks to express the foundation and source of the human religious response of faith. Of course this attempt is only tentative, and because of the transcendence of its concern, it has to be expressed in symbolic language. It is not therefore a question of a pattern of 'two worlds', ours and another. *Our own* reality is itself different from and more than what we believe; this reality itself, and not another higher world, is a surprising revelation of what has never been conceived of by man. For the believer, the very existence of man and the world is a symbol or a manifestation of the divine, but always in such a way that there is a necessary identity between the revelation and the concealment of the divine. For when confronted with any manifestation of the divine, God's essential reserve is always experienced: God can never be reduced to one of the forms in which he is manifested. Reality continues to surprise us. That is true in turn of both religion and the religious language of faith, which both reveal and conceal God and thus in their *own* symbols speak of the God who has already appeared in symbols – man, the world and history. However, the inadequacy of our talk of God is no reason for silence (any more than it is in the sciences). Unless linguistic expression is given to the reality which escapes us but grounds our being, even though this may only be through the 'poverty' of symbolic expressions, it threatens to disappear into forgetfulness. Out of sight, out of mind. Creeds and liturgies are therefore a necessary (and dangerous) form of anamnesis or remembrance. Relationship to the unconscious and the inexpressible is an essential part of critical human reason; 'dogmatism', on the other hand, identifies reality with what is expressed adequately, whereas scepticism falls silent because of our our ignorance. By contrast, critical knowledge of our own ignorance does not give up the will for truth, but rejects any absolute knowledge. It has the courage to express the inexpressible clumsily, knowing that this comes nearer to reality than dumb silence or the dogmatic attitude of knowing better.

In philosophy since Kant this problem has been discussed in terms of the difference between the 'thing in itself' and the 'object for me' – a distinction which is unavoidable, even if it cannot be realized.[42] It is unavoidable, because reality cannot in principle be comprehended by the consciousness; it cannot be realized, because man cannot distinguish what he does not know; for in that case he would have to recognize the 'thing in itself' precisely in the way in which it is distinct from the 'thing for us'. On the other hand, this distinction occurs again in our consciousness, at least in so far as this distinction *leaves room for* that which does not come to conscious awareness, 'a space which we can fill neither through possible experience nor through pure understanding', as Kant himself puts it.[43] The difficulty is as follows: how can we describe the way in which reality, under the aspect in which it does not enter our consciousness, can still be *thought of* by this consciousness? This knowledge of our own ignorance is part of the very structure of critical reason, and here the relationship to the unconscious is constitutive of man's finite thinking, which keeps being overtaken by reality. Reality and truth are 'given' to human, articulative knowledge in so far as in them man also experiences and takes into account the inadequacy of his own thought and language. From this it emerges in turn that the supra-rational is part of the structure of human rationality, without our having to think in terms of 'two worlds'.

Now if that is the structure of human thought, we cannot do justice to the inexpressible element which can be found in the human tradition of experience by remaining silent about it – even if our talk in this direction is clumsy and always open to criticism. Moreover, this religious, symbolic language is experienced by believers as a gracious gift from the one whom they confess. The believer experiences the living God as the source which enables and makes possible such language. Thus however human it may be, this language is not an autonomous human initiative, but derives from an authority and mandate, by virtue of reality. Man is not master of reality, but only its steward. From this it emerges in turn that this talk of God and his revelation is indissolubly bound up with our interpretative experience, as believers, of the reality of man and the world. Any religious statement about the God who reveals himself is in fact a statement about man and his world, but understood in such a way that any religious statement about man and the world is also in fact a statement about God. Theology is not anthropology, but a theological statement is *at the same time* an anthropological statement. In other words: in the self-understanding of religion there is, right at the beginning, a particular, i.e. religious, view of the world and man. God is always greater than the way

*[margin note: Theological anthropology]*

in which he shows himself to man in our history, greater than the deliverance of the exodus from Egypt, greater too than the judgment of the Babylonian captivity. And even Jesus says that his disciples will do greater things than he himself has done.

Symbolic and 'negative theology' accepts the thousand names that men give to God; perhaps it will add to them new names that speak to our time. At the same it will say: none of these is wholly appropriate; it will leave room for the surprise that reality gives us. For many, the source from which we live has no name at all, but it is the task of believers and theologians constantly to name this ultimate reality and not leave it in anonymity, while at the same time being aware of their 'conscious ignorance'.

At the same time, were we to claim that this 'contemplation' rests purely on itself and does not develop any critical force of its own, we would be showing a wrong understanding of this 'contemplative' thematization of the inexpressible. Thanksgiving and praise in prayer are not in fact purposive actions; they are not 'useful for . . . ', but have a worth and value in themselves. But they also have a critical force. They make it clear that talk of the divine is only understood rightly to the degree to which it subjects itself to criticism, while at the same time urging the necessity of this discussability. Without it, man is abandoned in his isolation, doomed to talk to himself, to the great loss of his fellow men. Liturgical and symbolic language and theological thematization make it possible to express the unconditional without however speaking unconditionally. This language is neither 'dogmatic' nor sceptical. Liturgy and theology speak of the inexpressible, and in this they are a dangerous reminder to everyone, and also a counterbalance to the *exclusiveness* of all 'controlling knowledge'. What continues to function even in the sciences as a 'marginal condition' 'somehow' (here this word is appropriate) has to do with what becomes the theme of religious language. Reality is always different from what we think, while it as it were nevertheless grudgingly gives up its secret, so that even the completely new is never the negation of what it has already revealed of itself. Hope is surprised by the constantly unexpected, but never disappointed! The truth of religious language and the confidence of hope derive from the same source as the constantly recurring new element which surpasses all religious conceptions and expectations. Because of this, revelation finds its way through in this clumsy human talk, which must, however, speak in veiled terms about this revelation. This talk is not the truth; it is a sign of the truth. If we want to keep the difference between 'truth' and 'manifestation' expressly in mind, we may in fact speak of the truth or the illuminating force of the manifestation (in this context, this religious language).

Because of the predominance of scientific thought in Western culture, this symbolic thinking in religious faith is often connected with the infancy of mankind,[44] as the result of a one-sided predilection for what is often positivistic 'instrumental reason'. Religious language is allowed to have emotional, but not cognitive value. In that case 'cognitive' is identified, as by Piaget, with an understanding which is essentially directed towards regularities, causal explanations and deductions.[45] And symbolic knowledge has no cognitive or truth value[46] except as 'childish thought'. This evaluation follows simply and solely from the fact that symbolic thinking is not subject to any empirical control; for that reason it is said to be a 'mythical group-thinking of primitives'.[47] But Piaget does not describe religious symbolic thought as a 'senseless activity'; not all human activity can be reduced to science. The particular task of this ideological religious language is the co-ordination of values, which are then more important than their cognitive significance.[48]

No proof is needed that such a view of purely scientific and instrumental thinking cannot possibly have a feeling for the particular cognitive value of the symbolic thinking of religious language. It betrays a purely scientistic view of human existence, the special quality of which is never really expressed, and in addition a particular view of human rationality in which no account is taken of the supra-rational presupposition of the possibility of this rationality. In the last resort the sciences do not discover the psychological, social, religious phenomenon to which they want to bring rational illumination. The sciences do not create man-in-the-world with his social, psychological, ethical and religious dimensions. And the more objective part of man and the world investigated by the sciences is not the whole of man, the whole of nature and the whole of history. However, we would be naive were we to assume that views like those of Piaget were not held in a popularized form by many people in this age of (neo–) positivism, to the detriment of faith.

We might say that it is empirically demonstrable that man is alienated from his own nature if he thinks he has finished with the symbolic thinking of the religious consciousness; we have learnt this from the criticism of religion put forward by the philosophers Marx, Feuerbach and Freud. But in our one-track Western culture we can also demonstrate that the exclusiveness and absolutism of purely scientific and technological thought (which does not reflect on its own presuppositions) allows whole areas of our humanity to die out or become stunted, and precisely in so doing alienates man from himself.[49] It is illuminating that the man who does not worship a divine God automatically prostrates himself before a non-divine God.[50] The truth about man in his encounter with the world is not exhausted by his purposive control of the world in science and technology. Precisely this justified human attempt continually comes

*[handwritten margin note:]* ✳ ✳ Either we worship God or something less than God.

up against the resistance which this reality offers to any purely controlling
and manipulative knowledge. Yet science as it were compels reality to
speak. What is said, however, often does not come out as expected. The
resistance of reality and the recollection of suffering which cannot be
rationalized – the suffering of evil and injustice, the suffering of grief, the
suffering of love, and so on, therefore belongs to the structure of critical
human reason which in practice seeks to be liberating. The sciences are
in themselves by no means reductionist (though they often look that
way); they simply pose other, *limited* questions, to which the answer may
be right but, given the nature of the question, equally limited. They only
become reductionist when they are offered as *the* answer. For that reason
they can never express the nature of man and his religion (nor criticize
it); these are only accessible to philosophical, critical-reflective and theological thought.

*Relation between science and religion* [margin annotation]

## (*b*) Ethical expression of the inexpressible

It will already be clear from what has been said that religion is 'not just'
ethics and cannot be reduced to ethics. On the other hand, there is an
intrinsic connection between religion and ethics, of such a kind that it is
ethics which gives the density of reality to 'mystical' thematization.

Ethics uses a different language-game from religion.[51] The understanding of good and evil logically precedes understanding God and doing his
will. That means that we cannot define our moral obligations primarily
in terms of God and his will. On the other hand, the believer can and
may see the will of his God in what he has learnt to regard as good and
evil. For that reason the knowledge of the will of God is communicated
historically, and indeed essentially, without the seriousness of the divine
will losing any reality in the process. Hence although medieval thinkers
used a now obsolete model of 'nature', they were right in speaking of the
natural law as the indirect ethical norm and thus as a historical mediation
between the commandment and the will of God (*lex aeterna*) and our
ethical consciousness. Ethics has a certain independence, but the believer
or the religious man sees its deepest foundation, source and ground in
the reality of God.

Grace and religion are therefore essentially an ethical task. A religious
man cannot separate the life of grace and ethical life from one another:
'Be doers of the word, and not hearers only' (James 1.22); 'He shall be
blessed (*makarios*, as in the beatitudes) *in his doing*' (James 1.25c). 'So that
those who have believed in God may be careful to apply themselves to
good deeds; these are excellent and profitable to men' (Titus 3.8b). The
Letter of James attacks a religious monism of grace: 'What does it profit
if a man says he has faith but has not works? Can his faith save him?'

(James 2.14). This is as authentic a mark of the New Testament as its kerygmatic mysticism, and does full justice to the Tanach spirituality of Yahweh, who requires righteousness in *this* world. This practical and ethical 'thematization' of the mystery of God, the ground and source of religious experience, is a special and necessary 'interpretation' of the inexpressible mystery. What God is must emerge from our unrestrained involvement with our fellow man, between one man and another, and through building up liberating structures without which human salvation proves impossible.

However, it is also the case that man is limited even in his most responsible ethical action and that he experiences his limitations. Ethics demands too much of him (see Part Four). The rationality of human action is only rational to the degree that it also leaves room for the surprising event of reality, which transcends human ethical rationality. The future cannot be fully mastered by rational and ethically responsible planning (necessary though this may be). Thus the ethics of human liberation is the very context of experience in which the question of God can be expressed most clearly (see under Part Four). Despite its relative autonomy (on the basis of which ethics is possible for non-believers, and the non-believer cannot be identified with unethical people), ethics in the last resort itself points towards religion and the 'mystical' thematization of the astonishing world event.

### (c) The relationship between 'mystical' and ethical formation

In all religions two trends can be found combined or locked in polemical struggle.[52] They are connected with the formation or 'making explicit' of the source of revelation in human life. With a reference to terms from the Jewish religious tradition, these two trends can be called on the one hand the 'theoretical and symbolic', the hasidic trend (M. Buber) and the 'practical and ethical', the anti-hasidic trend (E. Lévinas). The mystical and ethical dimensions are family traits in almost all religions. Giving a personal name to the ultimate ground and source of ethics and calling on the name of God expresses, albeit in the only way possible to us, i.e. a symbolically real way, the source of all ethics. This happens in the religious liturgy of thanksgiving and praise. *Theological* thought is therefore less a theoretical thematization of this ground (except in the form of *theologia negativa*) than the 'theory' which must secure by argument the inexpressible transcendence of God as he is expressed in the history of religious men and which must discover the status and the context of human experience in which this history can be meaningfully preserved and activated. Theology is an outline sketch to secure the health of religious confession and liturgy, as rooted in a profoundly human experience, and to articulate contexts of experience in which God can be talked of in meaningful terms. The true 'thematization' of the real element of revelation in human experiences takes place both in the symbolic liturgy with its explicit naming and in worship ('mystical' element) and in ethical formation ('ethical' element).

We may ask which element has the greatest density of reality: the indirect and 'orthopractical' expression of God in ethical action or the indirect symbolic expression of the source of this practice in explicit nomenclature: 'my God', 'our God'. Both seem to me to be indispensable, but in view of the experiential structure of revelation, the symbolic-religious talk of God owes its density of reality to the *mediation* of *ethical existence*. In *this* perspective I would prefer to follow E. Lévinas: 'Tout ce que je sais de Dieu, et tout ce que je peux entendre de sa parole et Lui dire raisonnablement, doit trouver une expression éthique.'[53] We do not find salvation primarily by means of a correct interpretation of reality, but by acting in accordance with the demands of reality. We can act 'rightly' without having a correct theoretical model of reality, even if we are not professing Christians.[54] But being a Christian essentially implies liturgical praise and thanksgiving; however, these are robbed of their real basis and their density of reality if they lack the ethos of human, helping, healing and liberating love and righteousness. Religious thematization (which is always indirect or 'symbolic') forfeits that ground when it is detached from its basis in experience, i.e. the ethic or human action which, while feeling itself responsible for human destiny, does not look for the meaning, ground and source of historical success in its own autonomy, but in the unconditional mystery which directs all our experiences, overturns them and gives them a new direction: 'My ways are not your ways' (Isa. 55.8). This problem of religion and ethics recurs today in all its magnitude in the question of the relationship between redemption and man's concern for liberation and emancipation. I hope that this book will point a way towards a meaningful solution.


## IV. BELIEF IN AUTHORITY

If we allow so much room to human experience as a communication of divine revelation, it might be asked: what is left of 'faith from hearing' (Rom. 10.14, 17)? Everything – though not in the pre-critical sense of blind faith in an external authority. Religious faith is faith 'on the authority of God' and not on the authority of human projections. If experience – both everyday experience and 'scientific' experience – consists in a dialectical movement of drafting, observing and criticizing the outline through the resistance offered to it by reality, the authority of God is revealed precisely in the fact that the course he takes differs from that of our human plans. 'Reality' is revealed in human thought and in God's 'guidance'. Israel had to experience this constantly in its history. The important thing was not Israel's own plans and reflections on what salvation might mean – in that respect it came under judgment – but the surprising way in which Israel's God corrected these plans, destroyed them, moved them in a new direction and finally brought salvation in a completely unexpected way. While this salvation was the fulfilment of Israel's deepest expectations, it went completely beyond all ideas of that. This faith is faith in the authority of God.

Religion is not concerned with a message that has to be believed but with an experience of faith which is presented as a message. On the one hand the religious message is an expression of this collective experience, and on the other its proclamation is the presupposition for the possibility of its being experienced by others. Revelation takes place *in* historical human experiences *in* this world, but at the same time it summons us *from* what we take for granted in our limited world. It is therefore not to be found in any direct appeal to our so-called self-evident experiences within the world. As experience, it is the crossing of a boundary within the dimensions of human existence.

This experiential structure of revelation is expressed in an extremely evocative way in the Christian revelation, which had its beginning in a historical encounter of men with a fellow man: Jesus of Nazareth. In it, something that we men could never have conceived of appears in a most surprising way *in* our history. Nevertheless, what could not have been conceived of by men appeared in the immanence of our historical experiences. In the encounter with Jesus, the authority of the (Christian) experience which he called to life coincides with the authority of the divine revelation. In that case perhaps I have analysed the concept of revelation on the preceding pages less as it functions in different religions than as it is specifically understood in the Judaeo-Christian tradition.

## V.  A NEW CONTEXT OF EXPERIENCE FOR PRESENT-DAY EXPERIENCE OF SALVATION IN JESUS

As man changes, i.e. as his pictures of man and the world change in the light of significant new experience, so too what he experiences as salvation and happiness also changes. Of course there are formal 'anthropological constants' in all this change, but they continually take on different colouring. The problem, then, is: how can salvation in Jesus, i.e. why we now need Jesus in the twentieth century, be expressed in such a way that it can be presented as an articulation of our expectations of salvation (duly subject to critical analysis) and the world in which we live without shaping Jesus and his salvation according to the measure of our wishes and criticizable requirements?[55] The problem for many Christians, their crisis, is not so much that times have changed and that Christians might be accused of moving with the times and the new questions that they pose. On the one hand the crisis lies in the fact that Jesus is still regularly explained to us as salvation and grace in terms which are no longer valid for our world of experience, i.e. in terms of *earlier* experiences; and on the other hand in the fact that we seem no longer capable in words or actions to 'make a defence for the hope that is in us' (I Peter 3.15). Are we really what we confess in our creed of faith and hope?[56] Is there not a false adaptation here? For the service of Christians to the world is a divine service. In other words, only insofar as we give form to our specifically religious, Christian task do we *ipso facto* give a specifically Christian service to the world instead of merely duplicating what the world already does, and perhaps does well.

From what has been said so far it has become clear that revelation has a structure of experience. The good that particular men experience in Jesus was experienced in the process of identification as salvation from God. What was really experienced by Christians in Jesus was therefore neither a purely logical conclusion nor a 'direct' experience, but an interpretative experience: an experience of faith. Because of this surprisingly new element of their experience of salvation in Jesus, Christians therefore wanted to express this in terms of their Jewish tradition of religious experience, which they made to interpret Jesus in the way in which they in fact experienced him. This led to the automatic development of the so-called proof from scripture (from the Tanach); the concern was to make an explicit presentation of the *continuity* experienced within the *newness* of their experiences with Jesus, in a tradition of the experience of faith in God's covenant with this people. At the same time this led to a new interpretation of this history in the light of the experience of a renewal of history. This finally led to a religious conception of the whole of history: the unity of a divine plan, counsel or divine dispensation which is developed in and through history by men.

What the Christian community will be concerned to say in constantly changing situations, through constantly new forms of expression, even in philosophical concepts of a very complicated kind, is ultimately no more than that in Jesus Christ it experiences decisive salvation from God. When the old concepts or interpretative elements no longer relate to new situations and when needs and necessities change, interpretative concepts also change. But the original experience persists through these changes: in their own different situations people still continue to experience God's salvation in Jesus. These changes do not themselves cause a crisis. As

*[margin, handwritten]* The Xian experience of Jesus was not direct, but interpreted experience

long as the basis of experience – experience of salvation in Jesus – remains, any possible crisis takes place above all on the level of conceptual interpretation.

However, the situation becomes critical when the basis of experience is itself removed, when people are no longer clear why salvation should be sought specifically in this Jesus of two thousand years ago. In that case there is no longer any experience of salvation in Jesus. And in the end faith is undermined if it has to look for salvation from someone on the authority of others, if there is nothing that corresponds to it in the whole of their personal experience. Faith then quietly vanishes from life, dying through its own irrelevance and a short circuit of human experience.

Of course it could be argued that Christian faith is diametrically opposed to all human experience – that we believe contrary to all experience and that as a result there is no correlation and no connection between faith and life. But in that case God is so transcendentally the 'wholly other' that a really living man will immediately conclude that he himself has nothing more to do with this God because he is so far removed from man's own life. Such a view contradicts the whole event of experience from which Jewish Christianity has arisen and developed: it ignores the history of its own origins. Furthermore, it reduces human experience to its projective and productive elements and passes over what proclaims itself *in* experience to be an astonishing and overwhelming event in reality, correcting and crossing all our plans and achievements. It is that which makes someone an 'experienced person'.

If as a result we cannot affirm faith or talk people into it on mere external authority, Christians who continue to experience decisive faith in Jesus will be able to invite others to renewed possibilities of experience, if they search from their own Christian self-understanding for something in our present pattern of experience of salvation from God in Jesus. I sometimes wonder how, if we had never used the word 'God' before, it could be meaningfully introduced into our vocabulary? It is a thought which is worth an experiment. Besides, sometimes it is *the* event in a normal human conversation – at least if the word God is not used too early, or too late.

Chapter 2

# The authority of the canonical New Testament

*Literature:* The most important articles on the formation of the New Testament canon have now been collected in *Das Neue Testament als Kanon*, edited by E. Käsemann, Göttingen 1970. See also N. Appel, *Kanon und Kirche. Die Kanonkrise im heutigen Protestantismus als kontroverstheologisches Problem*, 1964; W. Bauer, *Orthodoxy and Heresy in Earliest Christianity*, ET Philadelphia 1971 and London 1972; P. Benoit, 'Inspiration de la tradition et inspiration de l'Ecriture', in *Mélanges M. D. Chenu*, Paris 1967, 111–26; J. Beumer, 'Die Inspiration der Heiligen Schrift', *Handbuch der Dogmengeschichte*, 1–3b, Freiburg in Breisgau 1968; H. Freiherr von Campenhausen, *The Formation of the Christian Bible*, ET London and Philadelphia 1972; J. Frank, *Der Sinn der Kanonbildung*, Freiburg im Breisgau 1971; J. Leipoldt and S. Morenz, *Heilige Schriften*, Leipzig 1952; O. Loretz, *Das Ende der Inspirationstheologie: Chancen eines Neubeginns*, I, Stuttgart 1974; K. H. Ohlig, *Die theologische Begründung des neutestamentlichen Kanons in der alten Kirche*, Düsseldorf 1972; Karl Rahner, *Inspiration in the Bible*, ET Freiburg and London 1961; A. Sand, 'Kanon. Von den Anfängen bis zum *Fragmentum Muratorianum*', *Handbuch der Dogmengeschichte* I, 3a, Freiburg im Breisgau 1974; B. Vawter, *Biblical Authority*, Philadelphia and London 1972; Faith and Order Report, *The Authority of the Bible*, Louvain 1971.

In my first book on Jesus, I described how, after their panic at the arrest and death of Jesus, the reassembling of the disciples (as the beginning of the formation of the church), the Easter experience and the sending of the Spirit were simply different aspects of a single saving event in which the disciples experienced Jesus as the risen one in their midst. The 'Jesus movement' which had begun during Jesus' life thus gained a permanent place in our history as the Christ movement. Its members ceaselessly described everywhere what this Jesus had done and what had happened to him and what had happened to them as a result and what can happen to all those who will listen to this story. That was their good news for all men.

The disciples' experience with Jesus was the dynamic origin of a religious movement and thus the actual founding of the church. This movement with its leaders was an echo of what Jesus himself had been, said and done. What enthused him began, for his sake, also to enthuse them. The message was handed on by personal example, and ultimately the movement and its leadership stood under the sole norm of Jesus of

Nazareth. This *religious* reference to the historical Jesus remained essential.

The history of this Christian movement which formed many scattered brotherhoods gradually crystallized in particular traditions and models. After a number of generations of Christian life, Christian practice and reflection, a whole Christian literature had arisen which amounted to an interpretation of the Christian experience on the basis of the Tanach (see p. 907), the Bible of the first Christians. At a later stage, because of the newness experienced in Jesus, this was called the 'Old Testament' and became an essential part of the Christian Bible. This Christian literature described what had happened to Jesus and his disciples in a great many ways, often very different. Because of this varied and increasingly different literature, which in the opinion of many people also gave rise to deviations from the original proclamation of Christ, one particular question eventually arose. In which of all these writings could the Christian movement recognize itself completely and authentically? For later generations no longer had any historical recognition of Jesus.

Some of these writings which bore witness to Jesus and his 'community' were used in the worship of many Christian brotherhoods. However, there were striking differences here between the Christian communities. Some communities refused to use in their liturgies certain texts which were held in high regard by other communities, although there was unanimity over many works. In a long maturing process, marked by mutual criticism, certain texts were finally chosen from a large collection of Christian literature which Christians began to recognize as 'Holy Scripture' (along with their Jewish or Graecized Bible). Under the impact of the historical Jesus, interpreted in the light of the Tanach, certain Christian writings were counted as 'scripture' and the New Testament was regarded as part of 'holy scripture' (though among Jews in the time of Jesus there was no unanimity over what literature was *graphe,* or part of the Tanach).

In other words, the chosen literature was canonized – as a norm for handing down the story of Jesus. This was the common foundation, above all, for the many Christian communities already scattered over the ancient world, who yet saw themselves as 'the one, universal or catholic church of Christ'. In this way it arrived at a normative, recognizable group identity, from then on at the same time on the basis of the canonical literature accepted in common by all the Christian churches (after a great many disputes).[57]

The starting point of the Christian movement was an indissoluble whole consisting on the one hand of the offer of salvation through Jesus and on the other of the Christian response in faith. And just as the living presence of the risen Jesus Christ among his own on earth was the beginning and the permanent stimulus to the Christian movement, so now particular Christian texts were elevated to the status of a canonical norm because of their content, while at the same time these many communities of believers, identifying themselves with reference to these texts consolidated themselves into a mutual group identity which was visibly recognizable for all believers. The Christian movement recognized itself fully and wholly in the content of this selection of literature. Just as the beginning of the Christian movement was the work of the community and its leadership, so too this later consolidation of group identity in and through the common recognition of the canonical value of particular Christian texts was historically the work of both the community and its leaders. These writings, which had already been used for a long time by the Christian communities in their liturgy under official direction, were finally confirmed by the leaders of the church as the only official texts. (This happened globally in the second half of the fourth century. For the East this was on the authority of Athanasius; for the African churches through synods at the ends of the fourth and beginning of the fifth centuries; the West followed Augustine's authority. However, these decisions by bishops or synods are only a sanctioning of much earlier traditions, and a discussion continued in the Christian churches which led to the concept of 'proto'– and 'deutero'-canonical writings which is still used today.)

The intrinsic logic of a group identity stabilized by canonical scriptures has far-reaching sociological consequences. As a result of canonization (though also because of their inspiring content) these texts took on a new significance over and above their content. This significance was *institutional;* it thus had social implications within the community. The texts give an institutional definition of the Christian group identity. Because of their official canonization, from that point on they apply much more stringently, because they provide the basis for a socially effective norm as a result of their endorsement by the group and its leadership. On the basis of their canonization or elevation to be the standard for the Christian gospel and life in accordance with the gospel of Christ, these texts are characterized by the fact that the process of education through which people are introduced to the message of the gospel and the conduct that follows from it at the same time becomes a process through which believers are integrated pedagogically, ethically and socially into a social group whose identity is defined by its relationship to these texts. The canonization of its own foundation documents is also a first institutionalization of the Christian message or the liberating truth of the Christian movement which now consolidates and guarantees its group identity. The true story of Jesus is thus given institutional protection against any possible distortion or falsification in the course of time. It is given official sanction.

Originally this historically spontaneous and necessary general recognition (which proved controversial in some marginal cases) did not cause any alienation. Rather, this process of canonization characterized the growing of self-understanding of an essentially 'evangelical movement' which, as it extended further, could not preserve its authenticity and identity without setting up at least a few ground rules and without introducing a number of institutional elements. For members of the Christian movement, the canonically binding effect of these texts did not involve any compulsion to believe, not even a formal prohibition on criticism and interpretation. *Within* this literature which was now called the 'New Testament' there is actually some mutual criticism (see below in Part Two). Existentially these communities could not do otherwise: this was the particular way in which they identified themselves with these texts. They identified themselves wholly and fully only with these models of Christian identity, and not any others (though many Christians were fond of reading non-canonical Christian literature, see Part Two). For Christians who had brought about this institutionalization and had recognized themselves in it, no serious problems arose. These only emerged when this already existing Christian 'institution' was handed down to new Christian generations who had not been involved in the origins of 'canonical scripture'. For them this institution needed some legitimation: it had to be explained and justified. Not because it had become less effective – on the contrary, institutions tend towards rigidification; for later generations the significance and self-evidence of the self-chosen institution are a 'historical entity'; it comes down to new generations *as tradition* (and not primarily as the expression of an experience which they themselves have had). As a testimony to the experiences of those who created it, scripture is an offer – a possibility that this experience can be extended to others. However, once it becomes a historical institution, it also presents new generations with a claim to authority, and is now detached, at least directly, from the process of a particular experience. Institutionally, the authority already exists as it were before the faith-experience of later believers. In other words, the authority does not reveal itself in the definition of a particular interpretative experience; before that, it has a 'juridical' precedence, even if this is only the *institutional* expression of the authority which had been recognized in *earlier* Christian *experiences*. During the period of the origin of the canon the authority of scripture is not in fact any juridical or formal authority (no external authority). At the beginning, the view of scripture was different from that which was to develop almost automatically on the grounds of its institutional canonization. Later, people argued that the holy scripture of the

New Testament had authority because it was inspired by God. To begin with, it was the other way round. A religious group of people, Christians, under the spell of Jesus, who was experienced and testified to as God's salvation, had recognized its own group identity in particular inspiring writings, as the expression of the faith experiences of fellow Christians within a developing tradition of Christian experience and an already existing *regula fidei* or norm of faith – the foundations of the later Christian creeds. Furthermore, they had already arrived at their Christian identity through the liturgical reading of these writings. For them the authority of this literature was existential, and derived from its content; in it they found an expression of their own understanding of Jesus and at the same time of their understanding of themselves as Christians. For this reason, in the end they were able with justification to formulate this existential authority in the language of faith and say, 'These writings are inspired by God', just as the whole Christian movement found its origin and its inspiration in Jesus, God's emissary. The beginning, however, was not the formal authority but the event of a new experience of salvation, narrated in texts the appealing and inspiring significance of which was experienced, acknowledged and affirmed existentially. What was involved here was the authority of the experience of Jesus himself, which the church at the same time recognized through the medium of this scripture as determinative for the meaning of its life; here it found meaning and discovered inspiration. Thus the original authority of the Bible lies in the element of revelation which has passed through the experience and interpretation of these early Christians. Within the church community it also has the special significance that in it the whole community found an authentic expression of what had happened in its Christian experience. In other words, here the element of revelation which keeps escaping us at last comes into its own; however wretched and human the expression may be, revelation is communicated in it.

Still, at the same time, in the explicit canonization of these texts which were called into life by Jesus, with their inward invitation which inspires life and gives it direction, there was also an 'institutional promotion'. For the church as an institution these now became a juridical and formal authority, a formal authority which can present some problems to later generations who had not themselves gone through this process of creating a canon. For the history of Jesus was sanctioned by the canonization of this literature. The normative sanctioning of certain stories which gives them an official character may have been an intrinsic necessity for a developing movement, but it represents a first possible hardening of the story of the living Jesus which has continually to be taken up by other Christians. There is a danger that new 'transformations' of the same story from now on will be regarded with mistrust, even if they are not ruled out altogether. In this way a dynamic group identity can become a social group stability. Christianity can change from being a movement around Jesus Christ into the religion of a book in which the direction of the community of believers is determined by 'scribes' rather than members of the community with their charismatic leaders. For this canonization gives some degree of independence to the responses made in faith to Jesus' offer of salvation, to the multiplicity allied with a basic unity which we find in canonical scripture. It isolates them, with the danger that they may be read or studied apart from the non-canonical literary context in which they stand. In the long run, all this can suggest that the rich and never completely exhaustible talk about Jesus allows only the responses of faith that we find in the New Testament and no others. Moreover, this blunts any feeling for the historical and contingent connections which exist with the earlier responses of faith and their ethical consequences – just as it is above all particularly easy to forget the tension between Jesus and the New Testament, which then becomes a 'little red book'. Its canonization should not make us forget that this particular literature has only laid down the basic story as a model. New stories of Christian experience remain possible, provided that they are a legitimate transformation of the original story in which the person of Jesus Christ is allowed a voice within the mediation of all kinds of other historical conditioning factors. In the centuries after the completion of the biblical canon the churches understood this well, and they saw their scripture not as the letter, but as spirit: inspiration and the indication of a particular direction. They wrote their history of Jesus within the contours of their different cultural world, in faithfulness to the original history, even if it was drawn and sometimes distorted by the spirit of their time. (Has it ever been otherwise with the 'images of Christ' in art over the course of the centuries?[58])

Without closing our eyes to the real dangers of an institutionalization of these Christian foundation documents, we should not forget that without such canonization the Christian movement would long since have faded out and vanished in eclecticism or even esoteric inwardness. Non-canonical Christian literature from antiquity already gives clear instances of this. We may not make Jesus into anything that we like if the element of revelation does not lie in the confirmation of our plans and reflections but in his refractory opposition to all our planning. We also have to concede that the boundaries between what the early church calls 'the New Testament' (as a book) and other writings from Christian antiquity are in marginal cases vague and uncertain. In terms of Christian literature, we could say that the early church made an extremely successful move. For those for whom this church is 'God's community' – for Christians – this Bible may therefore be regarded as a fragment of grace, or, to put it in religious terminology, like Jesus and his community, the Bible finds its inspiration in God.

Consequently the dialectical unity and tension between the church as a movement and the church as group identity, given institutional security through its holy scripture, belongs to the concrete historical reality which may in fact be called the 'church of Christ'. And it is worth noting that the element of 'movement' belongs both to the community of believers and to its ministry or its leaders, just as the 'institutional' element belongs to both ministry and community. In view of the history of the formation of the canon we can hardly put the *institutional* element in the church exclusively on the side of its ministry and its *movement* exclusively on the side of the community of faith. Furthermore, history teaches us that sometimes it is the ministers of the church who are more on the move while the community is stabilized to the degree of rigidity, and sometimes it is the other way round.

Chapter 3

# Do we begin with the New Testament or with present-day experience? A false alternative

At the beginning of our analysis of the authority of experiences and of the authority of the New Testament we saw that some people feel that theology should no longer begin from scripture and tradition but from contemporary experiences. I would regard this as a false alternative for anthropological, hermeneutic and religious reasons.

1. Men in fact live in the present, but they live from a past and are directed towards a future. The present is highly significant, precisely because it is the dividing line between past and future. But the present is not an absolute starting-point: as present, it is itself a tradition of experience. Even when we fight against our own past, whether individual or collective, we never get the better of this past, which is part of our own hidden present. At the very point where this resistance is most vigorous, this past proves to be an oppressive present.

One can never see the relationship to the future which prompts action and the hermeneutical and theoretical relationship to the past as alternatives. Relationship to the future is only possible by means of our relationship to the past, and conversely, our relationship to the past, in whatever form, traditional or critical, always already contains a decision about the future: that is why our relationship to the past is never purely theoretical and hermeneutical.

It is by no means impossible to reconcile a connection of Christian faith to the past history of Jesus and Christianity with a theological orientation towards the future – provided that, as I have said, the future is not simply *contrasted* in a one-sided way with the present and the past. Such a crude contrast usually ignores the fact that a definite orientation towards the future is *always communicated* through present and past experiences which have been handed down to us. The significance of the past for any new present is shown in the process of tradition. Whether the past becomes relevant for the present depends on our answer to the question how far the history of the past contains a future which we have not yet taken into account; in other words, how far it can illuminate the experience of a later present in its relationship to the future.[59] J.-B. Metz rightly concludes from this hermeneutic interrelationship that the loss of identity 'cannot be removed by a *theoretical* revival of Christian traditions'.[60]

Christian theology in particular is concerned with an interrelationship between an 'analysis of the present' on the one hand and an analysis of the historical experience of Christian life and hermeneutical reflection on this life on the other. Its concern is to distil from this totality a direction which Christians can responsibly take in the process of living towards the future. The present is in fact the 'hermeneutical situation' in which we live. But we cannot regard this present as the climax of history. This present has its own presuppositions and blind spots, just as it also has a sensitivity of its own which our ancestors never had. True, the present is an utterly original source of new experiences and new insights as an element in a new life-style. But here too it can be one-sided. So no present as such can be a criterion, a norm by which everything is judged. Our present experience is contextual, as limited as that of any people during the course of history. Yet it forms the horizon of understanding in which we contemplate, experience and interpret everything. An analysis and interpretation of this present is necessary, if we also want to have the critical strength which makes it possible to guard against presuppositions of our own time which we tend automatically to endorse.

Even if we are in opposition to it, the first requirement seems to me to be that we should not reject solidarity with our own past, but acknowledge it. Radically to reject the past results in loss of identity, for this radical rejection still does not liquidate the past: the surest way of becoming victims of our own past is to negate it or ignore it.

Furthermore, it is necessary to understand the *original* truth of institutions and traditions, particularly if they seem strange to us today. To begin with, most of them were not repressive or oppressive; they became so later, in other times. At first, they are almost called to life as an instrument of liberation and for the protection of the weaker. For that reason we need to investigate from what period and why an institution or tradition became false, ossified and oppressive. Jacques Ellul[61] has made a historical analysis of the way in which positive laws are really made by the ruling classes, but are seldom promulgated in order to favour the predominant position of the ruling class; on the contrary, they originally served bit by bit to keep the power of the ruling class in check and to prevent arbitrariness. They therefore originate in self-limitation – not for quite altruistic purposes, but simply as a requirement of the group if it is to be able to survive. Only later, in changed circumstances, do laws often acquire a reactionary significance – and are claimed to be unchangeable. Besides, the claim that the law – as a type of 'institution' – originally served to strengthen the power of the ruling class is more a positivistic argument than a Marxist one.[62] The greatest alienation consists in having no laws at all: in that case, the chaos of the power of the strongest emerges. All this means that alienation arises where laws made at a particular time are accorded a timeless authority. Then institutions fall under the criticism of Karl Marx: they then serve the interests of the powerful and the strong in the guise of 'absolute values'.

If we are to be able to grow out of the past, we have to know it. In this sense, historical study is a catharsis,[63] a liberation of the sociological unconscious in us; for our origins are hidden from us. Therefore a *creative* foundation in our own past is a presupposition for a new future.

2. On the other hand, a romanticism about origins is just as much an error in interpretation. People often play about with the term *primum* or *principium* in its double meaning, of beginning and principle (norm); in that case the origin is the all-controlling norm, the essence of a movement, tradition or institution – *norma normans, non normata*. There is a grain of truth in this.[64] When we are dealing with a historical movement, we find that its origin is in fact normative. But in this respect there are a number of hermeneutical implications that we need to take into account. It is illegitimate to absolutize any single historical epoch, even that in which a movement begins, and impute to it a one-sided normativeness. The beginning, considered as a canon or norm, is never a problem for the earliest period; it becomes a problem for later times. The putting of questions to the beginning, described as a norm or canon, will be intrinsically governed by the horizons of the questioner, who will belong to a later historical period. Paul and the evangelists did not themselves regard their writings as *graphe* or holy scripture; this was the standpoint of later generations, who were no longer original, when a long Christian tradition

had arisen in which there were many differences of opinion (the books of Karl Marx, too, only became a 'canon' at a later stage in the Communist party). Only then does the earliest period become the norm *en bloc* (and then there is always a degree of selectivity), and a particular theological tradition even talks of 'the end of revelation with the death of the last apostle'. This seems to be a sociological phenomenon of almost every group identity (for some orthodox Marxists, too, the 'Marxist revelation' ceased with the works of Engels and Lenin; any 'revisionism' then becomes treachery). 'Separatist communities' always come into being in attempts at a contemporary – called by others 'reformist' – interpretation of the ancient heritage.

That is already evident from the fact that any reference to the sources or to the origin is already involved in a hermeneutical circle, a circle in which the present and what lies between the past and the present (the whole Christian tradition) already exerts a *mediatory* function. True, we try to subject the present to the criticism of this origin, but in such an attempt we are always 'prejudiced'. We cannot *a priori* disqualify the intermediary period – the tradition – as apostasy (which is a particular tendency of Reformed theologians since A. Harnack); on the other hand we are no more justified in *a priori* pronouncing the tradition as legitimate (as Catholic theologians often tend to do). At all events, we cannot neglect the period between origin and present, because otherwise we never see what conditions in any age, even the earliest period, make possible a correct insight into the truth of Christian origins.

An idealization of origins often reveals a hermeneutical dualism, i.e. that of the nucleus or essence and the clothing or historical form. But even in the phase of the origin or the beginnings of Christianity there is a communication of faith and historical conditioning. Our problems are not solved by discovering through exegesis how, for example, church government functioned in the early church. Of course, as we put our questions our attention is also drawn to the way in which historical developments have carried on from this origin, simply by reflecting that this origin is itself historically conditioned. What was once a legitimate structure for the church (given the historical circumstances) can in changed social circumstances be seen to be illegitimate, to be a structure which is neither favourable to nor healthy for Christianity. In that case it is no longer a valid development from its origin. Therefore only an *indirect*, historically conditioned biblical foundation is possible: in any period contemporary experiences of man and the world and political and social structures find their way into the particular form of belief and the church. As Christians today, why should we not do what the church has always done? Neither the structures of the ancient church nor our demand for reformation of the church's structures can be based *directly* on the

Bible; we cannot therefore absolutize them in a one-sided way. One might even say that precisely because the religious dimension is one dimension of the whole of culture, any religion (even Christianity) has both a liberating and an alienating effect. There is no church in our world which consists only of the saintly and the 'pure'; indeed, in Catholic eyes that would even be a 'heresy'. But for that reason theology will always have to keep a watch in order to see how far religion can maintain the *critical* tension with culture as a whole in which it has its existence. The situation is full of dangers and risks, but no religion can escape them unless it wants to find itself in a ghetto and thus to have no influence on our history.

All this should be enough indication that the question 'must we begin with scripture and tradition or with our own contemporary experiences?' is a false alternative. Present and past are not 'two things' in juxtaposition. In reality, the message of the New Testament and our present experiences do not stand over against each other and alongside each other as two things. They already touch each other. At least in the form of the claims made by the church, this message is already among us here and present today. If we speak of the disruption of communication between the Bible and our present time, the problem arises as the problem of a *contemporary* claim of the church to meaning and truth which comes out of the past. As long as we regard the past as something that has to be sought somewhere in the distance, far away from our present culture and our present insights, we are at an abstract theoretical level which allows only formal analyses of the hermeneutical structure of our experience. The pattern of present-past already evaluates the gulf between present and past in a negative sense: there is a 'disruption of communication'. The starting-point is therefore that there must be communication and unity with the past. This scheme already works with an interpretation. But it is by no means clear why this gulf should be assessed *per se* in negative terms. For others might say that the past would do far better to remain past, finished and done with, precisely because of the present, and that the present is an emancipation from the past. But in this case we also begin from a presupposition and interpretation, namely that the influence of the past on the present by means of a particular communication hinders communication in the present and the future. In both instances it is impossible to maintain the abstract opposition of present and past: both arguments already draw a line between present and past, in a positive or a negative sense.

All this means that the problem of communication is always already presented from within the framework of a pattern of interpretation: either (*a*) in terms of a critical emancipation from an 'authoritarian pre-history' or (*b*) in terms of a prehistory which is normative for us in one way or another or (*c*) in terms of a deeper meaning which is offered to us among the normal chance phenomena of history.

Thus any talk of communication involves an interpretation. H.-G. Gadamer is therefore right in pointing to the fundamental position – the primacy – of language in our historical conversation,[65] and P. Ricoeur also asserts that it is the first task of reflection 'to recall itself in language'.[66] However, at this point language should not be elevated into becoming a metaphysical entity: it is merely a *model* of reality. Thus it is impossible to solve the problem of communication in purely theoretical interpretative terms.

3. Finally, there is a religious reason why the contrast between the 'New Testament' and 'present experiences' is an abstraction. It has emerged from the preceding analysis of the relationship between revelation and experience that religion needs the world to be itself, and that the world needs religion to keep its attention alive to the presuppositions of its own rationality which go beyond reason. I said earlier that theological statements about God are always communicated by anthropological statements (as elements of human experiences). Human history was already running its course before Jesus took up the threads of this history, and this history continues – with or without Jesus. The fundamental symbol or the manifestation of God is the worldly reality of man and his history in nature. Religious experience is in line with a particular interpretation of man and the world. Religious language is essentially bound up with a religious way of expressing our experiences of the world. This fundamental hermeneutics of man and the world also continues to be the matrix for the distinctive Christian interpretation of the New Testament and the great biblical tradition of Christianity. In the light of Jesus Christ, the gospel itself is a hermeneutic of fundamental human experience. What speaks to us in Jesus is his being human, and thereby opening up to us the deepest possibilities for our own life, and *in this* God is expressed. The divine revelation as accomplished in Jesus directs us to the mystery of man. Therefore, to ask people to accept the Christian revelation *before* they have learnt to experience it as a definition of their own life is an impossible and useless demand, which goes against the structure of revelation.

It is therefore essential to have a constant movement to and fro between the biblical interpretation of Jesus and the interpretation of our present-day experiences. We cannot begin with one without beginning with the other; otherwise the Christian succeeds neither in interpreting the Bible nor in interpreting our present-day experiences. The New Testament and the history of its influence help us to understand our present-day experiences as a realization of the eschatological remembrance of Jesus Christ or to reject them as humbug. In that case we can in fact 'begin' from a critical analysis of present-day experiences and then discuss them in the light of the gospel (though we shall also have to learn what the gospel is!). We can also begin from an exegetical analysis of scripture and tradition, keeping within their own socio-cultural context of experience in order to relate the message which emerges from them to our present experiences (though the way in which this message is formulated remains alien to us unless it is expressed in terms of contemporary experiences, critically interpreted). Thus the contrast between the two starting-points proves to be a false dilemma: the one does not work without the other. *Revelation* is brought about through *experiences*. The Christian revelation is given a hearing today (within the communication of the living proclamation of the church) in contemporary interpretative experiences.

The preceding analyses of the problem of the relationship between revelation and experience indicate that we will not make much progress either with a so-called 'purely theological' analysis of New Testament and church documents or with an undialectical reference to human experiences. In addition, other things are beyond question just as necessary:

(*a*) A study of the *reasons* why the faith was given a particular expression and underwent a particular development in the life of the early and later church. It is not that these motives were decisive, but that they give us a better understanding of the arguments used and allow us to assess the final result indirectly.

(*b*) An analysis of the foundations on which the arguments, say, of Colossians and Ephesians are based in contrast to the authentic letters of the apostle Paul, and in the light of which the final conclusions are drawn. Thus we seek to understand the reason why e.g. the deutero-Pauline epistles reject alternative interpretations in their polemic against tendencies in particular churches. These were in fact historical decisions. To refuse to choose a particular historical alternative at a particular moment in history can result in the abandonment of the meaning of the original Christian impulse.

(*c*). The discovery of the way in which new insights of faith are expressed, and an investigation of the way in which new insights of faith are incorporated into those insights which have already been achieved. Is this purely additive, or does it involve relating the whole of traditional faith to a particular present?

(*d*) Mixed up with this threefold study is research into socio-historical and political circumstances. Why, for example, did the first Christians adopt a comparatively loyal attitude to the occupying powers of Rome? Is this an intrinsic consequence of their view of grace – and normative for all Christians – or is it a piece of historically conditioned astuteness which made free evangelization possible in a situation of oppression?

(*e*) Only rarely will it be possible to make a study of the character of a New Testament writer. However, this is possible with the authentic letters of Paul. In fact Paul seems to have been difficult and aggressive, a black and white character who not only carried on a bloody persecution of Christians at the beginning of his career but was characterized after he became a Christian by his constantly aggressive attitude to opponents and by an inability to get on with almost all his fellow-workers (Mark, Apollos, Barnabas, Luke . . . Peter). His exclusive and almost aggressive view of grace evidently has something to do with his character. His letters are concerned with one norm, Jesus Christ, but this is 'Paul's Christ', *his* gospel (Gal. 1.18; I Cor. 4.15; Gal. 5.10; see I Cor. 1.12f.). In the New Testament tradition of faith, God's revelation is constantly communicated through and in human signs: in human language, which takes in everything that is characteristic of man – his experience, education and upbringing, his style and his form, his whole personality. The fact that each New Testament writer has left behind in his writings traces of his character, whether 'normal' or 'abnormal', is a feature of the profoundly human character of the revelation of God, which is free from any hocus-pocus.

✳ ✳  So for believers, *revelation* is an *action of God* as *experienced* by believers and *interpreted* in religious language and therefore expressed in human terms, in the dimension of our utterly human history. The all-pervasive, authoritative element of revelation in this complex context is not this interpretative experience itself but what can be experienced in it.

Thus the analysis given in these first three chapters leads essentially to the following conclusion. *In* our human experiences we can *experience* something that transcends our experience and proclaims itself in that experience as unexpected grace. 'My thoughts are not your thoughts' (Isa. 55.8). The prophets did not know that through a special telex link with heaven, but through their own interpretative religious experience.

So because in this book I 'begin from' the New Testament history in which Christians articulated their experience of grace, it does not mean that my starting-point in Christian theology contradicts a starting-point 'from the other end,' with our contemporary experiences. Furthermore, we are confronted with the inescapable fact that Jesus of Nazareth appeared in *our* history and that his appearance had an incredible after-effect which brought liberation to many men and servitude to many others. Be this as it may, Christianity is part of our present-day experiences! Both the Christian believer and the non-Christian must come to grips with this positive and negative effect of Jesus, whom Christians acknowledge as the Christ; it is our prehistory, and for all those who have come into contact with Christianity at any time, whether by means of Christian churches or by means of Western culture which has been influenced by Christianity, it is at least a hidden dimension of our own present. The fact that others can say something of the same kind from their religious traditions – Jews, Buddhists, Hindus, Muslims – is one more reason for considering the significance of our Christian claims. True, Christians are convinced that they have a message for all men, but they do not have a monopoly of the truth.

*Part Two*

---

# New Testament Theology
# of the Experience of Grace

In the New Testament, the word grace *(charis)* does not appear in the Gospel of Mark, which also does not use the kindred Greek Septuagintal term *eleos* (gracious mercy). Matthew has *eleos* three times, and does not have *charis* at all. The concept of grace (*charis* and *eleos*) is completely missing from the Gospel of John, apart from the four occasions on which *charis* appears in the prologue (where it is in all probability an element in the hymn from the tradition which John takes over and, in accordance with his method of editing, incorporates organically into his gospel). Nor does it appear in I and III John.

*Charis* appears in I Thessalonians and Philippians, but only in traditional greetings. In Luke the term occurs often (eight times; *eleos* occurs seven times and seventeen times in Acts) but usually not with a theological meaning (apart from *eleos*, where Luke follows the Septuagint). It is therefore striking that in the Pauline corpus *charis* occurs about a hundred times, sixty of them in the authentic letters of Paul.[1]

Statistics about vocabulary say very little, and sometimes nothing at all. They simply attract our attention. Be this as it may, this statistical survey[2] – if we also include the content of *charis* in the various contexts – shows that the explicit theological use of *charis* in the New Testament is restricted almost exclusively to Paul and his school. That does not mean to say that Paul gives us a theology of grace or that the beginnings of such a theology are absent elsewhere in the New Testament; far less that the rest of the New Testament would not know the reality which Paul calls grace. It is, however, evident that Paul uses the word *charis* often in his personal vocabulary; it seems likely that as far as he is concerned (in the New Testament) the word is associated with typical Pauline themes; this does not mean that they are exclusively Pauline; he could be taking over a particular theme from the inter-testamental period (see below).

If we compare these statistics with the theology of grace (*charis* and *gratia*) in the patristic writers, it is immediately evident that 'grace' did not formally become the centre of theological reflection until the later works of Augustine in his polemic with Pelagius. That does not mean that talk of grace consists of second-order statements, i.e. is a statement about a statement which says something else. In that case grace would not be a direct element of experience but a subsequent statement about a particular experience, i.e. the experience of Jesus as the Christ. The thematization or further reflection on grace as an element of experience is itself a 'second-order' undertaking, a kind of 'objectifying' reflection on what is already given in experience. Chronologically, this is always an undertaking which already presupposes a long tradition of experience of grace: thus one aspect of the experience of salvation in Jesus from God is analysed formally in the so-called theology of grace. In the New Testament we find only *the beginnings* of a theology of grace.

The experience of grace is not simply identical with the particular way in which it is articulated, but the use of particular words (e.g. *charis, eleos*) to express this experience does take us part of the way towards a better understanding of what the New Testament means by Christian experience. In Part One, I showed how experience and interpretation influence each other; the interpretative element in language has an effect on the experience itself. It is therefore quite important to investigate the vocabulary at the disposal of the New Testament writers in order to express the element of grace in their Christian experiences, so as to establish the direction in which the semantic field of these words could guide their interpretation of the experience of salvation in Jesus Christ. However, this particular influence is not decisive, because their new experience can prove stronger and more comprehensive than experiences which have been described previously. The tradition and the new development can coincide in the use of the same word (e.g. *charis*).

At the same time, this gives us a methodological pointer, above all because the Tanach or the Old Testament is the most important interpretative framework for the New Testament. We shall therefore first consider the semantic field of *charis* (grace) in secular and religious Hellenistic terminology. Furthermore, because Greek-speaking Jews translated the semantic field of the Hebrew conception of grace into Greek, and in so doing struggled with the problem of rendering Hebrew concepts in Greek words, we must also investigate the concept of grace in the Septuagint and before that the Hebrew vocabulary connected with grace, which also had a direct influence on the formation of the literature of the New Testament. However, just as we have already seen that by clarifying the formal structure of revelation we have also said something about its content, so too it is impossible to say anything meaningful about 'grace' without taking account of the content of salvation which is received as a gift. The question of grace in the New Testament must at the same time be an answer to the way in which New Testament Christians experience salvation in Jesus from God. To put it in traditional terms: the tractate of grace is in fact a 'second order' thematization in respect of the doctrine of redemption, a kind of formalization of it – which is one reason why we should not want to separate them.

# The field of meaning in vocabulary as a controllable expression of New Testament experiences of grace

*Literature*: H. J. Stoebe, s.v. *ḥesed*, in *ThHandWAT* 1, 600–21; id., s.v. *ḥanan* (and *ḥēn*), op. cit., 1, 587–97; H. Wildenberger, s.v. *'aman ('emet)*, op. cit., 1, 177–209. Also on the corresponding Greek words in *TDNT*, above all s.v. *charis*, 9, 359–87 (W. Zimmerli); s.v. *eleos*, 2, 477–87 (R. Bultmann); s.v. *aletheia*, 1, 232–7 (G. Quell); s.v. *hosios*, 5, 489–93 (F. Hauck); M. Bailly, s.v. *charis*, in *Dictionnaire grec-français* (Paris [9]no date), cols 2124C–2125B; W. F. Arndt, F. W. Gingrich, W. Bauer, *A Greek–English Lexicon of the New Testament*, Chicago and Cambridge 1957, s.v. *charis*, 885–7; H. G. Liddell, R. Scott and H. S. Jones, s.v. *charis*, in *Greek-English Lexicon*, Oxford [9]1940, 1978–9. Also: F. Ascensio, *Misericordia et Veritas*, Rome 1949; K. Berger, ' "Gnade" im frühen Christentum', *NTT* 27, 1973, 1–25; P. Bonnetain, 'Grace', in *DBS* Vol. 3, 701–1319; N. Glück *Das Wort Hesed*, BZAW 47, Berlin 1927; J. Haspecker, 'Der Begriff der Gnade im Alten Testament', in *LTK* IV, 977–80; A. Jepsen, 'Gnade und Barmherzigkeit im Alten Testament', *KuD* 7, 1961, 261–71; id., *''Aman'*, in *TDOT* 1, 292–323; W. Lofthouse, 'Cheen and Chesed in the Old Testament', *ZAW* 51, 1933, 29–35; U. Mäsing, 'Der Begriff Chesed im alttestamentlichen Sprachgebrauch', *Charisteria Iohanni Kopp*, Stockholm 1954, 27–63; D. Michel, 'Aemaet. Untersuchung über "Wahrheit" im Hebr.', *Archiv für Begriffsgeschichte* 12, 1968, 30–57; J. Montgomery, 'Hebrew hesed and Greek charis', *HTR* 32, 1939, 97–102; G. Morrish, *A Concordance to the Septuagint*, London 1974; H. H. Rowley, *The Biblical Doctrine of Election*, London 1950; H. J. Stoebe, 'Die Bedeutung des Wortes Haesaed im Alten Testament', *VT* 2, 1952, 244–54; T. Vriezen, *Geloven en vertrouwen*, Nijkerk 1957; G. P. Wetter, *Charis*, UNT 5, Leipzig 1913; J. Wobbe, *Der Charisgedanke bei Paulus*, NTAbh 13.3, Munster 1932.

Chapter 1

# Ḥānan and ḥēn: ḥesed and ᵉᵐmet: the concept of grace in the Tanach

## §1   Yahweh's activity of ḥānan

### A. Ḥānan: have a loving approach

Theologians (exegetes) who study the semantic significance of Hebrew words come up with very different interpretations. This is clear if we simply compare the studies of *ḥānan* and *ḥēn* produced by W. Zimmerli, A. Jepsen and H. J. Stoebe in the various theological word books. It is particularly the case if the etymological root-meaning of a word is unknown or uncertain, because in that case every context in which the word is used is essential for arriving at its basic meaning. Furthermore, the real significance of a word in a text is formally governed by this context, and in that case theological interpretation, which often has marked confessional connotations, especially when it is a question of the theology of grace, exercises great influence. The following analysis should be read in the light of these qualifications.

The meaning of the root (*ḥnn*) of *ḥānan* is: be gracious, have mercy on someone. The dominant notion here is not so much that of treating a person in a condescending manner (though there is still a good deal of discussion about this among specialists), as the idea of attention, approach. This approach is not only, or not primarily, a matter of inner disposition; it takes the form of a particular action in which good will is expressed in a specific way. In *ḥānan* (as opposed to the Greek *charis*), *turning towards* one's fellow man is primary. Hebrew is not familiar with the dualism of an inner disposition which is then expressed outwardly in acts of good will. Grace (*ḥānan*) is the kindness expressed by anyone in a gift or a present. Yahweh is good to Jacob *in* the gift of his children (Gen. 33.5); the gift of the Torah *is* God's grace (Ps. 119.29). So there is no dualism between an inner disposition or gracious benevolence and outward gifts of grace, or presents. The gift itself is someone's approach towards his fellow man. One might say: 'It's the little things that count,' and not just an inner disposition. The word *ḥānan* (be gracious to some-one) primarily has no religious significance. The semantic field of the word is derived from the sphere of human relationships, in which it has its original setting.

This concept of being gracious presupposes a lack on the part of the one to whom grace is shown; this can be expressed in a request which is so strong that *hānan* is sometimes replaced by a Hebrew word which means 'respond' (*'ānā*). Someone who does not have it – or has nothing – is given something by the kindness of another, with the secondary connotation that in this gift the one who does the favour turns to the other with all his heart, a gesture which at the same time is a response to the crying need of this other. Grace as expressed by the verb *hānan* is therefore a warm inclination towards another, at least as an implicit response to a crying need, whether or not this need has been explicitly formulated by the person who receives the gift. However, it emerges from this very structure that the person who gives is related to the person in need as a superior to an inferior. *Hānan* and its derivatives are therefore often associated with the attitude of the king towards his subjects about whom he must be concerned. *Hānan* means to look round for someone and therefore often 'look down on' from one's own height (though here it does not have any pejorative connotations). The content therefore includes taking account of someone, inclining towards him and, finally, granting him a favour.

In the wisdom literature, above all, *hānan* is given heightened meaning: to have mercy on the poor (Prov. 14.31) and lowly (Prov. 28.8), by giving them something (Pss. 37.21, 26; 112.5). The same thing is expressed in the *hānan*-attitude of the victor who 'spares' or 'lets off' those who are defeated in war. From this, *hānan* also acquires the meaning of 'grant forgiveness', 'be gracious', or 'show grace' (an aspect which is completely lacking in the Greek word *charis*, which is one reason why the Septuagint prefers to render the term *hānan* with *eleos* rather than *charis*).[3] After a war, pardon follows through the conclusion of a treaty (Deut. 7.2). Thus gracious love is also covenant love, with an accent on mutality. In purely 'secular' terms, therefore, grace and the covenant already call one another forth, though the term *hānan* is not *per se* related to covenant love.

Reference is made from the sphere of the experience of human relationships to this 'secular' interpretation in order to be able to express experiences with God. With this religious significance, throughout the Tanach *hānan* acquires a typical meaning which clearly influences the New Testament. *Hānan* is used in about sixty instances, and in more than forty of these, God himself is the subject; there are twenty-six occurrences in the Psalms, which thus become the chief witnesses to the grace of God in the Old Testament. Just as Paul, in the New Testament, sees God's relationship to man above all in terms of grace, so too in the Psalms we can discover a similar concentration. Here, too, the correlation between need and grace is significant: God answers the prayers of the pious. It is striking here that the term for petitionary prayer, as a prayer for a responsive attitude of *ḥānan*, is derived from the root *ḥānan* (above all in the psalms of lament).[4] Grace and a petition for grace (helplessness) are correlative and are therefore derived from the same root (*ḥnn*). The reflexive form of *ḥānan* means to pray for attention to one's own situation and for a realization of one's own state of misery, hence, generally, to ask for grace, and at least for an acceptance of prayer (even when it is not heard: see I Kings 8.30, 45; II Chron. 6.35, 39; Ps. 6.9). There is thus a twofold foundation to the prayer for grace. On the one hand is the need of the person who prays (for a situation of need see: Pss. 4.1; 6.2; 9.13; 25.16; the title to Ps. 52). In a number of cases this is specified: weakness (Ps. 6.2), loneliness (Ps. 25.16), oppression of different kinds (Ps. 31.9; 123.3), desperate misery (Ps. 86.3). On the other hand we find belief in God's grace or in his gracious favour (*ḥānan*).[5] Generally speaking, grace comes in answer to a prayer (Ps. 4.1), the details of which are given in particular cases: a healing (Ps. 6.2; 41.4), rescue from distress brought about by enemies or by misfortune (Ps. 9.13), freedom from anxiety (Gen. 42.21; II Kings 1.13; Job 19.16), redemption or delivery (Ps. 26.11), support (Ps. 41.10), the forgiveness of sins (Ps.51.1), strength (Ps. 86.16), being spared from the threat of death or being preserved from Sheol (in many psalms of lament) and so on. The 'grace' sought or prayed for is connected with 'human life'.

It is particularly important to note that according to all these texts grace is experienced as such in a situation of dialogue, in prayer. We find everywhere a specific expression of the assurance of faith that Yahweh cares for the weak, the poor, those who have been enslaved by their fellow men, those who are lost and oppressed. All this is as it were already implied in the religious use of the term *ḥānan*. This can be seen above all in the term *ḥōnēnī*, i.e. 'Be gracious to me', which occurs as a closing prayer after a particular request for a favour (Pss. 4.1; 6.2; 9.13; 27.7; 30.10; 41.4, 10; 51.1f.; 86.16). It also becomes a form of blessing, 'God be gracious to you' (Num. 6.25; Ps. 67.1). The insignificant and humble man finds grace; he is 'raised up' by God. That is what grace consists of. It is not unique to the spirituality of the Tanach: parallels to such petitions are part of the religious heritage of many people. This trust in God's gracious concern (*ḥānan*) only becomes specific as Israel and the Israelites who pray put all this within the covenant grace or the *ḥesed* of Yahweh (see below), and thus in the context of Yahweh's concern for his people (Ps. 51.1; 119.58; II Kings 13.23). In view of man's sinfulness, this situation of need is summed up in the words 'I have sinned against you' (Ps. 41.4), so that *ḥānan*, or God's care and concern for man, also includes the forgiveness of sins.

Against this background the 'priestly' blessing, in which there is a prayer for God's gracious concern, acquires its full significance. 'God be gracious to you (*ḥānan*), my son' (Gen. 43.29), says the patriarch Jacob to Benjamin. In Aaron's blessing (Num. 6.25; see 6.27) the name of Yahweh and his grace is laid upon the people. This is an indication of God's original gracious concern, promised to his people on the basis of a particular covenant. However, God's grace remains a free gift, as Moses, the mediator of the covenant, is told quite firmly: 'I give grace (*ḥānan*) to whom I please, and I show mercy (*raḥam*) to whom I please' (Ex. 33.19). *Ḥānan* in its theological significance should not therefore be connected too closely with the covenant (in contrast to *ḥesed*), because when all this has been said, in its religious significance, *ḥānan* points to God's sovereign freedom in his grace.[6] For all the inequality between divine and human partners, a situation of *ḥānan* implies mutuality. Grace is a matter of setting out together, as we discover from the subtle formulation of Ex. 33.12–23:

> Moses said to the Lord, 'See, thou sayest to me, "Bring up this people"; but thou hast not let me know whom thou wilt send with me. Yet thou hast said, "I know you by name, and you have also found favour in my sight." Now therefore, I pray thee, if I have found favour in thy sight, show me now thy ways, that I may know thee and find favour in thy sight.' Then Yahweh said, 'My presence will go with you, and I will give you rest.' And Moses said to him, 'If thy presence will not go with me, do not carry us up from here. For how shall it be known that I have found favour in thy sight, I and thy people? Is it not in thy going with us?' And the Lord said to Moses, 'This very thing that you have spoken I will do; for you have found favour in my sight, and I know you by name.' And Moses said, 'I pray, show me thy glory.' And he said, 'I will make all my goodness pass before you, and will proclaim before you my name Yahweh; for I will give grace (*ḥesed*) to whom I please and I will show mercy to whom I please. But,' he said, 'you cannot see my face; for man shall not see me and live.'

This text is characteristic of the view of grace held throughout the Tanach: election, favour, setting out together, mutual knowledge of each other's name, the use of familiar forms of address, God's countenance which is turned towards men, towards Israel – God, who looks upon Israel, whereas otherwise this gracious God remains a hidden God, who for the sake of his revelation keeps longing alive in his concealment of himself from Israel. The most intriguing sentence is: 'I will make all my goodness pass before you, and will proclaim before you my name Yahweh; for I will give grace to whom I please.' <u>The text indicates that the name of Yahweh means free and sovereign grace.</u>[7] The God of sovereign freedom is no longer God as arbitrary potentate in the ancient Near East, but the God of Israel, Yahweh, in grace and mercy. Here the Exodus name of God, 'I am who I am' (Ex. 3.14) is therefore explained as: I am there for man as king (*ḥānan*), and also as mother and father (*raḥam*: for the influence of Ex.33.19 see II Kings 13.23; Isa. 30.18; and also probably Isa. 27.11). He is a 'God of men'.

It is striking that the <u>great canonical prophets do not mention God's attitude of *ḥānan* in any way</u> (apart from Amos 5.15, which speaks of God's mercy on the remnant of Joseph after a threat of disaster as an extreme possibility).[8] This shows that for these prophets the central theme is a threat of disaster caused by unfaithfulness to Yahweh, and not God's grace. Judgment is the reverse side of God's grace.

Finally, the critical and productive strength of God's grace is sealed, in the Tanach, in liturgical worship. 'The gracious one' becomes a doxological attribute in the liturgy, to the praise of God, and is expressed in rhyming form: '*raḥūm weḥannūn*: he is a merciful and gracious God' (Ex.34.6). We find this rhyming formula in eleven passages: Ex. 34.6; Joel 2.13; Jonah 4.2; Pss. 86.15; 103.8; 111.4; 112.4; 145.8; Neh. 9.17, 31; II Chron. 30.9. Sometimes it simply appears as *ḥannūn*,[9] but sometimes it is expressed with more exuberance: 'A God merciful and gracious, slow to anger, and abounding in steadfast love and faithfulness' (in *ḥesed* and *'emet*; see also below, Ex. 34.6); this addition means that God's grace remains despite the failure of his people. Liturgical praise also appears in the festal proclamation of the name of Yahweh in the context of the covenant on Sinai (Ex. 34.6; which has influenced Num. 14.18; Joel. 2.13; Jonah 4.2; Pss. 86.15; 103.8; 145.8; Neh. 9.17; in that case, Ex. 34.6 is probably to be understood as a kind of aetiology or 'origin' of this liturgical prayer in the Temple).[10] <u>The experience of God's grace – in itself a matter of dialogue – comes as it were to an antiphonal climax, in liturgical thanksgiving and liturgical praise.</u> This aspect will also prove to be an essential part of the New Testament experience of grace.

### B. The most important derivative of *ḥānan*, the term *ḥēn*

No noun goes with the verb *ḥānan*. The noun *ḥēn* – a substantive infinitive form of the verb *ḥānan* – might best render the range of meanings of *ḥānan* in the noun form: *ḥānan* means to show someone *ḥēn* (favour). Originally this was also the meaning of *ḥēn*, as is clearly shown by a text of Zechariah,

'And I will pour out on the house of David and the inhabitants of Jerusalem a spirit of compassion (*ḥēn*) which will lead them to pray' (Zech. 12.10). However, it is striking that *ḥēn* (only in the singular) is seldom used in sentences of which Yahweh is the subject, and moreover that the Psalms, which are the chief witnesses to the use of *ḥānan*, do not use the word *ḥēn*, apart from a few instances which have no theological significance (Pss. 84.11; 45.2).[11] This detachment from the root meaning of *ḥānan* lies in the fact that with *ḥēn* attention is focused more on someone's attitude or disposition on the basis of which another – always a superior (above all the king: I Sam. 16.22; 27.5; II Sam. 14.22; 16.4; I Kings 11.19; Esther 5.2, 8) – is well disposed towards him. Hence it means to find favour 'in the eyes' of a superior (the royal court is probably the setting for the use of *ḥēn* – though at a later stage this is democratized, e.g. Gen. 32.6).

*Ḥēn* is usually followed by the words 'in the eyes' of: a man is found well pleasing in someone's estimation. The meaning 'look round for', 'take note of' is thus originally also associated with this word derived from *ḥānan*. But in contrast to *ḥānan*, the perspective is not that of the one to whom favour has been showed; it is reversed. Thus *ḥēn* is not always the result, but the object or the reason why someone has pleasure in someone (see II Sam. 15.25). Increasingly the possession of *ḥēn* becomes the reason why someone delights in someone's favour. In other words, the semantic development of *ḥēn* (as opposed to *ḥānan*) tends to exclude the subject who gives the *ḥēn*, expressing only the reason, or a characteristic, on the basis of which a third party is well pleasing to him. Above all in the wisdom literature, this development is taken to the point when *ḥēn* eventually expresses the characteristics of a particular person, and even of animals. It principally expresses charm and elegance, especially in the later wisdom literature, where 'a gazelle with *ḥēn*' simply means a charming, attractive gazelle; similarly with an 'attractive woman' or a glittering necklace (Prov. 11.16; 1.9; 3.22; 4.9) or the happy laughter on the lips of the bridegroom (Ps. 45.2; see 84.11).

True, scholars would want to point to various shades of meaning here, but we might say that the word *ḥēn* has a tendency to depart completely from the basic meaning of *ḥānan*, as the initiative in turning to someone. This is all the more remarkable because the word used by the Septuagint to translate the Hebrew *ḥēn* is in fact *charis* (grace as what a man receives, see below).[12]

Granted, the idea of a gracious encounter does not disappear altogether from the word *ḥēn*, but the focus shifts: *ḥēn* is not the gift of grace which is given in an attitude of *ḥānan*; on the contrary, the possession of *ḥēn* (wherever this may come from) becomes the reason why another person looks with favour on someone who thus finds favour with him. Hence, 'to find grace in the eyes of another', a third person,[13] usually a superior, and finally also God. 'Noah found grace (*ḥēn*) in the eyes of God' (Gen. 6.8; Ex. 33.12, 13, 16, 17). As a result of this shift, *ḥēn* can become a general formula, even a mere expression of courtesy, rather like 'please': if only I find favour in your eyes: 'Kill me, then, if I have found favour in your eyes' (Num. 11.15 = 'please let me die').

This use of *ḥēn*, grace, is very frequent in 'secular' language or in dealings between men. 'Joseph earned respect (approval; found favour, found grace) with him (Potiphar)' (Gen. 39.4); Jacob gives Esau a present so that he may find grace – find favour – with him (Gen. 32.5). What wins another's regard, i.e. *ḥēn*, can in reality be a gift of God, but the word itself does not express that any more. A typical example is that Yahweh grants the Israelites *ḥēn* in the eyes of the Egyptians who give them valuable vessels as presents at the time of the exodus (Ex. 3.21; 11.3; 12.36). In Ps. 84.11 Yahweh gives his people *ḥēn* and *kābōd*, grace and weight, i.e. respect with others (see also Gen. 39.21). There is always a third aspect: be in favour with someone. Thus the distinction between *ḥānan* and *ḥēn* is that even if God is the cause of the *ḥēn* that someone has with a third person, this word does not include the giver in its scope, but the estimation and favourable reaction of a third party. Thus *ḥēn* (*charis*, grace) is not completely detached from the root meaning of *ḥānan*, as being a gracious concern for someone (so Zimmerli); rather, the gracious concern *has shifted* and follows the recognition of someone's possession of *ḥēn*.

This semantic shift in the use of the word *ḥēn* demonstrates an interesting development. As there is no corresponding noun in the semantic field of *ḥānan*, another takes its place. That is the word *ḥesed*. Although it comes from quite a different root from *ḥānan*, it in fact serves as the substantive form of the verb *ḥānan*, be gracious, and means grace.[14] With a few later exceptions (see below), in the Septuagint *ḥesed* is not translated by the Greek *charis*, but by *eleos* (mercy), while on the other hand the Greek verb 'have mercy' (*eleein*) in the Septuagint is the usual translation of *ḥānan*. In other words, this translator clearly saw the connection between *ḥānan* and *ḥesed*, despite the fact that they come from different roots.

## §2   Israel's view of the *ḥesed* and *ʾemet* of God

Theological philologists argue over the term *ḥesed* in the same way that they argue over the real meaning of *ḥānan* and *ḥēn*; theological and confessional motives often have a hidden effect here. Does *ḥesed* point to an interrelationship between rights and duties? Or does *ḥesed* go beyond inter-personal obligations, even a covenant relationship? Furthermore, does *ḥesed* already presuppose a community relationship between two partners or is it the basis for such a community? The etymology of *ḥesed* is very uncertain and does not give any help; it is, however, certain that the basis of the word lies in inter-personal relationships and derives above all from mutual relationships in a fixed sociological group. In reality, *ḥesed* is the attitude and behaviour of members of a group by which the group is given firm cohesion. That does not, however, say much about the view someone has of the character of his own particular group. Since the fundamental study by N. Glück, which has been followed by many exegetes, more recent years have seen a notable swing in interpretation. Many people have followed Glück in saying that *ḥesed* does not mean spontaneous, unmotivated kindness and friendliness, but a way of behaving which results in a relationship which is regulated and governed by rights and duties, such as that between man and wife, parents and children, king and subjects. Applied to God, *ḥesed* then means covenant love. *Ḥesed* in the sense of generous friendliness and kindness would then be a secondary meaning, which arose above all through a connection with *raḥāmim* (kindness) and other more specific words, like *'emet*. *Ḥesed* is then loyalty to the community, i.e. it already *presupposes* a relationship between partners and within this community (say, by the making of a covenant); *ḥesed* is to be found within these parameters. More recent works have abandoned this exaggerated standpoint. As an inter-personal attitude, *ḥesed* is of course connected with community; but that is not to say anything about the nature of *ḥesed*. We should not understand the Hebrew use of *ḥesed* in a human community in terms of our modern conceptuality. *Ḥānan* is primarily concerned with an approach of one person to another and not with a demonstration of fellowship. In *ḥesed*, the perspective of the person showing *ḥesed* is likewise central, but the relationship is never seen in a one-sided way: in essence it calls forth mutuality. That is also the case with *ḥānan*, but the term does not have the same implication as *ḥesed*. There is *ḥesed* between host and guest (Gen. 19.19), between kindred (Gen. 47.29), between confederates (I Sam. 20.8) and also between anyone who has received a favour and the one who has shown the favour (I Kings 20.31; Judg. 1.24; Josh. 2.12, 14). However, the question whether *ḥesed* is the foundation of a community relationship or whether this relationship is the basis of *ḥesed* poses quite a false dilemma. In Gen. 21.23 Abimelech asks Abraham to give him *ḥesed*, as he himself has done in turn, so as to make a covenant with him. In I Sam. 20.8 David refers to the covenant which Jonathan has made with him, and appeals to him to show *ḥesed* now because of this covenant. It is possible to ask for *ḥesed* on the basis of a covenant, and also to ask for a covenant on the basis of the *ḥesed* that has been shown. While a covenant may also point to rights and duties, it does not embody the special significance of *ḥesed*, though it is also evident that this special significance obtains above all between partners who are allied or about to be allied. In other words, *ḥesed* looks for a response in *ḥesed*. This makes clear the mutuality, but not the special significance of it.

*Ḥesed* can be used interchangeably in both singular and plural, above all in later texts (Ps. 106.1, 7, 45; see also Isa. 55.3; 63.7; Pss. 17.7; 25.6, etc.). Thus *ḥesed* is a fundamental attitude which manifests itself in acts of kindness and friendship. Here *ḥesed* implies something special about the mutual relationship, and this special element in fact defines the *ḥesed*. It extends beyond what is obligatory and a matter of course to an inter-personal relationship. In the earlier narrative texts, *ḥesed* points to an unexpected, surprising act of kindness and friendship, to something which could not have been reckoned with (I Kings 20.31; also Gen. 39.21; 40.14; 47.29; 20.13; 21.23; Josh. 2.12; I Sam. 15.6; II Sam. 3.8; 16.17). Such *ḥesed* makes a covenant possible, but is not a presupposition for it. It goes beyond the pattern of action and action in response.

It is very difficult to render *ḥesed* as an inter-personal relationship in modern terminology. Grace and good will are inadequate. <u>By nature *ḥesed*</u> <u>is something that happens tangibly in a specific situation and yet goes</u> <u>beyond it; it is connected with devotion towards someone else's *life* and</u> <u>therefore implies the whole person of the subject of the *ḥesed*.</u> Even if it comes about within given social structures (parents towards children, king towards subjects or between partners in an alliance) it goes beyond the structure of rights and duties. *Ḥesed* is not just good will which proves itself openly in action, but in formal terms generosity, overwhelming, unexpected kindness which is forgetful of itself, completely open and ready for 'the other'. Similar *ḥesed*, i.e. surprising *ḥesed* that goes beyond all duty, may therefore be expected of the receiver of such *ḥesed* or loving devotion. *Ḥesed* is concerned not with mutual relationships but with the *nature* of such relationships: with an abundance of mutual love.

The religious and theological usage of *ḥesed* has its root in this vision of inter-human relationships. It is therefore really a very anthropomorphic usage, but at the same time the most adequate language for saying something about God's attitude towards man, and for hinting at the possible depth of man's response. The central meaning of *ḥesed*, that of expressing the relationship between God and his people, emerges from the fact that *ḥesed* is included in the great hymnic, liturgical predicates of God in which the Tanach celebrates the *nature of God* as that of a 'God of men': Ex. 34.6f.; God is 'a merciful and gracious God, long-suffering and rich in *ḥesed* and *'emet'* (this formula has influenced Num. 14.18; Joel 2.13; Jonah 4.2; Pss. 86.15; 103.8; 145.8; Neh. 9.17). The further elaboration of this *ḥesed* is significant: a God 'who keeps steadfast love down to the thousandth generation, forgiving iniquity and transgression and sin, but who will by no means clear the guilty, visiting the iniquity of the fathers upon the children and the children's children, to the third and the fourth generation' (Ex. 34.7). The contrast lies in the steadfast love 'down to the thousandth generation' (hence the connection of *ḥesed* with *'emet*: faithfulness), whereas punishment does not go further than the fourth generation at most. In the second commandment of the decalogue (Ex. 20.5b–6; see also Deut. 7.9), God's *ḥesed* is mentioned along with his jealousy; he is a jealous God, who is zealous for his rights and therefore punishes those who 'hate' God down to the fifth generation, 'but showing *ḥesed* to the thousandth generation of those who love me and keep my commandments'. *Ḥesed* thus points to the abundance of grace which is richer than the necessary punishment for evil (see Rom. 5.18–21). Furthermore, in this text stress is laid on the abundance of the grace of God, which had already been mentioned in the first commandment (Ex. 20.2), and connected with Yahweh's age-old demonstration of *ḥesed*: the salvation brought about by the exodus from Egypt. So God is, so he was and so he always will be: an abundance of grace. Genesis 32.9–12, a prayer of Jacob's, is an apt expression of this Tanach spirituality as seen by Yahwistic faith. Israel is confident in the faith that Yahweh will as it were imperceptibly accompany the course of the sinful world – we have already come across 'set out together' in connection with *ḥānan* – and will finally bring it into a secure haven. The whole of this belief is expressed by *ḥesed*. 'You meant evil; but God meant it for good' (see Gen. 50.20). This surprising and miraculous characteristic of God's *ḥesed* is expressed above all in the Psalms (of the 237 passages where *ḥesed* is mentioned, 127 occur in the Psalms). *Ḥesed* is therefore also associated with wonders (Ps. 107.8, 15, 21, 31), and the pious Jew prays 'for the wonder of the grace (*ḥesed*) of God' (Pss. 17.7; 31.21). The divine *ḥesed* is the wider background against which every individual demonstration of God's grace shines forth (and therefore it is also in the plural: Pss. 6.4; 25.6f.; 31.16; 44.26; 69.16; 109.21, 26; 119.88, 124, 149, 159). The Jew turns to this *ḥesed* in prayer in order to be heard (Ps. 119.149), for rescue (Ps. 109.26), and redemption (Pss. 44.26; 130.7), for support to life (Ps. 119.88, 159) and for forgiveness (Ps. 25.7). As a parallel term to *ḥesed* we sometimes also find *yᵉšuaʿ*, i.e help, or any form of salvation (Ps. 36.10; 103.17). Because man is sinful, God's *ḥesed* also acquires the meaning of mercy and the forgiveness of sins (Ps. 86.5; Ex. 34.7a; Neh. 9.17). Grace is also the forgiveness of sins.

This abundant and constantly faithful *ḥesed* of Yahweh is often expressed in a double formula which is also known in 'secular' terminology, but is used above all in connection with God. This formula is *ḥesed weᵉmet*, God's graciousness and faith or dependability (above all in the Psalms: 25.10; 40.12; 57.3, 10; 85.10; 89.14; 138.2; – Pss. 61.7; 86.15; 115.1; – Gen. 24.27; see 24.49; 32.10; 47.29; – Ex. 34.6; II Sam. 2.6; 15.20; – Prov. 3.3; 14.22; 16.6; 20.28). With the exception of Hos. 4.1; Micah 7.20; Ps. 89.24, *ḥesed* always appears in first place, which is one reason why W. Zimmerli[15] asserts that *ᵉmet* is a closer definition of *ḥesed*, i.e. promised *ḥesed*, *ḥesed* given under oath, God's everlasting love (this is probably the meaning of the double formula in Josh. 2.14; II Sam. 15.20; Prov. 3.3; 14.22; 16.6; 20.28). However, the arguments of A. Jepsen[16] and above all H. Wildenberger[17] seem more convincing. They do not always see the double formula as a hendiadys, but as a mention of two independent qualities of God, namely his love and his reliability (above all Ps. 85.10f., where *ḥesed* and *ᵉmet* meet each other and are clearly seen as 'two partners'); also Ps. 89.14, where *ḥesed* and *ᵉmet* stand before God's throne almost as two hypostases. When applied to man and God, *ᵉmet* means someone on whose words, acts and love one can rely; someone on whom one can build: reliability with the connotation of truthfulness (from the root *ʾmn*, giving firmness, security, and therefore also permanence). Because people are often unreliable and false, *ᵉmet* is used above all of God: he is an *ēl* *ᵉmet*, a faithful and reliable God, a God on whom men can rely (Ps. 31.5), even an eternal God (Ps. 146.6). God is rich in *ḥesed* and *ᵉmet* (Ex. 34.6; Ps. 86.14), and above all his words are reliable (II Sam. 7.28; Ps. 132.11, etc., chiefly Ps. 119 as a hymn of praise to the reliability and eternal validity of God's commandments). For this reason, in prayer man can also refer to God's *ᵉmet*: his *ḥesed* and *ᵉmet* are a shield and a protection (Pss. 91.4; 40.11).

The Septuagint usually translates *ᵉmet* as truth (*alētheia*) and less often as *pistis* (trust, reason for trust or reliability); rightly according to some interpreters, but wrongly according to more recent philologists. It is, however, the case that 'truth' (reason for reliability) is one of the root meanings of *'mn* and *"met*, and when used of men, it can often be rendered as truth. Used of God, *"met* always means faithfulness, eternal validity and reliability (also in Isa. 59.14f.; Pss. 25.5; 19.9; 119). Only in the book of Daniel does *"met*, used in connection with God, acquire the specific meaning of God's revealed truth (Dan. 8.26; 10.1; 11.2), indeed of God's being true (Dan. 8.12; perhaps Eccles. 12.10 and especially Ps. 51.6 already point in this direction).[18]

To begin with, there was little explicit reflection on man's consistent response to God's *hesed*, though this was specifically implied in connection with God's *hesed* in 'those who love me' (Ex. 20.6; Deut. 5.10). Hosea above all pays attention to this involvement, which he expresses in the image of Yahweh's bethrothal to his people (Hos. 2.19). Yahweh's 'steadfast goodness, mercy and faithfulness' are his dowry. Here we have a connection between *hesed* and *rahāmīm* which becomes more frequent as time goes on. (*Rehem* means a mother's womb, Jer. 20.17; the soft part in man, Gen. 43.30. *Rahāmīm* is its abstract plural, i.e. the attractive, natural, emotional love of a mother for her child, thus mercy; Hos. 11.8; Gen. 43.30; I Kings 3.26; Prov. 12.10; Isa. 63.15. It is regularly used of the relationship between a superior and an inferior.) Through its connection with *rahāmīm*, God's *hesed* acquires the meaning of a tender, almost vulnerable motherly love. This emerges above all in Hosea. But this connection in a double formula becomes more frequent (Jer. 16.5; Zech. 7.9; Pss. 25.6; 40.11; 103.4; Dan. 1.9; in a looser association, Ps. 69.17). Yahweh's free and heartfelt approach to Israel is the basis of the covenant (Hos. 2.19). For this reason he also expects *hesed* from Israel, as a grateful recognition of what Yahweh has done. In his speech against the people, this prophet cries: 'There is no *"met* (faithfulness) or kindness, and no knowledge of God in the land' (4.1f.); 'Your (=Israel's) *hesed* is like the dew that goes early away' (6.4). Thus a mutuality is required in *hesed*: grace, *hesed*, is a mutual bond of love between God and people. But on the foundation of Yahweh's dowry this mutality is itself a grace; and this mutuality seems to lie in *hesed* and *"met* towards the fellow man, the kinsman among the people.[19] God's *hesed* is a presupposition and at the same time a model for Israel's mutual *hesed* (Hos. 10.12); 'be as good as God'. Hosea also sums this up in a twofold formula: 'love and righteousness' (12.6). While the accent lies on inter-human relationships, this is realized as mutual *hesed* in the face of God (see also 'practise *hesed* and justice' in Micah 6.8).

Following Hosea, Jeremiah refers to the honeymoon period long ago (Jer. 2.2), a time in connection with which Deut 6.5; 11.1 also stressed Israel's love for God. Here it is evident that in itself *ḥesed* is not synonymous with faithfulness (since Israel forsook the love of its youth), but refers formally to the spontaneous generosity and involvement in the self-offering. Jer. 31.3 again stresses that God's *ḥesed* is always the presupposition of a human response. In addition to Hos. 6.6; 10.12; 12.6; Jer. 9.24; 16.5; 31.3 and Deutero-Isaiah (Isa. 54.8–10) refer to the mutuality of *ḥesed*. This is also the case with *ᵉmet*, or constant faithfulness: 'Fear the Lord and serve him with *ᵉmet*' (I Sam. 12.24; see also Pss. 15.2; 145.18; I Kings 2.4). But human *ᵉmet* is a rarity. Therefore mutual faithfulness is an eschatological vision of the future: one day Jerusalem will be called a city of *ᵉmet* (Zech. 8.3), a city on which God can rely (for Isa. 10.20 this relates to a remnant in Israel).

However, it is striking that the mutuality of *ḥesed* and *ᵉmet* rarely defines directly the relationship of man *to God*. The human response to God's grace and faithfulness is on the one side praise of God because of his *ḥesed* (this is also true of his *ᵉmet*), and on the other love, faithfulness and truthfulness towards one's fellow man (mutual *ᵉmet* connected directly with God appears only in individual later texts: II Chron. 31.20; 32.1). The question of human *ḥesed* as a response to God's *ḥesed* is put particularly sharply in Genesis 24 and the book of Ruth. If men live in the sphere of God's gracious love, they must also be prepared to show *ḥesed* to *one another* (Gen. 24.49; Ruth 1.8; 3.10). God's love for us is the basis of love for our neighbour in which mutuality between God and man takes on concrete form. That is why it is sometimes said that the human answer to God's *ḥesed* lies in *ṣᵉdāqā*, righteousness (in the Israelite community of faith: I Kings 3.6); this culminates in salvation and peace, wholeness of life for the community and within it. Still, the great commandment to love God with all one's heart (Deut. 6.5; 10.12; 11.13; 13.4; 30.6), which also indicates the completeness and profundity of the self-surrender suggested by the word *ḥesed*, also has to do with God's own *ḥesed*. In later texts this profundity and grace in God's *ḥesed* is often emphasized by a regular connection with *tūb* (goodness) or *tōb* (good) (Ex. 33.19 with 34.6; Isa. 63.7; Pss. 69.16; 100.5; 106.1; 107.1; 118.1,2,3,4,29; 136.1–26; Ezra 3.11).

However, in addition to remembering this *ḥesed* (Ps. 106.7), meditating on it (Ps. 48.9), understanding it (Ps. 107.43; grace and the knowledge of God belong together) and looking out for God's gracious help (Pss. 33.18, 22; 147.11), man's real response to God's love and faithfulness lies above all in the *doxology* in which he gives thanks and praise for

Yahweh's gracious *ḥesed* and *ᵉmet*. Grace culminates in liturgy, as this is to be found in a number of doxological formulae, above all in the antiphonal refrain 'for his *ḥesed* (overwhelming goodness) abides for ever' (Ps. 136; Ps. 107). According to the writings of the Chronicler, 'Give thanks to Yahweh for he is good; for his *ḥesed* lasts for ever' rings out in all liturgical gatherings (I Chron. 16.34; II Chron. 5.13; 7.3, 6; Ezra 3.11); this praise can be heard even in time of war (II Chron. 20.21). Consequently '*the* day' also, the day at the end of the ages, will be celebrated as a day on which the hymn of praise to Yahwe's *ḥesed* will break out (Jer. 33.11; see Sir. 51.12). God's gracious love is therefore a summons to joy (Pss. 31.7; 90.14; 101.1; 138.2). It is therefore possible to speak extravagantly in temporal and spatial images of God's grace and loving-kindness; of the greatness of the *ḥesed* which fills the earth (Pss. 33.5; 119. 64) and reaches to heaven (Pss. 36.6; 57.11; 103.11; 108.5); of an everlasting *ḥesed* (Pss. 89.2; 103.17; 138.8). Hence *ᵉmet* too (often together with *ḥesed*) is an object of praise (Isa. 38.19; Pss. 40.11; 57.10; 71.22; 108.4; 115.1; 117.2; 138.2).

This question of mutuality brings us to the relationship between *ḥesed* and *bᵉrīt*, gracious love and covenant, or covenant love. Characteristic of this is the infrequent expression *habbᵉrīt wehaḥesed*, the covenant and *ḥesed* (Deut. 7.9,12; I Kings 8.23; Dan. 9.4; Neh. 1.5; 9.32; II Chron. 6.14). There is specific reflection on the relationship between grace (*ḥesed*) and covenant above all in Deuteronomy (5.10; 7.9,12) and the texts dependent on it. However, it is not that *ḥesed* is an attitude resulting from the covenant (though in fact this too is the case), since above all in the earlier texts of Deuteronomy *bᵉrīt*, covenant, is subordinated to Yahweh's oath to the patriarchs; the covenant itself has its foundation in Yahweh's free resolve to love: Deut. 7.8 puts the love of God first. The link between *ḥesed* and covenant continues to occur in the Deuteronomistic literature. So *ḥesed* should not be translated everywhere as covenant love. In I Kings 8.21, 23 the covenant becomes 'the binding document of a historical covenant',[20] but that is already qualified in 8.23. In Ps. 89.28 and 89.2f. the covenant is based on the foundation of God's *ḥesed*, and not the other way round. The covenant is just one expression of the divine *ḥesed*, albeit a fundamental one.

However, the covenant is only realized completely in a mutual relationship: 'With everlasting goodness I have had mercy on you, says Yahweh, your Redeemer . . . so I have sworn that I will not be angry with you and will not rebuke you . . . My steadfast love shall not depart from you, and my covenant of peace shall not be removed, says Yahweh, who has compassion on you'; thus Deutero-Isaiah (Isa. 54.8–10). But this peace, which comprises *ḥesed* and *ᵓᵉmet*, implies Israel's conversion to God: 'On a foundation of righteousness you shall be built' (Isa. 54.14). The final realization of this conversion is eschatological: in the new covenant (Isa. 55).

In the last resort, the concept of grace in the spirituality of the Tanach comes up against a limit: 'Can man tell of God's *ḥesed* in death, or of thy faithfulness in the underworld?' (Ps. 88.11). As long as there is no prospect of eternal life, Yahweh's *ḥesed* seems to know a limit. However, the believing Psalmist does not feel this as a limit: 'Your *ḥesed* is worth more than life itself' (Ps. 63.3). This spirituality comes up against the problem of death where the love of God as a historical object has an end. However, as long as there is life, it is true that 'I will not look darkly upon you, for I am *ḥāsîd*' (Jer. 3.12), i.e. someone who exercises *ḥesed*.[21] Finally, in life or death, 'your hand will hold me' (Ps. 63.8). An unexpected perspective which even transcends death becomes the last and supreme possibility of the divine *ḥesed*.

*Conclusion: The spirituality of grace in the Tanach*

As a result of an investigation of the technical and linguistic forms in which Israel's experience of grace and salvation are expressed, we can say that God's loving-kindness and grace are seen primarily not as an inner disposition in God but as God's love towards men, which is revealed in acts which are surprising and unexpected demonstrations of love. Yet God's loving-kindness also transcends any individual demonstration of love, which is to say that God's *ḥesed* is above all his intervention for the whole of human life. Israel uses words from ordinary everyday conversation in order to express this. *Ḥānan* stresses God's gracious approach, in which the emphasis lies on God's concern for men, above all on his care for and solidarity with the weaker and the oppressed, with those in need. By contrast, *ḥesed* points above all to a love which is extended beyond any call of duty, to an unmerited abundance of love which is, however, taken as self-evident within a community relationship, both from the side of God and from the side of men, as an answer to the one who has first loved us. A historical response to the abundant loving-kindness of God's love must be given in our righteousness and love for our neighbours. Even in passages in which *ḥesed* retains the specific meaning of covenant love, the priority of God's initiative of love is strongly stressed (though sometimes there is also the subsidiary idea that God must reward the observance of his commandments with *ḥesed* or favour).

God's abundance of grace, his faithfulness and reliability, are so central to Israel's spirituality that 'grace and faithfulness' become the fundamental predicates of God in liturgy and doxology: God is gracious and reliable, a God who cares for men, a God of men. However, he remains sovereign and free. But this freedom is a freedom of love, not of whim; the other side of grace is therefore judgment. God's love and reliability – his grace – become as it were a hypostasis: Yahweh sends grace like an ambassador to men (Ps. 57.3); grace comes to meet men (Ps. 59.10, 16f.; 89.14; 85.10) and follows them on their ways (Ps. 23.6).

Grace is experienced; it can be found in a relationship of prayer. On the side of the man who receives grace, this dialogical structure culminates on the one hand in the true response of ethical and religious activity for the salvation, well-being and peace of the whole people of God – righteousness and love towards the neighbour – and on the other in doxological liturgy, that is in joyful thanksgiving and praise to God. Thus grace has both an ethical and a mystical-liturgical dimension.

Because man is a sinner, God's approach in grace also has the significance of mercy, mercifulness and the forgiveness of sins. But God's grace comprises more: God is ready for every help and every fragment of salvation or *yᵉšuaʿ* (see Pss. 36.10; 103.17).

Although the man who receives grace is somewhat confused by the perspective of death and the ultimate threat, despite everything he remains capable of believing in God's ultimate love of man and his reliability: 'Your hand will hold me' (Ps. 63.8; see 63.3).[22]

Chapter 2

# Early Jewish reinterpretation within the Hellenistic concept of *charis*

## §1   Hellenistic *charis*

Jews faithful to Yahweh, who lived in the Diaspora in a chiefly Greek-speaking environment and even used Greek as their own everyday language, felt obliged to translate their Hebrew Bible into Greek. As a result, the spirituality of the Tanach became closely connected with the religious terminology of Hellenism. With what Greek words were they to render the Jewish spirituality of grace? And what is the specific Greek significance of these words? The particular content of the meaning of Greek words can make the originally Hebrew Bible richer or poorer by the introduction of new meanings.

Strikingly, in the Septuagint *charis* is not the rendering of the Hebrew *ḥesed* (except in some later parts of this translation, see below), but of *ḥēn*, which has become furthest removed from the concept of grace, whereas *ḥesed* is usually translated by *eleos* (mercy, mercifulness). Thus in the Septuagint, *charis* is virtually insignificant as a theological term for grace. New Testament *charis* has little or nothing to do with *ḥēn* in the sense of the Septuagint *charis*; its connection is entirely with the Hebrew *ḥesed* (in the Septuagint, *eleos*). How does it happen that *charis* in the Septuagint does not render the concept of grace? To answer this question, we must first trace out the Greek meaning of *charis*.

In Greek, *charis* and *chairō* (delight in) have one and the same root, *char-*, that is, something which glitters or shines and which as a result delights men or moves them: something in which they have joy and pleasure. Thus in an objective sense *char-* is something or someone which seems pleasant; in the subjective sense, to find pleasure in, to desire something or enjoy something; to find it – whether words, actions, persons or things – attractive; to delight in it; to enjoy something or 'desire' it (which also involves the root *char-*); to be entertained by something. This basic meaning is to be found throughout the whole semantic field of *charis* in Greek. As a result, three fundamental meanings can be seen: (*a*) *charis* is something which brings, joy, whereas *chara* (joy) represents the reaction which is produced. Therefore *charis* is charm, attraction, 'grace', something that makes a pleasant impression. The point here is not so much that a thing, actions, words or persons are beautiful and attractive (though this is presupposed), but rather that this 'dazzling' is itself enjoyable; it is a matter of the enjoyable and attractive impression made by elegance, beauty and charm. In this sense *charis* is the expression of a typically Greek view of life. In connection with this meaning, *charis* also takes on the sense of the enjoyable favour of destiny (symbolized in the three *charites* or graces). (*b*) In direct association with this *charis* means affection, kindness, favour, benevolence, taking care of someone. This can be both active, above all when used of an emperor or official towards his subjects (this is where there is a real connection with the Hebrew *ḥānan*), and passive, i.e. *charis* is the favour received, the gift or the alms or the benefit or the sympathy received by someone from another – always as an act of goodness which brings joy. (*c*) The consequence of this is that, according to this Greek view of life, *charis* also looks for a response. *Charis* (a demonstration of love) summons up *charis*, which is gratitude, expressed in an active response to the graciousness of the giver. This leads to the more or less threadbare expression *tois theois charis*, or 'Thank God (the gods)'. In contrast to Hebrew *ḥesed*, with the Greek *charis* the idea of an obligatory recompense *(charis)* evidently comes more into the foreground, though this obligation does not seem to be primary. Thanks is *gratia reddita*, thanks-giving, returning the *charis* received as it were in the form of thanks (the recompense lies in the gratitude). Greek writers (and Paul, too) play on these two meanings of *charis* – as 'grace' (favour) and 'pay homage' (Sophocles; Aristotle).[23]

These secular meanings also go with a religious usage in Greek: the favour of the gods. However, in non-biblical Greek, *charis* is not a central religious concept, far less an explicit philosophical term. Only with the Stoics does the divine *charis* become a central concept: Cleanthes even wrote a book, now lost, with the title *Peri charitos* (On love as grace). From echoes of it we know that in it the emphasis lay on the disposition of benevolence. *Charis* adds to *aretē*, the Greek virtue which characterizes the strong and good man, the aspect of bringing joy, the attractiveness of virtue *(kalokagathia*, i.e. *kalos kai agathos*, the good paired with the beautiful which delights the eyes – the estimation); *charis* is the charm of true virtuousness. It is striking that the Stoa speaks of God's grace (the *charis* of God), but is unfamiliar with God's anger.

In the Greek of the later, imperial period, *charis* undergoes a striking development in two directions (which is not without its significance for the Greek New Testament'. (*a*) In the imperial period *charis* becomes a regular expression for showing favour or the promotion of someone by the emperor (e.g. a legal concession or subvention) or by a senior official. In this sense there is often also mention of the emperor's *philanthropia* (cf. Tit. 3.4). *Charites*, then, are favours shown,[24] whereas *charis* (in the singular) refers rather to a gracious or favourable disposition. One particular case of (imperial) favour or *charis*, albeit in the juristic sense, is 'clemency', bestowing grace, namely liberation or remission of a punishment. (In the New Testament, Barabbas is thus 'favoured' in the Gospel of Luke.) (*b*) A second but, in my mind, doubtful development is thought by many scholars to take place in the Greek of late antiquity: *charis* (grace; favour) becomes synonymous with power in the sense of a 'power from above', from other-wordly, supernatural spheres. True, classical Greek (e.g. Euripides) was familiar with the power of *charis* or the demonstration of love, but now things change; *charis* is a concept of power with an essentially religious significance: a power which comes down over certain men from the world above. In that case (in contrast to classical Greek), *charis* becomes a specifically religious concept. The *dynamis* of grace *(virtus gratiae)* is an ethereal power of grace which is said to be manifested above all through miracle-workers. In that case *charis* manifests itself as a supernatural power in miracles, acts of power and witchcraft. It is this last aspect which seems to be to be doubtful. Liddell and Scott do not give this meaning, but they recognize *charis* in the sense of an act of homage which men owe to demons.[25] There is talk of the power of grace in men of God in the later Hermetica and in gnosticism;[26] whether *charis* is used here in connection with miracles and witchcraft does, however, seem to me to be doubtful.

When we compare this Greek concept of *charis* with the semantic field of the Hebrew *ḥesed, ḥānan* and *ḥēn*, we can see striking affinities coupled with considerable differences. First of all, *charis* is not, like *ḥesed*, also a specifically religious term in classical Greek. But the affinity between the Hebrew *ḥēn* and the Greek *charis* is striking; that is one reason why the Septuagint prefers *charis* to *eleos* for translating *ḥēn*. The fact that it prefers to render *ḥānan* and *ḥesed* by *eleos*, indicates that it does not consider the classical Greek *charis* to be appropriate. In the divine *ḥesed* and in his showing of *ḥānan* to man, God is not influenced by the 'brilliant' properties which he sees in man, but his approach to man in love makes man 'well-pleasing'. Furthermore, this Greek *charis* never has the significance of the forgiveness of sins (only in the Greek of the imperial period does *charis* also have the meaning of acquittal; this influences the inter-testamental literature and also the New Testament). Imperial Greek in particular is more inclined to translate *ḥesed* with *charis*, and with the completion of the Septuagint that will also come to influence Greek-speaking Jews. Quite apart from that, however, the Greek *charis* seems to be too 'humanistic' to be able to render a high-sounding religious concept like *ḥesed*. Still, the specific question is: how did the translators of the Septuagint regard it themselves? And did the special character of the Greek terminology influence the spirituality of grace in the Greek-Jewish interpretation of the Tanach? Finally, after this translation did a further development take place in the literature of Greek-speaking Jews, which might explain the New Testament use of *charis*?

## §2    The concept of grace in the Septuagint and in early Jewish literature

We have already pointed out that the term *ḥesed*, which has strong religious connotations, above all in the Psalms, is not translated in the Septuagint by the Greek word *charis*, but by *eleos*, mercy. There are only three exceptions: Esther 2.9; 2.17 (in both cases 'find favour with someone'); Sir. 7.33 (*charis domatos*; favouring with a gift) and 40.17 (*charis* is like a blessed paradise). Seen in a wider traditio-historical context, these later Septuagintal texts are symptomatic. For it is striking that in later Greek translations of the Bible (after Christ, Symmachus and, say, Theodotion) as opposed to the Septuagint, the Hebrew *ḥesed* is very often translated by *charis* while at the same time it is a fact that a Greek-speaking Jew prefers to render *ḥesed* by *charis* and not, like the Septuagint, by *eleos*. These facts clearly indicate that at the time of the completion of the Septuagint, and even more afterwards, a Greek-Jewish tendency arose to translate the Hebrew *ḥesed* by *charis*, in contradiction to the Septuagint. This Jewish tendency finds confirmation in the New Testament, or better, as far as the usage of *charis* is concerned, the New Testament stands in a historical process in which *ḥesed* is increasingly translated by *charis* rather than by *eleos*. This must be connected with the historical fact that the Greek *charis* became popular in the religious sense only at the time of, and particularly after, the completion of the Septuagint. This certainly happened among Greek-speaking Jews, though it was not the case in classical Greek.

According to a somewhat dated work by G. Wetter (1913),[27] this shift in the Greek concept of *charis* is connected with the Emperor cult, which had arisen in the meantime: it runs parallel to the use of the title *Kyrios* for the Emperor. It appears from papyri of the time that Diaspora Jews, too, used *charis* in an explicit religious sense (unknown in classical Greek). According to this approach, the theological meaning of *charis*, grace (as a rendering of the strongly religious, Jewish, *ḥesed*), is said to have arisen as a result of foreign Jewish influences on Christianity. Is that really the case?

As we have already said, apart from some non-theological exceptions, *ḥēn* (Septuagint *charis*) was not used in the Psalms, which by contrast are the chief evidence of the spirituality of *ḥesed*, grace, in the Tanach. However, the use of *ḥēn* in this sense is all the more striking in the wisdom literature, which on the whole is much later. Here the term often appears in the meaning of a property or an attitude on the basis of which something or someone is attractive in the eyes of another, pleases the other and influences him favourably (a typical special meaning both of the Hebrew *ḥēn* and the Greek *charis*). True, in the Hebrew Tanach this meaning is repeatedly found in connection with God ('be well-pleasing in the eyes of God'), but it is striking that in the Jewish literature after the Septuagint, this term 'be well-pleasing to God' undergoes a special new development. 'Those who fear the Lord will find *charis*' (Symmachus: Sir. 32.16; but already Sir. 35.20 = 35.16: 'He who serves God according to his well-pleasing finds *charis* with him'). *Charis* is seen increasingly clearly as the *coming reward* for the God-fearers or the righteous. 'Those who trust in God will understand truth, and the faithful will abide in his love, because *charis* and *eleos* will be upon his elect' (Wisdom 3.9); also 'His soul was pleasing to the Lord, therefore he took him quickly from the midst of wickedness . . . *Charis* and *eleos* will be with his elect' (Wisdom 4.14f.) At another place in this wisdom literature we read, 'For *charis* was not given him by the Lord, since he is lacking in all wisdom' (Sir. 37.21). In significant manuscripts of Prov. 8.17 we read, 'Those who seek wisdom will reap *charis*'. It is already clear from these texts that *charis* and *eleos* are used in parallel, more clearly than in the Septuagint, and that both refer as it were to the eschatological reward of the elect.

This fairly new tendency is heightened in apocalyptic literature. On the one hand, *charis* is the eschatological reward of the righteous; on the other it is as it were the all-embracing word for 'coming salvation'. In the Greek Enoch it is said that the unrighteous have no *charis* (99.13). What *charis* means here is complicated, because on the one hand it is 'formalized', and on the other it becomes a term within a series of concepts relating to salvation: peace *(eirēnē)*, *eleos* (mercy), *sōtēria* (salvation), *phōs* (light), *zōē* (life), *agialliasis* (joy) and among them *charis* (Greek Enoch 5.4–8; cf. 1.8, a similar and shorter list). All are quite abstract but interchangeable terms, among which *charis* has a tendency to 'sum everything up'. The later Christian *Didache* is an illuminating witness to this; with a clear allusion to 'Thy kingdom come' in the Lord's Prayer, it remarks: 'May your *charis* come, and the world pass away' (*Didache* 10.6). In this interchangeable culture, abstract words like *eleos, charis* and *eirēnē* (peace) can easily be varied (as is also clear from the greetings contained in private or 'official' letters).

Another striking feature is the formation of quite particular combinations of terms: *charis* (grace), 'knowledge' (light and life) and sinning-no-more, keeping the Law or God's commandments, form a constantly recurring conglomeration which is certainly not a chance one. Above all, *charis* and *gnōsis* (knowledge), and *charis* and obeying the Law, sinning-no-more, attract one another.[28] This has been seen as an indication of Hellenizing intellectualism, but such a view overlooks the particular situation of religiously committed Greek-speaking Diaspora Jews who adopted an apologetic and proselytizing attitude to an alien world and found sympathizers among the Gentiles. Their apologetic and proselytism was based on the spirituality of the Jewish Tanach, but expressed in such a way that it could be made comprehensible to those who spoke Greek. This tendency begins clearly with Sirach and continues throughout Alexandrian Judaism. Stress is laid on the higher wisdom revealed by God, in contrast to the rational wisdom of the Greeks. Whereas Job 28 says that wisdom cannot be fathomed by men, but remains hidden in God, Prov. 8.22–31 asserts that wisdom can be found by those who seek her honestly. Instead of being God's exclusive favourite (Prov. 8.30), wisdom becomes a royal host, teacher of those men who heed her call (Prov. 9.13; 9.4ff.). Thus wisdom has a mediating role in revelation. The revelation of divine salvation takes place through the personal call of wisdom (Prov. 1–9). She is the mediatrix of revelation.[29]

Under the influence of Hellenism and at the same time in connection with the proselytizing apologetic of Diaspora Judaism, revealed wisdom becomes connected with wisdom at creation. Yahweh creates 'with wisdom and insight' (Prov. 3.19; see Job 38–42; Pss. 104.24; 136.5). Wisdom is created before everything (Sir. 1.4,9,10a; Job 28.27). In Sir. 24.5f. wisdom has a universal, cosmic significance; it becomes a kind of world Logos (an all-pervading wisdom which is the rational principle of the world and at the same time – in true Greek fashion – an ethical norm). However, the point of Jewish apologetic is that this universal wisdom is identified by Sirach with the Jewish Law, the Torah – God's *charis* or grace to Israel.[30] 'All this is the book of the covenant of the Most High God, the law which Moses commanded us as an inheritance for the congregations of Jacob' (Sir. 24.23). In other words, cosmic (Greek) wisdom is connected on the Jewish side with Israel's history and the gift of the Torah to Israel: this limits the universal accessibility of wisdom to all men, and is also a reason for the insertion 'for those who love her (wisdom)': 'She dwells with all flesh according to his gift, and he supplied her to those who love him' (Sir. 1.10). This tension between the universality of grace and Israel's exclusive possession of it can also be seen in Sir. 24.6–8. Contrast: 'In the waves of the sea, in the whole earth, and in every people and nation I (= wisdom) have gotten a possession' (24.6): and, 'I sought a resting place among all these . . . Then the Creator of all things gave me a commandment, and the one who created me assigned a place for my tent and said, "Make your dwelling in Jacob, and in Israel receive your inheritance' "(24.7f.). In other words, the wisdom which holds good for all men is given as the *charis* of the election of the God of Israel. Here an earlier datum, 'Keep them (Yahweh's rules and commands) and do them; for that will be your wisdom and your understanding in the sight of the peoples' (Deut. 4.6), is taken up and used in a wisdom context (see Pss. 1 and 119, which also probably come from the third century BC). The identification of hypostatized wisdom with the Jewish Torah is especially clear in the Septuagint translation of Prov. 8.22–31 (which differs markedly from the Hebrew text). Revealed wisdom is pre-existent and is at the same time the instrument by which God accomplishes his creation. The ways of *wisdom* are ways of *life* (8.35). This is really a reference to the Torah.[31] In a wisdom psalm incorporated into Baruch, which was originally written in Hebrew, Diaspora Judaism is addressed and presented with 'the law of life' (Bar. 3.9); Israel has 'abandoned the source of wisdom' (3.12). 'Where *understanding* is, strength and *insight*, there you find *life* . . . *light* for the eyes and *peace*' (3.14). 'Who has ascended to heaven to bring wisdom down from there, and who has brought her down here from above the clouds?' (3.29). '. . . All the ways to knowledge come from him (= our God): he has shown it to his servant Jacob, to Israel whom he loved. After that she appeared on earth (*ōphthē*) and lived among men' (3.37f.). 'She is the *book of the commandments of God*, she is the law which lasts for ever. Those who follow her attain life' (4.1). 'Happy are we, Israel! We have been shown what pleases God (we know what pleases God)' (4.4). This is a hymn to Israel's wisdom, which comes from God and far exceeds Greek wisdom. The Law is a light (Sir. 45.17; Bar 4.2; see also Test. Lev. 14.4; 19.1; IV Ezra 14.20f.; II (Syr.) Bar. 59.2).[32]

In this wisdom literature, wisdom, revelation, insight and knowledge, life, following God's commandments or the Law, light and peace are concepts which all have an inner connection. In the last resort they are associated with God's *charis* to Israel: the gift of the Law which can either be ignored or followed – for man is free. However, God recompenses every man in accordance with his works. In these Diaspora circles, which were open to the Gentiles with an eye to winning them over, proselytism or the entry of Gentiles into the Jewish synagogue was seen in the perspective of these speculations about wisdom = Torah. In this missionary-catechetical situation the older expression 'find grace with God' becomes as it were a theme or a typical expression for the gracious act of the divine election of the Gentiles, the 'God-fearers', who are converted to the Jewish religion. They are now given the grace of the wisdom of the revelation of God to Israel.[33]

The connection of *charis* with the revelation of mysteries hidden with God and consequently with a knowledge of revealed wisdom became a special theme for Jews in the Hellenistic period, both in the newer sapiential apocalyptic and in Hasidic or early apocalyptic[34] (the theme can also be found in Paul). However, it acquires a specific significance in the Graeco-Jewish missionary situation of the Diaspora. Non-Jews receive knowledge of and a share in God's revelation to Israel, Israel's creed and its ethics (good works). This event is seen in a special way as God's *charis*. Abraham, the father of all believers, becomes the model of election and justification 'by grace', even before the Christian period. *Charis* is the great grace of the conversion of a Gentile to the faith of Israel, to Israel's wisdom or revelation of God.[35] Thus a connection is drawn between *charis* or grace and justification through faith in the God of Israel – specifically, in the divine *charis*-gift of the Law, in Greek Judaism even in the period before Paul. *Charis* and conversion, or justification by grace, namely the grace of the Law, are expressed in this early Jewish literature by the formula 'find grace with God'. Thus *charis* or grace are preferred above all (without excluding further sanctification) to describe that one great moment in which a Gentile receives the revelation or 'saving doctrine' (creed and ethics) of the religion of Israel in faith (without excluding further sanctification). (Preparation is made here for the New Testament idea, which is especially characteristic of Paul, of the connection between election, conversion, justification and baptism into Christianity. However, here it is Christ, and not the Law, which is the decisive point. Nevertheless, the theme has already appeared in Judaism.) Thus *charis*, grace, becomes an equivalent of conversion from sin to Yahweh, the one true God of Israel and through Israel of all nations. In such a context *charis* essentially contains knowledge of the true revelation (in the sense of *gnōsis* or *epignōsis*).

In contrast to what Wetter once claimed, as far as the concept of grace is concerned, we can discover no alien Jewish influence in the New Testament. What we find is the influence of a more fully developed Jewish concept of grace which had its *Sitz im Leben* in the catechetical and apologetic missionary situation of Diaspora Judaism (a Hellenistic-Jewish concept of *charis*, the explicit religious significance of which was 'made easier' by the increasing religious significance of the Greek *charis* in the time of the empire).

In the same way, it was in the spirituality of Diaspora Judaism that there was increasing discussion of the conflict between 'from grace' and 'from works'. This was a typically Jewish problem area in these circles. True, Israel had been elected on the basis of the divine gift of the Torah or the Law; in this respect, Jewish sinners were essentially different from Gentiles, who do not know Israel's God and Israel's Law. However, within Israel there is only a small group of the 'truly righteous', who do 'works of righteousness' and will receive God's *charis* as a reward according to their works.[36] *But*: Israel's God is rich in mercy; he has mercy on those Jews whose hands are empty of good works, and above all he has mercy on the Gentiles who do not know any good works because they do not even have the Law. He justifies the sinners freely. The possession of the Law is election, the divine *charis* – an early Jewish version of the *ḥesed* of Yahweh which rests on Israel. In other words, what was formerly *ḥesed*, the grace of God, now becomes the *Law*. The fight against the rulers who wanted to do away with the Law in Israel by armed force was the very thing that made early Judaism attach itself to the Law. *Ḥesed*, *charis* and Law are identified. *This* Judaism knows no contrast between justification by grace and justification by the Law or by works of the Law. Consequently it will not make any antitheses, and will never be able to say 'justification by grace alone' (though this is indeed the case) and 'therefore not on the basis of works' (because this antithesis cannot follow). But justification *on the sole basis of belief* in the wisdom or revelation of God in the Law is essential for this early Judaism. Anyone who does not keep this Jewish conception in mind will almost inevitably interpret Paul's doctrine of justification wrongly.

Following this early Jewish feeling for God's transcendence, emphasis is laid on the fact that the Creator is also the only cause of salvation. That God alone grants forgiveness of sins is based on the omnipotence of his creative act. In this tradition the theme of the heroes of salvation history is very much alive: Noah, Melchizedek, Abraham, Isaac, Jacob, Esau found grace with God without having done any good work previously (cf. Heb. 11; Rom. 4; 9.20–22). According to Philo, 'everything is grace'. The world of man and of things are God's *dōrea, energeia, charisma*. God goes before all our willing, his *charis* goes before everything. In God's eyes no man is righteous (Greek Enoch 81.5). 'Before you the whole world is like a speck of dust on the scale. You have mercy on all because you can do all things, and you overlook the sins of men, so that they repent' (Wisdom 11.23). God's gracious election exists 'before the creation of all things'. The contrast between *kata charin* (from grace) and *kat'opheilēma* (indebted or deserved) is Jewish (and not original to Paul). This distinction has its context in the distinction between individual pious and righteous Jews, who follow the Law, and Jews as Jews who, by virtue of the gift of the Law, fall freely under God's gracious election.[37]

On the other hand, God's grace is above all visible where the Jew opens himself to the divine grace by a humble acknowledgment of his own creatureliness and sinfulness. '*Charis* goes before the modest man' (Sir. 32.10). 'Towards the scorners God is scornful, but to the humble he gives *charis*' (Prov. 3.34). The spirituality in accordance with which grace comes into its own in weakness is an element of belief in this line of tradition in early Jewish literature, 'for the lowliest man, *elachistos*, is *eleous*, full of mercy' (Wisdom 6.6: there are many echoes of this in Paul, with a christological accent).

In this literature, which generally speaking coincides with the last books of the Old Testament and the writings of the New, we find two themes concerning *charis* (which recur in Paul in a christological perspective): (*a*) on the one hand the early Jewish opposition between grace and works,[38] specifically in connection with the theology of creation and the theology of the covenant; righteousness comes from God's grace in election, though on the other hand there is an identity between 'faith' and 'works'; (*b*) in salvation history there is a contrast between *charis* and *hamartia*, between grace and sin: 'Where grace prevails, sin has disappeared' (Greek Enoch; Test. Patr.; see above).

According to early Judaism, salvation and the forgiveness of sins stem only from God's grace (that is a general Jewish view), that is, on the basis of the divine gift of the Law. This is the great exclusive gift of God to Israel. Thus in Qumran the eschatological time of salvation is also the time of the perfect fulfilment and following of the Law (4QFlor); the time of sin is followed by the time of the works of the righteous prepared for by God (II Bar. 27ff.). Justification by grace is put very clearly in the Alexandrian Jewish version in contrast to the Pharisaic version. On the other hand, there are individual Jews who follow the Law closely; therefore *charis* will be their reward. There is a difference between the views of this Judaism and the Pharisaic-Rabbinic view of Torah ontology in which the revelation of God through history is in reality replaced by revelation by means of the sacrosanct book of the Bible, concentrated in the Law (so that the historical and prophetic books only have an authority derived from the Torah).

The problem of 'grace and works' and 'grace and sin', grace and justification, is therefore antecedent to Paul – above all in the early wisdom tradition, which is a major influence in Alexandrian Judaism. The basic difference between Judaism and Christianity lies in the fact that the latter does not see the Law as the point of reference for justification through grace; that is replaced by Jesus as the Christ The central point is occupied by the contrast not between 'grace' and 'works', but between the grace of the Law and the grace of Christ. That is what we must now investigate.

# New Testament experiences of grace and their interpretations

*Introduction*

The formal structure of revelation already says something about its content. If revelation is recognized formally as revelation in the consciousness of believers through human experience, we have already been told a good deal about its content.

It is impossible to present a complete 'New Testament theology of grace'; at the same time it is irresponsible, at least for anyone who is in search of a biblical foundation for a contemporary understanding of the message of the gospel in the light of the demands and questions of the present time, to make an arbitrary selection from the New Testament material. I shall therefore have to work carefully with great blocks of New Testament tradition: Paulinism; Johannine theology; the theology of I Peter and the so-called Epistle to the Hebrews, which are akin to both trends while having a stamp of their own; the late apostolic letters, and finally the Christian apocalypse, Revelation. Because the synoptic gospels were the chief subject of investigation in my earlier book, *Jesus. An Experiment in Christology*, I shall not discuss them again, at any rate directly.

The purpose of the following analysis is to show how all authors as it were colour the same basic experience – of decisive and definitive salvation from God in Jesus – according to the horizon of their own experience and understanding, on the basis of difficulties and problems which arose in the Christian communities to which they wrote their letters or their Gospel (John); in other words, the way in which they go about *interpreting*. *Formative structural principles* then emerge from the variety of these interpretative experiences and a comparison of them,[1] which are an inspiration and a normative orientation for present-day Christians, encouraging them (in faithfulness to the apostolic tradition which has been handed down) to act as boldly as the New Testament writers in formulating a new contemporary interpretation of Christian experience within our own horizons of experience and understanding (which also need to be criticized). It will, however, emerge from Section Four of Part Two of this book that

112

this theological analysis is valueless unless at the same time the historical circumstances are also analysed.

## Chapter 1

# Theological theory of grace in Paul

If we take those letters of Paul which are certainly genuine – I Thessalonians, I and II Corinthians, Galatians, Romans, Philippians and Philemon – as an exegetical unit, we can see that in them the concept of *charis* undergoes a development. The normal use of *charis* which was at Paul's disposal from Greek vocabulary, first becomes a central term for describing the saving act of God in Christ at a particular point. This is already prepared for in Galatians, but Romans obviously marks the dividing line (here *charis* occurs most frequently – twenty-four times). For Paul, his own experience of a very specific act of divine love towards him, namely his call to become the apostle of the Gentiles, forms the transition to the technical designation of the saving event in terms of the grace of God.

*Literature* (esp. on ṣ*dāqā, righteousness*): K. Berger, ' "Gnade" im frühen Christentum', *NTT* 27, 1973, 1–25; J. Blank, *Schriftauslegung in Theorie und Praxis*, Munich 1969, esp. 129–87; id., *Paulus und Jesus*, Munich 1968; G. Bouwman, 'Gods gerechtigheid bij Paulus', *TvTh* 11, 1971, 141–57; H. Cazelles, 'A propos de quelques termes difficiles relatifs à la justice de Dieu dans l'Ancien Testament', *RB* 58, 1951, 169–88; L. Cerfaux and A. Descamps, 'Justice et justification', *DBS* 4, 1949, 1417–1510; A. Descamps, *Les justes et la justice dans les évangiles et le christianisme primitif*, Louvain 1950; id., *La justice de Dieu dans la bible grecque*, Studia Hellenistica 5, Louvain 1948, 59–92; J. Dupont, *Les béatitudes*, three vols, Paris 1973; A. Dupont–Sommer, *The Essene Writings from Qumran*, ET Oxford 1961; J. Eckert, *Die urchristliche Verkündigung im Streit zwischen Paulus und seinen Gegnern nach dem Galaterbrief*, Regensburg 1971; J. M. Fiedler, *Der Begriff der Dikaiosune im Evangelium des Matthäus, auf seine Grundlage untersucht*, Halle 1957; W. Grossouw, 'De vrijheid van de christen volgens Paulus', *TvTh* 9, 1969, 269–83; id., *De brief van Paulus aan de Galaten*, Bussum 1974; W. Grundmann, 'Der Lehrer der Gerechtigkeit in der Theologie des Apostels Paulus', *RQumran* 2, 1960, 237–59; R. Gyllenberg, *Rechtfertigung und Altes Testament bei Paulus*, Stuttgart 1973; E. Käsemann, ' "The Righteousness of God" in Paul', in *New Testament Questions of Today*, ET London and Philadelphia 1969, 162–82; O. Kaiser, 'Gerechtigkeit und Heil bei den israelitischen Propheten und griechischen Denkern des 8. –6. Jahrhunderts', *NZSTh* 11, 1969, 312–28; K. Kertelge, *'Rechtfertigung' bei Paulus*, Münster [2]1966; G. Klein, 'Gottes Gerechtigkeit als Thema der neuesten Paulus-Forschung', *VuF* 12, 1–11; K. Koch, Sdq *im Alten Testament. Eine traditionsgeschichtliche Untersuchung*, Heidelberg 1953; id., s.v. *ṣᵉdaqa*, in *ThHandWAT* 2, 1976, 507–30; T. C. de Kruyff, 'Justice and Peace in the New Testament', *Bijdr* 32, 1971, 367–83; S. Lyonnet, 'De iustitia Dei in Ep. ad Romanos', *VD* 25, 1947, 23–34, 118–21, 129–44, 193–203, 257–61; U. Luck, 'Gerechtigkeit in der Welt. Gerechtigkeit Gottes', *WuD* 12, 1973, 71–89; D. Lührmann, 'Der Verweis auf die Erfahrung und die Frage nach der Gerechtigkeit', in *Jesus Christus in Historie und Theologie*, FS H. Conzelmann, ed. G. Strecker, Tübingen 1975, 185–96; id., 'Rechtfertigung und Versöhnung', *ZTK* 67, 1970, 437–52; R. Mach, *Der Zaddik im Talmud und Midrasch*, Leiden 1957; C. Müller, *Gottes Gerechtigkeit und Gottes Volk. Eine Untersuchung zu Römer 9–11*, Göttingen 1964; F. Mussner, *Der Galaterbrief*, HThKNT 9, Freiburg im Breisgau [2]1976; F. Nötscher, 'Das Reich Gottes und seine Gerechtigkeit (Mt. 6, 33, vg. Lk 12,31)', *Bibl* 31, 1950, 237–41; A. Oepke, *'Dikaiosyne tou Theou* bei Paulus in neuer Beleuchtung', TLZ 78, 1953, 257–64; H. Reventlow, *Rechtfertigung im Horizont des Alten Testaments*, Munich 1971; K. H. Schelkle, 'Gerechtigkeit nach dem Neuen Testament', *BuL* 9, 1968, 83–94; E. Schillebeeckx, *Jesus. An Experiment in Christology*, ET London and New York 1979, 115–78; H. H. Schmid, *Gerechtigkeit und Weltordnung. Hintergrund und Geschichte des alttestamentlichen Gerechtigkeitsbegriffs*, BHTh 40, Tübingen 1968; G. Strecker, *Der Weg der Gerechtigkeit*, FRLANT 82, Göttingen [3]1971; P. Stuhlmacher, *Gerechtigkeit Gottes bei Paulus*, FRLANT 87, Göttingen 1975; P. Trude, *Der Begriff der Gerechtigkeit in der aristotelischen Rechts- und Staatsphilosophie*, Berlin 1955; *Rechfertigung im neuzeitlichen Lebenszusammenhang. Studien zur Interpretation der Rechtfertigungslehre*, Gütersloh 1974. Also the commentaries on the Pauline epistles.

## §1   *Charis:* A new way of salvation made known through revelation and not invented by man

I.   *CHARIS* AND THE GOSPEL OF PAUL IN HIS FIRST LETTERS

The background to the development of the concept of *charis* in the New Testament is the greeting at the beginning or/and at the end of the Christian epistolary literature. Even in his earliest letter from which the term *charis* is completely missing, Paul greets the Christians in Thessalonica at the beginning and end with the words: 'The grace (*hē charis*) of our Lord Jesus Christ be with you all' (I Thess. 1.1; 5.28). This greeting can be found in every letter in the Pauline corpus.[2] Greeks and Greek-speaking Jews began their letters with *chaire*, 'Hail' (see also Acts 23.26; 15.23). Jews often used a double greeting.[3] Many interpreters assert that it was Paul himself who adopted this greeting into Christianity. However, that is very doubtful, because the twofold expression 'Mercy (*eleos*) and peace' is frequent in Greek Jewish literature before Paul (Tobit 7.12 [Sinaiticus]; cf. II Sam. 15.20; II Bar. 78.2; Esther 9.30: 'peace' and 'truth'), whereas *eleos* and *charis* are used interchangeably in the same period (see above).

However, *charis* does not appear in I Thessalonians outside the greetings. In this letter Paul is as it were the faithful mediator of a very particular, very old – perhaps the oldest – pre-Pauline tradition, and also of Hellenistic Jewish terminology. From the beginning he speaks of 'the gospel of God' (I Thess 2.2,8,9), which is at the same time 'the gospel of Christ' (3.2). And he begins his letter by referring to 'our gospel' (1.5), whereas in 2.4 he speaks absolutely of 'the gospel' which has been entrusted to him by God. This gospel embraces the confession of 'belief in God' and 'belief in Jesus Christ who is to come'. They have turned 'from idols to God, to serve the living and true God', and 'to wait for his Son from heaven, whom he raised from the dead, *Jesus* who delivers us from the wrath to come' (1.9f.). This is the pre-Pauline, monotheistic and christological kerygma to *Gentiles* – in which the perhaps more original expression 'Son of man' has been replaced by 'the Son of God' (presumably a baptismal confession). Here the christological message is directed eschatologically towards the parousia, though also on the basis of the resurrection of Jesus from the dead which has already taken place. 'We believe that Jesus died and rose again; even so, through Jesus, God will bring with him those who have fallen asleep' (4.14). That is the gospel of God, of Christ, our gospel, says Paul. His proclamation and its acceptance are based on God's love in election (1.4), a 'call to his *basileia* (or his kingdom) and his glory' (2.12). All this is an expression of pre-Pauline primitive Christianity, albeit that of Greek-speaking Jewish Christians (the Christianity of Stephen). This gospel, 'the divine word of proclamation' (2.13) is 'not a word of man but . . . the word of God himself' (2.13b) which Paul preaches 'in power and in the Holy Spirit' (1.5).

Throughout this letter we hear nothing of *charis* and justification, Paul's later key terms. The key term here is Jesus' coming parousia (2.19; 3.13; 4.15; 5.23; apart from this letter it appears elsewhere in the authentic Pauline letters only in I Cor. 15.23). Nevertheless, it already emerges from this letter how difficult Paul found preaching among the Gentiles

(2.16). His proclamation of salvation to the Gentiles contains the principles which he will develop later.

The immediate reason for the letter as a whole seems to be to give an answer to the problem which has come up in the community: *Christians* have died (4.13–18; see also 5.10: 'whether we wake or sleep'). Paul proclaims the primitive Christian expectation of the imminent return of Jesus; his own contribution is to give an answer to a community which is disturbed about the fate of Christians who have died, because it is feared that they will not be able to experience Jesus' parousia. Paul gives his answer within a framework of Jewish apocalypticism (4.15–17): Christians who have already died ('the dead who are in Christ', 4.16b) will rise and thus go to heaven along with those Christians who are still alive, or will be 'caught up' 'to meet' Christ (4.16f.). Thus for some there will be resurrection and for the others (who are still alive) a 'transportation'. The parousia is evidently expected very soon. This passage shows clearly how historically conditioned situations can influence even a basic dogma like the resurrection. Later Paul will speak differently about it. However, the Christians already have the eschatological gift of the Spirit (4.8; 5.19).

In both of Paul's letters to the Christians of Corinth (chronologically the letter to the Galatians is usually put between the two), the word *charis* occurs frequently (ten times in I Corinthians, eighteen in II Corinthians). It is used in its various Greek meanings: as thanksgiving (I Cor. 10.30; 15.57; II Cor. 2.14; 9.15), and above all as a demonstration of favour or a work of love, specifically the work of love (alms) performed by the Christians of Corinth for the poor of the Jerusalem church (I Cor. 16.3 and above all II Cor. 8.1,4,6,7,9,16,19). Such a generous gift of love (*charis*) is at the same time a demonstration of God's favour towards these Corinthians, who indeed have everything that they need, so that they can give some of it to the poor (II Cor. 9.8). Here the term *charis* in the sense of a debt of honour plays a role, and Paul gives it a christological foundation: 'For I need not remind you of the (*charis* or) act of love of our Lord Jesus Christ, that, although he was rich, for your sakes he became poor, that through his poverty you might become rich' (II Cor. 8.9; cf. Phil. 2.6–11). *Charis* is further used in those letters in the sense of God's help, support or demonstration of favour (II Cor. 9.8; 12.9, but – see below – it is God's *charis* towards the apostles).

Now it is already striking that in these letters there is a connection between grace and the office of apostle (I Cor. 3.10; 15.10; II Cor. 1.12; 12.9), so that here too grace has the technical meaning of the revelation of God's salvation in Christ and, an essential concomitant of that, the election of Christians: 'the grace of God which is given us in Christ' (I Cor. 1.4), the call to the Christian life. Grace is also used absolutely: 'See that you do not receive his grace in vain' (II Cor. 6.1). Here the accent lies more on the general election of Christians than on the election to the office of apostle, through which this revelation of salvation is made known. Throughout, grace has the Greek meaning of being 'richly endowed with all gifts' (I Cor. 1.5f.), as Paul goes on to define more closely the grace which he mentions in 1.4, so that the rich Corinthians 'are not lacking in anything'. Therefore grace still does not have its technical Pauline meaning here, any more than it does in II Cor. 9.8: 'God, within whose power it is to provide you with every gift.' The parousia still occupies the central point within these rich gifts of grace, as it does in I Thessalonians: 'as you wait for the revealing of our Lord Jesus Christ' (I Cor. 1.7b). However, there is already more stress on the 'fellowship of his Son' (I Cor. 1.9) which has been achieved in the meanwhile through the resurrection of Jesus: 'We preach Christ crucified' (I Cor. 1.23). In contrast to I Thessalonians, emphasis is laid on the foundation of the parousia: on Jesus' death and resurrection, on the basis of another pre-Pauline tradition (which is not, however, that of the parousia of the Son of man). Its nucleus is in I Cor. 15.3b–5a or 15.3b–7 (also the pre-Pauline element in Rom. 1.3f). From now on death and resurrection are the heart of Paul's gospel (see I Cor. 1.23; II Cor. 2.12; 5.18–21, etc.) On the whole the two letters to the Corinthians are principally concerned with the apostolate as the 'service of reconciliation' (II Cor. 5.18–21; for this pericope see further below).

It is striking that what in I Cor. 1.9 is described as: 'God is faithful, by whom you were called into the fellowship of his Son, Jesus Christ our Lord', is expressed in Galatians with the term *charis theou*, the grace of God (Gal. 2.19–21). For Paul, *charis* becomes a technical theological term. 'The gospel' is now identified with what Paul terms in Galatians *the gospel of justification*. Here the content of Paul's gospel is the foundation of Christian existence on the *charis* of God and therefore a rejection of 'the way to salvation' by means of human righteousness on the basis of works of the Law. 'The truth of the gospel', its content, is now justification of the sinner by virtue of the mystery of Christ (Gal. 2.14). Paul's gospel is *to euangelion tēs akrobystias* (2.7), just as that of Peter is *euangelion tēs peritomēs*. In other words, Paul proclaims the gospel to the uncircumcised and Peter to the Jews (circumcised). Both do this on the basis of the one divine commission.

It is this divine commission which plays a decisive role in the use of *charis* in Galatians. Paul understands himself to be the mediator of something which he has received from God in Jesus Christ. Throughout his letter, the apostle hands on what he has received from God.[4] For in early Jewish literature *charis* means the grace of a revelation which has been received and is to be handed on. In beginning his letters with a greeting of grace, Paul has already expressed his understanding of the apostolate. There is a historical connection between the old expression 'The Lord be with you' and the New Testament 'grace be with you', because in early Judaism the name of God is often replaced by 'grace' (following the increasing use of abstract nouns). Thus the use of *charis* is less directly inspired by the Old Testament term *ḥesed* than by colouring from apocalyptic and wisdom literature which the word had since acquired. *Charis* is the knowledge and teaching (concerning salvation and ethics) *received through revelation* (for Paul: in and through Christ). This also explains the first technical use which Paul makes of this word. He speaks of a very special favour of God. 'The grace which is given me' is from the beginning an indication of Paul's divine call to be an apostle among the Gentiles (Gal. 1.15f.; 2.9; I Cor. 3.10; Rom. 1.5; 12.3; 15.15; see also I Cor. 15.10). For this reason his apostolic visit to the community is also a *charis* or a delightful event (II Cor. 1.15; perhaps also in Phil. 1.7; cf. Eph. 3.2; 3.6f.). Over against the general usage of *charis* in the formulas of greeting, here God's gracious revelation of salvation (*charis*) is *personalized* for Paul and at the same time connected with a very special service to others: the apostolic preaching of the gospel by Paul to the Gentiles. Grace has been given to him, Paul, 'to proclaim Christ among the Gentiles' (Gal. 1.15; Rom. 1.5; 12.3; 15.15; cf. Eph. 3.2: 'in respect of you'; also Eph. 3.6f.; see I Cor. 3.10). In Gal. 1.15 we have what amounts to a definition of this term *charis*: the elect apostle is called by *charis*, on the basis of the fact that the Son of God, the content of the gospel, has been revealed to him. In this first technical use of *charis* this terminology is unmistakably associated with *the office of the apostle*. Here, as throughout apocalyptic, *charis* means the communication of a supernatural (even visionary) knowledge (on the basis of a vision at the time of his call). Paul's grace is recognized by 'the pillars in Jerusalem' (Gal. 2.9). They recognize Paul's *charis* and thus the legitimacy of the vision in which he receives his call and the gospel which it contains. Following the early Jewish understanding of *charis*, the term here refers to the vision in which Paul receives his call to be apostle to the Gentiles. Grace is correct, revealed teaching (as opposed to alien, false teaching), see e.g. Heb. 13.9; in I Tim. 1.13f. and Titus 3.7–9 *charis* and *pistis* are contrasted with false teaching). 'To fall from grace' (Gal. 5.4) is go to over to another gospel (Gal. 1.6). Thus *charis* represents the true doctrine that is received by Paul in revelation, above all on the basis of Gal. 1.6; 1.15 and 2.21. *Charis* is an *apokalypsis*, revelation, of which Paul is the apostle. In Galatians grace has the early Jewish significance of a new revelation of salvation from God: there is a connection between *charis* and *(epi)gnosis* or the knowledge of revelation, typical of wisdom literature and apocalyptic (see above all also II Peter 1.2f. and 3.18): Jesus Christ as the light on the way to salvation – *lumen gentium*.

'I would have you know, brethren, that the gospel which was preached by me *is not man's gospel*. For I did not receive it from man, nor was I taught it, but it came through a *revelation* of Jesus Christ' (Gal. 1.11f.). What is called *charis* in certain circles within early Judaism is not human wisdom, but a wisdom derived from revelation. Not from man – without conferring with men (1.16c) – 'I went up by revelation' (2.2) – 'the truth of the gospel' (2.5; 2.14) – 'they perceived the grace that was given to me' (2.9); all these are expressions which refer to *charis* as the divine truth of revelation. In Paul's first technical use of the concept of grace, grace is the doctrine of salvation which is handed on from the Father by Jesus through the apostles, and for Paul that is the doctrine of the election of all men in Christ Jesus. With this doctrine Paul 'does not nullify *the grace of God*', i.e. Israel's election (2.21). Therefore in early Christianity 'grace' is essentially revelation in and through Jesus, the Christ and the Son; Jesus is the only teacher (cf. John 1.14–17: 'grace and truth' in the early Jewish sense). Jesus is the new revelation which transcends the Mosaic revelation. Therefore in essence this concept embraces the election of those to whom this revelation is given.

## II. GRAECO-JEWISH *CHARIS:* GALATIANS AND LUKE/ACTS

It is striking that the term *charis* hardly appears outside the Pauline corpus and the New Testament writings influenced by Paulinism. Luke, that is, the Gospel of Luke and Acts, is the great exception to this. Here it is important to note that the Lucan concept of grace similarly has its root in the early Jewish milieu of those Diaspora Jews who carry on a mission among the Gentiles.

The predominant feature in Luke is the Septuagint meaning of *charis* as a rendering, not of the Hebrew *ḥesed*, but of *ḥēn*. This meaning comes very close to the genuinely Greek *charis*: to give joy to someone else, to be truly friendly towards them, 'to find grace in the eyes of someone' through attractiveness or particularly pleasant or ethical properties. Thus the Christians find *charis* among the whole people (Acts 2.47); i.e., they enjoy popular favour (also Acts 7.10, which is a quotation of the Septuagint of Gen. 41.40f.; and Acts 7.46; Acts 4.33 probably also has the same significance). Another characteristic expression is that Stephen was 'full of *charis* and power, did great wonders' (Acts 6.8); here the later significance, characteristic of the time of the empire, seems to play a part. *Charis* is a supernatural power (see above), but it can also be used as an equivalent to *ḥēn*. When Luke 1.30 says that 'Mary has found favour *with* God' (in the eyes of God), this is not formally a matter of *ḥesed* but of *ḥēn*; i.e., God is well pleased with Mary and therefore favours her. The same is true of Luke 2.52: Jesus increased 'in wisdom and *charis* with God and man'; literally: the growing boy pleases everyone, God and man, because of his wisdom and his engaging nature. Similarly Acts 18.27: Apollos 'greatly helped the believers through his *charis*; for he powerfully confuted the Jews in public, showing by the scriptures that the Christ was Jesus'; earlier it was said that Apollos was 'an eloquent man, well-versed in the scriptures' (Acts 18.24; see Prov. 22.11). Here, too, *charis* is *ḥēn*, being respected by others for particular characteristics or talents (perhaps here the meaning of power, *virtus gratiae*, *charis* from the time of the empire, plays a part). Attractive speech is often described by the term *en chariti* (see e.g. also Col. 4.6; thus this is not a question of Apollos' 'gifts of grace'). Luke 2.40 fluctuates between *charis* as *ḥesed* and *charis* as *ḥēn*: 'Jesus was filled with wisdom, and the *charis* of God rested on him'; this is a matter of the grace and benevolence of God. In other words, the *ḥēn* that Jesus possesses (Luke 2.52) in fact finds its source in the *ḥesed* of God (Luke 2.40). Luke also uses *charis* in the Greek meaning of gratitude (Luke 6.32; 6.34; 17.9) and in the general meaning of favour, gracious gifts or demonstrations of favour (Acts 24.27; 25.3; 25.9).

However, the real *theological* significance of Luke's use of *charis* lies elsewhere. Jesus speaks 'words of *charis*' (Luke 4.22), 'the gospel of God's *charis*' (Acts 20.24), 'the word of his grace' (Acts 20.32), and finally: they bear testimony to 'the word of the Lord's grace' (Acts 14.3). Here are four texts in which *charis* and word or gospel are closely connected, a typically Lucan concept of grace in the New Testament. Paul usually associates *euangelion* (gospel) with *dynamis* or power, and not with *charis*. What does *charis* mean in these four texts? Luke 4.22 gives us some indication. The Lucan Jesus begins his public life with a homily in the synagogue on Isa. 61.1f.: the Spirit of God which rests upon the anointed one who is sent by God to bring good news to the poor (*eu-angelisasthai*), to heal the blind, to bring salvation to the oppressed and to proclaim God's year of grace (in which the unjust concentration of possessions is altered). This generally corresponds to the picture of Jesus given by Luke (7.21). According to Luke, the reaction of Jesus' audience to his words was: 'All . . . wondered that words so full of *charis* came from his mouth. They said: Is not this Joseph's son?' (Luke 4.22). Here is something more than *charis* in the sense of a 'winning nature'. It is clear from the context that *charis* is clearly meant in the original Greek meaning of 'something that brings joy'. The word *charis* is as it were brought to life by *eu-angelion*, a message which brings joy: *charis* is the gospel to the poor. The good news is for them. In fact the word *charis* in this context really explains the *eu* (what is good and gladdening) in *eu-angelion* or the gospel. Luke uses the word here in its original Greek meaning (*charis* is 'what brings joy' – and therefore goes more closely with Hebrew *ḥēn* than with *ḥesed*). With his use of *charis*, Luke thus stresses the element of joy in the gospel, what touches the human heart (see also Acts 4.33).

However, this specifically Lucan, genuinely Greek conception of *charis* is at the same time Hellenistic and characteristic of early Judaism. I remarked earlier that *charis*, in the Hebrew sense of *ḥēn* (not of *ḥesed*), was used often in Hellenistic Judaism, which was characterized by traits of wisdom. I also pointed out that in the Graeco-Jewish inter-testamental literature, *charis* as supernatural wisdom and *revelation* as it were formed twin concepts. It is also striking that 'wisdom and *charis*' are twice used in juxtaposition (Luke 2.40 and 2.52) in Luke, as in the wisdom literature. Whenever Luke uses *charis* in a theological sense (Luke 4.22; Acts 14.3; 20.24; 20.32), he does so in connection with the *proclamation of the word*, either the word of Jesus or that of the apostolic tradition. It is about this word, the gospel, that Jesus' audience wonders. Is he not the son of Joseph (Luke 4.22)? Thus the *charis* of the words of Jesus points to supernatural wisdom: revealed wisdom – wisdom from above, not rational human wisdom nor the product of human knowledge. Here Luke's concept of grace has roots in the same ground as that of Paul's concept of grace in the letter to the Galatians: the Hellenistic concept of *charis*, to be found in the Jewish Diaspora, which sees it as a supernatural, revealed wisdom (which delights men and brings them joy – that is the particularly Greek emphasis which Luke introduces). This also explains why in Acts 11.23 Luke describes the extension of the church as 'the *charis* of God', with the consequence that 'he (Barnabas) was glad' (11.24). For Luke (in formal terms) *charis* is not so much 'an unconditional demonstration of grace' (as for Paul in Romans) as the joy brought by the divine wisdom which is communicated to men in Jesus and the church's gospel. Therefore Luke, like Paul, can combine *charis* and *dynamis* – the power of grace (Acts 4.33; 6.8; 20.32; see 14.26; 15.40; 18.27 etc.).

The word *euangelion*[5] (with a history in Judaism and the Hellenistic world) principally belongs in the context of pre-Pauline and pre-Marcan, Greek-speaking Jewish Christianity (which is open to the Gentiles). *Charis* has a similar setting: it refers to the Jewish-Christian 'wisdom from above', unknown to the Gentiles, which is communicated through Jesus to the elect and handed on by these in the gospel or the proclamation of the church to anyone who is prepared to hear them. Luke can therefore say in almost Pauline terminology: 'But we believe that we shall be saved through the *charis* of the Lord Jesus, just as they will' (Acts 15.11, in a report in which Paul's views are being discussed; see also Acts 13.43; 14.26; 15.40). It is this concept of *charis* that is predominant in Paul's letter to the Galatians.

## §2 Justified through faith in Christ: Galatians and II Corinthians 5.18–21

The concept of *charis*, as it has so far been analysed, does not of itself produce a contrast between 'grace' and 'Law', because for the Jews the Law was a *charis* or a gracious revelation of God which was reserved for Israel; here too, election and grace as revelation of a higher wisdom went hand in hand.

Thus without any polemic against the Law, Paul can put forward his doctrine of justification as he does in II Cor. 5.18–21: 'God was in Christ reconciling the world to himself, not counting their trespasses against them' (5.19) and 'God made him to be sin who knew no sin, so that in him we might become the righteousness of God' (5.21). The death of Jesus is an expiatory death, through which our sins are blotted out and God's own righteousness, or *ṣᵉdāqā*, becomes ours. This concept of the *dikaiosunē tou theou*, which is central to Romans, cannot be found anywhere in Galatians; in my view, however, in its essential formula it *presupposes* Paul's doctrine of justification as found in Galatians. In II Corinthians, this pericope about reconciliation and justification does not, however, stand in a context of polemic against the works of the Law, but is related to the 'service of reconciliation', which is Paul's special apostolate. However, this apostolate is an apostolate to the Gentiles, the uncircumcised, the non-Jews. And in that case the question inevitably arises whether the *charis* of the revelation of God in reconciliation through Jesus Christ does not exceed the *charis* of the Torah. For if God reconciled the world to himself in Christ, so that this reconciliation is really the forgiveness of sins and a way to divine salvation, then the *solus Christus* principle comes into play. In that case the *charis* of the Law is surpassed by the grace which has been manifested in Christ, and no *Gentile* who has become a Christian can be obliged to be circumcised and observe the Law. Paul calls any opposition to this 'apostasy from *grace*', i.e. from Christ as the only way of salvation. With Jesus, a new revelation, and thus a new authority, has appeared. 'If justification were through the law, then Christ died to no purpose' (Gal. 2.21; also 5.4). In that case the dilemma is indeed 'salvation in the law' (5.4) or 'salvation in Christ'. The question is that of the decisive and definitive authority of the revelation of God, or *charis*: the law or Jesus Christ?

In Galatians, a new conflict developed. At an earlier stage, the apostles had agreed that Paul's sphere of mission was the Gentiles and that Peter's sphere was to be confined to the Jews (including the Diaspora Jews) (Gal. 2.6–10); consequently the first great conflict was solved, at least in principle. However, in the Galatian community something different was afoot from what was to be found within the Christian community at the time of the Judaizers. Paul found himself in conflict with certain people who affirmed that circumcision was necessary even for Gentiles, if they wanted to become Christians. However, these people observed a kind of 'calendar piety' (depending on the state of the moon or the sun) and all kinds of cultic usages (Gal. 4.10). As a result of this they exerted pressure on fellow Christians and caused confusion (1.7; 5.10). Paul interprets their thesis in a polemical fashion and as a result claims that they defend the need to fulfil the Jewish Law, although they do not observe it themselves (5.2f.; 6.12f.). In Gal. 2.15 Paul considers his opponents as 'Judaists' in a Pharisaical sense (as is meant in Acts 15.5; see Gal. 2.15), 'Judaizers' who want to combine Christian faith with the Jewish religion, which Paul explains as wanting to be justified through the law (4.21; 5.4). This he calls apostasy from Christ (1.6f.; 5.4), a consequence which his opponents perhaps did not want and did not even see. I think that in Galatians we have a form of syncretism which was to become even more marked in Asia Minor and in which Jewish *peritomē* (circumcision, which at that time was also 'in' with non-Jews) played a role (Colossians; Ephesians; Hebrews; the Johannine writings). In my view, the Galatian error lies in this direction (see Gal. 3.19f.; 4.8–10, whereas in Colossians there is mention of 'the powers of the cosmos' which have something to do with the law – both Torah and *nomos* [law] – which rules men). Paul thinks in apocalyptic terms: Christ has given himself up for our sins in order to rescue us from 'this aeon' in accordance with the will of our God and Father (Gal. 1.4). The age to come is already present in the risen Christ, and we with him: the Jerusalem from above is already in one sense present in the Christian community on earth (4.26); they are a 'new creation' (6.15). Paul expresses this with the words: God calls man *en chariti*, i.e. he calls in grace. Here *charis* describes God's call as gracious (other than in 5.4). Here grace is used in an absolute way (1.6; 5.4); it is a system of grace as opposed to a system of the law. The expression *charis Christou* appears only once (Gal. 1.6), and *charis Jēsou* never; what we find is the *charis* of 'our Lord Jesus Christ' (Gal. 6.18; see Rom. 16.20,24; I Cor. 16.23; II Cor. 13.13; Phil. 4.23; I Thess. 5.28; Philemon 25; cf. II Thess. 3.18 and II Cor. 8.9). In other words, for Paul the *risen* Christ is the *charis* of God. Nowhere will he call the historical Jesus a *charis* (in contrast, say, to Luke and even to the Deutero-Paulines). In Galatians *charis* is a qualification of the call of God (1.6; 1.15), or a kind of isolation of the grace of the saving act of God (2.20c–21; 5.18); on the other hand it is also a grace achieved in us (5.4), in the sense of Christian existence as a gift of God. Above all, Paul calls his apostolic ministry a *charis*. All in all, in Galatians the term grace acquires the significance of a 'regime of grace', a system of grace, in contrast to the regime of the Law (see Gal. 5.4). This contrast is expressed in the 'truth of the gospel' (2.5,14), characterized as a gospel *apart from the Law* (see 2.15–21). By its polemical context, God's gracious calling acquires the meaning of 'independent of our works of the Law', without any merit on our part (2.15–21, where Paul gives a short, sharp account of his doctrine of justification). This grace is given to both Jews and Gentiles, though Paul also sees a certain difference in the sinfulness of them both. The Gentiles are sinful 'anyway' (*physei*, by nature, by birth); so are the Jews, but not by birth, because by their birth God's promise rests on them (this is not made explicit here in Gal. 2.15, but it is in Rom. 3.2). However, this distinction is significant, and that was also seen by many early Jewish movements. In connection with the question of the relationship between grace and works there are two traditions in early Judaism: (*a*) God does not give grace on the basis of man's own works, but on the basis of the election of Israel and the covenant with the patriarchs; (*b*) God rewards men according to the works. According to the first view, all Israelites are the elect, righteous; the promise rests on them even when they sin. Only the Gentiles are the real 'sinners' (see Gal. 2.15). They lack the great grace of the Law. However, the new question with which Christianity was faced was: is election given with the possession of the Law or with the gift of the risen Christ? Paul and his opponents are agreed about the essential connection between grace and election. The decisive point lies in the question whether election has its focal point in the Law or in Jesus Christ.

God's call through grace means that 'Man is not justified by works of the law but through faith in Jesus Christ'; therefore 'even we have believed in Christ Jesus, in order to be justified by faith in Christ and not by works of the law, because by works of the law shall no one be justified' (Gal. 2.16; also 3.2,5,10). Here Paul argues on the basis of the Pharisaic and rabbinical conception of justification. All Jews stand firm on the view that only God justifies men and brings them to salvation.[6] Here it is simply a discussion of the *manner* of this justification by God's grace.[7] For the Jews this takes place through faith in the grace of the Torah; for Paul through faith in the grace of Christ. Paul contrasts these two ways of salvation. For the Pharisaic and rabbinic, the so-called 'orthodox' Jewish trend, faith and works form a whole; for them faith in God is a work of the Law, even the first commandment of the Law. The doctrine of justification by faith comes from the Old Testament

(Gal. 3.6–9). Abraham 'introduced' this great commandment of trust in God (see James 2.20–24). For Paul, on the other hand, 'faith in Christ' is not an *ergon*, a work of the Law, although it is an intensive human activity (Gal. 5.6). Faith and work are contrasted (Gal. 2.16; 3.2,5,10). Paul rejects obedience to the Law as a *principle* of salvation. As a principle of salvation, Christ too requires a consistent ethical life with works (2.17–19; 5.13–15). It is clear that Paul sees the Law as a *system* or a regime, a 'law under which we live' (4.4), a power system. And 'the elements of this world' have been destroyed by Christ (4.3,9). The power of the Law and thus the tutelage of the Law have been broken by Jesus on the cross (3.13; 4.5; see 2.21). To believe that the power of the Law has been broken by Christ is to believe in God's grace (2.21). Therefore his death on the cross is the sole source of salvation (3.1b). However, that is not really the point under discussion. The striking thing is that the concept of 'God's righteousness', which is central to Romans, still does not appear here in Galatians. Paul argues in 'Jewish' terms: to be justified means that man is no longer taken into account (see Gen. 15.6; Ps. 32.2). It is a question of God's eschatological judgment (see Gal. 5.5); God alone justifies or acquits. Faith in Christ therefore gives us a share in the Old Testament promise: God's blessing to Abraham, Jewish pride in the name 'son of Abraham',[8] was a matter for proselytes too.[9] Abraham's blessing thus applied to his sons, as did the prospect of the inheritance which was promised him (Gal.3.6–14): the *klēronomia*, the portion or the inheritance (*naḥᵃlā*). This is a concept from the Priestly and Deuteronomistic tradition. 'The heritage of Israel' is 'the land which Yahweh your God will give you' (Deut. 4.21,38; 12.9; 15.4; 19.10, etc.; also Jer. 3.19; 12.14f.; 17.4; and Ps. 105.11; 135.12; 136.21f.). On the other hand, for Jeremiah, Israel is God's heritage (Jer. 2.7; 12.7–9; 10.16; 50.11; also in Ps. 68.9). Anyone who lives in this heritage or this communion with Israel has fellowship with Yahweh (I Sam. 26.19; 11 Sam. 14.16). In Judaism Yahweh's heritage is synonymous with messianic salvation. Through the fact that God announced the promise of the heritage to come it is irrevocably valid. Now the Law came after this legal decision on the part of God, and therefore too late to be able to change anything.[10] Paul speaks of the *charis* of this promise (3.18), that is, of God's gracious will. In Paul's time, 'heritage' in the last resort also meant everything that could not be achieved by one's own work;[11] that being so, the term *klēronomia*, heritage, is in fact appropriate for underlining the contrast between grace and work (Gal. 4.7; see Rom. 8.17 and Matt. 21.37f.). Paul therefore calls Christians *hoi ek pisteōs* (Gal. 3.7,9): men of faith, 'men for whom faith is the starting point, source and origin of their whole life.'[12] As a result of this interpretation of the text Paul can connect all nations with the promise to Abraham.[13] For him the Old Testament already speaks of 'justification by faith for all nations' (Gal. 3.8,14). Now faith takes the place of Law as a ruling force or a system: 'Since the coming of faith' (Gal. 3.25; 3.23a). However, there is a difference between the two systems: the Law 'came' (*genomenon*); faith, on the other hand, 'is revealed' (Gal. 3.23,25), i.e. faith is a mystery which is hidden in God for all centuries and has now been revealed with Christ in time.

For Paul, 'Jew' and 'Gentile' are primarily *religious* concepts, which means that according to Paul, both Jewish and Gentile religions are done away with in Christ: 'There is neither Jew nor Gentile . . . you are all one in Christ Jesus' (Gal. 3.28); or Christianity forms a *tertium genus* alongside Jews and Gentiles ('Jews, Greeks, the community of God', I Cor. 10.32). Faith in Christ as salvation from God frees the Christians from what in both apocalyptic Judaism and in Greek religion was seen as man's tutelage under cosmocrators or heavenly spirits (Gal. 4.3,9), who ruled the Jews through the Law (3.19: the mediator of the Law is not Moses, but a spiritual cosmocrator; for Gentiles that is the *nomos* or the law of nature, Gal. 3.23; for both, 4.9). To deny Christ means to put oneself once again under the tutelage of these spiritual cosmocrators, whether they are evil or not. Paul is concerned with the Law as a state of dependence under the rule of cosmocrators: he is not against the Law as subjection to Christ (*ennomos Christou* I Cor. 9.21). Thus Paul defends himself both against a subjection to the Law and against a spiritual libertinism (Gal. 5.13–15). The two poles are really therefore not: works of the Law or grace, but *election* (grace) on the basis of the gift or the possession of the Law (which looks for works), *or* on the basis of the gift of Jesus Christ and faith in Jesus Christ (a faith which must come to fruition in action, above all in brotherly love and other works). This emerges clearly enough from the great final conclusion which Paul draws from his conception of grace (Gal. 3.28).

## §3  Paul's theory of grace: Romans

It cannot be a coincidence that Rom. 15.25–29, which discusses the collection for the poor of Jerusalem (see I Cor. 8), does not use the term *charis* for it. That could of itself indicate that in Romans *charis* is used consistently in a very specific significance. In reality this gift of money to the brethren in Jerusalem is in the last resort a kind of debt of honour (Rom. 15.27). This Greek emphasis on a debt of honour no longer allows the word *charis* to be used in such a context after everything that Paul has said in Romans about *charis*.

After Paul has demonstrated that everyone, Jews and Gentiles alike, are sinners and alienated from God, he says: 'They are justified by his *charis* as a gift, through the redemption which is in Christ Jesus' (Rom. 3.24). 'Through his grace' is further emphasized strongly by 'as a gift': *dōrean tē autou chariti*. *Dōrean* means in the form of a gift with the possible connotation of its being an unreciprocated gift, even if the giver does not receive anything back in return and thus has been as it were good 'in vain' (e.g. in the Greek Job 1.9; see II Cor. 11.7, where Paul preaches 'without cost', i.e. without wanting financial support from his community). In Romans the term grace points to the special mode of the divine saving action: the gratuitous generosity of God to sinful humanity. Paul calls God's outgoing and beneficent love grace or *charis* because of its generosity which is unmerited, sovereign, superfluous and in and of itself almost vain. Here *charis* is an outgoing love which does not lay down any conditions. Grace is made absolute, so strongly that some people see in it a kind of *carte blanche* for libertinism (Rom. 6.1). That it is not Paul's purpose for grace to remain 'in vain' already emerges from I Cor. 15.10: 'His grace toward me was not in vain'; however, the fact that this grace is not in vain is itself a further grace: 'I have worked hard. . ., not I, but the grace of God with me.' Also II Cor. 6.1: 'Do not accept the grace of God in vain.' Paul defines *grace* as follows: 'But if it is by grace, it is no longer on the basis of works; otherwise grace would no longer be grace' (Rom. 11.6).

Paul uses other adverbs alongside the adverbial expression *dōrean*, as a gift, in order to express unmerited favour. Above all, *kata charin*, as it appears in Rom. 4.4: 'Now to one who works, his wages are not reckoned according to grace (*kata charin*) but according to merit (*kat'opheilēma*)'. 'From grace' describes the relationship between man and God (see also Rom. 4.16); *charis* is here so to speak still not a substantive but a property of God's relation towards man: generous, and without laying down any conditions.

The theme of Romans is: 'the *gospel* . . . the power of God *for salvation to everyone who has faith*, to the Jew first and also to the Greek. For in it the righteousness of God is revealed through faith for faith '(Rom. 1.16f.). There it is said literally that in this gospel God's righteousness is revealed *through* faith *for* faith. In a context which is not immediately concerned with the dynamic growth of the life of faith in person and church (as in Colossians and Ephesians), but with the system of salvation of either the Law or grace, the 'through (*ex*) . . . for (*eis*)' means fullness; that is, justification belongs entirely within the ordinance of faith. To translate the passage 'through faith and faith alone' might seem to be a Targum, but it renders accurately in good English the full significance of the Greek. In this letter Paul wants to develop a Christian theory of grace. I shall sum up the structure of his train of thought (in the light of the *theological* interest which we have in this text) as follows:

(*a*)   Neither paganism nor Judaism give salvation in the sense of the righteousness of God (1.18–3.20).

(*b*)   The revelation of the righteousness of God (3.21–31) is explained through:

    1. A Pauline version of a traditional, early Jewish 'Abraham Midrash' (4.1–25).

    2. A Pauline version of a similarly early Jewish 'Adam Midrash' (5.12–21).

    Rom. 5.1–11, as a summary of 3.21–31, forms the transition between these two parts.

(*c*)   God's righteousness, realized in conversion to belief in Christ: Christian baptism (6.1–11).

(*d*)   Christian paraenesis: a Christian attitude to life as a consequence of the righteousness of God (6.[1,]12–23); with an account of the law of the flesh and the spirit (7.1–25 and 8.1–27), a description of the Christian struggle (7 and 8.1–27) and a concluding hymn of praise to the grace of God in Christ.

(*e*)   In the light of the manifestation of the righteousness of God in Christ, Paul asks what the purpose of God's election of Israel is (9.1–11.35); (This part is dealt with more thoroughly later on in the present book, in the chapter on 'Israel and the New Testament church', pp. 602ff.).

## I. NEITHER PAGANISM NOR JUDAISM GIVES SALVATION OR *CHARIS*

In Rom. 1.18–3.20 Paul demonstrates how, despite a fundamental difference in the divine plan of salvation for Jews and Gentiles, all are sinners and need to be reconciled with God.

What was said in Gal. 2.15 remains valid: 'We ourselves are *Jews* by birth and not Gentile sinners.' Israel has the true knowledge of God, of Yahweh; it is not *a-theos*, i.e. without Yahweh, like the Gentiles (see also Ephesians: 'You [Gentiles] were dead through the trespasses and sins in which you once walked, following the course of this world, following the prince of the power of the air, the spirit that is now at work in the sons of disobedience', Eph. 2.1f.). This is not primarily a Christian view: it is traditionally Jewish: in the Torah, Israel possesses the knowledge of God and his will; the Gentiles are excluded from this. True, Israel sins, just as the Gentiles sin, but Israel is nevertheless the elect. Therefore God considers his election and his covenant, on the basis of which he is merciful towards the sinfulness of Israel. That was the pre-existing, Jewish conception of the sin of Israel and the Gentiles which Paul had before him.

Now Paul stresses the fact that there is no distinction between Gentiles and Jews as far as personal behaviour goes, despite the privilege which Israel enjoys. Early Judaism (after the exile) above all sees the world divided into two great blocks of peoples: 'Jews' and 'non-Jews' or the *'gōy'*, that is, the people of the Gentiles *(gōyīm)* in contrast to Israel as *'am, laos* or people of God[14] (though this contrast does not play any part in the earlier texts of the Tanach). The difference is above all a religious difference, on the basis of which the Gentiles are regarded as 'foreign' and 'enemies of Israel' (II Kings 17.33; 18.33; 19.12,17; Jer. 3.17; 31.10). The essential thing here is that the *gōyīm* do not call upon the name of God (Jer. 9.26; 10.2,25; 14.22; 16.19; Ezek. 23.30; Ps. 79.6); they are 'people who have been forgotten by God' (Ps. 9; Ps. 10), in other words *heathen* (as a Jewish term). Israel looks for its strength in keeping strictly apart from these people. Therefore even at the beginning of Deuteronomy there is no indication that Israel's election involves a mission to all peoples; at best these can wonder at Israel (Deut. 4.6). However, there are some texts (one line runs from Gen. 12 via Ex. 12 to Isa. 60) which put forward another conception: Israel has been *chosen* to bring *all peoples* to Yahweh. Exile and Diaspora in fact made a positive contribution to this development, in which finally there is mention of the Torah[15] and the 'servant of Yahweh' as the 'light of the *gōyīm*' (Isa. 49.6).

In reality, however, Gentiles and Jews sin: Paul puts this right at the beginning (Rom. 1.18), and goes on to analyse this universal sinfulness, among the Gentiles (1.19–32; 2.14–16) and then among the Jews (2.1–13; 2.17–29). As far as the Gentiles are concerned, although they do not know God's will through the Torah, they have a conscience (Rom. 2.15) which by means of the world of creation is in some way a consciousness of good and evil (2.14f.) and thus also of the absolute mystery of God (1.19–23; a theme of wisdom literature: Wisdom 13–15; Job 12.7–25). They know God, but do not acknowledge him in their way of life (Rom. 1.21); they have erred and become idolatrous (Rom. 1.23; see Wisdom 13–15). Here Paul is clearly referring to the principle of the *yēṣer* or man's power of free decision (Sir. 15.14f.: see below) which is to be found in the wisdom tradition: 'They are without excuse' (Rom. 1.20b = Wisd. 13.8). But God rewards them according to their works (Sir. 4.5f., 9f.; 21.5): for Paul, therefore, the immorality of the Gentiles which he sees in the cities of the Diaspora is an expression of the wrath of God, an intrinsic consequence of failure to recognize the one true God. Anyone who does not acknowledge God makes an idol for himself and regards the created world as the be-all and end-all (1.24–32). The basic condition for the entry of Gentiles to Christianity will therefore be conversion to the one true God (I Thess. 1.5; see Acts 14.15; 17.22–31; see later in the chapter 'To bring all to unity', pp. 515ff.).

Yet despite their knowledge of God and his will in the Torah, the Jews still sin. They cannot appeal to God's *ḥesed* and *'emet* (see Rom. 2.4) to excuse their sinfulness. (This too is a feature of the wisdom tradition: Sir. 5.1–6, for the other side of *ḥesed* is God's anger: Sir. 5.6. Sirach had a great deal of influence on the Pharisees, to whom Paul belonged.) God will reward everyone according to his works (Rom. 2.6: which is also a principle found in Sirach). Retribution for evil and the wrath of God thus affect both Jews and Gentiles and, because of the preferential situation of the Israelites, 'Jews first and then Gentiles' (Rom. 2.9). This also applies, with the same nuances, to recompense for good (2.10f.). Despite Israel's privilege of the Law (called by Jews the *charis* of the Law), God recompenses every man according to his works, without partiality (2.11f.). For 'it is not the hearers of the law who are righteous before God, but the doers of the law who will be justified' (2.13). Here the Christian Paul is arguing in *purely Jewish terms*, and agreeing with them. He is thus affirming the Jewish principle of reward in accordance with works. That should not be forgotten in any analysis of Rom. 4–5. Paul cannot use a principle in Rom. 2 which is useful for him in his discussion of universal human sinfulness and then attack it in Rom. 4–5. In other words, after what Paul has said in Rom. 2, it cannot be his purpose to attack this Jewish principle of recompense in Rom. 4–5.

In the light of this universal sinfulness Paul then goes on to ask what the advantage is in being a Jew. Here he again seeks to take up the early Jewish view of the Torah as the 'embodiment of knowledge and truth' (Rom. 2.20b), and thus of Israel as the 'light of the *gōyīm' (lumen gentium)*: 'Light for those who are in darkness' (Rom. 2.19). But Paul says, 'You who boast in the Law, do you dishonour God by breaking the Law' (2.23), surely a bad example for the *gōyīm* (2.24, with a quotation from the Greek Isa. 52.5). Does being a Jew, with the mark of circumcision, then offer any advantage at all? Yes (2.25), given that man follows that of which circumcision is a sign, namely the Law of God's covenant. But in that case the converse follows: a Gentile who follows the content of the Torah without knowing this formally 'is regarded by God as though he were circumcised' (2.26). A Gentile who leads a morally good life is a condemnation of the sinful Israelite, even if he has the book of the Law in his hand (2.27). Following a view which was already widespread in early Judaism and above all in the Diaspora, Paul says, 'He is a Jew who is one inwardly, and real circumcision is a matter of the heart, spiritual and not literal' (2.29.). This whole description is Jewish, and Rom. 1.18–2.29 could just as well have been written by a non-Christian Jew. It is also worth noting here that when Paul speaks of man's universal sinfulness he does not have individuals so much in mind (though only individuals sin) as blocks or collectives, for both the people of God and the *gōyīm* or pagans sin; there is only incidental mention of the actual doing of the Law by individuals – a Gentile (2.14f.) or a Jew (see 2.25 and 2.28f.). It is a question of the status of being a Jew or a Gentile as such: and here we see sinfulness on both sides. What Paul means to say is that the two blocks (the whole of humanity: Jews and non-Jews) live under one system in which sin reigns, literally: 'We have (namely I, Paul, have – but this is a statement with which anyone will agree) already put forward the accusation (Rom. 1.18; 2.9) that all, Jews and Gentiles, are under *hamartia* (sin)'(3.9b). In other words, before the advent of Christ mankind lived under the *power* of sin. Here Paul is thinking in 'apocalyptic' terms of a *succession of ages*: a new age has been introduced by the appearance of Jesus and his death, the age in which *charis* prevails.

But: what advantage does the Jew have over others (Rom. 3.1)? Paul replies in Jewish fashion: 'Much in every way' (3.2).

First of all: the *logia tou theou*, God's words, have been entrusted to Israel. And the unfaithfulness of the Israelites does not make God's faithfulness to Israel of no effect (3.3f.). 'God alone is justified' (Rom. 3.4b) is reminiscent of Sirach: '*Kyrios monos dikaiōthēsetai*' (Sir. 18.2: 'the Lord alone will be found righteous'; see Ps. 51.4b: 'You are righteous, unassailable in your judgment').

Furthermore, the sin of the Jewish people brings out God's mercy even more (3.5) provided that this is not misused and the statement is not put in a false light (3.5b–8). In conclusion (in 3.20b), Paul adds: 'The law allows sin to be recognized (formally as sin).'

But apart from these two ways in which Israel has an advantage over others, 'we Jews are not any better off' (3.9). And Paul repeats the conclusion that he has already drawn: the accusation against all, Jews or non-Jews; humanity is a history of sinfulness. Human history lies under the power of sin (see 3.9b), despite the human conscience (or human *sophia* or wisdom) which can arrive at a certain distinction between good and evil, and despite the *nomos* or the gift of the Torah to Israel which Paul, for all his critical remarks about the Law, counts as the 'covenant of the promise' (see Rom. 9.4; it is 'the law of God', 7.22,25; 8.7; it is holy, 7.12; righteous and good, 7.12; and it is given by God for life, 7.10; see Gal. 3.12). But 'flesh and blood', man as *sarx*, is not in a position not to sin; neither *sophia* and *nomos* give him sufficient strength (see Rom. 8.3; Gal. 3.21). And this experience of reality as expressed in the wisdom tradition is something which Paul already finds in the Tanach, since he concludes this account of the universality of sin (in the sense indicated) with a series of biblical quotations. These are meant above all to silence the Jews, because it is for them that the Tanach is intended (3.19). Therefore once again: 'The whole world *(pas ho kosmos)* is guilty before God' (3.19). And finally, with a biblical quotation (Ps. 143.2: 'in your sight no creature is justified'), Paul prepares for his subsequent account by the insertion of 'by the works of the Law'; 'for no human being (the weak *sarx*) will be justified in his sight by works of the Law' (3.20). *That* is a conclusion which *in no way* follows from the whole account in Rom. 1.18–3.19! Therefore Rom. 3.20 is on the one hand a conclusion of 1.18–3.19, but on the other hand it is not a direct consequence, but a preparation for what is to come. At the same time it means that throughout the whole of the previous section another 'new' concept of *righteousness* has been brought into play, differing from the official Jewish concept of the 'acquittal of the *ṣaddīq* or the one who is faithful to the law'. This will emerge from the following analysis.

## II. REVELATION OF THE 'RIGHTEOUSNESS OF GOD' IN JESUS CHRIST

### A. *Ṣᵉdāqā*, righteousness, the transition from Judaism to Pauline Christianity

The term righteousness – in the masculine *ṣedeq* and in the feminine *ṣᵉdāqā* (in the Septuagint *dikaiosunē*) – had a remarkable history in Israel and in early Judaism: the religious, even sacral, term developed out of the secular sphere and then split in two directions within early Judaism: on the one hand a justification on the basis of the grace of God alone, and on the other hand human righteousness towards God through obedience to the commandments. This development has to do with social conditions as well as with Israelite spirituality. After a secular usage of *ṣᵉdāqā*, the religious concept of righteousness was developed in a time of theocratic, nationalistic popular conceptions in which authority and the force of law were sacral. In Israel at that time all authority was exercised in both religious and temporal matters in the name of Yahweh, the only true king of Israel. Human righteousness was connected with God's righteousness. Religion and society were one: the people of God. Later, however, even at the time of Jesus, the Jews no longer had any independence. Authority and society, authority and religion, split apart. The people of God came under a strange authority which now had control over the exercise of righteousness. The consequence of this was that the concept of righteousness was desacralized and often forced to the periphery in the religious life of the Jews. Paul wants to attack this vigorously. It is, however, striking that in so doing he follows an early Jewish apocalyptic trend which was not the official Jewish and Pharisaic conception (even called by some 'heterodox Judaism'), but which from the middle of the second century BC to the end of the first century AD represented a very virulent tendency in Jewish spirituality (even in the Qumran community).

It is sometimes said that the Old Testament concept of *ṣᵉdāqā* is closely connected with the ancient oriental idea of a cosmic order which is guaranteed by God.[16] In the Tanach, however, the root *ṣdq (ṣᵉdāqā)* is nowhere connected with the world order (for which other terms are used). Rather, the term righteousness has its context of experience in the whole complex of human action and the good or bad consequences which are connected with it for the community and the subject of that action.

We find the term first in connection with the king, who sees to it that righteousness prevails among the people and for the people (II Sam. 8.15; I Kings 10.9; Jer. 22.3,15; 23.5; 33.15; Ezek. 45.9; see Deut. 33.21). As the righteous one, who is *ṣaddīq*, the king must be as it were the life-giving sun of the people (II Sam. 23.3); he is the protector of those with few rights and must declare the right, i.e. pronounce *ṣaddīq*, anyone who is wrongly accused (II Sam. 15.4). Conversely, the subject is righteous if he does not rebel against the king (I Sam. 24.18; 26.23). If he is loyal to the king he has *ṣᵉdāqā* with him (II Sam. 19.28). That means that righteousness also includes the public recognition of the good actions of a man; this recognition is essential if righteous action is to retain its full significance.

However, there are also relationships of righteousness between masters and servants (Gen. 30.33). In that case *ṣᵉdāqā* is the true devotion of the servant to his master, quite apart from any hope of a reward. Precisely by his faithfulness the servant gains 'righteousness' in the eyes of the master. Thus, above all in the use of *ṣaddīq*, it is a question of righteousness between those with equal rights (II Sam. 4.11; I Kings 2.32), whereas there can be no talk of *ṣᵉdāqā* between blood relations. (In the only text which is relevant in this respect, Gen. 30.33, there is a working relationship between Jacob and his father-in-law.) There is also righteousness between host and visitor (Gen. 44.16). Moses says to his helpers: 'And I charged your judges at that time, "Hear the cases between your brethren, and judge righteously between a man and his brother or the alien that is with him" ' (Deut. 1.16), 'for the judgment is God's' (Deut. 1.17c).

Thus righteousness has to do with specific community relationships. It is connected with a particular form of 'fidelity to the community'. G. von Rad defines as *ṣaddīq* someone who recognizes and fulfils claims which come to him from the community to which he belongs.[17] But in what respect? It is striking to note that *ṣᵉdāqā* is destroyed where two parties are in dispute. But it does not emerge in Hebrew thought that both parties might be wrong. In conflicts there is a polarization: one is good, the other acts badly. But in that case there is no longer any *ṣᵉdāqā*, with either the one or the other. Righteousness must be restored by justice. For even a righteous man whose conduct is questioned in public, e.g. by an accusation, loses his *ṣᵉdāqā*: he becomes an object of popular derision (Ex. 23.7f.). The righteousness of the judge (Lev. 19.15) is not the focal point in such a treatment, but the restoration of the righteousness of either the accuser or the accused. Only punishment of the truly guilty can restore *ṣᵉdāqā*. The acquittal of one party is thus at the same time the punishment of the other, and thus *ṣᵉdāqā* prevails (Deut. 25.1–3; 19.19).

*Ṣᵉdāqā* is thus a situation in which personal and social life is not only undamaged but irreproachable. Such a condition of well-being, salvation and happiness is connected with the good actions of a man which earn happiness, prosperity and salvation. However, even the *ṣaddīq* loses his righteousness through the accusations of others; in that case he becomes the innocent sufferer, whose righteousness is questioned publicly. Thus the term *ṣᵉdāqā* points to the inner connection between good deeds and the state of prosperity, happiness, salvation and good fortune, in other words, life. By what he does, man creates for himself an atmosphere or a field of force which as it were surrounds him as salvation or disaster, even in the eyes of others. This very characteristic, 'in the eyes of', makes up the whole complex of problems associated with the concept of *ṣᵉdāqā* and calls to life the concept of the 'suffering righteous' in a way which will finally produce a crisis within Jewish religious feeling. For the righteous is not only oppressed by false accusations. He will also discover that the connection between good actions and a happy, healthy life is not in fact achieved in real life: this is the problem of Job. The connection between good, ethical life and a happy, healthy life-in-salvation, so long taken for granted, became a religious problem in the long run, above all at the time when Israel's spirituality was completely 'this-worldly' and did not know any future after death.

Nowhere in the time before the exile do we find *ṣᵉdāqā* associated with a divine norm, and even later this word will only rarely be associated with the Torah (it is, however, in Deut. 4.8; Ps. 19.10 and Ps. 119). The concordances which give details of the statistics of terminology show clearly that two thirds of the occurrences of the root *ṣdq* (righteousness) in all texts are to be found in Isaiah, Ezekiel, the Psalms and Proverbs; in other words, in writings which derive from Jerusalem and the cult, and also in the wisdom traditions. In these writings above all the connection between divine and human righteousness comes into the foreground. Here righteousness is like an atmosphere which surrounds God and his action (Pss. 89.16; 97.2). It comes down from heaven in order to make good the damage in human righteousness (Pss. 85.10–13; 99.4). Human conduct must constantly be renewed (Pss. 118. 19f.; 24.5f; 68.2f.). In one particular tradition, the priestly tradition, this renewal takes place above all through the cult, presumably through sacrifice in the Temple (Pss. 4.6; 51.19; Deut. 33.19). This is not the justification of a sinner but that of a *ṣaddīq* or an already righteous man.[18] According to the entrance liturgy[19], only the *ṣaddīq* may cross the Temple threshold (Ps. 118.19f.); the sinner must remain in the outer part of the Temple (see the story of the righteous Pharisee and the sinful publican in the New Testament, Luke 18.9–14). The priest declares the man who presents himself as *ṣaddīq* to be righteous: 'not guilty within the terms of the Law'; therefore, '*ṣaddīq hū, ḥayō yiḥye*', 'he is righteous, he will live' (liturgical model in Ezek. 18.9; cf. Ezek. 33.12–14 and Pss. 15.5b and 24.5).[20] Leviticus 18.5 had said: 'You shall therefore keep my statutes and my ordinances, by doing which a man shall live. I am Yahweh.' In the entrance liturgy the priest can only establish the situation of the *ṣaddīq* externally and thus confirm it 'forensically', juristically. Here the essential connection between righteous behaviour and life which is obedient to the Law (healthful life-in-salvation) becomes clear. Yahweh himself is 'the God of *my* righteousness' (Ps. 4.1; see Pss. 35.27; 31.1f.; 71.2; 143.1; also 36.6–10), that is, God is my salvation and my prosperity, also in the sense of: I have him to thank for my prosperity. Or, when I am suspected, God will do justice to my real state of being *ṣaddīq*. Divine and human righteousness are intrinsically bound up together so closely that it is often difficult to establish who is the real subject (Ps. 146.8). However, it always has something to do with a basic meaning of *ṣᵉdāqā*, namely, to be recognized as such by others as well. In that case, in a religious conception of righteousness, being right 'in the eyes of God' is the all-important element, which the *ṣaddīq* who is under suspicion or threat in the last resort rates higher than what people think of him. In the royal psalms, the king is the mediator between Israel and the righteous judgment of Yahweh (Ps. 72.1–6).

Because righteousness has its religious foundation in Yahweh, the connection between good works, prosperity and the respect of others, typical of *ṣᵉdāqā*, is not disrupted (see Pss. 72.7; 92.12; 58.11; 75.10; 112.3,9),.since when the religious man is reviled by his fellows he can set his hope on God's righteousness or justification; this is decisive. However, the idea that God does not 'justify' the sinner but the righteous remains unchanged. The *ṣaddīq* finds righteousness with God (Pss. 69.27f.; 143.1). That is the chief note struck by the *ṣaddīq* who is disturbed by misfortune or suspicion in the individual psalms of lament.

The term *ṣᵉdāqā* does not appear often in the prophetic literature. According to the Babylonian prophets, righteousness has vanished from the people through the sin of the northern kingdom, Israel (Jer. 3.11; Ezek. 16.51f.). But God remains *ṣaddīq* (Jer. 12.1); in this way hope arises and a search for a new righteousness (Jer. 4.1f.; Zeph. 2.3). Ezekiel is the first to associate *ṣᵉdāqā* with the observance of the commandments (Ezek. 14.14; 18.5–9, 14–17,20). With Jeremiah, righteousness becomes eschatological and is connected with the king of salvation to come (Jer. 23.5) and the renewal of Zion (31.23; 50.7). However, outside the priestly tradition of Ezekiel no connection is made between *ṣᵉdāqā* and the cultic conception of it in the Priestly and Deuteronomistic traditions.

According to Deutero-Isaiah, righteousness is coming in a very near future (Isa. 46.13; 51.5); as in the Psalms, this is God's 'saving righteousness' (Isa. 46.12; 48.1; 51.1.7). However, for Trito-Isaiah this righteousness is still a long way off (Isa. 59.14). In this literature divine righteousness is clearly a force which pours over the true people like a flood (Isa. 48.18). *Ṣedeq* (masculine) comes from heaven, so that *ṣᵉdāqā* (feminine) can take root on earth (Isa. 45.8). The Messiah to be sent by God is therefore the *ṣaddīq*, the righteous one (Ps. 45.4; Jer. 23.5), the man who gives form to the divine righteousness in human righteousness. Finally, in a perspective of final or eschatological salvation (Isa. 41.1–7; 46.12f.), *ṣᵉdāqā* becomes synonymous with a condition of salvation. In a verse from the prophet Habakkuk which is later quoted twice by Paul (Gal. 3.11; Rom. 1.16f.), a connection is made between *ṣᵉdāqā* and a life of salvation in believing trust (in the prophet's word): 'The *ṣaddīq* who has trust (faith) will remain alive' (Hab. 2.4, to be interpreted along the lines of Ezek. 33.12–14).

In the introduction to his Greek translation of a Hebrew text written by his grandfather, the author of Sirach remarks: 'For what was originally expressed in Hebrew does not have exactly the same sense when translated into another language. Not only this work, but even the law itself, the prophecies and the rest of the books *differ not a little* as originally expressed' (Sirach, The Prologue). That is the remark of someone who is completely at home in both Hebrew and Greek. Greek-speaking Jews therefore found it difficult to translate the Hebrew term *ṣᵉdāqā*. The Greeks had their own particular concept of righteousness. Although *dikaiosunē* originally had a religious significance (finally the daughter of Zeus was called *dikē*), the function of this term in Greek thought acquired a completely different significance. Righteousness is a moral, above all a social and political human virtue or basic attitude: the word was hardly appropriate for rendering the religious *ṣᵉdāqā*. Therefore the Septuagint sometimes translates the Hebrew word as *dikaiosynē*, and then again – to stress the reduction which it contains – as salvation, redemption, etc., whereas on the other hand Hebrew terms like *ḥesed*, covenant love and piety can also be rendered with *dikaiosynē*. Thus in the language of certain Greek-speaking Jews, *dikaiosynē* takes over the very rich meaning which is characteristic of *ṣᵉdāqā*[21] – a semantic richness which the non-Jew would never read into it. Consequently, the Jewish-Greek *dikaiosynē* means that the man who is truly bound up with God in social and human relationships is involved in a world in which God's promises and law will finally be realized. This is the beginning of the tendency in which not only *ṣᵉdāqā* but also *dikaiosynē* can become the central concept for salvation, as a summary of the proper religious and ethical approach to life as a gift of God – though this tendency was only to be carried through in one trend of early Judaism.

We already find an indication of a first shift in the book of Proverbs. There *ṣᵉdāqā* means the righteousness which man creates for himself through his wise action; here Yahweh works as it were only from afar (Prov. 3.33; 10.3,6f.; 18.10). In a way characteristic of the wisdom tradition, righteousness is identified with acting in wisdom and with insight (Prov. 1.3; 2.9); instead of the connection between righteousness and the cult, there now arises a connection between righteousness and wisdom and insight. But the old connection between 'acting well' and life or salvation is retained. 'One who practises righteousness finds life' (Prov. 11.18f.; 11.30); and 'in the house of the righteous there are many riches' (15.6).

In this term, and therefore in Jewish religion, we can see signs of a crisis which is made clear in Job and Ecclesiastes, though in each case the solution is very different. In this literature the connection between righteous and good action and a happy and healthy life, which is taken for granted elsewhere, is in fact broken (Job 22.2f.; 36.6f.; 33.26; 35.6–8). Despite his disastrous state, Job is convinced in his conscience of his righteousness.

The story of Job is characteristic of this problem. Job, who in all his unmerited distress initially claims that God has not acted justly (Job 34.5), hears from a friend, Elihu, that God as Creator takes no sides. Each and every one is his creature: princes *(sārīm)*, noblemen *(sōwā)* and the poor *(dallīm)* are all the same to him (34.9). God's righteousness emerges above all, Elihu argues, in the fact that he casts down the mighty (*kabbīrīm*), when they become socially unjust by turning away from Yahweh, to such a degree that the injustice done to the poor cries out to heaven (Job. 34.28). However, man has no rights over against God (4.17; 9.2; 25.4). But that is precisely Job's problem: he believes that he is a *ṣaddīq*, i.e. 'innocent in terms of the Law'. The question of God's righteousness is posed in the light of contrasting experiences of unrighteousness in the world.[22] Job arrives at the view that there is no theological justification for the history of human suffering and that the theology of the connection between good deeds and earthly rewards is nonsense. In terms of the insights of the human conscience, he has nothing to blame himself for. But what is man when face to face with God? No man is *ṣaddīq* or righteous compared with the holy one (Job 9.2; 40.8). The ancient connection, then, is not completely disrupted; moral and religious action must be connected with salvation. But do we men have an accurate insight into true righteousness according to God's purpose? In fact Job questions the concept of God which is traditional to his religion. He brings 'God', as the guarantor of true recompense and harmony between a righteous life and above all material prosperity, before the forum of the critical examination of human experience. This God is not Yahweh, the living God, but a theological phantom. Against such a concept of God he looks for human rights.[23] In rebellion against a particular concept of God, this *ṣaddīq* in his wretched Job-like situation trusts in the true God who transcends human theological systems. For Job our human world is out of order; he refuses to justify the situation as such in theological terms; that is the mark of his rebellious attitude. A God who would desire such a ruined history could not be God. God's righteousness must be regarded in different terms from all these attempts at harmonization. He continues to believe in man's right to happiness and fulfilment, but at the same time he believes in the true God. He remains open for . . . God's grace. Job is as it were the Old Testament model for Jesus of Nazareth, with his proclamation of the kingdom of God in which righteousness dwells.

Koheleth (that means leader or speaker in a popular assembly) or the Preacher comes to a similar reaction from the same critical experience, but with a completely different, bourgeois solution. He begins his book with words which prove to be its motto: 'Vanity of vanities, says the Preacher, vanity of vanities, all is vanity. What does man gain by all the toil at which he toils under the sun?' (Eccl. 1.2) . . . 'All things are full of weariness, a man cannot utter it' (1.8). For this author, the traditional connection between a righteous life and human happiness and prosperity is completely shattered. Anyone who looks round can see that in this world a *ṣaddīq*, for all his righteousness, can come to nothing, whereas all

goes well with the wicked (Eccl. 7.15; 8.14). That brings this cultural
analyst to the prosaic conclusion: 'Be not *ṣaddīq* overmuch and do not
make yourself overwise; why should you destroy yourself? Be not wicked
overmuch, neither be a fool; why should you die before your time' (7.16f.).
Here is the so-called golden middle way: one hand for the ship, the other
for yourself! In his own way, and unlike Job, the author takes upon
himself the right to lead his own life as a man in the way he wants. Like
Job, he experiences a gulf between the individual and his surroundings.
He decides for the individual. The human person and his actions are seen
independently of nature and society; the harmony of a perfect world order
yields to the rights of the individual. That is clearly a sign of a general
cultural trend beginning at the middle of the third century BC. Social
problems are left as they are, and there is a retreat into inwardness – a
clear departure from the time of the prophets. 'What is crooked cannot
be made straight' (Eccl. 1.15). This was also a time in which the political
activity of the 'citizen' was extremely limited because of alien rule. The
Preacher sees the vast amount of injustice all too well, 'In the place of
justice, even there was wickedness, and in the place of righteousness,
even there was wickedness' (3.16; see 4.1). What is to be done about it?
'If you see in a province the poor oppressed and justice and right violently
taken away, do not be amazed at the matter; for the high official is
watched by a higher, and there are yet higher ones over them' (Eccl. 5.8).
Koheleth thus sees as clearly as the prophets. His social criticism is not
religious, but as it were precociously secular. It is based on an analysis
of what he sees. But he capitulates to facts; he does not see any point at
which to call a halt. A generally pessimistic attitude to the world and
society develops, with a certain despair over existence. 'So I hated life,
because what is done under the sun is grievous to me; all is vanity and
a striving after wind' (Eccl. 2.17). 'The life (of man) is full of pain, and
his work is a vexation' (2.23). Human action is criticized. The age-old
assumption that the righteous life is a good and happy life has vanished
on the basis of new experiences. The other side of this pessimism is,
however, an increasing universalism. Koheleth avoids the name Yahweh
and goes back to the general term Elohim, but does so in the sense of
'the Elohim' (with the article). He considers not so much the history of
Israel as the historicity of mankind, the *condition humaine*. This way of
thinking is not oriental, but is influenced by Greek thinking.[24] There is
a gulf between God's omnipotence and all the unrighteousness on earth.
The Preacher does not despair over God, but over all human plans.
Moreover, death makes everything meaningless (Eccl. 3.19–21). With
death, everything comes to an end, both for the good and the wicked.
For the author that is a bad experience. Like Job, he attacks the earlier

'theology of the wise men', who believed that they could unravel the mystery of life, and gave the impression of knowing what was *ṣᵉdāqā* and what was not. He regards this as pure theory, which is contradicted by one's experience of life. Here, too, we find criticism of the orthodox concept of *ṣᵉdāqā* and the concept of retribution which is used all too easily. The Greek criticism of the gods has had its effect on the Preacher, though he continues to believe in God's guidance of the world. If Job was a *religious* monument in the history of mankind, the Preacher is a *document humain*.

In one particular aspect, the later wisdom literature returns to the teaching of earlier wisdom. The *sōpēr* or scribe (see Sir. 38.24–39.11) Sirach (between 190 and 175 BC), living in Jerusalem, attacks the pre-Maccabean Hellenistic freethinking that is to be found there (see Sir. 37.19–26). In this, strikingly enough, he refers to experiences which he has considered critically (34.9–13 = Greek 31.9–13). He reveres the Torah and the old prophetic wisdom (in which Moses, too, is called a prophet, 46.1) (Sir. 38.34; 39.7f.). In the last resort, scribes like Sirach are on almost the same footing as the earlier prophets: they interpret scripture in terms of the present. As in Hellenism with its reverence for earlier heroes (*de viris illustribus*), at this time the theme of the great leaders of Israel also becomes popular among the Jews – it was evidently a favourite theme in synagogue sermons to warn and encourage believers. Furthermore, this leads to a kind of apostolic succession (Sir. 44.17; 46.12; 48.8):[25] the continuity of tradition gives this particular view authority.

Against this background Sirach asserts that good works really do mean life and salvation; anyone who denies that is stupid (16.22f.). He sharply attacks the oppression exercised by the rich (13.2–5), but not unconditionally, as the Preacher does: in his view excessive searching for riches leads to unjust action (11.10; 31.5). Like the prophets before him, he too ridicules the absence of conscience among those who nevertheless cross the threshold of the Temple and thus give themselves out as *ṣaddīq* (34.24–27 = Greek 31.24–27). Here Sirach refers to the principle of retribution: God rewards in accordance with works (4.1, 9f.; 21.5), an old Jewish principle. A new element here is the idea of compensation: supererogatory good works, e.g. charity, can be a kind of counterbalance for sins committed, i.e. *ṣᵉdāqā* expiates sin (3.30), which in no way means the forgiveness of sins through grace. Here the old idea of reward is given a completely new (Greek) foundation: God gave every man his own *yēṣer* or free power of decision, through which he can observe the commandments of the Law (Sir. 15.14f.; something similar to what will later be called Pelagianism within Christianity). Man himself has the power and freedom to choose between life and death (15.17), and therefore to choose between good and bad actions (in accordance with the principle of the intrinsic connection between righteous actions and prosperity). In thus returning to the ancient traditions of Israel, at the same time as a reaction against the Hellenizing upper classes in Jerusalem and therefore also with the help of Greek ideas, Sirach accentuates the piety of the Law. But this stress on human freedom to choose is a new note in Israel – coming from Hellenistic Judaism. Before this, Israel had looked for the ultimate basis of good and evil in the sovereign God, without too much reflection, and without supposing that God's holiness was affected as a result. For Sirach, the old *ᵉmūnā* or fidelity of faith lies in man's free decision: to follow the Law or to reject it in practice. What is called typically Jewish piety is here given a foundation in Greek philosophy. For the first time in Jewish history there is explicit discussion of a kind of doctrine of the two ways (Sir. 2.12); this is the implication of human freedom of choice (*yēṣer*). But that is from the start inclined to evil; so from now on the term 'flesh and blood' will also be used explicitly as a term for the creaturely weakness of man and his tendency to sin (14.18; 17.31).

Wisdom, fidelity to the law and *ṣᵉdāqā* are almost identified (see 1.14; 1.26). All wisdom is obedience towards the Torah (19.20,22–24; 1.26). In this way universal wisdom is limited to an exclusive gift of God to Israel – which is a view directed against the rational wisdom of the young aristocracy of Jerusalem with its Hellenistic Jewish views (Sir. 3.21–24). This exclusiveness is also expressed in the assertion that every people has its *archontes* or heavenly protectors (guardian angels, as a consequence of the end of henotheism, i.e. the view that every people has its own God), but Israel alone is directly God's own possession (17.17).

In view of the tendency towards libertinism among the rich of the time, Sirach attacks the favoured class which believes that God is merciful and will forgive sins (5.1–6). But God's grace has two sides: *ḥesed* and wrath (5.6), as Sirach argues. Paul, too, takes over this theme from Sir. 5.4–6: 'Do not say, "I sinned, and what happened to me?" For the Lord is slow to anger. Do not be so confident of atonement that you add sin to sin. Do not think, "His mercy is great, he will forgive the multitude of my sins".' For Sirach's opponents, a life of outward prosperity was the main thing, and experience taught that this prosperity was independent of a good or evil life. With this Sirach contrasts once again the old doctrine of recompense, even though in the meantime it has been strongly criticized by Job and Ecclesiastes (and Pss. 49;73). Followers of the Hellenistic fashion were evidently aware of this criticism and therefore took what they wanted from life. However, Sirach maintains the view that infidelity to the Law brings divine punishment (even in this life). There *is* an essential connection between good deeds and life in happiness and salvation (divine recompense) (see Sir. 2.8; 3.14f., 31; 4.10,13,28; 5.7f.; 6.16; 7.1–3; 9.11f.; 10.13f.; 11.17). Sirach's repeated insistence on the idea of recompense suggests that this argument is very close to his heart. It is less concerned than before with a kind of immanent righteousness and more with the 'Godness' of God: God is the guarantor that the good will be rewarded and the wicked punished, 'For he is a God of retribution' (35.13; 17.23).

This idea is essentially connected with Sirach's belief in creation. His reaction in one direction is striking. This is against a thought which evidently came to him (as a consequence of the experience that human life is a vale of tears), that God is not concerned with man or is himself the cause of evil in the world (a Greek idea of the time). In his hymns to creation Sirach therefore celebrates God's good and meaningful works (39.24–34). He associates the idea of recompense with this good creative activity on the part of God (40.10), as a kind of rational theodicy (see above all 40.1–41.4). He attacks the prevalent pessimism. Despite everything the world is good; human freedom is responsible for the evil in it, but in the end good triumphs on earth through reward and punishment. Thus there is a perfect harmony in creation (see Sir. 42.15; 42.22–25), even though this may be a dialectical counterbalance (hence the idea of 'bi-polarity', Sir. 42.24 and also 33.13–15). For Sirach, the bright colours and the dark specks in creation and history form a surprising harmony. Without evil it would be impossible to see the brilliance of the good!

Hence all Sirach's teaching can be summed up under the motto *Kyrios monos dikaiōthēsetai* (18.2): 'The Lord alone will be found righteous.' Here theodicy, in the literal sense of the word, enters Jewish faith. Man himself justifies God's behaviour through his speculative theory. The Lord fills everything with his glory, and like a Stoic, at least in terminology, Sirach exclaims: 'God is the all' (43.27). Sirach the scribe, going back to Israel's ancient traditions, adapts himself to fundamental Greek ideas for apologetic or missionary reasons.

Sirach's view of life is still 'this-wordly'; he still knows nothing of a life after death or a resurrection (ideas which are to appear soon after him in Daniel and the Maccabean literature). However, he maintains his principle of recompense. In this he differs from Hasidic literature, and in chronological terms comes before the splintering which produces the various 'religious parties' in Judaism. However, even with him we find many of the features which will later characterize these parties: 'Strive even to death for *righteousness*, and the Lord God will fight for you' (4.28). Here we detect a truly Jewish voice, albeit in the context of a way of thinking influenced by Hellenism, since the author is also writing for non-Jews. It is important not to underestimate the influence of Sirach's writing on the later Pharisees and the whole of the rabbinic movement, even if the rabbis did not accept his book in the list of 'holy scriptures'. In particular, Sirach's ideas of reward and retribution become a rabbinic dogma.[26]

Greek criticism of the gods, which evidently had some influence on the criticism of Ecclesiastes in particular, along with the new religious experience of Job with his criticism of the traditional image of God, gradually gave rise to a religious renaissance which developed from the increasing experience of human history as a single vale of tears with much injustice and many 'suffering righteous'. The rational human wisdom in Hellenism could give no satisfactory answer to this history of failure and disaster. But in reaction to Hellenistic wisdom, religious movements arose throughout the Hellenistic world from the second century on, which referred to a higher, revealed wisdom (see ch. 2, §2, on Ephesians). Soon after Sirach, this trend also made itself felt in Israel, despite the continuing influence of Sirach's ideas, above all in early and Hasidic apocalyptic. Religious *ṣᵉdāqā*, manifested as surrender to God's saving will in the gift of the Torah, becomes the central concept for the eschatological salvation which Yahweh brings (Dan. 9.24). Righteousness is also a central religious concept in early Essenism. Its founder is never mentioned by name; he is the teacher of *ṣᵉdāqā* and the elect Essene brotherhood contains the 'sons of righteousness' (1 QS 3.20,22; 9.14). Despite the heightened demand for obedience to the Torah, here there is a breach with the old tradition according to which God alone justifies the *ṣᵉdāqā*. On the contrary, it is the sinner whom God justifies. His righteousness is associated with the forgiveness of sins (1 QS 11.2–4; 1 QH 3.21; 7.30).[27] In later apocalyptic (first century AD), *ṣᵉdāqā* remains the fundamental concept of salvation (IV Ezra 7.114). At the end-time, no 'faith', no *ṣᵉdāqā* can be found among men (IV Ezra 5.11; see also Luke 18.8b in the New Testament). God's *ṣᵉdāqā* will then be manifested (see Paul: Rom. 3.21: 'But now the righteousness of God has been manifested'), not so much in retributive righteousness as in gracious mercy on those who have assembled no treasury of good works in heaven (IV Ezra 8.48f.). In that case it is a justification not by good works, but by grace! That is already a Jewish view. The difference from Christianity does not lie in the justification by grace but in the diacritical point: whether this gift of God is identified with the saving gift of the Torah or with the divine gift of Jesus, seen as the Christ.

However, this Jewish conception was not what might be termed the 'official Jewish' line. Within it there was a further development of the idea of reward and recompense, more along the lines of Sirach. The Jewish synagogue in particular reduced *ṣᵉdāqā* to human action, above all to 'good works' (the classic trio of alms, fasting and prayer), which accumulate a treasury of merit in heaven. The bewilderment of II Baruch can be understood in this spirit. He bitterly ponders how it can be possible that the fall of Jerusalem took place (in the year 70) when the Jews had accumulated such a treasury of merits (II Bar. 14.4–7). The good man begins to doubt God's promises and even more the significance of good works.[28] This history gives a good account of the official teaching of Judaism in the New Testament period. However, such 'official teaching' should not be described as the specific practice of the people and the pious. They knew that they lived only on God's mercy, and not on the basis of their own merits.[29]

This survey shows that at the time of Jesus and the origin of the New Testament there were two tendencies in the Jewish conception of *ṣᵉdāqā*. To put it simply, on the one hand there was the idea of a justification by grace, not by virtue of works, though this grace could also be expressed in obedience to the Law; on the other hand, God justifies or makes righteous the *ṣaddīq*, and not the sinner; this latter view was the doctrine of the leading classes in Israel (apart from the Herodians, the pro-Roman clerical circles). Here, moreover, there are two different themes which need not necessarily be thought to contradict each other.

It is striking that in another perspective – that of christology – both these Jewish trends can be found again in the New Testament. On the one hand, Paulinism: justification solely by divine grace and mercy. But outside the Pauline school and the sphere of Paul's influence, pre-New Testament primitive Christianity hardly followed this Pauline terminology, so on the other hand there was the concept of 'righteousness' as held in orthodox official Judaism. Strikingly, Matthew gives the three Jewish categories of good works, alms, prayer and fasting (Matt. 6.1–4, 5–14, 16–18), as being synonymous with Christian perfection. The virtuous man who follows God's commandments (Matt. 1.19; 13.17; 23.29; see Luke 1.6; 2.25; Acts 10.22) is 'righteous'. So here 'righteousness' does not mean the Pauline concept of salvation, but ethical virtuousness (Matt. 5.20; 6.1–33), though as a consequence of faith in the redemption of Jesus. Here Matthew is in no way reacting against the Jewish concept of righteousness, but he accuses the Jewish leaders above all of forgetting the essential commandment: mercy (Matt. 23.23f.); he charges them with hypocrisy, so that the heaviest burdens lie on the insignificant and the poor (Matt. 23.3f.) Luke, too, uses a similar concept: 'And will not God vindicate his elect, who cry to him day and night? Will he delay long over them? I tell you, he will vindicate them speedily' (Luke 18.7–8a). Here we find the old idea that God brings about justice for the (suffering) *ṣaddīq*. As a result, this term is often connected with the earlier Jewish idea of the 'suffering righteous' (e.g. Matt. 5.6–10). In this sense a particular tradition calls Jesus himself 'the righteous', *ṣaddīq* (but only in

Luke, who is later: Acts 3.13–15; 7.52; 22.14; here, however, there may also be a trace of the Greek conception of *dikaios*). The authentic Pauline concept of divine righteousness – from early Hasidism, apocalyptic and Qumran – is not to be found elsewhere in the New Testament, with one important exception: 'But seek first his kingdom *and his righteousness*' (Matt. 6.33; see Luke 18.14); in other words, here we find the eschatological concept of God's *ṣᵉdāqā*, the *justitia Dei*, which does not occur in the New Testament outside Pauline theology, at least with the *word* 'righteousness'. Granted, the New Testament is essentially agreed in its concept of the *grace of Christ* and his forgiveness of sins; nevertheless, as far as the use of the term *ṣᵉdāqā* is concerned, it is clearly influenced by two distinct *Jewish* tendencies and themes.

In his explanation of grace and salvation in Jesus Christ, Paul will refer to the old concept of 'God's righteousness' (which was also alive in his time in certain non-official circles), in contrast to the frequent use in official Jewish circles of 'righteousness' as a qualification of ethical human action (in obedience to the Torah). God will secure justice. In his own way, Paul had the same experience as Job. From his own experience he learnt that man can in no way rely on his assessment of his own good works, since he understood and had an existential experience of his earlier persecution of Christians as an act which was well pleasing to God! Later, he must have thought: how is that possible? This *religious* concept of righteousness, interpreted in human terms, must have been shattered by Paul's own experience of God's mercy in Christ. He sees the false element in his earlier career not so much in his ethical zeal for what he recognized in his conscience as a good thing, but in his mistake over its 'object': he fought against what proved to be the source of sanctification and grace. That was his fundamental mistake ('his ignorance', as the Pauline school puts it more gently, I Tim. 1.13). Through his reference to the old religious concept of righteousness, the righteousness of God, he now seeks on the one hand to make a connection between Israel and the church, while on the other hand he stresses the new element that has appeared in Christ. The eschatological saving gift of God is not the Torah, but Jesus Christ; it is he who from now on rewards every man according to his merits (Rom. 2.1–16; I. Cor. 4.3–5). For Paul, too, God's free gift of righteousness is manifested *in* ethical Christian conduct. If one were to delete the ethical admonitions from Paul's writings, not even half of them would be left. The problem with Paul lies in the fact that in his polemic, his renewal of the old religious *ṣᵉdāqā* of God (and also of the Hasidic, apocalyptic conception of *ṣᵉdāqā*) is put in the official Jewish context of the theme of 'human righteousness' or ethical action. There, in quite a subtle way, Paul reconciles the free character of grace with *Christian* merit or reward. Here two groups of problems overlap, and some fellow Christians have considerable difficulty in following him (see II Peter 3.15f.). Paul really has to give a new content to the term *iustitia* which is used by official Judaism; but such a semantic operation of one man within a semantic field which in fact (even among Jewish Christians) has a different character is always an awkward business. Either it is unsuccessful or it produces misunderstandings. James 2.24 expresses quite plainly the way in which Paul presents *his* view: 'You see that a man *is justified by works* and not by faith alone.' The important thing is to bring 'human righteousness', ethics into accord with the *dikaiosynē tou theou,* with God's righteousness or the life of grace. Later Augustine will be confronted with an even more difficult task. Faced with a more massive, Graeco-Roman, secularized concept of righteousness – one of the most humanistic and philanthropic elements in the culture of late antiquity – he has to make this profoundly human, 'pagan' concept of *iustitia* agree with the *iustitia Dei* or the grace of God. In the context of the intensely ethical, pagan humanistic *dikaiosynē* (the cardinal attitude at least of ancient, Graeco-Roman dogmatic ethics), he had to express the unmerited grace of God. A number of misunderstandings also arose between him and the pious priest Pelagius (who in fact was also critical of society; for Pelagius, the Roman *gratia* meant favour, which in the higher circles of the Roman empire of the time was tantamount to nepotism and corruption). This was to the detriment of both sides and led them to harden their positions.

Because (so far as we can reconstruct the situation) Jesus did not talk in terms of righteousness but of *the kingdom of God*, he avoided the problem which (in part) was raised more by the term *iustitia* than by the reality which was actually involved. This problem can obscure the heart of the question when we read Paul. Paul is less concerned with the problem of 'grace' and 'human activity' than with discovering decisive salvation either in the divine gift of the Torah or in the divine gift of Christ Jesus. The first problem is subordinate to this, and *outside* this context becomes a kind of conversation between two deaf and dumb people with the help of different sign languages. This will become clear from a further analysis.

B. The righteousness of God, revealed in Christ Jesus (Rom. 3.21–5.21)

When Paul describes the *charis* which God shows in Jesus Christ in face of the universal sinfulness of the world – Jew and Gentile – he contrasts the accusation that 'all stand under God's wrath' with Jesus as the Christ, an apostolic datum: 'But now God's righteousness has been revealed apart from the Law' (Rom. 3.21a). But Paul adds: 'the Law and the prophets (the Tanach) bear testimony to this' (3.21b). On the one hand newness in Jesus, attested as the Christ, while on the other hand the whole Tanach bears witness. Witness to what? That 'now the righteousness of God has been manifested through faith in Christ Jesus for all who believe, without any distinction' (3.21b–22), i.e. to both Jews and Gentiles.

The starting-point for the new argument is the conclusion of the previous chapter: 'Since all have sinned and fall short of the glory of God' (3.23). The contrasting, second part now demonstrates that 'all are justified by his grace as a gift, through the redemption which is in Christ Jesus' (3.24). 'Redemption' (*apolytrōsis*) is here concentrated in the death of Jesus on the cross: 'an expiation by his blood' (3.25). Here 'God's righteousness' is openly manifested (see 3.21); in other words, in this way it emerges that 'God himself is righteous and that he justifies anyone who lives by faith' (3.26). In these few sentences (3.21–26) we have the heart of what Paul seeks to demonstrate in Rom. 4–5 in terms of Jewish argumentation. In Rom. 3.27–31 he already anticipated the conclusion: there is no room for boasting (3.27). The living God is not only a God of the Jews; the contrary cannot be inferred from the Tanach. He, one and the same God, is 'also God of the Gentiles' (3.29). For unless the Torah is to be robbed of its salvation-historical significance as willed by God (3.31b), it has to be conceded on the basis of the Tanach that Yahweh will justify both Jews and non-Jews by faith (3.30). Having put forward this argument, Paul now seeks to justify it. It is important to make a clear distinction between two groups of problems in his argument: the Jewish contrast between grace and works (Rom. 4) and the contrast between grace and sin. This, however, has to happen in such a way that the second group of problems already makes itself felt in the first and the first has an influence on the second.

### (a) The Pauline version of the early Jewish Abraham midrash (Rom. 4.1–25)

In this section Paul is concerned with justification by faith: grace (*kata charin*) is here contrasted with 'what is owed' (*kat'opheilēma*) (Rom. 4.4). The analysis of Rom.1–3 has shown that because of the universality of sin, 'redemption', victory over sin or the forgiveness of sins, will be the gracious act of God, for Jews as for Gentiles. True righteousness is to belong to Jesus, to confess Jesus as the Christ, the one who has been raised from the dead. In Christ the *religious* opposition between the people of God and the *gōyim* or Gentiles is completely a thing of the past.

In order to prove this and to make it clear above all to Jews (the Christians in Rome, to whom Paul addresses this letter, were at that time predominantly Jewish), Paul seeks to draw a connection between the *ḥesed* or *charis* of God and the phenomenon of Jesus Christ. To this end he refers, in a specifically Pauline way, to an already existing Jewish Abraham midrash (Rom. 4.1–25).[30] The essence of this account is as follows. Even according to the Tanach, righteousness (*ṣ<sup>e</sup>dāqā*) is essentially connected with faith, just as in the Jewish tradition *ḥesed* (or God's grace) is connected with righteousness or *ṣ<sup>e</sup>dāqā*: from a Jewish point of view grace, righteousness and faith form a single complex. Therefore in Paul's argument two factors are combined: on the one hand the already existing complex of grace, righteousness and faith (at least in certain Jewish circles), and on the other hand the Christian apostolic datum of faith in Jesus Christ as salvation from God. This association of certain early Jewish concepts with the basic creed of traditional apostolic faith does not immediately give rise to the opposition between Law and *charis* or between Law and Christ, whereas that is precisely Paul's concern. Therefore he will alter the Jewish Abraham midrash in such a way that this contrast clearly emerges from it. A comparison of the Jewish midrash with Paul's version shows that Rom. 4.6–8; 4.13–15 and 4.21, 24f. reveal Paul's redactional intervention into the early Jewish, traditional material. The heart of these changes lies in the fact that Paul identifies the contrast between *charis* (grace) and *ergon* (work) with a contrast between grace and works of the Law (as is already suggested by the conclusion in 3.20, through the insertion of *ex ergōn nomou*, 'through the works of the Law'). Furthermore, almost imperceptibly, he moves here to a contrast between grace and sin. This change gives rise to the contrast between the *charis* of Christ and the Torah. I shall try to explain this more closely.

Romans 4.6–8 already indicates the distinctive version of the Abraham midrash which Paul gives: 'So also David pronounces a blessing on the man to whom God reckons righteousness apart from works: "Blessed are those whose iniquities are forgiven and whose sins are covered" (Ps. 32.1f.)' (Rom. 4.6–8). Grace is not just contrasted with an absence of *works*, but also with the presence of *sin*. This latter element points to the necessity of the death of Jesus; 'but for our [sake] also. It will be reckoned to us who believe in him that raised from the dead Jesus our Lord' (4.24). 4.13–15 also points to a Pauline intervention in the traditional Abraham *pesher*: the promise to Abraham is not founded on the Law, but on the righteousness of faith. The time of the rule of the Law not only hindered the realization of the promise, but provoked God's wrath in place of *charis* (4.14–16). Finally, 4.24f. demonstrates that the 'righteousness of faith' in essence includes the forgiveness of sins. It is not just a question of the works of the Law, but of sinfulness, of wrath because of the Law and *charis* for the sake of Christ. Here *charis* is at the same time the forgiveness of sins. Paul almost imperceptibly changes the

Jewish contrast between grace and works into a contrast between grace (the forgiveness of sins) and *sins*. The reason for God's mercy, namely election, no longer refers to the gift of the Law but to the new monopolistic position of Jesus Christ.

Paul understands election only through faith in Christ; therefore he seeks to abolish election which is based on the gift and possession of the Law. He takes up the traditional Abraham midrash, but alters it in this respect. The preferential position of Judaism, above all on the basis of the *charis* of the Law, must be undermined by the apostolic belief in salvation from God only in Jesus Christ, and Paul will have to show that, with or without the Torah, all men are sinners and need the beneficent forgiveness that comes from God. It is striking that in these first chapters the great contrast is made between God's anger and God's grace, and that the works of the Law do not occupy a central position. Instead we are reminded of the universal sinfulness of all men, even of Jews who do the works of the Law. The wrath of God is itself a product of the Law ('For the Law brings wrath, but where there is no Law there is no transgression', 4.15). If grace is thus contrasted with wrath, then *charis* comes to be contrasted with the Law.

The Pauline version of the Abraham midrash thus gives rise to the following diptych: *charis*, righteousness and faith *over against* wrath, Law and works. This produces an un-Jewish contrast between 'faith' and 'works', a conception which even many Jewish Christians do not understand. However, we must understand Paul's intention and conception properly. In his account both 'works' and 'faith' are given a special significance. 'Works' are associated with the Torah (works of the Law), just as 'faith' is identified with faith in *Christ*. For a Christian, salvation may be associated only with Jesus Christ: that was the heart of the tradition: 'There is salvation in no other' (Acts 4.10–12). In this way Paul had to show that it was impossible for the Law to be an eschatological gift of salvation. He certainly will not deny that faith must become effective 'in works' (above all in works of brotherly love, Gal. 5.6, and 'in all that is righteous', in 'all that is virtuous and deserves praise' Phil. 4.4–9, including an ethical dedication 'to all that is good, very good and perfect', Rom. 12.2; 12.21; II Cor. 8.7b, etc.). Paul is concerned with something else. Just as the Jew acknowledges his faith in the Torah through the works of the Law, so the Christian confesses Jesus as the Christ through faith. So Paul's conclusion from the Abraham midrash is as follows: 'That is why it depends on faith, in order that the promise may rest on grace and be guaranteed to all his descendants – not only to the adherents of the Law but also to those who share the faith of Abraham, for he is the father of us all, as it is written, 'I have made you the father of many nations'' ' (4.16f.). 'Abraham the father of us all' is not only the father of the Jews but the father of all nations; long before the Law came, the saving plan of grace and faith was inaugurated by God in him for all men. '*Dia touto ek pisteōs, hina kata charin*' (4.16a): Paul's stress is placed on exclusive faith *in Christ*, and '*in this way* full of grace' (since for many Jews the Law was the great *charis*). Stress is laid not on grace but on *this* grace: the grace of faith in Christ, since Jews too accepted that grace comes from God's *ḥesed* or gracious gift. The drift of Paul's argument is therefore that the Law represents a hindrance to the *charis* of God because it brought about wrath. With a reference to the figure of Abraham from the time before the Torah, Paul therefore breaks open the restriction of God's gracious election to the circumcised only (Rom. 4.10: 'At that time Abraham was not yet circumcised'). This is a new concept of election, without prior conditions (that is Jewish), and also without restriction to one people, but by means of Abraham as father of all peoples: salvation 'first for the Jews but also for the Gentiles' (Rom. 1.16; 2.10; see 9.1–11.35; see below on 'Israel and the New Testament church', pp. 601ff.). Thus to be a son of Abraham is dissociated from the Torah. The only *way of salvation*, intended from ancient times, is that of faith: Abraham's faith in the coming Christ, the descendant of Abraham. 'Follow the example of the faith which our father Abraham had before he was circumcised' (4.12b).

(*b*) The Pauline version of the early Jewish Adam midrash
(Rom. 5.12–21)

In 5.1–11, Paul sums up what has already been said; justified by faith, we live in peace with God through Christ. This life is a being in grace (5.2), a state of grace which on the one hand is not yet eschatological consummation but a justified expectation of that (5.2), and on the other hand is confirmed and established by the suffering and hindrances that have to be borne in the meanwhile. For if God already loved us 'while we were still sinners' (5.8b), how much more certain may we be 'now that we have been justified through his blood' (5.9), in face of the eschatological judgment. *Reconciliation* has been achieved (5.11); *redemption* (i.e. physical and spiritual salvation) is still to come (see 8.24).

After these musings about faith Paul continues with his explanation. He now discusses the contrast between grace and sin, so to speak as independent power blocks: the sphere of *charis* (grace) and that of *hamartia* (sin); the evil time in which the power of sin prevailed as compared with the time of the friendly rule of Lady Charis; the old age contrasted with the new, for in this letter Paul thinks less of individuals than in terms of 'ages': periods of disaster and periods of salvation, inaugurated by the expiatory death of Jesus. In Rom. 5f. the contrast between Jews and

Gentiles fades into the background. It gives place to the contrast between the first age, the kingdom of sin (for Jews and Gentiles) and the second age, the kingdom of grace 'first for Jews but also for Gentiles' (see Rom. 1.16). Paul is now concerned with the differences in the effectiveness and force of the power which rules the first age and *charis* as the power of the second age. But just as Rom. 4 imperceptibly moves from works of the Law to sin, so Paul does not forget the works of the Law in Rom. 5–6 in his contrast between grace and sin. For Paul sees these works, once they are *outside* the saving sphere of grace, as an expression of servitude to the law of power which is called sin. Adam typology, another midrash from early Judaism,[31] dominates this new account. Paul also uses this traditional midrash to bring into the foreground the eschatologically unique position of Christ as the only mediator of the grace of God. Only through association with Jesus Christ in faith does anyone stand under God's election and in the sphere of God's *charis*, which then has ethical consequences: life without sin. Now the ethic of the Torah is contrasted with the ethic of the one who is associated through faith and baptism with Christ and has 'died to sin' (6.11; 6.17f.; 6.22).

In order to explain his christological exclusiveness (*solus Christus*), Paul now associates the traditional Adam midrash with the Law (as he associated the Abraham midrash with the Law in Rom. 4) (Rom. 5.12–21). (The tradition which stands behind Heb. 2.6–9 also knows this Adam midrash in connection with Ps. 8.4–6 and Gen. 1.27f., as earlier with Paul, I. Cor. 15.45, but here with no reference to the Law.) Paul needs this feature for his new argument, so as to shed new light on the contrast between Christ and the Law. The Law gave the power of sin a good start for its regime, since formally sin is transgression of a Law. The Law makes sin manifest as sin, and also the overabundance of sin. Romans 5.13f. interrupts the argument in order to stress the universality of sin. Otherwise the relationship between sin and Law would not be expressed so sharply. Thus Paul wants to show why, in the period between Adam (who stood under a divine prohibition, Gen. 2.17) and the Mosaic lawgiving, in a time 'without laws', death nevertheless prevailed (as a punishment for sin). These men too were sinful, though not by transgressing an express command or prohibition: they died because of Adam's sin, which was the transgression of a law. Here, then, is the type and antitype of the diptych: the universality of disaster which is to be ascribed to the first Adam, contrasted with the universality of salvation in the second Adam, Christ. Typology culminates in the *abundance* of grace as contrasted with the *abundance* of sin. Just as in Israel's confession of faith God punishes sin to the fourth and fifth generation but shows *ḥesed* 'to the thousandth generation',[32] so in the universality of sin and grace Paul stresses the *all-transcending* manner of the abundance of grace: 'the free gift in the grace of that *one man* Jesus Christ abounded for many' (5.15b), that is, the new Adam or the new man. 'The abundance of grace through the one man Jesus Christ' (5.17). Grace immeasurably transcends the abundance of sin (5.12–21); 'his grace is stronger than this one sin' (5.16), 'so much more glorious . . . is the abundance of grace' (5.17). Romans 5.20 in particular seeks to stress the abundance on both sides so as to express the hyperabundance of grace. (It is difficult to translate the Greek into English: 'Where sin increased, grace abounded all the more', 5.20, is a rather weak rendering. The Vulgate is sharper: *ubi abundavit delictum, superabundavit gratia: epleonasen* as contrasted with *hypereperisseusen*.) Where the measure of sin is full, the measure of grace runs over. Here Paul unmistakably gives a Christian conception of the old Jewish *ḥesed* of Yahweh: the *multo magis* of the *ḥesed* of God in Christ. Here alone is there mention of the *charis* of God (5.15), in Christ.

However, there is also a second contrast between these two universal power blocks, that of sin and that of grace. In the power block in which sin and death prevail, men are tyrannically oppressed; in the power block in which grace prevails, man is freed and made free: 'Through sin death began to prevail . . . through the abundance of grace . . . it is men themselves who rule and live' (5.17). In this way the old connection between 'righteous action' and 'life' becomes an intrinsic and essential connection between grace and life (see 5.10; 5.17,18,21; 6.4) in contrast to the equally essential connection between sin and death; 'Whereas sin exercises lordship through death' (5.21a), 'grace rules through righteousness and for life' (5.21b).

The Adam-Christ typology is taken up again in 5.18f., now under the aspect of what comes at the beginning of the two power blocks or ages: on the one hand a single evil deed of one man – multiplied by the sins of each individual (5.20) – brought disaster to all, while on the other hand a single good deed by one man, Jesus Christ, led to justification or acquittal for all. This one good deed (5.18) of an individual man, by which *charis* and salvation are communicated, is for Paul the obedient sacrifice of Jesus on the cross (4.25; 5.6; 5.8; 5.9–11).

(*c*) Paul's own view of justification

In this long account (Rom. 3–5), *charis* is associated with Jesus' death on the cross, which is clearly seen as a death *to expiate sin*, and is even identified further with *the forgiveness of sins*, which in no way was expiation for sins in Jewish tradition. True, the expiatory offering was the 'canonical' requirement for forensic or juridical acquittal from sin, in the sense of being 'not guilty (any longer) in the eyes of the Law'; however, this juridical level says nothing in itself about the forgiveness of sins, which is reserved to God alone. In 'official' Judaism, anyone is acquitted of sin if he is *ṣaddīq* or if, having transgressed the Law, he makes good this transgression by a sin offering. In both these instances he is *ṣaddīq* on the level of the Law. That was felt to be enough, since it was 'in the name of God', 'thus says Yahweh' (Ezek. 18.9b), that in Judaism the priest declared someone righteous and gave him the right to live (Ezek. 18.9; Pss. 15.5; 24.5). The plane of the forgiveness of sins is another matter; it is God's own forum. And only in some so-called 'non-official' Jewish circles was the opinion held that God forgives not only the *ṣaddīq* but also the sinner. Early Christianity so to speak combined the two Jewish conceptions: God gives *forgiveness of sins* in Christ, who through his bloody death ('justified through his blood', Rom. 5.9) has made *atonement for sins*. In Christ, God and God alone brings about reconciliation (II Cor. 5.17–19). In my view, this combination of two different Jewish conceptions explains the remarkable division that we find in Rom. 4.25; 'put to death for our trespasses and raised for our justification' – expiatory sacrifice and justification and acquittal (after the sacrifice), this time no longer forensically but through the forgiveness of sins as 'dead to sin and alive to God in Christ' (6.11; 6.22); thanks to the *charis* of God (5.15). For Paul, to have oneself baptized and to enter the community of God is the forgiveness of sins and justification,[33] which in formal conceptuality coincide with conversion to Christianity, being bound in faith to Christ, a sign of God's gracious election. As a result, Paul arrives at a formal distinction between justification (*iustificatio impii*) and subsequent sanctification, a distinction which becomes irrelevant in practice in established Christian communities (already in Colossians and Ephesians). However, it emerges from Rom. 1–6 that redemption through Jesus, *charis* and the forgiveness of sins are essentially bound up with the demand to lead an ethically religious life: the works of grace are essential for an understanding of grace that is true to Paul. The life of grace is really 'sinless life' (as the Johannine writings will explain clearly; see below).

However, the consequence of the strong connection in Paul's writing between God's *charis* and the death of Jesus on the cross is that the concept of *charis* to be found in early Jewish wisdom and apocalyptic where it is used to denote a revealed wisdom which is communicated in a supernatural way (see above all in Galatians), fades right into the background. It does not disappear altogether, but it takes a back place in the technical interpretation of grace in Romans (and is first discussed properly in Rom. 8). This gives Paul's concept of *charis* a very specific significance: God's grace is the death of Jesus on the cross: 'Since all have sinned and fall short of the *doxa* or glory of God (*ho theos*: the Father), they are justified by his grace as a gift, through the *apolytrōsis* (or redemptive purchase) (which we have received) in Christ Jesus, whom God designated centuries before as a *hylastērion* – or expiation – for the one who believes – through his blood' (3.23–25b, in a literal translation). That means that the *charis* of the purely eschatological forgiveness of sins (in Judaism) is associated by Paul with a historical event, the sacrifice of Jesus. True, the resurrection of the believers is an event which is still to come, but the eschatological forgiveness of sins is a living actuality. So although salvation or being saved have not yet been completely achieved in the dimension of our history, a central part of this, namely sanctification, freedom from sin and life for God, is already a historically given reality. The eschaton is now already effective and present in history.

Important though this quasi-exclusive connection between *charis* and the *crucifixion* of Jesus is, it is a diminution of the general New Testament concept of grace. In other words, this *charis* concentrated on one point is put in a wider context of grace through the whole of the New Testament. It is here that the Pauline conception of grace has its complete and authentic significance. In Romans the problem of grace is largely limited to the problem of the *iustificatio impii*, conversion to Christianity, a happening which is not often the centre of interest elsewhere in the New Testament writings. It is a way of posing the problem characteristic of early Christianity, whereas at a later stage in the New Testament the concern is above all with the sanctification of Christians, their fidelity and their perseverance. On the other hand, in Romans, which in contrast to Galatians gives a synthesis apart from all the problems with opponents, the whole dogmatic account is put to the service of admonitory paraenesis (Rom. 6–7): the sanctification of Christians who are still constantly inclined to sin. For, while for Christians the specifically Jewish Torah may be done away with, the ethical consequences of the life of grace remain in force.

## III. ETHICAL AND RELIGIOUS CONSEQUENCES OF THE LIFE OF GRACE

In Romans 6.1–7.25 Paul bases the imperative of Christian ethics on the indicative of the reconciliation which has been achieved. Soteriology or the doctrine of salvation issue in a Christian mode of life.

## A. The indicative of the event of baptism in faith

'Sin may have no dominion over you' (6.14a), for 'You are not under the Law but under grace' (6.14b). 'But thanks be to God, that you who were once slaves of sin have become obedient from the heart to the standard of teaching to which you were committed, and, having been set free from sin, have become slaves of righteousness' (6.17f.). 'You are not under the Law, but under grace' (6.14). This transition from the power block and the age of sin into that of grace is accomplished by every Christian at baptism: 'through which we have become one with Jesus Christ' (6.3). By 'sharing in his death' the baptized person is 'dead to sin and alive to God in Christ Jesus' (6.11). Paul distinguishes two aspects: (*a*) 'dead to sin' (6.11) or 'freed from sin' (6.22) and (*b*) 'alive to God in Christ Jesus' (6.11) or 'become servants of God' (6.22). This distinction corresponds with what Rom. 4 has described as: 'Jesus was put to death for our trespasses and raised for our justification' (4.25, though elsewhere Paul usually sees death and resurrection as a whole which has saving power). This formal division of two aspects in the one saving act of Jesus provides a good basis for what Rom. 6 has to say: dead to sin and alive to God. For Paul, this formal distinction is all the more necessary since for him (in contrast to the deutero-Pauline epistles) baptism is *not* a rising with Jesus. Baptism is only dying and being buried with Jesus, dying to sin (6.3; 6.4; 6.6; 6.7). Jesus himself has been raised from the dead (6.9), but we have still to be raised. To follow Jesus 'in his resurrection' (6.5), in expectation of our own, has at first another significance. The resurrection life of Jesus 'is only concerned with God' (6.10b), that is, life in the true sense of the word is always connected with life for God, with a living fellowship with God. Therefore Christian baptism means: (*a*) no longer being servants of sin (6.6), to have settled up with sin (6.10), and therefore to 'live for God' (6.11) – (*b*) not yet being risen with Christ, but only in the spiritual sense, 'as men who have been brought from death (the death of sin) to life' (6.13), namely to life for God without sin. Anyone who lives thus 'has as his reward sanctification and finally eternal life' (6.22), i.e. physical resurrection; but this reward is at the same time and in effect a gift of God: 'the wages of sin is death, but the gift (*charisma*) of God is eternal life in Christ' (6.23, cf. 6.22).

## B. The imperative of the law of grace

The consequences of the fact that redemption as physical wholeness (or resurrection) is not yet complete means that life reconciled to God must be lived under the conditions of the old age, in a *sarx* which is not yet sanctified or in weak humanity, the exponent of which is 'the mortal body' (6.12).[34] 'To serve God in the new life of the Spirit' (7.6c) does not change the constitution of the *sarx* or mortal weakness, which sees the good and fundamentally seeks to do it, but, 'left to itself' (7.25b), cannot accomplish it (7.18b–21). Here (7.7–25) Paul takes up a Stoic theme of the anthropological split between *logos* (reason) and *sarx*, but he baptizes this anthropological split into Christianity by making it a conflict between 'the law of the spirit of Christ' (8.2) and the 'desire of the flesh' (8.6); here it is a question of *the whole man* who is drawn to the good and does what is good through the divine *pneuma* (8.2–4) and, 'left to himself', does evil against his better inclination (7.25b).

In this section *sarx* is man himself in his physical and ethical weakness on the basis of his lack of the Spirit of God in Christ. As the Spirit of God is the foundation of the coming physical resurrection – 'to live in the Spirit' (see I Cor. 15.29; II Cor. 5.5; Rom. 8.23; Phil. 3.21) – in Paul, certainly in Rom. 7 and 8, the human *sōma* or the body plays an essential role in this use of *sarx*; otherwise, expressions like 'mortal body' (8.11; 7.24) and 'members of the body' (7.5; 7.23) would not make any sense at all in this context. Without doubt the background is the Stoic contrast between the *nous*, understanding, which is directed towards the good, and the *soma*, the body, which cannot wholly be governed by the Spirit. The terms *sōma* and *sarx* are constantly interchanged in Rom. 7 and 8, and the whole account is dominated by the sign, 'Who will rescue me from the *sōma tou thanatou*?' (7.24), the body which, while subject to death, is still not a spiritual body. Paul sees the physical body, the body which has not been raised, as a focal point of sin: 'Nothing good dwells in the *sarx*' (7.18), and in 7.22f. he declares that this *sarx* is clearly connected with the human body (which is not risen). Romans 7.24 speaks of *sōma* and 7.25 ends with *sarx*. Above all, 'Let not sin rule in your mortal body' (6.12). Without doubt the 'body of sin' is the 'body of death' (7.24). Thus Rom. 7.14–25 unmistakably makes use of the Stoic division between *sarx (sōma)* and *nous*. *Sarx* or *sōma* is the body as it stands under the power of *hamartia* or sin – not yet redeemed. Both *nous* and *sarx* have their own forms of law: 'the law of the *nous*' (7.22f.) and 'the law of the flesh' (see 7.23), just as there is also mention of the 'law of sin and death' (8.2; 7.25) and 'the law of the members' (7.23).

However, this Stoic background is taken up by Paul in his contrast between *sarx*, i.e. the whole man without the possession of the *pneuma* and *pneuma*, man with possession of God's *pneuma* through grace. This emerges from a formula like 'when we were still in the *sarx*' (7.5); in other words, through the gift of the *pneuma*, the foundation for the resurrection to come (see 8.24), the human body is in principle taken out of its constitution as *sarx*. In principle, the Christian who possesses the *pneuma* may no longer sin (a notion which will find even more vivid formulation in Johannine theology). But in this argument 'a mortal body' is a body which is still under the power of death, as it is itself a fruit of the power of sin (5.21; 6.23; 8.10; see I Cor. 15.56). And for Christians death has not yet been conquered: it is the last enemy (see I Cor. 15.26), although for those who are baptized 'the law of sin and death' (Rom. 8.2) has been broken by the possession of the *pneuma* of God. Even in the body, therefore, a Christian must already live in accordance with the demands of the spirit. Laying aside the *sarx* at baptism is at the same time an ethical imperative for the whole of Christian life (8.13). The counterpart to 'in the *sarx*' is 'in Christ' (8.1) or indwelling of the *pneuma* (8.3; see 8.10; 13.4) or 'in the Lord' (Phil. 4.1). Through baptism man is a 'new creation' (see II Cor. 5.17). Therefore, 'Put on the Lord Jesus Christ and make no provision for the flesh, to gratify its desires' (Rom. 13.14; cf. Gal. 5.16). Thus *sarx* and *pneuma* (in the Christian sense) as it were emerge as living entities (see also Gal. 5.16f.; Rom. 8.5–14). This *sarx* sets itself at enmity with God (8.6; see 8.8; 7.14–25). Because the body is still mortal and therefore a possible entry for the attacks of *hamartia*, 'the Christian *sighs* for the redemption of the body' (8.23), that is, not *from* the body, but *for* a spiritual body. Even in Paul, the physical and the ethical cannot be separated – as throughout the culture of late antiquity. Without leaving aside its formal relationship to the mortal body, *sarx* is man without the *pneuma*; and because the body is still not spiritual, despite the gift of the *pneuma* in baptism, the fight against all sinfulness is still an urgent task for the Christian; the fight of the 'new man' against 'the old man' (see Rom. 6.6; cf. Gal. 5.24): 'Our old man was crucified with him so that the sinful body might be destroyed, and we might no longer be enslaved to sin' (6.6). In all this, 'physical sins' do not occupy the foreground, in a kind of hostility towards the human body, but simply sins of all kinds, though even in Paul's thought the mortal body remains the exponent of our redeemed physical nature. However, *ho thanatos*, death, is not always just physical death, although it is also and formally that (5.12–14); this death also has an ethical and religious significance (1.32; 6.16; 6.21; 7.5; 7.8–13; 8.6–13; see II Cor. 5.14; 7.10). The same is also true of the concept of *apōleia* or corruption (see Rom. 2.12; 9.22; cf. also 8.21; I Cor. 1.18; 8.11; 15.18; II Cor. 2.15; 4.3; I Thess. 5.3; Phil. 1.28; 3.19) and of the concept of *phthora*, transitoriness (Rom. 8.21; Gal. 6.8; I Cor. 15.42).

*Conclusion: Paul's doctrine of justification*

From all that Paul says about justification (Galatians and Romans, with
a short, sharp summary in II Cor. 5.18–21 and Phil. 3.8f.), it becomes
clear what he means on the one hand by faith and on the other by works
of the Law. Faith is putting oneself under the guidance of Jesus Christ
in grace; the works of the Law mean accepting the rule of the Torah,
which Paul has shown to stand under the rule of the 'law of sin'. Throughout the argument, Torah, Law, has almost imperceptibly become the law
of sin, so that the works of the Law also belong within the historical
sphere of the rule of *hamartia*. Paul's argument must sound strange to a
non-Christian Jew, but Paul is writing for Jewish *Christians* who in fact
experience decisive salvation in Jesus from God. First of all, he had said
that God's righteousness gives a reward according to works (works of the
Law) (2.6–10), and thus creates the righteousness that the Law accomplishes; in the later chapters (prepared for by Paul's insertion in the
quotation from the Psalms in Rom. 3.20) it is said that to be *ṣaddīq* in
accordance with the sense of the Law is in no way a manifestation of the
righteousness of God (see the announcement of the theme in 1.17 and
the proclamation of this event in Christ Jesus, 3.21–23). This manifestation has been revealed 'outside the Law' (3.21a), in fact in accordance
with the basic intention of the Tanach itself (3.21b). It is clear that Paul
contrasts the Law as a principle of salvation or way of salvation with
Christ as a way of salvation, and in the light of his belief in salvation in
Christ denies the Law as a principle of salvation (whatever the value of
this Law may have been). It is a question of the apostolic faith: 'Salvation
lies in no other' (Acts 4.12): no more, but also no less. The Jews have
interpreted their own Tanach falsely in that they concentrated on Law
and circumcision, whereas *Israel's own foundation* (see Rom. 9.30–33) is
laid in Abraham's faith in the seed promised to him by God, that is,
Christ Jesus (Gal. 3.16). So for all their 'righteousness based on the Law,
the Jews have not achieved the aim of the Law' (9.31). Paul interprets
this as follows: 'Being ignorant of the righteousness that comes from God,
and seeking to establish their own, they did not submit to God's righteousness' (10.3), that is, they did not hand themselves over to the new age in
which God's *charis* prevails (the new age which is identified by Hebrews
simply as the *charis* of God: see below). The *Didache* will say: 'May grace
– the new age – come and "this world" (the first age) pass away',[35] and
I *Clement* 7.4 will say – in Pauline terms: the blood which Jesus shed for
our salvation has brought the *charis* of *metanoia* (conversion) to the whole
world. The Pauline feature is *charis* as the universal salvation of mankind
as an act of God in Jesus the Christ. That is why Paul could write in
Gal. 3.22: 'Scripture consigned all things to sin, that what was promised

to faith in Jesus Christ might be given to those who believe.' Scripture is the promise to Abraham from the Tanach, and because God speaks in scripture, Paul can write in Romans: *'Synekleisen ho Theos tous pantas eis apeitheian, hina tous pantas eleēsē'* (Rom. 11.32): God has shut up (or imprisoned all men in sin ( = disobedience) in order to include all, both Jews and Greeks, in his mercy. In Jesus, from now on 'works' become the expression and the consequence of salvation in Jesus and no longer salvation in the Law, for despite everything Paul does not criticize the works of the Law, but only the works of the Law as a principle of salvation.

## IV. PSEUDO-PAULINISM AND THE LETTER OF JAMES

Literature (see also the literature of *ṣˤdāqā,* above): T. Boman, *Die Jesus–Überlieferung im Lichte der neueren Volkskunde,* Göttingen 1967, 196–207; M. Dibelius, *Der Brief des Jakobus* (Meyer 15), Göttingen [10]1959; F. Grosheide, *De brief aan de Hebreeën en de brief van Jakobus,* Kampen 1955; I. Jacobs, 'The Midrashic Background for James II, 21–23', *NTS* 22, 1976, 457–64; G. Kittel, 'Der geschichtliche Ort des Jakobusbriefes', *ZNW* 41, 1942, 94–102; J. Marty, *L'épître de Jacques,* Paris 1935; M. Meinertz, *Der Jakobusbrief,* HSNT 9, Bonn [4]1932; A. Meyer, *Das Rätsel des Jakobusbriefes,* Giessen 1930; J. Michl, *Die katholischen Briefe,* RNT 8, Regensburg 1953; F. Mussner, *Der Jakobusbrief,* HThKNT, Freiburg im Breisgau [3]1975; H. Rendtorff, *Hörer und Täter. Eine Einführung in den Jakobusbrief,* Hamburg 1956; A. Schlatter, *Der Brief des Jakobus,* Stuttgart [2]1956; J. Schneider, *Die Briefe des Jakobus, Petrus und Johannes,* NTD 10, Göttingen 1961; E. Tobac, 'Le problème de la justification dans saint Paul et dans saint Jacques', *RHE* 22, 1926, 797–805.

Man will be 'blessed . . . in his doing' (James 1.25): 'It is clear that man is *justified by works* and *not by faith alone'* (2.24). This *seems* to be an antithesis to Paul, but that is not the case. However, it cannot be denied that the impression we get from James 2.14–26 has something to do with 'Paulinism' as this was in fact understood, above all by a number of Christians from a Gentile background. Paul himself had to fight against pseudo-Paulinism (Rom. 3.8; 6.1; cf. Gal. 2.11).

The question whether Paul is attacking the group to which James belongs or James is attacking Paul depends, among other things, on the dating of this letter. For some scholars James is the oldest writing in the New Testament;[36] others date it around the middle of the second century;[37] that is surely a mistake, since after 70 the Jewish-Christian communities (to whom this letter is directed, 1.1) had lost all significance. Others put it about the time of Paul's letters to the Christians in Rome, i.e. about AD 60[38] (though the author does not know Romans). Everything indicates that James goes back to the circle around James the Less, the great leader of the mother church in Jerusalem, and that the letter was therefore written before 70 (say between 50 and 60).

In order to understand James' doctrine of justification, we must put it in the context of the *theology of the poor* which is so characteristic of this letter (1.9–11; 2.1–23; 5.1–6). The author is ignorant of any Pauline theology of the cross; he is evidently more interested in Jesus of Nazareth, the great prophet of love, and probably stands in the Q tradition; more-over, he is familiar with sources which are peculiar to Matthew and Luke. His theological model is that of humiliation and exaltation, of poor and rich. Furthermore, the 'poor of Jerusalem' is a technical term in the New Testament; they are 'Israel's remnant', the poor (Zeph. 3.12; see Gal. 2.10; II Cor. 8.9; Acts 11.29). It is well known that the Christians in Jerusalem drew their recruits from the poorest classes. For James, the Jews who persecuted the young church (Acts 17.5; I Thess. 2.14–16) are therefore 'the rich', who persecute the poor. James develops his theology of the poor above all in 2.1–13. The author attacks a worldly disposition; the very pronounced class distinction of antiquity threatens also to find its way into the church. Suppose that a man comes to a Christian meeting with a gold ring and fine clothing and 'a poor man comes in in dirty clothing'; if one says to the man with fine clothes, 'Sit here in the place of honour', and to the poor man, 'stand there, or sit under my footstool' (2.2), can such an attitude be reconciled with 'belief in our Lord Jesus Christ'? (2.4 and 2.1). Then James explains how God thinks otherwise: he prefers the poor and gives him the place of honour (2.5). God chooses what the world finds uninteresting (cf. I Cor 1.27f.). God calls the poor, but you humiliate the poor (2.6), whereas – James takes up an Old Testament theme – it is the rich who do violence to the poor (2.6b, see: Wisdom 2.10; 17.2; Hab. 1.4; Amos 4.1; 8.4; Zech 7.10; Jer 7.6; 22.3; Ezek. 18.12; Isa. 59.9; Micah 6.11f.; etc.). This is 'godless' behaviour (Jer. 5.26f.; Isa. 59.9), a stain on the name of Jesus which is spoken over Christians, the poor, in baptism (2.7): the humiliation of the poor whom God exalts (see also Prov. 14.21; Sir. 10.24[27]). James therefore calls love of neighbour and help for the poor the 'royal commandment' (2.8; see Lev. 19.18); this law of love has the supreme royal status among all the works of the Law. Not to follow this commandment to love is tanta-mount to despising the whole Law (2.10f.). To refuse to love one's neighbour and help the poor is like murder (see 2.11; see Sir. 34.26, which strongly influences the paraenesis in the Letter of James). The author names this 'the law of freedom' (2.12), 'the perfect law, the law of freedom' (1.25), that is, which leads men to freedom. The law of freedom is *eleos*, mercy (2.13), solidarity with the poor. Christianity is love of one's neighbour and, above all, solidarity with the poor and oppressed. Therefore James' judgment on the unsocial rich is extraordinarily sharp (5.1–6): 'You have laid up treasure for the last days. Behold, the wages of the labourers who mowed your fields, which you kept back by fraud, cry out; and the cries of the harvesters have reached the ears of the Lord of hosts. . . . You have condemned, you have killed the righteous man; he does not resist you.' This is doubtless a Jewish theme, but now it is connected with 'faith in Jesus Christ' (2.1). The synoptic Jesus, with his love of the poor and his attack on the service of mammon, along with the opening of the kingdom of God to the poor, the maimed and the blind, has a strong influence on this Jewish Christianity of the Jerusalem church (see Luke 6.20; 14.13; 14.21; Mark 4.19; 8.36 par.; 10.21 par.; Matt 11.5 par. Luke 7.22; Matt. 6.24 par.; 6.19f. par.; 10.9f.). When James thinks of works, he first of all has in mind the work of loving one's neighbour (see also John 4.34; 7.17; 9.31; 15.14).

In this connection he speaks of the role of faith and works in justification (2.14–26). 'Faith without works is nothing' (2.14–20). James does not attack Paul in any way, but a pseudo-Paulinism. Suppose, the author says, that someone is poverty-stricken and you give him a friendly pat on the shoulder and tell him to 'Keep your spirits up', or something similar – what is the use of that (2.14)? 'So faith by itself, if it has no works, is dead' (2.17) 'To have faith' can only be demonstrated in consistent actions; without works, faith can be pure illusion, a mere form of words (2.18; see Isa. 58.7; Prov. 3.27f.). For James, not showing mercy to the poor (2.1–13) is the occasion for attacking a false concept of 'justification through faith *alone*'. 'Faith without works' (2.26) is nothing, a torso; and for James, works are acts of loving one's neighbour. Paul says the same thing, 'Faith which expresses itself in love' (Gal. 5.6).

Now it is very striking that both Paul and James support their own view of justification biblically by referring to the same model: Abraham (Rom. 4; James 2.21–23), and moreover both of them quote Gen. 15.6!. Paul concludes from this exegesis, 'Therefore, without works' (Rom. 3.28), while James, on the other hand, argues, 'Thus, not without works' (James 2.24). True, as will transpire, there is really no contradiction between James and Paul, but from the whole context it can hardly be denied that James has something like 'pseudo-Paulinism' in mind. We must first investigate the biblical background to James 2.21–26. In the last resort, James 2.21 points back to Gen. 22.9, 10, 12, the sacrifice of Isaac (see Heb. 11.17), but connects this text with Gen. 15.6 (in accordance with the hermeneutical principle of the time: 'There is no "earlier" or "later", i.e. no chronological order in the Torah').[39] James 2.21 quotes Gen. 22.9

literally, with the exception of one word: it chooses 'offered upon the altar' (according to Gen. 22.2,13, *anapherein*) as technical sacrificial terminology. This readiness of Abraham to sacrifice Isaac, the son of the promise, this *ergon* or work, was the basis for his justification by God.

Genesis 22.16–18 in fact says: 'Because you have *done* this and have not held back your son, your only son, *therefore* I will richly bless you.' Thus James rightly reads an *ergon*, a work, into this 'what you have done'. On the other hand, Gen. 15.6 says: 'Abraham *believed* Yahweh, and he reckoned it to him as righteousness.' One Genesis text speaks of 'righteousness by faith' and the other of 'righteousness through works'. James now combines the two: in justification there is a *synergeia* of faith and works: *synergei (hē pistis) tois ergois autou* (James 2.22), that is, Abraham's faith helped his works (*synergei*); faith and work form an indissoluble whole. Faith itself is effective in 'work' and faith is 'completed' (2.22b), and in this way the truth of scripture becomes clear: 'Abraham *believed* in God' (Gen. 15.6), and therefore he was not only 'justified' but called 'friend of God' (2.23). Abraham's faith *showed* itself in his readiness to sacrifice Isaac. Thus faith justifies, but not 'by itself'; only when it shows itself in action. Abraham is not an example of *iustificatio e sola fide,* much less *e solis operibus;* he is an example of this synergy or combination of 'faith' and 'work'. The particular feature of this argument is that Gen. 22 is connected with Gen. 15.6. Now this is not an invention of James; the connection was already there in early Judaism. It is still rather vague in I Macc. 2.52: 'Was not Abraham found *faithful* when tested, and it was reckoned to him as righteousness?' (F. Mussner already noticed this);[40] more explicitly in Sir. 44.20f., where the sacrifice of Isaac (Gen. 22) was already bound up with God's oath to Abraham and consequently with Abraham's *faith* (Gen. 15); in addition to that, and more explicitly,[41] it is to be found in Pseudo-Philo.[42] Here Gen. 22 is simply 'interpreted' by Gen. 15 in accordance with a well-tried early Jewish pattern of exegesis. God himself – not James(!) – therefore declares Abraham 'righteous', the 'friend of God', on the basis of the *synergeia* or the combination of faith and works achieved by him (2.23). The general conclusion (which does not only apply to Abraham) is: 'You see that a man is justified by works and not by faith alone' (2.24), that is, indeed by faith, but a faith which expresses itself in action, a plausible interpretation.

Thus James does not in any way defend the principle of works; he is completely in agreement with Paul that faith must be effective in brotherly love; otherwise it makes no sense (James 2.14–17; Gal. 5.6). But for James, *ergon* means a *work of love,* whereas in Paul (in Galatians and Romans) it means a *work of the Law.* Paul could happily subscribe to James' 'justification', but *he* fights against people who tend to explain the law as *the way to salvation,* even for Gentiles who become Christians. The way to salvation by works of the Law is contrasted with the way to salvation through faith in Christ (which is made effective in love) (Rom. 3.20,27,28; 4.2,6; 9.11,32; 11.6; Gal. 2.16; 3.2,5,10). But this faith in Christ requires good works of the kind which James demands (Rom. 2.7; 13.3; Phil. 1.6; Paulinism: Eph. 2.10; Col. 1.10; 3.17; II Thess. 2.17). Furthermore, Paul accepts 'reward according to works' (Rom. 2.6; 14.10b; I Cor. 3.12–17; 9.23–27; 10.11f; II Cor.5.10; 6.1; Phil. 2.12; 3.8,14). By contrast, James directs his comments to Christians who call 'Lord, Lord', 'believe' (see Matt. 7.21), and at the same time oppress the poor. The later controversy between Augustine and Luther does not enter the picture here. For both Paul and James, faith is only *consummated* in brotherly love and solidarity with the despised poor. But both have to criticize other 'heresies'. Thus for James too, faith in Christ brings justification (2.14; 2.17; 2.18; 2.20; 2.22; 2.26), but this must always be a consistent faith which *makes itself manifest* in love: otherwise one never knows whether faith is there (2.18). James is evidently concerned with Gentile Christians who now believe in the one true God ('You believe that there is only one God . . . excellent!. . .', 2.19) and are fanatics about this new experience. But 'even the devils believe and tremble' (2.19c). The 'tremendous' element in monotheism[43] does not bring justification (here it is clear that James cannot have the real Paul in mind); this must lead to love shown by solidarity. A believer is 'a *doer* of the word' (1.25), 'a doer that acts' (1.25), 'a doer of the Law' (4.11), but Paul says that just as forcefully in Rom. 2.13!

As a second example alongside Abraham, for whom the justifying power of faith 'proves' itself in works, James mentions the case of the harlot Rahab (a favourite theme in early Judaism and Christianity; see James 2.25; Heb. 11.31). Rahab is a Gentile woman who is not only saved by acts of faith from the ruin of the city (Josh. 6.22–25), but according to a Jewish legend becomes the mother of a family which includes many prophets and priests;[44] according to Matt. 1.5, even Christ. Thus without works of love, faith is 'a corpse' (2.26).

In essentials, Paul and James are agreed: James criticizes the caricature of Paulinism which is produced by many people. However, there is a difference between the theology of the early Jewish Christian congregations in Jerusalem which are oriented on *Jesus of Nazareth*, and Pauline theology, which only knows 'the crucified'. There are two aspects of one and the same Jesus, but James experiences in Jesus not so much the one who has given his life as an expiatory offering as the great prophet of the kingdom of God for the poor, the prophet of radical love for one's neighbour. For Paul, however, this emerges most strongly from his sacrificial death. James stands in a tradition which intensively recalls the action and enduring of Jesus; Paul in a tradition which reflects on all the consequences of the death of Jesus. The consequences are the same. James is more oriented on Jesus, Paul more on Christ. The consequences are the same: Jesus of Nazareth *is* the risen crucified one. The orthopraxis of both Paul and James stresses one and the same orthodoxy.

Finally, James stands in the same line of tradition as I Peter. There are not only literary points of contact (James 1.1 → I Peter 1.1; James 1.10f. → I Peter 1.24; James 1.18 → I Peter 1.23; James 4.6 → I Peter 5.5; James 4.10 → I Peter 5.6; James 5.20 → I Peter 4.8), but the problem of suffering (typical of Mark, I Peter and Hebrews) is also central to James. Faith is trust in God (in the Jewish scene) (1.3; 1.6–8); it is a faith in the eschatological future and therefore a 'faith in Jesus Christ' (2.1), but a faith or an 'orthodoxy' which makes itself known in the orthopraxis of love (1.21–27; 2.14–26) and in the ethical obedience of faith towards God (1.27b; 3.18; 4.13–15). For James, too, 'the Law' is the gospel of Jesus Christ (1.21f.). But faith is put to the test of *peirasmos* (1.12–18); suffering tests faith. James refuses to say that God tempts us (1.13). Only good comes from God, the source of all illuminating goodness (1.13–17), the Creator of light. Christians are 'born of God' through baptism, and so 'a kind of first-fruits of God's creation' (1.18, just as Israel is 'God's firstborn', Ex. 4.22; Jer. 2.3; see Rom. 16.5; I Cor. 15.20; 16.15; Rev. 14.4), the first-fruits of the new creation of God (above all the Jewish Christians in Jerusalem). But this birth from God (see also Johannine theology, which has Palestinian sources) is bound up with the 'birth-pangs which lead to life': 'When he has stood the test he will receive the crown of life which God has promised to those who love him' (1.12). The author returns to this suffering before the parousia in 5.7–11.

In the Letter of James we recognize all the features of the primal (Aramaic and Greek-Jewish) Jerusalem community, *perhaps* through the mediation of the Hellenistic Jews from Jerusalem. It is striking that we have the first indication of the Letter of James in Egypt (Alexandria). Does this letter hint at the Jewish-Christian communities in Alexandria of which Luke says nothing? The author calls himself James (the Less), and writes his letter to the twelve tribes of Israel 'in the diaspora', the primitive community as 'the remnant of Israel'. Here we have a clear expression of 'exported' *Palestinian Christianity*, without a developed christology, which has nevertheless preserved Jesus' deeds and experiences as a 'dangerous memory'. It also gives us some insight into the misunderstanding that 'Paulinism' caused in the primitive church (see also II Peter 3.15f.). In the Letter of James we perceive a living echo of the peace-loving Q tradition, somewhat turned in on itself, looking out for the parousia and the final judgment, which then clearly bears the stamp of very definite Jewish Christian communities.

## §4 Transition from Paul to Paulinism: Philippians

*Literature*: F. W. Beare, *A Commentary on the Epistle to the Philippians*, London and New York [3]1973; G. Bornkamm, 'On Understanding the Christ-Hymn (Philippians 2.6–11)', ET in *Early Christian Experience*, London and New York 1969, 112–22; L. Cerfaux, 'L'hymne au Christ-Serviteur de Dieu', in *Miscellanea historica* I, FS A. Meyer, Louvain 1946, 117–30; J. Collange, *L'Épître de saint Paul au Philippiens*, Neuchâtel 1973; R. G. Hamerton-Kelly, *Pre-existence, Wisdom and the Son of Man*, Cambridge 1973, 156–68; J. Huby, *Saint Paul, Les épîtres de la captivité*, Paris 1947; D. Georgi, 'Der vorpaulinische Hymnus Phil. 2.6–11', in *Zeit und Geschichte*, FS R. Bultmann, Tübingen 1964, 263–93; J. Gnilka, *Der Philipperbrief*, Freiburg im Breisgau [2]1976; J. Jeremias, 'Zu Phil. 2,7, eauton ekénôsen', *NT* 6, 1963, 182–8; E. Käsemann, 'Kritische Analyse von Phil. 2,5–11', in *Exegetische Versuche und Besinnungen* I, Göttingen [4]1965, 51–95; A. Klijn, *De brief van Paulus aan de Filippenzen*, Nijkerk 1969; E. Lohmeyer, *Der Brief an die Philipper, Kolosser und an Philemon*, Meyer 9, Göttingen [10]1956; R. Martin, *Carmen Christi: Phil. II, 5–11 in Recent Interpretation and in the Setting of Early Christian Worship*, Cambridge 1967; G. H. ter Schegget, *Het lied van de mensenzoon. Studie over de Christuspsalm in Fil. 2:6–11*, Baarn 1975; J. A. Sanders, 'Dissenting Deities and Philippians 2,1–11', *JBL* 88, 1969, 279–90; J. T. Sanders, *The New Testament Christological Hymns*, Cambridge 1971; G. Strecker, 'Redaktion und Tradition im Christushymnus Phil. 2,6–11', *ZNW* 55, 1964, 63–78; E. Schweizer, *Erniedrigung und Erhöhung bei Jesus und seinen Nachfolgern*, ATANT 28, Zurich [2]1962; C. H. Talbert, 'The Problem of Pre-existence in Phil. 2.6–11', *JBL* 86, 1967, 141–53; K. Wengst, *Christologische Formeln und Lieder des Urchristentums*, Gütersloh 1973.

Exegetes do not dispute that this is an authentic letter of Paul. However, there is much to support the assumption that someone from Paul's school has combined two of his letters, relating to two completely different situations, into one, and to achieve this had to do some 'joining'. A legitimate division would then produce the following result: 1. 'Philippians A': 1.1–3.1a and 4.2–7, 10–23 (perhaps from the years 55–60); and 2. 'Philippians B': 3.1b–4.1, 8f. (of a later date: whereas the combination of the two parts by an editor would have to be put, at latest, in the nineties).[45] However, this problem is not really relevant to the purpose of our theological interpretation. I personally believe that the second part of this letter in fact has *deutero*-Pauline features; it presupposes a 'reverence for Paul' in the Pauline school (3.1–15).

## I. JESUS CHRIST AS *SŌTĒR*: BENEFACTOR AND SAVIOUR

In the second (late Pauline) part of his letter (Phil. 3.1b – 4.1, 8f.) Paul in fact adopts a sharper tone than in his first part. What has happened? Philippi, Paul's favourite community, seems to have fallen victim to some false teaching which can only be reconstructed from Paul's reaction.

The syncretism of late antiquity is beginning to disturb the apostolic faith throughout Greece, but above all in east Macedonia, through the pressure of certain propagandists in the Christian community. Jewish, Hellenistic and Asiatic elements are being combined with Christian faith. Paul interprets this phenomenon – wrongly – as a new form of the re-Judaizing of Christianity, because the propagandists argue for circumcision (Phil. 3.3), and do so in a predominantly Gentile Christian community. However, in Colossians 'circumcision' clearly means more a kind of mystery religion in which a man puts off 'the old man' and is filled with the divine through initiation. Circumcision (whether Jewish or non-Jewish) also enjoyed a high reputation among Gentiles within the syncretism of the time; it was part of the 'new fashion'. In Philippi, the heretics called themselves 'the perfect' (see 3.15), filled with the *pneuma*, although they did not espouse any libertinism of grace (3.15f.). However, they deny that suffering is the way to glorification. As Paul interprets the phenomenon, they reject the cross (3.18). Evidently Paul's opponents do this out of a spiritual enthusiasm for perfection (3.12–16). It is striking that Paul interprets their view as a denial of the resurrection, at least in the sense that these enthusiastic Christians claim that they no longer need the resurrection (cf. also I Cor. 15.12, or, as some will say later, 'We are already risen', see II Tim. 2.18). Philo had already spoken of a 'calling from above' to the divine as a special feature of men filled with the spirit, who are convinced that they are only sojourners here on earth, whereas their *politeuma* or true fatherland is in heaven.[46] These false teachers evidently speak of a *Sōtēr* or Saviour, pride themselves on an allegorical interpretation of the Tanach, and, as in Galatians (later, too, in Colossians), a piety based on observing times and seasons also plays a role. In short, theirs is an enthusiastic religious experience which, as Paul understands it, by-passes the cross and hope of a resurrection still to come and takes delight in spiritual experiences of perfection, fulfilment and completeness (3.12–16).

D. Georgi and J. Gnilka see here a sign of Hellenistic philosophy or the approach of the *theios anēr*, following the pattern of the Mosaic Sinaitism which we find, for example, in Philo.[47] The problem is that such a well-rounded philosophy of the *theios anēr* is a construction of scholars, above all, since we see 'miracle workers' as part of it.[48] However, it is certain that there was knowledge of 'men of God' in the sense of people with mystical connections with God. And in this sense the expression well reflects what was happening in Philippi (here, too, there is no mention of thaumaturges or miracle workers). It seems to me incomprehensible that the false teaching should be an overestimation of the historical Jesus, namely as a miracle worker, as J. Gnilka claims.[49] In that case these people would share a universal tendency of Greek Judaism of the time, according to which the earthly Jesus with his divine *dynamis* would be enough for human salvation; by contrast, cross and resurrection would be superfluous. In that case the divine power of Christ would make itself evident in the heightened sense of living and the powerful impression made by these Christians, which would stand in sharp contradiction to the weakness and sickly appearance of Paul (Paul was evidently a small, unattractive, sickly man, which is perhaps what made him so aggressive in character). For these men, suffering and weakness brought the power of proclamation and its herald into discredit. I have already criticized a *theios anēr* christology in my book *Jesus. An Experiment in Christology*.[50] No trace of it is to be found at Philippi. What we have is a so-called heterodox-Jewish mysticism of the 'perfect' who, by being filled with the Spirit, already live in heaven, who have 'true knowledge', and who make scripture serve to articulate their heavenly experiences by allegorical interpretation – as it were Pentecostalism in its least authentic form, a further stage of what was already developing in II Corinthians. In both cases these propagandists concentrate their activity on Greece. Here we have a conglomeration of what will emerge in an even more evocative form from this cosmopolitan melting-pot in Asia Minor. The *anō klēsis* or 'calling from above, or heavenwards', a term which Paul evidently takes over from his opponents, points to the habitation of heavenly spheres by spiritualistic Christians in ecstasy. Hebrews and Colossians will be critical of this phenomenon, but on the whole it is still regarded positively: they Christianize this tendency (see below). Paul attacks it sharply, because he fears that here the foundations of apostolic faith threaten to vanish into the mist. 'Look out for the dogs, look out for the evil-workers, look out for those who mutilate the flesh. For we are the true circumcision, who worship God in spirit' (3.2f.).

Over against the false teaching he briefly and tersely sets 'righteousness from God on the basis of faith' (3.9). Being joined to Christ in the Spirit – 'being in Christ' – finds its foundation in the 'righteousness of God' (*dikaiosynē tou theou*, the basic theme of Romans). For the Christians in Philippi know Paul's doctrine of justification. Paul sets against the false teachers' illusion of perfection the idea of being the church on the way (3.12–16; 3.17–21), and above all launches a sharp attack on the *de facto* misunderstanding of the cross (3.18), which is a threat in such mystical experiences. Thus Paul attacks an *experience* of 'realized eschatology' on the part of Christians who believe that they are already living in heaven. Philo had already written: 'They regard the heavenly sphere, in which *the wise men* live as citizens, as their fatherland.'[51] In a hymn which has perhaps been inserted, it is said, 'But our commonwealth is in heaven, and from it we await a Saviour (*Sōtēr*), the Lord Jesus Christ' (3.20). 'He will change our lowly body to be like his glorious body, by the power which enables him even to subject all things to himself' (3.21). Paul concedes that the fatherland of Christians is heaven, where the *Sōtēr* Christ lives, but resurrection and glorification and eternal life are still to come. Paul has not used the Greek religious word *sōtēr* before. It means benefactor, one who gives *sōtēria*, salvation, i.e. the forgiveness of sins, a protection against demonic powers and the gift of eternal life.[52] Evidently *sōtēr* and *politeuma* were favourite words among the false teachers; Paul quotes them critically, for the heavenly life of these Christians resulted in a kind of ethical indifference to the physical. Christ will transform our body 'by the power which enables him even to subject all things to himself' (3.21b); here the Greek Ps. 8.7 is transferred to Christ himself; that is more a deutero-Pauline feature than a characteristic of Paul himself. Paul always makes this attribution to God through Christ; he never makes Christ the active subject. However, Paul is no stranger to the idea that Christ is not just Lord of the church, but Lord of the universe (see I Cor. 15.25–28).

## II. THE HYMN TO TRUE GREATNESS, I.E. TO THE HUMILIATED ONE (PHIL. 2.6–11)

Of theological significance in the first part of this letter (1.1–3a and 4.2–7, 10–23) is the christological hymn – one of the many hymns to Christ which was composed by Christians from Hellenistic Judaism who were interested in the mission to the Gentiles. Paul has incorporated the hymn with manifestly paraenetical intent: 'Let that mind be in you which was also in Christ Jesus' (Phil. 2.5): then follows the hymn. The result is that whatever the hymn may mean outside this letter, Paul reads into it a model which he requires his Christians to follow: to exercise *tapeinophrosynē* towards one another, i.e. in modesty and humility to reckon the other person higher than oneself and to support the interests of others rather than one's own (2.3f.). In the hymn itself (2.8), the *tapeinōsis* of Jesus occupies a central place. In what does this humiliation of Jesus consist? He 'humbled himself, taking upon himself the form of a servant' (2.7). To call a man *doulos* in this culture of late antiquity is to refer to his subjection to supernatural, heavenly powers who determine human destiny (see also Gal. 4.3f., 8f.; Rom. 8.21; and outside Paul, Heb. 2.15 and passim, see below: Col. 2.20). *Doulos* is the human condition as inter-preted in late antiquity: the plaything of fate or destiny and all kinds of supernatural forces.[53] Being human is called humiliation above all in Hebrews (see below); it is even more so for a pre-existent heavenly being, because according to the early Jewish interpretation of Ps. 8.4–6, this was a demotion 'below the angels'.[54] In Philo, too, *tapeinōsis* means the worth-less, transitory existence of human beings who are condemned to death;[55] to be human means to enter upon man's difficult history of suffering. The fact that Jesus accepts this human life freely and is obedient to death as the nadir of the situation of *douleia* or human servitude, shows the great-ness of the man who has freely accepted this humiliation. Whether the status of Christ is an 'eschatological' (*res rapienda*) or a 'protological' (*res rapta*) pre-existence is incidental, at least as far as Paul is concerned: with this hymn he means to say that true greatness manifests itself in humility, in identification with enslaved and fallen man, and that such an attitude to life finally receives God's blessing. God himself will publicly proclaim the true greatness of this man, for before the eyes of the world it remains hidden. This is the moral lesson which Paul offers to his Christians from this hymn to Christ.

As a pre-Pauline hymn to Christ, the hymn which Paul has incorpor-ated into his letter does not necessarily have the intention which he assigns to it. In fact the author of the hymn means to present a christo-logy, a confession of Jesus Christ as cosmocrator, ruler of the world, to whom everything (upon, above and under the earth) has been subjected. But there is considerable dispute about the interpretation of the hymn. Its structure meets with quite general assent: (*a*) 2.6–7a; (*b*) 2.7bc–8b; (*c*) 2.9 and (*d*) 2.10f.: in other words, pre-existence, incarnation, exalta-tion, universal homage to the ruler Christ Jesus. Interpretations diverge because many interpreters continue to begin from a sharp distinction between 'Palestinian Jewish' and 'Hellenistic' influence, although this distinction is no longer historically tenable; above all in the first century AD, Judaism too was characterized by a syncretistic mixture of Jewish, Greek and Oriental Hellenistic influences, even in Palestine.

E. Lohmeyer and J. Jeremias think in terms of a purely Palestinian Jewish background: in that case the hymn is a combination of the suffer-ing servant of God (Isa. 53) with the Danielic Son of man (Dan. 7.13). E. Käsemann sees a Greek, even gnostic model here: the *anthrōpos* myth or the mythical history of the primal man who in wisdom literature and also in Philo was identified with wisdom or the Logos. In the hymn, Christ is then the antitype of Adam or the first, disobedient man; he is the obedient eschatological man who by freely and obediently subjecting himself to death has broken the power of death and redeemed man for freedom. This view has been adopted by many modern exegetes after a number of corrections, say as a combination of Palestinian and Greek traditions. This is especially the view of J. Jervell in his book *Imago Dei*, which has become a classic.[56] By contrast, D. Georgi wants above all to stress the influence of Isa. 45.23, in other words the influence of the Hellenistic Jewish Septuagint, as say in Wisdom 1–9, where wisdom enters into a wise man but nevertheless remains different from him. However, in the hymn there is an identification, and that is rather different! Still, Georgi is right to point to the fact that in Wisdom 3 and 4 the death of the wise man is an exaltation and that the doxology of Phil. 2.11 shows affinities with Wisdom 18.13. At an earlier stage L. Cerfaux had seen a close affinity between this hymn to Christ and the Greek Isaiah (Isa. 49.4; 53.8; 53.12; 49.7).[57] J. T. Sanders assents to this view but makes it more precise: he argues that the similarities with the Hebrew text of Isaiah are even more significant, above all those with Isa. 53.[58] Furthermore, J. A. Sanders sees affinities with Jewish apocalyptic, in which 'heavenly beings' are envious of men and want to make themselves equal to God and to rebel against God.[59] G. Strecker looks for a solution completely in this direction, following Phil. 3.20f.[60] E. Schweizer, L. Ruppert and G. Nickelsburg stress that the exalted 'suffering righteous man' of Deutero-Isaiah was already identified in early Judaism with the apocalyptic Son of man.[61] Finally, R. Hamerton-Kelly puts forward a fine abstract synthesis. Philippians 2.5–11 represents a combination of the heavenly redeemer from Jewish apocalyptic and the heavenly anthropos of the *Corpus Hermeticum* 1,12–14.[62] The correct insight in this position is that in the first century AD Jewish apocalyptic, Greek mysticism and the wisdom traditions come together syncretistically.

However, it emerges from this plethora of interpretations that the investigation has been more concerned with the background of the hymn in the history of religions than with its significance *within* the structure of Philippians. Of course the one cannot be detached from the other. The interest of this whole discussion lies in the question whether the *forma dei*, the form of God, mentioned in Phil. 2.5 is a *res rapta* or a *res rapienda*.[63] That is, is being equal with God a pre-existent state of Christ or something for which man strives (like the angels in Jewish apocalyptic)? In other words, it is a question of protological pre-existence (i.e. the divinity of Christ) or eschatological pre-existence. One can and, in my opinion, must first put the question how Paul himself has understood the hymn in view of his paraenetic purpose. He is not concerned with some temptation in pre-existence, but with obedience *in* the human state itself. The decision for humiliation is predicated solely of the *man Jesus*: '*Being found as man* he *humbled* himself . . . even to death', whereas on the other hand 2.7 speaks of a *kenōsis*, namely of the incarnation itself. There is a difference between this *kenōsis* or self-emptying, the incarnation as such, and the *tapeinōsis* or humiliation, which is a reference to death. The one who by nature has true greatness, not only 'emptied' himself in becoming man, but as man also accepted the ignominious fate of crucifixion. I therefore wonder whether, contrary to the claim of many exegetes, the phrase 'even to the death of a cross' does not belong to the original hymn. Otherwise the distinction between *kenōsis* and *tapeinōsis* would simply remain without an object; for the *forma servi* already embraces mortality and death, but not *per se* the humiliation of a crucifixion. In my view the *hyper-* in the term 'super-exalted' therefore refers primarily to the divine reparation for this twofold humiliation – *kenōsis* and *tapeinōsis;* not only the first but also this second 'degradation' is honoured, and more than honoured (*hyper-*), by God. In view of the spirit of the hymn and the way in which Paul understands it, there must therefore be a reference to protological pre-existence in the strict sense. In that case it is obvious that such an attitude of humble identification with the human condition of servitude was thought by people of the time to stand in marked contrast to what contemporary (inter-testamental) literature had to say about arrogant angels who were envious of men as the 'image of God' and 'lords of creation' (Gen. 1.28), and even ventured to build their throne in highest heaven,[64] or who wanted to bring down men, as the crown jewels of creation, by urging them to be 'equal to the *'lōhīm'* (Gen. 3.4).[65] In my view, in addition to the figure of the *'ebed Yahweh* (with which the hymn clearly has terminological affinities, as L. Cerfaux and J. A. Sanders have shown), the background to the hymn is to be found in early Jewish speculation about man as the *image of God* and *Lord of the world* (Gen. 1.26), which Jewish *pesher* exegesis connected with Ps. 8.4–6: 'What is man that you are mindful of him? and the son of man that you care for him? You made him little less than the angels, you crowned him with glory and honour. You have given him dominion over the works of your hands; you have put all things under his feet' (also quoted in Heb. 2.6–8). In this speculation the image of God (being man) and lordship over the world were correlative concepts,[66] just as throughout the New Testament Christ as *eikōn* of God is always associated with the mention of his mediation in creation. He holds the world in his hand (Heb. 1.3; John 1.3; Col. 1.15–17; II Cor. 4.4; see the wisdom tradition: Wisdom 7.21, 25f.; 9.12 with 16.21; Sir. 1.4; Prov. 8.30) – insights which were to be found above all in Hellenistic Judaism. Early Jewish speculation on the disobedient first man, Adam, and the eschatological 'heavenly man' to come (see Paul, I Cor. 15.22, 45; Rom. 5.12–21) unmistakably underlies this hymn, rather than a Hellenistic *anthrōpos* myth (despite the similarity in ideas). (In any case the chronological sequence is very difficult to determine.) The same idea occurs in Hebrews: incarnation is degradation 'below the angels', just as the exaltation planned by God from eternity is above these angels, his gracious reward for the temporary humiliation (see below). Genesis 1.26 and Psalm 8.4–6 as they were discussed in early Judaism can explain the whole of the hymn in its historical context. (It is not impossible that there was alien influence of Canaanite and ancient Near Eastern myths on this Jewish *pesher* exegesis, but in view of the difficulty of accurate chronology, there does not seem to me to be any proof as yet, despite *Corpus Hermeticum* 1, 12–14). Scholars often give the impression that the New Testament writers composed their pastoral letters in some great library! Every age is familiar with particular concepts and ideas which become common currency. (People who talk today of 'existential experiences' or 'human alienation' need not necessarily know anything about existentialism or Marxism.)

It is, however, important that the early Jewish view of man as the image of God and the cosmocrator, or ruler of the world, finds a historical setting in the Palestinian traditions of kingship. Many exegetes have already pointed out that the account of the prelude to the Yahwistic history of Israel to be found in Genesis, both the story of the patriarchs and ultimately the account of creation, is shaped in the light of the situation of the so-called united monarchy of Israel and Judah under David and Solomon.[67] In other words, Genesis 2–11 was written in the light of the social and historical conditions of the time of David. David, God's vizir and ruler in Israel, is the model in accordance with which 'the Adam' is depicted in Eden in the book of Genesis. 'The man' or Adam is portrayed by the Yahwist in accordance with the model of the later king of Israel. Adam is really 'the king'. Man has a royal status in creation, just as David was 'exalted out of the dust' – or out of nothing – to kingly status (see I Kings 16.2). Furthermore, even within the semi-feudal structure of Canaan, kings and courtiers were called 'sons of men' (gentlemen, *gentilhommes*), in contrast to simple 'man' (*homme* or *Mensch*), i.e. the ordinary people. This distinction in terminology was known throughout the ancient East (and almost every language has such aristocratic designations which were later democratized. For the first colonials, those who were 'black' or 'yellow' were also 'not men' – of course they were men, but not *white* men, *gentilhommes*, sons of men). Initially, son of man was a man with a very privileged, legal status: prince, king, nobleman, high born. David, a humble shepherd ('taken from behind the sheep') becomes prince (II Sam. 7.8; 7.9: 'one of the great ones of the earth' – a 'son of man', as they said at that time). In Ps. 80.17, David is called prince, 'the man at your right hand', a 'son of man'. That has important consequences. For in the Near East prominent men, princes, nobility and kings, formed as it were the royal court of the heavenly God with his heavenly council of *ʾᵉlōhīm*, even in pre-Israelite Jerusalem. When David becomes king, he too, along with his royal family, joins the heavenly court and its angels on Mount Sion (Ps. 89.5, 7). 'Sons of man' participate in God's divine council.[68] If they have to go to war, 'the stars' or the angels of heaven fight with them and with Israel (the Song of Deborah, Judg. 5.20). David, the king, is as it were 'an angel of God' (I Sam. 29.9; II Sam. 14.17,20). Israel's nobility, its 'sons of man', are therefore often called *ᵉlōhīm* because of their status and consequent membership of God's heavenly council (Ps. 82; 45.6; 58.1). But they are *only* 'sons of the Most High' or '*like* angels or stars'. Of Adam – a projection of king David on to the figure of the 'first man' – it is also said in Ps. 8.4–6 that God made him almost like an *ᵉlōhīm* or angel. To have further pretensions is then a kind of *robbery*. It is said of a 'son of man' like the prince of Tyre, who regarded himself as a God (Ezek. 28), and of the king of Babylon who planned to ascend 'beyond the stars (angels) of God' (Isa. 14), 'that they fell from heaven' (into the abyss).

Finally, the Yahwist and also Ezekiel democratize this term 'son of man'. Every man is a gentleman. But that means that every nobleman or 'man' is only a man; so the son of man finally becomes a 'maggot' or a 'worm' (Job 25.5f). It is also striking how the old story of the *nᵉpīlīm* – the great of this world (Gen. 6.1–4), i.e. the 'sons of men' – was interpreted in early Judaism. These are no longer dead noblemen, princes, vassals or notables from the past (as in the original story), but 'fallen angels' (who had intercourse with human beings from whom were born a race of giants). The idea that Israel's notable men were members of the heavenly council is thus given a mystical significance.

These very ancient ideas, which had died out in the meantime, were revived in early Jewish apocalyptic. With the help of Greek ideas people arrived at the notion of a 'two-storey universe'.[69] The whole elect people of God – and not just the noble leaders of the people – were associated with the angels of the heavenly council (thanks to the democratization of the concept of the son of man). Every country had its own heavenly leader ('the angels of the nations'). Just as David was 'like an angel of God' (at the time of the monarchy), so in more democratic times the whole of the elect people – in reality its holy remnant – were 'like stars' or heavenly angels (Dan. 12.3). The heavenly figure 'like a son of man' (Dan. 7.13) is at the same time the 'heavenly prince' in the heavenly council, in which he has his seat as the leader and representative of Israel on earth – a heavenly *eikōn* of earthly Israel.

Through its apocalyptic revival in the heavenly son of man, the protector of the earthly son of David and Israel as the people of God, this history of the concept of son of man, originally bound up with David and his sons – princes and notables, and in this capacity members of the heavenly council – acquired a fundamental significance for Christianity. In this way Son of David and Son of man overlap in early Christianity, and in primitive Christianity this entire early Jewish prehistory will bring christology and angelology closely together (see below on Hebrews and Johannine theology). That can tell us something about the Johannine identification of Spirit and Paraclete and about early Christian tendencies to call Jesus 'an angel' ('angel christology'). It explains why Hebrews is so concerned to show that a man and not an *angel* sits at the right hand of God (Heb. 1.5–2.9) and also illuminates one of the earliest 'trinitarian formulae': Father, Christ and angel (see below).

✳    In my view, this analysis makes it clear that the hymn to Christ in Phil. 2.6–11 can be fully understood in terms of the 'son of man' as understood in early Jewish interpretation of Gen. 1.26 and Ps. 8.4–6 in combination with the suffering servant of Deutero-Isaiah. If it is acceptable to others, this analysis would be one more indication of the difficulties encountered by Christianity, in the culture of late antiquity, particularly among the cultural *élite* of the time, in gaining acceptance for its proclamation of salvation and redemption *by means of a man* – not an angel or a heavenly hero – and a *crucified*, mortal man at that. What impression could this make on a culture oriented on heavenly spheres and heavenly beings, which looked longingly for a *heavenly* redeemer from above? This also represented a temptation for Christianity, namely to explain Jesus in terms of contemporary expectations. However, it is striking that especially outside Johannine theology (see below), the New Testament, and Pauline theology in particular, sees the heavenly character of Jesus principally in *eschatological* terms: the exaltation of Jesus *through God* after his death is indeed a plan devised by God from all eternity, in which Jesus is an eschatological gift, apocalyptically pre-existent with God and prepared for the times to come. This very old, early Christian concept of pre-existence did not, however, have any 'protological' character. In these Christian circles (outside Johannine thought), the pre-existence was *eschatological* (as understood in apocalyptic and wisdom).

In that case, Philippians says of this eschatological pre-existent Jesus that he joined the ranks of men(*anthrōpōn*): he entered our human history as a man. In contrast to earlier 'sons of men', Jesus accepted human destiny (*below* the angels or *ᵉlōhīm*) and did not want more than that. He accepted humble manhood. In this period of 'looking for' the help of heavenly beings, this was of course an act of self-emptying: Jesus is not, and does not want to be, an *ᵉlōhīm*. Even more, this self-emptying (*kenōsis*) is intensified by a *tapeinōsis*, an accentuated humiliation within an already lowly human existence. Jesus accepts the extremely gruesome tabu of a death on the cross. The man Jesus experiences this *kenōsis* and *tapeinōsis* as obedience, not to the powers of *heimarmenē* or fate, but to the living God. Herein lies his true greatness, which is made manifest by his super-exaltation by God (who values everything according to its true worth), at least for the heavenly being and those who believe in him, the people who sing this hymn to Christ. But the world does not yet see this; it sees only the shame: being a man – standing below the angels – and being crucified as well.

If we follow the line of this hymn to Christ we cannot say that God solely and only affirms and acknowledges what is already great and valuable in and of itself, in such a humbling solidarity with what (in the eyes of late antiquity) amounted to 'despised humanity'. The temptation in this direction was great, but it is *alien* to *this* hymn to Christ. All the more so, since this hymn is the only place I know in the whole of the New Testament in which it is expressly said that Jesus' exaltation is a *charis* or a favour on God's part *towards him*. Here it is primarily Jesus himself who is favoured: '*ho Theos . . . echarisato autō to onoma to hyper pan onoma*,' that is, God favoured him with the *charis* of a name above every name (Phil. 2.9b): the name *Kyrios* (the synagogue name for *Adonai* or God, Phil. 2.11b). In this exaltation God gives him his own name, so that believers can see that he, God, is a God of men and that therefore all beings on earth, above the earth and below the earth must bow the knee to this humble figure who from a cosmic point of view is only a son of man and not an angel; he is a 'subordinate'. Therefore, again according to the line taken by this hymn, although salvation comes from God it must lie in a particular kind of human life and a particular way of being a human being. For all the idea of pre-existence in the hymn, the emphasis is on the one hand on the *self-emptying* and *unjust suffering* of the historical manhood of Jesus, and on the other, on the fact that *this* is in no way the last word. Such a way of life has a definitive, irrevocable value, in and of itself. A man does not live in this way for the sake of reward; that would contradict the unconditional nature of the gift in *kenōsis* and *tapeinosis*. On the other hand, to be dead is to be dead. This even human irrevocability cannot be the *last* word – at least, if one is interested not only in 'values' but also *in the living man* who embodies them. In that case God's affirmation of the inner irrevocability and decisive, final attitude of Jesus must have some real significance *for the person of Jesus himself*. Were that not the case, in the last resort we would no longer be dealing with *people*, but with abstract ideals, values and visions, or with an abstraction, 'humanity' or the '*ben Adam*', to which all specific men must fall victim.[70] At all events, before we 'modernize' this hymn to Christ and make it topical, we must recognize that according to the line it takes about the son of man, God's *charis* is mercy upon the person of Jesus himself who comes to grief because of his ideals, and not just a divine affirmation of the value and the ideal for which he lived and for which in fact he was killed. According to this hypothesis, he would be a God of noble ideals, but *not a God of men*. The context may be that of late antiquity with a belief in angels, but in that very context we can see what is really at stake. The testimony of Philippians is that God is a God of *men*. Hieratic, Near Eastern, Hellenistic Jewish this Christian hymn may be, but it is an ode to God's mercy towards men precisely in their most grievous human condition. It is at the same time a hymn of praise to the true greatness of men, concealed in the unattractive form of humiliation.

This hymn also shows that its basic pattern is not Paul's pattern of death and resurrection, but a pattern of incarnation and exaltation. After his death Jesus is merely the 'object' of God's action, which is suggested by the model of *katabasis* (descent) and *anabasis* (ascent) (see e.g. Eph. 4.8–10; John 3.13). Jesus is 'super-exalted' by God (*hyper-hypsōsen*). Here a particular view of the spatial make-up of the world exercises some influence: Jesus comes into the *highest of all* heavens, beyond the heavenly spheres where angels dwell, right to God's own dwelling place (one can find the same idea in the Letter to the Hebrews, with which this hymn is closely connected). In other words: Jesus, who as man is placed *below* the angels, is exalted by God *above* all the angels, and set 'at the right hand of God'. True, the hymn to Christ does not make this last statement explicitly, but it is implied in his enthronement by God to be ruler of the world. Therefore both angels and subterranean beings (2.10b) must bow the knee to their new lord and master, the exalted one who was humbled: Jesus of Nazareth. The exaltation or ascension (there is formally no mention of a resurrection model) of Jesus Christ (see also I Tim. 3.16 and Heb. 1.3f.) is represented after the pattern of the enthronement of an earthly ruler, in the three phases that were traditional at that time: (*a*) presentation, (*b*) proclamation and (*c*) *proskynēsis* (bending the knee, or homage and reverence), and *exhomologēsis* (acclamation) of all bystanders. The background to this model is Isa. 45.22–25. But in Isaiah all the nations are invited by Yahweh to salvation, and the 'bowing of the knee and swearing of the tongue' (Isa. 45.23b) is offered to Yahweh as sole God (Isa. 45.22–25; see Rom. 14.11, where there is a direct quotation of Isa. 45.23). Philippians 2.10f. transfers all this to Christ: the whole world, all the powers above and below the earth, must do homage to the new ruler presented by God. This new ruler (and only now is his name given!) is *Jesus Christ*, Jesus the historical man, who has shared human destiny in solidarity with us. This universality becomes 'cosmic': everything in the universe which is not-God must acknowledge the sovereignty, the lordship of the exalted Jesus, the new cosmocrator; not a tyrant, but someone who knows what it is to be a man and has experienced it in his own body. The striking thing in Philippians is that this *kyriotēs* or lordship of Christ is not related to the community or the church of God, as is *almost* exclusively the case in Paul, but to the *universe*.

For Isaiah this tremendous inauguration was a coming, eschatological event – at that time a widespread conception: all demonic powers will be annihilated at the final judgment (see Rev. 19.20; 20.14; Matt. 25.41). However, according to Philippians the powers are not annihilated but subjected; their servile acclamation is an essential ingredient of the enthronement.[71] It is not said here that in the end the lordship of Christ will only be transitory (as is still hinted at in I Cor. 15.24), though Paul continues to stress the subjection of Christ under God. This is expressed here also in the additional doxology which in all probability Paul himself composed (for this purpose): 'to the glory of God the Father' (2.11b, see also I Cor. 15.24; 3.23; 11.3; Rom. 15.7). For Paul, the salvation of man and the glory of God are one; but God is God, and he alone. Paul makes this solidarity of Jesus with 'demeaned mankind' (as expressed in terms of late antiquity) the model for the ethical and religious life of Christians. That is why he quotes this particular hymn to Christ. The hymn cannot tell us how this solidarity of Christians is to be expressed in present-day situations. There are historical circumstances which the Christian himself has to analyse and interpret.

### Conclusion: The charis of Jesus Christ in the authentic letters of Paul

Paul repeatedly points to the *solus Christus* principle in an almost fanatical exclusiveness and a monism of grace. 'For Christ's sake I have suffered the loss of all things, and count them as refuse, in order that I may gain Christ and be found in him, not having a righteousness of my own, based on law, but that which is through faith in Christ, the righteousness from God' (Phil. 3.8f), 'and I will know Christ in faith and the power of his resurrection, and will share his sufferings, becoming like him in death, that if possible I may attain to the resurrection from the dead' (Phil. 3.10f.). That is Paul's theory of grace. No other principle of salvation than Christ Jesus. All other ways of salvation, even that of the Torah, are barred by this exclusiveness. This revelation of salvation is historically bound up with Jesus, above all with his crucifixion, and is given to the *elect*. That is implied by the early Jewish term *charis* as found in Paul. *Charis* is election. 'For those whom he foreknew he also predestined to be conformed to the image of his Son, in order that he might be the firstborn among many brethren. And those whom he predestined he also called; and those whom he called he also justified, and those whom he justified he also glorified' (Rom. 8.29f.). This exclusiveness centred on Christ also gives the Christian community its group identity. In that case, how can one talk of Christian universality? Paul solves this problem with a reference to the special *charis* of the apostolic proclamation: this revelation of salvation is made universal and communicated to all people by proclamation, above all that of Paul. *Charis*, the gift of the mystery of salvation revealed to the chosen, at the same time becomes universal through the special *charis* of the apostolate. 'God was in Christ reconciling the world to himself, and gave us the message of reconciliation' (II Cor. 5.19), 'so we are ambassadors for Christ, God making his appeal through us. We beseech you on behalf of Christ, be reconciled to God' (II Cor. 5.20). Through world-wide proclamation, *particularity* (association with the historical crucifixion of Jesus and the elect community of God) becomes *universality*. This tension is evident in Paul's concept of grace. If preparation has been made for the eschatological conversion of Israel by virtue of proclamation to all the Gentiles (Rom. 9.1–11.33, see below), the exclusiveness of *charis* in Christ is a universal event for all mankind. Universality is not an objectified datum, but a task to be realized through mission and presence all over the world by virtue of election or actually being a Christian (for that is what Paul means by election). Thus *charis* embraces both the *revelation* of God and the apostolic *paradosis* or tradition, namely the proclamation of the gospel apart from the law, which for Paul is the expression of what he means by grace. Jesus as the Christ is the light of all the *gōyīm*, 'the light of the world' – and by Christ Paul means the one who has risen from the dead and is alive. *Charis* is the revelation – in time – of the mystery of salvation and concern for salvation prepared through God from eternity, and at the same time the power to accept this mystery of revelation and to realize its ethical consequences in everyday life. In short, *charis* or grace as Paul understands it is a 'supernatural' *knowledge* of the mystery of salvation, or faith in the mystery of salvation, and an *ethical force*; through the forgiveness of sins and justification, sealed through baptism, both make man a new creation (II Cor. 5.17).

In the portrayal of the grace of God as an unconditional free gift, the emphasis is placed above all on its abundance and superfluity (Rom. 5.15, 20; 6.1; II Cor. 9.8,14). Because these riches given to men by God in Christ (I Cor. 1.4; I Cor. 2.12; II Cor. 9.8,14) concern sinners, *charis* is also redemption: rescue, salvation, reconciliation and emancipation (II Cor. 6.1; Gal. 2.21), God's own righteousness in man (Rom. 4.5; 5.17, 21; II Cor. 5.21b). The totality of God's grace as salvation for man means: the one man Jesus Christ (Rom. 5.11b; see 8.32), the crucified one, who is nevertheless risen. Therefore for Paul grace is essentially also participation in Jesus' suffering and death, by faith and baptism (Gal. 3.26f.; Rom. 6), a participation above all in his status, 'children of God through faith in Christ Jesus' (Gal. 3.26), *hyiothesia* or adoption (Galatians, Rom. 8.14f.), and therefore (Rom. 8.15) possession of the *pneuma* (Rom. 8.9), the foundation of the legacy which we shall receive with Jesus from God (Rom. 8.17; see 8.29; Gal. 4.5). For Paul, grace is communion with God through the mediation of Jesus Christ in the power of the spirit; it is liberation for brotherly love and for 'whatever is honourable, whatever is just, whatever is pure, whatever is lovely, whatever is gracious, if there is any excellence, if there is anything worthy of praise' (Phil. 4.8). 'Being of the same mind, having the same love, being in full accord and of one mind' (Phil. 2.2), above all being freed for love (I Cor. 13.1–13). The goal and the final end of this saving initiative of God's grace is the *salvation of man* as the *glorification of the Father* (Rom. 5.2; II Cor. 4.15). *Charis* (grace) requires *charis* (thanksgiving) (II Cor. 9.11): 'To the glory of God the Father' (Phil. 2.11b).

Chapter 2

# Paulinism outside the authentic letters of Paul: new interpretations

*Introduction: Christianity in Asia Minor*

There is much to suggest that after AD 70 the focal point of Christianity was shifted to Western Asia Minor, at that time the Roman proconsulate of Asia, and specifically to Ephesus. This city was in fact the capital and the seat of the Roman proconsul; in ecclesiastical terms, we might call it a see. In Ephesus, Pauline and Johannine theology would come together (at a later date the Johannine corpus was assembled in Ephesus, though manuscripts, indeed very old manuscripts, of the Gospel of John have been found in Egypt). At that time, of course, the whole of the ancient world was Hellenistic in culture, but the Hellenism of Asia Minor had strong oriental colouring; it was a melting pot for Eastern and Western cultures, each with its own social aspect (for example, the woman, and above all the widow, had a much higher standing there than in Palestine or even in Greece, at least the Attic part of Greece). The Christianity of Asia Minor even had its own grammar within the generally accepted Hellenistic *koinē* (the Greek *lingua franca* of the time). The oriental extravagances of Asia Minor, the need for experiences of being filled with the Spirit, the feeling of living amidst angels and demons, all this was an existential problem in the area. Good spirits were to be found behind good deeds, whereas evil deeds were prompted by evil, demonic world powers or cosmocrators, against whom protection was sought in various religious rites. Astrology and calculations based on the calendar, to see whether one was determined by the state of the moon or the state of the sun, formed an ingredient of many people's lives: recourse was zealously had to horoscopes.

In such a culture, which was in search of salvation and affirmation of life and protection for life, any new way of life had a chance – even Christianity. People in Asia Minor were looking for a *way*, a philosophy of life – and this was all the more significant because they were geographically at a crossroads of the world. As a result, New Testament writers who addressed this Christianity in Asia Minor on the one hand took this spiritual climate into account and had sympathy with it, while on the other hand they maintained a critical detachment from it, where syncretism attacked the principle of 'Christ alone'. In their reaction, perhaps these Christian writers did not always understand the needs of people in Asia Minor properly; perhaps they did not even see the implications of their desire to supplement the sober apostolic faith with something to meet the needs of people in Asia Minor for 'experience' and Eastern spiritual experience. However, it is certain that the authors of the epistles written in Asia Minor speak the language of these divergent Christians, while refusing to yield a millimetre if they feel God's exclusiveness of grace in Christ to be endangered. The letters to the Christians of Colossae and Ephesus are striking examples of this. At the same time they show how they can adopt the teaching of their master, Paul, while adapting it to new situations in the world and in the church. Thus – within the authority of the New Testament – they serve as models for any theological re-interpretation of the apostolic faith, and also for the transplanting of Christianity into another culture.

*Literature* (on Colossians and Ephesians): D. Amand, *Fatalisme et liberté dans l'antiquité grecque*, Louvain 1945; P. Benoit, 'Rapport litteraire entre les épîtres aux Colossiens et aux Ephésiens', in *Neutestamentliche Aufsätze*, FS J. Schmid, Regensburg 1963, 11–22; E. Best, *One Body in Christ*, London 1955; M. Dibelius and H. Greeven, *An die Kolosser, Epheser, an Philemon*, Tübingen [3]1953; C. Colpe, 'Zur Leib-Christi-Vorstellung im Epheserbrief', in *Judentum, Urchristentum, Kirche*, FS J. Jeremias, BZNW 26, Berlin [2]1964, 172–87; J. Dupont, *Gnosis*, Louvain-Paris [2]1960; A. J. Festugière, *L'idéal religieux des Grecs et l'Evangile*, Paris [2]1932; id., *La révélation d'Hermès Trismégiste*, 4 vols, Paris 1944–54; J. Gnilka, *Der Epheserbrief*, HThKNT X, 2, Freiburg im Breisgau [2]1977; H. Gross, 'Der Engel im alten Testament', in *Archiv für Liturgiewissenschaft*, VI, 1, Regensburg 1959, 28–42; H. Hegermann, *Die Vorstellung von Schöpfungsmittlern im hellenistischen Judentum und Urchristentum*, TU 82, Berlin 1961; J. Huby, *Les épîtres de la captivité*, Paris ²1947; J. Jervell, *Imago Dei, Gen. 1.26–27) im Spätjudentum, in der Gnosis und in den paulinischen Briefen*, FRLANT 76, Göttingen 1960; E. Käsemann, 'The Disciples of John the Baptist in Ephesus', ET in *Essays on New Testament Themes*, SBT 41, London and Naperville 1964, 136–48; id., 'Das Interpretationsproblem des Epheser-briefes', in *Exegetische Versuche und Besinnungen* II, Göttingen 1965, 253–62; id., 'Unity and Multiplicity in the New Testament Doctrine of the Church', ET in *New Testament Questions of Today*, London and Philadelphia 1969, 252–9; id., 'Kolosserbrief', in *RGG*³ III, 1727f; E. Lohmeyer, *Die Briefe an die Philipper, an die Kolosser und an Philemon*, Mcyer 9, Göttingen ¹³1964; E. Lohse, 'Christusbotschaft und Kirche in Kolosserbrief', *NTS* 11, 1964–65, 203–16; id., *Colossians and Philemon*, ET Hermeneia, Phila-delphia 1971; J. Meuzelaar, *Der Leib des Messias*, Assen 1961; J. Michl, s. v. 'Engel', *RAC* V, 53–200; F. Mussner, *Der Brief an die Kolosser*, Düsseldorf 1965; id., *Christus, das All und die Kirche*, Trier ²1968; P. Pokorný, 'Epheserbrief und gnostische Mysterien', *ZNW* 53, 1962, 160–94; id., *Der Epheserbrief und die Gnosis*, Berlin 1965; H. Schlier, *Mächte und Gewalten im Neuen Testament*, Quaestiones disputatae 3, Freiburg im Breisgau 1958; id., *Der Brief an die Epheser. Ein Kommentar*, Düsseldorf ²1965; id., *Christus und die Kirche im Epheserbrief*, Tübingen 1930; P. Schub-ert, *Form and Function of the Pauline Thanksgivings*, BZNW 20, Berlin 1939; C. H. Talbert, 'The Myth of a Descending-Ascending Redeemer in Med-iterranean Antiquity', *NTS* 22, 1976, 418–40; G. Thompson, *The Letters of Paul to the Ephesians, to the Colossians and to Philemon*, Cambridge 1967.

## §1 Christ, the fullness of God; the church, the fullness of Christ: Colossians

Colossians seeks to develop the universal significance of Christ by means of his triumph over cosmic powers and to determine the position of the church and the task of the apostolic ministry in it. The focal point of its Christian confession is the living presence of salvation from God in Christ, now already given, but this present salvation is itself oriented on hope for the eschatological future as disclosed through the apostolic procla-mation of the church for the world (1.5). Here the living reality of Christ is the foundation of the community and its hope (1.27) for the world.

Outside the formal greeting (1.2; 4.18), *charis* is used in the Pauline sense of the grace of the apostolic ministry (3.16) and also once again as an indication of the Christian calling: 'from the day you heard and under-stood the grace of God in truth' (1.6). Here grace evidently has the early Christian and early Jewish meaning of revealed wisdom or the truth of life, revealed to the elect and handed on through the grace of the apostolate, so that others will take part in this election (see above). This is followed by *charis* or thanksgiving for the grace received – classical in all Hellenistic letters and in Greek Judaism.

The community of Colossae has recognized the word proclaimed by Epaphras (1.7f.) as the truth and has accepted it; this is the 'grace of God' (1.6; see Gal. 5.4). In this sense the Letter to the Colossians has no distinctive concept of grace; rather, the author uses the term with a derived content, i.e. the content of the wisdom which was hidden with God as a mystery from all eternity, and now has been revealed in Christ and handed on in the church through the apostolate. The author knows nothing of the Pauline conflict between grace and good works. This problem is obsolete, and he stresses the demand for good works like all the Deutero-Pauline letters (1.10; 1.21; 3.17; see Eph. 2.10; Titus 1.16; 3.1; I Tim. 2.10; 5.10; II Tim. 2.21; 3.17). In Colossians, an author of the Pauline school is at work. For him, Paul's view of the definitive and exclusive salvation from God in Christ is the apostolic norm: 'Christ is our life' (3.4). But this view is realized in completely new situations.

## I. THE HERMENEUTIC BACKGROUND OF COLOSSIANS: A 'PHILOSOPHY OF LIFE' IN ASIA MINOR

In Asia Minor, above all in cities like Colossae and Ephesus, there were people from many countries, and people without a country of their own. They were in search of individual salvation and had a penchant for heavenly happiness.[72] These people were aware of a cosmic fault, a kind of catastrophe in the universe, a gulf between the higher (heavenly) and the lower (earthly) world. The problem of meaning and meaninglessness is experienced in cosmic terms and is expressed in a longing for salvation which will consist in the restoration of the unity of the cosmos. In this connection some people have spoken of a kind of 'pan-cosmic a-cosmism', a feeling for the unity of all things into which the earthly is as it were caught up. New views of life and patterns for living were called *philosophia*, but this was not the same thing as Greek philosophy. Philosophy of life is the Hellenistic expression for a religious way of life. Thus Hellenistic Jews called the whole non-Jewish approach to life a 'philosophy',[73] while Josephus usually calls religious groups within Judaism, like Pharisees, Sadducees and Essenes, 'philosophical schools'.[74] At that time even the mystery religions were called philosophies. (As a result, we cannot see the reaction of Colossians against 'philosophy' as a New Testament mistrust of philosophy or critical thought, as so often happens; it has nothing at all to do with that.)

We can only discover hints from the letter itself of the particular religious philosophy of life which Colossians has in mind. The philosophy which threatens the community (2.8) evidently refers to a venerable tradition (2.8) and seeks to communicate true knowledge and insight (*sophia*: 1.9,28; 2.3,23; 4.5; *synesis* or spiritual insight: 1.9; 2.2; *gnōsis* or knowledge: 2.3; *epignōsis*, deeper knowledge, though in Hellenism the word has a weaker meaning and simply means *gnōsis*: 1.6,9,10; 2.2; 3.10), above all a knowledge of the *stoicheia tou kosmou* (2.8,20) – an expression which occurs in a number of passages in the New Testament –, powers of the world, heavenly beings or angels (2.18), or cosmic (personal) forces (2.10, 15). *Stoicheia*, elements, literally means something that is arranged in a regular order (e.g. links in a chain); hence basis, foundation. The word is used above all for the elements of which the universe was thought to be composed: water, fire, air and earth. In Hellenistic syncretism these elements, of which the world was thought to be made up, were mythologized: they became living beings. The stars, too, are such 'elements', and they determine the course of the universe and the destiny of mankind. Hence the twelve signs of the zodiac were also called *stoicheia*;[75] this explains the great significance of horoscopes (of which a large number have been found even in Qumran). Those who know the course of the stars acquire power; and by magical arts or initiation people can make use of the power of these heavenly beings. For the Jews of the time the stars had already been stripped of their spiritual power, but every star was directed by a heavenly spirit being, an angel; the universe of all these movements of the stars was directed by the archangel Uriel (I Enoch). However, in this syncretistic period the stars, at least in popular belief, were worshipped as divine beings (the boundary between 'stars' and 'angels' is a vague one). Man is a being who is made up of the same raw material: he is a microcosm in a macrocosm (a concept which was made popular by the Stoics).

The key word of the philosophy of life which is attacked by Colossians is, then, the *stoicheia tou kosmou*, the heavenly powers who are worshipped in order to gain access to the (divine) *plērōma* or fullness (2.9). In other words, the aim of the angel cult was the experience of being filled with divinity (2.10). In Colossians the relationship between the *stoicheia* and the *plērōma* is left undefined: are these elements threatening forces which hinder access to the *plērōma* (fullness) if they are not given their due reverence? Or are they representatives of this divine fullness? At all events, man can only be filled with heavenly fullness by worshipping these cosmocrators. He voluntarily declares his readiness (*ethelothrēskia* 2.23) to pay cultic homage to these angels (2.8) and to observe the many tabus: 'Do not handle, Do not taste, Do not touch' (2.21) and to celebrate the calendar feasts (2.16). The initiate turns away from the world by adopting a strictly ascetic way of life (2.11; 2.23); he scrupulously observes the holy days and times as determined by astrology (2.16), and abstains from certain foods and drinks (2.16,21). In this way he organizes his life in accordance with the laws of the cosmos, which as the ordering of the macrocosm are also the norm for mankind as the microcosm.

In this way the world is as it were the *sōma*, the body of a single all-embracing Logos or 'Spirit' which permeates all things. A similar intellectual climate was to be found among the Stoics, who originally were not a specifically Greek phenomenon: the views which they represented had come into being as a result of the contact of Greeks living outside Greece with the spirituality of Asia Minor (however, they looked for the 'Logos', or reason, in these religious tendencies: we might borrow the title of Kant's famous book *Religion within the Limits of Reason Alone* to describe the Stoics). None of this is gnosticism, but the syncretism of late antiquity, from which later gnosticism was to develop. Its nucleus is the need for the experience of being filled with divine power from the 'soul' of reality, above all the reality of the *epourania* (the heavenly spheres with their mysterious inhabitants).

At that time it was possible to belong simultaneously to very different religious brotherhoods. The danger which resulted for Christians was that some people believed that they could find a kind of supplementary experience, an additional security, in one of these philosophies of life. (The whole problem thus has a certain affinity to the phenomenon of contemporary Christians who practise, say, Zen Buddhism.)

## II. THE REACTION OF COLOSSIANS TO THIS RELIGIOUS LIFE-STYLE

Colossians reacts to the demands of this philosophy of life in the spirit of Paul. Paul said, 'You have to choose between "the Law" and "Christ"'; Colossians points to the alternative: it is necessary to live either *kata stoicheia tou kosmou* or *kata Christon* (Col. 2.8). 'These angels' or 'Christ' – it is impossible to combine the two as two different ways to salvation, since in apostolic terms salvation is only to be found in Christ; there is only one way to salvation. But in the light of this new spiritual climate, what Paul calls 'the grace that is Christ' is given another interpretation. The unalterable criterion remains: salvation from God alone in Christ Jesus. The author expresses the grace of Christ in a new hermeneutical situation which also provides the new terminology with which Colossians speaks of present salvation in Christ. Of this Colossians says: in Christ alone the divine *plērōma* (fullness) dwells *sōmatikōs*, as in its own *sōma* – corporeally (2.9). The author takes over the key words of the philosophy of life. 'Fulfilment' is in Christ alone. To this end he quotes a hymn which is well-known to the Colossians: 1.12–20. It has long been an apostolic conviction that Christ is the Lord, *Kyrios* of the church, but now Colossians wants to give Jesus a place in the whole of the macrocosm with its heavenly spheres.

Christ is the *eikōn* of God, i.e. he is the one in whom God reveals himself to us (1.15), God as he is visible to us (see Wisdom 7.25f.: wisdom is the *eikōn* of the goodness of God). In this respect he is completely on God's side, over the cosmos: he is '*prōtotokos*, firstborn of the whole creation' (Col. 1.15b) and *pro pantōn* (1.17), before the universe was, pre-existent as wisdom (see Prov. 8.22; Sir. 1.4; 24.9; Wisdom 9.9; 9.4). Christ is the 'firstborn of creation', before all others (see also Heb. 1.6), because he is the mediator of creation. As Lord he stands over against the world of creation, although he is himself created. Created and yet pre-existent; that is an eschatological pre-existence, characteristic of wisdom and apocalyptic; that is, Jesus is the eschatological salvation prepared by God from eternity in order to be revealed in his time. (There is no mention in this text of pre-existence in the Trinitarian sense, of a prior existence of the second person of the Trinity.)

This apostolic confession of Jesus as *Kyrios* is then illuminated with a terminology which is derived from the Stoa and which was presumably used also in this philosophy of life current in Asia Minor (but not in fact for Christ): '*in* him all things were created' (1.16). God is the Creator, but 'in Christ'. A Stoic hymn of praise to all nature (or *physis*) contains the words: '*ō physis, ek sou panta, en soi panta, eis se panta:*'[76] 'O nature, everything comes from you, everything is in you, everything tends towards you.' This pantheism had already been eliminated in Hellenistic Judaism, but these terms also came into early Christianity by means of the Greek synagogue. Paul was already familiar with the triad *ex, eis* and *dia* (from, in and through: I Cor. 8.6; Rom. 11.36), but the *ex quo* (whence) is used of God alone (I Cor. 8.6), whereas *in quo* (in whom), *a quo* (*dia*: through the mediation of) and *ad quem* (for whom) are used of Christ alone. God alone is the Creator.[77] We should not forget that what is said about Christ in the first strophe of the hymn to him in Colossians is viewed from the perspective expressed in the second strophe: the *eschatological salvation* that Jesus has brought. For this reason he is present as counsellor at the *prōton*, before the beginning of creation, which exists for his sake. This is an expression of the universal and cosmic significance of Jesus (cf. I Cor. 8.6; also John 1.3; Heb. 1.3; 2.10). *Everything*, even the heavenly beings, is '*in* him'. Four kinds of heavenly beings are named: 'thrones and principalities' (*kyriotōtes* or heavenly hosts, see also I Cor. 8.5), and 'principalities (*archai*) and authorities' (*exousiai*), i.e. 'supernatural beings' (see I Cor. 15.24; Rom. 8.38; also Eph. 1.21; 3.10; 6.12).[78] Christ stands as Lord over all powers (in addition to Col. 2.10,15, see also Eph. 1.21; I Peter 3.22). The 'all things are created for him' means: in respect of him; Christ is the meaning of the universe. He holds the world in his hand; in him the world has its existence (*synestēkenai* is also a Middle Platonic, Stoic term which denotes the miraculous unity and interconnection of the universe). The framework of the world is held together by the Logos (see also Sir. 43.26; Heb. 1.3). The reason for this is given: *kai* (which here means 'for'); in my view this statement is not part of the second strophe but forms the end of the first strophe, which Colossians subtly alters (see below). In him everything has its existence, 'for he is the head of the body' (1.18; following 1.17): as head he holds the *sōma* or the body together. That was the view held in this spirituality current in Asia Minor: the Logos is the head of the cosmos, which is its cosmic body.[79] In this syncretism from late antiquity this idea of the cosmic body was connected with Iranian conceptions.[80] According to them, the supreme God became pregnant and thus brought the whole of creation into being: heaven appeared from his head, earth from his feet and so on. In this pantheistic milieu the notion of the cosmos as the body of the divine Logos and the elements as various members of his body was widespread. 'Zeus is the *kephalē* (the head) of the cosmos and permeates the whole world with his power' (from an Orphic fragment), was a fashionable way of putting it. The Stoa is also familiar with the idea: the whole cosmos is filled with God, and men are members of this one body as a macrocosm. The notion was also known in Hellenistic Judaism.[81] In Philo it is above all the super-terrestrial, heavenly world lying nearest to God's own dwelling that is the *sōma tou Logou*, the body of the Logos, which is its head: its life-principle.[82] The hymn to Christ is inspired by such Logos hymns: 'For he (Christ) is the head of the body.' In Hellenistic terms this must primarily mean that he gives life and existence *to the cosmos*.[83] Here, however, Colossians drastically *corrects* the ideas already current in the cultural background against which it is set. The basic notion is that salvation and the life-principle (the relationship between head and body) are to be found only in Christ. The correction made by Colossians is to understand 'body' as a reference to the church, *and not the cosmos*. This alters the whole perspective of the cultural and religious setting (or – and perhaps already – the hymn to Christ which is quoted in Colossians). The cosmic background is reinterpreted in terms of salvation history and ecclesiology. In fact Christ is already exercising his lordship over the world *now* (for Paul this was a future eschatological event); however, he is doing this only as the head of the church, his *body*, to which he gives life and strength. Thus Colossians claims that the church alone, rather than the cosmos, is the body of Christ. Or to put it another way: it is the *sōma tou Christou* at one point in the world, namely where it is the church.[84]

Contrary to what many people say, Colossians does not have a cosmic theology: it is centred on the church, or at any rate, the church's view of itself is seen in terms of Hellenistic conceptions of the cosmos as the body of the Logos, which gives life and existence. The consequence of this correction is that *through the church* Christ is exercising his lordship over the world, and is doing so *already*. Christ is Lord of all, and also 'head of the heavenly powers', as Col. 2.10 states expressly. However, these are not his body. And this cosmic lordship manifests itself in the fact that the church brings Christ *to all nations* through its proclamation (Col. 1.27f.). According to Colossians, the church is the place where Christ exercises his world-wide rule here and now: through the proclamation of salvation and reconciliation. Indeed the significance of the hymn – the way in which it fulfils its function in Colossians (and this, after all, is what we are concerned with) – has already been hinted at in 1.13f.: 'He has delivered us from the dominion (*exousia*) of darkness and transferred us to the kingdom (*basileia*) of his beloved son, in whom we have redemption, the forgiveness of sins.' *Exousia* (Hebrew *memšālā*) means 'sphere of influence'; Colossians thinks primarily in spatial rather than in temporal terms (in relation to the cosmic background; these spatial terms will become even more significant in later epistles). There is a change of rule: just as a king can uproot a whole people from its home and make it settle elsewhere, so Christ has uprooted Christians from the sphere of influence of 'this world', where supernatural beings determine human destiny by means of the horoscope, and has transported us into another sphere of influence, a kingdom *(basileia)* in which Christ alone is Lord. Paul speaks in future terms of 'the kingdom of God' (I Thess. 2.12; Gal. 5.21; I Cor. 6.9f.; 15.50): a 'kingdom *of* Christ' is mentioned only in I Cor. 15.23–28, but that proves to be a temporary and provisional rule which lasts until Christ restores his power to the Father; only then does the kingdom of God begin. For Colossians, on the other hand, Jesus' rule of the world is already in force: even now 'Christ is all in all' (3.11).

This spatial conception has many consequences. Not only have Christians already died with Jesus in their baptism; through their baptism they have already *risen with* Christ (2.12). They have been 'transported': they already dwell above in Christ's heavenly sphere of influence (1.13) – the *sōma Christou*. Only this 'higher world' is permeated by Christ's power. But that is the church! The consequence is: 'If then you have been raised with Christ, seek the things that are above, where Christ is seated on the right hand of God . . . Your life is hid with Christ in God' (Col. 3.1–4). Men are not to seek the *epigeia*, earthly things, but *epourania*, heavenly things. Thus Colossians goes along entirely with the spirituality of Asia Minor, but describes things by their Christian names: all this, a life filled with heavenly things, is possible only in Christ, who is truly risen and dwells with the Father. Colossians makes this one point about the apostolic faith – which is by no means new – and does so in a completely different setting. The *stoicheia tou kosmou*, the heavenly principles which direct this world, *are* still there, but Christians no longer live in this world (2.20): they live elsewhere, 'above'. So the author can show that the heavenly fulfilment which these men seek in 'philosophy' can only be given through Christ. He seeks to correlate 'apostolic faith' and 'human experience', in the same way as modern theologians attempt a similar correlation.

We must follow through this model in Colossians to the end. For this translation of Christians to the other side, as the 'body of the risen Lord', has a pure apostolic content; this is called *apolytrōsis* (1.14), redemption or liberation, which in Colossians is none other than the *forgiveness of sins* through *Christian baptism* (1.14; see Eph. 1.7). Paul saw sin as a power, a tyrant over men (Rom. 5.12), but a power which has been broken through the superior might of Jesus and his crucifixion (Rom. 8.3; II Cor. 5.21; see Rom. 5.15). Even for Colossians, the content of salvation is the forgiveness of sins and corporate fellowship with God in Christ; however, this comes about in such a way that the power of the heavenly beings which control good and evil in the earthly world is broken. This is achieved by the atoning death of Jesus. In another quotation of a fragment (Col. 2.13c–15) it is said: 'He has forgiven all our trespasses, having cancelled the bond which stood against us with its legal demands; this he set aside, nailing it to the cross. He disarmed the principalities and powers and made a public example of them, triumphing over them in the cross.' Jesus' expiatory death on the cross, which results in the forgiveness of sins (2.13c), is explained in 2.14f. Sin is explained in rabbinic, juridical terms: the sinner appears before God like a debtor before his creditor, with a list of debts in his hand. According to official Judaism, God only writes off the debts if they are counterbalanced by other merits, good works and sin offerings.[85] The Christian community confesses that as a consequence of the expiatory death of Jesus, God tears up the list of debts and forgives all sins; no one can prove anything against us because all the incriminating documents have been destroyed. Thus sins have lost their force. Here Colossians calls to mind the early Christian datum of the forgiveness of sins thanks to the crucifixion of Jesus, in which we are immersed by means of baptism in water. This is the way in which the power of the heavenly spirits who control the world is broken: they are led captive behind the chariots in the triumphal procession in which the *Sōter* or victor makes his great victory parade after a war; he has put the conquered leaders 'publicly on show' (2.14f.). Their defeat is visible to all, in the life of Christians, who are no longer concerned with all these supernatural spirits, demons and cosmocrators.

For Christians, they are 'nothing': in Christ there is no longer any reason for cosmic anxiety, the great problem of life in those days. This is the experience of grace which is peculiar to the letter to the Colossians, in which the forgiveness of sins opens up a perspective on a radical trust in Christ through which believers are free men who need no longer be afraid of anything or anyone. If salvation is only in Christ, the Christian is freed from 'serving angels' (2.18) and from all the tabus (2.21) which prevent us from eating and drinking this or that (2.20f.). The author adds that all these are God's gracious gifts (2.22). 'Christian life above' is therefore not as unearthly as ʰis model might suggest.

The real basis for the cosmic predicates of Christ is disclosed in the second strophe of the hymn (1.18b–20): Christ is the *archē*, i.e. *prōtotokos ek tōn nekrōn* (1.18b), the first born from the dead. In the wisdom literature, wisdom (and in the inter-testamental literature the Logos) is also called *archē* (Prov. 8.23). In Colossians it is not said that Christ is the *archē tēs ktiseōs tou theou* (the beginning and the principle of God's creation, see Rev. 3.14). He is *archē* as firstborn from the dead, as the first one to be raised, and therefore 'first-fruits', *aparchē*, of the coming resurrection (see I. Cor. 15.20, 23), 'the author (*archēgos*) of life' (Acts 3.15), 'firstborn of the resurrection of the dead' (Acts 26.23), 'the firstborn of the dead and the ruler of kings upon earth' (Rev. 1.5) – a primitive Christian tradition. Colossians says, 'that *in all things* he may be the first, he alone' (1.18), that is, in the order of creation and resurrection or salvation, as Christ, Jesus is the first (*prōteuōn*: who precedes everyone and everything; he possesses priority over all).

The reason is now given for this: 'In him all the fullness of God was pleased to dwell' (1.19: *pan to plērōma*). Here too the hymn to Christ takes up an expression which belongs to the cosmic spirituality of Asia Minor. The author (or the hymn) is not afraid of what might be called 'modernism', in comparison with traditional faith. Here the term *plērōma* certainly has nothing to do with gnosticism, because in second-century gnosticism it is not God himself to whom the term *plērōma* is applied; there *plērōma* is the totality of emanations which come forth from God; the supreme spiritual world closest to God, a world which is separated from the earthly world by a dividing wall. And in this later, Christian, gnosticism Jesus is the perfect fruit of the *plērōma*, the one who descends as redeemer from the *plērōma*–world to restore *in* this *plērōma* all that was originally spiritual. In Colossians, God himself is the *plērōma*, and in this perspective we have what is already an Old Testament concept: God *fills* heaven and earth (Jer. 23.23; Isa. 6.3). Here is a universal concept from the syncretism of late antiquity. The context determines the exact significance of this fullness. However, its background is the distinction between God and the world. *Corpus Hermeticum* 6.4 calls the world 'the *plērōma* of evil', and God 'the *plērōma* of good', while the cosmos, which is intrinsically bound up with God, is called a *'plērōma tēs zōēs'* (*Corp. Herm.* 12.15), a fullness of life. Syncretism arises from the fact that these same *Hermetica* call God 'the all' and that this fullness cannot be duplicated: it is one (ibid. 16.3). So God himself is the *plērōma*, as the one, all-permeating God.[86] What is said here might be taken to be the universal concept of God valid at that time. *Plērōma* is God, and Colossians also understands the word in that way. Paul used the word *plērōma* in the Jewish sense (Rom. 11.12,15; 13.10; 15.29; I Cor. 10.26). But this cosmic, theological term is transformed in Colossians so that it acquires a christological and soteriological meaning: 'It has pleased God . . . to dwell' (Col. 1.19). This is the old Deuteronomistic theology: Yahweh chooses a dwelling place for himself (Greek Deut. 12.5,11; 14.23; 16.2, 11; 26.2; II Macc. 14.35; also in III Macc. 2.16). In itself, *skēnōsis* or indwelling does not mean putting up a tent, but simply 'dwelling somewhere' (for a shorter or longer time: it was the similarity of consonants between the Hebrew *sh-k-n* and the Greek *skēnē* – which is in fact connected with a tent – which made the Septuagint translate the Hebrew 'dwell' by *skēnoun*, put up a tent; in Hebrew this is the case only exceptionally, see Gen. 9.27; Judg. 8.11).[87] The word is used in religious terminology to express God's 'dwelling among his people' (Num. 5.3; 35.34), above all in Israel (Ex. 25.8; 29.45f.; Ezek. 43.9, etc.), on Mount Zion or in Jerusalem (Isa. 8.18; Joel. 3.17,21; Ps. 135.21), or in heaven behind a cloud (I Kings 8.12). That God *only makes his name dwell* somewhere is a later interpretation. Colossians 1.19 (*katoikein*, also in 2.9), says: God dwells in Christ, and does so 'in order to reconcile all things through him to himself' (1.20). Colossians 2.9 makes the meaning of this indwelling in the hymn to Christ more precise: the *pan to plērōma* or the whole fullness is the fullness of God (not *theiotēs*, but *theotēs*, which means the being of God himself). The divine fullness is to be found only in Christ, and therefore it is senseless and useless to look to angel worship as a way of salvation. Colossians 2.9 makes clear not only what this fullness is, but also the nature of the indwelling: *sōmatikōs*. The use of this word has a great many connotations. *Sōmatikōs* indicates truthfulness, the reality of the indwelling of God in the man Jesus the Christ. *Sōma* is reality, as opposed to pseudo-reality or at least a mere copy of reality: a shadow reality. 'These are only a shadow of things to come; but the substance (*sōma*) belongs to Christ', says Col. 2.17. Thus in Col. 2.9 *sōmatikōs* already means that God's fullness *truly* dwells in Christ. However, this in turn is connected with Col. 1.18, where the church is called *sōma tou Christou*, the body of Christ. In other words, just as the church is the *sōma*, the body, of Christ, so Christ himself is the *sōma* of God. Being *filled with* God, *Christ* for his part *fills* the church. 'God dwells "corporeally" in Christ' (2.9).

In Col. 1.20 it is presupposed that the world needs reconciliation – why, we are not told. The starting-point is that the present situation is not in order, and that something has gone wrong. It is possible to detect a cosmic fault between the upper and the lower world, of which man is the victim: this can be traced through the human history of meaning and meaningfulness, suffering and guilt, a life under the compulsion of destiny; for men evidently often try to do good and end up doing evil. This was a problem throughout antiquity. In that case, reconciliation has to be a mending of this cosmic fault. The argument in Colossians, then, is that the universe is reconciled because through the resurrection and exaltation of Jesus at the hands of God, heaven and earth (humanity) are restored to the order given them in God's creation. The gulf between the world below and the world above, the cause of all misery, is bridged by the fact that an earthly man Jesus, in whom the fullness of God dwells corporeally, has brought reconciliation and is now enthroned above as ruler of the world. In the church as the community of those who believe in Christ, the universe once again stands under one head, Christ. Thus cosmic peace is achieved and is already manifest in the church (1.20).[88]

*Because* Christ is the mediator of reconciliation, of the *eschaton*, he is also mediator of the *prōton*, creation. The link between creation and Christ (the first strophe of the hymn to Christ) is given in the fact that as redeemer Christ is the goal and meaning, the *eschaton*, of creation. In Pauline terms, however, the author adds the words 'through the blood of the cross', thus linking a *theologia gloriae* (of triumph) in the hymn with a *theologia crucis* (through suffering and death: see also Col. 2.14f.). Peace is restored in the universe, not through a supernatural drama, but through the historical crucifixion of Jesus. The cosmic christology in the first strophe of the hymn to Christ can only be understood properly in terms of the soteriological statements in the second strophe. That follows from the identification of the body of Christ with the *church:* through the church, the exalted Christ exercises his role as peacemaker throughout the world, in that as head of his body, the church, he gives life. 'The peace of Christ' (3.15) is realized through the church and in the church in the world. In other words, cosmic peace has *now* in fact *already* been realized, but for the moment only in the community of the church, Christ's sphere of power.

I mentioned earlier that Col. 1.13f. shows how the hymn to Christ must be understood in this letter. It is striking that the cosmic dimension of Christ (his role in creation) is affirmed in a way unparalleled in the rest of the New Testament, but is not explained further. The only remnant of this cosmic dimension is the assertion that the Christian no longer has any cause for cosmic anxieties, for tabus determined by horoscopes or the forces of destiny (2.16–23). 'The mystery of God is Christ' (2.2), that

is, the Christ proclaimed by the world to all nations (see the context in
1.24–2.5: Paul's apostolic ministry) is *the hope* of the world and the foundation of the church as a community. The proclamation of this mystery of
Christ discloses its eschatological future *to the world* (1.5: see 1.23; 1.27).
The content of the message of the church is 'Christ' (1.27), our hope.

Colossians simply contrasts the 'philosophy of life' current in Asia
Minor with the apostolic faith, and translates the faith in terms of this
philosophy of life: the proclamation of Jesus crucified and risen. In
Col. 1.21–23 the author points out that the Christians of Colossae were
once Gentiles, from a Jewish point of view *atheoi*, not so much atheists as
living apart from the one true God. This is one more reason for those
who have now become Christians not to return to non-Christian doctrines
of salvation. Instructed by Paul, the author stresses that their conversion
to Christ has come about 'in faith' (2.12; 3.3). Here, however, 'faith' is
given a special, full significance; it is contrasted with the 'puffed up'
(2.18) experience of fulfilment alluded to by the 'philosophy' people, a
condition which is in the last resort not a matter of being full of God, but
of being full of oneself (2.18): 'Insisting on self-abasement and worship
of angels, taking his stand on visions, puffed up without reason by his
sensuous mind.'[89] For the author attacks the ecstatic experience of a kind
of 'vision' of the otherwise hidden ordering of the world at the moment
when the initiate (in this particular philosophy) has put off his old
garments and put on new ones. Colossians 2.23 adds: 'These have indeed
an appearance of wisdom in promoting rigour of devotion and self-abasement and severity to the body, but they are of no value (*timē*) in checking
the indulgence of the flesh'; instead of being filled with the spirit this is
self-satisfaction or self-deception (in the mystery religions *timē* means
election or deification). Evidently the experience of bliss played a central
role in the 'philosophy of life' (or religion) practised in Colossae. However, Colossians asserts, anyone who does not hold fast to Christ as head
(see 2.19) cannot be *fulfilled*, since life flows from the head to the body,
and God's fullness can be found *sōmatikōs* (corporeally) only in Christ
(2.9). Christians are those who are 'fulfilled in him' (2.10). Thus the
saving mystery of God is '*Christos en hymin*' (1.27), Christ in you, which
is the Christ *preached* among the Gentiles and *accepted* by Christ in faith
(see II Cor. 1.19: '*ho en hymin dia hēmōn kērychtheis*', the Christ who is
proclaimed by us among you). 'The mystery of God, which is Christ'
(2.2) is no subjective, blessed event, but a *belief* in Christ *proclaimed*. In
the New Testament there is evidently a certain restraint towards mystical
experiences which cannot be subjected to the criticism of the apostolic
faith. Paul, too, was critical of them.

## III. COLOSSIANS AND PAUL

Colossians is clearly a document which brings up to date Paul's Christian view in the context of a particular pattern of experience and understanding in Asia Minor. It has important points of contact with Paul: 'Yet for us there is one God, the Father, from whom are all things and for whom we exist, and one Lord, Jesus Christ, through whom are all things and through whom we exist' (I Cor. 8.6), and: 'Who will separate us from the love of Christ? . . . Neither angels, nor principalities, nor things present, nor things to come, nor powers, nor height, nor depth, nor anything else in all creation, will be able to separate us from the love of God in Christ Jesus our Lord' (Rom. 8.35–39). In the last resort, Colossians says the same thing. But the author has new perspectives. God really dwells in Christ, as it were in his own body (Col. 2.9). Christ is the head of all powers and dominions (2.10), not just apocalyptically, at the end of time, but already now. Paul does not speak of this rule in the present (1.15–20; 2.9f.; 3.1f.,11) – even though for him the distinction is more apparent than real. For in Colossians Christ exercises this present rule as head of the church, *his body* (1.24), by sending this church to the world (the Pauline element). These angelic forces are not his body, even though they are subject to him. Where the saints are gathered together in Christ (1.2), joined together through love as the perfect bond (3.14), there Christ reigns – in this world. The proclamation of the gospel (1.5,23,27) 'to every creature under heaven' (1.23; see 1.26f.; 4.3f.) points to the cosmic, i.e. universal dimension of salvation in Jesus. Hope for a future event remains untouched; the eschatological tension has not vanished and is indeed the nucleus of what is called 'the gospel' (1.5,23,27). However, even more strongly than in Paul the forward-looking perspective becomes a perspective directed upwards, spatially: there the heritage is already laid up (1.5). The *fides quae creditur*, the content of faith (see 2.7 and 1.23), is given a stronger accent than the *fides qua*. For Paul, hope is grounded on faith (Rom. 4.18), whereas in Colossians hope is the *content* of the gospel which is preached everywhere.

Baptism, too, is given a new meaning. For Paul, Christian baptism, as dying with Christ, is above all a dying to sin, an earnest of the *pneuma* and therefore the ground for hope in a later resurrection with Christ (6.1–11). In Colossians, baptism is no longer dying with Christ, but above all *rising with him* (Col. 2.12; 3.1, though even Colossians does not make the addition that we shall find in Ephesians: even now we are sitting with Christ at the right hand of God, Eph. 2.6). We still await the manifestation of what we already *are* now, hidden in Christ (Col. 3.3). Colossians goes as far as possible with the philosophy of life which it fights, but does so only to show that the heavenly fulfilment sought there is to be found only in Christ, the risen one. Paul orients his ethical admonitions on the coming resurrection, albeit on the basis of baptism; in contrast Colossians stresses the present reality: 'If then you have been raised with Christ, seek the things that are above' (3.1).

There is no longer any mention of Paul's doctrine of justification as such. Colossians is Paulinism in another situation, a theology which has been given new life independently of Paul – doubtless with special risks, just as Paul's view of the apostolic faith had special risks. The 'new man' put on in baptism (Col. 3.10a), who is created after the image (*eikōn*) of the Creator (Col. 3.10b), also amounts to a slight shift of accent in comparison with Paul. He talks of 'putting on Christ' (Gal. 3.27; Rom. 13.4), whereas Colossians talks of 'putting on the new man', which is formed after the image of God, i.e. after Christ. In matter-of-fact terms, the newness of this life in Christ's sphere of influence without the tyranny of heavenly powers specifically amounts to love and mercy, graciousness towards one's fellow men, concern for others and not for oneself, helping others in the right direction and being patient (3.12) – five virtues which are interrelated on earth in everyday human relationships. The author adds: readiness to forgive like Christ, in whom we are baptized (3.13), and above all, *agapē* or love (3.14), for this is the *syndesmos* (i.e. bond which ties loose parts together) of perfection (a final genitive). In other words, love is a bond which leads to perfection. It joins the members of the community together in the one body of Christ and in so doing creates perfection in the community. That is 'the peace of Christ' (3.15), which the author wishes for the community (cf. John 14.27; II Thess. 3.16). What this means is not so much a 'peace for the soul'; peace is as it were the sphere in which the new man lives, the body of the church – that part of the world which is already reconciled, where peace already prevails and from where peace-making activity must extend into the world (Ephesians in particular will make this a central point).

Consequently Colossians is a new version of the experience of salvation in Jesus from God – a new experience – and yet the same apostolic experience of faith. It is an ecclesiological soteriology, not individualistic, but communal, an applied christology. Grace, salvation in Christ, is developed further in terms of the church on the basis of apostolic christology, and in so doing is given a 'cosmic' significance, that is, a peace-bringing message for *all men*.

## §2 The peace of Christ among the Gentiles: Ephesians

*The setting of the letter*

According to Ephesians itself, it is Paul who writes this letter from prison. We can be certain that the author of Ephesians is an even more outspoken supporter of Pauline theology than the author of Colossians. On the other hand, the style, the exuberance, even the cultural background are so characteristic of Asia Minor that it is possible that this letter might be ascribed to Paul himself. The letter says that Tychicus (according to Acts 20.4, from Asia Minor) will bring the letter (is he the author?). The community to which the letter is addressed is not mentioned at all in the best manuscripts. Furthermore, in Eph. 3.1f. the author says that he does not know the readers of his letter, whereas according to Acts 19.10, Paul himself spent two years in Ephesus. There is no reference in the letter to the particular circumstances of a specific community. The author has a completely impersonal attitude to his readers.

Ephesians seems to me to be a version of Romans in terms of Asia Minor. The author sets out to present 'the hope to which Christians are called' (1.18) against the general cultural background of Asia Minor in late antiquity (towards which he adopts a critical approach). The letter is probably a kind of encyclical to the various churches in Asia Minor. We still find a trace of this in 1.1, where the mention of 'in Ephesus' was originally missing. We may supply 'to the believers in', and Tychicus will in that case have added the name of the church community in which the letter was to be read out (Laodicea, Hierapolis, Ephesus, etc.). Presumably the first 'editor' of the letter found it in Ephesus and added 'in Ephesus', or got hold of a copy in which these words had been inserted. Be this as it may, Ephesus was the chief city of the churches of Asia Minor.

In bringing up to date the ideas of Romans, Ephesians seems to have a good knowledge of Colossians (not vice versa; cf. Col. 1.5 with Eph. 1.13f.; Col. 1.23 with Eph. 3.6; Col. 4.3 with Eph. 6.19; the quotation from Isa. 52.7 in Eph. 6.15 – see Eph. 2.17 – is secondary in comparison with Colossians). Thus the author is writing as it were a new version of Colossians. (However, there might be another explanation of this relationship between Ephesians and Colossians: both might be based on *the same material*, and Ephesians might not have a direct acquaintance with Colossians.) The key concept of Ephesians is *eirēnē*, or peace; this is the content of its good news as the 'gospel of peace' (Eph. 6.15), i.e. the mystery of Christ, proclaimed to all through the ministry of the apostles and also by the whole church (6.15): peace, which is to be achieved by a hard struggle against the powers of darkness (6.12–17). For the author, these powers are of a mysterious heavenly kind. Victory over these heavenly powers which alienate men will do away with the gulf between the nations – Jews and non-Jews – through the peace in a church made up of Jews and Gentiles.

The portentous style can be explained by the pattern of thought and feeling in the culture of Asia Minor (by contrast, the style of Colossians is hieratic and terse). Thanksgivings in a sentence going on for several verses are interrupted by 'according to the riches of his grace' (1.7c), 'by grace you have been saved', (2.5b), 'out of the great love with which he loved us' (2.4), 'how great a hope', 'how rich a glory', 'how great his power' (1.18f.), 'the abundant riches of his grace' (2.7), etc. A partial explanation of this style is the influence of solemn hymnic material, whether the model is provided by the Old Testament (and the synagogue) or by already existing Christian hymns to God used at the baptism of the newly converted. Furthermore, the stress on predestination and the overabundance of grace shows close connections with the world of Qumran (a more indirect relationship, which interpreters have worked out increasingly over recent years). Furthermore, the author writes particularly good Greek. The first three chapters in particular are a gem of literary construction; unfortunately it is impossible to go into the details at this point.

Leaving aside the introduction, which gives the letter its orientation (an extended thanksgiving in the form of a hymn), the letter falls into two parts: (*a*) *a dogmatic part*: 'that you may know how great is the hope to which he has called you' (1.18): 'called to hope' (see 1.15–23), interpreted in Eph. 1–3; and (*b*) a paraenetic or *admonitory ethical part* built on the foundation of the preceding dogmatic section. 'Lead a life worthy of the calling to which you have been called' (4.1), given in more detail in Eph. 4–6. As a child of his time and its cultural environment, with its universal cosmic awareness, the author is sympathetic to the conceptions of his time, but feels that they are valid and permissible only if the historical responsibility of the church is taken seriously. A typical phrase is: 'To God be the glory *in the church* and in *Christ Jesus*' (3.20f.). If any book lays the foundations for a political theology in the New Testament, it is Ephesians, though the author himself does not see through its historical consequences or implications. This should emerge from the following analysis.

I. THE CULTURAL AND RELIGIOUS PRESUPPOSITIONS OF
EPHESIANS

In the years in which Ephesians are written, Jesus had already become
'part of culture', an element in the syncretism of late antiquiry. In other
words, syncretistic-thinking Jews and Gentiles had already been converted to Christianity. They brought the whole of their spiritual and
cultural heritage with them into the church. The critical question which
underlies the attempt in Ephesians is: How far is it permissible for
Christians to reconcile the spirit of the time with the perspective of the
apostolic faith, which here – as in Colossians – is identified with Pauline
apostolic faith and, beyond this Paulinism, with the mystery which has
taken place in Jesus? It is remarkable that in Ephesians we find something
that is unique outside the four gospels: in Eph. 4.20f., 'Jesus' is contrasted
with 'Christ'.[90] Does this represent a reaction to speculation about a
cosmic 'Christ' or a 'Christ principle' which was to develop within the
religious presuppositions of the culture of Asia Minor apart from Jesus
of Nazareth (in Pauline terms, that would be apart from his self-sacrifice
to the point of death) (see below)?

The constantly recurring problem of the 'community of God' (Ephesians) is: the church, which is not of the world, lives *in* the world. The
question then is, does the church maintain a critical and creative tension
towards and within this social and cultural environment, which is also
the atmosphere breathed day by day by its members? By comparison
with Colossians, Ephesians is not strikingly polemical (just as Romans is
not polemical in comparison with Galatians). Nowhere is there mention
of opponents, as there is in Galatians and Colossians. One might say that
Ephesians is to Colossians as Romans is to Galatians. The polemic has
already been incorporated into the placid thematic account. There is no
trace of angel worship in Ephesians (as there is in Colossians). The fact
that there is an implicit detachment in Ephesians, e.g. from a christology
which passes over into a kind of all-embracing cosmic atmosphere of
liberation and a unification with the universe, in a vaguely cosmopolitan
brotherhood which was developing at that time (and was encouraged
above all by the Stoics and the unity of the Hellenistic Roman empire),
must be read from the text of Ephesians itself. It seems to me more
difficult to establish the cultural background to the letter than that of e.g.
Colossians or Galatians, in which there are explicit references to remarks
made by opponents. Certainly, it is evident that the background is one
of the syncretism of late antiquity, but syncretism has many features.
Exegetical interpretations are widely divergent.

According to H. Schlier and E. Käsemann, the letter is based on a
gnostic model, mixed up with Stoic elements of a universal synthesis and

world-wide brotherhood. In the view of the Czech theologian P. Pokorný, the background is a milder form of gnosticism, whereas C. Colpe speaks of the myth of the primal man, a saviour who descends from the highest spheres to redeem souls sunk in the material earth. J. Gnilka looks towards the thought of Philo: the Logos as the head of the cosmos, which is depicted as a macrocosm. E. Schweizer is convinced that the model of the eschatological Adam has influenced Ephesians; moreover, it has had a triumphalist and quietistic impact, which is one reason why the letter lays emphasis on the necessity for good works. And J. Dupont, a specialist in gnosticism and Stoicism, simply sees Stoic speculations about the *sōma* and the *plērōma* in the background to the letter.

The fact that so many different interpretations are possible is the best indication that here we have a *syncretistic* cultural background, a melting pot for many originally different ideas which have come together, fertilized one another, and are difficult to bring together under any one heading. It is already clear from Colossians that the cosmos was seen as an *anthrōpos* (macrocosm of man as microcosm) and as the *sōma* or body of the Logos. Such thinking obviously plays a role here, but it does not amount to 'Philonism' (which is in itself a particular version of syncretistic ideas). Ephesians may also have these ideas from Colossians. I think that it is better to explain the presuppositions of Ephesians on the basis of the text (and not directly from our knowledge of religions in antiquity, which can only be auxiliary). Only then, if at all, is it possible to determine which concepts from this syncretistic culture are dominant in Ephesians. If we do that, three key concepts come to light.

## A. Spiritual heavenly powers

It is already said in Eph. 1.21f. that after his resurrection Christ was 'exalted far above all rule and authority and power', three designations or classes in the hierarchy of the heavenly spirits. We have already seen that the problem for man in antiquity was that his life was determined by astrology or by 'heavenly' forces. As in apocalyptic Judaism (I[Eth.] Enoch 56.5), discord between heavenly spirits and men was a *theme* of this culture. This view of the world had an existential breeding ground. Then, as at all other times, man did not feel that he was the master of his fate, his action and his experiences. We *want* good and *do* evil, as Paul said – and in so doing was in agreement with the Stoics. Men felt themselves subjected to forces and powers which they could not control – a general fact of experience in the *condition humaine*, for which people in every age have sought an explanation. People in antiquity found this in *heimarmenē, fatum*, destiny, which for some was an indefinable factor, while for most it was a living spiritual reality in the world above. (Even in the thirteenth century, Thomas Aquinas would devote an entire *Quaestio* not only to fate, *S. Th. I*, q. 116, but also to the angels who are the prime movers [*primi motores*] in the world of the stars, I, q. 53 and q. 110). These heavenly forces were at work in nature and history. In some way life and death were influenced by these cosmocrators, 'rulers of the world', as they were often called. The New Testament also lives with this view of the world, though it is not interested in the detailed classification of these heavenly angelic hierarchies (like the inter-testamental literature with its endless speculations on angel choirs). Furthermore, in this view of the world, no sharp distinction is drawn between good heavenly beings (angels) and evil (diabolical) beings, though there is some general idea of a kind of fall of the angels (this does not appear anywhere in the New Testament, apart from a quotation from an apocryphal book in the Letter of Jude and in II Peter, see below).[91] These beings dwell in the air immediately above our earth, 'in lower regions', the earthly atmosphere (see Eph. 2.2). That is where 'the God of this earthly world' (2.2) dwells, in a sphere which in ancient cosmology was regarded as 'chaotic' (the sphere of clouds, thunder, lightning and hail), in contrast to the eternal harmonious rest and the regular course of the starry world far above the earth. Despite the primitive geocentric standpoint, according to this spiritual view of the world everything revolves round the boundless world of the stars. (The earth was by no means the centre of the universe in this pattern of spirituality. We need only read I Enoch to find how for these people the heavenly spheres were the centre of all reality – particularly when this reality affected *men*.) Another tradition tells how some of the fallen angels were imprisoned in subterranean caves (Jude and II Peter, see below). This pluralism is connected with the 'transference' of the kingdom of the dead which took place in late antiquity, in the inter-testamental period. Earlier it was supposed to be in the underworld (Sheol or Hades), but later it was located in higher spheres (in that case dying becomes an 'ascent of the soul', an *anabasis*). In the view of others, these 'spirits of the air' only come down into subterranean caves at the end of time (see Luke 10.18; Rev. 12.9–12; 20.10).

This interest in the world of the stars (which was also influenced by scientific astronomy from the East) begins to show itself throughout antiquity from the second century BC on, and among other things is a reaction against the 'rationalism' of the Greek spirit which was then prevalent. It was in this situation that the bias towards the East, *ex oriente lux*, developed. At that time there was a flood of 'revelation literature' based on supra-rational wisdom, from all sides: Sibylline wisdom, Hermetic wisdom, Orphic wisdom, apocalyptic Jewish wisdom and astrological wisdom. Earlier fragmentary ideas began to develop into a variety of 'philosophies of life', even if datable literature about them often comes only from the second and third centuries AD (which is the reason for all our uncertainty).

At all events, for Jews and Christians these spirits were God's creatures, and in the last resort were subordinate to him. Jewish and Christian monotheism does not as yet know of any metaphysical dualism. Therefore salvation is possible, or at least not excluded. The rift in God's good creation must therefore have come about through some cause which is not of God. The ambiguity in our human world, that on the one hand it is created by God and therefore good, and on the other hand is in fact sinful and thus is hostile to God, is projected in this old view of the world on to the world of heavenly forces, in which a similar ambiguity of good and evil seems to prevail. If there are no angels or devils, then man himself is a devil – and man cannot accept that, for all his experience of meaninglessness; he has the experience that he is weak, but the spirit is willing. Something of this psychological mechanism was at work in this ancient view of the world. The most striking thing is that neither the Tanach nor the New Testament are interested in these heavenly spirits as such; they are concerned with their relationship to man and his world. Even Satan is of no interest, except insofar as he is 'the God (ruler) of this world' (Eph. 2.2; see Rev. 12.9–12; 20.10; Luke 10.18, etc.). The view prevails that 'the whole world lies in the power of the evil one' (I John 5.19). And all the cosmic powers seem to be confederates of the devil (Eph. 1.21; 2.2). For Christians, therefore, the earth is the arena in the struggle against the tyrannical rule of the powers of heaven: 'For we are contending . . . against the principalities, against the powers, against the world rulers of this present darkness, against the spiritual hosts of wicked- ness in the heavenly places' (Eph. 6.12; see Rom. 8.35–39; II Cor. 4.4; Hebrews). According to this view, to sin is to subject oneself to heavenly powers (Eph. 2.1–3; see II Cor. 4.4) The forgiveness of sins through the death of Jesus on the cross is therefore *ipso facto* a triumph over the heavenly powers. In antiquity, anthropology and ethics are seen against a cosmic background, i.e. one determined by heavenly spirits. Therefore Jesus' resurrection is *ipso facto* an enthronement of the Lord Jesus over all angelic powers. But the earthly world goes on. Therefore these heav- enly powers remain a real threat; above all, death, their last weapon, is still there (see I Cor. 15.24–28).

Apparently there is some uncertainty throughout the New Testament as to whether these powers are subject to Christ or not. Three factors can explain this. First of all, the literary genre, that of hymns in which God or his mighty acts are praised as though all had already been accomplished (from the certainty of hope: already in Pss. 97 and 98; Luke 1.46–55; 1.68f.; Rev. 11.17f.; Heb. 1.6–14). On the other hand, it can be explained from the ancient picture of the *basileus* or ruler: the king rules in and through conquering his foes (see Ps. 110). Therefore the universal rule of Christ, as a confession of the community of God, means that Christ rules in and through victorious resistance against evil, or in terms of late antiquity: against Satan and his followers. Although there is still active resistance, then, Christ nevertheless reigns. In the last resort, we have here the 'already now' and 'not yet' as factors in salvation which are typical of the New Testament.

The heart of this view of the world is that in human life there are powers and forces which determine human destiny in a way which cannot be understood. The fight against evil is not only a fight against human weakness (Eph. 6.12a), and therefore not merely a summons to be of 'good will'; more is at stake (6.12b). There is an essential connection between redemption through Christ and liberation from the (heavenly) power-blocks which alienate mankind.

## B. Redeemer myths underlying Ephesians

Two ways to salvation have evidently influenced the account of redemption given in Ephesians.

### (a) The breach in the dividing wall

Centuries before Christ, the Greeks had said that *polemos*, war, hostility and disorder was 'the law of things' (the pre-Socratics). Redemption myths came into being from this experience; in other words, people attempted to track down and identify precisely what in mankind was diseased and damaged in this experience of contrast. Such experiences at the least presuppose an implicit awareness of a perspective of meaning which was largely made explicit in original experiences of meaning and happiness. This totality leads to a projective expectation of universal meaning, which it was also hoped to identify. These interpretative identifications called redemption myths into being.

What was the myth with which Ephesians had to contend? Christian though its inspiration and interpretation may be, Eph. 2.14–17 betrays the latent presence of a pre-existent tradition which is slanted in another direction. In the context of Ephesians, the thought is expressed that in the church as God's community, Christianity appears as the new 'third race': a unity made up of Jews and Gentiles. The church is the sphere in which the breach between the nations is healed and the nations are reconciled. That is the particular soteriology of Ephesians. However, the terminology used bears traces of another myth. This presupposition is confirmed by Eph. 4.8f.: here there is talk of reconciliation on the basis of the fact that a divine mediator heals the breach between the world above and the world below by an act of descent and ascent, by a journey through all the worlds (above the earth, on the earth and below the earth), afterwards returning to the *epourania* or heavenly spheres. This redemption model was widespread at the time.

Here, however, we are reminded first of Israel's tradition (which at all events was influenced from Canaan). In the Tanach, 'descend' and 'ascend' (*'ālāh*, ascend, and *yārad*, descend)[92] have a theological meaning when they are used of Yahweh, from which one assumes that his dwelling place is above. In that case Yahweh's gracious appearance among men is a 'descent' (*katabasis*) and an 'ascent' (*anabasis*). This is not so much a matter of anthropomorphism as an indication of Yahweh's transcendence. Yahweh visits his people, 'descends' to free his people (Ex. 3.8; Isa. 31.4; 63.19; Ps. 144.5–8) or even to punish them (Gen. 17.7; Micah 1.3). Furthermore, there is also something special about the royal psalms (above all Pss. 47; 68; 97). Here we have mention of an ascension of Yahweh and of his enthronement as ruler of the world (Ps. 47.2 with 47.5; 47.9 and 97.9). In Ps. 68.18 Yahweh takes prisoners with him on his ascension who pay him gifts of homage: this is a sign of God's rule over the world (Eph. 4.8f. quotes this very psalm). The ascension of God and his universal rule over the world coincide. In this capacity he is called *'elyōn*, the Most High, either above all other gods (who later become *'elōhīm* and angels, Ps. 97.9), or above the political and military authorities on earth (Ps. 47.9). As *'elyōn*, God is ruler of the world (e.g. Ps. 7.17; 9.2; 50.14; 92.1), who must be praised for his majesty. This ancient name for Yahweh went out of favour in the time before Christ and in the inter-testamental literature: 'the Most High' with 'his kingdom without end' (Dan. 4.17, 25, 32; 5.18; 7.18–27), Yahweh's universal rule.

What was more obvious than for Christian belief, for whom God had visited Israel in the person of Jesus, to use the model of Yahweh's *anabasis* and *katabasis* and to connect the resurrection of Jesus with these royal psalms: the enthronement of Christ as ruler of the world, as victor over all heavenly powers? Granted, the theme comes from ancient Canaan, although it has been baptized into Yahwistic faith, but Jewish Christianity could drawn on its own resources for *this* model of *katabasis* and *anabasis*.

This plays a prominent role in Ephesians. However, it was easy to connect this Jewish theme with non-Jewish myths. Thus in I Enoch (14.9), 'the saviour', on his journey through heaven, comes up against a crystal wall which separates the heavenly world from earth. Testament of Levi 2.7 and the Greek Apocalypse of Baruch (III Bar. 2.1f.) also talk of a cosmic dividing wall. On his ascent, this saviour and hero comes upon a gap in the wall. This is not gnosis, though later gnosticism will use these categories in its view of life. In Hellenistic Judaism the gulf between the two worlds has already become a characteristic theme (Eth. Enoch 56.5). Furthermore, in gnosticism there is no reconciliation of the two halves of the world; it is a question of being rescued from them. Only in the *Corpus Hermeticum* is the earthly world called the *plērōma* of evil and God the abundance of all grace (*CH* 12.15). Cosmic reconciliation consists in the fact that the division of these two halves of the world by an impregnable wall is shattered by a heavenly hero and that these two worlds are reconciled: in one man, the great macrocosm. A cosmic drama on high brings redemption and salvation for men. Similar ideas were to be found throughout the Mediterranean world. The author must have heard some of them; at any rate, that would explain the terminology of the 'dividing wall' and 'one man'; however, instead of a mystical drama we have a historical crucifixion (see below).

(*b*) All is one: *panta hen*

At the same time, the Stoics propagated a completely different way to redemption with great success. The Stoics did not deny the need for redemption, but for them it was not a mystical event. Everything had already been reconciled from all eternity and was one. There was a hidden harmony in the world in which everything had its place to the benefit of the world. The good Logos permeates all things, and gives everything life, regularity and a place of its own. The whole of the angelic world is swept away; there is nothing supernatural. The supernatural is the soul of everything that lives. What we have is the transcendence (which is also the immanence) of the principle of life which makes all things one. The Stoics continued to 'tolerate' the many 'spirits' of popular thought, but they were no longer significant. God is everything, and yet in one sense above all, Father of all. The whole cosmos is a body, with one pneuma or one Logos as its soul. 'All things are one.' But we need to be led to this deeper insight, and then we see the harmony of the world and are redeemed. Thus redemption is liberation of the self through insight. Without doubt, this Stoic notion (reinterpreted in Christian terms) underlies the terminology of Eph. 4.3–6: 'Eager to maintain the unity of the Spirit in the bond of peace. There is one body and one Spirit . . . one Lord, one faith, one baptism, one God and Father of us all, who is above all and through all and in all.' The *panta hen* terminology plays its part, as it was already incorporated into Greek-speaking Judaism and interpreted in terms of Yahweh: 'one God, one Temple, one Law, one people'. The formula of Eph. 4.5f. shows influences from Hellenism and Judaism, yet retains its Christian characteristics, both exclusively and inclusively. For Ephesians, God is the Father of all; he is not simply the one common origin of all religions, which express what the Stoics mean by 'the one God and Father of all' through a mythical form and a variety of divine names; nor is he bound up with just one nation or people: he is 'the Father of the universe and above all' (Eph. 4.6, see 1.10,23; 3.9f.,15). This cultural background explains the stress of Ephesians on unity and peace and universality. However, this unity and peace are not based on the cosmic Logos, the soul of the world: nor are they based on Roman rule, or on a redeemer myth, but on the historical crucifixion of Jesus and his exaltation to be the 'Father of all'.


## II.  THE CHRISTIAN WORK OF PEACE

What does Eph. 1.10 mean by 'the union of all things in Christ', which the author sees as the content of the mystery or the divine counsel? The meaning of this statement is explained in 2.1–21. For Ephesians, one historical fact stands in the foreground: the gulf between the nations, or more precisely, between Jews and non-Jews. The Gentiles were excluded from the promise to Israel given through Abraham; for that reason they were alienated from God, *atheoi* (4.18; see Col. 1.21). They had no access to the one true God; their exclusion from the holy of holies in the Temple was the clearest indication of this. The Torah had been raised like a dividing wall between the nations. This is not a Christian interpretation, but a statement made by the Jews themselves.[93] The law kept the Jews apart, and separated them from the Gentiles. This made the Jewish law an obstacle to peace among the nations. This was the Jews' view of themselves, and the Gentiles' view of the Jews. Above all in the world of late antiquity, in which Stoic *philanthrōpia* or benevolence towards all mankind tended to be a kind of international solidarity, the attitude of the Jews tended to arouse an almost universal feeling of rejection (even in the book of Esther).

Along with other works, Ephesians is convinced that the Jewish Law is the reason for the disquiet and hostility between the two groups which make up the population of the world (2.14f.). Furthermore, the point of the description in Ephesians is that the Law makes it difficult even for the Jews to find access to God: according to the Law, they too are sinners. The law as a dividing wall is given symbolic expression in the Temple of Jerusalem, where a heavy curtain divided off the place which non-Jews were prohibited from entering on pain of death (see the accusation against Paul: Acts 21.28f.; 24.6). For this very reason Gentiles were *atheoi* (Eph. 2.12), excluded from communion with the God of Israel (2.12f.). 'But now in Christ Jesus you (= the former Gentiles) who once were far off have been *brought near* in the blood of Christ' (2.13). The author adopts a Jewish standpoint, with an allusion to Isa. 57.19, 'Peace, peace, to the *far* and to the *near*, says the Lord.' Those who enjoy full rights as Israelites are called 'the near', whereas Gentiles and open Jewish sinners (like publicans) are called 'the far'. 'To bring near' therefore becomes a technical term in Jewish proselytism, namely to accept someone as a preferential member of the Jewish community (which included circumcision). In Ephesians, the term is also used for Christian baptism. By the death of Jesus, Gentiles have achieved access to the God of Israel, the one true God (see 2.1–3). Therefore 'Christ is the peace' (2.14), the bringer of eschatological peace which has already been spoken of by Isa. 57.19; 52.7; Zech. 9.10; Micah 5.4. Instead of strangers (*xenoi*) and sojourners (*paroikoi*) they have now become 'fellow-citizens' (Eph. 2.19). These too are Jewish legal terms. The rabbis applied the law in the Tanach about foreigners (Lev. 19.33f.) to religious proselytes. Resident foreigners (*paroikoi* or sojourners) received limited Jewish rights of citizenship. In the New Testament they received full rights of citizenship through baptism.

But the Temple, the dividing wall between Jews and non-Jews, was itself already an earthly symbol of the heavenly dwelling place.[94] Architecturally, and by means of representations of the starry universe on the curtain (see below on Hebrews), the Temple reproduced in 'shadow' form the structure of the universe. Thus the Jewish image of the dividing wall in the Temple could be seen against a cosmic background: a cosmic wall which separated the heavenly dwelling-place of God with its courtiers from the world of men. The two sets of imagery go into one another and act on one another. No one ascends above from the world below through his own strength. In the last resort the cosmic gulf is the diastasis between the inaccessible transcendent God and sinful creatures, symbolized on earth by the people of God, Israel, with the holy of holies in the Temple, into which no non-Jew was allowed to enter, and Jews, only through the high priest. (Hebrews will go on to analyse this theme in more detail.) The divide between Jew and non-Jew on earth is the symbol of the holy transcendence of God over against everything that is creaturely. Christ has torn down both dividing walls and brought about universal peace: (in the church) he has brought both groups (Jews and non-Jews) together, and thus makes it possible for both of them to have *access to God*: 'For he is our peace, who has made both (*amphotera*, neuter) one and has broken down the dividing wall of hostility, by abolishing in his flesh the law of commandments and ordinances, that he might create in himself one new man in place of the two, so making peace, and might reconcile us both to God in one body through the cross, thereby bringing the hostility to an end. And he came and preached peace . . . for through him we both have access in one Spirit to the Father' (Eph. 2.14–18). This text, which

sounds like a hymn, is full of allusions to the Old Testament and early
Jewish literature. Ephesians 2.17f. combines Isa. 57.19 with Isa. 52.7:
after the conclusion of peace, peace has to be 'proclaimed'; in other
words, the service or the proclamation of reconciliation is part of the
essence of reconciliation (see II Cor. 5.17–21). While it is possible to see
a 'cosmic myth' behind Ephesians, little of this myth is left in the letter:
Ephesians is concerned with the event of the establishment of peace
among men and with God: in Ephesians *the church* is the new humanity
in which all hostility has vanished away – all together form one body
(1.23). Ephesians is a 'gospel of peace' (6.15), through which 'the unfathomable riches of Christ' are preached to the Gentiles (3.8). And the
author says that God has so ordained everything that 'through the church
the manifold wisdom of God might now be made known to the principalities and powers in the heavenly places' (3.10). The cosmic *model*
certainly has a part here, but Ephesians thinks in *historical* terms: the
proclamation of 'baptism for the forgiveness of sins' and the 'new life'
makes it clear to the evil powers that men can escape sin, that is slavery,
which is brought about by evil powers, and gain free access to God (3.12;
see 3.4). Reconciliation among all men *is* free access to God (2.18; 3.12).
Following this argument, it seems that the evil spirits want to prevent
the access of all earthly men to God, a thought which already plays a
part in this literature through the figure of the serpent in the book of
Genesis. Man is prevented from having free access to Eden, in which he
was able to walk unhindered with God in the garden, as a punishment
for sin. Cherubim watch over the entrance – as they do before the ark of
the covenant and the holy of holies in the Temple. Ancient ideas and
newer ones derived from them were current in Hellenistic Judaism, which
also came across other myths in the melting-pot of the syncretism of the
time. In fact Ephesians 'demythologizes' all this, as the author says in a
matter-of-fact way that access to God is denied us only through sinfulness.
However, this sinfulness stands under the power of evil spirits who are
set over us (2.1–3).

However, the cultural and religious cosmic background does not disappear altogether. 'Therefore it is said, "When he ascended on high he
led a host of captives, and he gave gifts to men" [Ps. 68.18]. In saying,
"He ascended," what does it mean but that he had also descended into
the lower parts of the earth? He who descended is he who also ascended
far above all the heavens, that he might fill all things' (4.8f.). Both
Eph. 2.14–16 and 4.8f. betray the background of a cosmic model of
redemption with which Ephesians was evidently confronted. At all events,
the author interprets this model in a radically new way – unless there is
some non-Israelite or non-Jewish model behind it. The model of descent
and ascent is unmistakably present in Eph. 4.8f. It is a model derived

from ancient Israel and early Judaism, though it has grown up in this way either in its antiquity or in its Jewish form. The idea is that *universal salvation* must fill all things. But these people also think in spatial terms, in cosmic spheres: the realm above the earth, on the earth and below the earth all make up the universe. A universal saviour has therefore visited all these places and 'filled' them with his arrival (though the author does not speak of an underworld; for him, our earth is the lowest level). Despite all this imagery, however, in the last resort Ephesians simply says that universal salvation is given 'through his blood' (1.7), his death on the cross: and his triumphal procession through all the spheres of the world in fact amounts to the forgiveness of sins (1.7). This is pure Pauline theology in the setting of the Asia Minor of late antiquity. Thus the cosmic element in Ephesians is that on the one hand sin is regarded as (freely affirmed) life in the devil's sphere of power (2.1), whereas God's decision for salvation was the *anakephalaiōsis* or restoration of all things – *ta panta* – in Christ (1.10). What is this *anakephalaiōsis*, the heart of this letter? In Greek the word has nothing to do with 'bringing under one head', in other words with *kephalē* (head); it is connected with *kephalaion*, i.e. summing up, or recapitulation, in the sense of a repeated, evocative summation (see also Rom. 13.9; Heb. 8.1). The term comes from Greek grammar; the grammarian Quintilian writes: *'Rerum repetitio et congregatio, quae graece anakephalaiosis dicitur. . . .'*;[95] to bring together parts which have been scattered and separated is *anakephalaiōsis*, or a recapitulation. That is completely in accord with the heart of Ephesians, i.e. with 2.14–16. There is no mention of bringing all things under one head (*kephalē*), Christ (even though this is what it amounts to); Christ brings all things together, in making peace.

Because Ephesians on the other hand speaks of Christ as *kephalē*, head (1.22), some exegetes believe, despite all the rules of Greek grammar, that in using *anakephalaiōsis* the author is thinking of 'bringing everything together under one head' (which is how many translations of the Bible have it). In my view this goes against the tenor of the whole of Ephesians.[96] Ephesians 1.22 says: 'God has laid all things under his feet'; Christ is the *Lord* of all. There is a quotation from Ps. 8.6: the exaltation of Jesus above all things. Nowhere, however, in Ephesians is it also said that Christ is the *kephalē*, the head of all. In contrast to Colossians, Ephesians goes against this: 'God has made him *head* of the *church*, his body' (1.22; also 4.15b and 5.23). In Colossians Christ is 'head of all', because he is head of the body, the church. Therefore Ephesians *reserves* for Christ the function as *head* of the church, and only for him (here Colossians is inconsistent). Otherwise in this one context we have to attribute a double meaning to the word 'head': as 'head of all' (so Colossians) he is only *Kyrios*, Lord, to whom all things are subjected (in fact this is an Old Testament concept: Greek Judg. 10.18; 11.8,9,11; Isa. 7.8f.), whereas 'head of the church, his *body*', has a Hellenistic, Stoic significance: the principle of unity which permeates everything with life and force. In my view, the term *'Christus, caput omnium'*, head of all, is alien to the spirit of Ephesians, and if the author is familiar with Colossians, he is correcting Col. 2.10. Ephesians is therefore more Pauline than Colossians. Christ is risen and exalted; so he is the *Lord*, universal, over all: 'far above all rule and authority and power' and 'above every name that is named, not only in this age but also in that which is to come' (1.21). But Christ is *head* only of the church: for that means the forgiveness of sins and life. The spiritual powers are subject to Christ, namely in the community of the church, to the degree that there is forgiveness of sins and new life in the Spirit. Therefore this forgiveness of sins calls for a constant fight against the powers of evil (6.12). The matter-of-fact and by no means 'cosmic' insight of Ephesians is that these powers are subject to Christ as long as men do not sin any more. In this view only the church, and not the world, is a medium of salvation, 'Do not give the devil a chance' (4.27). In my view, therefore, *anakephalaiōsis* must be understood to mean bring together, make peace (which also fits Greek sensibilities better). The fundamental insight of the letter, as of 1.10, is that Christ is the founder of universal peace. The cosmic aspect of this establishment of peace is not denied, but it is concentrated into an ecclesiological approach. By the crucifixion and resurrection of Jesus, forgiveness of sins and access to God may be had by all men, without any distinction. 'A hallowed life' is possible. Consequently the power of sin – which here takes the form of evil spirits – is broken and subjected to Christ. That gives the church of God a cosmic, i.e. a *universal* task. Apart from the 'evil spirits', there is nothing 'cosmic' in the whole of Ephesians – much less than there is in Paul, who even makes the whole material creation sigh for the revelation of the final redemption of *mankind*.

A similar shift takes place in Ephesians over the term *kephalē*, or head. It differs from Colossians in saying that the church, rather than the *cosmos*, is the *body* of Christ. Christ is not the head of the church and *furthermore* head of the universe (as Gnilka asserts, along with many others); in Ephesians everything is subjected to Christ, but Jesus is head only of the church. His resurrection *is* his presence among us; this presence is the community of God and not a kind of cosmic omnipresence. In Ephesians, Christ is *Kyrios*, Lord of *ta panta* and *kephalē*, head of the 'church'. And precisely because *sōma*, body, and therefore also his *plērōma* (fullness) are reserved for the church, according to Ephesians Christ is not a *caput mundi*, ruler of the world, *except* through his work as peacemaker, which is carried on by the church.[97] It is also striking that Ephesians avoids the title Son of God; it occurs once (4.13) and is *perhaps* against a cosmic christology in which the world is called the body of the 'Son of God'. It seems to me that for Ephesians, the transformation of the cosmic concept characteristic of late antiquity, namely that the cosmos is the body of the Logos (which can already be found in Colossians), into ecclesiological terms is affirmative evidence (Eph. 1.23; 5.23); the author draws the consequences from this for his concept of the *kephalē* (which Colossians has not thought through to the end). Furthermore, Ephesians does not talk of Christ in terms of the creation (at any rate, we do not find such terms mentioned in Ephesians). It does, however, use cosmic expressions: 'the breadth and the length, the height and the depth' (3.18), the four dimensions of all possible objects, things and living beings in the universe. The terminology may well come directly or indirectly from the Stoa, but for Ephesians it describes the all-embracing love (and the all-embracing insight) of Christ (3.19).

As head of his church, Christ is called *redeemer* of the church (5.23b): 'He gave himself up *for her,* that he might sanctify her, having cleansed her by the washing of water with the word, that the church might be presented before him (= above) as a glorious bride' (5.25–27). Here the picture changes: 'because we are *members* of his *body*' (5.30). Members of the church, members of the Lord? Or, as members of the church members of his glorified body? The two images seem to overlap: both the church and the body of Christ are 'one flesh', like man and woman in Genesis (5.31f.). For Ephesians argues that Gen. 2.24 itself alludes to the relationship between Christ and his church, to the inner link between them.

This is why Ephesians introduces the term *plērōma*, which is already known from Colossians: according to Colossians it is the fullness of God which dwells in Christ. However, once again Ephesians is thinking in ecclesiastical terms: as the body, the church is itself the *plerōma Christou* (1.23; 3.19; 4.13; 5.18). Where Colossians was christological and christocentric (Christ is the *plērōma* of God), Ephesians is for this very reason ecclesiological; the author brings Colossians up to date in an ecclesiological direction: the church is the *plērōma* of Christ. The starting-point for this interpretation is Col. 1.19 and 2.9f.: Christ is the fullness of God and the Christians are 'those who are fulfilled in him' (Col. 2.10). Colossians is thus already familiar with the substance of the idea of the church as the *plērōma Christou*, but it only mentions this in passing. The soteriological content of Colossians (we are filled with the fullness of Christ) is taken further in ecclesiological terms in Ephesians. As the fullness of Christ, the church is the sphere filled with the power of Christ in which believers have a place. Thus *plērōma* illuminates the function of Christ as head in relation to the church as body. Ephesians therefore talks indiscriminately of the 'fullness of God' (in Christ) and the 'fullness of Christ' (in the church). That is why for Ephesians the church is already 'in the heavens', in the heavenly sphere (see 2.6). What Ephesians calls *plērōma* is evidently what Paul calls the *pneuma* or spirit.

Although Christ also 'fills the universe' (4.10), only the church is his *sōma* and *plērōma*, Christ's field of force, the sphere where God is at work in Christ *in the world*. Thus according to Ephesians, the church is not a self-contained sphere: Christ makes use of the church in order to fill the universe. Ephesians is concerned with a historical process in which the church emerges as the mediator of salvation and peace *for the world*. In the last resort this is equivalent to a modern conception: the church is the *sacramentum mundi*, just as Christ is God's saving medium. The church is the sphere of salvation: here Jews and Gentiles are reconciled and together form the new humanity, an example of what is to take place in the world.

Ephesians is also aware that Christians sin and deny the nature of the church (see Eph. 4–6). The church, 'the glorious bride without spot or wrinkle or any such thing' (5.27), is as it were given an independent status; it is extrapolated so that it becomes a 'being' and is therefore expressed in *imperative* terms. However, this being does not hover in the air as some kind of example; it takes shape among Christians (where and how?), though at the same time this church must also grow into Christ (4.15b–16) and needs to be built up as a community 'in love' (4.16b; see also 4.12b–13).

In my view, Ephesians achieves a drastic demythologizing of a 'cosmic christology' which was perhaps already in circulation. Ephesians seeks to impress upon Christians that the church must be a sacrament of peace for the world, an effective sign of the establishment of peace. It is clear from the cosmic tradition behind Eph. 2.15f. (cf. 4.8–10) that the author thinks in historical and ecclesiastical, rather than in cosmic terms. Consequently, *plērōma* must be understood predominantly in a passive sense. The church is *filled*, by the divine power of Christ. This approach is, however, supplemented by an active, mediatorial sense: 'the church, which is his body, the fullness of that which fulfils all in all' (*to plērōma tou ta panta en pasin plēroumenou*, 1.23). Thus instead of talking about the 'cosmic' dimension of Ephesians, we would do better to talk of the church's *responsibility for the world*, its universal work of peace, seeing that the 'peace of Christ' is given specific form in the body of Christ. Thus Ephesians does not proclaim any kind of individualistic or private salvation, even though its terminology may be that of the ancient world (see 4.12f.). Proclamations of Jesus as *Kyrios* – 'Lord, Lord' – should not force the realization of the historical *pax Christi* into the background, however fond Ephesians may be of 'spiritual songs' and hymns in praise of God (5.18f.).

As the *plērōma* of Christ, the church is the sphere into which the love of Christ flows (3.18f.). Christ exercises his saving power in the world through the love of believers (see also 5.25ff.), the very love with which he accepted his death (5.2 and 5.25b). It is the church's work of peace, which is achieved not by power, but by love.

## III. THE INWARD EDIFICATION OF THE CHURCH COMMUNITY

The Christians who are addressed in Ephesians are Gentile Christians. Gentile Christians are blessed, shown God's favour (1.3f.), called to hope (1.15–23), brought to life (2.8–10) and made fellow citizens of the church of God on earth (2.17–22); they are accepted into 'the peace of Christ', the community of God, and are therefore themselves peacemakers.

In Ephesians, the expression 'brought to life' in the last resort conveys what Paul referred to as justification. These authors have no predilection for particular words. In Ephesians, the distinction between justification (at the baptism of believers) and sanctification and even *sōtēria* or salvation as an eschatological event (the physical resurrection), which is so important for Paul, vanishes into the background. Christians are already risen with Christ through faith and baptism (Colossians), and Ephesians explicitly adds that they are already sitting with their Lord at the right hand of God (2.6). Ephesians therefore speaks of *sesōsmenoi* (2.8–10): we are already redeemed: 'by grace you are saved' (2.5,8), with a strong emphasis on God's action. In Christ God has blessed us (1.3), chosen us (1.4), given us grace (1.6), bestowed forgiveness (4.32) and involved us in resurrection.

'For by grace you have been saved through faith; and this is not your own doing, it is the gift of God – not because of works, lest any man should boast. For we are his workmanship, created in Christ Jesus for good works, which God prepared beforehand, that we should walk in them' (2.8–10). This is pure Paul, but the accent is in a different place. Justification at baptism is seen as a transition from death to life (see already Rom. 4.5). The term 'God's righteousness' has such Jewish overtones and reminiscences that Gentile Christians do not know what to make of it. It says nothing to them. However, they are very familiar with the word 'life', life which is not subject to the forces of destruction or dependent on them, life which is not the product of an ascetic mysticism but a gift in Christ which can only be received in a response of faith. To be baptized is to pass from death to life (2.1–3; see Col. 2.13). Paul said that it was to die to sin (Rom. 6.10f.; see Col. 2.12). In Ephesians justification is the bringing of the dead to life (2.5; 2.1–3; cf. Rom. 1.18–3.20; Eph. 2.3 and 5.6 with Rom. 2.5–11; also John 5.24; I

John 3.14 and Luke 15.24,32). That implies that man dies to sin – it implies holiness, God's own holiness. However, when Ephesians talks of being raised to life, it is not referring to the physical resurrection in the future (as happens in II Cor. 4.14; Phil. 3.11f.; Matt. 19.28; 26.29; Rev. 3.12), but to the spiritual resurrection which takes place in the present. Christians have died with Christ, are risen with him and already have their seat with him above (Eph. 2.6; see the parallels between 1.19–23, which refers to Christ, and 2.1-10, which refers to Christians). Eschatology is directed more strongly towards the present than in Paul, but there is no question of a demythologizing of the *eschaton*: the final redemption is still in the future (4.30; see 1.13f.), although certain Christians will always feel that they are already risen, hallelujah, and will convey this feeling in spiritual experiences which forget that redemption has yet to take place. Because cross and resurrection are inseparable throughout the New Testament, Ephesians, like Paul, can sometimes stress the crucifixion in order to talk about the resurrection, and at others put things the other way round (e.g. Eph. 1.17–2.10, contrasted with 2.11–22, or I Cor. 1.17–2.5, contrasted with I Cor. 15.12–19).

In Ephesians, the mediation of Christ at creation which we find in Colossians becomes eschatological: 'to unite all things peaceably' in Christ (1.10). Whereas Colossians says, 'In Christ we are created' (Col. 1.16), Ephesians says that God alone is the Creator of the universe (3.9b). Christ is the mediator in the ordering of salvation, but eschatological peace is brought to *the whole of creation*. However, Ephesians sees Jesus Christ as being more active in the communication of salvation than Paul, who often uses the passive (Rom. 1.17; I Cor. 6.11; 15.22; II Cor. 1.19f.; 5.21; active, II Cor. 5.19; 2.14). Thus in Ephesians, *charis* or grace as it were becomes the principle of salvation: 'By grace we are saved' (2.5,8), by grace we have the forgiveness of sins (1.7), and by grace Paul becomes the 'servant of the gospel' (3.7). Ephesians knows nothing of the polemical opposition of grace to works. For the author, justification is a disposition towards good works, which are themselves heavenly gifts (2.10). As a whole 'we are God's work, the product of his making : a new creation' (2.10; cf. II Cor. 5.17). To be brought to life therefore has a double meaning: (*a*) living, as opposed to dead; thus life is a gift of the Creator, and not a reward for good works; but (*b*) life is also a way of life (2.3; 4.1,17; in this sense the Greek Bible prefers to talk of 'walking' rather than 'living'). For Ephesians, this first meaning of 'life' is basic (Paul's justification), but once brought to life, the Christian must live, i.e. perform good works, 'be worthy of his calling' (4.1–6). New life is given by grace in order to make possible a new way of life.

Ephesians describes the work of salvation in terms of creation. 'We are *God's work*' (2.10) refers to the new creation in salvation, whereas Paul uses this term for being a creature (Rom. 1.20). Our state of grace is the work of God. So redemption is God's creative work, bound up with Christ. Thus for Ephesians (2.15; 3.9; 4.24; cf. Col. 3.10; 1.16), the link between 'creation' (*ktisis*) and Christ lies within the ordinance of salvation, which is one 'creation', the final meaning of the first creation. This places considerable emphasis on the creative supremacy of grace. The saving action of God can be *seen* on the level of our human history in and through the good works of the 'new man' (2.10; cf. II Cor. 9.8; Col. 1.10). Thus there is no contradiction between what God does in Christ and what the church does as the fullness of Jesus.

Christ is the model of this (new) creation of man by God. Unlike Paul, Ephesians speaks of the newly created '*kata theon*' (4.24), and not 'in the image of God'. In the Deutero-Pauline letters, people do not 'put on Christ' (Paul) at baptism, but the 'new man'. This is not 'Christ', but it is measured by the standard of Christ (see below). The shift from 'created *in the image of* God' (Col. 3.10) to 'created *after God*' does not seem to me to be simply the consequence of the influence of Gen. 1.26f. Of course the concept of the *eikōn* (image) in Col. 3.10 underlies the phrase *kata theon*. However, to stress the point again: Ephesians sees grace in terms of creation as it ought to be: the new man is himself the image of God and not made in the image of God; only now, through the redemption brought by Christ, is man *kata theon*; only now is he himself the image of God. Therefore 'be imitators *of God*' (5.1). Throughout, the author applies the terminology of creation solely to the gracious ordinance of eschatological salvation: the peace of the universe. The relation between *creation* and *salvation* is not the same as that, for example, to be found in the hymn to Christ in Col. 1.15–20 (though, of course, in connection with this I have said that the first strophe only acquires its protological meaning in the light of the second strophe). In this sense, the presentation in Ephesians is less mythological than that in Colossians (and texts related to Col. 1.15ff.). Only now does the paradisal man from Genesis come into being through Christ (see Eph. 4.21c; cf. Col. 3.10; 1.15; II Cor. 4.4).

It looks as though Ephesians sees what Paul terms the position of Jews and non-Jews, i.e. all people, 'under God's wrath', in other words history before the appearance of Jesus (Rom. 1.18–3.20), as the primal chaos before creation: as unrest. With Jesus Christ, everything is created . . . in peace. This is also expressed in the repeated allusions in Ephesians to the contrast between darkness and light (though these two concepts can also be used in other contexts in late antiquity: by apocalyptic, the Pharisees and Qumran). 'Once you were darkness, but now are you light through your communion with the Lord' (5.8–14). 'And God said, "Let there be light" – and there was light' (Gen. 1.3). 'And God saw that it was good.' Ephesians sees this as having taken place in Christ, not in

apocalyptic and mythical terms ('Christ as pre-existent wisdom', counsellor at the first creation, as e.g. in Colossians), but historically: in his
crucifixion and resurrection, as the creation of the new man, the man of
brotherly love (4.31f.), who 'maintains the bond of peace' (4.3), 'for-
bearing one another in love' (4.2b).

However, the creation of the new man (through baptism) does not
bring everything to a conclusion. This new creation must now come to
life and begin its new history: development and growth, the maturing of
the 'perfect man' (4.13) in the sense of the 'mature man' (in contrast to
the man who has not yet come of age): 'to the measure of the stature of
the fullness of Christ' (4.13b). The author once again expresses this in
spatial terms: God has appointed a certain place in his plan for the
church which has already been exalted to Christ in the heavens; the final
extent of the church is so to speak already established in the apocalyptic
pre-existence of salvation. The church must develop on earth to this
extent, *eis metron hēlikias tou plērōmatos tou Christou*, the extent of the perfect
age of the church as the 'fullness of Christ'. This is the vision of future
which brings strength on earth; it is a process which can be slowed down,
but which will be realized from the vision – a promise – as long as there
are 'new men'. Ephesians is thinking directly of a process *within the church*,
not only, or primarily, of the individual. Because the church is already
exalted, its growth is not a spatial movement upwards, but an inner
extension. Spatially it is 'the heavenly city' (2.19ff.; 2.5f.; 3.18), which as
it were needs to be filled with 'new men'.

## IV. MAN'S SALVATION TO THE GLORY OF GOD

The author brings the hymn which begins his work to an end with the
words: 'to the redemption of God's own people and to the praise of his
glory' (1.14). Grace must culminate in thanksgiving; this is of the very
essence of grace and is not some extravagant superstructure. Following
the model of the *b<sup>e</sup>rākā* or blessing in the Jewish synagogue (which is also
the model for the Christian eucharistic thanksgiving, see Ex. 18.10; I
Cor. 1.4–8; II Chron. 2.12; Num. 6.24–26), Ephesians describes God's
saving work in Christ in the hymn which opens the letter. The readers
have heard of it in their baptismal catechism (1.13); they are beginning
to believe in it (1.13b) and have been sealed into it at their baptism
(1.13c) with the promised eschatological Spirit, which even now is the
pledge of their later heritage, the perfect eschatological salvation (1.14).
After the opening praise, 'Blessed be the God and Father of our Lord
Jesus Christ', as was customary in every *b<sup>e</sup>rākā*, the reasons are given for
this praise and thanksgiving to God: . . . God has blessed us in Christ

even as he chose us in him – to the praise of his grace which he has bestowed on us in the beloved – making known to us the mystery of his will – namely, to unite all things in Christ, in whom we also share, we who first put our hope in Christ – in whom also you have been sealed with the spirit of promise (cf. I Peter 1.3–5, which suggests that in both cases the model for the hymn of praise is the conferring of Christian baptism). The hymn began with the insertion *en tois epouraniois* (1.3), in the heavenly places. As we have seen, this is a favourite idea of the author and also a favourite word (1.3; 1.20; 2.6; 3.10; 6.12). The gifts of grace are also called heavenly blessings (1.3). Some phrases are striking: 'Blessed be God, *the Father* '(1.3); '*in Christ*' (the heart of 1.3–14) and 'sealed with the *Holy Spirit*' (1.13c). The Christian hymn of praise or the *eucharistia* (*eulogia*) is evidently beginning to adopt the structure of a 'Trinitarian' doxology.

'In Christ', the Christian is elected to *hyiothesia* or adoption: to be a child of God (1.5) with a sanctified way of life (1.4); in him God continues to show his love, and in him he also brings his counsels into effect: 'which he had set forth *beforehand* in Christ, to be put into effect when the time was ripe' (1.10; the New English Bible is right here; the phrase does not mean 'to realize the fullness of time'; cf. Gal. 4.4; Mark 1.15). 'Redemption' (*apolytrōsis*, see the later synthesis) has been achieved in the crucifixion of Jesus; that is, Christians have been freed from sin (the forgiveness of sins) and been given the blessing of 'new wisdom' from above (1.8–10). Finally, at the same time the whole hymn explains what is meant by the word *charis* which is repeated constantly. It seems to me to be the definition of the concept of grace to be found in early Judaism (wisdom and the inter-testamental literature). *Mystērion* (1.9) is a rendering of the Hebrew *sōd*,[98] a word which is virtually limited to the Old Testament wisdom literature. It denotes the meeting of a confidential in-group in which decisions are made: resolutions following the discussion of a particular plan. Since anything discussed and agreed upon in secret cannot be allowed to leak out, *sōd* also means a secret, a mystery (Prov. 11.13; 20.19). Thus *sōd* is originally Yahweh's heavenly council ('in the assembly of the saints'; Ps. 89.7; 82.1; Jer. 23.18,22), and finally God's counsel. Different words were used to translate it in Greek, almost all of which appear in the opening hymn of Ephesians (and which for this very reason already indicate the influence of the synagogue), namely: *eudokia tou thelēmatos*, the well-pleasing of his will (1.5), *mystērion tou thelēmatos*, his secret counsel (1.9), *boulē tou thelēmatos*, the disposition of his will (1.11). This term presents us with the fully-developed meaning of the early Jewish, inter-testamental concept of *charis*: at a time in our history foreordained by God's decision, the revelation of a plan of salvation and of counsels hidden from eternity in God is entrusted to people who enjoy

God's favour or have been elected by him: they receive 'wisdom from above', and for their part hand on this mystery to others (in Ephesians for the first time not only through the apostolic ministry but also through the whole of the church community, 6.15). The content of this counsel, and therefore of 'the gospel', is peace: 'the gospel of peace' (6.15); in 1.10 this is expressed as 'to unite all things in him, things in heaven and things on earth'. This concept of grace is therefore essentially bound up with a profound wisdom which is brought to the fore in Ephesians.

### Conclusion: The 'political theology' of Ephesians

It is commonly claimed that Paul thinks in terms of salvation history and Ephesians thinks in cosmic terms. The analysis given above shows this conception to be completely false. In Ephesians, the church's responsibility for the proclamation of peace and the 'gathering together' of all the nations make up the specific perspective of the 'gospel of peace' (Eph. 6.15), namely, world peace. Especially in Asia Minor, the melting-pot of many peoples, the idea of cosmopolitan brotherhood current in late antiquity was very well known. In this sense, Ephesians is not so much cosmic as cosmo-political: its foundation is not to be found in a cosmic, romantic sense of unity, so much as in the redemption brought to all men by the cross of Jesus, forgiveness of sins and renewal of life, the basis of all peace. Ephesians calls this liberation *apolytrōsis*; through his death, Jesus paid the ransom for the release of mankind held in the grip of the terrifying, spiritual powers of heaven; anyone whose sins are forgiven and whose life is renewed is free from these heavenly rulers of the world. They influence men only through sin and human injustice. The new man, shaped through Christ, is a free man, no longer a slave and no longer held captive. However, men remain men! To this extent the supernatural powers of evil remain the great opponents of the peace-bringing vocation of the man who is created anew in Christ, and must therefore have his 'loins girded with truth, and have put on the breastplate of righteousness, and have feet shod' (6.14). He goes out to fight 'not against flesh and blood, but against the principalities, against the powers, against the world rulers . . . ' (6.12). We do not need any 'materialistic exegesis' to revive in very different historical circumstances, in different times and in a different climate, the powerful appeal which is contained in this gospel of peace among the nations. A modern reinterpretation of Ephesians (just as Ephesians is itself a reinterpretation of both Colossians and Romans) opens up wide perspectives, albeit always of a religious kind: reconciliation and peace among men through a common access to one and the same God. Ephesians provides a biblical basis for a political theology and a theology of liberation, but at the same time it provides a religious criticism of those phenomena which only duplicate what the world already does. The *religious* element – with its particular *liberating* and *critical* force – is the essential nucleus of the liberating theology of peace which we find in Ephesians. Ephesians cannot tell us how it is to be realized in modern times, but the letter does provide us with stimuli, signposts and critical features which we must take fully into account in attempting to relate Ephesians to our time if we are to come to a firm decision as a result of and in the context of the apostolic faith: salvation from God in Christ. Of course the terminology of Ephesians and its general approach are firmly rooted in the culture of late antiquity; many concepts which it uses are akin to those found in Qumran – why, I do not know; perhaps the link is not direct, but both go back to common traditions. (Or might it be that after AD 70, people from Qumran became Christians? At that time many travelled to Egypt, Syria, Transjordania and Asia Minor.) At all events, Ephesians is radically different from the spirituality of Qumran, for all its affinities (because of the apostolic faith which is expressed in it). In particular, the conception of 'being a remnant' is completely alien to apostolic Christianity, for all the gratitude shown by the first Christians at their election. In fact, this sense of election was experienced as a call to help everyone to share in the election.

In the last resort, the most striking feature of Ephesians seems to me to be its great courage in the face of the future. At a time when Christian communities were invisible cells in the world of their time, minority groups in the great cities of the ancient world, without any prospect of influencing the wider world or the society in which they were set, a *quantité négligeable*, the author of Ephesians dared to call the 'community of God' the great *universal instrument of peace* in this world – a community which takes up the fight against what he calls the 'rulers of the world' and the powers which cause unrest. This Christian community had no fear of these great powers, against which it put up a defence.

## §3   A community with questions about 'the true faith': II Thessalonians

In this analysis of Paulinism, it is important to discuss the Pastoral Epistles as well as II Thessalonians. However, I shall include them in another chapter (after Hebrews), because along with Jude and II Peter the Pastoral Epistles tend to reflect, rather, a 'late apostolic', indeed post-apostolic situation in the church.

In II Thessalonians above all we continue to hear echoes of the apostolic voice of the leader of Pauline theology; however, everything in the letter points to situations after the time of Paul. The author of the letter introduces himself as 'Paul and Silvanus and Timothy' (1.1a); this is also the beginning of a letter which is certainly genuine, namely I Thessalonians (in which the three appear as a single pastoral team). The letter is addressed 'to the church of the Thessalonians in God our Father and the Lord Jesus Christ' (1.1b).

*Literature*: P. Andriessen, 'Celui qui retient la venue du Seigneur', *Bijdr* 21, 1960, 20–30; L. W. Dewailly and B. Rigaux, *Les épîtres de saint Paul aux Thessaloniciens*, Paris 1954; M. Dibelius, *An die Thessalonicher I, II. An die Philipper*, HNT 11, Tübingen [3]1937; E. van Dobschütz, *Die Thessalonicherbriefe*, Meyer 10, Göttingen 1909; A. Oepke et al., *Die kleineren Briefe des Apostels Paulus*, Göttingen [2]1962; B. Rigaux, *Saint Paul, Les épîtres aux Thessaloniciens*, Paris 1956; K. D. Schunk, ' "Der Tag Jahwes" in der Verkündigung der Propheten', *Kairos* 11, 1969, 14–21; A. Strobel, *Untersuchungen zum eschatologischen Verzögerungsproblem*, Leiden 1961; W. Trilling, *Untersuchungen zum Zweiten Thessalonicherbrief*, Erfurter Theologische Studien 27, Leipzig 1972.

Just as Ephesians might be termed an updating of Colossians, so II Thessalonians might be termed an updating of I Thessalonians. The themes discussed reveal a community which is evidently distressed and uncertain about certain matters of faith. The community which had been instructed by Paul could not cope with the new situations with which it was confronted. II Thessalonians alludes to this, referring to the authority of Paul, the leader of the Pauline tradition.

Thessalonica was the most significant port in Macedonia, an important link between Rome and the Roman province of Asia Minor, at the same time the capital of the province of Macedonia. Such cities are always a melting-pot of ideas from every point of the compass. The Greek inhabitants were particularly attracted by Eastern ideas from Asia Minor, especially the 'oriental exuberance'. This is also clear from II Thessalonians. The most characteristic feature of this letter is the interpretation of the last judgment, from which according to I Thess. 1.10 Christians are spared. Paul taught that Jesus would preserve them from the wrath to come. By contrast, II Thessalonians stresses that the gospel of the last judgment includes a judgment on Christians. The important thing is the way in which they have reacted as Christians to the 'gospel of our Lord Jesus Christ' (II Thess. 1.8). This is a new development compared with I Thessalonians, at least in explicit terms. Evidently a tense eschatological expectation prevailed in the Thessalonian community (2.1f.). The Christians became 'adventists' of a special kind. If Christ is to come soon – as Paul taught – why should we go on working and bother with everyday matters (see 4.15)? Moreover, perhaps other members of this community were concerned with the question about the suffering of Christians: all goes well with the Gentiles, whereas we Christians are oppressed and despised (1.4–10). Is that Christian liberation?

The author deals with these problems. Christians are 'chosen from the beginning to be saved, through sanctification by the Spirit and belief in the truth' (2.13b). This is a good Pauline view, though Paul himself never spoke in absolute terms, without further qualification, of 'belief in the truth'. 'God . . our Father . . . loved us and gave us eternal comfort and good hope through grace' (2.16). The letter deals with this hope: the parousia or the imminent coming of Christ or 'the glory of our Lord Jesus Christ' (2.14). But, symptoms of psychological tension and unhealthy attitudes can be detected in Thessalonica in respect of this coming (2.1–17). The author reacts to this by saying that in fact we do not know this day of Christ's coming. Many people claim that it has already taken place, and that is one of the possibilities. However, although Paul has said that Christ will come like a thief in the night – and that can be at any moment – a number of conditions have to be fulfilled before that happens. There are signs which announce this coming, and nothing is to be seen of them. Thus II Thessalonians does not reckon with any immediate developments today or tomorrow. It gives two signs, two prior conditions which have to be fulfilled; first a massive apostasy, coupled with the appearance of 'the man of godlessness', God's opponent *par excellence* (2.8–12, a forerunner of the Antichrist), and secondly another 'restraining factor' (2.6a, 7b).

The first theme is derived from the biblical account of Antiochus IV Epiphanes, the model of 'the man of godlessness', the cause of a massive apostasy of Jews at the time of the Maccabean revolt (see I Macc. 1.41–58; 2.15–18). We find an eschatological reinterpretation of this as early as Dan. 9.26f. and 12.11. II Thessalonians recalls I Maccabees in calling this lawless man 'the adversary, who opposes and exalts himself against every so-called god or object of worship, so that he takes his seat in the temple of God, proclaiming himself to be God' (II Thess. 2.4; see Dan. 11.36 together with Ezek. 28.2). The meaning here is that this man, who tramples down every (Jewish) law (hence he is also called 'the man of lawlessness', 'the son of perdition'), attacks not only the God of Israel but religion in general, in all its forms, except those which concern his own petty person. This figure is Antiochus IV, who had his effigy erected in Israel's holy Temple. This was the climax of blasphemy and godlessness, an abomination to Jews faithful to Yahweh (Dan. 11.31; see also 9.26f., which is already given a Christian interpretation in the synoptic gospels: Mark 13.14; Matt. 24.15). This historical event had a traumatic effect on theocratic Israel. 'The godless man' became a stereotyped theme in early Judaism: he was Israel's anti-Messiah (I shall attempt a synthesis of this development in the chapter on 'The life of grace and political power in the New Testament', pp. 567ff.). The Jewish Christians took over this idea of anti-god and anti-Messiah (which had already been interpreted eschatologically in Judaism) when they became Christians. Nevertheless, II Thessalonians argues, however hard times may be (in this sense 'the mystery of godlessness' has already become a reality, 2.7), such an eschatological power, hostile to God and his Messiah, does not yet seem to have appeared. So despite the 'messianic birth-pangs', the parousia is not round the corner.

The second factor which explains the delay of the parousia is called *ho katechōn arti* (2.7b), literally, 'something that still restrains'. This is a factor which provisionally delays the appearance of the anti-godly and anti-messianic adversary. II Thessalonians says, 'You know what I mean' (2.5f.), and gives no further explanation. An inter-testamental 'apocryphal' feature plays a role here. Texts like Jude 6 and II Peter 2.4, which quote identifiable apocryphal literature (the book of Enoch), say that for the time being the fallen angels 'are imprisoned' in subterranean caves, watched over by heavenly angels, and awaiting the last judgment. In other words, this is a variant of the Jewish apocalyptic theme of the 'provisional binding of Satan' (see also especially Rev. 20.1–3, 7–10; 9.13–15; there is a faint echo of it in Luke 4.13). *To katechon* (2.6a) or *ho katechōn* (2.7b) is something, or someone, which restrains (the fluctuation between the masculine and the neuter might point to a collective element). So the one (the ones) who restrain(s) are angels who in the name of God have imprisoned the demonic forces hostile to God until the last days. Then this anti-Messiah will be released and the final eschatological battle will begin between Satan and God's anointed (in a Christian context, Jesus Christ). We cannot be certain whether II Thessalonians is referring to *this* feature of Jewish theology. For the author, the 'godless man' is not Satan but an instrument of Satan (2.9); furthermore, the expression is inappropriate and cryptic if it is meant to refer to an angel which restrains Satan: 'He (the angel) must first vanish from the scene' (*ek mesou genētai*, 2.7). Various inter-testamental models were available to describe this final eschatological battle, and II Thessalonians is evidently referring to one of them. The vagueness of expression might perhaps be derived from the vague formulations in these inter-testamental traditions. At all events, the author speaks of a 'special parousia (i.e. manifestation with power and mighty acts) of Satan' (2.9), so that the passage is certainly concerned with the apocalyptic confrontation between Satan and God's anointed (in whatever form). Jewish Christians took over this feature from Jewish theology. However, in this final battle Jesus Christ will slay Satan with 'the breath of his mouth' (2.8). Galatians, Colossians,

Ephesians and Hebrews regard what II Thessalonians (like Revelation) depicts as a dramatic eschatological event – Christ's victory over the powers (we would say 'of hell', but people in those days said 'of heaven') – as an event which in principle is completed at the death of Jesus. Christians in fact saw this as a pattern of resistance against the supernatural powers of evil which was spread over the whole of human history (see Eph. 6.11–17). (Paul himself could never have spoken in such apocryphal and mythical terms, even if he knew this theological feature as well as II Thessalonians.) However, II Thessalonians draws a very Pauline conclusion from this mythical history (which reflects a profound human reality). The author reminds Christians of their duties in the world (3.6–15). 'If anyone will not work, let him not eat' (3.10) – which was at that time a proverb of common-sense experience. That is the message of II Thessalonians to those who are expecting the parousia ('Jesus is coming'). And the author threatens ecclesiastical punishment – *excommunicatus vitandus* (see 3.6; 3.14) – even if a brotherly concern is evident in this excommunication (3.15).

Another problem in the community was the suffering of Christians, a problem which after some time posed a disastrous threat to those enthusiasts who were convinced that 'Jesus is coming'. Their heightened spiritual awareness tended to fade after a while – the abrupt descent to earth after feeling 'high'. However, the solution presented by II Thessalonians is in the classical rabbinic tradition, taking after Sirach (see II Thess. 1.6, the principle of an eye for an eye – the author does not seem to have seen the connection with the first problem): God punishes the evil and rewards the good (1.8f.). However, he also knows from Paul that the suffering of Christians is 'suffering for the kingdom of God' (1.4f.; of course Paul puts this in a different way, and always uses christological terms). A typical statement from II Thessalonians is: 'Inflicting vengeance on those who do not know God and upon those who do not obey the gospel of our Lord Jesus' (1.8), whereas the Christians who have accepted the gospel will be rewarded (1.5): in them 'the name of the Lord Jesus will be glorified' (1.12 and 1.10). These phrases and this terminology are certainly not Pauline; they are much more reminiscent of the Old Testament. The vigorous reaction against people who do not want to give a hearing to the gospel of the Lord Jesus is particularly striking, as is the reference to 'those who refuse to acknowledge God' (this last phrase is the classic description of the Gentiles). But to what does the first phrase refer: Jews who acknowledge God but deny the gospel of Christ? Is this category connected with those who persecute and oppress Christians (1.4b)? Or are they the Christian adventists from 2.1–3? That is hard to establish. However, the threat of 'excommunication' (3.6; 3.14) and the absolute expressions 'believe in the *truth*' (2.13b), 'love of *truth*' (2.10) and 'those who reject the *truth*' (2.12), always without any Christian apposition (e.g. 'the truth of the gospel', which occurs in other passages in the New Testament), and finally also the reference to arguments based on authority, those of Paul in particular, point to a situation later on in the church (of course Paul himself is familiar with an authoritative apostolic proclamation, but the reference to Paul in II Thessalonians has a different ring, see e.g. 2.5). Thus it seems most probable that the reference here is to Christians who obscure the gospel or draw false conclusions from it. Paul himself would have given a more vigorous and more profound answer to the new situation in the church in Thessalonica. He would not have referred to apocryphal details, but to the heart of the apostolic faith. II Thessalonians is not one of the strongest parts of the New Testament. That is theologically significant; not every New Testament author was able to give an appropriate pastoral answer to the questions raised by a particular situation with the same fidelity and the same skill as, for example, Paul, Ephesians and Hebrews. In the New Testament we are listening to believers, but all too human believers, who are interpreting their experiences of salvation in Christ Jesus.

Chapter 3

# Suffering for others: the future of a better world

*Introduction*

Considering the tone of both the so-called Epistle to the Hebrews and I Peter, I feel compelled by their content to discuss these two New Testament writings in the same chapter (3.1 and 3.2). A large number of details, large and small, suggest that the two writings are closely connected in spirituality and argumentation. In a way reminiscent of the Gospel of Mark, the ideas of the 'necessity' and yet the freedom of suffering for others, bringing salvation and opening up the future, and the disarming and yet vulnerable and wounded 'defenceless love', run through both writings like a golden thread. *For this very reason* one author – Hebrews – calls Jesus the *high priest*, and the other author – I Peter – deliberately speaks of the Christian community as a *priestly* people of God. What was once a cultic sacrifice is replaced by the 'spiritual sacrifice' of solidarity with the suffering of others.

Chapter 3.1

# The suffering of the innocent: the future for historical failures: I Peter

## §1 The gospel of suffering for others

*Literature*: R. Bultmann, 'Bekenntnisse und Liedfragmente im ersten Petrusbrief', *ConiNeot* 11, Lund 1947, 1–14; W. Dalton, *Christ's Proclamation to the Spirits*, Rome 1965; R. Gundry, ' "Verba Christi" in I Peter. Their Implications Concerning the Authorship of I Peter and the Authenticity of the Gospel Tradition', *NTS* 13, 1966–67, 336–50; H. Gunkel, *Der erste Brief des Petrus*, SNT 3, Göttingen [3]1917, 1908; J. N. D. Kelly, *A Commentary on the Epistles of Peter and Jude*, BNTC, London 1969; R. Knopf, *Die Briefe Petri und Juda*, Meyer 12, Göttingen [7]1912; J. Michl, *Die Katholischen Briefe*, RNT 8, Regensburg [2]1968; K. H. Schelkle, *Die Petrusbriefe. Der Judasbrief*, HThKNT XIII, 2, Freiburg im Breisgau [4]1976; A. Schlatter, *Die Briefe des Petrus*, Stuttgart 1965; id., *Petrus und Paulus nach dem ersten Petrusbrief*, Stuttgart 1937; J. Schneider, *Die Kirchenbriefe*, NTD 10, Göttingen [10]1967; E. Schweizer, 'I Petr. 4.6', *TZ* 8, 1952, 152–4; E. G. Selwyn, *The First Epistle of St Peter*, London [2]1947; C. Spicq, 'La prima Petri et le témoignage évangélique de saint Pierre', *StTh* 20, 1966, 37–61; id., *Les épîtres de saint Pierre*, Sources bibliques, Paris 1966; G. Thevissen, *De eerste brief van Petrus*, Roermond 1973; R. Thurston, 'Interpreting First Peter', *JETS* 17, 1974, 171–82; H. J. Vogels, *Christi Abstieg ins Totenreich und das Läuterungsgericht an den Toten*, FThSt, Freiburg im Breisgau 1976; G. Wohlenberg, *Der erste und zweite Petrusbrief*, KNT 15, Leipzig 1915.

I Peter has features characteristic of Paul and early Christianity – one might call it 'Pauline' –, yet it also has a particular theology of its own. There are a number of minor indications that it should be dated fairly late. 'As a Christian' (*hōs Christianos*, 4.16), is evidently already a current technical term. I Peter 1.12b, according to which the message has been brought to the churches by 'those who preached the good news', also points to a later Christian generation. In contrast to the early Christian view of redemption as the rescue of Christians from the wrath of God's last judgment (I Thess. 1.10), the attitude of Christians to the church's gospel becomes the object of God's judgment (I Peter 4.17, see the difference between the two texts and an almost parallel text in Paul, I Cor. 11.32), as in the late II Thessalonians (II Thess.1.8).

Nevertheless, recently there has again been a series of attempts to defend the Petrine authorship of this letter with new arguments (Schelkle, Kelly, Gundry, Spicq – see the bibliography). In my view these scholars do no more than point to an early Christian, 'Petrine' *tradition* behind this letter. Under the name of Peter, the author himself says that he has written his letter 'with the help of' Silas (Silvanus, 5.12). Now Silvanus was Paul's helper for years (see I. Thess. 1.1 and Acts 15.40; 18.5) and accompanied Paul on his missionary journeys. That explains the 'Paulinism' of this letter. On the other hand, *explicit* references to Deutero-Isaiah in the New Testament (as in I Peter 2.22–25, see 1.24) point to a much more developed stage of theological reflection.

The letter is addressed to various Gentile Christian communities in Asia Minor. To judge from numerous allusions, it was written at a time of pressure from the Gentiles (see 4.12; 3.16; 4.14f.; 5.7–9), symptoms of the beginning of a persecution of the church, perhaps before that of Domitian (81–96).

For the author, the content of the gospel is 'the salvation of your souls' (*sōtēria psychōn*, 1.9), on the basis of the preaching of the death and resurrection of Christ which he describes in a striking way on the one hand as *ta eis Christon pathēmata* (the many sufferings which came upon Christ) and *hai meta tauta doxai* (the glorification which followed, 1.11). Here the suffering and death of Jesus, understood as an expiatory death, are presented as a model for suffering Christians (e.g. 2.21–25; 3.17f., etc.).

## I. SUFFERING TO THE ADVANTAGE OF THE LIVING

The suffering Christ occupies the centre of I Peter, as a model for suffering Christians (1.6; 2.19f.; 3.9,14,17; 4.14–16, 19; 5.6,9f.). The reference is always to 'innocent suffering' as opposed to deserved suffering (2.20; 3.17; 4.15).

For the author, *charis* or grace is salvation from God in Jesus (1.10; 1.13). *Charis* acquires the significance of 'revealed mystery', hidden in God from eternity and eschatologically revealed: 'You were ransomed with the precious blood of Christ, like that of a lamb without blemish or spot. He was destined before the foundation of the world but was made manifest at the end of the time for your sake' (1.20; see 1.10; here too I Peter has many features in common with Hebrews). Its somewhat 'later' character can be seen from the fact that angels have attempted to look at the consequences of God's eternal council (1.12c), and that in all their writings the prophets have 'searched and inquired' in order to understand something of this divine mystery or counsel. But this *charis* was 'intended *for you'* (1.10; 1.12), for your sake (1.20), the elect. I Peter shows marked traces of the stress on the predestination of the chosen ones to whom the mystery has been revealed, which is so characteristic of wisdom and apocalyptic. The content of this mystery embraces two large spheres of interest: (*a*) the *death of Jesus*, seen as an expiatory death (I shall not be discussing the different meanings of this phrase in the context of my study of each author, but in the synthesis that will be made at a later stage of this book). 'He himself bore our sins in his body on the tree, that we might die to sin and live to righteousness' (2.24, in a passage, 2.22f., which is again strongly reminiscent of Hebrews, also 1.2b; 1.11; 2.21; 3.18a; 4.1). The price or the 'ransom paid for freedom from the futile ways inherited from your fathers' (1.18; the author is writing for Gentile Christians) is 'the precious blood' (1.19); (*b*) Jesus' *resurrection from the dead* (1.3c; 1.21b; 3.18c; 3.21c; 4.13c). There is a reason why 1.11 talks of his 'glories' in the plural (*hai doxai*). For the resurrection, exaltation or ascension comprises an entire journey: first a descent into the underworld, where 'spirits' are imprisoned (3.19; see 4.6). First Jesus preaches there the 'church's kerygma' of death and resurrection (the universalism of salvation in Jesus); then Jesus ascends through all the heavenly spheres (3.22): 'with angels, authorities and powers subject to him' (3.22b): having ascended into heaven, Jesus sits at the right hand of God (3.22a). On this ascension through all the heavenly angelic dwelling places (where they are in fact subjected), Jesus ascends to the holy of holies, alongside God's throne, which is also described in some detail in Hebrews.

Without question the expiatory death and resurrection of Jesus are the 'apostolic faith' on which the whole of I Peter is based. They are both presented in his letter as fixed, already established formulae – in Pauline terms. However, this in itself is not the *specific feature* of this letter; it has one characteristic which is not 'un-Pauline', but gives I Peter a flavour which is not really typical of 'Pauline' theology.

In this letter, the emphasis is not on 'suffering' as such, as for example in Pauline theology; it is markedly on *innocent* suffering, as opposed to a suffering that we *deserve* because of some kind of stupidity or sin. If asked, Paul and his followers would not reject this distinction, but it plays no role in Pauline theology. By contrast, it lies at the heart of the argumentation of I Peter, which is concerned with the *innocent sufferer*, with specific reference to the suffering servant of Yahweh in Deutero-Isaiah. This *explicit* reference points to a later stage in the Christian use of scriptural proofs; from primitive Christianity up to this point we find isolated reminiscences of the suffering servant of Yahweh without reference to scripture.[99]

I Peter speaks in two passages and almost with the same words of *agathopoiountes paschein*, suffering for the sake of good works (2.20f. and

3.17), in contrast to suffering as a punishment or suffering that is deserved (2.20; 3.17; 4.15). That is clear from 3.17, which mentions 'the better', *kreitton*. This first category is that of innocent suffering: 'For it is better to suffer for doing right, if that should be God's will, than for doing wrong.' *That* seems to me to be the hermeneutic key to the whole of I Peter.

In 2.19 the author calls such suffering – that of the 'innocent sufferer' – a *charis* and a *kleos*, i.e. a thing to be proud of. Here *charis* is clearly not interpreted in terms of *ḥesed*, but rather in terms of the Hebrew *ḥēn*, i.e. as something which is not given to us by God *per se*, but is rather that which God finds good and acceptable in us (see above on *ḥēn-charis*), i.e. what is 'pleasing in God's eyes'. Innocent suffering which does not come upon us as a direct act of God (the unjust slave-owner is censured; undeserved suffering is not a gracious gift of God but the injustice of others; somehow, the author goes on to say, the 'if God wills' of 3.17 is only a matter of God's *permission*, 4.19) is *charis* only in the sense that God himself stands behind it and identifies himself with it: it is 'acceptable in his eyes' (see 2.19 and 2.20b). Such suffering 'is a sign that the Spirit of glory, which is the Spirit of God, rests on you' (4.14). Therefore the author also adds, 'Take care that none *of you* has to suffer . . .' (4.15). The letter does not glorify any mysticism of suffering, but suffering *for the sake of* others and *at the hands of* others has a quite special significance for it. Why? Well-deserved suffering (the inflicting of legal punishment) is not a *charis*, nor is it anything to boast of (2.20); there is nothing special about it. This suffering serves to atone for offences committed by the person concerned: it makes good what has gone wrong. But innocent suffering (4.19), 'suffering for doing right' (2.20b and 3.17), 'suffering for the sake of righteousness' (3.14), 'suffering as Christians' (4.16), 'suffering for the good' (3.17), is suffering *for others* and atones for the evil that *others* do. That is the concern of I Peter.

Therefore the 'suffering servant of God' (2.21–25, with explicit quotations from the servant song in Isa. 53.9; 53.4f.), 'the suffering Jesus Christ' (3.18ff.) is the *hypogrammos* (2.21) of all Christians. This word literally means the letters, vowels and consonants, set down in a copy-book which pupils must learn to copy exactly. I Peter is concerned with the *imitatio Christi*, the synoptic pattern of 'following Jesus'. We already find some echoes of the idea that God can give positive value *for others* to innocent suffering in the inter-testamental literature,[100] and in the books which form part of the Old Testament in the Roman Catholic canon: in addition to the servant song of Isa. 53, some of the wisdom books and II Maccabees.[101] However, in the New Testament, in the light of the suffering and crucifixion of Jesus, this becomes a key reality. For I Peter 2.21 it is the calling of Christians to be prepared to accept this innocent suffering for others. The foundation and model of this calling is the fact that 'Christ has suffered for you' (2.21b). The author is not thinking of what is later called 'vicarious suffering' (see below), but of suffering which *benefits* others. That is the special *charis* and merit of such suffering. Jesus, the innocent one (2.22), 'bore our sins in his body on the tree' (2.24a; Isa. 53.4; see below, the summary about 'bearing sin'). Its value for others was 'that we should die to sin and live to righteousness' (2.24b; 2.24c; Isa. 53.6). The author is not talking simply of 'unmerited suffering' – the reaction to which might be angry and abusive. The point he is making is that 'He did not revile . . . did not threaten.' 'He trusted to him who judges justly' (2.23). I Peter 3.16 calls for 'gentleness and reverence' in the face of abuse, even in self-defence. It is important to follow the example of Jesus: 'Do not return evil for evil or reviling for reviling, but on the contrary bless . . .' (3.9). There is to be no vengeance and no anger with the 'suffering servant'.

I argued that there was no 'vicarious' suffering in I Peter, but suffering which benefits others. How does this come about? I Peter says of the Roman authorities who are making things difficult for Christians, 'Maintain good conduct among the Gentiles, so that those who *speak against you as wrongdoers* may see your *good deeds* and glorify God on the day of visitation' (2.12), and, through your innocent suffering and your good behaviour as Christians (3.16, taken in conjunction with 3.17), '*put to shame* those who revile your good behaviour' (3.16). 'Putting to shame those who revile good behaviour' is a matter of the innocent victim making his tormentor think and perhaps converting him. The intrinsic connection between living an exemplary life and praising God can be found throughout the New Testament (I Peter 3.15; 2.12; 2.14; 3.1; 3.16; 4.14; 4.19; see Matt. 5.16; see also the emphasis on keeping calm in adversity: Titus 3.2; II Tim. 2.24f.; also Gal. 6.1; II Cor. 10.1; James 1.21; 3.13). In the New Testament, righteous living and loving and gentleness are always mentioned in connection with the impact that they make on others. The self-control, patience, gentleness of the suffering servant, without any anger (2.22–25), have a *soteriological*, redemptive significance *for others* – well-deserved suffering only for the one who suffers (the expiation of his own sins). That is 'the better thing' of which 3.17 and 2.20 speak; here Jesus has gone before (3.18; 2.21). In 2.12 we have clear evidence of the theme of the 'righteous sufferer' who is put out of the way by his enemies; however, these have to bear the sight of the innocent sufferer in the heavenly council, thus recognizing their mistake. They are forced to acknowledge the true son of God. The innocent sufferer is rehabilitated before the heavenly court of justice, and those who once mocked him have to pay homage publicly.[102] This theme, which is connected above all with the wisdom tradition, underlies I Peter. However,

it amounts to more than that. It is an anticipation of the past judgment.
For I Peter, suffering for others has one particular result: it puts wrongdoers to shame (3.16; 2.12; cf. 3.1), and thus converts them. 'For Christ
also died for sins once for all, the righteous for the unrighteous, *that he
might bring you to God*' (3.18). Jesus' suffering for sinners (for others) makes
them think; it brings about their conversion: to God. The same thing is
true of the suffering of Christians for others: it is to their advantage, it
leads them to *metanoia*. Thus, 'Since Christ suffered (for others) . . . arm
yourselves with the same thought' (4.1). Here we have a clear echo of
the Gospel of Mark.

Thus it is no part of the argument of I Peter to say that undeserved
suffering is 'better' *for me*, since *I* shall be rewarded for it a hundred times
– in the world to come, and perhaps even now. I Peter sees 'redemptive'
suffering as benefiting *others*, *dikaios hyper adikōn* (3.18); the righteous
suffers on behalf of the unrighteous,but in such a way as to convert the
unrighteous (who probably deserve punishment or suffering and manage
to escape it) and bring them to God. The vengeful, furious anger of
apocalypticism, which can be seen in inter-testamental literature, like
Enoch, is convinced that the innocent victims of suffering will soon be
able to laugh at their oppressors, in the last day when they are exalted
and look upon the torments of their former oppressors (one of the verses
of the *Internationale* amounts to the same thing). This, however, is diametrically opposed to what I Peter implies and even says in so many
words. The overriding concern is not to make the oppressors into the
oppressed, but to convert them *to good*. Granted, I Peter concedes that
this suffering for others falls under the eschatological blessing of God's
power in the case of all innocent sufferers (1.6f.; 4.13), as with Jesus
(3.22). God exalts the lowly (5.5c–6), but *that* is not the dominant theme
in I Peter: the suffering servant 'trusted to him who judges justly' (2.23)
and 'entrusts his soul to a faithful creator' (4.19b). However, that implies
that he is already *justified* before this public judgment is given, and that
therefore his standpoint *intrinsically* – rather than from any external perspective – has *decisive* and *definitive* value which will *therefore* be confirmed
by God. This is certain, even if in the meantime, in the eyes of the world,
there will be uncertainty about his behaviour: ambiguity and even perhaps derision.

Of course I Peter does not present the kind of kerygmatic history that
we find in the four gospels: however, once we have posed 'the question
of the historical Jesus' with the help of these gospels (see my *Jesus. An
Experiment in Christology*), we shall have to acknowledge when reading I
Peter that it represents a perfect reflection of what must really have
happened in the person of Jesus of Nazareth, along with the way in which
this must have presented itself to the second Christian generation in the

experience of this Christian, the author of I Peter.[103] The discipleship of Jesus practised by these Christians illuminates the picture of what Jesus really was. (The most important passages for I Peter are: from the old Q tradition, Matt. 24.42–51 par.; 23.12 par.; 6.25 par.; 5.10–12, 16; and from the special Lukan tradition, Luke 6.33; 24.25f. and, in connection with I Peter 5.2, also Luke 12.32). Furthermore, I Peter demonstrates that men achieve salvation not only through the apostolic kerygma, the proclamation of the resurrection of Jesus from the dead, but through the Christian way of life, the historical witness of Christians which (where it takes place) is *seen* (*epopteuontes*, I Peter 2.12; 3.2) not only by Christians but by non-Christians, without any preaching of the word (*aneu logou*, 3.1). Their conduct as suffering servants breaks through the stubbornness of others, i.e. Gentiles, by presenting a vision of the men of the future – even when it is clear that this vulnerable love does not always disarm others or compel their respect, but brings down even more oppression upon the defenceless. Even then, I Peter says, this is the way to salvation. This defencelessness is not a sign of weakness and naivety: such Christians must also defend themselves, be able to give a reason for the hope that is in them, yet all the time 'with gentleness and reverence' (3.15f.).

The great difference between I Peter and Hebrews, which is so closely related to it (see below), is that while I Peter interprets suffering for others as an expiatory sacrifice, it does not understand it in a cultic sense (*sacrificium propitiatorium*). It sees it as an *invitation*, to vulnerable love for others. Herein lies *the hope* of which the author says that Christians 'must always be prepared to make a defence to anyone who calls them to account for the hope that is in them' (3.15). Christians must tell the story of this hope, but, the author adds, they must not do so in a triumphalistic way, but 'with gentleness and with reverence' (3.15). This is a hope which is grounded in suffering for others, so that these others may be led to reflect and even to be converted, 'to be brought to God' (3.18), just as through the suffering of Jesus, Christians and sinners are brought closer together.

## II. SUFFERING FOR THE BENEFIT OF THE DEAD

However, there is an even deeper dimension in the conceptions of I Peter, in its meditation on Jesus' suffering for others. In this context, Colossians and Ephesians thought above all in terms of angelic heavenly powers. I Peter mentions them only once, in passing: by nature, Jesus' exaltation to the Father is an exaltation above all other inhabitants of heaven (3.22b): it sounds almost like a cliché. The author makes use of the idea of depth. He is the New Testament writer who talks explicitly of Jesus' 'descent into hell' (3.19; this is also implicit in Acts 2.24; see Matt. 12.40; Rom. 10.7). Furthermore, he mentions something that Jesus did there: 'he proclaimed' – a word which is always used in the New Testament in connection with the message of salvation (there are New Testament parallels, but these are implicit: Matt. 8.11f. par. Luke 13.28f., Q tradition, and above all John 5.25–27: 'The hour is coming, and now is, when the *dead will hear the voice of the Son of God*, and those who hear will live'). Thus I Peter is clearly based on a pre-existing Christian tradition. Many exegetes (whose thoughts about purgatory are clearly also affected by their confessional convictions) who are widely acquainted with intertestamental literature, but in this case have failed to make a structural analysis of the function of 3.18–22 in the immediate and wider context of the letter as a whole, have created a whole Targum about a proclamation by Christ after his death to the 'fallen angels' imprisoned in hell. They are judged by Jesus. Some theologians see this as a proclamation of salvation (even for the fallen angels); others see it as ultimate damnation.

First of all, it is clear from the text that Jesus' descent to hell must be seen as a synonym for dying, i.e. descending to Sheol or the underworld (Gen. 37.35; Num. 16.30; Isa.5.14; 38.18; Ezek. 26.20; 31.14–17; Ps. 22.29; 28.1; 30.3, 9; 55.15; Job 7.9; 33.24; Prov. 1.12; 5.5, etc.). The expression used in I Peter is not intended to affirm, over against one or another alleged view of docetism or apparent death, that Jesus *really* died. No trace is to be seen of any danger of docetism. The translation, 'being put to death in the flesh but made alive in the spirit; in which he went (*poreutheis*) and preached to the spirits in prison' (3.18c–19), is ambiguous. Here the descent to hell seems to be an element in Jesus' ascension, as though it were the already glorified Jesus who was bringing this gospel to the 'imprisoned spirits'. In fact, for the author resurrection is a resurrection *ek nekrōn* (I Peter 1.3, 21), i.e. from the world of the dead. Thus the descent into hell is part of Jesus' death, and not of his resurrection. Now in some Jewish circles of the time the fallen angels were thought to be incarcerated not in the underworld, but in the lower spheres of heaven, and the place where the dead were to be judged was also transferred there. However, the decisive question is whether 'angels' are involved here; we are told expressly that those concerned are 'unrighteous'. The Greek *en hō* does not refer to 'the spirit, in which'; it means 'there'. In other words, as a result of his suffering and death Jesus went to the underworld where 'he preached to the spirits in prison' (even before his glorification). Who are these spirits?

In fact a myth of a fall of the angels was still current in early Judaism and Christianity (since the original meaning of 'sons of God' in Gen. 6.1–4 was no longer understood).[104] It was even connected with the Greek myth of the fall of the Titans.[105] According to one particular tradition these angels were imprisoned in the underworld. Even Jude 6 and II Peter 2.4 implicitly refer to I Enoch 6–11 (the Greek version), which deals with angels (the so-called apocalypse of Noah). It is not said here, however, that these angels were imprisoned. In a *vision*, Enoch is allowed to visit the angels in order to announce final damnation to them. Detached from its context, I Peter 3.19 might suggest that the author is simply transferring the role of Enoch to Christ. In that case, however, one has to forget the whole of the context in which it is set. Why does I Peter cite the church's kerygma of expiatory death and resurrection (3.18 and 3.22), and the verse from the hymn, *thanatōtheis men sarki, zōopoiētheis de pneumati* (killed in the sphere of the fleshly or earthly man, but raised to life in the sphere of the spirit, 3.18c)? The character of such fragments of a hymn to Christ and such kerygmatic formulae is to praise and celebrate God, but here they are cited with a paraenetic intent (as by Paul in Phil. 2.6–11). In that case 3.17 is the key to interpretation of this passage. By means of these quotations the author seeks to show that in fact it is better to suffer for others than to undergo well-deserved punishment, and he does this to encourage his audience to be steadfast in persecutions. He seeks to show by this quotation that the expiatory death of Jesus – the death of a righteous man for the unrighteous (3.18b) was in fact for the benefit of others: for us, Christians, and for the imprisoned spirits. In 4.1 he takes up his admonitions again; here the whole quotation (with the author's explanation) is enclosed on the one hand by *epathen* (3.18, he suffered or, according to a variant reading, he died) and on the other hand by taking up the thread again in 4.1: *Christou oun pathontos* ('Since therefore Christ suffered'). Suffering for others and to the benefit of others (as a model for Christians) is illustrated in 3.18–22 by various examples. At any rate, it emerges that the author means to say that Jesus' death was to the advantage not only of Christians but also of these imprisoned spirits (*kai tois pneumasin*). This 'dogmatic section' inserted in the paraenesis contains statements about both christology (3.18,22) and baptism (3.21). I Peter 3.20f. speaks of baptism in terms of type and antitype, then and now. On the one hand it describes how in the flood many perished and few were saved; now, however, in baptism, many are saved (3.21a), while 3.21b explains precisely what baptism means. I Peter 3.18–22 is doubtless meant to illustrate why suffering for others is better than well-merited suffering. In 3.18 it becomes clear that the death of Jesus is to the advantage of sinners. 3.19 takes this up and gives a new reason why the death of Christ helps sinners. 'Then he went and preached to the spirits in prison' (3.19), in other words, according to the context this preaching must have benefited the spirits. The undeserved suffering of Jesus and his glorification benefited not only us believers, who were once sinners, but also the imprisoned spirits to whom Jesus descended.

What is said in 3.18 (about the good effect of the innocent suffering of Jesus – for himself glorification and for Christians the forgiveness of sins) is clearly to the advantage of these spirits. The author wants to give a second example to illustrate 3.17. Thus 3.19 introduces a *new* soteriological element, which must be meant in this way because of the structural framework. Thus the purpose of 3.19 is, as in 3.18, that 'these spirits too should be brought to God' by the death of Jesus (3.18). Accordingly, the whole text and context require that we should see 3.19 as referring to a *redemptive* action of Jesus and not as a condemnation. This hardly shifts the perspective in the direction of 'fallen angels'. In fact, it is very clear from 3.20f. that *pneumata* simply refers to the dead who were rebellious at the time of the flood and were therefore punished ('in prison', that is, in early Jewish terms, in the part of the underworld allotted to the *unrighteous*): Jesus' death is also to their benefit. *Nun sōzei baptisma* – now baptism brings salvation – and not just the ark with the few that it can rescue (3.21). Jesus' suffering has atoning worth not only 'for you' (3.18), but also for the many who perished in the flood. People are now saved by the very means by which some were rescued from the flood 'in the midst of water' (3.20b; *dia hydatos*, as through water). 3.21 explains that this is the typology: baptism is the antitype of the ark at the time of the flood. The living are saved through Christian baptism, 'which is a *prayer* for a good conscience' (for the forgiveness of sins and sanctification) (3.21c: *syneidēseōs agathēs eperōtēma*; in the early church, baptism was associated with a prayer, an *epiclēsis*, rather than a baptismal formula in the indicative). This prayer bears fruit, thanks to the resurrection of Jesus (3.21c). Paul also said, 'Delivered over (put to death) for our trespasses and raised for our justification' (Rom. 4.25; see above): this submersion in water washes us clean 'from sins'; coming out of the water gives us a good conscience, that is, justification. I Peter says that by means of Jesus' proclamation when he descended to hell the benefits which come to living sinners now through baptism are extended to former sinners who did not heed Noah's admonitions and therefore perished in the flood and were punished. The death of Jesus also has expiatory force for sinners from the old covenant, an idea which, remarkably enough, can also be found in the Letter to the Hebrews, the atmosphere of which is so akin to that of I Peter: 'A death redeems them *from sins which were committed under the first covenant*' (Heb. 9.15). Thus I Peter is in no way concerned to limit this reconciliation to sinners from the time of Noah. 'In the days of Noah' is in fact a standard theme, an example for all the unrighteous of the old covenant (see also Matt. 24.27–39 par.; Heb. 11.7; II Peter 2.5): the Yahwist also depicts the flood as God's punishment on the whole of sinful mankind. Thus I Peter 3.19 describes the proclamation of salvation by the dead Jesus to the whole of the world of the dead (we are not told whether the dead responded to his call; see further below in connection with I Peter 4.6). The *pneumata* or spirits of 3.19 are the *nekroi* or the dead of 4.6. In Hellenistic Judaism (and even in the wisdom literature: Wisdom 2.3; 15.11; 16.14), *pneumata* is often used for the souls of the departed (whereas in Greek Enoch, to which reference is often made, angels are exceptionally called *pneumata* in the Noah apocalypse. There, too, *pneumata* often means the souls of the dead: I (Greek) Enoch 22.3, 6–9, 11–13; cf. Heb. 12.23 which is clearly concerned with 'the spirits of just men made perfect' from the old covenant). The fate of the 'souls' of those who perished in the flood is narrated in detail in Gen. 6.5–9, 24 (I Peter 3.19 refers to this text, using almost the same terminology, and not to the story of the sons of God in Gen. 6.1–4).[106] Furthermore, I Peter regularly uses other names for angels (see I Peter 1.22; 3.22). Finally, these spirits are also imprisoned; they are 'in a prison' (3.19), that is, in that part of Sheol or the underworld in which the unrighteous have their abode (see also Luke 12.57–59 par., to which there is a clear allusion; Greek Enoch 22 also speaks of separate abodes for the righteous and the unrighteous departed). The idea of the possibility, not of a conversion of the departed, but of their *reconciliation* through the good deeds of the living, gained force in early Judaism after II Macc. 12.43 (however, this 'purgatory' became a rabbinic dogma only in the second century AD). The idea of reconciliation already mentioned in I Peter 3.19 is made more precise in 4.6. First of all these dead are judged, i.e. segregated into good and bad, and then 'they live like God in the spiritual (heavenly) sphere' (4.6b). Jesus proclaims the message of salvation to them in order to bring about this crisis, this distinction (*hina krithōsin*). Here the author is thinking of the 'disobedience' of the Gentiles who persecute Christians. To this end he again cites an element of tradition: 'him who is ready to judge the living and the dead' (4.5). Christ is also ready to judge these Gentiles. The proclamation to the dead is first in order to judge them, but after that, they will live. This is obviously not a reference to the last judgment, as salvation is still possible: *krithōsi men, zōsi de* (4.6; see I Cor. 3.12–15, 'be saved as by fire'). Thus the author seeks to console the persecuted Christians and to warn their persecutors by referring to the inescapable judgment which they themselves will incur after death (4.5: the proof of this is the judgment on sinners at the time of Noah, 3.19f.). 'For this is why the gospel was preached even to the dead, that though judged in the flesh like men, they might live in the spirit like God' (4.6). We do not have *en sarki* and *en pneumati*, but *sarki* and *pneumati*, which in I Peter always has the same meaning (see 4.2: 3.18). *Sarx* is the natural sphere of unredeemed man, and *pneuma* is the spiritual sphere (3.18; 4.6). The reference is to the condition of the whole man after his death. 'Judged after the flesh' refers to punishment after death, which is, however, transitory: it purifies, for in the end they will 'live in the sphere of the spirit'. Here *kata anthropous* is contrasted with *kata theon*; that is, what all men experience (cf. I Peter 1.16). Both the dead and the living will be judged; but like God they will 'live in the sphere of the spirit'. The living are as it were the model for judgment on the dead, just as God is the model for the life of the departed after their purification.

Thus in I Peter 3.19 and 4.6 the author presents a purifying judgment on the departed, after the proclamation of salvation by the dead Jesus, with the possibility of a final chance of salvation. The essence of his dogmatic position is that he proclaims the *universal* efficacy of the expiatory death of Jesus. This death offers a future even for those who have sinned and failed in the past. By means of purification and forgiveness there is even a future for the dead, thanks to the infinite power of the innocent suffering of Jesus for others, for the living and the dead. Following the Christian tradition (see Rom. 6.10; Heb. 9.26–28; 7.27; 10.10), I Peter 3.18 also calls the power of the suffering of Jesus for others the *hapax*, the unique – once for all – in our human history: as a result, all 'innocent sufferers' can suffer for the benefit of others. Structural and terminological analyses show that there is not a chance of finding support in the text of I Peter for the theory of a final damnation of the imprisoned angels;[107] furthermore, it makes the insertion of 3.19–21 quite incomprehensible. Of course, the *form of the account* is another matter. On the one hand we have the *presentation*: descent to hell (i.e. dying) and the proclamation of salvation (by the dead Jesus), and on the other what is *meant*: the death of Jesus also has expiatory force for those unrighteous who died within the old covenant (i.e. for the dead who did not know Christ, then or now).

## §2   The holy, kingly and priestly people of God

The fruit of the expiatory death of Jesus and his glorification to the right hand of God can be seen quite simply in the *Christian community*, depicted as 'a royal priesthood, a holy nation, God's own people, that you may declare the wonderful deeds of him who called you out of darkness into his marvellous light. Once you were no people but now you are God's people; once you had not received mercy but now you have received mercy' (2.9f.; see 2.5, with Rev. 1.6 and 5.10, the only passage in which the Christian community is called 'the priestly and royal people of God' in the New Testament). This pericope is full of references to the Tanach: Ex. 19.6; Isa. 43.20; Hos. 1.9f.; 2.1; see Rom. 9.25f. Of course, the point at issue here is not the problem of the relationship of the church to Israel: the message of I Peter is that the Christian community is the *laos*, i.e. the people of God. Clearly the author is writing to a community which is made up of Gentile Christians: here the church and Israel are not a community problem. Hos. 2.23, 'not my people', who become the people of God, in I Peter refers to the Gentiles (2.10, like Rom. 9.25f.; see Acts 15.14; Titus 2.14).

As a holy people the church is 'taken out of the world' (1.1), sanctified (1.2), just as God is 'the holy one' (Num. 15.40; Deut. 7.6; 26.19) and so is Christ (I Peter 1.19). For this persecuted community, 'sanctified' acquires a special significance. These Christians are persecuted (5.9), have a constricted life as 'aliens and exiles' (2.11; 1.17; 1.1). This not only surprises sympathizers (4.3f.): they are mocked and reviled (2.12; 3.9,15f.; 4.14). However, as aliens Christians are nevertheless also at the service of the world: 'Maintain good conduct among the Gentiles; then they will . . . ' (2.12). They must overcome hate through good-and-beautiful actions (*kalokagathia*, 2.12). However, the community of God is not only holy, but also 'priestly'. The author explains this with the phrase 'offer spiritual sacrifices acceptable to God through Jesus Christ' (2.5b). Here again the idea of suffering for others comes into the foreground. This is a *charis*, not a grace (*hesed*) which God gives us (it is something that other people do to Christians), but it gives Christians *hēn*, well-pleasing in the eyes of God. *That* is a 'well-pleasing sacrifice'; in it this people is priestly 'through Jesus Christ' (here we find ourselves close to Hebrews): a priestly 'suffering servant', that means suffering for others. The author remains faithful in his basic conception, even down to points of detail. As a priestly people, Christians must also proclaim the mighty acts of God (*aretai*, probably a markedly Hellenistic term) which they themselves have experienced (2.9b). It was Israel's ideal finally to be Yahweh's priestly and royal people (Isa. 61.6; 62.3). For I Peter that is realized in the church. Now the whole people has direct access to God in Christ: all offer spiritual sacrifices (2.5) and all make the proclamation (2.9). So the author tells Gentile Christians, 'once excluded from grace and now having received grace' (2.10). Grace is 'access to God' through the death and resurrection of Jesus (3.18).

The church community is now itself 'the temple', the 'keystone' of which is Christ (2.6f.), who holds all things together (see Ps. 118.22 with I Peter 2.4 and 2.7; Isa. 28.16 with I Peter 2.4,6; and Isa. 8.14 with I Peter 2.8). The rejected stone is Israel, once despised and rejected *by the Gentiles* who are now persecuting Christians. The church is suffering Israel. But this people is now completely rehabilitated (according to Ps. 118.22; see Matt. 21.42; another application from that in I Peter). In Isa. 28.16 the people and their leaders are at war with Assyria; they do not trust in God but in the help of the pagan Egyptians; they forget that Yahweh alone is the keystone which holds together the building of Israel.

The rabbis also explained this text in messianic terms. So according to I Peter 2.6f., anyone who trusts in Christ will not be ashamed. Finally, Isa. 8.14 is a prophetic threat: if it fails to believe, Israel will come up against Yahweh as a stumbling-block – once again this passage was interpreted in messianic terms by the rabbis. In I Peter, Israel is accused of having failed to recognize Jesus as the Christ, the suffering servant, and thus of having failed to accept his death as a messianic event (2.8b).

The real fruit for which the community of God constantly hopes is the 'heavenly heritage', the land of the promise: eternal, incorruptible, unde-filed (1.4: here, too, closely akin to Hebrews and Greek in terminology). This ultimate fruit is *sōtēria*, salvation (1.9f.; also a Hellenistic term; see the synthesis below), a term which is messianic in the New Testament (Luke 1.69, 71, 77; 2.11; John 4.22; Acts 4.12; 5.31; 13.23; I Thess. 5.9f.; Rom. 1.16; Heb. 5.9; II Peter 3.15; Jude 3; I John 4.14; Rev. 12.10). The author says, 'You love Christ without having seen him' (1.8a); 'you believe in him although you do not see him now' (1.8b); 'how heavenly will be your joy when you attain the final goal of your faith – your *sōtēria*' (1.9, 'the salvation of your souls', a Hellenistic Jewish expression). The author calls this final goal simply 'grace' (1.10; 1.13); in other passages it appears as 'the blessing' or 'the grace of life' (3.9). Grace is salvation from God in Jesus, which will only be complete at the parousia (1.13).

For this persecuted Christian community, the intervening period between the ascension of Jesus and the parousia is an exodus into exile. At this time Christians must (*a*) be an example to the world through holy, good and fine actions (2.12); (*b*) follow Christ in his patient and innocent suffering for others (2.21–25; 3.18–4.6) and (*c*) offer Christian resistance against the emperor when God's rights are at stake (5.8f.), but when this is not the case, be respectfully loyal to the alien civil authorities (2.13–17; see further in the synthesis below). I Peter stresses the true greatness of the humble man; he stands under the grace of God (5.5c). 'Humble yourselves therefore under the mighty hand of God' (5.6). I Peter shares with Hebrews and much of the rest of the New Testament God's predilection for the suffering, afflicted and oppressed righteous. The author says this in connection with church leadership (5.1–4; 5.5). Everyone has a special role in the community, 'but all must be humble, one towards another' (5.5b). Whether they are church officials or simply church members, each must 'love one another, as good stewards of God's *varied grace* (*charis*) with the gifts (*charismata*) which each one has received' (4.10).

Thus the fruit of the atoning death and resurrection of Jesus is the Christian community as the people of God (2.9f.), a royal and priestly people, which has free access to God (3.18; 2.9f.), on the basis of rebirth (1.3; 1.23) through baptism (3.20f.), in faith and hope for God (1.21) and in brotherly love (1.22). This hope keeps the community directed towards its goal, salvation (1.10), the heavenly heritage (1.4), 'which is already prepared to be revealed at the end of time' (1.4–5b), since the consummation is eschatological (1.5b; 1.6; 1.20; 4.5, 7–17; 5.10). Thus here *charis* is also the divine counsel or the mystery hidden in God (1.12c, see 1.4f.) that angels want to know (1.12c), and that was searched for by the prophets (1.10–12). However, it has been revealed only to Christians through the proclamation in the gospel of Jesus as the Christ (1.12). But the prophets had already discovered that this divine mystery is a plan of salvation that comprises a way *through suffering* to glorification (1.11). This also implies that Jesus' suffering for others is 'according to the scriptures' and has thus been taken up into God's counsel (the 'divine necessity' of Mark). The death of Jesus is not a fiasco, but is included in God's unfathomable purposes (see 1.19f.). The author concludes: 'The God of all grace, who has called you to his eternal glory in Christ, will himself restore, establish and strengthen you' (5.10). Right at the end, he calls this short summary of Christian doctrine – above all that of the 'suffering servant', suffering for a good cause – which he has given in his letter 'the true *charis* of God' (5.12b), in which his readers must stand firm (5.12c).

Chapter 3.2

# The world of the future as God's great grace: Hebrews

*Literature*: P. Andriessen and A. Lenglet, *De brief aan de Hebreeën*, Roermond 1971; J. Bonsirven, *Saint Paul. Epître aux Hébreux*, Paris [6]1943; F. F. Bruce, *The Epistle to the Hebrews*, NLC, London [2]1967; id., ' "To the Hebrews" or "To the Essenes" ', *NTS* 9, 1962–63; A. Cody, *A History of Old Testament Priesthood*, Rome 1969; J. A. Fitzmyer, 'Further Light on Melchizedek from Qumran Cave XI', *JBL* 86, 1967, 25–41; G. Friedrich, 'Das Lied vom Hohenpriester im Zusammenhang von Hebr. 4, 4–5, 10', *TZ* 18, 1962, 95–115; R. G. Hamerton-Kelly, *Pre-existence, Wisdom and the Son of Man*, Cambridge 1973; A. T. Hanson, *Jesus Christ in the Old Testament*, London 1965; A. J. B. Higgins, 'The Priestly Messiah', *NTS* 13, 1966–67, 211–39; M. de Jonge and A. S. van der Woude, '11 Q Melchizedek and the New Testament', *NTS* 12, 1965–66, 301–26; J. L. Martyn, *History and*

*Theology in the Fourth Gospel*, New York 1968; W. A. Meeks, *The Prophet-King, Moses Traditions and the Johannine Christology*, NT.S 14, Leiden 1967; O. Michel, *Der Brief an die Hebräer*, Meyer 13, Göttingen [12]1966; H. W. Montefiore, *Rabbinic Literature and Gospel Teachings*, London 1930; G. Schille, 'Erwägungen zur Hohepriesterlehre des Hebräerbriefes', *ZNW* 64, 1955, 81–109; C. Spicq, *L'épître aux Hébreux*, two vols., Paris 1952; V. Taylor, *The Atonement in New Testament Teaching*, London 1940; A. Vanhoye, *La structure littéraire de l'épître aux Hébreux*, Bruges-Paris 1963; G. Vermès, *The Dead Sea Scrolls in English*, Harmondsworth 1962; R. Williamson, *The Epistle to the Hebrews*, 1964; id., *Philo and the Epistle to the Hebrews*, Leiden 1970; A. S. van der Woude, 'Melchisedek als himmlische Erlösergestalt in den neugefundenen eschatologischen Midraschim aus Qumran-Höhle XI', *OTS* 17, 1965, 354–73 (see also under M. de Jonge); Y. Yadin, 'The Dead Sea Scrolls and the Epistle to the Hebrews', *Scripta Hierosolymitana* 4, 1958, 36–55.

## Introduction

For many Christians, Hebrews has become an unknown text. This is partly because of its complicated synagogue-type exegesis, partly because many exegetes have given a negative evaluation of it, especially in the last generation,[108] and finally because of various anti-priestly tendencies in the culture and the churches of our time. This is wrong. For anyone who learns to understand the character of Jewish exegesis to some extent and escapes the presuppositions of certain exegetes quickly discovers that Hebrews is the most subtle human document in New Testament literature and at the same time unmasks the sacral images of priesthood, despite the frequency with which they appear. What one finds in Hebrews is not so much a sacral reinterpretation of Jesus as the Christ in terms of Judaism and a so-called radical Hellenizing of christology, as the beating of a Jewish-Christian heart. The Christian community to which the author addresses himself is well versed in Greek thought, and the author's sole concern is to articulate the apostolic experience of faith – the experience of decisive and definitive salvation from God in Jesus – in profoundly human expressions from the thought and the life of his environment, against the background of the threat of a considerable apostasy on the eve of a persecution. While the final pastoral admonition of Hebrews, 'let us go outside the walls' (13.13), raises critical questions for us today (which must at all events take into account the historical circumstances which influence the spirituality of this author), the writer of Hebrews has much to say to us as Christians, and often says it in a compelling way.

Unlike Paul, Hebrews is not particularly concerned with the contrast between law and grace, though the author is very much aware of it (10.1; see 8.5). Nor is it concerned with the contrast between the Old Testament and the New (8.6); the central point of interest is the conflict between the impotence and inadequacy of Jewish sacrifice or worship in accordance with the law of Moses and the effective grace of the ministry of Jesus, in faithfulness towards God and in solidarity with suffering mankind. Even this contrast is simply an ingredient in the more fundamental dialectic between what the author calls 'this world', or the present age, in the categories of Jewish Greek apocalyptic, and the *oikoumenē mellousa* (2.5), the world of the future or the future age. The perspective of the author of Hebrews is cosmic and ecumenical; the confrontation between the church and the synagogue is merely one striking instance of this – which is, of course, painful for the Jewish Christian who was evidently a diaspora Jew from Alexandria before his conversion to Christianity, familiar with a number of Greek ideas which were current in Egypt at the time, but particularly drawn to Jewish spirituality, above all the so-called 'Sinaitic spirituality' of the less 'orthodox' or mystical trends within early Judaism in the second half of the first century AD. The author seeks to present the apostolic faith without distortion in the context of this Jewish spirituality.

One of the most important reasons why the author writes this letter (in fact, it is not so much a letter as a kind of homily which is intended to be read in the context of some form of Jewish worship) is evidently the danger of apostasy. We discover this (in the wider context of the admonitions in 5.11–6.12 and 10.19–39) above all in 10.25 and 6.6. Some Christians who were originally Jews turned their backs on the church, either to return to their former faith or because they felt attracted to the religious atmosphere of late antiquity, with its syncretism and its emphasis on the spirit. Furthermore, one reason for the lassitude and frustration in the Christianity of the time seems to have lain in the attitude adopted by the church in connection with the relationship of angels to Christ, which many people found too matter-of-fact. The whole religious environment with its dominant interest in angels, which were of existential significance in the world of late antiquity, seems to have alienated some Christians from Christianity. This environment contrasted strongly with the matter-of-fact attitude of apostolic Christianity to the main problems of the time – fate and the spiritual heavenly powers. The concerns and interests of the culture of the time did not lie with human beings, much less with a crucified man.

For Hebrews, this attitude included a complete failure to understand the significance of the life of Jesus Christ. The author accuses these Christians of theological immaturity, as a result of which they are in such a sorry state that they are likely to apostatize (5.11–6.12). They do not distinguish between 'good' and 'evil'; in this connection, that is, between a healthy christology and a bad one. Above all, they fail to grasp the christological implications of the Old Testament; it is this omission which made it likely that Christians from Judaism would apostatize. So in his work the author seeks to show what it means for Jesus to be the *Christ*, that is (as far as he is concerned), the eschatological priestly Messiah. He seeks to create a solid basis for a proper understanding of this mystery with material from the Tanach. In an unparalleled way he seeks to secure the Jewish basis of Christianity and to show that the Tanach itself intended that the levitical priesthood should have a *provisional* character.

We do not have much idea of the social conditions which probably led to this apostasy. It is, however, certain that Christians of that time had severe social problems, and Hebrews indicates this. Because of the way in which pagan religion stamped the whole of public life (including even civic entertainments), Christians detached themselves completely from civic life. Hebrews in fact urges them to do so. Because of this attitude, the Romans called them 'misanthropists'. Tacitus wrote this in his account of the reign of Nero in connection with the years 54–68: *odium generis humani* characterizes the *Chrestiani*.[109] Hebrews also indicates arrests and confiscation of goods (10.32–34); furthermore, the problem of the suffering of Christians runs right through the letter like a scarlet thread. The rift between church and synagogue began to take its toll in social terms (Judaism was a recognized or permitted *religio licita* in the Roman empire). Christians were not allowed any civil rights. For some people, these hindrances must have been a reason for leaving the church; people began to fail to turn up at gatherings of the community (10.25).

Thus the author of Hebrews emerges as a Christian apologist who seeks to show that Jesus is the fulfilment of all the Old Testament promises: in other words, that Christianity has a genuine and solid basis in Judaism. He presents a christology on the basis of a personal study of the Jewish sacred scriptures along the lines current in the synagogue exegesis of the time. In my view, the letter does not give any kind of theological justification for the *de facto* separation of the church from the synagogue, a breach which is as it were officially confirmed in Heb. 13.10 ('We have an altar from which those who serve the tent have no right to eat'; this is wrongly – see below – interpreted as an excommunication of the Jews from the Christian eucharist). That interpretation goes against the whole tenor of the Hebrews, and against the complicated synagogue-type exegesis through which the author seeks to demonstrate the Jewish basis of Christianity. The harsh relegation of the Torah which we find even in Paul, in Galatians (see above), is quite alien to the author of Hebrews. True, the institutions of the Old Testament are inadequate and provisional, but at the same time they are prefigurations of the coming truth, Jesus Christ. In addition to the elements in the Old Testament that are imperishable (see e.g. Heb. 11), its contents are important to the author of Hebrews. He may be a Hellenist from Alexandria, but at the same time he is a Jew body and soul, and against this twofold spiritual background he sets out to show what Christianity seems like to a Diaspora Jew who has in the meantime become a Christian: salvation comes from God alone in Jesus the Christ.

If there is an opposition between the church and Israel in Hebrews, it is to be found in a wider cosmic and ecumenical framework. The author himself says that the *oikoumenē mellousa*, the world of the future or the coming age, is 'our real theme' (2.5). The religious and cultural background is the Hellenistic-Jewish apocalyptic of late antiquity – the assumption of the two world governments or two ages. In the Alexandria where the author lived, the pattern of two levels of reality had already been reinterpreted in Hellenistic terms. It had become a visible and transitory world which exists at the same time and over against a *kosmos noētos*, the super-sensible world of ideas (as in Platonism). As a Hellenist the author is familiar with this Greek conception of a two-storey world, but as a Jew (who also has a perfect knowledge of the Septuagint), he is more influenced by the Jewish 'historical' scheme of the 'present world' as compared with a future world, in other words with the pattern of (Hellenistic-Jewish) apocalyptic. In my view, R. Williamson has given a convincing vindication of this interpretation as over against the incomprehensible caricature of Hebrews given by C. Spicq, for all his valuable references. However, as so often, the pendulum can swing right over to the other side. Williamson forgets one very real aspect of the Jewish apocalyptic of that time. In it, what must be seen in history as *'now'* and *'to come soon'* exists already in the heavenly spheres.[110] Hebrews takes the same view: 'God's work was already complete before the creation of the world' (4.3c); as for apocalyptic, the whole of salvation is already stored up in a pre-existent form in the *epourania* or the heavenly spheres. To some extent, Williamson has misrepresented this aspect. There is an obscure connection between earthly history and this supernatural, pre-existent, timeless 'history'. As the end-time comes nearer, however, the boundaries between earthly and heavenly history disappear. Whatever is alive on earth at that point can already participate in festive gatherings in heaven (see also 12.22–24). Thus this apocalyptic of the two ages has both a *horizontal* historical dimension ('this world' as contrasted with 'the world to come') and at the same time a *vertical* dimension, comprising two levels (the *earthly* world over against *heavenly* eternal reality; these two dimensions are suggested above all in 8.5f. and 9.23–26). The particular standpoint of Hebrews is that of Hellenistic Jewish apocalyptic; this is one of the author's presuppositions, his spiritual context or his thought-world. (That is why we shall have to make a critical distinction between what the author wants to say about Christianity – salvation from God in Jesus – and the general cultural and religious presuppositions in which he sums up his belief.) Long before Hebrews, what we call Hellenism had already been given a Jewish stamp and had been incorporated into apocalyptic (whereas for another Alexandrian Jew, Philo, things are the other way round: here the Jewish apocalyptic pattern has been absorbed and neutralized by Greek philosophy). Consequently the author of Hebrews can quite happily take over a *terminology* reminiscent of Philo from his Alexandrian background, while keeping it within his particular form of Hellenistic Judaism, which is fundamentally different from that of Philo. There is no mention at all in Hebrews of any kind of Hellenizing of Christianity, much less of a priestly reinterpretation of it in Jewish terms. The author is in the tradition of Diaspora Judaism, which was already given a purely Jewish expression, for example, in the Book of Wisdom, albeit with the use of Greek categories.

We must leave open the question of the date of Hebrews. The letter is quoted by I *Clement* (which was written in 96). It must therefore have been written before 93/97 at the latest. On the other hand, it is striking that in Heb. 13.7 the author is already aware of Christian reverence for the apostles: Christians must keep before their eyes the former great leaders of the church, 'their life and the outcome of their life'; thus strictly speaking they are already living in a post-apostolic age. Furthermore, persecution of the church seems to be imminent. There were persecutions of Jews and Christians in Alexandria as early as 38 and 66, in Rome under Claudius in 49[111] and under Nero in 63–66[112] (in which tradition puts the death of Peter and Paul). Then follow the two great persecutions of the church; that under Domitian (81–96) and that under Trajan (98–117). Is Hebrews, then, to be dated immediately before Domitian? Or perhaps between Domitian and Trajan? We must leave these questions open (at least for the moment).

## §1   The cultural and religious presuppositions of Hebrews

### I. 'THIS WORLD' AND THE 'WORLD OF THE FUTURE'

The two worlds – this world, or our created world (9.1), and the *oikoumenē mellousa* or the world of the future (2.5, see 6.5; 9.9f.) – are on the one hand earthly realities, in that they are provisional and transitory, and on the other hand the heavenly, definitive and imperishable reality. The terminology is, as such, clearly Hellenistic. But Hebrews sees Jesus, the Son, as the great juncture – *in* our world – between the two worlds. As

Son, Christ stands over the ages, while at the same time the new age is subject to him alone: he has been set above all heavenly beings (1.4–9; 1.13f.; 2.2–4) and is the heir of all (1.2), Lord and Master (2.5–9). This breaks through the Hellenistic pattern of two levels. The author alters Hellenistic terms in order to make it possible to express a Jewish-Christian, apocalyptic picture of history.

1. The first age is 'this creation' (9.11): the visible (11.3), material and transitory (1.10–12; 7.12, 18, 23; 8, 7, 13; 12.26f.) world which according to the views of the time (above all in apocalyptic) was subject to 'heavenly rulers', that is, a variety of angelic heavenly beings (2.5). All human institutions also belong to this first age – the world in which we live: they are deficient (8.7) and earthly (9.1). Israel, with its priesthood, its law and its institutions also belongs to this first creation (2.2). There are also angels who have brought men the Jewish Torah and subjected them to this Law (2.2–4; cf. Ex. 19.16, 19; 20.18; also Acts 7.53; Gal. 3.19; Col. 2.14f.).[113] In Hebrews it is presupposed that this present earthly world of men is subject to angels (see 2.5–9; 1.4). This idea, which was widespread in antiquity, can also be found to some degree in Ps. 8.5f., which says that man was created 'a little lower than the *ᵉlōhīm*' or angels. In Jewish apocalyptic literature this 'a little' was reinterpreted and understood to mean 'a short while', i.e. provisionally: it was expected that these conditions would be completely changed or at least altered by a final apocalyptic event. At that time 'a little lower than' the angels was understood to mean 'for a short while' (see 2.7), and not for ever (see 12.2). It was then a common notion in Jewish apocalyptic circles that on his exaltation the 'Son of man' would have a new relationship to the angelic heavenly powers and would even be enthroned above them.[114]

The chief characteristic of this age is death, seen as subjection or servitude to evil heavenly angels, and above all to the devil (2.14–16). Within this culture, the existential anxiety of ancient man, torn between meaning and meaninglessness, was explained in terms of the subjection of men to various supernatural, spiritual powers which they could not control. These powers seemed to be able to make decisions over the heads of men and guided human destiny. The Christian interpretation of apocalyptic thought, that this system would not last for long and that circumstances would be changed by the Son of man – Christ, the seed of Abraham – is central to Hebrews. For the author, that is a sign of God's love for the humble, the oppressed, the weak, wherever they may be in the cosmos. This idea reappears regularly in Hebrews. Hence *charis* or grace in Hebrews automatically takes on the connotation of divine mercy for the weaker, the younger who do not have the rights of the firstborn, and for people like Rahab the harlot – for anyone who suffers. For God's *charis,* nothing is too insignificant, least of all those who are insignificant. They will be exalted.

This letter, so full of the ideas of Jewish priesthood, and with so many ideas that are quite alien to us, also has an immeasurably deep understanding of human nature, such as I cannot find expressed anywhere else in the New Testament. This feeling is expressed under the cloak of an external sacralism which Hebrews in fact seeks to unmask.

2. The second age of apocalyptic is contrasted with this first age: it is the *oikoumenē mellousa* (2.5), identified in Hebrews with Christ and his followers, along with all the inhabitants of heaven. It is the world of powerful realities (1.4; 7.19, 22), of a permanent and imperishable (10.34) reality which is beyond the senses (11.1), and indestructible (12.28) and everlasting. The astral sphere, the world of the stars, is not part of this invisible and imperishable world. In Hebrews it has evidently already been demythologized and become part of the perishable material world (see 1.10–12; 9.11; 12.26). However, the angelic heavenly beings do belong to the imperishable, second age, 'the heavenly fatherland' (11.16). According to Hellenistic Judaism they were created imperishable beings (where the Hebrew text of Gen. 1.1 spoke of the 'creation of heaven and earth', i.e. our cosmos, this was interpreted as 'our earth and the heaven of spiritual beings'; cf. Philo, *De opif. mund.* 27). Furthermore, these heavenly beings which had been created beforehand assisted God at his creation of the *cosmos* along with everything in it (see Job 38.7; Rev. 7.1; 14.18; 16.5). At the time this was simply current Jewish theology. So Hebrews stresses that it is the Son, Jesus, 'through whom all things are created' (1.2; not through the angels, 1.5); the world to come is therefore also subject to him (2.5).

Everything in our first age which is imperishable and thus of abiding value also belongs to the 'future world', as for example the faith of the righteous figures of the Old Testament (Heb. 11) and above all the brotherly love which belongs to those things which must abide for ever (13.1). Indeed, according to Jewish apocalyptic, the heavenly age was already secretly at work in the old age. Therefore *epourania* or heavenly things embrace everything that is invisible, incorruptible and not subject to the flux of time (3.1; 6.4; 9.23). And, as has already been said, 'God's works were finished from the foundations of the world' (4.3c); that is, according to apocalyptic, all the aspects of salvation – even more particularly, Christ – have been prepared and are pre-existent in the heavens.

This is not a metaphysical statement; it is intended to be in terms of wisdom and apocalyptic (which does not, however, make it any less 'real'). Therefore everything that has been redeemed historically by the sacrifice of Jesus belongs to the realm of the pre-existent which is both in our *chronos* or time and is at the same time part of the 'future world' of the *epourania* or heavenly things (9.23; 3.1).

Thus as far as Hebrews is concerned, anything in our present transitory world which has no relevant relationship to the future world has in fact served its purpose once Christ comes. Anything that still has significance is imperishable. So the men of faith from the Old Testament belong to the community of God which is 'heavenly' in Christ, as the *'ecclesia* from Abel' (this phrase does not appear, but its content is there, see 11.4); they belong to the world of the future. What the author of Hebrews means is that they are *in* the world but not *of* the world.

However, even for those who already have a share in the coming world on earth, the first world simply goes on (9.9). The new world is a *kairos* or a chance of life which leaves the old world behind it (9.9f.), but the *chronoi* – our time as chronology (see 3.13) – simply continue until the *telos* or end (see 3.14; 6.11). It is a striking feature of Hebrews that the *kairos* of the Jesus event is put on the plane of our earthly *chronos* (9.11). The humanity of 'the Son' (1.2) is not a mythical event or an event outside time; it appears within our *chronoi* or earthly history. Jesus died at the climax of the ages (*epi synteleia tōn aiōnōn*), and Christians live in the earthly time between ascension and *parousia* (10.13; 9.28). Thus Hebrews stresses the historicity of Jesus, but also emphasizes that everything that Jesus has done in history has eternal relevance (10.14). Thus in extraordinarily un-Greek terms, this author supposes that particular events within the chronology of our earthly age could be of decisive and final (eschatological) significance. For me, the fact that Christian material, the proclamation of the apostles, i.e. the fundamental reference to Jesus as a historical event, can be asserted in so uncompromising a way, against the spirit of Greek Alexandrian theology, is one of the clearest indications that a religious reference to the historical Jesus is an essential characteristic of Christianity and that to give up this reference is to attack Christianity from within. The essential characteristic of Christianity as a religion is its reference to a historical source, a historical individual and not primarily a reference to human experiences which serve as a model, essential though these latter may also be. The process of understanding Jesus as salvation, which serves to identify him, is only achieved in that act in which man also comes to grips with a fundamental problem of human life.[115] For that very reason, the story of human suffering is for Hebrews the great test of Christianity, for both Jesus and Christians (2.18). Here Hebrews stresses that Jesus is not simply the model for basic problems of human life (so to speak a mythical representative of human destiny); the whole letter shows that Jesus became a man among men, human in every respect (*kata panta* 2.17). Precisely as this specific man – not as a Greek *eikōn* or model, but in the human situation – he shared in experiencing all our inhumanity. Hebrews shows the Greek-thinking Jew who subjects Greek thought to the criticism of apostolic Christianity and yet at the same time can think for the most part in Greek terms, as will emerge from many passages in Hebrews. The Christian in Hebrews really looks upwards towards the invisible heavenly world of the angels, in which God dwells, but *at the same time* he looks forward, to the world of the future, the approaching parousia of Christ Jesus (9.28; 10.25, 27, 37; 12.26f.). And for him this world of the *parousia* is the coming *charis* in which the Christian already lives in the context of an 'already now' and a 'not yet'.

3. God is enthroned above both dimensions of reality – the transitory earthly world and the world of abiding reality which since Christ has been manifested in our history. (Because of the superiority of the 'heavenly-world' he is strikingly called 'the Father of spirits', 12.9; see also Rev. 22.6; the phrase was common at that time, e.g. I Enoch 37.4; 59.2; cf. Num. 16.22; 27.16).

As the great mediator between the first age and the future age, Christ, 'the Son' receives an equal all-controlling position (1.2; 2.5). As the point of juncture on earth between the two worlds he spans them both, 'appointed (as he is) the heir of all things, through whom he also created the world' (1.2). Therefore Jesus Christ is not only the point of juncture between the two ages but at the same time the connection between them; he is the bond between what is incorruptible in the world of creation, above all by virtue of belief in God, and the essential incorruptibility of the second age. For in our created world, too, there are people to whom the author movingly makes the testimony (characteristic of wisdom) 'They were too good for this world' (11.38).

## II. THE MELCHIZEDEK MIDRASH

In Hebrews 7 we come up against an argument which is extremely puzzling on a first reading. It is about Melchizedek and Jewish sacrifice. The cult of which Hebrews speaks is certainly not that of the Temple in Jerusalem – in the last resort, we are dealing here with the situation of Diaspora Jews – but of the sacrifice connected with the tent of meeting from the time of Moses and the founding of Israel: the journey through the wilderness, the lawgiving on Sinai and the inauguration of worship. As a Diaspora Jew, the author takes us back to the high point of the history of Israel, to Moses, the leader and guide of the people of God, and to Israel's journey through the wilderness on the way to the promised land. This theme lies at the heart of his writing: the new, greater Moses, 'the pioneer of faith' (2.10; 12.2), Jesus, who goes before us into the land of promise, our heavenly fatherland with God and the heaven of spiritual beings (see Heb. 3.1–6; 11.23–31; 13.20f.; 12.2; also in 2.14, 15, 18; 3.1; 4.15; 5.2; and implicitly in 1.2; 10.14; 12.23; 13.13). By means of a *pesher* type[116] exegesis (see p. 905) characteristic of the synagogue, Hebrews shows that the people have constantly failed at the high points of their history. Despite the insertion of Abraham and the figure of Melchizedek, it is Moses who holds the central place in the author's account. Of course this is a special Moses, a Moses who, from the Deuteronomistic tradition onwards, was increasingly glorified in later Judaism: the leader of the people becomes at the same time prophet, king and hierophant or high priest; furthermore, following the lines of Deut. 5.27; 9.9, 18, 26, he takes on the features of the suffering servant of God (see Acts 7.17–44, where Moses is seen as God's messenger who is misunderstood and rejected).[117] At the same time, among more orthodox Jews, he became principally significant as the great lawgiver of Israel, the man of the Torah. A Diaspora Jew like Philo even speaks of *divus Moyses*, the divine Moses.[118] Hebrews is certainly not unaware of this Alexandrian thought-world in which themes from the wisdom tradition came under the influence of what has been called the Sinaitism of early Judaism. The author follows this general tendency without taking over from it any of its particular forms, e.g. that of Philo.

Hebrews 7 mentions Melchizedek in a similar connection. The author's exegesis is based on two hermeneutical principles from biblical interpretation of the time: (*a*) *quod non in thora, non in mundo*,[119] i.e. whatever cannot be found in the Tanach or the sacred Jewish writings must be regarded as non-existent (a kind of *argumentum e silentio*), and (*b*) rabbi Hillel's hermeneutical rule from the synagogue: if two sections from different parts of scripture contain the same key word (in this instance Melchizedek), they belong together and explain each other.[120] This makes the allegedly puzzling exegesis of Hebrews quite clear. For both Gen. 14.18–20 and Ps. 110.4 speak of Melchizedek. Therefore these two texts must explain each other. However, Hebrews was not the first writing to see this connection. Philo explained the two texts on the basis of this exegetical principle[121] (thereby identifying Melchizedek with the Logos and the heavenly high priest), and a tradition is to be found in thirteen fragments from Qumran Cave 11 in which Melchizedek is identified with the eschatological leader of the heavenly hosts of angels.[122] I think that this must be put in the apocalyptic context of the two-storey universe.[123] The eschatological fight on earth carried on by the royal warlike Messiah is duplicated or anticipated in heaven by the fight of the good spirits against the bad. The leader of the good angels is Michael, who is at the same

time Melchizedek. Here the royal, warlike pattern of messianic expectation has the upper hand (a later phase in the Qumran community). This
conception of the kingly Messiah, Melchizedek, and Philo's conception
of the high-priestly Messiah, Melchizedek, are an indication of the syncretism of the time. At all events, in Qumran, Philo and Hebrews we
find the same midrash method of synagogue-type exegesis (see pp. 903f.)
with the result that the coming Messiah is seen as a figure like Melchizedek. However, in Hebrews, Jesus-Melchizedek is no angel, but the
'Son', man.

The facts from the Genesis account are as follows. After his victory
over four kings Abraham meets a fifth, who is presented as Melchizedek,
king of Salem, priest of the Most High. Hebrews interprets *melek sālēm*
(Gen. 14.18, where this refers to a vassal, a king, who is prepared to
submit) as king of Salem: king of peace, called Melchizedek, or *melek* of
*ṣedeq*, king of righteousness. This etymology serves as a prelude to his
Christian interpretation of Melchizedek=Christ, the king of righteousness
and peace.

As in early Jewish exegesis, Hebrews is particularly interested that in
Genesis Melchizedek disappears from history as unexpectedly as he
appears in it (in historical terms, we can see how the final redactor
incorporated some local legend or tradition, from a time before the Israelites took over Jerusalem, into the Genesis account). The first principle of
interpretation, that anything that is not in the Tanach does not exist, is
then applied to this discovery. Melchizedek is a being without beginning
and without end. However, he appears as king and priest.[124] So Melchizedek is a royal priest 'without father, without mother, without genealogy;
his life has neither beginning nor end. He is like the Son of God'
(Heb. 7.3).[125] This indicates at the same time that Melchizedek is merely
an antitype; the type to whom he is like is Jesus, the Son of God. Thus
Melchizedek is an eternal someone, a pre-existent being of heavenly
origin (as also in the Melchizedek exegesis from Qumran).

However, a reading of Genesis introduces even more into this perspective. For Melchizedek gives Abraham the priestly blessing, and not vice
versa. 'It is beyond dispute that the inferior is blessed by the superior'
(Heb. 7.6): this is evident for Jews (see also II Peter 2.19). Thus Melchizedek is higher than Abraham. The consequences of this idea are
enormous, since in return for this blessing Abraham pays Melchizedek
a tenth of all the booty that he has gained. Now a Jew was aware that
any child of Abraham had to pay a tenth to the levitical priests
(Num. 18.21–24; Heb. 7.5). Here, however, it is Melchizedek who
receives the tithe, and does so from Abraham, the ancestor of the Jews,
the father of the levitical priesthood and at the same time the bearer of
all the promises (Heb. 7.6). Thus in Genesis we are told not only that

Abraham, already rich in promises, now also receives the priestly blessing (he is as it were consecrated priest through the eternal high priest Melchizedek), but also that here Abraham is *subordinate* to Melchizedek. The conclusion of the midrash is obvious: the Jewish, levitical priesthood has a lower status than that of Melchizedek. A priest after the order of Melchizedek is a transcendent order, much higher than Jewish priesthood. True, at the time of Abraham there were still no levitical priests; but that does not spoil the argument, for they were 'in the loins of their forefather' Abraham (7.10). The Jewish priests themselves were in Abraham, paying the tithe instead of requiring it (7.10); they themselves recognized the superiority of the priesthood after the order of Melchizedek.

Hebrews read the Genesis account in the light of Ps. 110.4 and came to the conclusion that the priesthood of the coming messianic Melchizedek also far surpasses the levitical priesthood and leaves it behind. For in Ps. 110.4, in which the same Melchizedek is named, we read: 'Yahweh has sworn it – he will not take it back: "You will be a priest for centuries by virtue of my pronouncement: Melchizedek." ' This text from the Psalms shows that an eschatological priest will come in Israel (Qumran also interprets this verse of the Psalms in messianic terms, and the psalm itself is already a *pesher* interpretation of Gen. 14). Hebrews now brings the two biblical texts together, and it transpires that the promised eschatological messianic priest (110.4) is thus a priest 'after the order of Melchizedek', of whom Genesis has already said that he far surpasses the levitical priesthood: he is an *eternal* royal *priest*, who moreover stands outside the Aaronite, levitical succession. For the Jews regarded Ps. 110 as a psalm of David, i.e. from the time after the Law of Moses. This psalm therefore makes all Mosaic legislation about priests worthless (Heb. 7.12–14; esp. 7.8). Furthermore, it is clear for Jews that Jesus does not come from the tribe of Levi (7.13), but from Judah, a tribe which has nothing to do with priesthood (7.13f.; see Gen. 49.10; Micah 5.2; Ps. 110; Isa. 11.1, 10; also Matt. 22.43–45; 1.2; Luke 3.33; Rev. 5.5). Jesus is not a priest in the official Jewish way; from a Jewish point of view he is a non-priest, a layman (as the whole of the New Testament, apart from Hebrews, will say). However, Hebrews seeks to break through the Jewish distinction between priest and layman and calls Jesus the eschatological priestly Messiah through whom all now have direct access to God (whereas in Judaism only the high priest had access to the holy of holies, and then only once a year).

That becomes clear when one remembers (7.15) that Jesus is described as a priest 'after the order of Melchizedek', i.e. after a priesthood which is independent of any genealogy and any connection with the tribe of Levi (7.15–17). (The bread and wine as elements in the making of the

covenant between Melchizedek and Abraham do not play any part at all
in this whole comparison. That is a later Christian midrash which conflicts with the general tone of Hebrews, for while it knows of church
leaders and presidents, Heb. 13.17, it never calls them priests. The only
priest is Jesus.) 'After the order of Melchizedek' points to the eternal
character of this priesthood, which is thus something from the *oikoumenē
mellousa*, the second age or the future world: prepared by God before the
creation of the world, appearing in time and made fast for ever in heaven.
By contrast, the levitical priesthood can only continue by a succession
after the death of many individual priests (7.23f.). For anyone thinking
in Greek (-Jewish) terms, this multiplicity is itself a sign of imperfection
and transitoriness. The special character of the priesthood of Jesus-Melchizedek is particularly confirmed when we see that this appointment as
priest – in contrast to the Jewish priesthood – is accompanied by a divine
oath (Ps. 110.4) (7.20–22 – this is a Jewish argument).

Yigael Yadin[126] asserts that Hebrews wants to show that Jesus, who
did not come from a priestly tribe (7.14), is nevertheless high priest and
of a higher order than the Aaronite priesthood. Jesus is the royal and
priestly Messiah: Hebrews wants to impress this on a group of believers
who expect two Messiahs – a group like, say, Qumran. It argues that
Jesus combines both functions in himself. This does not seem to me to be
quite correct. Certainly the kingship of the Messiah is expressed at the
beginning of Hebrews in the exaltation of Jesus above the world and all
the angels, but in connection with the priestly Messiah there is never any
stress on the fact that he is also royal: the important thing is that his
priesthood is *everlasting*. Hebrews does not have the concern that Yadin
ascribes to it, though the problems indicated by Yadin did exist at that
time. Hebrews stands more in the tradition of priestly messianic
expectations.

Because the priesthood of Jesus is superior to the Jewish priesthood
and of another order, his service is that of a completely new covenant
(7.22; see 8.6–13; 10.15–18), a priesthood which has the power of an
eternal life (pre-existent and risen or exalted) which is indestructible
(7.16). No wonder that the work of this priest is called the 'source of
eternal salvation' (5.9), and 'consequently he is able for all time to save
those who draw near to God through him, since he lives for ever to make
intercession for them' (7.25).

All this seems to us to be a fantastic exegesis of the Tanach, but this
was not the case for the Jews of the time. Of course the author of Hebrews
retained his experience of Christ before embarking on an argument of
this kind. His experience is that decisive and definitive salvation is given
by God in Jesus; here he is at one with the whole of the apostolic faith,
which has now existed for decades; compared with it, everything else

pales into insignificance. Hebrews really does not need this argument from scripture; indeed it can go wrong in it. Genuine Christian experience has an authority of its own, and does not need to be grounded in ancient texts, however sacred they may be. On the other hand, no one has new experiences outside the tradition in which he stands and from which he creates new possibilities of articulating the new element. For all our critical questions, in this perspective the midrash exegesis of Hebrews becomes especially significant, especially against the background of contemporary Judaism and early Christianity.

## §2   A priestly conception of grace and salvation

### I.  THE FOUNDATION: JESUS IS 'FROM GOD' AND 'FROM MEN'

#### A. Jesus is the Son and not an angel

'In many and various ways God spoke of old to our fathers by the prophets; but in these last days he has spoken to us by a Son, whom he appointed the heir of all things, through whom also he created the world' (Heb. 1.1f.). This is the way in which the preacher begins his homily – in a solemn, almost oriental fashion. Perhaps its nucleus is the kind of Christian hymn that we find among the Hellenistic Jewish-Christian mission to the Gentiles (e.g. Phil. 2.5–11; Col. 1.15–20; I Tim. 3.16; I Peter 3.18–22; John 1.1–14).[127] More probably, however, this is the author himself, beginning in a solemn style. The message which has been given to us over the course of history by the prophets reaches its finale and its decisive expression in the Son, in these last days. 'The Son' is the centre of attention.

As the Son, *Jesus* is 'the reflection of the glory of God' and the 'stamp of his nature' (1.3, *charaktēr*, where II Cor. 4.4 and Col. 1.15 speak of the *'eikōn* of God'; the meaning is 'impression', cf. Wisdom 7.25f.). Jesus is the *charaktēr*[128] of the *hypostasis* of God (cf. Wisdom 16.21). That means that in Jesus we see what makes God God. Here the attributes of Jesus are those of wisdom (Wisdom 7.26; see Wisdom 7.25–8.1; and 9.12; cf. Ps. 110.1). The addition of these attributes to the mention of the Son is not just an expression of the exalted beginning of a solemn homily. At the same time the author is preparing for his image of the priesthood. As reflection and image of God and mediator at creation (Heb. 1.3b), Jesus is at God's side. The reality which is God had manifested itself earlier in many different ways (which for anyone brought up in the setting of Greek culture also meant fragmentary and incomplete ways); now, however, it was manifested 'once for all' in the Son, and in a man of flesh and blood

(2.14), who had suffered and had been tempted (2.18), and knew our weaknesses from his own experience (4.15; above all 5.7–9). In the humanity of Jesus we *see* (*charaktēr*) who and how God is. Thus more than any other New Testament writing, Hebrews gives concrete evidence of the way in which Jesus is the *eidos* or *charaktēr*, impression and expression, of God himself. Jesus' position at God's side is described in terms of *charaktēr*, i.e. in terms of what is visible to man; thus the term also indicates that Jesus is at our side in human life, which is the second aspect of his 'priesthood'. On the one hand, Jesus is the visible expression of God who manifests himself in faithfulness to God (see below); on the other hand, he is a man as we are: the Son knows 'days of his flesh' (5.7), a normal human, mortal life: here he is brother of men (1.5–2.18), the firstborn of many brethren (2.10). These two characteristics – that Jesus takes up God's cause and at the same time shows solidarity with mankind and defends their cause – makes the author of Hebrews realize that what apostolic Christian experience calls salvation from God in Jesus can equally well be expressed in *priestly* terms. Evidently he does not mean to say anything new. He seeks to articulate the apostolic faith in terms which for some reason are popular in the churches in which his homily will be delivered or read out.

Before it takes this theme further, Hebrews *quotes* (from an anthology?) seven texts from the Tanach, to demonstrate, by means of contemporary *pesher* exegesis, that the Son has a higher status than heavenly angelic beings.[129] Evidently it wants to avoid a particular misunderstanding in these churches and to drive home once again traditional faith in the exalted Jesus before making its own view of this exaltation or consummation of Jesus more precise. In some circles at that time the angels were the 'servants of heaven and earth'[130], who set all things in order; this heavenly liturgy is an essential element in early Jewish apocalyptic, and has its place in the context of the expectation of a high-priestly Messiah.[131] This excursus, in which the author in fact wants to demonstrate that Jesus is not an angel but a man and in the last resort is superior to the angels, is also connected with the figure of Melchizedek (a structural element in the letter), since it was in the Melchizedek tradition of early Judaism that this mysterious figure was seen as a particular angel.[132] Thus at the beginning, 'the Son', who became man and is not an angel, occupies a central place.

All the seven quotations from the Tanach go back to the Greek translation. They are as follows:

(*a*) Ps. 2.7 (Heb. 1.5a), which was also interpreted as a messianic prophecy in Qumran (1QSa 2.11). Primitive Christianity looked on this text from a messianic perspective, but originally only in connection with the resurrection of Jesus (Rom. 1.4; Acts 13.33): the quotation was later associated with Isa. 42.1, and in this form made up the 'words from heaven' believed to have been spoken at the baptism of Jesus (Mark 1.11 par.) or at his transfiguration (Luke 9.35).

(*b*) II Sam. 7.14 (Heb. 1.5b). This text, too, was interpreted at Qumran in messianic terms (4QTest). In II Cor. 6.18 Paul associates it with Isa. 52.11, and Rev. 21.7 connects it with Ps. 88.26 (LXX). Hebrews uses it to support the eternal, permanent status of the Son in his special relationship with the Father.

(*c*) Deut. 32.43 LXX (Heb. 1.6) is a tradition associated with Luke 2.13, which mentions the angels at the birth of Jesus. Deut. 32.43, originally used of God, is applied in Hebrews to Jesus: he is worshipped above all angels.

(*d*) Ps. 103.4 (EVV 104.4 cited in Heb. 1.7) was originally cited in connection with the Christian Pentecost (Acts 2.2). Hebrews uses this text to show that, in contrast to the Son, angels are 'created'.

(*e*) Ps. 44.7f. (EVV 45.6f. cited in Heb. 1.8f.). In this royal psalm, used at a royal wedding, it is said of the king that 'God is my throne.' Here Hebrews says indirectly that the Son is *ho theos*, God (Heb. 1.8b–9).[133]

(*f*) Ps. 101.26–28 (EVV 102.25–27, cited in Heb. 1.10–12), applied to Jesus: he is the creator and eschatological judge.

(*g*) Ps. 110.1 (LXX Ps. 109.1, cited in Heb. 1.13). This particular verse is also cited regularly elsewhere in the New Testament (Rom. 8.34; Eph. 1.20; Col. 3.1; I Peter 3.22; Rev. 5.1; Mark 12.35–37, etc.). Like wisdom, Jesus is pre-existent. Thus in Hebrews, what was originally a scriptural proof for the exaltation or resurrection of Jesus becomes an argument for his pre-existence.

This polemic about the angels is heightened and brought to a climax in Heb. 2.5–8, with the help of Ps. 8.4–6. Man is '*a little lower* than the angels'; *brachy ti* (a little) can also be understood temporally, 'for a short while', and this was the interpretation given to that particular verse of the psalm at the time. *For a while* humiliated man will be crowned with glory, and all other creatures will have to do him homage (2.5–8). The background to the whole of this argument (which can be found in the inter-testamental literature) is Gen. 1.26: man is 'God's image' and 'Lord of the world'.[134] Jesus is the last Adam, to whom everything is subjected. He is the exalted humiliated one. Here Hebrews gives an exegesis of Ps. 8 with the help of Ps. 110.1 (both also occur together in I Cor. 15.25–27, where Jesus is the man from heaven and the last Adam, I Cor. 15.22, 45). In Hebrews Adam is not mentioned explicitly, but there is mention of man and Jesus,[135] who are viewed on the same level (*autō* appears three times, and refers both to everyman and to Jesus: Heb. 2.5–7; see 2.10–18). Any man, even Jesus, is provisionally subject to the power of the angels; however, the risen Jesus is the eschatological man who is exalted above all angels who must now worship him. In becoming man, Jesus identifies himself as a priest with the people, 'his brothers'. Jesus, the Son – and not the angels – is the mediator between heaven and earth.

Hebrews evidently represents polemic against a form either of 'angel christology', of which we can find further traces in the early church,[136] or of the cult of angels, which is thought to be superior to the belief in Christ – a mixture of Jewish apocalypticism and Hellenistic-Jewish mysticism, a variety of notions which will have been current in a Greek-speaking synagogue in Alexandria, in which the influence of Qumran (or a similar mentality to Qumran) was combined with a Middle Platonic syncretism. We may well see this as the background to Hebrews. After this initial clarification, the author begins to develop his theme. The two aspects of the Son, namely the 'reflection and image of God' (standing at God's side) and 'brother of man' (standing on our side of life), above all in sacrificial service, bring the author to the idea of priesthood. This causes him to make a new interpretation of the full apostolic tradition in terms of a sacerdotal, i.e. priestly and messianic christology, soteriology and doctrine of grace. This philanthropic christology, which works with what in the last resort is a very simple concept of priesthood, is made difficult for us by the complicated comparisons with the Old Testament and Jewish sacrifices for the great day of atonement (Kippur) and the sacrifice connected with the Mosaic tent of meeting. However, for Hebrews what seems to us to be a sacral reinterpretation of the *layman* Jesus in terms of Jewish priesthood is a demythologization of the Jewish image of priesthood. For the author, the love of the human Jesus who suffers for others, in faithfulness to God and in solidarity with the history of human suffering, is priesthood in the true sense of the word: bringing men to God.

## B. The essence of the account in Hebrews

Hebrews 3.1–6 and 4.15–5.10 present the two aspects of the theme to be discussed, which are then developed further in 7.1–10.18.[137] 3.1–6 is concerned with Jesus' faithfulness to God; 4.15–5.10 deals in particular with his solidarity with suffering men[138] – the two aspects of the priesthood of Jesus. 'We have much to say on this theme,' the author confesses (5.11), whereas in 8.1 he says explicitly that the essence of his whole account, i.e. the many things that he has to say, is contained in the exaltation of Jesus to God.

As far as the author's view of the world is concerned, the fact that Jesus, the pre-existent Son (1.2), is man means that as a result of his humanity, like all his brethren he is 'made a little lower than the angels' (2.5–8; Ps. 8.4–6) – as we have said, at that time this was understood to mean 'for a little while lower than the angels'. Thus the true humanity of Jesus is stressed in very realistic terms: for this particular author, to be human means to be subjected to higher heavenly powers. This means that Jesus is a man who in all things can experience human destiny from the inside: he takes part in it (7.26). Because he lives in a world which is subject to good and evil spirits, and shows solidarity with all men, Jesus can be tempted (4.15) and suffer (2.10–14; 5.7; 2.16–18; 12.2f. etc.). 'That is why he is not ashamed to call them brethren' (2.11), just as 'God is not ashamed to be called their God' (11.16). The author has the ability to suggest a soteriological christology, often in a short, pregnant phrase. Therefore to lead the life 'of flesh and blood' (2.13f.) is a humiliation for the one who is the Son: for the Son, to become man is to be degraded below the angels. It was evidently the most difficult point for many of the Christians to whom Hebrews is addressed. Jesus becomes the lowly one, the inferior one – in Hebrews, a general theme of the synoptic gospels and the New Testament as a whole is set in a cosmic perspective in which the world of spirits belongs to a higher reality than the earthly world of men – at least for the moment. In essence, this is the same humiliation as, for example, in the christological hymn in Phil. 2.6–11, but Hebrews fills it out in a very human way. Granted, the author could have done this better by referring to the words and deeds of the earthly Jesus as presented in the synoptic gospels to the Christian churches. However, he does it indirectly, from scripture: here Moses is the model (who is surpassed by Jesus). For Moses was the 'adopted' son of Pharaoh (Ex. 2.10). However, says Hebrews, when he saw the suffering of his people (Heb. 11.23–27), he showed solidarity 'with his brethren' (2.11; 2.17; 5.1; see 12.2) and thus took up the cause of his brothers before Yahweh, the God of Israel (11.25; 3.1–6). Moses preferred the humiliation of life in solidarity with his brethren, rather than to enjoy the delights in store for him as the adopted son of Pharaoh (in Hebrews, the formal content of the *morphē tou theou* – the form of God – and the *homoiōma tōn anthropōn* – similarity with man – from Phil. 2.6–11 derives its significance from the model of Moses. In reality, of course, it is the life of Jesus himself which makes the author take up this model, which was very familiar to the Jews of his time). Moses turned his back on the fleshpots and the rich storehouses of Egypt in order to stand at the side of his tormented people (11.26). It is the same with Jesus. Although he is 'the Son', he shows solidarity with mankind and becomes a man of suffering (2.9–18; 4.15), in order to free his brethren from slavery (and thus from subjection to the angels) (2.15). It is clear from the fact that the author regards Moses' suffering as being a share in the suffering of Jesus (13.13) that Jesus, the new Moses, is greater than Moses himself (Jesus is the point of juncture and the link between the two ages!). Because God's cause was at stake in the Egyptian slavery of the Jews, his brothers, 'Moses turned away his eyes' (11.26: *ap-eblepen*) from the good fortune destined for him, in order to turn towards the suffering of his people. This interpretation of Moses shows on the one hand how the Christian experience of Jesus drove Jews towards such an approach, and on the other hand how the interpretative element, or the model, again coloured the way in which Jesus was experienced and presented in the New Testament. For with the picture of Moses before his eyes, the author goes on to say, 'Although he was God's Son, he learnt obedience in the school of suffering (i.e. in the lowliest possible situations) . . . and so he has become the cause of eternal salvation for all who obey him' (5.7–9). In view of mankind's actual history of suffering, Hebrews regards this so to speak as an *appropriate* course of action on God's part: 'For it was fitting that he for whom and by whom all things exist, in bringing many sons to glory, should make the pioneer of their salvation perfect through suffering' (2.10). The somewhat harsher, a priori *dei* (Christ had to suffer) which appears in the Gospels of Mark and Luke is here tempered so that it becomes an obvious course of redemption and liberation.

Two concepts are represented in Hebrews by the one concept of priesthood. These are, standing at God's side, i.e. for the Son who became man, faithfulness to God (3.1–6), and at the same time taking sides with man, i.e. compassionate solidarity above all with suffering mankind (4.15–5.10). The problem is: how can Jesus be mediator between God and man if he renounces his divine status and subjects himself to human destiny? How can this service be used 'for the consummation'? For the author does not reflect on the significance of the incarnation as such; his perspective is 'the world of the future' (2.5). Consequently he himself calls the consummation of Christ, Jesus' glorification to the right hand of God, the *kephalaion* or essence of his account (8.1). Only then is the concept of 'priesthood' fully analysed, and above all, then the humiliation or subjection of Jesus – below the angels – through the incarnation is done away with. In this way emphasis is laid on the *heavenly* priesthood of Jesus. For during his earthly life Jesus can only be understood to 'stand at God's side' in terms of the obedient faithfulness of a man towards God (3.1–6). His *charaktēr theou* manifests itself in this faithfulness; in other words, this faithfulness shows what and who God is: a God of men. The consequences of this are as follows. However much the sacrificial human existence of Jesus in obedient faithfulness to God is an essential aspect of his priesthood, the accent nevertheless lies on his perfect, i.e. heavenly priesthood. Only then is he exalted above all angels, in the highest sphere of reality, with God. The *teleiōsis* or consummation is in fact the heart of the whole account in Hebrews. For the consequence is that a man, one of us, has made his way to the supreme heights, beyond the seven heavenly spheres, beyond the angelic world, to the holy of holies, where the living God dwells. Only after that is man's cause pleaded at the highest level, before God himself, by a man. Only then is there an end to utopian futures, which are replaced by a real, well-grounded hope for men. 'He has entered heaven itself, now to appear in the presence of God on our behalf' (9.24); 'he is seated for ever at the right hand of God' (10.12) – in this way he can plead our cause before God (5.1), 'to intercede for our concerns before God' (2.17b).

At the same time, Hebrews seeks in this way to express God's preference for the insignificant and the lowly. He has chosen something lower than the angels: 'in the last resort God has not chosen an angel to sit beside him on the throne' (1.13; 2.16; 2.5; see Isa. 41.8f.)! God takes the lowly by the hand (2.16, *epi-lambanein*), cares for them, has mercy on them and himself shares in the fate of *men*, the descendants of Abraham: 'He himself likewise partook of the same nature, that through death he might destroy him who has the power of death, that is, the devil, and deliver all those who through fear of death were subject to lifelong bondage. For surely it is not with angels that he is concerned but with the descendants of Abraham. Therefore he had to be made like his brethren in every respect' (2.14–17). All this lies at the heart of Hebrews (8.1), and is the author's theological understanding of experience of salvation from God in Jesus. He then goes on to analyse its two aspects in detail; at least, he explains them in terms of the Jewish understanding of worship or sacrifice (in a way which would be obvious to Christian Jews).

Now in accordance with the model of Jewish sacrifice (Deut. 18.5; Num. 3.12, 41; 8.6), two functions of priesthood must be distinguished (without being separated): a priest must (*a*) represent man before God (Heb. 5.1), i.e. plead for man's concerns before God (2.17b), and (*b*) present 'gifts and sacrifices for their sins' (5.1b), i.e. 'atone for the sins of the people' (2.17c).

Thus if we connect what Hebrews calls the heart of its argument, the basis of its soteriological christology, with this Jewish understanding of the priestly cult, we are led to the conclusion that the author wants to present traditional apostolic faith in the earthly life of Jesus – as faithfulness to God in solidarity with man – and in Jesus' death and resurrection or glorification in the presence of God, and make it understandable for Jews who have become Christians and for whom worship was the most important thing in their religious life. At the same time he was writing for Jews who in the early Jewish syncretism of those days dreamed dreams of sharing in the 'heavenly liturgy' of the angels. The author tries to explain what he described in 8.1 as the crucial point of his account – Jesus' position at the right hand of God (a traditional item of Christian belief) – in terms of the 'heavenly liturgy' with which the Jewish sacrificial cult was replaced. Just as, according to Pauline theology, the grace of Christ robs the *Law* of its force, so in Hebrews it makes (Jewish) *worship* obsolete. The grace of the Law and the grace of worship must be replaced by the final *grace of Jesus Christ*. Both of them, Law and cult, have had a positive but provisional significance.

## C. Jesus is the eschatological high priest

'Every high priest chosen from among men is appointed to act on behalf of men in relation to God' (5.1). Priesthood or mediation presupposes election and appointment ('chosen from' is election and thus 'separation'); no one can appoint himself priest (5.4). Not even the eschatological high priest can do that. So he is appointed by God to priestly service (5.5). This happened, 'when God said, "You are my Son, today have I begotten you" ' (Ps. 2.7), and at another point, 'You are a priest for ever after the order of Melchizedek' (Ps. 110.4; Heb. 5.5b–6; 5.10). By combining Ps. 2.7 with Ps. 110.4, the author seeks to justify in biblical terms his association of traditional elements of belief (the sonship and resurrection of Jesus) with the concept of priesthood. This proves necessary if we remember that Heb. 5.5b–6 is the only passage in the New Testament in which a striking new argument is present. It goes as follows. If Ps. 110.1 is applied to Christ, namely to his exaltation to the Father (or his 'sitting at the right hand of God') as was *generally* the case throughout the early church (Mark 12.36; 14.62; 16.19; Matt. 22.44; 26.64; Luke 20.42f.; 22.69; Acts 2.34; 5.31; I Cor. 15.25; Eph. 1.22; Col. 3.1; Hebrews itself, 1.3; 1.13; 8.1; 10.12f.; 12.2; 5.6–10; 6.20; 7.3, 11, 15, 17, 21, 24, 28; see Phil. 2.9; I Peter 3.22), then it is essential to be consistent and also apply Ps. 110.4 to Jesus. The kingly exaltation (Ps. 110.1) of Christ *is* at the same time his exaltation as priest (Ps. 110.4, see also Heb. 1.5; 1.13; 7.21): 'Yahweh said to my Lord, "Sit at my right hand and I will soon make your enemies your footstool" (Ps. 110.1), and "Yahweh has sworn, he will not take it back. You will be a priest for ever by virtue of my pronouncement, Melchizedek" (Ps. 110.4).' The reference to Ps. 2.7 (in Heb. 5.5b–6, see 5.10), 'So I say of the Lord's resolve, he said to me, You are my Son, today I have called you to life,' connects the combination of Ps. 110.1 and 110.4 even more strikingly with Jesus as 'the Son' (see Heb. 1.2). It is without parallel in the New Testament here that the whole of this psalm has to be understood christologically and that more than a single verse is related to Jesus (110.1): nowhere else is Jesus or 'Christ' called (high) priest. Is this an invention on the part of the author of Hebrews? Something he simply thought of by himself? Or were there good reasons in Christian tradition for this new interpretation?

The latter is clearly the case. Even before Hebrews, the death of Jesus was expressed in *sacrificial* terms, i.e. with terms from the Jewish sacrificial cult. In Mark 10.45 the death of Jesus was called 'a ransom for many'. The redemptive work of Jesus is also expressed in terms from Jewish sacrificial worship in I Cor. 1.30; 7.23; Rom. 3.24; Col. 1.14; Eph. 2.18 and 1.7; I Peter 1.18; I Tim. 2.5f.; Rev. 1.5; 5.9. Furthermore, Paul spoke of Jesus as the slaughtered paschal lamb (I Cor. 5.7; see also the Deutero-Paulines, Eph. 5.2, and, under Pauline influence, I Peter 1.9; 3.18). John speaks of the 'Lamb which takes away the sins of the world' (John 1.29, 36; see John 19.36). Finally, we hear some twenty-eight times in the book of Revelation about the slain Lamb. In addition, Paul refers to the mercy seat (*hilastērion*, Hebrew *kappōret*) of the tent of the covenant (Rom. 3.24f.). Thus the theme that Jesus is a sacrificial offering can be said to be a general New Testament theme: he is sacrificed in the full meaning of the word. Indeed, this idea found its way into Christian liturgy from the period before the New Testament, i.e. in the so-called words of institution, in the eucharist, which is interpreted either as a covenant sacrifice (so in Luke 22.20a; Mark. 14.24; I Cor. 11.25) or as an atoning sacrifice (Matt. 26.26–28). Christ is the sacrificial victim: the author of Hebrews regards this simply as part of the apostolic tradition. Nevertheless, in this traditional apostolic faith it is not explicitly stated elsewhere that Jesus is the sacrificer and priest as well as the sacrificial victim. However, this idea is not an exclusive discovery on the part of Hebrews. In addition to Hebrews, there are two other New Testament texts in which Jesus' priesthood is at least hinted at, on one occasion rather vaguely, when Paul speaks of Jesus 'who, sitting at the right hand of God, makes intercession for us' (Rom. 8.34: the content is precisely what Hebrews calls the heavenly priesthood of Jesus, Heb. 7.25): it occurs clearly again in Rev. 1.13 where Jesus is represented as clothed with the *priestly* talar and girded with the golden girdle after the manner of a priest (see below in connection with the book of Revelation).

So we have good reason for claiming that the step taken by Hebrews, to move from Ps. 110.1 to Ps. 110.4 and understand both as christological statements, was quite a natural one, even in terms of the Christian tradition. It was also a help to this Christian interpretation that Ps. 110.4 was already interpreted messianically in early Judaism, e.g. in Qumran.[139] So we can understand why on the one hand no New Testament text other than Hebrews calls Jesus priest, while on the other hand the designation of Christ as priest seems quite obvious to the author of Hebrews. We can find the essence of the claim that Jesus is a priest throughout the New Testament, but Jesus is nowhere explicitly called priest in the New Testament outside the Epistle to the Hebrews. It was impossible for primitive Christianity to express the significance of Jesus in priestly terms,

because to the Jewish mind priest essentially meant levitical priest, someone from the tribe of Levi. Jesus did not come from the tribe of Levi; for
the Jews he was descended from a lay tribe, the tribe of Judah. The
author of Hebrews, on the other hand, can call Jesus priest without any
hesitation because throughout his argument (and above all in Heb. 7) he
has presented a picture of the priesthood which escapes the essential
Jewish requirement of levitical descent. Hebrews does not in any way
reject the other meanings or functions of priestly service, which are also
Jewish; these concern the essence of priesthood, namely, interceding for
men and bringing atonement for sins. These two functions are in fact the
pivots on which his whole account turns. So Hebrews can happily speak
of the priestly messiahship of Jesus without coming into conflict with the
rest of the New Testament. Hebrews does not in any way reinterpret
Christianity in terms of Judaism. It is more correct to say that it 'demythologizes' the priestly image, current in Judaism and throughout late
antiquity, of the pontifical priest. This is made more human by showing
how the priest has solidarity with suffering mankind, how God confirms
the validity of such a pattern of life, and how Jesus in heaven defends
men's concerns before God.

### D. 'Christ' means 'messianic high priest'

Our analysis also makes clear the particular significance which Hebrews
attaches to the traditional word 'the Christ'. Many exegetes have been
struck by the way in which Hebrews, unlike any other New Testament
writing (outside the gospels and Acts), often speaks of Jesus in absolute
terms, without adding 'Christ' (thus 2.9; 3.1; 4.14; 6.20; 7.22; 10.19; 12.2,
24; 13.12; 13.20; we also find Jesus Joshua in 4.8). On the other hand,
we sometimes find 'the Christ' used without any mention of Jesus: *ho
Christos* (5.5; 9.28; 3.14; 6.1; 9.14). Furthermore, apart from 11.26, where
'the Christ' or the anointed refers to the Jewish people, and three occurrences of Christ without the article (3.6; 9.11; 9.24), and finally the
expression 'Jesus Christ', which also occurs three times (10.10; 13.8;
13.21),[140] about ten passages in Hebrews stress 'Jesus', the historical
Jesus of Nazareth. This interpretation is attractive, above all for those
who regard the earthly Jesus of Nazareth as the norm and criterion for
christological thinking. However, I believe that this interpretation of the
so-called absolute use of 'Jesus' in Hebrews rests on an optimistic
delusion.

   In almost all the texts containing the word 'Jesus' that I have cited,
Jesus is immediately qualified by the term 'priest', understood in terms
of the priestly Messiah. In the tradition which takes this view of the

Messiah, the word anointed, or Christ, in fact means priest. So *'the high priest' Jesus* means precisely the same as *Jesus Christ*. In each occurrence of the so-called absolute use of Jesus we find the name Christ in some form. This is the case, for example, in Heb. 3.1: 'Jesus, the apostle and high priest', that is, Jesus the high priest sent by God. Also, 'seeing that we have a high priest (= a Christ), Jesus' (4.14). Or, 'whither Jesus has gone before us, now that he is high priest (= Christ)' (6.20). 'Jesus, the author and perfecter of faith' (12.2: Jesus as perfecter lies at the heart of the picture of the priesthood presented by Hebrews, see 8.1 and further below). Also, 'Jesus, mediator (= priest = Christ), of a new covenant' (12.24; the same in 13.20). A solemn explanation of the title Christ or priest for Jesus is given in Heb. 7.21 (see 7.22). This leaves only two texts in which 'Jesus' seems to be used absolutely: 'The blood of Jesus' (10.19) and 'Jesus, who suffered outside the city gates' (13.12), two texts which mention particular events connected with the *earthly Jesus*: his crucifixion on Golgotha, at that time immediately in front of the city gates of Jerusalem. In fact, here we find that subtle distinction between what happened to Jesus *on earth* and what happens through him *in heaven* (we find this distinction even in Paul, e.g. Rom. 8.11; II Cor. 4.10; Gal. 6.17). Hebrews calls what is referred to elsewhere in the New Testament as the appointing of Jesus as the Christ or the Son of God in power or the public recognition of this at the resurrection (Rom. 1.4; Acts 2.36) – the heavenly institution of Jesus (i.e. consummation or ratification) as messianic priest ( = Christ). Even Hebrews 5.5, 'So also Christ did not exalt himself to be made a high priest', a text in which we would expect to find Jesus: even *Jesus* did not high-handedly adopt the *title Christ*, confirms this rather than telling against it. Here we have *ho Christos*, i.e. even the one, only true high priest (the messianic priest) did not high-handedly claim this messianic dignity: it was graciously bestowed on him through his election. This whole line of interpretation, namely that for Hebrews 'Christ' means '(high) priest', is quite evident from the whole context in Lev. 4.1–5.13, above all in Lev. 4.3–12, where we have the mention of 'Christ', the priest as the anointed one who makes the atoning sacrifice (the framework within which Hebrews thinks). There is no mention in Hebrews of a *special* interest in the *earthly* Jesus that stands out from the rest of the New Testament; the author thinks in terms of the (Jewish) models which are familiar to his audience. The fact that he does this is connection with *Jesus* is doubtless a consequence of what he has heard about him in the apostolic proclamation. Nevertheless, he devotes his attention largely to the model of Moses and the lawgiving on Sinai which will have been known to his Christian Jewish audience in order to explain the significance of Jesus for salvation.

Hebrews takes up both the wisdom tradition and early Jewish speculations about the royal and priestly characteristics of the Messiah or Christ. Jews had been preoccupied with the question of the separation or combination of royal and priestly functions from the time of the Maccabees onwards;[141] even in Qumran the emphasis was constantly shifting. For a long time this Essene community laid stress on priestly messiahship, while the Pharisees emphasized the royal, Davidic Messiah. In the long run, however, a tendency developed in Qumran either to connect the royal (and therefore warlike) understanding of the Messiah with the high-priestly Messiah or to look for two Messiahs. As far as terminology goes, Hebrews has nothing to do with the warlike royal view of the Messiah; it is firmly in the line of the tradition of the priestly Messiah as this was carried on (or at least had been carried on) among believing Jews, even in the Qumran community, who wanted to 'live like angels', 'in expectation of the world of the future'.[142] True, this is not the main concern of Hebrews, but the author did combine the two messianic characteristics in one person *who came from Judah* (7.14); and that is quite unknown in Qumran and the apocryphal literature. For Hebrews, Jesus is the Christ, that is, the eschatological high priest, just as Melchizedek is king and high priest. The royal aspect is stressed only to demonstrate the eschatological superiority of Jesus Christ over the angels; but the author sees in this kingship more the heavenly, incorruptible and eternal character of the priestly messiahship of Jesus: 'after the order of Melchizedek' is *eternal* priesthood (see 5.10; 6.20; 7.8, 16, 17, 21, 24, 25, 28; 10.12, 14). Because of the image of priesthood to be found in Hebrews (the suffering believer, with a clear allusion to the servant of Yahweh), one might call it a priesthood along the lines of what Anglo-Saxon exegetes often call 'servant messianism'.

## II. THE MINISTRY OF THE MESSIANIC PRIEST JESUS

According to Heb. 5.1 and 2.17b, a priest defends men before God, and according to 5.1b and 2.17c he offers sacrifice to God to expiate sins. How and where does the author find this twofold function in the messianic ministry of Jesus?

### A. The solidarity of Jesus with human suffering. Jesus' sacrifice of his life

Hebrews says that Jesus can plead man's cause before God because of his divine vocation or election (5.5); however, this is elaborated in quite specifically human terms. 'We have a high priest who can sympathize with our weaknesses. He has been tested in many respects as we have, yet without sinning' (4.15). 'He can deal gently with the ignorant and wayward, since he himself is beset with weakness' (5.2). 'In the days of his flesh, Jesus offered up prayers and supplication, with loud cries and tears, to the God who was able to save him from death' (5.7). 'Although he was a Son, he learned obedience through what he suffered' (5.8). Hebrews – like Mark and I Peter – sees the priestly ministry of Jesus explicitly in terms of *solidarity with human suffering*. Hebrews calls Jesus' solidarity with mankind and his readiness for sacrifice the purpose of his life (10.5–7).

'In all things like to us, sin alone excepted.' It is unknown in rabbinic literature that the Messiah should be 'sinless', but it is a known factor in Jewish apocalyptic.[143] It is a widespread primitive Christian tradition (John 8.46; II Cor. 5.21; I John 3.5; I Peter 2.22). For all his readiness to sacrifice himself (10.5–7), Jesus knew weaknesses and temptations (4.15; 5.7). 'With loud cries and tears' can be an allusion to the synoptic account of Gethsemane, but it may have been suggested above all by Ps. 116 and Pss. 22.2, 24; 31.2; 39.12; 69.13 (which are, in fact, psalms which also play a role in the synoptic passion narratives). From a Jewish point of view, obedience is of the essence of any childhood (see Heb. 10.5–10; John 4.34; 5.30; 6.38–40), but Hebrews says, '*although* he was God's Son'. For it is specifically concerned with obedience in the lowly state of subjection to the angels, that is, to death (see Heb. 2.15), just as Moses, 'although he was Pharaoh's son', was obedient to Yahweh out of solidarity with his brothers (11.24–26). 'For the joy that was set before him he endured the cross, despising the shame' (12.2b). Thus Jesus had to learn obedience in suffering. *Emathen aph'hōn epathen* (5.8) is a Greek proverb from the educational theory of the ancient world: beating makes a person wiser: the Greeks said (with a play on words) *pathos* (suffering) brings *mathos* (learning or wisdom)[144] (see also Heb. 12.2–13). Thus the correct translation is that Jesus learnt God's purpose for his life in the 'school of suffering'. So he was faithful to God's cause (3.1–4.13): 'He was faithful to God who appointed him' (3.2) – again like Moses, but in a preferable way (3.2–6), for Moses was faithful '*in* the house of God', while Christ was faithful as Son, appointed over the house of God (3.6a).

Thus Hebrews locates the priestly ministry of Jesus, in faithfulness to God and in solidarity with suffering mankind, in the crucifixion of Jesus, which is interpreted by the author as a *priestly sin-offering* and *covenant-offering*. For the expiation of sins is just one of the two functions of a priest: 'to sacrifice for the people'. The technical formula in Lev. 4.1–5.13 runs (repeated several times): 'So the priest shall make atonement *for them* for their sins, and so they will be forgiven' (Lev. 4.20; 4.26b; 4.31c; 4.35c; 5.6b). These are ritual formulae. Hebrews refers the stereotyped formula, 'So the priest shall make atonement for them for their sins' to Jesus, the real 'anointed priest', or *the Christ* (as the priest is repeatedly called in Lev. 4.1–5.13). He analyses in detail this satisfaction made by Jesus for the sins of men, by contrasting it with what Jewish priests do.

Hebrews contrasts the 'many times' of Jewish sacrifice or the 'once a year' of the sacrifice on the great Day of Atonement with the final *ephapax*, the once-for-allness of the one all-sufficient sacrifice of Jesus the high priest (7.23; 10.1f., 11f). We also find here an echo of the Greek idea that 'the many' must naturally be fragmentary and incomplete by contrast with the perfection of 'the one' (see also 1.1). But the author sees more in it. As the more exalted priest after the order of Melchizedek, Jesus offers a perfect sacrifice which is completed by God (7.1–28): his life. This is described in 9.1–28 in terms of the ceremonial of the Day of Atonement. On this day, once a year, the Jewish high priest sacrificed a bull for his own sins and those of his priestly tribe (7.27); he then entered the holy of holies to offer incense on the mercy seat above the ark of the covenant;[145] then he went in a second time to sprinkle the ark with the blood of the bull. After this ritual he sacrificed a second victim, a goat, for the sins *of the whole people* and again sprinkled the mercy seat with blood. Hebrews 9.1–10 regards these two bloody sacrifices and the taking of blood into the holy of holies, where the ark or the throne of God is set, as parts of a whole; the author compares them with Jesus' crucifixion, to demonstrate the inadequacy of this ritual slaughter (9.11–22).

God's deepest purpose with Jesus and Jesus' learning in the school of suffering' are projected in Hebrews on to a conversation between God and the Son at the moment of the incarnation (but as it were already in our world): 'Consequently, when Christ came into the world, he said, Sacrifices and offerings thou has not desired, but a body thou hast prepared for me; in burnt offerings and sin offerings thou hast taken no pleasure. Then I said, Lo, I have come to do thy will, O God' (10.5–7). Psalm 40.7–9 is put on the lips of Jesus on his entry into the human world. True, Jesus cried and pleaded to be spared this death (5.7), but his voluntary acceptance of it was included *in his own career*, as faithfulness to the God who had sent him. Like Paul, Hebrews concentrates the redemption brought by Jesus wholly and utterly in his death (and resurrection). 'By his will we have been *sanctified* through the offering of the body of Jesus Christ once for all' (10.10). The significance of the life of Jesus lies in his crucifixion as *a voluntary self-sacrifice* (9.14; 9.22; 9.25. 26, 28) or a *sacrificial self-surrender* (10.9; also 2.10, 18; 4.15; 5.9) – this is in any case already a traditional Christian interpretation (I Thess 5.10; Gal. 2.20; Matt. 20.28; John 3.16; 12.23f., etc., and later I John 3.16; 4.10). 'Once for all' (7.27; 9.12; 10.10; see 9.26; 9.28), i.e. irrevocably, decisively and finally, no new sacrifices are needed any more. The author underlines the self-surrender of the person of Jesus in this sacrificial giving. These accents make relative, without negating, the 'theology of blood' which is to be found in Hebrews because of the framework of the Day of Atonement within which the author now puts the death of Jesus, and because of the theology of blood which is characteristic of Jewish propitiatory sacrifices in accordance with the interpretation in Lev. 17.11.[146] The crucifixion is also seen as a *bloody* sacrifice (1.3; 9.7; 9.18; see 9.25; 10.29; 13.12; 13.20). By means of the sacrificial love expressed in it, Jesus is 'the mediator of a new covenant with sprinkled blood that speaks more graciously than the blood of Abel' (12.24: here the imagery of the Day of Atonement shifts to the picture of the murder of righteous Abel); its fruit is above all inward forgiveness of sins and access to God (see below). Unmistakably, the accent is not so much on the blood as on the human self-surrender *in* this bloody death (see above; and also 2.6–10, 17, 18; 5.7; and the whole of chapter 9). The author puts the idea of the crucifixion of Jesus as an atoning sacrifice (the so-called soteriological pattern), which can be found throughout the New Testament,[147] in the context of bloody sacrifice by a Jewish priest. The picture of the 'precious blood' which is already well-known throughout the New Testament (see above all I Peter 1.19 and the references already mentioned) is in no way 'spiritualized' in Hebrews (with a stress on love and free will); rather, it is interpreted in more human terms as sacrificial service in solidarity with brethren who live in fear of death (see 2.15) and suffer.

Hebrews understands the crucifixion as a sin offering and a covenant sacrifice and thus integrates two traditions: the crucifixion as a covenant sacrifice (I Cor. 11.25; Mark 14.24; Luke 22.20a and Matt. 26.28a) and as a sin-offering (Matt. 26.28b).[148] The two sacrifices were sharply distinguished in the Tanach. The covenant sacrifice was offered with a view to communion with God; therefore it was concluded with the eating of sacrificial meat. By contrast, it was not lawful to eat the meat of the sin-offering; this meat had to be burnt to ashes outside the camp or outside the city gates (Lev. 16.27; Heb. 13.11). However, later all sacrifices were also seen as sin offerings, because man first had to purge himself of sins before entering into covenant community with God. So in Hebrews we should not interpret the model in a one-sided way. The author is concerned with the sacrifice of Jesus' life; the imagery of the covenant, of reconciliation and even of the blood of Abel (which has nothing to do with either covenant or reconciliation), run into one another. (In 9.18–22 it becomes clear how the idea of the Day of Atonement goes over into the idea of the covenant rite.)

However, the author is primarily thinking of the image of the sin-offering (and thus of the forgiveness of sins). The context of his account is the *yōm hakkippūrīm*, the great Jewish Day of Atonement (9.1–10). Outside priestly terminology, *kipper* means to bring about reconciliation by offering a gift; in priestly usage it acquires the connotation of bringing about reconciliation by performing a ritual prescribed by the law (Lev. 4.31–35).[149] In Judaism, even according to rabbinic theology, only God can forgive sins. The sacrificial rite has atoning force when the rite is performed in a way prescribed by God himself (Lev. 7.11); in that case sins are not counted. Thus atonement is taking away, not counting and expiating sins, and therefore atoning for sins (Heb.2.17; see Ps. 65.3; Sir. 3.3, 30). For Hebrews the one and decisive *kippur* sacrifice is the crucifixion of Jesus, through which all sins have been blotted out (9.15, 22, 26, 28; 10.17f.). 'The blood of his sacrifice is his own blood, not that of goats and calves. So he has entered into the sanctuary once and for all, and has secured an eternal redemption' (9.12). Because of the decisive and final character of this sin offering it is also the sacrifice for a new covenant: 'Therefore he is the mediator of a new covenant, so that those who are called may receive the promised inheritance, since a death has occurred which redeems them from the transgressions under the first covenant' (9.15). The sprinkling of the whole of the tent of the covenant by Moses – and not by Aaron, who had to offer the sin offering – was an act of consecration by which the tent and all that went with it was removed from the secular sphere and dedicated to God. So for Hebrews the crucifixion of Jesus is not only a purification from sins but also a *sanctification*, in the sense of a dedication to the God of the covenant. In this way Christians are no longer earthly, or of this age, but heavenly: they belong to the world of the future (see 9.21–23).

For Hebrews, purification from sin (10.2) and sanctification (*hagiazein*: 10.10; 13.12; see also John 17.19) does not exhaust or complete the full meaning of the true sacrifice; this sacrifice requires a *teleiōsis*, a perfecting by God (10.14). Important though the sacrifice of Jesus may be, without its completion by God Hebrews can only regard it as a *vain* sacrifice. It is concerned with this consummation: 'that is the essence of our account' (8.1), just as in 2.5 he has said, 'The world of the future is our real theme' (cf. 10.1; 11.1). What is this consummation?

## B. Advocate of man to God: access to God

In the summary (5.7–10) of what he will later be analysing in detail, the author mentions in technical terminology the three important elements which are present in a final and effective sacrifice: (*a*) being heard (5.7), (*b*) being brought to completion (5.9), (*c*) being called an appointed high priest with power (5.10).

'Now the heart of our account is that we have such a high priest who has sat down at the right hand of the throne of the Majesty in heaven' (8.1). The author has already repeatedly outrun himself (e.g. 7.19; 7.25b). What is to be explained in detail in 5.11–10.39 has already been summarized briefly in 5.9f. : (*a*) he presented prayers and petitions to God with loud cries and tears. . .; because of his piety (that is, his fear of God, *eulabeia*, and thus his humble faithfulness to God), he has been *heard* (5.7); (*b*) in him the *perfection* or *teleiōsis* of the sacrifice has been achieved (5.9), in contrast to the ineffective sacrifices of animals (8.1–9.28); (*c*) consequently Jesus is appointed high priest in the full exercise of his ministry (5.10), and he is the 'cause of eternal salvation' (5.9), since his consummation is to be 'called by God to be high priest after the order of Melchizedek' (5.10), that is, an *eternal* royal *priesthood* (7.1–28), like Melchizedek, but with a higher status (7.25); (*d*) the consolation of the gospel, which the author offers in a closing paraenetic section, is based on this dogmatic foundation (10.19–39).

## (*a*) Jesus' sacrifice perfected by God

'Although he was Son of God, he learned obedience in the school of suffering and being made perfect (*teleiōtheis*) . . . he is the source of eternal salvation for all, being designated (*prosagoreutheis*) by God a high priest after the order of Melchizedek' (5.8–10). The pericope makes a close connection between *teleiōtheis* and *prosagoreutheis*, both forms of a theological passive, in which God is the agent, though this is not explicitly said. Hebrews sees the *kephalaion*, the essence and the summary of what it means to convey by its argument as a whole, in the connection between these two (8.1). But what kind of a connection is it? This becomes clear from the Hebrew term, 'sacrifice', which forms the background to Hebrews.

The root meaning of *qārab*[150] is to approach or be near, whether in a spatial sense: 'approach something or someone', or a temporal sense: an approaching event (theologically, above all that of the time of salvation or judgment: Isa. 51.5; 56.1; Ezek. 36.8). Thus to approach someone 'spatially', in the theological sense, to approach God, means in general terms to draw near to Yahweh (Ex. 16.9; Lev. 16.1 ). The content of the phrase is the same as 'to come before God's countenance' (see Lev. 9.5; Deut. 4.11; Ezek. 44.15f.). In the earlier parts of the Tanach, the specific meaning of this is to go to the holy place (those holy places) where Yahweh is present (Ex. 3.5; Deut. 5.26f.; 4.11; Gen. 28.16f.; 32.30), especially to the holy mountain (Deut. 4.11), the tent of the covenant (Lev. 9.5; Num. 18.22), and above all to the sanctuary which contains the ark, the throne of Yahweh (Josh. 3.4 etc.). It is generally the case in these ancient texts that no mortal is allowed to approach Yahweh's dwelling; if he does, he dies (Ex. 3.5; Josh. 3.4; see Gen. 28.16f.). If the people are said to approach Yahweh, then they evidently keep their distance (Deut. 5.26f.; Ex. 16.10: separated by a cloud). Only Moses is allowed to go really close to God (Deut. 4.11; 5.26f.; Ex. 19.12). Later, only the priests will be allowed to approach God's sanctuary (at least in the priestly traditions: Num. 1.51; 3.10, 38; 17.28; 18.7). In later times the presence of Yahweh is not so specifically tied to sanctuaries: he is a God who is 'near' (Jer. 23.23), omnipresent and always close (Deut. 4.7; Isa. 55.6; Ps. 145.18). In that case, to approach God means to pray to him and present petitions to him, to call for his help (I Kings 8.59; Pss. 22.11; 69.18; 119.169). Apart from this general terminology, 'approach God' acquires a very specific significance in priestly and therefore cultic terminology. In the *hiphil* (*hiqrib*), *qārab* is the technical term for offering sacrifices (especially in the great blocks of tradition in Leviticus, Numbers and Ezekiel 43ff.) (the noun *qorbān* then means the sacrifice in a general non-specific sense, Num. 15.4; 15.25; 18.9; Lev. 22.18).

For the author of Hebrews, this general and priestly terminology reproduces the two aspects of what he regards as the Jewish priestly ministry: approaching God in the sense of pleading with him and interceding for men's concerns, and approaching God to offer gifts and sacrifices for the expiation of sins (Heb. 5.1;2.17). Both aspects together indicate that to approach God means to offer him sacrifice, to atone for sins and to ask for grace. 'To sacrifice' means to approach God or 'go up to the throne of grace' (4.16). As always, Hebrews thinks in the categories of the lawgiving on Sinai: of Moses, the mount of God and the tent of the covenant with the ark of the covenant in the holy of holies and the golden mercy seat (*kappōret*) above it (I Chron. 28.2; Jer. 3.16f.; Pss. 132.5,7), the real throne of God, 'the throne of God's mercy' (already in the Greek of Isa. 16.5), which is contrasted with his 'throne of judgment' (Pss. 9.4, 7; 122.5; Prov. 20.8). (The idea is that Yahweh sits on one throne or another, depending whether he is judging, or being gracious and giving *charis*.) Hebrews interprets the aim of all this Jewish priestly ministry as an entreaty for *charis, ḥesed* or grace from God by the offering of a sacrifice or by 'approaching God'. Thus in Hebrews grace takes on a sacrificial colouring – in this sense it is in fact 'officially' more Jewish than the Pauline concept of grace, despite the degree to which Paul also interprets the cross as an expiatory sacrifice. Hebrews speaks only of God's *charis* and never of the grace of Christ (though it does talk of his love and solidarity); however, it sees God's grace from the perspective of the sacrificial priestly mediation of Jesus. The context of the whole argument in Hebrews is therefore as follows: On the great Day of Atonement, the *yōm hakkippūrīm* (Lev. 23.27f.; 25.9), the feast of Kippur, the sacrificial blood of bulls must be brought into the holy of holies, where the high priest sprinkles the 'throne of the grace of God', the mercy seat of the ark of the covenant, with this blood (9.1–10). The sacrificial blood must *come to God* if the participants in the sacrifice themselves want access to God: Hebrews calls this *teleiōsis* or the fulfilment of the sacrifice: access to God. Despite the compelling symbolism – these sacrifices are 'copies of the heavenly things' (9.23), namely the heavenly liturgy, as the 'shadow of good things which are to come' (10.1; see also 9.8f.; 9.24) – the sacrifices of animals could not achieve this *teleiōsis*. 'The law has but a shadow of the good things to come instead of the true form of these realities', so 'it can never, by the same sacrifices which are continually offered year after year, make perfect those who would draw near' (10.1, see also 9.8–10). The author immediately goes on to conclude that 'it is also impossible that the blood of bulls and goats should take away sin' (10.4), a view which is obvious for Christians, but which in Hebrews is given a biblical foundation (Pss. 40.6–8, see Heb. 10.5–7). All these are 'external regulations for the body imposed until the time of reformation' (9.10b), namely with Christ. But 'now Christ has come' (9.11), 'Christ has entered, not into a sanctuary made with hands, a copy of the true one, but into heaven itself, now to appear in the presence of God on our behalf' (9.24). 'He sits at the right hand of the throne of God' (12.2b; see 1.3; 8.1); he has set himself there and will continue to sit there – *kekathiken* (perfect); this word sums up the whole of Hebrews, whose entire christology is concentrated by the author in Jesus' death and session at the right hand of God. Hebrews does not speak directly of the resurrection, and does not mention the 'descent to hell' at all; it does speak of the life of Jesus after his death, of 'redemption' and of 'being brought back' from death (see. 5.7; 13.20). It speaks only once of a 'better *anastasis* (resurrection)' (11.35b).[151] Hebrews presents a theology of suffering and of the heavenly victory or the heavenly 'rest'. The resurrection is presupposed, but is not noted as such. The heavenly high priest *sits*, and the Jewish high priest *stands* (see the word play in 10.11 in contrast to 10.12f.). That means that the risen Jesus, the Christ, celebrates the liturgy of the eternal sabbath rest. The holy of holies in Moses' tent of the covenant, and within it the ark of the covenant, or God's throne of grace, is also called 'God's rest' in II Chron. 6.41 and Pss. 132.8,14. Just as God, who created all things for all eternity, both 'this world' and 'the world of the future' (Heb. 4.3b–4), rested on the seventh day, so too Jesus completed his sacrificial ministry with the sacrifice of his life. From now on he rests by and with God: 'But when Christ had offered for all time a single sacrifice for sins, he *sat down* at the right hand of God, then *to wait* until his enemies should be made a stool for his feet' (10.12f.; for the further heavenly activity of Jesus see below). Hebrews contrasts the activity of the daily

Jewish morning and evening sacrifice, the business of the annual sacrifices on the Day of Atonement, with the one and only sacrifice of Jesus which is followed by the one eternal sabbath rest, that is, 'being with God' ('rest for the people of God' (3.7–19). 'Enter into rest' therefore means to have access to God. This is what the author is referring to with his term *teleiōsis*: access to the sanctuary, i.e. now, to God himself, no longer in shadows or in symbols. This is a free and confident (10.19; 10.35; 4.16; 3.6 – *parrhēsia*) access (10.19; 4.16; 7.19b; 7.25; 10.22; 12.22).

(*b*) Access to God

At a first reading one has the impression that Hebrews sees the ascension of Jesus along the lines of the Greek or oriental model of the journey of a hero through space and the various spheres of heaven to the highest heaven (9.11; 1.6; 4.14; 7.26; 8.1f.; 9.23f.). Access to God presupposes an ascension in which in the end Jesus arrives at the true 'holy of holies', at the real dwelling-place of God (9.11; 1.6), where he takes his place at the right hand of God (that is the place of honour, and at the same time the place of the eschatological priest and judge) (also 5.9; 7.25; 9.24). However, the question is on the one hand a simpler one, and on the other more complicated. The Semites, too, shared in the ancient view of the many heavenly spheres. Like many orientals, they symbolized this view of the world in the institution of the Mosaic tent of the covenant (and the later Temple in Jerusalem). This tent was made up of the 'holy place', i.e. the vestibule, and the 'holy of holies', the sanctuary or the holiest place in which there was the ark and the throne of God (see also 9.1–10). There was a curtain before the vestibule and before the holy of holies. The whole of the heavens was depicted on the front of the curtain. When on the Day of Atonement the high priest went through the curtain of the vestibule as far as the sanctuary with the sacrificial blood, it was as though he had to go through all the *epourania* or heavenly spheres in order to be able to come to God's throne. *Cherubim* were depicted on the other side of this curtain (Ex. 26.1,31; 36. 8,35). Behind them was the sanctuary, protected – like paradise lost – by *cherubim* with fiery swords (Gen. 3.24; indeed, this is a priestly reinterpretation of the tent of the covenant in terms of the history of creation). Thus the tent of the covenant as a whole symbolized the universe, with its *fanum* (sanctuary) and *profanum*, and therefore all the heavenly spheres in which the Inapproachable was enthroned, withdrawn from all eyes. Here was Yahweh, surrounded in concentric circles by the various dwelling-places of many hierarchies of angels and blessed ones.[152] Only the supreme archangels, 'the angels of the presence', dwell in the space reserved for God, as his attendants; the other angels have their abode in the lower heavenly regions and receive their commands through the dark cloud (or the curtain).[153] With a number of differences, this was the general oriental conception of the heavenly spheres, of which the sanctuary on earth formed a copy (also found by scholars for example in the codex of Hammurabi). Wisdom 9.8 says: 'You have commanded me to build a temple . . . a copy of the holy tabernacle which you have already prepared from the very beginning.'[154] Thus the view of the world and the way in which it is symbolized in the tent of the covenant, a copy of the universe, have a reciprocal effect on one another. Hebrews thinks of both the tent of the covenant and the real heaven. It sees the Old Testament sacrifices as being caught up in the symbolism, the human work, which belongs to the first age (9.11c). 'By this way the Holy Spirit indicates that the way into the sanctuary is not yet opened as long as the outer tent is still standing (the tent of the covenant), which is symbolic for the present age' (9.8f.). By means of his ascension Christ has gone through the real spheres of heaven and found a way to God, once and for all. The essence of this recognition is that Jesus lives in glory with the Father. So access to God has been opened up for Christians. But what is the meaning of this access, first of all for Jesus and therefore also for us?

*(i) The heavenly inauguration of Jesus the high priest at the right hand of God*

First of all, if only for a short time, Jesus was 'placed below the angels' (2.6–8; 2.7); now he has been exalted high above all heavenly beings (7.26; 1.3–2.16), 'crowned with glory and honour. You have subjected all things to him' (2.6–8; Ps. 8). 'Now in putting everything in subjection to man, he left nothing outside his control' (2.8), i.e. including the angels. However, '*We do not yet* see everything in subjection to him. But we see Jesus, who for a little while was made lower than the angels, crowned with glory and honour *because of the suffering and death*, so that by the grace of God he might taste death for every one' (2.8c–9). The subjection of the angels is an eschatological event: Jesus 'only waits for this moment' (10.13). On the other hand, they already seem to be subjected (2.6–8), and 'he himself likewise partook of the same nature, that *through death* he might destroy him who has the power of death, that is, the devil' (2.14). In Jesus Christ this death has already been conquered, but not yet in us. For Christians – through faith in Jesus' rest (3.7–19) – that means a true and encouraging certainty of faith. The result is assured: 'For to what *angel* did God ever say, "You are my Son?" . . . But again, when he brings the firstborn into the world (at the parousia), he says, "Let all God's angels worship him" '(1.5f.) . . . 'Are they not all ministering spirits sent forth to serve, for the sake of those who are to obtain salvation?' (1.14). From such texts we can see to what degree the ancient world was obsessed by a belief in demons and on the other hand looked longingly towards the exalted heavenly spheres where angels dwell – a mysterious world into which almost every man in late antiquity wanted to look. Thus belief in redemption through Jesus is a liberation from this cosmic and existential anxiety. Where Paul wrote, 'Neither death nor angels, nor evil spirits . . . nor any thing else in creation can separate us from the love of God which is in Christ Jesus our Lord' (Rom. 8.38f.), Hebrews says in the same spirit: 'God himself has said, "I will never fail you nor forsake you" (Deut. 31.6,8). Therefore *we* can say with confidence, 'The Lord is my helper, I will not be afraid, what can *man* do to me?' (Heb. 13.5b–6). (The author is thinking of a number of symptoms of a threat of persecution of the church – the work of the emperor which is, however, directed by the 'angels of the nation'; see Revelation and I Peter 5.7–9).

Thus the exaltation of Jesus to the right hand of the Father is the divine recognition of the 'power of sacrifice' (see 9.14), i.e. the sacrifice of Jesus, which has final and decisive value because of his love for man and his faithfulness towards God. However, in the author's view, this was not in and of itself, for 'through God's *charis* his death was for the benefit of all men' (2.9c); this sacrifice is the *death* of Jesus and as such not only the end of sacrifice but also the end of the one offering it. Only resurrection and exaltation bring the sacrifice to 'completion'. Only God's merciful action over the death of Jesus gives this death abiding, everlasting value.

### (ii) The heavenly liturgy of Jesus: eternal intercession

The sacrifice of Jesus on the cross is not just purification or the forgiveness of sins (10.2), and not just sanctification (10.10), but also perfection (10.14) – all three in the perfect: purified once and for all (10.2), sanctified once and for all (10.10) and perfected once and for all (10.14). The first two elements in this sacrifice are acts of Jesus; the third element, the perfection over and above the sacrifice (albeit on the basis of this sacrifice), is an act of the merciful grace of God, no longer an earthly but a heavenly event. Thus Jesus, himself perfected *(teleiōtheis,* 5.9), is also the perfecter *(teleiōtes)* for us: 'perfecter of our faith' (12.2). It was precisely at this point that the Old Testament sacrifices failed (7.18f.; 9.9): furthermore, the power of their purification and sanctification was in accordance with the Law (9.13f.), and this cannot bring any perfection or any access to God *(inter alia,* 11.39f.). Within this sacrificial framework (Ex. 29.9; Lev. 4.5; 8.33; 16.32, all in the Greek version), *teleiōsis* is an initiation, namely the official recognition of the priesthood of Jesus by God (see 5.9; 6.18f.; 7.26; 8.4). Anyone in Judaism who was anointed priest could enter the sanctuary of the tabernacle. What happened there symbolically had been accomplished literally in Jesus: his session at the right hand of God is the solemn inauguration of the heavenly priesthood of Jesus. It is not even an ascension: for Hebrews, it seems more like the acceptance of Jesus into heaven, 'being brought in' or 'taken up', as the author describes the resurrection of Jesus (see 13.20; however, this is inspired by the Greek text of Isaiah: Isa. 63.11f., where we find *ho agagōn*, God, who took Moses by the right hand). On the one hand Jesus was consecrated priest only after the sacrifice of his life, when he was exalted; on the other hand, this inauguration is the confirmation of Jesus' sacrifice and his priestly service by God (in contrast to later Socinianism, which claims that Jesus only becomes a priest in heaven – though some texts in Hebrews also suggest the same thing: 5.7f.; 8.4; 10.5–10). What is meant is that *perfect* liturgy is *heavenly* liturgy, real access to the heavenly God; priestly ministry to the world of the future, the second age (see 8.1–9.28). It is thus liturgy 'in a sitting position' (10.12 as contrasted with 10.11). We know of prayer in a sitting position from the Tanach only in II Sam. 7.14–19, in conjunction with Ex. 17.12: David sits down before the countenance of God. For Jesus, reconciliation is perfected by his sacrifice on the cross. In heaven Jesus *no longer sacrifices* (in contrast to later sacrificial theories for which support is sought in Hebrews). He does, however, perform priestly service. On the basis of the sacrifice which he has accomplished (aorist. 8.3; see 9.25f., 28), Jesus, now sitting (9.24; 10.12), intercedes for us with God, no longer by offering a new sacrifice or by means of a kind of heavenly continuation of his sacrificial action. He simply intercedes for me, *semper interpellans pro nobis* (2.5; 2.17; 5.1; 7.24f.; 8.1f.; 10.1; 11.1). True, this is stressed most strongly in Hebrews, but other New Testament writings are also familiar with the idea: 'an advocate with the Father . . . Jesus Christ, who is wholly without sin' (I John 2.1f.), see also Paul in Rom. 8.34. However, they avoid the term priest. Only one of the two priestly functions remains, because the sacrifice has been performed and is completed. So the heavenly ministry of Jesus consists in eternal intercession. He represents our interests before God (2.5; 8.1f.; 10.1; 11.1; see already in 2.17; 5.1; 7.24f.). Jesus' heavenly function is to continue to care for his people, to guide them, protect them and defend them. So Hebrews calls Jesus 'the great shepherd' (13.20, as in Isa. 63.11). As the exalted one, Jesus is 'perfected' in his priesthood or 'appointed with power'. He is the minister of the heavenly temple (8.1–9.28; see 1.7, 14; 10.11), *leitourgos tōn hagiōn* (8.2); that is the liturgy of the holy of holies, the heavenly sanctuary.[155] According to Sir. 24.6–14, Wisdom first had its tabernacle 'in the heights' and its throne in the clouds. Then God gave it Israel as a dwelling place; there it instituted *priestly* service in the Temple and exercised *kingly* rule in the city of Jerusalem. (Thus the whole tone of Hebrews follows the tradition of pre-existent wisdom, which in John 1.1 is identified with the Logos and in Heb. 1.3 with the 'the Son' as high priest. So too it is for Hebrews: after wisdom has returned to God in the incarnate Son – in the heavenly Jerusalem (see below) – Christ exercises priestly and kingly functions in heaven. The Tanach had in fact already identified the tent of the covenant or 'the tent' with the heavens (Ps. 104.2). Thus for Hebrews 'the tent' is not the *glorified* body of Jesus, as some people have interpreted it; rather, the earthly body of Jesus is the means of redemption (10.10). 'The tent' is heaven as the dwelling-place of the heavenly beings, where Jesus has now begun his heavenly liturgy and exercises his royal functions – 'the *true* tabernacle' (9.11f.). Sirach said, 'I have served before his eyes in the holy tent' (Sir. 24.10). In this heavenly liturgy Jesus has gone before us as pioneer and inaugurator (here in 12.2 *archēgos* appears in a different context from 2.10–13). In 12.2 Jesus is called *archēgos* and perfecter, that is, the one who sets everything in motion and perfects it in us: in 2.10, by contrast, he is the pioneer, the leader who goes before his people, or 'the great shepherd' (13.20), who brings the flock to its destination, to God. Jesus seizes the initiative which he brings to a good end in us (12.2); he goes before us through our life (12.2 with 2.10) and takes his own with him from their *paroikia* or wandering in exile to the place of rest (2.10; see below).

## III. THE RESULT OF THE PRIESTLY MINISTRY OF JESUS

The result of the ministry of the earthly and heavenly Jesus is salvation from God in and through Jesus, experienced as a unique priest (see 7.25). So he is the pioneer of our salvation (2.10) or 'the cause of eternal salvation' (5.9 and 10.1–8) by opening up access for us to God.

### A. The church of God on earth as participation in the heavenly liturgy of Jesus

Jesus has been brought to perfection by God himself (2.10; 5.9; 7.28); thus he has 'entered into the heart of the sanctuary' (6.19, see 9.3), he sits at the right hand of God. This perfection came about so that Jesus could perfect us; having been 'perfected', he becomes our 'perfecter' (12.2; 11.40). God alone granted him access to the holy of holies, but once Jesus is with God, he himself becomes the medium or the means of access to God. He is the *archēgos* and *teleiōtēs* of faith (12.2), that is, he was the first to find a way to God. He went before us and is thus our leader; at the same time he also brings us to God and thus gives us 'perfection' or access to God. That is the content of our faith. Through his sacrifice, perfected by God, Jesus has opened up a new way of life to God (10.20), the only way which leads to this final goal. *Hodos prosphatos kai zōsa* (10.20), that means a new way of life (in ritual language *prosphatos* means freshly slaughtered and therefore new; *zōsa*, living, is contrasted with the carcases of slaughtered animals).

This new way to God is depicted in a passage of oriental splendour (12.18–24). In contrast to the useless, horrific and terrying event on Sinai (12.18–21), it is represented as a gentle, peaceful and splendid event: a solemn procession in which Christians enter the *panēgyris* or heavenly festival of the assembled angels (12.22–24; the angels are also part of the scene at the Sinai event). Christianity is one great panegyric: 'Remember where you stand. For you have not come to what may be touched, a blazing fire, and darkness, and gloom, and a tempest . . . so terrifying that Moses said, "I tremble with fear." But you have come to Mount Zion and to the city of the living God, the heavenly Jerusalem, and to innumerable angels in festal gathering, and to the assembly of the first-born who are enrolled in heaven, and to a judge who is God of all, and to the spirits of just men made perfect, and to Jesus, the mediator of a new covenant, and to the sprinkled blood that speaks more graciously than the blood of Abel' (12.18–24) – an oriental gem of Christian solemnity and matter-of-fact faith, which at the same time reproduces the whole of the spiritual climate of late antiquity in which the author lives (the first and the second ages!).

This is without doubt no longer an assembly of the synagogue but an 'episynagogal' assembly (10.25, though it is uncertain whether Hebrews *means* this contrast; for in the inter-testamental literature *synagōgē* and *episynagōgē* are evidently used interchangeably and without distinction). At all events it is an *eschatological* assembly in which the church on earth is already taking part, albeit in confident expectation of the parousia (10.37–39).

Thus Jesus, who is exalted to God, is not just the minister in the heavenly sanctuary, where God dwells with his attendants and where from now on Jesus always intercedes for us. At the same time Jesus is the minister of the 'vestibule', i.e. the heavenly sphere of the ordinary angels, a sphere in which the church on earth is already involved (8.5f.). 'The tabernacle of his priesthood' (8.5f.; see 9.11f.) embraces both the tabernacle, or the holy of holies, and the vestibule in which the church on earth has already been incorporated. Thus in contrast to Rev. 21.2, 'the city of the living God' (Heb. 12.22; see 3.12; 9.14; 10.31) or 'the heavenly Jerusalem' (12.22) does not descend to earth; rather, the church ascends. Christians are already taken above into the heavenly Jerusalem, the vestibule. This embraces three categories: (*a*) the angels (12.22) – (*b*) the *ekklēsia tōn prōtotokōn* (12.23); *ecclēsia (qāhāl)* is (in the Deuteronomistic tradition) the solemn designation for the assembled people of God (see Ex. 4.22; also Acts 7.38). 'The church of the firstborn' means the Christian community on earth (though this is still disputed by some exegetes, wrongly to my mind), i.e. the Christians 'who are (already) enrolled in heaven' (12.23) and thus have their abode there: for they belong to the world of the future, the second age (see 2.5; 6.5; 9.11; 10.1). (*c*) Finally, 'the spirits (*pneumata*) of the righteous who have already attained the consummation' (12.22f.), i.e. the men of faith from the Old Testament (see Wisdom 3.1; 4.7–13) and those Christians who have died.[156] As minister of the whole of the tent of the covenant, the holy of holies and the holy place, Christ is also the chief minister in the church's liturgy on earth, the heavenly forecourt. The church's liturgy is a participation in the heavenly liturgy of Jesus the Christ or high priest, who sits in prayer in the midst of his heavenly hosts (9.24–28; 12.23). The church is that part of humanity which is already reconciled and redeemed, still a kind of heavenly limbo, but already 'taken up' into the dwelling places of the angels and the saints (12.22f.). 'The more perfect tent', 'the true tent' (9.11f.) (of which the Mosaic tent of the covenant is only a shadow) is thus the heavenly world of the angels, the world of the future or the coming age (9.11).[157] For the ecclesiology of Hebrews this means that the church on earth is the vestibule on the way to the holy of holies, the way of access which leads to God. Hebrews does not have the expression the church as the body of Christ (Pauline theology), nor does the author ever speak of the church *of Christ*. It is a community *of God* in which Christ is mediator and, like Moses, leader, guide and pioneer (2.10; 6.19f.) of the people of God. The Christian community is 'a house of God' (see 3.2–6), and, as Christ, Jesus is appointed *above* the house of God (3.6). The author adds: 'and we ourselves make up this house' (3.6b). For this reason Christians are *metochoi tou Christou* (3.14), partners of the high priest (with the qualification to which Hebrews keep returning: 'if only we hold our first confidence firm to the end', 3.14b; for the community of faith to which Hebrews is addressed knew of many instances of apostasy).

As a sharing of the heavenly liturgy of Jesus,[158] the church's liturgy on earth is, for Hebrews, a sacrifice of *thanks* and *praise* (13.15). Leviticus 7.12,15; II Chron. 2.9.31; Pss. 50.13–23; 107.22; 116.17 describe three kinds of peace offering. These were connected with the offering of unleavened bread and shewbread. In addition to sacrifices of thanks and praise, brotherly services *(koinōnia, eulogia* – in this context evidently a collection for the poor during the service) is a form of sacrifice. However, Hebrews never mentions the eucharistic liturgy by name, although it must have known of it. Is this an instance of the *disciplina arcani*, the injunction to silence? Some exegetes find a number of allusions to the eucharist in Heb. 13: (*a*) probably a collection for the poor during the Christian eucharist (13.16); (*b*) the 'confessing of the name' (13.15b); (*c*) the 'sacrifice of praise ' (13.15, which at the same time contains a reference to a meal with unleavened bread); (*d*) 'to sanctify the people through his own blood' (13.12; see 9.18–20; 10.10, 14, 29); (*e*) 'blood of the eternal covenant' (13.20, a liturgical formula which also occurs in the primitive Christian eucharist; (*f*) the context of Hebrews: this assumes that Hebrews was initially conceived as a homily during a eucharist along the lines of a synagogue reading (since Hebrews is certainly not a *letter*). In that case, 13.20f. would best be regarded as the end of a homily, which would come before the anamnesis and doxology in the eucharistic prayer that would follow. (*g*) Finally, 13.10 could be a latent, but very clear reference to the eucharist, from which non-Christian Jews would be excluded. While the whole of this argument is illuminating, it is not conclusive, least of all the last argument, which is thought to be the strongest. In fact Heb. 13.10 refers to the altar of Golgotha, Jesus' crucifixion outside the city walls – just as the sacrificial flesh from the Day of Atonement sacrifice also had to be burnt outside the city walls without the priests being allowed to eat it. There is a contrast to *kippūr* here, because Jesus had to give up his life as a sacrifice outside the city walls (13.12), 'to sanctify *the people* with his blood' (13.12b). As far as I can see, there is no mention in this text of excluding Jews from the Christian eucharist. In any case, this conclusion is provoked by 13.9: 'Do not be led away by any strange teachings; for it is well that the heart be strengthened by grace, *not by foods*, which have not benefited their adherents.' What is involved is the *final* character of the sacrifice on the cross, which makes food regulations and the sacrifice of animals quite superfluous. Hebrews is not thinking so much of the eucharist as of the crucifixion of Jesus, just as the so-called words of institution in the synoptic gospels are not really words of institution but a theological interpretation of the crucifixion of Jesus (though the church may justifiably see them as a biblical basis for its eucharist). In fact this meaning of the crucifixion is celebrated in the eucharistic praise and thanksgiving of the church, but as far as the New Testament is concerned it is wrong simply to transfer the significance of the crucifixion to the eucharist. Hebrews above all, which stresses the 'once for all' of the crucifixion so strongly and so often, will not have applied expressions and interpretations of the expiatory death of Jesus to the eucharist. (In the earliest liturgy they were accepted *as such*; this is the case above all with the phrase 'the blood of the eternal covenant', which refers to the cross and not to the eucharist itself.) Hebrews does not discuss the relationship of the crucifixion to the eucharist and vice versa; the author simply says that the church's liturgy is a participation in Jesus' heavenly liturgy, which is no longer a sacrificial cult, but eternal intercession before God on the basis of the historical sacrifice of his life made by Jesus. For Hebrews, the liturgy of the earthly church is a sacrifice of thanks and praise and a share in Jesus' heavenly intercession; this is the only form of reference in Hebrews to the church's eucharist – which is then made in consideration of the wider context. However, Hebrews 13 does not allude to the eucharist as it was interpreted in the later church. (This is not an argument *against* the later theology of the eucharist, but such theology cannot appeal to Hebrews.)

## B. THE 'NOW ALREADY' OF HOPE (6.19f.)

Many texts in Hebrews reflect the tension between 'now already' and 'not yet'; moreover, 'but now' (*nun de*) regularly appears in the text. 'What was' is contrasted with 'what now is'; and 'what now is' is held in tension with 'what is still to come' (see, *inter alia*, 2.8; 9.24; 9.26; 11.16; 12.26).

This dialectic is bound up with the idea, to be found in the wisdom tradition and apocalyptic, of the eschatological pre-existence of all the constituents of salvation, and with the tension in our history between the first and the second age, which is already there and yet is a 'coming age', a world of the future. What lies between the *prōton* and the *eschaton,* the first and the last, is the human history of suffering, atonement, guilt and unrighteousness. It is therefore in accordance with the character of God – who is absolutely the first and finally the last in creation – that in seeking to bring men to this *eschaton* in and through Jesus, he should make Jesus follow the same human career, the way of human suffering. He bears our sorrow, our anxiety, our burden of sin, in order to be the first to achieve perfection *by means of a human life.* In other words, he achieves eschatological communion with God, so that on the basis of his self-sacrifice, from now on supported by his intercession with God in heaven, we may be brought through him and with him to this eschatological communion with the living God, with the angels, and with all who have already gone before us and were dear to us. This is the ultimate result of the redemption in Jesus, thanks – literally (as Hebrews would have it) – to his *pioneering* service: a new way of life (10.20).

However, while the community of God already has its dwelling place in the heavenly tent, this tent is still pitched on earth. So it continues to look for Jesus' 'second *coming without sin*' (9.28c); in other words, his first 'coming with sin' was Jesus' coming to bear our sins and to atone for them. However, this redemption is final, made once for all; it has everlasting power (9.25f.; 7.28; 10.10; 10.14; 9.12c). His second coming is not to bring reconciliation – that is no longer necessary; at that time he will come only 'for the salvation' of those who long for his coming and 'for the judgment' of the rest (9.26–28). For the author, the result of this dialectical tension is that 'Here we have no lasting city, but we seek the city which is to come' (13.14), 'waiting for the Lord' (9.28; see also 2.5; 11.10, 14, 16, 39; 12,22; cf. Phil. 3.20; Col. 3.1f.). On the one hand, Christians on earth draw near to heaven: God (12.23b) and Jesus Christ (12.24); on the other hand, they are still on the way to Jesus. They *draw near*. Through encountering Jesus they encounter God: Christians 'draw near to the throne of God' (4.16), since they are 'children of God' (8.10–12) and thus already have a share in the constituents of salvation (10.34). They are already sanctified (*hēgiasemenoi*, 10.10); they are already 'at rest' (4.3) and therefore with God, their salvation. Nevertheless. . . .

## C. The 'not yet' of faith

Although they are already sanctified (10.10: *hēgiasmenoi*), Christians are on the other hand *hagiazomenoi*, on the way to sanctification (10.15–18), by virtue of the spirit in their hearts. Indeed they are at rest (4.3), and yet 'they have still to enter that rest' (4.11).

Jesus has 'opened a new way of life for us through the curtain' (10.20). He has gone from the earth, the *profanum*, through the *fanum* of the vestibule and finally 'through the curtain' into the holy of holies; he has already entered the sanctuary as a forerunner (6.19f.). As Christians, we have already arrived in the vestibule, but we have yet to pass through the curtain (6.19; 10.20); for us there is still the *katapetasma* (the curtain) of *faith*. However, *hope* is the sure and firm anchor of our souls. Hope has already penetrated to the holy of holies (6.19b), since Jesus has already made his entrance as forerunner (6.20; 9.12). Faith cannot get this far. For Christian faith the curtain between the vestibule and the holy of holies continues to remain intact (6.19).[159] Thus only in faith do we have access to God. God's community is heavenly, but not 'eschatological' in the sense of being 'still incomplete' (see 10.37); not for the world, because they are already 'in the vestibule', but not as yet in the holy of holies.

This situation of 'not yet' still leaves room for suffering in the world, since Christians still live on earth. As we have already said time and again, suffering has a central place in Hebrews (10.32–24; 12.1–3; 13.3; 5.7f. etc.). However, for Christians it is transformed into participation in the suffering of Jesus (13.13; 12.4–13). Such suffering is then seen as the educative disciplining of the son by his loving father, in accordance with the model provided by wisdom (Prov. 3.12f.; 13.24; 22.15; 23.13f.; Sir. 22.3, 6; 30.1, 3, 13; Job 5.17–22; see also Rev. 3.19 and I Peter

4.12–16). In Heb. 12.5–8, this pedagogical principle, to be found throughout late antiquity, is applied to God the Father, who is contrasted with 'the Son' and all Christians. So in theological terms a distinction must be made between the model used by Hebrews (instruction in human wisdom, which is a non-theological principle with cultural conditioning) and the theological principle of religious language: Christian suffering as participation in the suffering of Jesus. Jesus himself endured hostility (2.10; 12.2), so Christians do not need to fear any persecution of the church. Because the enemies of Jesus have been conquered only in principle, i.e. in Jesus and his ascension (2.14, where the death of Jesus is seen as a means of dethroning Satan; see 1.13; 2.8; 10.13), whereas our earthly life still unfolds in this age (see 2.7–9), our suffering can become participation in the suffering of Jesus, who has overcome suffering and death (12.4–13; 13.13). Furthermore, Jesus can console us in suffering (2.18), since he himself has been taught in the 'school of suffering' (5.8) and he is able to 'sympathize with our weaknesses' (4.15). To suffer as a Christian is, like the suffering of Jesus, to suffer outside the camp, on the way to the city of the future (13.13b–14, see below).

According to Hebrews, the life of Christians has one foot in 'this age' and the other in the 'new age'. That is the pattern of faith: Christians still stand in front of the curtain which has been penetrated by hope, with a faith which still lacks vision. This leads the author to introduce a long discussion of faith (Heb. 11), in which he introduces the great figures of the salvation history of Israel.[160] He is concerned with the heavenly city into which the men of faith from the Old Testament have already entered, a city which, though *invisible*, is nevertheless real (11.7, 9f., 13–16, 17). The things that Christians are promised in the future already exist in the present, apocalyptically, in heaven. They are real, but invisible. These figures were *believers* without ever having seen Jesus or heard of him: they believed in the invisible world of Jesus which was to come. Thus their faith should serve as an example to Christians who have seen the fulfilment of what was not granted to their ancestors (11.40; 6.12).

In this context, *faith* is faith *in God (pistis epi Theon)* (6.1; see 11.1ff.; above all, 11.6). In contrast to Paul's Jewish concept of faith, Hebrews (which here is more Johannine) refers more to the (Greek and) Hellenistic Jewish concept of faith. Faith is a matter of giving credence to what cannot be seen, of trusting in it. Faith is a *hypostasis* of heavenly things – the *epourania* – insofar as these are in the future, and it is an *elenchos* of heavenly things insofar as these are invisible (see 11.1; again one of those formulae constructed by the author). It indicates the double significance which he attaches to the 'coming age' (see above): this *oikoumenē mellousa*, or future world, is on the one hand something which is to come in time, and on the other hand has already been prepared for by God, in space, before all time. Therefore to believe in God's eschatological city is both a *hypostasis* and an *elenchos*. *Hypostasis* means something that is hidden, that exists below something else, in order to bear it and support it. Hence the meaning foundation, pledge, guarantee; also the right to property, an act of purchase, etc.; in other words, it is something which gives us *objective* certainty about something else; for example, on the basis of this *hypostasis* (e.g. a purchase), one can claim something which cannot be immediately seen and which is not immediately available. Thus in the end it can also mean the *subjective* aspect of this certainty, namely being convinced of something or trusting in something (e.g. in Heb. 3.14). Thus *hypostasis* can have both an objective and a subjective meaning; the context must indicate which. At all events, in the word *hypostasis* the subjective conviction or trust has an objective basis. This is what Heb. 11.1 seeks to stress. The firmness of this basis explains the subjectively strong confidence in faith to which these men of faith – or, more exactly, in the spirit of Hebrews, to which God himself bears witness in scripture. *Elenchos* – proof –, which can never have a subjective meaning, also confirms the interpretation that here in Hebrews *hypostasis* is primarily intended in an objective sense. Therefore, 'Faith is the assurance of things hoped for, the conviction of things not seen' (11.1). Faith gives *substance* to hope, and as a result for believers the future is not uncertain and disquieting, despite all the disappointments that may have been experienced. Faith is the matrix in which hope is cast; it does not make hope into any kind of illusion. Thus Hebrews also sets out to demonstrate that faith transcends what is outwardly tangible and obvious – whatever is at man's disposal. Because of this, men of faith are often the butt of mockery for people who build only on empirically demonstrable evidence; as a result they are persecuted people, sufferers, 'utopian'. They are mocked like Noah, who built an ark in fine weather (11.7). Hebrews stresses this aspect by means of a whole series of figures from the past. Thus Abraham had to leave his dwelling place, his possessions and his own land 'without knowing where he was going' (11.8); but God had promised him abundant descendants in the land to which he was to go (11.8b). However, his wife Sarah was old and barren. Nevertheless, Abraham believed (11.11). And when the son of the promise, in whom he believed, was eventually born, Abraham had to present for sacrifice the empirical proof of the first fulfilment of the divine promise. He was commanded to sacrifice his own son of the promise, Isaac. 'He who had received the promises was ready to offer up his only son (the son of the promise)' (11.17). However, it is possible to say, 'These all died in faith, not having received what was promised to them' (11.13). Still, this faith was not mere trust and acceptance or an announcement; it was an *experience,* a *veiled sight* of invisible things in faith: 'They saw salvation and greeted it only *from afar*' (11.13b). They remained on the way, on pilgrimage 'as strangers and exiles on the earth' (11.13). According to Hebrews, the land of promise to which they travelled was not a piece of land in 'this world'; it was already 'the world of the future', the second age; for them this world was the evidence of faith, more real than the earth which they were to inhabit. Again and again we have the same theme in Hebrews: God is concerned for those who suffer, who are mocked, for the helpless, for the barren, so as to bring his power to fruition in their weakness: 'Your weakness is made strong' (11.34b; cf. Paul, II Cor. 12.9). This election of the inferior, of the weak and the suffering, is expressed once again in Hebrews in the way in which it includes a prostitute in the ranks of the men of faith. This is Rahab (11.31, see Josh. 2.9): Matthew 1.5 includes her in the genealogy of Jesus; cf. the woman who was a manifest sinner in Luke 7.50; see also James 2.25. In other words, Rahab seems to have been a favourite topic for sermons in the synagogue and in the early church; see also I *Clement* 12.7. No man is too insignificant for God (besides, the early church drew its members above all from the lowest strata of society; it was a church of the poor, the insignificant, the slaves in the literal sense of the word). But this is a fixed datum in the Jewish-Christian tradition of experience. When Yahweh gives his blessing – through one of the patriarchs – then he often does so *cancellatis manibus* (as the Vulgate translates it); he often puts his arms crosswise, so that the true blessing – that with the right hand – rests on the younger and more insignificant and not on the firstborn whose due it is (see e.g. Deut. 21.17; Gen. 27.39f.; 48.14–16; 49.3f). Moses was also a model: he despised the right to be the son of Pharaoh and 'chose rather to share ill-treatment with the people of God' (11.24–27). There is a whole series of mocked, suffering men who nevertheless have an unshakable faith, of whom Hebrews profoundly says, 'They were too good for this world' (11.38); they were already men of the new age, the world of the future – 'yet not one of them saw the promise fulfilled' (11.39b). It was this that showed their faith to be so strong, and at the same time it shows what the author understands by faith. 'God had foreseen something better *for us*, that *apart from us* they (the Old Testament men of faith) should not be made perfect' (11.40). 'With us' and 'apart from us' refer to the community of God, the Christians. None of these great figures of faith saw the promise fulfilled, because the eschatological time begins only with the exaltation of Jesus to God (2.10; 5.9; 7.28; 10.14); only then is access to God free (9.11f.; 10.19f.). Only by means of Jesus' exaltation to God is this access opened up for the righteous of the pre-Christian Jewish past, who could not achieve perfection by the Law and the cult (7.19; 9.9; 10.1). In other words, it begins only with the heavenly church on earth, and is therefore 'not apart from us' (11.40). Now this implies that for Hebrews the righteous of the

Old Testament and the believers of the New are the *one people of God,* already introduced into or belonging to 'the city of the living God, the heavenly Jerusalem' (12.22; see also 9.15), 'the eternal kingdom (of God)' (13.14). Faith in this city gives substance to hope for the unseen and pre-existent, and for the world of the future which has not yet been realized for us.

The author of Hebrews introduced this extensive insertion about faith with the last verse of the preceding chapter: 'We have faith, and though faith keep our souls' (10.39b). For Christians in this world the interim between the ascension and the parousia is a system of faith – the curtain between the first and the second ages is still intact.

Consequently Hebrews repeatedly emphasizes the need for perseverance in the 'already now' and 'not yet' of Christian life (12.1–13; 3.12–14; above all 3.14b; 3.6c; 10.36). This has ethical consequences. Thus Hebrews sees a Christian life-style in conformity to the demands of what the synoptic gospels call the kingdom of God, in the following terms. If Christians make up 'the community of firstborn', 'inscribed in heaven' (12.23), they must also lead a *heavenly* way of life (12.14–13.9). But this 'heavenly way of life' is there in front of them; it consists above all in 'brotherly love, which is one of the things which must remain for ever' (13.1), namely the heavenly things of the second age which must already be realized *in* our historical world. Above all, the author admonishes Christians not to stay away from Christian liturgical gatherings (10.25). In that case 'we mock the spirit of *charis* (grace)' (10.29; *pneuma charitos,* see already Zech. 12.10). Here Hebrews is evidently referring to apostasy and calls this a sin which cannot ever be forgiven; it is a sin against the Holy Spirit, who is a Spirit of grace, and thus it is rejection of the grace of God which the heavenly Christ seeks for us from God and which God gives to him by virtue of Jesus' well-pleasing sacrifice on earth. This grace must not be 'put at risk' (12.15). In the background here (5.2 and 10.26), we doubtless have the assumption to be found in the Jewish (Num. 15.22–30) and New Testament tradition (Mark 3.28–30 par.), that 'sins against the Spirit' cannot be forgiven. However, Hebrews means something special by this: there is only one such sin. The argument is remarkable: 'A death has occurred which redeems them from *the transgressions under the first covenant*' (9.15; also 9.27f.). Thus on a first reading it seems that according to Hebrews there is no forgiveness for the sins of *Christians:* in that case there is 'no longer a sacrifice for sins' (10.26); there is only 'a fearful prospect of judgment and a consuming fire' (10.27). Some scholars wrongly see these texts as an indication of a phase in the church before there was any practice of *paenitentia secunda* or penitence (later narrowed down to private confession). This is confirmed by the author's view that Christians themselves do not offer any atoning sacrifice, but only praise and thanksgiving for the final and perfect sacrifice on the cross which has been made by Christ.

Here, however, Hebrews is concerned with something different. The author is well aware that Christians, too, must struggle (12.4), and even need instruction, admonition and forgiveness (see 12.1; 13.1–3; 13.20f.). On the other hand he speaks of an eternal redemption (9.12b). Christ saves us *eis to panteles* (7.24f.), i.e. everywhere and always and for all sins (see also 1.3; 4.15f.; 9.14; 9.27f.; 10.12–18). There is no need, therefore, to limit the forgiveness of sins. The passage is not directly concerned with the difference between serious sins, deliberately committed, and sins of weakness and ignorance, though the author also knows this already traditional difference (5.2; 10.26). It is exclusively a matter of apostasy, of falling away from the faith, since here things are different. When that happens, a person turns his back on redemption, denies the *principle* of redemption and the forgiveness of sins and there really is 'no longer any sacrifice for sin' (10.26). For 'it is impossible to restore again to repentance those who have once been enlightened, who have tasted the heavenly gift, and have become partakers of the Holy Spirit, and have tasted the goodness of the word of God and the powers of the age to come, if they then commit apostasy, since they crucify the Son of God on their own account and hold him up to contempt' (6.4–6). For in that case they deny and reject the very principle of all conversion. The author is *formally* right in what might appear as rigorism: anyone who rejects the principle of all redemption goes against redemption itself. Such a sin is unforgivable, not because God's mercy is limited, but because such a man himself rejects any such forgiveness. It is beyond the author's comprehension that apostates can come back to Christ in the community of God; he even seems to exclude this possibility (10.26). Those who had Jesus executed did so 'in ignorance' (Acts 3.17; Luke 23.34, just as Saul persecuted the Christians in ignorance, I Tim. 1.13b). But, Hebrews says, Christians know better; they know who Jesus is; after that, to depart 'once one has received knowledge of the truth' (10.26) is to sin against the light (12.15). For Hebrews this is by definition a deliberate and serious sin which in addition excludes the principle of conversion – and that is where the element of the impossibility of forgiveness lies. One certainly cannot profit from a principle which one negates. Men of late antiquity had still not come to the realization that our complicated human make-up and various social elements play a great part, above all in our silent, modern 'apostasy'. In fact Hebrews probably did not yet know any instance of repentance and restoration. In formal terms the argument of Hebrews is convincing to a believer; furthermore, it is by no means isolated in the early church. In the New Testament Christians are not judged by Christ in accordance with their sins – for these have been atoned for by Jesus (through Jesus,

Christians escape God's judgment, I Thess. 1.10). They only fall under the judgment of Christ in the case of a deliberate sin against Christ himself (e.g. the Gospel of John, passim; II Thess. 1.8), i.e. in the case of sinful apostasy (however, Hebrews describes any apostasy as *per se* sinful). For that very reason Hebrews issues regular admonitions to persevere: 'Do not hurl this trust overboard' (10.35); 'what you need is endurance' (10.36). Furthermore, 'Only a little while and he who must come will indeed come and will not delay' (10.37). One can hardly claim, as many do, that in Hebrews the eschatological tension with respect to the parousia – the *temporal* line – disappears, to make room for the Greek pattern of the two-storey world, the *local* line of spheres lying one above each other, the visible and the invisible world. In Hebrews, the Greek view of the world is incorporated into the Jewish conception of time, which runs between *prōton* and *eschaton*. Time and space are essential to the author's view of the world, just as they are in the Jewish apocalyptic of the two ages. Thus the author of Hebrews looks both upwards and forwards into the future. 'In search of the city of the future' (13.14), 'to meet the Lord' (9.28; see also 2.5; 11.10, 14, 16, 39; 12.22; cf. Phil. 3.20; Col. 3.1f.). The special element of this view of the world, which is very difficult for us to grasp, is that for this author, to look upwards is at the same time to look forward: the *oikoumenē mellousa*, our real theme (2.5), is the 'coming' world, the world of the future, which at the same time, like all eschatological elements of salvation, has been prepared from all eternity by God, and is apocalyptically pre-existent up above. It would not be very difficult to rewrite Hebrews for our time without using the author's view of the world. Only then would it become clear for modern man (with other – equally relative – views of the world) how much Hebrews is a human document with considerable religious profundity.

## IV. CHRISTIAN SPIRITUALITY, THE CONSEQUENCE OF A PRIESTLY DOCTRINE OF GRACE

Not only does Hebrews indicate the ethical consequences of its doctrinal view (10.19–39); in a number of characteristic and well-chiselled sentences it outlines its view of Christian spirituality: 'Let us go forth from the camp' (13.13), 'to the *"oikoumenē mellousa"* (2.5) or the future world' (13.14); and 'enter into God's rest' (3.7–4.11).

A.   The exodus community: 'Let us go forth from the camp' – to the
future world

On *kippūr*, the great Day of Atonement, 'the bodies of those animals
whose blood is brought into the sanctuary by the high priest as a sacrifice
for sin are burned outside the camp' (13.11). The priests are not allowed
to eat any of the sin-offering (13.10). Hebrews is not thinking of Herod's
Jerusalem, so it does not say 'outside the city gates' (as it does in 13.12
where there is an allusion to the historical crucifixion of Jesus outside the
city walls of Jerusalem, namely on Golgotha); it says 'outside the camp',
the 'city' of the people of God under the leadership of Moses on the way
to the promised land – that short stay in tents which is characteristic of
a pilgrimage.

Jesus also 'gave his life as a sacrifice outside the city gates' (13.12);
but he did that 'in order to sanctify the people through his blood'
(13.12b). *Hina hagiasē* (in order to sanctify) is reminiscent less of the sin-
offering (to which this term usually refers) than of the sacrifice of the
covenant (see 9.13; 10.29; 12.23f.) As is his usual practice (it almost
seems second nature to him), the author associates reminiscences of a
number of events from the distant past of Israel, summed up in the key
phrase 'outside the camp' (13.13), with the historical event on Golgotha.
Abraham too had gone out from apostate Haran (Heb. 11.8); Moses went
out from sinful Egypt (11.25). Thus all the great men of faith went out
from cities or fixed abodes and even from temporary camps and sought
out the wilderness (11.37f.) in search of the heavenly city – 'they were
too good for this world' (11.38). Moses set up his tent 'outside the camp'
(Ex. 33.3–7), since according to the story of the golden calf God refused
to go on dwelling 'in the midst of his people'. Consequently Moses set up
his tent outside the camp and called it 'the tent of meeting. Anyone who
wanted to ask Yahweh anything went to this tent outside the camp'
(Ex. 33.7). They then remained standing outside the tent; Moses went in
by himself and a pillar of cloud came down and remained over the
entrance. Moses had crossed through the heavenly spheres and behind
the cloud where Yahweh dwells: 'Yahweh then spoke to Moses face to
face, as a man speaks with his friend' (Ex. 33.9–11). Hebrews 13.3f.
alludes to this in the light of Jesus, the new Moses, when the author uses
the suffering of Jesus outside the gate (namely on Golgotha) as the
occasion for a pastoral spiritual conclusion: 'Therefore let us go forth to
him outside the camp, bearing abuse for him. For here we have no lasting
city, but we seek the city which is to come' (13.13f.): the church on earth
is a community engaged in an exodus to the city behind the mystical
cloud where Jesus already dwells with his God and ours. Thus the tent
outside the camp is the sanctuary into which the exalted Christ has

entered, at the right hand of God. The community must leave its established earthly dwelling and go out to this tent of Moses, immediately in front of the entrance through which the new Moses, Jesus, has already gone as their forerunner. In Hebrews, the city which the Christian has to leave is not simply the city of men, but the concrete, historical pagan society, the 'pagan city' of man. Christians are to leave the city 'in order to bear abuse for him' (13.13: the shame and abuse of all the men of faith; see Heb. 11); that is, in order to become insignificant. For Hebrews, the city with its city walls or, in earlier times, the camp, is clearly the image of 'this age', and the tent to which Christians go is 'the age to come'. Therefore the community of God is a *paroikia* ('parish' in the biblical sense), that is, an exodus community of those who are as 'strangers and sojourners' in this world as they travel to the future world. Given the whole tone of this spirituality, I cannot believe that Hebrews means 'outside the camp' to refer to *Israel*, as some interpreters claim, which would make 13.13 a kind of official endorsement of the separation between church and synagogue. The verse is meant in general terms: to leave this age and to go to the future world. Since what is transitory and provisional in Israel (as anywhere else) belongs to this age, in Heb. 13.13 there is implicitly also an appeal to the *Jewish Christians* (= Hebrews, who give their name to this work) resolutely to put aside the obsolete cultic practices of the Old Testament, and above all its food laws (see 13.9).

Thus, following the tradition of ancient Israel, Hebrews preaches the model of the church as an exodus community. This happens in all the New Testament writings, but Hebrews and I Peter are the most radical. The exodus is that of a community of God which lives on the periphery of this world and is critical of it; it lives *alongside* wordly society and inwardly builds up a new specifically Christian community (see my analysis of the social and historical conditions in a later chapter, which it is essential for us to understand if we are to establish what elements of this spirituality are historically conditioned and are therefore not a norm for all Christians). In view of the historical social conditions in which this exodus spirituality must be practised, these Christian communities must inevitably have given outsiders the impression of a mysterious, closed, isolated brotherhood – the sort of thing which always gives rise to mistrust, suspicion and finally malicious talk. Pliny, who knew Egypt and Asia Minor and had to report on Christians to the emperor, called this a society 'full of new and perverse superstition' and designated it (evidently because of its isolation and detachment from – pagan – society) a society of 'misanthropists'; see also Suetonius.[161] Hence the many allusions in Hebrews to the suffering of Christians. In those days its appeal did indeed sound like an 'Away from this earthly, pagan city! It will not last much longer, and Christians will literally go out into the wilderness' (the desert fathers). In the end, Hebrews says at length what the *Didache* puts quite expressly: 'Let *charis* come and this world pass away' (*eltheto charis kai pareltheto ho kosmos houtos*),[162] a passage in which *charis* or grace is clearly identified with the future world of Hebrews, for which the future world also includes God's *charis* or grace to men. This New Testament exodus community, in the spirit of Hebrews, is critical of society in its marginal position and its radical criticism of the world. But this exodus or Emmaus model of the church in Hebrews has a mystical and liturgical dimension and reflects a closed church – which was perhaps the only possibility at that time (see a later chapter).

## B. Entering the 'rest of God'

It has emerged time and again that the author of Hebrews is a Christian who has pondered the problem of suffering, above all the suffering of the righteous – the ancient problem of Job. For him and his Christians it must have been an existential and personal problem. Therefore, however brave and persistent he may be, he longs for *rest*. Here too he finds himself akin to a profoundly Jewish spirituality.[163] This is expressed in Heb. 3.7–4.11.

In the Tanach, God is the 'giver of rest' (Ex. 33.14; see Isa. 28.12). *Nāhat* or rest comprises many aspects: material, social, personal and religious. (*a*) There is rest after war: peace as rest (Josh. 14.15), free from oppression by enemies (Deut. 12.9f.); political rest (Isa. 28.12); a period without unpleasant incidents and misfortunes (Ex. 5.5; Ps. 94.13); finally there is well-deserved rest in bed (Isa. 57.2); (*b*) 'rest' or *menūhā* is the promised land as a place of rest, Canaan, with all the good things that it was to bring, did bring and would still bring in the future (Josh. 1.13, 15; Deut. 3.20; 12.9); (*c*) 'rest' is also sabbath rest – in the first place God's rest on the seventh day of creation (Gen. 2.2; Ex. 20.11; 31.17); thus for Heb. 4.1–5 'rest' is a pre-existent reality connected with Gen. 2.2, for this rest of God at creation is what will be brought to us by the 'world to come'. This rest has been prepared for us from eternity. Furthermore, 'God's rest' also means the holy of holies or the tabernacle in the tent of the covenant, the ark with the mercy seat, the throne of God (see II Chron. 6.41; Ps. 132.8, 14); (*d*) rest is also the weekly joy and rest of the Jew as he celebrates the sabbath (Ex. 16.23–30; 31.15; 34.21; 35.2, see Isa. 58.13f.; Ps. 92); (*e*) rest is only perfected in the world to come (Isa. 32.18); the sabbath is an anticipation of that. Thus in these last three meanings rest is sabbath rest: the rest of God after creation, the rest of Jews on the weekly sabbath, and eschatological rest. Hebrews adds the rest of Jesus 'at the right hand of God', his seated liturgy

(Heb. 10.12f.). (*f*) Finally, the term 'rest' is also bound up with redemption, above all with the great atoning at *kippūr* (Lev. 16.30f.) (according to many rabbis, on this day no sin was to be found in Israel). Thus rest is reconciliation, holiness and righteousness – which is also the meaning of sabbath rest.

Hebrews also takes up this line of tradition when it talks of rest. The first mention of 'rest' (3.11) is concerned with God's rest (with a reference to Ps. 95.11; also in 4.3; 3.18; 4.1; 4.4; 4.10). The Joshua who led Israel to rest, and thus into the promised land, could not, however, give Israel rest. This was possible only for the Joshua of the New Testament, Jesus (3.7–4.11; cf. Matt. 11.28; John 14.2). Only Christian obedience in faith gives access to God's rest (3.19; 3.12; 4.2; 4.3), thanks to 'the rest of Christ' (see 10.12f.). Hebrews 3.7–11 bases this promise of the rest to come on Ps. 95.7–11, and Heb. 4.4 on Gen. 2.2. Thus rest is both a place which has been prepared (Ps. 95) and a condition or status (Hebrews). Soon images like temple, city and so on will be used to suggest the same reality. What is promised by God is thus worth believing in: it will come to pass, as in apocalyptic terms it is depicted as existing already, and then temporal and local or spatial categories are used interchangeably at will (see e.g. 3.11; 3.14). In Hebrews rest always has a liturgical colouring. Thus Christian rest is both present (4.3) and still to come (4.11). But for Hebrews, rest also means 'rest on', to be able to support oneself on something or someone in order to rest. Just as Jews rest on the Law and animal sacrifices, so Christians – by virtue of the content of their faith, which gives substance to hope (Heb. 11), rest directly on God. For Hebrews, rest is the same thing as justification by faith; it is present and eschatological; it will only be realized fully after the *paroikia* or earthly pilgrimage of the 'strangers in this world' (4.3; 4.11). Therefore rest after this pilgrimage is not so much an *anapausis* (*dolce far niente*) as a *katapausis*, i.e. a rest after the hard struggle of life.[164] 'Rest' is not a matter of doing nothing (see Gen. 49.15), but the end and abolition of all alienation, all suffering and all disappointment. Therefore in Hebrews rest is never connected with atoning sacrifices. Rest at the right hand of God begins for Jesus only after the sacrifice which is offered up by Jesus and perfected by God. It is a rest like that of God (see 4.10), characterized by expansive *ḥesed* and *'emet*, love and faithfulness: grace – just as Christ resting never ceases to make intercession for us; rest, being there completely for others without any alienation, suffering and tears, without any thought of reward: simply being there for others.

Biblical rest, perfected in Jesus Christ, is in fact a human society free from compulsion, which only finds rest in selfless living; for others with God and Christ in their transparent midst.

*Conclusion: Imperishable* charis, *the only firm and abiding support for believers*

'Jesus Christ is *the same* yesterday and today, and will remain so for ever' (13.8); that is the literal translation. It means: Jesus the priest (= Christ) is the second age, new, abiding and imperishable, which has been prepared from eternity and is pre-existent with God, the *prōtos* and the *eschatos*, the *alpha* and the *ōmega* of all (2.10), and 'creator of the two ages', both the first and the second. In contrast to 'some diverse and strange teachings' (13.9), the teaching of Jesus and teaching about Christ is unalterable; he is *ho autos* – the same; the main accent is put on this in 13.8. He himself is not subject to the change of the ages. The author's warning to Christians not to return to the earlier food laws (13.9c), together with the mention of 'some strange theories' (13.9a), points once again to the danger of syncretistic religious practices, even in the Christianity of the last decades of the first century (see also Galatians, Colossians and I Peter). Hebrews contrasts the permanence of the grace of God with the transitoriness of these things; this grace of God has become effective in the heavenly exaltation of Jesus to be Christ in power: an everlasting priesthood. Consequently 'we rightly rely on the *charis* or grace of God' (13.9b, in the context of 13.9a and 13.9c). The fundamental problem for Hebrews was: what provides support, stability, a firm basis (see the definitions of faith and hope)? The author's answer is: the coming age or the *charis* of God (compare this with the *Didache* as quoted above): prepared from eternity, manifested historically in Jesus who now eternally makes intercession for us. Christ is the same yesterday, today and for ever: that means, in his pre-existence with God, in his historical manifestation among us and his subsequent exaltation to God.

Hebrews is a sacerdotal – priestly-messianic – theology of grace. The author does not know of priests in the church. On the one hand he speaks of 'your leaders' (13.7), but by that he means already dead apostolic leaders of the church: 'Remember your leaders, those who spoke to you the word of God, consider *the outcome of their life*; and imitate their faith' (13.7). Thus Hebrews was written when a degree of reverence for the apostles had developed. On the other hand, Hebrews also speaks of present church leaders who are still alive (13.17), who are working for the salvation of the community; however, they are not called priests. Nowhere in the New Testament is there knowledge of priests in the church (though there is mention of church leaders and overseers); for the New Testament, Jesus alone is priest (Hebrews, and to some degree Revelation), whereas the whole of the community of God is named *a priestly people of God* (though even then only in two passages, each of them a quotation from the Old Testament: I Peter 2.9f. and Rev. 5.10).

According to Hebrews, life in accordance with the gospel is the grace of a new way of life (10.20; sacrificial self-surrender in solidarity with all and in the service of all). The author contrasts this with the sacrifice of bulls, goats and heifers, sacrifices which are without grace, a helpless attempt to open up access to God. But Jesus Christ has opened up this access; he is therefore the pioneer, the leader and perfecter of our faith; he is access to God, the new way of life (10.20).

All of this comprises the *logos parakleseos* (13.22), that is, the consolation or encouragement of the gospel, which the author strives for with his writing. The foundation for this consolation is the dogmatic insight which he has given, a 'higher doctrine' (6.1). Jesus is the last and final, decisive and perfect image of God among us (1.1f.), particularly through his priestly service in the purification from sin (reconciliation) and sanctification and, after he himself has been perfected by God, through his eternal intercession: '*by the grace of God* he tasted death for everyone' (2.9). *In Hebrews* the death of Jesus has saving significance only as a result of his (resurrection and above all) his exaltation to the right hand of God, though this exaltation presupposes Jesus' sacrifice. Death and exaltation are two inseparable elements in Hebrews' theory of sacrifice. This Christian doctrine is a comfort in the gospel because the content of Christian faith is the source and the substance of hope (3.5; 4.14; 10.23; 11.1). The priesthood of Christ is *aparabaton*: indestructable and inalienable (7.24).

In all this we have a correlation with our humanity: 'It was fitting that we should have such a high priest' (7.26; see 7.25). It is *appropriate* that we men who are caught up in a history of suffering should be freed by someone who personally identifies himself with this suffering (2.10). For this author the important thing is not a doctrine, not even the earthly preaching and the living words of Jesus, but his way of life. This way of life is not filled out with a kerygmatic account of his career, as happens in the four gospels; it is as it were 'formalized' so that its deepest essence is presented. This is given evocative form in the account of the crucifixion: it is self-sacrifice in solidarity with suffering brethren. For Hebrews, words and messages only make sense if they are demonstrated in the course of a particular career: the way of suffering trodden by all men. The church of Hebrews does not talk; *it marches*, and stops now and then to *celebrate its liturgy* on the way. In this sense the work is one long argument against priestly verbalism, though the author himself needs a brilliant homily in order to make this clear to us. The exodus community of Hebrews is a praying church, giving thanks and praise: the context of Hebrews is therefore Asia Minor or, as I suppose, the Christian churches of Alexandria in Egypt.

Some exegetes claim that Hebrew talks more of a 'Christ principle' (along the lines of the idealistic christology of the nineteenth century) than of Jesus of Nazareth, who never seems to take concrete historical form in the work. And of course it must be conceded that for all the human terms that the author uses of Jesus, the categories he employs are nevertheless formal. The literary genre of Hebrews is clearly different from that of the synoptists, who for example condense the suffering of Jesus into the story of Gethsemane and the way to Golgotha and his testing in the story of the three temptations; by contrast, Hebrews is more thematic and speculative (5.7; 2.10–18; 4.15; 12.2). There is no 'narrative theology', as with the gospels; the theology of Hebrews is argumentative and thematic. Are the synoptics therefore more (or less) historical than Hebrews? In fact the author draws a complete picture of Jesus, though he does so from his faithfulness to God and his solidarity with human suffering. He does not give a photograph, but a signed portrait of Jesus, just as the synoptics have done. The author knows that Jesus came from Judah (7.14) and that Golgotha was outside the walls of Jerusalem (13.12). Hebrews 1.5 may be seen as an allusion to the stories of the baptism of Jesus found in the synoptic gospels, just as 1.6 is an allusion to what is portrayed in Luke by the angels' song of praise at the birth of Jesus (Luke 2.9–15; granted, this is thematized, but it does show that Hebrews is familiar with Christian traditions). Hebrews is also aware that Jesus endured resistance and hostility (12.3). True, the author quotes fewer 'facts' from the life of Jesus directly, and prefers to describe Jesus' life with words and events from the Old Testament (above all from the story of Moses); for him, however, this strengthens his argument rather than weakens it. 12.28 talks of the synoptic kingdom of God, though in the context of the view of the world held by Hebrews. Many small details indicate that Hebrews is familiar with the so-called Jesus tradition. It presupposes this tradition: 'It was declared at first by the Lord, and it was attested to us by those who heard him' (2.3); he himself seeks to give 'more mature instruction' (6.1). The author is concerned with access to God, and this is only opened up – albeit on the basis of the earthly life of Jesus – at the moment of his exaltation to the sanctuary of God. That is the focal point which binds him in Jesus the Christ and claims his attention.

Hebrews is not a gospel, nor even a letter, but a kind of lecture or homily. However, the author sets out to depict the Christian experience of salvation in Jesus from God in a particular framework of interpretation. Therefore Hebrews is one of the best New Testament examples of the problem presented by the relationship between *experience* and (theological) *interpretation*. The author *experiences* Jesus as *high priest*; for him this is not merely a superstructure which might be seen as extremely successful in relation to the world-view and the religious presuppositions of the author and his audience. It is an experience and an interpretation at the same time, in such a way that we can always understand why other New

Testament authors experience and interpret Jesus otherwise, although each one is aware that it is a question of one and the same Jesus. From a theological point of view this is liberating. It leaves open the possibility that, inspired by what we have heard in the New Testament about interpretative experiences of Jesus Christ, we should again be able to experience the same Jesus differently within a new and different horizon of experience. Indeed it lays this upon us as a task. This is what we can do while still remaining faithful to the apostolic tradition as embodied by the author of Hebrews in his new interpretation of Jesus as the high priest.

Chapter 4

# Churches in the process of stabilization speak of salvation-in-Jesus

The so-called Pastoral Epistles (I Timothy, II Timothy and Titus), the Epistle of Jude and II Peter are characterized above all by the fact that they are as it were encyclicals, written for all the provinces of the church or to their leaders, at a later period, namely during the transition from the second to the third Christian generation. The awareness of the beginning of a post-apostolic period begins to make itself felt in a tendency to hand on traditional material 'unaltered', without being brought up to date; it is also used as a criterion for judging a number of heresies. We also become aware of the significance of the church's ministry of the overseer, who had to lead Christian communities at times which chronologically were now at an increasing remove from the first apostolic spring in which people could still talk of their encounter with Jesus.

## §1  Jesus Christ, the personal manifestation of the grace of God: the Pastoral Epistles

*Literature*: N. Brox, *Die Pastoralbriefe*, Regensburg 1969; R. Deichgräber, *Gotteshymnus und Christushymnus in der frühen Christenheit*, Göttingen 1967; M. Dibelius, *The Pastoral Epistles*, ET, Hermeneia, Philadelphia 1972; G. Holtz, *Die Pastoralbriefe*, ThHNT 13, Berlin 1965; J. Jeremias, *Die Briefe an Timotheus and Titus*, NTD 9, Göttingen [7]1954; T. de Kruyff, *De pastorale*

*Brieven*, Roermond 1966; O. Merk, 'Glaube und Tat in den Pastoral-briefen', *ZNW* 66, 1975, 91–102; H. Roux, *Les épîtres pastorales*, Geneva 1959; G. Schille, *Frühchristliche Hymnen*, Berlin 1965; E. Smelik, *De brieven van Paulus aan Timotheus, Titus en Filemon*, Nijkerk ³1961; W. Stenger, 'Der Christushymnus in I Tim. 3.16. Aufbau – Christologie – Sitz im Leben', *TrThZ* 78, 1969, 33–48; E. Schweizer, *Erniedrigung und Erhöhung bei Jesus und seinen Nachfolgern*, ATANT 28, Zurich ²1962; K. Wengst, *Christologische Formeln und Lieder des Urchristentums*, Gütersloh 1973; B. Weiss, *Die Briefe Pauli an Timotheus und Titus*, Meyer 11, Göttingen ⁷1902.

These letters are addressed to the church leaders of Christian communities which increasingly consist exclusively of Gentile Christians and as a result are gradually becoming alienated from the spirituality of the Tanach and their own original roots – the great scar left by the church's struggle against the angel of God, the struggle of Jacob with his brother Esau. Like Israel itself at one time, now too the church is fighting against this evil.

However, there are still many Jews in the Christian communities, and that is clear from the reactions in this letter. Moreover, the communities live by the kerygma, Christian hymns and confessions, all of which were composed by *Jewish* Christians. Probably all three letters – I and II Timothy and Titus – were written by one and the same author, and, like Jude and II Peter, they presuppose a tension. *On the one hand* is the establishment of orthodoxy: 'faith on which God's guidance rests' (I Tim. 1.4c); 'the church of the living God, pillar and foundation of truth' (I Tim. 3.15b), 'the principles of faith and sound doctrine' (I Tim. 4.6), 'the sound principles of our Lord Jesus Christ and the teaching of our religion' (I Tim 6.3; II Tim. 1.13), 'the treasure entrusted to you' (II Tim. 1.14), 'sound doctrine' (II Tim. 4.3; Titus 2.1). On the other hand there is what in these letters is called 'hair-splitting' ( I Tim. 1.4), 'vain talk' (I Tim. 1.6; Titus 1.10); 'craving for controversy and for disputes' (I Tim. 6.4; II Tim. 2.14; 2.23; Titus 3.9), 'godless chatter' (II Tim. 2.16). The Letter to Titus makes it more precise and sums it up: 'Jewish myths' (Titus 1.14); 'especially among the circumcision party' (Titus 1.10). The disputes are evidently about the Law (3.9). However, this has nothing to do with the earlier Judaizers. The heretics referred to 'forbid marriage and enjoin abstinence from certain foods' ( I Tim. 4.3; and see also Titus 1.14f.). I Timothy 4.7 speaks in more general terms of 'godless and meaningless myths' or of 'myths and genealogies' (I Tim. 1.4; 4.7; II Tim. 4.4; Titus 1.14; 3.9; cf. II Peter 1.16). Once again these are forms of syncretism in the last decades of the first century. Furthermore, there are people who 'claim that the resurrection has already taken place' (II Tim. 2.18).

These letters contrast what they call 'subtleties' with the healthy apostolic tradition: 'the truth' (a term which occurs frequently) and which to a large degree has already been 'fixed in writing'. 'The saying is sure and worthy of full acceptance, that Christ Jesus came into the world to save sinners' (I Tim. 1.15 is here evidently quoting from what will later be called 'the New Testament', e.g. Matt. 9.13 par.; Luke 15.2; 19.10; cf. II Tim. 2.11; Titus 3.8). Also, 'The saying is sure: If we have died with him, we shall also live with him . . .' (II Tim. 2.11–13; the reference is to Christian texts, perhaps Christian hymns, in which we recognize Rom. 6.5; 8.15; Matt. 10.33; I Cor 1.9). As such, these letters, which are intended to give guidelines to church leaders (they are addressed not to the communities but to their leaders, which in itself is something new) have little doctrinal content, but they do contain brief dogmatic formulations, albeit in stereotyped form, in which the person of Christ Jesus is himself called 'the grace of God': the man Jesus is the personal manifestation of the grace of God among us.

'The goodness and loving kindness (*philanthrōpia*) of God our Saviour has appeared on earth (Titus 3.4: *philanthrōpia* is a Hellenistic word which is sometimes the translation of *ḥesed* in the Septuagint instead of *eleos* or mercy). 'In virtue of his own purpose and the grace which he gave us in Christ Jesus ages ago, and now has manifested through the appearance of our Saviour Christ Jesus' (II Tim. 1.9b–10). '*His* grace' is the grace of God (Titus), that is, his grace (II Timothy) has been manifested in the appearing of Jesus Christ. In Titus 3.4; 1.3; 2.10 and I Tim. 2.3 God is called 'our Saviour'; on the other hand, Christ himself is also called 'our Saviour' (II Tim. 1.9f.; Titus 3.6). In Titus 2.11 we find, 'The grace of God, source of salvation for all men, has appeared on earth' (literally, 'the salvation-bringing grace of God appeared to all men'). Thus the heart of the doctrine of the Pastoral Epistles seems to be contained in Titus 3.4; 2.11; II Tim. 1.9b–10; we should also add I Tim. 2.5: 'There is one God, and there is one *mediator* between God and men, the *man Christ Jesus*.' The man Jesus Christ is the manifestation of the grace of God on earth, or to put it more pointedly, he is personally the manifestation of the grace of God on earth, as Titus 2.13b speaks of 'our great God and Saviour Christ Jesus', with the whole expression under a single article (*tou megalou Theou kai sōtēros hēmōn Christou Iēsou*), that is, the unity of God and Christ seems to be stressed more strongly here than Paul himself would ever have ventured to do. Christ seems to be 'the great God and Saviour' (so also II Peter 1.1). It is, however, grammatically possible to take the two genitives together as an instance of hendiadys; indeed, I think that it is even the case that we must read *Christou Iēsou* as the predicate of *doxa*, namely the epiphany or parousia of the glory of the great God and Saviour in Jesus Christ: 'We look for the revelation of the glory of our great God and Saviour', and the revelation of this glory of God is Jesus Christ at his parousia. Just as Jesus on earth is the manifestation of the *charis* or grace of God, so his parousia is the manifestation of the *doxa* or glory of God. This seems to me to be the real argument of the doctrine of all the Pastoral Epistles. 'God and Saviour' is a Hellenistic hendiadys from Greek religion. It is not the Pastoral Epistles, which are still strongly oriented on Paul, but II Peter, an even more markedly Hellenistic work, which goes one step further and perhaps names Jesus Christ himself 'God and Saviour' (1.1, see below); at all events, in II Peter, in a quite un-Pauline way, Jesus Christ himself is the subject of the doxology. The *grace* and finally the *doxa* of God appear in the 'mediator between God and man, the man Christ Jesus' (I Tim. 1.15–17; 2.3–6; 6.14–16; II Tim. 1.9f.; 4.1; Titus 1.2f.; 2.11–14; see 3.4). II Timothy in turn does not speak of the 'grace of Jesus Christ', but (according to the Greek) of 'the grace (namely of God) which is in Jesus Christ' and also of the 'salvation which is in Christ Jesus' (II Tim. 2.10). All these Pastoral Epistles – in loyalty to Paul – constantly bear in mind the mediation *between* God and man. These dogmatic 'formulae' in the Pastoral Epistles also give the impression of being liturgical formulae.

At the same time, even in formulae, after a mention of the appearing of the grace of God in Jesus Christ, we continually find a mention of the death of Jesus, as a ransom or an atoning sacrifice: 'mediator . . . the man Christ Jesus, who has given himself as a ransom for all' (I Tim. 2.5f.); 'Our Saviour Christ Jesus, who abolished death and brought life and immortality to light through the gospel' (II Tim. 1.10); 'The appearing of the glory of our great God and Saviour Jesus Christ, who gave himself for us to redeem us from all iniquity and to purify for himself a people of his own who are zealous for good deeds' (Titus 2.13f.). God's grace has appeared in Jesus to redeem us through his death; therefore, 'the saying is sure: . . . Christ Jesus came into the world to save sinners' (I Tim. 1.15). We have a share in this through baptism: 'The loving kindness of God our Saviour appeared on earth and he has saved us, not because of deeds done by us in righteousness, but in virtue of his own mercy, by the washing of regeneration and renewal in the Holy Spirit' (Titus 3.4f.). Here the marked distinction which Paul draws between 'justification' and 'redemption' (see Rom. 5.9f.) is completely obliterated: 'God who *saved* us and called us with a holy calling, not in virtue of our works but in virtue of his own purpose and the grace which he gave us' (II Tim. 1.9; see, however, Titus 3.5–7, which mentions 'redemption', 3.5, and 'justification', 3.7). Just as God's saving grace has appeared to all men (Titus 2.11), so the crucifixion of Jesus is testimony to the eternal saving will of God: 'God our Saviour, who desires all men to be saved and to come to the knowledge of the truth' (I Tim. 2.3b–4; the author bases this universalism on monotheism and on the one mediator, the man Jesus Christ, 'for . . . ', 2.5). In another passage we find, 'one Saviour for all men, especially for believers' (I Tim. 4.10).

If in all this we take into account hope for the coming parousia in which God's glory (and not just his grace) 'will appear' (Titus 2.13, and all the texts on hope), we have the explicit essence of the christology of these three letters. The resurrection is not a distinct theme, but it is presupposed everywhere (clearly in II Tim. 2.18). The unapocalyptic, doctrinal matter-of-factness of these letters is striking.

Finally, the way in which a hymn to Christ is cited in I Tim. 3.14–16 is particularly noteworthy. A grammatical analysis shows that the author cites the hymn unaltered, just as it has been handed down (whereas Paul does not hesitate to work over such a hymn in order to make it serve the purpose of his letter completely). Here we have the literal citation of a hymn which is at the same time a confession, the norm of faith for the community and the criterion by which false teaching is to be judged. The christological hymn consists of three strophes, each of two lines, and is preceded by a sentence from I Timothy in which the quotation is introduced as a quotation: 'Great is the mystery of our religion (or piety)':

16b He was manifested in the flesh,
16c vindicated in the Spirit,

16d seen by angels,
16e preached among the nations,

16f believed on in the world,
16g and taken up in glory.

The contrasts in this hymn[165] are striking: flesh/spirit; angels/nations; world/glory, while the whole of the hymn is in turn dominated by the contrast of flesh and glory. The pattern of exaltation and humiliation controls the structure of all three strophes, which as a whole are governed by the tension between 'revelation' in the flesh and 'taken up in glory'. The principle on which the hymn is built up is the contrast that we have come across so many times before between the earthly realm of the *sarx*, flesh, and the supernatural realm of the *pneuma*, the heavenly, or the sphere of the divine. In Hellenistic Jewish terms the hymn thinks of the two great spheres of the world, that of the *sarx* and that of the *pneuma* (the heavenly sphere). Christ has appeared in the sphere of the *sarx* (v.16b), but he has been taken up into the spiritual sphere of the *doxa* or glory of God (v.16g). That is the content of the opening and closing verses. To understand everything that lies between these two all-inclusive verses we must think back to the Israelite royal psalms (see above, in connection with the analysis of Ephesians). When there came to be a greater awareness in Israel that Israel's God was the Creator of heaven and earth, this idea was linked with that of God's rule of the world, and this in turn helped to develop Israel's awareness of being the 'light of the world' (Isa. 49.5–9) with a mission to all nations. In monotheistic terms, Yahweh's rule over the world was therefore an exaltation above all *ᵉlōhīm* (a remnant of ancient polytheism, Ps. 97.9). At the same time, this heightened understanding of creation made Yahweh even more transcendent: Yahweh is seated up there in highest heaven, above all the angels, and at the same time his glory fills heaven and earth and all the nations (Isa. 66.18f.; Ps. 72.19; 57.5). This background gives us the key for understanding the hymn, since the earthly Jesus is taken up to God's throne: like the glory of Yahweh, the lordship of Christ fills heaven and earth and all the nations. That is said in a poetic, hymn-like way in v.16c–f.

'Vindicated in the spirit.' The earthly Jesus, mocked and put to death, an 'innocent sufferer', is rehabilitated in the heavenly sphere. He is 'vindicated'; i.e., his rights are restored. The condemned man emerges triumphantly from this process (*dikaioun*, see also Luke 7.29; Rom. 3.4, which quotes the Septuagint version of Ps. 50.6 (EVV 51.4): that has *nikan*, emerge from the trial triumphantly as victor). 'Seen by angels' and 'preached among the nations' points to Christ's universal rule over the world: in the heavens the angels acknowledge Christ's heavenly exaltation over them, and 'the Lord Jesus' is preached everywhere on earth. 'Believed on in the world' (vv.16f.): Here again the Greek has *kosmos*, the world of the flesh as contrasted to the spiritual world of God's glory. Although he has been taken above into God's heavenly world, Christ is 'believed in' on earth. In other words, the exalted Jesus binds the heavenly spiritual sphere with the earthly sphere of the *sarx*, in his person and in the belief of Christians. However transcendent he may be in his exaltation to God, *in faith* Christ's 'glory of God' fills the whole cosmos. The gulf between the *epigeia*, the earthly, and the *epourania*, the heavenly, has been bridged in Jesus Christ (this is also the theme of Ephesians and Hebrews). A *man* has been glorified to be *with God* and by him has been appointed Lord of the universe, over both angels and the nations. This is the hymnic confession of faith in praise of God which is contained in this hymn to Christ, which unmistakably originates in Greek-Jewish communities with wisdom traditions (cf. Sir. 24.2–22; and I Enoch 42.1–3).[166]

At the same time, I Timothy uses this liturgical hymn as a criterion for the Christian community, 'the pillar and bulwark of the truth' (I Tim. 3.15c), against possible heresies. From this we can see how these late apostolic churches continued to stress their foundation in the apostles and to live by faith in the exalted Jesus Christ, who was once the manifestation of the *charis* of God on earth, now 'witnessed to in faith' and soon – at the parousia – the manifestation of the glory of God. That is the christology presented by these three Pastoral Epistles. However, only II Timothy stresses the suffering of Christians, and regards it as a normal occurrence. 'All who desire to live a godly life in Christ Jesus will be persecuted' (II Tim. 3.12; see 2.3). Appearing in the *sarx* (humanity: in this hymn there is no direct mention of pre-existence) is clearly seen as a 'sarkic' situation, i.e. as helplessness and suffering. In this respect, this hymn has a primitive Christian stamp: a hymn to the truly great, the suffering righteous, which is the tenor of almost all the ancient hymns to Christ.

In conclusion: these Pastoral Epistles apply Paul's concept of *charis* – *charis* as the election of Paul to the apostolate (see above) quite generally to the church's ministry as such: 'the gift of God that is within you through the laying on of my hands' (II Tim. 1.6); 'Do not neglect the *charis* you have, which was given you by prophetic utterance when the elders laid their hands upon you' (I Tim. 4.14: see the synthesis on 'Differentiations in grace "to the good of all" ', pp. 532f.).

## §2 'Our God and *Sōtēr* Jesus Christ': Jude and II Peter

*Literature*: (Jude and II Peter)
(*a*) See the bibliography given in ch. 3.1, §1 above on I Peter, which also takes II Peter into account.
(*b*) Also: V. Luz, 'Erwägungen zur Entstehung des Frühkatholizismus. Eine Skizze', *ZNW* 65, 1964, 88–111; W. Marxsen, *Der 'Frühkatholizismus' im Neuen Testament*, Neukirchen 1958; F. Mussner, 'Frühkatholizismus', *TrThZ* 68, 1959, 237–45.

Both letters are dealt with together here, because they have the same atmosphere, attack the same heresies and often have verbal correspondences. Internal criticism shows that II Peter as it were rewrites the letter of Jude and even corrects it.

### I. THE STABILIZATION OF THE CHURCH AND CHARISMATICS

It becomes clear from these two letters that the basic lines of the apostolic faith have been canonized and that a New Testament canon is already beginning to form. II Peter 3.15f. knows of a collection of the letters of Paul, and these, along with the Bible, the Tanach, already have the status of 'holy scripture' (see II Peter 3.16c). From this moment on, in addition to the question of the exegesis of the Old Testament, we also have the problem of the hermeneutic or interpretation of what will soon be called the 'New Testament' (II Peter 1.20f.), since II Peter points to difficulties in the interpretation of the letters of Paul. Furthermore, the author is concerned to reconcile the authority of Peter and Paul, both of whom are called great pillars of the church. The apostolic teaching is a possession of the church (Jude 17, see II Peter 3.2). The authority of oral tradition is gradually giving way to what will be called the 'New Testament'. A number of Christian generations have already passed away (II Peter 3.4), and once again many have left the church (II Peter 2.20–22). The authors of these letters, church leaders in their time, deliberately write their letter as an encyclical to the whole of the universal church (II Peter 3.2, 16), and even for coming generations (II Peter 1.15), on the basis of a heritage which has already been set down in writing (II Peter 3.15f.). This includes not only Paulinism (II Peter 3.15b), but evidently also synoptic traditions (II Peter 3.16). The function of the church's teaching ministry is growing, as the church has the task of interpreting these writings (II Peter 3.15f.; 1.20f.). The demarcation between what is Christian faith and what is not has been laid down as it were canonically and in writing (II Peter 2.21). The essential *paradosis* or tradition is coming to an end (Jude 3), and now it alone – 'the most holy faith' (Jude 20) – is becoming the norm (II Peter 1.1; 2.21; 1.12f., 15; 3.1f.; Jude 3, 5, 17). Scripture is called inspired (II Peter 1.20f.); the reference is still to the Tanach (see I Peter 1.19), which is not to be interpreted in any arbitrary way. Now it has become a book of Christians: 'You must understand this, that no prophecy of scripture is a matter of one's own interpretation, because no prophecy ever came by the impulse of man, but men moved by the Holy Spirit spoke from God' (II Peter 1.20f.; cf. Mark 12.36; Acts 3.21; II Tim. 3.16).

Christology is expressed in a few stereotyped formulae; these must be accepted as a Christian commandment (II Peter 1.11; see 3.2), whereas eschatology is privatized and made an inward event (II Peter 1.19), although it is still bound up with an apocalyptic cosmic expectation of a universal conflagration (II Peter 3.10–13; this conflagration, the end of our earthly world, was an essential element of the world-view of late antiquity). The obverse of growing orthodoxy was the eagerness with which Christians read Jewish and Christian apocryphal writings (at that time Jewish apocrypha were often revised and had Christian interpolations). Even these two official church letters refer to the apocryphal book of Enoch, explicitly (Jude 14) or implicitly (II Peter 2.4f.). We also find implicit allusions to the Christian Jewish apocryphon the Assumption of Moses (Jude 6 and 9; II Peter 2.10f.; 3.5). The Reformation was suspicious about recognizing the New Testament canonicity of these letters above all because of their use of apocryphal literature, and some church fathers rejected the Epistle of Jude for this very reason. Legends also found their way into the New Testament because of references to apocryphal writings (and did not lose their legendary character as a result). However, we should not overlook the fact that II Peter makes some corrections to the all too ready use of apocryphal writings in the Epistle of Jude (see the synthesis below on 'Victory over alienating demonic powers', pp. 499ff.).

Furthermore, we should not lose sight of the fact that this stabilization of the church towards the end of the first century is not a specifically Christian phenomenon. At that time the whole of civilization showed a tendency towards fixed norms, towards stability and 'orthodoxy', whether in pagan religion, Judaism (the growth of rabbinic orthodoxy in this period) or Christianity. Signs of a universal cultural pessimism began to make themselves felt, above all after the splendours of Stoicism. This led to the consolidation of the positions achieved throughout the culture of the Roman empire. The stabilization of ecclesiastical Christianity was just one element or variant, though on the basis of internal Christian criteria it was set in an increasingly larger church.

This situation also explains the kind of heresies attacked in the two letters. Some Christians have ecstatic experiences (Jude 8), as a result of which they are 'fulfilled' and claim to have arrived at a deeper knowledge of divine matters (II Peter 1.5f.; 1.2, 3, 8; 2.20; 3.18). They call themselves *pneumatici*, those who are filled with the spirit, whereas the simple church people are *psychici*, without the inspiration of the *pneuma*. This was a charismatic spiritual movement of the kind which was to be found regularly in early Christianity. II Peter explains that it is the result of arrogance (II Peter 2.18), characterized by an individualistic and evidently arbitrary and fantastic interpretation of scripture (II Peter 1.19–21; 3.16). These people evidently misuse 'the gospel of freedom' (II Peter 2.19; Jude 4), and above all Paul's optimism over grace and his principle of 'by grace alone' (Jude 4; II Peter 3.15b–16). In contrast to earlier groups (or groups elsewhere) which overestimated the angelic powers, and in which church leaders showed that these heavenly beings were subject to Christ (Paul, Colossians, Ephesians, Hebrews, I Peter), these spiritual Christians thought themselves to be above the angels (Jude 8–10, 16; II Peter 2.10f.), as indeed they had been told at an earlier stage! Perhaps they interpreted this in a similarly free way. Both letters admonish these Christians to pay rather more attention to these angels (Jude 8–10; II Peter 2.10f.). In the first flush of freedom the spiritual Christians evidently criticize what had traditionally been called 'God's ordinances of creation' (Jude 8, 16, 25), as though there were a conflict between the ordinance of creation and the ordinance of salvation (forerunners of Marcion?). In their spiritual exultation they effectively deny the parousia, the 'not yet' of being a Christian, in favour of an 'already now' (Jude 4, 18; II Peter 2.2; 3.3f.). Has 'Christ is the Lord' become a myth by which they live (II Peter 1.16)? Unlike earlier spiritual Christians, these people mock the parousia, which is always said to be 'very near' but in fact never comes (II Peter 3.3). They are clearly no spiritual adventists. They evidently deny even Christ's lordship (which is here designated by means of a Greek word *despotēs,* ruler: Jude 4; II Peter 2.1). These phenomena interpreted by the authors (but to what extent?) evidently contain themes which will develop only at a later stage, in the second century, into what will be called Gnosticism, though this takes over a number of tendencies and themes from the culture of antiquity and late antiquity and develops them into a completely new philosophy of life. At this stage, however, it is not yet syncretism. Furthermore, there is no schism. II Peter and Jude are still talking about Christians within the community of faith, who participate in table fellowship (II Peter 2.13; 2.14; Jude 12, 2, 4); for both authors, however, these are expressions of heresy (Jude 19; II Peter 2.1): in reality these Christians have already left 'the true way' (II Peter 2.15) and they regard this situation as more serious than if these people had never become Christians (II Peter 2.20–22).

The authors are obvious attacking a tendency to make Christianity into a 'myth' and to separate kerygma and ethics. An 'anti-theology' is beginning to develop against the official theology of the church, which feels itself to be bound to Jesus. Perhaps in the first place these people wanted to revive and re-establish 'hidden truths' which were being passed over by the official church. Perhaps this is a first symptom of what in the second century will develop into a breach with the mainstream church: the separation of Christianity from its origin in Israel and in the Old Testament. A church which is made up only of Gentile Christians loses contact with its Jewish foundation. By means of its kerygma, its proclamation of Christ, which in the last resort is grounded in the Old Testament, the official church seeks to rescue what can be rescued, but the seed of the 'anti-church' of the second century is evidently already beginning to sprout, though in a hidden way, and the ground already seems to be shifting.

## II. FROM THE 'GOD OF JESUS' TO THE 'GOD CHRIST'?

One striking fact is that the doxology, which earlier writers always directed to God the Father through Christ in the Spirit, is now directed to Christ himself (II Peter 3.18). It is 'Lord and Saviour' (II Peter 1.11; 3.2), with two Hellenistic titles, *Despotēs* and *Sōtēr,* both of which are applied to the Roman emperor – which at the same time contains criticism of the divinized emperor. Now Christ himself becomes Lord of the eschatological kingdom, which has been shifted to the world to come (II Peter 1.11). While the *charis* of grace of God remains the origin of the whole of Christian existence (Jude 21, sec II Peter 1.3), the Christian way of life is given a markedly ethical character so that it becomes a moral way of life (II Peter 1.10f.), and what was earlier called *charis* now becomes commandment (II Peter 2.21; 3.2). The vocabulary is now more strongly Hellenized (no longer by Greek Jews but directly by converted Gentiles) (see above all II Peter 1.4). The official church also loses the contribution from the Jewish element and the spirituality of the Tanach. We find the first beginnings of 'patristics'. Jude 3 speaks of the *sōtēria koinē*, the redemption or salvation which is common to the whole of the world church. II Peter 1.1 begins the letter with 'our God and *Sōtēr* Jesus Christ', joining God and Saviour under one article. In other words, the God Jesus is our Saviour. This is the only passage in the whole of the New Testament where Christ himself *seems* to be called God and Saviour. 'God and *Sōtēr*' is a double term for God in pagan Hellenistic religion, and II Peter is doubtless referring to that. The question remains, however, whether 'God and *Sōtēr*' are referred directly to Jesus. At another point II Peter speaks of *Kyrios* and *Sōtēr* (1.11; 2.20; 3.2, 18) in the same sense. However, the question is whether it is so strong there: '*tou Theou hēmōn kai sōtēros Jēsou Christou* (1.1); 1.2 has: *tou Theou kai Jēsou tou Kuriou hēmōn*. In v. 2 there is evidently a difference: 'God (= Father) and Jesus our Lord'. Grammatically, however, a second reading is possible: 'our God and Saviour Jesus Christ'. But 1.2 reads the phrase in the first and not in the second sense (as is also the case in the Pastoral Epistles); in the light of 1.2, then, 1.1 means 'our God and Saviour Jesus Christ'. The Hellenistic expression 'God and Saviour' is used deliberately, but with the necessary Christian correction. This is obviously also its meaning in all the other instances where we have a mention of 'God and Saviour' in the New Testament (Titus 1.4; 2.13; 3.4), and where there is always *Kyrios* and *Sōtēr* in passages which deal only with Jesus.

A second expression from Hellenistic religion is also taken over by II Peter, which will exert considerable influence on the patristic churches. Salvation in Jesus from God – the central experience of the New Testament – is here interpreted by means of the expression *theias koinōnoi physeōs*, 'achieve a share in the divine nature' or in 'God's own being' (II Peter 1.4; the famous *consortium divinae naturae*). As such, the term comes from Greek philosophy and in particular from the Stoics, but it had already been taken over in Diaspora Judaism. In Stoicism man was as it were a part, a member of the one great divine nature or *physis*. In Hellenistic Judaism, with its clearly expressed concept of creation, this had long since been transformed into a *gift* of participation in the divine being.[167] 'Sharing in the divine nature' was already a common expression for Greek-speaking Jews. Despite the Hellenism of the terminology, the content is Jewish and Christian. The literal expression, which is not put particularly well, is: 'So that as a result (namely as a result of God's gracious promises) you attain a share in God's nature, thus escaping (*apophygontes*) the corruption of the world in selfishness' (as a consequence and at the same time as a presupposition of sharing in the divine). There is no question here of a natural affinity with the divine nature. The author says that from of old, as a result of the fulfilment of God's promises, and therefore through grace, Christians attain a share in God's own being and in so doing escape the corruption of a *selfish* world. Although the terminology is Greek, this passage is concerned with what in the apostolic tradition is referred to as 'dying to sin' and 'access to God'. And the author makes this more specific. This participation in the incorruptibility of God is faith bound up with virtue, knowledge, self-control, steadfastness, piety, brotherly love and above all charity (1.5–7). Anyone who acts and behaves in this way has access to the kingdom of our Lord and Saviour Jesus Christ. So even Greek pagans can understand what this Jewish Christian tradition really means. II Peter is simply doing what Romans, Colossians and Ephesians had already done for Christian communities: it is trying to give an explanation to particular readers. The Jewish-Greek 'kingdom of God' is here explained to Greeks. And it is very clear what they understand by it: a man can only be said to participate in the divine nature if he lives a religious and moral life. The interpretation of experiencing salvation in Jesus is not bound up with the language of Canaan, as salvation is meant for all, including Greeks. They may relate their experience of salvation-in-Jesus *in their idiom*.

Of course this brings dangers with it. The Jewish expression of the experience of Christ was also full of dangers. In expressions which can be understood by Greeks, II Peter says that this participation in God (*a*) is a grace, the fruit of Yahweh's ancient promises: (*b*) is expressed in a virtuous religious and ethical life; and (*c*) is diametrically opposed to a selfish life. Can anything be more characteristic of Jewish Christianity?

II Peter contrasts this event, which has been accomplished by Jesus Christ, with 'myths' (1.16). God said to a historical person, 'This is my beloved Son' (1.17). Here the letter alludes to a synoptic tradition, that of the transfiguration of Jesus (which was originally perhaps a resurrection appearance). God affirms officially that this Jesus is the Son of God; as such he will come again, as has been prophesied (1.19) in the Old Testament (without any reference to a particular passage; the Tanach as a whole becomes a single prophecy about Christ). This parousia has obviously become a problem in some communities. There are mockers who say, 'Where is the promise of his coming? For ever since the fathers fell asleep, all things have continued as they were from the beginning of creation' (3.4). And where is the end of the world which is supposed to be coming soon? The author replies, 'With the Lord one day is as a thousand years, and a thousand years as one day' (3.8). God has patience for our sake 'as grace to salvation' (3.15b). The author depicts the end of the world as a great conflagration – a Hellenistic conception of the end of the world which can be found throughout the non-canonical literature, a pagan theme that was associated with the prophetic theme of the eschatological fire of judgment (Isa. 33.11f.; Joel 2.3; Zech. 12.6). This cosmology is not part of the statement of the faith; it is a human assumption. The conflagration (3.7) is an event in which the four elements melt in an inferno and the stars are destroyed in a great tumult (3.10; 3.12). They are replaced by a new heaven and a new earth (3.13). However, in this imagery the author is speaking of God's judgment on our history (3.10c; 3.12c): a new world 'in which righteousness will dwell' (3.12c). The more holy and righteous the life of the community of God, the more quickly will this vision be realized (3.11).[168] (Thus in Acts 3.19f., the conversion of Israel is the presupposition for the parousia, whereas for Paul the conversion of the Gentiles is the presupposition for the conversion of Israel and the coming parousia.) Despite late apostolic features and clear fixations, these Christian leaders on the one hand remain faithful to the apostolic belief, while on the other hand they are less courageous than their predecessors in reinterpreting it creatively. For them the importance of the tradition *qua* tradition becomes more a 'commandment', a must, than a permanent concern for a reorientation on new problems. The norm of the apostolic faith, which requires allegiance and seeks orientation, takes on the form of an 'orthodoxy' in the sense of what is a quite restricted reinterpretation compared with its creative predecessors in the same apostolic faith.

Chapter 5

# Jesus, the witness of God-is-love: Johannine theology

General literature
Specific literature on particular themes is given at the beginning of each section. I list here only the great commentaries on John of more recent

date, and literature which is concerned with the whole of the Gospel of John, or at any rate its basic features.

C. K. Barrett, *The Gospel according to St John*, London 1958; J. Blank, *Krisis. Untersuchungen zur johanneischen Christologie und Eschatologie*, Freiburg 1964; F. M. Braun, 'Saint Jean. La Sagesse et l'Histoire, *Neotestamentica et Patristica*, FS O. Cullmann, NT.S 6, Leiden 1962, 123–33; R. E. Brown, *The Gospel According to John*, AB 29 and 29A, two vols, New York 1966 and 1970; R. Bultmann, *The Gospel of John*, ET Oxford and Philadelphia 1971; H. van den Bussche, *Het vierde evangelie*, four vols, Tielt 1959, 1960, 1955 and 1960; O. Cullmann, *The Johannine Circle*, ET London and Philadelphia 1976; C. H. Dodd, *The Interpretation of the Fourth Gospel*, Cambridge 1953; A. Feuillet, *Études johanniques*, Paris-Bruges 1962; E. Käsemann, *The Testament of Jesus*, ET London and Philadelphia 1968; R. Kysar, *The Fourth Evangelist and his Gospel*, Minneapolis 1975; H. Leroy, *Rätsel und Missverständnis. Ein Beitrag zur Formgeschichte des Johannesevangeliums*, Bonn 1968; B. Lindars, *The Gospel of John*, NCB, London 1972; G. W. MacRae, 'The Fourth Gospel and Religionsgeschichte', *CBQ* 32, 1970, 13–24; J. L. Martyn, *History and Theology in the Fourth Gospel*, New York 1968; W. A. Meeks, *The Prophet-King. Moses Traditions and the Johannine Christology*, NT.S 14, Leiden 1967; id., 'Am I a Jew?', in *Christianity, Judaism and other Greco-Roman Cults*, ed. J. Neusner, Leiden 1975, Vol. 1, 163–86; L. Morris, *The Gospel According to John*, London 1972; U. Müller, *Die Geschichte der Christologie in der johanneischen Gemeinde*, SBS 77, Stuttgart 1975; T. Pollard, *Johannine Christology and the Early Church*, Cambridge 1970; G. Reim, *Studien zum alttestamentlichen Hintergrund des Johannesevangeliums*, SNTS 22, Cambridge 1974; J. A. T. Robinson, 'The Destination and Purpose of St John's Gospel', in *Twelve New Testament Studies*, SBT 34, London 1962, 107–25; J. Robinson and H. Koester, *Trajectories through Early Christianity*, Philadelphia 1971; J. N. Sanders, *The Gospel according to St John*, London 1968; R. Schnackenburg, *Das Johannesevangelium*, HThKNT IV, three vols, Freiburg im Breisgau 1965, 1971, 1975; ET of vol. I, *The Gospel according to St John*, London and New York 1968; id., *Die Johannesbriefe*, HThKNT XIII, 3, Freiburg im Breisgau ⁵1975; S. Schulz, *Das Evangelium nach Johannes*, NTD 4, Göttingen 1972; T. C. Smith, *Jesus in the Gospel of John*, Nashville 1959; S. van Tilborg, ' "Nederdaling" en incarnatie: de christologie van Johannes', *TvTh* 13, 1973, 20–33; W. C. van Unnik, 'The Purpose of St John's Gospel', *StEv* 1 (=TU 73), 1959, 382–411; B. Vawter, 'The Gospel According to John', *JBC* 2, London 1968, 414–66; J. Willemse, *Het vierde Evangelie. Een onderzoek naar zijn structuur*, Hilversum-Antwerp 1965; *Studies in John* (for Professor J. N. Sevenster), NT. S 24, Leiden 1970.

*Introduction*

For a while now, some people have been reading the Gospel of John as an example of liberation theology,[1] while others have regarded it as the expression of a Christian Buddhism[2] – an indication that one often looks in scripture for confirmations of one's own longings, ideas and prejudices.

As in the preceding analyses, I am here concerned with the *theology* of the Johannine writings; I am not immediately concerned with a literary analysis of the text (though this will have to be presupposed). For John, too, the essence of the apostolic faith is that 'God so loved the world that he gave his only-begotten Son that all who believe in him should not perish but have everlasting life' (3.16). This is primitive Christian tradition, even if it is expressed in Johannine terminology. Paul already said, 'He even did not spare his own Son but gave him up for us all' (Rom. 8.32), 'But God shows his love for us in that while we were yet sinners Christ died for us' (Rom. 5.8). The allusion to Abraham's readiness to sacrifice Isaac, the son of the promise (Gen. 22.16), cannot be denied. But in Johannine theology this original datum of the primitive Christian tradition is developed in a particular way, above all because those who handed on the Johannine tradition were originally *Palestinian Jewish* Christians, not from orthodox, official Jewish circles, but from those which are nowadays called 'heterodox' marginal communities with a Jewish spirituality within the Jewish syncretism of the first century AD. However, before we emphasize this Jewish heterodox milieu of Johannine theology, we must first stress the roots of the Johannine tradition in the tradition of the earliest church, indeed in that of *Jerusalem*. So first of all we shall look for some keys which will open up an understanding of the Fourth Gospel to us. After that we shall analyse Johannine theology, partly by means of the specific construction of the Gospel of John, partly, and more especially, on the basis of specific themes within Johannine theology.

## §1 Keys for understanding the Gospel of John

*Literature* (in addition to the general literature mentioned above): J. Beutler, *Martyria. Traditionsgeschichtliche Untersuchungen zum Zeugnisthema bei Johannes*, Frankfurt 1972; J. Bowman, *Samaritanische Probleme*, Stuttgart 1967; J. H. Charlesworth, *John and Qumran*, London 1972; G. Wesley Buchanan, 'The Samaritan Origin of the Gospel of John', in *Religions in Antiquity* (in Memory of E. R. Goodenough) (NumenS), Leiden 1968, 149–75; C. Colpe, *Die religionsgeschichtliche Schule. Darstellung und Kritik ihres Bildes vom gnostischen Erlösermythus*, Göttingen 1968; R. A. Culpepper, 'The

Odes of Solomon and the Gospel of John', *CEQ* 35, 1973, 298–322; R. Le Déaut, *La nuit paschale. Essai sur la signification de la pâque juive à partir du Targum d'Exode XII, 42*, AnBibl 22, Rome 1963; K. M. Fischer, 'Der Johanneïsche Christus und der Gnostische Erlöser, in Gnosis und Neues Testament', in *Studien aus Religionswissenschaft und Theologie*, ed K. W. Tröger, Berlin 1973, 245–67; E. Freed, 'Samaritan Influence in the Gospel of John', *CBQ* 30, 1968, 580–7, and *NTS* 12, 1970, 241–56; T. F. Glasson, *Moses in the Fourth Gospel*, SBT 40, London 1963; J. R. Harris and A. Mingana, *The Odes and Psalms of Solomon*, Manchester 1920; J. Jervell, *Imago Dei. Gen. 1.26–27 im Spätjudentum, in der Gnosis und in den paulinischen Briefen*, FRLANT 76, Göttingen 1960; H. Jonas, *Gnosis und Spätantiker Geist*, two vols, Göttingen [3]1964 and [2]1966; H. B. Kuhn, 'The Angelology of the Noncanonical Jewish Apocalypses', *JBL* 67, 1968, 211–9; H. Kipperberg, *Garisim and Synagogue*, Berlin 1971; A. Lacomara, 'Deuteronomy and the Farewell Discourse (John 13:31–16:33)', *CBQ* 36, 1974, 65–84; R. Longenecker, *The Christology of Early Jewish Christianity*, SBT II 17, London 1970; B. L. Mack, 'Wisdom Myth and Mythology', *Int* 24, 1979, 46–60; id., *Logos und Sophia. Untersuchungen zur Weisheitschristologie im hellenistischen Judentum*, Göttingen 1973; M. McNamara, 'The Ascension and the Exaltation of Christ in the Fourth Gospel', *Scripture* 19, 1967, 65–73; id., *Targum and Testament*, Grand Rapids 1972; id., *The New Testament and the Palestinian Targum to the Pentateuch*, Rome 1966; G. W. MacRae, 'The Jewish Background of the Gnostic Sophia Myth', *NT* 12, 1970, 86–100; id., 'The Coptic Gnostic Apocalypse of Adam', *HeyJ* 6, 1965, 27–35; W. A. Meeks, 'Moses as God and King', *Religions in Antiquity*, NumenS, Leiden 1968, 354–71; Juan P. Miranda, *Der Vater, der mich gesandt hat*, Bern-Frankfurt 1972; G. W. Nickelsburg, Jr, *Resurrection, Immortality and Eternal Life in Intertestamental Judaism*, Cambridge, Mass. and London 1972; L. Perlitt, 'Moses als Prophet', *EvTh* 31, 1971, 588–608; G. Quispel, 'Qumran, John and Jewish Christianity', in *John and Qumran*, 137–55; H. M. Schenke, *Der Gott 'Mensch' in der Gnosis*, Göttingen 1962; F. Schmutenhaus, *Die Entstehung der Mosestraditionen*, Heidelberg 1958, typescript dissertation; M. Simon, *St Stephen and the Hellenists in the Primitive Church*, London and New York 1958; C. H. Talbert, 'The Myth of a Descending-Ascending Redeemer in Mediterranean Antiquity', *NTS* 22, 1976, 418–440; H. M. Teeple, *The Mosaic Eschatological Prophet*, JBL Monograph Series 10, Philadelphia 1957; H. A. Wolfson, *Philo*, two vols, Cambridge, Mass. [2]1948.

## I. JESUS, THE ESCHATOLOGICAL PROPHET GREATER THAN MOSES

### A. Jesus, God's eyewitness

All the witnesses to Jesus already appear in the literary unit made up of John 1.19–51. There are John the Baptist (1.19–33), the Father (1.32–34; see 8.18), Jesus himself (1.31, 47, 51; see also 8.14, 18), the 'works' of Jesus (1.46; see 10.25), the Tanach or scripture (1.45), the 'Holy Spirit' (1.32, 33, see 15.26), the disciples (1.35–51; see 15.27; 12.41, 45) and the evangelist who writes 1.19–51 (see 19.35 and, in the additional chapter, 21.24).

It is worth paying special attention to the so-called 'call' of the first four disciples. John the Baptist himself brings two of his disciples to Jesus; these become disciples of Jesus (1.35–37) as a result of John's testimony. This also confirms that the church to which the gospel is addressed derives from the followers of John the Baptist (see below); however, John has primarily theological concerns. One of the two disciples, Andrew, in turn brings his brother Simon Peter to Jesus, who immediately calls him Cephas, rock (1.41f.). Then Jesus himself calls Philip (1.44), who comes from the same city as the two brothers Andrew and Peter. Philip in turn seeks to convince Nathanael (1.45). John has a particular purpose in telling this story. The first two disciples, disciples of the Baptist, follow Jesus after the Baptist's remark 'Behold the Lamb of God' (1.36). These first disciples asked Jesus, 'Rabbi, where do you live?' (1.38). Jesus replies, 'Come and see' (1.39). Philip for his part says to Nathanael, who at first does not believe, 'Come and see' (1.46b). Finally, Jesus says to Nathanael: 'You will *see* heaven opened and the angels of God ascending and descending upon the Son of man' (1.51). The 'calls' prove to be an invitation 'to see'. Only to Philip does Jesus simply say 'Follow me' (1.43), as it were without seeing first. This Philip will later also ask, 'Show us the Father,' whereupon Jesus says, 'Philip, he who sees me sees the Father' (14.9).

'Seeing and believing' and 'believing without seeing' (see 1.50f.; 20.29) play a special role in the Fourth Gospel. The disciples 'believe in Jesus' from the beginning (2.11). But they are really called to be future *witnesses*: they must therefore also have 'seen' so that those who have not seen Jesus and his works can also themselves believe (see 19.35; 20.29, 31). True, 'the Jews' also see Jesus' signs, but they do not believe (12.37). In the Gospel of John there is 'seeing' (often *blepein*) and 'seeing' (*idein*). For disciples who are soon to be witnesses it is important that they 'see and believe' whereas the Johannine community (the second and third generation of Christians who have no longer seen the historical Jesus) is told, 'Blessed are those who do not see and yet have believed' (20.29b). However, the disciples bear witness in faith on the basis of their role as eyewitnesses (1.34; 3.11; 3.32; 15.27; 19.35; 20.30; see also I John 1.1–3; 4.14). Here we can already see connections in the tradition between the Gospel of John and Luke (Luke 1.2; Acts 1.21f.); these are not direct, but come from a tradition common to both: 'You shall bear witness, for you have been with me *from the beginning*' (John 15.27; see Luke 1.2). John has good reason for putting the story of the call of some disciples (four of them) before Jesus' first sign (2.2–11). After the Easter experience, Peter, who has already been called the rock (1.42), becomes the norm for the replacement of Judas, the apostle who has fallen out. He is someone who was the witness, 'beginning from the baptism of John' (Acts 1.22).

The four disciples 'follow Jesus', that is, they *believe* in him (1.37, 38, 40, 43) once 'they have seen' (1.35–51). They see and believe – so that others later can believe without seeing. Quite apart from the historicity of the Johannine account (which has every chance of being historically true) the two *disciples of John* are theologically necessary, in order to give a guarantee for the testimony of John the Baptist himself (1.19–34). Otherwise there would be a gap in the chain of witnesses.

All this is important for John, because Jesus also bears *witness*, namely about what he has seen and heard with the Father (3.11, 32, 33f.; 4.44; 5.31; 7.7; 8.14,18; 13.21; 18.37). The continuity of all these testimonies must be guaranteed. For Johannine theology, bearing *witness* means not speaking on one's own authority but saying what one has seen and heard; saying the words of the sender. This is true of the disciples (17.8; 17.14; see 16.12–15; 17.6–8; 17.16–18). It is also true of John the Baptist: 'I myself have seen and bear witness' (1.34; see 1.33). It is even true of the Paraclete, the Holy Spirit: 'He will not speak on his own authority, but whatever he hears he will speak' (16.13). He simply recalls what Jesus has said. Finally, it is also true of Jesus himself: 'The Son can do nothing of his own accord, but only what he sees the Father doing' (5.19,30; 3.11; 8.28; 14.10,24; 17.4,8). To bear witness means to speak of what one has seen or heard (3.11; 12.50; 5.19,30; 8.26,28,38,40; 16.13; 1.32f.,34; 19.35; I John 1.1–3).

However, it is true of all the witnesses but Jesus that 'No one has ever seen God' (1.18). 'No one has seen the Father except him who is from God; he has seen the Father' (6.46; 3.31f.; see 7.28f.; 8.26f.). In the last resort, any religious testimony goes back via Jesus to God's own truthfulness (7.28f.; 3.31–33). John is ultimately concerned by means of all testimonies to demonstrate their foundation in God's own truth and truthfulness. The pre-existent Logos who is from the beginning 'with God' is the ultimate foundation of all testimony. Jesus was there 'from the beginning': 'In the beginning was the Word and the Word was with God' (1.1): thus he can be a witness. So the chief witness says to his disciples: 'You also are witnesses, because you have been with me from the beginning' (15.27). The *in principio* of the Word is continuous with the *in principio* of the present experience of the disciples of John, later to become disciples of Jesus, with John the Baptist and with Jesus. That is significant in itself. 'In the beginning was the Word' (1.1) serves as a guarantee of Jesus' testimony: he was there, with God, from the beginning; he is an eyewitness. He has good grounds for telling us what he has seen and heard from the Father: '*I am he who bears witness . . .*' (8.18), namely, the Word of God. He was in the beginning with God, to be able to bear witness to God. He speaks only 'the words of the Father' (see 5.20b,23,36; 14.10; 3.34). That is why he became *sarx* (1.14a). His *sarx* is the *skēnē tou martyriou*, 'the tent of witness' (see Greek Num. 4.3f.): the tabernacle of God, the place where God dwells in our midst. John 1.14–16 stands in the Sinai tradition (see below: though this is also by way of an early Jewish interpretation). Jesus' manhood, the incarnation of the Word, is the realization of the promise of 'God's abode among his people' (Lev. 26.11f.; Ex. 25.8; Ezek. 37.27; 43.7; 48.35; Joel 3.21; Zech. 2.10; 8.3, etc.). It is not a question of a 'tent' – though his human habitation among us is transitory (see above). The allusion in 1.14ab is to the tent of the covenant, 'the tent of testimony' (see also Rev. 15.5; Acts 7.44; Heb. 8.2,5,9). As early as John 2.19–21, the Johannine Jesus speaks of 'the temple of his body'; 'he dwelt among us' (*eskēnōsen*, 1.14b): in his *sarx*, Jesus is the tabernacle, the tent of witness. The book of Revelation will say, 'Behold the tabernacle (*skēnē*) of God is among men. He will dwell (*skēnōsei*) with them' (Rev. 21.3). John 1.14 says that in Jesus God dwells in our midst. The *sarx* is the tabernacle of the Word among us. 'We have seen his glory' (1.14c), 'full of grace and truth' (1.14e). Jesus has come 'to bear witness of the truth' (18.37). He is the only one (*monogenēs*, see below) to have seen God (1.18). And this event is in continuity with 'We bear witness to what we have seen' (1.18; 3.11). The 'we' form, which Jesus himself uses by way of exception in 3.11, makes the testimony of the leader of the Johannine community, through original eyewitnesses, fuse with the testimony of Jesus, God's eyewitness: from the beginning 'with the Father' (1.1f.). 'He who comes from heaven . . . bears witness to what he has seen and heard' (3.31f.). He *is* the word of God: he *is* what he has heard from the Father. Therefore he can say: 'I am the one *who bears witness to myself*' (8.14); and that is the same thing as – though different from – 'the Father is greater than I' (14.28c), or 'the Father, who has sent me, bears witness to me' (8.18b).

The theme of bearing witness will recur almost monotonously in the Fourth Gospel, even when the word itself is not always used. Jesus can do nothing by himself; he does nothing by himself; he does not pass judgment by himself. He speaks only the words of the Father, does only the works of the Father and speaks the truth which he has heard from God. A witness is *sent* to bear witness to what he has seen with his eyes and heard with his ears: Jesus has been sent by the Father (3.17; 4.34; 5.36f.: 6.38f., 44,57 etc.). The Holy Spirit, who bears witness to Jesus, is then sent by Jesus or, at the request of Jesus, by the Father (14.26; 15.26; 16.7). John the Baptist has been sent by God (1.6, 33); finally, the disciples are sent by Jesus (17.18; 20.21). This primal Christian theme of sending is made specific in the Gospel of John in two ways: first in terms of the eschatological prophet like Moses, greater than Moses, and then in terms of the model of 'descending' and 'ascending'.

## B. Jesus, the eschatological, final prophet-greater-than-Moses

'The word which you hear is not mine but the Father's who sent me' (14.24). Jesus himself is 'from God' (16.30; 16.28; see 8.47; 13.3). The whole of John's view seems to me to be inspired by the great claim made by Yahweh in Deutero-Isaiah: '*You are my witnesses*' (Isa. 43.10). In Isa. 43ff. 'God's cause' is as it were discussed before a great world tribunal: 'All the nations come together, and the peoples have assembled . . . You are my witnesses – this is the Word of Yahweh – and my servant whom I have chosen, so that they come to realize and believe in me and known that *it is I* . . . I, I alone am Yahweh, and apart from me there is no helper . . . I, and no strange God in your midst. You are my witnesses . . . I alone am God, the Creator of all. . . Apart from me there is no God who is righteous and who saves. . . Every knee will bow before me. . .' The Gospel of John demonstrates the same exclusiveness in respect of Jesus, and this is emphasized by many witnesses. There is no salvation and no redemption apart from the Father and the Son. 'I am', says Jesus (see below). This whole argument in the Gospel of John brings us close to the eschatological prophet-like-Moses, greater-than-Moses, a popular expectation in early Judaism, which goes back to a Deuteronomic conception (Deut. 18.15, 18f.; 34.10; Ex. 23.20–23; 33.2).

This tradition of the eschatological prophet was originally separate from the expectation of Elijah (Mal. 4.5f.; see also Sir. 48.10f.): it belongs with the Moses tradition,[3] as it is clear that the forerunner, Elijah, is a secondary introduction in Mal. 4.5f. (see Mal. 3.1, which is connected with the original prophet-like-Moses). In fact the figure of Elijah takes on the function of a forerunner of the Messiah in early Judaism.[4] But this secondary tradition is based on an earlier, Deuteronomic tradition. For Deuteronomy, Moses is a preacher of the word, a prophet. Deuteronomy is essentially composed as a speech of Moses (see Deut. 5.1, 5,14; 6.1): he is the mediator between God and people (Deut. 5.5). However, at the same time Moses is a suffering mediator; he is not an intercessor for his people (Deut. 9.15–19; 9.25–29), he also suffers for his people, for Israel (Deut. 1.37; 4.21f.). For Deuteronomy, Moses is the *suffering prophet*.[5] Later prophets therefore readily come forward with the prophetic characteristics of Moses (see Jer. 1.7, cf. Ex. 4.10; Jer. 1.9, cf. Deut. 18.18; Jer. 15.1, which mentions Moses explicitly; see also Elijah and Elisha, I Kings 19.19–21; II Kings 2.1–15, cf. Deut. 34.9 and Num. 27.15–23: the duo of Moses and Elijah). It is striking that this prophetic model of Moses is above all a tradition from the northern kingdom (rooted in the Sinai and Horeb tradition, with the sanctuary of Shechem as a focal point), and not from the land of Judaea (see below for the nuances which this lends to the Gospel of John). In the northern tradition we find, 'If there is a prophet among you, I the Lord make myself known to him in a vision, I speak with him in a dream. Not so with my servant Moses, he is entrusted with all my house. With him I speak mouth to mouth' (Num. 12.6–8), 'as a man speaks with his friend' (Ex. 33.11), 'face to face' (Ex. 33.11). Deuteronomy says time and again that the prophetic Moses is the 'Ebed Yahweh', the servant of God (Ex. 14.31; Num. 12.7f.; Deut. 34.5; Josh. 1.2,7; Wisdom 10.16; Isa. 63.11). Furthermore, Moses is a *suffering* Ebed Yahweh, 'who bears the burdens of the people' (Num. 16.47f.; see Isa. 53.4). Moses is the suffering servant of God who atones for the sins of his people.

Various more recent investigations have made it probable that the theme of the 'innocent sufferer', itself an independent theme, has been fused in Deutero-Isaiah with the theme of 'Moses, the suffering prophetic servant of God', the Deutero-Isaianic Ebed Yahweh (above all in Isa. 42.1–4; 49.1–6; 50.4–11a; 52.13–53.12). It is wrong to put Proto–, Deutero– and Trito–Isaiah side by side as three disparate blocks in the final 'Isaianic' redaction. Structural analysis requires us to consider the whole. The prophetic, kingly Moses, who bears the burden of his people, *is* the suffering servant of God in Deutero-Isaiah: royal (see Isa. 41.21; 43.15; 44.6; 52.7), but with the emphasis on his *prophetic* character. Thus Deutero-Isaiah is said to have spoken of the suffering servant of God in a terminology which is strongly reminiscent of the developing picture of the eschatological prophet like Moses.[6] Like Moses, the servant mediates the Law or instruction (*tōrāh*) and justice (Isa. 42.1f.), but now he does so world-wide: this suffering Ebed-like Moses is 'the light of the world' (Isa. 49.5–9; 42.1–6). Like Moses, he is mediator of the covenant (Isa. 42.6; 49.8), leader of the new exodus, this time from the Babylonian exile. As a result of this exodus, the twelve tribes are reassembled (Isa. 49.5f.; 40.3). In this exodus the eschatological prophet like Moses will again strike water from the rock and offer his people 'living water' (Isa. 41.18; 43.20; 48.21; 49.10). The suffering servant of God is the

Moses of the new exodus (Isa. 43.16–21): the Mosaic servant of God who atones for sins and suffers for his people, who in fact has all the features of the one who in early Judaism was called the messianic eschatological prophet like Moses (see also Hebrews, which some people regard as 'Johannine', with some degree of justification).

After Deutero-Isaiah, the theme of the eschatological prophet like Moses developed in early Judaism into a 'Moses mysticism', a phenomenon which is also called 'Sinaitism' in exegetical literature. We already find something of this mysticism in Jesus Sirach: 'He . . . was beloved by God and man, Moses whose memory is blessed. He made him equal in glory to the holy ones, and made him great in the fears of his enemies. By his words he caused signs to cease: the Lord glorified him in the presence of kings. He gave him commands for his people and *showed* him part of *his* glory. He sanctified him through faithfulness and meekness; he chose him out of all mankind. He made him *hear his voice*, and led him into the thick darkness, and gave him the commandments face to face, the law *of life* and *knowledge* . . .' (Sir. 45.1–5; this passage seems to contain a number of Johannine themes). But the Moses mysticism continued to grow in early Judaism. The death of Moses is already an exaltation and *anabasis*, an ascension to heaven (just as the death of Jesus is for John).[7] Furthermore, the Moses who is glorified with the Lord mediates, through the grace of a new rebirth, access to the vision of God. In this tradition Moses is a *messianic*, royal figure.[8] For Philo, Josephus and the later rabbis Moses is in fact a *messianic king*; at the same time the suffering Ebed Yahweh – *divine* ('*theos*', not '*ho theos*', see also John 1.1c compared with 1.1b). This Moses mysticism was particularly marked among the Samaritans, to such a degree that some historians speak not only of Sinaitism, but also of Samaritanism. True, the connection between the Johannine tradition and Samaria has still to be illuminated satisfactorily, but most exegetes see strong connections between the Johannine community and the Samaritan mission (see John 4). Though the last word has yet to be spoken on the subject, the connection between Johannine theology and the Samaritans can hardly be denied.[9]

I therefore found the basic ideas of my book *Jesus. An Experiment in Christology* confirmed by the analysis of the specifically Johannine tradition. In this tradition, too, Jesus was originally seen as the eschatological prophet like Moses who far surpassed Moses, an early Christian tradition of which the earliest gospel, Mark, bears clear traces. Mark 1.2 begins the gospel with an implicit reference to Ex. 23.20; Mal. 3.1 and Isa. 40.3 (at the time of Jesus the source of inspiration for the concept of the 'eschatological prophet'). 'See, I send my messenger *before* you' (Mark 1.2). 'Before you', that means before Jesus, John the Baptist is sent who is to announce 'the prophet who comes after Moses and is greater than Moses': 'a prophet *from your midst* and *from your brethren*' (cf. Deut. 18.15–18 with Mark 6.4). Mark 6.14–16 also rejects three false prophetic identifications of Jesus: (*a*) Jesus is not John the Baptist *risen* from the dead (Mark 6.14), whose body has been laid in the tomb (Mark 6.29); (*b*) still less is he Elijah, who has already identified with John the Baptist (Mark 1.2; 9.11–13); (*c*) finally, Jesus is not 'a prophet *like the others*' (Mark 6.15). No, he is the 'prophet-after-Moses', 'like Moses and greater than Moses', the eschatological prophet: Elijah, then Moses, then Jesus (Mark 9.2–9), from which there follows almost automatically: 'Listen to him' (Mark 9.7: an implicit reference to Deut. 18.15, which at the time of Jesus was also understood in the complex of the tradition of the eschatological prophet after Moses). In all the gospels we find the theme that Jesus is the prophet, but 'not like the others'. Nowhere do they present any polemic against the conception of Jesus as the prophet; they attack the conception that he is a prophet '*like all the rest*'.

We hear exactly the same thing from quite a different side, the Johannine tradition. This is all the more striking as the Johannine community (for 'the disciple whom Jesus loved', see below) evidently had its earliest roots among the Greek-speaking Jewish Christians in the mother church in Jerusalem who were associated with Stephen; these later fled from Jerusalem to Samaria and then went on to Syria or Alexandria (though I can produce no compelling arguments for assuming their presence in the latter). In this particular context Stephen's speech according to Luke's version in Acts 7 is extremely interesting (if only because some affinities have been established between the Gospel of John and certain Lucan traditions). In my view, this speech of Stephen's, Acts 7.22–53, is unmistakably concerned with Jesus as the eschatological prophet like Moses, greater than Moses. Moses was 'powerful in word and deed' (Acts 7.22). But the *Ioudaioi* (the Jews) do not understand that God wanted to bring them salvation (*sōtēria*) through Moses (7.25), who, as '*leader (archōn)* and redeemer (to atone with a ransom for much suffering, *lytrōtēs*)' had been sent 'to the people' by God (7.35), and 'by working signs and wonders' (7.36). 'This is the Moses who said to the Israelites, "God will raise up for you a prophet from your brethren as he raised me up"' (7.37, thus with an *explicit* reference to the classical text of the eschatological prophet like Moses, Deut. 18.15, 18f., as interpreted in early Judaism). In these groups focussed on Stephen, who were originally in Jerusalem (and to whom the Johannine 'beloved disciple' refers), Jesus is seen as the eschatological prophet like Moses, *sent* by God and *rejected* by his people (Acts 7.17–44), which is the Johannine theme. (It should become clear later that the Johannine concept 'Lamb of God' also comes from the tradition of the *Mosaic* Ebed Yahweh, in Deutero-Isaiah's version.)

All this means that the one 'anointed with the Spirit of God', the *messianic* significance of the *Mosaic servant of Yahweh*, already existed in early Judaism before Christianity, as a result of the combination of Deutero- and Trito-Isaiah.[10] In addition to the tradition of a *messianic* son of David, there was also the tradition of a *Mosaic* messiah, the eschatological prophet.

The Johannine tradition expresses not only the special relationship of the eschatological prophet-like-Moses to God but also the specific relationship between Moses and the elect people of God. In fact the Gospel of John defends the messiahship of Jesus from the beginning (even immediately after the prologue, in the pericope about John the Baptist: 1.41). However, anyone who looks closer will see that John in no way defends *Davidic* messiahship; he defends *Mosaic* messiahship, the messianic eschatological prophet like Moses, a theme which was current in particular Palestinian and Samaritan circles.

The specific character of the *Mosaic Messiah* seems above all to be the original background to the Johannine summary of the ministry of Jesus (John 12.44–50; cf. John 3.2; 3.14a; 6.14; 7.31, 40; 9.17). Exegetes from various traditions have to recognize that in this pericope the Gospel of John presents the basic features of Johannine theology. In this section, which is a retrospective view of the public ministry of Jesus, John summarizes Jesus' revelation of himself. John 12.44–50 forms a literary unit, but this is simply one ingredient which is integrated into the final pattern of the Fourth Gospel. Within this gospel it has the purpose of expressing the essence of Johannine christology. And this Johannine gospel – the message of the Johannine Jesus – is: anyone who believes in Jesus, really believes in the Father who has sent him. Whoever sees Jesus, sees the Father. 'I have come as light into the world, that whoever believes in me may not remain in darkness' (12.46, see the prologue). Jesus has not come to judge, but to save the world (12.47). He speaks only words of salvation, life-giving words. To reject him is to reject the Father who sent him. This is the summary. Even so careful an exegete as R. Schnackenburg dare not deny that the so-called Sinai-tradition underlies this theme.[11] In John 12.50, as in Deut. 32.47, a connection is made between a commission from above and eternal life: 'Moses said to them, "Lay to heart all the words which I enjoin upon you this day, that you may command them to your children, that they may be careful to do all the words of this law. For it is no trifle for you, but it is *your life* ..."' (Deut. 32.46f.). In early Judaism the Torah was called *light* and *life*. But, John says, 'What Moses gave you was not the bread from heaven' (John 6.31–53): '*I* am the bread of life' (6.35). Jesus is the one who speaks on the basis of a personal converse with God (8.26; 3.32): the tradition is one of the identification of the one *who is sent* with the one by whom he is sent, 'for my name is present in him' (Ex. 23.20–23).[12] 'A servant is not greater than his master, nor is he who is sent greater than he who sent him' (John 13.16): 'For I have come down from heaven, not to do my own will, but *the will of him who sent me*' (6.38): 'he who seeks the glory of him who sent him is true' (7.18; see 8.18, 26, 29, 42). Jesus is the final, eschatological ambassador of God; 'in him is the fullness of grace and truth' (1.14; 1.14–18 can be found even in the early Jewish tradition of Sinaitic theology, see below). This insight is significant because although pre-existence is in fact a Johannine notion, nevertheless it is not always possible to identify 'coming forth from God' (e.g. 13.3; 7.28f.; 8.42) with pre-existence. 'To be sent from God' does not mean pre-existence in itself; as such it has a different content. Finally, it is important to take seriously the statement of John that 'the Father is greater than I' (14.28). 'He who receives me receives him who sent me' (13.20).

'Moses' speaks to his people *out of* his own intimate, unique converse with God, as a result of his meeting 'face to face' (see above). John composes the whole of his gospel – Moses and the eschatological prophet like Moses – in accordance with this model. We have already remarked that this eschatological figure of Moses is also a structural principle of the Gospel of John.[13] On the other hand, a whole series of exegetes have repeatedly expressed the hermeneutical significance of the Jewish festivals (precisely as they are understood in Mosaic terms). Many exegetes have also been struck by the fact that in the Gospel of John, Galilee and Samaria 'receive Jesus', whereas Judaea, Jerusalem and its surroundings – whose inhabitants John calls the *Ioudaioi*, the Jews – *reject* Jesus. It is also striking that the Johannine Jesus performs 'Mosaic wonders', including the miracles performed by the prophets from the northern kingdom (the Galilee of the time), above all Elijah and Elisha (John 2.1–11; see I Kings 17.1–6 and II Kings 4.1–17). The sympathy of the Johannine community for Samaria emerges from a number of details (John 4.7–28; 1.47–51). Furthermore, the Fourth Gospel does not know any concept of the Son of David (which is a Jerusalem tradition). In addition, specialists recognize some Samaritanisms in the Gospel of John ('Ephraim', John 11.54; Mount 'Garizim', 4.20, etc.).

In particular, the flight of the groups focussed on Stephen to Samaria must have something to do with the earliest roots of the Johannine tradition (4.31–38). There is much to suggest that the Jerusalem 'Hellenists', the Greek-speaking Jews from the earliest community of the Jerusalem church – the so-called Stephen groups – have everything to do with the *earliest* roots of Johannine theology. We have already pointed to Stephen's speech, in which the Mosaic Messiah occupies a central position. I remarked that this concept of the eschatological prophetic Messiah like Moses was also bound up with the concept of the 'innocent sufferer'. In this same Stephen's speech, the 'Mosaic Jesus' is also called 'the righteous one who was murdered' (Acts 7.52). But there are further affinities between this speech and the Gospel of John. First of all, there is the position of the group focussed on Stephen, who reject the Temple as a fixed place for worship and are therefore persecuted by the Jews, unlike other Jewish Christians (Acts 8.1). Stephen compares the building of the Temple with the apostasy of worshipping the golden calf (Acts 7.41–48). John, too, detaches the worship of God both from the Temple in Jerusalem and from Mount Gerizim (John 4.20–23): 'The hour is coming, when neither on this mountain nor in Jerusalem will you worship the Father ... But the hour is coming, and now is, when the true worshippers will worship the Father in spirit and truth' (4.21, 23b). God now dwells in transient *sarx*, which can move from Galilee to Judaea and back again (1.14a), Jesus, 'the tent of meeting' (*eskēnōsen*, 1.14b). Stephen's speech also speaks expressly of the 'tent of witness' (Acts 7.44: *hē skēnē tou martyriou*, see *skēnōma*, Acts 7.46). 'But the Most High does not dwell in houses made with hands' (Stephen's speech, Acts 7.48). God's final revelation is no longer bound up with a country or a place, but *with the movements of the person of Jesus*.

Another striking feature is the discussion in John 7.42–52. In the view of one party the Messiah cannot come from Galilee (7.42). It says in scripture that the *Davidic* Messiah comes from Judaea from Bethlehem, the birthplace of David. Here we have an instance of the opposition inherent in the role which John assigns to *hoi Ioudaioi*, the Judaeans (see below): there is a contrast between Galilee and Judaea. But this geographical opposition has *religious* overtones. 'So there arose a division (*schisma*) among the people' (7.43). For Jews (high priests and Pharisees, 7.45), to believe in Jesus is roughly the same as 'to come from Galilee' (7.52), with the reaction, 'Search and you will see that no *prophet* is to rise from Galilee' (7.52b), so say the opponents of Jesus. In other words, John sees Jesus as the prophet from the north, the *Mosaic* eschatological Messiah, not the Judaic *Davidic* Messiah. The traditions about the wonders performed by Jesus also come from Galilee,[14] and the signs which Jesus performs in the Gospel of John point to Moses, Elijah and Elisha. Moses is not only the suffering Ebed Yahweh, but also the king. The kingdom of Jesus is not of this world; it lies in his personal converse, face to face, with God; he is no worldly Son of David. In this context, John 1.51 is significant: 'Truly, truly I say to you: You will see the heavens open and the angels of God ascending and descending on the Son of man.' The allusion to the place 'Bethel' as the location of the revelation of the glory of God (Gen. 28.12) is clear. Near Jerusalem Jacob saw the ladder, the place of contact between the heavenly and the earthly. But for John this place is only the Son of man, and not Jerusalem: Jesus – his body as *temple* (John 2.21; see 1.14b) – is from now on the place of the revelation of God, the place where God is worshipped in spirit and in truth (4.23).

Furthermore, Stephen's speech also speaks of the Son of man as '*standing*' (Acts 7.55f.); that is, Jesus, who takes his place 'at the right hand of God' as Paraclete or advocate for the cause of Stephen, the 'innocent sufferer'. It also says that Jesus, like Moses before him, brings about a separation of spirits: acceptance or rejection is continually brought up in Stephen's speech. God was to 'redeem the people through the mediation of Moses', but '*they* did not understand' (Acts 7.25): 'our fathers did not want to listen to him; no, they rejected him' (Acts 7.39).

Thus there are numerous affinities between Stephen's speech and the Gospel of John. Now the Christians associated with Stephen fled from Jerusalem after the death of Stephen . . . to Samaria (Acts 8.1), where they were able to register great success with the first large-scale Jewish-Christian mission (Acts 8). The Samaritans also rejected the Jerusalem temple cult (though they did attach themselves to Mount Gerizim; in this they were less radical than the heterodox Jewish circles, above all those Christians associated with Stephen). However, as a result of these same heterodox Jewish, syncretistic presuppositions (which perhaps explains the success of this Christian mission), and above all their focus on Sinai, they had much in common with people from Jerusalem like Stephen and Philip – the group focussed on Stephen.

Acts clearly seeks to emphasize the role of Peter in the mission to Samaria,[15] but Luke himself reveals that this whole initiative comes from Philip, a man from the group around Stephen (Acts 8). The Gospel of John shows the same interest in the mission to Samaria (John 4). John therefore seeks to show that the church's mission to Samaria is willed *by Jesus himself* – in accordance with John's usual model of the two planes: seeing the life of the Word incarnate, Jesus, on the same plane as the life of the church, Luke gives an apt description of the extension of the gospel 'in Jerusalem and throughout Judaea and Samaria and to the end of the earth' (Acts 1.8). He knows from a special tradition that it was the heterodox-Jewish 'Hellenists' from Jerusalem, who had become Christians, the group associated with Stephen, which took the initiative in this mission. It is impossible to deny a *certain* tension between this group of primitive Christians and Peter and 'the twelve' within the Gospel of John (ch.21). This 'Johannine' group completely and utterly recognizes the authority of the twelve (there is no question of opposition to Peter, as some interpreters claim), but it does argue for its own Christian uniqueness. Peter has to acknowledge the destiny of the 'beloved disciple' (which is at the same time the special Christian character of the Johannine community, John 21.15–23); however, Peter and his followers had supervision of this missionary group (Acts 8.14–17). (The tension can also be seen from Matt. 10.5: 'Do *not* go into the cities of Samaria'; Judaeans in particular made a detour so as not to have to go through Samaria to Galilee.) The Johannine Jesus says in connection with the story of the Samaritan woman: 'Lift up your eyes and look on the fields; they are white for harvest' (John 4.35). John 4 indicates that Jesus sows while the Samaritan mission carried on by the group around Stephen reaps (see John 4.37–39; cf. Acts 8.34–40).

This already tells us a good deal about the earliest, *Palestinian* roots of the Gospel of John: Christians from non-official Jewish so-called 'heterodox' Jewish circles within the one church proved to have special characteristics from the very beginning, even in Jerusalem. This circle focussed on Stephen had to flee from Jerusalem, whereas the more orthodox Jewish Christians among the Jews did not suffer in any way and remained in Jerusalem (8.1), though nursing resentment against the Christian 'outsiders'. 'Heterodox' Judaism, the group of Christians in Jerusalem focussed on Stephen and Samaritan theology, provides the first great roots of the Gospel of John.[16] To put things cautiously, this is the trend in Johannine scholarship over the last ten years (I say, to put things cautiously, because some scholars go much further and claim, among other things – wrongly, as far as I am concerned – that a converted Samaritan was responsible for handing down the whole of the Johannine tradition).[17] Thus the pattern of 'Jewish Christians' and 'Gentile Christians', which in theory is already superseded, is duplicated by another break, namely that many more distinctions ought to be drawn with *Jewish* Christianity than has previously been the case. *Palestinian* Judaism (and Christianity) was more Hellenistic and more syncretistic than had earlier been supposed, and yet it was truly Jewish. To denounce the Gospel of John as a strange, 'Hellenistic' cuckoo in the nest is an obsolete historical view. The originally Palestinian character of Johannine theology is only one of many indications of this.[18]

However, all this confirms the standpoint which I am taking up in this discussion (in view of the researches into John carried on over the last decade). The Johannine tradition has deeply Jewish, *Palestinian* roots, but these are to be found less in Jewish 'orthodoxy' than in the unofficial, non-Pharisaic communities which, while being on the periphery of Judaism, are nevertheless truly Jewish (which is why some historians call them 'heterodox'). The Johannine tradition is in the tradition of early-Jewish Sinaitic theology (with a distinct colouring from Samaritanism); in other words, it is in the same tradition as *early Jewish Moses mysticism* (which from now on, for the sake of brevity, I shall call *Sinaitism*).

The reaction of the Gospel of John (against its own Johannine traditions) is living proof that this Sinaitic Moses mysticism could also be a danger for Christians. Although that is not its main concern, the Fourth

Gospel combats the intrinsic dangers of Johannine theology to an ever increasing degree: from the Gospel of John via I John to II John. Although the Gospel of John itself has this focus on Sinai, it makes 'Moses' argue against the Judaeans in the same way as Paul makes Abraham argue against the Jews. 'It is *Moses* who accuses you, on whom you have set your hopes' (John 5.45). 'Jesus' is contrasted with 'Moses' as early as 1.17. For John, Jesus is the supreme and final fulfilment of the eschatological prophet-like-Moses (Deut. 18.15, 16–19; see John 4.25; 8.28; 12.49f.). For John the kingship of Jesus is real, but he is not a *Davidic* king. He is a Mosaic king. In early Judaism and in Samaritan theology people talked about 'King Moses'.[19] For John, Jesus *is* the royal prophet like Moses (cf. John 3.14 with Greek Num. 21.8f.; see also John 19.18 in conjunction with Ex. 17.12; and the time spent by Jesus in the wilderness in the Johannine version: John 6, also Jesus and Moses as the shepherd, John 10). Some authors, above all T. F. Glasson, also see a parallel between 'Moses and Joshua' and 'Jesus and his disciples'[20] (however, in my view this is much less clear, if not downright improbable, as is the hypothesis of A. Lacomara that Jesus' farewell discourse(s) in John have been modelled on Moses' farewell discourse).[21]

Here I would defend the viewpoint that the first inspiration of the Johannine tradition lies in the identification of Jesus of Nazareth with the eschatological prophet like Moses who exceeds all expectations (see Stephen's speech in Acts), and, moreover, that this identification of Jesus as the new Moses who spoke with God 'face to face' as with his friend has called forth another theme, namely that of the descending and ascending heavenly redeemer figure, though this model also has Jewish roots.

## II. THE JOHANNINE MODEL OF UNDERSTANDING: DESCENT AND ASCENT

The model of ascending and descending is made an explicit theme in the discussion between Nicodemus and Jesus in the final redaction of the Gospel of John. This model has its own function in the conversation with Nicodemus, but first of all (for theological purposes) we must detach 'the model' itself.

A fundamental feature of the Gospel of John is evidently the distinction between the earthly or the sarkic (*ta epigeia*) and the heavenly (*ta epourania*) (3.12). We already know this distinction, above all from Hebrews (which has many other points in common with Johannine theology); it also appears in Rom. 7 and 8 (though again in a more anthropological sense). John gives an exact explanation for this distinction. 'God is *pneuma*' (4.24). He goes on to explain: 'What is born of the flesh (*sarx*) is flesh, and what is born of the spirit (*pneuma*) is spirit' (3.6). The *origin* of something determines its *nature*. By origin, only the heavenly sphere is 'spiritual', whereas the earthly sphere is of the *sarx*. Therefore, by nature man has nothing to do with the spiritual, even though he is also God's good creation (1.3). (There is certainly no trace of gnosticism here.) So if man wants to participate in spiritual realities or spheres, he must be born again, of a virgin or through the Spirit, 'of (water and) Spirit' (3.5; see 1.13); otherwise he cannot enter the kingdom of God (3.5), i.e. the kingdom of the God who is *pneuma* (4.24). Although he is God's creature, man is not-*pneuma*, not-God and therefore has no essential spiritual nucleus. Yet the *pneuma*, God, Creator of the world and man, is in someone (1.2) who as such is without 'grace and truth' (1.14e), that is, without wisdom from above. The Fourth Gospel becomes comprehensible against this background.

Salvation, man's eternal life, will only be possible as the result of an initiative from above, from the kingdom of the *pneuma*. The light which belongs with the spiritual world must appear *in* this world of the *sarx*. The Gospel of John will go on to develop all this in *spatial* conceptions, of descending and ascending. In so doing (see below) it will radically shatter these spatial categories through the *reciprocity* of the relationships of love between the God who is *pneuma* and believing man, thanks to Jesus Christ who is sent by this God as *pneuma*. The greatest 'mythologist' among all the New Testament authors is at the same time an exponent of 'demythologizing'.

Descending and coming down are primarily connected with the picture of the world drawn in antiquity: above, here, below. Heaven, that is, where God dwells, is the highest storey of our universe (Ps. 29.3, 10; 104.3). This conception itself replaced a more primitive one according to which God's abode was bound up with a rock, a thorn bush, a cult place. If God dwells 'up there', any theophany or revelation of God is experienced as his 'descent'. Thus for the Old Testament, descent (*katabasis* or *katabainein*) is revelation terminology, whereas *anabasis*, ascent, indicates the end of the divine revelation (see Gen. 17.22; Ps. 47.6; 68.19). Strikingly enough, here again Stephen's speech also has an allusion both to 'the *appearance* of the God of *glory*' (Acts 7.2) and to the God who '*descends, to free the people*' (Acts 7.34). Thus for the Old Testament, descent and ascent are connected with *revelations of God* (cf. Ex. 24.16 with Ezek. 9.3; 11.23; see also Isa. 13.4f.; Prov. 30.4). However, it is particularly relevant in this connection to recall the angel which brought Tobit salvation from God. After the event, the angel said, '*anabainō pros ton aposteilanta me*', '*I ascend to the one who sent me*' (Tobit 12.20) – Johannine terminology! From a Jewish point of view, ascent and descent had long been a common conception even before there could be any question of gnosticism. In the world picture of the time, 'descend' and 'from God' were simply synonyms. We can now analyse John 3.13–21 and 3.31–36 against this background.

(*a*) John 3.31–36. 'Jesus comes from above' (3.31) and is consequently 'exalted above all' (3.31b), not only at this resurrection but because of his sending from above. In 3.13–21 the Gospel of John really argues the other way round: it argues from another end (the standpoint of the ancient Christian hymns after the experience of Easter): only he ascends who has first descended (3.13; cf. Eph. 4.8f.). Therefore on the basis of the pre-existence of Jesus, John ascribes to the earthly Jesus characteristics which elsewhere in the New Testament are assigned to the risen Christ or are put on the lips of the earthly Jesus by the exalted Christ. Because Jesus comes from above, he can 'bear witness to what he has *seen* and *heard*' (3.32), namely during his life with God. That is a new feature in the New Testament. Because of his pre-existence (see also 1.18; 6.38, 46; 8.26, 40; 15.15) the Johannine Jesus can reveal himself – *'Ego eimi*, I am' – and thus the Father, with authority, as salvation, the goal and the way of life for all (14.4–11): access or 'the way to the Father' (14.6b). Therefore the Son can communicate with fullness – 'of his fullness' (1.16) – to others who believe in him what he possesses in unique fashion from the Father: the knowledge of God (17.6), life (5.26; 6.57), glory (17.5, 22). (This is once again like Moses in Stephen's speech: 'Moses received *living oracles* to give to you. But our fathers would not listen to him' (Acts 7.38f.).

In speaking of this *katabasis* or descent from heaven, that is, of the sending of Jesus by the Father, John is not presenting a theology of the Trinity but a christology. Because of his pre-existence, the *earthly Jesus* has the gift of the knowledge and power of salvation. 'He whom God has sent utters the words of God, for it is not by measure that he (in my view this refers grammatically to Jesus himself and not to God) gives his Spirit. The Father loves the Son, and has given all things into his hand' (3.34f.). The accent is not placed first on his death and his resurrection, but on his sending itself, though this does not mean that the special significance of the death is forgotten. On the contrary! As a result it acquires a special Johannine significance.

Thus in the earthly ministry of Jesus in Galilee and Jerusalem we do not find the exalted Christ projected back on to the earthly Jesus, as happens in the kerygmatic history of the synoptic gospels; the earthly Jesus speaks of his 'pre-existent' experiences with and by God. He speaks with the full awareness of his origin 'from above' (3.31a). Although he is one with the Father, on earth he is not '*with* the Father' (the implication of 17.5); Jesus is only *with* the Father in his pre-existence and postexistence (3.13, 31; 6.62; 13.1; 16.28). However, on earth the Father is *in*

him and he is *in* the Father (14.10; 14.11; 14.20; 10.30, 38; 17.21) and
the Father is *with* the Son (16.32). Therefore anyone who, during the
earthly life of Jesus, 'believes in the Son, has eternal life' (3.36). In the
Q tradition we find that to adopt an attitude to Jesus, for or against, is
a decision with far-reaching, eschatological (i.e. *future*) consequences
(Matt. 10.32f. = Luke 12.8f.); the synoptic gospels already give this their
own particular interpretation, Matt. 12.32; Luke 12.10; also in Mark
3.28f., probably going back to a saying of Jesus, 'blessed is he who takes
no offence at me' (Q Luke 7.23=Matt. 11.6). This tradition is interpreted
in John 3.36 in terms of an explicitly present christological reference.
Anyone who does not believe during the life of Jesus, in contact with him,
*is* already judged; anyone who does believe, has eternal life. Not to see
life is not to see the kingdom of God (3.3).

(*b*) John 3.13–21. Whereas 3.31–36 speaks of the *katabasis* or the heavenly
origin of Jesus, 3.13–21 is concerned with the *anabasis* or the return of the
Son to the Father: 'No one has ascended into heaven but he who
descended from heaven . . . (3.13). *Ho katabas* (aorist, a unique event,
namely at the incarnation), and on the other hand *anabekēken* (perfect),
that is, the one who has descended, has *ascended*. Now he dwells in the
heavenly spheres. According to the Gospel of John, the pre-existence of
Jesus explains the real and complete signficance of the final phase of the
life of Jesus: his exaltation (death) and his resurrection or glorification.
However, the return of Jesus, the Son of man (3.13; 6.62; 13.31; 12.23)
to the place whence he came, the Father (13.1; 14.28; 16.5, 28; 17.11, 13;
20.17), takes place by means of his death. The Gospel of John already
regards this as the beginning of the final exaltation. 'As Moses lifted up
the serpent in the wilderness' (3.14b), so the Father lifts up his Son on
his death. This analogy with the lifting up of the serpent (Num. 21.8–10;
II Kings 18.4) is a feature which can be found elsewhere in primitive
Christianity, but only John connects it with the *death* of Jesus as a life-
giving exaltation. Elsewhere in the New Testament this takes place only
*after* his death, at the resurrection (of course John does not deny this
aspect: see below). As salvation (for those who believe), the death of
Jesus is at the same time eschatological judgment (*kekritai*; 16.11; 12.31)
for those who do not believe. In the critical situation of the Johannine
communities, in which 'the Jews' rejected the idea of a humiliated and
executed Messiah, the Gospel of John never speaks openly of the kenotic
or humiliated state of the Son of man. On the contrary, the life of Jesus
is that of the incarnate Word. The cross itself becomes the supreme
manifestation of the love of the Son and the Father (3.16): the hour of
glorification (12.23; 17.1; 13.1). Perhaps John found a reason for this
view in Isa. 52.13, where both the typically Johannine words 'exaltation'
and 'glorification' also appear (*hypsothēnai* and *doxasthēnai*, Isa. 52.13). He

has come from heaven, 'not to condemn the world, but that the world might be saved through him' (3.17). Life is contrasted with corruption and salvation with judgment: 'He who does not believe *is* judged already' (3.18; 3.36); the believer is not judged (3.18a; 5.24; see also I John 3.14). John concludes the summary of his brief account of *katabasis* and *anabasis* with an illusion to the prologue of his Gospel: 'And this is the judgment, that the light has come into the world, and men loved darkness rather than light, because their deeds were evil. For every one who does evil hates the light, and does not come to the light, lest his deeds should be exposed. But he who does what is true comes to the light, that it may be clearly seen that his deeds have been wrought in God' (3.19–21). The incarnation itself is a judgment on the world in that this world does not recognize the light which shines in darkness. In the Gospel of John, salvation and judgment are bound up with the manifestation of the person of Jesus in our world.

It emerges from this summary of the Johannine model of interpretation (3.13–21; 3.31–36) that the Gospel of John uses material from the Christian tradition: (*a*) the pre-existence of Christ is itself pre-Pauline (Phil. 2.6–11) and, along the lines of the wisdom tradition, Pauline (sent: I Cor. 10.4; 8.6; Rom. 10.6f.; Gal. 4.4–6; Hebrews 1–3 is also expressed in terms of wisdom). The Gospel of John gives some indications of this (6.62; 8.14, 58; 17.5, 24), namely Jesus' utter awareness of his own pre-existence (protological pre-existence); (*b*) the notion of the exaltation of Jesus above all; for John this can be found as early as the incarnation in a first, dynamic beginning. It does not in fact achieve a climax after the death of Jesus; it already *begins* with his death, which is then followed by the return of Jesus to the Father; (*c*) there is also a point of contact between the Gospel of John and the synoptics in the concept of the 'kingdom of God' (3.5; see 3.3), although for John this means entering into the higher, heavenly world of the *pneuma* (3.12,13,31; 8.21); (*d*) the 'Son of man'. John knows the Davidic Son of man (John 5.27), and also the primary synoptic significance of the Son of man who comes in judgment (Luke 12.8 par.; Mark 8.38 par.; 13.26 par.; 14.62 par.; Luke 11.30 par.; 12.40 par.; 17.24, 26, 30 par.; Matt. 13.41; 19.28; 25.31; Luke 18.8; 21.36). In the synoptic gospels the glorification is also bound up with the eschatological Son of man (Mark 8.38 par.; 13.26; Matt. 25.31), but John sees this glory already at work in the earthly Jesus (however, there are already hints of this in Luke 22.69; 23.42f.; 24.26; Acts 7.55f.). John has incorporated the concept of 'sitting at the right hand of God', which can be found in the synoptic gospels and elsewhere in the New Testament, into his concept of 'exaltation'; thus it is not a second act, following on a phase of humiliation. The crucifixion is itself an exaltation (John 3.14; 8.28; 12.32–34). Furthermore, the second group of sayings about the Son of man, those connected with his suffering, death and resurrection (e.g. Mark 8.31 par.) can also be found in the Gospel of John (3.14, though there they do not have this duality). Among other passages, Isa. 53 and 52.13 underlies both the synoptic gospels and the Gospel of John. Here in John then, earlier concepts simply take on another colouring (12.23f. and 32, 34c; 13.31f.; 17.1f.). Only when it comes to the third group of synoptic sayings about the earthly Jesus as Son of man can no connection be shown between John and the synoptic gospels.[22] A non-synoptic type of the Son of man can be found in 3.13; 6.27, 53, 62; 12.23 and 13.31f.: a descending and ascending Son of man. However, even more than in the synoptic gospels, in the Gospel of John the *earthly* Jesus is the 'Son of man', but in content and terminology John speaks about him in quite a different way. Here John develops a theme of his own, independently of the pre-synoptic material. Evidently there is no common ground between the synoptic gospels and John here. And the difference seems to come from the particular christology of the Johannine model: *katabasis-anabasis*, the content of which is not a model for John, but reality, in connection with Jesus Christ, the Son of man. In John, primitive Christian material is given another significance, because it begins from another christological model. In the Gospel of John, synoptic proofs from scripture for the resurrection and exaltation of Jesus, along with other New Testament scriptural proofs, become indications of his protological pre-existence.

In itself, this gives us a first, preliminary insight into the Gospel of John. The Gospel reinterprets primitive Christian traditions in terms of the *katabasis-anabasis* model. All this was an occasion for Bultmann to see John 3.13–21, 31–36 as a *gnostic* part of the myth of the *salvator salvandus et salvatus*, a redeemer figure, a kind of mythical prototype of man's need for redemption and the way in which 'man' can achieve redemption, just as 'Adam' in Genesis is a prototype of what mankind ultimately is in its positive possibility and its actual reality. Since Bultmann, who simply relied on the current state of research in the history of religions school, more recent historical research has established that the gnostic myth of a redeemer descending from heaven was in fact known in the second century AD, but shows signs of both Jewish and perhaps Christian influence.[23] Furthermore, the God *'anthrōpos'* (primal man) is intrinsically bound up with the gnostic understanding of the world and cannot be separated from it. Therefore the Gospel of John has no connection with Gnosticism. On the other hand, second-century Gnosticism did not fall from heaven. It worked with pre-existing traditions, and the tradition in which the evangelist stands is the spiritual milieu which will provide the *Hermetica* and later Gnosticism with a whole mass of raw material. A further question is whether this 'redemption myth' is constitutive of later Gnosticism. Quite apart from all the discussions of Gnosticism, we can hardly dispute that the existence of some descending and ascending redeemer figures is an undeniable fact before Christianity and even before Gnosticism, both in the Graeco-Roman world and in Judaism. Gods who descend in order to bring about redemption are a theme to be found in Graeco-Roman writings before the formation of the New Testament,[24] and this theme is familiar above all in Hellenistic Judaism. We already find a mention of the *anabasis* and *katabasis* of a feminine wisdom (Sir. 24; Bar. 3.27–4.4; Wisdom 9.10; 7.27 and 8.10; 6.18–20; 8.13, 17) in the wisdom literature; the ultimate aim is always redemption (Wisdom 9.18; see 10.1, 4, 6, 13, 15). It also appears in apocalyptic literature (I Enoch 42.1f.; II Bar. 48.36; II Ezra 5.9f.). In addition, pre-Christian Judaism is also familiar with the model of *katabasis* and *anabasis* within its angelology. It first appears in connection with the *mal'āk* Yahweh or the angel of Yahweh (Gen. 19.1, 13; 22.11–18; 16.13a; Ex. 23.20f.): 'three men' who are one 'angel of God' (Gen. 18.2–22; see also Gen. 32.24f.; Hos. 12.4; Judg. 13.6, 8). We also hear of a 'coming and going of angels' (Ex. 3.8; Judg. 13.20) who are always concerned to help, save or redeem (Gen. 19.12ff.; 22.11; 48.15f.; Judg. 6.11ff.; Ex. 3.2; here even to save Israel from Egypt). The 'angel of the presence' is also a saving angel (Isa. 63.9). In Tobit 3.16f., 21; 8.3; 9.8–16; 12.3, 14f., 19f., the archangel Gabriel is a descending, saving angel. There is also mention of descending and ascending angels in the non-canonical Jewish apocalypses.[25] The theme of a descending, saving angel is similarly to be found in Qumran.[26] The wisdom traditions then became fused with this angelology, and this gave rise to identifications like Wisdom=Logos=angel. According to I Enoch 42.1f., Wisdom descended in order to find a home in Israel, but, failing to achieve its aim, it had to return and took up its abode in heaven, among the angels. In Wisdom 10.6 it is Wisdom who, as Yahweh's angel, saved Lot. Wisdom freed Israel from Egypt (Wisd. 10.15f.), whereas in Wisdom 18.15 this was achieved by the angel of Yahweh. Furthermore, in Wisdom 9.1f., Wisdom is the Logos (see Sir. 24.3) which then proves to be an angel again in 18.5. Finally, we have a connection between Wisdom and the Holy Spirit in Wisdom 9.17. Thus the conception of a heavenly redeemer and Saviour, more or less precisely identified with Wisdom, Logos, an angel and the Holy Spirit, can be found in Judaism before the time of Christianity. It is an element of the spirituality of so-called unofficial but nevertheless authentic Jewish groups. Philo, too, can only confirm this: we find the same identifications in his writings: Wisdom, Logos, *pneuma*, angel.[27] This suggests to me that we must look for the background of the models used in the Gospel of John to *Jewish* circles in which wisdom traditions were fused with Jewish angelology. It is a characteristic of the whole of this early Jewish (and Hellenistic) age that heavenly transcendent realities were given many names. The heavenly redeemer too was given different names: Wisdom, Logos, angel, Son, man, high priest. This syncretism was increasingly resisted in more official Jewish circles. However, the Odes of Solomon,[28] which come from about the time of the Gospel of John, represent a complete break with angel christology, though the redeemer Christ is still depicted in accordance with the *katabasis-anabasis* model.[29] Although they are Christian, these Odes were written in an early Jewish milieu.

It follows from all this that the model of *katabasis* and *anabasis* was already known in unofficial circles in the early Jewish and pre-Christian period and was associated with redemption and deliverance by a heavenly figure: Logos, Wisdom, angel – a terminology which we also find in the so-called 'angel christology' of the first church fathers.[30] As such, the 'model' is early Jewish.

Therefore this model is already implicitly at hand for Paul: pre-existence, descent, ascent, parousia (Rom. 8.34b; I Cor. 15.24–27; Phil. 3.20; see even I Thess. 1.10; 4.16f.), though the *anabasis* is mentioned only implicitly, in the exaltation. Galatians 4.4f. speaks of the *'sending* of the Son' with a view to redemption (cf. John 3.17; I John 4.9; also Rom. 8.3, with its *pempein*, send, which is so typical of John). Also 'he *gave* his Son' (Rom. 8.32: *paredōken*; John: *didonai*, e.g. John 3.16). These formulae of sending and sacrifice also have their roots in Jewish wisdom (Wisdom 9.10; 9.17 – Wisdom 9.17a. The angel of Yahweh is also *sent*: Gen. 19.13; Ex. 23.20f. etc.). The conception of 'sending', associated with the title 'Son of God', is perhaps typical above all of Egyptian Judaism.[31] We even find some trace of a connection between 'Christ' and 'angel' in Gal. 4.4–14.

The model is to be found more explicitly in Hebrews: (*a*) pre-existence (Heb. 1.2; 9.11, 26); (*b*) descent (2.17; 2.9, 10, 14, 15; 5.8; 10.10); (*c*) ascent (7.25f.; 9.12–24); (*d*) parousia (9.28; 10.37). It is interesting to note here that the main titles which are associated with this model of ascent and descent are 'Son' (Heb. 1.2; 3.6; 4.14; 5.5, 8; 6.6; 7.3; cf. 11.17) and 'high priest' (4.14–16) and also that the Son is called the *apaugasma*, the image of God (1.3; Wisdom 7.26). It is clear that Hebrews, which we analysed earlier, carries on a degree of polemic against angels: Christ did not become an angel, but a man (1.4–2.16). Angel worship was unmistakably a pressing problem in early Christianity (*inter alia*, see also Col. 2.18). Like the Odes of Solomon (and Tertullian, at a later date), Hebrews is an attempt to remove the element of 'angel' from the complex of Son, Logos, angel, high priest, Wisdom.

The Gospel of John unmistakably uses the same Jewish model:
(*a*) *Pre-existence*: John 1.1–3, 10; 1.30f.; 3.31; 6.51; 8.58; 17.5, 24.
(*b*) *Descent for the purpose of redemption*: sending (3.17) or 'gift' (3.16; 6.38; 8.23, 42); so the Father is *seen* in the Son: 14.9; 1.18; the one who has

descended 'baptizes with the holy spirit' (1.33; 20.22, see below), takes away sins (1.29), gives eternal life (3.16; 5.21, 25, 26; 6.27, 51; 17.2f.) and overcomes 'the prince of this world' (12.31).

(c) *Ascent for redemption*: 'go to the Father' (13.3, 33, 36), 'be exalted' (in a double sense) (12.32; 12.28); be glorified (12.23; 13.32; 17.5), 'go away' (16.7); give the spirit (14.16f., 25f.; 15.26f.; 16.7–11, 13–15), prepare a place for believers 'in heaven' (14.3).

(d) *Parousia*: 5.28f.; 14.2f. ('farewell') and in the additional chapter (John 21.22); 'the last day' (6.39; 6.40) in contrast to 'on that day' (14.20; 16.23; cf. 20.19f., that is, at Easter, see below).

The titles used in connection with this pattern are Logos, Son of God, Son of man. These titles are typical of this early Jewish model. As has already been said, the title Son of man is the only one to create any problems, because in the Gospel of John we come up against two different complexes of thought: 1. the synoptic type of the Son of man (John 1.51; 3.14f.; 5.27; 8.28; 12.34) and 2. a non-synoptic type (3.13; 6.27, 53, 62; 12.23; 13.31f.), namely a descending and ascending Son of man. Are we to see in the Gospel of John, as in Hebrews, a kind of anti-'angel christology', above all in 1.51 (cf. Rev. 19.10; 22.8f.) and 5.1–9? The Paraclete is the 'spirit of truth' (14.16; 15.26; 16.13, see below). According to G. Johnston, John thus rejects the pre-Johannine indentification of the angel Michael with the 'spirit of truth'.[32] In Qumran, too, 'the spirit of truth who bears witness' is an angel (I QS III, 18–25), and the Paraclete is most probably the angel Michael.[33] Thus there must have been something like an early Christian Jewish christology which regarded Christ and the spirit as 'two angels', which was then opposed by the Gospel of John. Given this assumption, it is surprising that in its account of the empty tomb the Gospel of John detaches belief in the resurrection completely from any angelic appearances (it does not know this tradition and does not want to accept it). Like the Odes of Solomon and later Tertullian, the Gospel of John is also an attempt to detach 'angel' from the complex of ideas which includes Logos, Wisdom, Son, Spirit and angel.

If this analysis is correct, than we have a very clear indication that the Gospel of John has genuinely Hellenistic-*Jewish roots* which originally may even come from Baptist circles in Palestine (John 1.6–8; 1.35ff.). Albeit for other reasons, in the researches carried out over the last ten years, this tendency is beginning to gain the upper hand over early Gnostic interpretations of the Gospel of John.[34] We may find it striking that John prefaces the whole pericope in which he as it were presents his model with 3.12: 'If you do not believe when I speak to you of earthly things (*ta epigeia*), how will you believe when I speak to you of heavenly things (*ta epourania*)?' The book of Wisdom had already said: 'We can hardly guess at which is on earth (*ta epigeia*) . . . but who has traced out what is in the heavens (*ta epourania*)?' (Wisdom 9.16). In connection with this contrast between the earthly and the heavenly (the spiritual sphere), the book of Proverbs says, 'Who has ascended to heaven and come down? . . . Who has established all the ends of the earth? What is his name, and what is his son's name?' (Prov. 30.4). And already Deuteronomy: 'The commandment which I command you is not too hard for you, neither is it far off. It is not in heaven, that you should say, "Who will go up for us to heaven, and bring it to us, that we may hear it and do it" ' (Deut. 30.11f.). Finally: 'Who has gone up into heaven and taken her, and brought her down from the clouds? . . .All the ways to knowledge come from him: he has shown them to his servant Jacob, Israel whom he loved. Afterward she appeared on earth (*epi tēs gēs ōphthē*) and lived among men (*en tois anthrōpois synanestraphē*)' (Bar. 3.29, 37f.). In fact, in a number of writings Wisdom returns from her visit to earth without having accomplished anything; she finds no dwelling place on earth (I Enoch 42.1f.) or for that reason returns to bring punishment (above all in the rabbinic pattern of descent and ascent).[35] However, no one would want to deny the affinity of the Gospel of John with all this or the affinity between John 3.12–31 and Isa. 55.8–11: 'My thoughts are not your thoughts and your ways are not my ways . . . for as the heavens are higher than the earth, so are my ways higher than your ways and my thoughts than your thoughts. For as the rain and the snow come down from heaven and return not thither but water the earth . . . so shall *my word (rēma)* be that goes forth (*exelthein*) from my mouth; *it shall not return to me empty*, but it shall *accomplish (suntelesthein) that which I purpose*, and *prosper in the thing* for which *I send it*.' The thought categories of John were provided by Judaism, and the heavenly personal existence of heavenly beings was similarly provided by early Jewish angelology. In Johannine theology, eschatological pre-existence as found in the wisdom tradition and *heavenly* existence of *personal* heavenly beings come together. This particular thought-complex could provide something like an 'angel chris-tology' in the pre-Johannine tradition, which is in all probability (though only incidentally) attacked by the Gospel of John, as by Hebrews (*inter alia* in its christological version of the concept of the Paraclete: see below). The fundamental conception in the Gospel of John is that the history of salvation has its origin, not in Bethlehem (7.41f.), nor in the house of Mary and Joseph (6.41f.), but *in heaven* (1.18; 3.13; 6.32f.; 7.28f.; 17.5, 25): Jesus has been sent by God from heaven. Here we have the most important key which opens up our understanding of what John intends with his gospel, and also his so-called 'dualism', which *primarily* indicates the transcendence of the *pneuma* of God over all earthly elements in the Old Testament tradition. This is expressed sharply in the text from

Isa. 55.8–11 which I have just quoted. 'No one has seen God at any time' (1.18; 6.46; Ex. 33.20). For that it is necessary to be 'from God'.

The consequence of being 'from God' and therefore of the descent of Jesus is that the Johannine Jesus speaks on earth of what he has 'seen and heard' (3.32; 3.31). 'We speak that which we know and we testify to that which we have seen' (3.11). He does 'all that he sees the Father do' (5.19), and 'I judge according to what I hear' (5.30). 'What I have heard from him I tell to the world' (8.26). In another passage we find: 'I have not spoken on my own authority, but the Father who sent me has himself given me commandment what to say and what to speak' (12.49). It emerges from this that seeing and hearing is the same thing as being sent by the Father to make a proclamation. Jesus speaks in the name of the Father. He also does this in the synoptic gospels, but in the Gospel of John this is given special significance within the model of descent and ascent.

### III. JESUS CONFRONTS MEN WITH A DECISION: BELIEF OR UNBELIEF

*Literature* (in addition to what has already been cited): G.. Baumbach, 'Gemeinde und Welt im Joh.', *Kairos* 14, 1972, 121–36; J. Beutler, *Martyria*, Frankfurt 1972; J. Blank, *Krisis*, op.cit.; O. Böcher, *Der Johanneische Dualismus im Zusammenhang des nachbiblischen Judentums*, Gütersloh 1965; K. L. Carroll, 'The Fourth Gospel and the Exclusion of Christians from the Synagogue', *BJRL* 40, 1957, 19–32; E. Grässer, 'Die antijüdische Polemik im Johannesevangelium', *NTS* 10, 1964–65, 74–90; E.. Käsemann, *The Testament of Jesus*, ET London and Philadelphia 1968, 65–7; H. Leroy, *Rätsel und Missverständnis*; J. L. Martyn, *History and Theology in the Fourth Gospel*, New York 1968; T. H. Olbricht, 'Its Works are Evil (John 7.7)', *Restoration Quarterly* 7, 1963, 242–4; R. Schnackenburg, *Das Johannesevangelium* II, 328–46; L. Schottroff, *Der Glaubende und die feindliche Welt*, WMANT 37, Neukirchen 1970; G. Steinberger, *La symbolique du bien et du mal selon saint Jean*, Paris 1970; W. Wilkens, *Zeichen und Werke. Ein Beitrag zur Theologie des 4. Evangeliums in Erzählungs- und Redestoff*, AThANT 55, Zurich 1969, 114–21.

### A. Jesus and 'the Jews'

On the very first appearance of Jesus as the heavenly bringer of salvation on earth and throughout the Fourth Gospel, his arrival leads to a 'crisis' between believers and unbelievers. Some accept him, others reject him. Jesus brings about a division among the spirits, in the same way as (so

John recalls), God's words 'Let there be light' (Gen. 1.3) bring about a division between light and darkness, day and night (Gen. 1.3–5). The 'dualism' arises only in and through the human decision to accept or reject Jesus as light. In the Gospel, dualism does not precede this decision (and if the result is *positive*, in view of our circumstances in the flesh, it is above all the consequence of 'the Father's drawing'; in other words, it is a matter of grace, 6.44–46). The dualism or the division of the spirits only comes about through the attitude which a person adopts to Jesus (however, John is thinking of this decision and not directly of people who have not yet been confronted with the Jesus event; these are 'potential' *believers* or *unbelievers*, as Jesus sends his disciples 'into the world', 17.15, 18).

The crisis or the division of spirits which also takes place in relationship to Jesus, already plays a fundamental role in the prologue to John: (*a*) 1.9–11, the block of unbelievers, who will not recognize the light; (*b*) the believers, who recognize Jesus as light by virtue of the grace of God: the children of God or the Christian community. Alongside the testimony of John the Baptist to Jesus as the 'heavenly redeemer' there are three more important witnesses: the testimony of Jesus' own ministry, the works of the Father which Jesus does (5.36); the testimony of the Father himself (5.37); and the testimony of holy scripture (5.39). However, all these witnesses simply seem to confirm the division of the spirits. Thus it is John's concern to show that Jesus calls forth belief and unbelief – that he therefore not only gives 'life', but at the same time confronts unbelievers as their judge (5.16–30; 7.15–24). Believers are not judged, but non-believers on the other hand are already judged in their unbelief (3.36; 9.39); by their own decision. Every 'I am' statement (see below) is followed by a discussion of belief and unbelief (6.41–47; 6.52–58; above all 6.60–71; 7.25–36; 7.40–52; 8.12–59; 10.19–21; 10.22–39; 11.45–54). This also happens after each of Jesus' wonders (e.g. 5.9b–47; 9.35–41). It is already evident after the healing of the lame man (5.1–10) that 'the Jews' want to kill Jesus (5.18). The Johannine Jesus always defends himself in the same way: he does nothing of himself (7.18; 8.28; 14.10); he does the 'works of the Father' (5.19f.); he does only what the Father has commanded him (10.18; see 4.34). The healing of the lame man is therefore life for the lame man (5.24–26), but judgment for the one who does not believe (5.27–30). Every symbolic action is moreover also a pointer, a reference to still greater works (5.20–22): the resurrection of Lazarus, itself again a pointer to something greater, to the resurrection of Jesus and the final judgment.

The statement that Jesus is the 'bread of life' (6.35, 48, 51) also brings about belief and unbelief. Just as the Jews in the wilderness murmured against Moses, despite the miracle of the manna (Ex. 16.7–9), so 'the

Jews murmured about him because he had said, "I am the bread which has come down from heaven" ' (6.41). The Jews know the origin of Jesus: he is the son of Joseph; they know his father and his mother. 'How then can he say, "I have come down from heaven?" ' (6.42). They know Jesus' earthly origin. Jesus' real, heavenly origin remains hidden from 'the Jews'. Jesus replies to their murmuring that the knowledge of his real origin cannot be discovered by flesh and blood; for that they need to be drawn by grace from above (6.44); a man must be 'of God' (6.46b) to recognize the true origin of Jesus. The subsequent representation of the eucharist (6.51b), 'The bread that I shall give is my flesh for the life of the world', also causes division among the Jews. 'He who eats my flesh and drinks my blood abides in me and I in him' (6.56). Nonsensical talk (6.60,71), but this time 'many of his *disciples*' (6.60f.), evidently believers find this so. Jesus is food, eternal life for men, because his origin is a heavenly one: 'The *pneuma* (the heavenly) brings life, the *sarx* (the earthly) is of no avail' (6.63). Faith that heaven has come among the disciples in the *sarx* of Jesus is what gives life. Not to believe means not to understand anything of Jesus: that is unbelief. 'After this many of his disciples drew back' (6.66). That *also* points to the situation in the Johannine community. I John gives a sharper picture of the situation: these false teachers *were* members of the community (I John 2.19), but now they have evidently separated from it (*schisma*) (aorist); however, they are still active *among* the members of the community; they 'lead astray' the faithful Johannine community. 'The Twelve' suddenly appear in the Gospel of John in this context (6.67); they make the Christian confession of faith from the mouth of Peter: 'We believe and know that you are the Holy One of God' (6.69). There is even a division of spirits within this group of Twelve (6.70f.).

There is also discussion after Jesus' saying, 'My teaching is not mine but the teaching of him who sent me' (7.16). 'No one knows of the Messiah whence he comes' (7.27) – this is a current Jewish tradition. But 'some people from Jerusalem' say, 'Yet we know where this man comes from' (7.27a). While they are arguing like this, Jesus preaches in the Temple: 'You know me and you know whence I am' (see 7.27a), 'but I have not come of my own accord; he who sent me is true, and him you do not know' (7.28). The argument is: the Jews do not know God, so how can they know the true origin of Jesus? Indeed they all know Jesus' origin according to the flesh, but he has been sent by the Father, and this vital point they have not grasped.

The statement that Jesus is 'the light of the world' (8.12) underlines the fact that Jesus is from above, whereas the others are from below (8.23). 'I am not of this world' (8.23b). There follows one of the most vigorous discussions between Jesus and 'the Jews' (8.33–59), in which

Jesus accuses them of not being true children of Abraham. They are liars, and therefore really children of Satan, as Satan is the Father of all lies (8.44). Only the Son can really give men freedom, and not Abraham (8.36); he is 'the truth that will make you free' (8.32). For their part, the Jews retort, 'Now we know for certain that you are possessed by the devil' (8.52). Jesus reacts in familiar fashion: You do not know God, 'but I know him' (8.55). Were Jesus to deny that, he himself would be a liar (8.55b). Jesus *is* the forgiveness of sins, and that is not a matter of being a child of Abraham. 'Truth' is Jesus' revelation of salvation (prologue), which gives divine life and thus the forgiveness of sins: the freedom of the children of God (see 8.36; cf. Gal. 4.4f.). Jesus alone leads to true freedom. As Son he is the free one (8.36), spiritually or from above (see 8.23). In 8.37–47 the tension between 'from below' and 'from above' is accentuated so that it becomes a contrast between children of God and children of the devil. Here the Johannine Jesus distinguishes between 'ethnic children of Abraham' (*sperma Abraham*, 8.33, 37) and the *tekna*, children who are born of Abraham but act in the spirit of their father (already a vision of Jer. 4.4; 9.25; Ezek. 36.26f.). Thus the Jewish distinction between 'Jew' and 'non-Jew' is replaced in the Gospel of John by the distinction between 'being from God' (for Jews and Gentiles) and others (Jews and Gentiles) who cannot hear God's voice in Jesus.

Therefore Jesus stands above Abraham (8.58; see Ex. 3.14). Thereupon 'the Jews' want to stone him (8.59). But Jesus *'leaves* the Temple', the place of the presence of God in Israel. He leaves a vacuum behind him.

In John 9 the discussion shifts to the healing of the man born blind and the Pharisees, 'Why, this is a marvel! You do not know where he comes from, and yet he opened my eyes. . . . If this man were not from God, he could do nothing' (9.30, 33). But the healed man is excommunicated and cast out of the synagogue. Later he believes 'in the Son of man'.

'I am the Son of man' (9.35–37; cf. 4.23–26). In 9.39 this is bound up with a function of judgment, 'to judge (*krima, krisis*) I am come into the world'. After Jesus has healed the darkened eyes of the man born blind, he gives him the light of true faith; faith in Jesus, the Son of man, who leads men into the glory of God (see 12.31–36; here also in connection with the Son of man). The Pharisees, on the other hand, though seeing, are 'blind'; the blind man is not (9.41).

At the feast of the dedication of the Temple there is again a discussion about Jesus as Messiah and Son of God (10.22–39). There had already been a discussion about his messiahship (7.40–44). Some people think that Jesus is truly the prophet (7.40), for others he is the Messiah (7.41), the Son of David and thus the national Messiah; a third group, on the other hand, objects that the Messiah does not come from Galilee (7.41b–

43), since according to scripture, as Son of David he comes from Bethlehem (Micah 5.2). Thus there is a 'schism' about Jesus among the people (7.43a). Now (10.22–39) the discussion about the Messiahship of Jesus is in fact a controversy with 'the Jews' (10.24). Jesus repeats, 'I and the Father are one' (10.30). They call that blasphemy (10.33). Jesus therefore argues from scripture, where it is said, 'You are gods' (Ps. 82.6). Thereupon Jesus calls himself 'Son of God' (10.36). For the one who does the works of God is his Son (10.37f.). Now Jesus does none other than the works of the Father; thus 'the Father is in me and I am in the Father' (10.38). 'Child or son of God' points back to 'born of God', 'children of God' (1.12f.; 8.35b, 36, 47). If every one of Jesus' 'signs' aroused vigorous discussion, the last sign, the raising of Lazarus, seems to be the last straw. 'The high priests and Pharisees' (11.47) summon a session of the Sanhedrin: 'From that day on they took counsel how to put him to death' (11.53).

This dialectic of belief and unbelief dominates the whole of the Fourth Gospel. Who are these unbelievers whom John calls 'the Jews'? The question has been discussed for a long time. The starting point of the discussion was simply the fact that John is the only one to use the expression '*hoi Ioudaioi*' in a special sense. After that, four usages were often distinguished in the Fourth Gospel: 'the Jews' are (*a*) simply the Jewish people (with reference to 2.6, 13; 3.1); (*b*) the Judaeans, inhabitants of Jerusalem and neighbouring Judaea (11.8f.); (*c*) people hostile to Jesus; in other words, 'the Jews' becomes the symbol for 'unbelievers' (6.41, 52, etc.) and (*d*) the Jerusalem authorities or the leaders of the Jewish people (1.19; 2.18, 20). However, a new purely semantic study of the word *hoi Ioudaioi* in contemporary literature, made by M. Lowe, has convinced me that John is simply following the *Palestinian* usage of the time: in that case *hoi Ioudaioi* are the Judaeans (not 'the Jews'), Jews from Judaea as opposed to those from Galilee. By contrast, the Diaspora Jews used *Ioudaioi* in a general sense: the Jews. The four gospels (apart from Luke 7.3) know only the Palestinian usage; and, to confirm the rule, the pericope about the Samaritan woman (John 4) is familiar with the Samaritan use of *Ioudaios*, because the Samaritans also regarded themselves as children of Jacob and thus belong to *Israel*.[36] For John, then, the Jews are the people from Judaea who had Jesus crucified because of their unbelief, and particularly because of their narrow conceptions of the Law; in other words, John attacks religious *Judaism*, which he also sees represented in the synagogue of his time, with which the Johannine community was confronted. That is official synagogue Judaism (Lowe neglects this important aspect in his study, which is semantically correct). John thinks on two planes. The *'Judaeans'* of the time of *Jesus* are a model of what the *synagogue Jews* do in John's time. So we need not in any way see 'the

Judaeans' and 'the Jews' from the time of John as a symbol of unbelief (an application of the text to the present might require that, but it is surely not the meaning of the text itself). For John, 'the Judaeans' in the historical sense, from the time of Jesus, are the symbol of what the Jews from the synagogue are doing in his own time; here type and antitype go over into one another in history.

As we have already remarked, in the last ten years, Johannine research generally tends to interpret the Fourth Gospel as a dialogue between the *Johannine community* and the *synagogue*.[37] This conception seems to me to be only half true. The drama that John narrates in fact takes place on two levels: the level of Christian tradition about the life of Jesus and that of the present conflict in the Johannine community. The question, however, is: Who are the parties which are in conflict with one another? J. L. Martyn claims, with many who follow him here, that the conflict is between the Johannine community and the synagogue. There must have been an active synagogue, hostile to Christianity, in the immediate vicinity of the Johannine community. The opponents of Jesus are, suddenly, both the Jewish leaders in Jerusalem in the first decades of the first century and also the Jewish synagogue leaders in the days of the evangelist. The two perspectives run into one another. Thus John 3.5, 6, 7, 9 tells us more about the situation of the Johannine community than about the historical Jesus. Many Jews left the synagogue and became Christians. They were – and the anachronism compared with the time of Jesus itself speaks volumes – 'excluded from the synagogue' (*aposynagōgos*: 9.22; 12.42; 16.2)[38] Furthermore, there were Jews who were secret Christians: the Nicodemus figures from the Gospel of John. In the Gospel, Nicodemus is clearly the representative of Christians who do not give up their Jewish connection with the synagogue, i.e. 'the secret disciples' (12.42f.; 9.16; 2.23–25). In 3.1–12 John relates a conversation between *Jesus* and Nicodemus, but this conversation is at the same time a discussion between the Johannine community and the Nicodemus figures in the community. This is clear from the otherwise incomprehensible form of expression. Here Jesus suddenly speaks, contrary to all Johannine custom, in the first person plural: '*We* speak of what we know and bear witness to what *we* have seen' (3.11). This implies both: 'What I have heard from him, that I say to the world' (8.26; 5.30; 12.49), and on the other hand: '*We* – the Johannine community – we have seen his glory' (1.14c). Thus the community can itself bear witness to what Jesus has seen and heard from the Father. The two historical planes (Jesus and the community) overlap.

The synagogue near to the Johannine community is evidently also in the tradition of Sinaitism, which was a characteristic of many Diaspora synagogues: this was a type of Moses mysticism.[39] In this contrast

between the church and the synagoguge, 'the Judacans' are for John the
type of those who reject the Christian gospel on the basis of the Law of
Moses. 'The Judaeans' represent a failure to accept the truth as it has
been revealed in the person of Jesus. Thus they are examples of unbelief
in John's time. The expulsion of Jewish Christians from the synagogue
is projected back into the time of Jesus. The Gospel of John is therefore
not a missionary document, as was earlier assumed, but the document of
a community which shuts itself off from the world and above all from the
attacks of the nearby synagogue. In their great commentaries on John,
R. Schnackenburg and R. Brown also speak of the high priority accorded
to anti-Jewish polemic in the Fourth Gospel: 'the Jews' are contemporaries of John, leaders of the (nearby) synagogue who are militant in
rejecting the Christian method. However, R. Brown does not see any real
ethnic, geographical or even religious content in 'the Jews'; they are a
*symbol* of all those who reject Christian belief. (While the Gospel may now
be interpreted in these terms, it does not really seem to have been meant
in this way.) John certainly does not use this terminology 'symbolically'.
'Moses' disciples' are contrasted with 'Jesus' disciples' (9.28), whereas
for John the Christian community is the new Israel.

It can hardly be denied that despite all the Jewish, even Palestinian
roots of the Johannine tradition, the Gospel of John detaches itself from
official Judaism. Scripture is cited polemically (e.g. 5.45), and the debates
about Jesus' messiahship dominate the whole Gospel (see e.g. 7.27, 41f.;
12.34). The synoptic gospels also do this, though in a less defensive and
aggressive way. If, as I assume, the Gospel of John has deep Jewish roots,
but these lie more in the unofficial, so-called 'heterodox', syncretistic
Judaism of the first century, then we can already understand why there
should be something of a gap between it and Pharisaic Rabbinic Judaism
from the time after AD 70. But John's repudiation goes further. I personally believe that Wayne Meeks has a true insight when he says, 'The
Fourth Gospel is most anti-Jewish just at the points it is most Jewish.'[40]
In fact John is using a familiar Old Testament theme in his sharp attacks
on the Jewish leaders or shepherds. John is decidedly Jewish, precisely
in the sharpness of this attack on 'the Jews'. In the course of this study
I shall show how John takes over the traditional Jewish prophetic criticism and applies it to the *leaders* of the people of God. That of course
leads to more serious consequences when a Christian (even if he is a
Jewish Christian) is critcizing non-Christian Jews.

Thus in the literature on John which has appeared over the last decade,
above all in the Anglo-Saxon world, there is increasing unanimity among
exegetes about the background of the Gospel of John: the Johannine
church is putting up apologetic and defensive resistance against a powerful, militant Jewish synagogue. However, I ask myself whether that still

covers the full concerns of the Gospel of John. This contrast seems undeniable, but here John is less concerned with the non-Christians than with the consequences of this conflict for and within the community itself, namely for the Jewish Christians. The Gospel seems to me less concerned with a defensive church facing hateful attacks from the synagogue (which is an undeniable fact); in my view the very striking and repeated admonition *to preserve unity*, which extends right down to the farewell discourse(s) of the Johannine Jesus, also points in the direction of a conflict between Jewish Christians and Gentile Christians *within* the community itself. John is thinking of the danger to the inner unity of the church: Christian Jews overestimate the ethnic sonship of Abraham (1.12c,13, where there is clearly a Johannine attack in the Logos hymn; also 8.33–59). Evidently the *Jewish* Christians in the Johannine community had a feeling of superiority over Gentile Christians. John sees this as a threat to the unity of the church: 'I have other sheep which are not of this fold. Them also must I bring, and they will hearken to my voice, and there shall be one flock and one shepherd' (10.16): and 'Jesus should die for the *nation* (Israel), and not for the nation only, but to gather into one *the children of God who are scattered* abroad' (11.52). The accent seems to me to lie on polemic between *Jewish* Christians and *Gentile* Christians, these Jewish Christians being Hellenistic Jews who are familiar with Moses mysticism or Sinaitism. This carried with it the inherent danger of seeing Jesus as bearer of the Logos alongside Moses, the bearer of the Logos, the prophets and John the Baptist. In that case Jesus may be the greatest, but he will be *in a line* of bearers of the Logos, above all including Moses (see 4.12; 5.43; 6.32; 8.53). The problem then is: can one follow both Jesus and Moses? This dilemma occurs in various forms throughout the New Testament. The exclusiveness of salvation in Jesus is damaged as a result, and John is clearly concerned with this *exclusiveness of Jesus*.

In order to understand this purpose of the Gospel of John better, we must remember that in the days when the Fourth Gospel was written, the gulf between church and synagogue was not only a reality, but had also been made official, if not legal. Round about the 90s, an excommunication of Jewish Christians was added in the Shemoneh Esreh, the Eighteen Benedictions: they were officially excluded from the synagogue.[41] The church and Israel were in confrontation. Because for John, 'belief' is belief in Jesus Christ, for him that means that belief and the church are in one place and unbelief and the synagogue in the other. John uses the traditional material about the disputes between Jesus and the Jewish authorities which led to the final rejection of Jesus and to his crucifixion, but he projects the situation of his time with all its crisis into the time of Jesus. The disputes about the (Mosaic) messiahship of the Johannine Jesus reflect the situation of the church at the time of John, though John also brings up to date details from the Jesus tradition. John's polemic about belief and unbelief in the time of Jesus must therefore be set against the background of a polemic between Johannine christology and Pharisaic Rabbinic Judaism, which above all after AD 70 became the only leading party in Judaism, and at the same time became the representative of Jewish orthodoxy.

Therefore the Fourth Gospel appears as a witness to Jesus' revelation of himself, the Word incarnate, which brings about a crisis between believers and unbelievers.[42] Hence the two blocks: on the one side *hoi Ioudaioi* (71 times, the Jews), and on the other side the disciples of Jesus – 'the church' in embryo – who *from the beginning* believe in Jesus as the Christ; that is, they already believe (in the Johannine concept of belief) *as Christians* (albeit still immature and with a good deal of misunderstanding) in the earthly Jesus as the saviour sent from heaven by God. The Johannine concept of *faith* already includes the synoptic demand for *metanoia* or conversion. To believe means to affirm Jesus' revelation of himself and personally to follow the figure of Jesus Christ: it is the recognition of the claims of Jesus as the Son of the Father who comes down from heaven for the salvation of all. In contrast, unbelief is the denial of the Messiahship of Jesus or of eschatological salvation (6.64 with 6.41f.; 7.5,26f., 31, 41). To believe means to believe in Jesus as the only bringer of salvation. Thus the *personal attachment* to Jesus (*pisteuein eis*) also includes a *christological confession (pisteuein hoti. . .*; see above all 17.20b with 17.8; 17.21d). To believe therefore means 'to come to Jesus' (5.43) or, as the Prologue already has it, 'to receive Jesus' (1.12; 5.43; 13.20). The first disciples 'come to Jesus' (2.11; 1.37, 47), that is, they become his disciples because they believe in him. It is not really Jesus who calls them (see 1.35–51); they are sent to him by the Father (17.2, 9, 12; 6.44).

For John, pre-Easter faith can already be *Christian* faith because the death and resurrection of Jesus, important though they are, are not the only facts of salvation: the event of salvation already begins with the appearance of the incarnate Word on earth, though even on earth Jesus cannot yet give eschatological salvation or the Holy Spirit (7.39), but only the pledge of salvation (see below). For John, to believe in the person of the historical (the earthly) Jesus is itself Christian faith. The disciples proper have this faith in Jesus (2.11; 6.67–69; 13.19; 14.1, 10; 16.27,30f.; 17.8; 20.8, 25, 29), but it is also used more generally for a still imperfect belief on the basis of belief in the divine signs performed by Jesus (4.1; 6.60–66; 7.3; 8.31; 9.28; 19.38). However, in contrast to the synoptic Jesus, the Johannine Jesus requires faith *in the person* of Jesus himself, whereas for example with Paul the object of *Christian* faith is really the death and resurrection of Christ (see Rom. 4.24f.; 10.9 etc.). John, however, looks for belief in the *historical manifestation* of Jesus; for in that case Jesus is already the eschatological presence of the Father among us: 'Whoever sees me sees the Father' (14.9; 7.16f.). The new existence and the new self-understanding begin in contact with the earthly Jesus: the Paraclete who is to come will later simply lead them into the fullness of the understanding of faith (14.26). In this the first testimony of the earthly Jesus and the later testimony of the Holy Spirit are agreed (15.26f.).[43] Thus Jesus knows that his disciples believe in him even before Easter. Although they are still so prone to misunderstanding (4.33; 14.5,8; 16.17f.; 11.8, 16; 18.10f.; also 13.37; 16.29f.), *they believe* in him in a personal connection: 'To whom then should we go?' (6.68; 16.27). The disciples have already done the most important thing: they accept Jesus as the one sent by God for salvation (16.27; 17.8; 17.14, 25; also 8.14; 7.16f.). Before his passion Jesus strengthens their faith against the tests to come (13.19; 14.1, 29; 16.31f.). But Jesus continually first tests this faith (2.3f.; 4.48, 50; 11.25f.; 6.6; 6.67: 'will you also go?').

From the beginning the disciples are the flock entrusted to Jesus (10.3f.; 10.14f.). God has given them to him (17.6; 17.9–12, 24a; see 11.52; 17.2; 18.37). To these disciples Jesus says, 'The Father himself loves you, because you have loved me and *have believed that I came from the Father*' (16.27). In the light of the pre-existence of Jesus, on the basis of which the earthly Jesus is the eschatological presence of salvation, Johannine christology for the most part brings up to date materials used by the synoptic gospels and projects it in this form on to the time before Easter (not formally in the light of the resurrection, but in the light of the *pre-existence* of Jesus).

## B. Light and darkness

However, there are still more profound reasons for the 'dualism' of the decision between belief and unbelief; they are bound up with the model of *katabasis* and *anabasis*. This is the breach which we have already come across in Hebrews between the *epigeia*, the earthly, and the *epourania*, the heavenly or the spiritual sphere. In the Gospel of John we constantly find contrasts like 'from below' – 'from above', light – darkness, truth – lie, life – God, God – 'the prince of this world'. And these positive or negative qualifications are interchangeable within their category. However, it is striking that all these contrasts relate to the acceptance or the rejection of the revelation of Jesus (e.g. 15.22, 24; 9.41). Here there is an existential dualism, really a form of the monism of grace. The only reality is the power of the good and the true, manifested in Jesus Christ.

The earthly world 'is under the power of the evil one' (I John 5.19), 'the prince of this world' (John 12.31). It emerges from the Prologue to John that this Logos hymn has deep roots in wisdom literature. Although this wisdom literature itself calls creation a good gift of God, it is nevertheless sceptical about a world of creation in which the light of the *revelation* of God cannot be found (Prov. 30.1–14; Job 28; Ecclesiastes; Wisdom 7; 9; John 1.4). Man has no salvation in himself, he possesses no knowledge which goes beyond the boundaries of the world (Wisdom 9.13–17). Man is 'flesh and blood', *sarx* a being who has the need of the gift of wisdom from above: for revelation (Wisdom 7.1f.; 10.17ff.; see also 1 QH 15.21f.). Wisdom is not innate in man (Wisdom 7.1–30), it 'comes from God' (Wisdom 9.6). 'We can hardly guess at what is on earth . . . who has traced out what is in the heavens?' (Wisdom 9.16; see John 3.12!). Without heavenly wisdom the world is *skotia*, darkness. This darkness is in no way a cosmic power, but creation without illumination, mankind without revealed wisdom. In itself the world is 'no-God', no-light, darkness. Seen in this way, there is a gulf between 'the earthly' and 'the heavenly', unless man receives illumination from above. Wisdom must as it were come from heaven and take up its abode among us, if there is to be light in the world. The lack of wisdom or revelation is no-light, creaturely darkness (see John 9.4f.; 11.9f.; 3.19– 21). Here John, like the 'wise men',[44] is not thinking of demonic powers; therefore in contrast to the synoptic gospels, his own gospel does not have any healings of those possessed by the devil. In the Gospel of John, the devil is the image of the essence of unbelief (8.44), as in I John the Antichrist is the picture and the name for the unbeliever or heretic: I John 4.3; 2.18–27; also II John 7. He is the prince of this world, not in the sense that the world is his sphere of power, but that it is his sphere of *law*; in other words, he has a claim to a world which rejects the light. Jesus denies him this right (12.31; 14.30; 16.11). For John, to sin means 'to reject the light'; in that case the 'world' is synonymous with 'darkness' (cf. 1.10 with 1.5). That is a feature of wisdom (Sir. 1.9f.; 24.6f.; Bar. 3.36– 39; Prov. 8.1–36; 11.1–31; also I Enoch 93.8; 69.8; 101.8 and 11 QS XVIII 5f.) For Wisdom appears among men, but men reject it (Sir. 24.7; Prov. 1.24f.,29f.,32; Bar. 3.12f.; 4.1; I Enoch 42.1f.; 93.8; 94.5). 'In the waves of the sea, in the whole earth, and in every people and nation I (Wisdom) have gotten a possession. Among all these I sought a resting place, I sought in whose territory I might lodge. Then the Creator of all things gave me a commandment, and the one who created me assigned a place for my tent. And he said, "*Make your dwelling in Jacob*, and in Israel receive your inheritance." *From eternity, in the beginning,* he created me, and for eternity I shall not cease to exist' (Sir. 24.6–9). 'I came forth from the mouth of the Most High, and covered the earth like a mist. . .' (Sir. 24.3). Thus Wisdom came above all to Israel, to God's possession

(Ex. 19.5; Deut. 4.20; 7.6; 14.2; 26.18; Ps. 135.4; Isa. 43.21; Mal. 3.17; see Sir. 17.17; 24.1,2,12; Bar. 3.36f.). But even the people of God rejected wisdom (Prov. 1.24f., 29, 32; Bar. 2.12f.; 4.1f.). Therefore individuals – the remnant – are chosen from Israel to be dwelling places for wisdom (Sir. 24.19–22; 1.10–20; Wisdom 6.12–16; 7.27f.; 8.21; 9.2,17; Prov. 8.17, 21). The wise 'gain the friendship of God' (Wisdom 7.27); they are 'sons of God' (Wisdom 5.5). For wisdom is a 'reflection of eternal *light*, a spotless mirror of the *working* of God and an image of his goodness' (Wisdom 7.26). Wisdom is 'initiated into the knowledge of God' (Wisdom 8.4), and it brings the wise 'into the circle of the children of God' (Wisdom 9.4; 5.5; 7.27; see John 1.12f.). Much in this sounds 'Johannine'.

Even in the wisdom literature, this tradition is combined with the innocent sufferer and the 'suffering prophet', who are 'counted among the sons of God' (Wisdom 5.5).[45] The theme of the innocent wise man, who endures hostility and is surrounded by 'enemies', comes strongly into the foreground in Wisdom 2.12–17a. Disputes arise, but the 'Son of God' or righteous man unmasks (*elenchos*, see John 16.8–11) his adversaries (Wisdom 2.14a). Who is the deceiver and liar: is it he, or his enemies (see Wisdom 2.21; 5.6; cf. John 7.12; 12.19b)? Wisdom 2.13, 16, 18; 5.5 is particularly concerned with the authority and the wisdom of the 'Son of God' who is 'glorified' in the face of his adversaries. For the outcome of this dispute is not decided by the killing of the wise and innocent man. God's glorification of the one who has suffered injustice rehabilitates him in the face of those who say him nay, and is therefore an offer of the grace of conversion (Wisdom 3.1–9; 5.1ff.). This glorification by God does not *make* the rejected and hated righteous and wise man the 'son of God', but it *proves* that he already was 'son of God', and that he already possessed eternal life before his death.

Thus these traditions already flourished in early Judaism and were combined with apocalyptic conceptions. Without doubt the analogy between their structure and the Gospel of John is a striking one. It is the horizon of experience in which John will articulate his gospel – the experience of salvation from God in Jesus. As we have already noted, other traditions also played their part, above all early Jewish angelology, with its affirmation of the saving purposes of descending and ascending angels, a tradition which we also find in the wisdom literature. In Wisdom 10.6 wisdom comes to save Lot in the form of an 'angel of Yahweh'. Furthermore, wisdom is identified with the Logos (Wisdom 9.1f.; see Sir. 24.3), which in Wisdom 18.5 again seems to be an 'angel'.

Wisdom splits mankind; it brings a 'crisis'. The idea of crisis therefore appears before John and can be found throughout the wisdom tradition (Prov. 8.17; 1.28; Wisdom 6.12; Prov. 1.20–33; Sir. 6.27). John takes over a Jewish complex of tradition. The background to his gospel is therefore a 'dualism', not so much of good and evil as of *salvation* and *damnation*, of a *decision* for or against the light of revelation. This will be confirmed by the meaning of 'truth and grace' in the Prologue to John: a life-giving gift of God which reveals itself in Jesus as God's saving wisdom. To accept Jesus as the one who has been sent by God, that is, the one who comes from heaven, is salvation: to reject him is already judgment and corruption. Salvation comes from above: from God. Thus all salvation begins with a descending movement from above. John is given all this as a *model*. It will make possible the Johannine community's *own* experience with Jesus Christ. For John, Jesus of Nazareth is God's descending gift of salvation to the world, but only some – a remnant of Jews and Gentiles – accept this eschatological and final saving gift of God, which is then a judgment for others. Therefore the opposition between 'light' and 'darkness' remains at the coming of Jesus, the incarnate Word. John describes this historical drama on two planes: the historical Jesus in Jerusalem and Jesus Christ in the situation of the Johannine community.

## IV. THE JOHANNINE TRADITION AND THE 'HISTORICAL JESUS'

It has become clear from what has been said that Johannine theology shows links with those people who were associated with the group focussed on Stephen, Greek-speaking Jewish Christians from Jerusalem. In other words, the deepest roots of the Gospel of John are to be sought in *Judaism* and not among Christians from the Greek Gentile world. Its Palestinian roots can be even more closely defined; they lie in Jerusalem, not in the tradition of official Judaism, but in so-called unofficial Judaism. *This* Jewish Christianity had a *special character* even in Jerusalem. Even Acts reveals a certain tension between 'the Twelve' and those whom Luke calls the seven deacons, though Luke seems to make light of the conflict: 'The Hellenists began to murmur against the Hebrews' (Acts 6.1): the reference in both instances is to Palestinian Jewish Christians, of whom the 'Hellenists' are the Greek speakers. Those whom Luke calls 'the Hebrews' are for John 'the Jews'. Acts says that to smoothe over the dispute, seven 'Hellenists' are named as *'deacons'*, but what they do (at least according to Acts) in fact goes far beyond the work of the diaconate. They preach the faith like the apostles, with a certain degree of independence, though they are supervised by the Twelve. Here we have an indication of an orthodox Christian community, which *fully* acknowledges the authority of the Twelve, but at the same time fights for the recognition of its own *Christian characteristics*. It is not separated from the wider church and does not in any way have separatist tendencies: it does, however, have its own view of the Christian gospel. Therefore its members are evidently on the defensive, because the official Christian leaders mistrust them somewhat, above all in their missionary ambitions towards Samaria. For the most part the synoptic tradition goes back to the traditions of the Twelve. In the Gospel of John, on the other hand, the Twelve from Galilee are mentioned expressly only once (John 6.70). In addition to friends in Galilee, Jesus evidently also had friends in Jerusalem, in other and 'higher' social circles. These also belonged among his 'intimates'.

The additional chapter, John 21, can illuminate the situation somewhat. Peter, who represents the Twelve and is explicitly recognized in this capacity (21.15–17), nevertheless stands in a somewhat tense relationship with 'the disciple whom Jesus loved' (21.20–23). Thus this beloved disciple is not one of the Twelve. Furthermore, the character of the Christians associated with Stephen emerges from the fact that they are persecuted by the Jews and have to flee from Jerusalem (Acts. 8.1), whereas the other Christians are not persecuted because they evidently do not criticize the Temple. The Christians associated with the Twelve seem to have had some suspicion of the missionary activity of the Christians associated with the Seven in Samaria (Acts 8.5–8; 8.14).

The question now is whether the beloved disciple has anything to do with the circle associated with Stephen. In John 21.24 the 'author' of the Gospel of John is identified with the 'beloved disciple', i.e. with someone who has a rather tense relationship with Peter as the spokesman for the Twelve. Thus the 'author' is not one of the Twelve (that is already suggested by the Fourth Gospel itself; and this author is certainly not John, one of the sons of thunder; the Gospel of John itself excludes this: cf. John 21.2 with 21.7). It is also striking that the Johannine traditions are historically and geographically more reliable about events in Jerusalem and Samaria than the synoptic gospels, and that in this respect the Fourth Gospel sometimes refers explicitly to an eyewitness, the beloved disciple (see John 19.34); on the other hand, what John says about Galilee is evidently not based on eyewitness, but on traditions which partly correspond with the synoptic gospels and partly diverge from them.

Thus 'the beloved disciple' has a good deal to do with the Christian character of the Johannine tradition. Some authors think that he is a symbolic figure: the Johannine community itself. But in that case the evocative contrast with the *historical* figure of Peter is hardly comprehensible. *Behind* the theme or the idealized figure of the 'beloved disciple' there lurks a historical disciple of Jesus, a disciple who did not, however, belong to the Twelve. This disciple is mentioned explicitly in 13.23–26; 19.26f.; 20.3–10; 21.7, 20–23, 24. We may accept the probability that the evangelist does not call himself Jesus' 'beloved disciple'; this happens, rather, through the Johannine 'school' or group (just as the Deutero-Paulines are acquainted with reverence for Paul). This disciple sits beside

Jesus in the place of honour at the Last Supper (13.23–26; perhaps in his own house); he is said to be an eyewitness of the crucifixion (19.26f. and 20.3–10). It emerges from all this that according to the Gospel of John itself, the first bearer of the Johannine tradition is the beloved disciple himself, who lived in Jerusalem and had access to the high priest because of his contacts there (John 18.15). He belonged to a different group of Jesus' disciples from that of the Galilean fishermen. In other words, we can infer from John 21 that the Johannine tradition and the Fourth Gospel are based on the eyewitness testimony of a disciple who has already died, the 'beloved disciple' (it is no longer possible to discover his real name). The Gospel of John (2–20) has been written in his terms: 'This is the disciple who is bearing witness to these things, and who has written these things, and we know that his testimony is true' (21.24). 'We', that is the leaders of the Johannine church, know that the Johannine tradition goes back to the beloved disciple, who was above all the witness of what took place in Jerusalem. That does not mean to say that the beloved disciple is also the *evangelist* (the Deutero-Pauline epistles, which are only written in the spirit of Paul, go *under the name of Paul*). Evidently John 21 was written after the death of the beloved disciple, about whom a rumour went round that he would not die. It is clear from 21.24f. that he has died in the meantime; in this passage an earlier Johannine tradition is corrected. The disciple 'remains' (*menein*), but not in the way talked about earlier in Johannine circles. Unlike Peter, the beloved disciple is not a martyr, but as an eyewitness he has authority for the Johannine community. John 21 sets out to stress this authority after the death of the old guarantor of the Johannine tradition. One can see the evangelist, or the author of the Fourth Gospel, occupying a position analogous to the authors of Colossians and Ephesians in respect of Paul. However, the writer of the Fourth Gospel connects *theological* concerns with the beloved disciple: Mary is entrusted to him (19.26f.); in the Gospel of John he is the first to believe in the resurrection of Jesus; he is the type of the true believer (20.8). In other words, for the evangelist this disciple is not only a historical person but – in true Johannine fashion – at the same time an ideal figure of faith (the founder of Qumran also remains anonymous and in that tradition is revered as 'the Teacher of Righteousness').

We can, however, ask whether it is true that the Gospel of John introduces the beloved disciple only at the last supper (John 13). Anonymous mention is made twice elsewhere of 'another disciple' (1.35, 40; 18.15), though without the addition 'whom Jesus loved'. R. Schnackenburg bases his argument that the beloved disciple comes from Jerusalem on the fact that he enters the story for the first time in John 13 (the last supper). However, it is striking that Nathanael, who has even less claim to be one of the Twelve, plays an important role in the pericope about the call of the disciples (1.45–51). John is evidently interested in 'intimates' of Jesus who do not belong to the Twelve. Thus in John 1.35–40 and 18.15 'the other (disciple)' is evidently the disciple who is later called (by the Johannine school) 'the disciple whom Jesus loved'; he is one of the first two disciples of Jesus and before that was a disciple of John the Baptist (1.35–40). According to the Fourth Gospel, (*a*) the beloved disciple only appears in stories concerned with Judaea; (*b*) was initially a disciple of John the Baptist and attached himself to Jesus when Jesus was still a disciple of John; (*c*) was there at the end when Jesus died; (*d*) was known to the high priest in Jerusalem; (*e*) is the spokesman of a 'Johannine group' (John 21); (*f*) is an eyewitness of various events in the life of Jesus.

This provides a link between the Baptist's circles, Jerusalem and Samaria. Furthermore, in suggesting how the Gospel of John should be understood, I have pointed out that the Judaism in which it has its roots is not official rabbinic Judaism, but the 'heterodox' circles of Palestinian spirituality.

In my book *Jesus. An Experiment in Christology*, I suggested that early Christian creeds were echoes in which could be heard a particular aspect of the historical Jesus (pp. 403ff.); the question of the relationship between Jesus and Johannine theology can be understood in the same way. As a disciple of John the Baptist (3.22ff.), Jesus evidently also had contact with Jewish marginal groups (like this 'Baptist' movement). As well as the Gospel of John, Luke also gives indirect evidence of Jesus' interest in Samaria, which was despised by official Judaism. There is the parable of the Good Samaritan (Luke 10.25–37); moreover, 'once when Jesus was going through the borders of Samaria and Galilee' (Luke 17.11), he healed ten lepers. The only one who came to Jesus and thanked him was a . . . Samaritan (Luke 17.16). Acts 7 and 8 connect the Stephen group with the mission in Samaria. Alongside the Twelve, Luke also knows a tradition about seventy (seventy-two) disciples; granted, this is inspired by the Old Testament, but it accords with the Johannine tradition that there was another circle of Jesus' friends apart from the Twelve. And the Lukan tradition, like John 4, gives some inkling of Jesus' open attitude towards the Samaritans. Moreover, in Matt. 11.25–27 we are confronted with a tradition which is often described over-hastily as an 'erratic block' of Johannine character in the synoptic tradition: 'All things have been delivered to me by my Father; and no one knows the Son except the Father, and no one knows the Father except the Son and any one to whom the Son chooses to reveal him.' Certainly it sounds very 'Johannine' indeed, but that does not prove that it has come directly from the Johannine tradition. It may come from early Christian traditions of which Johannine theology is one echo among others. If Jesus experienced God so intensively as *the Father* and thus saw him as a father figure, as is attested by both the synoptic gospels and Pauline as well as Johannine theology, it can hardly be denied that (within this pattern of experience) Jesus experienced himself as *the Son*, even if we have no direct proof of this (though Matt. 11.25–27, which is perhaps independent of Johannine theology, could be an echo of it). In that case, Johannine theology, despite its special character, will have to be seen as a real echo of particular historical sayings and events from the life of Jesus himself, as are the synoptic gospels and Pauline theology. To see the Gospel of John as a non-Jewish, Greek-Gentile interpretation of Jesus in no way corresponds with the historical insights of Johannine scholarship over the last ten years; it seems to me to be outdated criticism.

The special character of Johannine theology as compared with both the synoptic gospels and Pauline theology lies in the fact that what the synoptic gospels still do quite 'unconsciously' becomes John's deliberate purpose. He seeks to *make present to the church* the reminiscence of what Jesus had said and done. John shows that in any happening the historical Jesus is at the same time the one who is present in his church. John himself explains this in his view of the Paraclete or Holy Spirit: he makes Jesus say, 'I have yet many things to say to you, but you cannot bear them now. When the Spirit of truth comes, he will guide you into all the truth' (16.13). John 15–17 is the best example of this. In it, the evangelist himself, under the guidance of the spirit, leads Christians into a *deeper understanding* of the Jesus event. Thus the whole of the Gospel of John is a 'recollection' (14.24) and at the same time a 'deeper understanding in faith' or a presentation of what has been recalled. The 'we' form in 3.11, 'We say what we know' (although Jesus is speaking), is the clearest indication of that. True, in that case the Gospel of John does not present us with a Jesus who talks to us about the coming kingdom of God, like the synoptic gospels, but in reality the author knows that the gift of the Spirit enables him to proclaim a deeper understanding of faith: for him Jesus Christ is this kingdom of God. So he too, is speaking of this kingdom when, for example, he makes Jesus say, 'I am the way, the truth and the life'. John does precisely what the synoptic gospels do. What they do unsystematically, he does systematically, by virtue of the spirit which alone can show him what Jesus himself said and did. For John the historical Jesus is 'the fullness of grace and truth' (1.14e), i.e. the final climax of the revelation of God in which both the pre-history (from the creation of light onwards) and the 'effective history' of the exalted Jesus come together in the church. It is the claim of Johannine theology, as of the synoptic gospels and Pauline theology, that the Johannine tradition goes back to *Jesus*, on the one hand through the eyewitness who is the guarantor of this tradition, the beloved disciple, and on the other through traditions which are partly related to the synoptic tradition about Jesus and partly diverge from it because of the way John has selected them, and also because they have a different origin (in particular they show some affinity to Luke's special tradition). Therefore, in principle the Gospel of John has as much value as the synoptic gospels as a source for historical knowledge of Jesus; indeed, it is in all probability historically more reliable than they are for events in Judaea – though for the most part detailed historical substantiation is impossible here.

Furthermore, the Johannine tradition has gone through a whole process of development. The acceptance of converted Samaritans into the Johannine community strengthened the 'heterodox' Jewish element even further. So we can see in the Gospel of John not only a reaction against official Judaism but in the last resort also an indication of the dangers inherent in the Johannine tradition with its spiritual impulses from syncretistic Judaism. These dangers became even more marked when after AD 70 the Johannine tradition found itself in a more syncretistic environment, perhaps in Syria. The Jewish Christianity which we find in the Pseudo-Clementines (and has many affinities with Johannine theology) fell victim to this syncretism. Therefore the Fourth Gospel defends itself against tendencies within the community to which it is addressed, which could threaten the exclusiveness of Jesus Christ. Thus in a later phase of the Johannine tradition (to which the Gospel and the Epistles testify), polemic arose against the dangers inherent in Johannine theology (even in the prologue, see below); I John stresses even more sharply than the gospel the atoning value of the death of Jesus (4.6f.; 2.1f.; 3.5, 8 etc.), while II John 7 attacks Johannine Christians who 'deny that Jesus Christ *has come in the flesh*'. In other words, this a manifestly anti-docetic polemic, quite apart from the fact that the author understood well enough what his opponents meant by their evidently *early-Johannine* talk about Jesus. (Still, it emerges from this and from other converging factors, that what has been called 'docetism' in the wider history of the church does not have its roots in the Greek Gentile world, but *in Jewish* circles. Thus for example we know from Tobit that heavenly beings, angels, could assume human form and then *put this aside* when their mission was accomplished.)

The fundamental characteristics of the Gospel of John can all be understood against a Palestinian-Jewish, syncretistic background which proved to be one of the sources of second-century gnosticism; this was the same kind of heterodox Jewish atmosphere as we find, say in Qumran. These are the *forerunners* of what G. Scholem calls mystical Judaism.[46] Moreover, it transpires that the Gospel of John makes use of pre-Johannine traditions or sources, above all the so-called 'book of signs' and a passion narrative. There is an increasing consensus that there was reciprocal influence (though no literary dependence) between the material in the synoptic and Johannine traditions.[47] It is assumed that the written synoptic tradition influenced the pre-Johannine tradition even at the oral stage, and vice versa. It is thought above all that Luke was influenced by an earlier form of the developing Johannine tradition. This research is only beginning, and is being carried on above all by Anglo-Saxon exegetes. When all is said and done, though, the evangelist is an *author* and not a compiler, and he is to be distinguished from the final redactor or from a Johannine group of 'editors'. At all events, John 21 and the Johannine epistles, compared with John 2–20, clearly demonstrate that we can beyond question talk of a *Johannine tradition*. Generally speaking, we may say that Johannine theology is not a variation on other New Testament *texts* but a *special form* of the primitive Christian confession, distinct from Pauline theology and the synoptic gospels. It is perhaps the tradition of a minority group which had to fight for its distinctive character, while feeling that it too was a legitimate part of the one great community of God in Christ which it affirmed. The roots of this form of a Johannine Christianity are as old as the Christianity of the Twelve, and in all probability it goes back to the group associated with Stephen in Jerusalem. Bearing this in mind, we can now go on to analyse Johannine theology.

## V. THE STRUCTURE OF THE GOSPEL OF JOHN

Before ending these preliminary remarks on the Gospel of John I must say at least a few words about the wider structure of this Fourth Gospel.

I have already remarked that theologically John sees two planes – the earthly ministry of Jesus and the life of the church – in a single perspective. He does systematically what the synoptics do perhaps less consciously: he looks on the earthly Jesus in the light of the later situations of the church. But precisely this special Johannine consciousness includes a sharp distinction between the fellowship of the disciples before Easter and that after Easter. Therefore the great turning point in the Fourth Gospel lies in the twelfth chapter. The earthly ministry of Jesus, the preexistent one, is concluded with a mention of 'the Greeks' who want to see Jesus (see my comments on this episode, below), i.e. the desire of the Gentiles to be allowed to experience salvation in Jesus (12.20–36) and on the other hand with the final judgment on 'the Jews' (12.37–43), which is followed by a summary of Jesus' preaching (12.44–50). This brings the first part of the gospel to an end and at the same time opens the second: the hour of Jesus' departure, which issues in 'that day', the day of the sending of the spirit through the risen Jesus and the beginning of the church (7.39; 16.7). However, there are already eschatological anticipa-

tions in the first part (John 2–11), by means of which, with the help of
the transition in John 12, the first part is seen in continuity with the
second.

Before 'that day' the apostles have not yet prayed in the name of Jesus
(16.26). At that time the spirit had not yet been given to the disciples
(7.39; 16.7). Only Easter Day (the gift of the Spirit) brings the disciples
deeper understanding (14.20; see 2.22; 12.16; 13.7) and enables them to
do 'greater deeds' (5.20; 14.12). Only then does the true 'discipleship of
Jesus' begin (13.36; cf. 12.26; 14.4–6). Furthermore, this period localizes
the significance of Jesus *within Israel*, though he is also sent to the world:
'Israel as the light of the world'. In this time before Easter in which Jesus
confines himself to Israel, it is already possible to see some anticipations
of the eschatological time of the church. For the mission of Jesus to Israel
is a mission to the world (3.11–15); above all, Jesus' visit to Samaria
(4.1–42) is an anticipation from which it emerges that what Jesus wills
is that the salvation which he brings from God should be salvation *for the
whole world* (4.42b). A time will come when people no longer worship God
on Mount Gerizim, as the Samaritans do, nor even on Mount Zion
(Jerusalem), but in spirit and truth (4.24). 'The time is coming, and now
is' (4.23a). Here in Samaria, Jesus' hour is clearly anticipated, as it was
in the miracle at Cana (2.4, 11). Thus the hour that is to come is 'the
day' (16.26): the departure of Jesus to the Father, when the Spirit of
truth will be given, the beginning of the time of the church under the
guidance of the spirit of Christ. That day, Easter and the time of the
church, beginning with the death and resurrection, is at the same time
also the time of the calling of the Gentiles: they will then be drawn into
the flock of 'true Israelites' (12.32); for this is said in connection with the
question put by the Greeks (12.20–23), to which Jesus in fact replies,
'The hour has come' (12.23). The crucifixion of Jesus introduces the call
or the 'drawing' of the Gentiles into the sheepfold in which the true
Israelites, like Nathanael, already find themselves (1.46–51). Even if 'the
Jews' misunderstand Jesus' departure, in the Gospel of John that misunderstanding has a grain of higher truth. They assume that Jesus will
go to the Gentiles (7.35), just as from the start they misunderstand the
voluntary sacrifice of this life as suicide (8.22). In fact Jesus' departure
to his Father is also a matter of his going to the Gentiles: 'I have other
sheep which are not of this fold' (10.16), and in connection with that: 'I
give my life for the sheep' (10.15b), 'not for the people only (Israel), but
also to bring together the scattered children of God' (11.52; see 18.37).
Thus the situation of the church from Easter onwards is anticipated in
Jesus' ministry before Easter. Despite his sharp awareness of the difference between the two periods, John sees them in an essential unity and
continuity: the earthly Jesus is the glorified Christ, at work in his church,

who makes the 'true Israelites' and the 'scattered children of God' from among the Gentiles into one flock. The Johannine view of the church and Israel is hardly different from that of Pauline theology (Rom. 11.16–22; Eph. 2.11–22). For John the divide falls not between Jews and non-Jews, but between faith in Jesus and rejection of his person.

With a number of anticipations, which indicate the fundamental unity of the two periods of Jesus' life, the Gospel after the prologue thus falls clearly into two great parts: John 2–11 and, after chapter 12, which concludes it and provides a new introduction, John 13–20 and 21.

## §2 Jesus' coming and his time on earth as the incarnate Word

### I. THE PROLOGUE TO JOHN

Literature (in addition to the commentaries on John already cited):

1. *Logos; structure of the Logos hymn; 'Incarnation'*: C. K. Barrett, 'The Prologue of Saint John's Gospel', in *New Testament Essays*, London 1972, 27–48; K. Berger, 'Zu "das Word ward Fleisch", Joh 1,14a', *NT* 16, 1974, 161–6; M. E. Boismard, *Le prologue de saint Jean*, Paris 1953; P. Borgen, 'Observations on the Targumic Character of the Prologue of John', *NTS* 16, 1969–70, 288–95; F. Christ, *Jesus Sophia. Die Sophia Christologie bei den Synoptikern*, ATANT 57, Zurich 1970, 35ff.; C. Demke, 'Der sogenannte Logos-Hymnus im Johanneischen Prolog', *ZNW* 58, 1967, 45–68; C. H. Dodd, 'The Prologue to the Fourth Gospel and Christian Worship', in *Apophoreta*, BZNW 30, 1964, 109–34; A. Feuillet, *Etudes Johanniques*, Paris 1962; R. G. Hamerton-Kelly, *Pre-existence, Wisdom and the Son of Man*, Cambridge 1973, 197–242; M. D. Hooker, 'The Johannine Prologue and the Messianic Secret', *NTS* 21, 1974, 53ff.; id., 'John the Baptist and the Johannine Prologue', *NTS* 16, 1969–70, 354–8; E. Käsemann, 'The Structure and Purpose of the Prologue to John's Gospel', *New Testament Questions of Today*, ET London and Philadelphia 1969, 138–67; G. Klein, 'Das wahre Licht scheint schon', *ZKTh* 68, 1971, 261–326; J. S. King, 'The Prologue to the Fourth Gospel: Some Unresolved Problems', *ExpT* 86, 1975, 372–5; P. Lamarche, 'Le prologue de Jean', *RSR* 52, 1964, 497–537; B. Lang, *Frau Weisheit, Deutung einer biblischen Gestalt*, Düsseldorf 1975; H. Langkammer, 'Zur Herkunft des Logostitels im Joh.', *BZ* 9, 1965, 91–4; B. L. Mack, *Logos und Sophia*, SUNT 10, Göttingen – Zurich 1973; M. McNamara, 'Logos of the Fourth Gospel and Memra of the Palestinian Targum (Ex. 12, 42)', *ExpT* 79, 1968, 115–7; U. Müller, *Die Geschichte der Christologie in der johanneischen Gemeinde*, SBS 77, Stuttgart 1975; T. E.

Pollard, *Johannine Christology and the Early Church*, Cambridge 1970; G. Richter, 'Die Fleischwerdung des Logos im Johannesevangelium', *NT* 13, 1971, 81–126 and 14, 1972, 257–76; M. Rissi, 'Die Logoslieder im Prolog des vierten Evangeliums', *TZ* 31, 1975, 321–36; J. T. Sanders, *The New Testament Christological Hymns*, Cambridge 1971; K. Schubert, 'Einige Beobachtungen zum Verständnis des Logosbegriffs im frührabbinischen Schrifttum', *Judaica* 9, 1953, 65–80; S. Schulz, *Komposition und Herkunft der johanneischen Reden*, BWANT 5, Folge 1, Stuttgart 1960; D. M. Smith, *The Composition and Order of the Fourth Gospel*, New Haven 1964; C. Spicq, 'Le Siracide et la structure littéraire du Prologue de St Jean', in *Mémorial Lagrange*, Paris 1940, 183–95; L. P. Trudinger, 'Prologue of John's Gospel', *Reformed Theological Review* 93, 1974, 11–17; H. Zimmermann, 'Christushymnus und johanneischer Prolog', in *Neues Testament und Kirche*, FS R. Schnackenburg, ed. G. Gnilka, Freiburg 1974, 249–65.

2. *The Johannine concepts of 'truth' and 'grace'* (*doxa*, glory is investigated below in more detail): S. Aalen, ' "Truth", a Key Word in St. John's Gospel', *StEv* 2 ( = TU 87), Berlin 1964, 3–24; K. Berger, ' "Gnade" ' im frühen Christentum', *NTT* 27, 1973, 1–25; J. Blank, 'Der johanneische Wahrheitsbegriff', *BZ* 7, 1963, 163–73; Yu Ibuki, *Die Wahrheit im Johannesevangelium*, Bonn 1972; L. J. Kuyper, 'Grace and Truth. An Old Testament Description of God and its Use in the Johannine Gospel', *Int* 18, 1964, 3–19; J. M. Myers, *Grace and Torah*, Philadelphia 1975; R. Schnackenburg, *Das Johannesevangelium* II, 265–81; U. Müller, *Die Geschichte der Christologie*, 36–45.

In the prologue to his gospel, we hear that for John, Jesus of Nazareth is proclaimed in the church from the beginning as the incarnate Word. From and within this insight of faith, John presents what he knows of the 'Jesus tradition', beginning with the baptism of Jesus in the Jordan, and including his signs and works, his words or 'logia', his death and his resurrection. John sets these early Christian traditions in the context of the *katabasis-anabasis* model. The Baptist, the words, signs and works of Jesus, and above all his death, become 'testimony' to his heavenly origin and his deepest personal identity: his special unity with the Father. The Johannine community, which lives by the Holy Spirit, but at the time of John was no longer a direct eyewitness of all this, *re-actualizes* the whole of the 'Jesus tradition' (according to the tradition which is known in John's community) in terms of the specific situation of the church and within a model which was popular within the community and had been taken over by it. This model was of the messianic prophet greater than Moses and had the model of *katabasis* and *anabasis* superimposed on it. The evidence, the force and the validation provided by *witnesses* was, of course, particularly significant for the second generation of Christians, or perhaps the beginning of the third. An existential question had arisen for the Johannine community. What is the basis of Christian faith for those of us who have not seen Jesus or experienced his physical presence?

## A. SOME PRELIMINARY CONSIDERATIONS

John 1.1–18 forms a prologue to the Fourth Gospel, with its particular problems. When I analysed the necessary presuppositions for understanding the Gospel of John I pointed out that it was common in early Judaism to use many names for one and the same reality. *Wisdom* and *Logos* were already identified. 'Logos' was used by Greek-speaking Jews to make their tradition more accessible to those with a Greek background. Just as 'wisdom' was used absolutely at that time, so too it was also possible to speak of 'the Logos', the Word.

Wisdom 9.1f. already spoke of wisdom and word (Logos). Wisdom was the Torah, the Law, which was called 'the Word of *God*' (Ps. 119; Wisdom 3.37f. with 4.1f.; Sir. 24.23–34).[48] The Law of Moses was the Logos (in John 1.17 the title Logos has disappeared, but in reality the Logos Jesus Christ is contrasted with Moses). In other words, even in early Judaism a connection was made between Jewish wisdom speculations and the Hellenistic Logos concept, so as to open up Jewish wisdom in the direction of Hellenistic wisdom. That is also the reason why the prologue speaks of 'wisdom' instead of 'the Logos' (a term which does not occur elsewhere in the Fourth Gospel and is thus peculiar to the pre-Johannine hymn to Christ).

The syncretistic milieu of the Gospel of John is perhaps an inadequate explanation of this evidence. Jewish wisdom speculation is also mixed up with so-called Sinaitism or Moses mysticism.[49] Here Wisdom or the Logos is identified with the 'original light' of Gen. 1.1ff., with conceptions which can be found again in the Palestinian Targums.[50] The terminology of John 1.5 is particularly illuminating: the light shines in the darkness, but the darkness *cannot overcome* it *(katalambanein)*. This is the only instance in which the Logos hymn does not use the expression 'did not accept it'. The verse is clearly an allusion to the light from Genesis which shines out over the darkness of primal chaos: this darkness *had to give way* to the light of creation. At all events, all these *Jewish* traditions are enough to explain the absolute use of the term 'the Logos' in the prologue to the Gospel of John. As such it is a pre-Christian, Graeco-Jewish element. Even if some exegetes think it useless to attempt any kind of scientific reconstruction, none of them fails to recognize that the prologue represents the revision of a pre-Johannine hymn to the Logos. However, the question is whether such scientific reconstructions help us any further, and whether what they bring to light cannot be discovered more quickly by an analysis of the prologue within the gospel. Furthermore, this reconstruction involves a certain danger, because it is governed by various presuppositions on the basis of which one exegete calls a redaction what another exegete takes to be a tradition. Whereas there are verses which some exegetes are unanimous in accepting as pre-Johannine, over others – the most important ones – there is considerable dispute. In the most recent substantial commentaries and studies on John one can see significant differences over practically every important verse. Furthermore, it is often forgotten that even the verses which can be certainly assumed to be pre-Johannine are at the same time redactional, in the sense that they derive their meaning from the prologue and the Gospel of John and not from the pre-Johannine hymn. The consequence of difficulties in such reconstructions has led most recently to completely new attempts. Thus M. Rissi[51] has recently proposed that the prologue should be seen as a combination of two individual hymns to Christ (1.1–12 and 1.14, 16, 17): others[52] came to the conclusion that the hymn to Christ is unfinished and must be supplemented by John 3.13–21, 31–36, which is a nucleus detached from the hymn. It cannot be denied that in practice, Rissi's solution solves many problems, but it cannot be substantiated. To end the hymn at 1.12, as E. Käsemann and many others do, does not explain the many terms in 1.14–18 which are not used elsewhere in the Gospel of John (*charis*, grace; *skēnoun*, dwell or set up a tent; *plērōma*, fullness). Rissi combines the fact that 1.12 unmistakably makes a good conclusion with the hypothesis that another hymn to Christ has been taken over in 1.14–18 (consisting of 1.14, 16, 17). I think that any reconstruction with a chance of success must begin with a comparison, not between the prologue and possibilities from the pre-Christian wisdom tradition, but between the Gospel of John and I John, two witnesses to the Johannine community, from which it emerges that the problems within the Johannine community only posed a serious problem in the situation reflected by I John. In that case we can get a better idea from the Gospel of John (which is concerned with the unity of Christians and clearly attacks certain tendencies in the community) of the *beginnings* of tendencies which at the later stage represented by I John are represented as heretical. For if we take into consideration the insertions into the hymn made by John, these first beginnings must be connected with the particular tendencies of the pre-Johannine hymn to Christ which are evident both from the Gospel of John and from I John 1:

'In him (the Logos) was life'
(John 1.4)

'The Logos who is life'
(I John 1.1c)

'The Logos was with God' (1.1,2)

'The life that was with the Father'
(1.2)

'The Logos became *sarx*' (1.14a)

'The life appeared' (1.2; see 4.2)

'We have seen his glory' (1.14b)

'We have seen it (the Word)'
(1.1).

Both passages are concerned with the pre-existent Logos who is life and appeared among us historically (John 1.14a; I John 1.2), whereas 'we' – that is the Christian (Johannine) community – have 'seen him'. The self-revelation of God in the incarnate Word, for man's salvation, the *visibility* (*sarx, phanerōsis*) of the saving Word, is unmistakably the nucleus of the liturgical hymn which the Johannine community sang as praise and thanksgiving. This hymnic confession of faith in the Johannine community must have given rise to a variety of interpretations which caused disunity in the church. We can get a vague idea of what this disunity was from the Gospel of John: it launches a strong attack on 'the Jews'. I commented earlier that while John is concerned with the disputes between Jesus and the Jewish leaders of his time, at the same time he sees this 'crisis' through the prism of what is taking place in the Johannine community: John is attacking a particular interpretation of Jesus by *Christian* Jews within his community. They claim to be superior to Gentile Christians by virtue of being children of Abraham and thus bring about discord in the community. And that is connected with Sinaitism and Moses mysticism; it is a Sinaitic 'vision of God'. These tendencies have become even more marked in I John. Not only does he call these disturbers of the peace within the church 'Antichrists' (I John, above all 4.2f.; also 2.18–22), but he insists even more strongly than the Gospel of John on 'brotherly love' (2.9–11; 3.11–24; 4.7–21), with a sharp attack on the 'Sinaitic vision of God' as found in Moses mysticism: 'He who does not love, does not know God' (I John 4.8). 'No one has seen God at any time' (see also John 1.18), 'but if we love one another, God dwells in us' (I John 4.12). 'If he does not love his brother whom he does see, then he cannot love God whom he has never seen' (I John 4.20); and finally, 'We know that the Son of God has come and has given us understanding to know him who is true' (I John 5.20). Jesus, the Son, and brotherly love are the only way to the vision of God: 'And by this we may be sure that we know him, if we keep his commandments' (I John 2.3), and these commandments coincide with the commandment to brotherly love (I John 2.7–11; this identity is stressed even more strongly in II John 6).

The Sinaitism of an immediate vision of God (which is also attacked in the Gospel of John: 1.18; 5.37; 6.46; 14.8), also had consequences for the Jewish-Christian view of the significance of the death of Jesus. In fact there is no reference at all to the death of Jesus in the prologue, unless, as might be expected, this is included in the humanity as creaturely, finite, earthly *sarx*. In the hymn, however, the prologue as it were passes over this death: the Logos has appeared as man and we – the later Christian community – have seen his glory. This 'swallows up' death, which evidently has no significance in this view of the hymn. This is a feature of Sinaitism. In the Targums we find an Aramaic word which means both 'die' and 'be lifted up' (*anabasis*),[53] the double meaning which we also find in the Gospel of John in connection with the death of Jesus: 'elevation' (of the cross) and 'exaltation' to God. The Targum on Ps. 68.18 speaks of the death of Moses as an exaltation or an ascent to heaven ('transportation theme'). In the view of early Jewish, Sinaitic Moses-mysticism, death has no significance; it is swallowed up in and by glory, which Moses possesses from God. It is therefore striking that the Gospel of John does not pass over the suffering and death of Jesus, and even calls Jesus 'the Lamb of God' (1.29b, 36), but on the other hand describes his death as the climax of the visibility of the glory of God in Jesus – a correction to the Christ hymn, but taking the same line. This particular tendency increased alarmingly in the situation of I John; this author therefore repeatedly stresses the atoning value of the death of Jesus (I John 3.5, 8; 5.6), above all that Jesus has come or has been sent 'to atone for our sins through the *sacrifice* of his life' (I John 4.10). I John unequivocally attacks any underestimation of the death of Jesus; a view which is quite understandable in Jewish, Sinaitic Moses-mysticism.

If the roots of the Johannine community are ultimately to be found in Palestine, then we can understand the reaction of John to a particular form of reverence for the Baptist in his community. That may also have something to do with Sinaitism. For in that case there can be many bearers of the Logos: Moses, the prophets, John the Baptist, Jesus. The uniqueness of Jesus as 'the Son' can in that case be misunderstood.

The particular tone of the pre-Johannine hymn stands out strongly against this background (which can be discovered from the Gospel of John and I John: in II John we even discover that there are heretics who deny that 'Jesus has come in the flesh'). The hymn celebrates the *visibility* of the glory *of God in* the man Christ Jesus. The very appearance of Jesus among us is salvation and grace. The incarnation is redemptive and brings salvation. Both the Fourth Gospel and I John *at the same time* stress the death of Jesus, but this is not mentioned in the hymn. The humanity of Jesus is itself God's grace among us. This is evidently the fundamental enthusiasm of the Johannine community. This theology represents a correction within the New Testament to the *exclusive* Pauline stress on cross and resurrection. On the other hand, it carries within itself the danger of ignoring the special significance of the death of Jesus. I John in particular attacks the one-sidedness of this theology of incarnation (*theologia gloriae*), and *within it* lays stress on the atoning death of Jesus (*theologia crucis*); the Gospel of John also makes a beginning of doing this.

If we take into account the particular, threefold reaction of the Gospel of John to certain tendencies in the community which sings this hymn to the Logos, then by leaving out those verses which are clearly an expression of this reaction, we can read the pre-Johannine hymn to Christ as follows:

I    In the beginning was the Word (1.1a)
and the Word was with God (1.1b)

And God was the Word (1.1c)
this was in the beginning with God (1.2)

II   All things were made through him (1.3a)
and without him was not anything made that was made (1.3b)

In him was life (1.4a)
and the life was the light of men (1.4b)

III And the light shines in the darkness (1.5a)
but the darkness could not overcome it (1.5b)

IV  It was in the world (1.10a)
yet the world did not recognize it (1.10c)

V    It came into its own (1.11a)
but its own did not recognize it (1.11b)

But to those who did accept him (1.12a)
he gave power to become children of God (1.12b)

VI  The word became flesh (1.14a)
and dwelt among us (1.14b)

and we have seen his glory (1.14c)
full of grace and truth (1.14c)

Of his fullness have we received (1.16a)
and grace for grace (1.16b).

This is in fact a very meaningful hymn to Christ. Given the state in which it has come to us, it makes sense to assume that before the Johannine stage, two hymns (1.1–12 and 1.14, 16) have been fused into one. John 1.12 gives the unmistakable impression of being a conclusion to 1.1–11 (E. Käsemann *et al.*). The combination of two independent hymns (so M. Rissi) thus remains a plausible (though abstract) possibility. Without 1.14–16, John 1.1–12 could even be a perfect hymn to the Torah from the wisdom tradition – the Book of Wisdom in the form of a hymn. However, sung by a Christian community, 1.1–12 would also be understandable as a genuine hymn to Christ. But in any case, the three-fold reaction of John turns this hymn into something completely new: from a literary point of view we have not only *insertions*, but a new composition of the whole hymn. So before we analyse the so-called 'insertions', we must look rather more closely at what is supposed to be the 'hymn of the Johannine community'.

The pre-Johannine hymn is clearly inspired by wisdom, with the influence of speculations based on Genesis for which the Palestinian Targums provide examples. The hymn thinks in *phases*, but in the last resort these all relate to the incarnate Word: darkness, the world, his own, *sarx* and 'we' all make the coming of the Word which is identified with Jesus Christ more precise and gradually more particular. Again and again we have mention of 'he was not accepted' (recognized), except in 1.5, where we have *ou katelaben:* the darkness could not overcome the light. 'The light which shines in darkness' (1.5) is thus an allusion (not yet to 'the world', but) to the darkness of primal chaos (Gen. 1.2), which was overcome by the word of God at creation: 'Let there be light' (Gen. 1.3): the darkness had to yield to the light of creation; it could not overcome it. 'God divided the light from the darkness' (Gen. 1.4b). Since then it shines on every man who comes into the world (John 1.9b).[54] But although light was in the world from creation, the world did not recognize it (1.10a, c). Then it came (*ēlthen*, as contrasted with 'being' in the world) into 'its own'. If this community hymn derives from a Christian community with Palestinian roots, we need not understand 'his own' either in terms of Philo (the world as 'Son of God') or in terms of Greek wisdom: the world as the work of God's own hand, the Logos (though this reading can be defended in the context of Johannine theology); it refers rather to the coming of the Logos in Israel: in Moses, in the Law, in the prophets and perhaps also in John the Baptist (in view of the various aspects of Sinaitism to be found in the community). So we must retain the ambiguity of 'his own', in the sense that the Johannine Jewish Christians saw it as Israel, Christians from a Gentile background the world as God's gift at creation. But even 'his own' did not accept him. Still, the work of wisdom or the Logos was not in vain: a remnant accepted him, and they are children of light: 'children of God' (1.2; see Wisdom 7.27). Then the Logos entered the *sarx*, a particular man, Jesus (1.14). *We*, that is, Christians – the Johannine community – we have seen God's glory in him and he was full of grace and truth, that is, the revelation of wisdom (see below). We belong to these 'children of God'. For of his fullness *we have received* grace and *continue to receive* yet more grace (1.16).

This seems to have been the inspired tone of the Johannine community's hymn. And it is possible that this originally Palestinian community in fact transformed an existing Jewish Logos hymn in honour of the Torah or Wisdom so that it could be applied to Jesus Christ, and that the evangelist added John 1.14, 16, to make the whole hymn into a hymn to Christ. But all the *phases* of the salvation-historical manifestation of the light come together in Jesus. *He* is light on primal chaos, the light of the world, the light of Israel; through his incarnation, in which we have recognized God's glory.

In view of the tendencies which had developed in the community and which were disrupting the unity of the church, the author introduces corrective insertions from the Johannine theology which to some degree was community theology even before the final redaction of the Fourth Gospel. All this can be understood if we are correct in seeing that the Jewish Christians in the Johannine community were under the influence of Sinaitism.

(*a*) John 1.6–8; 1.15. In these verses of the prologue, John stresses that the true light is not John the Baptist, but someone else – Jesus (1.9). The Baptist was not this light; he came to bear witness of the light. The insertion of 1.6–8 and 1.15 in particular leads R. Bultmann (and some authors who follow him) to describe this hymn to the Logos as a hymn which originally arose within a Baptist movement with a gnostic orientation: it is a Logos hymn to John the Baptist. We know from the somewhat later Pseudo-Clementines[55] that in the second century there was something like a movement originating from John the Baptist which revered John as its own Messiah. And in fact there are some features in the Gospel of John which point to polemic against veneration of John the Baptist. But this does not of itself prove that there was such a Logos hymn in honour of John nor that this veneration of John was a competitive movement *outside* Christianity in the time of the Gospel of John. (From a historical point of view, it may just as well have developed within the Johannine community, when we think of the schism which is either threatened or has already come about in I John.) But Bultmann was on the way towards a true insight, which is now more generally accepted,[56] namely that the Johannine community itself has Palestinian roots and that these lie in circles associated with John the Baptist (John 1.35ff. indicates that John the Baptist himself brought the first disciples to Jesus, so that the Gospel itself so to speak locates the origin of the Johannine community in circles associated with the Baptist: see also the discussion with disciples of John in 3.24–30). But the prologue and the Gospel of John are not concerned with a 'Johannine movement' outside or alongside the church; it is within the community itself, and consists of Jewish Christians who are involved in Sinaitism. The insertion of 1.6–8 corresponds with the insertion of 1.15; 1.18. The pre-Johannine tendencies which go back to the community's hymn in that case seem to lie more in the fact that Moses, John and Jesus were put on roughly the same level as bearers of the divine Logos. So the evangelist makes John the Baptist the first witness to Christ, the prototype of the Christian disciple or the church (1.15; 1,27), who points to the true light and is the friend of the bridegroom (3.30).

The interruption caused by the insertion 1.6–8 also made the Johannine transitionary verse 1.9 necessary; here John again takes up the interrupted thoughts of 1.4f., at the same time perhaps making them more precise (governed by 1.6–8): 'the *true* light that illuminates every man' (1.9) again takes up 1.4b (perhaps, for I John 2.8 also speaks of 'the true light', evidently without any allusion to John the Baptist).

(*b*) John 1.12c–13. Because of the difficulties in the Johannine community above all from Sinaitic Jewish Christians, we can also understand the insertion of 1.12: 'Born not of blood nor of the desire of the flesh nor of the will of man, but of God' (1.13). This insertion required a repetition of the theme (see the position in the Greek text) 'to those who believe on his name' as a closer Christian definition of 'all' and 'them' from 1.12ab. Being a child of God (1.12, which as a result of the insertion of 'believe on his name' is clearly being a child of God in *Christ*) is not based on an *ethnic* blood relationship or being a child of Abraham in the physical sense, but on a spiritual birth from God. The fact that this insertion comes here suggests that John knows that some Jewish Christians in fact read vv. 11f. of the community's hymn as the coming of the Logos into the world and as a specific coming of the Logos in Israel, 'his own' (in Moses, the Law and the prophets), which was completely clear in terms of wisdom. All those who have accepted this light may be called 'children of God' (see also Wisdom 5.5; 7.27). But here John immediately adds: ethnic blood relationship does not give any priority (1.13).

(*c*) John 1.17f.; 1.14d. In these Johannine insertions Jesus is called *monogenēs*. This word betrays a specifically Johannine interest (in addition to 1.14d see 1.18; 3.16; 3.18) and itself indicates that 1.14d and 1.18 are Johannine insertions (the somewhat distorted construction of 1.14c, d, e is best explained by taking 1.14d as an insertion). *Monogenēs* does not mean 'only-begotten' (*monogennan*), but 'unique', the only one of his kind (*mono-genos*), and thus the only beloved.[57] *Doxan hōs monogenous para Patros* (1.14) literally means the glory which he receives as the only beloved of the Father from the Father ('the Father of glory' is a liturgical predicate for God in early Christianity; see Eph. 1.17; II Peter 1.17; cf. I Peter 1.21; Rom. 6.4 and even Mark 8.38 par.). In Jesus the community sees the glory of God (which is otherwise unattainable).

I mentioned Sinaitism and Samaritanism (both of which are closely connected) in the pre-Johannine community. Moses was revered as prophet, king and priest, leader of the people of God, suffering servant of God and 'mystagogue'; after his suffering for the people he was 'transported to God'.[58] By mystagogical initiation one was 'born of God', and this was connected with a particular 'vision of God'.[59] 'The Jews' set their hope on Moses (John 5.45); they believe in him (6.32) and are his disciples (9.28f.). In the Johannine community this Moses mysticism evidently exists alongside belief in Jesus, particularly among Christians from Judaism (see Wisdom 7.22).[60] John wants to stress the unique character of Jesus as bearer of the Logos over against bearers of the Logos like Moses, the prophets and John the Baptist. Hence also the insertion in 1.17f. Above all: 'No one has ever seen God; the only beloved Son who is in the bosom of the Father, *he* has made him known' (1.18). Here John repeats the expression 'the only-beloved', but now makes it specific as relating to the unique, dear *Son*. According to the best manuscripts the passage reads 'only beloved *God*' (*theos*); elsewhere, however, John knows only the expression *monogenēs hyios*, the only beloved Son (3.16; 3.18), and this is to be preferred above all because the contrast between *Theos* (God) and *ho Pater* (the Father) is not Johannine. John means to say that the Son is in the bosom of the Father.[61] The Son is *ho ōn*, the one who is in the bosom of the Father. This does not point to the return of Jesus to the Father, but to the fact that the Father never leaves Jesus 'alone', even in his *sarx* situation. 'I am in the Father and the Father is in me.' As 'only beloved' refers to the love of the Father for the Son, the 'lying of Jesus in the bosom of the Father' is seen as the Son's loving response to the Father. The unity of love between Father and Son remains in the incarnate Word, the Son. 'Be in the bosom of . . .' or 'lie in someone's bosom' is a Semitic expression for a loving relationship (e.g. in marriage: Gen. 16.5; Deut. 13.6; 28.54, 56; a suckling on its mother's breast, I Kings 3.20; also God's care for Israel, Num. 11.12; see 'in Abraham's bosom', Luke 16.22f.). In 1.18 John stresses the reciprocal love between Father and Son because of which only the Son can tell us of the Father, of God: Jesus is the final revelation of God. Moses only gave the law, whereas Jesus gave grace and truth, the eschatological revelation of wisdom (1.17). As John takes up in his insertion 1.17 a formula from the original hymn, namely 1.14e, 'grace and truth' (*charis* cannot be found elsewhere in the Gospel, but it appears four times in the Prologue), this latter is not a criterion for detecting the passage as a redaction by John. In the original hymn, 1.14e read: 'We have seen the glory of the Logos, full of grace and truth.'

It seems to me that U. Müller gives an incorrect explanation of the expression 'grace and truth', on the basis of his assumption that the theology of the community before John involved a christology which interpreted Jesus as a *theios anēr* or wonder worker;[62] he follows the investigation of *charis* made by G. P. Wetter,[63] which sees it as the supernatural power of the man of God, on the lines, as he puts it, of 'full of grace and power' (Acts 6.8, on Stephen). But if it is correct to assume that Sinaitism was to be found among Jewish Christians in the Johannine community, here if anywhere we may expect the influence of the exodus and Sinai tradition on the Johannine community: Ex. 33; 34, with the typical Sinai concepts which can be found there: 'glory' (Ex. 33.18, 22), 'grace and truth' (*ḥesed* and *ᵡmet*, Ex. 34.6, 9; 33.12f.; 33.16f.), 'God's dwelling in a tent' (Ex. 33.9–11) and his accompanying the people (Ex. 33.14–16; 34.9).[64] However, in that case we must immediately go on to add that *ḥesed* (grace) and *ᵡmet* (faithfulness, covenant love) are read with early Jewish, Hellenistic Jewish eyes. In my analysis of these two Hebrew terms for grace (see above), I pointed out that in the later Old Testament texts *ᵡmet* has largely lost the meaning of faithfulness and covenant love and simply meant truth, revealed wisdom. In this Greek, early Jewish usage (above all in the wisdom literature and apocalyptic), *charis*, grace also acquired the meaning of the grace of revealed wisdom and the sinless life that this conveys (this is also a central theme in I John 3.4–10). The Sinai themes, including *ḥesed* and *ᵡmet*, are no longer directly understood in the early Jewish usage, above all in Sinaitism, as loving care and covenant faithfulness (a concept which is in fact alien to the prologue), but as a love which is expressed in the gift of truth, revealed wisdom. In my view, however, it makes no sense to deny the underlying Sinai and Exodus tradition for the sake of these semantic shifts. For Sinaitism, it was Moses above all who had brought the divine revealed wisdom through the gift of the Law of God; for Jewish Christians who held to Moses mysticism in the Johannine community, Moses too (and John the Baptist) was a bearer of the Logos (Philo says this explicitly). John sees a danger here. Hence the insertion: 'the Law was given by Moses, but grace and truth (of which the hymn in 1.14a speaks) came through Jesus Christ' (1.17), that is, the full, final revelation of wisdom was given us by Jesus, who is greater than Moses. This is clearly an 'insertion' of John's despite the fact that he uses a non-Johannine word (*charis*), since he takes this from the pre-Johannine hymn in 1.14e. That is also the reason why in 1.15 John once again mentions the Baptist, this time to make him bear witness to the absolute priority of the heavenly Jesus.

Thus all these insertions can be explained by the fact that John sees the dangers which Sinaitism posed to the community. John is concerned with the 'grace and truth', that is, the truth of the doctrine or revelation of Jesus, the light, the life, which is given in all fullness by the Father in the Son, in Jesus Christ.

## B. The prologue itself

Despite the need to see the Gospel of John as a whole, in the light of which all the parts are to be understood, and vice versa, from a literary point of view the Gospel of John poses one particular problem. From this point of view, some passages are masterpieces (e.g. John 5; 17; 20), but others have been written carelessly; this would seem to indicate that the Gospel is made up of individual units which have already been edited and have grown together and been made into 'one gospel' during the development of a community theology. It emerges from a comparison between the Gospel of John and the Johannine epistles that for all the differences, 'both authors' have their roots in the same community theology. Anyone who wants to make a literary investigation of this Gospel will have to begin with the analysis of individual literary units *within* this gospel. This is the only way towards an overall view. It is indisputable that various 'hands' have been at work in the composition of this gospel in the form in which it has come down to us, though they have been governed by an overall Johannine theology. So it will not always be possible to resolve the 'tensions'. The Gospel is not one man's composition, though in the last resort it is a completely new composition.

If we look upon the prologue as a literary unity, it is clear that it is concerned with Jesus Christ, who is revered as the Word with God. Throughout this Gospel the evangelist is not interested in the salvation-historical phases of the manifestation of the Logos: over primal chaos, in the world, in 'his own' and finally in Jesus. Yet at the same time it is impossible to ignore these phases. They come together only in the prologue (even more strongly than in the community hymn) *along with* the historical manifestation of the Logos, Jesus of Nazareth. This particular kind of thinking on a variety of levels is peculiar to the Fourth Gospel. The whole event expressed in the prologue *is* the event of the appearing of Jesus on earth. The Gospel of John speaks of *Jesus of Nazareth* when he appeared on earth. This Jesus on earth is pre-existent with God (1.1f.), the origin and future of all that is created (1.3f.). He came to us as a light over primal chaos, that which is not divine; he was the light of the first day of creation through which day and night, light and darkness were separated (Gen. 1.3–5), 'the light of the world' (from Genesis: see John 9.4f.), and which lightens all men coming into the world (1.10). He came into the world, 'his own', the work of his hands (a Jewish Christian would perhaps understand this as Israel, God's own people, 1.11). Not only did he come from above into this earthly world (or better, this world below the heavens); he appeared in real fleshly form, i.e. in the form of what as such is 'from below', transitory and creaturely (1.14). In this *sarx*, the Logos, Jesus Christ (cf. John 1.1 with 1.17) shines as a light in the darkness (1.5), a light which lightens all men (1.4, 9b *lumen gentium*). John the Baptist bears witness to this (1.6–8). It was Jesus who came into the world (1.10), 'to his own' (1.11)[65] and who gives all who accept him, that is (John makes it more precise) those who believe on his name, the capacity of becoming children of God (1.12), through a birth from God (1.13), which is a spiritual birth or birth from a virgin (1.13). But Jesus' coming into the world is surrounded by belief and unbelief. We – the Johannine community – however, were able to recognize God's glory in his fleshly manifestation among us, a glory which he received as the only beloved of the Father (1.14). He is the fullness of the final, divine revealed wisdom (1.14). John the Baptist bore witness to his pre-existence, and so the content of his own revelation is quite different from that of Jesus (1.15). The community *lives* from the abundance of grace in Jesus and will *continue to live* by it day by day.[66] The law given by Moses fades away in the light of this final and complete revealed wisdom of Jesus Christ (1.17). Salvation comes from none but him. For salvation is *pneuma*-God: to know him. For men who are 'from below', the God 'from above' is inaccessible and unapproachable (John 6.46; 5.37; see also Hebrews and Paul). To approach him and thus to know him one must come from above and thus have descended. And this is only the case with the dear, only-beloved Son, who also himself loves the Father (1.18b; 7.29; 8.55 etc.). By virtue of his unity with the Father he alone can bring us to know God. Jesus Christ is the eschatological revelation of God (1.18).

Jesus Christ is the coming of the Word-with-God to us ('I am never alone, the Father is always with me', 16.32; 8.29), as light in the darkness: 'I am the light' (8.12; 12.46; 3.19), the new day of creation. Where Jesus appears, the darkness of our primal chaos vanishes, as it did at creation; it yields before the light that shines at God's word in the darkness (Gen. 1.3–5): 'God called the light day, and the darkness he called night' (Gen. 1.5): 'Are there not twelve hours in the day? A man can walk by day without stumbling, because he sees the light of this world. But if anyone goes by night . . . As long as I am in the world, *I am the light of the world*' (John 9.4f.; see 8.12; 12.46; and 1.4f., 7, 8, 9; 3.19, 21; 5.35; 8.12; 11.9f.; 12.35f., 46). In Jesus, the Word also comes as life for men: 'I am the life' (11.25; 14.6). His descent is a coming into a world which is his, the world of creation. This coming is also an incarnation: the word came as creaturely *sarx*, as man like we are. 1.14, the incarnation, is by no means central for John (as it is, say, in Hebrews); the all-important thing is his coming, his being sent as light and life for all. But the one thing is the other: through and in his *sarx*, light and life have come among us. His being sent is expressed in the *sarx*. The incarnation is another expression for 'the coming of light' in earthly spheres, in our darkness. The Gospel of John seems to pay less attention to Jesus' being *sarx* as such than, for example, the synoptic gospels, I Peter and Hebrews. Nevertheless, it is only in and through the *sarx* that the heavenly – the Word – has come among us, and only *as long as* there is this *sarx* (see below). What John 1.14 calls *egeneto*, the word *became* flesh, is termed *ephanerōthē* in I John 1.2, 'has appeared'; both have the same meaning. In other words, the terminology as such has yet to indicate precisely how the incarnation is understood in theological terms; Johannine theology is concerned with the *manifestation* of the Logos in the man Jesus. Thus there is still no express indication of the christology presented by the Gospel of John; that can only emerge from an analysis of the way in which the Fourth Gospel understands the relationship between *sarx* and *doxa* or glory; but the word *egeneto* as such cannot give us any information. John 1.14 sees in the appearance of the Logos in the flesh the realization of the promise of 'God's dwelling among his people' (Lev. 26.11f.; Ezek. 37.27; 43.7; 48.35; Joel 3.21; Zech 2.10; 3.8 etc.). Elsewhere the Johannine Jesus calls himself an *anthrōpos*, a man, it is true, but 'a man who communicates the truth (of revelation) to you' (8.40). We may not play off *sarx* against *anthrōpos*. He is therefore the only access to the Father (John 1.18): 'I am the way' (14.6; 10.9). Therefore, 'Any spirit that confesses that Jesus Christ has come in the *sarx* is from God' (I John 4.2), 'child of God' (John 1.12), 'born of God' (1.13). Thus the darkness can no more overcome Christians than the darkness of primal chaos could overcome the light of creation (12.35; the same verb as in 1.5). Jesus is the only beloved Son who also loves the Father; the Father is with the Son (16.32), in the Son (17.21), one with the Son (10.30); both are the same 'life' (1.1; 5.26; 11.25; 14.6; 17.3). 'The Father is in me' and 'I am in the Father' (14.10; 14.11; 14.20; 10.30–38; 16.32; 17.21).

From John 1.1 to 1.18 the hymn has been transformed into a new literary entity: into the prologue to John, the introduction to the Fourth Gospel. Exact knowledge of the community's hymn (from elsewhere) would in fact lead to a better knowledge of the prologue and the Gospel of John. As we do not have this historical information, a scientific reconstruction cannot produce more than can be obtained by literary-critical exegesis from the Gospel of John and I John. In other words, this reconstruction does not help towards a better exegesis of John; at best it can be its *result*, and therefore does not add anything new. However, the division between 'redaction' and 'tradition' (which in turn is once again 'redaction' *within* the prologue) helps us to recognize certain reactions which are present in the Gospel of John.

In all this it is striking that John's attention, like that of the synoptic gospels, is directed towards the *earthly Jesus* and not immediately towards the risen Christ. For John the light that is Jesus shines only during his earthly life. Jesus says to his disciples, 'The light is with you for a little longer. Walk while you have the light, lest the darkness overtake you . . . While you have the light, believe in the light . . . ' (12.35f.). 'As long as I am in the world, I am the light of the world' (9.5). The earthly Jesus is the presence of the spiritual light world among us; at his death *this* presence of the light vanishes. So when Jesus is no longer there he will send the spirit (14.16f.; 25f.; 15.26f.; 16.7–11, 13–15). As long as *he* is visibly there, 'the pneuma is not yet' (7.39b), nor is it necessary: the light of the spiritual world *is there*, with Jesus, albeit in the dimness of the *sarx*, and not yet as *pneuma*. When he has gone away, another Paraclete will come from above to remind the disciples of all that he has told them about the spiritual world, about God (3.32; 3.11; 8.26). However, I John will speak of the abiding of the light after the death of Jesus: 'The darkness is passing away and the true light is already shining' (I John 2.8).[67] For John himself the true light is there as long as Jesus is in his *sarx* among us. Here, too, 'the division of light and darkness' (Gen. 1.4b) plays a part: 'God called the light day, and the darkness he called night' (Gen. 1.5). The light that is among us only 'for a short time' in the *sarx* of Jesus (see also 7.33; 13.33; 14.19; 16.16–22) lasts as long as it is day (9.4): 'as long as I am in the world, I am the *light of the world*' (9.5).

However, in the prologue John does not talk of Jesus' going away. Many exegetes read the *anabasis* or return of Jesus to heaven out of John 1.18, perhaps because of the notion suggested by *eis ton kolpon* (the usual expression is *en tō kolpō*, in the bosom of, but one can also say, to lie towards (*eis*) someone's bosom, that is, to love someone and be loved of them). I cannot therefore find any *anabasis* here. Nor would this fit the function played by the prologue in the gospel. This prologue or introduction deals with the *katabasis*, Jesus' coming (from above) among us. Clearly the perspective is that of the Christian church and thus an insight from the time after Jesus' death and resurrection: in reality this perspective presupposes the return of Jesus. But (as a Christian) John speaks from the perspective of the *pre-existence of Jesus*: the Johannine Jesus also speaks from this perspective in the Fourth Gospel. That is the fundamental difference between the Fourth Gospel and the synoptics, which also put into the mouth of the earthly Jesus words of the Lord, the Christ who is already risen and present in the church. But John makes the earthly Jesus speak, in the light of his pre-existence with the Father, of what he has 'heard and seen there' (3.11, 31f.; 8.26; see also 5.19; 5.30; 12.49). What John knows of the 'Jesus tradition' – and that is a good deal, as we can prove even in detail – is seen in his gospel from the perspective of the faith that Jesus is from above. The evangelist says this so many years after the death of Jesus, obviously on the basis of the experience of the Johannine community (1.14b, c) which has come down to the author of the Fourth Gospel through the first eyewitness and by a living tradition, becoming in the spirit a contemporary experience in faith by the community (hence in 3.11 the remarkable first person plural: '*We* speak and testify to what *we* have seen'; here Jesus speaks in the first person plural. The two planes, 'Jesus' and 'the community', seem to fuse into a 'we' which John does not use elsewhere for Jesus, who speaks in the first or third person singular, see e.g. 17.2). But the *prologue* still does not think forward to the *anabasis*: it paints the first wing of the triptych of revelation: the coming of the Logos as *sarx* among us. It is then followed, in the gospel itself, by a kerygmatic history of Jesus' life: from the baptism of Jesus to his return to the Father via the exaltation on the cross, through which the *doxa* of God in Jesus first comes completely into its own. The prologue is simply the opening of the gospel and therefore not an independent literary unit which discusses the *katabasis* and *anabasis* by way of anticipation. In the *sarx* of Jesus we have a progressive historical revelation of the *doxa* or glory of the Father (1.18; above all 12.28), though this is visible only to the eyes of the believer. For the moment, then, nothing need in fact be said about the death of Jesus. (Of course this was rather different in the case of the pre-Johannine Logos hymn in honour of Jesus: here we have a compact hymn to Christ which does not mention the death of Jesus, at least explicitly. That is no longer the case in the hymns to Christ that we find in the New Testament and which go back to an earlier stage before the New Testament. This fact in itself does not as yet say anything about the value which the Johannine community places on the death of Jesus.)

Thus John uses a spatial model typical of the whole of the thought of late antiquity: the *epigeia* or earthly spheres and the *epourania* or heavenly spheres, at that time *the* reality. But without abandoning this spatial conception it expresses real existential *relationships*. Life in the true sense is 'heavenly' or spiritual life. Anyone who is from above bears 'life' in himself (see 8.23). Hence the repeated expression in John: Jesus has descended *from (apo)* God, from *(apo)* heaven (6.38), and has entered *(eis)* the earthly sphere, the cosmos. As well as *apo* (from, in a local perspective), John also speaks of *ek* (from): having come from heaven (3.13) and having come from *(ek)* the Father (16.28). Finally, he also comes 'from God' *(para*: 6.46). Jesus comes to earth from the heavenly spheres. However, this spatial conception sets out to say something about the *nature* of Jesus, for when he too leaves the Father's side *(para)*, the Father does not leave Jesus alone (8.29; 16.32): in the earthly Jesus 'the Father is in me and I in the Father'. The earthly Jesus *is* of a heavenly nature. His coming is an initiative from the Father. Hence Jesus has been sent by the Father (3.17, 34; 4.34; 5.23, 24, 30, 36, 37; 6.29, 38, 39, 44, 57; 7.16, 18, 29; 8.16, 18, 26, 29, 42; 9.4; 10.36; 11.42; 12.44, 45, 49; 13.20; 14.24; 15.21; 16.5; 17.3, 8, 18, 21, 23, 25; 20.21); he does nothing in his own name, but everything in the name of God (5.43). He has come to do the Father's will (4.34; 8.29; 10.18; 12.49f.; 14.31; 15.10), the work of God (4.34; 5.20b–23; 14.10; 17.4), and he speaks the words of God (12.49; 14.10, 24; 17.8). These are the technical words of any prophetic mission. But the *katabasis* model makes these statements radical: in Jesus the heavenly, spiritual reality is present in the *sarx* or a piece of our cosmos. The vertical 'above' is now to be found horizontally, indeed frontally, 'here below', in the person of Jesus Christ. Anyone who sees him sees the Father (14.9). In Jesus God has manifested himself as a God of and for men. In John, a general feature of the New Testament is given a very special form of expression.

In the Gospel of John, the gradual revelation of the true identity of Jesus, which elsewhere, e.g. in the Gospel of Mark, is called the messianic secret, is expressed in the repeated questions about the origin of Jesus: *the origin* of anyone determines his nature. This is made clear again and again in the accounts of the signs: where does this delicious wine come from (2.9)? Where do we get bread from (6.5)? Where must this living water come from (4.11)? And above all at the trial of Jesus. Pilate asks: 'Where do you come from?' (19.9). In this spatial model, a person's origin determines his nature. Jesus keeps saying, 'I know *where* I come *from* and *where* I am going' (8.14b; 7.28f.; see 9.29f.). That will emerge from the whole of Jesus' *kerygmatic* history, as narrated by the Fourth Gospel.

## II. JESUS IS PRESENTED TO ISRAEL THROUGH JOHN THE BAPTIST (JOHN 1.19–34)

Before the incarnate Word, Jesus of Nazareth, appears to reveal himself, he is solemnly presented to Israel by a prophet sent by God (1.31), namely the messiah coming from heaven or the eschatological bringer of Holy Spirit: of salvation, life and light. Throughout his gospel John puts special stress on witnesses on which Christian believers have good reason to rely.

It appears from the account in 1.9–34 that John knows the primitive Christian tradition which began the public ministry of Jesus at his baptism by John. Even more, it is striking that the Fourth Gospel has geographical information about the place of the activity of John the Baptist, namely the east bank of the Jordan, 'in Bethany' (not 'Bethany' near Jerusalem), that is, 'the house of the boat', the place where one could move over from the west bank of the Jordan to the east (1.28). We know from the synoptic gospels that many people came to the Baptist (Luke 3.7; Mark 1.5; Matt. 3.5; cf. John 3.23); a river crossing was an appropriate place for baptisms, especially as it was also (as the synoptic gospels point out) a desert place: Transjordania (Peraea, near Judaea). In all probability this information about John is historically reliable.

However, from the very beginning John has worked the traditions known to him into the perspective of his christology. The historical characteristics of the activity of John the Baptist, which are already overpainted in the synoptic gospels in a Christian style, disappear completely in John. The Baptist's task and activity are seen completely in Christian terms: he bears testimony to Jesus as the Messiah from above which ultimately comes from God (1.6–8, 19–23; 3.23–30; 5.33–35). The Baptist is no longer even a foreunner; he runs *alongside* Jesus and is active at the same time as he is (1.29, 34–36; 3.22–30; but John goes on to say in 3.28 that the Baptist was sent to go before Jesus.) John the Baptist is the first disciple of Jesus, an image of the true church. What is the concrete task of John the Baptist in the Gospel of John?

(*a*) Negative. John refuses to give himself any messianic significance (1.20; 3.28); he even denies that he is Elijah or the forerunner (1.21). In the end he denies being 'the prophet', the eschatological prophet greater that Moses, who was generally expected at the time of Jesus (1.21b). It is historically certain that baptist movements worshipped John as Messiah at least at the beginning of the second century.[68] At best the Gospel of John appeared a few decades earlier; in all probability, such tendencies must have been visible at this time. John makes the Baptist himself attack them.

(*b*) Positive. (1) The Gospel of John knows the traditional, primitive Christian datum that the Baptist pointed to Jesus as being stronger and greater (John 1.27, 30; Mark 1.7 par.). This too is revised in terms of Johannine christology: Jesus is the pre-existent one. 'The one who comes after me is before me, since he was earlier than I' (1.30, see the prologue, 1.15). (2) But the Baptist has a distinct function as 'forerunner' even in John. He is someone who prepares the way of the Lord (1.23). However, this raises the question why the Baptist still took the initiative towards this practice of baptism if he is neither the Messiah, nor Elijah, nor the eschatological Mosaic prophet (1.25). John the Baptist gives the answer to this in the Gospel of John: 'For this I came baptizing, with water, that he (Jesus) might be *revealed* to Israel' (1.31). That had already been announced in the prologue: 'He was not that light, but came to bear witness of the light' (1.8). Therefore the Johannine John the Baptist baptized only in order to be able to be God's witness to Jesus as the Messiah of Israel. For the Gospel of John, the significance of the baptism of Jesus by John lies in the fact that this baptism is as it were the solemn presentation of Jesus to Israel as Messiah in the name of the prophetic voice of the Old Testament. Nevertheless, the Baptist makes his attitude to Jesus more precise. The Johannine churches evidently found it difficult to understand that the heavenly Jesus allowed himself to be baptized by John. 'He who comes after me, I am not worthy to loosen the thongs of his sandals' (1.27). *Ho opisō mou*, 'he who comes after me', is a rabbinic expression for 'my disciple'. On the other hand, 'not be worthy to loose someone's sandal' is also a rabbinic expression for 'be someone's disciple' – this was too lowly a task even for a disciple, which the master always refused. John 1.27 in fact says, 'I have a disciple, Jesus, but really I am his disciple'. In the divine perspective (1.6; 1.33), John is at Jesus' service; his task is to present Jesus to Israel as the Messiah who comes from heaven (1.30), thus as a bringer of salvation, utterly filled with the spirit from above: 'He baptizes with the spirit', that is, he communicates (from his fullness, 1.16) the spirit or the heavenly (1.33). Thus the baptism of Jesus by John (the Fourth Gospel never once says explicitly that Jesus was baptized by John) is not in any way a humiliation; on the contrary, it is the solemn recognition of his saving mission from the Father. (3) Furthermore John the Baptist brings Jesus his first disciples (1.35–39; see 3.29). At the same time, John indicates by this that the competition between the disciples of John and the disciples of Jesus which seemed to be a feature of his time (perhaps as a result of tension within the church, 1.15, 20; 3.25–30) was not to be found with John and Jesus. (4) John has the Baptist already presenting Jesus as 'the Lamb', as the suffering servant of God, the Lamb of God (1.29f.; 1.36, perhaps with Easter colouring in 19.33f., see below).

Jesus makes his public appearance thanks to this christological testimony by John the Baptist (1.31). So in the Fourth Gospel his baptism by John is given a different significance from that in the synoptic gospels. The 'heavenly event' which in the synoptic gospels concerns only Jesus, as a kind of inward event between Jesus and heaven – the voice from heaven – is also experienced by John the Baptist in the Fourth Gospel. He now becomes himself the voice from heaven: he bears witness to the heavenly origin of Jesus. John the Baptist himself sees a dove descending on Jesus, and this dove *abides* (the Johannine *menein*) on him (1.32): this Jesus possesses the Spirit permanently (see Isa. 11.2; 61.1). There is no mention of the heavenly voice; on the contrary, John the Baptist himself expresses what it has to say: 'I myself have seen and bear witness: this is the elect of God' (1.34; *eklektos*, Isa. 42.1, quoted even more literally than in the synoptic gospels; see Mark 1.11; Matt. 3.17; this can confirm that in the synoptic tradition the heavenly voice is a dramatic representation of the word of God). The testimony of John, which the prologue has already mentioned, thus culminates in the fact that Jesus is the pre-existent bringer of salvation who comes from heaven and takes away the sins of the world; he alone can give men the gift of salvation, the *pneuma*, and therefore eternal life (3.34; 6.63; 7.37–39). The whole significance of the baptism of Jesus by John is to bear witness to this. As a result, it becomes clear that while John bases his gospel on primitive Christian traditions, he brings these up to date in terms of the community which he is addressing.

Three elements stand out in the literary unit 1.19–51, which are fundamental to the Gospel of John as a whole: the 'definition' of the identity of Jesus, the witnesses to the identity of Jesus (who have already been discussed above) and finally the crisis or failure to believe that Jesus is the Messiah.

(a) Jesus is 'the Christ' or Messiah (see 1.41), 'the Lamb of God', which 'takes away the sins of the world' (1.29–36), that is, the Deutero-Isaianic servant of God (1.29, 36; see Isa. 53.7; 53.11), 'on whom the Spirit (of God) rests' (1.32f.), 'the elect of God' (1.34; Isa. 49.7; 42.1), the anointed one foretold by the Tanach (1.45), 'the Son of God', 'king of Israel' (1.49), finally the 'Son of man' (1.51). All this is said of Jesus, 'the son of Joseph from Nazareth' (1.45); he is the Messiah. The first disciples say: 'We have found the Messiah' (1.41), that is, 'the one who is anointed with the Holy Spirit' (John 1.33b; see Acts 10.38). In other words, the Baptist presents Jesus to Israel as the Messiah (1.31), though from the beginning in the form of the suffering servant of God: 'the Lamb of God'.

(b) However, we must not forget the other side of all this. Jesus brings a division among the spirits. That is already prepared for in the presentation of Jesus by John the Baptist (1.9–34). The witness of John the Baptist already produces its own lines of demarcation: 'the Jews from Jerusalem' (1.19a), the 'priests and Levites' (in reality 'from the group of the Pharisees', 1.24), are sent as inquisitors (1.19b). In the call of the first disciples of Jesus which follows, Nathanael is termed the 'true Israelite in whom there is no guile' (1.47). On the one hand, at this point 'Israel' is already contrasted with 'Judaea' (the Jews from Jerusalem: cf. 18.3, 12; 11.47; 18.14; 9.22 with 11.57); on the other hand, these Jews from Jerusalem are the opponents of Jesus from the beginning (they come to act as an inquisition), whereas 'Nathanael' is the true Israelite. In comparison with 'the Jews', the testimony of John the Baptist is very restrained; for even though they pretend that they have come because of the significance of John's baptism, it soon transpires that they are critical of *Jesus*. The Baptist simply says to them: 'One stands among you whom you do not know' (1.26). Only when 'the Jews' are evidently on their way does John the Baptist say more precisely what he has said in cryptic terms to 'the Jews' (1.27): 'Behold the Lamb of God, who takes away the sins of the world' (1.29). John shows that 'the Jews' cannot have understood this: they do not know him (1.26).

John the Baptist evidently came to present Jesus to Israel (what is meant is not the 'northern kingdom', as opposed to Judaea, but the whole of the Jewish people as the people of God, 'Israel'). However, the people 'from Judaea' (Jerusalem and the surrounding area) clearly appear in the Fourth Gospel as those who *a priori* reject Jesus: in that case the true Israelite who 'sees' is in some way contrasted with the 'Judaean who does not see'. The light in the darkness (see the prologue) has already been given a specific form before Jesus appears and has been announced by John the Baptist. The introduction of Jesus itself produces a division of the spirits. The Gospel of John then goes on to relate in kerygmatic fashion the messianic career of Jesus.

## III. THE APPEARANCE OF JESUS HIMSELF: SELF-REVELATION IN WORD AND DEED

John takes up a good deal of his account in showing how Jesus bears witness to himself. In addition to seven 'I am' sayings (Jesus' revelation of himself 'in the Word'), John relates seven great wonders of Jesus. Both the 'I am' sayings and the signs which Jesus performs are implicit references to the time of Moses and the exodus, though John sees them through the perspective of the early Jewish wisdom tradition. Here Jesus emerges in word and deed as the one who brings about a division of the spirits. Some believe in his words and deeds; others – for John, these are always 'the Jews' – do not believe.

### A. Jesus' revelation of himself through 'wonders' and 'works'

*Literature* (in addition to the literature already cited, and above all the three more recent substantial commentaries on John: those of R. Brown, B. Lindars, and R. Schnackenburg): J. Becker, 'Wunder und Christologie', *NTS* 16, 1969–70, 130–48; R. Bultmann, *The Gospel of John;* J. Montgomery Boice, *Witness and Revelation in the Gospel of John,* Grand Rapids and London 1970; P. van Diemen, *La semaine inaugurale et la semaine terminale de l'évangile de Jean. Message et structures,* three vols, Rome 1972; R. T. Fortna, 'Source and Redaction in the Fourth Gospel's Portrayal of Jesus' Signs', *JBL* 89, 1970, 156–65; J. Gaffney, 'Believing and Knowing in the Fourth Gospel', *ThS* 26, 1965, 233–6; J. C. Hindley, 'Witness in the Fourth Gospel,' *SJT* 18, 1965, 319–37; S. Hofbeck, *Semeion, Der Begriff der 'Zeichen' im Johannesevangelium unter Berücksichtigung seiner Vorgeschichte,* Münsterschwarzbach 1966, esp. 158–60; Morris Inch, 'Apologetic Use of "Sign" in the Fourth Gospel', *The Evangelical Quarterly* 42, 1970, 35–8; W. Nicol, *The Semeia in the Fourth Gospel,* Leiden 1972; P. Riga, 'Signs of

Glory: The Use of *semeion* in St John's Gospel', *Int* 17, 1963, 402–10; H. Schneider, ' "The Word was Made Flesh". An Analysis of the Theology of Revelation in the Fourth Gospel', *CBQ* 31, 1969, 344–56; L. Schotroff, *Der Glaubende und die feindliche Welt*, Neukirchen 1970, esp. 247–57; C. Traets, *Voir Jésus et le Père en Lui selon l'Evangile de Saint Jean*, Rome 1967; A. Vanhoye, 'Notre foi, oeuvre divine, d'après le quatrième évangile', *NRTh* 86, 1964, 339–48; R. Walker, 'Jüngerwort und Herrenwort. Zur Auslegung von Joh. 4.39–42', *ZNW* 57, 1966, 41–54; W. Wilkens, *Zeichen und Werke*, Zurich 1969.

Above all in this complex of problems we are confronted with the discussions by exegetes of the so-called 'book of signs', a tradition of perhaps even a source which is said to be reinterpreted by the Fourth Gospel in John's distinctive christology and soteriology (in the same way as Matthew and Luke used the Q tradition or the Q source). The hypothesis that John made use of an already extant collection of wonders performed by Jesus is commanding increasing assent.[69] 'Now Jesus did many other signs in the presence of the disciples which are not written in this book; but these are written that you may believe that Jesus is the Christ, the Son of God, and that believing you may have life in his name' (John 20.30f.) in fact seems to conclude something; it is an ending (although the Gospel goes on). Regardless of the mistaken terminology, 'a christology of the man of wonders' (as *theios anēr*), one can concede that the 'book of signs' is more a collection of traditions about wonders performed by Jesus (just as Q is above all the collection of logia of Jesus). Jesus is seen as a miracle worker, who helps men. Here his manhood is the focal point: the son of Joseph of Nazareth (1.45), someone whose parents are known (1.45; 2.1, 12; 7.2–5). That does not mean that this tradition of wonders will have been as it were the christology of the pre-Johannine community. The fact that the Logos hymn was sung in a different form from that which we find in the prologue itself makes this impossible. The pre-Johannine community believes in the 'incarnate Logos', which is then seen above all as a miracle worker, a 'benefactor' in whose actions one can see God's glory. However, the Fourth Gospel seeks to show that this glorification of Jesus comes to a climax in the crucifixion. All that we can say of John's reaction to a tradition of wonders is that he seeks to stress the significance of the death of Jesus. The various exegetical explanations of the function of the signs and works in the Gospel of John[70] therefore derive less from a direct terminological and structural analysis of the text and context in which the words *sēmeion* (sign) or *ergon* (work) occur in the Gospel of John than from what so far has been a quite arbitrary reconstruction of a *theios anēr* christology which is said to characterize 'the book of signs'. In that case, precisely those features which may be taken as characteristics of the pre-Johannine community are often regarded as John's polemic against this one-sidedness. According to Fortna, Brown, Lindars and, with some qualifications, Wilkens and Schnackenburg,[71] the book of signs defends a 'belief in signs' (believing because one sees) which the Gospel of John accepts and yet believes to be surpassed by a 'higher faith': to believe without having seen. According to J. Becker,[72] John rejects belief in signs; the faith is to believe the words of Jesus. Wilkens and Schnackenburg[73] and above all F. Schnider and W. Stenger[74] adopt the standpoint that the signs give a deeper insight into christological belief: signs confront us with the decision between belief and unbelief, but the aim remains belief in the words of Jesus. So belief in Jesus' words is a presupposition for being able to see the signs in faith: a man sees because he believes. Faith in Jesus' *word* leads to *seeing* the signs, and this leads to knowledge, that is, a deeper knowledge in faith. Luise Schottroff[75] sees inner contradictions in the Johannine concept of belief in signs (above all John 7.31; 4.48): according to her, John combined two traditions, a tradition in which the signs served as legitimation and a tradition in which Jesus refused to take signs as the means of initiating faith. In that case John is concerned with the nature and character of seeing signs: this distinguishes true faith from false. Belief in signs is rejected unless this leads to belief in the heavenly origin of Jesus. However, if the sign has this effect, then it in fact has a function of its own. W. Nicol[76] (and also Wilkens and Schnackenburg) asserts that John wants to correct the one-sided and trivial christology of the book of signs: John stresses the visibility of the *doxa* or glory in the *sarx* or the human deeds of Jesus. John wants to examine the divine dimensions of the story of Jesus under the guidance of the Holy Spirit as Paraclete: the believer sees his glory in the signs of Jesus. Finally, according to R. T. Fortna,[77] John wants to bring his source up to date: the believer must recognize in the signs the messiahship, sonship and glory of Jesus, of which the most extreme expression is his death. Instead of stressing the resurrection as the proof of the messiahship of Jesus, the Gospel of John stresses the life-giving death of Jesus. J. Becker[78] and R. Schnackenburg[79] affirm this. It is generally assumed (the exception is Nicol, for whom this is thought to be a blind spot) that the Fourth Gospel wants to correct the one-sidedness of the 'wonder man' christology of the so-called book of signs: John is said to enrich the christology of his source, spiritualize its soteriology and contrast faith in signs with a richer and more complete faith. This may be described as the result of the last decade's Johannine research. In view of the fact that the more recent investigation by C. R. Holladay, beginning directly from the sources, has confirmed a number of conceptions about the *theios anēr* men which are on the other hand so different that to talk to a *theios anēr* christology is simply a scholarly construction,[80] I am convinced that any reconstruction of the so-called 'book of signs' which has so far begun (always excepting the work of W. Nicol) from a *theios anēr* christology, is doomed to failure. In any case, whatever the specific theological direction of the so-called 'book of signs' may have been, it is enough for our particular concern (or for any 'dogmatic' concern) to read the text of John as we find it, with the tensions which are perhaps inherent to it (and which in fact can only be illuminated through form criticism and redaction criticism, i.e. by the separation of tradition and redaction in the Gospel of John).

## (a) The symbolic actions of Jesus

John enumerates seven wonders of Jesus: the miracle of the wine at Cana (2.1–11), the healing (at a distance) of the son of a high official (4.46–54), the healing of a lame man (5.1–9), the miracle of the loaves (6.14), the walking on the water (5.16–21; the term 'sign' does not occur here), the healing of a man born blind (9.1–41), the raising of Lazarus (11.1–44). The Gospel of John calls them *sēmeia*, signs (2.11; 4.54; 6.14, 26; 9.16; 12.18; see 11.47) and sometimes also *ergon*, a work (5.20, 36; see 7.21). Both terms are also used quite indiscriminately (cf. 7.3 with 7.31; 9.3f. with 9.16; 10.25, 32, 37, 38, with 10.41; and 12.37 with 15.24).

Clear connections can be established between the Johannine concept of the sign and that in the synoptic gospels. In both we find Jesus' rejection of the Jewish demand to perform signs (which in the synoptic gospels are usually called *dynameis*, mighty works) (John 2.18; 6.30; Mark 8.11f.; Matt. 12.38f.; 16.1, 4; Luke 11.16, 29). The expression *sēmeia kai terata* (John 4.48) is characteristic of the Old Testament; it goes back to the Deuteronomistic conception of the prophet (Deut. 6.22; 7.19; 13.2f.; 26.8; Ex. 7.3; Jer. 32.20f.; Isa. 8.18; 20.3; Ps. 78.43; Neh. 9.10. Acts 4.30; 5.12; 14.3; 15.12; Rom. 15.19; II Cor. 12.12; II Thess. 2.9. Acts 2.19–22, 43; 6.8; 7.36).[81] In general, *teras* indicates the astonishing aspect of an event, while *sēmeion* or sign points in or by a miraculous event to God, whereas *dynameis* (e.g. Gal. 3.5; Acts 2.22) means powerful actions. (The three occur together in Heb. 2.4.) John uses what is elsewhere a technical term, *sēmeia kai terata*, only once (4.48). 'Signs' goes back via this pre-Johannine tradition of wonders to the biblical *'ōt* (*'ōtōt*), since the seven signs in the Gospel of John are all connected with the signs performed by Moses at the time of the Exodus, as interpreted in Wisdom.[82] In the Septuagint, *'oyt* is translated *sēmeion*, sign, *testimonies* of the God of Israel; *'ōt* is a revealing sign. The signs which the prophets performed are as it were symbolic actions communicating revelation in visible or tangible reality,[83] symbolic actions as creative anticipation of things to come. Thus according to Isa. 60ff. the eschatological messenger does not bring cosmic glory, but he does show this forth in symbolic actions.

Symbolic actions take on a deeper significance in the Johannine view of Jesus, the incarnate Word. The signs performed by the Johannine Jesus *do not anticipate* but introduce eschatological salvation here and now in Jesus' *present* actions. Here is more than a prophet. Despite this fundamental difference of content, the Johannine concept of the sign has formally the same significance as the prophetic symbolic action; it is a revelatory action. In all probability both the wonders done by Moses at the Exodus – signs of the great Moses – and the prophetic symbolic actions (in the early Jewish period there is also talk of 'the prophet' or 'the lamb' Moses) form the background against which the Johannine concept of the sign can be elucidated.

In the Johannine understanding of 'signs', a *sēmeion* serves to lead men to a *deeper insight* and is not meant to make them believe *because* they have seen signs. As early as the time of the calling of one of the disciples, Nathanael, who, as was the wont of Pharisees, 'was sitting under a fig tree', that is, studying the Torah – John warns against 'believing because one has seen' (1.50; see also his remark to the doubting Thomas: 'Because you have seen me, do you believe? Blessed are those who have not seen and yet have believed', 20.29). In the Fourth Gospel, sign has a *christological* relevance; signs stand in a different perspective from 'works'. As events which are seen and which cause astonishment (2.23; 6.2, 14), signs stimulate reflection (3.2; 7.31; 9.16; 11.47). But if they are perceived only in their capacity to cause wonderment, they in fact remain ineffective for christological faith, even more when they are sought after as sensations (4.48). Their real meaning can only be grasped through faith in the Christ (3.11; 6.26; 11.4, 40). Thus the 'sign' is different from the typical Johannine concept of testimony which leads to a well-founded faith: 'signs' show to those who truly believe the glory of the Logos in Jesus which is at work in the *sarx* or in manhood on earth. 'We have seen his glory' (1.14b), namely also in the wonders that Jesus does. For the weak, those who do not believe in the Christ, these signs are merely miracles which can be perceived externally without any further significance (see 12.37). As 'signs' in the Johannine sense, the mighty acts of Jesus have an exclusive christological orientation; as 'works', on the other hand, they are *messianic*, that is, a testimony with a certain degree of validity, which brings about a distinction between belief and unbelief.[84] In the Gospel of John, however, it is never possible to make a precise distinction between the two.

However, this formal distinction has the consequence that 'signs' and works' each open up a different perspective on Jesus. Signs remain limited to the *earthly* life of Jesus, and therefore cease after 12.37 (they are mentioned briefly once again in 20.30). Thus the signs embrace the earthly activity of Jesus in revelation. However, Jesus promises his disciples that they will perform 'still greater works' (14.12), but there is no mention in the Gospel of John of 'signs' performed by disciples. Signs are an expression of Jesus' work of revelation as the incarnate Logos on earth. They are all *preliminary signs* of what will happen at Easter. *Works*, as a motive of belief, are on a lower level than the words of Jesus (10.38; 14.11), with which the signs are comparable; these are spoken, expressive revelations of God (6.35, 48, 51; 9.5; 11.25f.), albeit on the presupposition that believers understand their character as signs and do not just stop at the element of wonder. As revelation they correspond to a christological answer of faith. Therefore in Johannine terms the appearance of the risen Jesus are not signs, at least not in the sense of preliminary signs; they do not occur on the plane of Jesus' revelation of himself to the *world;* they are christophanies to his own disciples (14.22), and like the death and resurrection, belong to the sphere of 'truth' (see below).

In the signs, Jesus shows his glory to those who believe: that he is the incarnate Logos (see 2.11, the miracle at Cana; 11.40, the raising of Lazarus: here God's glory can be seen): 'This illness is not unto death; it is for the glory of God, so that the Son of God may be glorified by means of it' (11.4).In the *sarx* of Jesus his *doxa* or glory becomes visible to faith; above all in symbolic signs or mighty works – the miracle of the loaves, the healing of a blind man through Jesus, the light, the resurrection of the dead – this aspect comes most fully to the fore. In short, John's purpose with the report of the signs of Jesus is to show that these point to the 'today' of eschatological salvation which is present in Jesus because of his heavenly pre-existence. The signs illustrate what the prologue has said: he is *sarx* and yet Logos. The *sēmeia* have an earthly, *sarkic* form, but they reveal a christological depth.

## (*b*) The 'works' of Jesus

When John calls the mighty acts of Jesus 'works', these works *bear witness* to Jesus as the one sent by God (5.36; 10.25, 37f.; 14.11; 15.24); they are certain (10.38; 14.11), as it were compelling (15.24) testimony to the fact that the Father has sent Jesus (5.35; see 9.4) or that 'the Father is in Jesus' (10.38; 14.11). Jesus performs his works in the name of the Father; he works with the Father (4.34; 5.17, 19) or his Father works through him (14.10). The works of the Johannine Jesus thus appear in the context of the historical sending of Jesus by the Father.[85] It is the 'works' which bring about the crisis between belief and unbelief; they arouse faith and put unbelief under judgment (10.25f.; 15.24).

The works of Jesus culminate in 'the work' that he has accomplished in his crucifixion (17.4; 19.30): an obedient and free accomplishment of the works which the Father has given him to fulfil. In this understanding of Father and Son which is characteristic of Judaism and above all of wisdom, the Son does the works of the Father, that is, the work which the Father has given him to perform, even and above all when this is a matter of delegation; the Son acts in the Father's name. From the perspective of the one who sees them, the works are motives of faith in the sending of the Son by God. 'If I am not doing the works of my Father, then do not believe me; but if I do them, even though you do not believe *me*, believe the *works*, that you may know and understand that the Father is in me and I am in the Father' (10.38): 'Believe me that I am in the Father and the Father in me; or else believe me *for the sake of the works themselves*' (14.11). One should really take Jesus at his word ('I am . . .'), but if one cannot produce this trust in the person of Jesus, there are still the works that he performs. The Johannine Jesus does not reject faith because one 'sees the works' (20.29; 1.50), but at the same time the reference here is never to a mere belief in wonders (4.48; 6.26,36). The decisive thing is to grasp the saving significance of the person of Jesus (8.14; 7.16f.). The works that Jesus does can lead a man to believe that the Father is in Jesus, that is, that God performs these works through Jesus (3.33f.). Hence the charge, 'You have seen and yet have not believed' (6.36). For the Johannine communities which had no longer known the historical Jesus it was a matter of 'not seeing and yet believing' (20.29). John is therefore concerned not to reject faith on the ground of seeing, but he regards it as less significant than 'not seeing and yet believing'. The Fourth Gospel seeks to show that the Christians of the second and third generation do not find themselves in a less favourable position than the first disciples during the life of Jesus. Jesus himself already referred to the connection with his person; for John that means *to believe*, and while Jesus does not object to faith 'because they saw his works', he constantly remarks that this is not true, complete Christian faith. On the other hand, John indicates that the faith of Jesus' beloved disciple is really *the model* of faith for the community: at the empty tomb 'he saw and believed' (20.8). But here there was nothing to see but an empty tomb.

The Johannine churches were confronted with the problem: how can the historical life and death of Jesus be the object of faith for later generations? In the Gospel of John, too, the historical Jesus is evidently the only norm, but later generations do not see him or hear his voice directly. For John, past history takes on universal validity in a special way, namely by a form of historical mediation. He therefore lays stress on the reliable witnesses who act as intermediaries (19.35; 21.24; I John 1.1–3), but not in such a way that later generations can find support in the personal conviction of these intermediaries; for somehow in the last resort there must be an objective testimony to God. Therefore at the time of John, testimony to God had become a central question. Hence the significance of the testimony which shows that Jesus is sent by God: John the Baptist (1.8; 1.19–34; 5.33), the works which Jesus does (5.36; 10.25; 10.37f.; 14.11), the teaching which he proclaims (7.17) and his words (10.38; 14.11; see 12.48) and finally also scripture (5.39). As a believer, John is aware that the words of Jesus act as proof in and of themselves (8.14); it is, however, quite different for outsiders (see 5.31f.). But the Johannine Jesus rejects the testimony *of men* to himself (5.34); at least, he has no need of it. Jesus himself accepts only the testimony of his Father (5.37; 8.18) and also the coming testimony of the 'Spirit of truth' (14.17; 15.26; 16.13), the Paraclete (15.26) and finally the truthfulness of his testimony to himself and his revelation of himself. For he is pre-existent and can thus speak from his own experience with God.

Thus the Johannine concept of faith always rests on a testimony, and here John seems to put forward the Jewish notion of valid testimony: when evidence is heard, at least two witnesses must agree in their testimony (John 8.17; see Deut. 17.6; 19.15); in that case the testimony is 'true' (*alēthēs*), reliable. It is therefore striking that in I John we have mention of three witnesses which agree together, first the spirit, then water and blood (I John 5.7f.). John himself speaks in 19.34 of the flowing of water and blood from the pierced side of Jesus on the cross. Christian baptism (John 3) and Christian eucharist (John 6.51b–58) are said to be undertaken in 'the spirit'. For the spirit is the principle of life from which these sacraments of initiation draw their force (3.6; 6.63). Supported by the Holy Spirit, the sacraments of the church bring the historical testimony of Jesus to the later communities which did not know the earthly Jesus. The saving action of God which took place in the sending and finally in the death of the Son who historically became man, are continued in the living church which brings life to later generations through preaching and the sacraments, the same life that Jesus brought when he was present on earth as a preliminary sign, to those who at that time believed in him (see 19.34 with I John 5.8). Thus God's testimony about Jesus during his earthly life *remains in force* (*memartyrēken*, perfect, I John 5.9): Christians have (*echein*, as a typically Johannine concept in the sense of *menein*, have permanently) the testimony of God: they have received it in Jesus and still have its living presence in the church's sacraments.

## (c)  Believing, seeing (or hearing) and knowing

How can 'signs' – really preliminary signs – and the works of the Johannine Jesus be legitimation if they themselves already presuppose belief?

John uses various words for seeing: *idein, theōrein, blepein*. Seeing or perceiving (*theōrein*) can be a physical seeing (9.8; 10.12; 20.6), a spiritual seeing (4.19; 12.19), a seeing in faith (14.17–19) and a direct, heavenly vision (17.24). So too there is external hearing (6.60; 9.27,40; 10.20; 12.29; 19.8) and an inner hearing or a hearing in faith (5.24; 8.43,47; 18.37; cf. 10.3,16,27). One can often sense in the Gospel of John an transition from outward seeing of signs and works (2.23; 6.2;7.3), publicly accessible for anyone to *blepein* (see) to a seeing in faith which is accessible only to believers (14.17,19; see 6.62).[86] Therefore John can talk of 'seeing' (*theōrein*) instead of 'believing' (cf. 6.40 with 12.45). Believing is believing that Jesus has been sent by the Father (5.24a; 6.35b; 13.16; 17.8,21 with 17.22f.). John rejects mere belief in wonders (2.23). But the signs and works of Jesus direct attention to the person who performs them; they can arouse a first interest in the person of Jesus himself and bring men to a 'crisis': to decide for or against Jesus who personally claims that he is doing all this by virtue of his unity with the Father. After the account of the first signs performed by Jesus, John says: 'This, the first of his signs, Jesus did at Cana in Galilee, *and manifested his glory*; and *his disciples believed* in him' (2.11). John had spoken of 'glory' in the prologue: '*We have seen his glory, the glory which the only beloved receives from the Father*' (1.14), and later the evangelist says that 'these signs are written that you may believe that Jesus is the Christ, the Son of God, and that believing you may have life in his name' (20.31). In the signs *we*, that is the Johannine community, see the glory of the Father in Jesus. Signs reveal the union of Jesus with the Father – a union which is the content of all that Jesus says in words: we hear little or nothing about any more content.[87] In fact the Gospel of John gives the impression that what Jesus says or does has as its exclusive content the fact that he is one with the Father; for believers this faith means life, salvation (20.31): to believe that Jesus is one with the Father is a life-giving gift which brings salvation. The Gospel of John does not say more than that. Perhaps the whole mystery of the Gospel of John lies in John's identification of the synoptic kingdom of God with Jesus of Nazareth.[88] Just as for the synoptic gospels the whole content of salvation is summed up in the term 'kingdom of God', so in the Gospel of John salvation is summed up in the person of Jesus: the kingdom of God *is* Jesus as one with the Father, and thus as salvation for us. The Gospel of John needs to be read in the light of this identification in faith. What for the synoptic gospels, as they present their account, is a cautious intimation which only breaks through fully at the death and resurrection, stands in the foreground for the Gospel of John. This is already the confession of the prologue. When John the Baptist appears, when Jesus preaches and does miracles and dies, the reader already knows that in Jesus we have an appearance of the incarnate Son of God, the Word. Some believe, but others do not.

Those who believe see the glory of the Father *in* Jesus. 'Philip, . . . he who sees me, sees the Father' (14.8–10), 'Believe me, I am in the Father and the Father is in me. Or at least believe it for the sake of the works themselves' (14.11). It is really necessary to believe in Jesus on the basis of this word (10.38; 14.11). If that is impossible, there are also Jesus' works, which point in the same direction: here God is effectively present (10.38). The signs that Jesus does can lead to true belief, they are a support for the initial beneficent openness (14.11; see 10.37f.). According to John, what Jesus says *is* revelation, since he speaks from his consciousness of being one with the Father. And the works of Jesus are similarly a form of divine testimony about Jesus. Where the kingdom of God is – and that is Jesus – there are the signs and the way of life of the kingdom of God. The glory of God, once manifested in the great miracles of the exodus, is now living and present in the Johannine Jesus. The signs that he does represent this present, and at the same time they are a gesture of introduction to Jesus who is one with the Father. To believe means to recognize this union and to live by it. The signs both reveal and veil. They reveal God's glory in Jesus (2.11; 11.4,40), but they veil this glory for unbelievers (6.36; 9.39,41; 15.22–24). So John comes to talk about *seeing* God's glory in Jesus. First of all this involves a perception: one sees what Jesus does. But for believers, this seeing is bound up with the way in which the Father 'draws' them to faith: 'No one can come to me unless the Father, who has sent me, draws him' (6.44): 'no one can come to me unless it is granted to him by the Father' (6.65).

In my view, John never calls this drawing by the Father an *inner* testimony (as many authors maintain).[89] True, John 5.37 says: 'The Father who sent me has himself borne witness to me', but this witness is evidently to be sought 'in the scriptures' (5.39). Is the testifying by the Father (5.37) to be connected with 'being drawn by the Father' in 6.45? John sees *complete* faith in connection with being born again from above, from the spirit which is given first at Easter (see below). To believe in Jesus as a teacher who is legitimated by God in signs is only the beginning of true faith (2.23–25; 6.26–33); truly to believe is to believe in the deepest nature of Jesus: in his unity with the Father (3.36 and 3.18). To *see* Jesus in the sense of *idein* is to recognize who he personally is, to believe in his name (1.12f.). To be taught by God (see Isa. 54.13) is to be drawn by God through teaching (3.31–36), that is, to be born of God (see 8.47;3.5).

This drawing (*helkein*) only appears in one place other than in 6.45; that is in 12.32, which speaks of the crucified one who draws all men to him.

Faith is grounded both in Jesus' testimony to himself and his works (5.36) and in being taught by the Father (6.45). So for John, faith is a grace of election (6.39; 17.2,6,12,24): 'those whom you (the Father) have given me'. On the other hand, unbelief is a man's own fault (5.44): 'If I had not come and spoken to them they would not have sin: but now they have no excuse for their sin' (15.22). Seeing, bound up with being drawn by the Father, sees the mystery of the person of Jesus in the events of his earthly life. Thus John speaks of 'seeing God' and 'seeing his glory'. The experience of divine salvation, in the communion of life and love between Jesus and the Father, takes place in human perception. The 'Johannine seeing' is a matter of understanding the historical life of Jesus in his presence as Lord in the church. We need not read our modern distinctions into the varied terminology of the Gospel of John – see, believe, know: for John, these are different descriptions of one and the same act of faith. Despite all the manifestations 'in signs' (2.11; 11.40) and the self-revelation of Jesus in word and 'works' (14.10; see 10.38), the pre-existent Jesus can be grasped only in faith. However, there is a distinction between faith in Jesus before and after the giving of the spirit at Pentecost: the Holy Spirit leads believers 'into all truth' (16.13). Therefore in the (final) farewell discourse, John 17 speaks more of 'knowing' than of believing (17.7f.): the hour is near when your faith will come 'into all truth'. 'This is eternal life, that they may know you, the only true God, and Jesus Christ whom you have sent' (17.2f.).

I John has put this aspect more precisely: 'That which was from the beginning, which we have heard, which we have seen with our eyes, which we have looked upon and touched with our hands, concerning the word of life' (I John 1.1), 'the life was made manifest, and we saw it, and testify to it, and proclaim to you the eternal life which was with the Father and was made manifest to us' (I John 1.2f.). As in the prologue of the Gospel, here we have the heart of the faith of the Johannine community. But certainly no one who had known the historical Jesus was still alive in the Johannine community. In that case, who are these 'we' who bear witness that the eternal and divine can be perceived and touched in the man (*sarx*) Jesus? I John does not mean all believers but 'the witnesses': they *bear witness* to what they have *seen* (see John 1.34; 3.11; 3.32; 19.35; I John 1.2; 4.14). For John, bearing witness is based on having seen and heard. And what one sees is an object of faith, 'the life' (I John 1.2) which 'appeared' to eyewitnesses. But in the meantime these have died. The church community goes back to the historical Jesus: the source is there. I John clearly seeks to connect the *community* with the *historical Jesus*, the only mediator between God and man (I John 5.11f.;

John 6.57; 14.6). Johannine theology does not want to know of any direct divine mysticism; this is communicated through a unique historical human figure who is the divine logos. This union is the real object of faith. Therefore the first immediate eyewitnesses of this event have a special task. The ultimate norm remains the person of Jesus of Nazareth. But how can this past event become the object of the faith of later generations? In Johannine theology, Jesus himself refers to witnesses for his claim to be one with God and to have been sent by God; to John the Baptist (John 5.33), to his own works (John 5.36; 10.25; see 10.37f.; 14.11), to holy scripture (John 5.39), to his teaching (John 7.17) and his words (John 10.38; 14.11). Jesus rejects the witness of man to himself (5.34). The only testimony that counts is that of his Father (5.37; 8.18) and the future witness of the Paraclete, the Spirit of truth (15.26). I John also stresses the testimony of God (I John 5). There are also differences from the Gospel of John. With a view to Jesus as the Son of God who has appeared in history, I John speaks only of the outward testimony of the proclaimer (I John 1.2; 4.14), and in I John 5.9f. the testimony (in the perfect) refers to a historical event. I John 5.10a, 11, says: 'He who believes in the Son of God has the testimony in himself . . . And this is the testimony, that God gave us eternal life, and that this life is in his Son.' Furthermore, 'There are three witness: the spirit, the water and the blood, and these three agree in one' (I John 5.8). Thus the testimony of God is evidently different from these three. It is three: *'memartyrēken'* (perfect), 'he has borne witness', with the object, the Sonship of Jesus (5.9f.), whereas the testimony of the spirit in baptism and the eucharist is in the present. This is clearly not an inward testimony of God, but a matter of taking to heart an outward testimony.[90] The believer takes God's testimony to himself and bears it in his heart; the unbeliever does not do this and therefore does not have life (5.10). The testimony of the spirit re-echoes in the preaching of the church (I John 5.7f.) about the life and death of Jesus, and continues to be effective in the sacraments of baptism (water) and the eucharist (blood). So the meaning of I John 5.9–12 is: the believers have taken to themselves the testimony once given by God about his Son, and it is an abiding reality (*menein*!) in word and sacraments. In this way Johannine theology explains the problem of 'not seeing and yet believing' among the second and third generations of Christians. A *spiritual* encounter with Jesus is possible, and this is in continuity with the historical Jesus, thanks to the Spirit that is at work in the church.

B. Jesus' revelation of himself 'in the word'

(*a*) 'I am' sayings

Literature: (*a*) *'I am' sayings*
R. Brown, *Gospel of John* I, 533–8; R. Bultmann, *The Gospel of John*, 225f., note 3; D. Daube, 'The "I am" of the Messianic Presence', *The New Testament and Rabbinic Judaism*, London 1956; C. H. Dodd, *Interpretation*, 93–6; A. Feuillet, *Études johanniques*, Paris ²1966, 72–83; id., 'Les *Ego Eimi* christologiques du quatrième Évangile', *RSR* 54, 1966, 5–22, 213–40; P. H. Harner, *The 'I am' of the Fourth Gospel*, Philadelphia 1970; R. Kysar, *The Fourth Evangelist*, 119–27; G. W. MacRae, 'The *Ego*-Proclamation in Gnostic Sources', in *The Trial of Jesus*, ed E. Bammel, SBT II 13, 1970, 123–39; I de la Potterie, 'Je suis la Voie, la Vérité et la Vie (Jn 14.6)', *NRTh* 88, 1966, 917–26; R. Schnackenburg, *Das Johannesevangelium* II, 59–70; H. Zimmermann, 'Das absolute *Ego eimi* als die neutestamentliche Offenbarungsformel', *BZ* 4, 1960, 54–69, 266–76.

(*b*) *I am the bread of life, the living water,* etc.
J. Blank, 'Die johanneische Brotrede' and 'Ich bin das Lebensbrot', *BuL* 7, 1966, 193–207 and 255–70; P. Borgen, *Bread from Heaven*, Leiden 1965; id., 'Observations on the Midrashic Character of John 6', *ZNW* 54, 1963, 232–40; R. Borig, *Der Wahre Weinstock*, Munich 1967; G. Bornkamm, 'Vorjohanneische Tradition oder nachjohanneische Bearbeitung in der eucharistischen Rede Johannes 6?', in his *Geschichte und Glaube*, Munich 1971, 2, 51–64; J. D. Derrett, 'The Good Shepherd: St John's Use of Jewish Halakah and Haggadah', *ThS* 27, 1973, 25–50; K. M. Fischer, 'Der johanneische Christus und der gnostische Erlöser, in Gnosis und Neues Testament', in *Studien aus Religionswissenschaft und Theologie*, ed. K. W. Tröger, Berlin 1973, 345–67; O. Kiefer, *Die Hirtenrede*, Stuttgart 1967; T. Preiss, 'Étude sur le ch. 6 de l'évangile de Jean', *ETR* 46, 1971, 144–56; G. Richter, 'Zur Formgeschichte und literarischen Einheit von Joh 6,31–58', *ZNW* 60, 1969, 21–55; R. Schnackenburg, 'Zur Rede vom Brot aus dem Himmel: eine Beobachtung zu Joh. 6, 52', *BZ* 12, 1968, 248–52; A. J. Simonis, *Die Hirtenrede im Johannesevangelium*, Rome 1967; J. Whittaker, 'A Hellenistic Context for John 10.29', *Vigiliae Christianae* 24, 1970, 241–60.

As pre-existent Son in humanity, the Johannine Jesus bears witness to what he has seen and heard (3.32). The 'I am' sayings are important in this respect. The seven I sayings can be divided into three categories: (*a*) the absolute usage, without the predicate, 'If you do not believe that I am, you will die in your sins' (8.24); 'When you have lifted up the Son of man, then you will know that *I am he*' (8.28); 'Before Abraham was, I am' (8.58); 'that you may believe that I am' (13.19); (*b*) with an indirect predicate: 'Whom do you seek? – Jesus of Nazareth. Jesus said to them: I am he' (18.5, 6, 8); so too, according to the context, 'I am, fear not'. If we take note of what is grammatically an absolute form, the sacral and heavenly nature of the 'I am' reflects the first category. More ordinary uses of 'I am' can be included here (like 4.26; 8.18; 8.23; 7.34, 36; 12.26; 14.3; 17.24); (*c*) finally, with an (allegorical) direct predicate: 'I am the bread of life – the living water – the true vine – the door and the good shepherd – the resurrection and the life – the way, the truth and the life' (6.35, 51; 8.12; 9.5; 10.7, 9, 11, 14; 11.25; 15.1, 5; 14.6).

Absolute 'I am' sayings are rare in the Old Testament. The most likely direct sources for John are Greek passages in Deutero-Isaiah, above all Isa. 47.8, 10, 'Yahweh says: *'anī hū*' (I am: in the Septuagint *egō eimi*), but also Gen. 28.13, 15; Ex. 3.14; Ezek. 20.5 etc.[91] Yahwistic monotheism is strongly affirmed in these statements: there is only one God (Isa. 45.5, 6, 18, 22). Really this is a hint at the name of Yahweh. So the Johannine Jesus seeks to stress both monotheism – the one Father – and his only ultimate ambassador, Jesus. Finally, Jesus makes this 'I am' the content of Christian faith (8.24; 13.19) and the Christian confession of faith (8.28).

On the other hand, the expression *'anī w'hū*, 'I am the one who', is to be found above all in the liturgy, particularly in the liturgy of the feast of Tabernacles, where it replaces the divine name:[92] various 'I sayings' of Jesus are put within the liturgical framework of this feast (see below). Furthermore, there are parallels to the wisdom literature in which Wisdom presents itself as 'I am' (Sir. 24; Prov.8), and also in later 'early Jewish' texts (IV Ezra 5.1; 1 QS 4.16–30).[93] 'I am' is therefore unmistakably an Old Testament formula of revelation.

However, exegetes will keep discussing the question whether the Old Testament and Jewish literature can fully explain the remarkable Johannine use of 'I am'. The affinity between this usage and pre-Mandaean, if not Mandaean literature, above all Coptic gnostic texts, seems to a number of scholars to be very striking.[94] In my view the presence of a syncretistic, Hellenistic *Judaism* is almost undeniable in Johannine theology.[95] But I pointed out earlier that in recent times, on the basis of texts, scholars are increasingly coming to see that certain Greek Jewish ideas underline both the Johannine terms and also later gnostic terms, and not vice versa. Moreover, one can ask what use it is to speak of pre-gnostic elements when virtually all the key sayings are markedly not gnostic! In John, the redeemer Jesus himself gives his life for believers (10.11, 17); he is a real historical man who is God's word. Though they are intrinsically connected, redeemer and redeemed remain distinct

(10.14), nowhere is the taking up of the redeemed into heaven presented as a return *home*; on the contrary, Jesus has to prepare a place for believers, since 'as men' they do not belong by nature in the heavenly realm (14.1–4); finally the ascension of Jesus is nowhere visualized.[96] John uses terms from unofficial so-called 'heterodox' syncretistic Judaism, from the last decades of the first century AD, from which *later* gnosticism derives.

John puts the 'I am' sayings with allegorical predicates in the context of the liturgical festivals which are important for Jewish identity; in them the Old Testament 'I sayings' were given particular prominence (however, these festivals are not the principle which gives the gospel its literary structure). After the author has explained his plan: 'the Law was given by Moses, grace and truth came through Jesus Christ' (1.17), what is said by Moses and the Law in the Old Testament is referred by the Johannine Jesus to himself in heightened form. While in the present redaction of the Gospel of John one cannot strictly maintain the framework of the Jewish festivals on which John builds his gospel from chapters 5 to 10, several exegetes have found it striking that the 'I am this or that' sayings of Jesus are uttered *on Jewish festivals* ('festivals of the Jews'; 2.6, 13; 4.45; 5.1; 6.4; 7.2; 11.55; 18.20; 19.40, 42; however much John also maintains the salvation-historical connection with Israel: 4.22; see 1.31, 49; 3.10; 12.13).[97]

5.1–47 are concerned with the Jewish sabbath and the Christian reaction to it (although there are no 'I sayings' here); 6.1–71 is concerned with Easter; 7.1–8.59 with the Jewish feast of Tabernacles and 9.1–10.21 with its aftermath; finally there is the festival of Hanukkah: the dedication of the Temple. On these feast days Jesus presents his unique and overwhelming particularity over against the theme of salvation brought through these festivals. It is also striking that in these 'I am' sayings which bring about belief and unbelief, the Johannine Jesus makes an appearance in Jerusalem. In John's view, the battle over belief and unbelief is decided in Jerusalem. It is here that the final decision is taken (7.25f., 32, 45–52). For John, 'Jerusalem' is the symbol of not believing in Jesus, of 'the world' which has not accepted Jesus, the light that has shone in the world (1.10; 15.18–25).

Before analysing the seven 'I am' sayings I shall discuss the sabbath (5.1–47). This characterizes beforehand the atmosphere in which Jesus will say 'I am'.

The Johannine Jesus works on the sabbath (5.9b), for the salvation of the helpless, who are more victims of this day of rest than beneficiaries of it. By the sheep gate in Jerusalem, in the baths, Jesus heals a lame man on the sabbath (5.1–9: the location of the baths in Bethesda near Jerusalem has been confirmed by modern archaeological discoveries).

The sick man, who is exactly thirty-eight years old, is perhaps a symbol for the thirty-eight years that the Jewish people were on the way in the wilderness (Deut. 2.14). Jesus brings him healing. This leads to a dispute (5.10–47). Jesus replies: just as my Father is constantly at work, so 'I too do not cease to work' (5.17). God's loving work continues always: so too does that of Jesus. Because Jesus presents himself here as Son of the Father, the Jews say, 'He makes himself equal to God' (5.18c). Jesus reacts by saying that he acts on the basis of what he has experienced with the Father (5.19). 'Truly, truly, I say to you, he who hears my voice and believes him who sent me has eternal life: he does not come into judgment, but has passed from death to life' (5.25). 'As the Father has life in himself, so he has granted the Son also to have life in himself' (5.26). John gives a commentary on what the prologue said, 'The Word became flesh . . . we have seen his glory' on the basis of the 'life' that Jesus gave to the lame man on the sabbath. Jesus' glory can be seen in the wonders that he does, a glory which the only-beloved receives 'from the Father' (1.14c); he is 'full of grace and truth' (1.14d). For these the unity of the Father and the Son is a gift: in *himself* (i.e. in abundance) Jesus, like the Father, possesses fullness of life, but for Jesus this is a gift and a being sent by the Father. Father and Son, although one, nevertheless stand over against one another as two persons. Jesus 'can do nothing on my own authority; *as I hear*, I judge, because I seek not my own will but the will of him who sent me' (5.30). The testimony given about Jesus by the Baptist (1.15; 1.19–51) is valuable (5.33–35), but who Jesus is emerges more clearly from his works (5.36) and from the testimony of the Father himself (5.37). This pericope already characterizes the atmosphere of the seven subsequent 'I am' sayings.

1. John 6. Almost on the feast (6.4) which in another passage is called 'the Pasch of the Jews' (2.13), the Johannine Jesus calls himself the 'bread that comes down from heaven' (John 6). The remembrance of the manna, the 'bread from heaven' which provided food for the Israelites, despite the grumbling of the people (Ex. 16.7, 8, 9; John 6.41, 43, 61) is part of the commemoration of the exodus at the Passover. In the Jewish tradition there were a number of midrash stories about the manna, for use in sermons in the synagogues. Furthermore, the Jewish passover was also connected with the theme of the messianic feast (Isa. 25.6; 27.13) and with themes from wisdom: those who 'eat [wisdom] will hunger for more, and those who drink me will thirst for more' (Sir. 24.21). Furthermore, in rabbinic Judaism the manna was connected with the nourishment provided by the Torah.[98] Against this background Jesus calls himself the bread from heaven: this is made *visible* in the miraculous feeding (6.1–15). First of all the sign is performed, and then Jesus explains it (6.22–71), because the Jews do not recognize the significance of the person of

Jesus in the signs (6.26f.): 'the one whom God has sent' (6.29). Therefore Jesus says: 'My Father gives you the true bread from heaven. For the bread of God is that which comes down from heaven and gives light to the world' (6.33). The person of Jesus himself, come down from heaven, is salvation for all men – salvation expressed in the symbol of the life-giving bread or manna which is recalled on these Jewish festivals. Again, Jesus is the new, but greater Moses (see 1.17). He gives the true bread (6.33). Jesus says quite openly: 'I am the bread of life' (6.35, 48). In various ways Jesus has patiently prepared the Jews for this self-revelation. In contrast to the Jesus of the synoptic gospels, the Johannine Jesus appeals directly to belief *in his person* as the only saving way to life (6.35; 6.36–40). As in the exodus under Moses, 'the people murmur' (6.41). They murmur against this idea of pre-existence. Jesus then explains that 'to come to Jesus' – that is, to believe on him – presupposes a grace or a 'drawing' from the Father (6.44; 6.65). He then takes up his self-revelation again, 'I am the bread of life' (6.48), to show that the support which this bread gives is eternal life (6.48, 51a). Only then does the thought of the eucharist actually emerge: 'The bread that I shall give is my flesh for the life of the world' (6.51b–58), 'unless you eat the flesh of the Son of man and drink his blood, you do not have life in you' (6.53–56). Again the historical places of the life of Jesus and the present situation of the Johannine community intertwine (John 6.51b–58 need not therefore necessarily come from another hand). Bread and paschal lamb, the symbols of the Jewish passover festival, are clearly interpreted here by Jesus in eucharistic terms. Jesus said all this 'when he was teaching in the synagogue at Capernaum' (6.59), when the Passover festival was near (6.4). It is typical of John that what the synoptic gospels present as three temptations of Jesus in a dramatic encounter with Satan, are in his gospel depicted as *scattered*, undramatic events (6.15; 6.31; 7.3).

2. John 7.1–8.59. This pericope is put in the context of the Jewish feast of Tabernacles: Jesus' going up for the feast (7.1–13), Jesus in the midst of the feast of Tabernacles (7.14, 25–36), Jesus on the last day of the feast (7.32–52). The feast of Tabernacles took place six months after. Originally it was a harvest festival in the autumn: *sukkōt*, the feast of Tabernacles, because it was celebrated in the open air in the vineyards, where booths had been set up. Later this festival was historicized: it became a remembrance of the time when the Israelites lived in tents in the wilderness, above all the Mosaic tent of the covenant, in which the ark of the covenant was placed: God's presence among his people. At the time of Jesus, the festival (which lasted seven days, and even had a couple of days' further celebrations afterwards) was marked by great ceremonies with *light* and *water*. The first nocturnal celebration was a feast of light, to commemorate the pillar of fire which went before the Israelites at the

time of Moses (Ex. 13.21; see Zech. 14.7; in Wisdom 18.3f. the pillar of fire is identified with the Torah, 'the light of the world'). During the night four golden lampstands were lit in the temple 'in the chamber of the women' (see John 8.20); the whole of Jerusalem was then aglow with the light burning in the various baths. For water also played a great part in this festival (originally an expression of prayer for life-giving rain). According to the Mishnah the festival was 'the joy of drawing water' (*Sukkah* 5.1). In the light, ritual dances were performed by prominent men. When the cocks crew in the morning, people went in a solemn procession to the spring of Siloah. Water was drawn there with a golden reed, and the procession went back to the Temple through the water gate. The high priest held up the golden cane of water for a while and then poured the water into a large basin, from which it flowed down various channels deep into the ground (*t'hōm*). Finally, because the cycle of reading the Torah was concluded at this festival and was begun again with the account in Genesis, there were various ceremonies with the scrolls of the Torah: wisdom is the Torah (Sir. 24.23–29), and wisdom or Torah was 'living water'. In other words, *light, water, doctrine* or *wisdom* (the Law) were the three key concepts of this festival which at the time of Jesus was also associated with an intensive messianic expectation.

'Now the Jews' feast of Tabernacles was at hand. . .' (John 7.2), and the 'brothers' said to Jesus, 'If you do these things, show yourself to the world' (7.4b) – a request for national, sensational messianism. 'These brothers' had not yet understood Jesus (7.5; see 6.26). The answer is clear: Jesus refused, 'for my time has not yet fully come' (7.8). Later, however, Jesus goes up, 'not publicly, but in private' (7.10), to the feast of light and water and the wisdom of the divine Torah; however, he does not go up to Jerusalem in the sense that his brothers understood this going up to the festival. Jesus does not want an 'epiphany': he goes up incognito. Jerusalem is full of 'rumours' about him (7.11–13).

Three key concepts are presented in John 7 and 8: Jesus the teacher; Jesus the water of life; Jesus the light of the world.

Jesus, who goes up secretly to Jerusalem without his brothers knowing it, is found *teaching* in the Temple (7.14). However, the disciples went up to the festival of Torah wisdom, water and light. Jesus does not – though he too can be found in Jerusalem: *he* is wisdom, the water of life and light. He is wisdom, the teacher. The Law was already interpreted in early Judaism as pre-existent wisdom, which took up its abode in Israel, above all on mount Zion. In the prologue of John this pre-existent wisdom is the Logos who became man: Jesus of Nazareth. The teaching of Jesus is the pre-existent divine wisdom of the Father. The Johannine Jesus reacts to the incomprehension of the Jews, so to speak commenting on the prologue to John (7.16–24): 'My teaching is not mine, but his who sent me' (7.16): he is the incarnate Logos; that is now applied to his teaching and his doctrine. What he teaches is the Father's teaching. Jesus is the new Torah. But the account continually makes it clear that people do not understand the pre-existence of Jesus and his being sent by the Father (7.25–36). Jesus therefore already talks of 'his departure' (7.31–36). The Jews believe that he will go into the Diaspora, away from the Jewish people, to the Gentiles, 'the Greeks' (7.35f.). That means that the Jews discuss Jesus' interest in a mission which goes beyond Israel's borders. Here we come up against the comments of '*Christian* Jews' from the Johannine community. In 8.21f. this misunderstanding goes so far that Jesus' departure is thought to be a suicide. Here John is thinking of his community, which consisted of Christians from both Judaism and the Gentile world (see 11.51f.; 12.20ff.).

The great ceremony with water takes place on the last day of the festival (7.37). Jesus says that he himself is the 'source of living water' (7.37–52). The water that Jesus gives is the *pneuma* (7.39, but Jesus gives this spirit only when he is exalted). Living or flowing water, spring water – significant above all in baptist circles in Asia Minor – had long been a symbol for God's salvation (Jer. 2.13; 17.13; Isa. 12.3; 43.20; 44.3); Moses too struck water from the rock (Ex. 17.6), and there is the eschatological Temple fountain (Ps. 78.16; Ezek. 47.1–12; Zech. 13.1; 14.8; see Rev. 22.1, 10): finally this theme is taken further in the wisdom literature, in which water and spirit are associated (even more explicitly than in Isa. 44.3; Ex. 36.25; see Sir. 15.3; 24.30ff.; Bar. 3.12; see Wisd. 7.25; Song of Songs 4.15). For rabbinic Judaism both Torah and spirit are the 'water of life'.[99] Jesus says: 'I am the water of life'. True, as said by the earthly Jesus this is only a promise; he gives the holy spirit only after his glorification (see 17.1f.; 20.22), although Jesus is now already the bearer of the spirit (Sir. 1.32f.): for the others, 'there is still no spirit' (7.39b). Only after the glorification of Jesus will the Christians 'draw water from the fountains of salvation' (Isa. 12.3; John 7.37). But once again, no one believes Jesus (7.40–52).

Immediately after this (8.1–11), Jesus takes up the third theme of the feast of Tabernacles: 'I am the light of the world. He who follows me will not walk in darkness, but will have the light of life' (8.12; 9.15). Jesus comes from the heavenly world of light into earthly darkness (8.13–20): 'as long as I am in the world, I am the light of the world' (9.5). But the 'darkness did not receive him' (1.5; 3.19).

In the images of teaching, the water of life and light, the Johannine Jesus proclaims himself as the pre-existent, incarnate redeemer or saviour of the world: he leaves behind him the saving significance of the Law as the water of life and the light of the world. Jesus does not go *to the feast of tabernacles,* but to Jerusalem, to proclaim himself the only true feast of tabernacles: the wisdom of the Father, the water of life and the light of the world. Salvation is in Jesus from God – this sounds somewhat monotonous, but the Gospel of John does not know what else to say. Jesus is 'I am': Yahweh also spoke of himself in the same way. Salvation is in Jesus alone, for God alone is the salvation of man; and Jesus is sent by this 'I am' God. As the one who is sent, he identifies himself with him by whom he has been sent. He accomplishes his will, brings his teaching and says nothing of himself that he has not heard from the Father. So revealing himself, he reveals the Father: God himself.

3. John 9.1–10.21. We find ourselves in the days of celebration after a feast of Tabernacles. The fact that Jesus is 'light' is now made manifest in the healing of a man born blind (9.1–41, also on a sabbath). 'Seeing', the Jews do not believe (9.41). Jesus therefore explains how he has been sent for man's salvation: 'I am the door of the sheep' (10.7), that means access to the heavenly Father (10.1–21). Like a shepherd, Jesus leads his flock home (10.4). 'I am the good shepherd' (10.11), a shepherd who gives his life for the sheep (10.11b). In early Judaism, Moses was the shepherd and leader of Israel; and Israel is the flock, just as the suffering prophet is called a lamb (in the sense of Isa. 53). 'Moses said to Yahweh, "Let Yahweh, the God of the spirits of all flesh, appoint a man over the congregation, who shall go out before them and come in before them, who shall lead them out and bring them in; that the congregation of the Lord may not be as sheep which have no shepherd" ' (Num. 27.16f.): thus Joshua became Moses' successor. In Ezek. 34, Yahweh is the shepherd of Israel (Ezek. 34.12). Here too, Jesus is the new greater leader and shepherd of Israel: he gives his life for his own.

4. John 10.1–6 and 10.22–29. The context in which Jesus reveals himself here – 'it was winter' (10.23) – is the so-called feast of Chislev, the December festival of Hanukkah, in Greek *enkainia* or renewal (dedication of the Temple, *dedicatio*), three months after the feast of Tabernacles (see II Macc. 1.9). According to II Maccabees this festival is not just a feast of the purification of the Temple under Judas Maccabaeus, but also a celebration of the miraculous kindling of fire on the altar of burnt offering under Nehemiah. Josephus calls this festival *phōta*, the lights: the festival of illumination.[100] The connection between the feast of Tabernacles and the feast of the consecration of the Temple was a long-standing one in Israel. According to I Kings 8.2; II Chron. 5.3; 7.10, Solomon chose the feast of tabernacles for the consecration of the new Temple; for the sanctuary of Bethel was also consecrated on this festival (I Kings 12.32). According to Ezra 3.1–4 the altar of the Temple which had been destroyed was rebuilt on the feast of Tabernacles. So in the long run this festival also became associated with the fire of sacrifice, the Jewish lamp of God, which was kept burning constantly in the holy of holies as a sign

of Yahweh's dwelling in the midst of his people – a fire which according to legend was of *heavenly origin* (that means the kindling of a sacred and completely new fire only by the power of the sun in the heavens). This festival was therefore celebrated 'in the manner of' the feast of Tabernacles, as a commemoration of the victories of the Maccabees, the festival of the purification of the Temple after it had been desecrated by the Syrians in 167–164 BC; and finally it became the festival of God's dwelling among men, celebrated on 25 December (I Macc. 4.41–61), the day on which Christians later came to celebrate the birth of Jesus.[101] On the feast of the holy fire, the priest prayed this prayer: 'O Lord, Lord God, Creator of all things, who art awe-inspiring and strong and just and merciful, who alone art king and art kind, who alone art bountiful . . . who dost rescue Israel from every evil, who didst *choose* the fathers and *consecrate* them. Accept this sacrifice on behalf of all thy people Israel and *preserve thy portion* and *make it holy*. Gather together our scattered people, set free those who are slaves among the Gentiles . . . Plant thy people in thy holy place, as Moses said' (II Macc. 24–29).[102]

John does not apply it directly to Jesus. First of all another I saying is woven in. Jesus is the shepherd. It was natural to talk of this, because as early as 10.19–21 there was mention of a 'schism' over the words of Jesus. In the evening, flocks belonging to different owners were driven together into one sheepfold. In the morning, each shepherd came and 'called *his* sheep'. These knew his voice and came out through the opening one after another. Then the shepherd went out to the pasture at the head of his flock. John shows the connection between shepherd and sheep (10.3b–4), which in Palestine each had their own names. The sheep spontaneously follow their shepherd. The believers go 'after Jesus', and the shepherd does not abandon his sheep, as hirelings often do (10.12). To non-believers Jesus' voice sounds 'alien'. John attacks the false shepherds of Israel who lead the people astray. They are 'thieves and robbers – hired shepherds – strangers'. Jesus is not only the true shepherd; he is also the opening or door of the sheepfold (10.7–10); the way to abundant life (10.10); other ways lead to damnation. (Sayings like 'I am the gate' are legion in later gnostic literature: see also 'I am the way', John 14.6, to which 10.9 is similar.) Jesus leads the sheep 'to rich pastures' (abundant life, see Ps. 23.2; Ezek. 34.12–15). He is 'the good shepherd' (10.11–15). But this shepherd, Jesus, also has sheep outside this fold (10.16). Jesus gives his life for the sheep (10.11b), but these others will hear his voice. There will be 'one flock and one shepherd' (10.16b). All the scattered children of God in the world (11.52; see 17.20) will be gathered by Jesus into one church community, which also contains Gentiles and Samaritans. The church community is now Yahweh's flock, made up of Jews and Gentiles – 'born of God'. And this union is the fruit of the death of Jesus (10.11 and 10.17).

In 10.22–30 the picture of the shepherd changes to themes taken from the festival of the consecration of the temple (10.22–30). 'Give his life for the sheep' was a good occasion for that. The theme of the shepherd is also repeated in 10.26–30, in the pericope about Jesus' stay in Jerusalem during the Jewish Temple feast (10.22). In 10.36 the mention of *hagiazein* (sanctify) is a typical expression from the festival of the consecration of the Temple. (See Greek Num. 7.1; there it is used for the consecration of the tent of the covenant by Moses, whereas in Greek Num. 7.10f. we find *enkainizein,* strictly speaking 'renew', hence *enkainia*-feast or feast of the consecration of the Temple). Jesus is in the Temple, in the 'hall of Solomon' (the place where according to Acts 5.12 the first Christians held their meetings). The Johannine Jesus speaks 'with Jews', with Jews from the time of Jesus, but at the same time, in John's view of two planes, with Christian Jews from the Johannine community. The subject is in each instance the saving significance of Jesus' death.

The dispute with 'the Jews' over Jesus' messiahship (10.24–30) gives us to understand that historically Jesus did not speak too clearly about his messiahship (as it appears in a Johannine context). John is aware of this 'synoptic trait'. But he is writing from faith to faith. Yet still people do not understand Jesus completely (see Luke 22.68). But for John this means that they have not been chosen by the Father, they have not been given to him by the Father. The sending of Jesus into the world is a sanctification by the Father (10.36). Jesus is God's Temple among us; he replaces the Temple altar, as he has been initiated into his manhood by the fact that as Jesus he is the Christ and Son of God (10.22–29). Hence (unlike 17.19) the sanctification of Jesus is bound up with the sending into the world. Again the Jews are scandalized because 'you, a man, make yourself God' (10.33). Jesus is the new sanctuary, the altar consecrated by God himself: he gives freedom to those who live in slavery among the nations: he gives 'eternal life' (10.28) – God's presence among us.

So in the context of the Jewish high festivals which expressed the religious identity of Israel as God's elect, Jesus says that he stands over the sabbath (5.1–47), that he is the true manna from heaven (6.1–71), that he makes known the Torah or teaching and the will of God, living water – giver of the Holy Spirit – light of the world, so that the feast of tabernacles, the feast of the Torah, water and light, is obsolete (7.1–8.59); he himself is personally in his manhood the sacrificial altar consecrated by God (10.22–39) – all this because by virtue of his pre-existence with the Father in his manhood (*sarx egeneto*) he is heavenly light in the darkness of the world. But only a few recognize the light, namely those 'to whom he gave the possibility of becoming children of God' (1.12f.), 'born of God' (1.13): only the spiritual knows the *pneumatica* or *epourania* (the heavenly). But many do not acknowledge him: 'He came into his own, but his own did not receive him' (1.11).

In another context, outside a liturgical Jewish context, the Gospel of John has three other 'I am' sayings (from which it again emerges that the Jewish festivals are not a regular literary framework, any more than they are in John 1: the first, second, third day after the first day on which light was created; it lies in the background, but is in no way a structuring principle).

5. John 11.25. ' I am the resurrection and the life. He who believes in me shall live even though he dies, and whoever lives and believes in me shall never die' (11.25f.). This is probably the strongest 'I am' saying outside the absolute 'I am "I am" ' sayings. In the presence of Jesus, death is no longer death. Jesus *is* life, even for the dead. He is the giver of life (see 5.21, 26; 4.50–53), above all of inner, divine life; but physical life, resurrection, is the visible sign of that. For the life became *sarx* or man (see John 1.14 and I John 1.1–3). He who believes that Jesus *is* life could know from that very fact that Lazarus would be raised to life at the appearing of Jesus – in John's narrative this is not something that becomes clear only from the coming resurrection of Jesus. But at the same time this resurrection of Lazarus is a 'work' of God in Jesus, a *sign* of Jesus' coming resurrection.

Jesus is 'the resurrection and the life' (11.25). These are not simply synonyms. Precisely because Jesus *is* the life – 'in him was life' (1.4) – life that became man (as I John comments on the Logos hymn of the Johannine community: 'The life was manifest and we saw it, and testify to it, and proclaim to you the eternal life which was with the Father and was made manifest to us', I John 1.2), he is also life for the body. Paradoxically the physical resurrection is given in the aspect of the divine life of Jesus in humanity as *sarx*, and is thus a sign of this divine life. Hence John's bold paradox: whoever believes in the life, Jesus, lives, even though he dies; anyone who believes in the life will not die (11.26). In this Semitic parallelism it is said that anyone who believes in Jesus lives; that is, he lives even if he dies; and anyone who believes, does not die! Death is banished from such a life in faith. In other words, in faith, physical dying is not final death; physical death takes on another significance; it is limited. Communion in faith with the life that is stronger than death. 'Do you believe that?' (11.26c), whereupon Martha, like Peter at one time, makes her confession of faith: 'I believe that you are the Christ, the Son of God, he who is coming into the world' (11.27); 'the one who is coming into the world' is a Johannine addition to the classical creed: 'You are the Messiah, the Son of God' (John 20.31).

6. John 14.6: 'I am the way and the truth and the life. No one comes to the Father but by me' (14.6). The emphasis in this pericope falls on 'I am the way'; Jesus is the way, that is, to truth and life. Jesus reveals the truth which leads to true life, and so leads believers to the Father. He is the only way which gives access to the Father. If John sees Moses above all in the background, we can rightly think of Deut. 1.29–33: 'Do not be in dread or afraid of them. Yahweh your God goes before you . . .(as) in the wilderness, where you have seen how Yahweh your God bore you, as a man bears his son, in all the way that you went until you came to this place. Yet in spite of this word you did not believe the Lord your God, who went before you in the way to *seek you out a place* to pitch your tents. . .'. John 14.1–4 also begins with, 'Let not your hearts be troubled. You believe in God – see Deut. 1.30 – *believe also in me*' (14.1). As Moses, with Yahweh before him, goes in search of a camping place, so 'Jesus goes to prepare a place for you' (John 14.2b,3). 'And when I go and prepare a place for you, I will come again and will take you to myself, that where I am you may be also. And you know *the way where I am going*' (14.3f.). Just as Yahweh earlier went before the people, so Jesus goes before his own to prepare a camping place, a place in heaven. He himself is this way. Thereupon Philip says, 'Show us the Father' (14.8a), and the answer follows: 'He who sees me sees the Father' (14.9b). Jesus is the only way to God. He brings the Father to us in his own humanity and his human appearing. 'Believe me' (14.11a), and if you cannot believe me on the basis of my word, 'then believe me for the sake of the works' that I do (14.11b).

7. John 15.1–10. 'I am the true vine, and my Father is the vinedresser' (15.1). According to Jewish evidence, a great golden vine stood immediately in front of the entrance to the 'holy place' in the Temple of Herod, to which Jesus also came: this symbolized Israel, the vine which God himself cherished.[103] In the wisdom literature wisdom says of itself, 'I am like a vine': 'Like a vine I caused loveliness to bud, and my blossoms became glorious and abundant fruit. Come to me, you who desire me, and eat your fill of my produce. . . Those who drink me will thirst for more' (Sir. 24.17, 19,21). Wisdom also presents itself in Sir. 24: 'I came forth from the mouth of the Most High. . . I took root in an honoured people. . .' (Sir. 24.3–12). Israel is the vineyard of the Lord, and Jewish wisdom is like wine. 'Yet I planted you a choice vine' (Jer. 2.21), 'Thou didst bring a vine out of Egypt; thou didst drive out the nations and plant it' (Ps. 80.8). 'Turn again, O God of hosts! Look down from heaven and see; have regard for this vine, the stock which thy right hand planted, and for the son whom thou hast reared for thyself' (Ps. 80.14f.; in the Septuagint 'son of man'; see also Ezek. 2.21). Israel, God's son, is a vine which Yahweh has planted and cherished. In Ezek. 17.6–8 this image is

transferred to Israel's king Zedekiah. Only in the extra-biblical literature is the image transferred to the Messiah.[104] In John, however, the stress on 'true' is striking (Jesus is 'the vine which is the true one'). The Johannine Jesus is himself the true Israel; the representation in terms of the church is given a christological foundation. The background of wisdom literature in which wisdom says of itself, 'I am like a vine' (Sir. 24.17), is sufficient explanation of the 'I' form.

What does a good vinedresser do? In the winter he cuts off the dry twigs, and in the spring he removes superfluous shoots on the branches (see John 15.2); he cuts them away and trims the vine so that it will bear plenty of fruit. John (like Sirach) thinks of the vine in terms of its many fruits, and not just of the nourishing strength of the wine. Jesus is the vine, the Christians are the grapes which are 'in him' (15.4). Here John is alluding to Christians who, because they have become dry, have already been removed (15.6; see I John 2.19). The trimming of the vines in spring gives John occasion to say (within the farewell discourse) that the disciples of Jesus have already been purified, 'thanks to the (life-giving) word that I have spoken to you' (15.3b: in the Gospel of John the disciples of Jesus are at the same time the Johannine Christians who have been purified by the water of baptism in the name of Jesus). The presupposition for bearing much fruit is 'to remain in Jesus' (15.4). 'I am the vine, you are the branches' (15.5); the immanence of the vine in the branches and the branches in the vine (15.4,5,9). John stresses the mutuality in love (15.9f.), as this brings perfect joy (15.11): 'Without me you can do nothing' (15.5c). To bear fruit is in the last resort to practise love for Jesus and his commands, just as Jesus loves the Father and follows his commands (15.9f.).

Thus John has seven 'I am' sayings. As he also records seven works of Jesus, the number seven is not accidental; it is meant as an expression of 'perfection'. A perfect soteriology on a christological basis (but this is not a structural literary principle; it is simply an expression of Johannine thought on various planes. To keep to one of these levels damages the pattern of Johannine thought.) Jesus is not the Father, but he is the eschatological revelation of God who has sent him for that purpose. He speaks from his own experience (3.11, 31f.; 8.26; 12.49); therefore he is the only access to the Father (14.6). To believe in him is to participate in the salvation, the life, that he has received from the Father: he has come that we might have life, and have it abundantly (10.10), because he himself is this abundance (1.16; 5.25f.; 6.57). He is what he *gives*, says John finally; to put it in modern terms: he is the primal sacrament of God. Because of this, even in the Johannine community – and in the process of growth leading up to the final redaction of the Fourth Gospel – a number of texts in John have been revised further in terms of the church's sacraments. A typical example of this is John 6.51c–59: these verses are wrongly – in Johannine terms – referred to as doublets. Here one can divide the exegetes into 'sacramentalists',[105] exegetes who claim that John interprets the sacraments in spiritual terms,[106] and finally the exegetes who claim that the original John mentioned neither the sacraments nor their spiritual interpretation, simply because we cannot assume that to begin with the eucharist was practised in all the Christian communities.[107] However, all are convinced that Jesus reveals God in human form, in other words, that *Jesus* is the sacrament of God; he is God's gift to this earthly world (3.16; 6.32). However, the Gospel of John makes this fact *present* in the Johannine community, in which baptism and eucharist carry on the historical Jesus in terms of Christ Jesus present and at work in the community.

### (b) The last 'public' words of Jesus 'to the world'

The Gospel of John had earlier informed the reader that the Sanhedrin had resolved to kill Jesus: 'It is expedient for you that one man should die for the people, and that the whole nation should not perish' (11.50). John sees this already as a remark about the redemptive death of Jesus, 'not for the nation only, but to gather into one the children of God who are scattered abroad' (11.52, see 1.12).

Jesus is in Jerusalem for the last passover feast. Some *Greeks* asked Philip if they could 'see Jesus' (*idein* does not simply mean to 'speak to' Jesus). Johannine 'seeing' is the *beginning* of possible *faith*. These Greeks want to know who Jesus really is. The question about wanting to believe is brought by Philip and Andrew to Jesus. But in this Johannine account Jesus incomprehensibly answers quite abruptly (at first sight): 'The hour has come for the Son of man to be glorified . . . Unless a grain of wheat falls into the earth and dies, it remains alone; but if it dies, it bears much fruit. . . Now is my soul troubled. And what shall I say? Father, save me from this hour? No, for this purpose I have come to this hour. Father, glorify thy name' (12.23–28). Some Greeks want to see Jesus, and . . .he begins to talk about his death as a crucifixion (12.32,33). Is this a meaningful train of thought? John 12.20–22 is an episode which continues to remain obscure. But Jesus' answer is immediately concerned with the religious quest of these Gentiles (in fact probably Jewish proselytes): only through his death does Jesus become important for Gentiles. The glorification of Jesus makes him universally accessible. At his death Jesus will 'draw *all* men to him' (12.32), including the Gentiles. (John has good reason for making 'the Jews' misinterpret Jesus saying about his 'departure' as 'departing to the Gentiles', 7.35. Jesus' departure to the Father is also a departure to the Gentiles.)

Suddenly in this story 'the people' are again with Jesus (12.29). And John adds here what is known from the synoptic gospels as the Gethsemane story. 'Now is my soul troubled. What shall I say, "Father save me from this hour?" No, for this purpose I have come to his hour. Father, glorify thy name!' (12.27f.). This has been explained earlier in Jesus' conversation with Andrew and Philip through sayings which we also find in the synoptic tradition: the grain of wheat must die if it is to bear fruit (12.24),[108] and 'he who loves his life loses it, and he who hates his life in this world will keep it for eternal life' (12.25), and finally, 'If anyone serves me, he must follow me' (12.26). What the synoptic gospels call 'following Jesus' in John becomes 'serving Jesus' (12.26; 13.13,16; 15.20). Jesus himself speaks, first to a few disciples, then to the people, about the *necessity – dei –* of his death. For Jesus, dying means 'going home' (see 7.34,36; 8.21f.; 13.33,36; 14.2–4; 17.24), going to the Father. It is the hour of glorification (see below). Jesus is perplexed by the prospect of his death (12.27), which he knows will be a violent one (12.32f.). But the Johannine Jesus knows that this perspective is in fact the significance of his whole life: the will of the Father (10.38) who gives him this cup (18.11). For John, dying is the attack of the 'prince of this world' (12.31; see 14.30; 16.11) – a datum which is widespread in early Judaism and in the New Testament ('the God of this age': II Cor. 4.4; Belial: II Cor. 6.15; see also Eph. 2.2; 'to dethrone the prince of death, the devil, through his death': Heb. 2.14b). The darkness is the sphere in which death rules, from which only the Son can bring liberation (5.24), since Jesus' light is life (12.50a; prologue). But because Jesus is one with the Father, this Satanic attack is at the same time the overthrowing of the prince of this world: 'he is cast out' (12.31). From where? Not from heaven (as in Rev. 12) nor even from the world, which for John remains darkness (12.25; 13.1; 15.18f.; 16.33; 17.15f.; see 'the whole world lies in the power of the evil one', I John 5.19). For John, to cast out means to reject, repudiate: for *believers* who look up to the cross (see 3.14f.; 19.37) and are 'drawn' by the crucified Jesus (12.32), Satan loses all his power. From now on Satan has no more influence on believers. John sees in the death of Jesus his community of life with the Father, through which this death is overcome and passed on for the salvation of many (12.32). Jesus draws all men 'to him' (14.3): the spatial conception of a being raised up to heaven (exaltation on the cross) is a personal event: Jesus is the one who mediates communion with the Father. His last admonition to the world is, 'Believe in the light' (12.36).

Jesus' last words in public 'to the world' give us a view of his crucifixion as glorification and victory over death and Satan and the beginning of his saving 'drawing' of all men to himself. For that he has come into the world (12.27c). But even these words come up against resistance (12.34).

'The world' does not understand Jesus: 'When Jesus had said this, he went out and hid himself from them' (12.36b). From now on he will speak only to his own (13.1) and not to the world, which has written him off (see 18.20). Now he hides from the world until he is again confronted with the leaders of the Jews before the judgment seat of Pilate the Gentile. Neither the Jews nor Pilate – the world – understand him; they cast Jesus out.

The evangelist concludes the first part of his gospel with a retrospect: (i) 'Though he had done so many signs before them . . . yet they did not believe in him' (12.37–43) and (ii) with a short summary of Jesus' revelation of himself (12.44–50).

John seeks to understand this universal rejection theologically, from the Old Testament. Evidently the evangelist wants to overcome objections in his community: if it is so clear that Jesus is 'from above', how does one explain this rejection? John refers to the doctrine of 'hardening' the heart, to be found in Judaism and throughout the New Testament: this is a divine disposition which does not, however, take away the freedom of human guilt (12.38–43). The eschatological revelation of God in Jesus confronts every man with a definitive existential decision. But John is also concerned with the inability of some people to believe. He revises Isa. 6.9f. in a special way. His doctrine of hardening the heart is harsher than that of the synoptic gospels (see Mark 4.12; Matt. 13.13–15; Luke 8.10; Acts 28.26f.). John takes less pains to connect both the good and the evil that man does with the all-decisive God. Jesus' suffering and death also seem to him to be a positive will of God (18.11). Jesus *is* the Saviour of the whole world (4.42; 12.47); those who cannot be saved are judged (3.17f.; 12.47). But even John does not have a divine decision of rejection, for many Jews, including their counsellors, believe in Jesus (12.42; see 3.1; 7.50f.; 19.38f.). Anyone who does not believe is guilty (9.39–41) and John seeks the ultimate reason for this in God. These texts reflect the anti-Christian propaganda of a militant synagogue against the Johannine community. In the summary of Jesus' revelation of himself (12.44–50), the evangelist finally gives a resumé of the Johannine christology (3.13–21, 31, 36) which he puts into Jesus' mouth as a last public confession ('with a loud voice', 12.44, though there is no indication of any bystanders). The pericope is as it were an independent literary unit. Anyone who believes in Jesus really believes in the Father who has sent him. Whoever sees Jesus sees the Father. 'I have come as light into the world, that whoever believes in me may not remain in darkness' (12.46; see the prologue). Jesus has not come to judge but 'to save the world' (12.47); the judgment is only the other side of the rejection of this grade (12.48). He speaks only words of salvation – from God; to reject him is to reject God, the Father. Everything Jesus does and says he does as one who is sent, and not on his own authority; this commission means 'eternal life', salvation. However, it is striking that the *katabasis-anabasis* model in the radical sense is missing from this summary. Here we find an expression only of the 'sending' model, in which the one who is sent is like the one who sends him (see also 6.32f., 38, 46; 7.18, 28; 8.18, 26, 29, 42). We also find this model elsewhere in the New Testament;[109] it is a prophetic identification of the one who is sent with the one by whom he is sent: it is the model of 'God's messenger'. But there is a special feature in the Gospel of John: the person of the one who is sent is decisive. He is the *eschatological* messenger of God, who requires belief in his own person, and not just in the words that he speaks in the name of God: his person itself is 'from Gôd', the presence of God among us. 'You believe in God, believe also in me' (14.1): one must believe in Jesus in order to have communion with God (see also 14.8–11). Jesus is a light: in him believers see the Father. So John wants as it were to 'justify' Jesus: Jesus cannot show of himself what he is; he does nothing by himself, indeed he is unable to (5.19): he does the works of the Father. All one can do is as it were to blame God, but for the Jews that is ruled out (see 12.47f., 49f.). His words are therefore only purifying (15.3), sanctifying (17.17), life-giving (8.51) and liberating (8.31f.). That they also bring *judgment* is experienced only by unbelievers (17.6, 14, 17). Those who do not believe are judged already: their unbelief judges them (3.18), and eschatological judgment (12.48) is simply the eternal confirmation of that. Jesus does not *judge* in this sense (8.26a; 12.47). In Jewish terms, God is the final judge. True, the Father hands over 'judgment' to the Son (5.22), but nevertheless he only judges according to what he has heard from the Father (5.30). John evidently wants to provide theological and christological support for his own harsh judgment on unbelieving Judaeans. All this clearly betrays the tension of the time between Judaism (perhaps even Christian Jews) and the Johannine community.

So for the Gospel of John, a summary of the public ministry comprises the facts that Jesus is the light of the world (12.46, 35f.; see 1.9), that he speaks of the Father (12.49f., see 1.18) and that he has a message of life for us (12.44–50; see 1.12f.). Now Jesus restricts his talking to 'his own'.

(*c*) Conversation with 'his own': farewell discourses

John 13 begins with the last supper (which in the Gospel of John is not the Jewish passover, as it is in the synoptic gospels). The farewell discourse proper is 13.31 to 14.31, concluded with 'let us go hence' (14.31). In fact this is followed by two other farewell discourses and a solemn prayer (John 17) in the presence of the disciples. Different strata are clearly visible here. There is growing agreement among exegetes that

John 15 brings the basic ideas in the evangelist's farewell discourse (13.31 to 14.31) up to date once again in terms of the contemporary situation of the Johannine community, whereas John 16 is a new version of John 13.31–14.31, the farewell discourse 'proper'. As we can recognize from the various seams, John 15–17 was worked into the first outline of the gospel at a later stage, even if the whole of the gospel reflects *Johannine* theology. This redactional question is not particularly important for our purposes. We are concerned with the theology of this canonical gospel and not formally with the complicated history of its origin.

In John 13–17 Jesus speaks to 'his own' (13.1; see 10.3, 12; 10.14; 17.6, 10) 'whom the Father has given him' (17.2, 12, 24) and whom the Fourth Gospel now for the first time calls *teknia* (13.33), little children (a term which is frequent in I John). In 15.14f. the Johannine Jesus says, 'No longer do I call you servants . . . but . . . friends' (just as Moses talked with God 'as with a friend', Ex. 33.11). By 'his own' and 'the disciples' John understands all believers, the Christians; in 13–17 Jesus' disciples are clearly not regarded as 'officials', but as representatives of the Christian community of believers. The expression *hoi idioi*, his own, is reminiscent of what John said about the good shepherd: 'The sheep listen to his voice; he calls them by their name' (10.3), 'they know his voice' (10.4b). 'The good shepherd gives his life for his sheep' (10.11); he knows his own. The farewell discourse(s) and the solemn prayer (John 17) are therefore words of a good shepherd who is there to give his life for his own. (To call the prayer 'high priestly' is un-Johannine, because the Fourth Gospel sees Jesus not as a high priest, but as a Mosaic shepherd, greater than Moses.) Despite the way in which it originated, this chapter comprises a whole: conversations of Jesus with his own, *hoi idioi* (13.1), on the one hand with the disciples (13–16) and on the other with the Father (John 17), who is in fact the *Patēr idios* (5.18): 'my own Father'. All these conversations are dominated by a sense of the love of the Father for Jesus and his disciples, the love of Jesus for the Father and the disciples and the love of the disciples for the Father and Jesus. They are those who are 'not of this world' (17.14, 16): God or 'born of God' (1.3): this in itself brings about the division of spirits. 'Now is the judgment of this world' (12.31).

John begins the farewell conversations with a reflection: 'When Jesus knew that his hour had come to depart out of this world . . . having loved his own who were in the world, he loved them to the end' (13.1). For *during* the farewell meal Jesus gets up to perform a 'symbolic action': the washing of the disciples' feet. He does this, the evangelist says, 'knowing that the Father had given all things into his hands, and that he had come from God and was going to God' (13.3; see 7.28, 33; 8.14, 21f.; 16.18–30). The time for appearing in the world (9.5) is past (17.11, 13). If one

takes the context into account, the authority which the Father has given
to Jesus *here* (13.3) means the freedom of Jesus, who is not sent to his
death against his will; for though this death is the work of Satan, 'the
prince of this world' (14.30), the ruler of this world 'has nothing against
me' (14.30b; see 7.30, 44; 10.28f.). For Jesus 'has come from God' (13.3),
he 'is over all' (3.31; see 8.42). In other words, Jesus' dying is the last
'work' that he does at his Father's bidding. The foot-washing is in this
perspective, and John interprets it in two ways : (*a*) as a model for
Christians, who must serve one another (13.12–17); this is the purpose
for which they have been sent into the world (13.20; see 17.18); (*b*) as a
prior indication of the saving significance of the death of Jesus (13.6–10):
Peter still does not understand this last aspect. It had already become
clear in earlier sections that Jesus' 'going away' had not only been
misunderstood by the Judaeans (7.33f.) but had also been misunderstood
by the disciples (7.36; 13.36). Jesus had even spoken in a riddle (*māšal*,
see 16.29; 16.17–19), namely *hypagein* (ascend, go away). You will seek
me, . . . but where I go you cannot come (7.34), at least for the moment
(13.36). 'And when I go and prepare a place for you, I will come again
and will take you to myself, that where I am you may be also' (14.3).
With this expectation Jesus makes known his testament, the new commandment of love (13.31–35; 14.15–24; 15.12–17; 16.27; 17.21–26). The
'new' element in this testament is not contrasted with the 'old' testament,
which also recognized love as the greatest commandment (Lev. 19.18
with Deut. 6.4f.). It is new because the love of Jesus gives it a new
foundation to the point of death (see 15.13). I John will say, 'By this we
know love, that he laid down his life for us; and we ought to lay down
our lives for the brethren' (I John 3.16). I John itself considers why the
commandment to love is called a new one in its particular community
(I John 2.7f.; also II John 5). In the Johannine community, brotherly
love is based on its experience of the love of Jesus which is the measure
(*kathōs*, like) of brotherly love (John 13.34). And *such a* love is the hallmark
of true Christianity (13.35): 'We know that we have passed out of death
into life, because we love the brethren. He who does not love remains in
death' (I John 3.14). In 17.21–26 this commandment is brought up to
date in terms of the situation of the Johannine church in an even more
explicit way: 'that all may be one'; its foundation is given christological
support: 'As thou, Father, in me and I in thee: that they too may be in
us, in order that the world may believe that thou hast sent me.' For John,
love goes round in a circle: 'He who loves me will be loved by my Father,
and I will love him' (14.21). 'For the Father himself loves you, because
you love me' (16.27); the Father has loved me before the creation of the
world' (17.24), 'that the love with which thou hast loved me may be in
them' (17.26): 'I in them and thou in me, that they may become perfectly

one, so that the world may know that thou hast sent me and hast loved them even as thou hast loved me' (17.23) And the criterion for this love is: 'laying down his life for his friends' (15.13). The origin of this circle of love lies with the Father and is manifested in the Son: 'You have not chosen me, but I have chosen you' (15.16), which I John puts as follows: 'In this is love, not that we loved God but that he loved us and sent his Son to be the expiation for our sins' ( I John 4.10). The community of love between Father and Son is extended to included the mutual connection of believers (14.10, 20; 17.20–23). 'Between' God-in-us and we-in-God stands Jesus the Son. In the last resort, the token (13.25; see 17.23) of Christianity is based in the mutual love of Christians as the reflection of the mutual love of the Father and the Son and as participation in it: Christians are taken up into this love on the basis of Jesus' surrender to the point of death. Brotherly love has a *christological* and a *religious* basis; it is a religious event. *Such* a love is a spiritual activity; it is not 'of this world', since this world is not capable of receiving it (see 14.22–24). Brotherly love and church unity are grounded in a fellowship of life with God in Christ (17.23; 10.38; 14.10f., 20, 23; 15.4f.). So in the last resort the glory which Jesus has from God is also shared by Christians (17.22). This brotherly union is so strong that John, in contrast to 10.16 and 11.52, no longer talks of a church made up of Jews and Gentiles; this distinction is obsolete: they are one. All this is illustrated in John 15 by means of an image: 'I am the true vine . . . you are the branches' (15.1, 5), 'Abide in my love' (15.9b), which at the same time means 'keep my commandments' (15.10, see I John 3.24; II John 6). It emerges from this whole account of love that for John the *innermost nature* of Jesus lies in his *personal association with the Father* and that this makes up the mystery of Christian redemption: *Abba!* Furthermore, the spatiality of the Johannine imagery (proceed from God, return to God) is as it were 'demythologized' by means of the mutuality in these formulae (I in you, you in me, we in them), as will at the same time become evident from the Johannine concept of 'heavenly dwellings'.

Before we come to the testament of love, the farewell discourses and the shepherd prayer of Jesus are 'preceded' by an interpretation of the content of the event which the Johannine Jesus calls 'going to the Father'. When the disciples are dismayed at Jesus' coming death (John 14.1), Jesus says: 'You believe in God, believe also in me' (14.1b). Belief in Jesus must have the same unconditional character as trust in God. Or, more precisely, through their belief in God the disciples must also continue to put their trust in Jesus. It is 'good for the disciples' (16.7; 14.28) that Jesus goes away. Of course he does not simply go away. He goes away *in order to do something* for the disciples, who do not belong to the spiritual, heavenly sphere 'from the beginning': he goes 'to prepare a place for his own' (14.1–3).

At that time people thought of heaven as a place with different areas.[110] Jesus speaks of 'my Father's house' (14.2), where he is really at home. There is no mention here of a gnostic 'homecoming' of men, whose souls would be by nature 'spiritual'. Jesus, who has come forth from God, must reserve a place for them; of themselves they are 'of the world' and not of the *pneuma*. So the first thing that must happen is for Jesus to send down *pneuma* from there. That is the significance of his departure. However, *in the last resort* John is referring to a place in heaven after death, though *directly* he envisages something else, which only becomes evident in John 20. Still, 14.3 already shows some signs of it: 'I will come again' (see also 14.8). In his updated eschatology John is not referring here to the parousia at the end of time but to the *Easter gift*. Then, on Easter day, Jesus and the Father will come to the disciples and 'take up their abode with them' (14.23). 'I will not leave you desolate; I will come to you' (14.18). 'On that day' (14.20; 16.23), that is, on Easter day (see below), 'you will know that I am in my Father and you in me and I in you' (14.20). The *monai* or dwelling places which Jesus is to prepare are connected with the Johannine *menein* (abide):[111] the 'abiding in Jesus' and the abiding of Jesus in the disciples, as an Easter gift. Precisely through his dying and his going to the Father, Jesus makes it possible for himself to take up an 'Easter abode' (*menein*) with his disciples. For John, what in the early church is ascribed to the parousia of Jesus is already an Easter event (but still with a further view towards the time after his death). Then the disciples already are 'where Jesus is' (14.3; see 12.26; 17.24), because Jesus himself returns and 'dwells in them'. In that case *they themselves* are the 'heavenly places'. For Jesus already begins to ascend, i.e. to draw men to himself, from the cross onwards (12.32). You know the way to the heavenly places (14.4), says Jesus: 'I am the way, the truth and the life' (14.6); that is, Jesus is the way to the full revelation of salvation and wisdom, which gives life. 'No one comes to the Father but by me' (14.6b). Just as Moses once asked God, 'Show me your glory' (Ex. 33.18), so Philip asks, 'Show us the Father' (14.8). But John 14.9–11 recalls the prologue, 'We have seen his glory, a glory as of the only beloved of the Father' (1.14c): 'Philip, whoever sees me, sees the Father' (14.9). 'For God so loved the world that he gave his only Son' (3.16).

If Jesus is this way of life, the disciples must turn to him exclusively: 'If you ask anything in my name, I will do it' (14.14; expanded in 16.23f., 26f.; see also I John 5.14f.; 2.1). For his part Jesus, who even during his earthly life was a good shepherd, a helper or Paraclete, will send after his death 'another helper, who will abide with you for ever' (14.16), 'the Spirit of truth' (14.17) which the world cannot receive 'the Holy Spirit'

(14.26). John comes back to this again five times (14.12–17; 14.26; 15.26; 16.7b–11; 16.13, 14), each time with new nuances (for the functions of the Johannine Paraclete see below). At Easter the Father will give the Spirit to the disciples at the behest of the risen Jesus. At Easter, then, not only will the Father and Jesus come to abide with the disciples, but the Holy Spirit will also enter into them. 'We – the Father and Jesus – will come to him and take up our abode with him' (14.23). Then the old expectation will be fulfilled of 'God's dwelling with men' (Ex. 25.8; 29.45; Lev. 26.22f.; Ezek. 37.27; 43.7; 48.35; Joel 3.21; Zech. 2.10 etc.) 'And by this we know that he abides in us, by the Spirit which he has given us' (I John 3.24). The incarnation of the Word (1.14a) was indeed already a 'dwelling of God among us' (1.14b), but for John christology is a *soteriology*, salvation: the dwelling of God *among us* only becomes a reality *in us* at Easter.

Glorify me, raise up the cross for me, 'that I may glorify you', i.e. by drawing all men to myself from the cross (17.2; 12.32); for the Father has given Jesus all authority over men (5.27), to give them eternal life (17.2). 'Power over all flesh' (*pasa sarx*) (17.2, to be compared with 5.27, the power of the Son of man) evidently associates 'power' (*exousia*) with the term Son of man (see Dan. 7). Therefore this shepherd prayer of Jesus (John 17) is clearly concerned with the enthronement of the Son of man. John 17 gives the answer to the question 'Who is this Son of man?' (12.34c): this is Jesus, who returns to his glory. Jesus prays for the glory (17.5) which, according to the prologue, John 1.1–4, he had 'with the Father'. Thus the Son of man is the Logos.

For John, actual eschatology begins only *at Easter* (20.19f.), and not with the incarnation as such, though the incarnation is its foundation. During the earthly life of Jesus, only the pledge of salvation is given; Jesus bestows the life-giving gift of the Spirit only at his exaltation on the cross and his resurrection.

Thus John does not say in any way that Jesus comes *in* the Spirit. Jesus himself comes, and apart from this gift, the Spirit too, is a coming gift of the risen one (20.22). The coming of Jesus and the sending of the Spirit stand side by side in the Gospel of John without any connection between them and without any synthesis (14.17f., repeated in 16.16, 19, where Jesus' going away is compared with birth pangs: brief pain, followed by joy: new life, 16.20–22). The death of Jesus is only a brief interruption: then 'I will come to you' (14.18), 'you will *see* me' (14.19), namely in the Easter appearances: 'they *saw* the Lord' (20.20), 'we have *seen* the Lord' (20.25; see also 20.18, 29).

To encourage his own during his short absence, Jesus gives and promises 'peace' (14.27, repeated in 16.33), not peace from here below, which is 'of this world' (14.27b), but peace as eschatological salvation (Isa. 52.7;

Ezek. 37.26) – the first gift that the risen one will offer to his disciples on
Easter day (20.20, 21). So the disciples should now be glad (14.28),
because Jesus is going away for a while: 'for the Father is greater than
I' (14.28b): glorified by the Father, Jesus will return with richer, ultimate
gifts. Therefore 'it is good for you that I should go away. For if I do not
go away, the helper (Paraclete) will not come to you' (16.7). Jesus' going
away is the sending of the Holy Spirit (see 16.7b; also John 20). Again
it emerges from this that for John, Jesus' humanity (1.14) is not of itself
redemption and the gift of salvation: his death as exaltation to the Father
is an essential complement, without which the eschatological gift of salvation is impossible. It runs contrary to the nature of the whole of the
Fourth Gospel that the Gospel of John should be thought to minimize
the saving significance of the death of Jesus. The *earthly life* of Jesus is a
preliminary sign: the *sign* is his death and the *reality* (that which is
denoted) is his resurrection, the Easter gift of the exalted Christ.

However, the peace and love of the markedly 'inwardly oriented'
Johannine community are subject to the hate of the world (15.18–27).
'Know that it has hated me before it hated you' (15.18). The evangelist
seeks to comfort his community with his view of Jesus Christ. The nearby
synagogue from which the Johannine community had to suffer a good
deal, posed problems to the Christians. The Johannine Jesus encourages
them, though he has sharp words for those who do not believe. He holds
them to be guilty and in the last resort to be hostile to God: 'they hate
my Father' (15.22–25). But once again appeal is made to the Paraclete,
who will also appear as the official accuser of 'the world' of unbelief: he
will bear witness to Jesus (15.26) in and through the witness of the
disciples (15.27). He will convict the world of its injustice (16.8). 'The
Jews' will finally banish the disciples from their synagogue (16.2; see also
9.22 and 12.42 – typical features of the time of the Johannine community);
indeed there will come a time when people will kill Christians believing
that they are pleasing God by doing so. However, the Christians are to
know that they do this 'because they have not recognized either the
Father or me' (16.2f.).

Finally, in 16.16–33, Johannine christology is accentuated to some
degree: 'I came from the Father and have come into the world; again, I
am leaving the world and going to the Father' (16.28). This is an explicit
formulation of the *katabasis-anabasis* model which in the process of the
development of the Gospel of John has been added to the model of the
eschatological prophet like Moses, incomparably greater than Moses, at
a time when people were becoming increasingly aware of the divinity of
Jesus. Hence the reaction of the disciples: 'Ah, now you are speaking
plainly, not in any figure' (16.29): 'we believe that you came from God'
(16.30) – the confession of the Johannine community. In the account,

however, it is a new formulation of earlier words of Jesus, now seen in the light of the imminent Easter event. We should not forget that Jesus always spoke of the Son of man in the third person, even in the Gospel of John. For the Gospel, his person was still shrouded in mystery.

The disciples may now be able to confess this in their enthusiasm, but John reminds his readers of their panic at the arrest of Jesus. They will be 'scattered in all directions' and will leave Jesus alone (16.32; though in 18.8 it is Jesus himself who as the good shepherd takes the initiative so that his own may be freed: 'Let these men go', 18.8f.). In Johannine fashion Jesus adds: 'But I am not alone, for the Father is with me' (16.32b).

The cohorts which will arrest Jesus, the instrument of the 'prince of this world' are on the march (14.30). 'Arise, let us go hence' (14.31; this was 'originally' followed by the passion narrative, 18.1). But in bringing the account up to date, John has yet more to say.

## §3   The return to the Father: the gift of salvation

### I.   THE LAMB OF GOD

The Gospel of John speaks twice of Jesus as the 'Lamb of God' (1.29; 1.36; with the word *amnos*, in contrast to the *arnion* from Revelation), i.e. only in the pericope about John the Baptist.

From earliest times, in the Old Testament the lamb was the image of *innocent* (II Sam. 24.17) and *helpless* suffering (Ps. 44.11, 22). Even in the nomadic period of Israel, the people of God was called a 'flock of sheep', with a polemical slant against agricultural life (Abel's sacrifice of the fruits of the field). A sheep or a lamb *is* the sacrifice that is well pleasing to God. Shepherds are also God's favourites: Moses was called from looking after the flock to become a prophet and shepherd, and the young shepherd David was called to be king of Israel. 'I was like a gentle lamb led to the slaughter': this text from Jer. 11.18f. was the inspiration for Deutero-Isaiah when he compares the 'suffering servant of God' with a lamb which is slaughtered (Isa. 53.7). The new element here (in comparison with Jeremiah) is that the idea of suffering for others is fused with the idea of the 'lamb'. None of this has any intrinsic *messianic* significance. The suffering servant does not call forth the notion of a messianic figure, but the image of the suffering prophet: at least, the term can be connected with this. In Ethiopic Enoch 89–90, Israel is called a shepherd and *David* a *lamb*; perhaps 'the lambs' here are even originally prophets (in a notable way, Matt. 7.15 calls the false prophets wolves in sheep's clothing, which in fact *presupposes* the image of prophets as lambs).

However, the basic idea is that 'the lamb' is the image of the *suffering prophet*. And that seems to be the way in which prophets understood themselves in earliest Christianity. The Markan and Matthaean accounts of the Last Supper cannot be understood apart from the background of Isa. 53 (even if they never cite it *explicitly*). It is typical that in Acts 8.31–33 it is Philip, one of the circle around Stephen and leader of the mission to Samaria, who interprets Isa. 53.7f.: 'He was led like a sheep to the slaughter, and like a lamb . . .'

If, then, the eschatological prophet like Moses, the suffering servant of God, is the background to the Gospel of John (as I have already suggested), it seems obvious to see the Johannine Lamb of God primarily as the suffering servant, the *Mosaic Messiah*. The expedient of explaining the *messianic* character of the servant in Deutero-Isaiah (Greek Isa. 53, *pais Theou*) by way of the Aramaic *talyā*, which can mean both lamb and son and servant, seems to me to be unnecessary from the point when 'the suffering servant of God' is seen in the perspective of the Mosaic suffering servant of God, which is the eschatological prophet. The suffering *"bed* has *Mosaic*-messianic, rather than *Davidic*-messianic features. Quite apart from the question whether the *"bed Yahweh* and the eschatological prophet like Moses are already explicitly associated in Deutero-Isaiah, a tendency in this direction can clearly be seen throughout Isaiah as we have it now. Thus the Mosaic messianic character of the *"bed* can hardly be denied. 'The Lamb of God that takes away the sins of the world', just as the suffering Moses bore the burdens and sins of the people, is thus the prophet who was led like a lamb to the slaughter (Isa. 53.7).

Now because early Christianity identifies Jesus with the Easter lamb (*inter alia*, I. Cor. 5.7; less clearly in I Peter 1.18f., which is a more general reference to the sacrifical lamb), we may concede that the Johannine Lamb of God is also, *at a secondary stage*, given the subsidiary meaning of the Easter lamb (at least the sacrificial lamb). This happens in John 19.14, 36: John makes Pilate pass the sentence of death about the sixth hour, at the time when the Easter lambs were slaughtered, and with a reference to scripture he sees that the regulations about the Easter lambs, 'not a bone of him shall be broken' (19.36), are fulfilled in the case of Jesus. However, these two allusions do not explain the use of 'the Lamb of God that bears the sins of the world' in John 1. Behind this we find the lamb of Deutero-Isaiah, perhaps already identified in Isa. 53 (within the wider context of the Book of Isaiah) with Moses, the shepherd, who gives his life for his sheep, the people. At all events *John* sees in Jesus the *"bed Yahweh* as identified with the Mosaic messianic eschatological prophet, 'who bears the burdens of the people' (Num. 11.14; see Isa. 53.4). The Fourth Gospel can therefore see the death of Jesus itself as an exaltation along the lines of the Sinaitism of early Judaism. There are at least some pointers in this direction in early Judaism.

## II. THE EXALTATION OF THE CROSS

The cross of a crucified man was raised up. For John, that is the image by which he expresses the fact that the death of Jesus is itself already an *exaltation*, a glorification. Jesus' exaltation and glory are already accomplished in his death. To some degree this is a new development as compared with the synoptic conception of Jesus' death.

There are repeated allusions to the death of Jesus even before the passion narrative in the Gospel of John: 2.17; 5.18; 7.1, 19, 25; 8.38; 12.23, 27; and to the exaltation on the cross: 3.14; 8.28; 12.32f.; see 18.32; 19.37. Above all, there is the anointing of Jesus in Bethany (12.1–11). Six days before the Passover, in the presence of Lazarus, who has been newly restored to life, Mary anoints the feet of Jesus with costly ointment of pure nard. According to John's explanation, this showed that she had recognized Jesus' true, sacred nature. The anointing which preceded Jesus' death was so abundant that this action was an expression of belief in Jesus' glory, even in death.

But the death of Jesus is seen as an exaltation as early as 3.14f., in which the image of 'raising up' is also used: 'And as Moses lifted up the serpent in the wilderness, so must the Son of man be lifted up, that whoever believes in him may have eternal life' (see Num. 21.8f.). The death of Jesus is an exaltation that brings salvation. However, this death remains a grim prospect, even for Jesus (12.27; see Ps. 43.5). In the Gospel of John this scandal of the cross is not taken away, but incorporated in the exaltation of the person of Jesus, through which death is as it were *ipso facto* overcome. His death is 'the Father's hour' (7.30; 8.20; 12.23; 13.1; 17.1), the hour of glorification (12.23; 17.1; 13.1). The reason for looking at Jesus' death in this way lies in the Johannine concept of the 'Lamb of God', the fundamental significance of which stems from Deutero-Isaiah. In Isa. 52.13 we find the two terms used by John: 'be *exalted*' (*hypsothēsetai*) and 'be *glorified*' (*doxasthēsetai*). In a departure from the approach of other New Testament Christians, John uses two categories: on the one hand lifting up or exaltation 'on the cross', and on the other resurrection and glorification after death. Is this connected with the two categories that we find in earliest Christianity, 'exaltation' and 'resurrection', a distinction (at least in form, if not in content) whose problems have been given a different solution in John from that in non-Johannine Christianity?

If my analysis of 'Lamb of God' and Mosaic Sinaitism in early Judaism is correct, the Gospel of John is primarily (though not exclusively) concerned with the exaltation and glorification of the Mosaic suffering servant of God. Jesus only communicates his full saving power when he has been raised up on the cross: he will then draw all men to himself (12.32) and will become the source of 'eternal life' (3.14f.). Here God gives his most precious gift possible, his Son (3.16), so that 'the world may be saved' (3.17; see 4.42b).

Before his suffering, the Johannine Jesus says, 'The hour has come for the Son of man to be glorified' (12.23). And Jesus prays, 'Father, glorify your name' (12.28). 'Then a voice came from heaven, "I have glorified it, and I will glorify it again" ' (12.28b), whereupon Jesus remarks: 'This voice has come for your sake, not for mine' (12.30). In the 'glorification' John is thinking of the fullness of Jesus' saving power: 'We have seen his glory . . . full of grace and truth' (1.14c,e; 13.32; 17.1f.). In John, christological statements are always also soteriological statements: the communication of Jesus' glory to believers. 'Father, the hour has come; glorify thy Son that the Son may glorify thee, since thou hast given him power over all flesh, to give eternal life to all whom thou has given him' (17.2; in his prayer with the Father, Jesus speaks of the 'Son' in the third person), that is: the real and ultimate *significance* of the glorification of Jesus is the Easter gift of eternal life to the believers. Jesus' life bears fruit for men only through his death (12.24). Here Jesus prays for 'the glory which I had with you before the world was made' (17.5). And again and again we find, 'Glorify me *now*' (17.5: see 'now' in 12.27, 31a, b, 23; 13.31): now, in the hour of suffering (12.27); now, in the hour of betrayal (13.31); now, in the hour when the cross is raised up (12.31); now, in the hour of glorification (12.23). All this is 'necessary' (*dei*, 12.34). To die to the world is to live (12.25). The hour of glorification is partly already the time of Jesus' death, which is experienced as the will of the Father (18.11). If Jesus has come 'that they may have life, and may have it more abundantly' (10.10), he has come to endure this hour (12.27c), for only the glorified crucified one can bestow the gift of life from the Father (3.14f.; 7.39; 16.7; 17.1–5). It emerges from this that John does not see Jesus as a 'god walking on earth' in borrowed form (as with the appearance of angels). So why could he not give any divine life when he was on earth (7.39; 16.7)? Still less than someone who at his death would again lay aside all humanity to become merely the 'pre-existent Son'. Why then did he appear as man, when he can only bestow the Spirit at the time of his departure (7.39; 16.7)? And in that case how does one explain Jesus' 'resurrection from the dead' (20.9)? There is no basis anywhere in the Gospel of John for the assumption made, above all by E. Käsemann, that the Gospel contains a naive docetism which culminates in a subsequent existence without humanity.[112] This is already contradicted by the image of the grain of wheat – the unity of death and resurrection (12.24) – and the statement, 'I lay down my life, that I may take it again' (10.17f.), and finally the primitive Christian resurrection terminology in connection with Jesus (above all 2.22; 20.9).

Therefore the *incarnate* Word in the Gospel of John can only give a sign of the salvation to come: his great saving work begins only as he 'draws' men from the cross (12.32). The response to this drawing is to be found in 19.31–37, among those who look up at the pierced Jesus on the cross (see 19.37).[113] 'Glorify your name' (12.28; see 17.2): show that you are God for us; exalt your name – sanctify it (cf. Ezek. 36.23; 28.23; Ps. 138.2). The name of God is the side of God that is turned towards men,[114] God as revelation. But in the Gospel of John this name – what is revealed – is the union of Father and Son (see *inter alia* 13.31; 17.5; 5.36; 10.38; 11.4, 40; 14.10); the Father reveals himself in the Son as glory or *doxa*. Jesus has revealed this name to his disciples (17.6) and 'they have received and know in truth that I have come from you: and they have believed that you have sent me' (17.8b): 'The glory which you have given me I have given to them, that they may be one even as we are one' (17.22); 'I have revealed your name to them' (17.26): 'We therefore believe that you have come from God' (16.30). This is the great difference from the belief of Nicodemus, who saw in Jesus only a teacher legitimated by God in and through signs, and no more than that (3.2; see also 2.23; as compared to 3.36: 'believe in the Son', in the unity of Father and Son, 3.35b). Glorification is therefore the *revelation* of the union of love between the Father and the Son who has been sent. Jesus has revealed this name: the holiness of God ('*holy* Father', 17.11), the righteousness of God ('*righteous* Father', 17.25), the love of God: 'I made known to them your name, and I will make it known, that *the love with which thou hast loved me* may be in them, and I in them' (17.26): 'God is love' (I John 4.8, 16) (at the same time an echo of the early Christian 'Hallowed be thy name', Luke 11.2; Matt. 6.9).

'I have glorified this name' and 'I will glorify it again' (12.28): these are the words of the heavenly voice, the message from the Father. John 13.31f. (after the departure of Judas) gives a very detailed picture of this, both of the 'past' (aorist) and the 'coming' (future) event: (*a*) *Now* is the Son of man glorified, and (*b*) God is glorified in him. (*c*) If God is glorifed in him, (*d*) God *will* also glorify him in himself, (*e*) he *will* soon glorify him (13.31f.). First of all it is clear that this passage is concerned with mutual glorification (in the past and in the future): of the Son of man and of God. In (*b*) and (*c*) it is said that Jesus glorifies God; in (*d*) and (*e*) that God will glorify Jesus. God himself is glorified (*b*) and (*c*) in the person of the Son of man (see also 14.13; 17.10); in (*d*) it is said that for his part God glorifies the Son of man in his person. Glorification and Son of man belong together. In that case the 'glorify again' from 12.28 refers to the whole of the Easter event: death and resurrection and the sending of the spirit. But when has the Father already glorified Jesus? He has done that among others and above all in the 'signs' that Jesus performed (2.11; 9.3), above all in the great preliminary sign, the raising of Lazarus: 'This illness is not unto death: it is for the *doxa* (glory) of God, so that the Son of God may be glorified by means of it' (11.4). Finally, with 'I have already glorified him' John is referring to the whole of the earthly work of Jesus (see 17.4); as the Father was always near to Jesus, Jesus was never alone (8.16, 29, 54; 16.32). The Father is also glorified in Jesus in that his own have received his words (17.6, 8–11). The whole of Jesus' life was a *revelation* of God as the Father of Jesus. To glorify means at the same time to rehabilitate and to justify someone, to show that he was right, and not all his enemies. The death of Jesus is triumph and judgment on 'the prince of this world' (12.32). Only 'from on high' can Jesus lead men away from the darkness, the world in which Satan rules. The darkness remains, but believers (who still themselves belonged to this darkness) are transplanted into another sphere of life (see also Col. 1.13: 'delivered from the dominion of darkness and transferred to the kingdom of his beloved Son', that is, away from sin, see also Hebrews). John vividly says of the elevation of the cross that it is 'lifted up from the earth' (*ek tēs gēs*, 12.32). to heaven. The movement upwards is a saving movement (see also 3.14f.). 'They will look up to him whom they have pierced' (19.37). Here John is citing Zech. 12.10–14: a lament of Israel over a man who was murdered with the connivance of the people (see also Isa. 53); there the looking up is an expression of the penitence and insight of the inhabitants of Jerusalem. Then they will have to confess their guilt: we have murdered a 'suffering servant'. They then see their crime.[115] Here John indicates not so much damnation as the last chance of salvation. People looked up to the serpent which was lifted up (3.14), 'in order to remain alive' (Num. 21.8). In 8.28, John says, 'When you have lifted up the Son of man, then you will know *that I am he*', and 'then I will draw all men to me' (12.32). When John thinks of the pierced side of Jesus from which flow water and blood (19.34f.), he also thinks of 7.38: 'as scripture says, streams of living water will flow from within him', and John adds here: 'This he said about the Spirit which they were . . . to receive' (7.39; see 4.14; 7.38). To look *in faith* (7.39) on Jesus who has been pierced (19.37) is a grace to eternal life; for non-believers it is a judgment. Faith is the only condition (3.15, 16; 6.37, 40; 6.45b, c).

A suffering Messiah was unthinkable for Jewish belief in a Davidic Messiah. John associates the *death* of Jesus above all with 'Christ' (Messiah) and King (12.12–34; 19.13–42), whereas for the risen one he uses 'the Lord' (20.18, 20, 25), but most of all he uses 'Son of God' (2.13–22;

5.1–18; 9.1–44; 20.1–23). But the Son of man, Christ and Son of God is Jesus of Nazareth. John himself indeed recognizes Jesus as Messiah, but not as Davidic Messiah; Jesus is the Mosaic Messiah, a concept which, as I have already pointed out, had already developed in Sinaitic theology and in the Samaritanism that was associated with it: the messianic Moses (Ex. 16.7,8, 9 plays a part here). The messianic prophet would be a new Moses figure; Jesus is the fulfilment of Deut. 18.15–19 (see John 4.25; 8.28; 12.49f.; 6.14; 7.40, 52; 5.44–47). For John, Jesus *is* the kingly Messiah; he is, however, not a Davidic but a Mosaic Messiah who is himself already called 'the suffering servant of God'. One cannot say that 'Moses' is a structural principle of the Gospel of John, any more than one can attribute this function to the Jewish festivals: the Fourth Gospel is characterized throughout by a mixture of various models, called forth by reminiscence of the Jesus tradition.

'The world' cannot recognize the exaltation on the cross, but for believing eyes it is the enthronement of Jesus. As in later Byzantine representations of the royal Jesus on the cross, for John the cross is a throne: 'Behold your king' (19.14; see 19.19). Here John makes Pilate involuntarily express a deep truth. For Jesus, his death is the last 'work' of all, the consummation of his whole task: 'It is accomplished' (19.30).

John makes Jesus give one last revelation, in a discourse before a kind of world tribunal, as in Isa. 40ff. In the praetorium of Pilate, the representative of Gentile unbelief, and before the high priests (whom John also has brought before Pilate), the representatives of Jewish unbelief, Jesus is put on trial. As 'king of the Judaeans', Jesus concedes that he is king (18.33–38a), but his royal dignity and his royal appearance are not 'of this world'. Yet he is king, Pilate confirms (18.37). However, Pilate too is 'of this world' and not 'of the truth', and therefore does not understand (18.37f.). He is not 'of God'. After the mockery and the flogging by the soldiers, Pilate wants to set Jesus free, on the one hand because he has seen through the motives of his accusers, and on the other out of a pagan religious fear (19.8, 9–12). 'Here is the man!' (19.5). The accusation is directed against 'these men' (18.29). Pilate himself does not intend any deeper meaning here, but only contempt for the Judaeans: this man, in his ridiculous royal costume, is only a man, without any regal ambitions: their accusation is idiotic. Shortly beforehand he had said, 'Behold, your king' (19.14). The account is shaped in such a way that the high priests (there is no sign of the Jewish *people* throughout this scene before Pilate in the Gospel of John) can only cry out in a most un-Jewish way, 'We have no king but Caesar' (19.15). After AD 70, in the eleventh blessing of the Eighteen Benedictions, the Jews prayed every day: 'Be thou, O God, our king, and thou alone.' Pilate may have not intended any deeper meaning with his *ecce homo*, but John does. For him, this man is the royal

Son of God. The cross, a nadir in the flesh, is for John a high point in the earthly manifestation of what Jesus really is: a king from the sphere of the *pneuma*, not of this world. John 19 has great theological depth.[116] Pilate finds Jesus not guilty of the accusation that he set himself up to be kind of Judaea within the jurisdiction of the procurator Pilate (Jerusalem and its neighbourhood). But he passes the death sentence so as not to lose Caesar's favour (19.12), and does so on the legal ground that Jesus is 'king of the Judaeans' (19.19). In the last resort Jesus *is* king. In the Gospel of John the whole trial is a royal epiphany: an hour of glorification. Now the Judaeans say, 'He has made himself the Son of God' (19.7), and Lev. 24.16 requires the death penalty for that. Having first laid political charges against Jesus, in this new accusation they charge him with a religious misdemeanour. In so doing they betray themselves: their first charge was only an alibi. John's account is markedly ironical: the *Gentile* hesitates to have this king of the Judaeans crucified; he realizes his innocence and detects something numinous in this man; by contrast, the *high priests* (18.35; 19.6; 19.15) call for his crucifixion.

John concludes this royal theme in 19.16b–22. The dying Jesus entrusts his mother, as representative of believing Israel in search of salvation, to the care of the Christian community, 'the disciple whom Jesus loved' (19.26f.; cf. the theme of the 'beloved disciple': 13.23–26; 20.3–10 and the final chapter of the Fourth Gospel: 21.7, 20–23, 24). This disciple is the great, original bearer of the tradition in John's community, on whose testimony and tradition the evangelist relies. He appears explicitly in the Gospel of John for the first time at the Last Supper (13.23–26); presumably he was a Greek-speaking Jew from Jerusalem, from the so-called Stephen group, which soon fled from Jerusalem, probably to Samaria. For the Gospel of John, the beloved disciple is as it were what Paul is for the Deutero-Pauline letters. According to the formula of adoption (declaring someone a brother and a sister, see Ps. 2.7 and Greek Job 17.14: John 19.26f.), the Johannine community is to accept all those who, like Mary, see messianic salvation and trust in Jesus (the miracle at Cana: 2.1–11). This is the abiding task of the Christian community. But Mary also accepts the beloved disciple.[117]

Finally, John shows that 'yielding up the spirit', or the death of Jesus, is a last sacrificial action. He uses an extraordinary term, *paredōken* (19.30b) for this, in contrast to the usual terminology of 'giving up the spirit' or breathing one's last (thus Mark 15.37; Luke 23.46 and, with a similar word, Matt. 27.50). In John this becomes a gift and a sacrifice. Jesus surrenders his life. 'For this reason the Father loves me, because I lay down my life, that I may take it again. No one takes it from me, but I lay it down of my own accord' (10.17f.). John expresses all this in the word *paredōken*: 'He bowed his head and gave up his spirit' (19.30b).

'Shall I not drink the cup which the Father has given me?' (18.11). Therefore the Johannine Jesus also says, 'I thirst' (19.28), namely to drink this cup of the Father, just as elsewhere he says, 'My food is . . . the will of the Father' (4.34). Jesus wants to accomplish his work. He is given a bitter drink (at that time a form of refreshment), but this is to fulfil scripture: Ps. 69.21, where the innocent sufferer is given vinegar to drink in a hateful gesture of scorn: suffering. Then Jesus says, 'It is accomplished' (19.30). The task appointed by the Father is at an end (see 14.31; 17.4).

## III. THE GLORIFICATION OF THE FATHER AND THE SON: RESURRECTION AND THE SENDING OF THE SPIRIT AS AN EASTER GIFT

Literature (in addition to the commentaries on John): J. E. Alsup, *The Post-Resurrection Appearance Stories of the Gospel-Tradition*, Stuttgart 1975; J. Baumbach, 'Gemeinde und Welt im Johannesevangelium', *Kairos* 14, 1972, 121–36; O. Betz, *Der Paraklet. Fürsprecher im häretischen Spätjudentum, im Johannesevangelium und in neugefundenen gnostischen Schriften*, Leiden-Cologne 1963; J. Blank, *Krisis: Untersuchungen zur johanneischen Christologie und Eschatologie*, Freiburg 1964; P. van Boxtel, 'Die präexistente Doxa Jesu im Johannesevangelium', *Bijdr* 34, 1973, 268–81; R. Brown, 'The Paraclete in the Fourth Gospel', *NTS* 13, 1966–67, 113–32; W. H. Cadman, *The Open Heaven. The Revelation of God in the Johannine Sayings of Jesus*, Oxford 1969; G. Caird, 'The Glory of God in the Fourth Gospel: An Exercise in Biblical Semantics', *NTS* 15, 1968–69, 265–77; W. Grossouw, 'La glorification du Christ dans la quatrième Evangile', in *L'Evangile de Jean*, Bruges 1958, 131–45; E. Haenchen, 'Der Vater, der mich gesandt hat', *NTS* 9, 1962–63, 208–16; R. G. Hamerton-Kelly, *Pre-existence, Wisdom and the Son of Man*, Cambridge 1973, 197–242; J. Heise, *Bleiben. 'Menein' in den johanneischen Schriften*, Tübingen 1967; G. Johnston, *The Spirit-Paraclete in the Gospel of John*, Cambridge 1970; E. Käsemann, *The Testament of Jesus*, ET London and Philadelphia 1968; T. C. de Kruyff, 'The Glory of the Only Son (Jn 1,14)', in *Studies in John*, Leiden 1970, 111–23; J. Kuhl, *Die Sendung Jesu und der Kirche nach dem Johannesevangelium*, St Augustin 1967; G. N. Locher, 'Der Geist als Paraklet', *EvTh* 66, 1966, 578ff.; J. P. Miranda, *Der Vater, der mich gesandt hat*, Bern-Frankfurt 1972; J. McPolin, 'Mission in the Gospel', *Irish Theological Quarterly* 36, 1969, 113–22; I. de la Potterie, 'L'exaltation du Fils de l'homme', *Greg* 49, 1968, 460–78; id., 'L'onction du Christ', *NRT* 80, 1950, 225–52; id., 'L'onction du chrétien dans la foi', *Bibl* 40, 1949, 12–69; id., 'Le Paraclet', in I. de la Potterie and S. Lyonnet, *La vie selon l'esprit, condition du chrétien*, Paris, 1965, 85–

105; F. Porsch, *Pneuma und Wort. Ein exegetischer Beitrag zur Pneumatologie des Johannesevangeliums*, Frankfurt 1974; P. Ricca, *Die Eschatologie des vierten Evangeliums*, Zurich 1966; H. Schlier, 'Der H. Geist als Paraklet nach dem Johannesevangelium', *IKZ* 2, 1973, 97–103; J. Schreiner, 'Geistbegabung in der Gemeinde von Qumran', *BZ* 9, 1965, 161–80; W. Thüsing, *Erhöhung und Verherrlichung Jesu im Johannesevangelium*, Münster ²1969; B. Vawter, 'Ezekiel and John', *CBQ* 26, 1964, 451–8.

John speaks of ascending (6.62), of exaltation (8.28; 12.34) and of glorification (12.23; 13.31), without using the theme of a 'heavenly journey'. He simply thinks in terms of the ancient view of the world: God lives above, on the highest level of the universe (see Ps. 29.3, 10; 104.3, etc.). Within this view of the world, *katabasis* and *anabasis*, descent and ascent, are connection with *the revelation of God's doxa*, of God's glory ('God descends' means that he shows his glory: see Ex. 24.16; Ezek. 9.3; 11.23; Isa. 14.13f.). John uses three terms in particular for this return to the Father: (*a*) *hypagein*, ascent to (7.33; 8.14, 21, 22; 13.3, 33, 36; 14.4, 5, 28; 16.5, 10, 17): (*b*) *poreuesthai*, go to (7.35; 14.2, 3, 12, 28; 16.7, 28); (*c*) *anabainein*, ascend (*inter alia* 3.13; 6.62; 20.17). First of all we should note that the synoptic gospels also speak of *hypagein* in connection with the death of Jesus (Matt. 26.24; Mark 14.21), and of *poreuesthai* (Luke 22.22f.); Luke also uses the third term as a word with a double meaning: *anabainein*, go up to Jerusalem, but in order to die there (Luke 18.31). In Luke, too, the disciples do not understand the meaning of this going up (Luke 18.34, as in John 16.16–19). Thus 'go up to' is an ambiguous word: it is a 'riddle'.[118] Only in John 16.29 do the disciples say that they are beginning to understand something of it, namely, 'I came from the Father and have come into the world; *I am leaving the world again* and going to the Father' (16.28). Thus going away includes the death of Jesus, but that does not make the *anabasis* fully comprehensible. We must now look closer at the other aspects of this return.

First of all it must be said that the death of Jesus, his departure, is a *final* farewell to the world and therefore a judgment on the world: the world, and unbelievers, 'will not see me again' (14.19; see 7.34–37), but that is also their death (8.21f.). For 'his own', the disciples, on the other hand, Jesus' death is only a brief parting: 'But you will see me again; because I live, you will live also' (14.19): for them Jesus will come again (14.3, 18, 28; 16.16f.). It is this aspect which finds expression in the final element of the glorification.

After Jesus' death, on their visit to the empty tomb, no one – apart from the 'beloved disciple', who 'saw and believed' (20.8) – not even Mary Magdalene or Peter, thinks of Jesus' resurrection. John explicitly states, 'For as yet they did not know the scripture, that he *must* rise again from the dead' (20.9: *ek nekrōn anastēnai*). Thus throughout, John uses the primitive Christian resurrection terminology, as he already has done elsewhere in connection with Jesus (2.22, *ēgerthē*). The idea of a glorification in the form of once more laying down his human figure is quite alien to John. It is a completely un-Johannine idea that the humanity of Jesus should be only temporary and provisional, even though with the death and resurrection Jesus is no longer ruled by the *sarx*. For John this *sarx* is a temple – 'the tent of meeting' (1.14a): as early as 2.21 he makes Jesus speak of the temple of his body, which the Judaeans will destroy but which Jesus will build up again in three days (2.19f.). This is Jesus' answer to the *sign* required by the Judaeans (2.18); it is no preliminary sign, like all the other signs that the earthly Jesus did, but the event that was prefigured by all these signs: it is what was denoted in all the signs, and in this sense is, '*the* sign'. After inspecting the empty tomb, 'the disciples returned home' (20.10) as though nothing had happened. There is no belief in the resurrection without Easter grace, and an empty tomb is still not an Easter experience. On the other hand, they are not terrified and have no fear because of the empty cave in the rock. On the contrary, in John's account Peter behaves like someone who is making a careful inspection and notices that the linen cloth has been neatly rolled up. John is evidently countering the legend which was going round 'among the Jews' in the years 70–90, that thieves had stolen the body of Jesus. Thieves would certainly not have left the grave clothes so neat and tidy. But this inspection of the tomb does not have more significance for John than that. At the same time, 20.9 shows that John knows the primitive Christian tradition: Jesus had (according to the scriptures) to rise from the dead (the divine 'must' emerges from the scriptures: I Cor. 15.5–8).

The appearance of Jesus to Mary Magdalene, a recognition scene in which Mary recognizes the master as the good shepherd by his voice, calling his own by their name (10.3f.; 19.27), 'Mariam', is significant because John makes the ascent of Jesus to the Father more precise. 'Do not hold me, for I have not yet ascended to the Father' (20.17). Does John, then, make a distinction between 'resurrection' and 'going to the Father'? In his appearance to Mary, is Jesus indeed risen, but not yet ascended, whereas in 20.19, on the same evening, Jesus bestows Easter grace on his disciples which evidently comes from the Father? At this very point it is evident that from a Johannine perspective these are not real problems. For John, 'going to the Father' is a single event: death, resurrection, Easter gift. What else could be the significance of the fact that Jesus is 'risen', but not yet 'glorified', while this is the case that very same evening? In fact, the evangelist is making his thinking more precise. Mary must tell the disciples (not, as in the synoptic gospels, that Jesus is risen, but): 'Go to my brethren and say to them, "I am ascending to my Father and your Father, to my God and your God" ' (20.17b, c). The Johannine Jesus deliberately calls 'his own' *brethren*, and explains the reason why: my Father is now your Father. The Easter gift has already begun. For Jesus departed to prepare a place in 'his Father's house' (14.1–3), and now, through Mary Magdalene, he tells the disciples: 'My Father is now also your Father.' This preparation was the whole purpose of his departure. 'On this day – Easter – you will know that I am in my Father and you in me and I in you' (14.20), and 'We will come to him and take up our abode with him' (14.23b). Jesus is not yet completely 'risen', because he is specifically fulfilling this promise. 'I am not yet risen' (20.17a) and 'I am arising' (20.17b) are in that case spatial conceptions, but are concerned with the one Easter event: resurrection and glorification, as accomplished in the person of Jesus, and the Easter grace, as perfected in the disciples.[119] Easter grace is the gift of the promised Paraclete (14.16f., 26; 15.26f.; 16.7b–11, 13–15), the hearing of prayer (16.23–26), the performing of greater works (14.12), the coming of the Father and the Son (14.21–23) and thus the experience of the great love of God (14.23: see above). 'I am ascending' is an ongoing process, the abiding and ever-new Easter gift of the risen Jesus to his community, the *process* of the sanctification of his followers whom Jesus now already calls 'my brothers'. The double element in the tradition, of 'ascension' and 'exaltation', is given a surprising solution in Johannine christology, i.e. a soteriological one: Jesus is also glorified *in* his disciples (by their Easter experience), just as the Father is glorified in the risen Jesus (see 17.22). For John, 'going to the Father' is Jesus' suffering and death, his glorification in the resurrection and his enthronement with God and the Easter grace of the Spirit to the disciples. The sending of the Spirit is part of the concept of 'going to the Father'. As long as the Spirit has not yet been explicitly given, Jesus is 'still ascending'. It becomes clear from this that John himself is aware that the whole concept of 'ascending' is a model or a conception. Magdalene goes to the disciples and says to them, with the Easter formula which was already being used in the church, 'I have *seen* the Lord' (20.18).[120]

So we may not separate the 'exaltation' at Jesus' death from the exaltation at the resurrection. The whole of Jesus' life is a process of 'being glorified': the cross is the climax of the glorification through the whole earthly life of Jesus and at the same time the beginning of the glorification through the resurrection. John sees the death and resurrection together, after the pattern of the grain of corn which dies *in order* to bear fruit (12.23f.). The fact that Jesus prays for the glorification which he possessed when pre-existent with God (17.5) implies that he does not possess this in his earthly life. But John sees this whole earthly life as a dynamic and progressive process of glorification. Thus the *doxa* or glory of God already appeared in the sign of Cana (2.11) and in the raising of Lazarus (11.40). John does not therefore need any special transfiguration, such as we find in the synoptic gospels (Mark 9.2–10; Matt. 17.1–9; Luke 9.28–36). The life of Jesus is itself a single dynamic event of revelation of the union between Father and Son, an event of glorification in life, death and resurrection. Here the dying and death are not a *precondition*, to be followed by the resurrection in the form of a reward. The 'exaltation on the cross' (*hypsothēsetai*, 12.34) is not the same thing as the 'glorification' (*doxasthēsetai*, 12.23), but at the same the two are not to be separated. For John, in fact, death itself already has an effect which elsewhere in the New Testament is ascribed to the resurrection, but it remains a view of death in the light of the resurrection and nevertheless, from there, in the light of pre-existence. For John, glorification is the revelation of the unity of love between Father and Son. This can be seen most clearly in the cross: in the Father, who has given his Son for us (3.16), and in the Son, who in his death has shown his obedience to the Father (17.4; 10.30; 14.20; 17.1ff.).

On the evening of the same day – Easter day (as we are to conclude from the subsequent happening) – Jesus appears to his disciples (20.19–23). The anxious disciples, hidden behind bolted doors for fear of 'the Judaeans', are suddenly filled with joy, when Jesus stands in their midst and wishes them the Easter joy (20.20f.) which they have been promised (14.27). Jesus shows his hands and his pierced side. John means to say: the crucified one is the risen one (20.20b). The risen Jesus then sends forth his disciples and for this gives them the Holy Spirit. 'As my Father has sent me, even so I send you. And when he had said this, he breathed on them, and said to them, "Receive (the) Holy Spirit" ' (20.21, 22; see Wisd. 15.11 and above all Gen. 2.7). The allusion to 'breathing in the spirit of life' is stressed, because John omits the article: 'Holy Spirit'; receive the new breath of life from above; as a result of this the disciples are caught up into a spiritual, heavenly sphere of life: they are 'from God' (see 1.13), 'children of God' (1.12; see 3.5–9). For the disciples, Jesus' going to the Father means that they are sent to be in the world, for which they are equipped with the Holy Spirit. In other words, resurrection is completed in the sending of the spirit and is indissolubly bound up with it. All the appearances of the risen Jesus in the synoptic gospels are also bound up with the sending of the disciples into the world (Mark 16.15; Luke 24.47; Matt. 28.19f.). John had alluded to a sending earlier (13.20: especially in Jesus' farewell prayer, 17.18), and above all to the sending of the Spirit: 'Streams of living water will flow from his heart.' By this he meant the Spirit which would be received by those who believed in him, 'for there was not yet "Spirit", because Jesus was not yet glorified' (7.39). The Christian community, which is not 'of this world', is sent by Christ into the world. In this passage John calls this sending with the help of the Spirit primarily a sending of reconciliation: 'If you forgive the sins of any, they are forgiven; if you retain the sins of any, they are retained' (20.23). In associating Spirit and the forgiveness of sins John is following a theme from the Old Testament and early Judaism (Ezek. 36.25–27), but above all an early Christian tradition: baptism is the forgiveness of sins and the gift of the Spirit (see I Cor. 6.11; Acts 2.38; 22.16; Heb. 10.22). John's bond with tradition is clear from the fact that elsewhere in his gospel he virtually never speaks of the forgiveness of sins (only 1.29; 8.24; see 8.34; 9.34). But Christian baptism was also bound up with 'baptism in the Spirit' (Mark 1.8; Acts 1.5; 2.38; 11.16). This tradition is clearly set against the same background as John 3.5f. and 20.21–23. John the Baptist had said of Jesus, 'the Lamb of God who takes away the sins of the world' (1.29): 'He will baptize with Holy Spirit' (1.33: here too there is no article). 'If anyone is not born of *water* and *spirit*, he cannot enter the kingdom of God' (3.5): 'What is born of the flesh is flesh, and what is born of the Spirit is spirit' (3.6). This birth from the Spirit is the Easter event of the disciples. It is the virgin birth, the birth from the Spirit, of which the prologue has already spoken (1.13). Thus a man's *being* is determined by his *origin*. For these disciples Easter is baptism with the Holy Spirit through the Lamb which takes away the sins of the world; but they themselves are further sent to continue this service of reconciliation elsewhere in the world.[121]

Although John only connects the gift of the Spirit here with the forgiveness of sins, we must also remember the promise of the Spirit which is repeated five times (14.16f., 26; 15.26f.; 16.7b–11, 13–15). In these texts he is called *paraklētos*, 'helper', above all the advocate at a trial, and therefore also intercessor; in a religious context, intercessor with God. In the first text in which he speaks of the Paraclete, Jesus says that he will send 'another Paraclete' (14.16f.). This means that Jesus, too, was a Paraclete during his earthly life, a good shepherd (by contrast, I John 2.1 calls the *heavenly* Christ a Paraclete, alongside the Spirit). But this Paraclete is 'the Spirit of truth' (14.16f.), 'the Holy Spirit' (14.26), so that the content and the functions of the Spirit are transferred to the term 'Paraclete'. In the Gospel of John, what is the function of the Spirit in the Christian community, and, perhaps, towards the world?

In 14.16f. it is simply said that the Spirit is an Easter gift (see also 7.39); sent (in 15.26; 16.7) by the Father at the request of Jesus (14.16). Jesus sends it, but because of the Father (15.26). Here the Paraclete is called 'the Spirit of truth'. As has already been said, in Johannine theology 'truth' has the meaning of *revealed* wisdom: 'from above' (14.17b; see 7.16f., 28; 8.28). 'To be of God' (8.47) and 'to be of the Spirit' (18.37) are synonyms (14.17b): this Spirit giving insight into revelation 'remains with you and will be in you' (14.17b). I John makes this more specific: the Spirit which bears witness to the truth (I John 5.7) and preserves the community from untruth and lies (I John 4.6). Thus the Spirit leads the church into truth (John 16.13; this too is a feature of Sinaitic theology).[122] His task is to 'teach' and 'call to remembrance' (14.26), that is, after the departure of Jesus the Spirit calls to remembrance for the disciples all that Jesus has said and done; it recalls Jesus' revelation of himself (16.13–15). He leads them 'into all truth', as is said later (16.12f.), in contrast to mere 'remembrance' (14.25f.). For Jesus had said, 'I have still many things to say to you, but you cannot bear them now' (16.12). Thus John suggests, not only that the community, directed by the Spirit, is a community which interprets the revelation of Jesus, but also that the Spirit 'leads them into all truth'. The community is as it were the *continuation* of the revelation of God in Jesus; it is always there as a reference to the one Jesus: 'He will take *what is mine* and declare it to you, because all that the Father has is mine' (16.14f.). Thus what God himself will do with the Spirit has to do with Christ himself. In this sense, *new* revelations of the Spirit are impossible. But it cannot be denied that John also recognizes *initiatives* of the Holy Spirit; he leads 'into all truth', 'whatever he hears he will speak, and he will declare to you the things that are to come' (16.13). In other words, the Christian community is bound by the Spirit to Jesus of Nazareth, the Christ. The Spirit is the guiding principle of the church's tradition. He confirms and completes the revelation of Jesus. It bears witness to Jesus (15.26). I John 5.7 therefore calls it 'the Spirit which bears witness', whereas he convicts 'the world' of its injustice, and thus of the justice of Jesus (John 15.26; 16.8–11). The Spirit provides the connection between the self-revelation of Jesus and the 'teaching' of Jesus in a world which cannot understand the Spirit or 'the truth'. The Spirit is the interpreter of Jesus' revelation of God: 'You will *understand* later' (then you will 'know', 14.20). Just as the sending of the Spirit has an intrinsic connection with the sending of the disciples into the world (20.21f.), so too Jesus had promised: 'When the Paraclete comes, which I shall send you from the Father – he will bear witness of me.' But 'you too must bear witness' (15.26f.); *through the church* the Spirit speaks to the world. For John the Spirit is only in the church, and is only effective in the world through the church. The Gospel of John does not know of any direct activity of the Spirit in the world; the Spirit merely convicts the world of its injustice, but does that through the community (also through the Gospel of John).

In this connection, I John speaks of *chrisma*, which has the same function as the Spirit in the Fourth Gospel (I John 2.20, 27). John, too, had said that a man's origin was the deepest determination of his being (John 3.5f.). For I John the *pneuma* is a heavenly, pneumatic principle, bestowed 'at' baptism, through which man is born again as a child of God (I John 3.1; 3.24; 4.13); John 20.17 speaks of 'brothers of Jesus'. For Johannine theology, the Easter gift of the Spirit is most profoundly the gift of a divine principle of life through which a person is born as a child of God – a divine gift of life. Now 'to be born of God' is at the same time 'to be of God' (I John 3.9f.; see 4.4; cf. 5.4). 'This is the proof that we remain in him (God) (as he remains in us), that he has given us *of* his Spirit' (I John 4.13), that is, that he has given us a share in his Spirit. Therefore the Spirit is the Christian principle of life (see the 'life-giving Spirit', John 6.63). Hence I John dares to speak of *to sperma to Theou* (I John 3.9), 'a divine seed of life'. Those who are reborn by virtue of this not only have all their sins forgiven; the spiritual man or the 'child of God' no longer sins: 'He cannot sin, since he is born of God' (I John 3.9, which goes on to warn against drawing false conclusions from this). In this connection, I John speaks of *chrisma* or being anointed with the Holy Spirit: 'But you have been anointed by the Holy One, and you all know' (I John 2.20); here too the function of the Spirit is to 'teach': 'The chrism which you have received from him abides in you; you need no other teacher. His anointing instructs you in all things' (I John 2.27). It is also a characteristic feature that one can recognize whether anyone possesses the 'Spirit of God' (I John 4.2) by the correct, orthodox confession of Christ: 'Every spirit which confesses that Jesus Christ has come in the flesh is of God' (I John 4.2b). Thus I John brings up to date the Johannine doctrine of the Spirit in the specific situation of the community in which false teachings had arisen: these men are filled 'with other spirits' (see I John 4.1). Through the inner instruction of the Holy Spirit people evidently feel that they are directed in all things and filled with the Easter grace of the Holy Spirit, which was connected with the grace of baptism (John 3.5f.). Furthermore, one can claim that the Johannine church used the early Syrian form of baptism. Here baptism is preceded by an anointing which communicates the Holy Spirit; this is then followed by baptism with water and then the eucharist: I John speaks of 'Spirit, water and blood' (I John 5.8) in that sequence: pre-baptismal anointing, baptism and eucharist.[123] The Spirit is bestowed before baptism; the purpose of this is that the Spirit makes the word heard by the catechumens into a perfect act of faith: the understanding of what they have heard. This is Johannine (but see also Acts 10.44; cf. with Titus 3.5; I Peter 1.23; James 1.18). Baptism is bestowed on people *who are already believers*. Thus fellowship with the Father and the Son is bestowed on those who already believe (14.23). The risen Jesus, too, shows himself only to believers, and not to 'the world' or to unbelievers (14.19). (All this would then point to a shift in the earliest Johannine tradition: Greek Jews in *Jerusalem* going by way of *Samaria* and its environs to *Syria*. For some scholars the movement goes from Syria *either* to Asia Minor *or* to Alexandria in Egypt. In my view, neither of these two hypotheses can be proved. Moreover, the question is whether this early Syrian baptismal model was not the original *Palestinian* model of baptism.)

Therefore in Johannine theology the Spirit is Easter and baptismal grace, which is connected with the nature of being a Christian – the principle of fellowship with God in Christ. That means that it is connected with the historical revelation of God in Jesus, with which the Spirit guarantees continuity, and finally is connected with the eschaton. The question remains, however – for those interested in the history of religion – why, John identified the Paraclete and the *pneuma*. According to G. Johnston,[124] there is a double concept of the Paraclete in the Gospel of John. On the one hand there is a polemical usage against early Jewish speculations about an angel Paraclete, an advocate with God. In Qumran, this angle, this Paraclete, is called the 'Spirit of truth', and the angel Michael is identified with the patron of Israel. To stress the exclusive significance of Jesus for salvation, John is said to have called the Holy Spirit, the Easter gift of Jesus, the *Paraclete*, who is completely independent of Jesus. On the other hand, John is said to have identified the active power which is present in certain prominent members of the community with the Spirit of God. By combination of these two, the spirit of Christ becomes that which is present and effective in the teachers of the church, and which is meant to guarantee continuity with the faithfulness to the original revelation of Jesus. According to R. Brown,[125] John gives the Holy Spirit the name 'Paraclete' only in one particular respect; in so far as the Spirit must guarantee the presence of Christ to and in the Christians in the time after Easter, the Spirit is called 'Paraclete' (Brown assumes – wrongly – that John 14.17–23 speaks only of a coming of Jesus *in* the Spirit and not of a coming of the Spirit *and* of Jesus). He bases this on the fact that everything that is said in the Gospel of John about the Paraclete is also said of Jesus in other passages in this gospel. The term Paraclete became necessary to bridge the gap between Jesus and the church which was opened up after the death of the eyewitnesses. The twofold theme of Moses-Joshua and Elijah-Elisha plays a part here, as typifying a successor-relationship, namely Jesus and the Holy Spirit: the one dies, and his 'prophetic spirit' passes over to his successor (see Deut. 34.9; II Kings 2.9, 15).[126] I. de la Potterie[127] calls it a theological identification. Thus John is said to want to distinguish the two phases of salvation history: on the one hand the earthly work of Jesus, and on the other the time of the life of the church in which the Spirit is at work as the spirit of Christ. R. Schnackenburg[128] does not deny a variety of other influences; however, he sees the content of the term in reality as being already provided by the early Palestinian Christian community (both in the Markan tradition, Mark 13.11, to be compared with John 15.26f., and also in the Q tradition: Luke 12.11f., par. Matt. 10.20; see also Luke 21.14f.). Bruce Vawter[129] makes the interesting observation that the Johannine Paraclete is dependent on Ezekiel; the term has a double function: on the one hand the '*prophetic* witness' of Jesus (see John 15.26f.; 16.8–11), and on the other the '*priestly* function' of an intercessor with God (15.26). (However, is not this to argue too much in terms of Hebrews? Nevertheless, it cannot be denied that Revelation, too, knows the heavenly Christ as high priest; see below.) Other authors[130] assume that for John the term Paraclete is a means of giving a christological interpretation of the *pneuma*, the Spirit of God, thus making it completely 'dependent' on Jesus. Finally, among exegetes there is a particular tendency to regard the term 'Paraclete' as an attempt by John to *Christianize* the *general* concept of *pneuma*. The Paraclete is said to be a christological interpretation of the *pneuma* in order to provide a continuous link between the historical revelation of Jesus and the contemporary hermeneutical situation of the Johannine community. But why did John need the concept of the '*Paraclete*' for that? He could just as easily have Christianized the *pneuma* directly, as happens in Pauline theology and elsewhere in the New Testament. So other factors must have been at work here. At all events, the 'Spirit of truth' (a favourite expression of John's: 14.17; 15.26; 16.13) is also a frequent term in Qumran (QM 4.23f.). That means that 'the Spirit of truth' was a common formula in certain circles of early Judaism. As Spirit of truth, the Paraclete here had above all a legal significance: advocate.[131] Such intercessor figures play an important role in Qumran.[132] Early Judaism used the term Paraclete as an adviser and advocate of the innocent sufferer in a world in which the good above all had to suffer and evil seemed to triumph (a 'dualism' which is not alien to Johannine theology). I therefore believe that we can hardly avoid seeing the early Jewish Paraclete figure Michael as the model which John had in mind when speaking about the 'Spirit of truth' as the Paraclete (and therefore not in *literary* dependence on Qumran). I do not see any gnostic influence on John, but a so-called 'heterodox' early Christian influence. Therefore in my view the work of G. Johnston must be taken more seriously. In the analysis of the Letter to the Hebrews I pointed out that the author of this homily lays great emphasis on the fact that it was *not an angel* but *the man* Jesus, the Son, who was put at the right hand of God. There was unmistakably some resistance in early Christian circles to a kind of angel christology. Furthermore, the Greek word *paraklētos* was so widespread throughout the Hellenistic world, and even in early Palestinian Judaism, that Hebrew simply used the Greek loan word (*p'raklīṭā*, alongside the Hebrew *mēliṣ*). The angelic mediator and intercessor already appears to be a common concept from the book of Job. On the basis of his christol-

ogy, John therefore also seems to oppose the concept of an 'angel-para-
clete', a spiritual leader of the Christian community, as Michael was a
spiritual leader of Israel. However, we must agree with the point made
by R. Brown, G. Johnston and O. Betz that the Johannine concept of the
'Paraclete' was on the one hand provided by early Jewish angelology and
on the other hand is used polemically by John (or is the result of an
earlier problem which had already been solved in the Johannine community before the gospel was written). The hypothesis of 'gnosticism'
seems to me to be quite superfluous.

The five Johannine texts about the *pneuma* convey the way in which
the Johannine church and therefore also the Fourth Gospel understood
their position: it is a well-thought-out and *thematic updating* of the message
of Jesus *for the church.* John sees the authority for this in the Easter gift of
the Spirit, which leads the church into all truth. The Gospel of John is
aware of the development of tradition or dogma which is brought about
by the Johannine community itself. And with an appeal to Jesus, John
asks for official recognition of this view of Jesus himself (John 21): Peter
must acknowledge the particular destiny of the 'beloved disciple'
(21.21f.). Johannine theology rewrites the traditional apostolic faith by
bringing it up to date in terms of the community within which it is set.
John does not speak on his own authority; in speaking *of* Jesus, the Holy
Spirit does not speak 'of itself': 'He will proclaim to you what he has
received from me' (16.15). In this awareness John *ventures* to write a
Gospel *of his own,* though the earlier tradition about Jesus continues to
influence it (albeit in a new interpretation). From this perspective of
John's updating of Jesus' message about the kingdom of God in terms of
the Spirit, we can understand the closing words of the Fourth Gospel.
'But there are also many other things which Jesus did; were every one of
them to be written, I suppose that the world itself could not contain the
books that would be written' (21.25). For in the spirit of Johannine
theology every community throughout the world has to write its own
history of the living Jesus. In all these histories Johannine theology is *one*
view of Jesus alongside those of Pauline theology and the synoptic gospels.
The mainstream church has recognized it as a legitimate conception;
John 21 fights for this conception.

This account may have made it clear that John presents a very much
updated eschatology, made personal in the figure of the glorified Jesus,
who 'dwells' with the Father and the Spirit in the Christian community.
The believer already *possesses* eternal life. Judgment and eternal life have
begun with the death of Jesus, seen as a departure to the Father. Death
is already the beginning of glorification – not really in and of itself (not
even for John) but as *an element in* the ascent to God. John does not do
away with the disconcerting reality of death, but this death is undergone

by the pre-existent Son. Thus death itself can hardly be separated from the resurrection. For John the resurrection (20.9) – which the world cannot see – is the other side of the death of Jesus. But in that case resurrection means that it is also as man that Jesus wins back his pre-existent glory (17.5). What he lays aside is not his humanity, but the transitoriness of the *sarx*. In this sense there is a radical difference from contemporary conceptions of heavenly beings (e.g. an angel like Raphael in the book of Tobit), which assume the 'form of a man' and discard it completely on their return to heaven. Were that John's view we would have to do away with the whole of John 20. The Johannine Jesus shows his hands and his pierced side (20.20), not to combat docetism, but to stress the identity between the historical Jesus and the heavenly Christ.

However, for John, *'eternal life' does not coincide with the resurrection* as it does for Paul. Eternal life has already begun now, but for that reason, thanks to their sharing of the life of God in Christ, death cannot harm Christians any longer: death is a matter of going to the Father. I cannot see any compelling reasons for attributing the outstanding, futurist aspect in the Gospel of John (which can be found there, despite the personalized, and therefore updated, eschatology) to the intervention of a later censor on behalf of the church, despite the fact that there are also obvious tensions between tradition and redaction in the canonical gospel. Experience of the eschatological 'now' is predominant in the Johannine community, to such a degree that a reaction against a kind of anticipatory vision of God clearly derives from the evangelist himself (1.18; 5.37; 6.46; 14.8). Although he himself is in a Sinaitic tradition, John can moderate it, though at the same time the 'heavenly dwellings' which Jesus went to prepare (14.1–4) are 'inhabited' from Easter onwards by Christians, since 'we shall come to them (namely at Easter) and take our abode (*monē; menein*) with them' (14.23). The mutuality of love – I in you, you in me and finally I-in-you-in-me – abolishes the spatial categories of descent and ascent. However, even *this* heavenly life of Christians on earth still has a future. John, too, knows of a future for the dead. 'For the hour is coming when all who are in the tombs will hear his voice and come forth' (John 5.28). John distinguishes between 'that day' (above all 14.20), i.e. Easter, and 'the resurrection on the last day' (6.39b). The distinction is made quite explicitly: 'He who eats my flesh and drinks my blood has eternal life, and I will raise him up at the last day' (6.54; though *this* occurs in a so-called doublet, in which what has already been said is now developed in a 'sacramental' way; see also 12.48); however, the evangelist himself makes the same distinction in 6.40. John *christologizes* universal eschatology, but he does not de-eschatologize the Christian eschaton. The 'now already' and the 'not yet' are preserved, but in a community which lives in the present of the Easter grace. The tension is reproduced in what is clearly an authentic Johannine text: 'I am the resurrection and the life; he who believes in me, *though he die*, yet shall he live, and whoever lives and believes in me *shall never die*' (11.25). It is at this very point that we find the Johannine paradox of the eternal life of the Christian which has already begun; since Easter he is 'from God' (like Jesus), and nevertheless still knows that he is to be raised at the last day – a grain of wheat, like Jesus!

## §4 The person of Jesus in Johannine theology: the Son

For John, Jesus is a gift of the Father: the true bread for all men (6.32). God sends his Son (3.16), the unique, most precious possession of the Father (1.14, 18; 3.16, 18; I John 4.9). Consequently John often speaks of 'the Son' in the absolute sense (3.16, 17, 35, 36ab; 5.19b, c, 20, 21, 22, 23ab, 26; 6.40; 8.35f.; 14.13; 17.1; and the disputed text 1.18); sometimes he speaks of 'the Son *of God*' (3.18; 5.25; 10.36; 11.4; and in the confessions: 1.34; 1.49; 11.27; 20.31); also 'the Father and the Son' (5; 3.35; 6.40; 14.13). It is the exception to find this absolute usage in the New Testament outside John (Matt. 11.27 = Luke 10.22; Mark 13.32 par. Matt. 24.36; Matt. 28.19; also I Cor. 15.28; Heb. 1.2, 8; 3.6; 5.8; 7.28). In the history of the tradition the predicate 'Son of God' is originally clearly associated with the exaltation/resurrection of Jesus (Rom. 1.3f.; cf. the messianic titles in Acts 2.36; 4.25f.; 5.30f.; 13.23), only later is it connected with the baptism of Jesus in the Jordan (Mark 1.11; Matt. 3.16f.; Luke 3.21f.; John 1.34). After that the predicate is applied to the pre-existent Jesus (Gal. 4.4; Rom. 8.3; I Cor. 2.7; 8.6; Phil. 2.6ff.; Gospel of John) and at a still later stage to his conception and birth (Matthew and the Lucan infancy narratives). The confession of the community that Jesus is the Son of God then also becomes a baptismal confession (see Acts 8.37, the so-called Western text; Heb. 4.14; cf. Col. 1.12f.). Therefore, just as Jesus originally appears as the Son of God in connection with his baptism, Christians also appear as 'sons of God' in connection with Christian baptism (Gal. 3.26f.; 4.6; Rom. 8.14f. with I Cor. 12.13).

Even in the pre-Pauline passage Rom. 1.3f., we have testimony that Jesus was descended from David according to his human origins, but had been appointed Son of God by virtue of his resurrection and after it. Here the resurrection is seen as God's confirmation of what was said in the first clause, namely of the status of Jesus as Davidic Messiah. In early Judaism it is extremely uncertain whether the Messiah was in fact even called 'Son of God'. In that case, how did early Christianity come to call Jesus Son of God?

First of all is the fact that Jesus himself addressed God as Abba in prayer. As in the synoptic gospels (above all Mark 14.36), so too in John Jesus addresses God as Abba, 'Father', *in prayer* (John 11.41f.; 12.27f.; 17). It is historically certain that God as Father completely filled Jesus' consciousness.[133] Granted, we have no clear information about this in the New Testament, but from the firm fact that Jesus was so strongly aware of God as Father we can understand how, in a similar way, he also felt himself to be *Son* of this Father. For the one amounts to the other. Therefore the Christian confession has a basis *in* the self-awareness of Jesus himself before Easter – we find this expressed also in a Q saying: 'All things have been delivered to me by my Father, and no one knows the Father except the Son and any one to whom the Son chooses to reveal him' (Matt. 11.27 = Luke 10.22; cf. John 10.15, though here we can hardly talk of a direct dependence on John). This is an early Jewish idea, from the wisdom tradition. This Q tradition indicates that the *Son-christology* was a very early stage in the Christian interpretation of Jesus and was not an invention of Johannine theology. Both the Q tradition and the Gospel of John point to a *Palestinian* tradition, probably above all of a wisdom character, though other lines of tradition also come together here, above all apocalyptic speculation about the Son (see below). In reality, the Q saying makes Jesus' self-awareness explicit in connection with his experience of God as Abba. Other New Testament sayings point in the same direction: Jesus is 'the beloved' (Mark 1.11; 9.7; 12.6 par.), 'the only' (John 1.14, 18; 3.16, 18; I John 4.9), 'the firstborn Son' (Rom. 8.29; Col. 1.15, 18; Heb. 1.6).

Then there is the argument from scripture. In the last resort Jesus was condemned to death by Pilate under the title 'king of the Judaeans'. That, too, is a historical fact. The event of the resurrection, already attested in I Cor. 15.3ff., was seen by the Christians as God's confirmation of Jesus' messianic claim. But it was here that the Jews found their great stumbling block: a crucified man, accursed because he had been nailed to a cross, was said to have been confirmed by God! That is why Christians were concerned to find proofs in scripture which showed that according to God's purpose the Messiah had to suffer, and on the other hand that the same scriptures make a connection between resurrection and sonship of God (II Sam. 7.12–14). This particular text from II Samuel underlies a variety of New Testament expressions: Rom. 1.3f.;[134] Luke 1.32f.; Heb. 1.5; Acts 13.33f., all texts which go back to earlier traditions. Furthermore, above all in Acts 13.33f. and Heb. 1.5 the scriptural proof from II Samuel was combined with that from Ps. 2.7. And Ps. 2 and Ps. 89 demonstrate a close connection between *Messiah* and *Son of God*. Luke virtually calls the 'sons of the resurrection' 'sons of God' (Luke 20.36): 'They cannot die any longer' (20.36a).

Above all there is the continuation of the wisdom tradition. In the book of Wisdom, the 'son of God' is described as the one who has 'eternal life' (Wisdom 2.23; 6.19; 1.15; 3.4; 4.1; 8.13; 17; 15.3). At the same time this brings the servant of God from Deutero–Isaiah into a wisdom context (Wisdom 2.13).[135] Because eternal life is promised to them, martyrs too are called 'sons of God' (II Macc. 7.34). One might think of the passage already quoted earlier: 'Who has ascended to heaven and come down? . . . What is his son's name?' (Prov. 30.4). It is said of the son of God, Jesus Christ, that his resurrection *manifests* or makes manifest that he is and already was the Son of God (Rom. 1.4). So it is also in the book of Wisdom: the exaltation of the wise and righteous by God demonstrates that he already was the 'son of God' when others were despising him and rejecting him. Because this is what he was, it could be made manifest at his exaltation: his hidden identity is then revealed. The significance of the New Testament *appearances* also becomes clear in this connection: it then becomes evident to believers that Jesus in fact was and is the Son of God and that he has eternal life. The 'Son of God' is revealed here as the living one (see Gal. 1.12, 16; Acts 9.3ff.). This is a recognition of the sonship of God which does not come 'from men' (Gal. 1.1, 16; Matt. 16.16–18) but is a revealed (Gal. 1.16; Matt. 16.17) knowledge of the sonship of Jesus (Gal. 1.16; Matt. 16.16). The theme in Wisdom 2–5, the synoptic gospels and Paul (Gal. 1.12–16) can clearly be recognized: the Son of God is first hidden, and to begin with his real identity is not known; it is, however, seen in his exaltation or resurrection. The Gospel of John, too, begins from this apocalypse or revelation at the resurrection of Jesus, but it intertwines the perspectives from before and after Easter: despite misunderstandings, even before Easter the disciples recognize the Son of God in the historical Jesus and the Jews do not. Like the law (Isa. 51.4–6), like Moses (Sir. 24.27), like the prophet (Isa. 42.6, 7, 16; 49.5f., 8f.), *Jesus*, as Son of God, is 'the light of the world' (Luke 2.32; Gospel of John). Thus quite apart from Jesus' own understanding of himself based on his experience of God as Abba, there were also a number of starting points in Old Testament and early Jewish traditions which suggested that the Messiah Jesus might properly be called 'Son of God'.

Finally, there is also the apocalyptic tradition, which has itself influenced the Son-christology. However, so far as I know, the *title* 'Son' does not occur anywhere in apocalyptic literature as an expression for the eschatological bringer of salvation; in later apocalyptic the term Son of man has become fused with the terms Messiah and Son of God, above all in I Enoch 48.10.[136] At the time of Jesus the term Son of man was current chiefly in unofficial, so-called 'heterodox' Judaism. There is also mention in the Odes of Solomon of a descending and ascending redeemer figure, most often called Logos (12.16, 29, 37, 41), Son of God (36, 41,

42) or Son of man (36, 41). Furthermore, the absolute usage of 'the Father' and 'the Son' can also be found here (Odes 3.7; 7.7, 12, 15; 19.2; 23.18, 22; 31.4, etc.). True, these Odes have been influenced by Christianity (though in all probability this is not yet Johannine Christianity), but they are evidence of the complex of terms Son, wisdom, Logos and man or Son of man in Palestinian Hellenistic Judaism.[137] In these circles the Son of man is a being who comes down from heaven. The Son of man also plays a role in the Stephen group (Acts 7.56). I have already pointed out that in early Judaism, partly under Greek influence, people expressed God's transcendence by giving him many different names. This multiplicity of names expressed someone's uniqueness. The awareness grew, above all in the group around Stephen, that in Jesus God's final revelation of salvation had taken place and that the revelation of salvation surpassed the wisdom in the Torah. However, this Torah and the wisdom of God which speaks of it had already been regarded as pre-existent. Jesus' superiority to the revelation of salvation in the Law thus almost automatically implied the notion of pre-existence,[138] in the sense of existing before all creation, and finally also in the sense of being mediator at creation – designations which had earlier been applied to the revelation of wisdom in the Law. By taking over these predicates, Christians had demonstrated that for them *Jesus* was the eschatological, i.e. the full and final, revelation of God's salvation. This is also the fundamental purpose of the whole of the Gospel of John. Paul had already said the same thing: 'Through him you are in Christ Jesus, who has become *our whole wisdom from God, our righteousness, sanctification and redemption*' (I Cor. 1.30). For John, Jesus himself is the gospel, the message, 'the word'. For John, the kingdom of God which Jesus preached is *Jesus himself*: in the gift of Jesus of Nazareth, the one and only Son, God's love has offered God's salvation once and for all to all men, a salvation which does not come from the world but *from God* in and through the man Jesus, who identifies himself with the saving will of the Father and at the same time identifies himself with the men whose burdens and sins he bears: the Lamb of God. As Son of God, this 'saving being', Jesus, has his origin in God: Jesus is God's own initiative which is not dependent on any human striving. In his *sarx* or human constitution he has shown us who God is for us and what man must mean for God. That is John's message, expressed in the key concepts of Palestinian heterodox Judaism. The unseen – the unattainable God – came visibly near in Jesus. Behind Jesus of Nazareth there stands a divine purpose and a divine plan which have to do with God's own purposes at creation. The nucleus of Johannine theology is that Jesus is not simply a chance, historical religious phenomenon which can in fact inspire man, but the historical embodiment of a quite deliberate purpose of God, the Creator and our salvation. Jesus is 'the re-

deemer of the world' (John 4.42; I John 4.14). Therefore he can only be understood in *terms of* God (6.46; 7.29; 9.33; 16.27f.; 17.8) or the spiritual world (4.24; 3.6). A more fundamental initiative is at work *in* the free initiative of this man Jesus, that of the Father. Jesus is *sent* (3.17, 34; 4.34; 5.23, 24, 30, 36, 37; 6.29, 38, 39, 57; 7.16, 18, 29; 8.16, 18, 26, 29, 42; 9.4; 10.36; 11.42; 12.44, 45, 49; 13.20; 14.24; 15.21; 16.5; 17.3, 8, 18, 21, 23, 25; 20.21). That is why the Johannine Jesus repeatedly says: I do nothing of my own accord (5.30), and cannot do so (5.19); I do the works of the Father (3.35b; 5.20b, 23, 36; 14.10); I say and do what I have seen and heard with the Father (8.28, 38, 40; 12.50; 15.15; see 5.20; 3.11). I do only the will of the Father (4.34; 8.29; 10.18; 12.49f.; 14.31). The Father grants that Jesus may be what he really is, 'his name' (17.11, 12). He gives Jesus his own *doxa* or glory (17.22, 24). He puts his own words in Jesus' mouth (17.8); he gives him everything (4.34; 13.3). Above all, he grants that Jesus can have 'life of himself' (5.26), fullness of life that can be communicated to others. The Father also gives Jesus those who believe on him (6.37, 39; 10.29; 17.2, 6, 9; 18.9). In other words: God gives his Son (3.16). He gives himself in Jesus as salvation for the world. In this generous saving initiative the action of the Father and the action of Jesus coincide: the Father is with Jesus (8.29; 16.30); although the Father is greater (14.28), they are one (10.30; 17.11, 22) in a mutual immanent love (10.38; 14.10, 11, 20; 17.21, 23). Jesus is at one with and dependent upon the Father, *ho Theos*.

From all this it becomes clear that John puts forward a *functional* christology, but not in the modern sense of this word. John's preference for *verbs* over nouns is very striking. He sees the relationship between Jesus and God in functional terms, as emerges clearly from the arguments put forward by the Johannine Jesus (10.34–38). For John, Jesus is really man, but in a unique, all-surpassing relationship with God. Anyone who knows him, knows the Father (8.19), and anyone who sees him sees the Father (14.9). What Jesus says and does reveals his person,[139] that is, the mystery of his unity of life with the Father. In this sense the function *is his person itself*. The Father and Jesus are *two persons*, one in love and will and work: Jesus reveals God, the Father, by revealing himself. Even Johannine theology does not make this duality precise in the unity of the Father and the man Jesus (1.14; 1.30; 4.29; 8.40; 9.11, 16; 10.33) who is the Son. In this unity of two intimately connected persons, even for John the Father remains 'the greater' (14.28): the Father is the goal of Jesus' career (13.1; 14.12, 28; 16.10, 27f.; 17.11, 13; 20.17). In Jesus, God himself has come to us. In this person, this life, death and resurrection, God has revealed himself as a God of men: 'God is love' (I John 4.8, 16). 'He who does good is of God; he who does evil has never seen God' (III John 11b).

It emerges from all this that the alternative of christology either 'from below' or 'from above' is a spurious modern dilemma; that is the reason why I have never wanted to take over this terminology myself, either in this book or in my earlier book on Jesus.

Chapter 6

# Christ, the witness of God-is-righteous: the Apocalypse

*Literature:* H. Bietenhard, *Das Tausendjährige Reich. Eine biblisch-theologische Studie,* Zurich [2]1955; O. Böcher, *Die Johannesapokalypse,* Darmstadt 1975; J. Bonsirven, *L'apocalypse de saint Jean,* Paris 1951; C. Brutsch, *La clarté de l'Apocalypse,* Geneva [5]1966; L. Cerfaux and J. Cambier, *L'Apocalypse de saint Jean lue aux chrétiens,* Lectio Divina 17, Paris 1955; J. Comblin, *Le Christ dans l'apocalypse,* Bibl. de Theol. III.6, Tournai-Paris, 1965; O. Cullmann, *The Christology of the New Testament,* Philadelphia and London [2]1963; A. Feuillet, *L'apocalypse. Etat de la question,* Studia Neotestamentica 3, Paris-Brussels 1963; A. Gelin, *L'Apocalypse,* Paris 1938; T. F. Glasson, *The Revelation of John,* Cambridge 1965; T. Holtz, *Die Christologie der Apokalypse des Johannes,* TU 85, Berlin 1962, [2]1970; M. Kiddle, *The Revelation of Saint John,* London and New York 1940; H. Kraft, *Die Offenbarung des Johannes,* HNT 16a, Tübingen 1974; E. Lohmeyer, *Die Offenbarung des Johannes,* HNT 16, Tübingen [3]1970; E. Lohse, *Die Offenbarung des Johannes,* NTD 11, Göttingen [2]1966; U. Müller, *Messias und Menschensohn in jüdischen Apokalypsen und in der Offenbarung des Johannes,* StNT 6, Gütersloh 1972; H. H. Rowley, *The Relevance of Apocalyptic,* London 1944, [3]1963; A. P. van Schaik, *De Openbaring van Johannes,* Roermond 1976; A. Visser, *De openbaring van Johannes,* Nijkerk 1965; P. Volz, *Die Eschatologie der jüdischen Gemeinde im neutestamentlichen Zeitalter,* Tübingen [2]1934.

Once again, I shall analyse only the so-called theological implications of this remarkable 'hymnic gospel', as the book of Revelation has been called. How does Revelation view salvation in Jesus from God? Of course, this Christian apocalypse has had a marked influence on the imagination of Christians, even academics. Otto Böcher's short book gives a readable, if somewhat superficial survey of interpretation of it since 1700. [140]

The author of Revelation presents a Christian apocalypse which stands in a Jewish apocalyptic tradition and works with existing traditions. He sees the struggle of the human community, the church, for good and against evil – the struggle for righteousness – in the light of the apocalyptic-eschatological struggle between God, Christ the sacrifice and Jerusalem on the one hand, and the dragon, the beast and Babylon on the other; and finally, between Christ and Satan. The *eschaton* offers us a perspective on the make-up of our history. It is not as if the apocalyptic view seeks to portray the specific course of human history; what we have is, rather, a great apocalyptic scenario: the sovereign power of the Christ, dead and risen, who has ascended for ever the throne beside God (the heart of the Christian kerygma) and who effects God's righteousness in the world. In the literary genre of apocalyptic, earthly history is so to speak played out on two planes: in the heavenly spheres by the *archontes* or heavenly guardian angels of the nations,[141] and on the other hand in our earthly history. The apocalyptic seer looks as it were into the heavenly spheres and this gives him his view of human history.

The special feature of this Christian apocalypse is that it is not ascribed to a great figure from the Old Testament, like Enoch, Moses or Elijah; the author represents himself as 'John, your brother, who shares with you in Jesus the tribulation and the kingdom and the patient endurance' (1.9), as a 'servant of God' (1.1; 22.6) – he is evidently a church leader, as he feels himself called and authorized to write to the churches (10.7); he possesses the charisma of prophecy (19.10; 22.8) and sends a message to seven local churches of which Ephesus, the capital of the Roman proconsulate of Asia, is as it were the metropolitan church.

Although it was already known throughout the church between 120 and 150, remarkably enough this book, which is addressed like a letter to the churches of Asia Minor, was recognized as canonical in the West before it was canonized in the East, where it was finally accepted only in 691 (Trullan Synod). The final editing of the book of Revelation is usually dated in the years between 81 and 96 (end of the reign of the Emperor Domitian), by virtue of the fact that Christians are evidently compelled to take part in emperor worship. It is a historical fact that the Emperor Domitian had temples built for the imperial cult in Asia Minor. Christians refused to offer worship (Rev. 13.4, 12; 14.9, 11; 16.2; 19.20). In its final form, Revelation was probably written after the murder of Domitian, i.e. at the beginning of Nerva's peaceful reign (96–98).

The plan seems originally to have been limited to the book with the seven seals, in which God's appearance, resurrection and universal judgment were to take place. In fact, a series of new visions begins after the seventh seal: the visions of the seven trumpets and the seven bowls. The great themes of apocalyptic expectations of the end are absent here: the appearance of the eschatological prophet, the great trials at the end of the time and the attack of the nations on Jerusalem, along with the return of all the Jews in the dispersion. Events under Domitian evidently moved the author to alter his original plan. Under the pressure of circumstances he sees Domitian as the figure in whom Satan is finally manifested. What was originally intended as an event of the last days (the content of the book with the seven seals) now becomes a prelude to the final judgment. Only then is the last time introduced through the figures of Satan, Antichrist and the false prophet, the adversaries of God, Christ and the eschatological prophet. Thus we have a somewhat 'dualistic' pattern: the church community, too, has a counterpart in the great whore, the 'earthly city'.

The seven letters (2.1–3.22) are connected rather loosely with the book of Revelation, but at a later stage have been incorporated organically. Thus the christophany, which originally occurred before 4.1, now has a double function: over against the seven letters (1.9–11) and – in the original plan – over against the apocalypse of the events of the last days (1.19). So Rev. 2.1–3.22 interrupts the real significance of the christophany. Evidently the vision of the appearance of Christ originally referred only to the apocalypse, and was then revised in such a way that it became a charge to warn the seven churches of Asia Minor.

It is often assumed that the author is a Jew, originally not even a Diaspora Jew. However, this assumption cannot be based on the fact that the author evidently thinks in Hebrew and writes inadequate Greek. In apocalyptic circles people often deliberately wrote bad Greek (even the everyday *koinē*). The apocalyptists are 'exegetes' of the Old Testament; they did not seek to present a new message, but to make the Old Testament itself say something about contemporary and eschatological events by means of a combination of various Old Testament texts. In fact they do not really *quote*, but actually *think* in Old Testament texts. For these apocalyptists, even Jewish Greek is too ordinary to express these exalted, eschatological things. This can be done only in the 'language of Canaan'. All these Semitic 'barbarisms' do not find their way into their Greek through lack of literary skill; their introduction is deliberate.

Like any apocalyptic book, Revelation is a book representing the spiritual resistance of Christians. The author seeks to encourage believers: Christ is coming soon. The end is in sight. Revelation comes from about the same time as the great Jewish apocalypses, IV Ezra and Syriac Baruch, all written in a new resurgence of early apocalyptic after the climax of the persecution of Jews and Christians under Domitian.

## §1 Illustrious titles for Christ and the identity of the person of Jesus which for the moment remains unknown

There is much discussion among exegetes about the relationship between the terms 'Son of man', 'royal Messiah' and 'the Lamb' in the sense of the Ebed Yahweh of Isa. 53 or the Paschal Lamb, throughout the book of Revelation. Some attribute this vagueness to the discrepant sources used by Revelation (U. Müller), others to two scribes whom the author is said to have employed (A. Feuillet), while others do not see any discrepancies at all, finding rather a synthesis of the terms Son of Man, royal Messiah and *"bed Yahweh* (the Lamb) (J. Comblin). Yet others explain the discrepancies in terms of the fidelity of the apocalyptic author to the Old Testament traditions, which cannot always be harmonized (H. Kraft), and so on. The genre of apocalyptic is ill-fitted to systematic and logical treatment; it has a logic all of its own. The author himself prefers a lamb-christology (see below). Christ, who has died and been exalted, is now already Lord of the community: this is contrasted with a Messiah christology in Jewish national terms, a warrior figure who conquers the peoples of the world. The author finds this last tendency in his Old Testament sources (as they are still *current* in the inter-testamental literature of his time) and includes this tradition, subordinating it to his lamb-christology. Discrepancies have to be put up with here. Palestinian Jewish apocalyptic was particularistic and national, whereas Diaspora Judaism was universalistic. These tendencies, which were not synthesized, were carried over into early Christianity. But above all the lamb-christology comes into the foreground in the book of the seven seals.

On his first appearance in Revelation Jesus Christ is presented as 'the faithful witness, the firstborn of the dead, and the ruler of kings on earth' (1.5). The background to these three titles seems to be the church's kerygma of the death of Jesus, his resurrection and exaltation to the right hand of God. The term *martyrs* or witness is applied in Revelation both to all Christian believers (all will prophesy, Joel 2.28–32) and also, even more, to the prophets, just as the title 'servant of God' (1.1), by which the author introduces himself, applies both to charismatic prophets and to all Christians. Servant of God is an early prophetic title (Amos 3.7). As a witness (before the exile), a prophet is above all a 'prophet of disaster'; that is why the suffering of the prophet (in contrast to the prophets who worked wonders) is regarded as a legitimation of their prophetic word. Therefore in Revelation *martys* is not necessarily a person who has given witness through blood, but the *suffering prophet* (see further in connection with the Lamb). 'Testimonies of Jesus' refers to the suffering prophet Jesus who has borne witness to the general resurrection through his death and resurrection. This turned into the term 'prophet' at the time of the New Testament. In Revelation, too, the term witness comprises both prophetic suffering and belief in the resurrection (1.5; 3.14; 2.13; cf. 10.11 in connection with the eschatological prophet, also 17.6: the idea of the murder of the prophets). Jesus gave his life on the cross for the sake of the kingdom of God; therefore he is the 'faithful witness'. He is also the 'firstborn of the dead', not, say, in the sense of Heb. 1.6, but simply as the first one to be raised (though Revelation never uses the term resurrection apart from 20.5f.; it prefers 'who was dead and is now alive again') (cf. Rom. 8.29; Col. 1.15, 18). Thus the title 'firstborn' (1.5f.) indicates Christ's relationship to the church community. He is Lord of the community. The third paragraph goes on to speak of Christ's lordship over the world. The echo of Ps. 89 is striking: 'And I will make him the *first-born, the highest of the kings of the earth*' (Ps. 89.27). The same psalm also contains the idea of the *faithful witness* (89.36). Christ's exaltation is not seen here in formal terms, as e.g. in Hebrews, as an exaltation above the angels, but above earthly kings and emperors who in reality persecute the community of Christ and exercise power over it – though the author sees demonic and Satanic forces at work behind these earthly powers which oppress Christians (17.18; 19.19; cf. 21.24).

'Lord of lords and kings of kings' (1.4; see also 17.14 and 19.16) is originally a predicate of God (see Deut. 10.17; Ps. 89.27; 136. 2f.; II Macc. 13.4; and throughout the inter-testamental literature, e.g. I Enoch 9.4; 63.4; III Macc. 5.35. At another place in the New Testament: I Tim 6.15).[142] Like God, Christ has the *basileia tou kosmou* (11.15), that is, he exercises rule over the world now.

This threefold set of titles (1.5) expresses the basic Christian creed, brought up to date in a quite particular situation of persecution within the church. By virtue of this resurrection from the dead, through which he has gained his community, Christ also becomes ruler of the world, which means (see below) that he exercises rule over the world through his church on earth, fighting against the evil powers and their satellites, the Roman empire. Thus the sequence in this kerygma is: the (expiatory) death of Jesus, his institution as Lord of the church, and finally as Lord of history (1.5; see Rev. 5). In my view, a significant feature of the christology current in Asia Minor is the fact that here, in contrast to Ephesians and Colossians, we have an apocalyptic drama.

In the christophany (described in 1.12–20), this witness, the Lord of the church and ruler of the world, appears to the author *as the Son of man* (having previously been said to be 'coming with the clouds', in 1.7, a deliberate reference to Dan. 7.13–15; 7.27; 10.5f.). Son of man is a central term in apocalyptic, and in Revelation it is used in precisely the way it appears in Jewish apocalyptic, for all the Christian interpretation. True, *in Jesus Christ,* terms like Son of man, messianic king and servant of God or Lamb are identical, but Revelation keeps the term separate and does not confuse the term Son of man with messiahship or with the Lamb. So the 'Son of man' is not the coming judge any more than he is in Daniel, where judgment is reserved solely for God (see Rev. 1.14, 16). As Son of man, Christ appears in Revelation only in the capacity of Lord and guardian of the Christian community. In the christophany in 1.12–20 he appears as the Lord of the community and therefore charges the author to send letters to the Christian churches. The Son of man appears between seven golden lampstands (1.12; see Moses' vision of the seven lampstands in Ex. 25.31–40; also Zech. 4.2–6, where the lampstands are a symbol of the Holy Spirit), and that is, as the author himself explains (1.20; see 2.5), the seven churches, 'between whom the Son of man travels'. Perhaps he is thinking of the seven-branched lampstand in the Temple (Ex. 25; in Rev. 11.1f. the Temple is 'the church'.). Furthermore, in his right hand the Son of man carries the seven planets (1.16), and according to 1.20 these are the 'seven angels' of the seven churches. This picture hardly allows us to see the 'angels of the churches' as official messengers from the churches (servants and representatives of subordinate churches in the main church at Ephesus), as H. Kraft supposes. Perhaps they are really angels, *archontes,* guardians of the churches and as it were identified with the church. (This apocalyptic identification does away with the illogical element that the Son of man gives the seer the task of writing to an angel.)

Thus Christ is the Lord of the heavenly ikons of the seven churches on earth. The apocalyptic seer therefore sends his letters in the name of the Son of man or the Lord of the whole church to each of the seven (heavenly) leaders of the seven churches, that is, to the whole church (after 70, the centre of Christianity lay in Asia Minor). Because the Son of man is Lord of the church, Revelation depicts him also as high priest (1.13; less clearly in Dan. 10; Ex. 28.4, 27; Ezek. 9.2). He wears priestly garments and (not the princely girdle, as is often said, but) a girdle decorated with gold which is folded over the breast, *in the style of a priest.*[143] After Daniel, the Danielic Son of man without doubt became a redeemer figure; in Revelation he is described as the one who controls the sevenfold spirits, that is, the Holy Spirit (1.13). Thus Revelation further emphasizes the priestly character which was only hinted at in Dan. 10.5 – although otherwise the author is not at all interested in priesthood or cult. Insofar as the *Son of man* is given a judicial function here (2.18, 23), it relates only to the church community and not to its enemies. Even the theme of the two-edged sword, the symbol of judgment (1.16, taken up again in 2.12, 16), points to judgment on the churches (see Isa. 49.2; 11.4; cf. Isa. 27.1; 34.5; 66.16). Finally, when the term Son of man recurs in later parts of Revelation (14.14–20), the Son of man is the 'harvester of the faithful'. In short, Revelation uses Son of man in the Danielic sense: the Son of man with 'the saints of the most high' (Dan. 7.13, 18, 27), with whom the Son of man identifies himself – the elastic 'collective' and yet 'individual' concept of the Danielic Son of man. That is an indication that for the author the fate of the church stands at the centre of his whole work. All the sections which do not make use of earlier Jewish traditions and in which the author speaks formally as a Christian (above all 1–3; 5.1–14; 7.13–17; 14.1–5; 22.6–21, to mention just the larger Christian fragments) are concerned with the churches: the promise to the tortured Christians (7.13–17), those sealed with the name of the Lamb (14.1–5), for the perseverance of Christians (14.12f.), the community as the bride of the Lamb (19.7b–8; 21.9; see also the whole of ch. 5; the promise to the faithful Christians, 22.7f., 12, 14, 17 and the admonitions to the seven churches, chs. 1–3). Revelation is concerned with a church-oriented eschatology.

*Christ's* saving action for the benefit of his community is illuminated in a threefold perspective. Towards the community, Jesus Christ is 'the one who loves' (1.5f.). In this love are rooted both the gifts which he has given to the community (cf. 3.9; 3.19 and perhaps 20.9), namely, (*a*) redemption through his blood and (*b*) transference of the lordship of Jesus to the Christian community (1.5b–6).

(*a*) The death of Jesus is seen as a victory over Satan and death and therefore as the forgiveness of sins: *redemption* with the blood of Jesus as ranson (for this term see the synthesis below). For a ransom, Jesus has redeemed his community, bought from the earth (14.3), and therefore rescued it from the sphere of demonic powers (see also 5.9; 7.14; 12.11; 14.3f.). This means not only the forgiveness of sins but also the freedom to resist the absolute divinization of the imperial power. In fact Revelation sees three aspects in redemption: triumph over death *(esphagēs)*, redemption *(ēgorasas)* and appointment as the priestly people of God *(epoiēsas) basileian,* 5.9f.). As in Hebrews (see also Rom. 3.25; 5.9; I Cor. 11.25; Eph. 2.13), 'his blood' (probably a theme from the Christian eucharistic tradition) means Jesus' death in the sense of its atoning worth. As a result believers are 'the first-fruits of man before God and the Lamb' (14.4), they are 'washed in the blood of the Lamb' (Rev. 7.14); in Christ they have put on new, 'white robes' (also 6.11; 7.9, 13; 22.14). That is true not only in eschatological terms (3.5; 6.11), but even now (3.4; see 3.18; also 7.14, which refers not only to the 'full martyrs' but to all the members of the community). This white robe, which was also actually put on in Christian baptism, is the purification from sins. Hence the hymn of praise, 'Blessed are those who wash their robes' (22.14), which is the basis of eschatological heavenly citizenship (22.14b). The 'washing white of robes' is also an intrinsic element of sanctification in Ex. 19.10, 14. Thus Revelation does not think, like e.g. Hebrews, in cultic categories. The author does not mention the redeeming death of Jesus in connection with the term Son of man, but does so *often* in connection with the title 'the Lamb' used for Christ, with which other Christ events are also connected (see 7.14; 7.17; 12.11; 13.8; 14.1, 4; 15.3; 19.7, 9; 21.9, 27). Thus the saving death of Jesus is the foundation of the whole of this Christian apocalypse.

(*b*) By virtue of this death in love, Christians become 'a royal race of priests before God, the Father of Christ' (1.6; see also 5.9f.; 20.6; see 7.15; with I Peter 2.5–9 the only passage in the New Testament where Ex. 19.6 is applied to the Christian community). In Ex. 19.6, the goal of the covenant is the establishing of a royal kingdom of priests. Evidently the author is thinking directly of Isa. 61.6; but what is intended here eschatologically is now already reality in Revelation. In Revelation, not only the people of God as a whole, but also each member of the community is 'royal and priestly'. Christians have a share in the lordship of Christ through his love. Here Revelation is closer to Pauline theology (e.g. Rom. 8.34f.; II Cor. 5.14f.; Gal. 2.20) than is Johannine theology, which stresses above all the mutuality of love, and in which Christ's love is more comprehensive (John 13.1) and is not concentrated so narrowly (also John 15.13; I John 3.16) on the cross. Rather, Revelation stresses the initiative of the love that comes forth from Christ; in this sense, too, it is also Johannine. '*He* (first) loved us' (I John 4.10, 16).

Thus as a priestly people of God the Christian community is now already the realization of the Old Testament vision. It reigns. That implies the fall of Satan and his earthly satellites whom the community resists, thanks to the 'blood of the Lamb': 'For the accuser (= Satan) of our brethren has been thrown down, who accuses them day and night before our God. And they have conquered him by the blood of the Lamb and by the word of their testimony, for they loved not their lives even unto death' (12.10d–11). Christ is now already triumphant, in the dimension of our earthly history, over Satan and Caesar, because *Christians* are opposing the imperial cult and as witnesses for God's cause (the exclusive rule of God) are already triumphing over evil in their martyr deaths. Christ exercises his lordship through the church. Satan has already been cast down *from heaven* through Jesus' death and exaltation (12.12), but he is now going around on earth (an apocalyptic conception) and oppressing the church. But the church is defending itself, i.e. it is triumphing, albeit as a suffering witness in the power of the testimony of Jesus' blood.

This indicates the relationship between Christ as 'Lord of the church' (Son of man) and Christ as 'King of kings' (messianic King). The two terms are connected by the concept of 'the lamb'. What does the author mean by *arnion*, the lamb? This title is used some twenty-eight times, though it is certainly not an early Jewish messianic title. Really, *arnion* means a little lamb (diminutive of *arēn*), or a ewe or battering ram; but in time *arnion* simply came to mean sheep or lamb. Apocalyptic has a tendency to depict eschatological figures in the form of animals, because of quite definite and particular animal characteristics. In Revelation, the apocalyptic lamb appears as a counterpart to the apocalyptic beast (the Roman empire) (Rev. 12–14). If one were to use an apocalyptic animal to represent Christ over against the other apocalyptic figures, the image of the lamb would be an obvious one. In the analysis of the Gospel of John above I pointed out that the lamb was an Old Testament symbol of unmerited and helpless suffering and in reality became a name for prophets and witnesses; it is more than probable that in the last resort it was also applied to the Mosaic eschatological prophet (see there). However, it was above all by means of Jesus, recognized as the Messiah, that the identification of Jesus with an innocent sacrificial lamb took on real messianic significance. Furthermore, the Gospel of John has the bold imagery in which the shepherd is identified with his flock, a good shep-hered who lays down his life for the sheep, Yahweh's flock. In this way there comes into being the concept of the 'Lamb of God' which 'takes away' not only the sins of Israel but 'the sins of the world'.[144] In the book of Revelation, too, the 'Lamb' on its own has a 'messianic' significance. When the Lamb is first introduced in Revelation, it is said to be '*as* slain' (5.6); 5.12 says 'the Lamb *that* was slain' (also in 13.8). This *hōs* (as), e.g. '*as* a Son of man' (Dan. 7.13), is merely a stylistic device in apocalyptic, to express 'heavenly' things which are scarcely visible to men. Thus the author sees the atoning death of Jesus as the focal point of the title 'the Lamb' as used for Christ. By virtue of this death Christians have become 'people of God', just as Israel became the people of God through the exod·us from Egypt – as celebrated in the Passover (it is typical that in 15.3 Moses is called *"bed Yahweh*). The suffering servant is rehabilitated by God: 'God's righteous judgments have been made manifest' (15.4c, in the song of Moses, Ex. 15.1). Moses, the *"bed Yahweh*, the suffering prophet, eschatological prophet and sacrificial lamb all come together in Jesus Christ.

Jesus, who as the Lamb has given his life for his own and now, exalted to God, is Lord of the church *qua* Son of man, is in the last resort also ruler of the world. On the basis of what Jesus Christ has done for the Christian people of God through his death, he receives the universal rule of the world from God (1.17b–18). In addition to the seven stars – the Christian communities – which Christ holds in his hand, he also has 'seven *spirits* of God': 'The words of him who has the seven spirits of God and the seven stars' (3.1; see also 4.5; 5.6 and 1.4). It emerges from 4.5

and 5.6 that there are seven angels in the service of Christ, perhaps originally the seven assistants at the throne of God, the archangels (see 1.4; Tobit 12.15); in Revelation, however, they are simply 'the Holy Spirit' in his sevenfold strength and gifts (see Zech. 4.2–6; Greek Isa. 61.1f., though because of the traditions of which they make use the two conceptions are quite similar; God is so utterly transcendent that he can only be spoken of with the help of higher, heavenly beings). We have a 'trinitarian' formula in 1.4: grace to you from God – from 'the seven spirits before his throne', evidently the Holy Spirit – and from Jesus Christ, the earliest sequence in the trinitarian formula. At another point in the apocalypse we still have 'ternary' formulae like 'God, Christ, angel' (3.5). Like God, Christ has 'the seven archangels' at his command. He gives God's spirit to Christians. The only other mention of these 'seven spirits of God' is in 5.6 (Zech. 4), where they are the seven eyes of the Lamb which are sent out into the whole world. They are therefore servants of Christ: Christ at work on earth through his spirit. In this way the 'divine force' of Christ is transferred: he is Lord of God's saving action in the world. In 6.10 the author calls God 'sovereign Lord, holy and true'; in 3.7 he calls Christ 'the holy one, the true one'. Nowhere in Judaism do we hear that the Messiah is called 'the holy one'. Only God is 'the holy one' (Isa. 40.25; Job 6.10; Hab. 3.3; see Isa. 1.4; 41.14). Revelation transfers this divine name to Christ. In addition he is given the title 'the *archē* of creation' (3.14; cf. *archē* in 21.6; 22.13). This can mean 'first-fruit of creation' and also 'mediator at creation' (e.g. Prov. 8.22; Wisdom 6.22; 9.2; Sir. 24.9; also Col. 1.15–17). It is striking that the author writes this to the church in Laodicea, which clearly has contacts with Pauline theology. Revelation hardly gives us enough evidence to decide whether the author also means a mediation at creation; however, the more ecclesiological concentration of the seven letters seems to point in the direction of the 'first-fruits of creation' (and this is confirmed by the fact that the author reserves the name 'ruler of all', *pantokratōr*, for God; see below). Thus the conjecture that we should read *'āmūn*, (i.e., in the context of wisdom, 'counsellor' at creation and thus mediator at creation) instead of *'āmēn* (Isa. 65.16), is mere hypothesis. In Enoch too, the Son of man appears before all creation, but he has no intermediary role at creation.[145] Here pre-existence is eschatological: as the exalted one, Christ is the first-fruits and the head of creation. Christ is not only 'amen' and 'the first-fruits of creation'; he is also 'alpha and omega'. The threefold pattern of the formulae which Revelation keeps using are the result of Greek influence; in early Judaism they were generally used to express God's eternity over and above the present, the past and the future. It is now said of Christ that he is 'the first and the last' (see 1.17; 22.13). When the Hebrew phrase 'the first and the last'

(Isa. 41.4; 44.6) from Isaiah is put into Greek in the Septuagint, the term 'the last' is always omitted. It is impossible for a Greek Jew to call God 'the last', since 'last' is essentially a temporal term (in Job 19.25 the Hebrew 'the last' is put into Greek, typically, as 'the eternal one'). But a man thinking in both Hebrew and Christian terms did not hesitate here. However, this presupposes that our history has an end, a goal, to which it is subordinated, and this totality, beginning and end, is in God's hands and also in Christ's. In 1.17f., 'beginning and end' is supplemented with the words 'the living one. I died and behold I am alive for evermore'. 'The living one' is also a divine predicate (Ps. 42.2; 84.2; Josh. 3.10; see Deut. 32.40; Dan. 4.34; 12.7). However, in early Christianity and Judaism 'life' has become an expression of the totality of the eschatological gifts of salvation (above all the Gospel of John: Rev. 2.7; 2.10; 3.1; 7.17). Christ possesses all the eschatological gifts, 'the seven spirits', in fullness; he is 'the living one', and therefore has the keys of the kingdom of the dead (1.18b): in the Old Testament an authority which is reserved to Yahweh alone (I Sam. 2.6; Wisdom 16.13; Job 14.13). One of the last of the eschatological events will be the time when 'death and Hades' are themselves annihilated (20.14).

In the letter to the church of Philadelphia it is said of Christ, the Son of man, that he has the key of David (3.7). In Isa. 22.22 the steward has the golden key, the sign of the power of King David; he has the power 'to open and shut'. This power of the keys means that Christ has the power to admit anyone to the kingdom of God or to exclude them from it (cf. 3.8) (in the New Testament: the power to admit to baptism or to refuse baptism to anyone; see Matt. 16.18f.; Acts 8.20–25). It is precisely because Christ, the Lord of the church, has this power of the keys that neither death nor the underworld can overcome the church.

Only in one passage does Revelation call Christ 'Son of God', and that is in a quotation from Ps. 2 (2.18; cf. 2.26f.). On the other hand, however, God is spoken of as 'the Father' only in relation to Christ (1.6; 2.28; 3.5, 21; 14.1). This 'restraint' towards the title 'Son of God' is perhaps to be explained in terms of the Jewish traditions used by the author: Judaism does not know of 'Son of God' as a specifically messianic title.

In apocalyptic proper it is said of the anointed one, the Jewish messiah, that he is clothed in a garment 'washed in blood' (19.13). This is not the blood of the Lamb, but the garment of the warrior Messiah stained from his bloody battle. The name of this messianic warrior is 'the Word of God'. The significance here is that God's triumphant action is seen in him. Word is not the name or the 'person' of Jesus but a designation: we have *keklētai*. This is what he is called, this is the name which he received at his exaltation to God, so he is the 'King of kings' (19.16). However, it also means 'faithful witness'. In 1.2, 9; 6.9 and 20.4, the title 'the word of God' always appears in connection with the 'testimonies of Jesus' (*martyria Iēsou*). The author never speaks in absolute terms of 'the Logos', as does the Gospel of John. It is as a particular person that Christ is the manifestation of God's saving activity. He is the revelation of God. In contrast to the Gospel of John, it is nowhere said in Revelation that the Logos of God is mediator at creation. As word, in Revelation Christ is the only bearer of the revelation of salvation.

On a number of occasions, not only God (some thirteen times), but also Christ is called *Kyrios*, the Lord (11.8; 14.13; 22.20f.; it is unclear whether 11.4 refers to God or Christ). However, it is striking that this primitive Christian title of Christ really occurs only in a traditional formula (14.13). In the really apocalyptic part of Revelation, only God is called Lord. The author is familiar with the traditional formula *maranatha* (*erchou Kyrie Iēsou*, 'Come, Lord Jesus', 22.20f.). He himself reserves the name *Kyrios* for God, even in an anti-imperialist sense. Where Domitian has himself called 'our Lord and God',[146] Revelation calls God '*ho Kyrios kai Theos hēmōn*' (4.11).

Although Revelation assigns various divine predicates to Christ, the author is still very restrained when it comes to particular divine names. Only God, and not Christ, is the *pantokratōr*, the ruler of the universe (1.8 and eight other instances). In the Septuagint, *pantokratōr* is always the translation of the Hebrew 'God of hosts' (Deus Sabaot), the divine predicate used by the later prophets. However, nowhere is Christ called *pantokratōr* or ruler of the universe. God alone is Creator, evidently without any intermediary at creation. However, Christ is exalted above all creatures, even the angels. And this exalted position was given to him at his exaltation after his death. His kingdom – he has 'received his power from the Father' (2.28) – extends through the order of salvation: beyond his community and the nations. God alone is 'the one who is and was and is to come' (1.8; 4.8c). In the view of a variety of exegetes this divine attribute is deliberately chosen *over against* a current motto about the *Nero redivivus*, of whom the rumour ran that 'He who was, and is not, and will appear' (see further the comments in the synthesis: 'The life of grace and political power in the New Testament', esp. pp. 578f.). People believed that the dead Nero was still alive somewhere, submerged in the East, whence he would return with an army to punish Israel and to reign in triumph in Jerusalem. Finally Nero became the eschatological anti-Messiah, and for Christians the antichrist: Satan in Nero's form. This Roman legend, which was Judaized and taken over by Christians, unmistakably plays a part in the book of Revelation (see 17.8; 13.3,14). That indicates that Revelation is concerned with the church in the face of the imperial power of the state under which it suffers persecution.

Even now the world and the churches are subject to Christ. The reason for this is his expiatory death. Who is this 'Christ' in Revelation? It is striking that this book never uses the name Jesus as subject of the real apocalyptic drama. The author uses the name by itself eight times (always in the genitive). What it then means is Jesus, whose coming the community awaits (1.9; 14.12; 17.6), for whom men hope and in whom they trust by faith, for whom and to whom they bear witness even to the point of martyrdom (1.9; 12.17; 19.10; 20.4). Thus the name is always used to depict Jesus as the object of an action of the part of the church. When Christ himself becomes the subject of an action, Revelation never uses Jesus. Outside the great apocalyptic corpus of Revelation, where 'Jesus Christ' is the subject of the action, he appears as the one who brings the revelation (1.1), promises peace and grace to his disciples (1.5; 22.21), and after a while will come again (22.20).

This indicates that the formal meaning of the terms used by Revelation in the great apocalyptic centrepiece of the work is determined by the Old Testament and Judaism: the Christ or the anointed. As a scribe, the author is evidently making a personal attempt to apply Jewish concepts to Christ Jesus; in other words, he is making a personal attempt to interpret Jewish apocalyptic in Christian terms (sometimes, too, even already existing passages of tradition like Rev. 12). From the point of view of method, therefore, this means that this Christian apocalypse must be interpreted primarily on the basis of presuppositions drawn from the Old Testament and early Judaism, of a clear and relatively unadulterated apocalyptic stamp.

All these illustrious honorific titles which are applied to Christ do not exhaust and express his nature. His true name will only be revealed at the parousia, when the revelation of God reaches its fulfilment. The author already says in 3.12: 'I will write on him the name of my God, and the name of the city of my God, the new Jerusalem, and my own *new name*'; the words are spoken by the Son of man. But this new name is not given. Evidently the seer himself does not know it. It is also said of the victorious Christ in 19.12 that 'on his head are many diadems; and he has a name inscribed *which no one knows but himself*'. We Christians now call him 'the Word of God' (12.13), but that is still not his final name. What that is will only become evident at the parousia. Person and name are identical. Thus Revelation explicitly maintains the mystery of the eschatological identity of the person of Jesus. It can only be made manifest at the consummation of the revelation. Even the apocalyptic seer is not given any knowledge of this 'new name'. Christ's innermost being is still hidden from us. We only know what he means for us as salvation from God; that is the experience of Christ's church. We do not know the real name which identifies his person. We only know that he reveals God to us. The author evidently means to *suggest* that the nature of Christ is intrinsically bound up with that of God himself. How this is so will be shown at the parousia. We must therefore try to remain modest: not out of minimalism (the author indicates something even greater than is to be expected after all these honorific titles), but out of religious reverence and above all because God's revelation is finally given only at the parousia. We cannot anticipate it.

## §2 The vision of a new world

After the messages to the seven churches of Asia Minor, the author goes over to an apocalyptic interpretation of history. The seer gazes into the heavenly spheres. What he sees first is the heavenly liturgy, in which the whole court of heaven sings praises to God as *pantocratōr* (4.8), Creator of the universe (4.11). What elsewhere in the New Testament is called the counsel of God is here depicted in apocalyptic terms: praise for the Creator God who holds the world and history in his hand. Only then does the aim of the divine plan for creation come to be put into effect. For at that point the glorified Lamb appears.

What is confessed elsewhere in the New Testament and expressed in the form of hymns is depicted in Rev. 5 in a great vision: the glorification of Jesus after his death. Christ has conquered, and therefore it is in his power to open the great book of history, the apocalyptic event. He is the Lord of history. The seer sees his enthronement. Appearing before the heavenly council, the Lamb 'takes' power from the right hand of the one opposite him, who sits 'invisibly' on the throne (5.7). This is followed by an acclamation from all present (5.9–13); the whole creation joins in it (5.13). (Here we find expressed in a vision what appears elsewhere in quotations from hymns, e.g. Phil. 2.9–11; I Tim. 3.16.) Here (after the christophany of 1.9–19, which is separated from this passage by the letters of 4.1ff.) is the beginning of the account of the apocalyptic vision: it also takes place in the heavenly spheres. Revelation 5 gives as it were the dogmatic (christological) basis (in the past) for what now follows: for 'all that must take place' in the right sequence (1.19). The death of Jesus, the basis of his exaltation and his eschatological rule, is the dogmatic nucleus of this vision. (A past event, namely the birth and life of Jesus, also becomes an apocalyptic vision in Rev. 12.) The basis for Christ's rule of the world is that 'The Lion of the tribe of Judah, the Root of David, has conquered, so that he can open the scroll and its seven seals' (5.5). This victory (*enikēsen*) is made more specific in 5.9: 'You ransomed them for God with your blood.' That means that because Jesus has won for himself his community from all nations and tongues through his death, he becomes the Lord of history (5.9). Thus Jesus' redemption of his community is his triumph, and his death itself is the victory: he is 'the victor' (Rev. 2;3). He conquers as 'the lion from the tribe of Judah' (Gen. 49.9), combined with the *virga Jesse* or the Root of David from Isa. 11.10. (By way of example, e.g. in IV Ezra 12.31f., the Messiah is called 'the Lion from the seed of David'.) As messianic victor, Christ fulfils the Old Testament promises. The reason for the use of the term 'victory' for the redemptive expiatory death of Jesus seems to lie in the early Jewish and early Christian conception of the world as Satan's sphere of power in his fight against God and his people. The victory over the world is at the same time an entry into God's sphere of power, the guarantee for the historical victory in Satan's eschatological fight against God. In heaven, however, victory is already won with the crucifixion of Christ.

Apocalyptic is always concerned with an interpretation of history: past, present and future; in it the present is seen as the initial time immediately before the last days. As Lord *of the church*, for believers Christ is also the all-determining power of the church's present. Revelation gives a preliminary view of this vision before the author looks back on earthly history: what has already taken place in the past with Jesus Christ *is determinative* for what is happening in the present. The 'book of history' is the apocalyptic symbol for Christ's rule over the world. It may be the case that the book is a document of the kind that was familiar in antiquity: a document in duplicate, in the sense that the text on the inside is sealed, whereas the duplicate on the outside is not sealed;[147] however, this does not play any part in the apocalypse. The author is thinking of the 'sealed book' of Isa. 29.11f.: 'And the vision of all this has become to you like the words of a book that is sealed. When men give it to one who can read, saying "Read this," he says, "I cannot, for it is sealed." ' This is an expression of the Old Testament theory of 'the hardening of the heart'. Because of their sinfulness, men cannot gain insight into God's counsel and rule of the world. No one is open to the (Old Testament) prophecies: they are all listed in the book with the seven seals. However, this book can be read by the charismatic exegete, the seer. He understands what the prophets meant and what they prophesied about the events of the last time. This is why the christophany was needed: the Lord of history gives the seer this insight; the author does not know it of his own accord. Thus his visions are filled to right and left with odds and ends from the Tanach, the word of God. As *seer*, he is the *interpreter* of the Old Testament prophecies. Only the Lamb 'with seven horns and seven eyes' (5.6), i.e. with all power and omniscient vision, is worthy to open this book. As he does so, the seer looks on.

Thus the content of the sealed book is also clear. It would be quite wrong to follow O. Roller in seeing it as a form of accusation – so to speak after the fashion of Col. 2.13–15. For guilt *is* already forgiven by Christ's death; and this provides the presupposition for the opening of the book, namely the forgiveness of sins which the community has come to share through the blood of the Lamb (5.9f.). Thus the sealed book cannot be any form of accusation. Why, then, are the heavenly courtiers so afraid that no one will be found who is capable of breaking the seals? Because they look forward longingly for the end of mankind's sorry history, i.e. for someone who is worthy to open the book. In apocalyptic logic, the last events take place in a certain order and according to a certain pattern. The final woes cannot begin before they have been announced; one event determines the other (II Thess. 2.5–8 is also an allusion to this, in connection with the *katechon*: 'something that still delays the arrival of the antichrist'). Thus the beginning of the last events cannot come before the seal of the record of these last events has been broken.

The Lamb is given this book: Christ is the Lord of history by virtue of his exaltation after his death. Through the opening of the book – in which one seal is broken after another – history becomes *eschatological* history, to the comfort of the persecuted and suffering community, which is now on the brink of the last days: Christ is coming: Maranatha. Thus the content of the book is the last events: 'Everything which happens after this (*meta tauta*)' (4.1: *specifically*, this is the content of 6.1–22.5). Thus the possession of the book is at the same time the symbol of Christ's rule of the world (see 5.9 with 5.12). In the last resort, doxologically, Revelation 5 celebrates the supremacy of the Lamb (5.9). He, the Christ, has the key to all history in his hands, for he has already settled all debts in his blood. He makes mankind's vale of tears an event in which God himself will wipe away all tears (7.17c; 21.4).

Every time the author speaks of Christ's rule over the world, this rule is associated with his character as the Lamb (apart from the block which is concerned with the 'Jewish Messiah'). This Lamb is not only the subject of the exaltation (thus T. Holtz); on the contrary, in Revelation 'the Lamb' is rather both *slain* and *exalted*. Exaltation is part of the significance of the Lamb (as it is part of the concept of the servant of God who, though suffering, is yet exalted). There therefore follows, on the basis of the killing and exaltation of the Lamb: 'You have made them a kingdom and priests to our God, and they shall reign on earth' (5.9f.). The servant figure of Deutero-Isaiah, the Lamb, is at the same time both 'individual' and 'collective', like the Son of man: the Son of man and the 'people of the saints of the most high'. All this confirms the view (characteristic of the theology of Asia Minor) that as Lord of the church Christ also rules over all human history. In Revelation, the Jewish apocalyptic picture of history – which is itself already concentrated on the people of

God – is focused on the church, and attention is directed on the whole of world history only from the church outwards. Thus the very heart of Jewish apocalyptic is baptized into Christianity. For Revelation 'the people of God' (without any contrast between Israel and the church) is quite simply the people whom God has won to himself through the death of Christ (5.9). Jesus' foundation of this people of God, a fulfilment of the ancient promise, through his death, is the *presupposition* of the enthronement of Christ as ruler of the world: this ruling in the world is already *provisionally* becoming manifest in time in the '(co)-rule' of Christians (5.10; see 1.6; 7.1–17; 14.1–4), through Christian resistance to the powers of evil. Here, even now, is the basis for a universal praise and thanksgiving, all the more since Christians are called 'from every nation, from all tribes and peoples and tongues' (7.9; see 10.11; 13.7; 14.6; 17.15). Christians 'will rule on earth' (5.10). The breaking of the first seal already shows that the church, 'the twelve tribes of Israel', occupies the centre of Jesus' rule of the world (7.1–8). Because Christ died an atoning death and has thus gained for himself a people of God, homage is paid to him as Lord of the world and of history. Christ's rule of the world which frees all men is realized by the *sending of the church* into the world; in Revelation this is made specific, not so much in proclamation through the word, through the kerygma or gospel, as through resistance by virtue of the gospel against the absolutized power of the emperor. Provisionally in history, the rule of the Christian community is its resistance – as a suffering witness – against the absolute power of the emperor. This conception is not alien to Eph. 2.14–18, albeit in a difficult church situation, nor even to Matt. 28.18f., where all power is and has been given to Jesus, but where as a result the church is sent into the world. In this apocalypse the messianic event, Christ, is not the *eschaton* of time but the *centrepoint* of our real history, the significance of which will only become manifest in the eschaton, at the parousia. *This* is an un-Jewish, specifically Christian view of messiahship, although the author assumes that this centrepoint is the eve of the last days. However, it does make room for the harsh progressive reality of earthly history.

Now this Lamb has 'seven horns and seven eyes, which are the seven spirits of God' (5.6), the power and wisdom of the Holy Spirit. In the resistance of the community, embodied in martyrdom, Christ already *reigns* over the world by virtue of the power of God. In heaven Satan has already been overcome and cast out by the death of Jesus, but now he is active against the ransomed people of Christ on earth. According to Rev. 5, this victory of Christ is seen in prophetic visions.

Before that the final victory of the Lamb (along with God) is celebrated in a doxology; for through his death and his exaltation Christ has already won for himself the royal priestly people of God (5.9). This event, which has already taken place, is even affirmed in a universal 'amen' from all creation (5.13). One cannot look for an exact chronology in an apocalypse, nor need one do so. An apocalypse looks for the last and deepest sense of history. The seer's gaze may already dwell on the heavenly spheres, but the apocalyptist knows all too well what is happening to the people of God on earth. If the heavenly rule of Christ, the Lord of the church, in this first aeon is primarily still the resistance of the church on earth, heavenly and earthly events are intermingled in inevitable confusion. That is the very nature of apocalyptic. It is said of Christ: 'he *has* conquered' (5.5). On the other hand it is said, 'They will make war on the Lamb, and the Lamb will conquer them, for he is Lord of Lords and King of kings, and those with him are called and chosen and faithful' (17.14). This apocalyptic dialectic permeates the whole book of Revelation. Even now, through his church, Christ is ruling over the world, but only at his parousia will he rule directly over the whole world; even then his community will remain in the centre. It reigns. Thus temporarily the church is under the sign of the 'now already' and 'not yet'. It is persecuted by enemies, as will become evident after the breaking of the seals on the scroll. Quite different enemies attack the community of Christ. The church is persecuted. On the breaking of the fifth seal one can see that many fallen martyrs are already longingly waiting from heaven for the end of all these trials. They cry out for God's retribution because so much blood has been shed (6.10; see Ps. 79, 5, 10). They are given white robes, but 'they are told to wait a little while longer' (6.11); there are still more martyrs to come (6.11c). Thus it is evident to the seer that the great eschatological testing is still to come. From this we must assume that the already fallen martyrs here are the Old Testament martyrs. They are already present for the 'heavenly history' and have an insight into it (7.14–17). On the breaking of the sixth seal (6.12–17) it is clear that the climax will also be reached in earthly history (6.12–7.17). However, before the bitter blow comes, in apocalyptic, to console and admonish the church, it is important to say who will be spared. Hence the vision of the sealed servants of God. The author sees those who are saved through Christ as a priestly people of God (see above). The 'sealing' of those designated follows the same line. The high priest wore a kind of breastplate with seals on which the names of the twelve tribes of Israel were written (see Ex. 28.11, 21; 39.6, 14 = Greek 36.13, 21). Furthermore, on 'the front of the head-covering' (Ex. 28.37), i.e. on his forehead, he wore a seal with the words 'consecrated to Yahweh' (Ex. 28.36; see Ezek. 9.4). Thus the author is thinking of Israel's holy remnant, which is identified with the Christian 'priestly people of God'. Of the various lists of the twelve tribes of Israel (Gen. 49.1–28; Num. 13.4–16; Ezek. 48; Deut. 33.6–29; I Chron. 2.1–8.40), the author took that of Gen. 49. Here the tribe of Dan is 'a serpent in the way, a viper by the path' (Gen. 49.17), the reason why Revelation does not mention it (according to a Jewish tradition this was the tribe of the antichrist, and Christians reinterpreted the tradition: Judas Iscariot came from Dan). In addition to the holy remnant of Israel, those who are finally saved also include a countless multitude of the Gentiles (7.9), who are dedicated to Yahweh (cf. 5.9). The interpreter angel then explains this vision (7.13–17): these are to the baptized, who have been cleansed from their sins in the blood of the Lamb: the priestly people of God consists of Israel's holy remnant and the church community.

At the opening of the last seal, which was originally meant to introduce the final apotheosis, 'there was silence in heaven for about half an hour' (8.1). This goes back to I Kings 19.11f., which describes the appearance of God to Elijah on Horeb: God was not in the storm, nor in the earthquake, nor in the fire, but in the calm of a gentle breeze (see also Hab. 2.20; Zech. 2.13). But the author gave up this first editorial plan. The final apotheosis is postponed. So the silence acquires another function: now the breath-taking events of the savage final battle between the powers of God and the powers of Satan are described in the new visions of the seven trumpets and the seven seals. A certain 'dualism' between good and evil is now evident. The first four trumpets announce many devastating cosmic phenomena (8.2–12). Things get even worse with the next three blasts of the trumpet (8.13–11.19). The earth is ravaged with almost all the ancient Egyptian plagues, even more seriously than at the time of the exodus. Between the sixth and the last trumpet blasts there is a special theophany, that of an angel of the Lord (10.1–7); this is followed by the call of the eschatological prophet (10.8–11.2; here the prophet appears with a twin, so as to be able to give legally valid evidence; cf. 11.4 with Zech. 4.3, 11–14). But at that time a beast will also arise from the abyss (11.7), the antichrist, the Roman empire as Satan's agent. After the seventh trumpet he is opposed by 'his anointed', the Christ, the Messiah (11.15). This marks a new phase in the eschatological period: the Messiah, who is preceded by the eschatological prophet, and on the other hand the anti-Messiah, the beast, whose own eschatological false prophet will also soon appear.

From Rev. 12 onwards we have 'apocalyptic' in the full sense. The war between good and evil is waged on two levels: the metaphysical struggle between Satan and God (Rev. 12), to which on earth there corresponds a political struggle between the beast (the emperor) and his false prophet, and Christ and his church (Rev. 13). All this is repeated in the *last struggle of all* (the author keeps widening his perspective by means of new comments): on the one hand on earth the annihilation of earthly political powers opposed to God and his anointed (Rev. 19), and on the other hand in the heavenly sphere the annihilation of all demonic and chaotic powers who have fought against God, Christ and his church under the leadership of the dragon (Satan).

In the apocalyptic section Rev. 15, the author incorporates a Jewish tradition of the fight between Michael and the anti-Messiah. All the events are still taking place 'in heaven' (see 12.1). Satan is scheming against the pregnant woman, Israel, who is carrying the anointed one. The messianic child (see Isa. 7.14; 26.17; Micah 4.10) is born, but (in accordance with a Jewish tradition) is 'caught up' to God (12.5f.). His role is purely eschatological. The author simply inserts this tradition into his narrative (with all the unevennesses which that causes). His intention is to show that the messianic birth-pangs are beginning (see Isa. 66.6–8). But in heaven, Michael is triumphing over Satan (12.7–9), 'the old serpent' (12.9: 'old' means 'think of Gen. 3.1'; the serpent is already identified with Satan in the Greek of Isa. 27.1). Now he is descending to earth from heaven and will carry on his battle here. In this context the (pen)ultimate struggle begins with Satan's fall to earth (see also Luke 10.18; John 12.31): 'Woe to you, O earth and sea, for the devil has come down to you in great wrath, because he knows that his time is short' (Rev. 12.12). In heaven, however, the song of praise over Satan's fall rings out (12.10–12). At the same time it is indicated that the number of the designated (6.11) is now complete. 'The brothers' of the Old Testament martyrs, namely the Christians, have fulfilled the number of the 'predestined' martyrs 'through the blood of the lamb and the word of their testimony' (12.11). Now salvation can finally begin.

But not for an apocalyptist. On earth Satan is now attacking Zion ('for a while' the Messiah, who is already born, is being concealed in heaven). But the woman (who is Zion and the church community in one) is escaping into the wilderness (12.14). *'Satan stood on the sea shore'* (12.18: in the Old Testament, the sea is the symbol for the powers of chaos). This is an ominous sign.

The battle in heaven (in Rev. 12) now acquires an earthly, political dimension (Rev. 13). A beast comes out of the sea: Satan's minion, the Roman empire, the seven-headed monster. Satan gives Rome 'his power and his throne, a great authority' (13.2b). The author parodies the Roman imperial cult by boldly describing it in expressions drawn from the heavenly enthronement of Christ and the ensuing doxology. The 'dualistic' scheme requires this procedure (cf. II Thess. 2.8f.). However, it is then said here, in Palestinian Jewish terms, that specific imperial authority is given *by Satan* (this is quite different from Paul in Rom. 13.1, where the imperial authority comes 'from God'). Just as Christ is like God, the anti-Christ – a beast, a diabolical counterpart of Christ – is at the same time like the one who sends him: Satan. Of the seven-headed beast (it is no longer possible to make out which seven emperors these are) the author says: 'One of its heads seemed to have a mortal wound, but its mortal wound was healed' (13.3). This is once again a parody, in terms of the resurrection – perhaps an allusion to the legend of Nero *redivivus* which was widespread at that time (see below), or perhaps an allusion to the murder of the emperor Domitian which had just taken place. The one emperor dies but the other is on his way! The solemn transference of power is concluded in almost blasphemous biblical terminology with a Satanic doxology (13.4).

To round off the contrasting picture, the Roman beast is given its false prophets, just as the Messiah has his forerunners: 'a second beast comes from the land' (13.11–18). (Job 40 also spoke of one beast from the sea and one from the land: Leviathan and Behemoth.) Therefore Satan, the anti-Christ and the false prophets are counterparts to God, Christ and the eschatological prophet (from 10.8–11.2). (So here Christ is no longer 'the prophet' or witness or the Lamb, but the Jewish Messiah, who has a prophetic forerunner. Another tradition is involved. The Lamb is not mentioned here, either.) The picture of the Satanic false prophet has been developing along the lines of the *earlier* interpretation of Christ as the prophet. The lamb is a prophetic figure. So the second beast also appears 'as a lamb' (13.11), i.e. like a prophet, 'but it spoke like a dragon' (13.11c), i.e. a false prophet. The second beast, the false prophet, is evidently not a political figure: it stands by itself. Perhaps the reference is to anyone who makes a compromise with the first beast, 'worships it' (see 13.12); he makes people fall victim to the emperor cult. (False Christs and false prophets are part of Christianity from the start; see Mark 13; Matt. 24.24.) There are *false* prophets: they do not *suffer*, but perform amazing wonders (see above, p. 435, on Rev. 1.5; the false prophets make statues talk – an ancient theme, 13.15; and perhaps I should have deleted 'ancient'). Anyone who sacrifices to the emperor is marked in some indelible way or tattooed (13.16f., evidently with the number 666, which was comprehensible to the reader – but no longer makes sense to us: was it the name or the abbreviation of the name of the emperor of the time?).

Revelation 14 then introduces the Lamb again: this is the phase of final deliverance (14.1–5), the announcement of the final judgment (14.6–13) and the 'harvest' (14.14–20). 'the first-fruits of mankind' (14.4b) sing a new song which is known only to them (14.3), gathered round the Lamb on Mount Zion. 'They are redeemed' (14.4b; 14.4f. seems to be a gloss, not in the direction of asceticism, which is alien to Revelation, but perhaps along the lines of the 'five wise virgins', the community; see Matt. 25.1–12; Col. 1.22). 14.6–13 proclaims judgment on emperor worshippers and urges Christians to persevere. Soon will come the harvest and the gathering of the grapes (14.14–20; see Joel 3.13; also probably Dan. 7.13).

This part comes from a tradition in which 'one like a Son of man', 14.14, seems to be an angel alongside other angels. However, the author keeps close to his traditional material and allows discrepancies to remain.

An apocalyptic theologian never seems to be able to arrive at an apotheosis. It is as though he wanted to draw the sigh, 'Maranatha, Come Lord', from his readers in and through his account. The apotheosis is delayed for a second time. First come the visions of the seven bowls with God's wrath (Rev. 15; 16; see Ezek. 9; 10; and again a series of Egyptian plagues). But the author consoles the community. The well-known song of Moses is now sung again as a hymn of praise to the Lamb (15.1–4; Ex. 15; Deut. 32).

We find another example of 'dualism' in Rev. 17: Babylon, 'the great whore', probably the goddess Roma, to whom the emperor Augustus had erected a great temple in the middle of Asia Minor, in Pergamon (in the Old Testament whoredom is an image of idolatry). Rome is 'Babylon, the great city, the mother of whores and the abomination of the whole earth' (17.5); she was 'drunk with the blood of the saints and the blood of the martyrs of Jesus' (17.6): 'The woman whom you have seen is the great city, which rules over the kings of the earth' (17.18): Rome and the Roman empire. From 14.7 on (a later addition), an angel explains 'the secret' (that is, a code or an image to be deciphered, not a mystery). At first hearing it is even more puzzling for us to decipher. Evidently, however, it is based on the legend of Nero *redivivus*, which was well known at that time. The woman sits on a beast 'with seven heads and ten horns' (17.3), 'it is the city with the seven hills' (17.9), clearly the city of Rome: there are also 'seven kings' (17.10a): 'Five of whom are fallen, one *is*, the other has *not yet come*, and when he comes he must remain only a little while. As for the beast that *was* and *is not*, it is an eighth but it belongs to the seven and it goes to perdition' (17.10). We know, principally from Suetonius, Tacitus and the Sibylline Oracles (see below on 'The life of grace and political power in the New Testament', esp. pp. 578f.) that after the death of the tyrant Nero, as often happens, a legend grew up: Nero was not dead but had escaped to the East, and would return to take vengeance on Jerusalem and the Jews. Thus Nero became the anti-Messiah, taken over by Christians in the form of anti-Christ. So Nero knows his parousia, namely the return of the anti-Christ ('the eighth, who belongs to the seven', 'who was and is not but is to come'). We cannot discover anything more about the 'seven' emperors, as seven is an apocalyptic number and is not 'historical'. After the murder of Domitian (to which 13.3 is perhaps an allusion) there was probably a general expectation that the Roman empire would collapse. For a while the murder of this emperor brought peace to both Jews and Christians. The last phase begins with the parousia of the anti-Christ. Revelation 18 already raises a lament over the fall of the great city (18.9–20), which has suddenly taken on another appearance. Here another tradition appears, which is directed against the city: 'Come out, my people, *leave the city*, lest you take part in her sins, lest you share in her plagues' (18.4; see Jer. 51.45; also Heb. 13.13). This city no longer seems to be concerned with emperor worship: the city is simply a 'great city' of merchants, seafarers and kings, an 'evil' port (see 18.9–20, where these three categories are matched by saints, apostles and prophets).

In Rev. 19 we have a hymn of thanksgiving for the destruction of the great whore. The seer also perceives that two beasts – the Roman empire and the false prophet – are destroyed by the messianic general (19.11–16). This 'military messiah' plays only a subsidiary role in Revelation, but the author finds him in his tradition and includes him: he is 'the anointed', 'the rider on the white horse' (19.11, 19), the Messiah of national Jewish expectation. This Messiah destroys the anti-Christ and the false prophets. This is perhaps an allusion to the murder of Domitian, which was followed by a period of peace for the church. The Messiah 'judges and wages war with righteousness' (19.11; see Isa. 11.4). There is no trace here of a distinction between the judgment on the church and the judgment on its enemies. It is a question of the opposition between the Jewish Messiah and 'the nations' (see Ps. Sol. 17, where the Messiah also appears in the blood-stained garb of a warrior). Revelation 19.11–16 (or 10.11–21) takes over a Jewish tradition. The christology of Rev. 19.11ff. does not correspond with the author's ecclesiological lamb-christology. Here the Messiah does not have a single characteristic of the Lamb. It is simply said of him that he bears a name which is unknown to all mortals (19.12; see Isa. 62.2b).

According to apocalyptic logic, the fact that the church on earth had a respite after the death of Domitian also meant that something must have happened to Satan; were that not the case, this respite on earth would be inexplicable. In fact the seer sees how a great angel (perhaps Michael) seizes Satan and imprisons him in the depths of hell, sealing the lock (20.1–3, 'afterwards he must be loosed for a short time', 20.3b; see also Jude 6 and II Peter 2.4). From Rev. 12 onwards Satan had been cast out of heaven on to the earth. Now he is taken away from the earth and banished into the underworld. Later he will be freed 'for a short time', i.e. for the last struggle of all. The question why the dragon who has been so firmly shut away will be freed for the final battle is ignored by the author. Apocalyptic (the fight between good and evil) simply requires this, and the final battle of the chaos monster against God is a theme which is widespread in antiquity. Just as creation was the triumph of God over the powers of chaos, so the world of creation is constantly threatened by these chaotic powers. The background of Rev. 20.1ff. is an

old myth about the 'fall of the angels'. One of the angels has taken hold
of the key to the subterranean powers of chaos, who were put under
constraint at creation, and now opens up the abyss of hell so as to launch
a violent attack on God's good creation in the last days (which are a
counterpart to the first days of creation). This theme was associated with
various Old Testament traditions in early Judaism (see Isa. 24.21f.).

Now if Satan is shut out for a while, this indisputably means a respite
on earth as well. So the author has the opportunity to insert another
theme from the tradition: the thousand-year messianic kingdom. The
respite referred to lasts a thousand years: the allusion here must be to
Ps. 90.4; a day of creation, or God's day, lasts a thousand earthly years.
Thus the reference is to the seventh day of creation, on which God rests.
It follows from this in early Jewish tradition that while God rests, the
Messiah takes over God's rule of the world in this age: this is the intermediate messianic kingdom. (One also finds echoes of this in Paul: at a
later stage Christ returns his lordship to God and the kingdom of God
proper begins only after this reign of Christ, I Cor. 15.27f.) Revelation
20. 4ff. envisages this intermediate rule. There is no clear indication of
who sits on the ruler's throne (20.4) (as in Dan. 7.9; 7.26f.; cf. also
Matt. 19.28: the apostles will sit with Christ on the throne and judge the
twleve tribes of Israel). The reference is to 'the last judgment' at which
'some' will take part in the kingly rule of Christ. Who? All those who
have been beheaded: 'The souls of those who had been beheaded for their
testimony to Jesus and for the word of God' (20.4b), 'and who had not
worshipped the beast or its image and had not received its mark on their
foreheads or their hands' (20.4c). These 'came to life again' (20.4d). They
are no longer dead; they live and reign with Christ for a thousand years.
'That is the first resurrection' (20.5b). That means that witnesses, martyrs
for God's cause (from Israel and the church), are given preference: they
rise before the general (or 'second') resurrection takes place. Here the
twofold concept of the resurrection from the Old Testament has its role:
the *individual* resurrection, 'the righteous are in God's hand', with God
(Pss. 16.8ff., 49.5; 73.23ff.; Job 19.25), and the resurrection of the whole
people (Greek Isa. 26.19 → Ezek. 37.1–14 → Dan. 12.2). To distinguish
the fact that the righteous, the witnesses and the martyrs are 'now already
living with God' from the resurrection of the whole people (the general
resurrection as a precondition for universal judgment), the author talks
of 'the first *anastasis* (resurrection)'. (Here he is thinking more of a form
of 'transportation to God' than of a physical resurrection: 'the *souls* of
those who have been beheaded'; corporeality remains outside his sphere
of vision.) But the others are *dead* (20.5a) until the judgment in the last
days. Only the living are 'priests of the Holy One' (20.6; see Isa. 61.6).

The intermediate messianic kingdom here is thus the consequence of two early Jewish messianic conceptions.[148] For one the victory of the Messiah over the enemies of Israel was the beginning of the final time of salvation, which knows no end. Alongside that there was a second, which saw the whole kingdom of God as being completely transcendent. In that case, earthly history has an end which is followed by the general resurrection as a precondition of 'being judged'; only after that does the new age begin. The two trends came together (e.g. IV Ezra 7.28ff.). In these circumstances the final kingdom of God is preceded by a messianic kingdom which is not final, but only transitory (IV Ezra speaks of four thousand years). According to IV Ezra 11;12, the Roman empire will be brought to an end by the empire of the national Messiah of Israel. There was a widespread view that the Messiah was already alive somewhere and would soon make a public appearance. It emerges from Rev. 12 that the tradition of the Jewish Messiah had already been connected with the tradition of the 'heavenly Son of man', through the concept of 'transportation' (see IV Ezra 13 and II Bar. 53). The insertion in Rev. 20.1–6 should therefore be understood in terms of the combination of two early Jewish messianic conceptions of salvation. In IV Ezra 7.26ff., after the messianic kingdom the Messiah vanishes for ever; then begins the sole rule of God. However, Revelation gives the Messiah an ultimate significance, precisely in the new age: the heavenly Jerusalem is the bride of the Lamb (21.9). In Revelation the thousand-year kingdom is a period of heavenly transition: the life of the saints with God before the general resurrection. (In dogmatics this became the direct vision of God by the saints after death, even before the general resurrection. In essence, this is the meaning of Rev. 20.4–6.) Under the names of chiliasm or millenarianism, the 'thousand-year kingdom' later had a considerable effect on the imagination of Christians. One particular theology, to which the historical background of this concept and the purpose of Revelation was unknown, neutralized this fact by identifying the era of the church between the death of Jesus and the parousia with this thousand-year kingdom. In Revelation, however, an early Jewish tradition simply becomes a theology of the final destiny of witnesses and martyrs.

In fact, Rev. 20; 21 is composed after the model of Ezek. 37–40 (the messianic kingdom, Ezek. 37; Gog and Magog, Ezek. 38; 39; the new Jerusalem, Ezek. 40ff.). After the thousand years, Satan will be let loose again (Rev. 20.7). Gog is the prince, the leader of the enemies of Israel; Magog on the other hand was originally the name of a land of people (Gen. 10.2; I Chron. 1.5), but in the course of time 'Gog and Magog' became a prefiguration of the later anti-Christ. The 'dualistic' pattern continues to exert its influence, and because Revelation sets out to take up all traditions, the composition of the book now becomes somewhat confused as a result of a number of doublets. On the other hand, the apocalyptic logic is firm. Because there are *two* periods of salvation as a result of the insertion of a thousand-year kingdom, the final, transcendent time of salvation must now be preceded by new eschatological woes. Time and again, Satan too is present just as salvation is about to appear. So he is again let loose immediately before the final act of all. This is the reason why the author takes up the tradition of Gog and Magog: the final attack of the nations of God's holy city (20.9). Here are all the demons of the subterranean powers of hell who have been freed by Satan and now seek to force the final decision under his leadership. But the author of Revelation has this Satanic rebellion crushed at a stroke: the devil and all his satellites are annihilated (apparently without any real action from God's side); they are thrown 'into the lake of fire and brimstone' by which the two beasts have already finally been swallowed up (20.10). In the author's view this is not annihilation but 'eternal torment' (20.10b), in contrast to the sinners who seem to be *annihilated* by this fire (20.15).

This final battle is followed by the universal judgment (20.11–15) and thus the apotheosis (foreseen in the original plan as events after the opening of the seventh seal, 8.1). The theophany is not described (God is too transcendent): there is a throne of judgment and '*the one who* sits on it' (20.11). His appearance is mentioned in passing: 'From his presence earth and sky fled away, and no place was found for them' (20.11). There is no world conflagration and no cosmic collapse of sun, moon and stars as in the earlier account of the visions of the trumpets (8.5–12; 9.1–21). The disappearance of the old vale of tears is simply the consequence of the appearance of the living God. God comes to judge. From a Jewish point of view, the final judgment is left to God alone: in rabbinic literature the Messiah is not the eschatological judge of the world,[149] nor is he even in Revelation. At this judgment Christ is merely the advocate of his own (see 3.5). the judgment takes place exactly and justly on the basis of books. There are two of these (20.12): on the one hand the book in which is written what everyone has done or not done: 'reward according to works'; on the other hand is 'the book of life', i.e. in which are written the names of the elect by the grace of God – the two great Jewish traditions: 'justified by works' and 'justified freely by grace'. Here too the author does not make a synthesis: now there are simply these two trad-itions. Both are given their place: righteousness and love. The last judg-ment is universal: death and Hades must surrender all their dead (20.13), and they themselves, death and the underworld, will now be cast for ever into the fiery abyss (see Isa. 25.8; cf. I Cor. 15.26: death as the last enemy): 'that is the second death' (20.14). Along with death and Hades, all those whose names are not written in the book of life are 'cast into the lake of fire' (though in contrast to 20.10, which is concerned with the devil and the two beasts, it is not said that they are tortured; here the lake of fire is evidently a place of annihilation). Thus in the last resort grace, 'the book of life', is decisive. Not to be included in the book of life is the real end: these people disappear. With 20.11 one can say, 'And no place was found for them'. Revelation does not seem to know of any 'hell for sinners'.

Then the apotheosis can begin: the new heaven and the new earth. There were two views about this in early Judaism: the old earth (and the old Jerusalem) is itself renewed (because people started from the new insight that God's works know no end and God does not destroy his work of creation, and on the other hand that the old world is so corrupt that a completely new creation must come, whereas the old world will pass away). As a true apocalyptist the author defends the 'new creation', but without the dramatic annihilation of the old world: this almost automatically disappears at the appearing of God (20.11). The author is inspired by Isa. 65.17, where the two conceptions are already combined; the Hebrew text speaks of a completely 'new creation' (I will . . . *create*), the Greek version omits 'I will create' and translates, 'so that people will no longer remember what was before'. The man of the future is like a child on Christmas Eve. He has asked for a model train and has pictured it to himself vividly with every detail and every possibility. But when he gets the long-awaited train on Christmas Eve, it is quite different. It is so beautiful that all earlier ideas about it are long since forgotten. The author suggests something of this kind. The 'new creation' is at the centre of apocalyptic.

Finally, the new creation is the descent of the heavenly Jerusalem 'to earth' as the 'radiant bride' of the Lamb (21.1f., see 22.17): the heavenly Jerusalem now becomes an earthly reality (for the earth is no more). As early as 19.7, 9, it was said, 'The marriage of the Lamb has come and his bride has made herself ready', 'Blessed are those who are invited to the marriage supper of the Lamb '(cf. II Cor. 11.2; Eph. 5.31f., but in Revelation this is a purely apocalyptic event). The marriage of God with Israel is a traditional conception (from Hosea, in Jer. 2.2; Ezek. 16.1–63; Isa. 50.1; 54.5f.; 62.4f.; cities are regularly personified). Early Judaism, too, knows only God, and not the Messiah, as bridegroom – an image of the inauguration of the final eschatological time of salvation. Here too there were two conceptions: the eschatological renewal of the old Jerusalem, though in accordance with the heavenly model (e.g. Tob. 13.10–18; 14.5; Isa. 52.1ff.), and on the other hand the completely new Jerusalem (later apocalyptic: II Baruch 4.3; IV Ezra 7.26; Enoch 90.29; see Heb. 12.22), a Jewish conception which comes above all from the time after the fall of Jerusalem in AD 70. The new Jerusalem is the perfect community, 'the beloved city' (20.9). The author does not imagine it in terms of Rome, but like a great Babylonian city in the form of a cube (cf. Ezek. 40; 48.31–35).

There are some particularly striking features in the visionary account of the heavenly city (21.9–22.5; cf. Isa. 60.1–11): the lightness and brightness (21.22–27) and the water, which was of such vital importance in the oriental world (21.6; see also 7.17; 22.17). Water is the saving gift of life (God is the source of the water of life, Jer. 2.13). 'Let him who is thirsty come, let him who desires take the water of life without price' (22.17; 21.6). In contrast to John 4.7, in Revelation this is an eschatological event: the paradisal river of the eschaton (Rev. 22.1; Ezek. 47.1). However, the river no longer comes from the temple, but directly from God and Christ: here is salvation without any cultic intermediary.

This lack of intermediary is expressed above all through the lack of a temple in the city of God: 'And I saw no temple in the city, for its temple is the Lord God and Almighty and the Lamb' (21.22). In early Judaism and also in Qumran, the restoration of the Temple is usually the eschatological event:[150] but there is also a certain degree of hostility to the actual Temple. We also find both views in early Christianity (sometimes connected: I will break down this temple, but in three days I will build it up again; cf. Isa. 66.1f.; Acts 7.49). In Rev. 3.12 and 11.1f. the community itself is called the temple, or at least its pillars. Furthermore, there was also mention of a heavenly temple elsewhere (thus another tradition: 7.15; 11.19; 14.15f.; 15.5, 8; 16.1, 17).

Now the former things have passed away (21.4; cf. Isa. 43.18f.). Everyone sees God and Christ (22.3f.). The earth itself has become heaven. There is a throne on which God and Christ, the Lamb, sit. Both are objects of *latreia* or worship (22.3c). Then is brought to pass the demand of Deut. 10.12: to worship Yahweh 'with all your heart and all your soul'. *Worship* fills the heavenly city *from the presence of God.* Israel's dream that in the last time Yahweh will again come to dwell with his people is fulfilled (Lev. 26.11: 'I will make my abode with them'; Ezek. 37.27; Zech. 2.10; see also Isa. 52.8; 60.2; Zech 8.8; 9.14; Ps. 102.16; Greek Isa. 37.33). *Opsontai to prosōpon autou* (Rev. 22.4): 'they will look on his countenance' (see Pss. 17.15; 42.2; also I Cor. 13.12; II Cor. 3.18, etc.). Encounter with God in the Temple in worship was also a Jewish conception. But here there is no longer a temple. The basic event in the final time of salvation is the radiant presence of God through Christ among his people. From this comes the brightness of the whole city, its splendour of light (21.22–27). The illumination of heaven and earth no longer comes from the sun and moon: through Christ, 'the light', 'God's splendour falls on everyone and everything' (21.23: so Christ does not give back his lordship to the Father; he shines in glory with the Father'). Sun and moon have fled at God's appearing: they are no longer needed as lights for the day and night. 'There will be no more night' (21.25; 22.5; see Isa. 60.11; Zech. 14.7). 'Behold, the dwelling of God is with men. He will dwell with them, and they shall be his people, and God himself shall be with them; he will wipe away every tear from their eyes, and death shall be no more, neither shall there be mourning nor crying nor pain any more, for the former things have passed away' (21.3f.; see 7.17b; the passage contains an accumulation of biblical texts, see above: 'I will make my abode with you'; also 'wipe away tears', Isa. 25.8; pain is past, Isa. 65.16; the former things have passed away, Isa. 43.18f.). God's voice had rung out, 'Behold, I make all things new' (21.5). The whole of the Christian apocalypse is directed towards this new event (1.8, 17 → 21.6; 3.12 → 21.2; 7.17 → 21.4; 19.20 → 21.8), the large-scale fulfilment of Isaiah's vision (Isa. 65.17): a new mankind without a history of suffering, without evil and tears – God's saving will from before all time. The demonic waters are no more (21.1), there is just the holy and righteous city of God (21.2; see Isa. 65; 64.10–12; 60.10–14; Hag. 2.7–9; Zech. 2.1–5). Then there is direct converse with God as once there was in the garden in the early days of creation. Here is the city of righteousness and love.

That is this apocalyptic writer's vision of the future; he takes it from the kerygma of the church and the death and exaltation of Jesus, and transforms this kerygma into an epic made up of an amalgam of Old Testament texts: the epic of the man of the future whom God has foreseen from all eternity.

It is evident that a number of hands have been at work in this closing section of the book of Revelation (22.6–21). Apocalyptic writers constantly go round in circles and cannot manage to end. The heart of this final passage is the sigh of the 'Spirit and the Bride', 'Come' (22.17). The author has in mind the liturgy of the community in which someone reads out the text, 'Come, Lord Jesus' (22.17a) and the community *hears* the reading and *responds* with 'Come' (22.17b) (see *Didache* 10.6, 'If anyone is worthy, let him come'; cf. Isa. 55.1). Here 'the Spirit' is evidently a figure who supports the community and prompts its prayers and passionate cries (see Rom. 8.26); precisely because of this characteristic, the Gospel of John calls the Spirit 'another Paraclete'. In the letters, too, it is a 'Spirit' which passes the message on to the community (cf. John 16.13). In fact what is said here amounts to the same thing as the Paraclete of the Johannine community. Christ is at work in the earthly church only through the Spirit (though in Revelation the Spirit is evidently an angelic figure, just as we also find many features of a tradition of angel christology in it).

In this perspective on the future there is hardly any mention of the people for whom it is destined. The seer is overwhelmed with what he is allowed to see: God and Christ, who make all things good through a completely new creation. Of men, all that the seer says is that all rule (22.5b), and *no one is enslaved*. The powers of evil have simply vanished away, like the old earth with its tears and sorrow: 'No one will ever find their place.' The last book of the Jewish and Christian Bible makes the vision of grace, the *ḥesed* or *charis* of God, once spoken over Israel as a priestly blessing, reach its fulfilment: 'May the Lord spread *the radiance of his countenance over you* and *be gracious to you*' (Num. 6.25; see Ps. 118.27). Even more, the prayer of Moses to be allowed to see God's *face* as well, at the time refused (Ex. 33.12–23), is now given a positive answer: *opsontai prosōpon autou* (Rev. 22.4): they will see his countenance and rule 'for all eternity' (22.5b). The humble and the oppressed, the suffering and the persecuted, all are exalted.

The imagery of the book of Revelation is often incomprehensible to us (though it will have been fully understood at the time), but the book as a whole is a rich interpretation of faith in Christ 'sitting at the right hand of God'. Hebrews had depicted this earliest Christian dogma in terms of a great heavenly liturgical ceremony. Revelation portrays it as a dramatic battle between the powers of good and the powers of evil, in which the good win the day. The onslaughts of evil are depicted in lurid colours: Christ and God seem to do little or nothing. They simply triumph (apart from the Jewish tradition of the messianic rider on the white horse; he returns from battle with bloodstained garments – on the outside, the blood *of others*). This is the faith by which the persecuted community lives. The seer has in mind only the church and the evil powers. So this book is the most ecclesiocentric in the whole of the New Testament.

However, this Christian belief and this hope of the minority groups of Christians who were to be found at that time throughout the empire eventually brought the Roman empire down (apart from some other factors, or taking these factors into account). For us, Revelation is not only a gospel of hope but at the same time – in the situation of our time – a real basis for a *Christian* theology of liberation which also provides a theology of *martyrion*: bearing witness to the sole right of the good to exist, even to the point of death. The furthering of all good, resistant to all evil as a dream of God: a new creation, as a struggle against the primal monster Leviathan, the unfathomable possibility of the deepest depths of our humanity. If the book of Genesis depicts God's beginning with creation, the last book of the New Testament depicts the final future of this world of creation. There is no good creation without repeated struggle against the powers of evil, in whatever specific figures they may make their historical appearance. For Revelation, this was above all slavery through the Roman empire as a power which persecuted *Christians*. The book of Revelation still has no eye for powers which persecute *human beings*. When the Christians were no longer persecuted by the Romans, like the Roman citizen Paul they were loyal to what at that time, above all for Christians *in Rome*, was not an occupying power but the local political authority (as is already evident from I Clement).

In the book of Revelation the apocalyptic seer is so overcome by what he sees that he almost forgets man himself. Perhaps that is the secret of this whole apocalypse. The one who loses himself will find himself again. The city of God *is* a city of *man* because it is 'from God'. In a historically conditioned fashion, appropriate to its time, Revelation is an inspiration and a landmark for Christians today – provided that we refrain from projecting back on the book of Revelation what *for us* is a matter of *updating* for our own time.

# The experience of grace and its interpretative elements in the New Testament

It is impossible to arrive at a fully consistent synthesis from the preceding detailed analysis. However, a fundamentally identical experience underlies the various interpretations to be found throughout the New Testament: all its writings bear witness to the experience of salvation in Jesus from God. This experience not only has geographical and cultural colouring, but also varies according to the difficulties which arose in the many different local churches. However, our analysis does permit a descriptive and summary synthesis. From it we can then extract the formative structural elements which still give us, as contemporary Christians, the bearings for formulating our experience of the decisive salvation in Jesus.

Chapter 1

# The concept of grace and the reality of salvation to which it refers

## §1  The concept of *charis* or grace

I.  THE NEW POSSIBILITY OF LIFE GIVEN AND TO BE ENJOYED

Corresponding to the key Old Testament concepts *ḥesed* and *ḥānan*, in the New Testament grace means the benevolent and merciful (and at the same time free and sovereign) love of God for men. This is not, however, to be understood exclusively in an internalized sense, as a benevolent disposition of God and in God, but rather as a benevolence of God which in fact brings salvation that manifests or reveals itself freely in the favours of redemption and liberation shown forth in history and experienced by men in faith (for Jewish Christians the Old Testament concept of *ḥesed* and *ḥānan* rules out any dualism between inwardness and its outward expression).

Grace is a *new way of life* prepared for us by God in Jesus Christ, and offered to us on the level of our own earthly history, freely (Paul) and to make us glad (Luke) (see Heb. 10.20; II Peter 2.15; John 14.6; a way of salvation: Acts 16.17; 9.2; 19.23; 24.14; I Cor. 12.31; 'the way' is an oriental expression, also to be found in late antiquity, for a particular practice and viewpoint which leads to salvation). Thus grace is a new human possibility for life, a particular mode of existence through which and in which man really experiences salvation and redemption, liberation and renewal of life, happiness and fulfilment. For the New Testament, 'the way' means following the life of Jesus with God, expressed in his concern for men, in solidarity with our experience of God's care for all: a way of life or mode of existence through which God's own concern, his merciful love and faithfulness – *ḥesed* and *\*met* – on which we can rely, are continued by man in our earthly history.

God himself equips man for this. For although this new possibility for human living, proclaimed by Jesus in his preaching and in his parables, demonstrated and put into practice in his way of life and his death, is given a variety of names in the New Testament, they all fundamentally express a single reality. Pauline theology calls it adoption *(hyiothesia)*, Johannine theology *birth from God*. Both conceptions seek to express that the Christian has a share in the particular relationship which binds the man Jesus, as the Son, through the Spirit with the Father – three concepts (Father, Son and Spirit), which in the New Testament point to God, but *in* his attitude towards men.

The concept of grace therefore points primarily towards a *call* to this special living community with God: the Christian vocation as a consequence of a prior decision made freely and graciously by God, who calls men to the way of the gospel (Gal. 1.6; I Tim. 1.11). On the other hand, by virtue of this call, namely as the obedience of faith (Gal. 3.5; I Cor. 2.12; Rom. 6.16; 5.15, etc.), the concept points to Christian life itself: existence in grace, in being and acting, through which this responsible action is experienced as being supported, guided and directed by the power of Jesus which, as divine *dynamis* (Acts 4.33; 6.8; 20.32; 14.26; 15.40; 18.27; I Cor. 1.18; 6.14; II Cor. 4.7; 12.9f.; II Tim. 2.1; Rom. 1.16; Eph. 2.7f., etc.) 'fulfils everything in us' (Col. 1.6f.), 'through faith which is at work in our love (of neighbour)' (Gal. 5.6).

This divine calling has appeared to us personally in Jesus and has taken shape in his personal call: to be converted, to take a different course from the one that we have been on, since the kingdom of God is now near (Mark 1.14f.). Therefore for those who have not themselves heard this historical call of Jesus, there is the good news of this event given by the Christian community in the world which is itself grace and power (Acts 5.20; 20.24, 32; Luke 4.22; I Cor. 15.2; James 1.21; II Tim. 1.1; Eph. 6.15, etc.). In addition, there is above all the event itself, Jesus' personal appearance in our history, the grace of which the New Testament particularly speaks. Individual texts, taken from a wide variety of New Testament writings, seek to express in brief formulations what these Christians have experienced as salvation from God and how they have experienced God as salvation.

'Grace and truth have come to us in Jesus Christ' (John 1.17)

'The great gift of the grace of God: the one man Jesus Christ' (Rom. 5.15, with 5.17)

'God's saving grace appeared to all men' (Titus 2.11)

'The goodness and loving-kindness – *(philanthrōpia* as an exceptional Septuagint translation of *ḥesed)* – of God our saviour has appeared' (Titus 3.4)

'God made all fullness dwell in him' (Col. 1.9)

'For in him the whole fullness of deity dwells bodily, and you have come to fullness of life in him' (Col. 2.9)

'One mediator between God and man, the man Christ Jesus' (I Tim. 2.5)

'He is the access to the Father' (Rom. 5.2)

'He has richly poured out the Spirit upon us through Jesus Christ our saviour' (Titus 3.6)

'In this the love of God was made manifest among us, that God sent his only Son into the world' (I John 4.9); and, 'See what love the Father has given us that we should be called children of God; and so we are' (I John 3.1)

'God who has called us ... to receive a share in God's own being' (II Peter 1.4c).

It is already clear from these texts how religious experience, the religious experience of God, has its focal point in the New Testament in its connection with the man Jesus Christ. Is Jesus here the symbolic point of reference of a kind of *mysticism of being?* Or is a *historical* event really the specific Christian access to God? The New Testament defends the latter point of view, sometimes with great stubbornness. Johannine theology, which most markedly demonstrates a degree of God-mysticism, nevertheless attacks any *lyein ton Iēsoun* (I John 4.3), that is, any attempt to do away with Jesus of Nazareth in favour of a heavenly or spiritual Christ principle (see also the deliberate use of 'Jesus' – not 'Jesus Christ' – in Eph. 4.21). Here we find the same interest as that from which the first three gospels were written.

There is a prelude to this appearance of God's grace in Jesus Christ, which gives us his and God's Spirit. But as the New Testament lives under the spell of Jesus' experience of grace, it shows less interest in God's revelation of grace outside Christianity. From a psychological point of view, this results in a certain narrowing of perspective and at a very early stage in a pattern of thinking in terms of thesis and antithesis. Nevertheless, at the periphery of this enthusiasm engendered by the Spirit over what has been experienced and continues to be experienced in Jesus Christ, these Christians are aware that universal grace had been revealed in a great many ways even before Jesus Christ: fundamentally in the history which embraces all men, as the event of men in nature, which arouses an ethical and even a religious consciousness (above all Rom. 1.18–22), and especially through Israel's own history in the melting-pot of the history of the nations of the surrounding world (Heb. 1.1; Rom. 2.1–3.20). Jesus of Nazareth makes his appearance against this general and specific historical background (Rom. 3.21–4.5), as God's 'amen' to all his promises to Israel and thus to all peoples (II Cor. 1.20).

## II. JESUS AS GRACE: THE RISEN CHRIST AS GRACE

All the parts of the New Testament assert that the earthly appearing of Jesus is the grace of God. But there are marked differences of accent. In the four gospels the whole event of and around Jesus is a sign of the grace of God. For Mark this is true from the baptism of Jesus on, and for Matthew, Luke and John from the first moment of his coming into the world (John 1.14; 3.16; 12.46f.; see also I John 4.9, 14). Not only his death and his resurrection but also his message of God's kingdom, intended for mankind, and his whole way of life are gifts of grace; his dealings with people, above all in eating with them, his care and concern and especially his contact with sinners, the poor and the oppressed who were despised by the religious and suffered the social consequences of this discrimination. It emerges above all from the supposition to be found even before Easter, that to take up an attitude for or against Jesus has to do with a decision about one's own destiny: a decision for or against the coming kingdom of God.[1]

The all-embracing sign of grace, however, both in the four canonical gospels and above all in the whole of the rest of the New Testament, is Jesus' love to the point of death: his suffering and dying as a breaking of the life which he entrusts to his God, in grief, but with all his heart (see Rom. 5.9–11; I Cor. 15.2f.; II Cor. 3.17f.; Heb. 10.29; I Peter 2.21; II Tim. 1.10b, etc.): 'He who did not spare his own Son but gave him up for us all, will he not *also give us all things* with him?' (Rom. 8.32). 'God so loved the world that he gave his only begotten Son that all who believe in him should not perish but have everlasting life' (John 3.16). Above all in Paul and in the New Testament traditions influenced by Paul, the grace of God in Christ is so strongly concentrated in the death and resurrection of Jesus that there is a tendency to concentrate and to limit *charis* as it has appeared in Jesus exclusively to his death and resurrection. So Paul himself never connects the term *charis* with the message and the appearing of Jesus of Nazareth, but only with Christ Jesus who has risen from the dead. Paul never associates *charis* with *Jesus* but only with (Jesus) *Christ*, the risen one (Gal. 2.19; see I Cor. 1.30; II Cor. 5.21). Only the *Lord* Jesus is grace. Without the resurrection from the dead, the earthly appearance of Jesus in fact remains open, even problematical. However, the four gospels avoid this exclusively *kerygmatic* conception of the dead and risen Jesus; in their proclamation *of the gospel* they also recognize the grace to be found in the message of Jesus and his way of life (albeit in the light of the resurrection).

It is, however, true of the whole of the canonical New Testament that death and resurrection are the determinative climax of the grace of God in Jesus Christ. Only after Jesus, dying, has firmly held God's hand and in turn has known himself to be sustained in this impenetrable situation,[2] is he confirmed by God: 'By the grace of God Jesus tasted death for everyone' (Heb. 2.9). Hebrews above all emphatically stresses that an exclusive divine act on the part of the Father gives 'perfecting' constitutive significance to the reality of Jesus' sacrifice. This in no way removes the element of Jesus' own love to the point of death, indeed it even presupposes it, as it is this that is confirmed and sealed by God in the resurrection or glorification of Jesus. Jesus' resurrection is thus a free and sovereign action on the part of God, even if it manifests itself as already beginning *in* Jesus' personal communion with God into which he has incorporated his suffering and dying. From God's perspective, this very communion is already a manifestation of *grace* to Jesus, a grace which simply reveals its inner dynamic in his exaltation or resurrection and is brought to a final consummation. Only at this final consummation – which Phil. 2.9 expressly calls a grace for Jesus himself: *echarisato*, see also Heb. 2.9, can one say that Jesus 'is the cause (source) of eternal salvation' (Heb. 5.9). In connection with the historical Jesus, the Gospel of John also says (while putting stress on the grace which already became manifest through the earthly Jesus): 'The Spirit was not yet because Jesus was not yet glorified' (John 7.39, a text which radically excludes the possibility that after his death Jesus again became a post-existent Logos *asarkos*, not incarnate as in his pre-existence).

Thus the New Testament conception conveys that only the risen Jesus bestows eschatological salvation: the *pneuma*, his, God's own Spirit

(Rom. 8.14–18; 8.29; Gal. 4.4–7; Eph. 1.3–5; Titus 3.6, etc. see below); the Spirit through which the Christian, thanks to the grace of faith and baptism (Rom. 6; Gal. 3.26f.; Titus 3.5), is conformed to God, i.e. receives a share both in his relationship to God and also in his 'brotherly' (Rom. 8.29) radical service and his dedication to his fellow man.

## §2 The saving content of the concept of grace

### I. ADOPTION AND NEW CREATION (PAULINISM) AND BIRTH FROM GOD (JOHANNINE THEOLOGY): THE GIFT OF THE *PNEUMA*

Salvation from God, which is given to us through the life of Jesus and culminates in the death and resurrection, is presented in thematic form as: (*a*) being a child of God and (*b*) the gift of the Holy Spirit. Before we summarize what the New Testament means by the 'riches of the grace of God' (Eph. 1.7b; 2.4–7; 3.8), these fundamental gifts must be analysed in more detail, as they form the basis for all the other expositions.

### A. Being a child of God

The synoptic gospels already talk of being a child: 'Blessed are the peacemakers, for they will be called children of God' (Matt. 5.9), 'that you may be children of your Father who is in heaven' (Matt. 5.45). In itself, this is a concept from general human religious awareness. The specific feature of the New Testament is that this particular communion with God is communicated through Jesus of Nazareth, the Christ, the Son of God, 'of whose fullness we have all received' (John 1.16; see Col. 2.9f.). In accordance with which model does the New Testament interepret this new, gracious relationship with God?

In addition to the passages which simply talk of being children of God without making the matter more precise (e.g. Matt. 5.9; 5.45; Eph. 1.5, etc.), we find two models which both present the same Christian experience: the more *juridical* model of adoption and the more *ontological* model of being born from God. To these we must add the model of creation, as being a more precise indication of the content of the juridical model of adoption. The first model comes from the Old Testament and Judaism. 'They are Israelites, and to them belong the sonship, the glory, the *hyiothesia*' (Rom. 9.4). Only in the Hellenestic period did Israel also begin to speak of God as also being the Father of *individual* believers (above all,

Wisdom 2.13–16; 12.21; 14.15; Sir. 23.1 4; 51.10; see III Macc. 5.7; 6.8; 7.6). Even before this there was talk of *the people of God* being the son of God (Ex. 4.22f.; Hos. 11.1–11; Isa. 43.1–7; 63.8f.; Mal. 1.2f.), but this was not based on natural origin or birth from God, which was the way in which neighbouring peoples often portrayed God's creation. The basis was election in grace (Deut. 14.1f.; Isa. 1.2–9; Mal. 1.2f.): this happens through the covenant, which in and of itself is more of a juristic concept, however deep and real life in covenant with God may be. Israelites are made sons of God by the Father (Deut. 32.6–43; Isa. 43.6f.; 63.16f.; Mal. 2.10). It is not a matter of being born from God, though we often find an echo of this conception from neighbouring peoples in the Old Testament; even Deut. 32.6 says, 'Is not he your father, who created you, who made you and established you?'[3] In the early Jewish period, being a child of God, like the Spirit, is an eschatological benefit of messianic times (Mal. 3.17f.; see also Wisdom 2.18; 5.5; and in the inter-testamental literature).[4] When Matt. 5.9 combines the eschatological beatitude with being a child of God, it is referring to this form of childhood.

Pauline theology will take up this tradition and speak of *hyiothesia* or adoption (Rom. 8.14–17; 8.23; 9.26; Gal. 3.26–28; 4.5–7). Johannine theology, by contrast, goes in quite a different direction; it never speaks of '*hyioi tou Theou*' (sons of God), but of *tekna tou Theou* (John 1.12f.; see also 'little children', John 13.33; and often in I John). *Tekna* are those who are born. So the Johannine literature knows nothing of adoption, but only of birth from God (John 3.3–8; above all I John 2.29 with 3.1; 3.9 with 3.10; 5.1 with 5.2; also 4.7; 5.4, 18, cf. also I Peter 1.3; 1.23; Titus 3.5). As the terminology *sperma tou Theou*, seed of God (I John 3.9), suggests, the author is not thinking of an adoption, but clearly of being born from God. Human begetting serves as a model here (I John 5.1). However, this is no human or earthly birth, but a *spiritual* birth; 'But to all those who believed in his name he gave power to become children (*tekna*) of God, who were born not of blood nor of the will of the flesh nor of the will of man, but *of God*' (John 1.12f.); in other words, they have a spiritual birth. They are conceived by the Holy Spirit. Being born is better symbol than adoption for what is involved here, i.e. for what it is to be a Christian. For 'what is born of the flesh is flesh and what is born of the spirit is spirit' (John 3.6; cf. Rom. 8.5, 9; without the concept of birth). Thus 'to be born of God' means 'to be of God' (I John 3.9 with 3.10; see also 4.4 with 5.4). In the expression 'be born of the spirit' (John 3.6), *pneuma* primarily has the meaning of the effective power of God, which is to be found in the Old Testament and the inter-testamental literature, i.e. spirit as power from above or the characteristic nature of the heavenly spheres (the *epourania*, see John 3.12). Thus in an exceptional, transcendent way, it can come to be used of God: 'God is *pneuma*'

(John 4.24), or as Paul will say at one point 'Christ is *pneuma*' (II Cor. 3.17), also in the universal (traditional) sense. The risen Jesus belongs completely to the 'heavenly' spiritual sphere, to the otherness of the divine as opposed to the earthly. The pneumatic (higher) world is contrasted here with the earthly, even human world. By being born of the Spirit, Christians also *receive* a 'heavenly' spiritual nature. The Spirit is therefore like a chrism, an anointing of our humanity so that it takes on a spiritual mode of existence (I John 2.20, 27). In content, the *sperma tou Theou* (I John 3.9) is identical with our new, spiritual mode of being; in effect it means the same thing as John 1.12f. ('not born of the will of man'). As Christians we are all 'virgin born', i.e. from the Spirit. Perhaps this *terminology* already comes from the Graeco-Jewish syncretistic environment of Johannine theology, but the Johannine *sperma pneumatikon* is in radical contradiction with the Stoic significance of this term and the other meanings to be found in late antiquity. Man does not have a spiritual nucleus to his being by nature, on the basis of his spirit; only through rebirth is he of spiritual, 'heavenly' divine nature, by virtue of grace. Only this new mode of being brings eternal life for that very reason: for Johannine theology it does so already. This is God's own life (John 3.16–18, 36; 5.24; I John 3.14; 5.11–13). The Spirit is 'a lifegiving Spirit' (John 6.63; II Cor. 3.6; I Peter 3.18), since real life is life in the Spirit, 'from above' (here Paul will stress the 'not yet' rather than the 'now already', cf. e.g. Rom. 8.2 with 8.11).

Those who are born of God, the *tekna* or begotten children, are endowed with the divine principle of life, the Holy Spirit. Therefore both Pauline adoption and Johannine birth from God[5] transcend purely juridical or even moral adoption: 'And so we *are*' (I John 3.1), even through grace. Therefore it becomes clear, above all in I John, that Christian action (I John 2.29; 3.9f.; 4.7; 5.1f.) has a more deep-seated, spiritual *foundation* (3.9). Here we find a concept of grace which comprises both (spiritual) exaltation and saving grace, in the sense of the principle and force of the ethical action of a Christian in a still unredeemed and threatened world.

Perhaps we can even find a third model in Pauline theology, one that deepens the significance of the model of 'adoption' which is meant in realistic terms, even if it derives from the law courts. This is the model of creation: grace as the new creation of man. It is absent from the Johannine model because the model of birth is itself already quite realistic. Paul also uses this model of creation alongside that of adoption: 'If anyone is in Christ, there is a new creation' (*kainē ktisis*) (II Cor. 5.17; Gal. 6.15). This model is also used in the Deutero-Pauline epistles: 'created in Jesus Christ' (Eph. 2.10), 'created for a new man who is in the image of God' (Eph. 4.24), 'the new man who renews himself in accordance with the image of his Creator' (Col. 3.10). The fact that this model of creation is peculiar to Pauline theology indicates that it is meant to make the model of adoption more specific. It also indicates that redemption is a creative work of God, linked with Christ, so that 'creation' and 'salvation' in Christ are combined (Eph. 2.15; 3.9; 4.24; Col. 1.15f.; 3.10). All this makes up a basic concept which will provide the structure for the later theology of grace: *creation, new creation, consummation* and all in God's special plan with man. Grace as man's redemption is taken up in an all-embracing ordinance of peace.

Precisely because they are grace and are not human by nature, adoption and a new creation in grace (Pauline theology), or birth from God in grace (Johannine theology), are accomplished in baptism and through the Spirit (John 3.5 with 3.6; I Peter 1.3; 1.23; Titus 3.5; see Rom. 6) – by virtue of faith (John 1.12), and in Paul justification by faith. Although in the New Testament Christian baptism was originally connected with the forgiveness of sins (see e.g. Acts 2.38; 22.16; I Cor. 6.11; also Heb. 10.22), because at an equally early stage in Christianity baptism was understood as baptism in the Spirit (Mark 1.8 par.; Acts 1.5; 2.38; 11.16; 19.2f.), there was also stress on the conception of baptism as birth: 'the washing of regeneration and renewal in the Holy Spirit' (Titus 3.5).

So although the adoption model as such is minimal and the birth model maximal, what is meant in both cases remains equally realistic: 'being formed in accordance with God' (Johannine theology, John 5.18; Pauline theology, Phil. 2.7). In other words, Pauline theology, also thanks to the creation model, fills adoption with a reality which transcends the juridical nature of this model, whereas Johannine theology reduces the ontological model to a birth through grace (also refraining from using the *ktisis* or creation terminology); it does not in any way see birth as a natural regulation of the mode of human existence. All this is confirmed by the fact that for both interpretations (thought patterns) divine sonship is the work of the Spirit of God and implies the possession of the Spirit.

## B. The gift of the Holy Spirit

As the basis of all other gifts, the gift of the Holy Spirit given with the status of being a child of God is God's greatest gift of salvation in and through the risen Jesus (Gal. 3.5; 4.6; 5.18, 25; I Cor. 2.4; 2.10–12; 6.11; 7.40; II Cor. 1.22; 4.13; 5.5; 13.14; Rom. 5.5; 8.9–11; 8.14f., 23; 12.11; 15.13, 19; Phil. 1.27; 2.1; I Thess. 4.8; Acts 1.5; 2.4, 17, 38; 4.31; 5.32; 6.3; 8.15, 17–19; 10.44, 47; 15.8; 19.2; John 3.6; 6.63; 14.17; Eph. 1.13f.; 2.18, 22; 3.16; 4.30; 5.18; Col. 1.8; II Thess. 2.13; I Tim. 3.16; Titus 3.5; Heb. 6.4; 10.15, 29; I Peter 1.2; 4.6; I John 3.24; 4.13).

The link which Johannine theology makes between birth from God and possession of the Spirit, and which Pauline theology makes between adoption and *pneuma*, leads in the latter instance to the formula *pneuma hyiothesias*, the spirit of adoption (Rom. 8.14–17; 8.23; 9.26; Gal. 3.26–28; 4.5–7. Cf. Matt. 5.9; 5.45; John 12.36; Eph. 1.3–5). Here Paul, in contrast to Johannine theology, will lay stress on the fact that we have received only a foretaste or pledge, an *arrha* (*arrhabōn*) of the Holy Spirit (II Cor. 1.22; 5.5; see Eph. 1.14).

Consequently the New Testament calls life in communion with God (I Peter 1.4), through adoption or birth, in succession: (*a*) a 'communion (*koinōnia*) with the Father' (I John 1.3; 1.6; expressed more frequently by John with the word *menein*, abide in, see below); (*b*) a 'communion with the Son' (I Cor. 1.9; Col. 2.6; I John 1.3; 2.24); (*c*) a 'communion with the Holy Spirit' (II Cor. 13.14; Phil. 2.1; Heb. 6.4); (*d*) a communion among men, a human brotherhood rooted in the Spirit (John 17.11, 21f.; I John 1.3, 7 and passim; II Cor. 9.13, etc.). In this living communion with God we are 'sharers in Christ' (Heb. 3.14), and in addition, 'partakers of the Holy Spirit' (Heb. 6.4), which II Peter 1.4 describes in terms already known from the Stoics as a *consortium divinae naturae* (*theias koinōnoi physeōs*). However, it detaches this from its Greek significance (see the ethical context) and means by it what Pauline theology means by adoption or Johannine theology means by rebirth from God. However, we should note here that more and more religious concepts derived from the Hellenistic Near East are used; this procedure is justifiable in itself if the salvation in Jesus is meant for all men and not just for those who speak the 'language of Canaan'. But if the church is formed almost exclusively of Christians from the Gentile world, difficulties will arise which will prove all the greater as Christianity becomes alien to its Jewish, Old Testament origins. For the New Testament presupposes the whole of the Old and moreover limits itself to experience with Christ. Without the Old Testament tradition, the New Testament, as a book by itself, is a torso.

The living communion of the Christian with God is like an unmerited, gracious sharing in the relationship and mutual communion between the Father and Jesus Christ, the Son (John 14.20; 17.21, 23; see ch. 10 and the whole of the farewell discourse, above all from 13.31 on). Only through the bond with Jesus, and not without Jesus Christ, is communion with God possible (and this distinguishes this communion from any Greek participation in the divine nature). 'Between' God in us and we in God (the Gospel of John) there is always the mediating man Jesus, the Christ and Son. Johannine theology speaks of this communion with God above all in expressions like 'abide in' (*menein*: I John 1.10; 2.14; 1.8; 2.4, 6, 24, 27f.; 3.6; 3.24; 4.13, 15f.; in the Gospel of John: John 15.4f., 7; 14.17; 15.9, 10, etc.), or 'have' God or the Son (I John 2.23; 5.12; II John 9), or 'be in God' (I John 3.10 with 9; 2.5; 5.20), always with the accent on the mutuality ('The Father in me, I in the Father') (John 6.56; 15.4–11; 14.20; 17.21, 23, 26; I John 3.24; 4.13, 15f.). (These formulae are often not Johannine constructions but evidently come from the Jewish-Greek and Jewish syncretistic religious culture in which the Johannine churches lived. In my view they are most likely to correspond with that mystic trend which issues in so-called Hermetic mysticism; here too there is talk of a 'birth in the Spirit'.[6] Moreover, the conception of birth from God had long been widespread in the East.) In John, 'knowledge of God' (for which in any case a foundation has already been laid in the Old Testament and Jewish concept of 'knowing God'), is an alternative expression for communion with God (e.g. John 17.3, and repeatedly in I John). However, in Johannine theology there is no mention of salvation through knowledge, and John even seems to attack false teaching in the Johannine community, according to which there is already some kind of 'blessed vision of God' on earth (John 1.18; 5.37; 6.46; 14.8f.; I John 4.12) and then even more a kind of identity mysticism in which Jesus does not appear (esp. John 1.18; see also 14.9; 12.45).

### C. The experience of the Spirit: religious and ethical insight

This communion with the Father through the Son in the Spirit is in fact a living communion that *can be experienced*. The spirit of adoption, or our spiritual mode of being through rebirth from God by virtue of the indwelling of the Holy Spirit, gives the experience of our being children of God, since it is this spirit which enables us, like Jesus, to say 'Abba', Father, to God (Rom. 8.15; Gal. 4.6). At the same time, however, we only experience the Father *in* the man Jesus (John 1.18; 6.57; 14.6–9; 16.26f.; I John 2.23; 5.11f.; John 8.19; 14.19f.), though a man needs the Spirit to recognize him as the Christ or the one sent by God (I John 4.2f.; I Cor. 12.3). Therefore for later Christian generations the Spirit provides the link between the apostolic and contemporary witness to Jesus Christ and the historic Jesus event. The Spirit is at work in the Christian rememberance of the historical Jesus. (See John 14.26; 15.26; 16.13f., to be compared with I John 1.1–3: 'What we have heard and seen with our own eyes' – although here it is not a matter of direct eyewitnesses but of what is experienced here and now in the community on the basis of earlier eyewitnesses and on the basis of the apostolic tradition. The Spirit is at work in this whole process.)

Communion with God is mediated through Jesus Christ. Thus living communion with God in faith can be experienced thanks to the gift of the spiritual mode of being of the baptized believer, an implication of the indwelling of the Spirit (Rom. 8). At the beginning, the stress was laid principally on the possession of the spirit which was expressed in a number of extraordinary charismatic experiences (Acts 2.38; 8.15f.; 10.45; 19.6), experiences of a more external kind, though not without a quite intensive inner movement. In time, however, in New Testament Christianity the experience of the Spirit becomes more and more a sober, real and yet intensive ethical emotion: 'God's love has been poured into our hearts through the Holy Spirit which has been given to us' (Rom. 5.5), 'All who keep his commandments abide in him and he in them. And by this we know that he abides in us, by the Spirit which he has given us' (I John 3.24), 'By this *we know* that we abide in him and he in us, because he has given us a share in his own Spirit' (I John 4.13; the Greek text runs: 'He has given us of his Spirit'). The fruit of the Spirit is love, joy, peace, patience, friendliness, goodness, faithfulness, gentleness, morality (Gal. 5.22), 'a spirit of power and love and self control' (II Tim. 1.7), 'a spirit of wisdom and revelation' (Eph. 1.17).

Thus the living communion with God which can be experienced through the Spirit in faith gives the believer a special knowledge of *ta tou Theou*, the spiritual or 'heavenly' things, a knowledge of 'what is of God' (I Cor. 2.11), i.e. of what is in accordance with the nature of the heavenly Spirit (I Cor. 2.10–17; see I Cor. 12.8; Eph. 1.7f.; Col. 3.1f.). Grace runs over into 'wisdom and insight' (Eph. 1.8), and it is an 'illumination of the inner eye' (Eph. 1.18). This spiritual insight is theologal (i.e. pertaining to God), but also ethical: God's *pneuma* in us, our spiritual mode of being born of grace, leads 'to the *works* of the Spirit of God' (I John 4.2), for this Spirit enables us to 'discern the spirits' (I Cor. 12.10; I John 4.1–6; above all 4.1 and 4.6c; and I Thess. 5.20f.), a capacity to distinguish between what is ethically good and ethically bad (Col. 1.9 with 3.10; Rom. 12.2). Thus the Spirit in us is the foundation both of a certain 'mystical' (theologal) knowledge of God and also of a spiritual-ethical insight; furthermore it gives a certain *sensus fidei*, a meaning of faith which can distinguish between true and false Christian statements of faith (at least if, as I suppose, Heb. 5.14: 'The faculties [of the mature] are trained by experience and practice to distinguish between good and evil' must be understood in this way; the main concern of Hebrews is the question of the capacity to distinguish between a proper christological interpretation of Jesus and a false interpretation). See also I Cor. 12.3: 'No one can say "Jesus is the Lord" except through the Holy Spirit', which should be compared with I John 4.2f.: 'Every spirit which confesses that Jesus Christ has come in the flesh is of God, and every spirit which does not confess Jesus is not of God'; in both cases it is a matter of a christological capacity for distinction (among other things, the later church doctrine of the *sensus fidei* of the community of faith is based on these texts). In other words, by virtue of his spiritual way of living, the Christian has a certain capacity for distinguishing on the basis of an experiential knowledge (in the Middle Ages this was called a judgment on the basis of experienced co-naturality) in respect of the divine and the demands of a consistent Christian mode of life. This capacity is essentially given with the Spirit, which is of divine origin, so that the man who has received the Spirit can judge what comes from God and what comes from elsewhere (see especially I John 4.1–6) (however, here we must remember that this capacity for distinction works certainly and correctly only on the basis of an analysis of historical circumstances, which the New Testament does not take into account).

## D. Being formed in the image of Christ: 'following Jesus'

Living communion with God, through the mediation of Christ, makes believers 'conformed to Christ' (Rom. 8.29; Gal. 3.27; 4.19; Col. 3.9). This is expressed by various images: putting off old garments and putting on new (Eph. 4.17–32; Rom. 13.12; Col. 3.8–11; Heb. 12.1). Colossians 3.10 speaks of renewal 'after the image of the Creator'; Eph. 4.24 of new creation *kata Theon*. Whereas according to Paul Christians 'put on Christ' (like a new garment), the Deutero-Paulines speak of putting on the 'new man', which is not necessarily identical with Christ, but is measured by the standard of Christ. What we have here is a new presentation of man in paradise, and this renewed Genesis man is made possible through Christ (see also Col. 3.10; 1.15; II Cor. 4.4; Eph. 4.21c). Conformity with Christ is therefore at the same time 'conformity with God' (Phil. 2.7; John 5.18). It causes believers to participate in the *ḥesed* and *'emet* of God: 'Be merciful like your heavenly Father' (Luke 6.36). Here Luke writes *oiktirmos*, the Septuagint translation of the Hebrew *rᵃḥāmīm*, that is, God's tender motherly love towards man, for *rᵃḥāmīm* (tender love) gives the concept of grace (*ḥesed*) the connotation of love and tenderness. Matthew 5.47 here uses a special Matthaean term: 'Be *perfect* like your heavenly Father', but he too knows Luke's idea of tender and concerned love: 'Learn from me: I am gentle and lowly of heart' (Matt. 11.29). Thus the two enlarge on the Pauline and Johannine 'conformity with Christ and God' by specifying that the Christian must demonstrate the same care for his fellow men as Christ, the personal manifestation of God's love and faithfulness among us. In another passage this is expressed by the admonition to 'cherish the same thoughts' as inspired Christ (Phil. 2.5; I Cor. 2.16); for 'those who are directed by the Spirit reflect on the things of the Spirit' (Rom. 8.5b–6). In a word, 'life in the Spirit', is 'life in accordance with the Spirit' (Gal. 5.25), and because the Spirit indicates the special nature of the divine realm, all this, in accordance with the world view of the time, is stated in expressions like, 'Seek what is above, where Christ is seated at the right hand of God. Reflect on heavenly things and not on earthly things' (Col. 3.1–4, etc.). However, this is enlarged on in specific terms by brotherly love and the consistent ethical conduct of Christians (see the paraeneses in the New Testament, which almost all can be summed up in ethical demands and in concern for fellow men).

### E. 'Now already' and 'not yet' in the kingdom of God. Access to the Father

Sharing Christ's destiny as a way to communion with God makes believers partake in 'the inheritance of Christ' (Gal. 3.29; 4.7; Rom. 8.17; Titus 3.7; Eph. 1.14–18; Heb. 1.2; 9.15; I Peter 1.4), as a consequence of childhood through adoption or birth. The Holy Spirit is a first pledge of this inheritance, which is 'to enter the kingdom of God' (Gal. 5.21; I Cor. 6.9; Col. 1.13f.; Eph. 5.5; James 2.5; I Peter 1.4; 1.5b; I Thess. 2.12; II Thess. 1.5; II Tim. 4.1; 4.18; II Peter 1.10b–11; Heb. 12.28; Rev. 12.10; John 3.3, 5; 18.36; and the idea of the kingdom of God among the synoptics). Through the 'pledge of the Holy Spirit', this entering into the kingdom of God is achieved both actually and eschatologically (i.e. eschatologically in its actuality), and therefore oriented in the present on a final consummation to come. Grace in the New Testament is involved in the tension between the *'now already'* and the *'not yet'*, even in Johannine theology, in which eternal life is already a present reality, but nevertheless waits for the final consummation of the resurrection. Christians are redeemed or hallowed (*hēgiasmenoi*, Heb. 10.10; *sesōsmenoi*, Eph. 2.5, 8), and on the other hand on the way to sanctification (*hagiazomenoi*, Heb. 10.15–18; 'sealed for the day of redemption', Eph. 4.30; see Eph. 1.13f.). They are 'at rest' (Heb. 4.3) and they will 'enter into rest' (Heb. 4.11).

This present communion with God is described in many places as 'access to the Father'; for Hebrews this is even the specific expression for the gift of grace in Christ (Heb. 4.16; 7.25; 10.22; 12.22; 13.15, etc.), but the expression also occurs regularly elsewhere (Gal. 4.6; Rom. 8.15f.; Eph. 1.3; 2.18; I Peter 1.5–7). In contrast to the Old Testament, in which only the high priest has access to the holy of holies where God dwells among his people, and then only once a year, the Christian has free access to God without any other mediation than that of Christ (Heb. 4.16; 10.19; Eph. 3.12; I John 3.21; here Hebrews compares a *ritual* event from Judaism with an 'inner' event in Christianity and keeps quiet over the deeply religious experience of God in Israel, so that the comparison is faulty and can have a damaging effect). Thus the Christian community is itself a priestly people of God (I Peter 2.9f.; Rev. 20.6). This free access – that of children going in and out, to and from their Father – characterizes the *parrhēsia*, the fearlessness of children who feel at home with God. Alongside doxological prayer (see below), this access is the basis for New Testament intercession or petition: 'The Father will give you all that you ask him in my name' (John 15.16b; 16.23b): 'Hitherto you have asked nothing in my name; ask, and you will receive, that your joy may be full' (John 16.24, and the synoptic gospels).

## II. THE SPECIFIC ELABORATION OF THIS FUNDAMENTAL GRACE

The New Testament calls this fundamental grace an adoption or a birth from God and describes it as redemption and liberation. From what and for what are we freed? The thematic development of this question in the New Testament is also dependent on the way in which damnation was experienced then (for example, the fear of demons in late antiquity, which was a heavy burden on the life of the time). Moreover, the salvation brought by Jesus was not directly depicted as a birth from God or an adoption, but first and foremost as a new way of life and a fulfilment, as redemption and the forgiveness of sins. Only later did people begin to reflect on the origin and the basis for all this: they tried to identify its source with the models of 'adoption' and 'birth from God'.

If we investigate all the New Testament aspects closely, we will certainly be able to find a great many variants. However, sixteen key concepts, which occur repeatedly in all parts of the New Testament, are enough to give us a good idea of the New Testament understanding of what redemption through Christ Jesus is from and what it is for.

### A. Salvation and redemption

In the New Testament, the salvation which Christians experience in Jesus is often expressed by the Greek word *sōtēria* (Luke 1.69, 71, 77, quotations from the Greek Bible: Acts 4.12; Rom. 1.16; 10.1; 11 Cor. 7.10; Eph. 1.13; Phil. 2.12; I Thess. 5.8–10; II Thess. 2.13; II Tim. 2.10; 3.15; Heb. 2.10; 5.9; I Peter 1.9f.; 2.2; II Peter 3.15; Jude 3; Rev. 12.10b; Titus 2.11), or with the verbal form *sōzein* (Matt. 1.21; 9.21f. par; 27.42 par.; Mark 5.23; 16.16; Luke 8.12; 8.50; 19.10; John 3.17; 5.34; 10.9; 12.47; Acts 2.21, 47; 4.12; 11.14; 14.9; 15.11; 16.30; 27.40; Rom. 5.9; 8.24; 10.9f.; I Cor. 1.21; 3.15; 5.5; 15.2; Eph. 2.5, 8; I Thess. 2.16; I Tim. 1.15; 2.4; Heb. 5.7; I

Peter 3.21). The verbal form (*sōzein*) clearly seems to be preferred to the substantive *sōtēria*. This latter is more a term from religious Hellenism, where it means the forgiveness of guilt by virtue of ritual initiation, and at the same time protection against demonic dangers (also those from the underworld of death), and therefore finally immortal and eternal life. *Sōtēria* or salvation thus understood can already mean the forgiveness of sins, victory over Satan and eternal life. Paul, above all, fills this concept with Christian meaning; here 'eternal life' becomes the salvation of the physical resurrection. In that case, as in the synoptic gospels, redemption has a purely eschatological significance, whereas the forgiveness of sins and victory over the demons at least fade into the background in this concept of *sōtēria*. However, the forgiveness of sins in the gift of the Holy Spirit is in fact the basis of this coming salvation. In other words, for Paul salvation is essentially victory over death. For Johannine theology, on the other hand, *sōtēria* or salvation is at the same time 'eternal life' and therefore victory over death, but in the gift of the Holy Spirit this eternal life is already a present reality. In that case salvation is more closely related to the new life in Christ, here already. The Deutero-Paulines give *sōtēria* or salvation an already present significance, so that with them the forgiveness of sins plays a central role. In the later New Testament writings the noun *sōtēr*, i.e. Saviour, bringer of salvation or benefactor, is also taken over from Hellenism.[7] It is first applied to God and later also to Christ (Luke 2.11; Acts 5.31; 13.23; I John 4.14; Titus 1.4; 2.13; 3.6; II Tim. 1.10; II Peter 1.11; 2.20; 3.2, 18). The implication then is that God in Jesus Christ, rather than the emperor, is the true bringer of salvation and benefactor to mankind. Above all, *sōtēr* adds to the concept of *sōtēria* or salvation the connotation of 'salvation for the whole world' (just as the emperor was called the 'benefactor of all humanity' or the whole commonwealth).

However, the Hebrew meanings of salvation are more strongly echoed in the verbal form *sōzein* than the Hellenistic ones (*sōtēria*). In the Septuagint *sōzein* is usually the translation of *yāšī'* (in the *hiphīl*)[8] and also of *pālaṭ* (in the *piel*).[9] The first verb means 'help' in general, often in the meaning of legal support, that is, to help someone who asks for help and thus save him from distress. (Hence the SOS call of all the needy: *hōšī'ā* [help], above all in the psalms of lament, Pss. 18.27; 72.4; 109.31; also Job 5.15). God is 'the God of my help' (Pss. 40.17; 25.5; 79.9; 85.4). He is *yēša'* (Ps. 12.5) or *y'šū'a* (Pss. 9.14; 13.5; 21.1; I Sam. 2.1; Isa. 25.9; Pss. 20.5; 35.9; 'from Zion comes *y'šū'ā* for Israel', Pss. 14.7; 74.12). In later texts, especially after the exile, God's help becomes eschatological and apocalyptic (Isa. 25.9; 33.22; 35.4; 60.16; 63.1; Zech. 8.7, 13; 9.16). It is this concept of *y'šū'ā* which the New Testament also renders with the Greek word *sōtēria*, in which Hellenistic religious overtones can then be found, above all in *sōtēr*. The second verb *pālat* (in the *piel*) means 'allow to escape' and thus bring to safety: rescue (Pss. 18.48; 22.8; 31.2f.; 71.2; 82.4; in the Psalms God is always the subject of this verb-form).[10] This meaning can also be found in the New Testament; redemption is also liberation in the sense of escaping from dangers or oppression. It is deliverance.

## B. Being freed from forms of servitude and slavery

In the New Testament various Hebrew words are rendered by words like 'being snatched away' (*ryesthai* – or active; *ryomai, exagein, exairein,* 'lead out of'), which (with God as subject) refer to a particular form of divine liberation, above all *yāṣā* (in the *hiphil*) and *nāṣal* (also in the *hiphil*).[11] The first Hebrew word has the root meaning of 'to leave a place in order to undertake something'. In the *hiphil* it means to rescue someone in the sense of 'lead out': rescue from the hand of enemies or from various dangers; from nets or snares and oppressions (Pss. 68.6; 107.14; 31.4; 107.28; 143.11), from prison (Pss. 68.6; 107.14; 142.7). Along with *'lh* and *g'l*, this word is one of the three technical terms which describe the liberation from Egypt, the primal confession of Israelite faith,[12] often with the meaning, 'liberation from the house of slavery.'[13] The Septuagint and the New Testament use *exerchomai* and *ekporeuomai*. The word *nāṣal* (in the *hiphil* with *min* – from) means 'to rescue from something which holds fast or keeps away', and hence to save from a variety of constraints[14] (*ryesthai; exairein*).

We already find redemption as rescue in the earliest text of the New Testament: 'Jesus, who rescues us (*Iēsoun ton ryomenon hēmas*) from the wrath to come' (I Thess. 1.10); in the Lord's Prayer, 'deliver us from (the hand of) evil' (Matt. 6.13). The Saviour or redeemer is *ho ryomenos* (Rom. 11.26), i.e. the one 'who snatches us from': 'It is God who has saved us from this dangerous death' (II Cor. 1.10), or who has 'extricated us from the curse of the law' (Gal. 3.13), or 'who has delivered us from the dominion of darkness and transferred us to the kingdom of his beloved son' (Col. 1.13), 'who gave himself for our sins to deliver us from the present age' (Gal. 1.4). In that case redemption through Christ here means being protected from eternal judgment, escaping the hands of the devil (see below), avoiding death, being freed from the constraint of the precepts of the Law and being translated from this age into the better world of the future – a new exodus, liberation from various forms of slavery.

### C.  Redemption as liberation through purchase or for a ransom

There is repeated mention in the New Testament of liberation in the sense of *apolytrōsis* and *lytrōsis* (Luke 1.68; 2.38; 21.28; Rom. 3.24; 8.23; I Cor.1.30; Eph. 1.7; 1.14; Heb. 9.12, 15), or of the verb *lytrousthai* (Luke 24.21; Titus 2.14; I Peter 1.18).

Some secular Hebrew terms which have been taken over into theology underlie this New Testament formulation of redemption through Jesus Christ. Their general meaning is: to bring about freedom of many forms of alienation and slavery, but for the payment of a ransom. The terms in question are *pādāh* and *gō'ēl*.[15] (The Septuagint usually translates *pādāh* with *lytrousthai*, but this is often the translation of *g'l*, whereas sometimes *ryesthai* is also the rendering of *pādāh*; exceptionally it is also rendered by *sōzein*, save.)

*Pādāh* (noun *pidyōn*, *lytron*, is then the purchase price or the ransom, Ex. 21.30; Num. 3.49) is a term from slave law (Ex. 21.7–11), but it also has a more general meaning: the freeing of a poor man who cannot pay his debt (Job 6.23). In the cultic sphere redemption means the paying of a ransom for the firstborn of a man or beast (Ex. 34.19–26; Num. 18.16). No one can redeem himself from dependence on God (Ps. 49.8). But because all things are possible for God (Ps. 44.36; see 49.1–9a), God can redeem men and so save them, both the individual (II Sam. 4.9; I Kings 1.29; Isa. 29.22; in the present as in the future: Jer. 15.21; Hos. 7.13; 13.14 etc.) and the whole people (Deut. 7.8; 9.26; 13.5; 15.15; 21.8; II Sam. 7.23; Micah 6.4; Pss. 25.22; 78.42; Neh. 1.10), especially in the eschatological future (Isa. 35.10; 51.11; 50.2; Jer. 31.11; Zech. 10.8). From what is Israel or the Israelite redeemed by Yahweh? From the hand of the powerful (Jer. 15.21), from the power of the kingdom of the dead, 'ransom from death' (Hos. 13.14), 'from all distress' (II Sam. 4.9; I Kings 1.29), 'from what encloses Israel round about' (Ps. 25.22), 'from domination' (Jer. 31.11), but above all from 'the oppressor' (Ps.78.42), that means (see Ps. 78.43) Pharaoh, Egypt, the house of slavery (Deut. 7.8; 9.26; 13.5; 15.15; Micah 6.4).

In Deuteronomy the liberation from Egypt (which, see above, was first translated by *'lh* and later by *yāṣā*) is also understood as redemption (*pādāh*, Deut. 13.5; 15.15; 21.8; 24.18; 7.8; 9.26). The question to whom and how Yahweh then paid the ransom is meaningless: 'redemption' from slavery (for which in fact a ransom had to be paid) becomes an image which expresses the fact that from a religious point of view we live in slavery and have to be freed. As soon as one develops the picture in detail and 'for itself', it becomes illogical. An image is touched on, and no more, otherwise it goes beyond itself. Therefore we can repeatedly find the expression 'I have redeemed my people' in the absolute (both with an allusion to the liberation from Egypt and also in straight eschatological terms: Deut. 21.8; II Sam. 7.23; Isa. 29.22; 35.10; 50.2; 51.11; Neh. 1.10; Zech. 10.8).

Precisely because in Deuteronomy the liberation from Egypt is also rendered by *pādāh*, which includes redemption and thus ransom (this was not the case with other expressions used to describe this liberation, namely *yāṣā* and *'lh*), the liberation from Egypt could finally also be described by the root *gō'ēl*. This term derives from family law. It is connected with the sabbath and the year of jubilee, in which possessions had to be restored to their earlier, original condition (Lev. 25.8–55). The *gō'ēl* or redeemer of relatives in need then had to pay the purchase sum in order to restore the land to the previous owners; the *gō'ēl* is a close member of the family who has to intervene in order to buy back the 'family possession' which has been lost[16] (see Jer. 32.6–15; Ruth 4). In the theological sense, *g'l* then comes to mean liberate and rescue, often in the cultic sense (Lev. 27). Finally, not only the verb but also the noun *gō'ēl* are transferred to God in the sense of the protector of the weaker ones (Prov. 23.10f.; Jer. 50.34), advocate or intercessor (Job 19.25; Pss. 72.13f.; 119.154; Lam. 3.58). Because it originally had the meaning 'replace lost possessions', *g'l* could finally also be used for the liberation from Egypt (Ex. 6.6; 15.13; Pss. 74.2; 77.15; 78.35; 106.10; Isa. 63.9). In that case exodus is the regaining of enslaved Israel for its lawful owner, Yahweh, and with it the restoration of the freedom of Israel. Deutero-Isaiah can therefore render the return from the Babylonian captivity with *g'l*, and not, like Deuteronomy, with *pādāh*, redemption: it is the return of Israel to its original owner (Isa. 48.20; 43.5f.; 49.12, 18, 22f.): Yahweh is the *gō'ēl* (Isa. 44.6), the redeemer of Israel, which is his possession. In Isa. 43.1–7 the ransom is made more precise: 'I give Egypt as your ransom, Ethiopia and Saba in exchange for you. Because you are precious in my eyes, and honoured, and I love you, I give men in return for you, peoples in exchange for your life' (43.3f.). Trito-Isaiah also uses the concept of *gō'ēl* (Isa. 59.20; 60.16) and finally combines it with the Fatherhood of God: 'You, Yahweh are our father, from of old you are called our redeemer' (Isa. 63.16). The redeemed (*g'ʾūlīm*) are then the members of the people of God who have been gathered from the Diaspora (Isa. 62.12).[17]

All these meanings are echoed in the New Testament (*apo)lytrōsis*, but as in the later literature of the Old Testament, in the New Testament too the distinction between 'redeem' and free, and release from slavery on payment of a ransom (*pādāh*), and finally repurchase of a lost possession, has almost disappeared (Luke 24.21; 1.68; 21.28: Rom. 3.24; I Cor. 1.30; Heb. 11.35). Still, we cannot deny that the Hebrew meaning continues to have an effect, and here the way in which Jesus died – an execution

– was the cardinal factor. 'You have been redeemed, and the price has been paid' (I Cor. 6.20; I Cor. 7.23); Mark 10.45 and Matt. 20.28 speak of the *lytron* that has been paid, 'as a ransom for many'. 'You know that you were ransomed from futile ways not with perishable things such as silver or gold, but with the precious blood of Christ, like that of a lamb without blemish or spot' (I Peter 1.18f.). 'Redemption through his blood' (Eph. 1.7). However, it must be said that the use of the words 'save' (*sōzein; sōtēria*) and rescue (*ryomai*), etc., words in which there is no mention of ransom, far exceed the terminology connected with ransom. Furthermore, the mutual influence of experience and interpretation emerges from the variety of the soteriological vocabulary in the New Testament. It brings us to a new block of interpretations, to those which have to do with the forgiveness of sins and justification, redemption and sanctification.

## D. Reconciliation after dispute

Throughout the New Testament, only Paul also calls redemption reconciliation in the specific sense of the words *katallagē* (reconciliation), *katallassein* (reconcile someone with oneself) and *katallagēnai* (be reconciled) (II Cor. 5.18, 19, 20, 21; Rom. 5.10, 11; 11.15), whereas the Deutero-Paulines express this content in a neologism: *apokatallassein* (Col. 1.20, 22; Eph. 2.16).

Before the reconciliation, both parties are at odds; they are enemies or separated (as emerges from the secular use of the same word: estranged couples must 'become reconciled', I Cor. 7.11): 'whereas we were enemies, we have been reconciled with God' (Rom. 5.10; see also the dividing wall in Eph. 2.14), 'And you (Gentiles) who once were estranged and hostile in mind, doing evil deeds, he has now reconciled' (Col. 1.21f.). Although this hostility between God and man is mutual (God's wrath: Rom. 1.18–32; 2.2, 5; 3.5; 8.8), it is not God who is reconciled to man, but only man to God: we are reconciled with God (Rom. 5.10; II Cor. 5.20), God reconciles us with himself (II Cor. 5.18–21; Col. 1.22; Eph. 2.16) and therefore men with one another, because the hostility between Jews and Gentiles (Eph. 2.16; 2.14) is done away with in the church (Eph. 2.16). This implies that reconciliation with God is not the diminution of the wrath of God through some soothing action, e.g. the death of Jesus, which is well-pleasing to God. (We shall discover later, in connection with the forgiveness of sins on the basis of a sacrifice, that this idea also occurs elsewhere in the New Testament and the meaning it has there.) It does not play any role in the idea of reconciliation. Where the word reconciliation (*katallagē* and its derivatives) is used in the New

Testament, it is never said that *God* is reconciled. 'We receive reconciliation' (Rom. 5.11). There is no difference in this respect between Paul and the Deutero-Pauline epistles, except that for Paul, God alone is the subject of the reconciliation, albeit in and through Christ; for Colossians and Ephesians Jesus can also be named as the subject who achieves reconciliation (Col. 1.22; Eph. 2.16), though in the last resort this reconciliation through Christ also proceeds from God (see Col. 1.20). Paul will never make Jesus independent as the *subject* of redemptive activity: God, and that is the Father, is at work *in* Christ bringing about (II Cor. 5.19).

The special meaning of reconciliation (which in this sense does not have any Old Testament parallel) is to make other or renew (in accordance with the root of the Greek word: *katallassō*, make another, *allos*, of someone). The relationship between God and man, and among men, is changed through our reconciliation by God: we are no longer enemies, godless, helpless (Rom.5.6 in conjunction with 5.10); we are no longer sinners (Rom. 5.8). 'So if any man is in Christ, there is a new creation . . . All this comes from God. He has reconciled us through Christ with himself' (II Cor. 5.17f.), 'he does not count man's trespasses' (II Cor. 5.19), for 'the love of God is shed abroad in our hearts' (Rom. 5.5); so 'we have access to the Father' (Eph. 2.18). Thus reconciliation means more than justification: it makes us friends instead of enemies of God, new men. 'To be reconciled' means to appear sinless before God's judgment (Col. 1.22), to live in peace (Col. 1.20; Eph. 2.15), a new man (Eph. 2.15), a new creation (II Cor. 5.17), finally in Col. 1.20 even the reconciliation of the heavenly beings with God.

Is reconciliation already fully achieved? Striking features are on the one hand the expression 'reconciliation of the world' (II Cor. 5.19; also Rom. 11.15), whereas elsewhere Paul always says, 'We (Christians) are reconciled' (Rom. 5.9f.; II Cor. 5.18 – in the *confessional* sense, not as an objectifying assertion), and on the other hand the complicated expression, '*Theos ēn en Christō kosmon katallassōn*, literally, 'God *was* in process of reconciling the *world* in Christ' (II Cor. 5.19), whereas in II Cor. 5.18 it had been said, *ek tou Theou tou katallaxantos hēmas*, all this comes from God who has reconciled us. Over against 'the world' it was God who 'is in process of reconciling it', but we, the Christians, are 'already reconciled' (aorist: II Cor. 5.18; Rom. 5.9f.). <u>Reconciliation has only taken place where men have reconciled themselves with God through Jesus.</u> For others, this reconciliation has still to take place; hence the service of reconciliation and the word of reconciliation which the church has received for the world (II Cor. 5.19).

## E.  Redemption as satisfaction: peace

As far as content is concerned, in Pauline theology 'reconciliation' (in the sense of *katallagē*, change) and 'peace-making' are of course close together, but both terms are very different in their connotation, especially against the Jewish background of *šālōm*. Reconciliation as *šālōm* comes from a completely different world from that of the Greek *katallagē* (reconciliation as change, a concept which, as far as I have been able to establish, really has no parallel in Hebrew, at least in the Tanach). The Greek rendering of *šālōm* by *eirēnē*, peace, in fact results in a quite noticeable limitation of the concept.

The root of *šālōm*[18] formally does not contain the meaning of salvation or being whole or peace, but of 'satisfaction', 'the making good of damage', and 'paying', and the basic significance of these words exercises an influence in all the other derivatives. For instance, if someone has left a well uncovered so that some beast of burden falls into it, the owner of this well must 'pay *šālōm*' (Ex. 21.33f.), make good the damage or render satisfaction. *Šālōm* points towards the realm of duties, claims or promises; it is concerned with giving satisfaction, whether in the positive sense (fulfilling promises) or in the negative (punish), in other words recompense (I Sam. 24.20; Deut. 32.41). Thus a man pays his debt (II Kings 4.7) or a thank offering (Ps. 56.12). Whether juristic or not, the term is therefore connected with the regulation of damage: for one party this means having satisfaction, 'having enough', being content, and for the other, bearing the damage or the punishment, atoning. Therefore outside the sphere of punishment, *šālōm* can simply mean 'make an agreement' or come to an understanding (Deut. 20.12; Josh. 9.15; 11.19; Isa. 27.5). Anyone who can satisfy his needs adequately is therefore 'content', happy (Gen. 33.18). Hence the noun *šālōm* does not so much mean peace, salvation or being whole, as 'recompense', above all in the positive sense, being in a state in which one has enough (an adequate sufficiency), outwardly as well as inwardly, i.e. inner satisfaction, pleasure or joy. Therefore as a greeting *šālōm* really means: may things go well with you (Judg. 6.23; 19.20). If the accent lies on the condition through which the act of recompense is achieved, then *šālōm* means peace, i.e. the condition which results from mutual achievements or from an agreement, above all after a war (i.e. peace). Therefore in the concept of peace there is always the idea of a peace treaty or agreement. Hence covenant of peace (*bᵉrit šālōm*: Num. 25.12; Isa. 54.10; Ezek. 34.25), a covenant in which the making good is regulated and thus the victor is given satisfaction. So, too, of God giving satisfaction (Joel 2.25). Thus the 'prince of peace' first of all really means the prince of recompense (Isa. 9.6), who rewards the good and punishes the evil. This often goes on to embrace the condition of subjection, e.g. of a vassal king (*melek šālēm*) under a higher king, hence a 'paying' or subject heart, readiness.

Thus the Hebrew term *šālōm* is connected with the general Jewish view that God guarantees the connection between good or evil actions and the prosperity or misfortune which results (see above, in the analysis of the term *ṣedāqā* or righteousness). God is the one who rewards good and punishes evil, and therefore is a God of peace. 'The work of *ṣedāqā* will be peace' (Isa. 32.17), or even, '*ṣedāqa* and *šālōm* embrace each other' (Ps. 85.10). *Šālōm* finally means 'be good' ('so everything is good'); not in the sense of a subjective experience so much as of an objective ordinance. It is striking here that Jewish thought begins from mistakes which are put right: righteousness has to happen. The Septuagint translation of *šālōm* by *eirēnē*, peace, therefore removes the typically Jewish connotations of the term.

Hence the New Testament also looked for other terms in addition to the term peace (*eirēnē*) borrowed from the Septuagint in order to express the ideas of satisfaction and reconciliation on the basis of recompense. So the term is distinct not only from *katallagē* (reconciliation), but also from *apolytrōsis* (liberation), in which one pays a ransom (for a slave, a poor man, etc.). It means, rather, to 'be in agreement with' God and men, even if something must be 'paid' for this. Paul's remark 'Your grace is enough' (II Cor. 12.9) is closely connected with this understanding of *šālōm*, 'recompense', and thus with being satisfied or having enough: 'so it is good'. In that case, reconciliation also means the state of subjection under God after a state of sinfulness, where in accordance with the Jewish conception something *has to be made good*. The so-called doctrine of 'satisfaction' in the New Testament has Jewish roots. That the New Testament should interpret the redemption brought by Jesus as satisfaction is already determined by the interpretative concepts which the Jewish Christians brought with them from their own history of experience and interpretation. Above all, the making good of our sins through the death of Jesus proved a suitable theme to prompt the application of a number of Jewish concepts to Jesus' utter self-sacrifice. That also emerges from the following concepts.

F. Redemption as the expiation for sins through a sin-offering

In Judaism, as in the New Testament, the forgiveness of sins and the expiation of sins involved two different semantic fields. The death of Jesus, out of solidarity with men in faithfulness to God (as presented above all in Hebrews), suggested an interpretation (for Jewish Christians) in terms of *k-p-r* (*kippūrīm*) or the sin-offering (here is the great difference from reconciliation in the sense of *katallagē* as the exclusive action of God). So we must give separate treatments to redemption as a sin-offering for sins and redemption as the forgiveness of sins.

*Kippūrīm*, which in the Tanach is entirely limited to the Priestly traditions, means 'reconciliation', but through the presentation of a sin-offering.[19] In the Hebrew *piel* form the root *k-p-r* means *atonement for sin* through a sin-offering (*expiatio*). It is striking that, statistically, only a tenth of the texts which speak of sin-offering come from the time before the exile: furthermore, three-quarters of all texts come from the Priestly tradition, and then from Ezekiel, Isaiah, Deuteronomy and the Psalms.

The basic meaning of the word in the Priestly – and above all cultic – tradition is to bring about expiation '*for* someone', an individual or the people, by the offering of a sacrifice (the word *hyper*: for someone, but not in the sense of vicariousness, is essential for the sin-offering which is performed through the priest, when a sinner has brought him some sacrificial animal prescribed by the Law). The atonement itself is performed through the priest (Lev. 16.32, see above). It is a universal Jewish belief that God alone can *forgive* sins. However, to '*atone for* sins' lies in a quite different sphere, that of the cult and the Law. The technical formula is, 'The priest makes atonement *for* him' (individual or people: Lev. 4.26, 31, 35; 5.6, 10, 13, 18; 6.7; 14.18, 20; 15.15; 19.22); that is the nucleus in Lev. 4.1–5.13, in connection with sacrifice as atonement for sins. A formula with a similarly cultic stamp follows: 'and he (individual or people) will be forgiven' (ibid.) After the sacrifice has been offered, there is a forensic or juristic declaration of purity by the priest: this man is 'no longer guilty in the eyes of the Law', he can live (see Ezek. 18.9). The basic thought here is that atonement requires a compensation (for the sin committed: Lev. 5.16; Lev. 16; Num. 5.7, 8), through which the relation to God disrupted by sins (against the Torah) is restored. To atone for sins therefore includes both 'purification' (from sin) and also 'sanctification' or dedication to God (Ex. 29.36f.; 30.10; Lev. 8.15; 16.18). Furthermore, if sacrifice is to be effective it must be 'well-pleasing to God',[20] i.e., God must find it good, must be satisfied with the sinner and accept him: 'You may live.' We saw earlier that Hebrews calls this aspect *teleiōsis*, or the consummation of the sacrifice through God. Thus atonement for sin is *not* the forgiveness of sins; this sacrifice is offered with an eye to the forgiveness of sins, but such forgiveness remains dependent on God's sovereign freedom. In that case, of course, the danger of a sacrificial formalism is great. We can see the sacrifices of the Old Testament as parallels to the 'canonical penance' of the church, which, in accordance with church order, was imposed in a purely legalistic manner. The precise performance of the penance imposed says nothing as such about inner repentance or *metanoia*, but it is assumed that this takes place. I already pointed out in my comments on Hebrews that Jewish 'blood theology' has a part in all this, because of the priestly theology in Lev. 17.11. Only in some later texts does atonement for sin simply coincide with the exclusive divine act of the forgiveness of sins (Pss. 65.3; 78.38; 79.9), where the verb *k-p-r* (in the *piel,* 'offer a sin offering') in the last resort coincides with the New Testament *katallagē* or atonement as the exclusive action of God (also Ex. 32.30; Deut. 32.43; Isa. 27.9; Dan. 9.24). It must therefore be said that the Old Testament does not have any clear theology of atonement, and that in any event it is illegitimate to identify this directly with the priestly conception of sin offerings. Whatever sacrificial theories there may in the Tanach, it emerges from both the earlier and the later texts that only God *forgives* sins. Furthermore, nowhere, not even in the priestly theories of sacrifice, is there mention of a 'substitution' in the sense of representation or the transference of a person's own sins to sacrificial or slaughtered animals.

Both the Septuagint and inter-testamental Greek Judaism render the Jewish idea of *kippūr* with *hilaskesthai* (atone for sins). In the Greek canon of the Jewish Bible (as in the apocryphal literature), stress is laid on the effective power of the sin-offering, even for those who have died (having sacrificed their lives in Israel's cause: II Macc. 12.45; see Sir. 45.16, 23). Finally, above all in the inter-testamental literature, the idea of atonement for sins through vicarious suffering comes into the foreground (IV Macc. 6.29; 17.22). In the Old Testament, it is possible to cite only one passage which can be interpreted in the same direction: the fourth Servant Song (Isa. 52.13–53.12, but even here the *kippūr* terminology is not used). We may rightly claim that the whole of the Jewish apparatus of sacrifice with its *kippūrīm* terminology had already ceased to have any meaning outside priestly circles even before the Fall of Jerusalem (AD 70). In Qumran (1 QS 9.4f.) and in the other early Jewish inter-testamental literature (e.g. Test. Lev. 3.6), all the stress is laid on the *sacrificium laudis,* the sacrifice of praise or the 'bloodless sacrifice of prayer'. Atoning for sins becomes *metanoia,* prayer, fasting, almsgiving, for this notion must also lie at the heart of the bloody sacrifice of beasts for the atonement of sins (see already in the deutero-canonical Old Testament Sir. 3.30; Tobit 4.10f.; and also the prophets' criticism of ritual sacrifice without righteousness: Amos 5.22; Micah 6.7f.; Jer. 6.20; Hos. 9.4 and even without 'the sacrifice of praise' or 'the hymn of the lips' [Ps. 104.34], i.e. the true praise of Yahweh).

The New Testament carries straight on with this newer inter-testamental devaluation of sacrificial-priestly theories, and for Christians lays stress on 'life' itself as a 'spiritual sacrifice' (I Peter 2.5; Phil. 2.17; 'the liturgy of your faith', Rom. 12.1; and the greatest sacrifice of all is brotherly love, Mark 12.33). Nevertheless, the redeeming death of Jesus is also understood as a sacrifice in terms of the Old Testament theology of sacrifice and this happens in all traditions of the New Testament: his death is an atoning sacrifice, and we are redeemed through his blood (see above: the Epistle to the Hebrews and the references to the general Christian tradition mentioned there).[21] The great difference from the Old Testament theology of sacrifice is that this sin offering is at the same time the forgiveness of sins, because it is accepted *automatically* by God and is found well-pleasing in Jesus' resurrection. Only Hebrews is to retain the sharper distinction – in this sense formally Jewish – between the atoning sacrifice, as purification and sanctification, and the act of well-pleasing acceptance through God or the 'perfection' of this sacrifice: 'that *by the grace of God* he might taste death for every one' (Heb. 2.9c).

## G.  Redemption as the forgiveness of sins

Forgiveness of sins (*aphesis tōn hamartiōn*; also *hilaskesthai*, atonement for sins here in a weaker sense) repeatedly appears in the New Testament as the fruit of the death and resurrection of Jesus (Matt. 18.11; 26.28; Mark 1.4; Luke 1.77; 4.18; 19.10; Acts 2.38; 5.31; 10.43; 13.38; Rom. 4.5; 5.6; 11.32; Gal. 3.22; Eph. 1.7; 2.5; Col. 1.14; see I Tim. 1.15; James 5.20; I John 1.9; 2.1f.). The death of Jesus, and therefore also Christian baptism, is a 'dying to sin' (Rom. 5.6; 6.2; 6.6–8, 10, 18). Only in two passages is the forgiveness of sins connected with the ministry of Jesus, i.e. before his death (Mark 2.10 par.; 2.15–17).

It is already an experience attested in the Old Testament that salvation or redemption essentially also means the forgiveness of sins.[22] *Sālaḥ* is the only real expression for 'bestow forgiveness', and only Yahweh can be its subject (though the term is also connected with priestly intercession: Lev. 4;5; 19.22; Num. 15.25f., 28). The precise meaning of *s'līḥā*, forgiveness of sins (Ps. 130.4; Dan. 9.9; Neh. 9.17), is covering sin, atonement for sin, purification or (in cultic terms) no longer remembering sin; hence metaphorically it comes to mean leaving sins behind one (Isa. 38.17) or casting them into the depths of the sea (Micah 7.19). Yahweh is a God of forgiveness (Neh. 9.17), 'good at forgiveness (ready to forgive)' (Ps. 96.5). As in the Tanach the forgiveness of sins is purely eschatological, actual atonement becomes 'forensic'; it is regarded externally and legalistically, in terms of a priestly acquittal. But this really does not involve a so-called forensic *forgiveness of sins*: the legalistic element is connected with the priestly declaration of cleanliness after the sacrifice has been made. In other words, on man's side everything is now legally in order *so that* God's forgiveness of sins may be sought. In that case, the sinner is no longer guilty 'in the eyes of the Law'. But even then God (who searches out the heart and reins) is left free to bestow the forgiveness of sins (which in that case is not forensic). It is not the forgiveness of sins, but atonement or repentance for sin, that is legally and formally a forensic process.

The New Testament also knows the expression 'bear or take away sins' (John 1.29; I John 3.5). This goes back to a Hebrew term *nāśā'*[23] (raise something, bear it or take it away), hence 'bear sins' both in the sense of taking sins on oneself, i.e. sinning, and also in the sense of bearing the consequences of sins, namely atoning for them (Lev. 5.1, 17; 7.18; 17.16; 19.8, 17; 20.17, 19, 20; 22.9; 24.15; Num. 5.31; Ezek. 14.10; 18.19f.). However, this word is in the same legalistic or 'canonical' sphere of the performance of the penance for a sin prescribed by the Law. For this very reason, substitution is possible *here:* the priest can bear 'the sin' of others and take their penance on himself (Ex. 28.38); the prophets also do this (Ezek. 4.4–6), or sons for their fathers (Num. 14.33), and finally also the servant of Yahweh (Isa. 53.12). Only in this sense, in the Old Testament, does 'bearing or taking away sins' mean the forgiveness of sins (Gen. 4.13; 18.24–26; Lev. 10.17; Josh. 24.19, etc.), i.e. to 'declare someone innocent' because of penance (which has been done by someone else: Num. 14.18f.). This Semitism (bear sins) is taken over in the New Testament but in the sense of the forgiveness of sins, albeit thanks to the atoning sacrifice of the cross: 'The Lamb of God which takes away (bears) the sin of the world' (John 1.29). An important feature of the New Testament use of many of these Jewish concepts is that redemption is essentially also the forgiveness of sins, and that this forgiveness is essentially connected with the crucifixion of Jesus. In other words, the saving significance of Jesus cannot be fully defined without his death and resurrection.

Precisely because the forgiveness of sins is mentioned in only a few passages in the Tanach, whereas all interest is directed towards 'canonical' atonement or expiation of sins (albeit with the focus on the forgiveness of sins), hardly any account is taken of the real *iustificatio impii* or the divine acceptance of the sinner and not just of the righteous or *ṣaddīq* (the one who is declared innocent 'in the eyes of the Law' because he is righteous, or because he has performed the prescribed penance). Only in a few texts (Ps. 65.3; 78.38; 79.9; Ex. 32.30; Deut. 32.43; Isa. 27.9; Dan. 9.24) do we hear of this, and then above all in extra-biblical, early Jewish groups, e.g. in Qumran (see above, in the analysis of *ṣᵉdāqā*). This acceptance of the *sinner* by God is the heart of New Testament redemption as the forgiveness of sins, above all in the Pauline and Johannine experience of Christian salvation: Jesus Christ *is* God's forgiveness, he *is* 'life'; in him life is made possible for us: we may *be*. That the legalistic meaning is still echoed in a number of New Testament texts must be attributed to the use of Jewish terms taken over from the juristic priestly acquittal from sin, rather than to the New Testament experience of salvation in Jesus from God.

## H. Justification and sanctification

Only in Pauline theology does the *iustificatio impii* or justification become a technical term for redemption (though not exclusively so). Redemption is understood as entrance into the 'community of saints' at baptism, in faith. 'We are *justified*' (aorist) and 'we shall be saved' (*sōtēria, sōzein* in Paul refer to the resurrection of the body: Rom. 8.23f.). Paul makes a distinction between justification and sanctification. Even the Deutero-Pauline epistles do not really maintain it. Sanctification (*hagiasmos; hosiōtes*, as a Septuagint translation of $s^e d\bar{a}q\bar{a}$ or righteousness) and *eusebeia* are both terms from the world of Greek religious sensibility: Rom. 6.16, 19, 22; I Cor. 1.30; I Thess. 4.3f.; 7; 5.23; II Thess. 2.13; Eph. 4.24; I Tim. 2.15; 6.11; I Peter 1.2; II Tim. 2.21; Heb. 12.14; *eusebeia:* I Tim. 2.2; 4.7f.; 6.3, 5f., 11; II Peter 1.3, 6f.; II Tim. 3.5; Titus 1.1. Christians are called holy, saints or 'those on the way to holiness' (Rom. 1.7; 8.27; 12.13; 15.25, 31; 16.2, 15; I Cor. 1.2; 6.1; 14.33; 16.1, 15; II Cor. 1.1; 8.4; 9.1, 12; 13.13; Acts 9.13, 32, 41; Eph. 1.1, 15, 18; 2.19; 3.8, 18; 4.12; 5.3; 6.18; Philemon 5; Col. 1.2, 4, 22, 16; I Thess. 3.13; II Thess. 1.10; Heb. 3.1; Jude 3; Rev. 11.18; 13.7, 10; 20.9). I analysed the term justification in some detail in my discussion of Paul and in connection with $s^e d\bar{a}q\bar{a}$, so I need not do so again in this synthesis.[24]

## I. Salvation in Jesus as legal aid

In Hebrews, the saving activity of the heavenly Jesus is understood as an everlasting intercession of Jesus with the Father. Jesus is the advocate and defender of the human cause with God (Heb. 7.23–25; 9.24; 4.14–16; 2.17). However, this notion can be found throughout the New Testament. I John 2.1 says of the exalted heavenly Christ that he is 'Paraclete', intercessor and advocate with God. When John 14.16 says that Jesus 'will send *another* Paraclete', this implies that during his *earthly* life (I John differs here) Jesus himself is a Paraclete. The notion of intercession and the Paraclete has legalistic contours, i.e. the judgment of God is depicted as a legal process in which the sinner appears as one who is accused. The heavenly Jesus is then the defender (and, according to Rev. 12.10, the devil is the *katēgoros* or accuser). Paul, too, knows of this intercession by Jesus (Rom. 8.34), and so does the Gospel of John (John 16.26; I

John 2.1). The basis for this can be found in the synoptic Jesus (Matt. 10.32f. par.; Mark 8.38 par.).

The special feature of the Gospel of John is that it also describes the earthly Jesus as defender and Paraclete (John 14.16), and what for I John 2.1 is the exalted Christ is for the Gospel of John the Holy Spirit as Paraclete (John 14.16, 26; 15.26; 16.7). 'Paraclete' (in the Greek an advocate at a trial) is clearly explained in the Gospel of John: the Spirit, sent by God and Christ, not to the world (John 14.17) but to the disciples of Jesus, is the accuser of 'the world' before God, in order to bear witness to the fact that Jesus is in the right (15.26) and that the world is in the wrong (16.8–11). The notion that the Spirit is an intercessor or provides legal support can also be found elsewhere in the New Testament, without the term Paraclete (Rom. 8.26f.; see Mark 13.11 par.; Luke 22.32).

The idea of Jesus' intercession for men, understood in the form of legal aid, has roots in the Old Testament. Moses above all is seen as the one who intercedes and protects Israel (Gen. 18.23–33; 20.7, 17). The concept of a heavenly intercessor appears with increasing frequency (Jer. 5.28; Job 29.16; above all Job 33.23); the references have a particular archangel in mind (Job 33.19–25; 5.1). In the Old Testament Pseudepigrapha the heavenly intercessor is either 'the great Moses' or the heavenly Enoch,[25] or particularly some angel,[26] above all Michael.[27] A new element here is that 'the Spirit of truth' becomes the great intercessor in heaven, the Paraclete.[28] We find a move in this direction in the deutero-canonical Old Testament. First of all there developed the notion of solidarity, in the sense of the obligation to intercede for one another before God (II Macc. 1.2–6; 8.14f.; 12.39–45). This solidarity with men was also presupposed in some heavenly beings. 'I am Raphael, one of the seven holy angels who present the prayers of the saints and enter into the presence of the glory of God' (Tobit 12.15). In this early Jewish period, in which God was conceived of as being unapproachably transcendent, a world of heavenly beings who mediated between heaven and earth came into being almost of its own accord. This new conception was connected with God's grace and judgment and with the forensic and legalistic character of many Jewish concepts: as a sinner before God, man is accused before God's forum, and as well as an accuser he also has an advocate before God. In Hebrews, this heavenly intercession takes on more of a cultic than a legalistic character. The notion of the *gō'ēl*, the helper and saviour, may also have contributed to calling the redeemer Jesus not only intercessor but finally Paraclete. Under this aspect, to be redeemed means to go through life in the encouraging awareness that the Christian is always assured of a powerful legal defence.

It is sufficiently clear from these descriptions of the nature of Christian redemption that the New Testament authors took their model of interpretation from the simple processes of everyday experience, processes from which men draw strength to cope with life. Men can venture out on life boldly with Jesus the Christ as with none other.

## J. Being redeemed for community

According to the New Testament, 'redeemed mankind' is the community of the church, i.e. that part of the world which sets its trust and hope on Jesus as the decisive salvation for man. Grace is not just seen as a gift to the individual. Just as in the Tanach, the notion of the covenant included a communion of God with his whole people (Lev. 26.11f.), so the Christian community binds individuals in one all-embracing whole, into a community, an *ecclesia* or *qāhāl*, the solemn Deuteronomistic designation for the people of God as officially assembled. Jesus himself addressed each individual personally with a view to their decision about the coming kingdom of God. Anyone who does the will of God is the brother, sister or mother of Jesus (Mark 3.35). This breaks down the connection between God, the people and the land which in one sense had been central to Judaism.[29] Belonging to a people, even to the chosen people, was by no means enough to ensure escape from God's judgment. Furthermore, it would only emerge at the day of judgment (Matt. 25.31–46) who really belonged to the 'elect of the Father' and to those for whom the kingdom of God had been prepared from eternity (Matt. 25.31–46). The criterion for this is the attitude which a man has adopted to the least brother (of Jesus, Matt. 25.40) and towards Jesus himself (Mark 8.38). The consequence of this pronounced personal confrontation is that terms like 'people of God' and 'covenant' make no sense at all in the context of Jesus' preaching. Even the term *laos*, people of God, is rare in the synoptic gospels; in Mark it appears only once (Mark 11.32; in Mark 7.6 it is a quotation from the Greek Isa. 29.13 and in Mark 14.2 it simply means a crowd). The word also occurs in Matt. 1.21; Luke 1.68, 77; 2.32; 7.16; 24.19 (Matt. 2.6 is a quotation from II Sam. 5.2). The idea of grace being directed only to one people is quite alien to the New Testament. Hence its avoidance of expressions like 'chosen people': anyone who believes in Jesus the Christ, from any people, is chosen. By virtue of the simple fact that Jesus' message is addressed to the human person, the kingdom of God is detached from the 'people of God', thus giving its content a universal human application (though this does not yet imply any individualistic view of salvation, see below).

Only after Jesus' death do his disciples, who see his resurrection as an eschatological event, as the beginning of universal eschatological happenings, begin to understand themselves consistently as the eschatological community. In so doing they refer back to Isa. 61 and Jer. 31; thus the Christian *ecclesia* becomes the subject of the new covenant with God (above all and almost exclusively in Paulinism and the Epistle to the Hebrews). Outside Pauline theology *diathēkē* occurs only four times in the synoptic gospels and twice in Acts. This same Pauline school speaks later of the Christian congregation or community as the *sōma Christou*, the body of the Lord, in terms which come more from Stoic thought (Col. 1.18; 2.19; 3.15; Eph. 1.23; 4.4, 12, 16; 5.23). However, there are also mystic tendencies in the New Testament which point in a more private direction; above all in I John there are conceptions which move towards what will later be called a mysticism of being, though these too (in Johannine theology) are within a fundamental experience of grace. But throughout the New Testament this is connected with the building up of community and 'the renewal of the world', albeit for the moment within a perspective which is limited to the church (for the reason for this, see below).

Those who are 'assembled together' in Christ form what the New Testament generally calls 'the church *of God*' (Acts 20.28; I Cor. 1.2; 10.32; 11.16, 22; 14.33; 15.9; I Thess. 2.14; I Tim. 3.5; 3.15) and sometimes also the 'church *of Christ*' (Rom. 16.16), finally a church or assembly which is 'in God and the Lord Jesus Christ' (I Thess. 1.1; II Thess. 1.1). The subject of redemption is not the individual in himself but the person who is accepted into a new community, a new brotherhood. Only in two passages is this termed (with an Old Testament expression) a kingly and priestly people of God (I Peter 2.9f.; Rev. 1.6, see 5.9 and 20.6), the *ecclēsia* or 'assembly of the firstborn' (Heb. 12.23). In our history this church is the historical *sōma*-manifestation of the glorified corporeality of Jesus, that is, the real life of Jesus with the Father made manifest here on earth (Colossians; Ephesians). Hence the Christian community, the church, is made into a visible unity and nourished through 'communion with Christ', that is, through participation in the one bread and the one cup of the eucharist, which at the same time is already an expression of a certain unity and mutual love which has been achieved (above all I Cor. 10.16; 11.27).


### K. Being freed for brotherly love


The natural way in which all the New Testament traditions speak of Jesus as 'the Son', even in the earliest New Testament evidence (I Thess. 1.10), taken with the early Christian (pre-) Johannine interpretation, with its quite different orientation, gives the reason for an equally original New Testament practice. The term *adelphos* (brother) is naturally used to refer to fellow Christians. The occasion for this New Testament usage seems to be Matt. 23.8, which takes up a saying of Jesus: do not allow yourselves to be called 'rabbi'; you have only one master, 'you are all brothers' (a text which can certainly be regarded as genuine).

On the other hand, early Judaism was familiar with many communities in which all the members of the group were called brothers. Christianity took over this custom, but gave it a specific basis of its own in 'the Son', our fellow and brother. On close inspection I would also interpret John 20.17 in this way: '*my* Father, who has now also become your Father', i.e. not in the perspective of later dogmatic theology, which was interested in drawing a distinction between the 'sonship' of Jesus *vis-à-vis* the Father and our own sonship. The sonship of Jesus is itself the foundation for specifically Christian brotherhood.

In addition to a number of passages in which 'brother' is used unmistakably in the sense of 'fellow Jew' or, more generally, in the customary and profound sense of 'fellow man', the New Testament knows the frequent use of 'brother' in the sense of a group identity: the fellow Christian. In the New Testament Jesus is 'the firstborn among many brethren' (*inter alia*, Rom. 8.29; Heb. 2.11, 17). In many pericopes 'the brethren' means 'members of the household of faith', Christians (Acts 1.15; 9.30; 10.23; 11.1, 29; 12.17; 14.2; 15.1, 3, 22, 32, 33, 36; 16.2; 17.6, 10; 18.27; Rom. 16.14; I Cor. 5.11; 6.5f.; 6.8; 7.12; 8.11; 15.6; 16.11f.; II Cor. 8.18, 22; 8.23; 11.9; Gal. 1.2; I Thess. 4.10; 5.26f.; II Thess. 3.6, 15; I Tim. 4.6; 6.2; Heb. 2.11–17; James 1.9; 4.11; I John 3.13; III John 3, 5, 10; Rev. 6.11; 12.10; 19.10; I Peter 2.17; 5.9). In I Peter 5.9 the expression 'the brotherhood' is simply used to mean 'the Christians' or the Christian community. However, because of the special and subtle approach of I John, it remains uncertain whether in I John 2.9–11; 3.10; 3.16f., 'the brethren' refers specially to Christians (this is nevertheless quite probable). It also emerges from I John that there is a tension between 'your brothers' in the sense of all men, and brothers in the sense of fellow Christians (or members of the household of faith; see also I Thess. 4.9f.; 5.5; Gal. 6.10). For although the Christians cannot expect any love from the world, they must themselves be prepared to show love towards all men to the utmost (I John 3.16–18). Thus in I John 3.13, 'brother' is the fellow Christian, whereas in 3.14 it is all men, even non-Christians, while 3.16, 18 again becomes an admonition to show love to one's fellow Christians. In Johannine theology, love of the brethren and general love of one's neighbour (shown to all men) coincide and yet stand in a certain tension with one another. However, despite this tension, even in Johannine theology the New Testament does not know of any hate of the Christian in-group for the out-group, of the kind that is demonstrated say in Qumran.

We may say that at the heart of the New Testament lies the recognition that we are redeemed for brotherly love. It is superfluous here to analyse the central concept of *agapē* in the New Testament. As a summary, it is enough to quote three passages: 'We have passed from death to life because we love the brethren' (I John 3.14); 'that we should believe in his son Jesus Christ and love one another' (I John 3.23); 'he who says he abides in him ought to walk in the same way in which he walked' (I John 2.6). Redemption is freedom for self-surrender in love for fellow men; that is abiding in God. Ethics, and above all love of one's neighbour, is the public manifestation of the state of being redeemed: 'By this it may be seen who are the children of God, and who are the children of the devil: whoever does not do right is not of God, nor he who does not love his brother' (I John 3.10). Alongside *agapē*, the New Testament knows the Hellenistic word *agathosynē* (Eph. 5.9; Gal. 5.22; II Thess 1.11; see also the catalogue of virtues in New Testament paraeneses or admonitions, e.g. Eph. 4.2b; 4.3; 4.31f. (on the other hand goodness, *tūb*, was also a Hebrew word which was often connected with *ḥesed*, grace, and *ṣᵉdāqā*.)

## L.  Being freed for freedom

In a terminology drawn from late antiquity and inspired by the Stoics, which at the same time has a direct and 'modern' ring about it, New Testament Christianity speaks of salvation in Jesus from God in terms of freedom and liberation from all alienation and slavery. For anyone who remains open to it in faith, the grace of God in Jesus has as a result 'the freedom of the children of God' (Rom. 8.21; I Cor. 10.29). 'Where the spirit of Christ is, there is freedom' (II Cor. 3.17): 'freedom in Christ' (Gal. 2.4). With a characteristic solemnity about freedom, Paul says, 'For freedom Christ has set us free; stand fast, therefore, and do not submit again to a yoke of slavery' (Gal. 5.1). Through Christ we are freed from the ancient existential fear of demons and other powers that enslave us (Paul: Eph.; Col.; Heb.; Rev., etc.), from the determinisms of an astrological kind and from heavenly spirits which determine human destiny. Thanks to this cosmic and ethical liberation, Christians may enjoy the things of this world in sovereign freedom, as they are free from taboos (Col. 2.16–23). Believers who are redeemed in Christ are 'called to freedom' (Gal. 5.13). God's 'children are free' (Matt. 17.26): 'For if the Son makes you free, you will be *free indeed (ontōs eleutheroi)*' (John 8.36). 'The Jerusalem from above is free; and that is our mother' (Gal. 4.26; see 4.31). Christian freedom is therefore essentially different from the circumstances which in fact prevail in secular social situations: in Christian experience the differences between Jew and non-Jew, man and woman, slave and free man, simply fall away (I Cor. 12.13; 7.22; Gal. 3.28; 4.7; 5.6; Col. 3.11; Rev. 13.16).

But in the New Testament this Christian charter of freedom, the intrinsic consequence and implication of grace, is accompanied by a warning: 'Live as free men, yet without using your freedom as a pretext for evil' (I Peter 2.16; Gal. 5.13–15; I Cor. 6.12–14; 10.23–25). The freedom of grace is no unbridled arbitrariness, but 'subjection under God and Christ' (Rom. 6.22; 7.3). As 'the law of freedom' (James 1.25), it stands under a 'new law', *en-nomos* in Christ; that means, as freedom it stands under the norm of Jesus Christ, a law of love. Jude and II Peter above all criticize misuse of what is called Pauline freedom (Jude 4; II Peter 2.19; 3.15b–16); they attack a charismatic enthusiasm which boasts that it is above all fear of demons, as though it knew nothing of any kind of alienation. This is countered by the admonition not to misuse the Christian kerygma of freedom (Jude 8–10, 16; II Peter 2.10f.), or better, not to understand it wrongly.


## M.  Renewal of man and the world

A second New Testament concept which also seems to us to have a modern ring is that of 'newness' ('*kainos*' and '*neos*'). The experience of newness is characteristic of the whole of the New Testament. There is mention of a new covenant of love (Matt. 26.28f.; Luke 22.20; I Cor. 11.25; II Cor. 3.6; Heb. 8.8, 13; 9.15, 18), a new teaching (Mark 1.27; Acts 17.19), a new commandment (John 13.34; I John 2.7f.; II John 5), of 'newness of life' (Rom. 6.4f.; 7.6; Eph. 2.15) and also of newness of spirit or mentality, 'other men with a new code' (Rom. 7.6; 12.2), a renewal of thinking (Eph. 4.23), and finally a renewal which embraces the whole man and makes him 'a new creation' (II Cor. 5.17; Gal. 6.15; Eph. 2.10; Rom. 6.4f.; 7.6), in other words 'a new man' (Eph. 4.24), which removes the difference between Jew and non-Jew (Eph. 2.14f.). For those who have been redeemed in Christ, 'everything' becomes 'new' and different (II Cor. 5.17; Rev. 21.5). There comes 'a new heaven and a new earth in which righteousness dwells' (II Peter 3.13; Rev. 21.1), a new society without alienation, a kingdom, a dominion of grace and life in which all receive 'a new name' (Rev. 2.17; this is a Semitic way of saying that men will become completely new, transformed beings), who will then also be able to 'sing a new song' (Rev. 5.9; 14.3) – the song of their grateful new existence, as praise of God.

In the gospel account this newness in Jesus is expressed in parables, in Old Testament symbols of salvation like the 'new wine' at the eschatological feast (Mark 14.25), new wine which therefore is not to be put

into old skins (Mark 2.21f.) This newness is depicted in Jewish eschatological terms in the image of the 'new Jerusalem' (Rev. 21.2; Heb. 12.22)
or 'the city of the living God' (Heb. 12.22); the realized rule of God
among all men. In short, 'Behold, I make all things new' (Rev. 21.5):
this is the transformation of humanity (I Cor. 15.51; II Cor. 3.18); eschatological new creation of all existing conditions (Rev. 21.1; Matt. 19.28);
'a rebirth' (I Peter 1.3; 1.23 and Johannine theology) even now.


## N.  Life in fullness

Now, however, we come up against the basic human question: Is life
meaningful? Is it possible? Can I cope with life? And what am I to make
of my death? Consequently the concept of 'life' plays an important role
in the New Testament (*zōē*, life; *zōopoiein*, bring alive) (Matt. 7.14; 19.16f.;
25.46; Mark 9.43, 45; 10.17; Luke 10.25; 12.15; 18.18; John 3.15; 3.16;
3.36; 4.14; 4.36; 5.21, 24, 26, 29; 5.39f.; 6.27; 6.33, 35, 40, 47–50, 53, 63,
68; 8.12; 10.10b; 10.28; 11.25; 12.25, 50; 14.6; 17.2f.; Acts 3.15; 11.18;
13.46, 48; 17.25; Rom. 2.7; 4.17; 5.10, 17f., 21; 6.4, 8, 10f., 13, 22f.; 7.10;
8.2, 6, 10f.; 11.15; I Cor. 15.19, 22; 15.36, 45; II Cor. 2.16; 3.6; 4.10; 6.14;
Gal. 3.21; 6.8; Eph. 2.5; 4.18; Col. 3.4; I Tim. 1.16; 6.12; 6.19; II
Tim. 1.10b; James 1.12; I Peter 3.7, 18; II Peter 1.3; I John 1.2; 2.25;
3.14; 5.11–13; 5.16, 20; Jude 21; Rev. 2.10; 7.17; 11.11; 21.6; 22.1, 17 (the
cross of Jesus as the 'tree of life', Rev. 2.7; 22.2, 14, 19).

It became clear in our study of *ṣᵉdāqā* that in the Tanach righteousness
always has an intrinsic connection with a flourishing and happy life, and
that this principle of Israelite and early Jewish belief led to a crisis which
is expressed above all in Job. However, Job continued to believe in the
mystery of God and in the mutual interconnection between life in accordance with God's will and the human concern for happiness and fulfilment.
The New Testament knows a similar intrinsic connection, but makes it
between *the life of grace* and human *life*, so that suffering and misery in
themselves need not contradict this connection; indeed, in the context of
grace they can even acquire a new significance. However, communion
with God in grace implies that in the last resort nothing can separate us
from God: neither man (Heb. 13.5f.), nor death, nor powerful beings
(Rom. 8.38f.), and that this has eschatological consequences for human
nature itself: eternal life, physical resurrection and 'a new heaven and a
new earth' with just conditions, a life without alienation, without suffering
and tears.

There is also an 'evangelical consolation' in such a Christian view and
way of life, which has nothing to do with an escape into illusions and
projections. II Thess. 2.16 summarizes this as follows: 'Now may our

Lord Jesus Christ himself, and God our Father, who loved us and gave us *eternal comfort* and *good hope* through grace, comfort your hearts and establish them in every good work and word.' Salvation in Jesus means from God (Rom. 15.5; II Cor. 1.3), through Jesus (Phil. 2.1; II Thess. 2.16; II Cor. 1.5; 1.7; 7.4; 8.4), in the Holy Spirit (Acts 9.31; 15.31), a *paraklēsis*, i.e. consolation, 'abundance of consolation' (II Cor. 1.5; 1.7; 7.4; 8.4; see I Thess 1.10; Heb. 6.18; 12.5), a consolation which is the source of constant confidence and thus produces free and profound boldness *(parrhēsia*: II Cor. 3.12; Eph. 3.12; Heb. 3.6; 4.16; 10.19; 10.35; I John 3.21; 5.14). The foundation of this consolation is hope: 'Christ is our hope' (I Tim. 1.1; see I Thess. 1.3), 'God is our hope' (Acts 24.15; Rom. 15.13), a 'hope against all hope' (Rom. 4.18), 'a joyful hope' (I Peter 1.3; see II Cor. 3.12). It is a hope which lends substance to faith (Heb. 11.1), and 'a love which hopes for all things' (I Cor. 13.7); 'that you may not mourn like those who have no hope' (I Thess. 4.13) or who 'live without hope and without God' (Eph. 2.12). Faith, love and hope are the pillars of 'the life' of which the New Testament speaks (see also Gal. 5.6, 13, 22; Rom. 13.8f.; II Cor. 8.4f.; Eph. 4.7–15; I Tim. 1.14; 2.15; 4.12; 6.11; Titus 2.2; Philemon 5; I Peter 1.21f.). We are redeemed for faith, hope and love; therefore despite many negative experiences, life is not without consolation.

Such life – 'he who has the Son has life' (I John 5.12) – is in the last resort a life in joy. The New Testament is therefore fond of linking *charis* (grace) with *chara* (joy). This connection (which is also a feature of the Greek concept of *charis*) is the feature of the *charis* of Jesus, and particularly of his message, which Luke tends to single out. For him the gospel of Jesus is something joyful and new, especially for the lowly – in word and deed – a joyful new thing bringing radical change and renewal. Luke is fond of seeing joy in many events of Jesus' life. For him the announcement of the birth of Jesus is already good tidings (Luke 2.10). Grace is the forgiveness of sins; therefore there is joy over every sinner who repents (Luke 15.7); grace is the resurrection of Jesus, so there is joy at this event (Luke 24.41). This is also expressed in other passages in the New Testament. Jesus' mere presence is already joy and grace (John 3.29), and lamentation and fasting are no longer existentially possible (Mark 2.18–22 par.). Grace is also ethical renewal of life; therefore following God's commandments (John 15.10) is sharing in Jesus' joy (John 15.11; 17.13). Meeting Jesus is like the happiness over the birth of a child (John 16.20–22). The kingdom of God proclaimed by Jesus as inaugurated in his resurrection is an event of 'peace and joy through the Holy Spirit' (Rom. 14.17). The 'God of hope', who is the God of Jesus, is 'joy and peace' (Rom. 15.13, etc.). 'The fruit of the Holy Spirit is love and peace' (Gal. 5.22; I Thess. 1.6). All this is the occasion for doxological boasting:

'You will rejoice with unutterable and exalted joy when as the outcome of the faith you obtain the salvation of your souls' (I Peter 1.8f.). However justified this enthusiastic Christian experience of grace may be, even within this early Christian enthusiasm, with its inbuilt self-criticism, Jude and II Peter advise moderation and caution in the face of such a triumphant alleluia mood.

## O. Liberation in the context of late antiquity: victory over alienating 'demonic powers'

A historical discussion of belief in demons in early Judaism and late antiquity is necessary if we are to understand why the New Testament speaks in a number of passages of redemption as *nikē*, victory or triumph, specifically over Satan and a number of demonic powers. This historical explanation is all the more necessary because many believers do not know what to make of this state of affairs in the New Testament, and are disturbed at this particular point.

*Literature:* J. Becker, *Das Heil Gottes, Heils- und Sündenbegriffe in den Qumrantexten und im Neuen Testament*, SUNT 3, Göttingen 1964; M. Black, *Apocalypsis Henochi graece*, Leiden 1970; O. Böcher, *Dämonenfurcht und Dämonenabwehr. Ein Beitrag zur Vorgeschichte der christlichen Taufe*, BWANT 90, Stuttgart 1970; G. B. Caird, *Principalities and Powers, a Study in Pauline Theology*, Oxford 1956; *Conc* 11, 1975, no.3 (Dämonen sind Nichtse); A. Dupont-Sommer, 'Exorcismes et guérisons dans les écrits de Qumran', *VTS* 7, 1960, 246–61; T. Glasson, *Greek Influence in Jewish Theology, with Special Reference to the Apocalypses and Pseudepigraphs*, London 1961; H. Haag, *Teufelsglaube*, Tübingen 1974; M. Hengel, *Judaism and Hellenism*, ET London and Philadelphia 1974; H. W. Huppenbauer, 'Belial in den Qumrantexten', *TZ* 15, 1959, 81–9; B. van Iersel, 'Jesus, duivel en demonen', *Annalen van het Thijmgenootschap* 55, 1968, 5–22; O. Neugebauer, *The Exact Sciences in Antiquity*, Providence [2]1957 (in connection with astrology and angelology); B. Noack, *Satanas und Soteria*, Copenhagen 1948; P. von der Osten-Sacken, *Gott und Belial*, SUNT 6, Göttingen 1969; B. Otzen, s.v. *beliyya'al*, *TDOT* 2, 131–6; B. Reicke, *The Dissonant Spirits and Christian Baptism*, Copenhagen 1946; J. Reider, *The Book of Wisdom*, New York 1957; J. A. Sanders, 'Dissenting Deities and Philippians 2, 1–11', *JBL* 88, 1969, 279–90; H. Schlier, *Mächte und Gewalten im Neuen Testament*, Quaest. disp. 3, Freiburg 1958; W. H. Schmidt, *Die Schöpfungsgeschichte der Priesterschrift*, Neukirchen 1967; Strack-Billerbeck, Excursus 21, Vol. IV/1, 1928, 501–35; M. Testuz, *Les idées religieuses du livre des Jubilés*,

Geneva-Paris 1960; J. Thomas, *Aktuelles im Zeugnis der zwölf Väter*, BZNW 36, Berlin 1969.

Before the exile, Israel saw no problem in ascribing everything to God: God brings about good and evil, hardens men's hearts, and so on, but in such a way that man himself is responsible for sin. Ideas of tormenting spirits in popular belief from neighbouring lands reached the periphery of this belief in Yahweh. But such popular beliefs were either vigorously contested in the name of Yahwistic monotheism or neutralized by integration. During and after the exile, however, the image of God changed. Yahweh was thought to be utterly transcendent. The consequence of this was that he was no longer thought to dwell in the tent of the covenant; only the tablets of the Law were preserved there (Deut. 10.1–5; Heb. 9.4). Yahweh's name alone still dwelt there (Deut. 12.11), and Yahweh occasionally appeared there to reveal himself. Thus Yahweh's Word, Wisdom and Spirit became independent; they gradually so to speak detached themselves from the transcendent God, although they remained identical with him (for this trend see Deuteronomy and the Priestly Writing). This tendency became even stronger after the exile (see Isa. 55.10f.). The Word of God became as it were a messenger who carried out his task independently. The same phenomenon appears everywhere in the middle of the last millennium BC. On the one hand a completely transcendent conception of God makes a universal appearance – in Israel, in Persia with Zarathustra; in India with the transition from the Vedas to the Upanishads, in Buddhism and in Jainism; in China in Confucianism (Taoism) and the 'hundred schools'; in Greece in the transition from Homer and Hesiod to the pre-Socratics and classical philosophy[30] – on the other hand, as a counter-effect of this conception of God as wholly other, various 'intermediary beings' between God and the human world keep making an appearance, first in accordance with the theory of the various 'emanations' from God (his Word, his Spirit), also in Zarathustra; later the demiurge in Middle Platonism, etc., then in the Persian-Hellenistic period by the explosion of a whole world of myriads of angels and demons. After the exile, in Israel the demonic world, which earlier had been sharply contested in the name of monotheism, gained universal significance precisely because of this transcendent monotheism: 'intermediary beings' became necessary in order to prevent such a transcendent God from coming into contact with our insignificant earthly world.

However, the Old Testament does not know of any real Satan. True, the words 'Satan' and 'Belial' occur. In Hebrew, *śāṭān* simply means enemy or accuser in the secular sense of the word, e.g. the prosecutor in a legal dispute (Ps. 109.6). By contrast there is a good deal of argument over the etymology of Belial: it is connected with the kingdom of the dead. In the Old Testament, sons of Belial are often anti-social people; anyone who disrupts the social order is an enemy of God. The monarchy above all is a social institution; sons of Belial undermine the monarchy and thus Belial becomes as it were the counterpart of the just king; he is a priest of unrighteousness, a bad king. And because the cult, too, is a social institution, the 'anti-social Belial' also becomes the one who leads men astray into idolatry. These secular concepts are only later applied to heavenly beings, angels.

There are three passages in the Old Testament where 'the Satan' is mentioned in connection with 'heavenly circumstances' (Zech. 3.1–7; Job 1.6; 2.1; I Chron 21.1–27, especially 21.2). In the first passage (Zechariah) where 'the Satan' appears in the Old Testament as a heavenly being, he is the accuser at the heavenly court of judgment (Zech. 3.1–7). This angel has the task of being concerned for order in the world *in the name of* God, and an accuser (Satan) must bring all those who disrupt this order before the judgment seat of God. '*The* Satan' (with the article) is not a proper name, but indicates the official function of the accuser. It is a title (*haśśāṭān*). In Zech. 3.1–7 he is rejected by the defender: 'Go away from me, Satan' (3.2; taken up in Mark 8.32f.; Matt. 16.22f.). In the face of God's plan of salvation, the accuser (Satan) represents the purely human conception of things; at this point he is still far from being a demonic counterpart of God (nor is he in Job 1.6; 2.1).

In I Chron. 21.1, what in II Sam. 24.1 is called 'God's wrath against Israel' is turned into 'Satan against Israel' (Satan, without the article; in other words, it is turning into a proper name). Satan is now the enemy of Israel; not one who leads Israel astray into sin, but someone who prevents it from reaching its goal. This is the only passage in the Old Testament in which Satan has something to do with what becomes the concern of the New Testament. Until about 180 BC, the problem of sin is resolved without recourse to Satan. Sirach, who is deeply concerned with the problem of evil, like Job before him, says that evil cannot come from God (Job still looks for it somewhere in God), but only from man (Sir. 15.11–13, 15–17), and solves the problem by retribution (to come: 16.1–14).

After 180 BC, however, a number of things had happened in Israel which made the solutions to the problem of theodicy given by Ecclesiastes and Sirach seem no longer adequate. There was too much meaningless suffering. This problem became acute for hasidic, apocalyptic circles after the desecration of the Temple by Antiochus IV Epiphanes, the bloody persecutions of those who remained faithful to the Law and, somewhat later, the disillusionment which arose over the Maccabean resistance fighters, who went wrong after they had come to power. All this was too much for the faithful in Israel. There had to be deeper reasons for evil.

A new conception began to develop in the extra-biblical, pseudepigraphical writings, on the basis of various popular legends. The theory is developed with increasing acuteness in I Enoch, the Book of Jubilees, the Testaments of the Twelve Patriarchs, the Life of Adam and Eve, and then above all in the early Essene writings from Qumran (though with the idea of a double predestination which was alien to Israel). All these works come from the time round about 150 BC, though the works mentioned first have later sections (even from the Christian era), alterations and revisions, and sometimes even Christian interpolations, as they were popular reading in early Christianity. The works were originally written in Hebrew or Aramaic (and therefore originated in Palestine); later they were translated into Greek and other languages (these versions are all we have left today).

*I Enoch* ( = Ethiopic Enoch, because we know the complete text only in an Ethiopic translation). It was a canonical book of the Bible in the Christian churches in Ethiopia; some Hebrew and Aramaic fragments were found in Qumran. The book is quoted in the New Testament, in Jude 14f., where there are also a number of implicit references.[31]

An important feature of the book of Enoch is the legend from Gen. 6.1–4: the fall of the angels and the consorting of angels with beautiful earthly women, who give birth to a race of giants. On the one hand this fall of the angels is not a feature of the Bible but a popular legend which came into being to explain evil. The fall of the angels is connected with the astronomical phenomenon of *falling stars*. Throughout antiquity these were seen as living beings (see already Judg. 5.20; Job 38.7; protest against star worship, Deut. 4.19; 17.3; Jer. 8.2; 19.13; at a later stage of spiritualization, as in I Enoch, each heavenly body and each material substance was assigned a guardian angel, so that there was a special angel for rain, wind, hail, etc. and each nation also had a guardian angel; for Israel this was Michael). The phenomenon of falling stars underlies the legend of a fall of heavenly beings (see also I Enoch 21.1ff.; 86.1ff.; 90.21–24). It was a legend which was universal in antiquity. In the Hellenistic syncretism of Judaism and Hellenism, Gen. 6.1–4 was also connected with the Greek myth of the fall of the Titans. In the meantime it had been a firmly accepted element of the ancient view of the world that there are angels; in Israel they are the depotentiated relic of ancient Canaanite polytheism ( *ᵉlōhīm*).

The demons on earth are simply the 'spirits' of deceased Titans, descendants of the consorting of angels with the children of men (I Enoch 18.13ff.; 21.6ff.; 86–88; 90.21), just as in Greece the good demons are the spirits of men from the past golden age.

By and large these notions show no consistency. The prince or leader of the evil spirits is sometimes called Semyala (I Enoch 6.3; 9.7; 10.11;

69.2) but sometimes – more often – Azezel (8.1f.; 10.4–8; 13.1). The sin of the angels, the cause of their fall, was sometimes their consorting with earthly women; but as this had now become difficult to conceive of in theological terms, their sin became the betrayal of heavenly astral secrets and heavenly knowledge to men (I Enoch 9.6; 16.3. One might think of the Prometheus myth in Aeschylus). Men learned from them astrology, the techniques of war, the means of abortion, and so on (7.1; 8.1–3; 69.4ff.). Finally, there were demons even before there were fallen angels (19.1). Chapters 37–71 speak of one or more Satanic figures (but that comes from a later time). The sin of angels now consists in the fact that they obey Satan and later lead men astray into sin (54.6). So Satan already exists even before the fall of the angels. In other words, the course of the origin of evil spirits is as it were forgotten, but the consequences remain valid. There are devils. These are no longer fallen angels, but satellites of Satan (intensified dualism).

In the *Book of Jubilees* the prince of the evil spirits is called Mastema, i.e. prince of enmity; his name itself becomes 'the enemy' (also in the New Testament). Adam's fall is narrated in 3.17–22, but Adam's sin has no consequences for mankind. So-called 'original sin' only occurs in the angels: they come to earth with good intentions – a kind of general inspection – but weaken under the influence of beautiful women (here the Book of Jubilees takes up the theme of I Enoch). As a punishment, these angels are imprisoned in deep chasms in hell until the last days; but Mastema asks of God that a tenth of them shall remain free to tempt men. God assents, but allows this only for a specific time (10.9–11). These evil spirits lead men to sin and are the cause of various sicknesses among men. This explains the problem of evil: evil does not come from God, but God allows it to happen (by means of the evil spirits: *voluntas permissiva Dei*). The remaining tenth will only be conquered in the last days: 'then there will be no more Satan and no evil to hurl mankind to corruption' (23.29). The prince of the evil world is also called Belia*r* (the Greek form of the Hebrew Belia*l*: *bᵉlīyyaʿal*) in the book of Jubilees; along with his satellites he makes men sin and then accuses them before God. It is these demons above all who urge men to wage war (11.2–4).

There are twelve farewell discourses in the *Testaments of the Twelve Patriarchs*, given by the twelve sons of Jacob (the original version is Jewish; there was a later Jewish revision and finally it had Christian interpolations). The fall of the angels is simply presupposed, but the consorting of angels with women is no longer mentioned. In other words, the existence of evil demons is detached from the legend of the sin of the angels; they are now simply a part of the socio-cultural picture of the world. There are evil spirits who incite men to envy (Test. Sim. 4.9), unclean spirits (Test. Benj. 5.2f.), false teachers, above all the origin of the eight deadly sins (Test. Reub. 2.1–3.6), spirits of the prince Beliar (Test. Iss. 7.7), 'angels of Satan' (Test. Ash. 6.4; Test. Dan. 5.6). Over against them stands 'the angel of peace', who helps men (guardian angel) (Test. Ash. 6.5f.; Test. Levi. 3.2). They plague and torment men, these evil spirits (Test. Benj. 3.3). Sometimes Satan or Beliar is called 'the devil' (*diabolos*) in the sense of the 'spirit of deception' and the lie (Test. Sim. 2.7). However, Satan avoids those who are faithful to the Law (Test. Dan. 5.1; Test. Napht. 8.4). The Messiah to come will fetter Satan (Test. Levi. 18.12) and cast him into the fire for ever (Test. Jud. 25.3). When people die they are raised either 'by an angel of the Lord' (*in paradisum deducant te angeli*) or by an angel of Satan (Test. Ash. 6.4). In this way, the doctrine of the 'two ways' finds an intensified echo (Test. Ash. 1.3–5): God confronts man with a distinction between good and evil. In the last resort the decision lies with man himself (Test. Jud. 20.1f.). It is remarkable that the origin of evil spirits (the fall) is no longer a matter for speculation; they are simply there. So the excess of suffering and evil in the world can be explained by reference to a principle subordinate to God, Satan. A diminished dualism serves as theodicy.

The *Life of Adam and Eve* goes back to a Hebrew original dating from the first century BC. We have only the Latin translation; the Apocalypse of Moses is to a large extent a copy of this. It is an extra-canonical popular book, but in it events are portrayed which have influenced almost the whole of Western Christian culture, sometimes more than the Bible. Adam's fall is not ascribed to the devil (the view that the serpent in Gen. 3 was a devil comes from elsewhere). Expelled from the Garden of Eden and punished, Adam seeks to do penance. He suggests that Eve should stand in the Tigris up to her neck for thirty-seven days and that he himself should do penance in the Jordan for forty. Satan, garbed as an angel of light, takes Eve out of the water after eighteen days and takes her to Adam in the Jordan. Adam immediately recognizes Satan (*Vita Ad.* 11). 'Alas, why do you fight against us?', asks Adam. Then he perceives something completely new: Adam himself is the cause of Satan's punishment. Here for the first time we have the legend which is based on a particular 'exegesis' of Gen. 1.26f., in which in P (the Priestly tradition) man is called the image of God. Thus man is even more beautiful than the angels. These have to reverence man, the crown jewel of creation, as God's image. Michael and his followers obey; Satan and his followers refuse. They are punished and are expelled from heaven *to earth*. But Satan is jealous of man's happiness in Paradise and wants to make men sin, so that they will be expelled from Eden. Hence the serpent in Gen. 3.1–7 is identified with the devil (which is certainly not what Gen. 3 itself intended). As a punishment, Satan, too, is now expelled *from the earth.* We also find the theme of *envy*, like an 'erratic block', in Wisdom 2.24, where it probably comes from the Greek theme of 'the envy of the gods' (so this exegesis of Gen. 3.1–7 is not so much exegesis as a midrash).

Finally we come to *II Enoch.* (This is the pre-Christian Slavonic Enoch, because we have only the Slavonic version of a Greek translation of a Hebrew original; III Enoch, on the other hand, is the Hebrew version.) In this book there is yet another explanation of the fall of the angels. One of the angels has the idea of setting his throne above the clouds, in order to become equal to God. However, he is cast down, and with his satellites from that point on he floats around 'in the air' (II Enoch 29.4f.). Here, too, we find Satan's envy of man as lord of creation(31.7f.).

In the *early Essene apocalyptic* from Qumran, all this is shaped into a theological system within an un-Jewish dualism; this dualism is, however, bridged by God. Two central passages illustrate this pre-Christian Essene theology: 1QS 3.15ff. and 4.26 (from the Rule of Qumran, written between 150 and 130 BC). This theology aims to guide men to a universal knowledge, both of 'all being' (creation) and of 'all words' (history) (the confrontation of Jewish thought with Greek ontological thinking). Without any meditation of 'wisdom' or 'the word', God's own perfect organizing and predestining knowledge has established everything unalterably beforehand, down to the individual destiny of all men. The 'children of salvation' are predestined to salvation and the 'children of darkness' to damnation by God, 'who created the righteous and the godless' (1QH 4.38). However, *two great spirits* stand between God and man as God's executive powers, each with its own sphere of influence: the 'angel of darkness' (1QS 3.21–24), also called Beliar (1QS 1.17f., 24; 2.5, 19), and 'the spirit of truth', who is none other than Michael (1QM 17.5ff.). (We find the same model in Zarathustra: God, at once 'the Father of the holy spirit', and the principle of the evil spirit, twins each with its own sphere of influence, both emanations of the one God who holds within himself the *coincidentia oppositorum.* However, this changes in later so-called 'Zoroastrianism', *c.* 400 BC, into a radical dualism between God and the evil spirit.) The struggle between the two spirits extends into the human heart, so that man is a split being (1QS 4.24–26). The suffering of those predestined to good is also seen as the work of Beliar (1QS 3.21–24).

However, God's predestination also appointed a temporal limit: the end-time, which the accumulation of suffering shows to be very near. In an eschatologically heightened final struggle, Michael directs the decisive blow against Beliar and conquers him. Seen in cosmic dimensions, this final battle is concerned with men: their salvation – specifically the salvation of the eschatological remnant formed by the Qumran community, the sons of light; all the rest are sons of the 'devil'.

This whole historical outline constructed by the Essenes is an attempt to answer the problem of evil, the question of meaning, the origin and the end of all evil in the form of apocalyptic. The solution offered goes further than the fatalism of Koheleth or the optimism of Sirach with his view of earthly recompense; it takes a different direction from the book of Job, for which evil remains an unfathomable mystery hidden in God's counsels. However, this solution falls short of its goal because of an excessive dualism. Qumran sought a *rational* solution, albeit in the light of a wisdom 'from above'. As in hasidic apocalyptic (e.g. Daniel), the question of evil becomes a question of the meaning of the whole of human history and thus of eschatological liberation from the sphere of influence of the 'prince of this world'. Specifically, this was the theological answer to the bitter challenge of the difficult times after Antiochus IV: the Jewish experience of the supremacy of evil and at the same time a deep struggle for *metanoia* and the experience of salvation (1QH 2.6ff.; 3.33ff.). In the last resort, righteousness is the deepest meaning of the universe: the earth and the heavenly spheres; human, collective and individual history.

As 'prince of this world' Satan is thus an *extra-biblical* Jewish figure, generally accepted in Palestine from about 150 BC onwards. We should not forget at this point that belief in Satan is completely lacking from wide areas of extra-biblical, non-canonical, Jewish religious writings (there is no trace of it, for example, in III and IV Maccabees, the Testament of Abraham or the Psalms of Solomon) and in the Old Testament works which were written at about the same time (deutero-canonical writings like Sirach; Wisdom – with the exception of one erratic text, Wisdom 2.24ff.; I and II Maccabees; Baruch; Judith). In Tobit (which takes place in the country of the Medes), there is mention (Tobit 3.18, 17) of an Asmodeus who is known to us from Zarathustra. In other words, the Old Testament and even large parts of the extra-biblical literature have no satanology at all. This is not a part of traditional Jewish faith; it became a part of popular Palestinian belief and also (though perhaps to a lesser degree) that of Diaspora Judaism in pre-Christian, inter-testamental, syncretistic literature on the basis of a number of legends. However, in psychological terms, Satan has powerful symbolic force as the expression of the supremacy of evil in a world which so often goes wrong, in spite of all good intentions. The religious significance of these conceptions lies in their symbolic force.

Compared with this extra-biblical literature, the New Testament remains very matter-of-fact, at least in terms of the content of its demonology and satanology. 'The Satan', the prince of this world, is simply taken for granted (e.g. John 12.31; 14.30; 16.11; I John 5.19; 2.13). The devil or Satan and the demons are an element of the cultural and religious consciousness of all the New Testament authors. When we enumerate the texts which speak of the devil, we may be struck by the large number of them that there are, even in the four gospels.

The *devil* or *Satan:* Matt. 12.26; 13.39; Luke 8.12; Acts 5.3; 10.38; Mark 1.13; 3.23, 26; 4.15; Luke 10.18; 13.16; 22.3; 22.31; Rom. 16.20; I Cor. 5.5; 7.5; II Cor. 2.11; 11.14; 12.7; I Thess. 2.18; II Thess. 2.9; Eph. 4.27; 6.11; John 13.27; 6.70; 8.44; 13.2; I John 3.8, 10; I Tim 1.20; 3.6f.; 5.15; II Tim. 2.26; James 4.7; I Peter 5.8; Heb. 2.14; Jude 9; Rev. 2.9; 2.13, 24; 12,9; 20.7.

*Beelzebub* (or Beelzebul): Matt. 10.25; 12.24, 27; Mark 3.22; Luke 11.15, 18f.

'*The enemy*': Matt. 13.39; Luke 10.19.

'*The prince* (*archon,* ruler) *of this world*'; John 12.31; 14.30; 16.11; I John 5.19 (see 2.13); or 'the god of this age': II Cor. 4.4; Eph. 2.2.

*Belial* (Beliar): II Cor. 6.15.

*The tempter:* I Thess. 3.5. The main cause of sin in the world: I Cor. 7.5: II Cor. 2.11; Eph. 4.26f.; I Tim. 3.6f.; John 3.19; 7.7; hence 'the evil one': I John 2.13, 14; 3.12; 5.19; a murderer and liar from the very beginning, John 8.44, see I John 3.8. Anyone who does evil is therefore a child of the devil: I John 3.12; John 6.70; 13.2, 27; 8.44, and so is anyone who fails to love his neighbour: I John 3.11–18; he is one who leads believers astray: II Thess. 2.9; I Tim. 3.6f.; 5.15; II Tim. 2.26; James 4.7; I Peter 5.8. (In Johannine theology, which is inspired by wisdom, the devil is not the tempter; he has no 'sphere of influence' only a sphere of competence: the devil has a right to men who reject the light, see above.)

*The devil of death:* death as a sphere of the devil's influence: Heb. 2.14 (which at the same time means 'sinfulness').

*The cause of possession:* Mark 3.23–30; Luke 13.16; Acts 10.38; Heb. 2.14; Rev. 2.9, 10–13; 3.9; 12.9, 12f.; he is 'the dragon', who stands behind the beast (the emperor) which persecutes Christians: Rev. 12.3f., 9, 13, 16f.; 16.13; 20.2; 11.7; 13.1; 13.4–7, 11, 12, 16f.

*The fall of the angels:* only in Jude 6 (with an implicit reference to I Enoch) (John 8.44 is not relevant here). So the only passage in the New Testament about a fall of the angels is a reference to the legend in I Enoch, whereas II Peter 2.4, which follows Jude here, omits this reference and critically removes mention of a union between angels and giants; it simply retains the fact of the fall of angels (which is then 'unexplained').

The New Testament is not interested in the pyramidal hierarchy of myriads of heavenly beings. However, various kinds are mentioned in passing: *archai* (powers), *dynameis* (forces) and *exousiai* (heights) (Eph. 1.21; I Cor. 15.24; Eph. 6.12; 3.10), also *kyriotētes* (rules) (Eph. 1.21; Col. 1.16) and *thronoi* (thrones) (Col. 1.16); then again simply *archai* and *exousiai* (Col. 2.10, 15), where Col. 1.16 spoke of *thronoi, kyriotētes, archai, exousiai.*

This does not seem to be particularly important. The gods of other religions are also called idols or demons (I Cor. 10.19–22). *Kyrioi* (lords) and *kyriotētes* (rules) seem to be more general, non-hierarchical names; in I Cor. 8.4f. they are called *theoi*. Finally, there is the generic name *stoicheioi tou kosmou* (Gal. 4.3, 9; Col. 2.8, 20), i.e. (in contrast to II Peter 3.10, which is concerned with the fundamental elements of the cosmos, though previously these were also divinized) the cosmocrators, heavenly beings which rule our world, for good or for evil (Eph. 6.12). Doubtless these were also felt to be at work behind and in the actual human political rulers (see above all the whole of the book of Revelation).

Mentions of demons are relatively more frequent (about twenty times) in the later New Testament writings (Jude; I Peter; II Peter; Pastoral Epistles; Revelation; II Thessalonians) than in the earlier New Testament writings (the 'later' character is already evident from I Peter 4.16, where we have simply the term 'as a Christian', *hōs Christianos*).

The New Testament (apart from Revelation) is not concerned with the good and evil spirits with their particular satellites, but with Jesus Christ and Satan (in the last resort, this is also the perspective of Revelation). In the New Testament, Jesus' saving activity is depicted as a fight against the demonic powers of evil (Mark 1.23–25, 39; 4.39; Luke 13.16). Jesus himself is portrayed as being tempted by Satan in person three times, though these attempts fail completely (Matt. 4.1–11; Luke 22.3; see I Cor. 2.8f.; 15.55; Rev. 12.13f. and implicitly also in Heb. 4.15).

The New Testament takes it for granted that Satan and all the demonic powers have been conquered by Christ. Their power has been broken even at the coming of the kingdom of God in Jesus (Luke 10.18; 11.20). After their return from their first apostolic journey, the disciples say to Jesus, 'Even the devils were subject to us in your name' (Luke 10.17), whereupon Jesus answers that he has seen Satan falling like lightning from heaven (Luke 10.18; again the image of the 'falling star'). Above all, however, the resurrection and exaltation of Jesus are seen as the exaltation and complete victory over all heavenly beings (I Cor. 15.24; Rom. 8.38; Eph. 1.21; 3.10; 6.10; Col. 2.10, 15; I Peter 3.22; Heb. 1.5–14; 2.8f.; Revelation). Paul sees this as a completely eschatological event which is still to come (I Cor. 15.24). In the Deutero-Pauline epistles this depotentiation of all devils is on the one hand something that has already taken place, and on the other a task still to be fulfilled. Jesus' victory (Eph. 1.21 and 4.8–10) does not do away with the need for us to fight against all the evil powers of heaven in our midst (Eph. 6.11–17). Johannine theology expresses this state of affairs in dualistic terms: 'We know that we are *from* God (i.e., are born of God) – whereas the whole world lies under (the power of) the evil one' (I John 5.19), and, 'You have overcome the evil one' (I John 2.13). In other words, Satan is still at work in the world, but the community of faith, the church, is the place where he has already been conquered in this world. For Christians, devils are *nothing*, they no longer exist. The power of Satan has been broken (I John 3.8); he has already been judged and thrown out (John 12.31; 16.11) and, as in the inter-testamental literature, now no longer dares to attack those Christians who are born of God (I John 5.18). Now there are particular Christians who destroy the true Christian understanding of Jesus and who are called the real Satan, Antichrist (I John 2.18–22); however, 'Do not fear, since this enemy too will be overcome' (I John 2.13f.).

In Johannine theology the whole of popular belief in Satan and demons stands under the *nenikēka* of Christ: 'I have overcome the world' (John 16.33; see I John 2.13; 4.4; and above all 5.4, where the 'victory over the world' is presented as a sure promise – an implication of the spiritual mode of existence of man born of God who is baptized in faith). The same is true of I John 5.5 (*ho nikōn ton kosmon* = the believer): the believer conquers the world of Satan. In Revelation the believer who overcomes is always called 'the victor' (Rev. 2.7; 2.11; 2.17; 2.26; 3.5; 3.12; 3.21; 21.7). Jesus, the Lion of Judah, and also 'the Lamb', *nikēsei*, 'will conquer' (Rev. 17.14). Thus the concept of *nikē* is an essential element in Johannine theology (and is concerned with the demons and Satan).

Finally, Jude and II Peter have a special feature. These late New Testament letters, from a stage when the church has already been established to some degree, have a good deal in common (II Peter is evidently a corrected version of the Epistle of Jude). The Epistle of Jude is full of reminiscences of I Enoch and perhaps also of the Assumption of Moses. So in Jude 6 and II Peter 2.4 there is an allusion to I Enoch 10.4–12; 18.11–19.3, where the leaders of the fallen angels along with their satellites are held captive by good angels in the depths of hell (in other passages in the New Testament they fly around 'in the air', e.g. Eph. 2.2). Jude 8 (probably uniquely in the New Testament) attacks Christians 'who despise lordship and scorn heavenly powers'. These are evidently Christians who are convinced, along with the teaching of the New Testament, that demons are of no account for Christians, but draw false conclusions from this. The author argues from a legend which was connected with Deut. 34.5f., where God himself buries Moses. Even for the Septuagint, this anthropomorphism about God was too gross, and its translation runs: '*They* buried Moses'. In Philo, it is 'immortal heavenly beings' who bury Moses (*Vit. Mos.* II, 291). In the Apocalypse of Moses, which has now been lost and is known only through the church fathers, it is Michael who buries Moses, though the devil gets in the way. Michael does not judge Satan and leaves the judgment to God. This legend is taken up as an argument in Jude 9: even the archangel respected the diabolical heavenly being. However, II Peter 2.4 deletes the whole of this apocryphal insertion. Jude 13 also mentions wandering stars (the fall of the angels, I Enoch 18.18–21) in connection with the godless and the heretics (an almost literal quotation from I Enoch 60.8 and 1.9 is Jude 14f.); by contrast, II Peter 2.17 deletes this apocryphal quotation.

If we compare II Peter 2.4 with Jude 6, II Peter 2.11f., with Jude 7f., and II Peter 2.10b-11 with Jude 8f., it becomes evident that Jude is corrected by II Peter (*within* what is now canonical scripture), and this criticism within the New Testament is connected with extra-biblical angelology. The legend of the begetting of a race of giants by angels from earthly women (Jude 6f.) is deleted in II Peter 2.4 and reduced to 'those *angels who sinned*'; the extra-biblical legend is detached from conceptions which are too adventurous for II Peter, though it too preserves the popular conception of a fall of angels (without giving any cause). (It is therefore hardly possible to use this *one* New Testament text – which is itself a quotation from an apocryphal writing – to provide a basis for the reality of a fall of angels.)

This is contradicted by the general New Testament protest against any interest in heavenly powers outside God and the risen Christ. 'How can you turn back again to the weak and beggarly elemental spirits, whose slaves you want to be once more?' (Gal. 4.9–11), and Col. 2.8–23 is one great Christian plea against 'purely human inventions which glorify the powers of the cosmos – cosmocrators or other heavenly beings, but fight against Christ' (Col. 2.8), 'Christ has disarmed the principalities and powers and made a public example of them' (2.15). 'Let no one disqualify you, insisting on angel worship' (2.18). Even more, it is not angels who will judge us but *we* who will judge angels (I Cor. 6.2–3a). Jude 8f. is the only passage in the New Testament which expects Christians to pay a little more attention to heavenly angelic beings; however, this passage is censored by II Peter.

One final question, which is by no means unimportant – though not decisive – is, how did Jesus of Nazareth himself regard belief in Satan and demons? It is not decisive, because even Jesus, true man, himself lived in a socio-cultural religious situation; he could not provide a supra-historical solution to all problems. So he speaks like any Jew of his time: '*Moses* has said,' although Moses often had said nothing about this problem; the 'whole Law' was ascribed to Moses. So Jesus can equally well speak of Satan and demons, within a particular religious and cultural situation.

Luke 10.18, 'I saw Satan fall like lightning from heaven', is presumably one of the 'authentic' sayings of Jesus about the devil (even according to Bultmann). At all events, this text means that from now on Satan is insignificant; all is up with him. According to all that we know of Jesus, for him evil lies *in* men. Even in the face of the widespread Jewish view that sickness and the like are the consequence of sin, however hidden it may be, and thus in the last resort derive from a demon, Jesus says that neither he nor his parents are guilty; the only relevant thing is that this man has achieved salvation thanks to God (John 9.3).

A second passage which may lay claim to being an authentic saying of Jesus is the so-called dispute over Beelzebub (Q: Matt. 12.22–28, 30 and Luke 11.14–20, 23 and a tradition in Mark: Mark 3.22–30).[32] From this alone it emerges that those who have long been active for man's salvation in God's name are all too ready to brand as children of Satan those 'newcomers' who do the same thing, and are from a different group: 'Jesus does all this by virtue of Beelzebub!' To this Jesus simply retorts, 'In that case, by whose power do you work?' None of the other texts about Satan in the New Testament can be considered as historical sayings of Jesus, at least in their present form. In other words, whatever ideas there may have been about Satan during the time of the appearance of Jesus in Palestine, Jesus sees his own appearance as the approach of God's salvation. He is not interested in Satan, but in man with his weaknesses and sicknesses, his lack of faith and his sinfulness which God seeks to remove – and that emerges from Jesus' ministry.

However, above all in the charge that Jesus is acting in the power of Beelzebub, we see once again at work the human mechanism which imputes doubtful motives to the good deeds of outsiders. The outsider who does good is 'of the devil'. The book of Revelation is guilty of this, as we can understand from the difficult situation of persecution: the author only speaks in passing about the positive significance of suffering for the sake of Christ (as do I Peter 2.12, 15, 18–21; 3.1f., 9, 15–17 and Hebrews). His slogan, often repeated, is a hard one: persevere and overcome the evil enemy (Rev. 2.7, 11, 17, 26; 3.5, 12, 21; 21.7). Throughout Johannine theology in particular, these inward-looking, mystical church communities show a degree of harshness towards the out-group, i.e. towards those Jews who do not believe in Jesus (even the Johannine Jesus is aggressive towards this unbelief). In I John, Christians who follow false doctrines are forthrightly branded as antichrists. In Johannine theology and Revelation we can detect something like anger at the non-Christian out-group, which is blamed for all the suffering of Christians, with a somewhat triumphant undertone: ours is the victory. In other words, a true datum of faith can sometimes begin to function in a suspicious way (however, we should not forget the bitter persecutions of the church, above all in Revelation).

### III.  GRACE AND PRAISE: GRACE LEADS TO CELEBRATION

The final dynamism of this rich variety of the gift of grace in Christ and his Spirit, which is fundamentally one and yet is given many different names, is the *salvation of man* as the *glorification of the charis* of God (Eph. 1.6): 'for the redemption of God's own people *and* for the praise of his glory' (Eph. 1.14), 'that we may spread the praise of his glory' (Eph. 1.12; Rom. 5.2; II Cor. 4.15). Irenaeus will say at a later stage, *gloria Dei vivens homo*. That is common biblical currency: praise of the *ḥesed* and *ᵉmet* of God; both are liturgically celebrated predicates of God, so that the praise and thanks of the one who has received *ḥesed* and *ᵉmet* is as it were part of the *concept* of this divine reality of grace.[33]

In the perspective of the New Testament experience of Jesus as the Christ, and of his Spirit, which is the origin of the Christian experience of *abba* (Rom. 8.15; Gal. 4.6; I John 3.24b), human existence is in the last resort a joyful (Col. 1.12) hymn of grace. It is grateful recognition and praise of God's overwhelming grace (see I John 3.1), both in and through moral and religious action in this world and through explicit *eucharistia*: celebration and thanksgiving and praise of God, which are reason enough for Paul to be particularly fond of associating *charis* with *chara* (joy) and with *eucharistia* (e.g. I Cor. 1.4; II Cor. 4.15). This is also one reason why he often plays on the double meaning of *charis* (grace and gratitude, e.g. Rom. 5; Rom. 7; I Cor. 1.4; cf. Col. 3.16f.), 'give thanks to the Father with joy' (Col. 1.12). Instead of theological discussions of grace and redemption, in the New Testament we find above all hymns to Christ and to the greatness of God's grace. According to the New Testament, in the last resort the life of grace is 'a heart overflowing with gratitude' (Col. 2.7). Grace achieves its inner consummation through praise; there grace is in fact expressly the experience of grace.

### Conclusion: Freed from what and for what?

The first thing that emerges from the preceding survey of the fundamental 'interpretative elements' with which New Testament Christianity has filled its manifold 'interpretative experience' of salvation in God through the mediation of Jesus is that it is not content with generalities and vagueness, or slogans about 'we are free'. The New Testament adds specific detail to the Christian experience of redemption, salvation and liberation, by defining what Christians feel themselves to be freed from and for what they know themselves to be free. Nowhere is this described 'objectively', but witness is given towards it, and the testimony is illuminated by argument.

Freed from what? From sin and guilt; from all kinds of existential anxieties, which men of antiquity experienced above all as the fear of demons, the grip of fate or *heimarmenē*, a complex of anxieties which are concentrated around the problem of death, 'to deliver all those who through fear of death were subject to lifelong bondage' (Heb. 2.15); freed also from existential cares and all kinds of everyday concerns (Matt. 6.19–34); from sorrow, despair and hopelessness, from dissatisfaction with fellow men and with God; from a lack of freedom, from unrighteousness; from oppressive and alienating ties; from lovelessness, arbitrariness and egotism; from credulity (Mark 13.5–7; Luke 17.22–37); from exploitation of credibility (Mark 9.42; Luke 17.1–3a; Matt. 18.6f.); from merciless condemnation of others (Matt. 7.1–5); from concern over problems of reputation, trying to be someone or to cut a good figure (Mark 10.35–45); from panic and absence of pleasure; to be freed from a life like that of men 'who have no hope' (I Thess. 4.13), etc.

Freed for what? For freedom, righteousness, peace among men and peace with God; for confidence in life; for new creation and the restoration of all things; for joy and happiness; for living and for life in eternal glory; for love and hope; for sanctification; 'freed from all unrighteousness, made his own people, purified from sin, full of zeal for all good things' (see Titus 2.14); for ethical commitment 'to all that is good, very good and perfect' (Rom. 12.2), to 'all that is true, noble, just, pure, deserving of love and attractive, that is called virtue and merits praise' (Phil. 4.4–9), 'to be generous and warm to one another' (Eph. 4.32), 'to overcome evil with good' (Rom. 12.21; I Peter 2.15); to bring about 'a certain equality' (II Cor. 8.14; what is meant is the sharing of goods and resources, albeit in the conditions of late antiquity; see the whole context of 8.1–24; the attitude of well-to-do Greek Christians towards the poor in Jerusalem. Here Jesus' attitude is recalled: 'How though he was rich, yet he became poor for your sakes, so that you might become rich through his poverty', II Cor. 8.9). In short, freed for salvation for the healing and making whole of each and every individual; to be 'imitators of God as beloved children' (Eph. 5.1), 'to walk in love as Christ loved us' (Eph. 5.2).

Liberation from various forms of human slavery and the fear of death is both the *consequence* of the adoption of grace or birth from God and also the *requirement* of this grace. In other words, liberation is not only liberation from unjust conditions *for* something good; what men are freed *for* is itself in turn a command to free men from unjust circumstances. For it is redemption within a world which is still damaged and sick. All this indicates that redemption and liberation in the New Testament are both a gift and a task to be realized. – Where are these redeemed? Nietzsche's objection is historically understandable and indeed justified, but it misunderstands the particular New Testament spirit of redemption, the dialectic of which was given only a formal solution by later scholasticism when it made the almost meaningless distinction between 'objective redemption' and 'subjective redemption'. The author of Hebrews (like the rest of the New Testament) saw this dialectical tension, though he expressed it in terms of the world of his time: 'Now in putting everything in subjection to man (i.e. by virtue of the fact that man no longer experiences slavery and alienation), *he left nothing outside his control. As it is, we do not yet see* everything in subjection to him' (Heb. 2.8f.). The 'already now' and the 'not yet' are in marked tension with one another, in a double perspective: everything has been *given* and everything is *to be done*. In addition to this, there is a tension between what is given and already done and its eschatological fulfilment. Christians can and may go to work as a result of a *metanoia* or change of conduct made possible through grace on the basis of the communion with God which they have attained, knowing that it is meaningful, knowing that even what is vain in human terms is not in the last resort in vain, even if we see how little the face of the earth and mankind is renewed, despite every effort. So joy is brought even in negative suffering, in failure and helplessness. That, too, is a form of liberation, albeit in a world that is still unhealed.

In the New Testament, this tension in liberation through Christ stands under the promise of *nenikēka*, 'I have overcome the world' (John 16.33; see I John 2.13; 4.4. and above all 5.4 where victory over the world is presented as a sure promise – as an implication of the spiritual mode of existence of believers or those who have received grace). Despite the objective foundation of this hope, namely what has already been achieved in the life, death and resurrection of Jesus, liberation remains a task which is to be realized in the dimension of our history. That it is concerned with more than an appeal to good will and co-humanity is shown by the fact that powers of slavery are at work *in* our world which (in accordance with the world-view of the time) are identified with the world of heavenly demons: 'For we are not contending against flesh and blood, but against the principalities, against the powers, against the world rulers of this present darkness, against the spiritual hosts of wickedness in the heavenly places' (Eph. 6.12). We can hardly say that the New Testament has not given specific expression to its understanding of the experience of 'freedom from' and 'freedom for', in the specific situation of the world of the time.

Chapter 2

## 'To bring all to unity (peace)'

### §1 'All is grace.' Creation and grace in the Old and New Testaments

*Literature*: K. Barth, *Church Dogmatics* III, 1, ET Edinburgh 1958; H. Baumann, *Schöpfung und Urzeit des Menschen im Mythos der afrikanischen Völker*, Göttingen ²1964, 1936; P. Beauchamp, *Création et Séparation. Etude exégétique du ch.1 de la Genèse*, Paris 1969; H. Berkhof, *Christian Faith*, ET Grand Rapids 1980; H. A. Brongers, *De scheppingstradities bij den profeten*, Amsterdam 1945; G. Fohrer, *Theologische Grundstrukturen des Alten Testaments*, Berlin 1972; J. Haspecker, 'Natur und Heilserfahrung in Altisrael', *BuL* 7, 1966, 83–98; id., 'Religiöse Naturbetrachtung im Alten Testament', *BuL* 5, 1964, 116–30; G. von Rad, 'The Theological Problem of the Old Testament Doctrine of Creation', ET in *The Problem of the Hexateuch and Other Essays*, Edinburgh 1966, 131–43; id., 'Some Aspects of the Old Testament World-view', ibid., 144–65; id., *Old Testament Theology* I, ET Edinburgh 1962, reissued London and New York 1975, 136–9; id., *Wisdom in Israel*, ET London and Nashville 1972; W. H. Schmidt, 'Schöpfungsgeschichte, Mythos und Glaube', *Kirche in der Zeit* 21, 1966, 260ff.; C. Westermann, *Schöpfung*, Berlin 1971; id., *Das Loben Gottes in den Psalmen*, Göttingen 1963; id., 'Genesis 17 und die Bedeutung von Berit', *TLZ* 101, 1976, 161–70; A. S. van der Woude, 'Genesis en Exodus', *Kerk en Theologie* 20, 1969, 1–27. Also the authors of *Mysterium salutis* (ed. J. Feiner and M. Löhrer), Einsiedeln 1965ff.

The object of the investigation here is not biblical faith in creation as such, but the biblical theology of grace. As in the Christian tradition, however, so too in holy scripture the central question is that of the relationship between 'nature' (creation) and grace: creation and covenant. This group of problems is the subject of exegetical and theological dispute, and is often complicated by confessional prejudices.

Terminologically speaking, *nature* as opposed to *grace* is not an independent concept in the primal documents of the Jewish-Christian tradition of revelation. There is no Hebrew equivalent for *natura* or *physis* in the Tanach. In the few places where we come across the term nature, *physis*, in the deutero-canonical book of Wisdom (7.20; 13.1; 19.20), as indeed in the New Testament, it does not have any specific theological meaning. The term found an entry into Christian theology when theologians began thinking about the revelation of the grace of God with the help of categories drawn from Greek philosophy: first of all from the popularized concept of nature current among the Stoics, and later in systematic terms drawn from Aristotelianism. Terms like 'nature' and 'creation' (created nature) did not completely coincide. What God has created is not merely a neutral nature which man can analyse by means of natural science, but created nature, i.e. the expression of a divine plan which extends beyond 'nature'. In that case, this nature cannot, theologically speaking, be separated from the divine plan. To speak theologically about the natural world, therefore, does not just mean that this nature is contingent, did not need to be 'in and of itself', and could have been otherwise, in other words, that it is transitory; this nature is also the living expression of a divine decision which in the last resort proves to be a will for salvation. Creation and consummation are embraced by one great divine plan. In this sense the theological, philosophical and scientific usages of the term nature differ from one another.

People of earliest times and of antiquity, including the Hebrews, the Israelites, and the believers of the Tanach, lived in a world in which everyone began from the assumption that God – a god or gods – had made or created this world with the people in it. For them, this was something to be taken for granted, an ingredient of their world-view. There was no alternative at that time. However, this accepted state of affairs was misunderstood by the important studies made by G. von Rad; and with his conception of creation and covenant he marked the beginning of the development of a common view which is almost ubiquitous among both Protestant and Catholic exegetes and theologians. Belief in creation is said to be a derivative extrapolation of belief in salvation, and has only a marginal significance in the Old Testament: 'Creation is part of the aetiology of Israel.'[34] This conception, which has been widespread since Karl Barth and Gerhard von Rad, begins from the observation (which is substantially correct) that nowhere in the credal statements of the Tanach is there an expression of belief in creation. The experience of the covenant is said to be the origin of the constituent parts of Old Testament belief in creation. According to this explanation, to the Israelite consciousness Yahweh was not so much the God of creation as the living God, i.e. the God of the grace, election and the history of Israel. 'Thus obedience towards the commandments, precepts and requirements of Yahweh is not required because the Creator has the right to make certain demands of his creatures by virtue of his creation of them, but exclusively because in ancient times Yahweh redeemed his people from alien captivity.'[35] The fundamental creed of Israel is the confession of God's deliverance of Israel from Egypt (Deut. 26.5–9). Israel explained its history and brought it up to date on the basis of this creed, and it was this that, in the course of time, also gave rise to Israel's belief in creation. Only then were accounts of creation put at the beginning of the holy books. Of course, these also took up earlier creation narratives; but it was peculiar to Israel that this belief in creation was seen only in the perspective of the covenant of Yahweh with Israel. Thus creation was thought to be subordinate to the covenant, and not to be an independent theme in the Tanach. However, these authors concede that in a number of passages, above all in Ps. 8, but also in Pss. 19; 104 and throughout the wisdom literature, we find independent creation hymns; the explanation of these is either that they are litanies in which creation and covenant are celebrated side by side or one after the other, or that they are the consequence of alien influence on Israel. In fact, Ps. 19 is certainly part of an ancient hymnic fragment from Canaan, and Ps. 104 shows striking similarities to the famous Egyptian hymn to Aten. By and large, the same kind of Egyptian influence can be detected throughout the wisdom literature; the influence of Egyptian didactic poetry is especially discernible in the later wisdom literature. Instead of a theology of creation embedded in salvation history, we find here an almost metaphysical, independent concept of creation. Creation is treated as an independent theme, apart from salvation history, in Job 28; Prov. 8; Sir. 24.

However, this fairly widespread interpretation has come up against sharp criticism from studies by C. Westermann and A. S. van der Woude which to my mind is completely justified. G. von Rad in fact conceded at a later stage that his approach had perhaps been too one-sided, but his successors did not take note of this;[36] he therefore assigned the belief in creation evidenced in wisdom a relatively special place *alongside* belief in Yahweh's mighty acts in salvation history. More recent criticism certainly accepts that Israel's faith is structured on salvation history (above all Deut. 26.5–9), and that nowhere in it does creation function as a special element of faith (as, for example, in the Christian Apostles' Creed). However, it rightly charges the von Rad school with having failed to see that because creation was an element in the world-view of the time which was completely taken for granted, it did not become an article of faith in Judaism. At that time there was no alternative solution to the question of the origin of man and the world.[37] Creation was not in Israel's own confession of faith, because the *awareness of creation* was an ingredient in the world-view of all men of antiquity and prehistoric times, including the Israelites. Theologians often used to posit a 'primal revelation' (supposedly substantiated by historical facts), *inter alia* on the basis of a wrong interpretation of Rom. 1.18–20. This primal revelation was said to have been obscured among non-Jews by the ravages of time, but in such a way that their history still contained some trace of belief in a Creator God. There was therefore no surprise that creation stories could be found outside the Jewish Bible – these were relics of a primal revelation. However, this theology forgot that in antiquity cosmic experiences were the matrix or basis of experience for all kinds of creation stories; in other words, that the awareness of creation was an essential ingredient in the self-understanding of the men of earliest times and of classical antiquity, and also of men who believed in Yahweh, who had experienced the exodus as a quite special event and for Israel. This ushered in the end for the notion of the primal revelation which was said to have remained current in a pure form only in Israel. Babylonian and Assyrian, Canaanite and Phoenician traditions of creation which were older than the Israelite traditions now provoked an opposite question. Was Genesis 'dependent' on these alien accounts? There was even the discovery in Memphis of a creation story in which God creates *solo verbo*, merely by virtue of his word, as in the Priestly tradition of creation, which had been regarded as a unique element in Israel's divine revelation. Babylonian and other myths had also mentioned the creation of man from clay and by the divine infusion of the breath of life through his nose (as in Gen. 2.7). Finally, H. Baumann could point out that there were agreements between biblical creation accounts and primitive African myths which were quite independent of one another: with a fall, stories about the origin of suffering and death, of culture and technology, symbolized above all by the building of a tower (the tower of Babel).[38] As a result of all these discoveries, critics became aware that these creation stories, with their parallel themes, had arisen throughout the world quite independently of one another, not from a so-called primal revelation but from cosmic experiences and interpretative experiences which necessarily led to myths with a similar structure. In other words, modern criticism began to evaluate the positive significance of myth all over again. In myths man seeks to secure his existence against the meaninglessness and chaos in existence; in the face of constant experience the question 'Why?' was answered through belief in an ultimately and originally good world because of its divine creation.[39]

The Israelite was not a different kind of man. He simply integrated this general belief in creation, current in his time, into the monotheistic Yahwism of Israel and above all into its conception of God's history with his people Israel. However, the fact that this awareness of creation was not a *credo* but a presupposition of the ancient view of the world has significant consequences. In that case, in the first place how God created the world and man is not a matter of faith. It could be imagined in different ways (both synchronously and diachronously). Thus even in Genesis we have two different accounts of creation. All in all, there are four versions current in antiquity and prehistoric times of the way in which God went about creation: (*a*) through making, working, modelling;

(*b*) through procreation or birth from God or gods; (*c*) through a battle between God and a chaos monster; (*d*) simply through a word ('He spoke, and there was light'). In Gen. 2.4b–24 we find the model of the sculptor. There is a weak echo in Gen. 2.4a of Sumerian, Accadian and also Egyptian cosmogonies through birth from the gods: 'these are the *tōl'dōt* (literally the births) of heaven and earth' (later again interpreted by many exegetes in terms of salvation history. See also the genealogy of Jesus according to Matt. 1.1 in which *biblos geneseōs* – the book of coming to be – corresponds with the *tōl'dōt* of the world in Genesis.)

Because he misunderstood this general mythical structure which was peculiar (exclusive?) to the archaic consciousness, Gerhard von Rad and his numerous pupils came to some very problematical conclusions. For example, in the Priestly account of creation, Gen. 1.1–2.4a, he finds the sabbath commandment, the sign of the covenant on Sinai (Ex. 31.12–17), grounded on the structure of creation. His argument is that there were originally eight works of creation in the creation tradition which P uses, and therefore eight days of creation. The course of the day was governed liturgically by the morning and evening sacrifice, which commemorated the covenant on Sinai (Num. 28.6). Genesis now limits the whole event to six days, and God rests on the seventh. The author clearly wants to depict the sabbath ordinance as an 'ordinance of creation' in an earlier account of creation – 'and there were evening and morning – the first day'. The difficulty in this interpretation, however, is that non-Israelite, early creation stories also speak of the *otiositas* or God's day of rest after creation, and similarly 'manipulate' what is evidently an earlier tradition of 'eight days of creation'. All these one-sided interpretations of belief in creation in terms of salvation history are inspired by a particular *a priori*, whereas we must ask whether the most obvious factors may not often be left out of account. It is hardly responsible criticism now to argue that 'creation' occupies only a marginal position in the Old Testament.

Furthermore, form criticism demonstrates that in both the first (Gen. 1.1–2.4a) and the second (Gen. 2.4b–24) biblical accounts of creation we have a combination of two originally independent myths – a frequent phenomenon in mythology.[40] In the first account, the creation of man (Gen. 1.26–31) was originally a separate story: in this fragment man is 'made'; in other parts of the P account we have 'divide', Gen. 1.4, 7, 9; 'create' Gen. 1.21, 27, and not create 'by a simple word', as in the other parts of the account. In this Priestly account man expresses his joy over his links with the whole of creation: he makes God say, 'And God saw that everything that he had made was very good' (Gen. 1.31). We find a similar expression of this human delight in creation, for example, in Psalms 104 and 148. In antiquity it was impossible for people to talk about the totality of 'everything that is' apart from creation, in which we have an expression of the connection between man and the universe. It is remarkable that in this account God first creates 'a sphere of life' (Gen. 1.10), and within this, first inorganic beings, then organic beings and finally man (1.11–19; – 1.20–25; – 1.26–31). In the same way, the second, Yahwistic account of creation (Gen. 2.4b–24) combines two myths.[41] The first tells how God placed man in the garden of Eden and then forbade him on pain of death to eat from one particular tree. Man allowed himself to be seduced by the serpent, and God expelled him from the garden. The second myth tells how God created man from clay into which he breathed the breath or spirit of life. However, God saw that man was lonely. So he created animals. Man was still lonely (perhaps this is also criticism of contemporary preoccupation with animals or with totemism). Then God created woman from man's rib. Only then did man feel happy. The Yahwist combines the two accounts, (*a*) to show that God created man 'good' and that the disorder in the world is man's fault; and (*b*) that human relationships are essential for man. The anthropology presented here is that man's relationship with God ('walking with God in the garden') and with his fellow man is *fundamental*. The model of the potter comes to the fore in this account (see also Isa. 45.9–13; Job 4.19; 10.8; Ps. 103.14; 104.29 and 146.4); this is a model which can be found in many creation narratives.

In the light of these interpretations, the biblical exegesis of Deutero-Isaiah put forward by G. von Rad and H. Brongers must also be revised. However, it is a fact that here creation and covenant are more closely connected than anywhere else in the Tanach. Still, one cannot meaning-fully claim that 'belief in creation' appears in the context of salvation history. Nevertheless, the prophet connects belief in the God of the cov-enant (Israel's *credo*) with the God of creation, in order to summon Israel-in-exile to trust in this God with his strong arm. The basis of this firm trust in God is his *omnipotence*, which is emphasized in his act of creation which is evident to all men (see above all Isa. 51.9f.). A. van der Woude rightly says that it is remarkable 'that Deutero-Isaiah does not describe exodus and election in terms of the ancient historical credo, but in terms of creation. Salvation history – what has already happened and what is to come – tends to be connected with the saving act of creation rather than vice versa.'[42] Deutero-Isaiah uses the word *bārā*, create (in the *qal* and *niphal*), for an action of which only God can be the subject, and in particular to express God's action in creation and covenant (Isa. 51.9f.; 43.1; 45.18f.; see 40.22–24; 44.24–28).[43] He points to God's mighty act which creates something completely new: creation and salvation. The *mighty act* of the one God who creates this new thing combines both creation and salvation. Rahab, the primal monster, who is defeated by Yahweh's creativity, is at the same time Egypt, just as the *t*ʰ*ōm* or the water of chaos of primeval times, ordered by Yahweh's creation, are at the same time the Red Sea through which Israel could escape Egypt and thus be saved.

The Psalms provide the same imagery. In his great work on the Psalms, C. Westermann makes a distinction in the biblical psalms or *tᵉhillīm*, i.e. songs of praise (the name given by Jews to their psalms), between 'informative and cognitive praise' and 'descriptive praise'.[44] In these psalms God's praise is celebrated either because of his creation or because of his liberation of Israel from Egypt. Thus, *on the one hand*, in Psalms 33, 136 and 148, there is praise of Yahweh because he shows his power and majesty on earth in creation or exodus or liberation. However, what connects creation and salvation history is not Yahweh's saving acts, but the *mighty wonders* which he has accomplished in both creation and liberation. *On the other hand*, for example, in Psalms 8, 9 and 104 there is praise only of God's marvellous acts in creation as a quite independent theme. The latter also often happens in the wisdom literature. In Job 36.27–37.13, and Job 38, the praise of God leads up to a summons to trust the omnipotent God and finally to the awareness that man cannot decipher the riddle of life and the world (Job 28), and that life must be accepted as it is from God's hand (Koheleth).

The conclusions drawn here are therefore more subtle than in von Rad's 'school'. There is no need to deny the fact that there is more emphasis on the concept of creation in the literature from the time after the exile, above all as a result of contact with other people from the Near East (and later also with Hellenism). (Is not the *bᵉrīt* terminology equally common oriental currency?) However, this cannot disguise the fact that the Hebrews and Israel had long possessed oral traditions about creation;[45] belief in creation on the basis of primitive and ancient natural experiences is a common feature of the history of religions. Nor need we deny that creation was not part of the distinctive creed of Israel (leaving aside early Judaism), though this is on the basis of the fact that it is an element of the view of the world which is taken for granted. On the other hand, creation is not seen as a presupposition of the covenant. Salvation and covenant occupy a central place (which can even be recognized in the structure of the Pentateuch as a whole); from this standpoint there is a retrospect on the history of the patriarchs and finally on the 'primal history'. However, creation was not derived from salvation history; on the basis of its own belief, Israel set salvation history against the background of the universal human experience of the time that in this world we are God's creatures, that we live in God's own world. As a result of this, the belief in creation which was taken for granted was refashioned in the style of Yahwism and Israel's experience of salvation, while maintaining its independent character. Thus Israel saw and experienced even in nature its God, the God of the salvation history of Israel, Yahweh, the Creator (Ps. 33.6–9; 139.13–15). Israel experienced God's creative power, the power of Yahweh, the God of Israel, the Creator of heaven and earth, in darkness and light, rain and snow, in camel and hippopotamus, moon and stars, in the power or beauty of flowers, plants and animals, in the birth of a child.[46] For Israel, the created world is the expression of the power and majesty of God, the basis of security, of trust, of communion with all things, in thankfulness and faith that chaos and meaningfulness do not come from God and need not have the last word. However, in the Tanach the question remains open whether creation is also an expression of the *ḥesed* of God, i.e. his merciful love of man which is ready to forgive and to redeem. Job struggled with this unfathomable mystery of creation. In this sense we already find implicit in the Old Testament something of the later theological distinction between 'nature' and 'grace'. This distinction rests on the relative independence of the theme of creation as over against the theme of salvation. The Tanach does not explore further how these relatively independent themes are in the last resort to be seen as a unity.

We can sum up the Old Testament conception of creation and covenant in the following way. (*a*) Everything is created by God. The way in which this happens is left open; in other words, it can be looked at in different ways. (*b*) This consciousness of creation is relatively independent over against belief in Yahweh's saving acts towards Israel. (*c*) Nevertheless, the power and the reliability of God as they are expressed in the created world are cited as a reason for trusting the God of history and salvation. 'O Lord, Lord, King who rulest over all things, for the universe is in thy power and there is no one who can oppose thee if it is thy will to save Israel. For thou hast made heaven and earth and every wonderful thing under heaven, and thou are Lord of all, and there is no one who can resist thee, who art the Lord' (Esther, supplement D to ch. 4, see Vulgate, 13.9–12). Creation is therefore a reason for conscious dependence on God and for trust, thankfulness and obedience (Isa. 17.7; 22.11; 40.26ff.; 43.1; 44.2; Ps. 103.22; 119.73; Deut. 32.6, 15, etc.). Faith in God's creative omnipotence is even a reason for hoping in the realisation of the mercy of the God of salvation: 'Yet thou, O Lord, art our Father; we are the clay and thou art our potter; we are all the work of thy hand. Be not exceedingly angry, O Lord, and remember not iniquity for ever. Behold, consider, we are all thy people' (Isa. 64.8f.), and, 'Yahweh, God of Israel . . . thou hast made heaven and earth. Incline thine ear, Yahweh, and hear . . . save us, we beseech thee, from his hand (the hand of the enemy), that all the kingdoms of the earth may know that thou, O Lord, art God alone' (II Kings 19.15f., 19). This passage is clearly concerned with Israel's God of salvation, but with an appeal to his omnipotence which emerges from creation (see Isa. 43.1–3; 40.12–14; 40.26; 42.5; 45.18; also 43.1, 15, 21; 44.2, 21, 24; 45.11; 51.13; 54.5; 40.22–24; 44.24–28; 51.9f.). (*d*) Finally, *Yahweh*, the God of Israel, and no other, is Creator of heaven and earth (Jer. 10.12–16; 51.15–19; Isa. 44.24; Sir. 1.8; Pss. 96.5; 115.3f.; II Esd. 9.6). This insight introduces tension between 'universalism' and 'particularism' in the religion of Israel. At the same time, the universalism of belief in creation will enlarge the Israelite conceptions of salvation. That God has created everything 'with a purpose', with insight and wisdom (Prov. 16.4; Sir. 39.21, namely 'to the praise of God', Sir. 42.23–25; Pss. 147.5; 148; 150; 95.1–5, and Ps. 8; Song of the Three Young Men 52ff.; Isa. 43.21; 45.18; 43.7) points not so much in the direction of creation *as the presupposition* for saving action as in the direction of creation as the foundation of a religious relationship to God in which creation and salvation are subsumed under the higher concept of 'miraculous acts of power' or God's activity of *bārā*. Wisdom 11.24–26 says that God gave existence to everything out of love; by virtue of God's creation, all creatures are good (Gen. 1.12, 18, 21, 25, 31; 8.22; Deut. 32.4; Jer. 5.22–24; Sir. 39.21; Ps. 104.31–35; Koh. 3.11; Prov. 16.4, Hebrew text). So-called necessitarianism is denied here. God creates of his own free will, as it pleases him (Ps. 115.2f.; 135.5–7); from love, and therefore not in order to destroy or annihilate creation once again (Pss. 102.26–28; 103.19; Deut. 32.3f.; Wisdom 11.26; see Koh. 3.14).[47] (*e*) It is true that everything has been created by God, but we cannot and may not think that 'because of the Lord I left the right way, for he will not do what he hates' (Sir. 15.11–20; Deut. 30.15–19). (*f*) In early Jewish synagogue spirituality, creation became a *dogma of Jewish faith*, which was taken up in Israel's creed of salvation history (see below).

We can hardly talk of an 'orthodox doctrine' in the Old Testament. Granted, there is a clear basic creed, but we can hardly claim that Israel had a uniform orthodoxy at different times and within different contemporary trends of spirituality. So there is not just one 'Old Testament' conception of covenant and creation. This also has consequences for the New Testament.

Just as the Tanach was primarily interested in Israel's *own* faith – Yahweh's dealings with his people – so the focal point of the New Testament lies in experience of salvation in Jesus, a salvation which, however, is essentially salvation from God. The New Testament says nothing about the inner nature of the world of creation; belief in creation is simply taken for granted and is the background for the whole of the Jesus event (Mark 10.6; 13.19; Matt. 19.4, 8; 13.35; 25.34; Luke 11.50; Rom. 1.20; II Peter 3.4; Rev. 3.14; 13.8; Heb. 1.10; 4.3; 9.26; II Thess. 2.13; I John 1.1; 2.13f.; 3.8; John 17.24; Eph. 1.4; I Peter 1.20). 'Creation' is often regarded as the first moment in which the world began (*creatio ab initio mundi,* John 8.58; 17.5, 24; Eph. 1.4). It is taken for granted that everything has been created by God (Col. 1.16; Eph. 3.9; Heb. 3.4; Rev. 4.11; 10.6; Acts 4.24; 14.14f.; 17.24; John 1.3). Acts 17.28 even suggests that this is something which all men take for granted. The same is true of belief in God's providential guidance (Matt. 6.25–34; 10.29–31; Luke 12.22–31; 12.6f.; I Peter 5.7, see also Matt. 5.45). The life of the created world is not seen as a system of natural laws, but directly as the work of the living God, though on the other hand men are not blind towards a degree of autonomy in nature (see Mark 4.28: *automatē*). As in the Tanach, for us the created world is the foundation for the praise of God (Acts 4.24; Rev. 4.8–11; 10.6; 14.7).

Along with all ancient peoples, and above all with the Old Testament, both Jesus and the New Testament presuppose belief in creation as living spirituality. Furthermore, in Jewish inter-testamental literature, above all in connection with proselytes – the access of Gentiles to the synagogue – creation (in contrast to the Tanach) became a feature of Jewish faith and not just an element in an ancient view of the world. Belief in the one Creator God is put as the first article of faith in the Jewish *šᵉmā:* 'Hear, O Israel, the Lord, our Lord, the Lord is one'. Granted, creation is not mentioned explicitly here, but this monotheism is supplemented with belief in creation in the *bᵉrākā* and the *haggādōt,* in praise and thanksgiving. During prayer in the synagogue, people turned to God, the omnipotent Creator. Here primitive Christianity stands in the tradition of the spirituality of the early Jewish synagogue, in which creation had become a *dogma of faith.*

In this connection a very early Christian kerygma which Paul mentions in I Thess. 1.9f., and which we similarly find in Acts 14.15; 17.22–31 and Heb. 6.1f., is particularly striking. It is a pre-Pauline kerygma to Gentiles which goes back to the Hellenistic-Jewish model of a mission sermon or an instruction for Gentiles who want to enter the synagogue. In the early Jewish model we can recognize a tripartite creed for proselytes: (*a*) belief in one God, the Creator; (*b*) belief in judgment on those who are not prepared to repent; (*c*) eschatological hope for the newly-converted:[48] creation, judgment, salvation. The model is even more evident in its Christian version: 'We bring you good news, that you should turn from these vain things to a living God who made the heaven and the earth and the sea and all that is in them' (Acts 14.15). In other words, belief in the Creator God becomes an article of faith in the Christian gospel as it is preached to the *Gentiles*. In the Areopagus speech in Acts 17.22–31 we find: (*a*) 'I proclaim a God who has created the world and everything that is in it, who is the Lord of heaven and earth. . . .' – (*b*) 'he has appointed a day on which he will judge the world according to righteousness. . . .' – (*c*) 'through a man whom he has appointed for that purpose, and of this he has given assurance to all men by raising him from the dead.' Here is a striking Christian adaptation of the early Jewish missionary confession of faith. At the same time, the primitive Christian function of the resurrection of Jesus becomes clear; he is risen in order to judge; here is judgment and salvation. In Hebrews 6.1f., the foundation of Christian life is said to be: (*a*) turning away from dead works, i.e. in reality from pagan idolatry; belief in the one true Creator God; (*b*) the eschatological judgment through God; (*c*) the function of the risen Christ at this judgment. Thus in two passages which are not dependent on Paul we find the kerygma which Paul takes up in I Thess. 1.9f.: 'How you turned to God from idols, to serve a living and true God, and to wait for his Son from heaven, whom he raised from the dead, Jesus who delivers us from the wrath to come.' Creation – judgment – salvation: the same pattern as with the Jews; in other words, protology, eschatology, christology. The early Jewish pattern of protology and eschatology is given christological substance by Christians. In the New Testament, the bond between creation and salvation is tied by means of the concept of 'eschatological judgment', on the basis of the essential connection between *prōton* and *eschaton:* God himself is alpha and omega, the beginning and the end of creation. Jesus is involved in the eschaton of creation, so precisely because of that Colossians in particular also gives Christ a role at the beginning of creation, just as wisdom dwelt with God as a counsellor when he created the world (see below). In another connection, namely in order to make Jesus' suffering comprehensible, Hebrews refers to the same bond between creation and eschatology: 'It was fitting that he, the origin and end of all things, in bringing many sons to glory, should make the pioneer of their salvation perfect through suffering' (Heb. 2.10; see Heb. 1.1–4). Here, too, the early-Jewish missionary confession of faith continues to exercise its influence, in a Christian interpretation. According to this Christian creed, Jesus is incorporated into God's plan for creation as the risen Christ who at his parousia will judge those who are unwilling to repent, and will bring salvation to the converted by granting them access to the Father. In this kerygma, redemption is understood in explicitly eschatological terms. Paul calls this tripartite credo 'our proclamation of the good news' (I Thess. 1.5). Here faith is faith *in God* (I Thess. 1.8f.), and christology is an ingredient of faith in God. There is as yet still no express mention of *faith* in Jesus Christ; this is the object of eschatological *hope*, whereas one's fellow man is the object of *love* (I Thess. 1.4; 2.8f.; 3.12; 4.9). Faith in God – hope for Christ – love of one's neighbour: this is the characteristic primitive Christian structure of the life of grace (the 'three divine graces' later grew out of this structure).

Hebrews 11 is also constructed on the basis of a Hellenistic Jewish

model, and venerates the great figures of faith from the past. Here too
the account of precisely what faith is begins with a mention of the
fundamental act of faith: faith in the Creator God: 'By faith we understand that the world has created by the word of God, so that what is
seen was made out of things which do not appear' (Heb. 11.3; this is at
the same time the Christian adaptation of a Greek notion); it is summarized in Heb. 11.6, 'Whoever would draw near to God must believe
*that he exists* and *that he rewards* those who seek him' – once again the
Jewish model of faith.

When the New Testament proclamation of faith is addressed to Jews,
there is hardly any mention of belief in creation; there was no doubt at
all about this among Jews (see Acts 4.24). When speaking to non-Jews,
however, Christians (like Jews themselves) had to stress the one true
God, the Creator of heaven and earth. Thus in the New Testament, belief
in the Creator God became the matrix of belief in the God of grace who
had revealed himself in Jesus. Just as Yahweh, the God of the salvation
history of Israel, is the omnipotent Creator, so in the New Testament,
belief in the Creator is transformed into belief in the Creator God, the
God of Abraham, Isaac and Jacob and the Father of Jesus Christ (see
Matt. 25.34; I Cor. 8.6; Col. 1.15–17; Rom. 11.36; Heb. 1.2f.; 1.10; 2.10;
13.8; John 1.1–5; 1.10; 5.17, 19; 3.3; 9.3; I Cor. 15.28; Rev. 22.13). The
living God is the Creator both of everything that exists and also of
salvation. Creation and salvation come together in the man Jesus Christ.
The specific divine activity is one of creation, in the sense that the
sovereign freedom it brings into being something *completely new* (*bārā'*).
The coming of a Gentile was not only a conversion to Christ, but also
conversion to a monotheism centred on the Creator, the one living God.
Thus creation was an element taken from the ancient view of the world,
purified by Israel's salvation history and by the historical ministry of
Jesus – to become the first article of faith in the Christian kerygma (it
was later incorporated into the Apostles' Creed) as a matrix of faith in
God's grace in Christ.

As a result of this eschatological position of Jesus in creation, in the
New Testament Jesus Christ is also often put at 'the beginning' of creation. True, this is expressed in almost stereotyped formulas. Nowhere,
however, is the theme developed further. These text have a hymnic,
liturgical character. Jesus is *eikōn*, image of the invisible God (Col. 1.15;
II Cor. 4.4), or *charaktēr*, i.e. stamp or image of the nature of God
(Heb. 1.3). He is then called mediator at creation, above all in this
capacity. 'In him all things have been made' (Col. 1.16), 'the universe
has been made through him' and 'for him and in him all things have
their existence' (Col. 1.16b–17). 'He reflects the glory of God and bears
the very stamp of his nature, upholding the universe by his word of

power' (Heb. 1.3), 'All things were made by him and without him was not anything made that was made' (John 1.3). Paul himself said, 'One Lord Jesus Christ through whom are all things and through whom we exist' (I Cor. 8.6). In such texts, which continue an earlier wisdom tradition in a christological perspective (see Wisdom 7.21, 25f.; 9.12 with 16.21; 8.6; 9.2. 18; 14.2; Sir. 1.4; Prov. 8.30), Pythagorean, Platonic and Stoic expressions are combined with a Jewish and Christian heritage: 'Adam' from Gen. 1.26, who is called both the *image of God* and the *Lord of the world*,[49] is, in his eschatological form, the man Jesus Christ (see the typical transition from 'him', man or Adam, to 'him', Jesus, in Heb. 2.8). Paul will take this theme further in his typology: the first and the last, the eschatological Adam (Rom. 5.12–21; 1 Cor. 15.22, 45).

Because Jesus Christ has an essential saving function in the 'eschatology' of creation, he must have already beeen incorporated into God's plan of salvation at the beginning of creation. Christ is 'the origin of God's creation' (Rev. 3.14), in the sense of the 'counsellor at creation' who is found in the wisdom tradition. Creation, salvation and consummation are connected in Jesus.

In Colossians and in Ephesians, redemption through Christ is depicted as an *apokatallassein*, the great reconciliation of the *universe* (Col. 1.20a; Eph. 2.16). Only in these two epistles is an intrinsic connection made between creation and the forgiveness of sins (this connection can also be seen in Heb. 1.2–4, but there it is weaker). In other words, the connection between mediation at creation and the forgiveness of sins is peculiar to Ephesians and Colossians and arises from a special background. Romans 4.17 and II Cor. 4.6 show that creation and redemption were already connected in Judaism.[50] However, there is more behind it than that, namely the conception of the *polemos*, the struggle or lack of harmony in the universe, taken up in *Jewish* Pythagoreanism, which is probably the 'philosophy' contested by Colossians. Even according to Heraclitus,[51] reality consists of war and strife (*polemos kai eris*). The human spirit wanders through these unfettered elements of the world in search of rest and peace. It is possible to escape the vicious circle only through purification, above all asceticism, through reverence for gods and demons, through baths of purification, washings and sprinklings and abstinence from particular foods and drinks[52] – the very philosophy to which Colossians refers and which had found its way into the Christian community. By means of this whole initiation one escaped the natural struggle or *polemos* by abiding in a 'higher world' of harmony and peace. These Christians could very well join in the hymn which underlies Col. 1.15–20. For them the healed world is above with Christ. However, the author of Colossians has something against *the way* that these Christians choose to escape the diabolical world. Such practices are unnecessary for reaching this world above; with Christ the Christian already sits 'above' (Col. 2.12), but thanks to the forgiveness of sins, that means not through a cosmic but through an anthropological reconciliation, and therefore through an ethical life in this world. The original hymn, Col. 1.15–20, stands as it were in the middle between the views of the author of Colossians and the 'philosophy' which he attacks. The hymn praises God, the Creator, in whom everything has existence, peace and harmony; however, God does this through the mediation of Jesus Christ by virtue of the resurrection of Jesus. This is the way in which the author interprets the hymn: only as *reconciled sinners* will we take part in a reconciled world. It is finally concerned with total peace in the world, but in and through the ethical and religious reconciliation of man with God and – as Ephesians in particular says – of men with one another. 'To bring all (*ta panta*) to unity and peace (*anakephalaiōsis*) in Christ' (Eph. 1.9f.), 'through him to reconcile the universe with itself and to create peace' (Col. 1.20): 'to reconcile all things in heaven and earth through him alone' (Col. 1.20). In the background is the ancient sense of reconciliation and the removal of the breach between the *epigeia*, the earthly world, and the *epourania*, the heavenly spiritual world, but all this happens in the New Testament in and through the forgiveness of sins, and when man lives an ethical and religious and not a cosmic life. However, in Jesus Christ, who is called mediator at creation, creation, redemption, grace and consummation come together. Thus in the light of a Creator God in fact all things can become grace ('Tout est grâce', said Thérèse of Lisieux, a remark which Bernanos often quotes). In only one passage in the New Testament do we also find the cosmic and corporeal aspect of redemption (that is, of course, leaving aside the resurrection): this is where Paul describes how the material world of creation sighs for the revelation of the freedom of the children of God (Rom. 8.20–22). This is fully in line with the Old Testament notion of the community of destiny between man, animals and nature. In Colossians and Ephesians the pan-cosmic effects of redemption are discussed against the background of late antiquity – which had a great interest in the 'cosmos' – and in the light of spiritual enthusiasm about the risen Lord, 'the all in all' (see Col. 1.23).

The consequence is that the Stoic autarchy of the man who is master of himself and inwardly free is transformed into a freedom of deliverance through grace which in Christ is as unassailable in any direction as is claimed by the Stoic boast of inner freedom: 'If God is for us, who will be against us?' (Rom. 8.31b), 'who will separate us from the love of Christ?' (Rom. 8.35; see Heb. 13.6), 'not even death' (Rom. 8.36–39), 'I will not leave you alone, I will never forsake you' (Deut. 31.6, 8), So we can say with some confidence that, 'The Lord is my helper, I have nothing to fear. What can *a man* do to me?' (Ps. 118.6; Heb. 13.5b–6), what can *demons* do to us? (Rom. 8.36–39). It can be said that, above all in Colossians and Ephesians, all is grace, apart from sin, and that too is blotted out by God's forgiveness. True, sometimes Paul himself does not know what to make of an enthusiasm which is characterized above all by ecstasy and speaking with tongues, but he will not go so far as to condemn it out of hand, except when it threatens a true conception of Jesus Christ as the Lord (see I Thess. 5.20f.; also I Cor. 12.10; 14.1–25, 26–33, 39f.; and above all the sharp reactions to an eclectic religious enthusiasm by Christians who revere a false monism of grace, in Jude and II Peter).

In this New Testament perspective in which creation and salvation are components of a single plan of salvation in Christ and therefore in which everything can become grace, failure, disaster and particularly unnecessary and alienating suffering (above all in the tradition of Mark, I Peter and Hebrews) are given a dimension of grace in Christ (Mark; I Peter 2.22–25; 3.13–4.6, 16; the whole of Hebrews; also James 1.2; Matt. 5.4, 10f.; Phil. 1.29; 3.10; 4.11–13; Rom. 8.17; II Cor. 4.10f. etc.). Although suffering as such is a negative experience, it can be transformed into 'a participation in the suffering of Christ' (Rom. 5.3; 8.17; ch.6; Gal. 3. 26f.; II Cor. 1.7; Phil. 3.10; Col. 1.24; I Peter 4.13; Heb. 12.5–13, where it is said to be a sign of sonship; see Heb. 2.10), and thus into the way to sharing in Jesus' glorification. Christ himself shared in our suffering (Heb. 12.7; see 1.9; 2.14; 3.1, 14; 6.4). For Hebrews, this wanting to share in our human history of suffering is as it were the project of Jesus' life on the threshold of his entry into our history (10.5–7; 2.14).[53]

This mysticism of grace, which embraces creation and salvation, issues in the certainty of faith: 'won strength out of weakness' (Heb. 11.34b), 'my strength is perfected in weakness' (II Cor. 12.9; see Rom. 8.26; II Cor. 4.7; 13.4b), in accordance with the model of Jesus. 'He was crucified in weakness but now lives through the strength of God' (II Cor. 13.4a). 'But we have this treasure in earthen vessels, to show that the transcendent power belongs to God and not to us' (II Cor. 4.7).

It transpires from this survey that we need not exclude a certain independent religious experience of God from natural experiences. In this sense, too, belief in Jesus can be strengthened by the experiences of the senses – perhaps it is even possible that in his protest against pollution modern man finds his way back to natural experiences as a kind of preamble to faith, an openness for deeper experiences of the senses. On the other hand, both the New Testament and early Judaism understand belief in creation as the all-supporting basis for the Jewish-Christian kerygma. We should not forget within our horizon of experience that despite the real difference between cosmos and history, nature has an increasing part to play in our human history. Still, there is an impassable barrier between the two; nature retains a remnant of independence and therefore also of resistance; it refuses to be incorporated entirely into the plans of our human history. Herein lies both our insurmountable human sorrow (the dialectical tension between nature and history) and a degree of protection for men from a merely technical domination of nature. That points us – even in ecological terms – to the permanent and relative independence of nature over against human history.

At the same time this raises the question of a transcendent principle which goes beyond nature and history through immanence – the question of salvation, or the wholeness and making whole not only of our history and our humanity but also of the material world. In the last resort, this is the question of the universality of Christian redemption, which is ultimately grounded in the one God of all men, the Creator of heaven and earth.[54] Paul rightly makes the whole of creation sigh for the revelation of the glory of God in perfect human salvation (Rom. 8.19–22). Consequently the concept of creation is of fundamental significance in any theology of grace. If man is left alone with a world for man which is not at the same time and more fundamentally the world of God, the assurance of faith remains in the subjectivity of man and is therefore constantly exposed to the suspicion of being a pure projection. The God of the universe, and also of nature, is one of the elements which can keep open the religious subjectivity of 'subjectivism'.

## §2 Grace as a moral and religious or an ontological category?

Because he has been shaped by philosophy, Western man in particular finds it striking that in the New Testament, *charis* or grace is not set *over against* nature or creation (like 'nature' and the 'supernatural' in later scholastic theology), but over against sin and helplessness (Galatians and Romans); as what is established and permanent in contrast with what is unholy, earthly and transitory (the 'first age'. Heb. 12.15, 28; 13.8f.); as rest and cheerfulness in comparison with fear and anxiety over life and death (Heb. 2.14f.) or the fear of demons; in contrast to standing under the Law (Rom. 6.14; 5.2; Gal. 5.4, 18); in contrast to all the taboos, 'Do not touch, do not eat, keep away' (Col. 2.20–23); in contrast to self-righteousness, autonomy by virtue of a self-confident nature on the basis of personal achievement or merits in the Pauline sense (Rom. 1.5; 9.12; 9.16; 11.6; Gal. 1.15; 2.21; 5.4; Eph. 1.4; 2.8; II Tim. 1.9; Titus 3.7); finally as an abundance of grace in Christ as opposed to the gentle grace of the Tanach (e.g. Heb. 13.9; John 1.17). Where grace is clearly contrasted with 'the world' (above all in Johannine theology), the world is understood to be the hybrid, ambiguous and in the last resort sinful world which is deprived of the light (John 1.9; 3.19; 6.14; 9.39; 10.36; 11.27; 12.46; 16.28; 17.18; 18.37; I John 2.15–17; 4.9).

It emerges from this that in the New Testament grace is a moral and religious concept from the language of faith or religious speaking about reality. Grace is not thematized so that it becomes a metaphysical concept (this will be the preoccupation, above all, of medieval theology). Nevertheless, even in the New Testament grace is more than one particular, religious way of speaking, which only makes sense within an absolutely closed language system. Or more correctly: what we are concerned with is not only *speaking about* grace, but with an experience of reality which can only be expressed in the language of faith. As a living reality of and from God – which appears to us in Jesus and comes to us through the risen Jesus in the gift of the Spirit – grace in the New Testament is also a reality from and in us (the Middle Ages termed it 'created grace', *gratia creata*, within a metaphysical frame of reference, as a *consequence of* and at the same time a *disposition to* uncreated grace or grace indwelling divine persons). For God's grace makes man a truly 'newborn being' (John 1.13; 3.3, 6,8; I John 2.29; 3.9; 4.7; 5.1, 4, 18; I Peter 1.3, 23), thanks to faith and the 'bath of rebirth' (Titus 3.5; John 3.5; I Peter 1.3; 1.23; see 2.2; John 3.3–8; I John 3.9; 5.8; cf. Rom. 6.4; II Cor. 5.17). Grace makes us 'new creatures', 'created in Christ' (Eph. 2.10; Col. 3.10; II Cor. 5.17; Gal. 6.15; Rom. 6.5f; 7.6); it transforms life (Rom. 6.5f.; 7.6), our whole *psychē*; our thought (Eph. 4.23); our spirit (Rom. 7.6; 12.2); our senses (I Cor. 2.12–16); it makes us 'other men with a new outlook' (Rom. 12.2), in short 'new men' (Eph. 4.24; individual, but at the same time collective; Eph. 2.14). Finally, by grace we receive a new name (Rev. 2.17; see 3.12); that is, only at the eschaton will we see what is the deepest identity of our being renewed through grace. It will even become manifest as identity, being ascribed glorified corporeality (*inter alia*, Rom. 8.11, 23f.; I Cor. 15.12–57), a public expression of perfect Christian identity.

Thus anyone who hearkens in freedom and the obedience of faith to this *charis* of God, lives in a *state* of grace 'stands in grace', (Rom. 5.1f.; 6.1–23; John 8.44; II Cor. 1.24; Phil. 4.1; I Peter 5.12), in which, however, the one who has been given grace has to persist (Acts 13.43; see Matt. 10.22, repeated above all in Hebrews). For men can also 'fall from grace' or 'forfeit grace' (Heb. 12.15; Rom. 11.22; II Cor. 6.1; Gal. 5.4; see 2.21) and thus 'abuse the spirit' (Heb. 10.29), 'quench the spirit' (I Thess. 5.19) or 'grieve the spirit' (Eph. 4.30: *lypein* is not so much 'disturb' as 'impair', 'damage', cf. Isa. 63.10; this is therefore a regular biblical theme). However, by persevering in grace, the believer personally accepts God's grace in Christ as a reality which is consistently affirmed, which becomes the basis of hope for resurrection (Rom. 8.11, 23f.) and eschatological consummation (Rom. 8.17; 8.29; Gal. 4.5; Titus 3.6; I Peter 1.7–10; 3.7; 4.10f.; 5.10; Rev. 21.23; Eph. 4.30).

At the same time the transcendence of grace appears, despite or precisely in, this realism of the New Testament conception of a grace which is not to be seen purely in forensic terms: 'independently of human actions and only dependent on the one who calls' (Rom. 9.12); 'So it depends not upon man's will or exertion, but upon God's mercy' (Rom. 9.16; cf. Eph. 3.20f.).

However, this grace must become fruitful for us in moral and religious action (Rom. 6.1–23; 7.4; I Cor. 15.10; II Cor. 6.1; Ephesians; Colossians; Hebrews, etc.). In a word, the theological and ethical life which man has to live is the work of God's grace through which 'the spirit helps us in our weakness' (Rom. 8.26). Even pleading for grace *is* already the work of the Spirit in us (Rom. 8.6b). 'Now to him who by the powers at work within us is able to do far more abundantly than all that we ask or think. . .' (Eph. 3.20). 'God is at work in you, both to will and to work for his good pleasure' (Phil. 2.13). Thus to allow the thought, the 'mind', of Jesus to come to fruition in us means to act and think like Jesus (I Cor. 2.16b), who, by emptying himself (see II Cor. 8.9 in connection with the collection for the poor community in Jerusalem, also Phil. 2.6–11), made others rich. Receiving grace always involves complete self-denial, openness to others, availability and readiness to learn, in joy at the value of the treasure that has been found, a pearl (the Eastern symbol for the mystery of life for which man surrenders everything else; Matt. 13.44). Here the Christian acts in the spirit of Jesus, 'who for the joy that was set before him endured the cross' (Heb. 12.2). Grace, the kingdom of God, the rule of God, the source and foundation of human and worldly peace, therefore require fundamental *metanoia*, a transformation of our natural and all too-human attitudes (see Mark 1.14f.; II Cor. 7.10, etc.). The new life with God in Christ requires a life for and with God in service towards one's fellow men: to have a share in the abundance of the *ḥesed* and *"met* of God which are personally present in Jesus (see John 1.17).

## §3   Differentiations in grace 'to the good of all'

Within the 'one grace which is common to all' (cf. *koinē sōtēria*, Jude 3) and the 'one spirit' as a gift to all (I Cor. 12.4), everyone – both individual and local churches (e.g. II Cor. 8.1) – receives a variety of special gifts of grace or *charismata* for a special service to the community, 'for the good of all' (I Cor. 12.4–31; Rom. 12.6; see I Cor. 12–14; II Tim. 1.6; Eph. 4.7, 11), each in accordance with his own calling and nature (I Cor. 7.7; I Peter 4.10). Medieval scholasticism and later theology call these gifts of grace *gratiae gratis datae* in contrast to the *gratia gratum faciens* or justifying grace (which according to the Council of Trent is called sanctifying grace or *gratia sanctificans*). The best way of understanding this is to imagine how the one grace as it were receives various extensive ramifications in the complicated and ramified structure of human nature and the human psyche.

However, it is striking that the word *charisma* occurs only in the Pauline epistles (apart from the text of I Peter 4.10, which is also oriented on Paul), and is always connected with the work of redemption. *Charisma* is connected on the one hand with *charis* and on the other with *pneuma*, because a number of spiritual phenomena in the church are also called *charismata* in Pauline theology. In particular, *charisma* simply means the fundamental gift of *charis* (II Cor. 1,11; Rom. 5.15f. bestowing *charisma* in *charis*) whereas the affinity with *pneuma* is expressed most strongly in the term *charisma pneumatikon* (Rom. 1.11; 6.23). The meaning therefore fluctuates, although anything which serves for mutual edification and the edification of the church may be called *charisma* (I Peter 4.10).

In I Cor. 12.4–6, Paul divides the special gifts of grace into three categories: *charismata, diakoniai, energēmata*, with a reference to the Spirit (*charisma*), or to the *Kyrios* or Lord (*diakonia*), or to God (*energēma*), although these references are not so clear in exegetical terms. The only relevant feature here is the multiplicity and variety of the gifts of the Spirit, which are all the work of the one Spirit (I Cor. 12.11). It is striking that these gifts of grace can as it were be cultivated (*zēloun*: in other words, they are connected with the psychology of each individual; I Cor. 12.31 in connection with 14.1).

A further development is evident in the Pastoral Epistles. They speak of a *charisma* of *office* in the church, which is attained by the laying on of hands (consecration: I Tim 4.14; II Tim. 1.6). It is striking here that these letters no longer speak of the *charismata* of the believers who do not hold office. (In accordance with the general trend in these later New Testament letters – the intrinsic consequence of the separation of the Christian brotherhood from the synagogue – the community must order itself internally, or create its own church order. In Jewish Christian communities the Jewish presbyteral structure was adopted, whereas in Gentile communities the structure tended to be the 'episcopacy' of Hellenistic society.) Soon after, that, the distinction between *klēros* and *laikos* begins to develop (outside the Bible).[55]

All this is perhaps connected with the new development in imperial times of the meaning of the secular Greek word *charis* (which has been mentioned above). It comes to mean power, authority from above, with the focus not so much on the gift as on the supernatural power. This is therefore a secular development of the word which is also manifested in the latest New Testament literature (and which will strongly influence later theological developments).

## Chapter 3

# God of grace, Jesus Christ and the Spirit

What the New Testament calls 'the gift of the Holy Spirit' (e.g. Acts 2.38; 10.38) presents a variety of problems. No difficulty is found in also ascribing to the Holy Spirit all the gifts of salvation which are ascribed to Christ – salvation, deliverance, redemption, justification, sanctification, access to the Father, etc. There is a *pneuma hagiasmou* (Rom. 15.13, 16; 1.4; II Thess. 2.13; Gal. 5.6; Acts 26.18; I Peter 1.2), a spirit of sanctification; a *pneuma dikaiosynēs*, a spirit of justification (I Cor. 6.11; Tim. 3.16; I Peter 1.2); a *pneuma apolytrōseōs*, a spirit of liberation (Eph. 4.30); a *pneuma zōēs*, spirit of life (Rom. 8.2, 6, 10f.; II Cor. 3.6; John 6.63; I Peter 3.18; Gal. 5.25); a *pneuma tēs pisteōs*, spirit of faith (II Cor. 4.13; Acts 11.24). Grace is also a *koinōnia pneumatos*, communion of the spirit (Phil. 2.1; II Cor. 13.14) which (like Christ) 'gives access to the Father' (Eph. 2.18) in 'a spirit of renewal' (Titus 3.5; Eph. 4.23). This is the 'spirit of joy' (Rom. 14.17; Gal. 5.22; I Thess. 1.6), 'the spirit of peace' (Gal. 5.22; Rom. 14.17; 8.6) and 'the spirit of love' (Rom. 15.30; I Cor. 4.21; Col. 1.8; see Rom. 5.5; II Tim. 1.7, etc.). Moreover, in the New Testament the spirit is understood on the one hand in terms of Christ (Rom. 8.9; I Cor. 15.45; Gal. 4.6), while on the other hand Christ is understood in terms of the Spirit: Jesus is the fruit of the Spirit, who begets him (Matt. 1.18; Luke 1.35); he is 'born of the Spirit' (Luke 4.18), which descends on him at his baptism (Mark 1.10 par.); Jesus is 'risen in the power of the Spirit' (Rom. 1.4; I Tim. 3.16). Finally, Christ means 'anointed with the Spirit' (Acts 10.38).[56] Hence the changing occurrence of expressions with the same content like 'in Christ' and 'in the Spirit', at least in Paul and the writings inspired by Pauline theology (this equation is impossible in Johannine theology because there the *pneuma*-paraclete has another significance and function). Finally, *hyiothesia* or adoption (Gal. 4.5; Rom. 8.15, 23; Eph. 1.5; see Rom. 9.4, *hyiothesia* as the privilege of Israel) is a gift of the Spirit, above all if we compare Gal. 4.5f. and Rom. 8.15f. Christians receive the *hyiothesia* as they receive the Spirit (see Gal. 3.2, 14; Rom. 8.15; I Cor. 2.12). The Spirit which we receive is the Spirit of the Son of God (Gal. 4.6). Is the Spirit poured out on us because we are sons of adoption, or does God pour out the Spirit so that we may become sons? I do not believe that we should pose this question with excessive theological concern: receiving sonship is receiving the gift of the Spirit; that becomes even clearer in Johannine theology which speaks of a spiritual birth from God. Sonship or adoption is realized specifically through faith, baptism and the gift of the Spirit; this forms a single (liturgical) event the elements of which can hardly be separated by analysis (hence the aorist: the Spirit is given at baptism). The 'spirit of the Son' is the Son himself in his spiritual presence (see Rom. 5.5). The Spirit itself therefore gives Christians the experience of the Father (Rom. 8.14; Gal. 4.6; see I John 3.24). The grace of the Father in Christ is the spirit of grace: *pneuma tēs charitos* (Heb. 10.29; see Zech. 12.10).

Through the grace of Jesus Christ, the *pneuma* is 'the Spirit that dwells in us' (II Tim. 1.14; Rom. 8.9, 11; I Cor. 3.16; James 4.5); thus the man of grace is 'an abode of God' (Eph. 2.22; see I Cor. 3.16; 6.19). The New Testament does not make more precise the relationship between the redeeming work of Jesus Christ and the same work of the Holy Spirit, and perhaps that is unnecessary. Apart from a few texts in the Gospel of John, it is therefore obscure whether the Spirit should be translated in the masculine or the neuter. The Johannine Jesus calls the Holy Spirit '*another* Paraclete' (John 14.16), while I John 2.1 evidently calls Christ himself 'our Paraclete with God', i.e. intercessor.[57] The identification of *pneuma* (Spirit of truth) with Paraclete is a feature of Johannine theology. John's purpose is perhaps to make the inter-testamental Paraclete completely dependent on Christ (see above). The concept of the Paraclete is the way and means by which John *Christianizes* the concept of *pneuma;* the term Paraclete makes the *pneuma* christocentric. So it is the Spirit which provides the connection between the historical Jesus of Nazareth and the contemporary life of faith of the Johannine community; the Paraclete provides the connection between the past and the present; he brings up to date the revelation which is accomplished in Jesus. The contemporary church is the place in which the saving work that God has begun in Christ is continued by the Spirit.

The Father gives us the Son (John 3.16), and the Father gives us the Spirit (John 14.16). The Spirit is both *pneuma* of God (the Father: Matt. 10.20; 12.28; Luke 11;13; Acts 5.32; Rom. 8.9, 13; I Cor. 2.11–14; 3.16; 6.11; 7.40; 12.3; II Cor. 3.3; Eph. 4.30; I Peter 4.14; I John 4.13) and the *pneuma* of Christ (or of Jesus, the Son, of Jesus Christ: Gal. 4.6; Rom. 8.9; II Cor. 3.17f.; John 14.16f.; I Peter 1.11; Phil. 1.19). According to the New Testament, Christ and the Spirit evidently perform the same function. This raises the question of the relationship between *christology* and *pneumatology*. Furthermore, God is also called *pneuma* (John 4.24); this is not an ontological definition, but a reference to his heavenly sphere of life and a way of denoting God in accordance with his active relationship to man, namely because he gives the Spirit (John 14.16; like 'God is light', I John 1.5; and 'God is love', I John 4.8, namely as the one who gives light and love to men). Like Christ, the Holy Spirit also 'brings about all things' (I Cor. 12.11). On one occasion Christ himself is called *pneuma* (II Cor. 3.17).

It follows from all this that, with the exception of a few Johannine texts, *pneuma* in the New Testament has a variable meaning which tends more towards the Old Testament and non-biblical Judaism.[58] *Rūaḥ* – wind and the breath of life – is a concept which was particularly appropriate for a number of derivative and symbolic meanings because of the volatile and explosive character of wind and storm (see the pre-theological meanings in the note).[59] The specifically *theological* usage of *rūaḥ* or spirit in connection with God is not as widespread in the Tanach as is sometimes supposed. R. Albertz and C. Westermann found only twenty passages (Judg. 3.10; 6.34; 11.29; 13.25; 14.6, 19; 15.14; I Sam. 10.6; 16.13, 14; II Sam. 23.2; I Kings 22.24 = II Chron. 18.23; Isa. 11.2; 63.14; Ezek. 11.5; Micah 3.8; II Chron. 20.14; Isa. 61.1). In these earliest texts the spirit of God is mentioned (*a*) in connection with charismatic leadership of the people and (*b*) in the case of ecstatic prophecy. Both instances involve the conception of a dynamic, explosive force which comes upon a man and enables him to perform special actions for a (short) time. In the first context, that of charismatic leadership, the phrase used is the *rūaḥ Yahweh*. In that case the 'spirit of God' indicates the particular way in which Yahweh brings about the salvation of his people in the time of the Judges, namely through charismatic leaders who are led by the spirit. Yahweh himself wages war in their military actions. The Deuteronomistic tradition had a clear view of the special character of this charismatic age of Israel; it prefaces the story of the Judges with an introduction which as it were reproduces the programme followed by these popular leaders (Judg. 3.7–11). In it the old pattern of apostasy, judgment, lamentation and deliverance (2.11–16) is changed: the *rūaḥ* of God comes upon Othniel (Judg. 3.10). This was originally not a particular office, but a transitory episode. The dynamic concept of the spirit underwent a marked change with the emergence of a permanent political institution, the monarchy (which proved a failure in the case of Gideon and a success in Saul's attempt, Judg. 8.22ff.; I Sam. 11.14). Originally it had so to speak run wild. In the stories about Samson, the hero is suddenly given great strength through God's power. The consequence of the *rūaḥ* seems to be a sheer demonstration of power (Judg. 14.6; 15.14).

In the second context, that of ecstatic prophecy, we hear of the *rūaḥ* *ᵉlōhīm* (an indication of Canaanite origin). God's spirit comes upon the whole group of prophets (*nābī'* – though this coming is as it were provoked by music, I Sam. 10.5f.). At a later stage this phenomenon is looked on in a negative way, in contrast to that of the *rūaḥ Yahweh* (I Sam. 10.10, 13a; 19.8–24: here 'spirit of God' and 'hand of God' are synonymous, II Kings 3.15; I Kings 18.46).

All this indicates that originally there was no connection between the 'spirit of God' and the communication of the 'word of God' by it. This connection is almost completely absent from the whole of the prophetic literature from Amos up to and including Jeremiah;[60] Ezekiel is the only exception. The explanation of this omission is that the whole of the prophetic literature is in contention with prophecies of salvation (see I Kings 22; II Chron. 18). The prophets of salvation understood their words as words of the *rūaḥ* or spirit of God; for the writing prophets, on the other hand, the only legitimation was the word of God without the mediation of the spirit. Only after the exile is the prophetic word 'interpreted afresh', and then quite naturally understood as the working of the spirit of God. In this period, in a survey quite in the Deuteronomistic tradition,[61] the prophetic word is also understood as the work of the spirit of God (Neh. 9.30; Zech. 7.12; cf. Micah 3.8; Ezek. 11.5 in a gloss). The work of the Chronicler sees all the prophets as being inspired by the spirit of God (II Chron. 15.1; 20.14; 24.20).

The emergence of the monarchy as an institution was a break with the old dynamic conception of the spirit of God. Now the spirit was a permanent gift to the anointed (i.e. king) of Yahweh; this gift points in a special way to the intimacy between the king or the 'Christ' and God, and to his special gifts (and that is true above all for the messianic king). The explosive character of the *rūaḥ* has disappeared: now it rests on someone (Num. 11.25f.; II Kings 2.15; Isa. 11.2); someone is 'full of' the spirit (Ex. 31.3; 35.31; Deut. 34.9; Micah 3.8). The gift of the spirit is connected with rites: anointing (I Sam. 16.13; Isa. 61.1) or the laying on of hands (Deut. 34.9); it is connected with a succession in office (Num. 11.17); at the anointing of David the *rūaḥ ʾlohim* leaves Saul (I Sam. 16.13f.); however, this is evidently only a later interpretation, above all in connection with the messianic king (Isa. 11.2; 42.1; 61.1). The promised Messiah is the bearer of the spirit of God (Isa. 11.2), and that is true of his whole rule, in wisdom, insight and strength (Isa. 28.6). The servant of God possesses the spirit (Isa. 42.1), and through his suffering he has to pronounce justice on all nations. In the Servant Songs we see a fusion of charismatic leadership (the old conception of the *rūaḥ*), prophetic office (the later interpretation of *rūaḥ*) and finally royal office. Trito-Isaiah expressly his message of consolation in the tradition of this promise (Isa. 61.1). In the same period, i.e. that of the exile, the leaders of Israel in earliest times, above all Moses and Joshua, were therefore interpreted as bearers of the spirit (Num. 11.17; 27.18; Deut. 34.9). At the same time, in addition to the mention of the gift of the spirit to preferred individuals, we also hear of the gift of the spirit to the whole of the people of God (Ezek. 36.27; 37.14; 39.29; see 11.19; 18.31; 36.26; Joel. 2.28–31; Isa. 32.15; 44.3; 59.21; Hag. 2.5) (here disparate conceptions come together, though as far as the gift of the spirit is concerned they seem to fit in a quite compact tradition). In both instances, in contrast to the original conception of the spirit of God, God's gift of the spirit is a *permanent* possession.

The eschatological gift of the spirit to the whole people is mentioned above all by Ezekiel (36.27; see 11.19; 36.26), in connection with a 'new heart' in men (11.19) and a (renewed) breath of life (Ezek. 37.14; 39.29), and by Joel (2.28f.), for whom this gift of the spirit is bound up with 'prophesying'. Now being a prophet is a permanent state, in the sense of a particularly close connection between God and his people (cf. Num. 11.29), which does away with all social differences (Joel 2.28f.). Spirit and blessing here become almost synonyms (Isa. 32.15–20; see 44.1–5). The spirit brings *šālōm* to Israel's community. In the late period of the Tanach, *rūaḥ* finally becomes a general theological term: it no longer indicates a specific action of God but God's activity in general. *Rūaḥ* and God are interchangeable (Isa. 34.16; 63.10f., 14; Pss. 51.11: 139.7; 143.10; Neh. 9.20; see also Micah 3.8; Zech. 7.12 and Neh. 9.30). This eventually gave rise to the expression *'the Holy Spirit'* (Isa. 63.10f.; Ps. 51.11).

In the New Testament we find the two competing lines of the late Old Testament prophecy of salvation: on the one hand the *rūaḥ* of the messianic king (the baptism of Jesus, Mark.1.10f. par.), and on the other hand the pouring out of the spirit on the whole people of God (Acts 2). It is only with John's distinctive association of 'Paraclete', a personal concept, with the traditional concept of the Spirit, that in Johannine theology the spirit unmistakably comes to be looked on in *personal* terms: *'another* Paraclete', different from God and at the same time different from Christ. In the other New Testament texts *pneuma* means, rather, the divine activity of salvation with man, the gift or the fruit of this divine saving activity in man, or simply God himself as a gift to man by virtue of the dead but risen Jesus. The gift of God, the possession of Jesus, is also shared by Christians. As in the later parts of the Old Testament, the Spirit points to the close connection between men who have been redeemed and through Jesus have been formed into the church and the living God. Therefore it is the Spirit of God which cries 'Abba' in the hearts of baptized believers (Gal. 4.6; Rom. 8.15; also I John 3.24b).

# The New Testament theology of grace and the life of Christians in the world

---

*Introduction: 'Materialistic' exegesis?*

In the introduction to this book (p. 22) I pointed out that a *theological* analysis of New Testament texts only made sense if at the same time it was connected with an analysis of *social and historical* conditions. In connection with this insight it is impossible to avoid saying something about the 'materialist' interpretation of the Bible which emerged a few years ago.[1] This is a new approach to biblical texts, one might say on the basis of the 'historical materialism' of Karl Marx and to a great extent particularly with help of 'structural analysis' of the text. The real results of this exegetical method are still too slight for us to be able to make a responsible assessment of it. However, a few comments are possible and appropriate.

On the one hand, it can be shown that a structural analysis of the text is *necessary* as a preliminary phase in order to limit the naturally subjective element in any hermeneutical analysis and to allow the hermeneutical interpretation to begin with the directions which are objectively indicated in the text itself. At the least this will eliminate hermeneutical *arbitrariness*.

On the other hand, a purely structural analysis of the text seems very banal and meaningless, especially when it is followed by a hermeneutical analysis. In that case one arrives only at anonymous typologies and codes and not at the authentic and original meaning of the text. 'Materialistic' exegesis of the text makes use of structural analysis, but does so in a particular way. I believe that it is correct, but I have one basic qualification to make. A purely 'ideological' analysis of texts which above all present a view of the world is in fact dangerously one-sided. So an analysis of socio-historical and even economic conditions is always necessary. On the other hand, from an anthropological point of view, it seems to me to be just as dangerously one-sided to deny that there is also an 'ideological history' within the system, i.e. in the light of the particular *structure of a problem*. Anyone who denies this, in the last resort rejects the original and personal element (which is at the same time socially and 'culturally' conditioned). Man is an alienated person and not an angel. In reality, and indeed in principle, as a consequence of their method, structuralist and materialistic interpretations of the text only investigate the (real) aspect of alienation and the wider connections with a larger social totality. So by definition they cannot say anything about the special quality and the originality of an individual text; they simply distil anonymous, universalist typologies. This is legitimate as a piece of scientific reductionism (and even the presupposition of their particular fruitfulness), as long as we remain aware of this *epochē* or abstraction. Furthermore, the danger of crossing boundaries is intensified (even in this materialistic method) by a fundamentalist principle that 'the Bible is right after all' (even, for example, in the socio-political sphere). In that case, for example, the widow's mite in the New Testament becomes a confirmation of insights which are justified today, but are in fact alien to the Bible!

Anthropologically speaking, this gives rise to a dialectical (rather than a simple) relationship between social changes and 'the history of ideas'. For this very reason, neither structuralist nor materialistic interpretation of the Bible can replace the historical-critical hermeneutical method or make it superfluous. However, if it remains true to itself, this latter method will have to make use of the more recent methods *in its own procedures,* and in so doing will become less subjective. However, to expect salvation only from structural-analytical and materialistic explanations of the text would be to sanction an increasing 'de-subjectification' of man; it would be the solemn exequies of the death of humanity, 'after the death of God'.

In the following analysis, I have not yet been able to make use of the valuable elements in a materialistic interpretation of the Bible. However, my analysis has been governed by the anthropological insight that the relationship between 'ideas' (in this case the New Testament conceptions of grace, salvation and redemption) and the socio-political context is not one-sided, but dialectical.

Chapter 1

# 'Seek first the kingdom of God and his righteousness'

'These things will be yours as well' (Luke 12.31; Matt. 6.33). These texts might be regarded as the central theme of the whole of the New Testament. They evidently come from the earliest stratum of the Q tradition and characterize the spirit of the historical proclamation of Jesus. The context of this New Testament interpretation emerges from Luke 12.22–31 and Matt. 6.25–33. This context is evidently that of the wisdom tradition.[2] Thus the Christian interpretation of the kingdom of God in the New Testament is primarily not apocalyptic, i.e., it is not to be understood primarily in terms of the pattern of a two-storey universe, though in the Hellenistic Roman period the wisdom tradition had fused with that of apocalyptic.

The prohibition against worrying about food and clothing is derived from a conviction of the imminence of the kingdom of God. It is a summons to believe in God, the creator of all things, the living God, who himself exercises his rule of the world 'without care'. Look at the lilies of the field, the birds of the air! That is an element of early Jewish theology, an expression of everyday experience, which is a source of the knowledge of God (Job. 12.7ff.; Prov. 6.6; cf. Deut. 32.1–3).[2a] This is apocalyptic from the tradition of wisdom and the Hasidim: 'See how all works in heaven do not alter their courses. . .; see on earth. . .; look at summer and winter . . . see. . . . But you have not persisted and have not observed God's law, but have fallen away' (I Enoch 2.1–5.4). The purport of all this is that God has done everything for the righteous, but they have not loved him in return. The conclusion drawn by the New Testament is that men should seek the kingdom of God and accord with its way of life. The birds and the lilies who do no work are not a model for idlers; they bear witness to God's care. God takes this everyday care upon himself, and it is our responsibility to seek the kingdom of God. But what does that mean for the New Testament Christians?

The proclamation of the kingdom of God or God's righteousness only acquires its significance in the horizon of the question of righteousness – the righteousness of God, of man, of the world.[3] The beatitudes turn the so-called righteousness of the world upside down. The antitheses which the community constructed out of these beatitudes also stand in the same perspective; they deprive me of the right to insist on my own rights, and they call my attention to the rights of others. They do not allow me to distinguish myself, mark myself out from and defend myself against others by seeking protection in the Law. On the contrary, they tell me that the Law protects others *against* me (see the Sermon on the Mount, Matt. 5, and the Sermon on the Plain, Luke 6.17ff.).

Finally, the parables too are concerned with this righteousness. They often contain what by human standards is 'injustice'.[4] But parables take their specific starting point from the context of everyday experience. That's the way the world is! At the same time, they quite deliberately contain a paradox: that's the way the kingdom of God is! The Jewish tradition often expressed the experience that God makes his sun rise on good and evil, that he makes rain fall on the just and the unjust, and that anyone who has worked for two hours receives precisely the same wage as someone who has toiled for seven hours at a stretch with a certain undertone of reproachfulness towards God who had evidently neglected to carry through his righteousness.[5] For Jesus, on the other hand, this everyday experience was the occasion for positive teaching: for the commandment to love one's enemy. Jesus does not brush aside doubt in God's rule over the world; he seizes hold of it in order to proclaim that this in fact is what God is like. He is just as we experience him, as someone who without care makes the sun shine on both good and evil. That God feeds and clothes the lilies of the field and the birds of the air, as he clothed Solomon and the Queen of Sheba, tyrants and Gentiles, is an experience which Jews often interpret as an incomprehensible attitude on God's part (Ps. Sol. 5) and therefore regard as a well-considered piece of divine pedagogy. Precisely that must make it clear why the godless often get on better in the world than the pious. However, Jesus draws other conclusions from the same experience. In the gospels, in the style of early wisdom teaching, the audience is asked to consider its everyday experiences and a type of wisdom which has been centuries in its formulation. Early Judaism had forgotten how to speak of God 'within the horizons of our experiences of the world'.[6] The Jesus of the New Testament once again restores God to the sphere of human experience. Precisely because people had forgotten this, a lack of a sense of reality had set in which led apocalyptic, in particular, to a two-storey world.

Jesus takes up the very experiences which seem to contradict God's righteousness. The human complaint about God's unrighteousness is taken 'literally', in order to make it possible to articulate God's righteousness. However, this implies that the standards of divine righteousness are quite different from worldly norms. The kingdom of God can also be experienced again in this world in the action and words of Jesus. Parallel to this in Paul is the separation of christology and eschatology. Christology is the presence of God in this world, but under the sign of weakness and the cross, of the curse and death. *This world* is and remains God's creation; God has not withdrawn from it. God's righteousness is *in* this world and at the same time puts this world in question, since it is often characterized by helplessness and failure. The conflict between belief in creation and empirical contradiction of everyday experience is the basic theme of belief in God in the Tanach, the New Testament and in the early church, in times when belief had not yet been reduced to the inner relationship between God and man, excluding the spheres of nature, the world and society.

The essential element in the proclamation of Jesus was that 'the *kairos* has been fulfilled and the kingdom of God is at hand' (Mark 1.15). This *direct* juxtaposition and intertwining of present and future is characteristic of the whole of the New Testament picture of Jesus. If we understand the present to be what is at hand and the future to be what is not at hand, such a simultaneity of present and future is of course absurd. But in that case we are speaking in banal concepts of time. Still, *this* temporal element in Jesus' understanding of the kingdom of God which is on its way should not be ruled out altogether. For Jesus, the *eschaton* is also a chronological reality.[7] In its original usage, 'it is time' always means that it is time *for something* (to eat, to sleep, to work). Thus there can be a 'contemporaneity' of many times: for one child it is time to go to bed and for another it is time to do homework. Time is filled time, and not just an external measure. It is precisely this original experience of time which makes it possible for present and future to coincide.

Now Jesus announces the time of the disclosure of the kingdom of God. That means that we must respond to it in the same way that we respond to the announcement, 'Lunch is ready!' Time is *kairos*, time to undertake something. Time takes us away from one thing and confronts us with another; withdrawing is the presupposition for devoting oneself to something else. This Heideggerian concept of time – which does not analyse time as an abstract mass, but rather the time of experience – gives us a clear view of the 'contemporaneity' of present and future in respect of the kingdom of God. 'The time is fulfilled and the kingdom of God is at hand' therefore means: now it is time for us to be open towards God's salvation; now we must grasp it. The coming of the kingdom of God – the lordship of the God who is concerned for man – is the time to realize salvation: the time of salvation. And it is the fulfilment of old expectations ('time is full'). *Metanoia*, to repent, is therefore the first thing to be done: to withdraw, in order to give one's attention to. And this demand for repentance becomes clear in one's encounter with Jesus: anyone who encounters him is confronted with the announcement, 'it is time to' . . . since anyone who adopts a standpoint for or against Jesus decides for or against the kingdom of God (Luke 12.8f. par; see Matt. 10.32f.). The criterion for the coming, eschatological judgment is one's present attitude towards Jesus (Matt. 25.31–46).

How did the Christians of the New Testament fill the time of the experience of salvation? Above all, from whom did they withdraw in order to turn towards salvation? What was their attitude towards the realities of this world: in general, towards society and its structures, towards political power, towards the ethical standards of their Jewish and Gentile neighbours, and finally towards the tree from which they were a late growth, Israel?

Chapter 2

# The New Testament churches as exodus communities in historically conditioned situations

As the New Testament experience of grace and its articulation also contains social and anthropological presuppositions from the culture of the first century, we must first look at that. Only then will we discover what was a typically Christian reaction and how far these Christians spoke critically or uncritically as children of their time.

## §1   Feelings and theories about life in late antiquity

*Literature:* D. Amand, *Fatalisme et liberté dans l'antiquité grecque*, Louvain 1945; P. Benoit, 'Sénèque et saint Paul', *RB* 53, 1946, 7–33; H. Bietenhard, *Die himmlische Welt im Urchristentum und Spätjudentum*, WUNT 2, Tübingen 1951; O. Böcher, *Der johanneische Dualismus im Zusammenhang des nachbiblischen Judentums*, Gütersloh 1965; E. Brandenburger, 'Die Auferstehung der Glaubenden als historisches und theologisches Problem', *WuD* 9, 1967, 16–33; W. H. Cadman, *The Open Heaven. The Revelation of God in the Johannine Sayings of Jesus*, Oxford 1969; F. Cumont, *Lux Perpetua*, Paris 1949; J. Daniélou, 'Odes de Salomon', *DBS* 6, 677–84; W. D. Davies, ' "Knowledge" in the Dead Sea Scrolls and Matthew 11.25–30', *HTR* 46, 1953, 113–39; W. D. Davies and D. Daube (ed.), *The Background of the New Testament and its Eschatology* (in honour of C. H. Dodd), Cambridge 1964; A. J. Festugière, *L'idéal religieux des Grecs et de l'Evangile*, Paris 1932; id., *La révélation de'Hermès Trismégiste*, 4 vols, Paris 1950–54; G. Friedrich,

*Utopie und Reich Gottes*, Göttingen 1974; H. A. Fischel, *Rabbinic Literature and Graeco-Roman Philosophy*, Leiden 1973; W. Harnisch, *Verheissung und Verhängnis der Geschichte. Untersuchungen zum Zeit- und Geschichtsverständnis im 4. Buch Esra und in der syrischen Baruchapokalypse*, FRLANT 97, Göttingen 1969; H. Hegermann, *Die Vorstellung von Schöpfungsmittlern im hellenistischen Judentum und Urchristentum*, TU 82, Berlin 1961; M. Hengel, *Judaism and Hellenism*, ET London and Philadelphia 1974; *Hermetica*, ed. W. Scott, 4 vols, Oxford 1924–36 (see also under Festugière); J. Jervell, *Imago Dei. Gen. 1.26ff. im Spätjudentum, in der Gnosis und in den paulinischen Briefen*, FRLANT 76, Göttingen 1960; H. Jonas, *Gnosis und Spätantiker Geist*. I. *Die mythologische Gnosis*, FRLANT 51, Göttingen [2]1964; II. *Von der Mythologie zur mystischen Philosophie*, FRLANT 63, Göttingen 1954; U. Luck, 'Das Weltverständnis in der jüdischen Apokalyptik, dargestellt am äthiopischen Henoch und am 4. Ezra', *ZKTh* 73, 1976, 283–305; J. Neusner, *The Rabbinic Traditions about the Pharisees before 70*, three vols, Leiden 1971ff.; J. Neusner, ed., *Christianity, Judaism and other Greco-Roman Cults*, Vol. 1, Leiden 1975; M. P. Nilsson, *Geschichte der griechischen Religion*, three vols, Munich 1955–61; E. Peterson, *Frühkirche, Judentum und Gnosis*, Freiburg im Breisgau 1959, 107–28; S. Pétrement, *Le dualisme dans l'histoire de la philosophie et des religions*, Paris 1946; M. Pohlenz, *Die Stoa*, two vols., Göttingen 1959; id., 'Paulus und die Stoa', *ZNW* 42, 1949, 69–104; H. C. Puech, *Le manichéisme, son fondateur, sa doctrine*, Paris 1949; G. Quispel, *Gnosis als Weltreligion*, Zurich 1951; E. Rohde, *Psyche*, Darmstadt [2]1961; M. Rostovtzeff, *The Social and Economic History of the Hellenistic World*, three vols, Oxford 1941; H. H. Schmid, *Altorientalische Welt in der alttestamentlichen Theologie*, Zurich 1974; W. Schmithals, *Die Apokalyptik, Einführung und Deutung*, Göttingen 1973 (see also the literature in *Jesus. An Experiment in Christology*, 116f.); G. G. Scholem, *Major Trends in Jewish Mysticism*, Jerusalem 1941; id., *Recent Trends in Jewish Gnosticism*, New York 1961; A. Strobel, *Kerygma und Apokalyptik*, Göttingen 1967; S. Schulz, 'Salomon-Oden', in *RGG*[3] V, 1339–42; G. Vermès, *Scripture and Tradition in Judaism, Haggadic Studies*, Studia Post-Biblica 4, Leiden 1961; U. von Wilamowitz-Moellendorff, *Der Glaube der Hellenen*, 2 vols, Darmstadt 1959; H. W. Wolff, *Anthropology of the Old Testament*, ET London and Philadelphia 1974.

In the New Testament churches, Jesus' summons to seek 'first the kingdom of God', after which everything else would be given to us (Matt. 6.33), a summons which on the lips of Jesus becomes a summons to act in accordance with the demands of God's rule which is concerned with humanity, was given concrete form, but not in historical circumstances which Christians – at that time in the minority – could direct in accordance with their wishes.

Almost all parts of the New Testament give evocative expression to the way in which in a non-Christian, pagan society, Christians with their experience of grace with Jesus Christ felt themselves to be strangers and pilgrims in this temporal and transitory, indeed sinful world (Heb. 13.13f. and passim; I Peter 2.11f., 13–17; 3.9, 15f.; 4.3f; 4.14; II Peter 1.11; Phil. 3.20; Col. 1.13; 3.1f.; Eph. 2.19; John 3.12f., 31; 8.21; I John 2.5c, 10; 5.20c, etc.). There is a dialectic at work here between Old and New Testament belief in God, along with Jesus' summons to 'seek first the kingdom of God', on the one hand and on the other the cultural and historical circumstances, the feelings about life current in late antiquity with its syncretistic attempts to find a way to salvation and life in a world which could only feel a deep sense of pessimism.

From the time of the rise of the Hellenistic empires, the Greek spirit had become accepted throughout the Roman empire along with the use of the Greek language, which had become universal. However, this spirit is not as homogeneous as is often supposed. Greek thought had a deep religious origin. This spirit was determined by a fundamental tension. On the one hand, 'man is the measure of all things' (Protagoras), whereas on the other hand, 'God is the measure of all things, even of man' (Plato), not so much as a limiting norm but as the goal of all humanity. On the one hand man is 'divine by nature', son of God (Plato; Stoa; Epictetus, Aratus). On the other hand, precisely in Greek religious feeling and poetry we can find the warning 'Do not seek to become like Zeus' (Pindar), and that was the real, primal Greek attitude from the time of the Homeric epics: God and man are two completely different races. Hence the permanent oscillation of the Greek spirit between the *condition humaine* and assimilation to God, the goal of both Greek philosophy and the Hellenistic mystery religions: the *Dionysiac* or mystical element in the Greek soul and the *Apollonian* element with its longing for ritual forms (it was this that made the Jewish requirement that Gentiles should be circumcised an 'in-thing' in this syncretistic culture). Yet there is a deep abyss between the two. Plato, above all, gives the ecstatic element its full rein in his *Phaedo*, full of veneration for the gods of Delphi (*logos* or *ratio*). It is not man, but the deity who is the measure of all things, says Plato (*Laws* IV, 716B, C). Ancient Orphism sought to get rid of the 'titanic' or 'earthly' element in man in order to get nearer to this divine nucleus. Plato, too, was concerned with *assimilation* to God, not deification. God's *eikōn* or image lies in man, and because of this communion with God, man must learn to be like God in form. There is only the *fascinosum* of the divine. God is not jealous of man, but man can go beyond himself. Aristotle rejects the old conceptions, for man merits only human things; however, he allows man a desire for divine immortality.

In typical Greek fashion this pride in humanity has religious roots: we are born of God. The Stoics will celebrate this theme in a special way. Humanism and religion coincide here, while 'the will of God' determines everything. Thus middle and later Stoicism in particular were an execution of Plato's testament which was popularized throughout the Hellenistic world in the form of Middle Platonism, a particular synthesis of Platonism and Stoicism. Seneca (born shortly before Christ) noted the universal rise of a new sense of pessimism. After the collapse of the institutions of the Greek *polis* with their democratic orientation and the rise of the sole rule of the emperor, philosophy lost its political function and its role of criticizing society. Stoic philosophy (which at that time dominated thinking and had been popularized) became de-politicized; it turned in on itself and took on a more profound religious character through which man was shown a meaningful way of life in the midst of the pessimism which was permeating culture and everyday living. As a consequence of the loss of political freedom there arose what Seneca calls a universal existential void (he found the *sibi displicere* to be generally typical of first-century man). At this time the Stoics worked out a completely new concept of freedom. Freedom is no longer civil and political freedom (which citizens had enjoyed at least in the *polis* or the republic). It was interiorized. Freedom is the inner independence which nothing and no one can take from us, and Seneca anticipates Paul when he writes that no one can rob us of this freedom, 'neither death nor poverty nor man nor the wrath of the gods' (Paul will simply develop this Stoic conception in Christian terms). Consequently the Stoa, at least in this phase of its development, finds that slavery need not be done away with, no matter how much it stressed human nature and the humanity of the slave and the necessity for humane treatment. Why should it be, if virtue and true humanity, internal freedom, are quite independent of external circumstances? Inner slavery can remain, even with extreme social freedom (Paul comes to the same conclusion). However, rather later, under Nero (who became emperor in 54 AD), the philosophers of the Stoa were the only ones who fought for freedom and offered resistance, putting up public opposition to the inhumanity of the emperor. In the years 70–72 (when the Jewish zealots were defeated in Palestine), Stoic philosophers were exiled from Italy. Many of them paid for their resistance with their lives. Seneca's principle, expressed earlier, acquired historical significance. He said: a true philosophy of life is politically relevant and must lead to political activity, *unless* something outwardly or inwardly keeps philosophers from it: outwardly, if political domination makes their work hopeless; inwardly, if duty requires a competent philosopher to remain in his study.

The rise of 'irrationalism' has often been interpreted as an anti-Greek reaction of the 'disposition' to the Greek 'rationalism' of those who were at the same time the occupying forces. This is clearly an instance of jumping to conclusions too rapidly, since this form of pessimism in fact originated in Greece! The scepticism of Ecclesiastes towards the traditional Jewish view that the promise of life is bound up with the law was already the result of Greek influence. All goes well with sinners, and those who long for righteousness are mocked. He pleads for simple middle-class pleasures. Jewish apocalyptic was born out of this experience of contrast and this pessimism. In contrast to the solution offered by wisdom, namely that wisdom is incarnate in the Law, here the Law and wisdom have gone their separate ways. Wisdom indeed came to Israel, but found no place there: nothing achieved, it returned and took up its abode among the heavenly beings (I Enoch [Ethiopic Enoch] 42.1f.). Any connection between 'righteousness', 'life' and 'observing the law' is radically contradicted by everyday experience. Trust in the divine ordering of the world had been shattered, and this was the trust that the apocalyptic writers sought to restore (I Enoch 37.1–5). To achieve their aims, however, they separate Law and wisdom, which is a new development over against wisdom literature. They want to give an answer to the burning desire for righteousness which the Law cannot provide. Wisdom is an 'esoteric' insight into the structure of the world that God desires. However, the question of meaning and righteousness cannot be answered in human terms. Because of this it is necessary to consider things *as a whole*. This is possible only through a special revelation through a mediator called by God, who surveys both time and space in a vision. Just as 'all things have their time' (Eccles. 3.1–8), so too righteousness has its times. In God's plan, the world order and ethical righteousness are closely connected; this is seen only by the apocalyptic writer, who in a state of ecstasy makes a journey through the universe and can look on the harmony of the stars with his own eyes (I Enoch 17–18; 41.3–9); at the same time he looks on the places of torment of the fallen angels, the abode of the dead, the paradise of the just (18.11–19.3; 22; 27; 32); he looks on history from the flood to the last judgment (83–90). In fact, right is triumphant (93; 91.12–17). None of this is accessible to normal experience, and even contradicts it. However, this world as it has been created is good, even if this will only become evident in the last days. The Stoics and the Enlightenment in the eighteenth century say roughly the same thing as this early apocalyptic, which has yet to arrive at the idea of a 'double' world. It was concerned with the deeper dimensions of our own world.

However, even this early apocalyptic approach did not provide a satisfactory answer to the problem of injustice and suffering. New apocalyptic, represented by the Fourth Book of Ezra (end of the first century AD, but preceded by an earlier development), poses 'tormenting questions'

(IV Ezra 14.14) which no one can answer. Here higher wisdom from above must come to man's aid (4.21). Human beings know only earthly things; only heavenly beings know what is heavenly. This apocalyptic is no longer concerned merely with what is 'still hidden' in our world, which is revealed in visions. This world is utterly helpless and held in captivity. Only a completely new creation, 'a new heaven and a new earth', brings righteousness (IV Ezra 7.10–14), and then through the death of *all*, including the coming Messiah. A new world comes into being only through resurrection (7.26–33).

It is striking that Ezra is the one who is chosen to rewrite the Law of Moses (which was destroyed in the universal conflagration). He completed ninety-four books in forty days. Only twenty-four of them were published (the twenty-four 'canonical books' of the Jews); the remaining seventy were kept back and only the 'wise men' had access to them (IV Ezra 14.47), because it was these 'non-canonical' books which contained wisdom! This form of apocalyptic could not express the break with wisdom literature – the Tanach itself *is* wisdom – more strongly than this. Only the *Law*, coupled with this esoteric *Wisdom*, results in the observance of the Torah in fact bringing life and salvation (IV Ezra 14.30). In the meanwhile, Israel and the Torah, at one time dwelling-places of wisdom (Sir. 24; Bar. 3.9–4.4), have lost their political significance; Israel and the Law are persecuted; there *is* no righteousness. This form of apocalyptic asserts, *'Nevertheless!'* The promise of life, associated with the Law (IV Ezra 4.27), remains in force, but the *present* world is too fragmentary to support this promise: in the new age to come it will become evident that the Law in fact brings life. There is righteousness only *through the Law* . . . but in the new age. This apocalyptic sets out to encourage those who at present are faithful to the Law: Keep your spirits up; despite all experiences to the contrary, the Law gives life, if only in the age to come. So the present is given a positive significance: take care that you belong among the number of the elect (IV Ezra 4.35f.). Thus the Law is not in the service of man; rather, man is in the service of a Law which apocalyptic has made independent! Apocalyptic culminates in the crudest 'positivism of revelation': the positivism of the Torah as over against all human experience of life and the world. Nothing can separate us from salvation – in the new age – if only we observe the Law: bear the yoke of the Law, put up with it: that is the great message of apocalyptic. *Through esoteric wisdom* the apocalyptist looks on the deepest significance *of the Law*, but the consequence of this conception (in contrast to the ideas of early apocalyptic) is a 'double world'.

These conceptions were already current in a syncretistic mixture even before IV Ezra. This unjust world does not seem capable of improvement. Hence an orientation on a completely different better world from this earthly system. As a result of influence from the East, all this was also influenced by astrology, which contrasted our earth with the 'higher heavenly spheres', seeing the latter as a more powerful and more exalted, more harmonious and better world. This was generally in line with the feelings of the time. On the other hand, the lowest spheres of heaven at least were inhabited by some demons who threatened this world and dominated human destiny in accordance with their wills. Thus the New Testament agrees with the early Jewish inter-testamental literature in speaking of 'the prince of this world' (Eph. 2.2; II Cor. 4.4; John 12.31; 14.30; 16.11). Hence a general desire to dwell 'in the higher spheres of heaven'. Apocalyptic described this as if part of the human world, that of the righteous, was 'taken up' into the heavenly spheres and 'made to dwell there'; on the other hand, others suggested that the better world prepared by God from eternity would descend to earth as a heavenly Jerusalem or a heavenly city (I Enoch 90.29). The drama of the whole book of Enoch, which was enthusiastically read by New Testament Christians and is even quoted explicitly in Jude 14, takes places in the *epourania* or heavenly spheres; it gives an exact description of all the phases of the sun and moon, a wisdom from the East which the author evidently perceives with a mystic amazement, an astronomical event which is perfectly regulated under the guidance of the angel Uriel (I Enoch 71–78; see also Bar. 3.33f.; IV Ezra 7.26 etc.). Above all, after the destruction of the Jerusalem Temple in AD 70, talk of the future 'heavenly Jerusalem' became a regular theme in Judaism; earlier, this heavenly city had tended to be the prototype in accordance with which the earthly city of Jerusalem had to be built.

We also find the same division between a 'world of darkness', the world below, and a 'world of light', the world above, in the so-called heterodox-Jewish world of Qumran. Here the cosmic pattern of two planes has above all an ethical and eschatological significance. Or rather, we would do better not to apply our modern sharp distinction between cosmic and ethical dualism to the world of late antiquity. At that time the ethical dimension was never separated from the cosmic dimension, because ethics is always connected in some way with the cosmos, even if only through the physical death of man, which casts a shadow on all his ethical efforts. Ancient culture always perceived this clearly. It makes no sense to describe all this as Gnosis (or Gnosticism); this only arose as a coherent system of life in the second century, as a result of first-century syncretism. However, in the *Corpus Hermeticum* we find a first synthesis of the various syncretistic elements in which there is a certain foretaste of Gnosticism, even if these *Hermetica* differ quite fundamentally from Gnosticism in their conceptions of the relationship between God and the world.

As far as I can see, only the Stoics defended a religion of reason against all popular religions and against the culture of a world on two levels; they escaped the allurements of the *epourania* or heavenly abodes. Nevertheless, they only achieved this by as it were intertwining these two planes (as Aristotle had done earlier in the face of Plato and his theory of ideas) and speaking of a Logos which was the nature of the universe without being completely identical with the transitory, material world. This Logos was the soul of all that exists, from which, through which and in which everything lives and moves. Here, too, the law of the cosmos is inseparable from the ethical law which includes man within the universal Logos of the cosmos (to live 'in accordance with the natural law' means to live 'in accordance with reason'). Here too, a cosmic dualism remains which becomes an ethical task for men: Logos or Spirit and materialism are involved in an intrinsic tension within the universe.

By contrast, the Epicureans concluded from this general sense of crisis in late antiquity and general feeling of helplessness that it was important to take advantage of what there was: *carpe diem*. They denied the crisis, ignored the history of human suffering, just as they called the tragedy of human death a pseudo-problem; for them this was asceticism.

However, people generally took refuge – a new way of life – in the various mystery religions, which initiated their followers mystically 'into higher spheres of life'. These religions gave them protection against demonic powers, and filled them with heavenly experiences and blessings: in the last resort the grace of redemption or *sōtēria*. The New Testament feels compelled constantly to attack Christians in the churches who feel attracted by a supplementary 'heavenly fulfilment', a *plērōma* fullness, which they did not seem to have been given by the somewhat matter-of-fact and ethically-oriented initiation of baptism (see above all Colossians, Jude, II Peter). This religious feeling was in fact oriented on inwardness, on the heart and the feelings; however, it would be incorrect to talk here of individualistic salvation, because this religious experience of late antiquity, under oriental influence, exercised strong pressure towards the formation of groups; from about 150 BC onwards there had been a widespread desire throughout the Hellenistic world for a religion of revelation (or a mystery religion). From this time until well into the first century AD many brotherhoods entered on a great period of expansion.

There was a different situation in the cities. Here academic scepticism and popularized 'cynicism' prevailed. Old and new religions were a matter for the *pagani*, i.e. the country population (though it is a fact that primitive Christianity made its greatest gains in the big cities). However, from the time that Augustus assumed power, various attempts had been made to bring new life to the old religions. We can hardly talk of a kind of religious *a priori* in the cities of the time. The ancient enlightenment – the de-divinization of the heavens, the mysterious world of plants and animals and finally of men – had dealt a hard blow to the natural tendency to take religion for granted. Above all in the cities, the world was largely secularized: this was in no way a consequence of Christianity, but the climate in which New Testament Christians already lived. The fact that the Christians were later called *atheoi* by the Gentiles, i.e. men without religion, certainly does not mean that they rejected the religious forms of the religion of antiquity,[8] though this is often asserted in some kinds of literature. These Christians defended themselves by claiming to possess the *true* religion. There was never an originally 'religionless' Christianity; this is a scholarly invention. It is easy enough to understand why the first Christians had no *specific* religious language and cultural forms *of their own*: they were *Jews*, and after their conversion to Christianity they simply continued to go to the Temple or the synagogues with their sacral religious forms. When they parted company with the synagogue, they replaced these forms with particular ones of their own. All this is clear from the Pastoral Epistles of the New Testament and from Jude and II Peter: there is a ministry, there is a norm of faith, there is an increasing recognition of specifically Christian holy scriptures, and so on. But it is a historical fable to suppose that before this Christianity knew a time of faith without religion; furthermore, this is to mistake the initial heyday of Christianity, however short, as a brotherhood within the *Jewish religion*. So there can be no question of talking about an 'early catholicism' or a repaganizing of Christian faith; this is an intrinsic consequence of the separation of Christianity from the Jewish religion and also the separation of Gentiles who became Christians from their sacral obligations. But we can hardly claim that the saving significance which Christians in the New Testament attributed to Jesus, his crucifixion and his resurrection was not just as sacral. It too was a 'religion', and as such was 'Christian faith'.

Against this background of the world-views of the first century we can now analyse what was specifically Christian, the elements which assumed specific form in the New Testament in a critical relationship with these religious presuppositions.

## §2   New Testament spirituality as a critical variant of feelings about life in late antiquity

When Paul says, 'Our homeland is in heaven' (Phil. 3.20) or 'our *politeuma* is above', and Colossians says, 'If then you have raised with Christ, *seek the things that are above*, where Christ is seated at the right hand of God. Set your minds on things that are above, not on things that are on earth' (Col. 3.1f.) they are using a language which was generally understood at the time and which echoed the deepest longings to be found in the culture of late antiquity. The same is true of many other authors: 'Here we have no lasting city, but we seek the city which is to come' (Heb. 13.14), as a result of which we must 'lead a heavenly life' (Heb. 12.14–13.9); Johannine theology talks of dwelling in a divine sphere, the realm of 'light' (I John 2.10; 2.5c; 5.20c) and James 1.17 says, 'Every good endowment and every perfect gift *is from above*, coming down from the *Father of lights*', while other passages say that we are merely exiles here on earth, 'strangers and sojourners' (Heb. 11.13c; I Peter 1.17; 2.11), but now already 'fellow citizens with the saints and members of the household of God' (Eph. 2.19). However, the model here is filled with a Christian content which points to a quite specific historical event. 'You are dead and risen with Christ, and with him you sit at the right hand of God' (Eph. 2.6; Col. 1.13; 2.12; 3.1–4; Heb. 12.22f.). For in the world picture of the time the heavenly spheres were the place where God himself dwells and thus the place where the risen Jesus, who lives with God, is to be found. That is why the world above had such attraction for Christians as well. Hence Hebrews summons men to go out of the city gates (i.e. out of this world: Heb. 13.13f; cf. Rev. 18.4) to the *oikoumenē mellousa* (Heb. 2.5), to the world to come, which has been prepared above with God from eternity for the righteous. This is a summons to rest or to the heavenly city of God's eternal sabbath (Heb. 4.3; 3.18; 4.1; 4.4; 4.10f.). What the *Didache* later expresses as 'May *charis* (or grace) come – *elthetō* – and this world pass away – *pareltheto*'[9] can be described as a fundamental theme which occurs throughout the spirituality of the New Testament: 'Maranatha' (I Cor. 16.22; Rev. 22.20b, c). The Christian community is an exodus community which departs from the earthly city of the Gentiles in order to go through the wilderness to reach the promised land, i.e. the heavenly city with its round of worship (Heb. 12.2f.; Rev. 18.4; also in Qumran), in which it is possible to join through the liturgy of the Christian community. The community sets out for the 'new earth and new heaven where righteousness dwells' (II Peter 3.13), the beginnings of which can already be seen and experienced in the concrete form of the new society which is called the Christian church.

The 'earthly vale of tears' and the 'world above' (even more than the beyond) is a feeling about life which is general throughout late antiquity and leads to a consistent view of the world. But even Greek Platonic philosophy with its world of ideas and shadows – often wrongly seen as the origin of the two-storey universe – is itself already the philosophical secularization of an existing religious attitude to life. However, quite apart from the critical variants which Christianity brings (see below), we should not be deceived by this model from late antiquity. For however much reality and model overlap in the ancient world, the *spatial* form of presentation should not allow us to forget that here apocalyptic at the same time includes the older Jewish *temporal* conception of a coming world which is better than the present one and even finds this world essential (this is clear, for example, in Hebrews). At an earlier stage, above all in the psalms of Israel, we find an 'appearance' of the rule of Yahweh who, perhaps on New Year's Day, was celebrated in the cult as the one who puts the powers of chaos and all enemies under subjection. The kingdom of God was *experienced* in the world order in which people felt themselves to be secure. However, right from the beginning this was experienced simply as hope, hope in a change in Israel's fortunes (Isa. 52.7).[10] Again, this hope remained bound up with the experience that things had once been different for the world and for Israel. The more radically this world deviates from God's creative ordinance and contradicts it, the less talk about the kingdom of God is talk about this world, because this world as people experience it is simply not 'in order'. In that case the kingdom of God increasingly becomes something which is not experienced in this world. Only in this way does the kingdom of God appear as an *alternative* to this world, an alternative the reality of which will only be revealed in the last days. This gave rise to the apocalyptic world of two levels, where everything that was to take place among men had been prepared for from eternity in a heavenly world. Despite all empirical experiences, Israel means to remain faithful to its belief in the Creator God, the protector and director of the whole world of creation. Israel also continued to believe in God's *just* ordering of the world. Israel's history is as it were a single great attempt to make everyday experience correspond with God's righteousness and with his promise to the righteous. It is therefore typical in the Roman empire and in Byzantium where the divine saviour was called *conservator*, i.e. the one who maintains the world order and the social order, Christians soon came to speak of the *salvator*, the *saviour* and the one who makes whole, the healer.

For the question of righteousness is in reality a question of the relationship between God and man, but is put the way it is because of men's experience of righteousness in this world. The story of Job is characteristic of this problem, as is the prophetic criticism of society.[11] Apocalyptic attempts to solve the same problem. Against the background of belief in God's rule of the world it is therefore a large-scale criticism of world and society. I Enoch (Ethiopic Enoch) is an illustration of this; its visionary story is played out almost exclusively in the heavenly spheres, but (in its final redaction) it becomes one of the most acute criticisms of ancient society that I know, quite impotent because the exploiters are simply threatened with eternal damnation in hell whereas those who do emerge happily in the end mock them with scornful laughter (I Enoch 98.4–8). These chapters are a kind of curse against all unrighteousness on earth:

almost exclusively against the political power which is bound up with riches and money. The author attacks (more sharply than any prophet before him) the rich who exploit the poor and 'build palaces with the sweat of others', monuments 'of which every stone, every piece of mortar, is made up of the sins of the powerful and the rich' (I Enoch 99.13). Finally, as a true apocalyptist, he says, 'But I say to you' (I Enoch 103), and then he utters a 'blessed are you' over the righteous who suffer now (I Enoch 104). However, here in fact the blessedness relates only to the last judgment in the beyond; this marks an essential difference from the beatitudes of Jesus which are meant in a present eschatological sense: the kingdom of God is coming now, with Jesus himself: 'the finger of God' (Luke 11.20). However, in apocalyptic too it is evident that what has been realized in our temporal world has already been prepared for 'above' from eternity; in other words, salvation and righteousness cannot come from our world, but only from above, though at the same time, *localization* (in heaven) and historical *temporality* cannot be separated in apocalyptic. The apocalyptic *eschaton* is a vague intertwining of ultimate and still earthly events, and post-historical circumstances: heaven and earth then seem to become one, the one reality in which God and all righteousness are experienced and from which all the unrighteous are excluded. In other words, God rules where unrighteousness vanishes.

So in this Jewish world we should not have any false conceptions about the general model of late antiquity as such. We must without question try to discover what in the New Testament really goes back to thinking in models and what is the Christian reality of salvation to which they refer; and therefore what is the Christian critical variant of this feeling current in late antiquity. So it is already remarkable that, say, in Ephesians, which puts a great deal of stress on this fact of Christians 'already sitting' with Christ in the heavenly places (Eph. 2.6) and points out that we are already 'fellow citizens with the saints and members of the household of God' (Eph. 2.19), ends its account by turning everything upside down (we are not up there, but God is down here): 'In him you are also built into it for *a dwelling place of God*' (Eph. 2.22), here and now, on earth, in this world. If we are to understand the New Testament we must give up our concepts of 'world' and 'heaven'; we must also be sparing with charges of Platonic or Middle Platonic influence – as though this Platonism (indeed by its own confession) were not a rationalization of the conception of the *religions* of heaven and earth.

What does the New Testament mean by '*this* world'? Hebrews has already taught us a good deal about that (see above). But as so-called dualism appears most strongly in Johannine theology, that is the best way of acquiring a better insight into what the New Testament means by its reference to the 'heavenly spheres' and its rejection of 'this world' and its flight from it. The concept of the *cosmos* in John is typical (John 1.9; 3.19; 6.14; 9.39; 10.36; 11.27; 12.46; 16.28; 17.18; 18.37; I John 2.15–17; 4.9); these are all passages in which grace and the world are opposed to each other in some way. 'The world' is in fact a dangerous sphere for Christians. In itself it is ambivalent or ambiguous in a way which is paralleled by wisdom literature before it is combined with apocalyptic. True, this world is created good by God (John 1.10b; see 3.17, 19), but the wise man is very sceptical about a created world in which the light of God's revelation cannot be found (John 1.4; see Prov. 30.1–14; Job 28; Wisdom 7 and 9; the whole of Ecclesiastes/Koheleth). Of himself man has no principles of salvation, no knowledge that goes beyond the boundaries of the world (Wisdom 9.13–17). Man is a being who has a need for the gift of wisdom (Wisdom 7.1f; 10.17; also Qumran: 1 QH 15.21f.). Therefore without the gift of wisdom or revelation the good world of creation lives 'in darkness'; in that case the world becomes *skotia*, darkness (John 1.10), not in the sense of a kind of cosmic power to evil but as creation without illumination. This is an expression of the fact that the creation is not God – an oriental Hellenistic expression for an Old Testament insight of faith which is expressed in the creation narrative (see Sir. 1.9f; 24.6f.; Bar. 3.37; Prov. 8.1; 11.1ff.; also in the non-biblical Jewish literature of the time: I Enoch 93.8; 69.8; 101.8; 11 QPs$^a$XVIII 5f., the Qumran Psalter).[12] In this inter-testamental literature the wisdom tendency is already mixed with apocalyptic, which merely strengthens the connections. Creatures are *not-God*, in the sense that they are not light and therefore already 'darkness'. God is the true reality. In itself the world is without 'revelation' (see John 9.4f.; 11.19f.; cf. 3.19–21). In the first place this is 'a wisdom-type experience of the *transitoriness* 'of this world' and not an evil power. It is also striking that this particular wisdom tradition (which in addition to other influences on John, like apocalyptic and so-called heterodox-Jewish mysticism of the kind that we also find in Qumran, has clearly left its mark on Johannine theology) did not think of demonic powers who led people astray to evil.[13] In contrast to the synoptic tradition, the Gospel of John does not produce any case of demon possession. However, this tradition too is familiar with the devil, 'the prince of this world' (John 12.31; 14.30; 16.11), and I John 5.19 even says, 'The whole (non-Christian) world stands under the evil one'. Still, at least in Johannine theology, the reference is to a sphere not of *power* but of *jurisdiction*; in other words, Satan has a claim to a world which rejects the light, but in this tradition he is not understood as a demonic power which incites men to evil. Therefore Satan is more an image and prototype of unbelief or the rejection of light (John 8.44). By virtue of the fact that Jesus brings light into the world, he deprives Satan of the right to anyone who accepts the light (John 12.31; 14.30; 16.11).

Thus it is the rejection of the light which makes the already finite world a sinful world. For Wisdom from God is continually offered to men, even if they do not accept it (Sir. 24.7; Bar. 3.12f.; 4.1; Prov. 1.24f., 29f., 32; I Enoch 42.1f.; 93.8; 94.5). Finally, Wisdom comes to Israel (Sir. 1.10–20; above all 24.3, 6–8; Baruch 3.36f.; see also I Enoch 42; 11QPs XVIII 20), but 'God's possession', i.e. Israel, is unwilling to accept it (Prov. 1.24f., 29–32; Bar. 3.12f.; 4.1f.; I Enoch 93.8; 94.5).[14] However, there is 'a remnant' which does accept wisdom – or revelation (Wisdom 6.12–16; 7.27f.; 8.21; 9.2, 17; Sir. 24.19–22; 1.10–20; Prov. 8.7–11; I Enoch 5.8). Finally the Wisdom/Logos appears corporeally in the man Jesus. The Christians accept him: they recognize in him the *doxa* or glory of God (prologue to John). As a result there is a renewed opposition in Jesus between 'the world' (unbelief) and 'grace' (belief). Thus from the perspective of the experience of grace with Christ, the world is the dwelling place of men, but a place which is obscured through the sin of man, through his rejection of the 'light from above', above all the light which is Jesus himself (John 3.19; 8.12; 9.5; 12.46).

Nevertheless it is precisely this sinful world which is an object of God's mercy: 'God so loved "the world" ' (John 3.16; also I John 4.9). Jesus is called *sōtēr tou kosmou* (John 4.42; I John 4.14), bringer of salvation for this world although it is under judgment because it persists in evil (John 12.31; 16.11; I Cor. 6.2; 11.32). Hence Johannine theology can also see the world as the dwelling-place of evil desires (I John 2.15–17), the evil world, as an *ethical* opposition to God: good against evil. Thus love of God is contrasted with love of the world, i.e. sin. This is a commonplace theme in earliest Christianity (James 4.4; 1.27; II Peter 1.4; 2.20; I Cor. 5.10; 7.31; Gal. 6.14; Rom. 12.2; Eph. 2.2). In this moral respect the world is the sphere of the jurisdiction of evil (I John 5.19; elsewhere in the New Testament it is the sphere of the power of evil). Because of this relativity – that wordly things (and also the sinful misuse of them) are not God – 'this world' stands under an eschatological proviso, the *hōs mē*: possess the world as though we did not (I Cor. 7.29–31); therefore worldly things may not be the ultimate concern of man under grace. Any ideology which makes the *secular absolute* stands under the religious criticism of grace. That is the reason for the contrast between the first and second aeons, a spatial opposition which is temporal at the same time.

Thus a deeply Christian conception of the world can be found alongside and in these spiritual circumstances. The New Testament makes special reference to the heart of the Jewish experience of Yahweh: 'Be holy as he is . . . for it is written: "Be holy, for I am holy" (Lev. 11.44)' (I Peter 1.14–16). That is, God is not the world and not man: he is the transcendent creator and the one who brings salvation and *precisely for that reason* he is not an outsider for a man in *the* world – ancient man will not say 'in *his* world', for this stands under a non-human alien power which has control of the destiny of man and the world (*heimarmenē*); even for monotheistic Jews (after the exile), 'our' world is rather the sphere of Satan's power (or, in wisdom, of his jurisdiction), and so too it was for Christians: 'the prince of this world'. Because Yahweh, the God of Israel, is holy, so too his people must be holy (Num.15.40; Deut. 7.6; 26.19), i.e. 'set apart' from the non-holy behaviour of the world. The New Testament takes over this concept. The church too is 'separate from the world' (I Peter 1.1), i.e. hallowed (I Peter 1.2; also Acts 9.32; Rom. 1.7; Eph. 1.4; Rev. 5.8), just as Christ is 'the holy one' (I Peter 1.15). 'You are not of the world, just as I am not of the world' (John 17.16) and just as Jesus' kingdom is not of this world' (John 18.36). The nucleus of these state-ments is the religious demand to live in ethical and religious holiness, which can only be experienced as a gift of God, in a world which does not have a use for this holiness. This gives rise to an actual *otherness* of the consistent Christian who does not apply wordly standards, but goes *another way* in the *world*. 'Father, I do not ask that you should take them from the world,' says John 17.15; 'I send them into the world' (John 17.18). For the Gospel of John above all shows how the division between the *epigeia* or earthly and the *epourania* or heavenly has been overcome by Christ. In the appearing of the *heavenly* Son of God, the Son of man, *on earth* in true humanity (*sarx*: John 1.14), the two-level world has been broken through and earthly men have access to God. The world, as standing under the jurisdiction of the 'prince of this world', has been conquered: 'I have overcome the world' (John 16.33c). From now on man can live a moral and religious life *in* the world, thanks to the forgiveness of sins, and that means – in terms of the world-view of the time – living a 'heavenly' life, but *on earth*. In other words, from now on some of the kingdom of God can be realized on earth.

The way in which this freedom and thus this practical otherness is experienced in the face of a sinful, unrighteous and captive world is bound up in the New Testament with the way in which the pagan world lived and is also determined by the historical possibilities open to the Christians of the time.

The critical variant which arose in New Testament Christianity as over against the cultural pessimism of late antiquity, in the search for salvation and happiness in higher spheres, makes it clear that historical circum-stances play their part here. These Christians clearly recognize that the summons 'to live in holiness and first to seek the kingdom of God can mean more than a question of the heart or an inner renewal of life (though the New Testament is often interpreted in terms of the salvation of the individual). In fact, every individual is personally addressed and chal-

lenged,[15] but this appeal to enter the kingdom of God was also concerned
with the creation of a better society *on earth*, a society in which righteousness prevails. In this respect, they had a good understanding of Jesus'
proclamation of the approaching rule of God. But the situation did not
permit this Christian minority group to make any alterations to the social
structure of the time in any way. On the whole, people forget that they
tend to do good where they are most capable of it, that is, within the
local Christian community. They build this up as a new society with just
structures and relationships, in which even the discriminatory distinctions
between man and woman, Jew or non-Jew, slave or free man have to be
overcome. In another, Christian context New Testament Christians practise what had been expected from his Stoic philosophy by Seneca: by
nature our gospel (for Seneca, Stoic philosophy) is relevant to politics
and society, and must become politically effective, except when historical
or particular situations make this impossible. However, where it is possible, it must come about. New Testament Christians really did want to
build up a *new world* in the small society of their own Christian communities. Despite all the tendency towards abstraction in the ancient
world, their critical view of the world and society was not a flight into
higher spheres, but an attempt to give form to the renewal of earthly
society, at least in one place and from one perspective which was accessible to them: among their own Christian members. Precisely because the
secular structures are un-Christian, they cannot be given a place within
the church community. One significant indication of this is Luke 22.25,
which in this respect has a good understanding of the spirit of Jesus'
message about the kingdom of God: 'Jesus said to them, "The kings of
the Gentiles exercise lordship over them, and those in authority over
them are called benefactors. *Hymeis de ouch houtōs*: but not so with you." '
Tormenting and afflicting structures and tyrannical power are not to
prevail in the Christian churches. Beyond question, the New Testament
recognizes that in addition to inner renewal of life, the life-style of the
kingdom of God includes a renewal and improvement of social structures.
These New Testament Christians practised this in the sphere in which
they were really able, in the structuring of their own Christian community, which for that very reason was experienced as part of the already
realized kingdom of God and a 'sitting at the right hand of God with
Christ'; the Christian community is 'the body of Christ', in other words,
the beginning of the realization of the kingdom of God on earth. Just as
the kingdom of God has appeared among us in the person of the man
Jesus, so the incarnation of man must be realized through the life-style
of the kingdom of God. The Christians of the time brought this about by
making a beginning in the church. For these Christians, nothing was
possible outside the church. To conclude from I Peter, we might even

affirm that the awareness of a renewed society *in* the church served *as a paradigm* for what had to happen in the world, since the author says, 'Maintain good conduct among the Gentiles, so that in case they speak against you as wrongdoers, they may see your good deeds and glorify God on the day of visitation' (I Peter 2.12). These Christians criticize the structure of the world, but given the circumstances, they cannot change it; they therefore live alongside pagan society and build up their own new society on the periphery. That this was the only meaningful, historically conditioned possibility at the time for giving form to the life-style of the kingdom of God is perhaps confirmed by the history of the unsuccessful enterprise of the Jewish rebellion and the protest of many Stoic philosophers, which was steeped in blood. However, it might be objected: is this public silence not complicity? Did Jesus keep silent? Jesus spoke out against all this and had to pay for it with his blood. Was that senseless and vain? Other ways were evidently open than those taken by the New Testament church, ways which, however, people knew in advance to be barred with bloodshed. However, might we not compare this ancient situation with similar modern situations, in which stubborn public resistance in the end gains the victory: 'We shall overcome'? Moreover, did not these Christians really, in their own way, follow this very course, as emerges from the bloody persecutions of the church? They refused to bow the knee to political power which gave religious sanction to its injustice by appealing to its sacralism. In fact, given the situation, these communities were 'subversive' religious groups, though they were characterized by a quite deliberate restraint because the resistance of the Zealots was historically senseless, and moreover because, inspired by Jesus, they saw no salvation in bloody violence, which did not seem to them to be the style of the kingdom of God. However, it must be conceded that the New Testament Christians had little feeling for the possibility of a secular humanist inspiration. 'Being a Christian' was contrasted with 'sinfulness', above all in the sense of 'atheism' (in the ancient sense); that is, not recognizing what Gentiles, Jews or Christians acknowledge to be the *true* God (see Eph. 2.1–3; 2.11f.; 'without God in the world').

The New Testament unmistakably impresses on us that the exodus character is an essential characteristic of the Jewish-Christian community. The form that this exodus has to take must continually be decided afresh within historical circumstances in Christian freedom. That is the *model* which the New Testament gives us for the building up of Christian communities in the world and for the forming of a better society. In reality the Christian Bible in practice already recognizes the Vatican principle: the church *is* (a performative 'is', i.e. must be) *sacramentum mundi*, a paradigmatic instrument in the unification and pacification of the world (we have seen that Ephesians in particular stresses this aspect). Here, despite the difference between God and the world of men, we are in no way tied to the apocalyptic, Middle-Platonic and ancient forms of a two-storey universe with its two levels, nor even to the many hyperbolic statements which are intrinsically bound up with it in the New Testament. But the same exodus idea must also find specific form in other historical circumstances as a consequence of a renewed, and yet abiding, eschatologically oriented experience of grace, in any community which in the future wants to call itself a Christian 'community of God'. New Testament Christianity can only be a model indirectly, and not directly. In an analysis of historical circumstances, the eschatological proviso expressed here is normative: the final consummation of the life of grace does not belong to this world, but *in our history* in every person and the whole of society, grace must find a recognizable content of salvation in continually new forms. In present-day situations, that implies that this attempt by Christians will recognize the historical circumstance of a pluralist society and that it does not have a monopoly in improving the world and caring for our human future; moreover, that this Christian attempt will lose credibility if this 'newness', 'freedom' and 'righteousness' does not prevail in the Christian churches.

Chapter 3

# The New Testament experience of grace and social structures

Inspired by the gracious experience of salvation with Jesus Christ, the New Testament Christian communities seek to organize themselves as a new society, *in* but *alongside* society or the non-Christian world. Here these Christians must be ready (over against this world) 'to give account of the hope that lives in them' (I Peter 3.15b), a hope which drove the Christians to a life-style so different from public (pagan) life. So we cannot assume that New Testament Christianity set itself apart from structural changes for the good or regarded these as secondary. Christians did what they could where they could, in building up Christian society, the community, in accordance with the norms of the coming kingdom of God. Many Christians wrongly assert that the New Testament is fundamentally uninterested in structures, and then go on, equally wrongly, to offer a theological justification for this attitude by claiming that it is a biblical demand. In that case they forget to analyse how this particular attitude of New Testament Christianity was communicated *in historical terms*. Jesus and Christianity seem to find structures unimportant because salvation and the message of the rule of God is really only an appeal to the heart, to the human person: an inner *metanoia*. It is taken for granted that salvation also includes an inner renewal of life as its consequence. In that case, however, why do New Testament Christians build up a 'new society', at least in their own communities? Why do they form a society which is not dominated by secular, unjust power structures? They do not in any way look on salvation in private and individualistic terms; in fact they look for a better world and a new society in which righteousness dwells. Thus the problem lies neither in a so-called New Testament type conception of salvation, nor even in a predilection for inner renewal of life and a relativization of the structural problems connected with it. In the New Testament, both the person and the structures are subject to the demand for repentance which is provoked by grace. The problem simply lies in the fact that these churches could realize this renewal of the person and the structures only within the church and 'on the periphery' of a wider society. Once again, this was a historically conditioned, specific choice or decision, if it is possible to speak of a real choice at all! As a minority group in the powerful Hellenistic Roman empire, the church had very few possibilities at its disposal. It is often objected that whereas, say, Spartacus led a slave rebellion, Christians – like the élitist Stoics, who were also critical of society – allowed slavery to continue, but this seems to me to be a piece of sophistry. The rebellion of Spartacus was born of a collective experience of contrast which inevitably led to an explosion. The slave status of Jews and Christians, who to begin with attracted many members of the lowest strata of the population, including numerous slaves, can hardly be compared with the slavery which Spartacus experienced. He was not concerned to break out of 'the status of a slave', but rather rebelled against quite specific and inhuman exploitation and torture.

The tendency of some Christians and theologians to make religion simply a matter of the heart cannot be based on the New Testament; furthermore, it presupposes a false philosophical personalism which *contrasts* the personal dimension with structures and the institution. It is a matter of course that the Christian message is directed to persons (to whom else would a message be sent?). But a man achieves his identity as a person also through the mediation of historical institutions on the basis of an anthropological constant: *identity* is fully realized only through the mutual confirmation of *person* and *institution* or through social consensus. The ancient world knew nothing of the modern, personalist dilemma which contrasts the person and the institution, nor did it recognize the priority of the personal sphere and hence the purely secondary significance of the institutional element in human life. For that very reason, the New Testament Christians understand the summons to *metanoia* or repentance as an implication of the coming of the kingdom of God, not simply as a mere internal renewal of life but also as a socio-political alteration in the structure of society. However, as we have already said, they do this only *within* the community of God, to which they give just structures with the norm of the kingdom of God in mind. The New Testament was not concerned with the dilemma of 'person' (heart) or structure, which in that case would be of secondary significance; it was concerned that the structure of a better world and a new society should be realized *alongside* the greater society in the 'enclosed garden' of the church communities. Relevant though it is for the New Testament, this distinction is hardly made in present-day exegesis (though it must be conceded that that the New Testament sometimes has a tendency to provide a theological support for particular situations). This is not to deny that the message and the reality of the coming kingdom of God – grace – also has a political and social significance. Only *the way in which* these Christians wanted to renew society is historically conditioned. Thus the New Testament indeed connects expectations, inspiration and orientation for the renewal of the social and political structure of our world with the gracious appearance of Jesus Christ. However, because of the historical situation, these begin only in the dimension of the church community. The church community is seen and constructed as part of wider society, whose structures and relationships are measured by the norm of the kingdom of God and realized according to the norm of the kingdom of God, 'the new heaven and the new earth, where righteousness will dwell' (II Peter 3.13). In that case we may also claim that (as a result of historical influence and thus indirectly) there is a biblical foundation for the fact that in other historical circumstances (above all when Christianity grows beyond the boundaries of its insignificant minority grouping) the essential relationships between grace and politics, between the Christian message and the improvement of the world, include the historical demand that this shall be realized not only in the church community but also in the world itself.

It may be asked whether in the New Testament there are already symptoms of this inner, ongoing dynamic as a consequence of the connection, so essential for these Christians, between grace as the renewal of life and grace as the improvement of social structures – an inner connection which in new socio-historical conditions also calls for a change in civil and social structures. The only text which seems to me to be primarily concerned with this is Paul's brief letter to Philemon.

Onesimus (a typical Greek slave's name, 'ready for service'), the slave of a well-to-do man named Philemon whom Paul had converted to Christianity and in whose house a Christian community gathered together for worship (Philemon 2), had (as often happened) run away from his master. Runaway slaves began to live the life of vagabonds, but could be searched for on the basis of an official notification. In some way that we do not know about, this slave came into contact with Paul, who was in prison (in Ephesus?). (At that time slaves had a right to asylum with certain recognized Roman citizens.). Under Paul's influence, Onesimus became a Christian. Paul, always a sick man, and getting older, would very much have liked to have kept Onesimus with him (slaves often wrote down letters that were dictated to them). However, Paul recognizes the civil rights of Philemon to his slave or house servant. For this reason he returns the slave to his master with an accompanying letter. In this letter, brother Philemon (Philemon 7) is first thanked for all that he does for the community. Paul then comes to the point.

He gives Philemon to understand that by virtue of his apostolic authority he could really compel him to release the slave. However, Paul prefers to forego this right and to appeal to Philemon's Christianity (8–9). For in the meantime the slave Onesimus has become a Christian, and therefore 'a beloved brother' (16). For that reason Philemon, too, must greet this slave 'as a man and a Christian' (16b), and even treat him as though he were meeting Paul, his good friend (17). If the running away of the slave has damaged his master in any way, Paul himself will make good financially the damage that has ensued (18). In fact this is only meant rhetorically (19), but Paul wants to make this brief comment to show Philemon that he is concerned about this Onesimus. Paul expressed his firm hope that the master will do more than is expected of him (21). In other words, Paul hopes that Philemon will not only greet the slave as a fellow-man and a Christian, but in addition will declare him to be a *socially* free man. He hopes that Philemon will draw the necessary civil consequences from the fact that this slave has become a 'free Christian' and that in Christianity the difference between slave and free man has been done away with.

At first reading, this seems to be in the intention of the whole letter – as indeed it is. However, the difficulty of this interpretation lies, on second reading, in the fact that in this instance Paul is not concerned with *any matters of principle*. His specific concern is really as follows: Paul has become attached to the young man and the feeling is mutual. Paul would very gladly keep Onesimus as his helper, but in view of Philemon's rights he is unable to (though in the background he threatens Philemon somewhat with his apostolic authority). Verses 13f. and 19f. therefore make it difficult to see the letter as one that raises a matter of principle. In that case it becomes only an occasional piece in which Paul wants to 'detach' a slave from his master with a good deal of diplomacy and 'for a good cause'. At all events, albeit for 'his own advantage', namely as a help in his apostolic work, *by referring to Christian principles* he also tries to make his fellow Christian Philemon free the slave in social terms. This is not to deny the master's rights of 'ownership' of the slave, as they were recognized at the time, though at least in *this* case (and therefore in not particularly 'harmless' circumstances) this right is devalued by the Christian conception that within the church there should be no discrimination between slave and free.

In another passage, however, neither Paul nor the Pauline school draws this fundamental consequence. Paul indeed even contradicts it emphatically: 'Were you a slave when you were called? Never mind. Even if you can gain your freedom, prefer to remain a slave. For he who was called in the Lord as a slave is a freedman of the Lord' (I Cor. 7.21f.) Here Paul speaks on the basis of a Christianized Stoic concept of inner freedom (like Sartre in what was originally a purely personalist concept of freedom: the inwardly free man is sovereignly free, even when he is caught up in external slavery). Therefore in principle Paul does not in any way draw civil and social conclusions from what in his view is an essential attitude for the government of the church. I would therefore prefer to see Paul's letter to Philemon as a 'business arrangement' between two Christians and (unfortunately) not as a discussion of Christian principles.

However, we should not minimize the honest concern to do away with all discrimination *within* the church community. In the church community slaves become free men (some of them even become bishops and popes). In the long run, as a result of historical circumstances, this social renewal within the church will also have outward consequences. Grace has political and social consequences (even if often this Christian stimulus is seen as socialized in culture, i.e. as *secularization* in culture, and is often brought to its social conclusions by non-Christians; that simply means that in the long run Christian redemption is also 'secularized', i.e. becomes an inner mainspring of the *saeculum* or is socialized).

In the meantime, however, the New Testament churches, including Paul's own, accepted the civil status of the legal relationship between slave and master which prevailed outside the churches. However, they did so only with a proviso which was significant for that time. The pagan ethical codes of the time (the 'house tables') are constantly concerned with the prevailing ethical norms between man and woman, authorities and citizens, and so on, but never with the ethical rules about the relationship of the master at least towards his *own* slaves. Here the master evidently had absolute rights. To all these valid ethical norms – to be applied 'in the Lord' – the New Testament regularly adds the ethical rule about the relationship of the slave to his *own* master, and vice versa

(Eph. 6.5–8; Col. 3.22–25; I Tim. 1; I Peter 2.18–25). From a purely social point of view, in itself this is already a new view of slavery. A subordinate relationship is assumed (obedience, authority), but the more painful side of this relationship must be mitigated by Christian love, both from the side of the master (if he is a Christian) and from the side of the slave. I Peter in particular is typical here of New Testament Christianity in recognizing that there are also unreasonable and unjust people who are the masters of slaves. The author is discussing the social suffering of slaves (I Peter 2.18–25); and he means *unmerited* suffering, at the hands of difficult masters, of slaves who have become Christians (2.18, 20). As in general (see 2.21–25; 4.14; 4.16, 19; 3.14; 3.17), so in this particular instance innocent suffering (see 4.19), 'suffering for righteousness' sake' (3.14) or 'suffering for the good' (3.17) is seen in the light of Jesus' example (2.21–25). The author calls 'suffering with God in view' a *charis* (2.19). The Greek text runs: *Touto gar charis ei dia syneidēsin Theou hypopherei tis lypas, paschōn adikōs.*' Merited suffering is nothing special, but 'to have to suffer for good deeds, that is well pleasing to God' (2.20c). Thus *charis* here is not used in the sense of 'grace', but in the sense of the Hebrew *ḥēn* (see above). As such, this term has no 'theological' significance. In antiquity the slave was his master's property, so that the master could never (according to this view) treat his *own* slave unjustly (though this is a qualification). This interpretation of *charis* (as *ḥēn*) *refuses* to see unmerited suffering, in this case of a slave, as a 'gift of God' *(charis* in the New Testament technical sense, which is the way in which some exegetes interpret this text from I Peter). It is, however, said that unmerited suffering with God in view is acceptable to him and is looked upon by him with favour – which indicates a very different attitude towards this suffering from the one that is condemned as being negative. The author says that Jesus, too, 'entrusted his cause to the one who judges justly' (I Peter 2.23). *This* suffering is in no way regarded as the gift of God: on the contrary, God's condemnation threatens those who impose this suffering. However, the author says, with a reference to God's sovereignty as creator, that God 'only allows' this suffering (4.19). Therefore innocent sufferers, in this case slaves, must 'entrust themselves to their Creator' (4.19b). But despite all the social criticism contained in it, the New Testament nowhere talks of social and political resistance against secular structures which in fact cause this innocent suffering – though it is condemned in the New Testament. It simply asks that such structures should not be found within the church. This as it were 'double' attitude is characteristic of New Testament Christianity as a whole: (*a*) things must not be like this in a society ruled by Jesus Christ, i.e. in the Christian churches; (*b*) in the world outside the churches these laws may apply in reality, but first-century Christians could do nothing to change them.

This latter feature characterizes the situation and thus in no way implies that Christians are uninterested in structures and institutional problems. Here we have an expression both of the permanent and normative Christian uniqueness of the New Testament experience of grace and also of the historically conditioned form (which is changeable and therefore always subject to change) in which Christians give their experience of grace concrete expression in respect of the structures given in society. The specific ethical form of the time certainly cannot be regarded as a norm for Christian life; it is a possibility determined by the situation, limited, understandable and perhaps even the only possibility in the situation of the time. As such it is a genuinely Christian attitude. However, it cannot serve directly as a norm for Christian options in completely different historical situations. The New Testament norm and orientation which can also be found in it for present-day Christians lies in the fact that in other historical circumstances the same Christian conception of grace can also direct and stimulate quite different Christian options – in view of a different historical situation with different specific features, both in the 'world' and in the 'church'. It may even happen that because of our historical situation this may become a Christian demand for our experience of grace. A Christianity which (in its official status) cannot in any way be termed sociologically a *'quantité négligeable'* in our contemporary world, however much the Christian community may be turning increasingly into a diaspora church, can play an active role as a 'cognitive minority'. In this respect it will be following the inspiration and the orientation of the New Testament.

Chapter 4

# The life of grace and political power in the New Testament

*Literature*: J. Blank, *Schriftauslegung in Theorie und Praxis*, Munich 1969, 174–86; S. G. F. Brandon, *Jesus and the Zealots, A Study of the Political Factor in Primitive Christianity*, Manchester 1967; O. Cullmann, *Jesus and the Revolutionaries*, ET New York 1970; id., *The State in the New Testament*, London 1957; P. J. Farla, *Het oordeel over Israël. Een Form- en Redaktions-geschichtliche Analyse van Mc.10,46- 12,40* (Dissertation, Nijmegen); G. Friedrich, *Utopie und Reich Gottes. Zur Motivation Politischen Verhaltens*, Göttingen

1974; E. Grässer, 'Der politisch gekreuzigte Christus', in *Text und Situation, Gesammelte Aufsätze zum Neuen Testament,* Gütersloh 1973, 302–30; M. Hengel, *Was Jesus a Revolutionist?* ET Philadelphia 1977; id., *Victory over Violence: Jesus and the Revolutionists,* ET Philadelphia 1973, London 1975; id., *Die Zeloten. Untersuchungen zur jüdischen Freiheitsbewegung in der Zeit von Herodes I bis 70 n.c.,* Leiden-Köln 1961; A. Hertz, E. Iserloh, G. Klein, J.-B. Metz and W. Pannenberg, *Gottesreich und Menschenreich. Ihr Spannungsverhältnis in Geschichte und Gegenwart,* Regensburg 1970; E. Käsemann, 'Was Jesus a "liberal"?', in *Jesus Means Freedom,* ET London and Philadelphia 1969, 16–41; H. M. Kepplinger, *Rechte Leute von links. Gewaltkult und Innerlichkeit,* Olten-Freiburg 1970; G. Kittel, 'Das Urteil des Neuen Testaments über den Staat', *ZST* 14, 1937, 651–80; H. W. Kuhn, 'Jesus als Gekreuzigter in der frühchristlichen Verkündigung bis zur Mitte des 2. Jahrhunderts', *ZTK* 72, 1975, 1–46; H. Kuitert, *Om en Om,* Kampen 1972, esp. 137–57; G. Petzke, 'Der historische Jesus in der sozialethischen Diskussion. Mk. 12, 13–17 par', in *Jesus Christus in Historie und Theologie,* ed. G. Strecker, Tübingen 1975, 223–35; H. Schlier, 'Der Staat nach dem NT', in *Besinnung auf das NT,* Freiburg 1964, 193–211; id., *Mächte und Gewalten im NT,* Freiburg 1958; L. Schottroff, 'Gewaltverzicht und Feindesliebe in der ursprüngliche Jesustradition, Mt 5, 28–48; Lk 6, 27–36', in *Jesus Christus in Historie und Theologie,* Tübingen 1975, 197–221; R. Schnackenburg, *Die sittliche Botschaft des Neuen Testaments,* Munich 1962, 88ff.; W. Schrage, *Die Christen und der Staat nach dem Neuen Testament,* Gütersloh 1971; G. N. Sevenster, 'Geeft den Keizer, wat des Keizer's is, en Gode, wat Godes is', *NTT* 17, 1962, 21–31; E. Stauffer, 'The Story of the Tribute Money', in *Christ and the Caesars,* ET London 1955, 112–37; A. Strobel, 'Zum Verständnis von Rom. 13', *ZNW* 47, 1956, 67–93; G. H. ter Schegget, *Het lied van de Mensenzoon,* Baarn 1975; A. Wlosok, *Rom und die Christen,* Stuttgart 1970.

Those Christians who favour liberation theology or political theology, or are generally critical of society, tend to call the biblical Christ *political*, whereas churches who want to adopt an apolitical or even neutral attitude find arguments in the New Testament for ascribing an apolitical attitude to Jesus. In both instances people put theological questions to the Bible in the light of a particular option which is already given, without making any analysis of historical conditions. The problem is often posed by theologians when they discuss the question of the political significance of the execution of Jesus on the cross. Exegetes may be said to be generally agreed that as far as the Romans were concerned this was a political execution. For some authors, however, it was a historical error;[16] in other words, the unpolitical life of Jesus came to a political end because of a historical error. On the other hand, other authors assert that the political crucifixion of Jesus was an inner consequence of his ministry, which from the beginning needs to be understood in political terms.[17]

It is striking that both approaches put their questions to the New Testament with a specific interest; some because they adopt the standpoint that the church today must take an unpolitical or a politically neutral stance (the church must stand 'between the fronts'),[18] while others want to ground their political theology on the Bible. Both positions seem to me to be a kind of fundamentalism – to the left or to the right; they forget to analyse historical conditions. This is not a fruitful way of putting the question; we cannot make progress as long as we are not clear about *why* this question is being put. If one wants to use it as a standard for one's own political position, the question immediately loses significance. Jesus was not a democrat! The question does not make sense if we seek to use it to solve the specific problem of our present attitudes for or against participation in revolutionary movements (i.e., the problem must be solved in other ways). They recognize in Jesus something that inspires them (for example pacifism or resistance). However, 'people try to use the question whether Jesus was a Zealot to answer quite a different question', namely what our attitude should be to the problems of institutions and structures.[19] On the other hand, Oscar Cullmann says that Jesus' expectation of an imminent end to the world was responsible for his lack of interest in structures and the institutional side of human life, whereas we no longer have this expectation. In that case the conclusion might be that the institutional side is indeed important. However, Cullmann does not draw this conclusion: the heart of faith remains a personal matter, a question of the heart. This approach to the problem has a twofold basis. Zealots are then people who in the first place want to overthrow institutions and structures, which is a matter of being a resistance fighter. The assumption is that even at that time there was already our distinction between person and structure. Why are O. Cullmann, M. Hengel and E. Grässer so interested in trying to show that Jesus was not a revolutionary? Even if he were not, that does not mean that a Christian today may not and sometimes even must not be a revolutionary now! We have a reason for putting questions to history. They are 'prejudiced'; we want to justify our own political decision by them and to condemn that of others.

Still, the question of Jesus' attitude to politics remains historically legitimate. In that case, however, we also have to investigate the question why the New Testament churches were so interested in showing Jesus to be 'politically innocuous'. For these Christians had every interest in depicting Christian faith in such a way that it also allowed a loyal attitude towards the pagan authorities, as long as these did not require Christians to recognize the sacrality of the political authorities. For it is striking that the New Testament enjoins Christians to be loyal to the authority and pray for those who hold secular office: '*that* we may lead a quiet and peacable life, godly and respectful in every way' (I Tim. 2.1f.). A concern to avoid the persecution of Christians is in any case one of the reasons why the New Testament is inclined to 'paint over' political aspects in the life of Jesus. Brandon's interpretation of Jesus as a political Zealot may be wrong, but his analysis of the tendency of the New Testament authors to make Jesus apolitical to avoid giving any occasion for reactions from the pagan authorities is indisputably correct.[20] Both the analysis of the passion narrative in the four gospels and the fourfold account of John the Baptist show that Jesus is increasingly presented as an apolitical, peaceful 'king of the Jews'. Luke 23.2 mentions a tradition according to which Jesus evidently did not want to pay any tax; Mark 12.13–17 either knows nothing of this or keeps quiet about it. For the Romans, from AD 66 onwards, 'Jews' had been almost synonymous with zealots, the 'robbers' – as they said – who had plotted a rebellion against Rome. In Rome it was well known that Christianity derived from Judaism.[21] Consequently there was in the Roman empire also a tendency to connect Christianity, at least after 66–70, with the Jewish Zealots, and there is an attempt especially in Mark (above all if he is writing his gospel for Christians in Rome) to depict Christianity and the Zealots as two completely different movements. Mark even deletes the Zealot-type name of one of Jesus' disciples, Simon (and transcribes it into the Greek consonants of this Zealot name, Kananaios, which would be incomprehensible to Romans). Mark attempts to disguise the fact that Jesus was executed by the Romans. What was a reputable death for Palestinian-Jewish Christians (a martyr's death, as a result of opposing the military occupation) was less so for Christians from the Gentile world. Mark therefore gives a new interpretation to the death of Jesus and puts the blame chiefly on the Jewish authorities; he builds up towards this from Mark 3.6 on. Pilate is compelled by the Jews to condemn Jesus (15.10f.). Following his source (which comes from Palestine), John has Jesus arrested by the Romans (John 18.12); in Mark Jesus is arrested 'like a thief' (Mark 14.48) by representatives of the Jewish authorities (Mark 14.43). Mark gives a new interpretation to the tradition: the Roman Pilate finds him innocent and wants to save him through the expedient of 'Barabbas'. It cannot be denied that the Gospel of Mark has a tendency to make Jesus an apolitical, even almost a pro-Roman pacifist (however, in that case we still do not know what Jesus' political attitude really was). Furthermore, it is not improbable that as one manuscript mentions *Jesus* Barabbas (Matt. 27.16f.: *Jēsous, ho legomenos Barabbas*), there were groups among the Romans who associated Jesus of Nazareth with a popular Jewish rebel leader. Mark wants to clear Jesus completely of any suspicion of Zealotism in the eyes of his readers. It is this particular tendency which makes it impossible for us to pass historical judgment on the real reason why Jesus was crucified by the Romans, though Roman crucifixion was clearly a political action. For Mark, the Pharisees are in fact the exponents of everything that the Gentiles found remarkable in Judaism; in his gospel they are therefore the enemies of Jesus *par excellence*. They join in a plot with the Herodians in an attempt to lure Jesus into a trap, in connection with the delicate question of paying tax to the Romans (Mark 12.13–17). But Jesus is a loyal subject (12.17). Mark seeks to detach Jesus from his historical context in Judaism; it is therefore a Gentile who for the first time expresses the official confession of faith: 'This man is truly the Son of God' (Mark 15.39; see 1.24–34; 3.11f.). In fact the Gospel of Mark represents a break with early Palestinian Christianity which had perhaps sought refuge in Transjordania and Egypt, whereas Pauline Christianity was predominant in Syria, Asia Minor and Greece. Mark also wants to impress upon his readers that blood relationships are irrelevant (3.20–30; 3.31–35), that Jesus was not accepted by his own family, indeed that they even said that he was mad (3.21; 3.31–35; 6.1–6). His 'Davidic origin', at least in a nationalist political sense, is a fantasy (12.35–37; see also 15.1f.; 15.31f.). Jesus is the break with Judaism: one can hardly deny that this is a tendency in Mark. Peter indeed recognizes Jesus as Messiah, but to begin with does not understand the Pauline doctrine of the saving significance of the death of Jesus (Mark 8.31f.). Mark gives the impression that while Palestinian Christianity, the Twelve, recognized Jesus as the one Messiah, it was incapable of accepting the Pauline conception of the soteriological value of the death of Jesus. In other words, Mark sets out to fill in the gaps in the Palestinian christology. At his death, Jesus is recognized to be Son of God by the confession of a *Gentile*, while in Jerusalem the curtain of the Temple is split in half; Christianity replaces Judaism, and therefore Jesus is detached from the concrete political context in which the Jewish people must have been situated, above all from 66–72 in the eyes of the Gentiles, and also for Jews outside Palestine.[22] All this indicates that (contrary to the prevailing view) Mark was only written after AD 70 and evidently *presupposes* that Judaism and rebellion against Rome are connected in the eyes of the Gentiles. Luke (both Gospel and Acts) says nothing about the church in Egypt and Alexandria (for a long time the sanctuary for Jews), i.e. about the Palestinian christology which continues to flourish there. The Christians had learned from the events of 66–70 that they had to behave as loyal subjects of Rome if they were to survive. 'He who is not against us is for us,' says Mark 9.40. When at a later stage the Christians themselves suffered severe persecutions and new ones threatened, the book of Revelation by contrast depicted Jesus as a fearful rider on a white horse, 'with eyes like fire, with blood-stained garments'; he was called 'the sword of God', and he sought to rule over all the nations with an iron rod; on his robes were written: 'King of kings and Lord of lords' (Rev. 19.12ff.), and he led the fight against Rome's bloody subjection.

It emerges from this that to begin with the New Testament had an apologetic interest in depicting Jesus as an apolitical figure, whereas Revelation sees him as the great eschatological fighter against unjust political powers. This does not yet mean that the New Testament deprives a political Jesus of political significance; it does, however, mean that it removed from the life of Jesus all those elements which might prove unacceptable to the Romans – certainly insofar as they would have given occasion to make a connection between Christianity and the events of 66–77 – in order to avoid a persecution of the church.

In antiquity, religion and the state formed an indissoluble unity; religion was the fundamental form of society. Worship of the gods stood at the head of the catalogue of civic virtues, since the well-being of the state (*salus reipublicae*) was dependent on the gods of the state. In this sense there was an identity between the state and religion, The same thing was true of theocratic Judaism, albeit in terms of Yahwistic belief.

However, with the rise of Christianity, this became a problem for Christians. A dualism developed, with the Christian community on one hand and political power on the other (the alien state with its integration by means of pagan religion). Furthermore, the authorities very quickly became anti-Christian. This gave rise to the dialectic between Christian faith and politics. Does the Christian experience of salvation in Jesus provide a perspective on this? It is striking that in Paul's well-known discussion (Rom. 13.1–7), there is no reference at all to christology. The particular attitude which Paul advises Christians to adopt towards (pagan) political power is not based on Christ or the message of the gospel, but draws its nourishment from other sources (see below). Furthermore, it is striking that Paul asks for loyalty towards the political powers 'for the sake of a good conscience' (Rom. 13.5). Thus he expressly raises the matter to an ethical level, without making any connection between the gospel and politics; Paul is concerned as it were with an autonomous ethical problem. The situation hardly allows anything else. So at this point we are particularly involved in the historical situation, before we can speak of the biblical understanding of political power.

What is Paul's view in this connection? He speaks of *archai kai exousiai* (Rom. 13.1), Hellenistic designations on the one hand of the higher and indeed supreme authority (*archai*: in Latin *imperia*), and on the other hand of the imperial authorities (*exousiai:* Latin *potestates* or *magistratus*).[23] Furthermore, the following technical terms occur in this pericope: the reference to the *agathon* ('the good') with which Paul begins the paraenetic section of his letter (Rom. 12.2; repeated a number of times in 13.1–7, which are concerned with political power); this is evidently meant in the sense of *kalokagathia*, i.e. the Graeco-Roman expression for public civic virtue. Paul also mentions direct tax (*phoros*) and indirect tax or toll (*telos*) (Rom. 13.6f.). *Leitourgos* (13.6) is a generic designation for someone who holds office in the Roman empire.

Paul begins his argument with the assertion that 'all authority comes from God': 'the powers that be are ordained by God' (Rom. 13.1: this is the view of Diaspora Judaism, see below; with considerable irony, Rev. 13.2, 4 will say that the authority of the Roman state comes from Satan). Therefore according to Paul, to oppose existing authority after the fashion of the Zealots is an offence against God. Those who hold state authority, government officials, are *'leitourgoi*, servants of God for your good' (13.4, 6). This ethical demand is given theological (rather than christological) backing (the deutero-Pauline epistles will add 'in the Lord'). Therefore the civil authorities are the guardians of the 'ordinances of God', and according to Paul the state is a divine institution. By this he means the pagan Roman empire (*hai de ousai exousiai*: the authority which *happens to be in existence* at present, and for many Christians outside Rome in fact an occupying power, Rom. 13.1c). Paul himself is a Roman citizen and is moreover a Diaspora Jew: two aspects which in themselves imply a loyal public attitude towards Rome. Because of widespread anti-semitism, Jews from the Diaspora in particular were greatly indebted to Roman imperial protection (Paul himself will appeal to the emperor, which will save him from the worst). The theologizing (all authority comes from God) is a theory which developed in Diaspora Judaism.

Some six centuries before, the problem of the relationship between synagogue and state had already arisen in these circles, since Judaism was not the universal religion of the empire. In the Babylonian exile the problem began to become urgent: Yahweh, the God of Israel, along with Israel, was subjected to alien gods. The prophets sought to give consolation and encouragement in this crisis of faith, Jeremiah above all: 'Thus says the Lord: . . . to all the exiles whom *I have sent into exile from Jerusalem to Babylon*: Build houses and live in them; plant gardens and eat their produce. Take wives and have sons and daughters . . . multiply there, and do not decrease. But seek the welfare of the city . . . and *pray* to the Lord *on its behalf*, for in its welfare you will find your welfare . . . I know the plans I have for you . . . plans for welfare and not for evil, to give you a future and a hope . . . I will restore your fortunes and gather you from all the nations and all the places where I have driven them – thus says the Lord' (Jer. 29.1–22). 'Yahweh, the Lord of hosts, the God of Israel', is the deliberate beginning. According to this view Yahweh extended his sphere of influence beyond Israel and Judah. Jeremiah asks the exiles to be prepared for a long absence and thus combats unrealistic, foolish dreams of an imminent return (Jer. 29.8). The prosperity of Babylon is to the exiles' advantage. Thus here for the first time there appears the prayer of the community of faith for the *res publica* in a new situation, namely in the situation of a *disjunction* between the *community of faith* and *political power*. In this way there arose the problem of the relationship between Jewish belief in God and political power. Jeremiah, and above all Ezekiel, the great religious leader of the exiles, give a first answer to this new problem: in this historical situation Ezekiel points to the necessity of an inner renewal of Israel's life as a believing community, which in that case, however, takes on the features of a ghetto community with a new form of religious practice, set aside from the world, namely the liturgical services of the synagogue, along with a kind of canonical legal ordering within the community (a situation which has much in common with the New Testament churches). Deutero-Isaiah (above all Isa. 40–55) goes more deeply into the problem. As a prophet of salvation he has a more positive view of the Gentile political power. He calls the Persian King Cyrus 'Christ' in the positive sense, an anointed of God (45.1), a king, a medium of salvation in God's hand (Isa. 44.24–28; 45.1–7). Paul's concept of the imperial powers that be as the 'servant of God' is thus already to be found here.[24] However, Cyrus is an instrument of salvation in God's hands for the sake of Israel and Israel alone. In other words, political power itself is not given any religious significance. The Persian government, which to begin with was very well-disposed towards the Jews, gave these prophets a positive attitude towards political power and led to 'collaboration'. In particular, Ezra, the official at the Persian court responsible for Jewish affairs, was sent to Jerusalem to regulate the relationship between the believing community and the political power 'in accordance with the laws of the Jews' (Ezra 7). It was precisely in this struggle to grasp the relationship between belief in Yahweh and political power that there developed among the Jews of the Diaspora the concept of Israel as the light of the world, *lumen Gentium* (Isa. 42.1–7).

The relationship between belief in God and political power is given a central significance in apocalyptic, above all in the Palestinian book of Daniel (in which contemporary situations are projected back into the time of the exile – it emerges from this that the author is taking up a Diaspora problem of the time). The Jew Daniel is very highly respected at the Babylonian court, yet nevertheless remains faithful to his ancestral beliefs. In him, Jewish wisdom surpasses Chaldaean wisdom. The God Yahweh stands above the four world empires (Dan. 2.20–22). And in Dan. 2.37 the principle is formulated that all authority comes from Yahweh: 'You, O king, the king of kings, to whom the God of heaven has given the kingdom, the power, and the might, and the glory.' But this power of the state has its limits (the three young men in the burning fiery furnace), for a *cult* of the authorities is an offence against belief in Yahweh (Dan. 3.16–18). The pagan authorities may require everything of their Jewish subjects, as long as it is not an offence against Jewish faith; when that happens, resistance is made to the point of death (as under Antiochus IV). Wisdom 6.3. puts it in the same way: 'Listen, O kings . . . for your dominion was given you from the Lord, and your sovereignty from the Most High'. 'All authority comes from God' is thus simply an expression of Yahwistic belief in only one God, the God of Israel, and is thus meant to put the non-Jewish authorities also under the threat of Yahweh's judgment. Their authority is subject to ethical norms. By virtue of this loyal attitude of the Diaspora Jews, Judaism in the Roman empire acquired the rights of a *religio licita*; it was protected by the state. After the year AD 70, the community prayer '*Domine, salvum fac regem*' became a rabbinic precept. The Diaspora Jews had set themselves apart from the Palestinian Zealots and the priestly resistance fighters.

Thus Paul's comments in Rom. 13.1–7 are simply the tradition of Diaspora Judaism, which is continued in the church (that is why there are no christological elements throughout the pericope). Above all when the Christians had withdrawn from the synagogue or had been exiled from it, the Christian community had lost almost all its rights – 'strangers and pilgrims' – in the great empire. However, in their attitude to the empire, the Christians took over the spiritual legacy of the Diaspora Jews. The community ordered itself in accordance with internal Christian jurisdiction (church order: see e.g. I Cor. 5 and 6), in which it was directed by models from Diaspora Judaism; and as a community its relationship to Gentile political power consisted: (*a*) in a relationship of civic loyalty; (*b*) in passive but stubborn resistance under persecution; (*c*) in all other respects in a positive observance of civic obligations (tax, excise, etc.), and later even in positive collaboration with state affairs. Political power was completely desacralized, but for Paul's Christian faith, the imperial powers are a 'divine ordinance'. At the same time this implies that Christians cannot claim any special rights in the state by virtue of their belief; they are just members of the state like everyone else. 'For the sake of a good conscience' (Rom. 13.5) and not for fear of punishment they must fulfil their civic duties; thus Paul sees this as an ethical question. In addition there is the *Christian* duty – Paul calls it 'a debt (of Christians)' – of mutual love, but this is not a civic duty as such (Rom. 13.8). Christians have a debt of love to the world.

We find the same attitude with a number of nuances in other passages in the New Testament. However, church persecutions threatening and already existing result in a sharper tone. Thus I Peter is more critical of pagan political power than Paul. For this letter the state is 'a human institution'; the author calls it a 'product' (*ktisis*, I Peter 2.13, though the use of the word *ktisis*, creation, is in some respects reminiscent of what Paul calls an 'ordinance of God'). Where Paul simply spoke of civil obedience 'for the sake of a good conscience', I Peter already spoke of obedience 'for the Lord's sake' (2.13). Here too the principle applies that authority is appointed by God (2.14b). Therefore official sanctions are almost *a priori* right and legitimate (2.14b). Civil obedience is not a lack of freedom, but free service for God (2.16). (Service here is seen as *douleia*, slavery, regarded in terms of Asia Minor and the Near East. In the East, man is a slave, i.e. God's possession; as a slave he prostrates himself before God. Romans and Greeks stand upright before God; they do not *serve* God.)[25] However, the author is also well aware that these authorities are anti-Christian (I Peter 3.14, 17; 4.1, 12–19; 5.13). He knows that there can also be 'unreasonable people' among state officials and governors (2.15). Therefore he does not issue an appeal to resistance, but to good actions, which can put to silence misunderstanding and unrighteousness (2.15b). Whereas Paul asks for 'fear' of God and the emperor (Rom. 13.7: this is also a feature to be found in the Near East and in Wisdom, in Diaspora Judaism: Prov. 24.21), I Peter draws a marked distinction: '*Fear* God, *honour* the emperor' (2.17b; see Matt. 10.28); i.e., a Christian does not fear the emperor! In this pagan milieu with its emperor cult, the 'fear of God' is not to be shown to the emperor. In the light of the Christian conception of grace, imperial power has its *limits*. The emperor cult is rejected by the whole of the New Testament (see Matt. 22.15–22; Rom. 13.1–7; I Tim. 2. 1–3; Titus 3.1–3, 8).

In the later writings of the New Testament, after or during bloody persecutions of the church, the tone is outspoken and sharp. Revelation 13 calls the Roman empire 'a monster', a beast of prey, and Rev. 17.18 calls Rome the great whore of Babylon, albeit in disguised form (perhaps this already begins in I Peter 5.13, where – if the author writes his letter from Rome, as seems probable – Rome is called 'Babylon'). Furthermore, in view of the general context, I Peter 5.8f. can have the same meaning. 'Your adversary the devil prowls around like a roaring lion, seeking someone to devour. *Resist him*, firm in your faith, *knowing that the same experience of suffering is required of your brotherhood throughout the world*', i.e. throughout the Roman empire. In my view this passage is clearly concerned with the suffering of Christians under persecution: like the Christian apocalypse, the author sees the devil behind these Roman persecutions.

The book of Revelation itself is the history of the final struggle of Jesus against the demons of this world, narrated in an apocalyptic and visionary style; on the one hand are the heavenly rulers, and on the other the imperial and royal political powers of this world; for in apocalyptic there is a prelude to the earthly fight against inhuman powers in the heavenly spheres, where good powers fight against evil. As it were through a visionary glimpse into the heavenly history, the author knows that the earthly fight against the powers of evil will also come out well: Christ, 'the faithful witness, the firstborn of the dead and the prince of the kings of the earth' (Rev. 1.5), is the guarantee of this. Where there is repeated mention in other New Testament writings of the victory and exaltation of Jesus above 'heavenly angelic powers', Revelation, in connection with persecutions of the church throughout the empire, describes the victory of Jesus over the dragon, the beast and the kings of the earth (17.4; 19.16), i.e. over all the earthly political powers, above all the great Roman emperor (the beast with the woman rider, the goddess Roma, see 17.18). The author sees Satan (the dragon) at work behind these persecutors of mankind and the church. Here Christ is depicted as the victor, with God's essential properties: alpha and omega (1.17f.). This apocalypse is a harsh *religious* criticism of the absolute and arbitrary imperial power. The emperor, at that time Victor – the great conqueror and benefactor or Soter (Luke 22.25f.) – must yield to the Christus Victor (a concept which will play a great part in patristic theology). *Nikē* or victory does not come from the Roman 'Caesar Victor', nor even from the Greek *psychē nikei* (the spirit overcomes), but from Jesus Christ. 'He has overcome' (Rev. 5.5: in this way the author takes up the well-known *nenikēka* of the Gospel of John, 'I have overcome the world', John 16.33c). True, he is 'the lamb once slain', but a lamb 'with seven horns and seven eyes', i.e. one who has all power and all knowledge, who looks into all things. The result of this heavenly and earthly struggle is the new creation and the new Jerusalem (Rev. 21.1–22.5). The evil powers of history – the dragon, the two beasts and Babylonian Rome – are swept away. Everything becomes new: the prophecy of Isa. 65.17 is fulfilled; a new mankind without a history of suffering, without evil and tears (21.4), in accordance with God's will from all eternity. With the apocalyptic Book of Jubilees, we could say, 'Then there will be no more Satan and no more evil one who will hurl mankind to destruction' (Jub. 1.20), but a 'heavenly Jerusalem' which comes down from heaven to earth' (Rev. 3.12; 21.2,10), 'God's abode among men' (21.3). Throughout its dramatic and apocalyptic scenario the book of Revelation is not only a gospel of hope but at the same time the basis for a religious criticism of society – again and again in a new historical setting – a theology of liberation with a Christian orientation, which is at the same time a theology of *martyrion* or martyrdom; for the whole of the New Testament sees God's righteousness under the sign of the acceptance of the cross.

Finally, under the perspective of the New Testament religious criticism of political powers, by a somewhat devious route the theological element of the *antichrist* comes into the foreground (explicitly under this name only in I John 2.18, 22; 4.3; II John 7; other passages speak of an eschatological anti-figure under other Jewish designations: Mark 13.14; Matt. 24.15; II Thess. 2.3–12; Rev. 13.1, 11; 16.13; 17.1; 17.17; Mark 13.22 speaks of 'false Christs', not however in the sense of *the* anti-figure in Mark 13.14).

The Jews were already familiar with the notion of a political power which was hostile to God, an anti-figure of messianism. The term 'the adversary' already appears in the history of Gog and Magog (Ezek. 38;39); above all, however, during the Maccabean struggles Antiochus Epiphanes was called 'the adversary', 'the son of corruption', 'the man of lawlessness', because he attacked Jewish customs and laws and declared that he himself was God (I Macc. 1.41–58; 2.15–18). However, Dan. 9.26f.; 12.11 already interpret this anti-figure in *eschatological* terms. He is the adversary of the eschatological bringer of salvation, the eschatological anti-godly figure, now designated as an individual tyrant (Dan. 7.25) who is a religious abomination (8.13; 9.27; 11.31; 11.36), and then again as a collective political power (Dan. 7), 'the fourth beast', namely the Seleucid kingdom, later also applied by Jews to the Roman empire (Ascension of Moses 10.8; Syr. Bar. 36–40; IV Ezra 12.11f.).

II Thessalonians 2.3–12, where this eschatological anti-figure is already regarded as an instrument of Satan, talks in the same terms (II Thess. 2.9f.). This too is a Jewish concept which is later fused with the Danielic anti-godly figure who makes himself God and therefore wants to root out any service of any gods outside himself (Dan. 11.36). For Satan (in the inter-testamental literature ultimately identified with Belial) in the form of Belial takes on the significance of an anti-figure; he is the prince of darkness, with his own supporters, hostile to God. Before he has to lay down his power at the end of time, he mobilizes all his forces in order to bring as many men as possible under his power.[26] The 'beast from the sea' in Rev. 13.1 also has the same features; he is a human anti-figure who receives his power from Satan (the dragon, Rev. 13.2, 4) and is against God (13.5f.), a figure who allows himself to be worshipped (13.8), but is finally conquered by the Messiah (19.19ff.). Here, however, the meaning fluctuates between an individual tyrant and a collective political power (therefore, the beast has many heads, one of which clearly relates to an individual, 13.5). In Rev. 13.1ff. this animal is clearly meant as an institution of power, whereas 'the beast from the land' (13.11f.), who makes ready the way for the first beast, refers to an individual (cf. 17.9ff.). The difference from II Thess. 2.3–12 lies in the fact that in the meantime a *third* element has been added to the figure of the anti-godly, individual or collective manifestation – already made a satellite of the anti-godly Satan, namely the saga of Nero *redivivus*. Popular feeling finds it difficult to accept the death of certain great figures, good or evil (he is still living somewhere: so of Hitler, John F. Kennedy). Both Tacitus[27] and Suetonius[28] record that popular belief was convinced that the dead Nero was still alive somewhere. The legend developed further. It was later said that he was hidden away in the East, from where he would return with an army to take vengeance[29] and to rule in triumph in Jerusalem.[30] The consequence of this was that often particular people gave themselves out to be Nero *redivivus*. The Jews, too, were familiar with this legend,[31] but they added Jewish elements to it (above all from Dan. 7): they fashioned it into the figure of God's adversary.[32] Christianity also took over this Jewish concept: Nero became the eschatological antichrist.[33] Thus the historical Nero became an eschatological and demonic figure as a result of the formation of legends and the fusing of other motives; he would be raised to life again by Satan to appear as antichrist.[34] He is Satan in the reform of Nero.[35] This legend about Nero plays a central role in the book of Revelation (e.g. 17.8; 13.3, 14).

Thus the three elements of the New Testament concept of the antichrist (which are used in a variety of ways by the New Testament authors) are already to be found in Judaism. The great adversary is: (*a*) a power hostile to God (Daniel; Revelation); (*b*) an anti-messianic, diabolical power (the inter-testamental literature); (*c*) a power hostile to Israel (according to the Nero legend). This anti-figure, interpreted in three ways, is as it were already prefigured in the creation myth, in which creation is depicted as a fight between God and the primal monster Leviathan. This thinking in thesis and antithesis is inherent in a people aware that it is set apart from all others and specially chosen; this dialectical thinking is then developed further in apocalyptic eschatology. The New Testament church which also knows itself to be chosen and also undergoes outward persecutions takes over this antithetical thinking. As well as 'Christ' there is the 'anti-Christ', a power hostile to God, the Messiah and the church, who above all in the end-time gathers together all his strength against the Christians (the apocalyptic conception of the final woes, which increase in severity) and will bring them to apostasy.

In the Johannine epistles, the only texts in which the anti-figure is expressly called *antichrist*, as a technical term, it also loses its mythical features. Anyone who refuses to confess Jesus as the Christ is 'anti-Christ': the unbelievers and Christian preachers of heresy in their time; for I John, Christians who preach heresies in the church. For him the danger of antichrist lies within the church itself (I John 2.18, 22; 4.3; II John 7).

Thus 'the antichrist' is not what one can call a 'datum of faith'. However, what stands behind it is theologically relevant: the stubborn struggle between good and evil on earth, in which man does not always have the power of evil under control; it is a power (though the Christian believer knows that as the power of good Christ has the last word). Furthermore, this power often takes the form of political powers; thus by speaking of the fight against the antichrist the New Testament, in the models and possibilities for action available at that time, summoned Christians to resist political powers which enslave men. Present Christian resistance against such powers can then be the concrete development of what was earlier belief in the antichrist. And it is also striking that since Christians have been led by the gospel to support those who seek to improve the world and to attack slavery, 'belief in the antichrist' in its mythical significance has become irrelevant and . . . disappears. Thus *Christian practice* has *taken over* the deepest purport of New Testament sayings about the antichrist. In this way orthodoxy in the form of myth becomes orthodoxy in the form of orthopraxis.

Hence a variety of historical conditions play their part in the New Testament conception of the relationship between the experience of grace and political power, quite apart from the inner dynamic of grace, the kingdom of God and the new way of life of the kingdom of God. These include above all the unproblematical statement that 'all authority comes from God' (in any case this was originally meant only in the sense of the supremacy of Yahweh over all earthly authority, which he uses as an instrument for his saving purposes with Israel) and the practical circumstance that the New Testament Christians could not alter given worldly structures and therefore moved away from them. All that could be said of these structures was: 'You Christians must not be like that.' This presupposes that at that time political power was completely in the hands of others, that no democratic conditions prevailed in which all men, including Christians, could work for an improvement of socio-political and economic conditions in the light of their inspiration and orientation. Precisely *because* these false secular structures had not found their way into the New Testament churches (as was later to happen when the church became a state church), the early Christian attitude was an ethically responsible, historically conditioned, authentically Christian option, though it is not a direct norm for all Christian behaviour in the face of political power. The basic difference between the present time and then is, moreover, that the particular churches have themselves become *part of* the world with its prevalent culture and its structures with their alienating effect, so that they fail in what the New Testament regarded as the first consequence of the way of life of the kingdom of God: making a portion of the realized kingdom of God on earth out of inner renewal of life, the church community itself. Therefore this New Testament Christianity implicitly involves some criticism of the church.

All this shows clearly enough the significance of the analysis of historical conditions for a correct theological hermeneutic of the New Testament. If this is neglected, the result is the danger of a reactionary ✗ fundamentalism which in the name of God and Christ establishes unjust structures and gives them theological legitimation on the basis of scriptural texts which derive from a quite different social and historical context, and therefore had quite a different intention from that which people now try to read into them. In that case no attention is paid to the New Testament insight that the way of life of the kingdom of God in essence also implies an improvement of the world (though New Testament Christianity could initially bring this about only within the Christian community which it sought to develop into a 'new heaven and a new earth in which righteousness dwells', II Peter 3.13). The politically coloured figure of the antichrist in the New Testament points to the struggle in which the Christians had to engage within society in the light of their gospel.

It is often supposed that John 19.8–12 means that the Johannine Jesus recognizes that the authority of the state comes from God. But Jesus does not say anything about this. When Pilate utters the threat that he has the power to free Jesus or to crucify him, Jesus, who 'comes from God', replies, 'You would have no power *over me* unless it had been given you *from above*' (John 19.11). Here John is not concerned with the royal or heavenly status of Jesus and the will of the Father (John 18.11) that Jesus should drink the cup of suffering. The Gospel of John does not make a single doctrinal statement here about the relationship of Christianity to the authority of the state.

One of the reasons for the Jewish revolt (66–72) was the introduction of special taxes even before the time of Jesus. But Josephus mentions the introduction of a tax (*phoros*) of two *drachmae* – later, under the Emperor Vespasian – which the Jews had to pay for the temple on the Capitol in Rome.[36] The new Emperor Vespasian and his son made a solemn entry into Rome in AD 71, during which there was a celebration of the victory over the Jewish rebels (and in the year 81 the triumphal arch of Titus was erected in the Roman forum). A pictorial description of the Jewish war was given in this triumphal procession.[37] Coins were struck with the inscription *Judaea capta* and an effigy of captive Israel. Along with other spoils of war, the purple curtain of the Jerusalem Temple was taken in the triumphal procession:[38] it had now become a symbol of the Roman entry into the holy of holies. At that time the whole of Rome could *see* the dramatic account and the record of the Jewish rebellion; this procession was like a televised account of the war. In the eyes of non-Jews, above all in Rome, in the first years after AD 70, Judaism and rebellion against Rome almost automatically went together. Furthermore, the Romans knew that Christianity was of Jewish origin. Mark 12.13–17 par. should probably be read in this context.

The problem of this tax is discussed in Mark 12.13–17, a text which has given rise to various interpretations. What is the relationship between Mark 12.13–16 and 12.17? A trap is laid for Jesus to give grounds for an accusation: 'Is it lawful to pay tax to Caesar?' Because of their theocratic understanding of the Jewish state, the Zealots repudiated the payment of any tax to the occupying power. However, Zealots are quite outside the horizon of the event in Mark 12.13–17. Still, Luke seems to know a tradition which says that Jesus prevented his disciples from paying tax (Luke 23.2, or is this a Lucan redaction?). Mark is concerned with the Pharisees and the Herodians (Mark 12.13; in Matt. 22.15 only the Pharisees appear, see also Luke 20.20–25). As collaborators with the Romans, the Herodian aristocracy clearly supported the payment of taxes to the Romans; the Pharisees offered only moral resistance and outwardly observed the Roman precepts (excusing themselves with a reference to Dan. 2.21, 37ff.; 4.14, 29ff.; the tolerance of alien rule in the hope of an imminent redemption by Yahweh).

In the Gospel of Mark, the account must be seen in the light of Mark's intention. He sets out to show that Jesus is involved in a fight to the death with all the Jewish leaders: with high priests, scribes and elders (Mark 11.27), with Pharisees and Herodians (12.13), with Sadducees (12.18) and finally once again with scribes in 12.28, 35, 38. Whatever the form of the account may have been in the pre-Marcan tradition, in the Gospel of Mark it is a matter of a controversy in which Mark keeps trying to show the superiority of Jesus to the Jewish leaders. Thus Mark 12.18f. is meant as a catch question, in which either a positive or a negative answer will compromise Jesus. If he says no, his opponents will accuse him of stirring up the people against Rome. If he says yes, then he will offend Jewish theocratic sensibilities. Seen in this context, then, the pericope will not help in clarifying any teaching of Jesus about the attitude that should be adopted towards the state. This lies beyond Mark's immediate purpose. The question he is concerned with is, how will Jesus demonstrate his superiority to his opponents in this tricky situation? How will he escape without compromising himself, while catching his enemies in the trap which they themselves have laid? So the pericope does not present any direct teaching (about the attitude of Jesus towards political power), but a controversy. This is clear from its stereotyped structure: the hostile attitude of the questioners (Mark 12.13), Jesus sees through their hypocrisy and recognizes the trap (12.15), he puts a counter-question (12.15, as he always does in such situations in Mark's Gospel: he never gives a direct answer to the question, see Mark 12.24; 11.33b). Jesus is quite uninterested in the content of the question, which is put with other ends in view. He wants to turn the questioners' intention back on themselves, with the result that we do not really hear anything *directly* of Jesus' own attitude towards Roman taxes. In a subtle way he shows that they themselves have already solved the question and are simply trying to catch him out. He says, 'Show me a coin.' One of the questioners immediately takes a coin out of his pocket. This already decides the question. 'What is on it?' 'The image of the emperor with his name' (12.16). 12.17a simply puts this result into words: 'Pay Caesar his due' (*apodidonai* does not mean 'give back', but is the technical term for paying tax, though this is sometimes doubted). The questioners have the coins; Jesus has more. In other words, they are caught up in the system; they are therefore to act accordingly: 'Give Caesar his due'. Jesus and his followers have given everything away; they have dropped out of the monetary system. So Jesus adds 'And give God his due.' There are no literary-critical reasons whatsoever why this statement should be declared to be secondary, as sometimes happens; it is an essential part of the history and above all the fundamental message of Jesus about the coming kingdom of God, in the face of which the question of taxes retreats right into the background. In other words, Jesus makes his hypocritical questioners understand that they would do much better to concern themselves with the kingdom of God than with such mean catch-questions. We hear hardly anything here about the payment of taxes, apart from the acknowledgment of the real power of the emperor, to whom in that case his enemies have completely surrendered; they have already decided for the world. Jesus asks them to be concerned for the kingdom of God. His indirect interest in politics is a *political* factor of prime importance.[39] In the light of the coming kingdom of God, for Jesus Rome is already *passé*. The power of Rome has been superseded by the end-time.

Thus the literary genre of the *controversy* in the Gospel of Mark prevents us from seeing Mark 12.17 as a *dogmatic* statement of Jesus about faith and politics (this is quite a different genre). Unfortunately, at a later stage Mark 12.17 was interpreted as an absolute, dogmatic statement and taken completely out of context. However, Mark and the New Testament cannot conceive of the separation between the religious and the social spheres which would follow as a result. One cannot serve two masters, God and mammon (Matt. 6.24; Luke 16.13). Even the social sphere of finance is seen in relation to God; and this confronts Christians with decisions.

If in his passion narrative Mark reveals a tendency not to blame the Romans too much in order to spare the Christians persecution, it seems

evident that at the same time he wants this pericope to show that Jesus
and the Christians are loyal citizens and that they do not see this as being
contradictory to their Christian faith. In that case Mark 12.13–17 agrees
with Rom. 13.1–7 (which is in any case earlier in date). This was the
general attitude of Christians, as emerges for prayers 'for kings and all
those in authority', 'that we may lead a quiet and peaceable life, godly
and respectful in every way' (I Tim. 2.1f.). All this implies that we do
not know everything about Jesus' own historical attitude towards political
power, except *by means of* a *church apologetic* which seeks to protect the
Christian community from persecutions.[40]

The New Testament simply continues the attitude of Diaspora Judaism
towards an occupying power (they themselves lived in a foreign land). It
was also the attitude of the Greek-speaking Jew Sirach, with a similar
motivation: 'Do not contend with a powerful man, lest you fall into his
hands' (8.1), and at the same time an attitude of Jewish traditional
wisdom (Sir. 4.7; 7.14; 8.10f., 14; 9.13; 13.9–13; 26.5). These Jews fear,
rather than revere, an alien authority.

Can we go further and reconstruct an original tradition behind Mark?
Of the many attempts in this direction, I find the reconstruction by P.
Farla most successful.[41] Generally speaking, he came to the conclusion
that the hypothesis of a collection of *controversy stories* existing even before
Mark is untenable. Mark himself often makes controversies out of miracle
stories or didactic stories, or even out of a logion. A clear piece of tradition
begins in Mark 12.14 (12.14–17). Since Jesus is addressed as 'master'
(*didaskale*), the purpose of the questioners in the pre-Marcan passage is
not hostile;[42] they are therefore not putting a catch question, but are in
fact asking Jesus what he thinks about the controversial question of
paying tax to the (Roman) emperor. (It follows from this that Mark 12.13,
15a, 17c are certainly redactional; they are a reworking into a controversy
story. The same is perhaps also true of the diplomatic 12, 14bc.) According to Farla, in that case the origin of this tradition goes back to the
catechesis of the Palestinian community, because the pericope hardly
makes sense as a doctrinal passage in discussion with the Jews, for whom
the tax was as burning a problem as it was for Christians. In that case
this catechesis takes up one incident from the life of Jesus or even a single
logion (Mark 12.17a, b). This reconstruction does not take us any farther
in discovering Jesus' attitude towards politics than we have already
shown: Jesus did not absolutize politics; his most burning concern was
the kingdom of God.

It follows from this that there is no direct evidence of either a 'political'
or an 'unpolitical' Jesus. It is therefore wrong to say that we could show
positively that Jesus was 'apolitical'. We can only say that Jesus was not
directly interested in politics, while remaining aware that his proclama-

tion of the kingdom and above all his practice of dealing with the oppressed had political implications. So anyone who wants to interpret Mark 12.13–17 in an apolitical way clearly has *quite a different intention* from that of Jesus, who proclaimed the imminence of the kingdom of God and uttered beatitudes about the poor and the oppressed. Jesus' eschatological and radical criticism of the world is replaced by a concern to adopt an apolitical and neutral attitude between the powerful and the oppressed, an approach which in effect helps the powerful, contrary to Jesus' express behaviour. In that case, where Paul and Mark save a Christian minority group from persecution and make it possible to proclaim the gospel without hindrance, modern Christians use a false interpretation of Mark 12.17 to arrive at a complete separation between faith and politics and in so doing reinforce existing power structures. 'The oppressed who attempted to protect themselves later became the ruling classes who, by referring to the same text, Mark 12.17, compromised with the power of the state and themselves exercised authority.'[43] It transpires from this that if biblical exegesis neglects the social and historical context, it can become reactionary and un-Christian. For such an interpretation of Mark 12.17 in fact runs contrary to the basic intention of the message of Jesus about the humanity whom God wants. Justin, the first great theologian of the established church, is in fact the beginning of an apolitical 'political theology',[44] when he interprets Jesus' saying in Mark 12.17 as a doctrinal statement, detached both from the literary genre of Mark 12 and from the social and historical context of New Testament Christianity.

The danger of referring to a 'political' or to an 'apolitical' Jesus consists in the fact that people feel that this removes the need for any political arguments! Even if Jesus was political – or apolitical – in his time, it does not tell us how we should behave in the light of the same faith in other historical situations. The social criticism which is to be found both in the New Testament and the Tanach is always a *religious* criticism of society; but that does not say anything for or against a non-religious social criticism and the necessary ethical consequences which emerge from this for a Christian.

We may conclude from this that the New Testament shows the attitude to politics of Paul and Pauline theology, of Revelation and of Mark. In other words, in it we find various *models* of the way in which Christians react to politics in given situations in the New Testament. It was the same with Jesus, but we arrive at his particular attitude only by way of the political models of the New Testament. The sum total of these models, as an orientation, tells us something about faith and politics. On the one hand, a complete identification with or an absolutizing of politics is unbiblical; on the other hand, the appeal in the gospels to *metanoia* concerns not only man's heart but also – in some circumstances – the renewal of social structures which enslave men (see above all Luke 22.25). However, there remains something of the 'game' in every model, and this attitude too is liberating. Christianity knows nothing of the wrath which seeks to improve the world through inhumanity. Eschatological restraint here means that there should be no ideologizing of politics. Every Christian generation, if it reflects at all, must determine its attitude towards the political situation by faith, above all if existing structures enslave men.

## Chapter 5

# The life of grace and socio-culturally determined ethics in the New Testament

The questions discussed above are intimately connected with the question of the attitude of the New Testament towards the relationship between the *kerygma* or the proclamation of faith and human nature, between grace and ethics, and between the kingdom of God as it was proclaimed by Jesus and has come near to us in his life and his ethical significance or the life-style of the kingdom of God. Therefore in this section we shall as it were open up the structural depth of the three problems I have just mentioned.

The question now is whether the New Testament has anything to say to us other than that a Christian must integrate the human ethical norms from his society into his experience of grace, whereas it has nothing to say to us about the ethics themselves. In this instance, theological interpretation of the ethical statements of the Bible would have only historical significance, namely the discovery of the ethical state of affairs in New Testament Christianity. This would not do for a hermeneutical approach which set out to relate the text to the present day. Some moral theologians claim that there is a specifically Christian hermeneutic of the New Testament, in other words, a specific New Testament ethics which therefore also has something to say to present-day Christians. By contrast, others affirm that the Bible simply accepts the ethical norms valid in the society of the time, which are then to be observed by Christians 'in the Lord'. But what is the exact position of the New Testament? We may distinguish a variety of aspects.

1. Both Old and New Testaments speak of moral norms and guidelines always against the background and in the context of a religious language which is concerned with God; in the New Testament this is related to Christ and the eschaton. Ethics is discussed in connection with the coming kingdom of God, and only in a christological or at least a theological perspective. In other words, grace and religion are also essentially an ethical task. The experience of God is *also* ethics: a religious man cannot separate the life of grace and ethical life. This is already a first and important fact: 'Be *doers* of the word and not *hearers* only' (James 1.22), *makarios en tē poiēsei autou*, 'he will be blessed through his doing' (James 1.25c). James attacks a religious monism of grace. 'What does it profit, my brethren, if a man says he has faith but has not works? Can his faith save him?' (James 2.14) 'Those who have believed in God must be careful to apply themselves to good deeds; these are excellent and profitable to men' (Titus 3.8b).

This has implications. Characteristic is a text like Phil. 4.4–9: 'Rejoice in the Lord always . . .; the Lord is at hand . . . Whatever is true, whatever is honourable, whatever is just, whatever is pure, whatever is lovely, whatever is gracious, if there is any excellence, if there is anything worthy of praise, think about these things? This is a stimulus on the one hand to observe the prevailing ethic; here we have the only passage in the whole of the New Testament in which the word *aretē* appears in the Hellenistic sense of an ethical civic virtue 'worthy of praise' (both terms, 'virtue' and 'respect', are typically Hellenistic with their slant towards virtuousness). On the other hand, this ethic is bound up with eschatology; for this very reason joy is a fundamental ingredient in Christian ethical action. For Christians ethics is more something that is graciously *allowed* than something that is firmly compelled. Ethics shares in the event of grace which makes man a new creature. In that case a very real question arises: what judgment is passed on the reality of human life in the light of Christian 'religious consciousness'?

However, as far as the specific content of ethical norms is concerned, the New Testament in fact nowhere contains a unitary principle, of the kind that can be found in the New Testament conceptions of grace. In other words, there is no distinctive ethical principle and therefore there is no fundamental ethical principle either. Nevertheless, ethical encouragement plays a large part in the New Testament literature, such a large part that if one took out all the ethical texts from, say, the Pauline corpus, it would only be half as extensive as it is now. However, ethical questions only come to be discussed against a religious and christological background.

2. The second demonstrable fact is that for the most part the New

Testament takes over the ethics to be found in the surrounding culture, namely in Judaism and Hellenistic Roman society, and assumes its validity for Christians as well. This is most evident in the acceptance of everything that – in German scholarship and now elsewhere – is called the 'house tables' or ethical code of the time, just as the old Greek popular ethic was glorified by the Stoa (see Col. 3.18–4.1; Eph. 5.22–6.9; I Tim. 2.1–15; 6.1f.; Titus 2.1–10; I Peter 2.13–3.9, all relatively later writings from a time when the Christian communities had already been in existence for some generations). By and large these house tables are the same as those which we find in Hellenistic Stoic society,[45] and also in Jewish society (which was itself already influenced by Hellenistic ethics from the time of the Greek and Roman occupation, see e.g. Job 4.3–21; Sir. 7.18–35, etc.). These New Testament house tables show that Christians at that time merely observed the existing ethical norms which related to the life of the family and the state. However, as in Graeco-Roman culture the worship of the gods of the state was a civic virtue, Christians left this divine worship out of their ethical codes, so that despite the intrinsic connection between the experience of God and ethics, the New Testament at the same time sees a clear distinction between ethics and religion and thus implicitly affirms the historical connection between religion and ethics.

3. A third demonstrable fact is that New Testament Christians observe existing human ethics 'in the Lord' (Eph. 5.22–33; I Peter 2.13f.; Col. 3.18); Paul himself does not use 'in the Lord' in an ethical context, but he makes a first move this way in I Cor. 7.39: 'marry a Christian', i.e. also for the sake of Christ and thus as a Christian.

However, there seems to be a tendency in Pauline theology to provide christological or at least theological support for the prevailing ethic and in this way to theologize the norms existing at the time and therefore make them absolute. Thus for example the patriarchal and androcentric ethical norm of antiquity that 'the wife is subject to the husband' (Eph. 5.21–33; Col. 3.18; I Cor. 14.34; I Tim. 2.11–15; I Peter 3.1 and Titus 2.5) is not just taken over and brought under 'the Lord', thus already doing away to some extent with social distinctions in the face of honest mutual love before which all are equal. However sometimes, and also in this case, this social norm is given an ideological basis, 'just as the church is subordinate to Christ'. Once again this statement could simply be interpreted as a synonym for 'in the Lord'. However, things change when Paul himself gives an exalted theological sense to the social fact that 'the husband is the head of the wife' (I Cor. 11.3; see Eph. 5.23), *paterfamilias*. Furthermore, in I Cor. 11.3 Paul seems to depict the fact that the man is head as a universal datum (not just in the hierarchy of the family), and to provide a theological reason for it. Ephesians, which takes up Pauline theology, simply says, 'as Christ is the head of the church' (Eph. 5.22–24; see I Cor. 11.8f.; I Tim. 2.13), but Paul says, 'Neither was man created for woman, but woman for man' (I Cor. 11.9, as a midrash on Gen. 3.16), and therefore she must be veiled.[46] If we compare Col. 3.18–4.1 (where 'in the Lord' is simply added to the secular elements) with I Peter 2.13–17 (where the Christian elements are emphasized) and with Paul's own tendency to provide theological support for the commonplace, we can see that the New Testament is still on the lookout for the right relationship between redemption in Christ and ethics. Paul even theologizes long hair for women and short hair for men (I Cor. 11.4) – an argument which can be found among the Stoics of the time; even the angels must take note of this (I Cor. 11.7–10). Despite all his theological arguments, however, Paul is not sure whether his case will convince the reader, since he adds: 'If anyone is disposed to be contentious, we recognize no other practice, nor do the churches of God' (I Cor. 11.16). So these are only honourable customs. However, in a worldly city like Corinth, this was not without significance. By means of its attack on women with 'braided hair or gold or pearls or costly attire', I Tim. 2.9f. (see I Peter 3.3f.) seeks to enjoin Christian moderation and at the same time to protect the much poorer fellow Christians (see very clearly in James 2.1–9, where Christian support for the poor is expressed very strongly). Paul's 'theologizing' should not be taken more seriously than he intended. It is already a feature of the Q tradition to appeal to experiences of human wisdom formulated in stereotyped narratives, stories like Adam and Eve, the flood, Sodom and Gomorrah, Jonah, the queen of Sheba and so on. These stories themselves keep on incorporating new experiences and make it possible to work in new experiences – just as for us the word Hiroshima is quite enough to evoke a whole situation. Such references to previous experiences compel the hearers to an agreement which they might not be so ready to arrive at of their own accord. When Hebrews 13.2 wants to impress hospitality on Christians, and says, 'it might be an angel', it already reminds the hearer of the story of Tobit (ch. 12), who was visited by an angel of God. The author by no means wants to provide theological support for his paraenesis with a doctrine of angels. However, his evocation makes the reader of the time think. The first Christians lived in and from the old biblical stories, which also preserved a treasury of humanistic and Jewish wisdom collected together over the centuries. I think that Paul's 'theologizing' must also be interpreted in this way. It is by no means intended as a theological support, but as an evocation of the admonitory wisdom of popular narratives. One can find this usage throughout the New Testament (see the large-scale example in Heb. 11; also II Peter 2.4–22, which even incorporates apocryphal narratives; and in every New Testament epistle). However, later Christianity detached itself completely from the wisdom of the Tanach; it thought more about a system – and not on the basis of evocative stories. Only then did people begin to read Paul in a different way and to find theological arguments in his writings, e.g. to provide theological legitimation for the androcentric masculine conceptions of a particular culture which was also the setting for the New Testament. As a result, this particular culture now continues to live on in the church and as a result wrongly, and unbiblically, receives a theological aura.

Be this as it may, the acceptance of culturally determined human ethics 'in the Lord' smoothed out the sharp edges of the social inequality prevailing at the time, through the demand for mutual Christian love. However, Christian love can exercise its critical force on society only on the presupposition of an analysis of social structures. Nevertheless, it is typical that New Testament Christians who wanted to build up a new society at least within their own church community retained a social hierarchy within the family of Christians. The family above all is the point at which secular structures enter the church.

So has the ethic which we find in the New Testament nothing to teach us? What emerges from this short analysis is that people themselves must look for ethical norms. By their very nature, ethical questions are in fact questions of the here and now, the present, and what is developed as an answer to an ethical question in the present may in fact be termed by the man of grace in his religious language 'the will of God', i.e. a matter of living 'in the Lord'. The answers to ethical questions which are given specific expression in the Bible are not normative. The important thing is the fact that the New Testament will not separate ethics from religion. Life in and from grace is also an ethical life. However, it is clear that many ethical guidelines in the Christian Bible go back to specific anthropological presuppositions, to socio-historical conditions and so on. When these presuppositions no longer apply, the answers to ethical questions governed by them lose their force; the conclusion becomes superfluous.

4. This is not, however, the whole story. As I have pointed out, there is a dialectical relationship between Christian ethics and socio-political reality. Nevertheless, moral theologians, who rightly defend the direct autonomy of ethics on a human basis, have a tendency to shift the distinction between 'natural' ethics and Christian ethics into the sphere of the disposition (disposition morality). Is there also specifically Christian ethics? In that case the question arises whether the New Testament in fact provides *ethical models* for it. True, many ethical questions of the Bible are no longer ours, but in them we find an ethical dimension which we might term specifically Christian (religious – with its foundation in

grace). We have already seen in general that the experience of grace also issues in a certain experiential knowledge, in a *discretio spirituum*, a discerning of spirits (which can be found in all spiritual gurus), both contemplative (mystical) and ethical (Thomas Aquinas calls this a *iudicium connaturalitatis*, i.e. the ability to make a fine distinction in and through the daily affairs of an ethically oriented life). Of course, such a judgment gives us no insight into social structures. When we speak of a *specifically Christian* ethic, we do not mean that it is exclusive to Christianity. Christian inspiration leads to a particular ethical judgment and ethical practice. However, this ethical insight can then be communicated and therefore universalized, i.e. its ethical content is accessible even to non-Christians (there is in fact no specifically Christian ethic capable of universal communication).

At this point, in the end we are not confronted so much with the problem of kerygma and ethics as with the New Testament life-style patterned on the kingdom of God as compared with secular ethics: we could say a confrontation between Christian ethics and secular ethics. It is striking that Catholic moral theologians often argue away the Sermon on the Mount (Matt. 5–7) in a hairsplitting fashion. They rob the Sermon on the Mount of its force by distinguishing between (*a*) *praeceptum* or commandment and (*b*) *consilium* or counsel in the sense of an ethical invitation which is not binding. The whole utopian critical force of the Sermon on the Mount, through which even the most modern ethic can come under the criticism of the gospel, is neutralized by this distinction. Furthermore, it would lead to a double category of Christians: second-rate Christians, who are content to follow 'the most modern ethics' 'in the Lord', and other Christians, who follow the counsels as well, i.e. in effect the nucleus of the New Testament ethic. Other theologians who do not allow the distinction between *praeceptum* and *consilium* speak of a disposition to which the Sermon on the Mount is supposed to bear witness – as though the Sermon on the Mount did not look for actions, a way of life which can renew the face of the earth!

The Sermon on the Mount, which (from a form-critical point of view) at least reflects the spirit of Jesus of Nazareth, does, however, show us that Christian ethics has its own source of inspiration. In this sense ethical 'nonconformity' is of the essence of discipleship: 'Do not be conformed to this world, but be transformed by the renewal of your mind' (Rom. 12.2, though here 'this world' clearly points to the apocalyptic 'first aeon': the *sinful* world). The Sermon on the Mount is of such a kind that its content cannot in fact be formulated in legalistic terms. However, this characteristic cannot be described, either, by means of a distinction between commandment and counsel or through a dispositional ethics. The Sermon on the Mount has the literary genre of a paradox and a utopia.[47] One cannot rob it of its binding ethical force in the light of the gospel, nor make it an elitist ethic. As a critical, utopian stimulus it applies to all Christians and is not just any kind of counsel. Like Matt. 5.48 (cf. Luke 6.36), 'Be perfect *as* God is perfect', the Sermon on the Mount also applies to all sinners under grace. It is an ethically binding task.

From form criticism we can see the essential connection between Jesus' message of the imminent coming of the kingdom (good news is preached to the poor) and the fact that the sick are healed and the blind see (Matt. 11.5; 10.1–8). Furthermore, the Lord's Prayer sees an essential connection between 'Thy kingdom come' and 'Thy will be done on earth' (just as in heaven the angels do God's will). The New Testament is concerned with God's rule which is focused on humanity (this biblical expression itself has a 'political' origin, political in its implication and consequence). Christian ethics are intrinsically bound up with the person of Jesus, who was able to break through both the specific laws of Judaism and the ethics prevailing at the time. Some examples of this 'biblical ethics' (as the source of a permanent model for Christians) may make this clear.

According to Paul, the apostle of Christ has the right to have a wife (I Cor. 9.5), and also the right to financial support from the community (I Cor. 9.2–27): 'these are not just human considerations, the Law itself says as much' (I Cor. 9.8; in that case this Jewish Law is evidently not as dead for Paul as he claims elsewhere. He refers to Deut. 25.4: 'You shall not muzzle the ox which treads the grain'). Paul restricts the whole of his argument to the second instance. This right is ethics. Then, however, comes an ethical Christian decision. 'Nevertheless, we have not made use of this right, but we endure anything rather than put an obstacle in the way of the gospel of Christ' (I Cor. 9.12) and 'will become all things to all men' (9.22); 'I can do no other' (9.15f.). Thus on the one hand Paul's inalienable ethical rights are established; on the other hand, however, of his own free will he can renounce these rights if his situation (as an apostle) requires it. We see here the utopian-critical force of the Sermon on the Mount, which for Paul is binding here and now, but which can never legalistically be codified in a commandment or a church law. For the believer, the gospel can exercise a binding power which leads to an ethical decision, but which can never be prescribed by a commandment or a prohibition. To express the Sermon on the Mount as a law is to misunderstand its literary genre. But once a Christian, like Paul, has made this choice, he can nevertheless make it clear and acceptable to non-Christians as well.

The problem of a second marriage after a marriage which has completely gone to pieces is just as clear an example. One has in fact to concede that such a marriage can hardly be made consonant with what can be called the 'Sermon on the Mount', i.e. the utopian-critical force of Christian ethical inspiration. But that cannot be encompassed in a canonical or juridical prohibition, or in legal form either. Jesus calls for mutual fidelity in a radical way (Mark 10.11), and in so doing even attacks the Law of Moses. In a fashion which runs quite contrary to the whole prophetic style of the proclamation of Jesus, which is expressed more in the light of the ideal of the coming kingdom of God, Paul already speaks of a *'command* from the Lord' (I Cor. 7.10f.). But Paul himself then singles out situations in which this commandment must be broken: a Christian can send away a non-Christian spouse if certain convictions (i.e. religious convictions) have radically changed, and this change has broken up the marriage. For – and the argument is relevant (though it is only appealed to as support for Christians) – 'God has called us to peace' (I Cor. 7.15). Here the complete breakdown of a marriage in fact serves as an argument for legitimate divorce. Canon law goes on to call this the *privilegium Paulinum*, but that again is an attempt to embrace in legalistic terms something that in fact transcends them. In other words, here too we have a model. We are not told precisely what makes up the marriage which the New Testament terms indissoluble. The 'nature of marriage' is a socio-historical cultural phenomenon, and this too is culturally conditioned. Therefore that which may not be dissolved is a culturally changing phenomenon. Therefore the past can never give a *direct* answer to ethical questions which are posed in terms of a different cultural model. So the exception clause in Matt. 5.32 is not a kind of dispensation, but another, Jewish-Christian interpretation, which turned out differently in this community from others.[48] One cannot ontologize marriage (even sacramental marriage), and the Christian community may not impose the 'commands' of Jesus as a law.

The ideal of Christian proclamation cannot be captured in any form of casuistic legislation. Consequently even the *search for* grounds for divorce already implies a surrender of the Christian ideal. A reluctance to marry again after a completely shattered marriage can in fact be a specific ethical response to the utopian-critical force of the Sermon on the Mount, which can therefore exercise a critical effect in two directions, positive and negative. Both the search for reasons for divorce and the canonical veto against a second marriage mistake the prophetic significance of the words of Jesus. All this also points to a deeper distinction between a religious and an ethical conception of evil. The religious conception in particular is concerned to *offer a future* to those who have failed. Therefore the Christian ethic connected with divorce is different in specific points from the pragmatic bourgeois ethic.

Finally, the New Testament offers another model in connection with eating meat offered to idols, a subject to which Paul devotes three chapters (I Cor. 8.1–11.1). Paul is talking about the eating of meat which could be bought in the market. In fact this was always sacrificial meat, which had been used in pagan worship. For Christians, did this not amount to a kind of tacit acquiescence in pagan cultic meals? The problem no longer exists for us, but the solution which Paul gives to it remains an ethical model for Christians and can always be adapted to new circumstances. Paul's answer is typical of the New Testament: what or who could prohibit me from eating this meat? (There is no mention of 'food laws' anywhere in the New Testament.) Whether we eat or drink, we do everything to the glory of our God. Colossians 2.20–23 delivered quite a sharp attack against some taboos: 'Do not handle, Do not taste, Do not touch (referring to things which all perish as they are used).' I Timothy 4.3f. attacks 'people who forbid marriage and enjoin abstinence from foods which God created. . . .' Evidently the matter-of-fact attitude of the free man Jesus still continues to exercise influence in this New Testament realism. Paul defends his *right* as a Christian to eat this sacrificial meat. His argument betrays his exclusive monism of grace, for 'we know that an idol has no real existence and that there is no God but one' (I Cor. 8.4, though he misunderstands the religious language of other religions here; the argument is historically conditioned). 'Food will not commend us to God. We are no worse off if we do not eat, and no better off if we do' (I Cor. 8.8).

However, from a Christian point of view this does not settle the matter for Paul. There is something that might be called the mercifulness of faith (I Cor. 8.7–13). This pericope is introduced by a general principle of Christian orthopraxis. Some Christians had argued from Paul's principle of freedom to various forms of libertinism or, perhaps more correctly, to an ethical indifference on the basis of a syncretistic Hellenistic conviction of their superior 'knowledge'. We indeed know better; this pagan idolatry is nothing and of no value; the fact that we Christians readily eat their sacrifical meat bears witness to our 'knowing better'. Paul now wants to say that the Christian knowledge that there are no gods apart from the God of Christ is not the only principle which provides an ethical ruling for the eating of (pagan) sacrifical meat. He adds other considerations to this intellectualism typical of a certain kind of orthodoxy: 'Now concerning food offered to idols, (you assert that) all of us possess knowledge. Knowledge puffs up, but love builds up' (I Cor. 8.1). For, 'if anyone imagines that he knows something, he does not yet know as he ought to know. But if one loves God, one is known' (8.2f.: Paul means to say, 'He is known by God', see Gal. 4.9). For him true orthodoxy takes shape in the orthopraxis of love. Certainly, on the basis of our Christian principles we have the right to eat this meat, but we must regard everything in the light of the situation, even as Christians. For, Paul continues, there are Christians among you who because of their pagan past are still unable to find this inner freedom towards eating meat offered to idols. The situation calls for an ethical decision made in the light of the mercifulness of faith: 'Take care lest this liberty of yours somehow become a stumbling-block to the weak' (8.9). Here Paul does not seem to be completely consistent, when one recalls his bitter reaction to Peter, who refuses to eat with uncircumcised Gentile Christians so as not to offend Jewish Christians – probably on the basis of the same principle of the merciful-ness of faith. 'Seem', though, is the operative word, for the issue here is the nature of a community made up of Jews and Gentiles. Your know-ledge, says Paul ironically – although he himself sets very great store on knowledge – is a mockery to these weaker brethren in the faith who have just detached themselves from paganism, 'these brothers for whom Christ died' (8.11). Paul's ethical argument then becomes clear: 'Therefore if food is a cause of my brother's failing, I will never eat meat, lest I cause my brother to fall.' In Corinth, in fact, only meat offered in pagan sacrifices was on sale in the *macellum* or the public market. Only a small amount of flesh was consumed in a cultic sacrifice; some was burnt, and by far the largest amount was put on sale in the market. So for Paul, 'I will never eat meat' was not just empty rhetoric; it was a consequence which followed from his ethical principles. Paul, who began his argument with respect for the sovereign freedom of the Christian towards all meat offered to idols, ends in a solemn commitment, deadly earnest for him as a Christian living in a particular historical situation, never to eat meat again if this means that some Christians will be deeply disturbed in their new faith as a result. This ethical situation has been given a name in the Christian tradition: *scandalum pusillorum*, giving offence to the weaker brethren. Leaving aside the historical circumstances, Paul's ethical prin-ciple of the *scandalum pusillorum* cannot be taken as an absolute; if it were, every Christian would be condemned to virtual inactivity because there will always be someone in the Christian community who will take offence at the conduct of fellow Christians, no matter what their justification. Today above all, there are particular political and social options which cause divisions among Christians. One can hardly advance the principle of the *scandalum pusillorum* to silence these political Christian options, far less if they are the historically conditioned expression of an attempt to draw the consequences of God's kingdom, which is intended to be for man. In that case Christian orthopraxis is at stake, which is evidently what Paul himself is concerned about. Nevertheless, his ethical model of the mercifulness of faith continues to be valid – at least if it does not contradict the New Testament demand for Christian orthopraxis; for in this latter instance, as in the conflict between Paul and Peter, the meaning of the community of God and its very justification for existence are at stake. For that very reason, e.g. the refusal of priests to marry, despite their recognition that ministry and celibacy may not be associated in legalistic, juristic terms by means of canon law, may be an expression of what Paul presents here as a general principle of Christian ethics – quite apart from the utopian critical force of the 'Sermon on the Mount', which can provide intrinsic grounds for holding office in the church as a celibate, for the sake of the kingdom of God. Here two principles of Christian ethics play a particular ethical role: on the one hand the personal ethical decision for celibacy, in order to be free for everyone (at least so long as this is not an immature decision), and on the other hand the Pauline *scandalum pusillorum*, in view of the whole of the predominantly Catholic Christian past. Despite all the criticism of the canonical association of ministry and celibacy in the light of the gospel, it is wrong to lose sight of these two gospel principles. Despite other ethical problem situations, the New Testament here continues to offer us normative models. The New Testament Christian knows himself to be a free man who is nevertheless under obligation: (*a*) as a result of the utopian-critical, prophetic perspective of the Sermon on the Mount; (*b*) as a result of the possibility of disturbing and offending a fellow believer (i.e. through irresponsibility); this is a reference to the fact that the gospel and its historically conditioned ethical demands can in fact damage particular expectations of Christians (members of the congregation or its leaders) and that in that case a Christian vocation to 'giving offence' can in fact become an ideology. In the New Testament itself, at first glance this emerges from Paul's contradictory attitude towards meat offered to idols and his conflict with Peter. Paul teaches us that knowledge (in theological terms, 'knowing better' than others) may not be our ultimate ethical principle. 'Being all things to all men' (I Cor. 9.22f.) may and must play a part here. Granted, the particular occasion for the presentation of this whole problem, namely, the offering of meat to pagan idols, is no longer an issue as far as we are concerned, but the ethical solution presented by Paul remains in force for Christians. The principle holds in general for Christians, and thus can be applied again in new historical circumstances. So we cannot dispense with the critical force of the New Testament ethic in any ethics which sets out to be Christian. As a result, the experiencing in the Lord of even the most modern ethics must be set in the utopian-critical perspective of what we call – in paradigmatic terms – the Sermon on the Mount.[49]

In the twentieth century we are confronted with completely new situations, but the ethical demand of the New Testament can still serve as a model for our new creative response. It is possible to refer to yet other biblical pericopes in which the ethical situation is perhaps a thing of the past for us, but which nevertheless give evidence of a Christian concern that can serve as a model for the historical and ethical decision of Christians in a changed historical situation. In its eschatological-critical force, New Testament Christianity also has a surplus which can never be adequately expressed in new structures and new institutions. It sets out to offer the 'comfort of the gospel' to people who are caught up in existing structures. This therapeutic concern of New Testament Christians with specific people will then logically – provisionally – strengthen existing structures to some degree; but the New Testament Christian is of the view that he cannot wait until there are more just structures in order to provide effective help for the innocent sufferer, the particular person whom he meets, and above all a person who in the meanwhile suffers oppression from these structures. He must do something himself. New Testament Christianity sees the particular man in need and refuses to sacrifice him for a better world, though he has a vision of this better world in the future. He sees it in terms of the kingdom of God which must begin to be given specific form even now, in our society, in a recognizable way. It is the general view of the New Testament that something of the eschatological kingdom of God is manifested historically in the society of divine communities which are critical of the world. In my view, this insight into the possibility of recognizing the Christian content of the proclamation of salvation in history is in fact a model of what we have to do now, in the twentieth century, in other historical conditions from those known by New Testament Christianity. So-called New Testament ethics is evidently socially and historically conditioned, and is therefore largely passé as far as we are concerned, but by and large it provides ethical models which a Christian cannot ignore. In them – albeit in a historically conditioned form – we find an ethical sensibility which, inspired by the Christian view of the grace of God, the faith and the disquiet of love, and driven by eschatological hope, becomes the realization of salvation in a lost world. Without being legalistic – it is prophetic – the New Testament 'Sermon on the Mount' is binding on Christians; it is the utopian-critical goad in every human ethic practised by Christians – it is binding, but can never be codified in laws. Modern church communities – above all as given shape by the Catholic church – which set out to be the guardians of the ethical 'natural law' have often in fact failed to show solidarity with what, in ancient terminology, the New Testament ultimately calls 'threatened humanity', threatened *humanum*. At the moment, the present crisis of so-called 'natural law' is at the same time a crisis of confidence in institutions which claim to be guardians of the natural law but deny it in practice. Today history itself accuses these institutions.[50] The New Testament understood the nucleus of Jesus' attitude in this respect rightly, above all in the story of the publican and the Pharisee: 'Two men went up into the Temple to pray, one a Pharisee and the other a tax collector. The Pharisee stood and prayed thus with himself, "God, I thank thee that I am not like other men, extortioners, unjust, adulterers, or even like this tax collector. I fast twice a week, I give tithes of all that I get." But the tax collector, standing far off, would not even lift up his eyes to heaven, but beat his breast, saying, "God, be merciful to me a sinner!" I tell you, this man went down to his house justified rather than the other; for every one who exalts himself will be humbled, but he who humbles himself will be exalted' (Luke 18.10–14: the story leads up to this last verse, which we also find in Matt. 23.12).

This story presupposes the Jewish liturgy used on entering the Temple.[51] When pious Jews went into the Temple, they had to make a kind of confession, in which the priest asked whether they had observed all the precepts of the Torah. If this was the case, then the priest made a declaration: 'He is justified, he will live', following the liturgical model in Ezek. 18.9: 'If a man walks in my statutes, and is careful to observe my ordinances – he is righteous, he shall surely live, says Yahweh the Lord.' In other words, the problem of ethics really confronts us with the question, May I live? Does life have ultimate meaning? Lev. 18.5 explicitly says, 'He who fulfils the law will live through the Law'; observing the Law brings justification, and all that the Jewish priest can do is to establish this and make a forensic declaration. True, this justification was not always understood in such legalistic terms, even in the Tanach (see Hab. 2.4), but this was clearly the case in official circles in the time of Jesus. What emerges from Luke's story is that Jesus turned this ethical relationship upside down: the publican and the Pharisee, in other words a notorious sinner and a professional pious man. The Pharisee had therefore 'crossed the threshold'; he had been declared cultically in the right. The publican remained on the other side of the threshold, at the back of the Temple; he was no *ṣaddīq*. But he was deeply repentant, whereas the Pharisee looked down disparagingly on publicans. Now, the Jesus of the New Testament of his own authority declares this publican to be *ṣaddīq* – in the eyes of the God of the Torah ('thus says Yahweh'). This story is about what Paul (at an earlier point in time, though not necessarily earlier than the tradition which Luke is perhaps taking up here) calls justification by faith, as opposed to the forensic justification of the one who has observed the Law and therefore may participate in the cult (such a man had rights in the divine covenant and in Israel).

The question of the young man was intended in the same sense: 'Master, what must I *do* to gain *life*?' (Mark 10.17 par.): for early Judaism, observing the Law, justification by the Law, and life all belong together. With the important exception of the Qumran sect, people began by presupposing that they were capable of observing this Law (even with the additions made by the tradition): they could 'do it'. Even Saul (see Phil. 3.6) thought that: he had earlier earned the right to be called *ṣaddīq*. Jesus turns the relationship around: 'This man went down to his house justified rather than the other'(Luke has already given this story a christ-ological colouring: *Jesus* declares the man righteous, Jesus acquits him from the Law). So another ethical standard is applied here. Christ says to the sinner: you may exist, you may live. Here we find a religious conception of evil which does not make light of evil or relativize it, but makes God greater than all evil put together. A penitent sinner is ethically better than selfish, self-glorifying ethical efforts. Ethics itself cannot give life. Only God can give life in the full sense of the word. Paul expresses the move made by Jesus in always prefacing his ethical imperative with an indicative. Post-exilic Judaism said, 'You must do that, and then you will live.' New Testament Christianity says, 'You have life – so do your duty. Being good is the source of good actions'. From this perspective people can say. 'New Testament ethics is not an ethic of the categorical imperative, of commandments and prohibitions; it is not even a value ethic or an ethic of virtue. It is an ethic which rests on the *iustitia Dei*, that is, on God's action in creating salvation,'[52] i.e. on God's right to bring about righteousness among men. Life as an eschatological gift is given to us as a new creation, and therefore we can also live in accord with the demands of the kingdom of God. Ethical life, in its micro- and macro-ethical dimensions, is the *recognizable* content of salvation, the historical manifestation or demonstration of the imminence of the king-dom of God. Therefore the kingdom of God and ethics are intrinsically connected. The religious manifests itself in the ethical, and as a result transforms the merely 'natural' significance of ethics. Thus through its ethical effects the kingdom of God is present in our history in non-definitive forms which keep on becoming obsolete. Ethical improvement of the world is *not* the kingdom of God (any more than it is the church), but it is an anticipation of that kingdom. In modern terms, this is what the New Testament describes as, 'You are dead and risen with the Lord, and now you sit at the right hand of God.' Therefore Christians must act in the world in conformity with this kingdom. Paul has already said this literally: 'Do not be conformed to "this world" (but to the "second aeon", the kingdom of God), but be transformed by the renewal of your mind, that you may prove what is the will of God, what is good and acceptable and perfect' (Rom. 12.2). The righteousness of God is God's definitive *yes* to men, a yes veiled in the human form of Jesus who went around doing good. Through faith in this 'Amen of God' (II Cor. 1.20), Jesus Christ, God's righteousness, is appropriated by men. The uncertain, broken, sinful man who is really capable of very little, is told, 'You may

live. Despite everything, life makes sense; despite everything, ethics, goodness, righteousness can be realized; despite everything, there is hope.
Abide in love, even if this love does not seem to get anywhere and is vain:
believe in this vain love and existing for others. Christian ethics has a
christological and an eschatological foundation: because of this it comes
under the perspective of effective hope, "of faith which is at work in the
love of neighbour" (Gal. 5.6). True, man under grace sees ethical evil
even more deeply than mere ethical consciousness, but his verdict on
history is gentler; he wants to participate in God's mercy.

Finally, it became clear above that the parable of the publican and the
Pharisee provided us with a religious perspective on ethics; it is concerned
with the realization of God's law, of righteousness among men. Grace
gives a future to human ethics that becomes the historical form of a way
of life in accordance with the kingdom of God. However seriously it may
be taken, Christian ethics will never become fanatical if it is going to
remain Christian. Ethics as such often finds it hard to forgive; it is
impotent to forgive. There are in fact instances when our feeling for what
is humanly permissible is so utterly violated that we become ethically
incapable of forgiving. Peter Berger says, 'Deeds that cry out to heaven
also cry out for hell.'[53] A fundamental violation of humanity which cannot
be made good does not allow of any relativizing; in that case there is the
'impossibility of forgiveness'. Indeed!

But the question is simply whether we accept this judgment and this
condemnation. Condemnation – in practice – is more the act of the man
who shuts himself off from love, and even from forgiveness, than it is a
positive act of God. It is much less the case that *we* can or may express
a final condemnation. God loved us, 'when we were still sinners'
(Rom. 5.8). So God's mercy is greater than all the evil in the world. I
Peter 3.18–20; 4.6 even speak of reconciliation for departed sinners.

Chapter 6

# Israel and the New Testament church

We do have some specific facts. To begin with, the church was a Jewish-Christian community, a Christian variant among the Jewish brother-hoods; it then became a church made up of Jews and Gentiles; later, in effect it became a purely Gentile church without any Jews (as it still is today). Are these historical facts theologically relevant? The question is, does this breach between Judaism and Christianity lie in the essence of Christianity, at least as far as the specific nature of Judaism, with its religious link between Yahweh, people and land, is concerned? Has the church taken over the place of the old people of God, or does Israel have its own irrevocable election and vocation to salvation alongside the church? And if that is the case, how can we reconcile 'salvation through the Jews' with 'salvation through Jesus Christ', when both appeal to one and the same God, 'the God of Israel, of the fathers . . . and the Father of our Lord Jesus Christ'? This latter statement in fact itself raises enor-mous difficulties for the mere juxtaposition of two parallel principles of salvation.

How does New Testament Christianity itself cope with this problem? For a Christian theology without a theology of the grace of Israel under-mines its own basic principle, that of the unrestrained and irrevocable faithfulness of God, 'whose gifts and call are irrevocable' (Rom. 11.29). That is a *Christian* theme: the 'theology of Israel' may not be neglected. But for us, even more than for the New Testament, there is a second reason: it must not be neglected because of the Jews themselves. In the course of their history, Christians have not been sufficiently grateful for their spiritual origin from Israel. Even worse, if not in the New Testa-ment, at least on the basis of references to this New Testament, they have not only discriminated against Jews in a terrible way but have even produced a Christian variant on the antisemitism which has existed for so long, even from before the time of Christianity. And since the Middle Ages,[54] high-ranking church dignitaries have framed discriminatory measures against the Jews, even in ecumenical councils (the Fourth Lateran Council of 1215).[55] There was an antisemitic explosion through-out the West after the eleventh century, chiefly for economic reasons, but also fuelled by the calumniations that Jews used Christian children for ritual murder and desecrated consecrated hosts. Societies often seek scapegoats for their own crises. In reality this explosion was connected with the origin of the feudal and the urbanized world.[56] The Jews were excluded from the new social systems, from feudal service and urban communities. The consequence was that there was nothing left for them to do other than to engage in marginal and often doubtful occupations (lending money on usury). However, it was only at the Council of Trent that the Roman Catholic church officially required the erection of Jewish ghettoes. This antisemitism was augmented by so-called Christian motives, to take a form which is now also an element in Western European consciousness.

In reaction to the Nazi extermination of the Jews, the new state of Israel was established. Here many Jews could once again celebrate the essential connection between their God, his land and people; but at the same time Israel was a state among other modern secular states. Its formation also produced the Palestinian question. This has posed a new problem for both Jews and Christians; for Christians there is no longer simply the relationship between church and synagogue, but also the question of the relationship between the Christian churches and the Jewish state and the Palestinian question.

Consequently, in our investigation of the New Testament conception of hope, it is intrinsically necessary to consider the question whether – quite apart from antisemitism, which is reprehensible purely on human grounds – the New Testament offers specifically Christian reasons for requiring the Christian churches to be particularly concerned about the Jewish people, or whether the New Testament gave grounds for the origin of a Christian variant of antisemitism.

In fact the New Testament does speak of old covenants or promises and a new covenant, but it was Marcion above all who at a later stage spoke simply of the New Testament *over against* the Old Testament, which he then deemed obsolete. He rejected the Old Testament even for Christians. This position was attacked by the church, which had interpreted its Jesus on the basis of this very scripture; for the church, scripture was both the Old Testament and the New: both were seen as the sacred books of the church. But part of this whole is and remains the Jews' own sacred book, the book of promises to the Jewish people. New Testament Christianity (which at that time did not officially have a canonical New Testament, but the *lex credendi* or norm of apostolic tradition) still recognizes this, and Jewish Christians discussed with Jews on the basis of the scripture which both held in common. Furthermore, we can hardly ignore the fact that most of the New Testament writings come from Jews, mostly Diaspora Jews. Antisemitism is therefore *a priori* hardly to be expected; in that case bitter accusations of *Jews* by Jews must have another source.

Consequently we must investigate the question how New Testament Christianity sees its relationship to Israel. And in that case, despite a fundamentally similar judgment, we can see how many different forms this judgment takes. We begin with Paul, who thought most deeply about this problem, because it was one which personally concerned him so deeply. He is the only New Testament writer who arrives at a synthesis in this problem and in so doing seeks to respect the *special nature* of the Tanach.

*Literature*: D. Crossan, 'Anti-semitism and the Gospel', *ThSt* 26, 1956, 189–214; P. J. Farla, *Het oordeel over Israël. Een Form- en Redaktionsgeschicht-liche Analyse van Mc. 10, 46–12, 40* (in preparation); D. Flusser, *De joodse oorsprong van het christendom*, Amsterdam 1964; T. F. Glasson, 'Anti-Phar-isaism in St Matthew', *JQR* 51, 1960–61, 316–20; J. Gnilka, *Die Verstockung Israels: Isaias 6.9–10 in der Theologie der Synoptiker*, Munich 1960; G. G. O'Collins, Die antijüdische Polemik im Johannesevangelium', *NTS* 10, 1964–65, 74–90; E. Grässer, 'Antisemitism in the Gospel', *ThSt* 26, 1965, 663–6; W. Trilling, *Das wahre Israel. Studien zur Theologie des Matthäusevange-lium*, Munich 1964 (see also above, in connection with the Gospel of John).

1. In his letter to the Christians in Rome, which is a hymn to *ḥesed* and *ᵉmet*, God's love and faithfulness, and at the same time a peaceful Chris-tian synthesis without personal reactions to identifiable opponents, Paul devotes three chapters to the problem of the Jews (Rom. 9.1–11.35).

   The pressing question is, has the grace of God in Jesus Christ reduced to nothing God's love and immutable faithfulness to his chosen people, which is attested and celebrated by Israel from of old? Paul the Jew and ex-Pharisee loves his people (see his heartfelt feelings in Rom. 9.1–3, which are not just empty rhetoric). Paul therefore maintains the Jewish principle that the Jewish people have in fact been promised adoption (*hyiothesia*: Rom. 9.4; see 3.2). Moreover, Jesus in whom God's promises have become 'Amen' and so have been realized for Christians (II Cor. 1.20), is himself a Jew (Rom. 9.5). 'Has God then rejected his people? Certainly not' (Rom. 11.1f.); 'it is not as though the word of God has failed' (9.6). For the Old Testament is constantly saying that in view of the unfaithfulness of many, 'only a remnant of Israel' inherits salvation (9.27; 11.5, 7). That is emphatically a Jewish view. A part always comes to grief (9.7; 11.7). Paul gives his own form of Christian explanation for this failure: the people wanted their *own* righteousness through their own observance of the Law, not through 'God's righteousness by faith' (9.30–10.5, 17) as Abraham and Habakkuk had already found out). Further-more, seen in the light of the great prophetic tradition, the assertion that purely physical descent from Abraham offers no guarantee of salvation is also thoroughly Jewish. 'It is not the children of the flesh who are the children of God, but the children of the promise' (9.8). Therefore non-Jews, too, may be admitted to the people of God as proselytes. 'He is a

Jew who is one inwardly, and real circumcision is a matter of the heart, spiritual and not literal. His praise is not from men but from God' (Rom. 2.29). This passage already contains a Christian interpretation; but we should not forget that this was also the view of many 'liberal' Diaspora Jews, whereas in Jerusalem things took on quite a different complexion. In other words, there is no specifically Christian relativizing of the ethnic matter of being a Jew.

Despite the rejection of the Christian gospel (9.30–10.1; 10.18–21) and the Jew Jesus by many Jews, the children 'after the flesh' 'are beloved for the sake of their forefathers. For the gifts and the call of God are irrevocable' (11.29; see also 3.3f.). This text is decisive. However much Paul interprets being a Jew as a religious reality, the children of Abraham are still the subject of divine election for him, 'the children after the flesh'; they have been called to this religious salvation.

Paul now goes in search of the meaning of 'this failure' (11.12) on the part of many Jews who did not recognize their own Christ. First of all he refuses to call this failure 'a stumbling so as to fall' (11.11). That means that their special vocation to salvation still remains in force. And just as once the prophets of old looked for the purposes of God when the people of God failed miserably, and went on to illuminate them by means of a prophecy of future salvation, so Paul does the same thing with the Jewish rejection of Jesus Christ. He looks for hidden meanings within the history of salvation. Through their failure 'salvation (also) *went to the Gentiles*' (11.11b). Their failure was 'riches for the Gentiles' (11.12). In fact, when he proclaimed Christ, Paul began with the Jews, and only took it to the Gentiles when the Jews rejected it.[57] The gospel is therefore 'a divine power for the salvation of all who believe, for the Jew first but also for the Gentile' (Rom. 1.16; also 2.10). Therefore it is fitting for non-Jewish Christians to be modest (11.12–24), because they are '*wild* branches, grafted on to an *alien* stem', and 'they thus share in the sap of the cultivated olive' (11.24), i.e. Israel, the people of God. Furthermore, it is therefore easier for Jews 'to be grafted back on to their own stem' after a momentary failure (11.24) than it is for non-Jews.

Paul sees all the complications in the problem. On the one hand, 'we Jews' 'in every respect' 'have considerable advantages' over the Gentiles; above all the divine promises (Rom. 3.1f.), but on the other hand, from the aspect of the actual relationship of man to God 'we Jews have no advantages over the others' (Rom. 3.9), for 'all, both Jews and Gentiles, are under the power of sin' (3.9; also 11.30–32). Election or the Gentiles cannot be regarded as values in themselves, however important this distinction may be in principle; the only thing that counts is the moral and religious life lived by any man. And then Paul says, 'We were all sinners'. Furthermore, the special character of the Christian proclamation offers no occasion for any kind of preference for Jews or Gentiles, for 'we preach *a crucified* Christ', who is 'for Jews a stumbling block and for Gentiles folly' (I Cor. 1.23). In this sense it is more difficult, rather than easier, for both of them to come to *faith in Jesus Christ*. 'Is God perhaps only the God of the Jews and not of the Gentiles also?' (Rom. 3.29f.).

This argument put forward by Paul who, although he is himself a Jew, is 'apostle to the Gentiles', is extremely subjective. Still, in the last resort he seems to deny the election of the Jews: God is a god of *all* men and not of a single people. However, Paul does not mean to rob his first statement secretly of its force: he accepts the *universalist* tendency which began to manifest itself in Judaism after the exile: God in fact does not know of any election of a single people 'in itself'; this people is chosen as a 'light of the Gentiles' to bring salvation to *all* people. Therefore the Jew Jesus brings salvation to all people. The idea of election is preserved, but is explicitly set in the perspective of universal service towards all men. For Paul, the faithfulness of the Jews to their own calling implies an affirmation of this universal salvation, to which the Jewish people was called by God as his instrument.

Still, Paul does not ignore the actual rejection of Christ. For the Old Testament often speaks of the many forms of disloyalty shown by the Jewish people, but always envisages a time when God and Israel will be fully reconciled. Paul still believes this as a Christian. He calls this rejection of the Jews 'a divine mystery' (Rom. 11.25); it is, as always in the Old Testament, 'only transitory', and Paul interprets: 'until the full member of the Gentiles come in' (11.25); then 'all Israel will be saved' (11.26). This is Paul's idea. The usual Jewish conception was that all the Gentiles would only come streaming into Zion once all the Jews had been hallowed and were gathered together on Mount Zion. Paul reverses this Jewish argument as a result of the actual situation, namely that the Christian churches had become less and less Jewish-Christian churches and above all contained members who had come over from the Gentile world (Gentile membership was later to become almost exclusive). He claims that Israel too will acknowledge Christ, but only when Christian salvation has been brought to all nations. Thus Paul was able to combine his universalist conception of salvation with his Jewish conception of the final and irrevocable election of Israel. That is evidently the result of his personal struggle with a problem which he himself has to call a divine mystery. This is the explanation of his feverish mission among the Gentiles, on the one hand 'so as to make Israel jealous' (11.11c) and on the other to hasten their salvation (see 11.13f. with 11.25). According to Paul, the church's mission among the Gentiles is the great hope for Israel. According to this conception of Paul's the Christianity of his time is *at the service* of the coming salvation of Israel. And so Paul suggests the divine mystery that there is no redemption and atonement *for Israel* without redemption and atonement *among all men*. (This acquires a special significance in the present conflict in the Middle East. As we are still unredeemed men, no one will bring this conflict to a peaceful solution except in righteousness and love, above all in sacrificial love.) Christians must therefore remember that 'if their (the Jews') rejection means the reconciliation of the world (= all men), their (the Jews') (final) *acceptance* can only mean life from the dead' (11.15): resurrection. In other words, Paul sees the Jewish people receiving a share in the resurrection of those who have been redeemed by Christ, that is, in the reconciliation of all nations. Thus the glory of God proclaimed *through Israel* from of old is *grace for all*, for Israel and the Gentiles (11.25–32; 9.24–29). 'Those who were not my people I will call my people' (Hos. 2.23; quoted by Paul in Rom. 9.24–29), but not-my-people here are the Gentiles, who with Israel become God's eschatological people. All have 'the same Lord, who bestows his riches upon all who call upon him' (10.12; see also Gal. 3.28; cf. Col. 3.11). 'I have been found by those who did not seek me; I have shown myself to those who did not ask for me' (Isa. 65.1), quoted by Paul at the end of his account (Rom. 10.20). Thus he has here reconciled both election and universality (of both sin and salvation). But there remains a mystery which is taken up 'into the counsel of God's election' (9.11f.) and therefore into praise of God at the end of his own theological reflections on the problem of synagogue and church (11.33–36).

In his very first letter (I Thessalonians), Paul is sharper against the Jews, which happens when he is involved in polemic. But in all probability this pericope is a piece of tradition which Paul has taken over: 'Brethren . . . you suffered the same things from your own countrymen as they did from the Jews, who killed both the Lord Jesus and the prophets, and drove us out, and displease God and oppose all men by hindering us from speaking to the Gentiles that they may be saved . . . But God's wrath has come upon them at last' (I Thess. 2.14f.). Paul is here alluding to specific persecutions of Christians by Jews, but describes them in accordance with a known Jewish model according to which Israel murdered its prophets (Neh. 9.26; Ezra 9.10f.; II Kings 17.7–20).[58] Striking non-Pauline phrases occur in the section (cf. also Mark 12.1b–5). The pericope indicates a pre-Pauline, Christian acceptance of a *Jewish* tradition.[59] Rabbis say the same thing. It would be sheer ideology to talk of antisemitism in this text.

In Paul's letter to the Galatians, written shortly before Romans, the tone is less peaceful, even vehement, and certain aspects of Romans do not reappear; in some passages what Paul says is even devastating for a religious Jew. But we should not forget that this letter is written to Gentile Christians who have allowed themselves to be seduced by 'invaders' into a syncretism of Judaism and Christianity; these invaders exert pressure on the Galatians to have themselves circumcised (6.12f.; 5.2f.). These are not Judaizers in the earlier sense of the word. This 'Judaism' is already bound up with syncretistic and perhaps even pagan elements, a kind of blurred transition from the teaching of the supporters of *peritomē* (circumcision) in Acts 15.5 to the *peritomē* religion attacked by Colossians which is specific to Asia Minor: in Colossae it is under oriental influence and in Galatia under Greek. It is uncertain whether Paul has summed up the situation in Galatia correctly; however, he reacts on the basis of his belief 'in Christ alone', and for that any syncretism comes from the evil one. The alternative is to be a Christian or not to be a Christian; he regards any association of paganism with other routes to salvation as a perversion of Christian faith. Therefore his reaction is particulary sharp, so sharp, in fact, that he denies the religious worth of the Torah and sees the worth of Israel as consisting only in the *epangelia*, in the *promises* of God to Abraham which have been fulfilled in Christ. This is unmistakably a *Christian* interpretation and not a Jewish interpretation of the Tanach. In Galatians, the radicalism of grace is absolutely Christian, and rightly so, but as a result, in this polemic it is difficult for Paul still to see how Israel continues to have its own religious value: apart from the promises (in which Israel has some advantage over the Gentiles, 3.15–21), he sees Israel as belonging to the past. Paul believes that the Law, which even Jesus himself still felt in his innermost being to be an expression of the will of God, was promulgated by cosmocrators, spiritual powers of the cosmos, who enslave men (3.19–4.7), just as they also have nature in their power. In Galatians Paul never says that the election of God permanently rests on Israel because of the promises of God. He does, however, say this in his rather later and more tranquil letter to the Christians in Rome, where many Jewish Christians lived. In Galatians he does not want as it were to say anything positive which might give his opponents some occasion for a possible compromise. For Paul a compromise is utterly ruled out. In other words, he keeps back some of his insights for tactical reasons. It is certainly a temptation to suppose that in his closing wishes in 6.16 he intends the wish of salvation 'for the Israel of God' for the Jews (in the sense of what he says in Romans about Israel's final conversion), but this letter, above all with its vehement conclusion, hardly allows such a reading. In that case we would already have here, for the first time, an explicit identification of the church of Christ with the 'true Israel'. However, in terms of content his whole Christian Abraham hermeneutic (3.6–14; 3.15–29) goes in this direction. The Deutero-Paulines and other letters of a Pauline character clearly understood this 'objective tendency' of Galatians and have given it expression. For Christians, the decisive question will always be: how must the exclusiveness of Christ (*solus Christus*), salvation only in Christ through the faith that is at work in love of the neighbour (Gal. 5.6), be understood in all concrete situations? (For example, would Paul regard a form of Christianity which made use of Zen Buddhism as a perversion of the *solus Christus* principle?) However, we learn from Paul that in any case Christian faith cannot be reconciled with an expectation of decisive and final salvation which rests on human achievements. Here the question of the precise nature of the salvation for which we need Jesus Christ is of fundamental significance. Salvation in Christ is an unconditional gift of God: everything that goes against that, in fact goes against the canon of Christianity. Paul's interpretation of religious Judaism, above all in the form in which it was seeking to find a footing in the church, suggested that he felt himself to be up against this essential contradiction. One should not forget that in Galatians Paul is not really writing polemic directly against Jews, but against Christians who thought it possible to compromise between the righteousness of the Law and the righteousness of faith; his criticism of Judaism applies only to its failure to accept Jesus Christ, though he sees the cause of that in their way of salvation, namely through their own efforts. While this may be a reflection of the official Jewish orthodoxy of his time, it is not the whole reality of Judaism. Judaism was very pluriform. Moreover, in Galatians we find a tendency which has been expressed more clearly in the Deutero-Paulines by the authors of Colossians and Ephesians than by Paul in Galatians: the predilection for the *nomos* or the Law is connected with the tendency in late antiquity for there to be a deep-seated fear of cosmocrators or world-rulers (at that time angels and demons), who use both the Torah and the natural laws as instruments of their spiritual domination of men. At that time the great alternative was: 'Christ or these heavenly spirits?', while some believed that they could harmonize the two. In I Cor. 2.8 Paul already comments: 'If the rulers of this age had understood this, *they* would not have crucified the Lord of glory.'

2. In Ephesians, which comes from the Pauline school, we already find another conception. 'Israel' is no longer a current problem in the historical situation. For the present is characterized by 'the third race', the Christian church (cf. I Cor. 10.32). Here a perspective of the future of Israel becomes irrelevant. With Paul, the author of Ephesians accepts that the old Israel possessed the promise (Eph. 2.12), but that the promise now applies only to the church, in which the promises are fulfilled (3.6). Thus the author has a positive attitude to the old Israel; however, during the time of writing of Ephesians the relationship with the Jews was no longer an acute Christian problem in Asia Minor. The churches consisted for the most part of Gentile Christians (see Eph. 2.11).

The author sees how in the past men were divided and at odds with each other: there was enmity between Jews and Gentiles (Greeks and barbarians – an old Jewish theme).[60] The Gentiles were excluded from the promises, which rested solely on Israel (Ephesians looks on the situation before Christ from a Christian standpoint, for the expectation of the Messiah is not a specific characteristic for Israel in Jewish belief). Here not only do we have an unfavourable verdict on the Law (though not entirely), but the author even forgets the universalistic tendency which could be found, even according to Jewish interpretation, in the promises that were in fact meant only for Israel (though this universalism also had Israel at the centre). By contrast, Paul wanted to bring the universalism of these promises into the foreground, albeit by way of Israel. The question is whether the author of Ephesians is a Gentile Christian and thus whether in fact he knew as much about ancient Israel as a Jewish Christian (though he was well schooled in Paulinism and in Paul's Jewish-Christian way of thinking). It must be allowed that most of the New Testament writers were Jewish Christians, even if they were Hellenistic Jewish Christians. When former Gentiles get a hearing, Christianity, while remaining authentic, takes on another tone. So Gentiles were excluded from Israel's *politeia*; they stood outside Jewish theocracy. In this way they were alienated from God (see Eph. 4.18; Col. 1.21). With Paul, Ephesians sees the essence of Israel not in the Law but in the *epangelia*, the promises (in the plural): the promise to Abraham (Gen. 15.7–21; 17.1–22), to the people under Moses (Ex. 24.1–11) and the prophetic proclamation of the new covenant (Jer. 31.31–34; 32.40; Isa. 55.3; Ezek. 37.26). The Law which made Israel a ghetto in the world of nations is seen here more as a cause of disruption and hostility among the nations (Eph. 2.14f.).

Excluded from the promises, 'the Gentiles had no hope' (Eph. 2.12); this was a general Jewish judgment on the Gentiles.[61] Yahweh alone gives reasons for hope (see Col. 1.5). Therefore Ephesians calls the Gentiles *atheoi*, i.e. men without God (see Jer. 10.25 Greek; I Thess. 4.5; cf. Gal. 4.8).

The great turning-point comes with Christ. As mediator of salvation through his death on the cross, he has brought the Gentiles near (Eph. 2.13). 'Bring near' is an expression from proselytizing; it means 'add to a community': the reference is to the Christian initiatory rite of baptism. 'Christ is our peace': through him the enmity between Jews and Gentiles is removed; he has reconciled the two peoples with one another and so with God in a universal church (Eph. 2.14–18), because he has broken down the dividing wall, the Law (Eph. 2.16: interpreted in another way, this is the same unfavourable verdict on the Law as in Galatians). According to Ephesians, the purpose of the coming of Jesus is the pacification of the world. He brought about 'the new humanity', gathered together in peace in one and the same church community: Jew and Gentile are reconciled; so too the community of nations has been reconciled with God (Eph. 2.16). It forms 'one body' in the church.

Ephesians does not reflect further on the continuing destiny of Israel. The promise which had been given to Israel has been fulfilled, namely in the church. In this sense, according to Ephesians, Israel has already fulfilled its role; for the author this role is therefore played out. The fact that the 'great church' really consisted only of Gentile Christians, though by nature it is a 'church made up of Jews and Gentiles' (this remains the standpoint of Ephesians), was the reason why there was no further reflection on Israel's future. The church itself was gradually seen as the new Israel in which Israel's promises were fulfilled, though the church is not explicitly called the new Israel in Ephesians. This notion gained general acceptance even in circles which lived in the spirit of Paul (like Ephesians). We must remember the historical factors which contributed to a failure to reflect further on the continuing destiny of Israel. Romans 9–11 soon became a forgotten truth even in biblical Christianity.

3. I Peter 2.9f. is even further removed from Paul's conception: the church is now the true Israel (2.9; cf. Phil. 3.3; Gal. 6.16). All the promises to Israel are fulfilled in the church. Deutero-Isaiah's prophecy (Isa. 43.20; Ex. 19.6 Greek) of 'an elect race, a royal priesthood, a holy people' is now applied to Christians (in principle a community made up of Jews and non-Jews). Israel's honorific titles become qualifications of the church (cf. Isa. 61.6; 62.3). The whole Christian people has access to God (= royal priesthood, also Rev. 1.6; 5.10). On the basis of Jesus' sacrifice on the cross (I Peter 1.19), the church is set apart to be the people of God (I Peter 1.15f.: 'the people chosen to be his own', Isa. 43.21; Mal. 3.17). And this people, the church, must now proclaim the mighty acts of God which it has experienced (I Peter 2.9). In 2.10, the text of Hos. 2.23, once spoken to Jews, 'Not-my-people become my people' is applied to Gentile Christians. *Laos*, applied in Judaism only to Israel, in contrast to *ethnē* (the nations), is now also used of Gentile Christians. In terms of contact, that means that the church is the true Israel. In these predominantly Gentile Christian churches the idea that by nature the church is a church made up of Jews and Gentiles (Paul and Ephesians) has become a dead letter. In the church the Gentiles, too, are the people of God, *laos* (cf. Acts 15.14; Rom. 9.25f.; Titus 2.14; Rev. 18.4; in the Tanach *laos*, people, is used almost exclusively for the people of God). Romans 9.25 also quotes Hos. 2.23; but we do not find this Christian reinterpretation of the term *laos* anywhere else in the New Testament than Rom. 9.25 and I Peter 2.10. Instead of being the holy books of the synagogue, the Tanach

has now become the book of the church: the Old Testament, which expresses the church's understanding of itself. It no longer matters whether a person is a Jew or a Gentile (I Peter is primarily concerned with former Gentiles, see also Phil. 3.20). 'Politically' speaking, being a Jew or a non-Jew is irrelevant: our *politeuma* or our homeland is heaven (for in the ancient world religion was the basis of the whole *politeuma*).

However, to all outward appearances Christians are a Jewish brotherhood. Antisemitism, which was widespread at that time, also affected Christians. For Gentiles, Christians resembled the Jews in being 'eccentrics', removed from all public life, which was steeped in pagan religion. Like Jews, Christians were in fact eccentrics in public life; they were mocked and hated by the people (see I Peter 4.3f.; also 1.1; 2.11). Because pagans were excluded from Christian assemblies, these assemblies became suspect. Tacitus wrote: 'Nero had many Christians arrested because they venerated a pernicious superstition and were hated by the people for their shameful deeds.'[62] All this had already been said earlier of Jews. In particular, Christians were accused of 'hatred towards the human race' (evidently because of their deliberate segregation).[63]

In Phil. 3.4a, circumcision simply becomes spiritual circumcision, i.e. Christian baptism in which the new people of God comes into being through faith (see also Gal. 6.15). Titus 1.10f. expresses its ill humour over the difficulties and heresies of 'insubordinate men, empty talkers and deceivers', and adds: 'especially among the circumcised'. These are evidently Jews from Crete (1.12), and the author attacks 'Jewish myths or commands of men who reject the truth' (Titus 1.14). These are certainly not the old Judaizers among the Christians, but Diaspora Jewish Christians who combine heterodox Jewish and syncretistic views, and in addition misinterpret Paul's slogan 'to the pure all is pure' (Titus 1.15) – a kind of mixture of extreme ascetic strictness and ethical indifference (not libertinism), characteristic of the religious syncretism of the time among a number of Diaspora Jews (see also Colossians, I John, I and II Timothy), all of which practise a similar kind of oriental syncretistic Hellenistic Jewish religion. There is no question of anti-Judaism here either, though there is an increase in Christian unwillingness that above all Jewish Christians should seem to obscure the Christian identity. Presumably these Jewish Christians still cherish a more general christological conception (as over against the christology which had already been developed further in the church) in which on the one hand Jesus was God's great and final prophet, and in which on the other hand there was an acceptance of a mystical contact with 'the heavenly' by means of other historical figures, above all Moses (the so-called Sinaitism of early Jewish theology). Heresies of this kind, Ignatius says later, have a demonstrable connection with Christians who have entered the church from Judaism (*Magn.* 9.8). These people evidently do not need redemption through the crucifixion of Jesus (see I John 1.7; 5.6) and suppose themselves superior to sinfulness (I John 1.8–10; see 3.6, 8; 5.18); thus they fail to understand brotherly unity (I John 2.9–11; 3.10, 14.f.; 4.8, 20; 5.2).[64]

4. The letter to the Hebrews perhaps contains the most radical expressions of the fact that Christianity has made the Jewish religion obsolete, although these are expressed in an extremely subtle way. This happens in a complicated Christian rabbinic hermeneutic of Jewish holy scripture, so that we Westerners can hardly understand the point of the final conclusion. This synagogue exegesis in fact presupposes that the author had already made his decision before he embarked on his interpretation of the Old Testament.

In contrast to Paul, for this author it is Jewish worship and not the Torah that occupies the central point (not worship in the Temple of Jerusalem, which is not mentioned once). He is concerned with the abolition of the cult (through Christ), which in the Old Testament is bound up with the Mosaic tent of the covenant, to which Israelite worship goes back for its foundation. The author as it were takes the Jews back to what he sees as the climax of the history of Israel: the people in the wilderness on their way to the promise. He seeks to impress on Christians that what the unwilling and grumbling people did then is an ever-threatening possibility for Christians, and that such an eventuality would be even worse (Heb. 2.1, 3; 3.8, 12f., 18; 4.1, 11; 6.6; 10.26). For the author, Christ brings true worship. He is the true sacrifice, the sacrificer and the victim in one, who is glorified and proclaimed to be eternal high priest by God for the sake of his suffering and death (5.7–10), and as heavenly high priest 'enters the presence of God for us' (7.24–25b; 9.24; 10.12), as the chief minister in the angelic liturgy, in which the earthly church also partakes (1.7,14; 8.6; 9.21; 10.11; see also 3.6; 10.21; and 7.25; 13.15; 9.24; cf. 12.22f.). One reason for this letter seems to be that Christians were beginning to stay away from Christian worship (10.25). This evidently betrays a slackening of faith or, in the religious syncretism of the time (see already Galatians and Colossians), the attractive force of a more spiritual religion of experience and fulfilment which at that time often went hand in hand with a 'Jewish esotericism' that had attractions for non-Jews. The author of Hebrews, who is an expert in rabbinic exegesis, must himself have come from Judaism. In his subtle way, in the last resort he seeks to confront his believers with the choice between Judaism and Christianity. Even if this is not expressly said, his whole letter seeks to demonstrate that only the Christian community is the true Israel, whereas Israel was simply bearer of the *promise*. Even this last, still Pauline, notion is to some degree devalued by Hebrews in an extremely complicated form of synagogue-type exegesis. The author relativizes the blessing through Abraham (Paul's exegetical argument), and by means of a very subtle exegesis shows that 'the unknown', the mysterious Melchizedek, without beginning, whose parents were totally unknown, himself gave his priestly blessing to Abraham (7.5f., compare Num. 6.22–27) and that Abraham paid tithes to him (7.4). Furthermore, according to Hebrews the priesthood is the foundation of the Law and not vice versa. Melchizedek, who had nothing to do with the priestly tribe and gave Abraham the priestly blessing, thus shows that the Aaronite priesthood is insufficient and transitory. This priesthood of Melchizedek, which in the view of many rabbis had passed over from Melchizedek to Abraham,[65] is identified in Hebrews with Christ (7.4–18). Access to God (7.19b; cf. 4.16; 7.25; 10.19; 10.22; 12.22; above all the great section 12.18f.) is the ultimate significance of any cult. Even the high priest could not achieve this goal in Judaism (12.18f.); he and he alone was allowed to enter the holy of holies (where Yahweh is enthroned) once a year on the Great Day of Atonement, but then only in the wake of a cloud of incense, so that he could not even see the ark (9.1–10). Therefore Jewish worship is only a shadow of the true worship of Christ (8.5; 9.4). Hebrews is not concerned with a renewal of the old covenant but simply with a new covenant. Through his glorification to God, Christ has opened up access to God in a way that was impossible for the Old Testament (8.9f.); this was finally realized by virtue of Jesus' self-sacrifice (9.22; 10.19f.), through his own blood, instead of through the blood of bulls and goats (9.12; see 9.7; 9.25; 9.14), by means of his voluntary sacrifice. This has given us liberation from our sins (9.18–23) and bestowed our heritage on us (9.15–17): the forgiveness of sins and salvation, reconciliation with God or access to God (10.19–25). This great promise or heritage is not reserved for the physical descendants of Abraham, but only for the one who is called (11.8, 18), namely the Christian (6.17). So Jesus is the sole source of everlasting salvation (10.1–18), 'once for all' (10.10). It is striking that throughout this account the high priest Christ ultimately emerges as 'the new Moses' who in early Judaism is not only the leader of his people but also 'prophet, king and priest' (along the line of Deut. 5.23; 9.9, 18, 26), even the suffering servant (Heb. 11.26); indeed, in Philo he is even the *divus Moyses* or 'divine Moses'.[66] It is precisely for this reason that Hebrews takes Mosaic worship rather than the Temple liturgy as a point of comparison. In Hebrews, alongside Melchizedek, Moses as high priest is the model for the high priesthood of Christ.

However, in the great hymn of praise to the faith of the great figures of Israelite belief, Hebrews sees believers from both Old and New Testament as the one people of God and adds: for these Christ was really the object of faith, Jesus 'the same yesterday, today and tomorrow' (13.8).

Following the line of the prophetic and Deuteronomistic tradition, Hebrews describes Israel as the elect people, though they refuse to listen to God's voice (12.18–21). As a Jewish Christian the author is very sensitive to this contemporary atmosphere, but in the end says that in Christ a man can find a hundredfold what he looks for elsewhere. Therefore, 'Let us go out' (13.13), just as according to the story of the golden calf Moses refused to remain in the midst of his people in the camp, and pitched his tent outside (see Ex. 33.3, 5, 7). 'And everyone who sought the Lord would go out to the tent of meeting which was outside the camp.' Moses only found God outside. Jews like Philo had already come to say something similar,[67] and the author of Hebrew doubtless knows the tradition which is expressed in Philo.

The author feels himself to be fully in accord with the *ecclesia ab Abel*, which in Hebrews 11 he describes as the one people of God who, along with the Christians, really confess the same Christ in Old and New Testaments. In this sense he does not in any way contrast the church of Christ as the true Israel with the Israel which has only transitory significance. Since Christ, however, Israel is a thing of the past. He does not go on to reflect, as Paul does in Rom. 9–11, on the Jews, who are now outside the Christian community of God.

5. Since the work of J. Louis Martyn,[68] there has been a tendency to describe the Gospel of John as the most acutely anti-Jewish document in the New Testament. At first reading this might well seem to be true. However, it is important for us to recognize the historically conditioned nature of the Johannine opposition to Judaism. His gospel – like the whole of the Johannine corpus – is in no way antisemitic. Over the last decade, interpreters from a variety of approaches have arrived at a growing consensus that the roots of the Gospel of John are to be found in Judaism – of the Old Testament and inter-testamental periods. John is seen to be based on both orthodox and heterodox, syncretistic Jewish traditions. The origin of the Johannine tradition even goes back to *Palestine*. One can hardly expect to find antisemitism in a Jewish tradition (even if it has been Christianized), but this does not rule out the sharpest criticism. Furthermore, in John 'the Jews' does not refer to what we would understand by the term; this is the designation used, not among Diaspora Jews but in the Palestine of the time, for the inhabitants of Jerusalem and its surroundings, the Judaeans (see my comments above on the Gospel of John).

In that case, what is the origin of the undeniable anti-Judaic tendency of this Gospel, despite the fact that (along with the whole of the rest of the New Testament) it preserves 'Israel' as an honorific title for the Jewish people (John 1.31, 49; 3.10; 12.13), and expressly acknowledges the salvation-historical connection between Christianity and Judaism (John 4.22)? For in this text John acknowledges (albeit through the mouth of others) that 'salvation comes from the Jews'.

It was pointed out above that over recent years there has been a growing consensus among interpreters that the Gospel of John works with very old pre-Johannine traditions about Jesus which show clear points of contact with the synoptic tradition, even if they are not directly dependent on that tradition. John does with this material what the synoptic gospels do with theirs: the tradition is understood in the light of the situation and the questions of the particular community to which the evangelist belongs, and is brought up to date on the basis of his own theological views. Thus we need a good knowledge of the particular situation of the Johannine churches if we are to interpret the gospel properly. For in the Gospel of John the drama is in fact played out as it were on two levels: the Christian tradition about the life of Jesus and the contemporary conflict in the later Johannine churches. So the two historical situations are interwoven in a very complex way. This theory is generally accepted by most interpreters today.[69] It identifies the situation of the Johannine communities as that of a Christian community which lives in the vicinity of a very aggressive Jewish Greek synagogue, so that the life of the community is characterized by polemic between the church and the synagogue. In that case the Gospel of John must be read essentially against the background of the polemic between Christianity and Judaism, between 'the disciples of Moses' and 'the disciples of Jesus' (John 9.27f.). In the Gospel of John the opponents of Jesus – on the basis of historical reminiscences of the life of Jesus – are really the Jewish protagonists of some fifty to sixty years later, namely the synagogue in the days of the evangelist. The whole of Johannine scholarship is now moving in this direction.[70] Meeks[71] thinks that from a sociological perspective the Gospel of John is under the trauma of the church separated from the synagogue. For the Johannine churches, belief in Jesus also means a change in their social situation, namely an isolation from their former Jewish environment and a new situation in a group which is now attacked by their former society. It seems to me highly probable that there was a Greek Jewish synagogue hostile to Christians in the immediate neighbourhood of the Johannine churches (in that case Alexandria would certainly seem most likely, or a large city in Asia Minor).[72] The Gospel of John is alone in the New Testament in speaking three times of being *aposynagōgos* (John 9.22 and 12.42 must be understood in the light of John 16.2), i.e. being thrown out of the synagogue. This presupposes a situation in the time after AD 70, when there began to be an official break everywhere between the church and the synagogue, which was as it were legalized, around AD 90, by the insertion of a curse on all heretics (*birkat hā-minīm*) in Jewish daily prayer by Gamaliel II.[73] I will not deny that specific historical friction between the church and the synagogue can be found in the background to the Gospel of John. But it seems to me that these interpreters have not demonstrated that it *governs* the whole spirit of the gospel. Although this background cannot be denied, the real problem of the churches from which the gospel comes lies in a tension *within the church*, between Jewish and Gentile Christians, a tension which threatened to destroy the unity of the church. This is the reason why the whole of the Johannine literature, in particular, stresses 'that all may be one' (e.g. John 17.11; 17.21; 17.23; 10.16; 11.52; 13.34f.; 14.12–17) and brotherly love. John is concerned with the purity of the Christian identity – faith is a personal link with the person of Jesus Christ (once again the *solus Christus* principle) – an identity which must not be endangered by an attempt to hang on to 'Jewish identity', whether secretly or in public. The Johannine figure of Nicodemus (and also of Joseph of Arimathea, 'a disciple of Jesus, but secretly, for fear of the Jews') in the Gospel is the type of the Jewish Christian who is a secret Christian for fear of the Jews while remaining publicly in contact with the synagogue (John 2.23–25; 9.16; 12.42f.; 19.38; 19.39). The Jewish Christians, at least in the Johannine communities, evidently overestimate their Jewish affinity as the people of salvation (see John's correction to the pre-Johannine hymn in the prologue: John 1.12c, 13; also 8.21–59). In the church they had a feeling of superiority over Gentile Christians, though these increasingly formed a majority in the church. So unity and love in the church were endangered. Paul in his turn had in fact warned 'the wild shoot' (the Gentile Christians) to be restrained towards those who had first been called to be Christians, the Jews. However, in the Johannine community this priority of the calling of the Jews, generally recognized in the New Testament, had become a cause of discord and lack of brotherly love. The Gospel of John attacks it sharply. That the local synagogue was very hostile emerges from the fact mentioned by John that there were 'secret Christians' (for fear of the Jews); but John sees this too as a danger to the Christian identity. Furthermore these (Jews and) Jewish Christians were evidently in the Jewish Moses tradition and that of Sinaitic mysticism (see above).[74] Highly esteemed though Jesus Christ was by these Jewish Christians, for them Moses had become an independent principle of salvation alongside him. For John, this puts the apostolic principle of *solus Christus* in grave danger, and he will tolerate no compromise. The Gospel of John also attacks a 'backward' Jewish Christian christology which with its low christological conception can easily join company with a Mosaic mysticism; it cannot, however, be reconciled with the high christological conception of Jesus as the Son and Son of man who lives with the Father from eternity, comes down to us and ascends again to the Father. I therefore see the polemic in the Gospel of John as being caused by tension with Jewish *Christians within the church* (although this is against a background of polemic between the church and the synagogue). The debates of Jesus over his messiahship reflect the situation of the later Johannine communities (see e.g. John 7.27, 41f.; 12.34). The sharpness of the tone in John 8.12–59 clearly betrays the cold war between the church and the synagogue in John's time.[75] There is one striking pericope in which Jesus alludes to his departure. 'The Jews then say, "Where does this man intend to go that we shall not find him? *Does he intend to go* to the Dispersion *among the Greeks* and teach the Greeks?" ' (John 7.33–36). This is evidently the suspicion held in *Jewish-Christian* circles about a church which increasingly becomes a church from among the Gentiles. In other words, the synagogue seems to be the reason why there is a certain tension *in* the Johannine church between the Jewish Christians and the other Christians.

The question, then, is what John means by 'the Jews'. According to E. Grässer,[76] 'the Jews' (for the time of Jesus this means 'Judaeans') are a model for all who reject the Christian gospel on the basis of the Torah (with a reference to John 1.17). Here 'Torah' stands for the opposition of the synagogue to the messiahship of Jesus as confessed by Christians. In my view, we have here the clearest expression of the 'two-level' approach of the Gospel of John. The Jews with whom *Jesus* enters into discussion in the report are in fact the Jewish leaders and Pharisees with whom Jesus was historically engaged in battle, but they are delineated and coloured with the features of Pharisaic rabbinism from the synagogue of John's time, and that happens *in connection with the presence of Jewish Christians* in the Johannine community (communities). By and large the leaders of the people (John 1.19; 2.18) are again the Pharisees, albeit in the same twofold historical perspective. According to John, these leaders are responsible for the unbelief of the Jews and for the failure of Jesus among the Jews; they are responsible for his persecution to the death (John 11.47–53). But in the time of John, too, they are the reason why Jews do not come to believe in Christ (John 16.1–4). John seeks to spare the Jewish *people* and lay all the blame on its leaders; so he continually lays stress on the manipulation of the people by their leaders and by the Pharisees (who after AD 70 became the leaders of the people, John 7.32, 47f.; 9.13, 15, 40; 11.46; 12.19 and 12.42). The pregnant use of 'the Jews' in the sense of the Jewish leaders (above all the Pharisees in the time of John) can be clearly seen from the section in which it is said that 'much was said secretly about him *among the people* (the Jews, of course!) . . . yet *for fear of the Jews* no one spoke openly of him' (7.12f.; see the same thing e.g. in John 9.22). The (Jewish) people does not dare to speak 'for fear of the Jews'! Furthermore, here we find the two historical planes interwoven in typical fashion: on the one hand, during the earthly life of Jesus, many of the Jewish people dare not sympathize publicly with him 'for fear of "the Jews" ', i.e. the Jerusalem leaders of the people, just as in the time of John many Jewish Christians did not break off contact with the synagogue, and like Nicodemus were secret Christians for fear of the synagogue leaders. Many pericopes became more understandable to anyone who reads the Gospel in this way. 'If we let him go on thus, every one will believe in him, and the Romans will come and destroy both our holy place and our nation' (John 11.48; in fact this presupposes the fall of Jerusalem in AD 70) takes into account both the anger of the synagogue over the loss of its members to the Johannine community and also that of the Jewish Christians in the same community who find themselves in the minority over against the Gentile Christians. Thus the so-called anti-Judaism of the Gospel of John has its origin in the church difficulties of the time, difficulties between Jewish Christians and Gentile Christians, which were for the most part caused by the activity and the powers of attraction of a neighbouring and hostile Jewish synagogue. In turn, the leaders of this synagogue (at that time the rabbinic Pharisees) become for John the *type* in accordance with which he delineates and colours the historical relationship between Jesus and the Jewish leaders; i.e., then as now the Jewish people are victims of their *leaders*. In itself this is not just a feature of the Old Testament and above all the prophetic tradition; it can also be found in Judaism of the inter-testamental period, and is a criticism from within Judaism. When Moses died, Joshua was appointed leader of the people 'for otherwise the community of Yahweh would be a sheep without a shepherd' (Num. 27.17). Soon, however, we hear Yahweh's lament over the leaders and shepherds of Israel, 'Son of man, prophesy against the shepherds of Israel, prophesy and say to them, even to the shepherds, Thus says the Lord God: Ho, shepherds of Israel, who have been feeding yourselves . . . I am against the shepherds; and I will require my sheep at their hand, and put a stop to their feeding the sheep . . . I will rescue my sheep from their mouths . . . I myself will search for my sheep. And I will set up over them one shepherd, and he shall feed them . . .' (Ezek. 34.1–31; a text which one can read afresh in the light of John's discourse about the 'good shepherd': John 10.1–21). Also, 'Woe to the shepherds who destroy and scatter the sheep of my pasture . . . You have scattered my flock, and have driven them away, and you have not attended to them . . . And I will set shepherds over them who will care for them . . .' (Jer. 23.1–8). In both cases the good shepherd to come is a 'righteous branch from David' (Jer. 23.5f.; Ezek. 34.23). Mark 6.34 had already taken up this theme: Jesus has compassion on the crowd and sees that it is a 'people without a shepherd'. Thus John takes over a criticism of Jewish leaders used purely within Yahwistic belief and uses it in Christian polemics. All the shepherds or rulers who came before Jesus 'are thieves and robbers' (John 10.8). This Ezekiel-like sharpness sounds doubly acute in the mouth of a Christian. The whole of the long description of Jesus as the 'good shepherd', the good leader of the people, is at the same time a vehement attack on the Jewish leaders (John 10.1–21 with 10.22–39). But what seems to us to be anti-Judaism in the Gospel of John in fact has deep Jewish roots. As such, all this has nothing to do with anti-Judaism; were that the case one would have to call all the prophecies of disaster in the Jewish prophets anti-Judaism. The (Jewish) Christians in the Johannine communities are victims of the diligence of the leaders of the local synagogue, just as the Jewish people was often a victim of its leaders, even as it was when Jesus of Nazareth came.

On the other hand, it can hardly be denied that if such a long-established pattern of criticism (from within Judaism) is applied to the Jewish leaders by a church which is either separate from or has been expelled from the synagogue, and which will consist more and more exclusively of non-Jews as time goes on, then it will have anti-Judaistic (if not antisemitic) overtones. However, at all events this so-called anti-Judaism in the Gospel of John has *Jewish* roots.

From the prologue onwards, the whole of the Fourth Gospel is constructed according to a particular pattern: Jesus, who as the Christ, the Son from on high, appears among us as the 'crisis' between belief and unbelief. He came to his own, and his own did not receive him. The Johannine Jesus is aggressive towards unbelief (John 3.19–21; 8.21–24, 40–44; 12.35, 46, 48). Given the situation of the Johannine communities, 'belief' and 'unbelief', always with reference to Jesus Christ, specifically becomes a contrast between Christianity and Judaism. And here the door is opened towards a certain anti-Judaistic spite in the Gospel of John which will have its effect on the church at a later date.

For the sake of faith or Christian identity (*solus Christus*), John always speaks in a detached way about the specific features of Judaism: '*your* Law' and '*your* father' (Abraham: John 6.49; 8.38). Finally, whereas Paul spoke of the Jews as the 'cultivated olive' and of the Gentiles as the 'wild branch' in Christianity, and of the fulfilment of the Old Testament promises of God, in John we find precisely the opposite: in comparison with Christians, who are 'green wood', the Jews are withered branches. The traditional Jewish theme of the people which is led astray by its leaders unmistakably becomes a cliché at John's hands – it becomes a deliberate *principle of redaction* (in it we clearly find the psychology of two rival religions within a religion). Presumably the Johannine churches are in an obvious minority in the great Diaspora cities where there were often large Jewish settlements. The Gospel of John maintains its good tone throughout. However, the controversial situation (of its time) makes it use, for example, the argument from scripture in a very aggressive way, while it presupposes that the Jewish rabbis who also study this scripture do so for their own honour and glory (John 5.42–44): they praise the law of Moses but do not observe it (7.19; 7.22; 8.39). Therefore the Gospel summons Moses to prosecute the Jews (5.45).

However, from John 13.31 to 18.12 (the trial of Jesus), 'the Jews' vanish completely from John's perspective. Throughout this complex Jesus as it were turns only to the Johannine community, 'the little children' (13.33, represented by the disciples who believe in Jesus). This move is characterized in a striking way if we compare John 13.33 with 7.33–36. In both cases we have a mention of Jesus' departure, but the first time Jesus had spoken to 'the Jews'. Now he is speaking to the 'Johannine church' (the disciples or 'little children'): 'As I said *to the Jews*, so now I say *to you*, "Where I am going you cannot come"' (13.33, where he adds, 'but later', 13.36b). The contrast between 'unbelievers' (the Jews) and the disciples as the community of Christian believers is striking. And it *is* a question of this believing community. The inspiration for this farewell discourse of Jesus perhaps came from the Deuteronomic farewell discourse of Moses.[77] Both farewell discourses take place before the death of the great leader, both groups of disciples are confronted with a new situation, and both speeches seek to establish and encourage the disciples and end with an appeal for mutual love.

Jesus prays 'that they may be one' (13.34f.; 14.12–17; 17.21–23). He warns the community that they will be persecuted as he is persecuted. However, the opposite pole is now no longer 'the Jews' but 'the world' – quite generally, the non-believing world (15.19), 'which hates you'(15.19), 'because you are not of the world' (17.14), just as Jesus is not (17.16), and just as 'his kingdom' is not (18.36): 'the world . . . which has not known the Father' (17.25). The persecutors are now repeatedly referred to quite generally as 'they' (15.20, 21, 22, 24, 25; 16.2, 3), but it is also said, '*They* will cast you out of the synagogue' (16.2, which is a clear reference to the situation of the Johannine Christians). However, Jesus tells his followers that they need not be afraid, 'I have overcome the world' (16.33c). The unity in the church for which Jesus prays is the unity between *Jewish* and *Gentile* Christians; there must be room in the church for both, 'In my Father's house there are many mansions' (14.2). Now, at this moment, Jesus does not pray for 'the world' (17.9), but for the unity of the 'church made up of Jews and Gentiles'. In these last sections the polemical note has completely disappeared from the words of the Johannine Jesus (in John's account it recurs only in his trial). True, the Gospel of John has sharp things to say against the Jewish leaders (following the line of the Jewish religious tradition), but it is nevertheless an appeal to unity and love among Jews and non-Jews in the one church of Christ.

6. In the book of Revelation the words of the Son of man in the address to the churches of Smyrna and Philadelphia (2.9; 3.7–13) are often regarded as the strongest anti-Jewish comment in the New Testament: 'the synagogue of Satan' (Rev. 3.9; see John 8.39–59). However, this text is usually interpreted wrongly, and not as Revelation intends it. On each occasion Revelation adds, 'I know the slander of those *who say that they are Jews and are not*, but are a synagogue of Satan' (2.9), and 'those of the synagogue of Satan who say that they are Jews and *are not, but lie*' (3.9). For the New Testament, Jew is never an insult but the *honourable name* of the people who are the bearer of God's promises. It is not 'the Jews' who are the 'synagogue of Satan', but the Jewish *Christians* who devalue the crucifixion and resurrection of Jesus, and in so doing endanger the faith of the Christian community. By calling themselves 'Jews' they escape the Roman persecution of Christians. The book of Revelation is referring to a syncretistic tendency among particular Christians who are collaborating with the Romans. They are the lying apostles of Rev. 2.2. Perhaps they are uncircumcised proselytes who become Christians, but had only accepted part of the apostolic faith (what comes to be known historically as 'Nicolaitism').[78] Thus there is no question of even a semblance of anti-Judaism in what is in any case a truly Jewish book, the book of Revelation.

*Conclusion and final considerations: the church and Zionism*

Biblical and New Testament antisemitism is sheer legend. On the other hand, there is unmistakably a *religious* tension between Jewish and Christian interpretations of Jesus.

Christians, however, do wrong if they assert that as a result of Jesus Christ any particular relationship between God and a people or an individual historical man has become outdated (in that case they would destroy the deepest meaning of their own religion: Jesus was a quite particular individual from an identifiable period in history and, moreover, a Jew). On the one hand, this assertion cannot be demonstrated by means of the New Testament: Jesus believed that he had been sent to Israel to be God's witness in the view of and for the benefit of all nations; he summons all Israel to faithfulness towards this task. On the other hand, the original Christian interpretation of Jesus is a Jewish interpretation, and to begin with Christianity was a brotherhood within Judaism which called the whole of Israel to be faithful towards its vocation: to live 'in holiness before God' for the benefit of all peoples (Deut. 7.6; 14.2; 14.21), just as God is 'the holy one of Israel' (Isa. 30.11; 41.14; 43.3, 14, 15).

What Christians believe Jesus to have made clear by his life and death, following in the tradition of Jewish prophecy, consists more in the fact that God's particular support and help are the objects of faith. They are not susceptible to empirical demonstration, nor do they offer empirical supports. In this sense, the prophets and above all Jesus of Nazareth have shattered all empirical guarantees and earthly 'definitions' to which the covenant with God and trust in God might want to lay claim or to which they might want to refer. One cannot identify the God of Israel with a single divine act of salvation. The history of God is not dependent on the history of Israel: even Israel does not have God at its disposal. In particular, the late, great prophets made it clear to this people that the future of Israel is not an automatic consequence of the saving action of God *in the past*. Even in the Jewish theocracy of the period after the exile, God's saving action did not come to a complete stop. The eschatological Jewish movements protested precisely against those who assumed this (by adopting an 'establishment' attitude). God is also the Lord of the 'Gentiles', and these do not have to become Jews for that to be the case. However, this is a high point in the understanding of Jewish religious feeling: the people of God as the forerunners of all. It took unexpectedly specific form in Jesus, and had already been prepared for by the Diaspora Jews outside Jerusalem who increasingly regarded circumcision as a matter of the heart. Pauline Christianity in particular continued an authentic Jewish tendency, albeit for other reasons.

In the end, non-Christian Jews and Christians who became Jews finally parted, with the result that they went their own ways as representatives of 'the Jewish religion' and 'the Christian religion'. This breach was inevitable as a result of these historical events and more profoundly (above all according to the convictions of the Gospel of Mark) as a result of what had been brought about in Jesus as the Christ. However, according to the basic tendency of Paul in particular, this has by no means done away with the vocation of Israel. Christian, and sometimes semi-official church interpretations, according to which the New Testament people of God has replaced the older people of God, cannot be justified theologically; here they also mistake the *theological* implications of Jesus' restriction of his universal message to the Jewish people.

To deny or to minimize the religious significance of the Jewish people of God is also essentially to deny the significance of Jesus Christ and Christianity, and thus to deal a death-blow to the universal demand made not only by Israel but by Jesus of Nazareth. On the other hand, to my mind it is a misunderstanding of Jesus to refuse to recognize a truly Jewish prophetic event in Israel itself, and following the line of the prophetic tradition of Israel, a misunderstanding of the dynamics of a typical Jewish line of tradition.

'Yahweh said to Abram, "Go from your country and your kindred and your father's house to the land that I will show you" ' (Gen. 12.1–4). The connection between religion, people and land plays an unmistakably large role in Israel's religious self-understanding. It is a basic theme of the official Jewish religion as a believing and *interpretative* response to God's actions with this people – in the last resort, and from the deepest religious perspective, seen not in egotistic terms, but as a *forerunner* in what will happen to *all* peoples. Part of the content of what a religion calls the progressive revelation of God is the interpretative response of the believer, and thus contingent human history and its interpretation (see Part One above). Here *this* religion and *this* people essentially belong together, while on the other hand it is hard to conceive of a people without a land. The essential connection between the Jewish religion and the Jewish people is also the reason why this religion never became a world religion and cannot ever become one in the future. Jewish religious understanding has only become a world religion by means of other real world religions, namely Islam and Christianity, both of which could not and would not give up their connections with Judaism, but broke the essential connection between 'religion' and '*this* people'.

*Israel* could not do this and (in view of its essential creed) can never do this for itself alone. But at precisely this point we are shown the *special feature* of the Jewish religion with which Christianity, for all its continuity, in fact has no continuity. We must simply establish this as a fact; it would be falsehood for the sake of a quiet life to obscure it.

From the nineteenth century onwards, and above all in Germany, Christian Old Testament and Jewish scholars have been intensively preoccupied in making the Jewish religion into a *confession* (just as nowadays in the Netherlands and elsewhere people talk about 'Israelite church communities'). From the point of view of civil rights this was a convenient solution for various problems of Jews in the Diaspora, and at the time an almost self-evident rule for civil society – one reason why many Jews accepted the situation with conviction. So in a number of Western countries it was possible to grant official recognition to the 'Jewish church community' alongside other church communities. However, according to later Jewish reflection, this was bound up with a degree of separation, within the Jewish religion, between land and people. So in accordance with the old Jewish self-understanding, in due course there was a return to the view that the covenant on Sinai represented not only a 'purely' religious reality, but at the same time a political and social reality. For non-Jews this may be a scandal or a stumbling block, but it is the living community of the Jews, rather than ourselves, who are the interpreters of the Jewish religious consciousness. In the view of many Jews today, even if they are secularized, the connection between 'people' and 'land' is a fundamental and extremely sensitive element of Jewish spirituality. 'Next year in Jerusalem' is not simply a conventional pious wish for many Jews.

The fact that by virtue of its innermost character Christianity had to break this connection between religion, people and land, but on the other hand recognized 'the scandal' of an intrinsic connection between salvation from God and the person of Jesus of Nazareth who was himself interpreted as 'Israel', 'called out of Egypt' (Matt. 2.15; see Hos. 11.1), indeed as *the* man, the second Adam (see Luke 1 and 2), brings Christianity into a fundamental but dialectical tension with the Jewish religion and its intrinsic connection with 'religion', '*this* people' and '*this* land'. Many elements – above all the Temple, but in certain prophetic movements also 'the land' – have undergone symbolic changes during the course of Jewish history; they have been spiritualized and generalized, and above all deprived of their eschatological dimension. This cannot be claimed without further ado of the theme of the 'land' of Israel, though it too has been reinterpreted in eschatological terms so that it becomes a future 'heavenly Jerusalem' on earth, the mount of Zion, to which all nations will be gathered at the end of time. However, above all after the trials of AD 135, the 'right to return' became a living reality in Jewish literature. Expectations of a third exodus after the exodus from Egypt and the second exodus from the Babylonian exile sprang into life. We have to take this seriously as the vision of a constant Jewish tradition if we do not want to make light of the biblical accounts of the first and second exodus (however much this may also apply to other nations). Religious Jews by no means see this as a *right*, but rather as a free *gift of God*, who is faithful to his own free goodness, and therefore they feel responsible for this land and its development, above all in the spirit of the so-called social righteousness of the Sinai covenant. However, it cannot be denied that, like all the Christian churches, the Jews too are aware of their 'quest for Jewish identity' (Rabbi E. Zerin) – in the crisis of all religions since the onset of the criticism of religion and the so-called process of secularization. We cannot anticipate the discussion of this problem. The fact is that even non-believing Israelis grow up with the Bible as the manifesto of their national ethos. These are realities of life and not abstractions.

Today, more than ever, we have arrived at the insight that any religious view falls under the suspicion of being an ideology if it is held at the expense of human rights. On the basis of the hermeneutic function of ethics for any understanding of faith, we may assert *a priori* that 'serving God' *at the expense of one's fellow-man* makes a religious view incredible and destroys it from within. No one can dispute this insight from the criticism of religion, whether he be Jew or Arab or Christian.

Moreover, in accordance with our modern understanding of problems, disputes among nations are resolved on historical and political grounds in accordance with the norm of social justice, the rights of peoples and human rights. Within the social and political order of our contemporary world, the contribution of a *theological* conception, according to which any people can lay claim to a particular land by divine right, without providing 'frontal' or horizontal justification in the dimensions of our earthly history, is seen as a foreign body. But *in itself* this says nothing for or against such a conception on the religious level.

Against the background of all this, and within the horizon of the modern understanding of the problem, what can a Christian theologian say when he is confronted with two different attitudes to the conflict between Jews and Palestinians in the Middle East? On the one hand, the first step is the solemn recognition that the Jewish people has a claim to a land and indeed to this particular land; on the other hand, the first presupposition is the solemn recognition that the Palestinian people has a claim to return as full citizens in their own land: present-day Israel? For these are the two most pronounced positions which are represented today by the parties in dispute.

To begin with, I should point out that I find the existence of the Jewish people just as compelling evidence as the existence of the Palestinians. The existence of the Jewish religion is equally evident. Finally, it is equally evident that the Jewish people has a right 'to land'. However, these factors have sometimes turned into incomprehensible theological dogmatism.

If we speak in political terms of a 'right to *this* land', we have not finished with abstractions. The state of affairs is the will of a people to dwell in *this* land, which many Jews in the depths of their hearts see as 'holy land'. There may be religious reasons for this, but *ipso facto* this will is at the same time a *political* reality. And this political reality is an unmistakable element in the problem. Furthermore, it is a reality for a number of Jews who no longer have religious feelings. As a collective political concern (with or without religious inspiration), this can rightly be termed Zionism (which in itself is no more a reprehensible word than 'Christianity', 'Islam' or even nationalistic movements, though they have all made serious mistakes in their history). Even – indeed above all – if as a theologian with a modern understanding of the problem one says that the question must be removed from the realm of theology and settled on a political level, it is impossible to by-pass the reality of political concern which is the consequence or (among many people nowadays) the secular remains of this religious conception. The historical reasons for this political will can be investigated, and there is a real element in the discussion which is susceptible to rational analysis; however, a *direct* reference to a *religious* demand introduces an inter-subjective element into the debate which is beyond discussion, because no rational grounds can be advanced in its favour. It must therefore be possible to investigate the historical reasons for this political concern and to introduce them into the debate. *In this sense* I am convinced that the theologizing of the 'Israeli-Palestinian' conflict is theologically false. Anyone who wants to speak in this context of the will of God – whether this is the God of the Jews, the God of Islam or the God of the Christians (and are these different gods?) – will have to look for it in the social justice, the specific human rights of all those who are caught up in this conflict, and will have to look for it in justice and love. 'God's rights' can never be to the detriment of human rights, while on the other hand suffering man and his suffering are no empty abstractions. Thus the political concern of the Jewish people must be reconciled with the rights of other parties and vice versa. And I think that no solution is in fact possible without real *reconciliation*.

However, false arguments must also be avoided because they obscure the problem. In my view, the appeal to greater responsibility in the *cultivation* and *industrialization* of this land as a special *ethical* claim to this land does not get us any further, because it is sometimes bolstered by Western presuppositions. It is a fact that the Arabs have not cultivated Palestine to the same extent. But on what grounds can one deny the right of a 'nomadic culture' (which at one time was also the ideal of the ancient Hebrews) to a meaningful existence, and then assert that nomads *thus* in practice have no responsibility for their own land? A particular responsibility concerned with controlling nature is indeed a real human possibility, but who can deny the right and the significance of the possibility of the nomadic way of life (even if it is gradually disappearing in the face of modern culture)? Consequently I believe that the principle of a greater or lesser responsibility for 'this land' which is sometimes adduced is a result of sociological and cultural conditioning, and must be left out of account.

Because of all this, the social and political level of the Middle East conflict must be clearly detached from *specifically theological* considerations. Unfortunately, we must also concede that the present conflict has for a long time involved more than the Israelis and the Arab countries, and now involves all the great Western powers, who are pursuing their own interests in it.

With all due respect to the character of Jewish spirituality and of the Moslem religion, as far as these play a part in the present complex of problems, I see the task of Christians and above all of Christian church leaders or church bodies as primarily consisting in the *demythologizing* of the problem in the political sphere. They must not attempt to solve it with a Bible interpreted in fundamentalist terms, finally bringing order into their own concerns. We can hardly forget that much of what is called '*sacred* history' in the Bible would bring many people out on the streets today in protest marches on the basis of the modern understanding of human and national rights, and some of the Old Testament prophets would be marching at their head. Moreover, the churches must stand up for the rights or protest against the infringement of the rights of all the parties concerned, and along with others make a constructive contribution in the search for a solution which is satisfactory to all parties within the demands of social justice. A *theologian* can hardly say more on this question. Theologians have a tendency to make a question even more obscure on the basis of their own theological problems; when it comes to theological questions, they have to remember that not only Christianity but also Islam found that the Tanach proved to be its most fertile soil. Furthermore, all this requires an expression of penitence on the part of Christians because of their own particular past (and present), in which an often destructive attitude towards both Jews and Moslems has been and continues to be supported by theological arguments. Religions make themselves incredible when they become the occasion for wars of religion. In reality, however, history shows us that there have never been pure wars of religion; there have always also been socio-historical, economic and political factors. For that reason too, the demand for a removal of theological factors from political conflicts is a pressing one, even when theological factors are also involved. These latter will then be judged in accordance with their socio-political implications, and will have to find their solution at this level. Here the saying holds, 'Do not be a Christian despite Jews and Moslems' (G. E. Lessing, *Nathan the Wise*, IV, 4).

# Part Three

# Structural Elements of the New Testament Theologies of Grace

*Introduction*

1. When it comes to defining more closely the character of the redemptive action through which God was in process of reconciling the world in and through Jesus (so literally II Cor. 5.19), it becomes necessary to point out that some key concepts of varying origin, deriving from the history of experience and interpretation in Israel and early Judaism, gave the New Testament the means of expressing in comprehensible terms the Christian experience of redemption through Jesus and salvation in Jesus, the Christ. What they had experienced in Jesus led Christians to make use of these pre-existing 'interpretative elements' from the tradition of their experience. In turn these key concepts coloured the content of their experience and provided them with new possibilities of development. This experience of salvation in Jesus from God drew its life-force from what they had experienced, Jesus of Nazareth, but also from their own progressive expression of their experience; it deepened this experience and in the light of experience revealed the subject of the experience more fully and more clearly. All the 'interpretative elements', i.e. (in the context in which I want to use this somewhat ambiguous concept) already existing and understandable elements of experience from life as they had lived it, taken over from the events of contemporary religious society, are used to describe experiences of Jesus. Everyone knew from his own experience how a slave could be redeemed. Everyone knew how important it can be in a human life to have a powerful advocate, to have legal support. Jews above all had a deep-rooted sense for the 'eye for an eye', not in the sense of vengeance, but in the sense of fair retribution (only one eye for one eye). Many arrangements, above all in the social sphere, which had been made over the course of centuries to protect the poor or the impoverished, e.g. the system of the *gō'ēl* or redeemer, were well-known national institutions. In particular, Temple worship, with its sacrifices to make good transgressions against the Jewish Law, was an essential ingredient of Jewish religion (though its prestige quickly declined in the first century AD). For a Jew, to give satisfaction, to have sacrifice made by the priests – expensive beasts from the rich and a pair of turtle doves from the poor – was a basic social and religious concern. The notion of *šālōm* (in the sense described above) essentially covers the making good of damage and satisfaction, given the unhealthy situation in which men must live together. Everything that had gone wrong in life had to be made good and

atoned for. In short, the fundamental concepts of Jewish society are used to show what had been experienced and was experienced in Jesus, above all with respect to the death of such a man. At that time, too, there were Jews and Gentiles who looked for their salvation in supra-terrestrial, heavenly regions, their mysterious spheres full of powerful spirits, the source of everything that happened or could not happen here on earth. For Greeks and Roman citizens, Christians from the Gentile world, there was also the great experience of the time in which the emperor was celebrated as *Sōtēr*, benefactor and saviour of the whole *oikoumenē*, and was praised in triumphal processions. All this was used in the New Testament to help to express something of what was experienced in the life and death of Jesus and his exaltation to the Father, and even to develop its significance.

However, above all after almost two thousand years, we must not allow this accumulation of different 'interpretations' to allow us to forget the reality that was interpreted in this way. In my introductory discussion about experience and interpretation, I pointed out that in our experiences there are interpretative elements which find their foundation and source directly in the experience itself, and that at the same time there are interpretative elements which are offered to us from elsewhere, and which in fact might be suitable for clarifying even more fully a first, already interpreted experience for others (or even for oneself). In fact, this is precisely what the New Testament authors do, and they do so with justification. They also do this in different ways, because they do not all look for the same 'interpretative elements'. Thus, for example, the Epistle to the Hebrews is the only New Testament writing which sees the redeeming work of Jesus as a priestly service; other writings in fact deny this, because for them priesthood is essentially a question of *levitical* priesthood. However, the content of what Hebrews sets out to state is in the last resort a basic creed to be found throughout the New Testament: Jesus' *solidarity* with suffering and sinful man as a result of a radical *fidelity* to God to the point of death, the giving up of his life, and God's creative and affirmative acceptance of such a life in solidarity and faithfulness. The particular concepts through which this reality of experience is expressed – e.g. satisfaction, bloody sacrifice, atonement and the dethronement of tyrannical heavenly powers – are to be taken at their face value, i.e., they apply in a culture in which these concepts are a living expression of everyday experiences. The mere fact that various New Testament authors look for other interpretative elements and images in order to express the saving significance, say, of the death of Jesus, makes it clear that the unifying factor is provided by what is to be interpreted and not the interpretative element. Not only the life, the message and the lifestyle of Jesus, but also his death in the context of his whole life, have a saving significance, a redemptive and reconciling value for Christians. This is the apostolic datum of experience, expressed in kerygma (proclamation), didache (catechesis and instruction), and finally in creed and dogma. The question is whether in our modern culture, which shrinks from sacral slaughter, this datum of faith has to be called a bloody sacrifice. However, that is not affected by the fact that, say, Hebrews tells its readers precisely what the Christian faith is all about. In the course of the post-biblical history of theology, more theories of redemption will indeed arise than those already offered by the New Testament, and these often, rightly, take up specific details of culturally determined sensibilities and contemporary expectations of salvation. However, one cannot compel a Christian who believes in the soteriological value of the life and death of Jesus, and his life with God and among us, simply to believe in all these interpretative elements; indeed for many people they can even endanger belief in the saving worth of the life and death of Jesus. On the other hand, I find it just as untheological to want to demonstrate by rational hermeneutic manipulations that for example Paul (or another New Testament writer) did not teach any particular conception of sacrifice – say providing satisfaction through the shedding of blood. That is clearly in the text and cannot be interpreted away. However, it is only a *problem* for the fundamentalist reader of the Bible (and in that case is not a problem at all). Another solution is that I take from the Bible only what suits me, and leave the rest where it is. However, this seems to me both Christianly and theologically irresponsible; for in that case, in the last resort we ourselves decide what Jesus might, could or would have to mean for us. In that case I ask myself why we really still need him. In any human life we find some kind of inspiration which guides our life and can make it better. However, that is not what the Bible and the whole of the great Christian tradition mean by salvation in Jesus from God.

In my view, all these conceptions also contain a philosophical error: a wrong insight into the relationship between experience and interpretation, and 'interpretative experience' and its further development. If all this is to be understood rightly (and I shall have to go into the problem more deeply than I did in the first part), then at least as a Christian one cannot simply make a selection from the biblical texts. The important thing is to attempt to *understand* all of them as a very human literary document which expresses the apostolic tradition of faith about Jesus as the Christ in a way which is normative for Christians and gives authentic expression to the real saving action of God in Jesus the Christ. In other words, Jesus is seen as the one who is experienced as decisive, final and eschatological salvation, both by virtue of his life and also by virtue of his death and God's merciful attitude towards his death. Such an event can and even must be articulated in an inexhaustible way, with a constant variety of images and 'interpretative elements', when people in constantly changing cultures want to give authentic expression to what the New Testament seeks to state, confess and proclaim. I would not call this demythologizing, since it is certainly not that; it is rather the *inculturation* of the one datum of the Christian faith; to put it more simply, it is a matter of keeping alive the content of the Christian faith. Therefore <u>the earlier pictures and 'interpretative elements' are not 'untrue' in their own context; however, they can become irrelevant for us.</u> An insight into the earlier history, the development and often also the social 'setting' of the explanatory terms (e.g. penitence, being reconciled through a bloody sacrifice, etc.) and the way in which they are used in the New Testament is also a factor which can contribute to our capacity for discernment. By that I mean a capacity to distinguish between the interpretation brought by the *Christian experience* itself (and this includes historical and social conditioning, though the experience of Jesus as the Christ or as decisive and final salvation can also include universal human experiences), and what I might call the subsequent culturally conditioned thematization and theoretical development of these Christian interpretative experiences. This insight leaves wide open the possibility of expressing in a new contemporary way and with due reverence what appears in Christian experience as the 'offer of reality'. One can only feel amazement at the often masterly inventiveness with which the New Testament writers – e.g. the Gospel of John, Colossians, Ephesians and Hebrews – dared to express, and succeeded in expressing, the raw material of apostolic faith in new patterns, without doing damage to its basic substance. Here, too, holy scripture is an inspiration and a guideline for us. At the same time, however, it is to be regretted how incapable present-day Christianity is of formulating this apostolic faith in the same way – just as faithfully and creatively – so as to bring joy and salvation to modern man as well. Is there a lack of truly living faith? Or a fear of heterodoxy under the pressure of orthodoxy experienced as a tabu, rather than as a liberating norm of the apostolic substance of faith? Or both? – a lack of faith.

2. <u>All the different New Testament conceptions of salvation, redemption and liberation, which are nevertheless *fundamentally* the same,</u> are held together by an intrinsic bond, namely the correlation between the providence of God or his sovereignly free initiative in salvation, and the experience of having found meaning in life, the discovery of the fullness of life among those who believe in Jesus. <u>The Christians of the New Testament found their self-determination, the definition of their humanity, in a personal relationship with God, as it had been revealed by Jesus.</u>

The saving work of God in Jesus Christ was experienced as grace in the explicit biblical Hebraic (*ḥesed*) and Jewish-Greek (*charis*) sense of a heart-warming *divine election*, including a *secular, marginal status (prothesis*, as the sovereignly free counsel or plan of God: Rom. 8.28; 9.11; Eph. 1.11; 3.11; II Tim. 2.10; I Peter 1.20, etc.). This predestination is based on love (II Tim. 1.9); it is a free *ḥesed* (Rom. 9.15), as Yahweh testified to Moses (Ex. 33.19). It is solely and uniquely dependent on God's own good pleasure (*eudokia*: Eph. 1.5, 9, 11; Luke 2.14; 12.32; Col. 1.19; Phil. 2.13), but a *eudokia agathosynēs* (II Thess. 1.11); i.e. it is no whim, but an expression of goodness. God's *calling* follows from this predestination (above all Rom. 8.30; also Eph. 1.18; 4.1, 4; Phil. 3.14; II Thess. 1.11; II Tim. 1.9; Heb. 3.1; II Peter 1.10). Christians are therefore called (Rom. 1.6f.; 8.28; I Cor. 1.2, 24; Jude 1; Rev. 17.14) or elect (Mark 13.20; Luke 18.7; I Cor. 1.27; Rom. 8.33; Eph. 1.4; Col. 3.12; II Tim. 2.10; Titus 1.1; Rev. 17.14), whereas Christ himself is *'ho hyios mou eklelegmenos'* (Luke 9.35), the elect son or the chosen one. According to Matt. 22.14, many are 'called' (*klētoi*), but few are 'chosen' (*eklektoi*). This predestination (as also in Qumran and generally in late Jewish literature) is expressed most strongly in Rom. 8.29f.; 9.1–11.35; Eph. 1.4f.; also Gal. 1.15; Rom. 1.6; 11.5; I Peter 1.2, 10; 5.10; 4.10.

Here the New Testament seeks to make clear that the meaning of human life is not simply chance and the consequence of destiny, nor is it dependent on a number of arbitrary, supra-terrestrial powers or demons. Life is directed by God in freedom and goodness. It is therefore the fruit of a caring love which seeks to turn all things to good for those who love God (Rom. 8.28). In other words, though we may not be able to identify God's will in detail, nature, history and in it above all Jesus are supported and directed by a transcendent divine purpose. There is a parallel between God's will and the ultimate purpose of human life. Faith is therefore both faith in the fundamental goodness of God's purposes with man and also faith in the ultimate meaning of human life – entrusting oneself and others to God. From a biblical point of view, that is an experience of grace.

Not in spite of, but because of this eternal divine counsel, however, the New Testament dares to say (without doing away with the tension between universality and election which comes into play here): 'God wills that *all* men should be saved' (I Tim. 2.3f.); 'God's saving grace appeared to *all* men' (Titus 2.11; see Rev. 21.3); he is 'the Saviour (bringer of salvation, benefactor, redeemer, *Sōtēr*) *of the world*' (John 4.42; I John 4.14), 'the Lamb of God who takes away the sin *of the world*' (John 1.29), 'the living God who is a Saviour for *all* men, and *especially* for believers' (I Tim. 4.10).

This notion of election expresses the deepest meaning of the religious language and confession of the New Testament. This confession is no arbitrary talk, it is a *homologia*: 'Speaking in agreement', 'saying the same thing' or *affirming*. In other words, the believer who is touched by God and has experienced his grace *returns* to God in thanks and praise what he has received and is allowed to experience from God. In gratitude he affirms what God has done for him. For the believer can only speak in religious terms (in which he takes leave of purely descriptive language) because God himself enables him to do so; in this sense God's grace in Jesus is not only the *content* but at the same time the *basis of possibility* for the *homologia* of the believer, his affirmative praise and grateful acknowledgement of God.

The divine, elective grace is given evocative expression above all in testifying and in confession, in proclamation. The New Testament proclaims what Christians have experienced in their encounter with Jesus, the one sent by God. However, in their proclamation they also experience rejection by others. This rejection of the testimony of Jesus and the Christian proclamation helps us to understand and experience even more sharply how unmerited is the grace of God. Rejection by others put Christians in an isolated position. Here they experience God's solidarity with marginal or peripheral people, all the more because early Christianity gained its adherents above all from the lower classes. All this made the notion of predestination, election, a central New Testament concept. Acceptance of the testimony of Jesus and the Christians allows their experience of salvation to be seen as election; not to their own glory but to the glory of God, as the New Testament repeatedly makes clear, understanding the deadly danger which can threaten people who have perhaps an all too human awareness of being elected and sent. However, this very real admonition, brought about by rejection through others (or the fact that they still do not know what has happened 'in these days' in Jerusalem), sharpens the consciousness of Christians and above all makes them aware that their 'yes' to Jesus as the Christ is not the consequence of blind destiny or fate, but is the fruit of God's care.

Paul and the Gospel of John in particular reflected on the mystery of this coincidence of God's gracious election and human choice and decision, but even they cannot cope with it completely. At all events, the grace of acceptance, faith, is at the same time a call to the 'ministry of reconciliation' (Paul, Ephesians) and not a stimulus towards the cultivation of one's own enclosed garden. This faith is a mission to the world, even for the somewhat introverted Johannine church (John 17.15–18). The New Testament knows nothing of the idea of a segregated remnant. Furthermore, even if it is also familiar with the unfathomable ambivalence of human freedom, an unspoken, underlying conception remains dominant: God loved us 'while we were still sinners' (Rom. 5.8). This insight is aimed directly at *Christians* who 'were still sinners' before their knowledge of the Jesus event, but it can hardly be denied that this New

Testament concept of grace (*ḥesed* and *charis*) continues to exercise a hidden influence, to such a degree that I Peter speaks of a chance of salvation or life for *departed sinners* (I Peter 3.19–21; 4.6; however, the author leaves open the question whether in fact they seize on this last of all mercies and the chance of life which it provides). This conception later fell under the suspicion of heresy as a result of Origen's teaching of the *apokatastasis* or final reconciliation of all (not so much because of the conception itself, as because of everything that was bound up with it: the pre-existence of souls, reincarnation, etc.) – one reason why I Peter was pressed in many other directions which cannot, however, find any support in this apostolic letter itself. The New Testament knows of only one deadly sin: that of those who deliberately and intentionally, against their better inclination, reject the principle of God's mercy in Jesus (Heb. 9.28 with 4.4–6 and 10.26–31); this is the sin against the Holy Spirit, which will not be forgiven either in this world or in the world to come (Matt. 12.32; Luke 12.10; Mark 3.28; cf. I John 5.16). The rejection of the merciful love of God is the only barrier which can be thrown up against God's mercy (we are not told whether there are people who do this quite deliberately). So quite independently of the context of Origen's *apokatastasis* we are challenged by the *New Testament* statement that God's merciful love *precedes* all our sins: 'He already loved us while we were still sinners.' The last decisive word is not with the sinner, but with God's mercy which grants forgiveness, freely. If righteousness and love are one in the unique mode of God's nature, we can only stutter when confronted with the question how righteousness and holy dismay at all that afflicts mankind, God's own creation, can be reconciled with God's mercy both towards those who are ill and towards those who are wretched and oppressed. Here human and divine justice evidently go their separate ways.

At all events, there is no mention in the New Testament of the election of an individual *from* a *massa damnata*: God's selfless and unbiassed love is directed towards sinners. This perspective in no way embraces the possibility of a *pecca fortiter, sed crede fortius* for those who are aware of God's mercy – on the contrary! The *divine* possibilities of this unrestrained solidarity with sinful mankind, unfree in the most profound sense, are the *mystery* of God's prevenient grace which is in fact effective in and of itself and will not break the bruised reed. Just a few righteous men could have saved Sodom (Gen. 18.23–32); a single righteous man would have been enough to save Jerusalem (Jer. 5.1); and 'many' are saved thanks to the prophetic 'righteous sufferer' (Isa. 53). In this light, the New Testament Christians are convinced that the whole world is saved by means of the one and only eschatological suffering prophet, Jesus Christ:

he is the 'Saviour of the world' (John 4.42; I John 4.14), 'the Lamb of God who takes on himself (takes away) the sin of the world' (John 1.29).

The New Testament relationship between God's universal will for salvation and the human experience of the ultimate meaning of life, the Christian experience of salvation in God in and through the experience of the fulfilment of one's own life, is a guideline in the attempt to articulate the structural elements of the New Testament theologies of grace and redemption with all their intrinsic ramifications. In this connection the basic datum is that it began with an encounter between the man Jesus and his fellow men. Salvation from God is revealed in the encounter of Jesus with his fellow men. Encounter, salvation and happiness are experiential concepts. They are not so much argued about, as narrated in a history which summons men to a critical and liberating way of life.

In the light of all that has gone before, we now arrive at *four structural elements* which Christians must take account of in any contemporary reinterpretation in which an echo of the gospel of Jesus Christ can be detected, if they want to preserve this gospel in its wholeness while at the same time making it speak to their own age in word and deed.

## I.  GOD AND HIS HISTORY WITH MEN

The Christian experience of an orginally Jewish group of people with Jesus of Nazareth developed into the confession that for these people, Christians, the bitter question, insoluble in human terms, of the meaning and purpose of human life in nature and history, in a context of meaning and meaninglessness, of suffering and moments of joy, has received a positive and unique answer surpassing all expectations: God himself is the guarantor that human life has a positive and significant meaning. He himself has made it his concern and has put his own honour at risk: his honour is his identification with the poor wretch and exploited man, with the captive man, above all the sinner, i.e. the man who is so at odds with his fellow man that this sickness 'cries out to heaven' (see Ex. 2.23–25; 3.7f.). Then 'God came down' (Ex. 3.8): 'God so loved the world that he gave his only begotten Son that all who believe on him should not perish' (John 3.16). In the last resort – and at the same time that is 'protological', from the beginning — God *decides* about the meaning and purpose of mankind, in man's favour. He does not leave this decision to the whim of cosmic and historical, chaotic and demonic powers, on whose crooked lines he is able to write, indeed whose crooked lines he is able to straighten. As Creator, God is the author of good and the antagonist of evil, suffering and injustice which throw men up against meaninglessness. In their experience of the meaning of life and its fulfilment, the disciples experience salvation from God in their trusting encounter with Jesus. This determination of life as an unmerited gift, as grace, is experienced as the initiative of God which surpasses all expectations. Here Old and New Testaments are agreed: Yahweh is a God of man, he is the 'He is' (Ex. 3.14), i.e. 'I am concerned for you' (Ex. 3.16). God's name is 'solidarity with my people'. God's own honour lies in the happiness and salvation of mankind. God's predestination and man's experience of meaning are two aspects of one and the same reality of salvation. Salvation is concerned with human wholeness and happiness, and this is in an intrinsic mutual relationship involving the solidarity of man with a living God who is concerned with mankind. This is God's history with man.

## II. THE NUCLEUS OF GOD'S HISTORY WITH MEN CAN BE FOUND IN THE PERSON AND THE LIFE OF JESUS

The meaning or the destiny of man, prepared for and intended from of old by God, has been disclosed and thus been made known in an experience of believers in the person, career and destiny of Jesus of Nazareth: in his message and his life, his life-style and the particular circumstances in which he was executed. Such a life and death have value *in and of themselves*. But for that very reason they also have a primary significance for God, who here shows his own solidarity with his people, their own calling and their own honour, and therefore identifies himself not only with the ideals and visions of Jesus, but with the person of Jesus of Nazareth himself. Thus the destiny of Jesus is fulfilled even beyond death in his resurrection from the dead, the Amen of God to the person of Jesus which is at the same time the divine affirmation of his true being: 'solidarity with the people', 'God is love' (I John 4.8; 4.16).

In general religious terms and in individual religions God may have many names, but he shows his *true countenance* to Christians in the unselfish involvement of Jesus as the good shepherd in search of his wandering and lost sheep. True, the Father is greater than his coming in Jesus Christ – 'the Father is greater than I' (John 14.28), but in Jesus 'the fullness of God dwells' (Col. 1.19). Anyone who sees him, sees the Father (John 14.9b). Jesus is God's countenance turned towards man, the countenance of God who is concerned for all men, especially and concernedly for the humble of the earth, all those who are crucified. 'Therefore God has exalted him and given him a name above every name' (Phil. 2.9), the Lord, 'I am' (Ex. 3.14; John 8.24; 8.58; 13.19), I am there for you. This can be followed only by a confession of faith, an affirmation, 'that at the name of Jesus every knee should bow' (Phil. 2.10).

In Jesus we have a complete portrayal of both the predestination of God and the meaning of human life: furthering the good and resisting evil. Therefore his destiny lay under a special divine care. He is God's only beloved as a gift to mankind. His career is the fulfilment and execution of divine care for man, albeit in and through the free and responsible, human and religious initiative of Jesus himself, in conflict and resistance at the same time through the historical occasion for his appearance as a pioneer in the fight for man's cause as God's cause.

This destiny shows the impotence of the still-necessary word, message or vision 'in itself'. Messages can be rejected, visions can be mocked as unrealistic dreams. However, anyone who as a martyr endorses his message with the sacrifice of his life 'for the sake of this message' 'as the service of reconciliation' thereby proves the *impotence* of those who can establish their rights only by murdering and doing away with the witness to the righteousness and love. Their brief victory bears the visible marks of self-destruction, even if their frenzy becomes the more violent the more it smells corruption. For the dying torch which they have quenched is taken over by others.

Suffering is not redemptive in itself. But it is redemptive when it is suffering through and for others, for man's cause as the cause of the one who says that he is 'in solidarity with my people', who has 'conquered the world' (John 16.33b). The New Testament does not praise suffering but only suffering in and with resistance against injustice and suffering. It praises suffering 'for the sake of the kingdom of God' or 'for the sake of the gospel' (Mark 8.35; 10.29), for the sake of rightousness (I Peter 3.14), 'unmerited suffering' (I Peter 3.17), 'for the good' (I Peter 3.17), 'suffering although you do right' (I Peter 2.20f.), in solidarity with one's brothers (Heb. 2.17f.). Suffering itself goes with the crooked lines which men draw. 'The hour is coming when whoever kills you will think that he is offering service to God' (John 16.2b) . . . 'but be of good cheer, I have overcome the world' (John 16.33b). Therefore instead of a 'divine must' or an apocalyptic necessity, Hebrews says in a more restrained way, more on a human than a divine plane, 'It was fitting that he for whom and by whom all things exist, in bringing many sons to glory, should make the pioneer of their salvation perfect through suffering' (Heb. 2.10). For the name of God is 'the one who shows solidarity with his people', and this people suffers.

III.  OUR HISTORY, FOLLOWING JESUS

In the sense of biblical *anamnēsis (zikkārōn)* or remembrance, remembrance
of the history of God with man in Jesus Christ is not just a matter of
reminding oneself what took place at an earlier stage. It is a return to the
past in narrative with an eye to action in the present. God 'reminds
himself' of his earlier saving acts in and through new acts of liberation.
So Christian faith is a remembrance of the life and death of the risen
Jesus through the practice of becoming his disciples – not through imi-
tating what he has done but, like Jesus, by responding to one's own new
situations from out of an intense experience of God. In the church community the future of Jesus, endorsed by his resurrection, is at the same
time a remembrance of his life. What we have is a living tradition directed
towards the future. Christian life itself can and must be a *memorial* of
Jesus Christ. Orthodox confession of faith is simply the expression of
truly Christian life as a *memoria Jesu*. Detached from a life-style in conformity with the kingdom of God, the Christian confession become innocuous and *a priori* incredible. The living community is the only real
reliquary of Jesus. 'Not everyone who says to me Lord, Lord, will enter
the kingdom of heaven, but he who does the will of my Father who is in
heaven' (Matt. 7.21; see 7.22f.) – often the attitude of those who rightly
want to hold high the orthodox creed of the resurrection of Jesus, but
destroy its credibility by their petty way of life. It is in Christian living
that one sees who really believes in the risen Jesus, the future of a more
hallowed world. The New Testament (above all Paul; also Colossians
and Ephesians, John, Hebrews) shows us that the church community,
the assembly of those who call Jesus to mind, is the public and living
memorial to Jesus and is thus 'filled with the fullness of Jesus' (Eph. 3.19;
1.23), and therefore with the vision, the life-style and the readiness for
suffering through and for others to which Jesus inspired them by identifying himself with the God whose name is solidarity with his people.

So in the man Jesus, the risen one, the history of God also becomes
our history, above all in and through the practice of solidarity with a God
concerned for humanity. By following Jesus, taking our bearings from
him and allowing ourselves to be inspired by him, by sharing in his *Abba*
experience and his selfless support for 'the least of my brethren'
(Matt. 25.40), and thus entrusting our own destiny to God, we allow the
history of Jesus, the living one, to continue in history as a piece of living
christology, the work of the Spirit among us, the Spirit of God and the
Spirit of Christ. So the Christian works in free responsibility for the
completion of God's plan to give ultimate meaning to human life. This
is the means of achieving the correlation between God's will for universal

salvation in Jesus and for human happiness or success for each and every individual.

Therefore we can only speak of the history of Jesus in terms of the story of the Christian community which follows Jesus. In particular, the Gospel of John (so often despised) is a model for such a history, in which the historical level of Jesus' own life is as it were fused with the history of the later community. Thus resurrection, the formation of a community and the renewal of the world in accordance with the life-style of the kingdom of God (in a particular set of circumstances) form a single event with a spiritual and a historical side. The present of the living Christ and his pneuma is at the same time the historical story of the community of faith in prayerful confession and action, in solidarity with man's cause as the cause of God.

## IV.  HISTORY WITHOUT HISTORICAL END

The end of this history of God with man in Jesus, handed on and put into practice by the 'community of God', cannot ever be completed or narrated right to the end within the narrow confines of our world-wide human history. The death of each individual keeps breaking the threads of history. In that case, is there no longer any salvation, not even for those who have handed on the torch of history and kept it burning among the living, and have perhaps met their death for that very reason? The final consummation of God's predestination and the realization of human meaning and purpose and thus of grace, redemption and liberation, is 'not of and from this world', although this liberating grace which makes men whole must take a recognizable, historically demonstrable form on the level of our earthly history in figures who constantly fade into the past and are superseded.

Although the definitive salvation is eschatological, and as such is obviously not experienced as the content of present experience, the awareness of this final perspective – the promise – in faith is given in an experience here and now, namely in fragments of individual experiences of salvation which bear within themselves an inner promise, as was the case in and through Jesus. The church's proclamatory announcement and promise of *final* salvation – the eschatological promise – takes on real significance only in the light of such fragmentary experiences of salvation. In fact, final salvation goes beyond our present experiences – in the last resort we do not experience actual salvation here and now – but the validity of this announcement in promise has its basis in a context of present-day experience of Jesus and the Christian life in this world. It cannot merely rest on a revelation through the *word* – besides, anthropologically speaking, 'word' is an expression of human experience and practice – nor on the *mere proclamation* of a final and universal salvation to come (on what basis?). Without the mediation of human experience and the realization of fragments of salvation transcending man's own limits, 'the Word of God' is not only not a metaphor, it is sheer illusion. However, in the context of fragmentary experiences of salvation we may rightly – metaphorically and with real depth – speak of the word of God and his promise of eschatological salvation which transcends all expectations of experience and is yet recognized as what is familiar and evident:

> Behold, the dwelling of God is with men. He will dwell with them, and they shall be his people [a reference to the old name of Yahweh, the one who shows solidarity with his people], and God himself will be with them; he will wipe away every tear from their eyes, and death shall be no more, neither shall there be mourning nor crying nor pain any more, for the former things have passed away (Rev. 21.3f.).

*Conclusion*

Put in the category of narrative – for the New Testament, that is the *euangelion, evangelium* or good tidings – these four fundamental perspectives seem to me to be the essential structural elements of the experience interpreted and thematized in the New Testament, the basis of the Christian confession of the experience of salvation from God in Jesus the Christ.

However, this report and the critical life-style to which it leads result in continually new consequences through and in the mediation of ongoing human history. The history of Jesus is not at an end when we have said what the New Testament tells us about it. At that point *we ourselves* have not yet been touched, we who here and now must hand on this history to coming generations. Or do we do this simply and solely by selling Bibles? The great question for many Christians is, where is the model of identification? Christian personal identity and church identity are correlates: they need mutual confirmation. Where this is lacking, and where only partial identification is possible – whether of believers with the church, or of the great church with believers, or of the Christian churches with one another – history undergoes a moment of crisis. It is not as though mutual confirmation would inevitably result in a uniform model. Even the Johannine church recognized the authority of the Twelve, but required that Peter should have confidence in his own destiny and that the Johannine community should have its distinctive Christian character (John 21.15–17, as compared with 21.20–23).

The way in which the New Testament has given specific form to the four structural elements which we have just analysed is doubtless bound up with the views about life current in the ancient world, the historical circumstances and the specific possibilities of the time. Many consequences which the New Testament has drawn from this for the behaviour of Christians (which are very varied indeed, even in the New Testament itself) are historically conditioned. And precisely because they are historically conditioned, they are not directly a norm for the contemporary *memoria Jesu*, even if they are models for the way in which we, in a different historical setting and with different possibilities, can add a chapter here and now to the history of Jesus, the living one.

# Part Four

# God's Glory and Man's Truth, Well-being and Happiness

God's glory consists in the restoration of the rejected, 'that they may have life, and have it more abundantly' (John 10.10).

*Introduction*

1. Some readers who have followed the argument of this book thus far may perhaps want to ask, 'So what? What do *we* do with this view of the Christian Bible in the year 1980, in our modern world? While two-thirds of the world population is crying out for justice and love, a powerful block made up of the remaining third, in East and West, is concentrating all its knowledge and its science, its power, its diplomacy and its tactics and means of subjection, on keeping what it has. *Personally*, people may not involve themselves in unscrupulous practices, but in reality and historically speaking they live at the expense of many others. It does not matter whether these large or small, but all-controlling power blocks, are called 'capitalism', Russia or China, multi-national corporations or whatever; nothing alters the fact that the *great majority* of those who may call themselves *human beings* here and elsewhere are kept down and oppressed, made slaves in practice, despite the all-too-similar slogans of all these power blocks. They promise freedom and happiness and true democracy, and at the same time themselves decide what is good for others. Using a dialectical tactic, one block protests to another that it has to act in this - inhuman - way *because* the opposed block still exists. If Western capitalism did not exist, then communist state capitalism would not have had to use tanks in its brutal suppression of the Prague spring. Were there no communism, in the same way American capitalism would not have wanted the senseless Vietnam war. It is always 'the other person's fault' that one has blood-stained hands. One acts 'under extreme pressure'. So this dialectic runs.

The existence of 'the other' seems to make a concern for humanity dialectically impossible. According to this line of argument, 'peace' would only be possible if 'the other' did not exist – in other words, if only one party had a say and ruled the world, and everyone else thought what this one party line or what financial technocrats and directors prescribed as the sole doctrine of salvation. This is connected with the slogan, 'Peace', yes, but under the sign of a one-party system, whether disguised or explicit; and whether Western, Eastern or of any other type. 'Peace' is based on the presupposition that 'the other' disappears or is liquidated.

However, since no one has a monopoly of the truth, it is necessary to establish some presuppositions for a socio-political system which will introduce and further the justest possible human society, securing truth, goodness and happiness for each and every individual. Here the minimal requirement (i.e. the least of all evils) is a two-party system which functions in a truly democratic way. It is impossible to talk with absolutists: they stifle anyone who thinks and speaks otherwise. A system (suppose we call it 'communism') which explicitly remains below this minimal level, or a system (suppose we call it 'Americanism' for convenience) which keeps below this level by virtue of *de facto* economic power structures, appropriates to itself an absolutism of truth which in the hands of finite man always has been and always will be fatal for humanity. Even when there is a burning vision which directs and goes along with all this, this vision is intrinsically no longer authentic; the dream then harbours in itself the really bitter consequences which the system produces. In that case they are not just fortuitous or avoidable, since they are inherent in any human absolutism of truth.

After the whole of the biblical analysis in which we have just engaged, some words of Luke's Jesus constantly keep ringing in my ears: 'The kings (rulers, or power blocks) of the Gentiles exercise lordship over them, and those in authority over them are called *benefactors*. But not so with you' (Luke 22.25–26a); in other words, this is no Christian way of life. This saying puts everyone to shame, unfortunately including Christianity, which since the fourth century (despite constant marginal protests at every level which have gone unnoticed) has succumbed to the temptation to exercise this worldly power and has done what 'the world' does, despite its sayings directed against the world.

It is a truism that one should not measure the ideal, the vision, of one trend by the *empirical* reality of the other. Still less should one ignore the question whether the actual empirical manifestation has anything to do with the breadth and character of one's own vision, or whether it contrasts grossly and inconsistently with that. That would be unrealistic. It seems to me to be quite superfluous to rejoice over the affinities between visions of different movements. Ever since mankind has existed, among the oppressed and their prophetic spokesmen a vision has arisen which is opposed to what people really do. *They* were always the authentic bearers of the vision, but perhaps it had to be put into words by others, because oppression robbed them of the capacity for speech. As a vision it is generally vague and similar – though continually given different colouring in accordance with particular cultural, social and geographical situations; a 'damp' eschatology in dry desert countries, a 'dry' eschatology in constantly inundated lands; a kingdom of justice for oppressed peoples, and so on; at any rate, the same theme comes over time and again: not the existing wretchedness. This vision of humanity: 'then it will be each and everyone for one and all', already the ideal of the primitive clan (albeit only towards its members), could sometimes be forgotten for a mess of pottage, i.e. for what people already in fact possessed in reality, certainly and abundantly. Even religious men often forget it as a result of what they themselves already possess, so that it is left to non-religious people to carry on the history of the old vision of humanity. However, no people, no movement has a monopoly. Again and again it will be the oppressed themselves, of all languages and colours, who hold high the vision in their humiliation. For Jesus too, as for Deutero-Isaiah, the poor are not only those who are addressed but also those who *hand on* the good news.

However, visions and utopias have a history. There have been murderous visions for which millions of men in our enlightened and secularized twentieth century, here as elsewhere, have been sent to their deaths (historians say six million Jews here, more than ten million anti-communists elsewhere). There has beeen fratricide even for religious visions of the future: Christians have murdered Moslems and Moslems have murdered Christians; Catholics have brought Protestants to the scaffold and Protestants Catholics; and today hold captive other burnt-out human wrecks as an expression of 'human' justice. All to the greater glory of a vision made absolute. A 'vision' has a dangerous Janus' head. Where the fanatical ideal of the *distant* absolute is held up in the hands of finite beings, somewhere *nearby* a Jesus of Nazareth is being nailed to the cross. Absolute ideals are fatal unless they are a vision *of love*, that is, of selfless involvement, even if they carry freedom and humanity on their banner. These concepts are already as stained with pollution as the name of God has been dishonoured down the ages.

2. Reflection on all this already makes anyone who thinks about it suspicious. For it implies that he has been 'freed' to reflect on it in tranquillity. He has not been deprived of the capacity to speak. *A priori* he already belongs to that third of the population made up of the privileged. This in itself makes his reflection suspect.

It was a criticism already made of Karl Marx studying in libraries, despite the fact that in his concern for humanity he there worked out in theory a new relationship between theory and practice, and could only do that because he could make this qualitative change from a life involved in practical work.

Western theologians can be accused of thinking up political theologies and theologies of liberation in comfortable studies, whereas for example their Latin American brethren come to them from suffering experienced in their own bodies, even from torture and a new communal human experience, that of 'marginal men'. This situation must certainly lead the 'old West' to restraint and to careful statements, but not to the pure silence of complicity. Repentance and conversion have their own intuitions, which derive from a different experience from that of the oppressed. The theology of the oppressed is not that of the converted. Both have something to say to us.

It is a fact that in modern times the real conversation-partner of Western theology has been the *unbeliever, the humanist*. One can hardly complain about this; this was the problem presented by its own tradition of freedom. Given the particular theme of theology, it was a topic of conversation between the believing citizen and the unbeliever whether God was the foundation and cause of their (civil) freedom or not. From Latin America we hear, 'Our "liberation" is not your "freedom" ' (thus e.g. G. Gutierrez, R. Alves, T. M. Bonino). The conversation-partner of this non-Western theology is no longer the unbelieving fellow citizen, but the fellow man who is despised, oppressed and held in subjection: the poor man (believer or unbeliever), the victim of our self-made systems. Latin American theology is the spokesman for these people. That in fact brings *another* theology to life.

Any theology is conditioned by its time and situation. Therefore, despite its deepest intentions, it is in fact 'regionalized', even if it was not aware of that before. That also means that where it was imported, it was really (seen in retrospect) a neo-colonialist undertaking, even if it could not have been experienced as such to begin with. It is an inevitable consequence of this fact that the new forms of liberation theology are now guarding themselves against the importation of regional Western theologies. Their theology has matured on another field of experience, though at the same time we must not forget that whatever its particular profile, in the last resort it is concerned with a general truth.

Furthermore, in our Western society times and mental attitudes towards biblical history have changed. The Bible speaks above all about the *innocent* sufferer. That was the burning problem of the time. True, it also spoke of the suffering *prophet*, with a concern less for his own righteousness than for suffering for the message of salvation or the judgment that he proclaims, but there is no direct discussion simply of suffering *mankind*, whether *ṣaddīq* or not, believing or unbelieving. It is precisely here that we have an oppressive problem in the present phase of the development of human consciousness. We are concerned with our *suffering fellow man*, who suffers under exploitation and oppression or rejection not only from individual human beings but above all from sociopolitical, economic and bureaucratic systems, anonymous forces which are none the less real. This constant exploitation seems to make it impossible from the start for the individual to find the strength or the time to become *ṣaddīq* or righteous. He does not suffer in any way *for* the kingdom of God or *for* a good cause. He suffers. And suffers above all *from* something, not *for the sake* of a cause. Dumb suffering. This is a new situation, at least a new awareness in comparison with what the Bible has to say. It is more reminiscent of the oldest biblical story of all: the mere fact of the lament of the Hebrews over their slavery (Ex. 2.23–25; 3.7f.). *This* caused God to come down to free his people (Ex. 3.8).

However, it is the heart of the Christian message of the gospel that God – who is by no means indifferent to holiness or sinfulness – *cares for men*, whether they are *ṣaddīq*, holy, or not; that the solidarity of God with man does not impose the condition that man must be *ṣaddīq* and not a sinner: 'While we were yet sinners he loved us' (Rom. 5.8). Here in the New Testament are impulses which have yet to be allowed full play, above all in view of the long time over which the church has concentrated more on itself than on the prophet Jesus, and has almost automatically identified itself, as 'the body of Christ Jesus', with Christ, a conception which fails to do justice to the real concerns of Ephesians and Colossians. Ephesians itself puts forward a vision of a humanity for which the dividing wall between the nations has been broken down by the advent of Jesus and his martyrdom for the message of peace among nations through the forgiveness of sins, of which all are in need, and through their anchoring in the one God of all men. The new modern consciousness therefore rightly articulates itself in what is called 'human rights' – not only the rights of those who are good and just, not only the rights of the 'household of faith'. The New Testament itself already rejects the one-sidedness of this 'only' and simply says: 'The living God who is the saviour of *all* men, especially of those who believe' (I Tim. 4.10).

The fact that at least in most recent times the historical impulses towards solidarity with suffering *men* (not only with one's neighbour, the member of one's own clan or party, not only with Christians, not only with saints, not only with the just) have stemmed above all from authorities and movements outside the church does not prevent Christians confronted with the situation from being able to experience a certain feedback as bearers of the tradition of the gospel, in which it becomes clear that they must also be able to perceive and understand their own tradition. In that case they will not only be able to have a good recognition of the solemn concern of others for the *humanum* in accordance with its own value, but will at the same time give a hearing to the echo, previously suppressed, of 'forgotten truths' and significant statements from their own experience of Christian belief. In this way the actualization and activation of impulses from the gospel become possible. Not through imitative repetition, but through the creation of new yet nevertheless Christian traditions: a tradition yet to come, albeit from wisdom already acquired!

The biblical vision of the coming kingdom of God envisages a humanity in which there are no more exploiters and no more exploited humanity, no more individual or structural servitude and no more slaves. For that

reason God's will to salvation is universal. His saving will does not know
of the transitionary phase of a temporary triumph of exploited men over
defeated and overthrown exploiters. This is an essential feature of Christianity, and must serve us as a criterion in the later stages of our discussion.
Otherwise, there is the danger of various pseudo-solidarities (in the direction of the right or the left), a modern repetition of what were earlier
called *crusades*, inspired by a similarly absolute vision. It is a matter of
men being true men, good and happy in the justest society possible. But
what is humanity and what is man's status?

# Between future and remembrance

In my analysis of individual New Testament writings I investigated not only the fundamental saving content of the Christian faith but also the historical circumstances in which it was set: the presuppositions of the New Testament authors, the movements and tendencies in the environment of early Christianity, the 'spirit of the time' which was also breathed by the New Testament Christians. All this was so that we could arrive at an exact understanding of the way in which these Christians continually gave new expression to the traditional message of the gospel or apostolic faith on the basis of new experiences and demands with which they themselves were in critical solidarity.

That then raises the question for us, what are the historical circumstances in which we, in the year 1980, must pick up the threads of apostolic belief? Where must our Christian *critical solidarity* find its focal point today, taking into account present-day experiences and demands? In what new experiences today do Christians hear an echo of their eschatological remembrance of Jesus Christ, and in what new experiences and demands do they see instead a distortion, blindness, paralysis or even alienation in their Christian identity? Here Christians naturally move on the level of historical decisions for which good reasons can be advanced and which are an expression of Christian responsibility here and now, even if history alone will judge whether in fact they were historically the most responsible decision. However, to refuse at a particular moment in our history to choose one of the possible historical alternatives can be tantamount to surrendering the impulse and the orientation of the gospel.

Today's demand is all the more difficult to respond to because there are more alternatives. I think that the urgent question which will prove decisive for the future of our world and of Christianity over the next thirty years is whether the most powerful impulse in world history will prove to be 'Marxism' or the 'Christian gospel' or the technocracy of humanistic 'critical rationalism' (along the lines of H. Albert and K. Popper and their many Western disciples). For these are the forces which are in question here and now as historical impulses towards an improvement of our secular society. For all the perceptible affinities and points

of contact, the concern for humanity and the 'vision' (dream, promise or
planning) which these three movements bring are *by nature* very different.
Not to realize this seems to me to be naivety or simple ignorance. Furthermore, given this judgment, a fundamental question is how far solidarity on the part of Christians with other historical impulses of the time
is a Christian demand – and if so, with which impulses? – and how far
it is not rather a blinding and alienation of Christianity.

Chapter 1

# Man and his future

## §1   The problem: man's responsibility today for his own future

In Part Four I shall attempt to do theologically what later New Testament
writers (e.g. the authors of Ephesians and Colossians, the Gospels of
Matthew and Luke) did in another historical situation, moving on from
earlier New Testament authors (e.g. Paul or the Gospel of Mark). In
conscious fidelity to the apostolic norm of the gospel, 'the faith handed
down', in the last resort, as we demonstrated in Part Two, they sought
to show critical solidarity with their fellow men who were believers. To
present this New Testament inspiration and orientation *for today* therefore
means not only making a theological analysis of the New Testament
without neglecting its non-theological, historical setting, but also having
a critical understanding of what is experienced and desired and thought
by men today to whom here and now the same good news is being
directed. This message is never given in a spiritual or socio-historical
vacuum, or on a clean sheet.

The urgent demands and responsibilities of man today are on quite a
different level from those of the men of antiquity and late antiquity who
became Christians and whose voices we hear in the New Testament. New
Testament Christians also spoke about 'human ethics' in their own socio-
historical circumstances, within their belief in Jesus as the Christ. That
is, they spoke of what also became an ethical imperative for Christians
as a result of their historical situation. A fleeting survey of the way in
which Christians have viewed their ethical responsibility over the course
of time can already offer us some first help here.

In the spirit of 'New Testament ethics' (the historical setting of which had not been analysed), ethics in the patristic period and the early Middle Ages – permeated with Stoic and later with Neoplatonic elements – was based directly on the Logos of God, on God's will and 'eternal law' as this was interpreted in detail by the church tradition. However, from the twelfth century on, and above all the in the thirteenth century, some theologians attacked this ethical extrinsicism and authoritarianism, which might properly (in modern terminology) be called a 'positivism of revelation'. Stimulated by the works of Aristotle, which were again becoming known in Europe, and by the medieval 'Eastern enlightenment' of Jewish and Arab philosophy, Thomas Aquinas in particular internalized the divine 'eternal law'; in other words, he mediated it by internalizing it within humanity itself, by incorporating as an intermediary between the law or the will of God (*lex aeterna*) and the human conscience the element of 'natural law' (*lex naturae*) in the form of man himself, as God's creation. Quite apart from this 'nature' terminology (a 'universal nature' for all men, even if Thomas already recognized a degree of historicity in this nature), in any case we can see quite clearly the intention to give ethics – which *in the last resort* is founded on God's divine nature – *indirectly* a humane basis in man himself. Thus for Thomas, human reason becomes the creative principle of human ethical norms: '*Lex naturalis est aliquid per rationem institutum*';[1] in other words, human reason presupposes ethical norms which are not arbitrary, but in accord with human nature, which at that time was seen as an ingredient of the cosmos as a whole: as a *natura*, while man is seen as an *animal rationale*. Here the relative independence of ethics on a human basis was decisively affirmed for the first time in the human tradition, albeit in an ultimately religious perspective.

This conception did not triumph for long. Shortly afterwards came a reaction on the part of the protagonists of the older tradition, though they had been stimulated by new insights into experience. In opposition to Thomas, Duns Scotus, later William of Ockham and finally the whole *via moderna* of nominalism defended the thesis that human reason was in no way capable of sustaining the burden of proof in laying a foundation for ethical norms of conduct. Norms are *transmitted* by the authority of a living tradition (they could produce a mass of material as pre-scientific knowledge, even if they could not advance theoretical arguments in support of this argument). As a result, the living tradition, in reality that of the church, again became the normative authority to which people had to submit, even if the commandment or prohibition seemed meaningless to them; in accordance with this conception, God's sovereign and free *will* was the only decisive factor here. In the sphere of the church, this was the nucleus of what in ethics is called 'modern positivism'. From now on the ethical norm, the expression of the sovereign *will* of God (Thomas says the sovereign *understanding* of God) makes itself felt, nominalistically and voluntaristically, in a purely 'external' way. Later, during the Counter-Reformation period, this 'living tradition' is *in practice* almost idenitified with the authority of the pope of Rome.

However, the Reformation exposed the authority of both the church's tradition and human reason to criticism. Ethical norms were bound up with *personal belief* on the basis of the word of God in the Bible. But precisely because Christian belief has become problematical as a foundation for a universally valid ethics from the time of the modern division of Christianity, since the Enlightenment people have looked elsewhere for the foundation and source of an ethical norm, above all in what is common to all men, hence in *practical reason* (albeit in a different interpretation from that of Thomas). In the course of this process of secularization, ethics has freed itself from its traditional theological context. Ethics with a vague religious tinge, or even without religion altogether, proves to be a concrete possibility and even an actual reality. It is effective into the bargain.

Christians responded to the new demand by saying that religion and ethics were not to be identified. Although this reaction was originally apologetic, it proved to be significant for the future. Religion is something more, something different, though at the same time it is ethical. Religions and Christianity arc not to be reduced to ethics.

Thus there came into being a purely ethical, non-religious, secular foundation for ethics, the basis of a universal, truly human culture. It is significant that precisely this emancipation of ethics from its former theological context demonstrated a *real* radicalizing of ethics in the modern consciousness. However, the historical background to this was also quite accidental.

It happened by chance that when ethics had become independent and had freed itself from Christian belief, it was confronted with completely new issues, namely with a cultural situation in which socio-political problems caused by the industrialization and technological development of social life began to throw up important and completely new ethical questions. These were problems with which the old Christian morality (which had been developed in other social infrastructures) had had nothing to do. True, in the sixteenth century, above all in Spanish neo-Scholasticism, Christianity had built up a large-scale colonial ethic which was fundamentally opposed to the theocratic tendencies of the colonizing countries, in the face of which it defended the natural right of other nations against the *sacrum imperium*: the sovereignty of all peoples and states was defended. But at a later stage, when the Enlightenment emancipated ethics from theology, the historical situation once again changed completely. The consequence was that the new, autonomous ethics came to the fore in contrast and in opposition to the earlier Christian morality, with its bias towards the sphere of the private individual. Broadly speaking, the older Catholic and Protestant ethics was principally a micro-ethics; by contrast, the emancipated, human ethics was, by a combination of historical circumstances, more of a macro-ethics. This heightened the opposition between old and new, and made even more intolerable the barrenness in contemporary situations of a 'Christian morality' which hardened its positions. Thus the burning ethical questions were only discussed *outside* the traditions of Protestant and Catholic moral theology. Christian morality was criticized for its reactionary tendencies in respect of new problems. Thus, above all from the time of Fichte, a rational ethic developed on a humanist basis and – in contrast to the ethics of Thomas Aquinas, which were on a similarly humanist basis – in the perspective of man's emancipated history of freedom. Ethical norms were recognized as a cultural creation of mankind in search of a higher humanity. Guided by his reason, man has to find a dignified way in history of building up a humane world. Thus quite apart from the question of the *final* grounds for ethics, this represented victory in the fight for an ethics which *at least directly* has its basis in what is universally human or worthy of mankind in constantly changing historical situations.

However, the emancipation of ethics from religion had even further consequences. For we see that the detachment of ethics from theology with the help of an ethics based on a purely human foundation itself begins to turn into an emancipation of *man* from *ethics* itself. In our society there is a clear call for an ethics which is free of norms. For many people, indeed, liberation from what are called 'repressive ethical norms' even becomes a basic postulate. In the meantime even in the 'Enlightenment', which thought itself to be so enlightened, what people understood by the slogans 'freedom', 'democracy' and 'humanity' had been made all too plain. Colonialism *proper* only began with the communication of the ideals of the Enlightenment, which Western man began to preach elsewhere. As a reaction to this past with its claims for 'absolute values' – made first by Christianity and later by the Enlightenment – not only has religion been banned from ethics, but even modern secularized ethics has been rejected. The watchword is: 'We must try to discover our own limits, simply by experimentation.' In fact, both in Christian and in secularized ethics, what was no more than the ideal of a liberal, (late-)capitalist, bourgeois society had often been elevated to the status of absolute and unchangeable norms, or biological laws had naïvely been elevated so as to become direct ethical norms.

We may certainly welcome a norm-free ethics if that is taken to mean that ethical norms may not have any alienating, external function, but must rather open up possibilities and perspectives which enable us to be as far as possible *true men* in specific historical situations; indeed, this was the special *concern* of St Thomas. Truly human ethics are not repressive, at least not for the man with a positive concern for ethics; however, they subject arbitrariness to serious criticism. Still, modern man does not seem to be able to cope by himself with the problems that he has produced, and with ethics is setting *our very humanity* at risk. One can be a Christian a Buddhist, or a Moslem, or have no religion at all, without the world visibly seeming to be shaken on its foundations. For many people, the *etsi Deus non daretur* (acting as though God did not exist) is unmistakably a significant experience which we should not make light of. On the other hand, however, even though its limits are blurred, ethics cannot simply be left to man's whim without undermining the basic structure of the world. For here we come up against the question whether man has the right and the duty in the last resort not to live like a dog, to borrow Ernst Bloch's phrase. In its fundamental concern, ethics bears the mark of a certain universal urgency and validity for humanity, however much that humanity may vary in time and space.

We can already draw some conclusions for Christian belief from this situation – namely the gulf between ethics and religion, and the danger of a gulf between mankind and ethics.

Like any religion, Christianity must accord *ethics a certain priority* over the religious (this is by no means to deny its reciprocal priority for believers). For ethics has the character of a really pressing urgency which cannot wait until there is unanimity among men over the ultimate questions of life. However, it is the case that ethics is essentially concerned with the basic question, 'What is man?', and therefore with the question, 'How is man in the last resort to live out his life?' 'For what kind of humanity must man finally decide?' This fundamental ethical question is also essentially concerned with world-views and religious options: as a Christian or a Buddhist, a humanist or an agnostic, and so on. It is a question of finality which is implicitly contained *in* every question of ethical immediacy and transitoriness.

Thus it can hardly be denied that ethics and one's view of life are intrinsically connected. Once again, however, we cannot postpone the answer to urgent ethical demands which confront us here and now until all men have arrived at a unanimous view of the final significance of human life. Despite the pluralism of religions and world-views, we must respond here and now to the specific inner demand and appeal of the ethical situation: this man, here and now – and in our time *mankind* (see below) – must be given effective and immediate help (directly, i.e. interpersonally, and through structures) in the light of our emergency situation. The situation itself makes this specific ethical demand on us as human beings, whether or not we are Christians, Buddhists, humanists or whatever.

Earlier, traditional scholastic ethics and even modern ethics based on natural law, or, to use a more modern expression, on the primacy of the reality called forth and experienced in the conscience, presupposed that 'order' was normally given; it is pre-existent, and gives rise to the command that we should not violate this order. Although the way in which this statement was articulated is correct *in the abstract*, such natural law was unreal. All too obviously, the starting point of this conception was an order already established on goodness, which in that case was not to be destroyed. However, if we look more closely we see that while man indeed is *potentiality-for-good*, the specific historical starting point for any ethics is not a pre-existing *order*, but *man who has already been damaged*: disorder, both in his own heart and in society. The *humanum*, threatened and in fact already damaged, leads specifically and historically to ethical demand and the ethical imperative, and thus to confrontation with quite definite, negative experiences of contrast. Therefore ethical invitation or demand is not an abstract norm but, historically, an event *which presents a challenge*: our concrete history itself, man in need, mankind in need.

Consequently, in *specific* terms, the 'ethically good' is that which overcomes evil, that which 'makes good' in the double sense of the words: (*a*) whatever realizes the good and as a result (*b*) puts right what is old, evil and awry, restores it to order and renews it: in other words, makes good in the sense of liberation and reconciliation.[2] Thus in specific terms ethics is concerned with redemption and liberation. What is called ethics, an ethical attitude, consists in resisting evil, furthering good and therefore bringing reconciliation in respect of the actual situation. So if the endangered *humanum* is the *immediate* historical impetus towards the ethically good action, in modern circumstances ethics also calls for a very exact, almost *scientific analysis* of the particular human situations in which we live. An analysis and *interpretation* of the situation is essential, in modern conditions, for a properly directed response to specific demands.

If we apply the term *orthopraxis*[3] – however dangerous the word may be – to man's specific ethically-good action in the world, insofar as this action is directed towards overcoming the threat to the *humanum* and furthering the possibility of human life in a given situation (which is only possible in the context of the question of meaning), we may and must say that orthopraxis is a fundamental hermeneutical principle, a pre-understanding in which the interpretation of the Christian message in a particular age first becomes possible and meaningful. For this message is good news of redemption and reconciliation, freedom and universal peace. In fact, this is precisely the way in which New Testament Christianity works in quite different historical circumstances. It is precisely in that way (and not in its literal content, without an analysis of its historical setting) that the New Testament serves as a model and as a norm, inspiration and guideline for Christians. This in itself enables us to understand the tendency of many religious people today to regard ethics, too, as a criterion of religious authenticity. A religious attitude can in fact be suspected of being an ideology if it is socially, politically and personally neutral in the ethical sphere. Man summoned in and through history to moral action is the subject to whom the Christian message is directed here and now. Man as *the subject of an ethical demand* is therefore the *presupposition for the understanding* of the Christian proclamation of faith. So unless there is consideration for and reflection on what is already present before faith, namely man as a subject who hears the message in his specific situation, Christian faith becomes incredible and incomprehensible. Ethics, as *the situation of* the believer, therefore has a hermeneutical or interpretative function even in the theological self-understanding of the Christian faith. Christians evidently need to go round by way of a secularized ethics in order to arrive at this self-understanding! But the challenge from outside is not yet at an end.

A great deal more has happened in the last few decades since the modern move from an ethics under the tutelage of the church to a rational ethics on the foundation of true humanity. As a result of the technological consequences of science, human action – and what has happened to mankind – has taken on such scope and significance that it is no longer possible to be content with ethical norms which regulate the life and society of individuals and smaller groups, with their requirement of a group relationship. In modern activity, what is at stake is no longer just the small group but often the future of all mankind. To give two examples: there is danger both from our use of atomic energy and also from the setting at naught of ecological principles of life by our technocratic and scientifically directed industrial society. In order to make clear the consequences and implications of human activity in the possible effects and side-effects of this activity, experts rightly make a schematic distinction between three clearly defined spheres (which in the end increasingly encroach on one another), namely: (*a*) the *micro-sphere*: family, clan, neighbourhood, district, etc.; (*b*) the middle or *meso-sector*: the effects above all of the policies of a country; (*c*) the *macro-sector*: the effects of our activity on an ever-increasing totality, and in the last resort on the fate of the whole of mankind. It is a fact that until recently, the ethical norms concerning men only related to the private and micro-sphere of human life; even in the middle sphere of state politics, impulses from group interests and demands for group identity often played their part. Only the great political decisions – after the particular group and state interests had been secured – were in reality left to the so-called ethically neutral reason of state.

As a consequence of the world-wide expansion of technological and scientific civilization, the effects of our action have a significance which affects *all men*. In other words, when one takes into account the state of science and technology, the consequences of present-day human action are to be located in the macro-sphere of the common interest of all men. Regardless of their specific group or their cultural and ethical traditions, all nations and cultures are confronted by our present civilization with a general ethical problem which applies to them all. That means that for the first time in human history, mankind as such sees itself confronted with the task of taking responsibility as a whole for the consequences of its action. The international solidarity, binding on all mankind, therefore calls for universally valid *ethical norms or basic principles which apply to all men*, if this situation is not to turn into a farce or a world catastrophe. The need for this combined responsibility is, of course, matched by the demand for an ethic of world-wide responsibility.[4]

Thus for the first time in our human history mankind is at the cross-roads, faced with the prospect of a critical change, in which through its action – or failure to act – it is deciding about the future of the *world* and thus also about its *meaning*. Moreover, the situation demands a human action which can no longer be the concern of the individual; it requires order on a socio-political basis. The situation thus calls for socialization. However, bearing in mind critically the history of the past and the present, this situation calls for a socialization which – and here I am well aware that personal ethical and religious values also have a part to play – on the one hand does not make the individual man isolated and absolute, and yet on the other does not push him to one side. In other words, the present urgent demand could be described as a call for *personalizing and democratic socialization*. The world situation requires *forces and impulses* which can guarantee not only human survival but also the meaningful survival of men.

But what is meaningful humanity, which will have to direct this common responsibility? The question arises whether there is a universally valid view on this question which is generally agreed and nevertheless not dogmatic – i.e. not imposed by *outside* authority, and which can be freely accepted by all. What can we see here that might be regarded as universally valid? Before answering this question, by way of exploring the ground we need to investigate man's actual concern with his future.

## §2  Man's utopian consciousness

*Literature*: F. Baumer, *Paradijs en heilsstaat, dromen van een beter leven*, Amsterdam 1967; E. Bloch, *Geist der Utopie*, Munich 1918, Gesamtausgabe 3, Frankfurt 1964; id., *Das Prinzip Hoffnung*, Berlin 1959, Gesamtausgabe 5, Frankfurt 1963; M. Buber, 'Pfade in Utopia', in *Werke* I, Munich-

Heidelberg 1962, 833–1002, ET *Paths in Utopia*, Boston 1958; F. Chirpaz, 'Aliénation et utopie', *Esprit* 36, 1969, 80–8; N. Cohn, *Pursuit of the Millennium*, Oxford [3]1970; M. Demaison, 'Les sentiers de l'utopie chrétienne', *LV* 95, 1969, 87–110; G. Durand, *L'imagination symbolique*, Paris 1964; C. Gremmels and W. Herrmann, *Vorurteil und Utopie. Zur Aufklärung der Theologie*, Stuttgart 1971; G. Kateb, *Utopia and its Enemies*, New York 1963; P. Ludz, 'Utopie und Utopisten', *RGG*[3] 6, 1217–20; K. Mannheim, *Ideologie und Utopie*, Frankfurt [3]1952; F. E. Manuel (ed.), *Utopias and Utopian Thought*, Boston 1967; H. Marcuse, *Das Ende der Utopie*, Berlin 1967; id., *Kultur und Gesellschaft*, 2 vols, Frankfurt 1965; W. D. Marsch, *Zukunft*, Stuttgart-Berlin 1969; id., *Hoffen worauf? Auseinandersetzung mit E. Bloch*, Hamburg 1963; T. Molnar, *Utopia: The Perennial Heresy*, New York 1967; J. Moltmann, *Theology of Hope*, ET London and New York 1967; L. Mumford, *The Story of Utopias*, New York 1962; A. Neusüss, *Utopie. Begriff und Phänomen des Utopischen*, Neuwied – Berlin 1968; G. Picht, *Mut zur Utopie*, Munich 1969; M. Plattel, *Utopie en kritisch denken*, Bilthoven 1970; W. de Pree, *Maatschappijkritiek en theologische kritiek*, Assen 1971; R. Ruyer, *L'utopie et les utopies*, Paris 1950; J. P. Sartre, *L'imaginaire*, Paris 1940; H. Schaeffer, ' "Politieke theologie" in een tijd van "religieuze renaissance" ', *TvTh* 12, 1972, 226–42; H. Schlette, 'Utopisches Denken und konkrete Humanitat', *Conc* 8, 1972, 355–62; J. Servier, *Histoire de l'utopie*, Paris 1967; S. Thrupp (ed.), *Millennial Dreams in Action*, New York 1970; P. Tillich, 'Politische Bedeutung der Utopie im Leben der Völker', *Gesammelte Werke* 6, Stuttgart 1963, 157–210; *Säkularisation und Utopie, FS E. Forsthoff*, Stuttgart 1957; *Temporalité et aliénation*, Centre International d'Etudes Humanistes de Rome, Paris 1975.

## I. CONSERVATIVE AND PROGRESSIVE UTOPIAS

In traditional cultures, people started from the assumption and the concern that the future had to be like the past (often leaving aside 'chance' deviations in the present). Given the circumstances of the time, this was in fact a sign of practical wisdom. The patriarchs had gathered together wisdom, and too many changes would endanger very existence (of the clan). The past was made a norm to provide protection against a destructive future. However, this was never the whole past. What was important was the *picture* that was made of this past; this was established as a norm, while other aspects were kept silent about or suppressed. Through the prism of collective memory, even in traditional cultures, a *selective picture* of the past was made a 'utopia' and a model. Thus a mystified past, such as there had never been, became the 'primitive' form of utopia, the *canon* of human society. This past is therefore an *ou-topos*, a no man's land; it never existed. It is *la belle époque* or 'the golden age' (golden for the top ten thousand, but not for the masses). From this we see that the past only serves and can serve as a norm when it is no longer 'the past', because people refuse to cut off a particular age in the past, and make it representative of the whole of history. A particular past is 'frozen' in an image. As a shining epoch, this past is a guarantee for the future, on the presupposition that people want to assimilate the future to this picture. However, such a will for the future and a corresponding way of life are essential for utopia (seen in conservative terms).

Thus in *this* utopian consciousness one can see the 'existing order' confirmed, both in nature and above all in society, whether on the basis of the normative value of patriarchal traditions or on that of classical culture or – in a religious interpretation *in* such a patriarchal society, or a society built on classical culture – through laws given by God (though in the meantime, despite this static picture of society, the emperor, feudal lords and kings can largely 'manipulate' the future in their own way). Briefly speaking, the following elements can be said to be the foundations of this conservative utopia with its static politics: particular patterns of social life, like the clan, and later cities and states with their particular values and laws; the family as the nucleus of this social order; the working community as an organic contractual alliance; the rulers as a natural *élite* called to leadership; finally the traditional cultural values which were regarded as normative: in the West above all the 'immortal' works of Greek art, the *philosophia perennis*, Byzantine Roman law, all this seen as a market-place and hereditary pledge of human sagacity and wisdom, an example for all nations. As a consequence, this static culture and politics had a claim to universality, and despite the degree to which it moved round a fixed nucleus, also a claim to immutability.

However, the conservative utopia does not allow any new meaning to develop; meaning is already given, and by its character as a model and norm for the future, excludes any new meaning.

In contrast to traditionalist utopias, our modern times know of futuristic utopias. The presupposition here is the concern that everything should be changed. For in the meantime people have experienced the mutability of society as a possibility. Our social structures are not necessities, but have developed through history; they are therefore contingent and changeable; indeed they need to be changed. However, the rejection of the past is by no means general here, except in the radical so-called 'great refusal'. And not even then. For people discuss the past or protest against it, *insofar as* our present is specifically the result of this past. Tacitly or explicitly, a selective image of the past also plays a part here, to inspire and activate; suppressed and misunderstood turning-points from the past

are taken up in order to alter the course of history here and now. People
are concerned with what in many countries is called 'anti-history': the
history of the conquered, of unsuccessful revolutions, exiled heretics and
millenarians, of unfulfilled expectations. People look for 'forgotten truths'
in the past, for everything that has been suppressed from our historical
memory by civic prejudice, rationalistic censorship and the church's
campaign against heretics. So here, too, people look for support and
inspiration in the past. Here, too, a single element from the past is also
elevated to be a norm for the future; here, however, people do not begin
from a golden past, but from a future yet to come. From this perspective
they look back on particular aspects in the past: the history of human
suffering. Here no past 'golden age' is taken as a model and a norm, but
people seek to *live for* a golden age, for the kind of society that has never
yet been. They refuse to create the future along the lines of the official
tradition. The future has a priority of the will, whereas the past can only
work by inspiration.

Instead of a pre-existing meaning, we have here the expression of the
'still open' meaning of history; meaning has still to be *created*.

Thus history lives from utopias of a traditionalist or futuristic kind. Really
the designations 'conservative' and 'approving of society', and 'progressive' or 'critical of society' are *modern* categories. One can only speak of
conservative politics from the moment when the particular possibility of
fundamental change becomes a real prospect; in that case conservatism
is a negative response to the demand of the possibility of fundamental
social change. There was a time when conservative politics could not be
given a name, not because it did not exist, but because there was nothing
else. However, in the light of modern situations we can rightly talk of
traditional and futurist utopias; both are forms of understanding and
wanting a *particular future*, which is not the same in each case (though
here to some degree I go outside current ideas to be found in the existing
literature about 'utopias').

In the utopian consciousness the past plays a basic activating role
either as a 'golden age', or, in critical remembrances, as a history of
suffering. Therefore both views are clearly subject to a *particular* concern
for the future. Either people *want* the future to be the way things were in
the past golden age (or as the patriarchal traditions viewed them); or,
people *want* the future to be different from the past and the present, in
other words, they want a golden age of the kind which has yet to appear.
In both cases, dreams of the future are connected with a selective remembrance of the past. This critical, selective remembrance is put at the
service of the future. Of course, images of the past and future have strong
emotional overtones; they are not neutral. *Because of their potentiality for the*

*future*, both the good things and the bad things from the past have emotive force which can direct action. Auschwitz and Buchenwald are disturbing for us, not only for the sake of what has happened, macabre though that may be, but because they might possibly be repeated in the future. Even yesterday's joy and love are only true happiness because it is hoped that they will be repeated and will continue into the future. The basic moods of human life – anxiety and despair, joy and hope – are evidently bound up with the temporal structure of remembrance and expectation. Therein lies their critical and productive force – in their remembrance and expectation.

Both the purely conservative utopia and the progressive utopia of the 'great refusal' are 'ideologies', a false consciousness – in other words a consciousness that has a broken relationship with the real facts of our human history. Man is not a *creator* of the future, nor does he possess its already existing meaning. He is an instance of situational and thematic freedom – and therefore has the possibilities and limitations of what is in fact a self-made history with human dignity. As a result, in their extremist and absolute one-sidedness, both trends conceal within themselves the germ of movements *hostile to man*, because they absolutize fragments and phases in our history – both past and future – and make them the norm of the whole of history. In this way, the valid priority of the future *is confused* with the *picture* that we make of the future (a confusion which dominates the whole of Heidegger's hermeneutics – and the use that has been made of them in many modern theologies). However, in both their extremes they in fact point dialectically to real dimensions of true humanity; on the one hand the critical remembrance of great traditions of humanity,[5] and on the other the concern for a better world to come, more worthy of men.

It is striking that both conservative and progressive utopias are concerned with particular *ideal theses* which relate to demonstrable and identifiable historical tendencies, and are effective precisely because they connect theory and practice. The utopian picture of man and society to which a man gives his allegiance becomes an ethical imperative. To take away the practical reference of a utopia makes it a mere *vision*, whereas its special force lies in its critical and practical influence. Thus the utopia which a man really advocates has a *hermeneutical* and *critical* value, and serves as an *orientation*; it combines rationality with fantasy. It is impossible to assess the influence which utopias have exercised in history (no matter in what direction), but it should not be underestimated. Utopias have a greater subversive force – either over against the existing order or over against those who want to change it – than people suppose.

Furthermore, it is striking that in the first stages of its history, mankind did not move from specific experiences of contrast to a better future, but rather to a retrospective utopia, a 'protology': the ideal picture of 'original innocence', the initial earthly paradise, in the Middle Ages characteristically called 'original righteousness' (*iustitia originalis*). The contemporary situation was illuminated in terms of the beginning (the myth of Adam): earthly paradise and the fall. Only later, in societies which had progressed further, were the *protological* myths, the myths of human origins, turned into *eschatological* myths, into promises that one day there would be a future which would bring complete fulfilment. Eschatological myths, or myths of the future, evidently presuppose a lengthy history, and a higher degree of reflection than protological myths. Thus the commemorative structure of human consciousness seems to be more primitive than its utopian structure, though paradoxically remembrance is a form of the utopia of the future!

## II.  A CRITICAL–RATIONAL 'UTOPIA' IN A VALUE–FREE SOCIETY: PROBLEMS IN PLANNING FOR THE FUTURE

Over against both 'critical' forms, I commented that in our day utopias which either confirm society or seek to alter it have been resisted by the claim of *critical science*. In fact, until recently it was impossible to imagine the future as an object of science. However, for about twenty-five years scientists, too, have had a methodical and systematic concern with the rational prognosis of the future and the rational planning for the future which follows from it. Man has arrived at the insight that he himself is reponsible for the future of mankind on earth – at the firm conviction that he himself can *produce* the future. So a new concept has emerged in our modern time: the future as the product of rational and deliberate human action. The growing awareness of this qualitatively different form of human existence has led to a systematic search for rational guarantees for human, individual and social survival. In contrast to science fiction and imaginative futurology, and in contrast to both conservative and progressive utopias, people today speak of a scientific or rational futorology (of which 'ecology' is only one ingredient). In so far as it is a product of man himself, in this futurology, the future of mankind in his world becomes above all a question on the one hand of science and technology and on the other of rational political action. In other words, it is a question of the critical, free and liberating use of human reason, which to this end also makes a critical investigation of the presuppositions, the social consequences, the ethical implications and finally the goals of science and political action.

In this scientific and futurological sense, the future of mankind therefore means a future which can be foreseen, calculated and even implemented. The three fundamental aspects of this futurological future on the basis of scientifically-grounded anticipatory thinking are prognosis, rational or 'enlightened' projections of the future, and planning.[6] *Prognosis,* that is, the forecasting of future situations made possible by scientific analysis, can be calculated with a high degree of reliability (though on the basis of a number of presuppositions which are not easily controllable!), for example population growth and its consequences for mankind; the problem of food resources and the conservation of water and energy; the consequences of environmental pollution, and so on. *Rational forecasting of the future* is a question of outlining those situations which can be brought about by deliberate action (e.g. through rational birth-control) and are said to be necessary on the basis of human reason. *Planning* is the concrete organization of measures which are necessary in order to realize future projects (e.g. a specific structural reform of instruction at all levels).

However, the problem is that the scientific conception of the 'value-free objectivity' of the sciences is incapable of providing a rational foundation for macro-ethics, whereas precisely since the detachment of ethics from its traditional religious, ecclesiastical and theological tutelage, ethical vision has been put on a human foundation and thus been given a *rational* basis. Since that time, however, people have evidently no longer been capable of creating ethical norms which are universally valid, binding on all men and yet non-dogmatic (i.e. are not to be accepted on external authority, but in freedom), and such norms are necessary to direct planning for the future. Therefore the separation of value-free objectivism from the sphere of convictions about ethics, religion and the world, which have been banished to the realm of existential subjectivism, make such planning for the future a difficult undertaking. In the Western democracies, ethical validity or normativeness has been forced out into the sphere of what is called irrational subjectivity. Here we can make a subjective distinction between three models of the future:[7]

1. The *decisionistic* (in reality, positivistic) model of the future. This model is based on a sharp distinction between science and technology on one side and politics on the other. The sciences simply offer alternative means, but the politicians decide on the ends and the particular choice of means. Subjective decisions of the conscience are as it were 'brought together' by means of various agreements reached through compromises (on the basis of parliamentary democracy); by votes they are finally established in the form of a law. In other words, the representative democratic combination of a variety of subjective decisions of conscience mediates between theory (scientific analysis) and practice.

2. The *technocratic* model of the future. Here things are the other way round. Scientific and technological means and possibilities determine the

(political) ends. In that case the politicians make only political decisions; they carry out the orders of a scientific and technocratic *élite*.

3. The *pragmatistic* model of the future (above all J. Habermas). The advocates of this model attack both decisionism and the direction of the world by technocrats. This model does away with the strict separation between scientific and technical knowledge and politics. There is a critical mutual interaction between the two, a dialectical relationship between values and scientific knowledge. Not only scientific knowledge, but also the values and aims to which this knowledge is related, become the object of a rational discussion. In this model the scientific experts do not have sovereign control over the politicians, but on the other hand there is no longer any scientific 'storm-free' or impregnable zone in which decisions are made only on the basis of political resolves. There is a collaboration between science and politics on a rational basis (at least this is the perspective hoped for, despite many specific problems).

By contrast with these three models in the Western parliamentary democracies, in the Marxist system, on the other hand, decisions of personal conscience are simply superfluous, because an *élite* of party leaders guarantees the union of scientific knowledge and ethical values on the basis of a dialectical super-knowledge. Insight into the rationality of the unavoidable historical process (which can be investigated by scientific analysis) here really *replaces* ethics; it mediates between theory and practice.[8] Thus in the last resort both the 'Western modern liberals' and the Marxist systems force the decisions of conscience back into the private sphere, where they have no inter-subjective validity.[9] In the one case, then, value-free scientific technocracy determines our future on the basis of a majority decision of politicians;[10] in the other, a nucleus of party ideologists enlightened by technocracy and science decides what will be good for man in the future. One cannot really call either of the two systems fully and completely worthy of mankind.

It emerges from the various kinds of utopias (which I have described somewhat schematically, but I hope nevertheless with sufficient accuracy), that man's concern for the future is based on *particular principles*, different though these may be.

The scientific utopia is *pragmatic*. One can hardly deny that its advantage is that at least part of human practice, above all the instrumental, technological and strategic part, can be 'objectified' and analysed by the value-free standard of science. *Given a particular goal*, science can in fact demonstrate what the technical possibilities of realizing it are; it can also demonstrate what will be the probable effects and side-effects of a particular human action. Even computers can be brought into use efficiently here. But this part of the interrelation between theory and practice which can be objectified by science and technology leaves out of rational discussion the goal itself. 'The open society' of K. Popper and the 'critical reason' of Hans Albert who is inspired by him – 'critical rationalism'[11], one of the chief tendencies of our time – provide as it were a paradigm of this tendency. In this model the decisions about the goal of human action are *presupposed*, i.e. left to the private sphere of subjective decisions. Thus this critical rationalism cannot give any positive criteria for the desirability, rationality and humanity of the particular goals aimed at. This of itself already reduces the utopian *humanum*, halves it through a scientistic and rationalistic connection between end and means,[12] which, it may be said in passing, is mostly governed by economic interests. However, in the present situation, faced with this theory it is impossible to avoid a discussion of the aims themselves. Furthermore, this ideal of freedom in critical rationalism leaves out of account the complex question of structural authority and does not see how often this freedom is a pseudo-freedom, which has already been manipulated by economic interests.

As compared with these 'rational utopias', the conservative and progressive visionary utopias are *dogmastistic*: they make absolute a single phase in the past or in the hoped-for future, a 'golden age' in the past or in the projected future – in both cases a kind of blueprint of the way in which society must look. These images or visions cannot be either tested or criticized. However one twists and turns, they are based on a particular dogmatic image of man, and this leads naturally and even intrinsically to an absolutizing of power.

In all this we must not forget that any rationally planned future is only half a history, a history understood along the lines of the model of a relationship between means and ends. For the rational 'future' does not coincide with what will really happen. *On the one hand* 'the future' is a wealth of possibilities, of which some in fact will be realized; some elements of this future can be calculated rationally with a greater or lesser degree of probability. Here the decisive question is already: which possibilities are men to take up and which not? This makes history a real adventure in which human decisions play a large part, quite apart from the fact that some imponderables will make the future turn out differently from what men had planned. *On the other hand*, mankind is not the universal providence of its own history. When the 'wealth of possibilities', which is what the future is for us today, has really become present, only one complex whole out of these many possibilities will have been realized, and this actual totality cannot ever be derived from the momentary 'historical trend' which we can in fact analyse. History does not evolve logically! But in that case past and present are interwoven with the future only through those thin threads of the particular complex event in which the future in fact becomes present in its foreseen and unforeseen, unexpected elements. The future is significant in determining the meaning of past and present only as it in fact comes to pass. *Future* is therefore in the last resort that which keeps *coming towards* men who are alive today, at once both thanks to and yet despite all prognoses, all projections of the future and all planning. The future can never be interpreted purely teleologically, technologically or in terms of the logic of development. The future transcends human rationality, not only provisionally, but in principle. From a purely human perspective (leaving religious views aside), man's future stands under the fundamental proviso of the *ignorantia futuri*, the unknown future (which may perhaps make men raise the question of God). The consequence is that a purely teleological conception of history in terms of the model of means and ends lands man in alienating frustrations, and in the last resort reduces him to despair and defeatism.

I said earlier that our relationship to the future which calls forth a particular practice is only possible as a result of our relationship to the past, whereas the (hermeneutical) relationship to the past already implies a decison for the future. This has also become clear from our selective survey of both conservative and progressive utopias, whereas on the other hand purely value-free and scientific planning for the future leads to a number of problems, to a gulf between scientific 'objectivism' and the subjectivism of the decisions of the individual conscience. The question therefore is: of what challenging realities, which cannot be controlled or theorized about by critical reason, must man take account in his concern for a good, true and happy future, a future worth living, and what must he do to secure such a future?

Chapter 2

# Critical remembrance of suffering humanity

> '*Si Deus est, unde malum?*
> *Si non est, unde bonum?*'

*Introduction*

Every man enters the world with a cry. And yet there is cause to rejoice! Suffering obviously has more than one face.

As Kant remarked, the lament 'The world is in the grasp of evil' is 'as old as our human history'.[13] He quoted scripture to this effect: 'The whole world is in the power of the evil one' (I John 5.19). In all cultures and societies known to us, men have used very different categories and human conceptions, theoretically, and above all in practice, in their attempts to cope with their experience of the history of human suffering. Even against the background of meaningful, joyful and satisfying experiences and hoped-for salvation, the history of suffering among man, and indeed in the animal world and throughout the universe, is the constant theme of every account of life, every philosophy and every religion; and today even of science and technology.

In order to come rather nearer to the problem of suffering man, we need to take counsel from more than today's critical thought. This problem is too vast for a single fragment in our history to be able to express the one liberating word about it. We are concerned here with human beings, and in that case *they* – and we among them – have the right to speak first. In that case it is right to take counsel from men's own experiences of suffering during the course of their history, from what they have thought about it, and from the way in which they have experienced *human salvation*. Here particularly, critical reason is not directed solely to its own reflection, but also and above all to the critical remembrance of the human history of suffering and the way in which people, in various circumstances and against a changing background, have attempted to cope with their own suffering and that of others. Even this survey of human history, in which something of what *humanity* is and means to be emerges, will naturally still be limited – perhaps even 'élitist'. The voices we hear are of philosophical and religious, Marxist and humanist 'thinkers', and not the suffering multitudes. Yet it cannot be claimed that these do not give evocative expression to precisely what is a living experience among all men.

The myths of both primitive and culturally more developed people have long been concerned with the impenetrable reality of suffering humanity. People have constantly expressed the conflict in human life in the projections of cosmic myths and vegetation myths (summer and winter), and they have sought to provide a practical insight into life which will serve as an orientation for action. Taught by what they have seen happening in nature around them, they have also as it were 'projected' (expressed hermeneutically) the history of their own humanity and interpretative reading of it in myths of the struggle of God (the gods) against 'the monster' (with varying names but the same function and significance, in all the old myths spread throughout the whole world and often independent of one another – down to the story of St George and the dragon, which is nearer to our own time).[14] There is the conflict between *erōs* and *thanatos*, experienced by mankind long before Freud gave a particular 'explanation' of it:[15] instincts of life and instincts of death, experiences of disaster and experiences of salvation. It is significant that really *no religion* – apart perhaps from 'critical reason' – has made light of suffering, and that in past history there has been more protest against suffering from religion than from critical rationality. Religions do not have their origin *in* suffering, but suffering becomes a problem only for the man who believes in God. This is already a lesson from the history of mankind of which we should take critical note.

## §1 Mankind in search of a way of life which will overcome suffering

I. AN EXCEPTION IN THE RELIGIOUS COMPREHENSION OF SUFFER-ING: DUALISM ('MANICHAEISM')

Different though the Jewish, Graeco-Roman, Christian, Hindu, Buddhist and Moslem religions may be in their treatment of the problem of suffering man, they all have one thing in common. They reject dualism, i.e. the existence of a twofold first and supreme principle, a principle of good and a principle of evil. This gives them all unmistakably the same basic intuition: the heart of reality is *mercy*. True dualism, if there has ever been a metaphysical dualism, is an *exception* in the life of religions and humanity.

However, there is one religion which (albeit with nuances) approaches the problem of suffering man from a dualistic view of the world. Not Zarathustra himself, but a later phase of Persian religion, Zoroastrianism, is strongly dualistic, as too is Manichaeism.[16] However, this religious exception is important precisely because of its influence on later Jewish religion, on Christianity, Islam and also on oriental religions. So we shall begin with a 'religious outsider' which has ceased to exist as a living religion, despite sporadic revivals.

According to modern experts in the history of religion, Zoroaster (or Zarathustra: about 630–550 BC) was himself a strict monotheist, though even with him the theory of 'two spirits', twin brothers, plays an important part. Both of these have their own sphere of influence, but they seem to be emanations of the one God who embraces within himself the *coincidentia oppositorum*. However, in the fourth century BC, in the Zenda-vesta version of Zoroastrianism, the twin brothers in fact became two first principles: the spirit of darkness and the spirit of light. Our world is the sphere in which both are at work, and therefore in it battle is joined between the children of light and the children of darkness. Thus this Persian religion does not set out to explain the problem of evil. The problem simply *exists*. This dualism is merely a duplication of the stubborn impenetrability of the experience of suffering and evil on the *theoretical* level. The theory simply formulates the problem. The great difficulty is, however, that put in this way it is by nature amoral. For if both good and evil go back to a particular absolute and first cause, it is impossible to discover any reason why one principle should be preferred above another. In that case 'Satanism' is 'just as good' as 'goodness'. However, people do not seem prepared to accept this consequence; they retain within their perspective the hope (which in dualism is unjustified) that in the last resort, in this cosmic and universally human struggle between the powers of good and the powers of evil, the latter will be defeated. The dualistic beginning turns into the eschatological priority of the good, which now already is productively at work. Here life is stronger than theory.

In this view, different and contrary functions are perceived in our world. This does not present any problem, but good and evil are by nature *antipodes*, not only contrary but contradictory: they destroy each other by being what they are. That is a fact of experience. The spiritual world, the origin of our earthly world, must therefore bear this dualism within itself. Thus the good Creator is confronted with an anti-being, for the good is the sole origin of everything that is good. The good God must therefore be pure positiveness, not a Lord over life and death, but the one and only source of life. However, there is suffering, even death. These phenomena therefore have an anti-creator, Satan, as their first principle.

This means that this phase in Persian religion includes a radical criticism of earlier forms of religion in which one and the same divine principle was the power which gave life and destroyed it. God becomes pure, saving goodness, and evil comes from elsewhere. The old places of worship in which people worshipped the 'God of life and death', of death and fertility, were systematically destroyed. If God is pure goodness, there is room for cultural activity and for the Persian concern for justice which was beginning to emerge at that time (these Persians are the ones who allowed Israel to return home from exile). Evil is the anti-godly principle and must therefore be fought against, by men as well. In a remarkable way, it was precisely this dualism which was the beginning of a dynamic development towards righteousness, the overcoming of suffering and delight in cultural works.

However, at a later date this dualism also took on other manifestations. Mani (Manichaeism) developed a dualism between 'spirit' and 'matter': he lived in Mesopotamia and was killed by the Persians around AD 276. What we know of him comes in most cases from Augustine, who himself had been a Manichaean for a while. Manichaeism was an eclectic system derived from Zoroastrianism and Christianity. God must remain free from all evil. But evil is simply a harsh reality among us. Therefore evil,

suffering, must be derived from the intervention of an alien power, hostile
to God. There was already a reality hostile to God before creation. When
God created his world, the divine and the anti-divine elements were as
it were mixed up in his creatures. Therefore the particular world of
human experience has something of both first principles in it. The world
is the great undertaking in which the good seeks to free itself from this
evil mixture. The blazing sun was like a hopeful promise; the waxing and
waning moon was a sign of fragments of light escaping from this hybrid
mixture. However, here too the perspective was that the shining sun
would triumph. This cosmic drama was played out within every individual. Thus Manichaeism embodies the great human struggle for emancipation and for the liberation of the good. Clear awareness of the reality
of these two essentially contradictory principles is necessary to begin
with, for success can only be achieved by acting accordingly. The way to
success is extremely strict asceticism, the demand that one should withdraw from 'the material'. The mere plucking of fruit from a tree makes
nature, the tree, weep. Augustine, who tells us all this had by this time
forsworn Manichaeism, but he nevertheless remained fascinated by the
theoretical consistency of the system and above all by its faithfulness to
real human experiences.

*Jainism*, a third 'dualistic' trend, particularly influenced India and the
East. Here there is certainly no longer any mention of a metaphysical
dualism (if there ever was). The soul or the ego is completely caught up
in matter. Salvation lies in liberation from this entanglement. Everything
in the universe has its own soul, to a constantly diminishing degree,
depending on whether it has five, four or fewer sense organs; the lowest
category has only the sense of taste (which, in Jainist terms, also includes
the inorganic world). Thus the universe is full of 'living beings'. Even
stones have their tears, although they cannot weep aloud. *Karma* (here)
is the entanglement of the good in evil. Suffering accepted voluntarily
breaks the accumulation of *karma* and frees the soul. Until that has
happened, the soul must constantly be reborn in the form of stones, trees,
iron and so on. It is sawn, melted, worked on with knives, dies a thousand
deaths. The whole world suffers.

It is therefore one's lifelong task not to impose suffering on others; one
may not even tread on insects unawares. Jainist monks go through the
world with a super-sensitive fear of damaging even a tree or a branch.
To die completely to the corporeal is the supreme task of life, in order to
make the soul free. The dualism involved here is a dualism between
'spirit' and 'matter', *jiva* and *ajiva*, spirit and non-spirit; but a metaphysical dualism, above all of the first two principles, is rejected as not being
in accord with human experience. In this respect Jainism is Indian (see
the discussion of Hinduism and Buddhism). Whatever reality may be in

itself, it is recognized in various forms from its manifestations. Absolute categorizing knowledge is therefore impossible. Each phenomenon has more than one aspect.

Jainism does not know of creation as the result of a divine plan. The existence of evil makes a creator inconceivable and impossible. Most of all, a *creatio ex nihilo* is utter nonsense. How can an eternal God suddenly hit on the idea of creating? In that case he would not be perfect; he would be No-God, and how could a No-God create the world? And if he created living beings purely out of love, why is there all this misery? God himself would sin if he inflicted sorrow and suffering on the children whom he created.

We must not forget the basic idea here: if God is really God, he is pure positiveness. This seems to me to be the correct intuition in any form of 'dualism', more correct than to say that God is ground of both the gift of life and the destruction of life. In the last resort, all religions will be concerned with this basic conception. Dualism is a false conclusion from what is basically a correct insight: if God is really God, he is love and mercy. But Jainism rejects a personal creator God. The 'existence' of good and evil is a kind of natural law.

Religions are only 'credible' if they take into account all the facts of human experience, suffering and joy, and if they do not claim that what is an all too harsh experience of reality is pure imagination. The religions which I shall now describe in all too sweeping terms have in common the fact that they give the last word to the *good*, and not to evil and suffering. None of them advocates a kind of dolorism; on the contrary, their deepest concern is to overcome suffering. (However, it should be said in advance that in all these religions there can be and in fact is a great divide between official orthodoxy and actual popular religion.)

## II.  ISRAEL'S PROTEST AGAINST SUFFERING AND ITS SUFFERING THROUGH AND FOR OTHERS

In Israelite religion, suffering man was a central problem of life. In a time of clan warfare there were also clan gods who fought against one another; the victory of one tribe over another was also the annihilation of the god of the other. However, in the long run Israel saw this differently. Even when Israel was defeated, Yahweh remained the mighty one, for while the people of God are dependent on God, Yahweh is not dependent on his people. In that case the suffering of the people is the consequence of the wrath of God over the sinfulness of the people, and Yahweh is therefore a principle of both the good that we enjoy and also the suffering of man. However, it was precisely this Yahwism of Jewish religion – Yahweh is the Lord of history – that made suffering, and above all unmerited suffering, a key problem in Israel, more significantly than in other religions.

The basic notion was that God created everything 'in good order' (Gen. 1.31; Ps. 104). It follows from this that disorder, and above all suffering, goes back to human sinfulness. Sin and suffering are closely connected in Judaism. This theory is developed above all in Deuteronomy and the Deuteronomistic tradition in the light of the idea of the covenant, in respect of both the people and the individual. The word *<sup>a</sup>wōn* (from the root crooked, bent) means both sin and also punishment for sin. Sin is a twisting, something 'twisted'; for that reason the term also includes the consequences of sin: the guilt of sin and punishment for sin. Whatever is crooked gives pain (see Gen. 15.16; I Kings 17.18; Isa. 30.13; 64.6; Jer. 13.22; Ps. 32.2–5, etc.). Anyone who does something perverse must bear the consequences (Gen. 4.13; Ex. 34.7; Ps. 85.4). Sin is therefore an action which calls forth punishment and suffering (Ezek. 18.30; 44.12; Isa. 30.13; Hos. 5.5; Job 31.11, 28 etc.). *<sup>a</sup>wōn* is also the Latin *poena*, which means both sin and punishment for sin, namely suffering. Furthermore, this connection is seen not only in individual but also in social terms: offspring are punished for the sin of their fathers (Lev. 26.39f.; Isa. 14.21; 53.11; Jer. 11.10; Ezek. 18.17, 19, 20, etc.). Thus the punishment for the sin of the 'first parents' is that every mother will bear children with birthpangs and that the husband will have to work for daily bread (Gen 3.14–19). The fear of the Lord prolongs life, but the years of the godless are shortened (Prov. 10.27).

Here many Jews turned the relationship round: they argued from the fact of suffering to the presence of some kind of sin, perhaps hidden. And this inevitably led to a number of dilemmas. Moreover, because of the connection between sin and suffering, it is always God who sends suffering as a punishment for sin (Hos. 4.9).

During the period of a more internalized individualism, some prophets attacked the theory of the collective connection between sin and suffering: 'You ask, "Why should not the son suffer for the inquity of the father?" When the son has done what is lawful and right, and has been careful to observe all my statutes, he shall surely live. The soul that sins shall die. The son shall not suffer for the iniquity of the father, nor the father suffer for the iniquity of the son; the righteousness of the righteous shall be upon himself, and the wickedness of the wicked shall be upon himself' (Ezek. 18.19f.). Thus Ezekiel sees the connection in personal terms; moreover, repentance will take away the punishment as well as the sin (Ezek. 18.21f.): 'Have I any pleasure in the death of the wicked, says the Lord God, and not rather that he should turn from his way and live?' (Ezek. 18.23). The response to the charge that God's ways are not just is: 'Hear now, O house of Israel: Is my way not just? Is it not your ways that are not just?.... For I have no pleasure in the death of any one, says the Lord God; so turn, and live' (Ezek. 18.25, 32). Thus not only does the *religious* understanding of suffering take on a more strongly personalistic tone, but divine punishment is seen in the perspective of *conversion*. God himself takes no pleasure in human suffering. Man attracts suffering to himself through his sinfulness, but God is always ready to forgive. This is clearly an attempt to provide a fundamental corrective to the older conception that Yahweh is 'a God who kills and makes alive' (I Sam. 2.6). God has nothing to do with suffering, except through man's sinfulness, and it is his concern to bring man life through repentance. At the same time Ezekiel defends himself against attempts to find an alibi for one's own suffering by pointing to the sin of others; he puts all the emphasis on man's own personal responsibility, but also allows this to have consequences for the whole people of God.

Deutero-Isaiah attacks his Persian contemporaries who favoured a certain dualism between good and evil. God is the Creator of light and darkness, of salvation and disaster (Isa. 40–55). But no matter how great the suffering of the people is, Israel reminds itself of the divine liberation from suffering in the slavery of Egypt. That is also Israel's hope for the future. Particularly in the Hellenistic period of Judaism, the Greek view that suffering is the school of life found its way into belief in Yahweh, above all in the Diaspora (Prov. 3.11f.; 6.23; 13.24; Ps. 94.12; Job 5.17; cf. Heb. 12.5f.; Rev. 3.19). True wisdom and wise humanity are the fruit of suffering.

However, old and new conceptions run together in Israel. Whereas prophets refute the people's lament that God does not concern himself with human justice (Isa. 40.27), for Israel suffering *as such* is not the problem, but the unequal and evidently unjust distribution of suffering between the pious and sinners. This is expressed in a loud lament throughout the Jewish Psalter, and Eccles. 8.10–14 gives an acute expression of the problem. Israel is confronted with the incomprehensible fact that even and indeed especially the righteous and the faithful suffer. The psalmist gives a forceful description of this situation: 'All this has come upon us, though we have not forgotten thee, nor been false to thy covenant. Our heart has not turned back, nor have our steps departed from thy way, that thou shouldest have rejected us' (Ps. 44.17–19). Israel has no problems with suffering which men bring upon themselves through their own sinfulness, but it protests and guards itself against unmerited suffering, quite independent of man's own folly. That, too, is a typically Jewish attitude. Israel knew how to cope with suffering in religious terms; but sinfulness apart, it did not simply want to accept suffering as a *given*. The concept of fate is alien to Israel. But how can this difficulty be solved if, given the distinctive character of belief in Yahweh, one cannot take refuge in the sheer 'facticity' of a fate that makes questions meaningless?

Because of belief in Yahweh, Israel did not hesitate to direct hard questions to God. 'Is God asleep?' asks Ps. 44.23, 26 first. This is an expression of human emotion, in revolt against innocent suffering. Then again, refuge is taken in the confession of the transcendent mystery of God. 'O Lord, how long shall I cry for help, and thou wilt not hear? Or cry to thee "Violence," and thou wilt not save? Why dost thou make me see wrongs and look upon trouble?' (Hab. 1.1f., see also 1.12). This vigorous lament is called forth on the one hand by the bitter wrong that man suffers, and on the other hand by the conviction of the believer that Yahweh is one who defends the good and attacks evil: 'Thou art . . . the victor over death . . . Thou art of purer eyes than to behold evil, and canst not look on wrong. Why dost thou look on faithless men, and art silent when the wicked swallows up the man more righteous than he? For thou makest men like the fish of the sea, like crawling things that have no ruler' (Hab. 1.12, 13f.). Israel fiercely attacks its own God when he is silent and Israel suffers unjustly. But again, in the last resort triumph appears on the horizon: 'If it seems slow, wait for it; it will surely come, it will not delay' (Hab. 2.3). The unjust besiegers will be shattered: 'Woe to him who builds a town with blood, and founds a city on iniquity' (Hab. 2.12). Finally, 'Yahweh goes forth to free his people' (Hab. 3.13). The power to hold on 'in the meantime' is Israel's faith: 'The righteous shall live through his faith' (Hab. 2.4b). In other words, faith in God, the author of good and opponent of all evil, i.e. faith that good has the last word, becomes the fundamental attitude of Israel, though at the same time it cherishes a protest because all this has taken so long. This is faith in the impenetrable nature of God, whose fundamental goodness is not doubted. In the last resort this is also Job's basic attitude: protest falls silent in the face of the mystery of God; furthermore, the point of the protest is to some degree 'blunted' because the story of Job comes rather too easily to a happy ending, though at the same time it perhaps already shows the *redemptive* force of suffering (Job. 42.10). In these conceptions we again find the old notion that the sinners receive their punishment – now with the addition 'sooner or later', with the accent on the 'later' (Prov. 24.19f.; Ps. 37.16f., 25, 28f.).

However, even this desperate statement is contradicted by particular experiences. In that case the tactic is sometimes adopted: do not make any comparisons. Do not look towards the sinner for whom all goes well, but cultivate your own garden (Ps. 101.2–4,6,8). However, this tactic does not do away with the undeserved suffering of the righteous. An earlier answer to this is: suffering is a test of true faith (Gen. 22.1–19;

Job 1.6–12; Prov. 3.11). The Preacher calls it 'vanity', an incomprehensible situation (Eccles. 8.10–14), also in the sense that men should not become megalomaniacs and want to experience all the good: it is a matter of the quality of what one experiences, of the 'small delights' of everyday life. There is a time for everything, birth and death (Eccles. 7.29; 3.1f., 9–14).

Jeremiah is the first to speak of the innocent sufferer as 'a blameless lamb led to the slaughter' (Jer. 11.19), and like Job, as someone 'who has laid his cause in God's hands' (Jer. 11.20). Here suffering emerges as part of a mission, the theme of suffering *for a good cause*, though this does not come to full expression. For Jeremiah, today's world is a *tōhūwābōhū*, a chaos as before God's first creation (Jer. 4.23). Something of a hope that God will draw a line under his first plan of creation and start all over again begins to come through (Jer. 4.23ff.). Jeremiah sees no solution other than to begin all over again – a *new* creation and a *new* covenant – an idea which will be developed further, especially in Jewish apocalyptic. Thus the problem is not really solved; it is merely contrasted with a vision in which the problem of suffering no longer exists. This reaches a climax in the Old Testament in the prophetic suffering servant of Deutero-Isaiah (Isa. 42.1–4; 49.1–6; 50.4–9; 52.13–53.12). Israel had to suffer because it was sinful (Isa. 40.2). The suffering servant is innocent, but he *suffers through and for others*, suffering accepted as a voluntary sacrifice of life for others. Here we have the notion of *redemptive* suffering. The prophet maintains the traditional standpoint that sin and suffering are linked (Isa. 40.2; 42.24f.; 43.22–28; 47.6; 50.1; 51.17–23; 54.6–9), but he takes on himself the suffering that others should have had because of their sins. Nowhere does the author say how this suffering can benefit others, but he evidently sees this fact as a 'way of God' which can bring sinners to repentance. However, in the perspective of faith in Yahweh as the Lord of life and not of death, this sacrifice, in Jewish eyes, cannot be the last word: the exaltation and glorification of the suffering servant is God's overwhelming approval of this solidarity with his sinful and therefore suffering people. Just as the people were once freed from Egypt, so too they will be freed from the Babylonian captivity: the new exodus will glorify Israel (Isa. 40.3–5; 49.7). Suffering has a redemptive significance; it is the basis for greater things. In the last resort, at the same time we have a perspective on the insight that suffering and even death do not have the last word, thanks to the faithfulness and solidarity which man shows in suffering.

But it is striking that Israel does not regard life after death as solving the problem of suffering. For this period it does not dawn on Israel that life after death is a postulate or a projection from man's particular situation of suffering: historically, that is simply untrue. Even in the later

parts of the Old Testament, where there is explicit mention of the coming
resurrection, this is not a 'supernatural' projection from man's helplessness to alter the situation of suffering humanity in any way. In it, rather,
there is a manifestation of God's yes to a life which is given for a good
and just cause. This is expressed above all in the trials of the Maccabean
wars. Suffering and dying for God's sake, martyrdom, show that belief in
God is stronger than death (Dan. 6.11; 11.32; I Macc. 1.54; 6.7; II Macc.
6.1–7.42) and they open up a life after death (resurrection: Dan. 12.1–3;
II Macc. 7.9; 7.28–41). In contrast to the 'Greek saints' of Cynicism and
Stoicism, there is no mention here of man's own contribution or of a
claim to be 'holier' than others. Suffering is seen *less* in its relationship to
sin (though that is not denied) and more as suffering for a good cause,
the most supremely relevant cause, God himself. Here, too, we have the
idea of sacrifice for a good cause, so that God 'will soon have mercy on
his people' (II Macc. 7.37a, 38), and so that the torturers will be converted (II Mac. 7.37b). Suffering, then, is an atoning sacrifice 'so that
God's anger against his people may cease' (II Macc. 7.38). Overcoming
evil with good – God's very being! Identifying oneself with this results in
martyrdom for mortal men in an evil world. The resurrection is not seen
as a happy ending despite everything, but as the implication of a life
lived in communion with God. As such, death separates man from God
(Ps. 6.5), whereas the martyr gives his life for God. That is the contradiction which the believer cannot accept; this contradiction would make
sacrifice for a good cause an illusion. The source of Jewish belief in the
resurrection, which is only attested at the end of the Old Testament, was
not suffering, but belief in God. The believer is 'in God's hand' (Wisdom 3.1–9). However, once this belief in resurrection does exist, it also
becomes a consoling thought for the martyrs among those who are faithful
to the Torah of Israel. Still, II Maccabees does not really refer to the
resurrection as the solution to the problem of suffering: 'Now I urge those
who read this book not to be depressed by such calamities, but to recognize that these punishments were designed not to destroy but to discipline
our people' (II Macc. 6.12–16). It is not the resurrection, but the earlier
Jewish theme of God's mercy even in suffering which is connected with
the problem of suffering man.

Only in the extra-biblical Jewish literature does life after death and
the punishment of the wicked after death become an ingredient in the
solution of the problem of suffering. I Enoch 102.6–11 (which poses the
problem) and 103.1ff. (which gives a solution) are a particularly good
example of this: heaven keeps strict account of all the good and evil that
men do. The Last Judgment restores this to a proper balance. But Enoch
knows this only through a quite special 'private revelation'. That is the
apocalyptic conception of suffering: the absolutely new future which at

the same time greatly relativizes present suffering and the problems of the world today, or at least puts them firmly in the context of later reward.

In particular, the fall of Jerusalem in AD 70 was a catalyst for the problem of the 'innocent sufferer', at least in apocalyptic. Righteous Jerusalem suffers and the godless Gentiles triumph (II Bar. 14.4ff.), but Jerusalem may take comfort: the crown of glory comes after suffering (II Bar. 15.8). Furthermore, great catastrophes are thought to hasten the triumphant coming of God (II Bar. 20.2); suffering represents the birth pangs of a new world. But here too the final answer is: who can explain God's unfathomable ways (IV Ezra 4.11)? People must recognize their own limitations (IV Ezra 4.13–19). This destruction made no impression on the Pharisees, who did not agree at all with the Sadduceean attitude over the Temple. Moreover, the effect of this destruction was to make the Pharisaic approach the dominant interpretation of the Jewish religion: rabbinic Judaism. (Here the fall of Jerusalem had something of the *déjà vu* about it – the Jews had already experienced this before.[17] Suffering also brings hardening of the heart.) Rabbinic Judaism simply repeats and refines the manifold Old Testament answers to the questions posed by suffering, but among themselves the rabbis continue to differ over the connection between suffering and sin. The medieval Jewish philosopher Maimonides will say: existence in itself is already a great good[18] (which makes Thomas Aquinas say, *melius est sic esse quam non esse*: existence, even existence in suffering, is always better than not to exist at all). Some things owe their origin to building up and breaking down; 'suffering' is one of these things. Beings subject to change are suffering beings. But there is also suffering which is caused by men to one another, and this form of suffering is in fact more frequent than the first form. Finally there is suffering which man inflicts on *himself*, and this suffering occurs most frequently of all; that is what people most often complain about. But it is their own stupid fault, says Maimonides. Rabbi Aha said, 'God wanted to give man four things: the Torah, suffering, sacrifice and prayer, but man did not accept these blessings.' And Rabbi Simeon ben Yohai said, 'The Holy One – blessed be his name – gave Israel three precious gifts: the Torah, the land of Israel and the world to come; but none of these things was given without suffering.'[19] For rabbinic Judaism, suffering has a purifying function, it is a way of life. Rabbi Huna asks, 'God saw that all was very good . . . Can suffering be "very good"? Yes, through suffering man achieves life in the world to come.' Suffering forgives sins. What these rabbis are saying is that saving suffering is as it were the soul of the Jewish people. Present-day Jews see the restoration of the state of Israel as one aspect of salvation, as the fruit of their suffering under Nazism: the Israelis, risen from the ashes of Buchenwald and Auschwitz.

The Jew rejects 'supernatural' explanations for suffering which cannot be understood rationally, but he has learned to deal with suffering in religious terms.

## III.  THE GREEKS AND SUFFERING MAN

Greek thought follows a pattern which all myths seek to express. Indeed, its reflective thinking is born from these religious myths. A deep pessimism about our humanity can be detected in Homer's *Iliad*: one thing is certain – that we die. 'The gods have so woven the fates of wretched mortals that they live in sorrow, while the gods themselves are untroubled' (*Iliad* 24,525). 'Creatures of a day! What is a man? What is he not? A man is the dream of a shadow' (Pindar, *Pythian Odes* 8.95). Usually, however, the Greeks make even their gods suffer[20] (cf. e.g. *Homeric Hymns* 2.445–7). Human and divine suffering are part of the suffering of the universe: there is no summer without winter. This mystery of the transition from decline to new life was celebrated especially in the Eleusinian mysteries. The great Greek dramas, above all the *Oresteia* and *Prometheus* of Aeschylus, know no other theme. There is a redemption from suffering, and this hope, this will for the future cannot be suppressed. But suffering seems to be a 'must' for true and final happiness. 'Wisdom is a child of suffering, born with many tears' (Aeschylus, *Eumenides* 517ff.). The golden rule is: no tyranny, and no anarchy either, but put yourself under the law (ibid., 526f.), and then suffering will be seen as a gift of God. So for the Greeks suffering is a school of wisdom (*pathos* gives *mathos*, ran the Greek proverb: suffering is a school, see Heb. 5.8). Taught by Socrates, the philosopher Plato went deeply into this problem of suffering. Both put suffering in a social context: democracy (Athens) or an oligarchy (Sparta) as the best form of government under which it is possible for men to live. Socrates was anti-democratic because democracy required too high a degree of virtue and knowledge; it was the capacity of spiritual aristocrats and not normal mortals. Undisciplined democracy only causes catastrophe. The man was condemned to death because he 'corrupted' young men disposed towards democracy. Although he had an opportunity to escape, he rejected this: 'I have accepted law and discipline when they were to my advantage; why should I run away from them when they turn against me?' Plato was to put this attitude as follows: 'It is worse to act unjustly than to have to suffer injustice' (a solution which I Peter developed in a Christian perspective). If virtue (*kalokagathia*) is the meaning of human life, why should this be connected with happiness and prosperity? This Greek emphasis sounds quite different from the Jewish problem: a *ṣaddīq* or righteous man must also have a happy life. The Greek relativizes the suffering from what is called the priority of the spirit. Bad action takes place in the spirit and is therefore unworthy of men; suffering affects the body and the *psychē*, but it is transitory and passes away; goodness and righteousness remain. Suffering and chastisement through life are the beginning of human wisdom, and therefore the righteous may expect suffering. Something like the idea of the 'innocent sufferer' is innate in Platonism. Suffering has a redemptive function, it is a transitionary phase. Therefore Aristotle will even describe suffering as something that does not exist, in the privative sense. And that implies that all positiveness can only be attributed to the good, in a clearly anti-dualistic sense. Good and evil may not be said to have equal rights; that would be to rob man of his worth.

After these 'classical' Greeks, the Cynics, the Stoics and the Epicureans reflected more deeply on suffering. True, these are three different schools, but they have a good deal in common. The Cynics, who take their designation from Diogenes' nickname 'the dog' (which is also the derivation of our term cynicism), were only cynical in a quite particular and limited respect. Their main concern lay elsewhere, in a quest for true humanity. They were the watchdogs for fundamental human values as these were interpreted in Greek terms. Renunciation and self-denial were their motto: renouncing everything and therefore also being citizens of the world, wedded to Mother Poverty. Diogenes 'abandoned everything'. His life itself was intended as a contemporary criticism of society; he was a hippie with an enjoyment of manual work, in which he engaged to mock the propertied classes who had been freed from it. The Cynic is the true, supremely human king in the form of a slave, suffering under the arrogance of the well-situated and powerful patricians. For the Cynics, the slaves are the ones who are subject to their passions, their aggressiveness and their sensuality. But the Cynics are also cynical because they know no compassion, because they deeply despise fellow men who are not as they are; they alone are the true but despised men, the supermen, who have moreover by their own efforts worked up to this height through discipline and asceticism. They have no compassion for their fellow-men, because even in suffering they are sovereignly free and above all suffering.

The great Stoic philosophers are influenced by the doctrines of the Cynics but have their own distinctive characteristics. As a result of a kind of pantheistic view of the world in which God is all in all things and all men, the present world, as it is, is the best of all worlds. This ontological optimism, in contrast to the fundamental pessimism of the Cynics, saw everything, even suffering, mysteriously integrated into the well-ordered universe, filled with divine reason. Evil and suffering can never affect the truly wise man, since he carries about the true and the good in his inner attitude like a precious treasure; wretched, even extreme, circumstances cannot change any of this. True, he feels sorrow, but his manly bearing lifts him above it. And if the external pressure becomes too great, for such 'Stoics' the door to suicide, freely chosen, is still open, by which the inwardly free man demonstrates his independence over against all disaster in a sovereign and royal way. In this pantheism, suffering is an aspect of the universal deity; it is thus well-ordered and good. Cleanthes' *Hymn to Zeus* is significant in this respect: 'Ah, you know how to make odd things even and to order what is disorderly, and to you the unlovely are lovely; you have so fitted everything together into one, good with evil, to make both one, in a single and eternal principle.' And Epictetus, a former slave with a crippled leg, regarded this impediment as an expression of the best of all worlds; he is a sacrifice for the good of the whole universe. He does not ask himself why and how this suffering serves for the good of all; for the Stoic sage, that *is* the case.

The decisive question in this Stoic wisdom is: if suffering is a form of illusion, is not this illusion then itself evil? And in that case why do men have such an abhorrence of all the sorrow which they imagine? Does this take suffering really seriously?

The Epicureans were not searchers after enjoyment and satisfaction in the way that our use of the term might suggest. They were ascetics modelling their life on the search for *ataraxia*, indifference and contentment. Once again this is Greek renunciation and inwardly free self-sufficiency (*autarkia*); being content with what one has and gets, does not have and 'lacks'. Epicurus began from the thesis that the original state of man was barbaric and wretched, but that man had raised himself above this level. That is his honour and his glory. Now he lives in the aristocratic sphere of the spirit. Real disastrous sorrow is only the suffering of desire, of craving for more. The wise man knows how to enjoy both the small and the great; he knows how to endure poverty and live in abundance (we also find much of this Greek wisdom – Cynic, Stoic and Epicurean, reinterpreted from the Christian perspective of grace, in the New Testament, especially in the Pauline writings). However, in contrast to Aristotle, the Cynics and the wise men of the Stoa, who disqualify attractiveness and above all compassion as a low human vice, for Epicurus, friendship and compassion are a supreme human virtue (according to the testament of Epicurus in Diogenes Laertius X, 16–21): one must be able to weep with those who weep, and suffer with those who suffer; only then does one attain to inner tranquillity. He is concerned less with the others as others than with the ascetic perfection of inviolable tranquillity. Suffering may never come to predominate over the enjoyment of life, but a certain dose of suffering can certainly be reconciled with this enjoyment. Why is all this? Epicurus does not ask; suffering is accepted as given: the question for him, as for all Greeks, is that of the significance that one attaches to it.


## IV.  THE ROMANS: *'PER ASPERA AD ASTRA'*

Although the Romans later were also strongly influenced by the Stoics (the Stoics of the imperial period are genuinely Roman, but refined by the Greek spirit), they had their own view of man's suffering (understood as the suffering of Romans), less reflective but an essential and effective ingredient of what they felt to be the vocation of the Roman people. Virgil put this sharply:

> Let others fashion from bronze more lifelike breathing images –
> For so they shall – and evoke living faces from marble:
> Others excel as orators, others track with their instruments
> The planets circling in heaven and predict when stars will appear.
> But, Romans, never forget that government is your medium!
> Be this your art: – to practise men in the habit of peace,
> Generosity to the conquered, and firmness against aggressors
> > (Virgil, *Aeneid* VI, 847ff., trans. C. Day Lewis).

The watchword for Roman wisdom is *virtus*: not 'virtue' as we would understand it, but strength, *vir-tus*, manliness, stubborn persistence (for Romans a markedly non-feminine quality) – the virtue of the hard worker, in good times as in bad, with a concern for his own family and above all for the Roman *respublica*; the virtue of fighting to the last for the good of Roman agriculture and above all for the Roman commonwealth. The Roman book *De viris illustribus* gives a clear picture of the Roman conception of suffering, summed up in the winged word: *moribus antiquis res stat Romana virisque* (Ennius): Rome's well-being stands and falls with the age-old Roman juristic experiential wisdom *and its men*, i.e. the *virtus* or stubborn manliness of the Romans. 'Even if the world should fall to pieces, its fall will find him (the Roman) unmoved' (Horace, *Odes* III 3.1f.). Here, too, the starting-point is the experience of hostility in our world. Such a world needs bold, hard-working and struggling men – good chaps. Suffering and tribulation are *given* in our world – here, too, there is no attempt to analyse the cause of suffering, but a powerful and brave attitude leads in and through these trials to praiseworthy, true *humanitas*. The Stoic elements give this 'hard', Roman soldier's outlook no more than a refined, cultivated Greek background, and with the Emperor Marcus Aurelius lead to a hitherto unprecedented level of personal, attractive and just humanity in one who as emperor himself chose above all not to 'lord it' over his people.

Without giving up the hard Roman look at the world, Virgil (who in his younger years had been an Epicurean) introduces a warm human tone into this approach. It can be summed up in his famous saying, *Sunt lacrimae rerum et mentem mortalia tangunt* (*Aeneid* I, 462), which given the possibility in Latin that a genitive can be both objective and subjective at the same time, means: there are tears in the heart of reality, and: the heart of reality is compassion (a piece of Eastern, and especially Tibetan wisdom), 'and transitory things touch the heart'. True, Virgil is describing his hero Aeneas in terms of a successful Stoic sage (Virgil lived from 70 to 19 BC), 'through suffering to victory', but he at the same time gives him the human touch of an Epicurean fellow man who has compassion on the suffering and destiny of others. Many classical scholars have pointed to a profoundly human trait in Virgil. 'Tell me, why did Aeneas . . . have to bear so much sorrow? Is there so much vengeance in the heart of the heavenly gods?' (*Aeneid* I, 11). And then his famous lament: *Tantae molis erat Romanam condere gentem* (*Aeneid* I, 33), so much sorrow and so much labour were needed to found the Roman people. The poet poses the problem of *labor improbus*, hard human work, above all in his *Georgics*. He never protests against it, but the bitterness of it affects him. It is a pity, a real pity, but it does not seem possible for things to be otherwise. To be a man is a hard task, a *durum genus* (*Georg.* I, 63), and it is never-ending (II, 397–401). Still, this is not pessimism. Jupiter himself arranged things this way: *per aspera ad astra*. Difficulties and suffering make men great. This emerges from the delight, after hard work, of looking on the smiling fertility of rich pastures. A friendly divine power underlies the real harshness of our human life. In his *Georgics*, Virgil pays homage to the mysticism of delight through hard work, Italy's greatness (*Georg.* II, 136–76). Difficulties are there to be overcome.

> *O socii (neque enim ignari sumus ante malorum),*
> *o passi graviora, dabit deus his quoque finem* (*Aeneid* I, 198f.),

'Friends, we have already suffered misfortune worse than this; even now God will give deliverance.' If the end is good, everything else is good: *forsan et haec olim meminisse iuvabit* (*Aeneid* I, 203): 'Take heart and do not be afraid, perhaps one day you will even be glad to remember these things.'

## V. SUFFERING IN HINDUISM

According to Hinduism,[21] one can look at one and the same thing from a variety of perspectives. Each view has its own justification, but none of them is exhaustive. Hindus suspect a 'universal' standpoint from the start – even a minority can be right. In the religious sphere this means that no religion may claim to be the one true religion. Each religion is *a reference to* the truth, but it is not this truth. From this there follows logically the tolerance of Hindus both within Hinduism and outside it. But that makes it difficult above all for Western man to understand Hinduism. It contains much that Western man would call contradictory. Every Hindu must search honestly for the truth and appropriate it for himself.

The caste system, in which each is different from the other but not therefore better than the other, is good, even if it means suffering for some people. A fisherman is a fisherman, a philosopher a philosopher, but both have the same God in them. Each therefore works out his own salvation. This view is made possible through *karma* and *samsara*.

*Samsara* is the cycle of death and rebirth in other forms of existence, the quality of which is dependent on *karma*, that is, the exact balance of action, in other words the quality of life that was achieved in the earlier existence. By and large the Hindu is not so strongly concerned with the ego: man must rather lose himself through concentration on his divine basis. Until this 'loss' has been achieved, man is bound up in an endless *samsara* process. Thus *karma* is the principle which governs our growing world: everything has its own, inner laws – the *law of being* of all things. The soul as it were takes on 'another garb' (body) in each new existence, tailored after the fashion of the former quality of life. Thus a true life according to the pattern and laws of a lower social caste will result in membership of a higher caste in the new form of life. That is, roughly speaking, the idea of *dharma*, the law. Thus the demand is that one should not do anything that is not fitting for one's own caste (*adharma*, lawlessness). Complete renunciation – 'giving oneself away' (*moksha*) – is the great law of life, and this loss of oneself leads to knowledge of the true nature of *atman*, the self. This true self appears in a variety of transitory forms, but is itself eternal.

In the last resort, Hinduism regards *atman* or the self as a manifestation of Brahman, being itself. Letting oneself go is accomplished when the individual 'realizes' (which is not merely a cognitive process) that he *is* the Brahman, that is, *atman is* a manifestation of Brahman. How? That depends on whether Brahman is understood in a theistic or a non-theistic sense. That worldly things seem to be different is in fact only an illusion, and not their true identity. What from a distance looks like a snake is in reality a piece of string or cord. So it is with the universe. It is filled with 'appearances', manifestations, *maya*, though this expresses something deeper and more subtle than the word 'illusion'.

Within these few key concepts, which moreover are not accepted by all Hindus (this seems to be a consequence of the Aryan invasion, which upset ancient Indian culture and influenced the Vedas), suffering receives its place. Suffering belongs to the world of *maya* (as a whole, the *samsara* process).For the individual, to be able to share in this relativizing is the ascetic way to *moksha*, or self-detachment.

Suffering is given a quite specific significance in the writings of the Hindus – the four Vedas, the Brahmanas and the Aranyakas and their developments in the Upanishads (Vedanta). The Vedas in particular represent a very ancient stage of religious consciousness, where natural forces are still personified as gods. A complicated system of relationships to these gods is arranged through sacrifices and rites ('theistic' Hinduism). Thus suffering could be understood as the repercussion of personal action on the part of the gods, with whom one achieves a better relationship by means of rites. Suffering is like the nature of things, when animals eat one another in order to live. Sacrifice was a kind of identification with reality, at the same time a way of controlling it to the advantage of the one making the sacrifice. Particular gods were originally identified with evil and the destructive forces of existence (Siva, Rudra, Kali). In other words, suffering derives from the fundamental conflict in the universe. In 'the gods', the massive, faceless and unportrayable world takes on a clearer countenance: *erōs* and *thanatos*, love and death, as the two principles in conflict. Yet this is in no way dualism, for both are aspects of one and the same reality, regarded from different points of view. The same gods (e.g. those of death) can also be considered from another standpoint and then they have a more attractive aspect: a smiling death, but a destructive death for the sinner. The Lord of death is also the destroyer of death. The god of tears, Rudra, is at the same time the god of loving joy and prosperity.

Suffering cannot therefore be defined colourlessly and objectively 'from outside'. It has as many meanings as there are suffering men. Thus suffering must be seen 'in perspective', and when freely chosen has a fundamental significance in the *moksha* process of self-renunciation.

This also contains the notion that suffering must be judged *in respect of the totality* (something that is also emphasized among the Stoics and in the Enlightenment): the idea of *maya*, the way in which things appear, is already present here, as is the idea of *karma*. These ideas of the Vedas are taken further and brought to an end above all in the Vedanta, though this also has polemic against the ritualism of the Vedas. The Upanishads seek a deeper understanding of the old myths and rites; they have a philosophical concern. Here, too, suffering is the result of a deep tension in reality, often described in the myths of conflicts between gods and demons, both of whom descend from Prajapati, the god of creation. The various creatures are aspects of the totality, Brahman, being itself. Duality *is* suffering, the consequence of a creation of duality in a non-dualistic situation. But the right view of the nature of things is a grasp of their unity, and for that very reason suffering cannot have the last word; if it too is reality, it is only relative. Suffering is the result of a human bond with transitory things, as though they were reality. Where our heart is, there we are; we become what we long for. That is slavery. Suffering is only a real problem so long as it is seen as the ultimate inescapable truth. Suffering can be a manifestation of Brahman, but it is not Brahman. Suffering is an element in a *karma* process.

In Hinduism, too, *morality* and *suffering* are essentially connected, but not in the same way as in Judaism. Here there is no Job's lament, for present suffering can be the consequence of our earlier form of life. Anyone who finds his identity in Brahman is beyond suffering and enjoyment; *atman* is then identical with Brahman, like salt in water: 'that is what you are.' Here suffering has not become an illusion, as though the actual experience of suffering were deceptive and non-existent. The body does in fact suffer, but not the self, which finds itself as it were in a dreamless sleep, in love and joy.

But this is no mere theoretical process. Men must see the world in the right perspective and act accordingly. Without such action, Hinduism would be a kind of intellectual escapism. It is essential to act accordingly in the world (the idea of *dharma*). Is this indifference towards the world and our tasks in it? Is there a Hindu compassion for the man who still suffers? Or is the prevalent feeling one of contempt for the still suffering slavery of others, as with the Stoics? Are these men who concentrate on themselves, condemned to inactivity, letting the world be what it is? And is all this an individualism of salvation?

That would be a caricature of Hinduism. Self-renunciation is tested precisely in and through engagement. For human development takes place in four general spheres: *dharma – artha – karma – moksha*. Without mentioning various (necessary) nuances, we can say: *dharma* relates to the sphere of the moral and spiritual needs of man, specifically the requirements of the caste system in Hindu society; *artha* is concerned with material needs and is particularly connected with the exercise of authority; *karma* relates to the sphere of the senses. These three spheres encompass everything but escapism and non-activity, and all three spheres require attention. Only the final stage is *moksha*, the achievement of self-renunciation, being one with Brahman, and 'that is what *you are*'. The only way to *moksha* is a right balance in relation to society and individual life. If the deeds of an earlier form of life keep following us, then *samsara* is a summons to a high level of responsibility for what we do – but along the lines of already existing social order (there needs also to be a critical sociological investigation of the socio-economic background of Hinduism as a form of spirituality). One must live as appropriately as possible within the caste in which one does live: a hunter must be a good hunter, a fisherman a skilful and competent fisherman, etc. (these men must kill – that is their duty). To cause *others* pain can thus be a consequence of the obligations of *dharma*. Moreover, a man cannot go many miles without killing various tiny insects and micro-organisms. Personal growth is dependent on social obligations, and not in any individualistic way. The social duties are the contribution that man makes to salvation and redemption. But the *Bhagavadgita*, which begins with the problem of suffering, stresses that all four castes must renounce imposing suffering in an 'unlawful' way (*adharma*) on others – people, animals, even things. In other words, *dharma* really requires a fundamental attitude of non-violence (*ahimsa*). In itself, suffering is not evil (it can even be sought through asceticism); however, it is necessary to trace the causes of suffering so that it can be alleviated and removed. The situation must be analysed and interpreted in a reasonable way. It is the *Gita* which pays special attention to the problem of another person's suffering, as a possible consequences of *dharma* obligations (on the basis of a historical struggle between two tribes, both of which had the same ancestor). The hero of the story refuses to fight against a tribe in which his own friends and his family live – the problem of a fraternal war. Krishna tells him that he must nevertheless take up arms, for two reasons: (1) the true and real self cannot suffer; (2) there is a *dharma* obligation. A warrior must fight in an obligatory or legal war: 'Blessed are the warriors.' On the one side there is detachment and on the other engagement. The *Gita* responds to this 'contradiction' as follows: there is not to be any 'attachment' to non-activity. Fortified in *yoga* or equanimity of spirit, the hero must go out to fight. This is typical of Hinduism.

In this non-dualistic duality, e.g. of suffering and enjoyment, the Hindu does not decide for one of the two poles as the supreme good; he looks beyond the duality to find identity with the Brahman: equanimity (= *yoga*) towards suffering and enjoyment. (This was also said by the Greek Stoics, who had non-Greek, oriental origins.) *Bhakti*, surrender to God, gives Brahman personalistic, theistic features (in the *Bhagavadgita*). The Advaita Hindu school in particular stresses that the gods, too, are manifestations of Brahman. In that case the worship and praise of God is not a transitory stage, but man's highest blessing. The self, one with man, does not lose its individuality: in God it *confronts* God in praise and intercession. The world of various individuals is then like the body of the one God, who is the one soul of them all. Thus the *Gita* knows of something like 'incarnations' (*avatars*). In incarnate form God can personally help and comfort suffering men. *Hari* is in reality Vishnu in the role of the victor over suffering. It is striking that the Hindu notion of God's incarnation is connected with the harsh reality of human suffering which nevertheless belongs to the ordering of *maya*. The specific danger inherent in Hinduism is in fact the shift from 'self-renunciation' to indifferentism and acceptance of the status quo. Many Hindus themselves put their finger on this special temptation and danger; contemporary Hinduism in particular attacks the false interpretation that existence in the world is an illusion. What use is an *escapist* attitude? It is no use to God, who has sovereign freedom, or to the world, for the flight of an individual into purely individualist salvation does not redeem the world from suffering. In that case there would be something in the individual which is neither of God nor of the world. In that case it is the flight of an illusory, non-existent I from an illusory slavery, into an illusory, non-existent world, as the highest good which this illusory being would search after.[22] In that case there is neither slavery nor liberation, nor a search for freedom. There is a legend about Buddha: when he stood on the threshold of Nirvana, he turned back and swore that he would never take the irrevocable step over this threshold as long as there was still a single being on earth who had not been freed from the entanglement of suffering and from the slavery of the ego. Nehru saw India's misery as the consequence of a false practice of Hinduism: indifference and acceptance of the *status quo*.

## VI. THE SUFFERING OF THE BUDDHIST

The problem of suffering is to be found at the centre of Buddhism more than in any other religion.[23] The four great truths are: the existence of suffering, its causes, the removal of all suffering by removing its causes, and the way to do so. This religion begins with the most universal of all experiences: suffering (*dukkha*).

There is suffering on three levels: (1) the suffering that is bound up with the process of life (above all, birth; sickness; growing old; dying); (2) suffering as a consequence of an awareness of the gulf or the distance between what we desire and what we obtain and the awareness of transitoriness; (3) suffering as a consequence of the actual nature and condition of humanity, 'human nature'. This leads Buddha to the question: what is this self that is caught up in all this suffering? The answer to that is that this ego does not exist. There is no 'I' which suffers. There is only a complex whole which altogether is called 'man', and is in a state of constant change. The Buddhist speaks of *anatta*, the non-I. This is con-

nected with *samkhara-dukkha*, suffering on the third level. Man is no more
a unity than the leaf of a tree. Nothing permanent can be saved from this
whole process of growth. There is no 'soul' in the body. For Buddha, this
was a shattering experience – a kind of experience of self-annihilation.
However, there is something permanent: 'the universe is this *atman*', and
after my death that is what I am for ever: *nirvana*.

Man is an accumulation of (five) ingredients: the corporeal, feelings,
perceptions, spiritual drives and consciousness. Thus there is suffering,
but no one who suffers. Everything is in constant movement and flux.
Thus human existence has no permanence; it is a sequence in a totality
of cause and effect. But man has an element ('spiritual orientation')
through which he is in a position to *guide* the stream of life to some degree
in a limited way. Buddha is concerned to show the direction in which it
is possible to still this constantly whirling stream. There is a *way* in the
middle of the stream of cause and effect. This is an 'order in the nature
of causality' or conditioned becoming. Through this, the unending cycl-
ical stream (of birth, death and life) is 'broken' as it were into twelve –
conditioned or conditioning – sequences, though the process continues
infinitely. Everything goes so quickly that we have the impression of a
continuity and thus of a 'self'. Buddha rejects the two extremes; on the
one hand complete annihilation, and on the other an eternal *atman*; there
is a *middle way*. If life is a kind of chain reaction, then the first moment
after death is the first link of the chain which goes on. Death is only a
moment which gives rise to a subsequent event. So there is no 'I reborn'.
At every moment there is birth and death – it is like lighting a candle
with another burning candle. A door is both an entrance and an exit; it
depends on one's particular standpoint. The whole stream is there at any
moment. *Karma* here is the precise effect of the previous 'event', and so
on. Human actions do not vanish into nothing without leaving traces.
Iron produces rust which itself eats away the iron. Anyone who acts
badly is like iron which produces devouring rust, i.e. suffering. All the
sequences of suffering are the immediate consequences of a preceding
cause (*dukkha, samsara, karma*). The chain of causality is inexorable. That
is why the direction which man gives it is so important, because it is
impossible to escape from the cycle. There is a chain of happiness, but
there is also a chain of accumulated suffering. The fleeting character of
happiness and joy is in itself already suffering. The first truth is: suffering
is a *fact*.

A second truth stems from this: 'thirst' or desire (*tanha*) is the cause of
suffering. Desire seeks to grasp something in the stream as though it were
substantial. But that is like trying to grasp water or air. A man longs for
*something*, for sensual enjoyment, now here, now there; he looks for his
own existence or his own annihilation. But 'desire' is itself already the

effect of some preceding cause. If we did not look at things in a possessive way, but renounced them, then we would not feel any grief or any disappointment in this eternal process of becoming. It is not the world, but we ourselves who are the cause of suffering because of our false attitude towards the world.

However, there is a third great truth. Suffering can be ended; the experience of this end is as real as the experience of suffering itself. As perfectly realized, this is *nirvana* (or *nibbana*), the ending of the stream of causality, though this state cannot be *described*, but only realized. However, it is the end of all thirst. *Nirvana* is not 'heaven' nor is it any state on which man enters after death. *Nirvana* is 'realized' by the quenching of all longing, as a result of which no new process of becoming arises. Etymologically, it is also a 'going out' – just as a candle goes out. Thus it can be described only as it were in negative terms.

The fourth principal truth lies *on the way to* the great 'quenching' and disappearance of all suffering. '*Nirvana* means stopping': not being carried along by the stream. Ceasing to desire means ceasing to hang on, and ceasing to hang on means stopping the development of *karma*; that in turn is the cessation of birth, of growing old and dying, suffering and despairing. The description is negative, but not *nirvana*, which is neither annihilation or absorption, nor eternal *atman*, but something in between. What is a fully *detached* person?. It is clearly difficult to explain this to people who do not know this state. The Buddha is not a nihilist, but he preaches the possibility of the end of all suffering, in such a way that this is a *real experience*. For *nirvana* is not even a state 'to come' after death. Supreme freedom, redemption and liberation, secure existence; a resting place, a secure haven, a cool cave, an island in the midst of the flood, emancipation, absolute stillness, security, supreme joy, the holy city. It is the inexpressible, *beyond* everything, that can be called 'negative' or 'positive'.

Are these day-dreams, utopias developed from the contrasting experiences of suffering? Here Buddhism can perhaps can perhaps criticize particular Western conceptions of the 'experience of contrast' in which only the negative aspect makes itself felt (e.g. T. Adorno). What is the guarantee of the possibility of realizing *nirvana*? The experience of Buddha, who proclaims what he himself has experienced. Others have experienced this as well, and this confirms his testimony. Experience and testimony to it through Buddha and finally personal experimentation give this guarantee. The promise is given because it was realized through Buddha; it is thus specifically possible: on the middle path (*majjima patipada*), which avoids exaggerated self-chastisement, but also concessions to enjoyment, two ways which the Buddha had first tried himself without any success. It is an eightfold path: right insight, right thinking, right speaking, right acting, right living, right striving, right attention and right concentration, summed up in (1) wisdom (*panna*), (2) ethical conduct (*sila*) and (3) spiritual discipline (*sumadhi*). 'Let the past be past, let the future be what it will, I will teach you *dharma*', says a Buddhist verse. The goal of all this is the *liberation* of man.

While the basic thoughts of Buddha were taken up by Buddhism, different interpretations arose (which we cannot investigate in detail; at least, only in one respect). Two principal schools developed: that of the 'great journey' (Mahayana) and that of the 'small journey' (Hinayana). Is this a question of an individualistic search for salvation, or is there also an interest in the salvation of the other person? Mahayana Buddhism works out the latter perspective in the Bodhisattva ideal, the attempt of a disciple to attain *enlightenment* (insight into his own nature) and in this way to become a 'Buddha'. But when he stands on the summit of the great realization of salvation, he turns back, and exposes his own last realization of salvation in order to be able first to help others on the same way of salvation. There is an expression of compassion here: 'Can there be blessing, if everything that is, suffers? Will you be saved, while the whole of the world groans?' The enlightened man does not forget his suffering fellow man (at all events, as in many religions, this official Buddhism distinguishes itself sharply from popular Buddhism). This solidarity of the Bodhisattva is also directed towards the suffering animal world and the suffering universe. An Indian prince (Buddha himself in one of his earlier forms of life) out of compassion offered his own body to a hungry tigress for food. 'Out of pity I offered my life.' Enlightened men become the redeemers of their fellow men: they identify themselves in solidarity with anyone who suffers. Buddhism is less concerned with diminishing this or that individual suffering in a 'reforming way', but rather with the overcoming of universal suffering through the removal of what is regarded as the cause of this suffering. The self-immolation of Vietnamese Buddhist monks is in no way independent of this ideal of Buddha of solidarity with suffering man; the action is meant as *construction* and not as *destruction*. By contrast, for the Buddhist real suicide is one of the most serious of crimes.

## VII. CHRISTIANITY AND THE SUFFERING MAN

It emerged sufficiently from the analysis in Part Two that the New Testament gave significance to the fact of the 'suffering Christian'. The New Testament does not produce any speculation on the problem of suffering, nor does it reflect on the fact of suffering man, but simply on the shocking fact that Christians are persecuted. All its attention is devoted to the 'suffering *Christian*'. Therefore we cannot look for any solution of the problem of the suffering man in the New Testament, at least directly: this problem simply is not raised. We can, however, find a number of general viewpoints.

First of all: the good news is for the poor. Strikingly, the signs for the coming of the kingdom and God's righteousness (Matt. 6.33), in the coming of the Messiah ('the one who is to come', Matt. 11.3) are: 'The blind see and the lame walk, lepers are cleansed and the deaf hear, the dead are raised and the poor have the good news preached to them' (Matt. 11.4f.). Jesus' interpretation of suffering is connected with his deep personal relationship with God, the heart of his life. God and suffering are diametrically opposed; where God appears, evil and suffering have to yield. So there is no place for suffering and tears in the messianic kingdom, not even for death; there is a deep community experience which has the power 'to heal' (Acts 2.43–3.10), until finally all evil, suffering and tears will disappear from this kingdom to come (Rev. 21.3f.). Furthermore, Jesus breaks with the idea that suffering has necessarily something to do with sinfulness. This is expressly stated in two texts. In the case of the man born blind the disciples ask, 'Who has sinned, this man or his parents, that he was born blind?' Jesus replies, 'Neither he nor his parents have sinned' (John 9.2f.); and when Jesus hears that Pilate had murdered some Galileans, according to Luke he says, 'Do you think that they were worse sinners than all the other Galileans because they suffered thus?' (Luke 13.1–5). Both New Testament statements finally show that it is possible to draw conclusions from sin to suffering, but not from suffering to sin. On the one hand suffering as a result of sin must lead to repentance (Luke 13.3, 4f.), but on the other, 'suffering' (apart from a connection with any sin) is something that God is concerned to remove (see John 9.3f.: healing as Jesus' 'work of the Father'). Here we already see a twofold possibility; given the nature of the Gospel of John, suffering 'reveals the work of God' because God heals and takes away suffering; it also reveals the glory of God because Jesus himself voluntarily accepts suffering through others for others. True, there were particular illnesses (in our time called psycho-somatic illnesses) which in accordance with the medical views of the time were called *demonic* possession (not 'being possessed' by the *devil*: see e.g. Mark 2.1–12; 9.14–29; Luke 5.17–26); we need not necessarily find in them the connotation that they were a punishment for sin.

On the other hand, the messianic coming of God, before which evil yields, is not a coming in power, which will shatter evil with nationalistic and messianic force of arms. It works through *metanoia*, repentance. It is a victory over evil through obedience to God, and not through human force. For anyone who seeks to achieve a kingdom of peace-without-tears by means of human force calls Jesus 'a Satan' (Mark 8.27–33 par.; see also Matt. 4.1–11; Luke 4.1–13; Mark 1.13). Jesus espouses the cause of redemptive and liberating love, which while not itself directly disarming and bringing the other to repentance – on the contrary – nevertheless eventually proves victorious over force. That Beelzebub cannot be driven out by Beelzebub also applies here. When two of Jesus' disciples wanted to call down fire on an inhospitable city, 'Jesus firmly rebuked them' (Luke 9.51–55). What applies to Jesus in the New Testament applies to all Christians: to follow Jesus to the point of suffering through others and for others. Jesus' way of liberation is suffering as the actual implication of total sacrifice for the sake of righteousness and as an accusation against unrighteousness (so that people must not lose their credibility by taking up the weapons of unrighteousness). Therefore in the New Testament suffering is seen as the birthpangs of a new time of true peace and true righteousness (Mark 13.8; Matt. 24.8; Rom. 8; cf. Isa. 26.17; 66.8f.; Micah 4.9f.; etc.). In this sense Jesus is not a 'liberator' but in fact a 'redeemer'. But the task to free men as far as possible from suffering remains a Christian task; according to Matt. 25.31–46, in the last resort man is judged by God in connection with this. The redemptive and ultimately truly liberating significance of suffering lies for the New Testament precisely in the suffering which man has to take upon himself in his responsible concern to overcome suffering. However, suffering which man himself imposes on others is anathema to the whole of the Christian Bible. Mere suffering through and for others does not have the power to separate man from God (see Rom. 8.35–39), and so the New Testament can even speak of joy in suffering (Col. 1.24; Rom. 5.2–5; James 1.2f.), not masochistically, but because of its redemptive force and because of the knowledge that God holds such a man silently by the hand: he is a participator in the redemptive suffering of Jesus (Phil. 3.10). This 'service of reconciliation' (II Cor. 5.18f.) is entrusted to all Christians. I Peter, Hebrews and the Gospel of Mark in particular stress this significance of *unmerited* suffering. The New Testament refuses to see this grievous suffering as imaginary or an illusion; its picture of God does not dissolve into a sense of oceanic unity. Rather, it holds high the picture of human righteousness. 'In the days of his flesh, Jesus offered up prayers and supplications, with loud cries and tears, to him who was able to save him from death' (Heb. 5.7). This is no Stoic wisdom! Precisely for that reason this suffering has a creative and productive force.

How did Christians practise and systematize this New Testament spirituality in the post-apostolic church?. To describe that would need a new book – a story of touching edification, of testimony to an incomprehensibly deep humanity, in which we must look above all to the many anonymous Christians, i.e. the true Christians who never go down in history. It would be a story also of Christians who *have* gone down in history. On the one hand there are those with the same true humanity as is shown in the gospel; on the other there are Christians whom history remembers all too well, and who tell us a story (under Christian colours, which were not even meant hypocritically) of what Christians today can only regard as an inhuman caricature of Christian evangelism: the misuse of the gospel story of 'redemptive suffering' by Christians. I will not record this long history here, nor even make some kind of apologia for it, excusing myself on the basis of the insight that what is evident for a later stage of human consciousness need not necessarily have been so in an earlier stage of human awareness – though there were always individuals who were ahead of their time.

In the post-apostolic period, persecution of the church was something which Christians had to expect. Sharing in the suffering of Jesus through martyrdom ultimately proved to be one of the greatest strengths of Christianity. Tacitus, who was by no means critical of the persecution of Christians, was nevertheless of the opinion that by his 'excesses' Nero actually gained Gentile sympathy for the Christians. Tertullian was to say later that 'the blood of Christians' was the seed which made Christianity spread in antiquity.[24] Here suffering is seen above all as martyrdom in the steps of Jesus, and as a fight of truth against force and lies; in other words, suffering as a conflict situation in the fight for truth.[25] Finally, stress was also laid on the redemptive power of this suffering, first of all for the martyrs themselves – martyrdom is 'a baptism of blood which forgives sins'[26] – but also for the benefit of those who made others suffer.[27]

As a philosopher and theologian, Augustine reflected on suffering. In particular, his theory of original sin and the role of the devil in the Fall was to be a strong influence on the whole Western conception of sin, suffering and redemption. *Salvation* is limited to the tangible aspect of the forgiveness of sins, being redeemed by Christ from the *massa damnata*, which is what all mankind has been since the Fall. This results in the following pattern. Man was created in supreme perfection, but he fell and thus obscured his humanity. This contrasts with the Greek model put forward by Irenaeus: man was created with many imperfections, and by God's grace he works towards the perfection which God has willed for man. For Irenaeus the Fall is not a mature act of grown man but rather a child's sin; for him, therefore, suffering is not a punishment for 'original sin' but a sign that good and evil are mixed in a humanity on the way to salvation; this is as it were the divinely willed 'ecology', the sphere of life within which man develops towards final perfection.[28]

Both these Christian conceptions contrast with each other; the Augustinian conception predominated (and was even given official sanction) in the Western churches, but 'Irenaeus' remained a legitimate Christian alternative which can be brought up to date in at least as good a way. Augustine is particularly fascinated by human freedom, which is willed by God as a freedom for the good. However, because the freedom is finite, the *possibility* for evil is intrinsically bound up with it. For the sake of freedom for the good, God has taken this additional possibility into account: God does not *compel* people to do good; he wants man to do good for the sake of the good, in sovereign freedom. Moreover, God bears the consequences of this risk which he has taken: in his Son he redeems mankind from the misuse of free will. Redemption is thus a freedom *freed for doing good.*[29] God knows how to put the evil of man in a saving perspective.

For all their opposition, the views of Augustine and Irenaeus converge in one fundamental conviction: it is better to have known *human existence* than not – this is a basic anti-dualism and a kind of delight in 'being a man', despite everything. This is expressed by Augustine, with all his sensitivity towards people, on one particularly memorable occasion. A young friend of his, with whom he had played and argued, laughed and fought, died in his absence. Then the theologian forgot all his thought-spinning. He found that the place where he had laughed and argued with his companion had suddenly become a prison. Without the friend, all his youthful memories had become sheer torment. And then came the profoundly human reaction: '*I* became a great riddle to myself.' And forgetting his own theories, Augustine realistically says, 'I did not know the answer.' Even the answer 'Trust in God' was not a solution, for the young man 'whom I had loved was nobler and more real than an imaginary God'.[30] This Christian would not think away the reality of suffering. This is one of the essentially Christian conceptions of suffering; it is not reduced to being an illusion. That is what makes it so impenetrable a grief: not wanting to 'swim' in a great all-embracing divine mystery, in which the I, the person, really disappear as illusion or sleep. Man himself is the first who has the right to speak where human suffering is concerned. But Augustine draws the conclusion from this that if man's being is created for goodness and happiness, then God is the only one who can give him salvation.[31] And then he arrives at a notion which is not far from that of Irenaeus: the process of human development. Faith in God, Augustine is really saying, is like love: having experienced love does not counterbalance the suffering of separation: the wonder of having lived, existed. The rest is entrusted to God. People do not *argue* against suffering, but tell a *story* and make statements on the basis of experience without giving an 'explanation': simply because as Christians they look to the suffering and death of *Jesus*. It must have a meaning,[32] even if no one knows how or why; the essential presupposition is that suffering should not be made light of. Faith in Jesus as Christ is an 'answer' without arguments: a 'nevertheless'. Christianity does not give any explanation for suffering, but demonstrates a way of life. Suffering is destructively *real*, but it does not have the last word. Christianity seeks to hang on to both elements: no dualism, no dolorism, no theories about illusion – suffering is suffering and inhuman – however, there is more, namely God, as he shows himself in Jesus Christ.

In the Middle Ages, when people did not read books but had to content themselves with tangible, visible things, this Christian conception was 'visualized'. Cradle and cross were an initiation into the 'suffering Jesus': a helpless child between ox and ass, and a Jesus who goes staggering up to Golgotha; Jesus experienced as the one who bears the suffering of mankind, prototype of the suffering masses of the Middle Ages. However authentic this experience may be, here the Christian interpretation of suffering enters a phase in which the symbol of the cross becomes a disguised legitimation of social abuses, albeit to begin with still unconsciously. The stigmatization of Francis of Assisi shows how deep the medieval identification with the suffering Jesus was, initially in solidarity with suffering man himself. Furthermore, with St Francis this was certainly no 'dolorism'.

However, at the same time this opened a way to concentration on one's *own* suffering, detached from suffering *for a cause*; in this way a cult of suffering could arise, detached from the critical and productive force of suffering. The suffering and death of Jesus were at the same time detached from the historical circumstances which brought him suffering and death. 'Suffering in itself', no longer suffering through and for others, took on a mystical and positive significance, so that instead of having a critical power it really acquired a reactionary significance. Suffering in itself became a 'symbol'.[33] Theologians began to 'systematize' suffering. First of all an attempt was made to overcome the theoretical difficulty by means of a reference to the difference between the good that God positively wills and the evil that he merely *allows* in respect of the good (however, the theologians, in contrast to the men of the Enlightenment, for the most part did not see this 'divine tolerance' as a metaphysical necessity in God). Really, however, this is a meaningless expedient for an experienced reality which could no longer be given a theoretical explanation. In so far as this distinction means anything, the expression 'divine tolerance of evil' simply means (and this is a tautology) that on the one hand evil is actually evil, has no ground of existence and therefore also no justification for existence, and that on the other hand God still remains God, i.e. author of the good and a fighter against evil. Therefore the expression 'God's permissive will' has no theoretical meaning as an *explanation*: it simply describes the dead end of human thinking when it is confronted with the incomprehensible history of human suffering. There is then the obvious danger that a fight between God and God will be transferred into God himself: between his universal will, which is concerned only for good, and the necessity of evil in a finite world.[34] Kant remarks that the concept 'of being compelled to permit evil on the basis of a fatalism, however necessary', is quite inconceivable 'for the supreme blessed Being'.[35]

However, theologians went beyond the theory of God's permissive will. From the moment when the death of Jesus took on independent significance, detached from the historical events which made it a suffering through and for others because of his critical preaching, people also began to theologize this death. The death of Jesus became a necessary ingredient in the reconciliation of sinful man with God, who was defending his divine honour. God laid the sins of the world on the innocent Jesus; he had to do penance for the crimes of others for which they could not do penance completely themselves. Thus suffering and death become 'a divine necessity', without which reconciliation is impossible. The various pictures which we find hinted at briefly in the New Testament, without any theorizing, later become a thought-out rational system. This both weakens and 'tames' the critical force of the crucifixion of Jesus. Suffering as suffering (in whatever way) takes on a positive theological significance: God's honour, as theologians imagined this honour, is avenged through suffering and blood. True, this is not the exact significance which Anselm gave to his theory of atonement, but that was the way in which in fact it lived on in many spiritual books. These are the books with which the older Christians among us have grown up, in both Reformed and Catholic churches – despite the fight between Martin Luther and Thomas Münzer and despite the polemic between Zwingli and Conrad Grebel.

The way in which suffering became a theme for preachers from the nineteenth century until well into the twentieth is clear from pastoral letters[36] – these are examples of the integration of suffering through the weakening of its critical force: the mysticism of suffering establishes the 'existing order' in church and society.


VIII.  SUFFERING IN ISLAM

Even more markedly than for Jews and Christians, for Moslems holy scripture, the Koran, is God's word for man: 'the book beyond doubt'. The Koran sees itself in the religious tradition of Abraham, Noah, Moses and Jesus of Nazareth. God is 'the one' and therefore there is only one revelation, only one piece of good news about him. For Moslems, the fact that Judaism and Chritianity have gone their separate ways, and thus have developed different religious conceptions, is also evidence that both of them have sullied the one unfalsified revelation of God. The Koran seeks to present this one revelation of God uncorrupted and without deviations: the Arab revelation of God, i.e. the Arab version of the one divine revelation; a *timeless* message, albeit bound up with the specifically Arab character of the life of the prophet Mohammed.

The Moslem problem of suffering therefore reflects the threatened existence of desert people in the midst of drought, lack of food and attacks by neighbouring tribes whose state is no better. The Koran is concerned with these particular situations of suffering and not with a theoretical problem – a general fact of life as experienced down to and in the seventh century: suffering as a concrete part of every human life. Suffering raises questions. But what questions does Arab suffering raise?

It is striking that in fact 'Arab suffering' does not raise any questions at all. The God of the Arabs is not only love, but also power: omnipotence. God is merciful and the Lord of the universe. For Islam, suffering is not a problem for the love of God but for his omnipotence: particular things seem to be outside the control of God. Thus the problem of suffering must be solved less in terms of the love of God than in terms of his omnipotence. It must be clear for the Arabs that even suffering is under God's omnipotent control of the universe. And therefore, given the *fact* of suffering, suffering must somehow be willed by God: it is part of his counsel.[37] Wherever one turns, to East or to West, 'there is God's countenance' (Koran II, 109); he is therefore also 'the Lord over life and death' (VI, 95; XXII, 5, 6). God created 'man along with all his works' (XXXVI, 94). To be religious is therefore to be subjected to God's almost 'arbitrary' omnipotence (III, 25). God does not tolerate any doubt about himself. Suffering therefore comes from God. True, Islam knows of the leprous Iblis, the devil, but he is under God's control: God makes Iblis do his own wicked work of temptation. This is not so much a matter of asserting that God *sends suffering*, but rather of affirming that it remains under his control. However, God's omnipotence willed *suffering* as an *element in* his creation. Therefore Moslems look for the many ways in which suffering can be fitted meaningfully into God's purposes.

First of all, there is the answer that suffering is a punishment for sin (IV, 80f.), and that is demonstrated above all by means of stories from the Jewish Tanach, examples of the rise and destruction of Arab cities and instances from Mohammed's own life. Victory in a battle is the fruit of Islamic struggle 'for God's cause' (III, 11); if a battle is lost, then the faithful have not to ask for God's reasons: 'God forgives whom he wills and he punishes whom he wills, and God is forgiveness, merciful' (III, 123f.)

Is there no discrimination in this suffering? In other words, can unmerited suffering be reconciled with God's will in the same way as merited suffering? The Koran refuses to argue from suffering *to* sin (XXIV, 60); suffering men are not *per se* under God's anger. Apart from being punishment for sin, suffering is also a touchstone of true faith (II, 150f.; XXI, 36; III, 134f.). Faith must 'be put to the test'; but happiness and success are equally a test (XXXIX, 50). Islamic faith seeks to be put to the test. Some ritual prohibitions are merely meant as a 'test' (V, 95). Suffering reveals the real nature and truthfulness of a man; only then does he show what he is worth. In Islam, suffering as a punishment for sin and a touchstone of true faith lies completely within God's meaningful rule of the world and he has everything under control.

If suffering is expiation for sin, the Moslem himself can take the initiative in the expiation of sins. Furthermore, situations in which the righteous suffers and sinners prosper in luxury are occasions to bring home the belief that God has both situations under control and knows what he is doing or permitting and why. Despair does not fit into this context, nor do Jewish lamentations about God's delay and reluctance to intervene (V, 69). Jews also look for human rights before God; the Moslem does not do this. *A priori*, man *bows* before God. Islam therefore know nothing of the perplexed and yet hopeful laments of the Jewish psalmist. The Leader is always right: there is no point in talking about human rights where he is concerned. Suffering, however, is also a way of resisting the evil of others (IX, 14).

In conjunction with human suffering, the Islamic conception of God leads to the only possible attitude, *sabr*, i.e. affirmative *tolerance*, the patience to 'bear it'. The only answer is, 'we belong to God, and to God we return' (II, 150f.). So 'God is our refuge' (VII, 199): 'subjection' (VI, 163).

Yet for Moslem faith this is not fatalism. This 'belief in predestination' takes away all concern for one's own small person. God knows what is good for me. The agnosticism over the content of this knowledge creates a personalistic relationship of trust in God through which all things are possible to the believer. To compare one's own life with that of others would then be a foolish action. Such a belief in God does not seem to exercise any 'criticism of society' of the kind that would improve it. But why should one have to *change* a society in which one felt happy? Islam is critical of society in this sense; in other words, it is a criticism of the concern of others – Westerners – who, without being asked, want to Westernize Arab society, or, in Western eyes, make it better. For the orthodox Moslem, this means the acceptance of *bad* things from Western culture.

Finally, the God of Islam produces exact eschatological rewards for the good and punishments for the evil (II, 286). God does not try anyone beyond his own strength (loc. cit.). However, this amounts to something like 'each for himself and God for all', i.e. not bearing one another's burdens (see XVII, 16). A Moslem is not his 'brother's keeper' (see the Arab version of Cain and Abel, V,30–34). Finally, Islam gives a 'supernatural' solution to the problem of suffering: the *beyond* restores the balance. In the last resort, the delights of paradise and the torments of hell solve everything. The reckoning takes place later. For Islam, the beyond is a decisive motive for living a good life in this world. That is certainly 'un-Jewish' and not originally Christian. 'If it pleases Allah', like the Christian 'If it pleases God', is not fatalism, but it can soon become that. However, *as such*, this fatalism is neither Moslem nor Jewish-Christian, though Moslems (and Christians) sometimes fall victim to it.

Despite this attitude to suffering, Islam knows both protest against suffering and the duty to alleviate human suffering as far as possible. In the society shaped by Islam, men must eliminate suffering and injustice as far as they can. The Islamic community must reflect God's mercy (II,172). In contrast to the time of Mohammed, the Koran condemns a war of aggression; only defensive wars are allowed, and 'war against evil', the 'holy war' (*yihad*) for God's cause.

Another characteristic of Islam is its assessment of the crucifixion of Jesus: it has no significance whatsoever. Jesus was a faithful servant of God: therefore those who put him to death condemned him falsely (IV,156). One of the many Moslem interpretations, perhaps the correct interpretation of this famous text (IV,156), is: in reality Jesus was not crucified, but someone who looked like him was executed in his place. Be this as it may, the death of the prophet Jesus, who is revered even in Islam, does not have any special significance. Islam knows suffering as a punishment and a trial of faith, but not 'redemptive suffering', though it knows of martyrdom for God's cause (II,148f.). However, this is not applied to Jesus, for that is the *Christian* interpretation. Jesus chose the cross; Mohammed, in a similar interpretation, chose the Hijrah, the way of success and power, the instrument of God in the fight against evil. Here the two ways depart radically from each other.

Later Islamic theologians sensed the problems to which the Koran inevitably led. God's omnipotence obscures man's free will. There was a theological reaction against the view of God's 'sole working' which seemed to make men into marionettes. Since then two schools have been at odds, but the Koran continues to remain the criterion.

In the eighth century there arose in Islam *Sufism*, a mystical movement which voluntarily took suffering upon itself in the succession of the early monks. A Sufi is 'someone who possesses nothing and is not possessed by anything' (Alkalabadhi), no slave of any desire. Suffering and grief make a man sensitive to God.

The first great schism in Islam between Sunni Islam and Shi'ah Islam

took place in connection with the legitimacy of the succession to Mohammed, which gave rise to fratricide. The three murders were the
foundation of the theology of the Shi'ah Moslems: the saving significance
of innocent sufferings, namely, the more suffering now, the more joy in
heaven. The murdered one becomes a universal mediator, the heavenly
intercessor for all sinners (a completely alien thought for Sunni Moslems)
a kind of Arab *apokatastasis* for all sinners at the intercession of the three
martyrs, above all Hussein. But the letter of the Koran constantly restrains such theological intermezzi. The Moslem is in God's hand, in
suffering and misfortune, in success and prosperity. God arranges everything for the best.

## IX. THE RATIONALIZING OF HUMAN SUFFERING BY THE ENLIGHTENMENT

The ontological optimism of the Stoa revived again in the seventeenth
century and in the early part of the *Enlightenment* at the end of the
seventeenth and beginning of the eighteenth centuries. The theodicy of
the Enlightenment systematized the notion of this world as 'the best of
all conceivable worlds'. The men of the Enlightenment wanted to justify
God in the face of the human scandal of our history of suffering by means
of human reason. Alongside the Stoa, the Enlightenment is the great
attempt to rationalize suffering *theoretically*, really to *explain* it and thus to
think it away in the literal sense of the word. However, in contrast to the
ancient Stoics, the men of the Enlightenment began from an initial experiential protest against the meaninglessness of suffering (a protest
which, however, was later shown up to be unreasonable). Leibnitz and
Christian Wolff, Shaftesbury and Alexander Pope (who devotes a whole
hymn to suffering), make light of real suffering in their speculations and
reduce scandalous evil to a form of intellectual deception brought about
by the senses. We have too short-sighted a view of suffering and evil, say
these systematic thinkers; we consider their own direct reality, which is
unclear and painful. We are wrong – and this is where our senses deceive
us – in not seeing this against the wide background of the best of all
conceivable worlds. Evil is only the consequence of a provisional, superficial view of things; for within the context of the whole of history,
suffering is wholesome and good:

> All partial evil, universal good . . .
> One truth is clear: whatever *is*, is *right*.

So Pope put it in 1734 in *An Essay on Man*[38], expressing the universal view
of the early Enlightenment. From the point of view of the history of

religion this is a unique problem which is limited to the Enlightenment (along with some academic offshoots in the later scholastic handbooks of theology, which are clearly under the influence of Wolff's metaphysics). The men of the Enlightenment in fact wanted to justify God by means of human reason, which now itself called God to answer for his apparently bad direction of the world and history. In 1710 G. W. von Leibnitz wrote his *Essais de théodicée*[39] against the *Dictionnaire historique et critique* written by the master of doubt and mistrust, Pierre Bayle, and published in 1697. The same reason which accuses God of bad government on the basis of the experience of human suffering also seeks to defend God's government. In the pre-critical period God was never accused directly; even Job does not accuse God; he simply laments to God about the incomprehensibility of the presence of so much meaninglessness in his life, and it is finally God himself who justifies Job and not vice versa. On the other hand, the same enlightened wisdom which accuses God also acquits him; i.e., enlightened wisdom continues to believe in a world which has been ordered well by an intelligent Creator. It understands God against the horizon of a metaphysically interpreted, created nature which has been well ordered by God, and not against a historical horizon of coming into being, tradition and eschatological consummation. *Reconciliation* is as it were given before all time in the *harmonia praestabilita*. The all-important thing is to become aware of this eternal reconciliation: *metanoia* consists in a renunciation of short-sighted thinking and the acceptance of the liberating insight which is provided by a realization of the reconciliation that has already been offered. By and large, the evil and meaninglessness in our history amount to almost nothing,[40] a simple presupposition for the good harmony of the world and an implication of it. The God whom Leibnitz and Wolff defend is in the last resort not 'the God of Abraham, Isaac and Jacob, and the Father of our Lord Christ Jesus', but the concept of God maintained by 'true reason', which is defended against the objections of sceptical reason. Here reason makes its own defence.

Voltaire attacked this, and to that end used the great event of 1755, the year in which the whole world was horrified by an earthquake which destroyed the city of Lisbon and shook the ontological optimism of the Enlightenment to its foundations. Even then many people continued unmoved to defend the view that everything that happens is good: *'Tout est bien'*. A few months later, Voltaire, who for a long time had been an opponent of this optimism, cried out his heart-rending veto to the whole of Europe:

> *Philosophes trompés qui criez: 'Tout est bien.'*
> *Accourez, contemplez ces ruines affreuses,*
> *Ces débris, ces lambeaux, ces cendres malheureuses.*[41]

Voltaire does not set out to accuse God or to open up a perspective towards atheism; he simply demonstrates the limits of human reason. In theory, reason cannot say anything significant about the scandal of human suffering. For the first time in its later phase, the Enlightenment will recognize the theoretical impotence of human reason in this sphere. Immanuel Kant will work out in more detail the almost demagogical view of Voltaire. He calls any attempt to justify God 'worse than an accusation' against God:[42] such a theodicy is a distortion of the true understanding of God and dangerous for human action in the world. In that case there is no holy and gracious God, in whom the moral human subject can trust and on whom man can set his hope for support and forgiveness. In short, in the theory of the Enlightenment about the harmony of the world, the human person becomes a means to a greater, universal end. And this argument goes against all forms of a theodicy which argues from an already existing harmony in the world. *Reason* cannot either accuse God or justify him.

## X.  MARXISM AND HUMAN SUFFERING

'And to you, speculative philosophers and theologians, I give you this advice: free yourselves from the concepts and prejudices of previous speculative philosophy if you also wish to attain to things as they are, that is, to the truth. And there is no other way for you to truth and freedom than through the Feuerbach (river of fire). Feuerbach is the purgatory of the present time.'[43] Thus said Karl Marx.

To go through the river of fire means to lay aside the idealism that Ludwig Feuerbach criticized sharply and to adopt a 'dialectical-materialist standpoint'. In his postscript to the second edition of *Capital*, Marx says: 'The mystification which dialectic suffers in Hegel's hands by no means prevents him from being the first to present its general form of working in a comprehensive and conscious manner. With him it is standing on its head. It must be turned right side up again if you would discover the rational kernel within the mystical shell.' For him dialectic is a scientific hypothesis which does not seek to be dogmatic, but needs examining.[44] It is a dialectic based on observation and analysis, in which the movement of the spirit is a reflection of the movement of reality, which for Marx is always the historical process of becoming.

First of all I would like to clarify some terms, above all the term dialectic. In contrast to the pre-Hegelian, scholastic philosophical concepts 'dialectic' and 'dialectical' (in the sense of 'argumentative'), the word takes on a new meaning, especially in Hegel and Feuerbach. For Hegel, dialectic is the whole process through which reality develops and therefore also the process of thought which seeks to know this reality as it is. Thought reflects reality. Hegel sees this reality as a *triadic* structure: progress or development through thesis, antithesis and synthesis. Here thesis and antithesis are related essentially as opposites, and both terms have an essential connection with synthesis, the higher transposition of both of them.

Karl Marx also uses the term 'dialectical' against this Hegelian background, though in a quite special sense, prompted by Feuerbach, whom he nevertheless criticizes. Marx, and Feuerbach before him, deny the *a priori* triadic character of historical dialectic.

Rather than having a precise triadic character, for Marx 'dialectical' is rather a more general indication of the notion of the natural, essentially mutual – interdependent – dependence of real phenomena. In *reality* – and for Marx this is always the process of human history – there is a mutual dependence which extends to all aspects of reality. Therefore Marx calls 'reality' itself a *dialectical* process, on the basis of this interdependence. In view of the epistemological classical theory of knowledge as a reflection of reality (*adaequatio rei et intellectus*), for Marx this thought, too, is dialectical. Dialectical thought is a way of thinking which is concerned to disclose and unmask mutual dependencies everywhere. Not only are historical reality and thought dialectical; men must look on the *method*, the nature and mode and the figure of thought in the same way. In that case, a dialectical method is one which takes account of the constant interdependent transformations of reality and in reality. In the last resort, *dialectical* becomes a synonym for *becoming*, the historical process of growth.

However, on closer analysis the word 'dialectical' in Marx has a quite special meaning which unmistakably plays its part, even though this is not always mentioned explicitly. Universal dialectic or the process of growth in history is also a dialectic in the sense that one phenomenon (e.g. capitalism) irresistibly (and yet freely) calls forth a counter-movement (e.g. communism). There is an inevitable and inexorable rational logic in history. The new elements which emerge in it are at the same time rationally necessary. Furthermore, it is clear to rational analysis that precisely because the opposition between thesis and antithesis is often not just a *logical* contrast between these two concepts but also a life and death *struggle* (e.g. class warfare), dialectic also signifies struggle and conflict. In itself struggle is already a dialectical concept. And as history is dialectical, history itself is a struggle (in reality a class struggle between the owners and the working class).

Finally, dialectic has one more specific nuance, by virtue of the fact that the synthesis mediates between the thesis and the antithesis. In Marx, however, this is a mediation of a quite special kind: mediation

above all through transposition of the two extreme concepts to a higher
level (dialectical mediation). Now in reality (by this he always means
historical process) there are often mediating concepts which escape in-
attentive men (those who do not think dialectically). Dialectical thinkers
are concerned to discover disguised connections. The transition from the
opposition of the two concepts to a synthesis often takes place suddenly,
by a leap, and does so in a twofold sense: (*a*) the synthesis is often
something new which is essentially different from the two elements which
have gone before, and (*b*) the synthesis appears suddenly in time. At a
particular moment a quantitatively gradual development can reach a
point at which a qualitative change takes place (e.g. water, which keeps
getting colder and then at a particular point becomes ice).

Furthermore, in Marx dialectical thinking is essentially bound up with
action, even in respect of knowledge itself. There is also a knowledge in
and through action. In this way Marx seeks to connect a theoretical
humanism with practical humanism. Humanity is confronted with the
task of transcending its 'original prehistory', i.e. its quite irrational prehistory, a period of private interests and class interest. This pre-history
of mankind is an epoch in which interests and the desire for possession
are objectified in their 'hypostatization' or in quasi-natural historical
forces so as to form an unalterable situation (as in the animal world).
The reification of man gets in the way of purposeful control of human
action and makes it impossible for men to take responsibility for human
history in international solidarity. In the coming period of history, as
Marx outlined it on the basis of a scientific analysis of the present
situation, the illusory freedom of action on the part of individuals and
groups fighting one another must be replaced by responsible human
action planned in solidarity.

Marx affirms the difference between what is and what must be (a
distinction worked out in the Enlightenment by Hume), but he does not
affirm it as a difference which is formulated in terms of an insurmountable
division between facts which can be ascertained by science and norms
which can be established subjectively. For orthodox Marxists retain the
postulate of teleological ontology (*ens et bonum convertuntur*), albeit in the
Marxist sense. In other words, rightly understood (i.e. in a Marxist way),
being and being good are identical, not in the Aristotelian and Scholastic
sense, but in terms of historical dialectic. For with Hegel, Marxism
understands historical reality to be rational and the rational to be real.
However, Marx goes beyond Hegel in so far as he seeks to understand
the unity of historical facticity (e.g. capitalism) and its specific negation
(antithesis) – the thesis and antithesis which make up the historical and
dialectical unity of rational reality – in more than speculative terms (i.e.
after the event). Marx believes that this unity of history (and thus also

the future which is still to be created by criticism and revolutionary action) can be the matter of an *objective-materialistic scientific analysis*. Thus in Marxism the connection between theory and practice is made by an objective scientific reduction (at this point there is a 'dogmatic' aspect).[45] The dialectical analysis and synthesis of the inevitable course of history seems *a priori* to remove the difference between what is and what must be in the whole of reality, understood to be rational. A super-science grounds and communicates the unity of theory and practice. And yet what we have here is a *total* mediation of objectivity and subjectivity, namely through dialectical science on the basis of scientifically objective analysis. Thus Marx puts forward the concept of the possibility of an empirically objective science of history as a totality ('scientific socialism').

On these presuppositions, how does Marx regard the problem of human suffering? He looks at the facts and analyses their causes. He thus arrives at the discovery that much suffering and above all superfluous suffering has its cause in objective forms of society in which we live, specifically in capitalism. Marx really approaches the problem of suffering from the perspective of an *economic theory* which enables him to present social suffering as it were in an addition sum as the final total of an economic system which is founded on the profit motive and competition. The suffering of many men is the calculable result of the conditions of production, which imply an inner logic, namely a development from barter to money and from money to capital, based on the wages of those who by definition are not the possessors of capital.[46] The result of this inner logic is the process of the alienation of the workers: alienated from their work and themselves, purely reified ingredients in an economic process which, moreover, does not belong to them and lies outside their control. The system is such as to compel men to eliminate their fellowmen by competition, in order to secure their own survival. In *this* economic system, suffering can be quantified and finally be formulated in an equation. Put in simplified form, the sum looks like this. A commodity is worth the cost of its production. That involves two factors: (*a*) All the finished products that are needed for the provision of a particular commodity plus the cost of all the material used (altogether this forms the 'constant capital', which may be represented as C). (*b*) All the wages that have to be paid for the production of the commodity in question (which do not go beyond keeping the worker alive) (that is the variable capital, indicated by V). The increase in the total value of the product as compared with the sum of the value of the individual factors is the increase in the new capital as compared with the original capital. The means of production on the one hand and the labour force on the other are simply different modes of existence which have taken on the value of the original capital, when it is transformed *from* money *into* the different ingredients

in the process of labour. This particular part of the capital, which is
represented by the means of production, the raw material, the additional
material and the machines, does not undergo any alteration in value
during the whole process of production (Marx calls this the constant
capital). But the part of the capital represented by the labour force does
undergo a change in value in the course of production. It produces both
the equivalent of its own value and also the surplus, the increase (S)
(which can vary depending on the circumstances). This part of the capital
is permanently being transformed from a constant to a variable factor
(Marx calls it variable capital). Thus the value of an article is specific:
C + V. However, in combination, both can produce a surplus value over
and above the strict costs of production. The equation is clear: C+V+S
= W (the worth of the article). Now what distorts the worth in capitalist
societies is, according to Marx, the surplus value which does not go to
the worker; it goes to the owner of the money. Now if we compare the
two processes of the production of worth and the production of surplus
value, it becomes clear that the surplus value is simply the extension of
the worth beyond a particular point. In the equation C + V + S = W,
the factor S (surplus value) is the alienating element which produces
human suffering. For this surplus value is not the same as the *profit* (for
an article must be sold at a profit, even if only to obtain new investment
to produce further articles). The surplus value is formed by *additional*
costs, and in a capitalist society these rest on the fact that the worker's
labour is *reduced* to an article of trade. An example will make this clear.
Assume that a labourer works seven hours a day, then he covers the costs
of his own labour in two hours and the cost of the raw material in one
hour (C + V). In the other four hours he is producing a surplus value
to the advantage of the capitalist. It is precisely this inbuilt exploitation
which in Marx's view robs the labourer of more than half of his product,
and as a result he is completely alienated from the product of his own
labour and effort and in this way from himself and his fellow man. The
surplus value (S) is the figure which produces the mass of human suffering
(*Capital* I, 9.1). Marx expresses this in the following equation:

$$\text{Ratio of the surplus value: } \frac{S}{V} = \frac{\text{surplus labour}}{\text{necessary labour}}$$

Both relationships express the same thing in different ways. The level of
surplus value here is in that case an exact expression of the degree of
exploitation of the working force through capital:[47] the numerical quan-
tification of human suffering.

   Thus Marx investigated the social and economic causes of suffering,
causes which could be removed. But in what direction did he seek a way

of overcoming this suffering? Marx knew very well that many people did a great deal to support the suffering man and to help him, but they left the causes untouched. In their overcoming of suffering, all religions primarily attacked its causes, but they did not take sufficient account of social and economic causes. The consequence of Marx's consistent approach is therefore to introduce a fundamental change in economic conditions themselves. In contrast to the French socialist utopians, Marx did not dream of an utopian future, to be achieved without first fighting hard for it, in which there would be no more suffering, but he was still certain that much suffering would disappear from our world as a result of another social and economic order. For Marx, revolution is the only way of overcoming this remnant of suffering. However, it is hardly to be expected that the owners themselves will go over to this revolution. The force can come only from the working class, which then have to surrender their own interests. They have nothing to lose but their chains, says the Communist Manifesto.

The problem is that the revolution not only means suffering for a good cause, but is also itself the cause of much suffering, because social change cannot happen without struggle: class struggle. Thus the means is a socio-political movement, but of a revolutionary kind, albeit intended in the last resort to arrive at a free society in which man can be completely himself. Before this result is achieved, however, in the interim there is conflict between thesis and antithesis. The power of the proletariat is the provisional antithesis, but not the final synthesis. The interim becomes a permanent state because (against Marx's own expectations) the thesis (capitalism) is tougher than Marxists had originally thought. New forms of inhumanity which are themselves a product of the revolution are ascribed to the still existing dialectic of thesis and antithesis, which has not yet been resolved in a synthesis (however, at least among European Communists, voices can be heard which simply say that the antithesis of the power of the proletariat is obsolete; in that case, an essential element is removed from Marxism, and the leading orthodoxy is not very pleased about this).

In practice this conception implies that anyone who is against Communism is against the truth and against true humanity. Within orthodoxy, those who think otherwise are regarded as 'abnormal', and put in psychiatric institutions. 'Social liberation' can be maintained only through a dictatorship. Marx undoubtedly had a deep concern for mankind, and his view derives from deep solidarity with suffering man. But he saw that the Communist liberation during the interim had to be protected against reaction and delay. However, the whole question is not concentrated on this long interim, in which we are at least given the impression that the end justifies all means. It is precisely at this point that a *confrontation* between Marxists and the religious traditions of humanity is supremely necessary.

The scientific analyses of Marx (which must, however, be heavily revised in a late- and almost post-capitalist age) do not imply atheism *as such*. But this is not the case with Lenin, who made Marx's scientific hypothesis into a metaphysical system. The developments from Marx and Engels to Lenin, Stalin and Maoist China cannot be pursued within the limits of this book. But we must remember that, like all religions, Marxism has called to life a movement which itself also undergoes a hermeneutical and actualizing process with at times the same oppositions: fundamentalism and 'heresy'.) By nature, Marxism is an *economic theory* which as such stands outside the pros and cons of religion. True, insofar as he speaks of religion, Marx also criticizes religion which conceals social injustice by means of hermeneutical interpretations. The young Marx pointed out that all religions had a correct intuition: they were a protest against human suffering. Marx simply criticized them for having sought a false solution, namely in a fictitious world above and in a beyond (historically this is incorrect; however, in all religions popular religion moves in this direction). For Marx it is more the case that when the social revolution has been achieved, religion dies *of its own accord* because its origin – suffering – has vanished. This conception includes a tendency to reduce all suffering to social and economic causes; but significant though these are, they are not the whole of man. Furthermore, suffering is not the origin of religion; belief in God was the factor that made suffering an acute problem in religions. True, all these great world religions arose at a time which was not ripe for the insight that Marx discovered after the Enlightenment and with the help of modern society: the objective form of society in which we live is one of the many causes of suffering – although (and this is something which Marxists easily forget) it is not the only cause and perhaps not even the chief cause (however decisive it may be). For example, Buddhism too looks concernedly for the cause of suffering: like Marx, it notes suffering in order to remove its causes. Marx did the same thing, except that he also saw causes where others had not seen them, or, since they too knew of social suffering, where the given form of society was regarded as an unalterable condition (sometimes even created by orders of creation).

In questions of religion, Marx, like many of the intellectuals of his time, was a Feuerbachian (despite his criticism of Feuerbach). For Feuerbach the absolute nature of 'God' is only a reflection of 'the nature of man'. God is the objectified nature of the genre man. The consciousness of God is the self-consciousness of man.[48] Religion is the solemn unveiling of man's hidden treasures. As a transcendental philosopher, Feuerbach says that self-consciousness is not accessible in a direct intuition, but only by means of the knowledge of the *object* of consciousness. It is self-consciousness by means of the object. By education and a change of heart man can arrive at the insight that he is simply projecting his own deepest nature on to God.

Thus Marx rejects Feuerbach's naive replacement of religion with education and also his transcendental philosophy of the objectification of the self which is not put in question. In his fourth thesis on Feuerbach he grounds the self-duplication of man in his world upon the cleavages and self-contradictions[49] within this secular basis. This is what must be understood in its inner contradictions and overthrown by means of revolution. In that case all the ground is cut away from under the religious projection. In Marx's view, Feuerbach was wrong in looking for the conditions of the objectifying of the self not in man himself. Feuerbach saw man as an abstraction inherent in each single individual (sixth thesis on Feuerbach), and not, as Marx does, as 'the total of social relationships'. Marx (here inspired by Feuerbach) regarded religion as 'the self-consciousness and self-awareness of man who has either not yet attained to himself or has already lost himself again'.[50] Religion is merely the 'appearance of sanctity' or the spiritual aroma of the human vale of tears, an expression of and at the same time a protest against real misery, a protest which, however, has not been sufficiently understood. Religion is in ignorance about its own nature and therefore in ignorance about the misery to which it owes its own existence. Therefore it is the opium of the people. Religion is a passive reflection of the economic conflicts in society.[51] In a letter of September 1843, Marx writes to Ruge what he really means when he says that religion (the mystical) has a false consciousness of itself: that 'the world has long possessed the dream of a thing of which it only needs to possess the consciousness in order really to possess it. It will be clear that the problem is not some great gap between the thoughts of the past and those of the future but the completion of thoughts of the past. Finally, it will be clear that humanity is not beginning a new work, but consciously bringing its old work to completion.'[52] Thus Marx does not want a radical break with human history. But does he reduce everything 'without remainder' to economic factors? Such a reduction understands the relation of the economic basis to the superstructure of ideas (whether philosophical or religious, and for all their repercussion on the basis) merely as a reflection of oppositions in the basis on the ideological superstructure. Neo-Marxist interpreters show that the relationship between basis and superstructure in Marx's view by no means implies a complete determination of the superstructure by the basis; it is more a matter of an interdependence which, however (under non-Communist conditions), is governed by the basis in an *almost normative* way.[53] Thus even Marx could attribute a certain relative independence to the superstructure, but in that case one which is trampled underfoot in Communism. If this is correct, one can hardly *a priori* deny the independent value of religion, despite what Marx terms its function in bolstering up society.

However, there is no avoiding the fact that even in the Paris manuscript about the abolition of economic alienation, Marx automatically expects the abolition of religions; thus for him these are merely an epiphenomenon or a subsidiary manifestation of real economic alienation. Therefore, at least for Marx himself, the real and direct object of his ideological criticism is not the criticism of religion but the criticism of society.[54] 'But since the existence of religion is the existence of defect, the source of this defect can only be sought in the nature of the state itself. Religion for us no longer has the force of a basis for secular deficiencies, but only that of a phenomenon. Therefore we explain the religious prejudice of free citizens by their secular prejudice. We do not insist that they must abolish their religious limitation in order to abolish secular limitations. We insist that they abolish their religious limitations as soon as they abolish their secular limitations.'[55] This sounds different from Leninist Communism when it puts forward the orthodox party line. For Marx himself, religion stands outside his Marxism, that is, real Marxism does not *per se* imply atheism. However, Marxism knows the additional assertion that when the socialist society is a fact, there will be no more need for religion. In other words, Marx gives an interpretation of what religion is *in addition to* that provided by his economic theory, but this interpretation is to some extent isolated from his theory (*unless* in fact he saw the ideological superstructure as a mere reflection of the infrastructure). It is, however, certain that Marx, in contrast to many Marxists, does not see religion as *the* source of all alienation but rather as a victim of social and economic alienation which precisely in being a victim then keeps this economic alienation firmly in the saddle.

That religion automatically disappears in a Communist run society will therefore have to be settled from the facts. Actual experience can then verify or falsify the Marxist theory of reflection. But despite Lenin, this theory of reflection can hardly be used as a dogma. Marx presented this theory of reflection at some length in *Capital*, specifically in connection with religion.[56] Religion is defined as merely the 'reflex' of non-reflected, alienated conditions of life. With the illumination (scientific analysis) which prompts revolutionary action, religion automatically disappears as a logically consistent consequence. Marx and Engels[57] say that, because they are not analysed scientifically, the religions do not see that social and economic forces display an other-worldly character precisely *because of their dominance*. God is 'the extraneous force of the capitalist mode of production'. Man proposes, but 'God' disposes.[58] However, as soon as the world of labour not only 'thinks, but also directs', this alien power which is now reflected in religion will vanish. The reflection, too, will vanish for the simple reason that there is nothing left to reflect. Salvation from God becomes meaningless if the prevailing regularities which men interpret as natural laws have been seen to be historical and contingent, i.e. changing and changeable.

However, the decisive question is how it can be proved that religions disappear in the (dissoluble) reflection of social and economic oppositions. Above all, the later Marx concedes that the removal of 'added suffering' inflicted as a result of the objective form of society (H. Marcuse) does not remove the suffering which results from other causes (e.g. nature, and ultimately death).[59] Marx has not proved anywhere that religion is a reflection of economic factors and not just a datum which simply arises out of *man himself* – albeit in specific situations. Man is not *exhausted* in the manifestations which have so far been realized. Any over-hasty verdict on the *nature of man* is 'unhistorical'. That religion has a value of its own in fact implies that humanity has dimensions which are not identical with the sphere of purely materialistic action. Ultimately, Marxism raises the question whether man is not reduced. For a Marxist view of man, talk about salvation from God is meaningless. But the decisive question is whether this conception does not contain an intrinsic anthropological reduction. Is man nothing but labour and the means of production? Marx speaks only of man's self-realization through labour. Is human identity an identity which can be controlled in this way through and for us?

## §2 The challenge of this history of suffering

In its wretched history, mankind has found many forms of action to overcome suffering without ever being able to give a successful rational theory to account for all suffering. Where a theory has been given, suffering is either made light of or reduced to particular forms of suffering (or, possibly without reduction, the theorizing has touched on only particular spheres of human suffering).

It would, however, conflict with the historical facts were we to claim that mankind has tended more to *think* about suffering – through gurus and wise men, philosophers, theologians and scientists – than to *do* something about removing suffering and its causes. All religions have made a zealous quest for the causes of suffering precisely in order to remove these causes by following a particular course of action; it has not been a question of hallowing suffering as a fact or giving it some kind of 'supernatural' significance. There is no difference here between, say, the religions and Marxism. The decisive question is simply, 'What do men see as the causes of suffering?' Their view of these causes, like any conscious attempt of mankind to understand, depends on the historical circumstances in which the believer or the critical reason are to be found. Not only are these historical situations ambiguous and thus capable of various interpretations; it is also possible to make a false assessment of one's time and situation. Fundamentally, the capacity for human reflection is dependent on the historical circumstances in which human reason is exercised. Not every time has an eye for everything. All this implies that both the believing rational thinker and the non-religious rational thinker can only be aware of particular dimensions of human life in particular historical circumstances. Thus Marx located the cause of excessive and unnecessary suffering in a quite specific social and economic structure, which he analysed; this is something which had not been perceived earlier. But the phenomenon itself, i.e., where one discovers causes of suffering, to search for an appropriate course of action to remove these causes, was characteristic of all religions. Where the causes of suffering were located in man's sinfulness, the way to overcome them was obvious: not to sin. Where religions saw suffering caused through greed and desire (Buddhism), or through covetousness, egotism, the pull of the lower elements (e.g. the Stoics and the Cynics), they developed an appropriate course of action to overcome greed and covetousness. Different causes require different responses, some ascetic and related to the person, others social and political. It is difficult to see why some have to be called 'religious' and others 'profane' and 'secular' when all religions see one of their tasks as being the overcoming of human suffering. However, it must be concluded from this that it is impossible to reduce the causes of suffering and the saving and redemptive action directed towards them *either* to merely personal *or* to exclusively socio-political action. In that case the saving action would in fact be only half redemption and half liberation; it would halve man by fixing spheres of non-salvation. However, it seems as though it is precisely this half-view of man which simply leaves the various forms of action aimed at overcoming suffering juxtaposed in a state of mutual mistrust.

The historical survey has already shown that no movement, not even religion, should be nailed down to its foundation documents, which despite their original impulse, their original inspiration and orientation, are also historically conditioned. It is illegitimate to give an unhistorical definition of any single religion, i.e. to leave out the conditions which accompanied its rise; or to ignore the present situation in which it must now be lived out, or to forget all the interim periods between then and now. That will apply just as much to a socio-political movement like Marxism, in which it is equally illegitimate to posit an 'unalterable essence'. Therefore religions can be open to the new discoveries of the social and economic causes of suffering, just as Marxism can be open to other than economic causes. If religions do not have the strength to integrate new human experiences, or experiences which are in fact already quite old, then they prove to have divided conceptions about the nature of human life and all become a danger to true humanity. For salvation means being whole, and threatens to be less than wholeness when people seek all salvation in only one dimension of humanity – whether this is socio-political or personal, along with everything connected with that.

It does not follow *per se* or directly from this that religions must *therefore* also be open to Marxist revolutionary action. This seems to me to be a naive delusion, above all for religions which refuse to overcome suffering by themselves causing suffering (even if this is a means to a good end); they refuse to drive out Beelzebub with Beelzebub. The suspicion which one can detect here in the consciousness of every religious believer (even if he sees quite clearly the presence of social and economic suffering) seems to me to lie in the intuition essential in almost all religions which oppose any form of dualism. I said earlier that in practice no single religion accepts 'dualism'. Consequently religion fears any movement which threatens to accept the form of a *social* dualism or Manichaeism, albeit in modern form, in which 'the realm of freedom' is described as merely future, 'eschatological', whereas past and present are seen as a naturalistic, animal 'prehistory'. For almost all religions, the beginning of the history of freedom lies in the first moment of creation by God and since then freedom has been already at work in many fragments of salvation amidst what is still a great deal of meaninglessness and suffering. As religions, they find it impossible to believe in a realm of freedom which will come only after the radical revolution. That would be a modern version of apocalyptic in which the 'old aeon' must first be shattered, so that the 'coming aeon' will finally triumph (even apocalyptic did not go so far in this dualism). Precisely because solidarity with suffering man is one of the deepest specifically religious experiences of all religions, they will show an instinctive abhorrence of Communist plans for totalitarian revolution and prefer to seek their own ways of giving shape to the socialist concern for humanity which Marx showed so clearly. Religious men rightly shrink by nature from *reducing* human suffering to a socio-economic problem, however much they must also look for a socio-political solution for this form of suffering.

On the other hand, it can hardly be denied that in their original form, many religions, and most prominently Islam, because of its concept of God, *start from* the given fact that there is suffering and then often look directly for what God's purpose may be for this suffering (without analysing social and historical conditions). In all the ancient religions, this in fact leads to a number of false conclusions. However, we must remember here that an insight into historical conditions and the 'pliability' of our world has entered deeply into the human consciousness only in modern times. On the other hand, this new experience poses the demand that all these earlier religions should be brought up to date if they want to be true to their *own* critical and productive impulse towards the problem of suffering man. At this particular point in all religions we often find the phenomenon of an inner struggle between 'fundamentalists' and 'progressives'. Conservative believers evidently have a concern for fidelity towards the original religious impulse similar to that of the so-called progressives. But the conservatives mistake the historical conditioning, while the progressives take into account these socio-historical conditions, in fidelity to the true religious impulse. (This does not mean *per se* that the progressives are right in detail. They are certainly right in their insight that faithfulness needs to be brought up to date, but the way they make an attempt in this direction is not automatically correct.)

The historical survey given above draws our attention to yet other aspects. Striking here is the fact that in cultures where critical rationality rather than religious reason predominates, man (in reality the intellectual) evidently comes to terms more quickly with existing suffering than is usually the case in religions. The *religious* consciousness in particular provokes a more vigorous protest against suffering, above all unmerited and helpless suffering, than has ever been the case with critical rationalism (Marxism excepted). (At the same time, this seems to imply that in Marxism there is something which amounts to at least a 'para-religious' concern.) Secularized Romans and Greeks and Europeans, above all the early Enlightenment, did not make much protest against human suffering. Marx's accusation against the religions in this respect applies historically more to 'critical reason' than to the religions (though on each occasion it is important to make a distinction between the 'foundation documents' of any religion and the way in which it is expressed in popular form). Religions regard the suffering of sinners (as in the last resort we are all egoists) as the most normal thing in the world, but they all struggle with the problem of *unmerited* suffering, which has not been provoked by human stupidity or complicity. This is the point at which protest arises. To begin with, those who are *aware of God* do not know what to make of it. A 'pagan' like Lucretius can feel as though he is sitting in a comfortable seat watching a tremendously gripping play when, safe on the coast, he watches seamen in distress during a hurricane which threatens to wreck their boat. He calls this a 'blessed experience' – *suave, mari magno* . . . Enlightened reason, too, has a tendency to see the tragedy which 'one' weaves round suffering mankind as really a fraud, a lack of insight. It is no coincidence that enlightened reason is the mother of our Western bourgeois society.

Greeks and Romans in particular tended not to be interested in the causes of suffering. Here their notions of fate play a part: for them, suffering is *given*. The only important question is what attitude one adopts towards it. What they regard as the causes of suffering emerge in the action which they call for in the face of it: in their view of what is noble humanity. For Israel and the Jews, suffering is to be explained above all from human sinfulness. The only problem is innocent suffering, which in the last resort – after a great deal of polemic – is experienced as suffering through and for others, for the sake of a good cause, and finally as atonement for the sins of others. From their understanding of mankind – the Greek priority of the spirit over the corporeal, the Roman priority of the prosperity and success of the family and the Roman state – the Greeks and Romans see suffering as an unavoidable harsh school (sometimes ordained in this way by God), which brings men to wisdom, true humanity and true fame and success. The Greeks and Romans (at least as represented by their intellectual spokesmen) certainly know of protests against injustice, but not of protests against suffering as such. True, suffering is not desirable (though there is a masochistic trait to some Cynics), but it is simply a fact of life: one does not protest against fate or against mother nature. However, people have to make sense of suffering. Greeks do this 'anthropologically': an ethical spiritual aristocracy relativizes all suffering; Romans do it socio-politically: suffering is one of the sacrifices which a Roman must make to have fruitful harvests, to grow up as a brave man, and above all for the sake of Rome. The 'suffering for the sake of' is thus interpreted in humanistic rather than religious terms, though it is also conceded that this is the way the gods have ordained it; but 'pagans' do not suffer for a god or for God's cause. By contrast, Israel sees innocent suffering, finally, as suffering for a just cause because it is God's cause. For both, Israel and the Greeks and Romans, good, rather than evil and suffering, has the last word. Israel shows great sensitivity to the suffering of others, of the people; but apart from the Epicureans and above all Virgil, the Greeks and Romans have little or no compassion: that is more of a human weakness and vice. By contrast, Israel's literature talks above all of the suffering of the insignificant, the 'oppressed'. What we hear about the Greek and Roman understanding of suffering is more the voice of 'aristocrats', not that of the suffering people themselves. The voice of the suffering slave Spartacus, who rebelled against dehumanizing forced labour, is silent. What we have is the suffering of 'philosophers' and aristocratic ways of living. At the same time, however, with the post-classical philosophers, above all the Cynics, but also with the sages of the Stoics and some Epicureans, the attitude towards suffering, in voluntary poverty, renunciation and a marginal social life, is a kind of social criticism of the patrician life of the time. In Israel and among the Romans the concern for right and justice plays a significant role; also among the Greeks, but there it is more as a result of an ontological approach to the universe as a whole than directly as a result of the human awareness of righteousness. Outside the Stoa, however, no one seems to argue away suffering as an appearance and an illusion, least of all the Jew who laments to God vigorously about it. Jews, Greeks and Romans have an eye for suffering which is the result of social structures or their misuse. The prophets of Israel launch a religious attack on it, i.e. on the basis of their concept of God. Greeks argue and discuss the best form of society and government in respect of more Greek humanity; they have a rational approach. Romans discuss the matter less: however, the old, familiar, truly Roman laws and the manliness of the people are a redeeming feature. But there is a degree of 'pessimism' about the nature of man, a sense of tragedy, with all these people, and above all with the Greeks.

Eastern religions see suffering as caused less through 'objective' situations than through the way in which people deal with objective situations. They doubt the objectively given, even the social situation, less than other religions. They make *the person of man* in all situations the object of their criticism, i.e. his 'attitude' towards these situations. They have worked out specific forms of a purposeful course of action aimed at really overcoming suffering. In this way suffering is overcome personally, though at the same time the objective situation remains what it was and is, and they have thought out this course of action against suffering *within a given system* which they do not criticize. Granted, an individualism of salvation (above all an élitist individualism) is a constant danger here, but the Eastern religions have associated this with a solidarity with the 'personal salvation' of others (which is sometimes difficult to express in Western terms). This is all the more striking, seeing that the Western experience of the ego – expressed in the concept of the 'person' – seems to be more strongly developed than the Eastern 'ego'. It seems to me that this is simply another expression of what the self, the ego, is for men of the East. However, one cannot escape the notion that for people of the East the socially given *status quo* is the inevitable framework of reference (*dharma*), in which the practice of the personal victory over suffering must take form. For these religions in particular the Marxist conception is a life-and-death challenge. The question is whether Hinduism and Buddhism are up to it and can at the same time remain true to themselves. Here Christianity seems more adaptable, which is one reason why to some people it seems instinctively to be 'unreliable'.

Arab-Islamic religion is a problem in itself. The a-priorism 'God is always right' (fundamentally an infallible religious truth) is suspicious if *men* express this truth. *Il Duce ha sempre ragione*, 'Our great Leader, Mussolini, is always right', was also a Fascist slogan. Few religions have accepted this a priorism uncritically, even in respect of their own God. Like all other religions, Islam knows the reaction of protest against unmerited and helpless suffering. The Arab *omnipotence* of God, who has everything under control (though we cannot quite see how), is an unshakable, rock-steady conviction. The Arab is 'patient', but his almost 'fatalistic' patience often proves stronger than some activistic impatience which the Arab (often contemptibly) regards as fickle pretence. However, this Arab wisdom is suspicious, not prepared to be its brother's keeper (desert circumstances give little occasion for that). Besides, there is even a Dutch proverb which says: 'One hand for the ship, the other for myself.'

In fact suffering has more rational and comprehensible aspects that people could have known of earlier. Both the religions and Marxism have come to accept this. Precisely for the sake of our humanity, a religious and rational enlightenment is urgently necessary. But suffering also has rationally inexplicable dimensions. There is also the suffering of our finitude, the abiding suffering of the irrevocable tension between *nature* and *man* (human history), the child born severely handicapped, the loneliness of many people, the suffering of death, the suffering of guilt. Here the believer and the secular man are confronted with extreme problems.

For the *believer in God*, Epicurus put the theoretical problem sharply (though also in a rather complicated fashion): 'Either God wants to remove evil from the world, but cannot. Or he can, but will not. Or he will not and cannot. Or he will and can. – If he will and cannot, he is impotent. If he can and will not, he does not love us. If he neither will nor can, he is not the good God and is impotent into the bargain. If he will and can – and that is the only thing that befits him as God – then where does evil come from and why does he not take it away?'[60] True, here the problem of God is approached in a coldly syllogistic way, and Epicurus works with a suspicious human a-prioristic concept of what God's omnipotence and love would have to mean, but his argument is a very impressive expression of the theoretical impotence of human reason in the face of evil and suffering. Kant, who refers to this well-known text, makes Epicurus himself go on arguing against the men of the Enlightenment, who want to bring evil and suffering into a theoretical accord with God by reference to what to us is a mysterious harmony in the world. 'If the harmony which you see in the world also requires a corresponding wisdom as its living ground, then you must recognize that for the most part the world does not depend on this wisdom, since more than half of its inhabitants find it full of discords and fearful deviations.'[61] Man's theoretical reason fails in the face of suffering. But if it is to maintain a critical and liberating influence, then critical thought must constantly subject itself to the challenging remembrance of the history of human suffering, and continually learn to listen to its own history of suffering men.

For the non-religious man, the challenge of suffering mankind is just as strong. In our secularized world, history is no longer *larva dei*, the mask of God. It is reinterpreted to become the mask of man, *larva hominum*; that is, man himself is urged to become the lord of history and creator of the future. Consequently man is called to responsibility, since he is constantly confronted with a history of suffering which has still not been brought to an end. Theodicy, the justification of God, then automatically turns into an anthropodicy, as happens in the *homo homini lupus* of Thomas Hobbes, and on the other hand the accusation of God or criticism of religions consequently becomes a criticism of man and society. It is not God who must be made responsible, said Jean-Jacques Rousseau, but man, for it is man himself who creates his own world for good or destroys it. In the case of a bitter experience like the Lisbon earthquake of 1755, one may not speculate in metaphysical terms, but must think historically and ask why men gathered together by the hundred thousand in a place like Lisbon.[62] An earthquake like Lisbon should not confront us with a problem of theodicy but, Rousseau says, makes us resolve to institute a different cultural policy.

But just as earlier the problem of theodicy concealed a subtle technique of making excuses and was the search for an alibi, so too in modern secular conditions a similar 'strategy of immunization' appears.[63] True, the consequences of the 'death of God' are accepted, as are those of the advancement of man to become the subject of history; now man himself becomes responsible for the human history of suffering. Now, however, and this is the new diversionary manoeuvre, 'man' – the doer of evil – takes on the face of the *other*, fellow man: the opponent and enemy. The ideal 'wholly other', God, on whom one could shift all final responsibility, has meanwhile disappeared from view. What could earlier be interpreted as a matter of 'transcendental foreign policy', as a battle of man with his God (whether this was made a theodicy or an accusation against God), now becomes a matter of 'domestic politics': a battle within the world of man against man, a conflict among men. For when there is no transcendental scapegoat, the immanent scapegoat comes into the foreground. This gives rise to the conflict between men who have made the world and history what they now sadly are, and men – which means ourselves – who want to create another, better world and blame 'the others' for having made our world into a history of suffering. Where suffering and evil emerge, the fault is now laid at man's door, but this is man in the form of the other, the enemy, the 'not me' or the 'not us'. However, the tactics of excuse, the constantly recurring alibi, are clear enough. Furthermore, this implies that the other is in fact the *dominant* opponent; for a history of philosophy which makes man responsible for the history of suffering and at the same time seeks to relieve him of responsibility cannot dispense with the still uninterrupted but gradually disappearing *rule* of 'the other'; that is its real *a priori*.[64] This emerges most clearly from particular forms of 'critical theories of society' which *identify* the scapegoat of the history of human suffering with late capitalism, still in a dominant position but now clearly in dire straits. People clearly go on looking for a culprit to be responsible for our history of human suffering. In so doing they do not seem to make it clear to themselves that the better, earthly future of coming generations for which they so hope for is just as much a 'beyond' for the generations now alive as was heaven for the oppressed of the pre-critical period. It emerges from this that the 'great refusal', the 'great alternative' or the 'radical revolution' is equally far from being a plausible solution for the scandal that the history of human suffering still in fact presents to us.

# Redemption and Liberation

Chapter 1

# God does not want mankind to suffer

Taught by our own specific experiences, we can accept that there are certain forms of suffering which enrich our humanity in a positive sense, which can even mature men so that they become thoroughly good and wise personalities. A man who has become mature through suffering compels wonderment, deep admiration, and reduces one to silence; one finds oneself enriched by the experience of such gentle wisdom which has grown through life. A world in which there was no place for suffering and sorrow, even for deep grief, would seem to be inhuman, a world of robots, even an unreal world. In almost all languages, people rightly speak of the 'school of suffering'. In our human world, great things are evidently born only in suffering.

Furthermore, a certain dose of suffering undergone can make us sensitive to other men. Love and attractiveness, as openness towards others, are at the same time the capacity to suffer: vulnerability. We found it striking that the wise men of the Stoa, who felt themselves to be above true sorrow, consistently rejected sensitive compassion for suffering men. They knew no sorrow, but also . . . no love. But believing love of God also knows its own fragments of suffering. Not all suffering is meaningless. That is part of the sum of human wisdom, as the whole of human history bears witness.

Furthermore, a certain amount of suffering transforms men, ourselves and others; not only in lesser things, but above all when it is suffering for a good, righteous or holy cause which is close to a man's heart. At the same time, however, human experience shows that this is not suffering which man chooses or seeks for himself. What man does choose is the cause for which he gives himself wholly. That is vocation: obedience towards the good which summons us and which we think worth the trouble: man is better than the suffering which can bring this sacrifice with it. Thus suffering takes on significance as the *actual* implication of

724

a call to, and a responsibility for, a true and good cause (fellow man, God). In *that* sense, this suffering is on the one hand not sought, and on the other freely accepted as an actual and possible consequence of a particular commitment. In this kind of suffering man is not concentrated on himself, nor on his own suffering, but on the cause which he takes up. All this is equally true of religious sacrifice. Such sacrifice is experienced as sacrificial love: for Christians that means 'participating in the suffering of Jesus Christ' (II Cor. 1.5).

Despite all these true considerations, however, there is an *excess* of suffering and evil in our history. There is a barbarous excess, for all the explanations and interpretations. There is too much *unmerited* and *senseless* suffering for us to be able to give an ethical, hermeneutical and ontological analysis of our disaster. There is suffering which is not even suffering 'for a good cause', but suffering in which men, without finding meaning for themselves, are simply made the crude victims of an evil cause which serves others. Furthermore, this suffering is the alpha and omega of the whole history of mankind; it is the scarlet thread by which this historical fragment is recognizable as human history: history is 'an ecumene of suffering'.[65] Because of their historical extent and their historical density, evil and suffering are the dark fleck in our history, a fleck which no one can remove by an explanation or interpretation which is able to give it an understandable place in a rational and meaningful whole. Or does someone perhaps want to give Buchenwald, Auschwitz or Vietnam (or whatever else) a specific structural place in the divine plan, which, as Christians believe, directs our history? No man, at any rate, who thinks it important to be a man and to be treated as a man will do so. And then we have still not said anything about the unmerited suffering of so many of the nameless among us, in our immediate neighbourhood. Perhaps including our own suffering that we do not understand. *We* cannot justify God. Of course we are not God, and we think of God's omnipotence and goodness with petty human terms. Yes, but that does not make the scandalous history of human suffering which we have to bear, with all its negativity, any less real.

Thus suffering and evil can provoke scandal; however, they are not a *problem*, but an unfathomable, theoretically incomprehensible *mystery* (unless one reduces it – against all human experience of suffering – to a *particular* sector of human suffering which we clearly have within our grasp, both scientifically and technologically). One can objectify a problem and take one's distance from it; this makes a detached explanation possible. But suffering and evil in our human history are also *my* suffering, *my* evil, *my* agony and *my* death. They cannot be objectified. In a moving passage in *The Brothers Karamazov*, Dostoievsky makes Ivan say that if this great universe, with its wonderful realities and splendid events, is bought at the cost of the tears of an innocent child, then he will politely refuse to accept such splendour from the hands of the Creator. Human reason cannot in fact cope with concentrated historical suffering and evil. Here the human Logos, human rationality fails: it cannot give any explanation.

If the powers of human explanation and interpretation are incapable of giving a meaningful explanation of suffering and evil, might not logic and everyone's dreams suggest that perhaps human *action* can provide a solution? In connection with this, it must first be conceded that if we cannot justify evil and the unfathomable mass of innocent suffering, or explain it as the *unavoidable* obverse of God's fundamental plan in his will for good, then the only meaningful reaction to this history of suffering is in fact to offer resistance, to act in a way meant to turn history to good effect. That is also urgently necessary. For one can refuse to allow evil the right to exist, on the basis of the insight that it has no justification for existence, and therefore refuse to give a theoretical answer to what is experienced as the darker reality of evil in its specific historical proportions and distortions. However, that is only consistent and coherent if this refusal is linked with a powerful involvement in resistance against all forms of evil. That means that *in practice*, too, people must refuse to allow evil the right to exist: they must espouse the cause of the good and refuse to treat evil on the same level as good.

In theory, people may not be in a position to *explain* suffering and evil, but the *remembrance* of what has happened in very specific suffering in a particular historical context also belongs to the structure of human reason or critical rationality.[66] The history of these specific remembrances therefore remains an inner stimulus for practical reason which seeks to be liberating and active. Human reason may not simply brush aside these admonitory remembrances if it still wants to remain *critical* reason.

The only question is whether at the same time this implies that the practical task with which men find themselves confronted as a result of the many accounts of contrasting experiences in our history of human suffering can also in fact be brought to a successful conclusion. For human action in resistance against evil is itself subject to criticism, at least in its claim to totality – not through any theory, much less through religious and Christian faith, but through a specific reality of experience, part of human life: the tension between 'nature' and 'history' which makes up man's transitory life and can never be removed, a dialectic of which death is merely an extreme exponent, the boundary situation. Thus at the deepest level, at the level of our outline of an earthly, human future, we are at the same time confronted with the final fiasco of our efforts at resisting evil. Death above all shows that we are deluded if we think that we can realize on earth a true, perfect and universal salvation for all and for every individual. However, human salvation is only salvation, being whole, when it is universal and complete. There cannot really be talk of salvation as long as there is still suffering, oppression and unhappiness alongside the personal happiness that we experience, in our immediate vicinity or further afield.

All this means that we cannot look for the *ground* of suffering in God, although suffering brings the believer directly up against God.

Some theologians want to base the necessity of a redemption by God on the theologically suspicious insight that God himself is the one starting-point of both the giving of life and the destroying of life; the permanent crisis of our human existence has its basis in the paradox of God – *fascinosum* and *tremendum*. The starting-point for the justification of our life is at the same time also that for the endangering of our life, namely God himself.[67] I do not want to deny that this is a fundamental conception in many religions, beginning with that of Israel. Numerous texts from the Old Testament could support this conception: Yahweh is a God 'who kills and restores to life' (II Sam. 2.6). However, I pointed out earlier that in the long run Israel itself rejected this primitive conception of God. God is pure positivity; he wills the life of the sinner and not his death. In the beginning, God was regarded as the principle of life and death. The correct intuition here was that the believer was thus guarding himself against a metaphysical dualism which ascribed the good to God and the evil to a 'first principle' of evil. Such a view cannot in fact be reconciled with a generally religious belief in God and especially with Yahwistic belief. If God is defined as equally the 'power of lifegiving' and the 'power of annihilation' in one, this undeniably cuts at the root of the critical and productive force of religion. For in that case, God's whim decides whether salvation or destruction has the last word. God's freedom, which is beyond human control, then becomes defined, in all too human terms, as a *finite freedom to decide* between good and evil.

If we recognize the correct intuition in the anti-dualism of this ancient Hebrew conception of God, which can also be found in religions generally, we must also recognize the correct intuition in Persian dualism, namely that 'God' cannot solely be pure positivity, the 'first principle' of good and in no way the *ground* of any evil. God is the author of the good and the opponent of evil, but in that case it becomes necessary to look for a non-dualistic 'ground' for evil.

It is well worth remembering that faith does not disqualify human reason and its liberating practice in order to claim the honour of being able to offer a correct solution once reason has conceded defeat. For religious belief does not blame man for his ultimate theoretical impotence and his practical failure in the face of evil and suffering. This bitter insight, this 'accusation', stems from our own human experience and critical reason. By contrast, religious belief seeks to rescue us from this fatal experience and give our action new meaning by breaking its impotence in the light of a new possibility *from* God: thanks to the proclamatory reminiscence of Jesus as the story of a crucified man who is now alive, through whom a future is given to those who have come to grief in history, even those who (for the moment) are victors at the expense of the defeated.

The Christian message does not give an *explanation* of evil or our history of suffering. That must be made clear from the start. Even for Christians, suffering remains impenetrable and incomprehensible, and provokes rebellion. Nor will the Christian blasphemously claim that God himself required the death of Jesus as compensation for what *we* make of our history. This sadistic mysticism of suffering is certainly alien to the most authentic tendencies of the great Christian tradition, at the very least. Nor can one follow Jürgen Moltmann[68] in solving the problem of suffering by 'eternalizing' suffering in God, in the opinion that in the last resort this gives suffering some splendour. According to Moltmann, Jesus not only shows solidarity 'with publicans and sinners', with the outcast and those who are everywhere excluded; not only has God himself identified him with the outcast; no, God himself has cast him out as a sacrifice for our sins. The difficulty in this conception is that it ascribes to God what has in fact been done to Jesus by the history of human injustice. Hence I think that in soteriology or the doctrine of redemption we are on a false trail, despite the deep and correct insight here that God is the great fellow-sufferer, who is concerned for our history.

I think that at this point it would be good to resort to Thomas Aquinas. True, in reality he is seldom understood and little studied, and he did not apply his fundamental philosophical or theological principle consistently to Christian soteriology. However, he does seem to me one of the few people who can give us some reasonably satisfactory viewpoints which at the same time leave all the darkness in its incomprehensibility. More than anyone else, Thomas stresses the priority of the all-determining, positive 'first causality' of God. On the one hand as a theologian he dares to write: 'The first cause of the lack of grace lies in us';[69] and on the other, as a philosopher: 'Although God is the creative cause of our (human) will – i.e. the one who calls up out of nothing – this will has this "being from nothing" from no one other than itself; and precisely for that reason the defects of the will which follow from a creaturely deficiency may not be carried back to a further or higher cause';[70] here we have finitude, as it were, as 'the first cause'. As soon as there are *creatures*, there is the *possibility* (not the necessity) of a negative and original *initiative of finitude*, if I can put it that way.

In a system of thought which seems somewhat alien to us, then, Thomas expresses deep insights into life which, without making the

history of human suffering understandable in theory – i.e., without harmonizing it with God's Godness or our positive humanity –, nevertheless
point to the unfathomable depths in which they have to be put. On the
one hand is the incomprehensible depth of the mystery of God, and on
the other hand the negative depth of what finitude and finite freedom
can involve. For Thomas, it is a senseless philosophical undertaking to
look for a particular cause, a ground or motive for evil and suffering in
God; these do not necessarily follow from our finitude, but they do draw
their fundamental possibility from there. *Negativity* cannot have a cause
or a motive in God. But in that case we cannot look for a divine *reason* for
the death of Jesus either. Therefore, first of all, we have to say that we
are not redeemed *thanks to* the death of Jesus but *despite* it.

On the other hand, it cannot really be claimed that the Creator God
remains as it were without awareness of what finite and free men can
make of their history in a finite world and nature. The enormity of the
fact confronts us: a history of suffering which has broken many human
hearts. The 'initiative' of finitude (I put *initiative* in quotation marks),
namely an initiative which at its extreme origin, albeit in deficiency, *begins*
*exclusively* from the finite without any contribution from God's side, such
a negative initiative which plays an *incidental* part *in* human life that is
positively supported by God, does not, however, checkmate God: in my
view, at any rate, we do not know this from a general 'concept of God'
but from the 'God of Jesus', namely from Christian belief in the *resurrection*
of Jesus. For it emerges that God transcends these negative aspects in
our history, not so much by allowing them as *by overcoming them*, making
them as though they had not happened. By nature, and in addition to
other aspects and meanings, the resurrection of Jesus is also a corrective,
a victory over the negativity of suffering and even death. From the point
of view of the Christian Bible, for anyone who thinks historically it is not
a question of 'divine permission' for evil and unmerited suffering (this is
the initiative of finitude), but of God's *victory* over this particular initiative
of the finite. Only *in* the overcoming of it can we say that the negative
aspects in our history have an indirect role in God's plan of salvation:
*God is the Lord of history.* That is why Mark 8.31 could say intuitively, 'The
Son of Man must suffer many things.' We shall never be able to give a
reason (any more than Mark could) for the significance for salvation
history of this improper expression 'the divine must'. On the one hand
it contains the insight that man is redeemed by Jesus *despite* the death of
Jesus, seen as negativity and the human rejection of Jesus from our midst,
one of the many exponents of our history of suffering. On the other side,
however, this 'despite' is so transcended by God, not because he permits
it in condescension but because through the resurrection of Jesus from
the dead he conquers suffering and evil and undoes them, that the

expression 'despite the death' in fact does not say enough. However, the terms in which we could fill this unfathomable 'does not say enough' in a positive way, with finite, meaningful categories, escape us. What this 'does not say enough' might suggest is expressed most clearly in the refusal of Jesus to look for a *culprit*. When the Jews ask, 'Rabbi, who has sinned, this man or his parents, that he was born blind?', according to John 9.3 Jesus replies: '*Neither he nor his parents* have sinned, but *the works of God must be made manifest in him.*' God overcomes the initiative of what 'finitude' can do purely of itself, without God's help – bringing suffering and evil into our history. The 'mystery of unrighteousness', which comes into tension with nature out of the unfathomable depths of our history of freedom, is evidently weaker than the 'mystery of the mercy' of the divine event that is God's nature itself: the Father who is greater than all suffering because he overcomes it in solidarity with our salvation. He is greater, too, than any theoretical and practical inability of creatures to experience the deepest reality in the last resort as an unconditionally reliable gift. But we are not in a position to arrive at a *theoretical* reconciliation of the two. For the depth of what the negativity of 'finitude' can (not 'must') mean, and the depth of what represents God's essential positivity, cannot be fathomed by human beings.

The insight that God does not want men to suffer but wills to *overcome* suffering where it occurs in our history (from a divine freedom of wisdom and will, whose divine nature and manner we cannot either define *a priori* or derive from his nature – do we know that so very well?), reminds us of *our own history* (in which Jesus himself also appeared), in order to be able to say something meaningful as Christians about redemption and liberation. God wants *men's salvation*, and in it victory over their suffering. The New Testament says with bold realism: 'Be imitators of God' (Eph. 5.1), whom we have come to know in Jesus as the champion of all that is good, as the one who brings happiness – makes whole – and as the opponent of chaos, evil and injustice: as the Creator and warrior against the beast Leviathan, under whatever form this may be manifested in history. What this talk means for Christians here and now will have to find its inspiring and orienting impulse on the one hand in the gospel of salvation from God in Jesus, and on the other hand from an awareness of the problem, at which we have now arrived, of true and good, happy and free humanity.

Chapter 2

# The height and breadth and depth of human salvation

## §1 What is humanity?

What is it to be a true and good, happy and free man, in the light of the awareness of the problem which mankind has so far developed, while it looks for a better future, the problem with which man has been confronted since his origins? What is a livable humanity?

Today we have become more modest in our positive definitions of what humanity is. Ernst Bloch writes: 'Man does not yet know what he is, but can know through alienation from himself what he certainly is not and therefore does not want to, or at least should not want to, remain false.'[71] We do not have a pre-existing definition of humanity – indeed for Christians it is not only a future, but an eschatological reality. However, there are people who give the impression that they have a blueprint for humanity. They have a fully drawn picture of man and a specific image of coming society, an 'entire doctrine of salvation', a dogmatic system which, paradoxically enough, seems to be more important than the people with whom it is really concerned. This totalitarian conception intrinsically issues in a totalitarian action, which is simply a question of application, of technology and strategy. Moreover, in that case those who neither accept nor apply this concept of true humanity are obviously regarded as the enemies of true humanity. Even Christians sometimes think in this way.

Our time has become more modest here. Nature, 'ordinances of creation' and Evolution (with a capital E) cannot give us any criteria for what is livable and true, good and happy humanity, and thus for what makes up the meaningful, ethically responsible action which furthers this true humanity. That cannot be either a so-called 'universal human nature' which, like plant or animal, is governed from within and is by nature oriented towards a pre-destined goal, nor can it be any of the modern versions of this: i.e. so-called natural law. Furthermore, no reflection on oneself can arrive at a crystallization of a kind of general substratum of rationality among all men, independently of time and space.

Structuralists have recognized constant depth structures in human society, but these say nothing about the specific peculiarity of a particular society. These structures do not relate directly to reality, but to the *model* which man has made of it. Thus while structuralism has opened up an aspect of human reality, namely that man is a model of projective being, any structuralism which is consistent in itself ignores the question how these models relate to reality. (At this point, however, there are a large number of inconsistent crossings of boundaries, as for instance when Lévi-Strauss asserts that the relative truth of all models consists in the fact that they are more or less successful human attempts to disguise the greyness and meaninglessness of existence. That is in effect a *philosophical* view of the world which goes beyond the boundaries of structuralism as a *science*.) Structuralism in fact excludes the human subject and therefore does not provide any criteria for human society.

Again, existentialism has analysed 'existentialia', that is, the basic determining features of human life: anxiety, despair and hope, suffering, death and happiness, finitude and guilt. And these aspects are extremely important in human life; they are connected with the *question of* what is ultimately worthy of man, but do not provide any answer to it as such. What is the basis of the hope for livable humanity within our finitude, our guilt and our suffering? Evidently it is only said here *what* we must be freed *from* and *for what*: for happiness. But how? And what is true happiness for each and every one?

Finally, we cannot make any better use of the positivistic conception of values and norms. Here an empirical analysis can certainly clarify what norms and value in fact hold in a particular group or society. This sociological insight is important, and even extremely relevant, say, for positive legislation; but to be capable of implementation it must, of course, be supported by quite a large consensus of all members of this society. However, it is impossible to raise 'the factical', i.e. the norms which in fact apply, those which represent the highest figures in a statistical survey, to the level of a universal norm for moral and meaningful action. Precisely as a result of that, after a certain time cultures with an initially high standing are dragged right down.

Man's critical awareness must therefore put us on the right road. If reason is the specific feature of mankind, then man's capacity for judgment, for assessing ambiguous phenomena in human history *on the basis of standards*, is his own critical task. Man is a being caught up in history. His *nature* is itself a history, a historical event, and is not simply *given*. So something of this nature can only be seen in the course of his historical history; in the history of humanity. He is a situated and thematic freedom, not a free initiative in a vacuum or an airless room. Salvation and humanity, being saved, integrity in a truly human and free way is in fact the *theme* of the whole of human history. Neither a materialistic nor an idealistic reading of this history can do justice to it.

Critical awareness is not only (*a*) the awareness that it is part of man's specific being that he is entangled in the surroundings of phenomena which do not *directly* show us the true and the good, but *at the same time* make it unrecognizable to us and conceal it, so that we need a standard of judgment; but also (*b*) the awareness that the critical force of human reason is dependent on the historical circumstances of human reason, so that the relationship between *reason* and *specific historical circumstances* must be taken into account as well; finally (*c*) also an awareness that both the past and the present and the time lying between the two can be judged wrongly, because they themselves are in turn involved in the ambiguity of all history. Human reason is only critical – and not 'dogmatic' or nihilistically sceptical (in an authoritarian way) – when it takes account of the ambiguity of phenomena which reveal and at the same time conceal the true and the good, in other words, when it takes account of the historical conditioning of human thought and also of the meaning of every epoch of time (which is often ambivalent or multivalent) – past, present and the intervening period. This is open to a variety of interpretations. As a result, human awareness is only critical when it not only passes critical judgment on given phenomena but in addition is capable of the *self-criticism* of *critical reason* – something which was evidently beyond the capacity of the Enlightenment in the eighteenth century.[72]

Thus what we have at our disposal is no more than a set of *anthropological constants*, rather than a positivistic outline, or a pre-existing definition of 'human nature' in philosophical terms (e.g. in Aristotelian and Thomistic or Spinozan and Wolffian terms) or, finally, a product which is provided in itself through the profoundly rational course of history in necessary historical terms (which would then be the Marxist definition of true and free humanity). These may present us with human *values*, but we must make a creative contribution to their specific *norms* in the changing process of history. In other words, in very general terms these anthropological constants point to *permanent* human impulses and orientations, values and spheres of value, but at the same time do not provide us with *directly* specific norms or ethical imperatives in accordance with which true and livable humanity would have to be called into existence here and now. Granted, they present us with constitutive conditions (given the analysis and interpretation of any particular contemporary situation) which must always be presupposed in any human action, if man, his culture and his society are not to be vitiated and made unlivable. Taking into account the particular socio-historical forms of a particular society, and in the light of these spheres of values recognized as constant (in our time-conditioned awareness of the problem), it is in fact possible to establish specific norms for human action over a middle or longer term.

I want to analyse seven of these anthropological constants. I see them as a kind of system of co-ordinates, the focal point of which is *personal identity* within *social culture*. I am concerned with views of man and his culture, with constitutive aspects which we must take into account in the creative establishment of specific norms for a better assessment of human worth and thus for human *salvation*.

## §2   The system of co-ordinates of man and his salvation

### I.  RELATIONSHIP TO HUMAN CORPOREALITY, NATURE AND THE ECO-LOGICAL ENVIRONMENT

The relationship of the human being to his own corporeality – man *is* a body but also *has* one – and by means of his own corporeality to the wider sphere of nature and his own ecological environment, is constitutive of our humanity. So human salvation is also concerned with this.

If we take no account of this human reference in our action, then in the long term we shall dominate nature or condition men in so one-sided a way that in fact we shall destroy the fundamental principles of our own natural world and thus make our own humanity impossible by attacking our natural household or our ecological basis. Our relationship with nature and our own corporeality come up against *boundaries* which we have to respect if we are to live a truly human life and, in an extreme instance, if we are even to survive. Therefore what is technically possible has not by a long way been an ethical possibility for men, which makes sense for them and to which they can respond.

This also applies to the physical and psychological limitation of our human strength. Although we may not be able (or perhaps may not yet be able) to establish by an empirical scientific method precisely where the *limits* of the mutability, conditioning and capability of humanity lies, we may be sure that such inescapable limits do exist. This certainty, which is *cognitive*, though it goes beyond the bounds of science, can also be seen manifested spontaneously in the individual and collective protests which emerge at the point where men feel that excessive demands are being made on them. The elementary needs of man (e.g. hunger and sex), their drives (e.g. aggression) and their corporeality cannot be manipulated at will without the realization that there is an attack on human goodness, happiness and true humanity (which will express itself in spontaneous resistance).

This first anthropological constant already opens up a whole sphere of human values, the norms needed for a relationship between our own corporeality and the natural environment of man worthy of our true humanity – norms, however, which we ourselves must establish in the context of the particular circumstances in which we now live. This already opens up the perspective of the relationships of mankind to nature, which are not exclusively provided by the human value of the domination of nature, but are also provided by the equally human value of aesthetic and enjoyable converse with nature. The limitations which nature itself imposes on the way in which it can be manipulated by man to man's advantage open up for us a dimension of our humanity which is not exhausted in the purely technocratic domination of nature.

On the other hand, the same constants warn us against the danger of an anti-technological or anti-industrial culture.[73] Scientists who reflect on what they are doing[74] emphatically point to the anthropological relevance of instrumental reason. Cultural philosophers have worked out that man is not really capable of remaining alive in a *purely natural* world. In nature man must create an appropriate human *environment* if he is in fact to survive without the refined instincts and the strengths which animals possess. A rational alteration in nature is therefore necessary. A 'meta-cosmos' (F. Dessauer) thus appears, which rescues man from his animal limitations and offers an opening for new possibilities. In times when this meta-cosmos' was hardly different from nature, only a small stratum of the population shared in the advantages of culture, and the mass of mankind had to work slavishly for the liberation of a few from material cares. (However, we can ask whether things are very different in a highly industrial 'meta-cosmos'. It emerges from this that the first, fundamental 'anthropological constant' is not enough in itself.) The meta-cosmos therefore offers man a better abode and a better home than the natural cosmos. So technology is not dehumanizing in itself, but is rather a service towards livable humanity; it is an expression of humanizing and at the same time a condition for the humanizing of man. Indeed, it is a fact that the establishment of a 'meta-cosmos' has been the historical presupposition for reflection on questions about the meaning of life. Furthermore, this humanization of nature has yet to be completed, though that might easily be assumed, given the advance in technology. However, man can have an influence on his ecological position in nature, though he depends on it, as becomes clear above all when he destroys the conditions under which he lives. Now the concern on the one hand to emancipate man from nature without on the other hand destroying his own ecological basis is an eminently human task, which cannot be accomplished without 'instrumental reason'.

Moreover, it is evident that the outlining of meaning and of particular pictures of the world and mankind is also communicated through instrumental and technological reason, and is not just an immanent development of ideas. Ideas about marriage, love and sexuality have shifted in our time (e.g. from biblical conceptions), for the most part solely because science and technology have been able to provide means which were not at the disposal of people of former times. With technological possibilities available, intervention in *nature* in fact looks different from those times when any intervention was felt to be an irresponsible and therefore evil attack on the divine ordinances of creation. However, at the same time there arises the human danger that simply because of the availability of technological possibilities and capabilities, people believe that they can and may provide a *purely technological* solution for all their physical and psychological, social and general problems of life. However, the technocratic *interpretation* of the ideal of a livable life worthy of human beings is not the same thing as the anthropological relevance of science and technology. What is in reality often the dehumanizing character of technology does not come from technology itself, but from the question of meaning associated it, which has *already* been solved in *positivist* terms. It is not science and technology, with their potentialities for improving man's condition, but their implicit presuppositions which are criticized.

Thus this first anthropological constant shows a whole series of partial constants – for example, that man is not only reason, but also temperament; not only reason, but also imagination; not only freedom, but also instinct; not only reason, but also love; and so on. Thus it is a matter not only of the active dimension of man and his control of the world, but also of his other dimensions, in contemplation, play and in love.

If Christian *salvation* is in fact the *salvation of men*, it will also have essential connections with this first 'anthropological constant'. To cite only one aspect from the past: Christian salvation is also connected with ecology and with the conditions and burdens which particular life (here and now) lays on men. To say that all this is alien to the meaning of 'Christian salvation' is perhaps to dream of a salvation for *angels*, but not for *men*.

## II.  BEING A MAN INVOLVES FELLOW MEN

Human personal identity at the same time includes relationships with other people.[75] This, too, is an anthropological constant which opens up a sphere of human value in which people have to look for norms which will provide them with salvation here and now.

The element of being together, of contact with our fellow men, through which we can share ourselves with others and even be confirmed in our existence and personhood by others, is part of the structure of personal identity: authorization by others and by society that we, that I, may be, in my own name, in my own identity, a personal and responsible self, however distorted this may be. A society which out of so-called self-protection (sometime euphemistically called 'the building up of society') leaves no room for the disabled person is not worth a fig.

This personal identity is only possible if I may be allowed by other fellow men, to be myself in my own inalienability, but at the same time in my essential limitation (*divisum ab alio*, as earlier philosophy put it), and if on my side I confirm the other. In this limited individuality the person is essentially related to other, to fellow persons. The human face in particular – a man never sees his *own* face – already indicates that man is *directed towards* others, is *destined for* others and not for himself. The face is an image of ourselves *for others*. Thus, already through his quite specific manifestation, man is destined for encounter with his fellow men in the world. This lays on him the task of accepting, in inter-subjectivity, the other in his otherness and in his freedom. It is precisely through this mutual relationship to others that the limitation of man's own individuality is transcended in free, loving affirmation of the other, and the person himself arrives at personal identity. The co-humanity with which we encounter one another as people, i.e. as an aim and an end and not as a means for something or other, is an anthropological constant which looks for norms without which whole and livable humanity is impossible here and now. This also implies that well-being and wholeness, complete and undamaged humanity, must be universal, must apply to each and every individual, and not only a few privileged ones – though it emerges from what has gone before that this wholeness will embrace more than inter-human relations on the *personal* level. No one can enter into a relationship of real encounter with everyone. Besides, there is more than the I-thou relationship. The presence of a *third*, a 'he', is the basis for the origin of *society*, which cannot be derived from an 'I-thou' and 'we' relationship. This has been clearly seen above all by E. Lévinas, and the insight brings us to a third essential dimension of humanity.

## III. THE CONNECTION WITH SOCIAL AND INSTITUTIONAL STRUCTURES

There is, thirdly, the relationship of the human person to social and institutional structures.[76] While we men bring these structures to life in the course of our history, they become independent and then develop into an objective form of society in which we live our particular lives and which again also deeply influence our inwardness, our personhood. The social dimension is not something additional to our personal identity; it is a *dimension* of this identity itself. When they become independent, these structures and institutions give the impression of being unchangeable natural regularities, whereas we ourselves can change them and therefore also their regularity. Independently of what men do, and independently of human reason and human will to preserve these structures, such highly praised sociological and economic regularities do not exist; in fact they are essentially subject to the *historical hypothesis* of the objectively given social and economic system. They are contingent, changeable and thus changeable by men (although sociologists and cultural anthropologists will perhaps be able to discover a deeper, almost immutable level and therefore structural constants in some perhaps even fundamental social changes).[77] The empirical sciences often do not take into account that this appearance of regularity depends on the hypothesis of our given (changeable) objective form of society: given the hypothesis, they rightly discover these sociological or socio-psychological regularities, but sometimes treat them as though they were a natural law or a metaphysical datum.

This constant, too, shows us a sphere of values, above all the value of institutional and structural elements for a truly human life. This is once again a sphere of values which needs concrete norms. On the one hand there can be no permanent life worthy of men without a degree of institutionalizing; personal identity also needs social consensus, needs to be supported by structures and institutions which make possible human freedom and the realization of values. On the other hand, actual structures and institutions which have grown up in history do not have *general validity*; they are changeable. This gives rise to the specific ethical demand to change them where, as a result of changed circumstances, they enslave and debase men rather than liberate them and give them protection.

## IV. THE CONDITIONING OF PEOPLE AND CULTURE BY TIME AND SPACE

Time and space, the historical and geographical situation of peoples and cultures, are also an anthropological constant from which no man can detach himself.[78]

Here, first of all, we are confronted with a dialectical tension between nature and history which cannot ever be removed, even by the best possible social structure. Nature and history come together in particular human cultures. Their dialectic is a given one, which is an element of our transitory human existence and of which death is only an extreme exponent, a boundary situation. That of itself means that apart from some forms of suffering which can for the most part be removed by man, there are forms of suffering and threats to life on which man can have no influence through technology and social intervention. This is where the question of the *meaning* of humanity emerges. The historicity and thus the finality of man, which he does not know how to escape so that he can adopt a standpoint outside time, makes him understand his humanity also as a *hermeneutical* undertaking, i.e. as a task of *understanding* his own situation and unmasking critically the meaninglessness that man brings about in history. Of course man can be helped in this attempt to understand himself, which also involves the question of truth and falsehood, by a variety of empirical, analytical and theoretical sciences, but at the same time he is conscious of the experience that the truth for man is only possible as *remembered* truth which at the same time is to be *realized*. If understanding is the original way in which men *experience*, this understanding is generally the same as history itself. That means that the presumption of adopting a standpoint outside *historical* action and thought is a danger to true humanity.

Numerous other problems are given with this constant. I shall only point to some of them (within the theme of this book). There can be historical and even geographically conditioned attainments which, although they appear late in human history and in particular places, and thus cannot be called necessary or universal *a priori* presuppositions, cannot be regarded *here and now* as random or arbitrary.[79] Here values have grown up requiring norms which apply, for example, to highly industrialized and advanced cultural conditions in which Western men live, and which need not apply directly in other cultures.

Some examples may be enough. Because of their general prosperity, Western men have a duty to international solidarity, above all towards poor countries (regardless of the historical question of how far they themselves are the historical cause of the poverty of these poor countries). (This obligation also arises from the duties resulting from the second and third anthropological constants.) It also follows on the basis of these same constants, which produce the historical and geographical limitations of any culture, that taking into account the limited potential of the imagination of men in a particular culture, critical remembrance of the great traditions of mankind, including its great religious traditions, will be a necessary stimulus in the search for norms for action which here and now further healthy and realizable humanity (this critical remembrance is an element in man's hermeneutical enterprise, in which he seeks illumination for his coming action).[80]

Finally, this fourth anthropological constant also reminds us of the fact that the explicit discovery of these *constitutive constants* has only come about in a historical process: their coming to consciousness is already a fruit of human hermeneutical practice.

## V. MUTUAL RELATIONSHIP OF THEORY AND PRACTICE

The essential relationship between theory and practice is likewise an anthropological constant. It is a constant in so far as through this relationship human culture, as a hermeneutical undertaking or an understanding of meaning, and as an undertaking of changing meaning and improving the world, needs *permanence*. On a sub-human level, i.e. in the animal world, permanence and the possibility of the survival of the species and the individual are ensured by instinct and the elasticity with which it can adapt itself to changed or changing conditions, and, finally, by the law of the survival of the fittest in the struggle for life. Now unless men want to make their own history into a kind of spiritual Darwinism, a history in which only will and thought, the power of the strongest and the victor, dictate to us what is good and true for our humanity, then on the human level a combination of theory and practice will be the only humanly responsible guarantee of a permanent culture which is increasingly worthy of man[81] – of what brings man *salvation*.

## VI. THE RELIGIOUS AND 'PARA-RELIGIOUS' CONSCIOUSNESS OF MAN

The 'utopian' element in human consciousness also seems to me to be an anthropological constant, and a fundamental one at that.

Here we are concerned with man's future (see above). What kind of future does he want? Under this utopian element I would place a variety of different conservative or progressive totalitarian conceptions which make it possible for man in society in some way to make sense of contingency or finitude, impermanence and the problems of suffering, fiasco, failure and death which it presents, or to overcome them. In other words, I am talking about the way in which a particular society has given specific form to the hermeneutical process in everyday life (see the fourth constant) or looks for another social system and another future in protest against the existing attribution of 'meaning'. These are totalitarian approaches which teach us to experience human life and society, now or in the future, as a good, meaningful and happy totality for man – a vision and a way of life which seek to give meaning and context to human existence in this world (even if only in a distant future).

Here we find 'totalitarian views' of both a religious and a non-religious kind – views of life, views of society, world-views and general theories of life in which men express what ultimately inspires them, what humanity they choose in the last resort, what they really live for and what makes life worth living. All these can also be called *cognitive models of reality*, which interpret the whole of nature and history in theory and practice, and now or later allow it to be experienced as a 'meaningful whole' (yet to be realized).

In most, though not all, of these 'utopias' man is understood as an active *subject* who furthers humanity, interpreted as being good and true, and the establishment of a good human world, though on the other hand individuals are not personally responsible for the whole of history and its outcome.[82] For some, this all-controlling principle is fate or *fatum*, for others evolution, for yet others humanity, the 'genre man' as the universal subject of the whole of history, or, less definitely, nature. For religious men this is the living God, the Lord of history. But no matter what form such a totalitarian view may take – unless one glorifies nihilism and professes the absurdity of human life – it is always a *form of faith*, in the sense of a 'utopia' which cannot be scientifically demonstrated, or at least can never be completely rationalized. And so in fact 'Without faith you're as good as dead.'[83] In this sense 'faith', the ground for hope, is an anthropological constant throughout human history, a constant without which human life and action worthy of men and capable of realization becomes impossible: man loses his identity and either ends up in a neurotic state or irrationally takes refuge in horoscopes and all kinds of *mirabilia*. Furthermore, faith and hope are strengthened as necessary human constants by the nihilistic claim which calls livable humanity an absurdity and thus has no faith and no hope. That implies that faith and hope – whatever their content – are part of the health and integrity, the worthwhileness and 'wholeness' of our humanity. For those who believe in God, this implies that *religion* is an anthropological constant without which human salvation, redemption and true liberation are impossible. In other words, that any liberation which by-passes a *religious redemption* is only a partial liberation, and furthermore, if it claims to be the *total* liberation of man by nature, destroys a real dimension of humanity and in the last resort uproots man instead of liberating him.

## VII. IRREDUCIBLE SYNTHESIS OF THESE SIX DIMENSIONS

In so far as the six anthropological constants which we have discussed form a *synthesis*, human culture is in fact an *irreducible autonomous reality* (which cannot be reduced either idealistically or materialistically). The reality which heals men and brings them salvation lies in this synthesis (and therefore the synthesis itself must be called an anthropological constant). The six constants influence one another and go over into one another. They delineate man's basic form and hold one another in equipoise. It may sound fine and even right to talk of the priority of 'spiritual values', but such talk can in reality at the same time destroy the material presuppositions and implications of 'the spiritual', *to the detriment of* these spiritual values. Failure to recognize one of these profoundly human constants uproots the whole, including its 'spiritual' component. It damages man and his society and distorts the whole of human culture. Whether consciously or not – even under the flag of the 'primacy of the spiritual' – this represents an attack on true and good, happy and free humanity.

On the other hand, it may have become clear from what has already been said that these anthropological constants, which open up a perspective on the fundamental values of 'humanity', in no way provide us with specific *norms* which must apply here and now, taking into account our objective form of society and given culture, in order to arrive at conditions more worthy of man. As I said, these constants simply outline, as it were, the system of co-ordinates in which specific norms must be sought through general considerations and after an analysis and interpretation of the position of the person in it. The minimum requirement for starting – and perhaps this too is an important factor in considering what is specifically 'worthy of man' – is that we should be at the *level of awareness of the problem which has already been achieved*. From that point we can then carry out an analysis of the gulf between ideal and reality, on the basis of negative experiences or experiences of contrast, and also on the basis of experiences which we have already had, in the light of what is seen to be 'utopia'. This differential analysis will show the *direction* which we must take (always in the form of different possibilities), a direction which we have to agree in defining and for which we have to make urgent specific norms which are valid here and now.

I said that there would always be different possibilities. For men have very different views both of the details of this utopian element in our human consciousness and of the analysis and above all the interpretation of the result of this analysis (for a utopian consciousness with a particular direction is always involved *in* the manner of this analysis). This gives rise, even in scientific analysis (which takes place in a conscious or unconscious framework of interpretation), to *pluralism* even in the sphere of specific norms – even when people recognize the same *basic values* to which the 'anthropological constants' draw our attention. However, the proposed norms which we ourselves adopt at our own risk must also be tested for inner logic and discussed in dialogue if we are also to challenge others with them. Even if their fundamental *inspiration* comes, say, from a religious belief in God, *ethical* norms, i.e. norms which make life more worthy of men, must be capable of being given a rational foundation in valid inter-subjective discussion, i.e. discussion which is accessible to all rational men. None of the conversation partners can hide behind a threadbare 'I can see something that you can't' and nevertheless compel others simply to accept this norm. All too often in discussions the initial situation can be of this kind: that one of the conversation partners sees something that others do not. But in that case the others must also be enlightened in a free and rational process of communication. No one can appeal here to a 'zone of tranquillity' (even if other conversation partners cannot *per se* arrive at a consensus on the basis of the arguments presented). One of the tasks of a livable modern humanity will be that of learning to live with different conceptions of specific norms for a worthwhile human life which is called for here and now. The pain of this pluralism is part of our *condition humaine*, above all in modern times; we must cope with it, and not by means of the dictatorial rejection of other conceptions. This art is also an element of true, good and happy humanity within the limitations of our historicity and transitoriness – that is, unless we want to become 'megalomaniacs' who have got it into their heads that they can step out of their human finitude. However, the concern for the salvation of each and every individual cannot on the other hand simply begin from 'politics' as the so-called art of the possible, what can be done or achieved. Politics, rather, is the difficult art of making possible what is *necessary* for human salvation.

Thus *Christian salvation*, in the centuries-old biblical tradition called redemption, and meant as salvation from God *for men*, is concerned with the whole system of co-ordinates in which man can really be man. This salvation – the wholeness of man – cannot just be sought in one or other of these constants, say exclusively in 'ecological appeals', in an exclusive 'be nice to one another', in the exclusive overthrow of an economic system (whether Marxist or capitalist), or in exclusively mystical experiences: 'Alleluia, he is risen!' On the other hand, the *synthesis* of all this is clearly an 'already now' and a 'not yet'. The way in which human failure and human shortcomings are coped with must be termed a form of 'liberation' (and perhaps its most important form). In that case that might then be the all-embracing 'anthropological constant' in which Jesus the Christ wanted to go before us.

Chapter 3

# Christian salvation

## §1   Individualistic descriptions

Some Christians are fond of asserting that the Christian gospel is merely a matter of the heart, a personal affair, and that Jesus and the New Testament called men to conversion of the heart, to inwardness, but not to the reform of structures. In so doing these Christians contrast persons and structures, and speak of the priority of the human realm and the merely secondary significance of the institutional element in human life. It is quite obvious that Jesus directs his message to *people*: to whom else can a message be directed? But it is also easily forgotten that the language of the gospel, and even the language of Jesus, is at the same time historically conditioned. Anyone who forgets this ends up immediately in a crude fundamentalism. And at that point people seem to be unaware that they are dealing with a false, namely abstract, personalism. Such Christians are then working with the concept of an abstract individual who in his free subjectivity is completely isolated from the objective form of society in which people live and from the power that prevails there. They forget how deeply and inwardly the individual is involved in society, above all how he or she is conditioned to the depths of their innermost being by a specific society, with the particular needs that it has created. One does not have to define man as a mere point of intersection or as the sum of socially determined roles (even if one still allows him a particular private sphere), but one does have to take into account the profound socialization of the I, the person. What existential personalism (as it has undergone a partial revival in certain charismatic movements concerned with inwardness) understands as the nature and inwardness of man is in reality determined deep down into his existential needs through his own dynamics and the objective form of society in which we live today. And this social system is based on profit, achievement and competition; or to put it less pleasantly, but just as realistically, on greed: on individual and group egotism. One can hardly say that such a system is commensurate with the gospel.

Under these conditions, a flight to inwardness is at the same time a flight into internalized 'society', and therefore a flight into the social *status quo*, instead of a criticism of the actual alienation of our inwardness. It is the 'God of pure subjectivity'[84] who has led to the modern forms of atheism. At present this modern subjectivity is being subjected to serious criticism, at least insofar as the secular and social presuppositions of inwardness or freedom are not being taken into account. When they are not taken into account, they acquire the *appearance* of being unquestionable and self-evident: the force of a kind of 'natural law'.

The problem which all this presents immediately becomes clear when we consider the character of what Christianity calls faith in salvation-in-Jesus from God. This faith is a free human action and is at the same time called a gift of God. Christian faith *presupposes* freedom and *discloses* freedom. The decisive question here is then whether in present social conditions self-liberation and emancipation are not a presupposition for a possible belief in the religious message of redemption and at the same time are not also a fragmentary sign of salvation. As a consequence of the extensive and intensive increase of a truly uniform society, personal identity and thus also Christian faith are increasingly being communicated *socially*. In that case the contrast between *person* and *social structure* to some degree becomes an abstraction with dangerous consequences. For Christians, affirmation of another's personhood, readiness to identify oneself with another and affirm his own subjectivity, is from the start a readiness to make the economic, political and social world habitable for humanity. Freedom (in faith) does not simply consist in a new *relationship* to our given secular situation which is then left to itself, as the Stoics and then Paul asserted. The question then is whether the freedom of the children of God is not pointed towards a social liberation as an integral ingredient of eschatological salvation from God. In other words, the question whether Christian freedom or redemption is not directed towards political and social liberation as a condition of its own possibility. It is of itself striking that our *religious* concepts of redemption imply *secular* concepts of deliverance, wholeness and liberation, and do so moreover in accordance with the forms of liberation longed for, which constantly change over the course of history. Before it is even possible to understand what Christians mean by liberation, it is necessary to have experienced some form of liberation. For what can love of God mean to anyone who has never been the 'object' of liberating love from a fellow man, who has never experienced human love? Completely hidden salvation, which is merely announced and promised, is what is now still the eschatological *borderline* case of Christian existence. In forms which will constantly become obsolete and in fact are obsolete, eschatological salvation must be made visible in fragments on the level of our human history: in human hearts and in structures, because (above all in our contemporary society) the heart or love is also communicated through structures. Essentially and substantially salvation is *love*, but not in such a way that everything else is merely the *presupposition* for salvation. Love is not sheer inwardness; the corporeal and the social elements enter into the substance of love in the mode of corporeality and society. However, the corporeal element, structures, never constitute salvation; therefore there can still be, for example, partial yet real experiences of salvation in love in circumstances of poverty and slavery (not that they give this slavery any legitimation).

However, for men who believe in God, any socio-political liberation is only partial; indeed, if it claims to be *total*, it essentially becomes a new form of servitude and slavery. Still, this Christian insight does not give us any cause to make light of political and social liberation. At the moment, the problem of the relationship between the ethics of human *liberation* and *eschatological* salvation is of central concern. Besides, in the history of religions, it is striking that illness and some forms of human alienation are always associated with religious conceptions, just as healing, recovery and liberation from powers which alienate men are always experienced as a sign of the coming kingdom of God.[85] This is also the case with the gospel. In both the Romantic and the Germanic language the root of the word *salus* or salvation is connected with *sanitas*, health; with being whole or with integrity. In other words, eschatological salvation is always expressed in terms of the integrity of human life. The Bible expresses this in terms of *šālōm*, which also includes the social dimension. Furthermore, it emerged in the analysis of the New Testament (Part Two) that the New Testament Christians also wanted to give expression to the salvation that they had experienced in religious terms in Jesus *in society* as well, so far as they could, given the circumstances of the time. This they did within their own Christian community, in which they did not tolerate any form of domination through power. In our changed situation today, this New Testament stimulus makes the question of the relationship between Christian faith and political action on the part of the believer an indisputable challenge to the Christian conscience.

## §2     Dispute over the relationship between 'history' and 'salvation history'

It is a well-known fact that the social and political attempts of men to bring about peace and justice in our history are often regarded in the name of the Christian concept of salvation as a humanistic and 'Pelagian' enterprise which threatens 'justification through faith alone'. Sometimes it is even described as 'godless activism'. Thus in almost all churches a wedge is driven between the so-called orthodox 'churches of redemption', oriented on contemplation, and the so-called 'churches of liberation', heterodox and oriented on activism.

The same problem has long been discussed in theology in connection with the question of the relationship between 'secular' history and salvation history, and between eschatological salvation and the building of a world fit for men to live in. Of necessity I can only make a representative selection here from a large number of authors. I shall therefore first analyse six modern solutions, in order to be able to put the problem in a more pointed form.

(a) In his book *Salvation in History*, Oscar Cullmann asserts that human history and salvation history are different. Salvation history deals with a special theme, different from that expressed in secular history. Salvation is contrasted with secular life: 'New Testament salvation history is radically different from all history.'[86] Cullmann bases this demarcation between salvation history and human history in general on a *selection* of particular events which enter into human history in general.[87] God himself simply chooses particular events which are interconnected by a particular context of salvation and thus form a special history against the background of secular history. God reveals this intrinsic connection to people he chooses – prophets and apostles. This divine act of revelation is an essential element in what Cullmann calls 'salvation history'.[88]

Thus salvation history is a thin thread in the complex totality of general human history. Cullmann is aware that this selection of particular events and their 'elevation' to the status of salvation history appears arbitrary, indeed meaningless, from a historical standpoint.[89]

It goes without saying that not all historical events have the same significance for salvation. Purely in anthropological terms, there is an evident difference between everyday human actions and 'basic human actions', in which man expresses his humanity in a concentrated way. The only question is whether this particular selection of events can be called the foundation of a special history. All historical research works selectively, and out of a chaotic whole chooses those data which are relevant to a particular historical project. Thus even a believer has the right to make a particular selection in the light of his religious programme. Here Cullmann is right. But there are no grounds for his assertion that there is a fundamental difference between this salvation history which is known from its own nature and universal human, so-called secular history. Every human action is concerned with salvation in a more or less concentrated way: with man's humanity and his wholeness, however this may be regarded and evaluated. And for the believer this implies that all divine action in nature and history – of whatever kind – is concerned with human salvation. Where, then, does one find a reason for making so radical a distinction between secular history and salvation history? This conception contradicts the reality that the whole history of mankind is concerned with *man* and thus with humanity, its wholeness or salvation.

We cannot begin from a divine counsel and plan – how do we know about it, anyway? – in order to recognize from it the thin thread of salvation history *in* secular history. Only from an interpretative experience of *our* history can we say something about God's plan with our human history, and not *vice versa*. Cullmann's theory has elements of a 'positivism of revelation', which is further paralleled by a decisionism of faith: the choice of those events which form salvation history is a matter of a decision of faith[90] which is not accessible to historical testing. Despite everything, and even against his own intention,[91] Cullmann falls into the trap of a dichotomy between 'experience' and 'interpretation' (see Part One). For him the element of interpretation is evidently an element *coming in from outside*, to be accepted on God's authority which escapes any critical control. In that case salvation history is a special, storm-free zone within the whole of human history: biblical history and its traditions.

(*b*) Wolfhart Pannenberg represents almost the opposite position to Cullmann.[92] For Pannenberg, all human history is concerned with man himself, with his salvation. Man is not the subject, but the *theme* of all human history – man, his wholeness and his salvation. The history of man *is* salvation history. But what is at stake for man in history is *thematized* in the religions. In other words, the various religions explicitly state what is implicitly to be found in history. So there is a certain difference between *universal* salvation history and *explicit*, thematized salvation history (the history of religions). Here Pannenberg denies that these religions (or one of these religions) can be an *infallible* and *authoritative* intepretation of the theme of salvation which is implicit in universal human history. But the various religions are *particular* interpretations of the theme of salvation in all human history, though only a comparison of religions can show which religion can articulate the theme of salvation implicit in universal history in the most coherent way. This removes even from Judaeo-Christian religious tradition the status of being Cullmann's 'storm-free zone'.

In this comparison of religions – thematizations of the salvation which is at stake in any history – Pannenberg notes that not all religions have arrived at the awareness that the salvation or wholeness of man must be realized *in history*, namely in a history in which man encounters his salvation 'as his future determination', which he can also forfeit, precisely because it is future. That is the Judaeo-Christian conception. For other religions, above all for those which speak of a mythical primal time, man's salvation is grounded in a primeval order of things. Mankind has fallen from this, and religious men seek to return to the primal state through the cult. Thus *history* has to be overcome by the *cult*, since history is change, and the further it moves from primal times the greater the decline it produces. In these religions, therefore, salvation is not to be found *in* history but in the cult which transcends history: in the liturgical life of the community. Only for Israel's nomadic faith in God as the ruler of the history of the people of God does history itself become the place of the self-revelation of God and the revelation of man's salvation. In contrast to the mythical spell of the primal period, the God of Israel, the Lord of history, the leader of Israel's exodus, brought to birth the consciousness that man is still unfinished, that his wholeness and salvation still lie in the future. According to Pannenberg, this consciousness found its evocative expression in Christianity in the image of the antitypical tension between the 'first Adam' and the 'second Adam' who appeared in Jesus; but for us this means a future which is still incomplete.

Thus Pannenberg avoids an arbitrary demarcation of salvation history from the whole of human history; at the same time he stresses that the totality of humanity – the hidden theme of all human history – is not thematized expressly everywhere. However, this explicit thematization does not take place through an authority of revelation coming to history from outside (thus Karl Rahner), but through each religious life. For Pannenberg, the sequence of particular events to which Cullmann attributes a quality of salvation history in the narrower sense is identical with the series of religiously relevant events which explicitly state the meaning of all history. The special character of Israel and Christianity does not come directly from above; it is a historical development of the religious life, a special feature the pecularity of which lies in the fact that it alone expressly formulates the *historicity* of the theme of salvation: God's revelation and thus man's salvation is accomplished in our normal human history. So here Pannenberg recognizes only the authority of history itself and of human reason. Whether that can be enough will emerge from the following theological interpretations.

(*c*) For Karl Rahner,[93] salvation history is not a selection of a limited number of events from the totality of human historical events (Cullmann). The whole of human history is the place where a decision is made on man's salvation or damnation. However, Rahner affirms a *special* salvation history within universal history, which is as broad and deep as so-called 'secular' history. It is specially revealed – namely, in that it expresses a *particular interpretation* – in the saving significance of all history. For Rahner, as for Pannenberg, there is only one history; one cannot discover within it a special, limited area which can be reserved as salvation history, while the other areas stand outside the history of grace or faith. Salvation is concerned with the totality of our humanity and not with a 'particular theme' to be detached from it. This is fundamental for Rahner's concept of 'salvation history'. History *is* salvation history (as for Pannenberg), but there is a difference between salvation history and 'secular' history, namely that salvation history provides an *interpretation* which cannot be arrived at otherwise. For, by and large, secular history 'does not of itself offer us any certain interpretation regarding salvation or damnation'.[94] Without what Rahner calls 'official revelation', any interpretation of our history in terms of salvation remains uncertain and ambivalent, on the one hand because man can never exhaustively see through his free actions ('reflect through' them), and on the other hand because salvation is dependent on a gift of God, on a grace which must also be explained as an inner transformation of the structure of human consciousness. What is changed through God's grace is in the first place the *'a-priori* formal horizon within which the intellectual life of man is enacted'.[95]

Thus the history of salvation appears as the hidden dimension of all history and to this degree coincides with the whole of secular history. However, this dimension can only be recognized within a particular salvation history which Rahner calls *'official* salvation history',[96] 'the history constituted by the Word of God which interprets and reveals'. This interpretation and revelation does not happen everywhere, but only in Israel and in the history of God's church community initiated by Jesus Christ. Rahner's views and those of Pannenberg (who develops his approach in confrontation with that of Rahner) have points of contact in many places: the religions interpret explicitly the hidden theme of salvation in universal human history. However, for Pannenberg these religious interpretations are not 'authoritative', but subject to a comparative rational analysis. For Rahner, only the Judaeo-Christian interpretation is authoritative and definitive, eschatological, sealed by the Word of God. For that very reason Rahner also goes on to make a distinction between the 'open' interpretation of the Old Testament and the definitively valid interpretation of the New. For in the Tanach 'there was as yet no institution which could act as a final court of appeal endowed with an absolute discernment of spirits which could have distinguished on every occasion between genuine prophets, legitimate religious renewal and criticism, on the one hand, and false prophets and perverted developments on the other'.[97] This capacity for distinction is given only by the absolute and indissoluble unity between the divine and the human in the person of Jesus Christ. Thus according to Rahner, what is interpreted in the (Judaeo-)Christian tradition is fundamentally really also present in universal history and in the universal history of religion, but the distinguishing characteristic of 'official salvation history' (in Israel and in Christianity) lies in its *authoritative* interpretation which is based on the eschatological definitiveness of the mystery of Christ. Thus within salvation history (the history of mankind) a distinction develops between salvation history in the broader sense and salvation history in the narrower, concentrated sense. Thus here too we find the element of truth which appears in both Cullmann and Pannenberg: the saving meaning of history is not equally explicit and clear everywhere. True, the whole of history is concerned with man's salvation or damnation, but this salvation or damnation is not expressed equally explicitly in all fragments of our human history as the real object, theme and content of our historical experience. In Jesus Christ the final, definitive meaning of all human history comes to awareness. That gives the Christian movement centred on Jesus and its further history in the world a special salvation-historical character, even according to Rahner, again distinct from the *religious* history of mankind, which has no authoritative, infallible arbiters of interpretation. Definitive salvation from God in Jesus Christ nevertheless gives the history of Christian faith a special character of revelation and thus the realization of salvation.

(*d*) Like the other authors, Johann-Baptist Metz[98] begins from the fact that *history* is the place where a decision is made about man's salvation or damnation. But in the interpretations which are given he misses the question of what salvation history is compared to the history of condemnation. He is less concerned, at least directly, to make precise what 'a history of revelation' is in connection with world history and the history of religions. In view of mankind's history of suffering it is clear to him that one cannot identify 'history' and 'salvation history'. There is too little salvation in our history. Metz does not consider so much the relationship between history and salvation history as the statement that specific history is a history of suffering. He therefore seeks to contrast the term 'salvation history' with the disastrous history of suffering mankind and therefore with the emancipatory liberation movements. Although he does not say as much, his immediate conversation partner is the Marxist, the (neo-) liberal and the positivistic, modern *homo emancipator*: the modern process of emancipatory self-liberation, whether in Marxist, neo-Marxist, liberal or neo-positivistic, 'technocratic' perspectives. In the light of the Christian view he wants to protect 'suffering man' in the face of these modern trends with their own conceptions of the future of man, and promise him a future. This *context* of Metz's thought also characterizes his theology, which as a result is 'regionalized' (as is any living theology).

For Metz, salvation history is not identical with human history (which contains too much disaster), any more than it is identical with the emancipating history of liberation which in so far as it seeks to be *total*, calls into being new histories of suffering.[99] Metz seeks a political outline of the future from the Christian eschatological remembrance of Jesus Christ[100] – a political outline that escapes the totalitarian tendencies which inherently threaten any Marxism; against the pragmatism and irrationality of any positivistic, liberal and neo-liberal political programme; against a future which could be created by technocrats.[101] So this theology clearly has a 'Western' colouring as a result of the choice of its implicit conversation partner. It is concerned with the question of how we understand 'freedom' and thus the liberation of men in a Western European context which has been governed by the Enlightenment. Here Metz does not attack the emancipatory history of freedom itself, but its positivistic and Marxist versions.

Metz emphatically stresses that the accent is not to be put on the *interpretation* of our existence, nor even on a 'value-free' and detached historical criticism. 'The essential dynamic of history . . . is accordingly the memory of suffering as a negative consciousness of future freedom and as a stimulus (with this freedom in our sights) to act to conquer suffering.'[102] However, for all the shift of accent, this is saying precisely the same thing as, for example, Pannenberg, when he talks of 'acting and suffering man', who is caught up in a struggle for human wholeness. However, Metz emphasizes that the history of suffering is not a transitory prehistory of mankind, but remains an intrinsic element of the history of freedom.[103] He is therefore concerned to express Christian faith in the resurrection in socially communicable symbols which have a critical and liberating force for us. 'The potential meaning of our history does not depend only on the survivors, the successful and those who make it.'[104] Metz calls total self-liberation through emancipation a 'historical Darwinism' in which the right of the strongest decides the future of our humanity.

Thus Metz opposes an attitude which can often be seen, in which a distinction is drawn between the history of suffering within the world and an other-worldly history of glory, and only in this way does he also reject the dichotomy between secular history and salvation history. World history itself must be made into salvation history. One cannot reconcile the two of them either speculatively or theoretically – nor, however, can they be formally contrasted. Therefore for Metz salvation history is in fact world history itself, in so far as in it salvation and meaning are found for the oppressed, rejected and suppressed expectations and the sufferings of humanity. Salvation history is 'that world history in which the vanquished and forgotten possibilities of human existence that we call "death" are allowed a meaning which is not recalled or cancelled by the future course of history'.[105]

Metz will not deny that our history is the place where the decision about salvation or disaster is made; so he is able to concede with Pannenberg and Rahner that salvation and damnation are brought about in the whole of our secular history. But he is not concerned with the theme 'salvation *or* damnation' with which our history in fact coincides, but with the elements in this history in which salvation is in fact realized;

only this history is salvation history and thus the history of revelation. Though in a quite different and even contrary context, he in fact sees salvation history *in reality* as a thin thread in our universal history which is salvation history only where salvation is realized in concrete terms. He is not concerned to give a theoretical and thematic account of history as the place where salvation or damnation are realized – that is quite evident – but to discuss the *realization* of salvation in this history: universal salvation for all, both living and dead.

Along with the whole Christian tradition, Metz affirms that God in his eschatological freedom is the universal subject and the meaning of history, and he goes on to conclude from this that consequently there is no universal subject of history which can be *identified politically* or *demonstrated socially.*[106] So where a party, a group, a race, a nation, a class, a group of technocrats, etc. attempts to define itself as this universal subject of history, a Christian will oppose it as an alienating political ideology.

Therefore Metz says that, in the light of the eschatological remembrance of the God of Jesus Christ, who suffered and died, yet rose again, political life (*a*) is 'set free', furthermore (*b*) it is protected against the dangers of totalitarianism, without, however, (*c*) becoming directionless (and therefore pragmatic). For this memory anticipates a quite *definite* future, a future which above all is a future for the desperate, the conquered, the victims, men without hope which is grounded in humanity. This is a future which must be created through solidarity with the weaker and the weakest among us.

Metz does not say what he means by 'salvation'; he does, however, repeatedly guard himself against the reduction of human suffering to socio-economic, political suffering. Furthermore he says that eschatological suffering cannot be derived from our political and social suffering. Above all in his fundamental article 'Redemption and Emancipation' (which in my view is the best expression of Metz's current theological thinking – though the construction of it is not at all easy to follow), Metz has posed the question whether there is a connection between 'salvation' (redemption) and 'history' in which (*a*) salvation and the history of suffering are not reconciled in a theoretical and rational way, and (*b*) the non-identity, i.e. the real negativity of suffering, is not denied, and (*c*) redemption or salvation is not seen solely in eschatological terms (without tangible realization in our history) and therefore is not reduced to a matter of sheer inwardness, and (*d*) redemption and salvation history are not juxtaposed unhistorically as a paradox. I think that these four questions are in fact fundamental to the present question of salvation. Metz himself sees the solution of this question of connection as lying in the narrative depth-structure of truly liberating critical reason. That means that the connection cannot be made rationally, i.e. theoretically or by argument, but exclusively through a narrative remembrance of the redemption by God in Jesus Christ. This history, as expressed in the non-identity or finitude of our clouded history of suffering, has a critical and productive force which prompts action. For Metz, this reference to narrative is not a lapse into the pre-critical period before the Enlightenment, because respect for the authority of the suffering man is part of the structure of liberating critical reason. In other words, for critical human reason to forget past suffering would be the beginning of its march into barbarism. Critical rationality is immanent in living history (not the historical sciences). Metz is therefore not concerned to present a vision of total liberation, but at the same time to provide a narrative remembrance of a very specific event: of someone who gives the future, who humanly speaking did not have the prospect of any future: Jesus Christ, who died and yet rose again.

Metz's political theology has been subjected to a good deal of criticism, in my view often unjustly, because his particular perspective and purpose has been overlooked. Moreover, Metz has put forward his views in increasingly precise stages, in which each preceding stage has been carefully shaped. One cannot object to this presentation of a vision in the making. However, I believe that Metz breaks off his reflections on the relationship between salvation history and the emancipatory history of freedom too abruptly with a reference to the communication of the narrative of the history of human suffering. He says that Christian redemption is not the transcendental aspect of the human history of freedom, any more than this is the immanence of Christian redemption. However, we do not really hear whether there is in fact a *positive* connection between the two stories. Nevertheless, along with many others Metz rightly and decisively rejects the dualism between our history and eschatological salvation. The decisive question, though, is whether the connection between the two is sufficiently articulated for one to be able to point exclusively to the history of human suffering. I myself am extremely sensitive to the history of human suffering – otherwise the whole programme of this Part Four would make no sense! But however barbaric it may seem, suffering is not the résumé of the life of every individual; even Metz will not deny that. It is, however, a brutal reality, a scandal, which moreover cannot be fitted into any theory and against which even a total way of life must come to grief, so that here at least suffering has the last word. At all events, this much must be conceded to Metz. He thinks – and I believe rightly – that non-religious emancipation movements either neglect this fact or sometimes cynically leave it out of account. It is the great merit of Metz's theology that he has remembered to take critical account of zones of human suffering which emancipatory freedom movements tend to ignore. Granted, the so-called 'warm stream' in Marxism, for example, also considers this specific problem, but one will hardly find the official Marxist reaction prepared to take account of this aspect of human life. Metz's purpose was precisely to draw attention to this. However, in my view he has not brought out sufficiently the positive connection between what is achieved in the experience of meaning and above all the changing of meaning, for good, in the history of human freedom, and has paid too little attention to eschatological salvation. In that case, however, the question in fact arises as to whether the narration of histories of suffering has this exclusive function of communication. Or, to put it rather better, the question is whether Metz has made an adequate analysis of their critical and productive force (which he accepts), down to the strategies which they require of us. Insofar as it relates to the histories of human suffering, his *memoria* thesis is above all inspired by philosophy (H. Marcuse, T. Adorno and finally, above all, Walter Benjamin – which is no bad thing in itself), whereas his reference to the story of the resurrection of course has a Christian, religious significance. But what I miss in Metz is a really *theological* consideration of the *memoria* thesis. Metz does not reflect on the concept of God as he is understood in the light of Jesus, as a God of pure positivity, as the author of good and enemy of evil. And this concept of God must colour what is in itself a correct theory of the narrative communication of the history of human suffering in a special way which Metz does not analyse.

Furthermore, Metz *seems to conclude from* the Christian recognition that God is the subject and the universal meaning of history that it is impossible for mankind or a group in it to be the subject of all history. I agree with this latter point, but I do not see how it can be derived from the insight of faith that God is the Lord of history. The human insight that 'humanity' (which in itself is an abstraction: what we have again and again is a number of men who are still alive) cannot be the universal subject of all history, and that it is theoretically impossible for mankind to free itself totally (because of the lack of a 'self' which would have to be the subject), seems to me to be the context of human experience in which the *question of* God as the Lord and universal subject of history (as this question is answered in the religions) can be meaningfully put. Here Pannenberg's starting point seems to me to be more consistent: *because* there is no 'universal subject' of history which can be shown to exist historically in politics or society, Pannenberg looks in the given fact of religions for the significance of their statement that God is the sole Lord of history. Differing somewhat from Pannenberg, Metz rightly does not want to give a theoretical account of the question of the total meaning of human history, but rather (with a word borrowed from the Frankfurt school), writes 'in a practical and critical intention', and therefore as a means towards a particular way of life.

However, sometimes one can hardly avoid the impression that for Metz 'suffering man' becomes something like the universal subject of human history. In other words, his political theology seems to be to be unfinished, and insufficiently worked out.

(*e*) In a recent article, 'The Peace of God and the Peace of the World', H. Kuitert[107] has taken up the problem of the relationship between eschatological salvation and human history from quite a different perspective from that of the authors we have considered so far. His argument, which seems to me to be a correct one (see Part One: The Authority of New Experiences), is that salvation is also an *experiential* concept. This provides a positive connection between eschatological salvation and 'social, economic and political peace which has been and needs to be built up by human effort'. The significant part of Kuitert's theory is his assertion that the Christian concept of salvation loses its rational significance, i.e. that it cannot be any rational concept of *salvation*, if there is no *positive* relationship between (to put it biblically) 'justification through faith alone' and the 'peace of the world'. He, too, begins from the Christian assertion that definitive salvation from God is only to be found in Jesus Christ.

Briefly, his argument is as follows. Christian salvation must be experienced as salvation, at least by those whom it affects. Salvation is an experiential concept, and therefore it must reflect at least partially what man *experiences* as 'saving'. The experience of salvation as saving is part of the concept of salvation. That does not mean that salvation is 'everywhere and fully and completely a reality of experience', but it must at least 'partially and at least sometimes' be experienced specifically by those affected as saving. However, not everything that men pass off as their own salvation is in fact saving; thus salvation is in fact announced to us in the name of God. God and salvation are not exhausted by our particular experience. Thus in the Christian concept of salvation there is an 'upper limit', a more, and a 'lower limit', in the following sense. In an upward direction it is impossible to discover any limit to the Christian concept of salvation, but there is a lower limit: 'Christian salvation is at least *salvation*, and salvation must at least correspond to a series of conditions if we are not to let the word salvation – and thus Christian salvation – die the death of a thousand closer qualifications.'[108] As a result of this 'distinction' it remains possible that on the one hand God retains the freedom 'to be God', i.e. a reality which cannot be tied to our concepts of salvation, and that on the other hand man is given the freedom to be man, i.e. a living man 'with a right to speak in everything that is or is not regarded as salvation'.

Furthermore, salvation must be experienced as salvation not only by those affected; it must be experienced as saving by 'historical men of flesh and blood who are referred to their natural environment and one another to build up a living world in which they can exist as people'.[109] If we call this 'earthly salvation', that means making *real people* whole. This is where we have what Kuitert calls the 'lowest limit' of the Christian concept of salvation. True, Christian salvation is also more, but it must *at least be earthly salvation*, i.e. salvation for men. Thus Christian salvation is not just a matter of saving souls.

The third argument produced by Kuitert is that 'to be able to be called salvation, salvation must be universal and complete';[110] the salvation of one can no longer be the damnation of others. Here, above all, we come up against the social and political institutions which 'are determinative in regulating the life of individuals for their salvation or damnation'. The consequence is that as a minimal presupposition, 'salvation in the sense of that which makes "whole" needs social, economic and political institutions which do not make one group whole at the expense of others, but make all men "whole" '.[111] That should not mean that Christian salvation is *reduced* to the ordering of a good society, but that this is a presupposition to which the concept of salvation must correspond, 'if it is still to be called a concept of salvation'. There can therefore be no inner peace 'detached from a social and political context'. On the contrary, 'The peace of God which passes all understanding [Phil. 4.7] . . . in the circumstances at present obtaining consists of inner disquiet';[112] 'bourgeois salvation is congealed salvation'.[113] His conclusion is therefore, 'As the lowest level of what can be called salvation I would like to claim here that salvation cannot amount to anything without institutions which ensure that everything necessary for a rounded, healthy and livable life is distributed in such a way that it is not just particular groups which get a place in the sun and that all men have a share in what makes whole.'[114] Kuitert rightly concludes that unless these minimal presuppositions are included in *the concept of salvation*, there is no possibility of making a positive connection between eschatological salvation 'and human efforts to make peace between social groups, races and peoples'.[115]

The special feature of Kuitert's view is that he fills a gap in the considerations of many theologians (Metz included): he locates the connection between history and eschatological salvation in the experiential concept of 'salvation' itself and so can give a better and clearer explanation of the fundamental political relevance of Christian faith and eschatological salvation than many other writers. His purpose was not to describe the whole of Christian salvation: he was only concerned with its 'lowest limit'; 'Whatever Christians may want to say about salvation, if their views fall below this limit, they are putting forward an impossible concept of salvation (ranging from the meaningless to the downright suspect).'[116]

(*f*) We discover something about Latin American theology from G. Gutierrez-Merino, J. M. Bonino and many others. These theologians of liberation[117] were originally inspired by the Western, principally European theologies of hope and revolution, and above all by the social sciences which are being intensively pursued in Latin America. However, very soon the ideas about development conceived in the West began to cause resentment in Latin America. As a result of the development strategy of the great powers, the situation of the developing countries got worse than before and they became even more dependent. Reflection on this made even the Western 'liberation theologies' seem suspicious. All this produced a breeding ground for a distinctive Latin American theological contribution. It is striking here that these theologians are not as afraid of 'totalitarianism' as Western theology. At the Louvain Congress of 1976, in his uninhibited, bold evangelical style Gutierrez mocked our Western horror of totalitarianism. These theologians are just as aware as Western theologians that God is the Lord of history, but they want to express this by 'conscientizing' a people who have been made fatalistic through centuries of oppression and by making it clear to them that things can be otherwise. This awareness of itself brings the people into a pre-revolutionary state. The political and social struggle for economic and social independence from local, national, international and 'multinational' control becomes the starting-point for their theology, which is inspired by the Old Testament model of the exodus. Here Christ is the consummation of this Old Testament theology of liberation. Such theology is often fragmentary, and in the last few years it has been especially critical of the West. Because the 'conversation partner' of theology is not the atheist or the man of the Enlightenment, or even the Christian from another confession, but 'enslaved man', this liberation theology takes on a completely untraditional character, as a result of which it stands so to speak on the opposite side to ecclesiastical and ecumenical theology, alongside and by suffering man. As far as it is concerned, collaboration with socialists, real Marxists and Communists is not the subject of critical reflection; it is simply a matter of necessity and is taken for granted. They are not afraid of an analytical Marxist approach to the analysis of social structures. Although there are many features in common, every Latin American country is a continent in itself, so that the particular way in which a theology of liberation is worked out is very different in each case. However, it is striking that the Christian approach to liberation seeks to embrace both the mass and the '*élite*', and in this sense wants to make the whole of society the vehicle of the impulse to freedom (thereby seeking in fact, and in its approach, to avoid the Western – and Christian – reluctance to mention a single subject involved in the improvement of the world).

It could be said that in these theologies of liberation practice has a certain priority over theory, though there is constant reflection on the practice of liberation. In this theology in particular, theory is the reflective element of a living practice. This contrasts strongly with American and European theology, which, detached from the practice of the official churches, is building up a 'modern' theology, in vigorous conflict with the theology which is *practised* officially. The result of this is that to some extent it exists in a vacuum. These liberation theologians, on the other hand, are supported not only by the practice on which they reflect but also by living Christian communities with a pastoral commitment. This liberation theology may be different from earlier 'church theology', but it is more related to the church, 'more community-centred', than any Western theology today (with its markedly academic approach). It is the theory of living church communities, if still only to a limited degree.

Gutierrez in particular defines theology as 'a critical reflection on action' because faith is on the one hand an act of trust in God and at the same time a sacrifice for one's fellow man.[118] He expressly says that by this he means 'the theory of a *particular* practice', which is therefore essentially critical of the church and society. In the spirit of the Letter of James, he stresses a justification by faith which becomes effective in a historically situated loving sacrifice for fellow men. 'Theology *follows*; it is the second step.'[119] Theology must look for the presence of the Spirit which inspires Christians to their way of life in the pastoral activity of the community. The community of faith with its life, prayer, activity and preaching is the *locus theologicus*, i.e. the quarry for all theology. The special feature of the Latin American view of this general theological datum is that 'oppressed man' is the starting point for theological reflection. This theology sets out to read the gospel message of a liberating practice all over again. Church proclamation is a political proclamation of liberation. It also has this function for Metz, but here it is not supported on the basis of a living community for which Metz is the 'theoretical catalyst' – as Gutierrez is. Liberation theology is not a theory looking for a church practice which it hopes will follow, but is called to life by the practice of a living community in reflection on its life. Thus the theologian is less the vehicle or the subject of the theological tradition: that function is performed by the 'church community' itself, for which the theologian is only as it were the critical interpreter.

The 'continental' theologians also *say* all this (and Gutierrez above all is aware that he is inspired by them), but for them it is in fact untrue. They speak *performatively*: it must be like this – but in reality it is not. In Latin America, however, despite a number of tensions with the official church, it is a living reality. And despite a number of 'Western' suspicions, which in themselves are quite justified, this gives this theology a

credibility which the modern 'Western theologians' essentially lack –
despite their *de facto* connection with the church. In Latin American
political hermeneutics the grass-roots community has in fact itself increasingly become the real and active vehicle. Here the theologian is as it were
a critical and reflective helper who speaks a language which is more
prophetic than academic; he is a *priest* theologian, a phenomenon which
is disappearing in the West (though here too advances are being made
by pastoral theology, the layman or the priest, over against 'academic'
theology).

Generally speaking, contemporary Latin theology is opposed to 'freedom' after the model of our Western world, a freedom which served as
a model in the initial policy of development. It therefore does not want
to hear any more about 'development', but only about 'liberation' from
inhuman dependencies, a liberation which is within man's own
capabilities.

One objection which might perhaps be made against this theology is
that it is concerned almost exclusively with macro-ethical, i.e. social and
political problems, and not enough with the problems which arise from
human finitude and mortality, which are not overcome by any political
undertaking. But to do that is to look at the situation too much through
Western eyes. True, these aspects hardly ever become a theme of their
theology of liberation, but for good or ill the Latin American soul has
long since come to terms with that in a *religious* way. It does not see the
focal point as being there. Besides, the micro-ethical problems have been
misused often enough in order to keep the Latin American population in
ethical slavery. Any reproach from the side of the West is therefore purely
'theoretical': it says more about the problems of the West than about
those of Latin America. For them the most urgent problem is that the
Latin American position of dependence is in fact an integral part of the
development and prosperity of Western countries.

Thus the same problem emerges in Latin American liberation theology
which we have already encountered in Cullmann, Pannenberg, Rahner
and Metz (and in so many others): an attempt is made to give an answer
to the question of the relationship between our human history and salvation from God in Jesus Christ. It is the old problem of the relationship
of the kingdom of God to our historical future or to the building up of
our world in love and justice.

True, Latin American theology no longer sees the victory of the church
as the only history in which salvation is realized. With for example
Pannenberg and Rahner, it breaks through the identification of salvation
history with the particular history of the religions of revelation. Gutierrez
expressly states that 'history' and 'salvation history' cannot simply be
contrasted.[120] To be involved in the process of human liberation is itself

already salvation history. Gutierrez in particular makes a distinction
betweeen three related levels of liberation: political liberation, liberation
of man to become the 'new man' in the course of his history, and liberation
from sin through community with God.[121] Christian redemption is therefore economic, social and political liberation, the creation of a 'new man'
within the solidarity of a society, and liberation from sin through communion with God and fellowship with all men. The former can in fact be
realized by man himself (as a task of creation); the latter is God's merciful
grace, and both – political action and Christian faith – are connected by
'utopia'.[122] Despite the real difference in level, all this is comprised in the
one aim in life which man has, the realization of *human salvation*. For
example, Gutierrez says that emancipatory self-liberation is the immanence of Christian redemption – God's gift in Christ reaches us through
the historical means of our liberation of ourselves – but he corrects this
by saying that the kingdom of God is *not completely* and utterly realized in
our history of self-liberation. At all events, eschatological salvation is
partly realized *within* our human history. These Latin American theologians obviously find it less difficult to regard the various forms of human
liberation as a fragment of God's grace than their Western colleagues,
who are aware of the centuries-old polemic about the theme of 'nature
and grace' and the *special* gratuitousness of grace in the light of the gift
of creation. They do not know of the inauthentic dilemma of a decision
between God and man, above all because they confess Christ in the
human form of Jesus who showed his solidarity with the oppressed.[123]
For them, the relationship between 'historical future' and 'eschatological
future' is not as complicated as it is for academic theologians. True, these
latter nuances are not important, but the often somewhat carefree Latin
American statements express a profound religious intuition. If God is a
God who cares for men, then everything he gives men through the
mediation of fellow men for their good and for their humanity is in fact
a gift of God, aimed at man's *salvation*. One cannot limit God's grace to
a special inner sphere, isolated from social life, even given that such an
isolated sphere exists of all.[124] Essentially, the Christian hope embraces
a hope for a better, just and human society. Liberation and Christian
redemption are not alternatives. The eschatological future which does
not lie in man's hands is mediated through sacrifice for a more humane
and more just earthly future which can be realized on earth. Human
action in doing good and fighting evil is the concrete historical means
which leads to the coming of the kingdom of God. Therefore Gutierrez,
for example, uses the concept of 'liberation' as a synthesis for what
comprises redemption and self-liberation.

So far I have pointed to the positive aspects of the Latin American
theologies of liberation. They do, however, have their darker side. Grant-

ed, the criticism made by these theologians of Western European political theology and the theology of hope is becoming increasingly vigorous (J. M. Bonino even speaks of a neo-liberal and technocratic ideology in the context of the EEC, without however producing any texts to support his view),[125] but *from a theological point of view* I have not found anything very different in all this literature from what has been said more precisely by J.-B. Metz and J. Moltmann, whom it attacks so vigorously, even if the theologies of liberation in fact have a more prophetic and vivid stress. Furthermore, their Marxism does not have any really Latin American features; here too they simply repeat what we have long been aware of from Western Marxist literature. However, the application of this analysis to Latin American conditions has hardly begun. All this simply confirms the general position of dependence of Latin America, which they denounce so vigorously. Despite all the promise, I have to say that there is not yet a specifically Latin American theology in contrast to the other non-European theologies, like for example Black theology, which in fact has a stamp of its own. In the West in particular we must look forward to the distinctive face of a Latin American church and theology which has come of age.

## §3   Salvation from God, experienced through man and the world

*Introduction: the story of Jacob and Esau*

And Jacob was left alone. And a man wrestled with him until the breaking of the day. When the man saw that he did not prevail against Jacob, he touched the hollow of his thigh; and Jacob's thigh was put out of joint as he wrestled with him. Then he said, 'Let me go, for the day is breaking.' But Jacob said, 'I will not let you go, unless you bless me.' And he said to him, 'What is your name?' And he said, 'Jacob.' Then he said, 'Your name shall no more be called Jacob, but Israel, for you have striven with God and with men, and have prevailed.' Then Jacob asked him, 'Tell me, I pray, your name.' But he said, 'Why is it that you ask my name?' And there he blessed him. So Jacob called the name of the place Peniel, saying, 'For I have seen God face to face, and yet my life is preserved.' The sun rose upon him as he passed Penuel (Gen. 32. 24–31).

To understand this story properly we must put it in the context of the whole of the account in Genesis. After serving his uncle Laban for many years, Jacob is returning to his homeland (Gen. 31). There he is to meet once again his brother Esau, whom he has cheated of the firstborn's blessing. In the meanwhile he had done considerable penance for his action, but now that he is on the way to Esau the severity of his former misdemeanour strikes him: he has sinned against both Esau and God (Gen. 32.3, 16, 20f.). The closer the meeting looms, the more his tension grows. Jacob is afraid of the face-to-face encounter, so he delays. And first he sends messengers ahead to make the coming confrontation easier. But there is also an increasing tension in his relationship with God as he pursues his way. He now experiences the face-to-face confrontation with the cheated Esau as a direct confrontation with God. God uses the same tactics as Jacob. First, he too sends a messenger (32.1). So we have a double story, first the confrontation of Jacob with the messenger of God, culminating in Jacob's nocturnal struggle with the man of God (32.24) and the face-to-face meeting with Esau. What in fact takes place in a single event is explained in two stories. The reconciliation of two men has something to do with reconciliation with God and from God's side. Jacob will later say to Esau, 'For truly to see your face is like *seeing* the face of God, with such favour have you received me' (33.10). This verse combines the two stories into a unity; it is here that the pearl in this story which we have to look for will be found.

In the story of the struggle with God we are first told of the *religious* depth of the laborious attempt of the imminent reconciliation of Jacob with Esau as an event 'in itself'. Jacob carries on the struggle to the end and finds harmony with God and with himself. In his most personal confrontation with God he has shown that he can stand the test (32.28). Instead of Jacob, which means sycophant, he is now called Israel, the fighter with God, someone who has reconciled himself with God and himself in a laborious inner struggle.

Now that his relationship with God is in order, his relationship with man, with Esau, is put to the test. Now Jacob voluntarily goes to meet Esau personally (33.3), face to face, without sending any further messenger. Blessed even by the nameless man of God with whom he had struggled all night, he returns the gift of the divine blessing to Esau (33.11). After some hesitation from Esau and pressure from Jacob, Esau accepts the blessing, glad to see his brother again. And with a masterly play on words the Hebrew text makes Jacob say: 'For truly to see your face is like seeing the face of God, with such favour have you received me' (33.10). The word-play lies in 'look up to someone' and 'see the face of someone'. On that very same morning Jacob had looked on God and finally been allowed to see God's face; that is, in a personal confrontation he had reconciled himself with God as he now does with Esau in a personal meeting. In the mutual acceptance and confirmation of one another in the personal, conciliatory meeting of Jacob and Esau, God's countenance itself shines forth like a *radiant sun* which had risen in all its splendour after the nocturnal struggle, 'as soon as Jacob had passed Penuel' (32.31). God's own countenance shines on reconciled men like the sun. That is why Jacob called this place Penuel, that is, 'face of God', for 'I have seen God face to face, and yet my life is preserved' (32.30). Those who have been reconciled have a right to exist, a right to live. Reconciliation means life, being able to live. It makes our life, within our history of suffering and injustice, worth living.


I. EARTHLY SALVATION, AN INNER COMPONENT OF
CHRISTIAN REDEMPTION

### A. Christian identity is connected with human integrity or human wholeness

On a physical, psycho-somatic and social level, factors which condition human personal identity and culture, much can be done by men towards the healing of our humanity, but we are still constantly confronted with suffering man: suffering from love, suffering as a result of guilt, because of our finitude and mortality, suffering through failure and inadequacy, and finally suffering over the invisibility and hiddenness of God. No human techniques of healing and emancipating practices can ever remove or diminish this suffering. Many forms of liberation are possible, through emancipation, through the help of our fellow men, through medicine, and through social and political means, and these forms are even *enjoined* on men in the name of the Creator God. However, such victories over suffering, often blotting out the guilt of our human history, are essentially partial and limited. Furthermore, for millions of men who in the past or the present have already been excluded because they have died or have been martyred, have been snatched away by illness and killed in road accidents or earthquakes, and so on, any form of liberation, however successful, will come too late. And if salvation means *perfect* and *universal* wholeness, do we then no longer include these in our modern conception of salvation? Are they the chaff in our history that we throw away? In that case, what is the significance of the sacrifice which emancipatory human liberation requires for this ever 'coming' (surviving) generation, which is to live in a state of salvation (and that, too, is not without its problems)? For past generations, put in this form this is a fictitious beyond, just as for the oppressed of the Middle Ages the beyond was a real beyond, transcending all their misery. Therefore there is no true liberation unless these forms of suffering which are not accessible to human liberation are also overcome.

However, it seems to me to be a disastrous false conclusion to argue from this that God's salvation in Jesus is limited to this restricted sphere and that the rest is to be left to an emancipatory process of human liberation. Moreover, that would also go against the New Testament itself, which sees the two saving actions of Jesus, apart from his good news, in the healing of the sick and the liberation of men from the alien domination of demonic powers!

If emancipatory human liberation[126] is essentially partial, non-universal and moreover transitory (if only because death puts a stop to every emancipated life), this implies that the deepest expectations which are to be found at the beginning of the process of emancipation are doomed to remain unfulfilled. That should not prevent us from showing solidarity with human liberation movements, since for mortal men as such no greater achievement is possible than to collaborate in the partial success of our history and in the removal of causes of suffering, wherever this lies within our power. It is worth while recalling here the humanistic saying of a great Christian, Thomas Aquinas: *'Detrahere perfectioni creaturarum est detrahere perfectioni divinae virtutis'*,[127] 'to vitiate human (creaturely) self-realization is to vitiate the perfection of God's power'. That implies that hope based on human creativity must be taken up into the Christian hope which is founded on God's own saving creativity. The unity of creation and covenant has often been destroyed in Christian practice. The Creator himself is the redeemer and he emerges as God even in his redemptive activity; that is, he is essentially creative, and there is no rivalry between what he does and what we who have our foundation in him do ourselves.

Where human liberation is possible, it remains a universal human task in the name of the Creator God, the redeemer. There is nothing specifically religious or Christian in its programme and its strategy, in its analyses and its approach. However, Christians sometimes make the mistake of identifying *Christianity* with what is *specifically Christian*, and in so doing restrict the sphere of human life. In contrast to the understanding of religion which only emerged at a late stage in the West, in all religions religion implies the whole of life, not an individual sector but a particular disposition – a way of being – of human, personal, social and economic life. In the West, on the other hand, people often thought in dualistic terms: religion (church) and world, reason (philosophy, science) and faith (theology), church and state, etc. One might even say that in the last resort two kinds of faith are concentrated here: faith in reason and faith in God. The tendency of the West to see religion as one part of life may be said to be striking. It helps us to understand three Western tendencies: (*a*) *The correlative conception*: culture and religion belong together, whether because (as in the Middle Ages) they are both connected by a Christian theory (church life and secular life are held together in a single, meaningful, social model), legitimated by revelation (two jurisdictions with a single model), or whether (as at present) in the form of 'juxtaposition': the two spheres are linked by a secular theory. The church as an institutional sector is not officially concerned with politics, and the state regards the church's task as a meaningful one. (*b*) *The exclusive conception*: this can be found in a positive or a negative form. Positively: belief in reason and belief in God are in fact two forms of belief, each with its own constructive inspiration (from the time of the Enlightenment). Negatively: religion is rejected, with the denial that it has any constructive significance for humanity (especially since the English 'secularism' of the nineteenth century). (*c*) *The inclusive conception*: this too, has a positive and a negative form. Positively, there is 'Christian secularity', as a reaction to the correlative and exclusive trends. What in the West is called the secular world is also the concern of Christianity. In other words, in concepts which are derived from dualistic Western thought, people attempt to define religion in terms which have always been accepted in non-Christian religions: as a quality of the whole of life. But that led to the distinction between religion (non-Christian religions) and faith (faith in Jesus Christ). It was thought that one could be a Christian without being 'religious'. The rejection of religion in favour of faith turned into iconoclasm. The *profanum* no longer recalled the *fanum*. The specifically religious with its own symbols lost its power of integration in the fact of the 'derived' religious sphere (the whole of life) and thus became unconstructive. Life, robbed of this specifically religious element, is impoverished and itself becomes destructive.

These three trends of dualistic religious thought (church and world, each with its own two sub-divisions) are, however, more of a schematic account of official religious feeling in the West as it has taken shape in theology and church documents. However, that is by no means all of Christian religion in the West. Alongside this official stream with its tributaries there has always been particular popular religion. This shows in the West what religion actually is in the East and everywhere else: a principle for orientating life, a programme for life which gives coherence, unity and direction to the whole of human life, individual and collective, without dividing it into a secular and a religious sphere. Even in the West, the man with a truly religious life has never recognized the official division into a religious and a secular sphere of life in theory and above all in practice, despite all the official theories. Therefore what is really 'dual' thought in official Western religion seems to have more to do with specific structures of authority, which have almost led to a split between the religious people and the religious leaders (regardless of the particular function which I in fact assign to 'church leaders' in Christian faith). That means that in popular religion in particular, religion – albeit often uncritically – has the same function that it essentially has everywhere, namely of being the totalizing, integrating principle which gives meaning to the whole of human life in the world and in society. For that very reason, religion is specifically constructive, though at the same time it has a destructive possibility (precisely because as religion it embraces everything). Theological reflection therefore also has the task of casting a critical eye on popular religion, in which the division between the secular and the religious is in practice rejected. This popular religion contains significant models which, when subjected to the *discretio spirituum*, could give us a guide. For these different experiences of individuals and of sub-groups are elements of specific historical Christian religion. Thus the forms of Christian counter-culture which we can see arising at present outside the great Christian churches are a *locus theologicus* for theological reflection, in the same way as popular piety and the anti-history of the so-called heresies. The important thing is to distinguish between the use and the misuse of popular religion.

One might say that the three tendencies mentioned were representative of Western religion (despite the permanent counter-history of suppressed protests) until (1) the present counter-culture; (2) political theologies (in a new, more critical form) and (3) the thematic difference between the official teaching of the church and popular belief both in America and in Europe (sometimes under other forms) found an emphatic hearing everywhere and became the subject of public reflection. This threefold reaction against prevailing culture (in the world and in the church) in fact took place simultaneously in its earlier and still latent phase, then in its first explicit expressions and finally in its breakthrough in words and action. It all stems from dissatisfaction with the representative, prevailing culture, the vehicle and transmitters of which are above all the great institutions (state, church, university, etc.).

As a human reaction it is 'culturally' conditioned in the form of a demand for a new culture, a *counter-culture*. Here 'counter-' relates to the one-sided, representative, prevailing culture, and 'culture' again reveals that the concern is for an alternative culture – not an un-culture or a non-culture (which men will never succeed in achieving, anyway, because un-culture simply leads to a ghetto culture).

Now it is essential for Christianity oriented on the gospel that it should encounter any culture (even its own – and even the cultural expressions of its own content of faith and church organization) in the light of the eschatological proviso (implication of faith in Jesus as an eschatological event). However, it is precisely this proviso that has its own special influence on culture. In Christianity, which people rightly experience as a unity of the religious and the secular, there is nevertheless an essential tension between the specifically religious focal point which is expressed in appropriate symbols (and in so doing is an essential element in forming a church and, in this sense, even forming a particular culture, for every specifically human expression is of a cultural kind), and the so-called derived religious element (i.e. the whole life of man in the world and society), whereas the whole forms a single integrated life. This double aspect cannot be avoided.

Without being specifically Christian, an emancipatory process of liberation can still be essential for Christianity, i.e. it can be a specific and historically necessary form of Christian love, faith and hope. Indeed, at a particular historical moment it can be a criterion of Christian authenticity, namely as a historical form of one of the fundamental criteria of the Christian religion: love of men. Whatever feature of empirical Christianity contradicts the demands of collective and personal human liberation must therefore be rejected in the name of Christian faith itself. Furthermore, the (critical) solidarity of Christians with the emancipating process of liberation must not be made dependent on the real chances of Christian proclamation or evangelization. Even when the church itself has no use for it, it has the duty to espouse the cause of men deprived of their rights, to press for a minimum of human salvation.

### B. The alienating claim of a total self-liberation

The believer and the Christian may see the limits of such self-liberation *in principle*, but this is not to deny the Christian legitimacy of the process of emancipatory liberation. However, every believer will oppose in principle any totalitarian claim to emancipatory self-liberation. In view of men's transitoriness and the fact that 'as humanity' they can only be the *theme* and *not the universal subject* of history, total liberation is moreover, suspect and alienating for them, and at best only partial liberation. It limits and reduces humanity, and this *ipso facto* has an alienating effect. In contemporary situations, the impossibility of a total, universal and final liberation through emancipation is the context in which the *question* of the ultimate meaning of human life can be put. Thus a fundamental question-mark is set against the project of emancipation, a question-mark which goes with the dynamics of any historical process of emancipation. It is not a question of temporary limitations, but of impassable ones. In this situation there are no longer any alternatives apart from the *religious* answer: redemption or salvation from God.

Of course even non-believers must recognize the absoluteness of this basic question, but for them it is more in accord with human dignity to recognize its limitations with open eyes (when they do this), rather than exceeding them in the direction that they call the illusion of religion.

However, it is striking that this theory of life is put forward by people who 'fortuitously' live on this, the Western side of our world, where people enjoy the greatest prosperity and where there is abundant possibility to transform the experience that our history is a mixture of meaning and meaninglessness above all into personally meaningful experiences. 'Fortuitously' they do not live on the other side, where meaninglessness, slavery and suffering determine the existence of many people. In other words, one can ask whether such a project, which 'reconciles' itself with our history as a mixture of meaning and meaninglessness, of sorrow and happiness, adequately takes into account the *suffering of others*. Does it not remove an essential part of our real problem of suffering? The question then arises whether such a concept of life, whether deliberate or unconscious, is not an egotistical view of life. At all events, the human experience of the mixture of meaning and meaninglessness which makes up our life raises the question whether in the last resort we can trust life. Is not our history cause for lament? Is there any kind of total meaning? For to evade the question of meaning, redemption and total liberation is certainly not liberation. The history of human suffering, our human experience, compels us to put this question. The non-believer rejects the *religious* answer to this question because he see a projection in the answer: the wish as father to the thought. But he himself does not give any answer. The believer has the experience of religious affirmation, an interpretative experience. So in present circumstances the religious problem stands very urgently in the centre of the emancipatory process of self-liberation, as a liberating human impulse which can only lead to partial, non-universal and provisional results, and in the last result finds itself confronted not only with the failure of any liberation which seeks to be total and universal, but also with the *alienating* character of any claim to total liberation. Such a total project unleashes enslaving and irrational forces.

Therefore the history of emancipation *cannot be identified* with the history of redemption from God, nor can the latter be detached from human liberation. For salvation from God is always salvation *for men* with all that that implies for truly human life – given the anthropological constants. Here the fundamental problem remains the reality of the human history of suffering, which even *remains* firm in an allegedly successful process of emancipation and is not just an ingredient of the 'pre-history' of mankind before emancipation (an aspect to which J.-B. Metz in particular has rightly called attention). Salvation cannot therefore be found *outside* suffering. Emancipatory liberation outside a perspective on religious redemption therefore takes on problematical and dangerous dimensions because it becomes blind to real aspects of human life and in this way reduces men. The history of freedom *remains* a history of suffering. That is a reality of being human which is taken seriously by religious soteriologies. Christian redemption is something more than emancipatory liberation, though it shows critical solidarity towards that.

Mediaeval theology above all – especially Albertus Magnus, Bonaventura, Alexander of Hales and Thomas Aquinas – emphatically pointed out that man is a being who cannot realize his own nature, promise and future in a complete process of emancipation.[128] *Quo magis creatura, eo amplius indiget Deo*, 'the higher creatures mount the ladder of reality, the more they need God', the more urgent and basic becomes the need to realize the promise of their own being with the help of God's strength. Complete experience of the promise of our humanity is grounded in the free, overwhelming gift of grace. A man is fully and completely man thanks to the grace of God. Above all for Thomas, self-realization is adoption and appropriation of God's salvation by man, active acceptance of a divine gift: an 'encounter'. Precisely because God's grace is mediated, and goes through man and the world, man has the possibility to resist it. Through this mediation, what is communicated historically partakes of the ambiguity of all history and is therefore never infallibly and unequivocally compelling; it always remains possible for people not to recognize the divine invitation and not to follow it (this is the way in which I would adapt the 'Thomistic doctrine' of the inner efficacy of grace, which is in itself correct). We must now analyse the implications of these historical mediations.

## II. CHRISTIAN FAITH AND POLITICS

### A. *De facto* pluralism among Christians

Theories and assertions about the political and social relevance of belief in God and especially the Christian gospel are a focus of interest everywhere today. But the range of their political colourings is very wide.

Because of this relevance, on the one side we see new parties arising with confessional connections, and on the other hand many Christians are leaving these very confessional parties in order to be able to realize their Christian inspiration and orientation in progressive parties. On the ground of the self-same gospel, yet others call for an alliance with Marxist and socialist movements as the only correct and compelling consequence of Christianity ('Christians for socialism'). Furthermore, there is also a political Christianity, which defends the argument that because of its transcendence and orientation on the specifically religious, Christianity must stand above all politics – which in view of the existing antagonism in social policy is in fact unmistakably also a *political* decision. It is a decision in favour of those in power and those who have the greatest economic strength (though in particular circumstances such abstention can also be aimed at giving progressive forces a chance: for example, the fact that the present Spanish bishops left Christians free to decide how to vote – in December 1976 – in contrast to what happened under the Franco regime is clearly not a matter of apolitical indifference, but rather the expression of a democratic concern after so many years of dictatorship). Furthermore, there are Christians (especially among students of the psychology of religion, who since Rudolf Otto have reacted against a functionalist definition of religion) who deny religion any function (even political), and yet stress that *as a man* the believer has ethical and political obligations. The reaction expressed in this last view is rightly directed against the old ideal of a *humanitas christiana*, which is governed by what should be the 'Christian social teaching' of the church. People thought that they could and must make a particular Christian order in the world. At that time Christians really believed that they had a quite distinct *view of society* all their own, at which unaided human reason could not arrive. In the meanwhile this view has rightly been unmasked as ideology. We find a similar 'Christian politics' among fundamentalist Christians who derive their politics immediately from the Bible, using it as a blueprint for a political programme. However, the decisive question is whether the justified refusal in this approach does not throw out the baby with the bathwater, if the political relevance of *faith* (and not an ideological, specifically Christian social doctrine) is denied on the basis of the assertion that faith is *non-functional*.[129] For resistance against the reducing of the religious to a function can open the door to unrecognized and concealed ideological functionalizing on the part of some political and economic forces which are very interested in the theory that religion is not functional (and are often very ready to support this lack of function, sometimes even without being asked). To refuse to adopt a critical attitude to the *function* of religion in man and society very soon means that people allow what are quite rightly non-functional religious experiences to be annexed to the non-religious aims of the social order. (Because of their particular psychological perspective, which may even be justified, psychologists can soon become blind to other approaches.) Above all in the light of the Jewish Christian tradition, which in solidarity 'with the least of mine' (Matt. 25.40) sees brotherly love (inter-subjectively and through anonymous structures) not only as ethics but as a 'divine virtue' (*virtus theologalis*), we could and should listen to a warning here against general religious pyschological approaches in which religious experiences of the gift of grace are classed with experiences under LSD, as some recent literature (taking up from what has been called the 'religious revival') would have us believe (however, we should not be at all horrified at what are in fact striking psychological affinities).

Quite apart from Christian views about faith and politics, sociological studies about the way in which religion actually functions in the political sphere also come to different results. However, sociology is still a long way from being able to give a satisfactory theory about the function of religions in the creation of the future. Still, a wide range of empirical data cannot be denied. It emerges from this that the function of religion is essentially ambivalent for the life of a society. We see that religions serve both to legitimate given conditions and also to provide motivation for reforms and even for revolutions. Thus from a sociological and a historical point of view, religion favours two contrary attitudes. Furthermore, we see that again and again, when there are static periods in history, in which little or no need is felt for revolution or reform, the religious world also has little movement and shows no power to criticize or to change society. In times of social and political change, on the other hand, it is striking that alongside a large group of believers tied to the church, who continue to maintain its stability, there are also very active church communities which attack existing conditions because of their religious convictions and press for change. Particular social and political options often govern the way in which Christians understand the gospel, whereas on the other hand a particular interpretation of the gospel also serves as an orientation for political attitudes. Thus the relationship is dialectical. The actual function of religion is therefore not only ambivalent, but social and political conflicts are further sharpened through polarization and religious conflicts in the congregations.

This widespread pluralism even among Christians in respect of the relationship between faith and social politics says a great deal in itself. Thus the relevance of Christian faith for a social and political world order does not prove as clear and simple as all that. These various conceptions are connected both with the pluralism in Christian belief itself and also with the everyday experience that conservative and progressive social policies have a positive influence on human emotions, non-religious frames of reference and specific achievements, or act as a critical spur towards them.

In political questions, faith should not be allowed to play too large or too little a part. Furthermore, even a critical theologian, if he is not to exceed his competence, can only speak in very general terms. For a specific indication of the direction in which a social and human politics has to go in order to meet Christian requirements of the action asked of believers to achieve human salvation here and now is *communicated* through the non-theological analysis and interpretation of the very specific conditions in which we live. In this analysis and interpretation the theologian has no competence, at least as a theologian (in this respect being like any other Christian in a higher or lower position). Therefore I am somewhat sceptical about any Christian who believes *as a Christian* that he has a clear, concrete, specific programme for action (whether such people call themselves 'Christians for socialism' or CDA, CDU or Democrazia Cristiana). They have worked all kinds of non-Christian and non-theological factors into their particular programmes (and rightly so – there is nothing else they can do). However, the decisive question here is whether they present their final conclusions based on Christian and non-religious factors as *the* Christian solution. (That is all that matters.) As a Christian and a theologian – and therefore not as a politician – I know that I can only make general statements, but they are worth consideration by politicians. At all events, these theological reflections can already reveal a good deal of ideology, even among Christians.

### B. How far can religion have any specific effect in politics?

The essence of all criticism of religion, no matter what form it takes, is really that religion proclaims man's inability to achieve his own liberation and in the face of that promises that God will bring salvation, although religion will in fact only confirm man's inability to achieve his own salvation. In modern circumstances, Christians have often come to use this criticism for their own ends, by suddenly reinterpreting the Christian religion. They point to the stimulus it provides towards political emancipation and its relevance for liberation, although the past history of this religion can only show somewhat shoddy credentials (apart from the 'heretical' arguments, which were often suppressed).

First of all, we have to concede that it is a characteristic of the structure of the development of Christian faith that believers begin to catch a glimpse of significant new dimensions to their own Christian tradition, precisely as a result of the introduction of new stimuli from outside, stimuli which were in fact alien to their religion. At an earlier stage, these insights may have been suppressed or simply ignored because of the prevailing social system. The message of Jesus calls for freedom and love for each and every individual, without any exclusiveness. This can hardly be questioned historically. But the consequences of this message by no means revealed themselves automatically and all at once, but only gradually, in the ongoing history of developing human consciousness. Christian, critical solidarity with the emancipatory history of freedom[130] and a coalition of theology with critical social theories about humanity[131] can therefore become here and now a necessary demand of historically situated *caritas* or Christian love and theology – the need to create new traditions. But in that case we must investigate how far Christianity and theology here develop their *own* religious and critical force, and do not just repeat what human movements and critical theories have said already. Do they simply *take over* views which are alien to Christianity, though justified in Christian terms, or do they become aware of their own original Christian impulse precisely as a result of these views (and there is no harm in that)? We must raise the critical question whether contemporary theologies of hope, emancipation and liberation, all with Jesus Christ as their fundamental basis, do not again perform the function of stop-gaps – not in the old way, but with an eye for the on-going malfunctions of our particular personal, interpersonal and socio-political action. In other words, whether these modern Christian attempts might not represent a new *sacralization*, this time no longer of the *status quo*, but of the political demand for *change* – and even revolutionary change.

However, the key question is whether believers and non-believers do not in fact *do the same thing*, namely renew the world. Perhaps the believer is simply giving another *interpretation* of this common action which *qua* interpretation has no consequences for what is done. For religion cannot of itself make any contribution to a practice which is indifferent to *religious* or *non-religious* interpretations. It follows from this that the claim of a religion to perform a unique and irreducible service for the world becomes problematical and seriously ambiguous to the degree that this service is understood in terms of *non-religious* goals. And vice versa, the claim of religion to offer its *own* interpretation of the world becomes just as problematical and seriously ambiguous to the degree that this interpretation remains irrelevant for *action*. Thus when we have a course of action which is common to believers and non-believers, and moreover with different theoretical interpretations of the world, we have mistaken the particular critical impulse which issues from the religious consciousness. For religion is not an interpretation of the world which remains alien to practice, any more than it is a practice without any reference to a particular interpretation of man and the world. Therefore in reality we often have the following experience. To begin with, people talk of inspiration provided by the gospel which stimulates them towards solidarity with liberation movements (which are in fact socialist). In a second phase, people see more accurately the particular rationality of this emancipation. In a third phase, they recognize the priority of emancipation in their own rationality over the proclamation of the gospel; and in a last, fourth phase all this often ends up with the rejection of orientation on and inspiration from the gospel, as being irrelevant to liberation movements. This development, which can in fact often be noted,[132] indicates that – although it is in fact possible to misuse religion, for anything at all – religion is *not usable* by nature, for anything at all. God cannot be used as a means for human ends, any more than man can be used as a means for divine ends. Religion and mankind transcend the category of the usable and the functional – which does not prevent religion in this respect being 'highly functional' for the advancement of human dignity generally. For religions are not inner dispositions; they *bring salvation*. They bring *salvation for men*. Only if we recognize the particular critical and hermeneutical force and impulse of religion as religion, can religion (as inner fullness, implication and consequence) show a service to the world which is both *specifically religious* and *practically effective* in the world (in politics as well). If specifically religious interpretation-and-criticism is lost sight of, in other words, if religion is made to serve non-religious ends, then *either* religious means are offered as means for non-religious ends and in fact religion becomes magic, *or* religion is merely forced into the role of being a teacher and instructor in morality.[133] (At an earlier stage, this morality was seen primarily as individual ethics, but now it is the macro-ethics of political and social society.) In other words, if religion enters the service of tasks imposed *from outside*, say by economic, social or political needs, it degenerates into magic, or it is undermined and reduced to mere ethics (though here it must remember that its specifically religious interest can be maintained only *within* the five *other* anthropological constants which were analysed earlier). True, religion implies an ethically good attitude, but it cannot be reduced to ethics. The only difference from the earlier position would then be that the alien service of religion to the world formerly showed a right-wing and reactionary tendency, whereas now it follows a left-wing and revolutionary course. In both cases, then, we have forms and manifestations of an out-dated 'Constantinian theology'. In that case, the appeal to Christian faith is often to serve the ends of a right-wing or left-wing policy, or to benefit a shrivelled, faceless party of the centre; it is merely an alibi for the lack of *rational arguments*. Therefore theology must stress the *specifically religious* form of the criticism of man and society; religion can do a service to the world in this respect if theologians do not just repeat and duplicate what critical sociologists have already said (perhaps rightly), but draw on *an experience of the holy*. Religions seek to bear witness to the holy, to God; it is there that they find the legitimation for their language and action. In their *service to God*, religions are also a *service to men*. If not, what we have is no more than a mere idealistic duplication.[134] For when we speak of religious consciousness (and its special critical force), we are speaking of a particular form of human consciousness. And the question then is, 'What is the *religious* element in this consciousness?' In other words, we then ask what knowledge and what reality so determine our consciousness that this consciousness becomes a religious consciousness. And at the same time, that means: how are we to judge the reality of man and the world in the light of the religious consciousness? Religion is concerned not only with God, but also with the *totality*, the support and hope of which is God.

Religion judges man and the world in the light of its experience of the holy or the divine. Every religious statement about the holy is in fact a statement about man and his world, but in the sense that every religious statement about man and the world is in reality also a statement about the holy, about God. In other words, the religious understanding contains – as it were from the start – a particular, i.e. religious, understanding of the world and of man. The question of God cannot be separated from the question of the nature of man, which in the last resort must also have a religious determination, so that man can be wholly and completely man. Religion does in fact express the existence of man and the world, but as an ambiguous manifestation of the holy, and not otherwise (though this does not mean that we can reject non-religious talk about the same phenomena). For the believer, man in the world is the fundamental symbol of the holy, of God as the champion of all good and the opponent of all evil, and therefore a manifestation of God as grace and judgment. In order to be able to appear, the holy must always conceal itself in images: it reveals itself in a veiled form in such a way that the holy cannot be attained outside these manifestations, although it is never itself identical with these manifestations. Therefore there is a *necessary identity* between *manifestation* and *concealment*. Religion under the aspect of a religious understanding of man and the world is indebted to this structure for a particular religious symbolism which, despite its special character, again points to the historical reality of man in the world.

From this critical-hermeneutical relevance of the religious consciousness there emerges: (*a*) the impossibility for a believer in any way to idealize any particular form of the world – past, present or future – giving it the status of a healed or reconciled world. For everything is only a *manifestation* of God, and is never identical with the holy, as man's salvation. But (*b*) at the same time religion forbids any escapism, because for the believer everything, everywhere, can be a manifestation of the divine. Because of that, nothing can be underestimated: reality is never completely outside salvation, as long as God is still there. So religion opposes *any theory of identity*, any sacralizing or absolutizing of any politics, right-wing, left-wing or centre, although political action is at the same time a *manifestation* of God among us for the good of men: indeed, concealment and manifestation are identical. In other words, religion, even Christian faith, is politically relevant, in that it opposes a *complete identification* of human salvation with politics. God's proviso, which for men takes the form of an eschatological proviso, makes it impossible for the believer to absolutize politics. Christianity *desacralizes* politics. For if the ground of the possibility of all existence lies in God, and on the other hand our human existence is threatened, not only from outside (by nature, by fellow men and by society), but also most profoundly from within (through one's own permanent possibility of being able not to be), then salvation in the full sense of the word is possible only where man can entrust himself to the ground of the possibility of his existence, that is, to the renewal of life through the holy, which is veiled in this permanent crisis of existence. The critical consciousness peculiar to the religious consciousness knows the validity of everything secular, and at the same time its radical crisis. That makes it possible to turn to man and the world *without* divinizing the world or idealizing and making absolute any particular policy of liberation: it makes possible radical criticism of man and society and the furthering of their good *without* recourse to a dreamed-up state of salvation and without the fiction of a healed or reconciled world in the limits of our history: in past, present or future. Thus religion criticizes both the *status quo* and also the absolutizing of a mere political and social renewal which men must undergo whether they want to or not. Nevertheless, following the God who is concerned for humanity, it seeks to support and further *men who are concerned for men*, and therefore also structures which make this possible, support it and further it.

This criticism based on religion is in fact religion's contribution to the world, but it is a contribution in and through *service to God*. We shall have to keep this firmly in mind in subsequent analysis, if we want to be able to talk meaningfully in *theological* terms about human liberation and not repeat like Christian parrots (under the flag of theology) what people worth taking seriously have said long before.

C. The political ineffectiveness of a purely formal 'eschatological proviso'

If we were only to take account of God's proviso, without also considering the specific *content* of belief in God, above all Christian belief in God, oriented on Jesus of Nazareth, the eschatological proviso could have a very reactionary function, to man's detriment. For God's proviso lies over all our human history and over everything that man brings to fruition in it. All political options are made relative by it. But that also means that if this real aspect of the revelation of God is taken *in isolation*, without considering what has come about for us in Jesus, this eschatological proviso can relativize any secular activity in such a way that both a conservative policy and a socialist policy demanding more justice for all can be neutralized *in the same way*. In that case Christian faith would not only desacralize politics and rob it of the threat that it might become absolute – which is the special justification and significance of the eschatological proviso or the freedom of God's divinity – but of itself it would not be able to give any inspiration, still less any orientation (pointing in one *particular* direction) in the choice of a social and economic policy to further growing humanity and a realizable state of human well-being. In that case God could just as well appear as 'salvation' in the sustaining and renewal of the human world as in its suffering, its servitude and its decline. It would make no difference. In that case the true Christian confession, which can in fact give decline, failure and suffering the form of salvation for the believer (who looks up to the cross of Christ), can be a sign of the silent presence of God; and in that case it can in fact be misused politically to establish and continue actual oppression. A merely formal use of the eschatological proviso would simply throttle the humanitarian impulse which is present in liberation movements, whereas at the same time by keeping silent one obviously cannot use God's proviso against the *status quo*. That, then, is the political consequence (and tacitly also the intention) of an appeal to the eschatological proviso in connection with political questions.

Thus the *content* of the confession of God also determines the particular action of Christians in this world. If one in fact begins from the way in which in primitive religions and in some others God is the ground and origin both of all positivity and also of all negativity – a God who kills and makes alive – then religion has no critical and productive contributions to make towards action for man's salvation on a personal, physical, medical, economic, social level – and so on. Human life and history are in fact ambiguous, ambivalent, so that they seldom say convincingly enough what is on the side of life and what is on the side of destruction, death and decline. But ambiguity is not the same thing as neutrality. If justice and injustice, joy and sorrow, equally have their ground and their source in God, it would be vain and meaningless for a believer to want to alter them. But precisely because of the particular critical and cognitive force of human experiences of suffering, many true believers would reject such a concept of God. Such a concept of God implies that 'God willed these conditions', that he willed to hold together both masters and servants, oppressors and oppressed, and the family of the holy hierarchy in the universe by means of commands and obedience. At all events, it emerges from this that religion *always* has political relevance. This relevance, wherever it may be, is not a matter for discussion. The only decisive question is: *what* political relevance does religion accord itself; i.e., which social and humanitarian policies will it support and which will it oppose?

But the God of Christians is 'not a God of the dead, but of the living' (Matt. 22.32). In other words, *this* concept of God assigns positivity simply and solely to God. 'God is love' (I John 4.8, 16); by nature he promotes the good and opposes all evil. And in that case, for the believer who seeks to follow God, the only orientation for action can be to further the good and to oppose evil, injustice and suffering in all its forms. This conception of God, which is not given to us as the result of a universal concept of God as found in the history of religions, but appears from and in Jesus of Nazareth, communicates to the Christian a quite definite orientation for action within what I have called the seven anthropological constants. In this framework he has the obligation, in faith, to further what is good and true for a realization of humanity; to fight energetically against everything which vitiates man's physical life, burdens his psychological life, humiliates him as a person, enslaves him through social structures, drives him into an irresponsible adventure through irrationality, makes the free exercise of his religious feeling impossible; and finally, to oppose everything which infringes human rights and reifies men as a result of their working conditions and the bureaucracy which shapes them. This productive and critical impulse, stemming from Christian belief in God, directed towards both activity which contributes to man's salvation and a well-determined political course of action for a better future for mankind, does not in fact neutralize the eschatological proviso. That continues to remain critical and productive, because mankind is not the subject of a 'universal providence'; and even then illusions, disappointments and failures, despite all the sacrifices and all the resistance, can in the last resort still be entrusted to God, the sole subject of universal providence. God's proviso reveals itself in the fact that humanity itself is not the subject of universal history and that its temporal providence is transcended by the Lord of history. In that case, this eschatological proviso, which therefore in no way neutralizes, but desacralizes and radicalizes the manifold human concern for the future of a true, good and happy humanity in the best possible social structures, is at the same time a basic criticism of all presumptions to identify salvation exclusively in specific terms. Salvation cannot be identified exclusively with political liberation; exclusively with 'being nice to one another'; exclusively with ecological efforts; exclusively with identifying oneself either with micro-ethics or macro-ethics or with mysticism, liturgy and prayer; exclusively with concerning oneself with education or geriatric techniques, and so on. *All this* is part of the concept of the *salvation* or *wholeness* of mankind, and is therefore also essentially concerned with salvation from God, which may be experienced as grace.

### D. The Christian and his choice of a political party

I have already pointed out that the future of our humanity, given the state of our present awareness of the problem, is also dependent on a political projection of the future in which believers are inspired by their experience of God as the champion of good and the opponent of evil and suffering, and Christians in particular by the concept of God which has taken tangible form in Jesus Christ.

Christian hope is not to be contrasted with prognosis, planning and political projections of the future, but with despair and defeatism. Christian hope incorporates the human activity of political involvement, but in so doing it issues in mystery. All in all, history and its total meaning is a mystery, so that the future also has hidden features which cannot be controlled. The foundation, origin and meaning of mankind is the living God, the Lord of history, a history which is nevertheless concerned with the salvation, the well-being and the happiness of mankind. The choice of a political party is therefore in some way connected with the Christian hope for man's salvation, because (as has already been said) a two-party system functioning in a truly democratic way is the minimal requirement (and the least of all evils), the first and basic presupposition for a social and political system which is to man's advantage. And in that case, believers and Christians are confronted with a specific choice.

Political theorists understand politics as the concern to give a predetermined form to future society through the exercise of power. Politics thus implies a reference to government, to the way in which it is formed and to its effect. Politicization can then be understood as the present-day increase in a conscious attempt to shape future society, 'on the one hand through the increasing degree of state control, and on the other by a similarly increasing attempt of citizens to influence the content and the formation of governments, along with an attempt to make the effectiveness of government much greater'.[135] From this perspective, in the political sphere of a democratic system and within a setting of social pluralism, the forming of political parties in fact amounts to a concentration of power, though this power – like any human rule – will have to be legitimated in the light of democratic criteria, by the politically liberating relevance of its content and the burden of suffering and oppression which it can impose on others.

Thus progressive politicizing is only possible where and insofar as there is an awareness that man can in fact himself shape future society through a political plan for the future; in other words, when people have become more aware that – to a certain and always relative degree – the future is also a product of human creativity, is a human work: the result of human prognosis, a political plan for the future and a specific form of planning. Only on the basis of this consciousness – which is new in history – is progressive politics possible.

It is worth noting at this point that progressive politics essentially involves a degree of scientific development within politics, at least in the sense that politics will have increasingly to fit in with science and technology, though without allowing itself to be governed by the primacy of science, technocracy and economics.

The political relevance of the Christian faith implies first of all that believers who live from the gospel must always have an active and constant concern for the integrity of the political sphere, a concern which they share with all men of good will. But above all and specifically it means that believers, as vehicles for the message of the gospel, have a prophetic and critical function in political questions, which encourages action. Because of their belief in the prophecy of a completely 'new earth and a new heaven' (the kingdom of God, that is, the community of God which has as its intrinsic consequence the *šalōm*, the peace and righteousness, the unity of all men), they will criticize any state already reached in a society which threatens to consolidate the injustices and disturbances in the system. In this sense believers criticize the social *status quo* to the degree that allows only as much new humanity and liberation to all as it thinks fit, in order to be able to ensure systematically and permanently that its own interests are safeguarded in new situations. Believers must make prophecy arising from the gospel into a prophetic-critical and ideological-critical force against the *polis* and its politics. Prophecy arising from the gospel requires all powers, governments and structures to become responsible for the suffering that they cause and for the oppression that they inflict on others. In its critical function, it is practical and critical, i.e. a prophetic criticism which serves as a spur to action.

It is essential for those convinced of the truth of the Christian faith to believe in the real possibility of a better future for all men in their personal and social dimensions; in a radically better future which, while being a gift of God, is *qua* gift at the same time a task, a task, now, to realize peace, justice and human unity in the historical dimensions of our social history. Belief in God radicalizes efforts for a better world. Christian belief in what is humanly impossible, namely a radically new improvement of the world, automatically drives Christians to quite specific political action. For conversion of the heart, on which Christian faith lays so much emphasis, is conditioned by the social structures in which human freedom is contained, and in turn the evil intentions of the human heart influence these structures. There is a *dialectical* relationship between conversion of the heart and the conversion of social structures, although even with the best possible structures the human heart can still cause disruption and injustice, and although even in unjust structures man personally can rise to the heights of human dignity. This latter does not exclude the fact that the ethical imperative to change unjust structures for the good remains a constant ethical and political demand, also inspired by the gospel message of liberation. In other words, the gospel inspires Christians to a *particular* political action.

Despite its social and political relevance, the gospel of Christian faith cannot of itself present us *directly* with a specific political programme of action. The impulse and inspiration, the degree of orientation (as a result of the exclusion of certain tendencies) which the gospel can provide for a political project, for the programming of political action and finally for political action itself, therefore runs dialectically, and indirectly: on the one hand, by means of experiences of contrast, and on the other, by the communication of a (scientific) *analysis* of social structures and their (hermeneutical) *interpretation*.

Scientific analysis and the interpretation of what is analysed are simply the necessary, time-conditioned continuation of social experiences. Therefore the impulse of the inspiration provided by the gospel is politically powerless and insignificant without the mediation of the analysis and the interpretation of these experiences and the society in which they originated. For in that case there is a vacuum between the demands of a politically relevant gospel of liberation and that for a specific definition of the content of political action. It is, however, significant that in the last resort it was not Christians who in their *caritas*, or Christian concern for fellow men, first and massively drew the attention of mankind to the institutional and personal suppression of the proletariat, although this concern is an intrinsic requirement of Christian *caritas*. True, then and earlier, Christians above all and almost exclusively did much to help the oppressed, at least with social therapy, as a result of their caring love for mankind; but they were not directly inspired to attack and change the structures themselves, the cause of this suffering. For this latter presupposes the insight that these structures can be changed, and this awareness in turn presupposes an analysis which shows that these particular structures had a historical origin, that they could have developed in a different way and that therefore they could have been changed. This fact clearly shows that in addition to its equally meaningful inter-personal effectiveness, Christian *caritas* is only fully efficient in contemporary conditions as a result of the mediation of political action. Only in this way does it become the specific imperative arising out of man's empirical experiences.

The conclusion seems compelling. Christian faith and its inspiration to *caritas* only becomes specifically relevant to politics, only becomes active when a historical *connection* is made between faith and political action through the analysis and interpretation of human experience and social structures (and thus also in the light of a political situation and forward-looking imagination in the planning of a programme for a coming society). The mediation of political imagination, a scientific analysis of time and society, and the interpretation of these and their ethos, is necessary to develop belief in the kingdom of God specifically on the level of human social and political history. Without this special, independent mediation, one only arrives at highly dangerous and naive false conclusions.

However, it should not be forgotten that the application of the apparatus of analysis is not a neutral undertaking. Whether consciously or not, there is already a political option between belief and the application of the techniques of analysis (or analysis itself). For the question is what one investigates, and to what ends. Is the intention to discover real freedom for all the power relationships which bring about conflict in our social contexts? Or is the intention to distil an abstract concept of 'common good' from social structures, thus by-passing the conflict situations and specific interests of some people, who must then submit to the so-called common good? (In reality the latter often simply means putting a different 'special interest' in the foreground under the guise of the 'general interest'.) In this instance a decision has in fact already been made before the analysis which, however, as such is not determined either by belief or by scientific analysis.

It emerges from all this that the immediate foundation of an effective policy is a *political programme for the future* which can be generally accepted by a large number of people. This political programme will make use of science and technology, without delivering itself up uncritically to the so-called (and falsely so-called) constraints and regularities of technological and economic processes.

The consequence is that the immediate foundation of a political programme for the future with priorities (hence, too, the formation of parties) cannot be Christian faith or a confession as such. In that case faith is not in fact the immediate basis of a particular policy, even if a party should be constituted on a confessional basis. For even in this case such a party will begin politically from criteria which are not derived immediately from the Christian religion as such; being a Christian cannot in itself then be a criterion for political decision. In that case, from a political and religious point of view there cannot really be any direct connection between the (confessional) party and Christian faith, or between this party and a particular social entity from which one draws members: Catholics or Christians (not Catholic faith or Christian faith), among whom there are unquestionably conflicts in economic interests!

As a *political* party, a confessional party has a historical right to exist only in situations in which a deficient political system does not allow particular citizens, namely Christians as state citizens, to enjoy their full rights; in other words, where the political system itself is already wrong. The so-called confessionalism of a political party is therefore never a matter of principle, but a question of historical opportunism. And there has in fact been occasion for this in the past. The basis for this whole argument remains the merely indirect and dialectical political relevance of the Christian faith and thus the necessity of the *mediation* of the analysis and interpretation of non-theological factors. The direct impetus for a specific political programme of action rests on the analysis (from a particular perspective) and interpretation of social structures. And even Christians will in fact come to different conclusions over the perspective and interpretation, as a foundation for political decision. One cannot build a political consensus directly on a religious consensus (except in fundamentalist and biblicist Christianity, which thinks that it can derive its programme for political action directly from the Bible). History also shows us that a political party whose political positions are based on a more or less agreed religious conviction can on the one hand sometimes be less inspired by Christianity as to its content than a non-confessional party, and – on the other hand is compelled often to show a certain restraint in its programme and its political practice because there is not in fact a political consensus among the Christians from whom such a party counts on recruiting its members. Anyone who wants to form a party which at least shows political unanimity over basic social and political questions (and thus can work effectively) will not gain members on the basis of an almost universal religious conviction, but on the basis of a *common political* conviction.

This brings me to a first conclusion. I regard the following formula for the moment as the most unobjectionable, both *theologically* and *politically*, on the one hand because it recognizes the political relevance of the Christian faith, and on the other because of the theological insight that this relevance is only of indirect political influence, namely through the communication of an analysis and interpretation of society, which in the last resort in many cases leads to a free and clear political option: *on the one hand*, a politically relevant or politically active *church* or community of faith which freely, without being tied to a political system or a political party, presents itself *qua* church as a critical consciousness of society and all its political parties from the point of view of both prophetic and ideological criticism; *on the other hand*, Christians combine with others who in common (fundamentally) share the same *political consensus*, in respect of a political programme for the future; in other words, Christians combine politically not on the basis of a Catholic or Christian conviction held more or less in common, but on the basis of a common political conviction.

The Second Vatican Council recognized the legitimacy of a political pluralism among Christians. In fact this was progress in comparison with the monolithic or uniform politics which had previously been imposed upon Christians. On the other hand, it carried with it the danger of political liberalism, as though Christians could think that any political option whatsoever was commensurate with Christian faith. However, it follows from Christian faith that certain political options (whether of the right wing or the left) can in fact be at odds with the gospel and that – if the general insight into the political relevance of faith is still to retain a real meaning – a *minimal consensus* in the *political* sphere is naturally a consequence of common belief in the gospel, which is good news of *liberation* for *all* (though this consensus of faith cannot form the basis for a confessional party unless it cannot be made effective in the specific sphere of politics in any other way). However, this free consensus cannot be enforced unilaterally from above and has to be fought for by a common effort. In the light of the gospel, therefore, through their specific political choice – even if this is through neutrality – Christians may not be party to a political system in which structural or personal compulsion sacrifices the weaker, and injustice becomes a permanent state. The Second Vatican Council clearly pointed in this direction in the Pastoral Constitution *Gaudium et Spes* (§§25–31; 34, 35). Christianity is essentially concerned with the progressive liberation of all men. In the light of the gospel, Christians must be partisans and advocates of the poor, those without rights, those who have no representatives anywhere. A political party which gives concrete expression to this aim in its programme will therefore be one of the first possible choices for Christians. The gospel summons the Christian to show solidarity with the historical process of human liberation; therefore he will give his vote for political parties which want to remove any discrimination and slavery, any personal or institutional exploitation from the world by means of a political programme for the future which responds to the situation without at the same time making men less than themselves. True, these comments are very general, but they do provide a first orientation.

A Christian who takes seriously the prophetic message of the gospel and its call for liberation can, however, discover some elements in particular parties which call themselves progressive that he cannot recognize as progressive. Or he can decide on other ways and means within the same progressive programme. For there can be different alternatives, and because of the nature of his Christian belief, the Christian can show a preference in deciding between alternatives (e.g. violence or non-violence). Finally, there is the view of man, the image of man, the answer to the question: 'For what kind of humanity am I deciding in the last resort?', 'What conception do people have of a good life?' Explicitly or implicitly, but unavoidably, the answer to this question takes shape in the specific social context of the society which man makes for himself. Thus a particular view of man can be a fundamental reason why Christians do not join a particular party which calls itself progressive. For a conscious or unconscious view of man always underlies the particular organization or articulation of a society and all its institutions, at any time. By analysing a particular society, one can in fact discover the image of man which serves as its model, and thus can unmask the limitations and constrictions of given social forms and institutions. This analytical and interpretative unveiling of an image of man which initially, at any rate, is often unconscious, and which underlies the divisions of wider social contexts, is even a necessary presupposition if we are to be able to transcend the limitations and constrictions of an established order with a view to a better future.

Now the picture of man which in fact exists, whether consciously or unconsciously, in a particular party-political programme for a future and in this sense progressive society can in fact seem to a progressive Christian to be no more than a torso, on which he does not really want to build a coming society. It is evident here that, after the analysis of social structures, fundamental differences can appear in their *interpretation* (as a basis for going beyond the *status quo* towards a better future). Anthropological conceptions and profiles of men play an essential role here. One example may be enough. For the Christian, man is not only a person, but is also essentially social; not only essentially social, but also an unassailable person. Therefore for him, as man and believer, both individualism and liberalism, and also totalitarianism, are unacceptable politically, even if they should appear in a more progressive form. Furthermore, man is not only a *homo oeconomicus* but also a *homo faber*; not only a *homo ludens* but also a thinker and researcher, *homo philosophicus* and a scientist; not only a *homo eroticus* but also a *homo contemplativus*, a *homo ethicus* and often also a *homo religiosus*, etc. Therefore it is in fact possible to give form to the torso of an image of man in a political party programme. The decisive question for Christians, as for the political ethos itself, is moreover which values are given priority in the programme: a priority not following an abstract scale of values from above downwards, but as a humane requirement posed by particular situations of human need (thus for example the need for somewhere to live can claim a high level of priority). Furthermore, it is also possible to 'functionalize' man completely, to reduce him to a future programme of scientific and technological planning, and simply to call this scientific technocracy progressive without being at all critical, when in fact one-dimensional technology represents a dangerous threat to our humanity.

I conclude from this that no one can responsibly claim on a Christian basis that as a Christian one must vote for this *particular party* to be consistent with the Christian gospel. I will not deny that particular circumstances can arise in which to vote in a particular way may be historically necessary in the light of the gospel; to give one example, as a Christian one can hardly vote for a party which propagates hatred against humanity and nihilism (along the lines of contemporary Satanist movements). Faith does not go with everything. Furthermore, contemporary assertions that the Marxist movement *must* be the one consistent choice of a Christian who is a supporter of the poor seem to me to be empty slogans which cannot be put forward on Christian grounds. Moreover, it is outdated critical sociology to claim that the Marxist analysis of society is the only instrument for analyses. As Christians, we do not need to become Marxists; and to call oneself a supporter of the poor does not amount to 'Marxism', any more than Marxism is the best way of giving specific form to one's solidarity with the poor and the oppressed. One can only say that Christians and Marxists have to learn from one another, and that we have to respect the honest decisions of others.

Because Christianity points to the necessity of a general and complete liberation, it can introduce a certain 'personalization' to the socialist struggle, and a resistance to hate, oppression and vengeance in this struggle. Christians can help to humanize this. The priest and Marxist Giulio Girardi says, 'Christians who decide for the revolutionary struggle often tend to stand on the extreme left. They no longer accuse the Communist party of being revolutionary, as they once did, but of being not revolutionary enough . . . One cannot deny the ambiguity which often lies in these hasty radicalizations, nor the ridicule to which men expose themselves who, on first becoming alive to the political dimension, think that they can give instruction in revolutionary purity to movements which have lived through a long and bitter experience.'[136] However, Marxism has also made Christians aware that the privatizing of religion has subjected them to the demands of society. Faith becomes 'ideological' when it is merely internalized, and thinks that it is then fully protected against science and political forces. It is certain that no one, not even the Christians, can ever decide for a party which corresponds fully to what he believes as a man and a believer in God to be true, good and happy humanity in the justest possible society. In that case one decides for a party which can present a mid-term programme in which the most pressing problems of man and society are given a juster and more humane solution for all, here and now, on the basis of *unselfish support* for those who are most oppressed. However, it is virtually impossible to find a party which does not describe itself as the supporter of violated and injured man! I spoke earlier of the need for a personalist and humanizing socialization. Of course this also includes a democratic socialization. But we can see how wherever socialism seeks to give itself a democratic and human face in countries where Communism prevails, any attempt in this direction is nipped in the bud. At the same time, in all honesty it must be said that wherever attempts are made to achieve 'capitalism with a human face', this is also destroyed by a variety of subversive means. This of itself already demythologizes the myth of 'subversive slogans'. For it can hardly be denied that the struggle for the *humanum* involves not only economic liberation from exploitation, but equally the democratization of all decisions in which the future of mankind is at stake. Realism requires that any socialization which limits human rights and freedoms already achieved (freedom of speech, freedom of the press, shared responsibility for political life and so on), even if these are not functioning as well as could be desired, can count on being resisted by any people who has once enjoyed these rights and freedoms. Socialism without personalism and democracy is an attack on the possibilities of realizing true humanity. At the same time, however, the call for freedom and democracy without socialism is in reality a disguised form of egotism and the expression of a requirement of free play for the profit motive. A Christian will therefore support those policies which in fact humanize economic conditions and for that very reason seek socialism for the advantage of all, while at the same time seeking to democratize social and political institutions. And democratization by no means coincides with a large degree of state control. True, 'humanity' is not the universal subject of history in general, but human history is made by men, and so they themselves must be the people, the subject of their own history, and not dictators on the right wing or the left, who think that they have grasped the truth. The fact that Christians are often confronted with political parties who to a greater or lesser degree neglect one of these two demands often makes it difficult for them to choose a particular party. A Christian will often be unable to feel at home in any one political party, though he will have to join a particular party because he is driven on by the idea of a humanizing, personalistic and democratic socialization.

In this context, a word ought to be said about the anti-Communist instinct, which for some people seems to be a characteristic of the specifically religious. It is a fact that the churches with all their institutions are an integral part of bourgeois society, with which they are linked by countless threads. The sociological 'law of institutions' is particularly clear at this point. In given historical conditions these churches can only continue to exist, economically, if in fact they borrow from this bourgeois society. In that case they become assimilated to prevailing political and economic systems. In this situation the possibility for development in any church institution, even if it means to be utterly in accordance with the gospel, is specifically dependent on the potentialities of late capitalism and is tied to those possibilities. That is a fact which is documented by the contributions made by capitalist sources towards so-called 'non-progressive' activities in the churches. The consequence of this situation is that it prevents these churches from speaking a liberating word at a time of crisis. Even if churches inwardly dissociate themselves from a system which makes the rich richer and the poor poorer, institutionally they are so tied up with the system that they have to keep their mouths shut. In order to be able to present their message, they have to keep quiet about this message! That is the vicious circle in this situation. In order to be able to continue to exist as a church, people keep silent about the demands of the gospel. Can the churches have forgotten that following Jesus can also cost them their lives? The primitive anti-Communism of many religious men (evidently there has to be a universal scapegoat somewhere) goes back to the same primal instincts of self-preservation: hang on to what one has. However, from a human point of view it seems to me to be just as much a basic feature of dogmatism as of primitive anti-Communism that 'anti-"anti-Communism" ' is here systematically defusing and ignoring the flagrant violation of social freedom and human rights by the Communist system. I reject any 'dogmatism', whether it comes from the right wing or the left or from any church.

However, I must concede that it is a double test for Christians if they are confronted with the fact that particular *Christian churches* have welcomed attacks on a government which seeks to introduce a humanizing socialization as *God's answer* to the prayer of many anti-Communist Christians, thus identifying mammon with the living God. This seems to me to be one of the most grisly examples of primitive anti-Communism. Such reactions call for counter-reactions, of which 'Christians for Socialism' is doubtless one. On the other hand, these people will have to remember that men cannot be *compelled* (except through a dictatorship) to juster economic conditions which are to the good of all. A dictatorship remains a dictatorship and is inhuman, even if it supports better economic conditions. I think that this was also the inner dilemma of the Enlightenment: can one compel people to emancipation and existence for others? To improve the world does not seem possible without an inner conversion! Perhaps here, too, the religions have an irreplaceable contribution of their own to make.

III.  ESCHATOLOGICAL OR FINAL, ALBEIT
UNDEFINABLE, SALVATION

### A.  God's glory is the salvation of the living man

*Gloria dei, vivens homo* (Irenaeus)

(*a*) The impossibility of defining man's complete salvation

It is a feature of the modern self-awareness of critical reason that despite its recognition of its own temporality and limitations it stresses its own value. Men see that their life in history is a mixture of meaning and meaninglessness and that there are limits to all human ethics. Among many people there is a growing consciousness that final meaning is either not yet given or still hidden or, as some believe, is simply not there at all.

Again, believers have arrived at the insight that social and political liberation 'is an integral part of salvation from God' (K. Rahner),[137] or a 'minimal presupposition' if we are to be able to speak of Christian salvation (H. Kuitert),[138] or that human liberation or 'healing must take place as a disclosure of a future horizon, if coming salvation is to be comprehensible at all' (J. Moltmann),[139] to mention theologians from three different confessions. These are signs of a growing awareness that theology cannot be built up on border-line cases, but must be constructed from the centre of human life, which manifests itself specifically as an emancipatory history of freedom. Believers who overlook this context in which we live are already exposed to the danger of standing in the way of human liberation and some of the present ways in which men are made whole: for fear that otherwise there would no longer be any area in which people could go on talking about salvation from God!

What earlier seemed to be only the interest of religious men is now the concern of a variety of humane sciences, technologies and activities: all strive for healing, making whole, or the salvation of man and his society. It cannot be denied that apart from the difference between faith and reason, the desire for a whole and livable humanity is more alive in humanity as a desire than at any other time, and that in our time the answer to it becomes all the more pressing the more we note on the one hand that people fail, fall short and are above all at a disadvantage, and on the other hand that we are already able to experience fragments of human healing and liberation. For the demand for healing and livable humanity is posed in particular situations of disintegration, alienation and all kinds of human violations. The *question of salvation*, the theme of all religions, is more than ever the great stimulus throughout the whole of present-day human existence, even explicitly outside religion. It is not just the religions that are an explicit thematization of general human salvation (*inter alia*, this is a qualification which has to be made to Pannenberg's basic thesis). The question of salvation is the great driving force in our present history, not only in a religious and theological context, but also thematically. It is becoming clear more than ever that human history is the place where the healing or the salvation of man will be decided, and people are now explicitly aware of this.

I said earlier that through and in the way in which they live, men themselves really confirm the nature of God where (whether or not they have a religious motivation) they further good and fight evil and suffering. For the believer's interpretation, God is the source and inspiration of all good and at the same time the origin of resistance against all forms of evil. Where good things are achieved to man's advantage – inter-subjectively and politically, within society – the believer sees salvation from God realized through man and the world. But divine freedom, the vehicle and source of human freedom, is not exhausted in our emancipatory history of freedom. On the one hand, finite freedom must leave God in his freedom, so that our concept of 'salvation' cannot be fixed on what we ourselves dream of and desire: it must remain open for the freedom of God which is surprising because it is absolute, and which in turn is familiar and 'a matter of course' to the religious man or the man who prays (even if it continually transcends his imaginings). On the other hand, for Christians this particular mode of divine freedom has become visible in Jesus Christ. As God's interpreter and one who practised a way of life commensurate with the kingdom of God, Jesus did not act from a well-defined concept of eschatological or final salvation. Rather, he saw a distant vision of final, perfect and universal salvation – the kingdom of God – *in and through* his own *fragmentary actions*, which were historical and thus limited or finite, 'going around doing good' through healing, liberating from demonic powers, and reconciliation. Understood in this way, Jesus did not live by a utopian, distant vision or by a consummation of all things in God which had already been brought about 'ideally', but he recognized in his specific action of doing good a practical anticipation of salvation to come. This confirms the *permanent validity* of any practice of doing good which is incomplete because it is historically limited.

Precisely because a perspective on final salvation comes to us only in historically broken situations of experiences of meaning or meaninglessness, the awareness of final salvation is provisionally a 'negative awareness'. However, this can be a powerful stimulus towards achieving meaning in our history. I pointed out earlier that both meaning already experienced and the experience of refractory meaninglessness have an emotional force which can direct actions and prove productive. Experiences of meaningless suffering have a critical force because of the disturbing possibility that they may be repeated in the future; experiences of meaning, of love and joy, are meaningful only because they may be possibly established in the future, which is not automatically a given. Conceptions of an unthreatened, final, perfect salvation applying to all are on the one hand to some degree formulated in a positive way because of partial experiences of meaning already undergone; on the other hand, however, within the real history of suffering within which we stand they can only be expressed negatively, in parables and visions: a world in which righteousness and love prevail, a world 'without tears'. However, our situation never allows us to define in positive terms what this will ultimately imply for human salvation, given the spiritual openness and the human 'self-transcendence' still to be realized in history and, moreover, in view of the absolute freedom of God as the 'God of men', a God whose glory lies in human happiness. Any positive definition runs the risk of either becoming megalomaniac in human terms or belittling God's possibilities. The Greek fathers in particular spoke of a *divinization* of man, in the sense of a gracious participation by man in God's own life.[139a] But this was simply another way of expressing the impossibility of defining the final future of human life in grace. For we do not have any term to describe the ultimate significance of our *humanity* which can be detached from our ongoing history, nor an appropriate unhistorical concept which means the Godness of God – as salvation for man. 'Divinization of man through grace' therefore simply expresses something positive and undefinable, that *God* is *the salvation of man*. Therefore the Old and New Testament say, 'These are the things of which scripture says, No eye has seen, no ear has heard, no man can imagine what God prepares for those who love him' (I Cor. 2.9; Isa. 64.3; 65.17b).

That does not in any way mean that final salvation will come upon us *from outside*, detached from and regardless of what men in fact make of it in their history. Eschatological or final salvation – let us call it heaven – takes shape (heavenly shape) from what men on earth achieve as salvation for their fellow man 'in brotherly love, which heeds the things that must abide for ever' (Heb. 13.1). We have biblical testimony to this effect: 'Come, O blessed of my Father, inherit the kingdom prepared for you from the foundation of the world; for I was hungry and you gave me food, I was thirsty and you gave me drink, I was a stranger and you welcomed me, I was naked and you clothed me, I was sick and you visited me, I was in prison and you came to me. . . Truly, I say to you, as you did it to one of the least of these my brethren, you did it to me' (Matt. 25.34–40). The Last Judgment is as 'atheistic' as that! However, there was a point in Thomas Aquinas calling love of neighbour a *virtus theologalis*, a 'divine virtue' (and not just ethics). It is to the human action of doing good that God gives an unexpected future in which his forgiveness plays a major role: 'He loved us (already) when we were still sinners' (Rom. 5.8). The fact that above all in Jewish-Christian spirituality the living God is witnessed to as merciful and ready to forgive, opens up a perspective of final salvation in which it would be presumptuous to attempt to provide a fixed and positive content. For in that case we run the risk of wanting to set limits to God's creative grace. Something of this undefinable mystery of God's mercy with our history is expressed in the practice of the Roman Catholic church which, while it has the courage to call exemplary brethren among us saints, happily does not venture to call any of the sons of men 'hellish' by name – not because no hellish things happen in our history, but because we men cannot fully fathom either human freedom or above all the freedom of the *creative* mercy of God. But that does not mean that we have to remain completely speechless about what happened to Jesus and what witness is borne to him through Christians. Faith in the risen Jesus gives us quite a *clear* perspective and not an indefinite one. Precisely here, the man Jesus is the revelation of what is possible with God.

## (*b*) Overcoming in death

The death of every individual puts radically in question the concept of human experience which is salvation *from man*. It seems to make complete and universal salvation impossible. From our point of view, any human salvation breaks off at death, which is the disintegration of every man. What ought to signify integration, unity and wholeness as the conclusion of human life is in reality the dissolution of a particular man in history. As a human event death is, to all appearances, the reduction of the individual to an element of society or history. But at the same time that marks the birth of human protest against the absurdity or 'the scandal' of death, above all and in particular with men who for justifiable reasons refuse to understand themselves, with name and surname, as a fleeting, personally insignificant and replaceable element in a history of meaning and meaninglessness. Nevertheless, the death of man is the exponent of his temporal corporeality.

The fact that Jesus became reconciled to this radical finitude, that in death he became reconciled with himself and with God, already makes it clear to us that within the limits of our history redemption can never be achieved by some heroic transcending of our finitude, but only in a readiness to refuse within our own limits, which can never be fulfilled in history, to accord evil the same rights as good. Therefore from a human point of view redemption essentially implies: reconciliation with one's own finitude, coupled with radical love, even when one sees that it is in vain, in terms of visible success, and is even an occasion for torture and execution. Evidently people only find their identity in losing themselves to others. However, men still find their own identity here – though this is not a motive for action (otherwise again the I – a person's own identity – and not identification with the suffering man, i.e. the transcending of the ego-centre, would be paramount). How is that?

Dorothee Sölle has rightly written: 'Jesus' love was radical in the sense that he was no longer concerned with the consequences for his own life.'[140] At precisely this point we see the critical barrenness of theological speculations which neglect the circumstances of Jesus' death and consider that death in and of itself, almost detached from the specific Jesus of Nazareth, then going on to ascribe to that death various world-embracing, universal saving meanings. It is when the message and life-style of Jesus which led to his death are neglected that people obscure the saving significance of that death. This happens above all when (as with Bultmann and others) the death of Jesus is seen as a tragic mistake, as a Jewish or Roman misunderstanding, and thus as a chance and regrettable combination of circumstances. Here this particular death in history is deprived of any saving significance and has to be given a meaning elaborated in mythical terms. The death of Jesus was no coincidence, but the intrinsic historical consequences of the radicalism of both his message and his life-style, which showed that all 'master-servant' relationships were incompatible with the life-style of the kingdom of God. The very radicalism of this proclamation as an intrinsic element in a consistent life-style provoked the fatal resistance of others. Seen in this way, the death of Jesus is the historical expression of the *unconditional* character of his proclamation and practice, in the face of which the significance of the almost disastrous consequences for his life fade right out of the picture. Jesus did not seek his own death, and he did not even want his passion – Gethsemane is a radical contradiction of that – but he identified himself so fully with his proclamation of a God who was concerned for mankind and with a life-style to match it that the disastrous consequences, as far as he was concerned, became unimportant to him. This radically universality of a will for salvation-for-all, without any exclusiveness, provoked the well-known and equally radical counter-reaction of 'this world'. At the end of his life, Jesus recognized the human, historical 'necessity' of this equally radical resistance to his message and his life-style. He assumed this human finitude, trusting in the non-finite God who has the last word. True, it is more than probable that the historical Jesus never *proclaimed* his death as a saving event, but in the dimension of our human history of suffering and injustice, *in these particular and specific circumstances* of his crucifixion, this death was an intrinsic consequence of his proclamation and life-style, which was more important to him than the saving of his life. Primitive, biblical Christianity therefore rightly expressed this inner consistency in the history of what in the gospels are called Jesus' predictions of the passion. Rightly, because in our human history of suffering and injustice this suffering and death are an indirect expression of the *unconditional* character of the proclamation of Jesus. Indirectly (in respect of our history of injustice), the unconditional character of the proclamation of a God concerned for man in fact became a proclamation of Jesus' own death!

In the life of Jesus, God's nearness shows itself to be *saving*, namely in the practical consequences of this nearness: the sick are healed, the lame walk, demonic powers are driven out (see Luke 7.22f.). In his goodness, God is also against evil and suffering. Where Jesus appears, salvation begins to live. His death was no historical accident. For him, the universality of the saving nearness of God was made present through a historical life of care for his fellow men, without exception, though also with a selfless championing of suffering men. Jesus was evidently little interested whether this suffering was the consequence of sin or was innocent suffering. He identified himself with the sufferer – *ṣaddīq* or not: neither piety nor lack of piety set any limits to his approach. Herein lies the universalism, without any exclusiveness, of his actual proclamation and practice (even when he limits this actual activity to the Jewish people). In his ministry, Jesus sees the suffering of others as his own task. The death of Jesus is the consequence of the incorruptible power of good: one either confesses oneself beaten by it *or* can only defend oneself against it by torturing such a man and putting him out of the way – an action by which his opponents testify indirectly, but in a very real way, to their own helplessness. That above all – even in the light of the Tanach – is the heart of the New Testament message: suffering through and for others as an expression of the *unconditional validity* of a pattern of doing good and resisting evil and suffering. Anyone who sets no limits to his sacrifice for the suffering of others will sooner or later have to pay with his life – even today. Jesus came to terms with this.

In Part Two I said that scripture interprets this way of life in various terms. There are many texts – including all the texts about the 'innocent sufferer' – in which it becomes clear that such a way of life has permanent validity *in and of itself*, and not just as the result of a later divine ratification. (This divine ratification is merely public recognition before the court of heavenly judgment, which discredits opponents, that the 'innocent sufferer' was always just and was 'Son of God' – see above.) In this sense the resurrection of Jesus does not provide ratification by correction of what has gone before, of what was still lacking from the earthly life of Jesus. In the resurrection of Jesus it becomes evident what Jesus was before and in his death. However, there are also texts in which the resurrection appears as a *divine corrective* of the *negativity* which is undeniable, above all in a violent death (even if this is – from Jesus' point of view – an expression of the unconditional character of his proclamation and way of life). 'By the *grace of God* Jesus died for all men' (Heb. 2.9). Philippians 2.9 puts it more strongly, calling God's exaltation of Jesus a *charis* or *grace* shown to Jesus by God (see above). In fact, if the resurrection (under the wider aspect which it embraces) is the manifest recognition of the permanent validity of what has come about in the specific act of crucifixion, this means that such an unconditional way of life which through the inexorability of history eventually leads to death (an 'inevitability' which leaves its stamp above all on Mark's account) has a permanent value *in and of itself* (for the whole of history), and not just as a subsequent ratification on the part of someone, even if this is on the part of God. In this former sense, belief in the resurrection is in fact a gospel *evaluation* of the life and death of Jesus: the recognition of the inner, irrevocable value of this proclamation and way of life which nothing can undo. It is belief in the irrevocability of all good, which men champion unrestrainedly, without taking any account of their own destiny. Thus the resurrection is an aspect of the unconditional character of Jesus' proclamation and the God who is concerned for man, an inner element of the specific historical career of Jesus in doing good (within the context of the historical conditions of the time), and at the same time the hidden side of the death of Jesus itself.

But this view is incomplete. *For whom* does such a crucifixion have definitive value as an intrinsic consequence of radical love? First of all, for all those who find in him inspiration and orientation for their actions in the equally finite and limited situation of their life. But as believers, can we leave *Jesus*, and above all *God*, out of this? Did Jesus simply introduce an ideal way of life involving boundless love, which can then as it were be detached from his person and continue to work as a ferment in our history? Without doubt that is also the case. And that is already to say a great deal. But if the nature of God's divinity has been revealed historically in Jesus' life, which involved a furthering of good and resistance against all forms of suffering, then the definitive validity of such a life (which evidently was not a roaring success) is in the first place valid *coram deo*, and not just as an inspiration and orientation for us men. God himself has the consummation of such a way of life very much to heart; it is his own being. 'God is love', says I John. The affirmation by God of the definitive validity of such an unconditional act of identification with the suffering of others is therefore divine, i.e. creative: the definitive validity of the person of Jesus himself. Resurrection is the continuation of the personal life of Jesus as a man beyond death. Not only is God 'ideally' called good: he is a God of man. God identifies himself with the person of Jesus, just as Jesus identified himself with God: 'God is love.'

## (c) Victory over death, the 'last enemy'

It is striking that wherever people talk of life after death this language always betrays a *religious* connection. Apart from some philosophies from the Renaissance and above all from the Enlightenment, when people thought that they could have life after death on purely anthropological foundations, the breeding ground of belief in life after death and thus in a certain victory over death was always seen in a communion of life between God and man. It was the same with the Greeks, for all their widely differing interpretations. Plato, who in fact took over his belief in immortality from Greek religion (*Phaedrus* 246d), maintains the (Greek) *religious* basis in his attempt to 'fortify' this belief rationally through philosophy. For him the spirituality of the soul is not in itself a foundation for a reasoned expectation of life after death; the essential factor is that the human soul 'participates in the *eternal* ideas' (*Phaedo* 78ff.).[140a] For Plato, communion with the eternally divine is the real basis of his conviction that there is a new life after death. Aristotle, who does not recognize this Platonic connection with the divine, and yet nevertheless affirms the spirituality of the soul, consistently argues that everything comes to a final end for man in death. This distinction between Plato and Aristotle compels reflection. The essence of the Greek argument is not *structurally* different from that of the Christian. The fundamental distinction from the Jewish-Christian tradition lies in the fact that the Christian does not see his living communion with God necessarily involved in the life of man; rather, it is the gracious happening of a free offer of saving communion presented on behalf of God, and a personal human decision through which one either accepts or rejects this offer, or puts it on one side out of lack of interest. The additional differences in the way in which people conceive of this life after death go back to differences between the Greek and the Judaeo-Christian image of man, above all to the different assessment which each has of human corporeality. Generally speaking, however, this is incidental (and in historical terms is often exaggerated). Living communion with God, attested as the meaning, the foundation and the inspiring content of human existence, is the only climate in which the believer's trust in a life after death comes, and evidently can come, to historical fruition (though this is not to deny that there are at least grounds in our personhood for human reason meaningfully to raise the question of a life after death). However, outside a *religious* perspective this possibility is rejected as ungrounded and meaningless, as a daydream: pure projection, which does not refer to anything because in fact the non-religious, human evidence of experience cannot offer any compelling proof for this perhaps desirable perspective. As far as I can see, there is no point in human history where one can see any kind of *non-religious* trust in a life after death, however this may be formulated (though in our time attempts are made in a scientific basis to say something about human 'survival' on the basis of so-called para-normal 'contacts with dead people', which are consequently regarded as a non-religious truth). For all its rationalism, even the Enlightenment's conception of immortality was still in a Christian tradition: Jean-Jacques Rousseau – and with him most of the representatives of the Enlightenment – maintained two fundamental religious convictions (albeit somewhat spasmodically): belief in God and in man's life after death.

The religious connection between a living communion with God and *life* after death indicates that the victory over death is never understood as any kind of human claim, but as a special gift of God. Such a conception of death is not purely anthropological, but has a religious foundation. It is concerned with a liberation, the opening up of a new sphere of life, through God: redemption from the negative; the gift of purely positive life.

However, this religious insight into the connection between living communion with God and life after death had a long history in Judaism. In a religious, and above all Jewish religious understanding of *life*, death is not merely a departure from the earthly sphere of life, a separation from close friends, and loved ones, but the end of everything and thus, by nature, a separation from God. It is the end of a living communion with God and, therein and consequently, of all inter-personal relations and enjoyment of creation.

However, as long as the individual man was thought to be taken up into the collective of the people of God, from a religious point of view death was nothing to worry about: individual men may have kept vanishing from the life of the people of God, but God's covenant, his communion with the people, was unchanging. The religious intuition into the unbreakable bond between communion with God and 'survival' remained intact. But from the moment when the awareness of personal individuality in a social context became noticeably denser, also as a result of a variety of historical circumstances, for believers death – which in religious terms was experienced above all as separation from God – was a bitter event beyond the bounds of comprehension: loss of God, the centre of religious life, the foundation, the source and the motive of their responsive conduct. For those who truly believed in Yahweh this was a tormenting, intolerable notion. Indeed, in the long run it was absurd. This utter finality of death, above all for the individual – for that is what it is in human (non-religious) experience – cannot be accepted by those who 'live with God'. As a result of a turbulent history, this gave rise, in Jewish religious traditions some centuries before Christ, to the belief that despite death, those who were faithful to Yahweh were in the hand of God. Some psalmists passionately expressed this trust in their God after the exile as a religious 'nevertheless' against the radical character of death (Pss. 49.15; 73. 24–26). Later, in some circles, this trust became faith in a personal resurrection at the end of time, and in other Jewish circles a faith in a personal acceptance by God, in some circumstances or others. The *religious* basis is always the same, but the *anthropological* picture of man can differ. The critical impulse in all these religious intuitions, which was directed against death, was that even death cannot destroy true, living communion with the living God: the kingdom of the dead does not have the last word about our history. Life with God is stronger than death.

This attractive and firm trust was given a new and unexpected confirmation in Christianity on the basis of the resurrection of Jesus from the dead. Insofar as the resurrection of Jesus is God's yes to the person and the life of Jesus, God approves of Jesus' fulfilment in his death of love for God and man. Insofar as the resurrection is God's corrective to the negative of death, God gives Jesus a renewed and exalted life.

It became clear to Christians through faith in the risen Jesus that the death of Jesus had no power to separate this Jesus from his God. The living earthly communion of Jesus of Nazareth with his God was even 'endorsed' by this God, and in this way the fellowship between Jesus and God which already existed was extended even beyond the bounds of death. In Jesus, God makes the negativity of this and any death into a permanent and perfect living communion with him. Even beyond death, Jesus lives among us from God in a new way. His communication with man is thus restored in a very real way, difficult though it is to describe. In essence, Christians say: over and above death there is a living communion with God and therefore also with men (*communion sanctorum*) in a completely new way – which may also be the specific fulfilment of this new life.

It can hardly be denied that from this perspective of faith death takes on a different meaning from that which it has on the evidence of nonreligious human experience. This is not denied in any way: in and of itself, death, even for Christians, remains impenetrable. No sense can be made of it either theoretically or in practice. Here the Christian will even be able to respect those who do not put the question of total meaning or, if they do put it, find it impossible to answer; consequently, fully aware of partial failure and partial success, they will look for partial and responsible solutions for human life and claim that with these they can live meaningfully and even die happy, without any further perspective, at least in personal terms. Outside a religious view of life, anthropologically speaking it is hardly possible to say anything more meaningful. However, to this the Christian adds that all this evidence, which also applies to him, is not the last word about death. It is contradicted by his experience, and above all his religious communion with God. Through the death of Jesus, seen in the light of his resurrection, the Christian has the assurance that suffering and death cannot separate him from God. And in that case, death – his death – takes on new meaning for him, even though he cannot in any way understand why a man 'has to die'. He does not make light of suffering; in that he shows solidarity with all his fellow men.

Here human experience is confronted not with an ungrounded, or at least unverifiable theory, but with experience *over against* 'experience', non-religious human experience over against human experience. On both sides people can and must judge these different experiences in accordance with their implications, consequences and functions in personal and social life. The Christian can only say to others, 'Look! This is the way in which I see it, in the spirit of the great Christian tradition in which I stand and want to stand: judge me by the way in which I live!'

If it is consistent, the Christian understanding of resurrection from the dead exercises a powerful force. Here the source of hope for a life after death is not a flight from the present; the source of every gaze towards this future is life *today*, in fellowship with God. Hope for life after death does not lure men away from the present: the *religious* depth of the present is in fact the only thing that can offer grounds for this expectation. One can understand how in former times this hope has lured believers away from their present, especially in periods when many people no longer had any worthwhile present nor any expectation of better times, and were therefore left with little more than trust in God, and, in this trust, a longing for an ultimately better future. (In such situations of helplessness the Christian hope acts as a kind of human healing.) In modern conditions, on the other hand, reference of belief in the resurrection to the present obviously takes on other historical forms. For what is done in the present is what will be confirmed by God on the other side of death because of its intrinsic goodness, or cannot be confirmed by him because of its inhumanity: sacrifice for fellow men, for our history (in the changeable expressions and conditions of our awareness of a particular contemporary problem), in living communion with God, witnessed to as the Lord of history. Belief in the resurrection gives Christians – assured in their conviction of victory over death – unshakable freedom, boldness in the face of the 'powers of this world'. (Things were just the same in similar situations in antiquity: Christians refused to bow down to any man, even though he were the emperor, who claimed for himself the total meaning of any human life.) Therefore Christian belief in the resurrection is a fundamental protest against the violation of personal freedom, because this Christian faith can only be born of the conviction that a definitive meaning is possible for human personal freedom within the total significance of the whole of human history. Therefore in the Christian understanding of death there can be no talk of individualistic salvation. Salvation is wholeness, and no man is made whole as long as disaster and oppression, injustice and misery, prevail around him. For Christians, the death and resurrection of Jesus, the man on whom they venture their lives – is the ground of hope for a general resurrection for all men. Put in terms of our modern awareness of the problem, for Christians this confession of the resurrection of Jesus means hope for all, a hope which is a stimulus to the healing of man and society and to a way of life which shows non-Christians that there can be living communion with God in Christ Jesus in a modern world, and what this communion looks like. Therefore concern for the salvation of others and for the good of society is inseparable from the Christian conception of death. There is not only an individual hope; the Christian opens up 'the divine virtue of hope' towards and to the advantage of his fellow man. Trust in God issues in a trust and a faith in one's fellow man – in man.

For believers themselves, the consequence of this Christian conception is that death is no longer a central event in their life, which claims all their attention. Death does not have that meaning for them, because of the fundamental message which they have been allowed to hear and can still hear from the death and resurrection of Jesus. The true Christian will therefore consider life not only from *boundary situations*, like death; for in that way one runs the risk of removing God from the complex of everyday life, the real centre of our human life, as a mixture of partial success and partial failure. For the Christian, the sting has been taken out of the history of human suffering and death. For him there is no ground for anxiety in life or death. Thus the Christian conception of death frees men for their work in this world, without anxiety, in true communion with God. This liberation from all anxiety may already be called a piece of *realized salvation.*

Whether Christianity also in fact *realizes* in the dimensions of human history, which are acceptable to all, what it *claims* in faith, must emerge from the life-style of Christians. That depends on whether Christians are in a position to give men enough light, expectation of the future and motivation for quite definite action, so that they are capable in our history, here and now, of living for and with each other in a meaningful and liberating way. In other words, the question whether Christian belief in the resurrection, through which death unmistakably takes on another meaning, opens up a real future for man, will have to be 'proved' again and again, here and now, from corresponding behaviour on the part of Christians, from their activities in this world. Without such consistency, what Christians assert is in fact incredible; furthermore, it has no power of attraction, and above all gives no hope to the world.

*(d)* Why Jesus Christ?

Why is all this seen in the light of Jesus Christ? Are there not many men,
right down to our own time, who have been tortured and done away with
because of their unconditional acts of righteousness and love, 'because
they were too good for this world' (Heb. 11.38)? Does not their way of
life have equal value in and of itself, and an effect on our history which
is not to be underestimated? Why pin all this on Jesus?

In fact, theoretically at this point we have a believing act of trust in
this man of Jesus of Nazareth, in which *no mediation is possible*: namely,
Christian faith. However, even if it is impossible to give fully convincing
and rational reasons for a single act of trust in anyone, such trust also
has rationalizable elements, good reasons as supports for the critical
reason of the believer himself.

First of all, there is the historical fact that down to the present day this
Jesus has been able to inspire men and provide them with guidelines –
the fact that he gave rise to a 'Christ movement'. In *Jesus. An Experiment
in Christology*, I pointed out that even the future or the historical influence
of a person is part of the identity of that person.[141] Thus today's living
Christian communities, a living remembrance of Jesus as the Christ, are
part of the full identity of Jesus. And this is no coincidence. For scripture
shows that Jesus in some way recognized his significance for the whole
of history to come (and may have also expressed this in some specific
way). Earliest Christianity expressed this by means of the concept of
'*eschatological* prophet', that is, the prophet who claims to bring a definitive
message which is valid for all history. That Jesus had a global conviction
that his person had a significance for the whole of history still to come,
open as it was, emerges from the texts in the Q tradition in which we can
hear a historical echo of Jesus' own understanding of himself: 'I tell you,
everyone who acknowledges me before men, the Son of man also will
acknowledge before the angels of God; but he who denies me before men
will be denied before the angels of God' (Luke 12.8f. = Matt. 10.32f.:
'Every one who acknowledges me before men, I also will acknowledge
before my Father . . . but whoever denies me before men, I also will deny
before my Father'; cf. Luke 7.18–23 = Matt. 11.2–6 and Luke 11.20 =
Matt. 12.28).[142] The claim that there is a connection between the decision
men make about Jesus and the final destiny of their life doubtless goes
back to Jesus' awareness of himself. That with the coming of Jesus, God
himself comes near to us, is a Christian conviction which in the first place
is grounded in Jesus' understanding of himself. One can hardly deny that
Jesus himself *puts his own person* in an *essential relationship* with the history
of mankind. In other words, in any case the historical influence of the
message and life-style of Jesus was also intended by Jesus himself. This

being so, the historical effect of his personality belongs in a special, unique way to the identity of Jesus of Nazareth. In and through what he *is*, he points beyond himself to history (which in fact continues). Jesus as the 'eschatological prophet'[143] or, as Johannine theology has it, 'redeemer of the world' (John 4.42; I John 4.14), and finally all the honorific titles which the church has given him, or the new ones which it will give him in the future, are simply a way of *making explicit* Jesus' *own understanding of himself*.

Of course, if one does not believe in Jesus, one can argue that Jesus was deceived about his eschatological significance and therefore his significance for world history, or overestimated it. There can never be compelling *historical* and *rational* proof that Jesus was right here. That is precisely the Christian act of faith, which cannot be communicated theoretically or apodeictically. Only through the actual life of Christians, the 'communities of Christ' in the course of the ages, can it be shown that as 'the service of reconciliation' (II Cor. 5.19), the liberating and reconciling life of the church is not a chance happening but is the realization in our history of the basic aim of Jesus, who in this way manifests its truth in history. No man and no prophet have ever made this claim. In Jesus, therefore, we *either* have a megalomaniac (which would go against the whole of his life and activity), *or* a claim which merits serious consideration even in theory, at least and above all to the degree that in the course of history his claim has had a clear effect in the actual redeeming, liberating and reconciling activity of all who confess this Jesus. Such historical significance, which Jesus himself attributes to an initiative of God towards salvation (in the last resort, that is the whole approach even of the Gospel of John), is rightly expressed in the basic formulation of the New Testament: definitive salvation from God in Jesus of Nazareth.

The universality of redemption from God in Jesus is therefore: (1) an affirmation *of faith* on the basis of an interpretative experience of Jesus through a particular, i.e. Jewish-Christian, tradition and not an 'objectively demonstrable fact', although Christians (albeit again *in faith*) are here expressing 'reality' and not merely subjective feelings. (2) It is also universal because in the failure of his life and in his unmerited suffering, as in the fact that he entrusted this 'fiasco' to his Father – whom he now also calls our Father ('my Father and your Father', John 20.17) – Jesus points away from himself and to a God who is the God of all men and all religions, and because in all this he addresses men about the problem of their own life and all the questions they cannot answer. (3) It is universal, because in Jesus, witnessed to as the Christ, *salvation* (the theme of the whole of human history) finds expression in the full sense of the word, as *perfect* and *universal* salvation or wholeness, for each and every individual, for man as a person, as a physical being, as a fellow man, and also for man as he is called to create liberating structures and institutions, for man as *homo faber*, as *homo ludens*, as *homo emancipator*, as *homo oeconomicus, homo contemplativus*, above all as man who longs for justice and love; salvation, finally, for all men, in present, past and future, living and dead. (4) It is a universal salvation which therefore can and must and above all may be communicated as 'good news' or gospel to all men, not only through proclamation but also through this proclamation as an inner element in the consistent practice of discipleship of Jesus, the way of practical reconciliation and liberation; a message which, moreover, can be proclaimed without any discriminatory action against anything that is good, true, fine and beautiful, even against anything religious which can also be found somewhere outside the Christian gospel. All this implies that, if it is lived consistently, the gospel of the Christian communities offers a way of life which by nature is an enrichment of human experience and our human world. Is not this the dogma of Chalcedon?

## B. Man's salvation is the living God

### (a) Political and mystical activity

When a Western European landed his plane among African natives who gazed unbelievingly at this enormous strange bird, he proudly remarked, 'In one day I have covered a distance which used to take me thirty.' Thereupon the wise black chieftain came forward and asked, 'Sir, what do you do with the other twenty-nine?' Here we have the twofold possibility of man's fundamental decision: on the one hand technological *rationality*, and on the other the question of the *meaning* of human action.

Almost twenty-five years ago, in his books on 'The Question of Technology'[144] and 'The Question of Being'[145], Martin Heidegger acknowledged the justification of the Western decision in favour of science and technology, but at the same time he pointed to the bewildering one-sidedness of this interest: it is in fact regarded as almost the only meaningful way of dealing with nature. As a result, in capitalist and Communist countries meaningful work (and that is taken to be productive work) is identified with meaningful existence, in three phases which have become classical: school as a preparation for later work, working life itself, and finally pensionable age as a rest from work. Everything which lies outside this system of work is consistently, and in a remarkable way, called 'free time'. Theologians, sometimes – indeed often – faithful servants of the *status quo*, have hastened to provide this system of work on the one hand with a *théologie du travail* and on the other with a *théologie des loisirs*, a theology of work and a theology of leisure time, without analysing the anthropological presuppositions of the system.

In our Western world, nature threatens simply to become energy that can be controlled and manipulated, and man himself nothing but the one who has control of nature. Now it is beyond denial that both in theory and in practice, acquisitive knowledge can be a truly human existential possibility, to which nature is in fact responsive and to which man is much indebted. To ridicule its *de facto*, even maximum, realization would be reactionary, naive and primitive. However, Western culture and Western society seem to be identified almost exclusively with this scientific and technical reason, taking for granted the sole pre-eminence of technological economy, often in a positivistic spirit. This totality is as it were the anthropological presupposition for the dominant cultural form, which is in fact Western.

As a result of this one-sidedness, modern Western man has become alienated from the sphere of his original experiences. Our capacity to see and hear, to taste and to smell, our perception and our spirit, our capacity for making one another happy, have been blunted by the one-sided uses of science and technology. As a result, an immeasurable part of reality has disappeared from the horizon of our possible experiences. Earlier it was possible for man to *experience* God. Faith was a special form of perception: man took his experience of God for granted and accepted evidence for it. He also lived consciously among angels and saints, in a different, but just as real a way, as a farmer lived among his cows and pigs, the farmyard and the field. If religious faith is in fact a particular form of *perception* (because I cannot imagine any form of real knowledge which has no basis in perception), then the world of a man who really believes is quite essentially another world – even psychologically – from that of a purely scientific and technological experience of the world. And this latter world has been culturally popularized among us modern men in a one-sided way; i.e., that is in fact our acculturation when we grow up into this Western world. That means that life in our one-sided Western society has in fact made faith more difficult than it used to be. At the same time, it means that under modern Western conditions faith, i.e. perception in faith, can no longer assume the shape and form of a 'first originality'. Thus this 'first originality' has become intellectually impossible for us as a result of the science, technology and criticism of religion put forward in the nineteenth century.

If, on the other hand, true human potentialities are forgotten or suppressed (although as the men we are, we nevertheless long, albeit unconsciously, for them to be actualized and will not be gainsaid), these neglected capacities become evident, even if in a hidden way, perhaps through neurosis and escapism. Many of today's syncretistic religious phenomena are primarily the concrete shape or sometimes the travesty of the protest of capacities which are suppressed or neglected by a one-dimensional culture; they are the expression, in protest, of other human epistemological possibilities which are not concerned with the control of nature: aesthetic, contemplative, playful, useless and aimless 'let it be'. This pantheon of counter-culture is the scene of more than the age-old, constantly recurring conflict between generations; an attempt is being made at an *alternative* life, on the basis of non-controlling, non-manipulative, more contemplative human possibilities of perception. Young people opposed to the Western model of society (a society which is fond of calling itself a secular society oriented only on science and technology, and which has proclaimed the death of God in a hymn to 'the secular city' by the mouth of its own theologian of secularization) are outraged in their rebellion against this society, and also from the depths of their human psyche, at the 'death of God' ideology and therefore shout provocatively, 'God lives, Jesus lives, Alleluia, Jesus loves me!' No matter what the religious content of these movements may be, originally and to the depths they are a protest of the human psyche, which also has contemplative possibilities, against the Western preference for the active capacity of this same psyche to control nature. It is primarily a reaction with a profoundly human origin, even when the specific form of this reaction is sometimes maimed and neurotic, or even reactionary and therefore once again alienating.

At first glance, the harmonizing of a contemplative approach with a concern for liberation seems to be an attempt to reconcile the irreconcilable. The two seem to be mutually exclusive.[146] Is any mediation possible here? For the moment, the dialectical tension between inner liberation and liberation from particular structures which enslave people has been shifted into the sphere of the church's liturgy. This was once the privileged place for prayerful intercourse with God in the loving presence of brothers and sisters. Today, many people experience the liturgy above all as the place where injustice, disorder and war are accused 'in the name of the gospel', where people pledge solidarity with suffering men, lost and deprived of their rights, and issue a summons to a better, more human, free world for all. Here the future is primary.

However, hardly was the monopoly of the future established both in theology and liturgy, and also in scientific futurology, than cultural critics came to us and warned us that not only longing for the past but also an over-hasty zeal for a better future could really be escapism. And now – after the establishment of the primacy and monopoly of the future and the correction in the argument that has already been made, namely that a programme for the future is a fatal venture unless it is accompanied by critical remembrance of the past[147] – we are hearing on all sides the cry that more importance should once again be attached to the present. Today the cry for 'life in the present' can be heard in an evocative form: in various scientific disciplines[148] and in new therapies. As far as these latter are concerned, the Freudian approach which analytically and hermeneutically stirs up the repressed past in order to free the patient from it, has been replaced by American *Gestalt* therapy,[149] which takes the opposite line and has been working spectular wonders in recent years. *Gestalt* therapy is oriented on the present and systematically excludes any attempt to escape, whether into the past or into the future. The aim of this therapy is to reconcile someone in the 'here and now' with themselves and with others, with everything that has been in the past and everything that the future will bring. One finds a similar concern in certain literary works: the people who among other things are terrified in their expectations of the future by the Club of Rome's best-seller, again want to put trust in the future and offer specific themes for it which suggest that despite many gloomy prospects, it will be possible to live a happy and meaningful human life, what can be called a real life.[150] All this may be true; indeed, I believe that to be the case: however, there is a considerable danger that these existential truths may be misused (sometimes against the intentions of their authors) in a more comprehensive sphere, that of social politics. Personal happiness is in fact decided in the present, but what is important in the last resort is the happiness of each and every individual (and not just of those who by chance happen to be in a favourable economic position); and given this universal concern, that implies the ethical obligation to work for a society 'in which human alienation is done away with and man enters a new relationship with himself, his work and his natural and social environment'.[151]

In view of the uncertainty of human life, even in Western society, which is beginning to recognize its inner contradictions, we must now pay special attention to the fact that man has a *temporalized* existence: in other words, exclusive emphasis, whether on future, present or past, runs the risk of narrowing or crippling truly human existence.

True humanity cannot dispense with any of these three dimensions. However, they are intrinsically held together by our time-conditioned humanity itself: a being that knows that it is on the way. In the last resort, we can only experience these three dimensions as meaningful if on the one hand we express our *temporal awareness*, and on the other hand also allow God a place in what we say here. We do not know precisely what God is for us. We do not have him in our hands, and of ourselves we do not understand our own humanity and its potentialities. Anyone who believes in God knows that, in some way or other, he holds us in his hand. In Hebrew, what we call belief is indicated by the root *'āman* (still recognizable in 'amen'). That means giving up our own uncertainty and insecurity and basing our existence on something else, on someone else who can provide a firm foundation. In that case to believe in God, to say 'amen' to him, means to base one's whole being, i.e. one's self, neighbours and world, in God. Thus the believer sets himself utterly at risk by trusting in the steadfastness of the one whom he does not see, the living God. 'If you do not believe, you will not be established', says Isaiah (7.9). Believing means being firmly established, trusting in what we believe to be a firm foundation. Therefore belief in God is the fundamental decision of a man who *entrusts* himself, others and the whole of history to God, and in so doing knows that he is reconciled with himself, with others and with history – present, past and future – because the believer has come to terms with God's incomprehensible actions. Faith is assurance in the message of God's *deity* as the ground and source of man's *humanity*.

However, I have been speaking quite spontaneously and with obvious naivety about God, as though I had met him and had had concrete experience of his reliability, whereas he is a God who provisionally refuses to present his credentials. When Moses asked God's name he was not given a direct answer; only 'I will be who I will be' (Ex. 3.14), that is, what I am will have to emerge in your own history. I am one with you. Believing therefore means putting one's trust in someone who to begin with still refuses to say who he is. We can only guess at his identity in a historical process. He is the one who cannot be named. We therefore describe him in a remarkably ambiguous way, as the one who is far and yet near, who is unapproachable and yet reveals himself, who is intangible and yet can be violated. *Our* identity as those who believe in God is little clearer: the believer is secure, and yet homeless, the orphaned seeker and yet the son who has returned home, 'in the world and not of the world'. Those who believe in Christ know that the reality which we mean when we speak of 'God' is not undialectically the ground of everything that is. It is the ground of what should be and will be, and so – dialectically – it is also the ground of present and past. Precisely for that reason God is not the ideological foundation of tradition and *status quo*, but represents a threat to them: he is a God of 'change *for the good*' and therefore judgment and grace, albeit in utter faithfulness.

Present, past and (unknown) future – humanity (or *homo absconditus*) in living relationship with the hidden God (*deus absconditus*): here we touch on what is perhaps the sorest point of the contemporary religious problem. Since in our time this relationship has been qualified in a different way, a great deal has been stirred up. We are concerned with what Dorothee Sölle (along with many others, and already as a corrective to the 'death of God' theology) has called the death of the 'immediacy' of God; that means that man has no direct relationship with God. This puts in question Augustinian theology, which has been a fundamental influence on the whole of Western Christianity, along with the attitude and 'piety' of the so called simple believer. It is precisely this break with an 'immediate' relationship with God in faith which has opened the doors of our churches to political theology, to the origin of critical communities and to a better, and above all a happy, world.

On the other hand, at present I see new symptoms of the old super-naturalism among us as a reaction against the tendency – which is unmistakable here and there – to reduce Christianity and belief in God to co-humanity, involvement, political action and change. Once again, some people are completely banishing grace into the inner life, which at the same time means that they regard society, the world and history as being so to speak outside the system of grace – and the *actual* consequence of this is a defence of the political *status quo*.

The heart of the problem therefore seems to be: Does the believer have a *direct* relationship with God or not? The decisive question here is whether both the men of the past and the so-called moderns have clearly formulated the scope of this problem. Perhaps both have seen part of the truth, and in each case have interpreted it in a one-sided way. Having carefully examined both the – let us say – traditional Western, Augusti-nian expressions and the newer Western Christian statements, I would venture to make the following comments. If by talking of the death of the 'immediacy of God', one means that man has *no unmediated* relationship with God, then I fully agree. However, things look different if we consider this same, i.e. mediated, relationship from the other side, for in my view there certainly is an unmediated relationship between God and us. The objection that immediacy on only one side of a mutual relationship amounts to an inner contradiction is untenable in this particular case. What we have here is not an inter-subjective relationship between two persons – two mortal men– but a mutual relationship between a finite person and his absolute origin, the infinite God. And that has an effect on our relationship to God. In other words, we are confronted with a unique instance, an instance in which the immediacy does not do away with the mediation but in fact constitutes it. Thus from our perspective there is *mediated immediacy*. Between God and our awareness of God looms the insuperable barrier of the historical, human and natural world of creation, the constitutive symbol of the real presence of God for us. The fact that in this case an unmistakable mediation produces immediacy, instead of destroying it, is connected with the absolute or divine manner of the real presence of God: he makes himself directly and creatively present in the medium, that is, in ourselves, our neighbours, the world and history. This is the deepest immediacy that I know.

'Mediated immediacy' seems to me to be the most appropriate way of expressing the mystery of God as the salvation of man, and also of coming as near as possible to the nature of prayer and liturgy; at the same time it can give us some insight into the relationship between the mystical and the political aspects of Christian belief in God. Here one can say that on the one hand the mystical element does not branch off into gnosticism, and on the other, that political involvement is realized, not on the basis of humanism, but on the basis of real belief in God.

I want to analyse this 'mediated immediacy' in two stages: with stress first on the mediation, and then on the immediacy (which nevertheless remains mediated).

## (b) Mediation in the direct, saving nearness of God

In Christian life the unity of creation and covenant has often been broken, whereas here above all it is true that what God has joined together, no man should put asunder. The Creator himself is the redeemer, and he appears as God even in his work of redemption. That means that he appears by definition as Creator, and therefore without there being any rivalry between what he does and what we ourselves[152] do on the foundation provided by him. Sometimes we have destroyed not only the unity between creation and covenant, but also belief in creation itself, and that means breaking the thread of life which links Christian *faith* with our *experience of reality*. In that case we have forgotten that God's salvation to us is accomplished in a reality which is ours, our own contingent world, and that God's salvation takes human form and is, moreover, given to us in a human way through Jesus as the Christ. I ask myself how great can be the content of *religious* experience and thus the reality in the experience of the real presence of God in the liturgy, if we have failed to learn to see ourselves, our fellow men and our world symbolically as God's real, though hidden, presence outside the liturgy as well. The language of faith and the language of the church become meaningless or empty to the degree that they no longer contain any recognizable reference to real experiences in the everyday world. Anyone who speaks of God and his salvation at the same time speaks of the world of our human experience and therefore uses understandable language. I do not see how anyone can recognize an experience of religious reality in the liturgy, which is a special field of experience of the real presence of God, unless the real presence of God is also experienced with others in the world outside the liturgy, by virtue of our historical status as creatures. For all this is an experienceable symbol of the real presence of God. That is the primary and fundamental experiential content of any form of the real presence of God.

The experience of creation, a historically variable experience of fortuitousness and contingency, seems to me to be the permanent breeding ground for any experience of the saving nearness of God, and also for example the special experience that is to be found in Jesus and in the liturgy. Liturgy *presupposes* this fundamental symbolic experience and intensifies it. Without this fundamental experience, no renewal or stylization of liturgy can give us a deepened liturgical experience which is true experience of the present and not just an experience of our own subjective reactions to what happens liturgically in the church. We cannot suddenly experience God in the church's liturgy if we can no longer see him anywhere outside the church. Were that to happen, then I fear that our liturgical sensibilities would have no *religious* content of reality; and this liturgical void cannot be filled, at least for the longer term, with a liturgical appeal to ethical action or a critical attitude towards culture. That would be to misunderstand the 'balance' on which the deepest ethical stimuli are based. In its changing historical forms, the experience of creation is the foundation which supports everything. It might equally well be called a fundamental 'experience of grace', or, rather more neutrally, an experience of the reality which prepares us and is therefore a norm for us – in other words, an experience of ourselves, our fellow men and the world in which we feel as a norm something which transcends at least our arbitrary control of ourselves. It is an experience of givenness, which is also the root of all religion as a mediated immediate relationship with what believers call the Creator God. This awareness is the gateway through which God enters our history, through which we ourselves really perceive God – mediated immediacy – and can express him in words. It is this that gives religion its fundamental character as reality and experience. On the basis of this, also, Jesus can be recognized as the manifestation of the universal love of God in the form of a human person, and on the basis of this, religious experiences are possible in the liturgy as well. In our historical experience of contingency, God temporalizes himself in historical truth, as past or remembrance, as present or trust, and as future or expectation.

The mediated immediacy of the saving real presence of God implies that our answer to God, our yes to God, has a similar structure of mediation, without however remaining stuck fast in this mediation. In other words, religion cannot be reduced to co-humanity and a sociopolitical concern for fellow men, though it cannot do without this mediation. Without this mediation, religious feeling would be chasing a void, since it is only in these forms of mediation that God makes himself immediately present. Therefore to look for him outside them would be to seek where he is not and never will be found. That becomes clear when Paul is talking about celebrating the eucharist. For him, sharing in the same cup, sharing in the same bread means the end of all discrimination between Jew or Greek, man or woman, slave or free in the sphere of the mediated real presence. The same Paul accuses the Corinthians of 'drinking judgment' in their eucharist, not because they profane the sacramental *divinum consortium*, the sacral converse with God, but on the contrary because they have violated the secular, human significance of the meal as a piece of brotherly sharing. Violence was done to the *koinōnia adelphou*, the brotherhood, when people adopted gnostic views and claimed to have an immediate share in the divine nature. Paul frees this Greek conception from its mystical and 'gnostic' connotations. It is striking that in the New Testament worship is often hinted at with the word *synerchesthai*, i.e. the brotherly assembling of the community of faith (I Cor. 11.17,20; 14.23,26). 'Brotherhood' is the concrete form which prevents thanksgiving and praise of God from being lip service, chasing a void. In our modern society, complicated as it is, this 'brotherhood' cannot just be realized in benevolent inter-personal relationships; it is equally necessary in the anonymous forms of socio-political institutions and structures. These need to be renewed and put at the service of freedom, for they are the modern political form of specific Christian *caritas*. Finally, it should not be forgotten that God's great acts for Israel, the *magnalia dei*, the saving acts which the liturgy does not cease to narrate, to hymn and to praise, were always accomplished through particular people, *per homines*, in Israel. It is therefore unbiblical to draw a contrast between the doxological or hymnic character of the liturgy and a so-called 'activism' which is concerned with the betterment of man, his world and society. Interest in social politics out of a concern for fellow men is not alien to liturgical celebration, just as it was also legitimate that the Jews should have historicized their originally agricultural spring festival into a liturgical commemoration of the exodus from the slavery of Egypt.

God's grace, that is, his saving real presence among us, is therefore not a special realm of inwardness, but the whole of reality in which we live and of which we ourselves are a part. If grace is removed from the world of creation, it is forced into the private and inner life of men: at the same time this makes the outward communication of grace an instrumental sign of invisible realities, and the world, history and society are forced into being an alien, extra-territorial sphere as far as grace is concerned. Beyond question, one can work out a socio-political order simply on economic and ethico-political principles, and through an analysis and interpretation of the situation with the possibilities which are constantly relevant to it. Here people start from human motives and undertake what is in and of itself a general human, ethical and political enterprise: all this seems to me to be self-evident. However, that does not rule out the possibility that what is done here in human terms to make a man whole can also in fact be a historical communication of grace, a foretaste of true salvation: the possibility of experiencing human salvation in the making.

For human freedom is not a purely interior matter. It is a freedom which also has its outward corporeal sign, and only comes to itself in the encounter of truly free men, in institutions and social structures which make freedom possible. Of ourselves we are only a possibility for freedom, and this freedom is still a vacuum; it has no content. Through culture, freedom creatively fills this void. However, no single form and level of culture can completely fill the void. Freedom realized in a specific way is always internalized freedom, that is: inner freedom must also be connected with the encounter with free men in social structures which make possible this freedom and protect it. The social dimension is an essential component of our inwardly free action; it goes to constitute the experience of ourselves and the world. Specific freedom or liberated freedom in grace thus transcends the dualistic distinction between inwardness and outwardness, and therefore also the equally dualistic theological application of it: the distinction between 'inner grace' and 'outward grace'. For from a sociological point of view it is evident that personal identity rapidly crumbles when someone finds no social recognition and a personal conviction loses its social plausibility.[153] The fact that a large number of Christians from the country quietly leave the church when they are transplanted into a large city indicates that their inner freedom is at the same time socially conditioned. The assertion that such people were never really true believers seems to me to draw too hasty a conclusion. The fact simply indicates that there is a constitutive relationship between personal identity and collective consensus and recognition, between inner freedom and social structures which provide freedom. It even seems to me to be the principal task of the church to form a free and liberating religious world of like-minded people in which personal freedom can flourish. That is the fundamental grace of the sanctifying and liberating world; from a sociological perspective it forms what theologians call 'habitual or sanctifying grace', a reality which in this way transcends the dualism of inwardness and outwardness.

Thus social and political improvements also form part of what may be called the grace of God, which can be internalized and as such becomes personal, liberated freedom. Furthermore, the humane sciences, like sociology, psychology, education and even the natural sciences are specifically creations of God, which have their place in the plan of grace. They help man on the way to truly human liberation. In them it is possible to experience God's gracious, saving nearness, in as real a way as Israel could and was allowed to experience, as a powerful saving act of God, a passage through the Red Sea under a favourable wind which forced back the waters. In fact God makes himself a 'cultural face', that is, he ex-

presses himself in terms of our culture. Therefore the experience of God
which is possible in a particular culture need not necessarily be able to
fulfil the same function in another culture. The fact that we are able to
experience God's creative and saving nearness, say, in an invention like
penicillin, does not tell against the reality of the Semitic experience of
God in the burning bush. There are many ways in which God allows
himself to be encountered through the medium of a natural (and in that
case I mean cosmic) or inter-personal act of beneficence. Modern believers can trace a forerunner of divine salvation in freedom which is realized
in socio-political action. Here the divine reality proves itself to be a *reality*,
as the one who wills good and opposes evil, the liberator from alienation.
Thus the history of human liberation can become a 'disclosure' in which
man learns to recognize God as the one who wills the *complete* liberation
of man.

### (c) Mediated immediacy: converse with God in prayer

Christianity without God is the end of all Christianity. True, one can
never avoid mediation, but *in* this mediation God himself really comes
near to us in salvation. Here the initiative is utterly his.

Salvation is in fact the conquest of all human, personal and social
alienations; salvation is man's wholeness, his world and his history.
However, the liberation of Christian freedom is not identical with the
emancipatory programme and process of human liberation. Person and
society are in an irreducible dialectical tension. And the 'void' or openness
of our freedom is never completely filled by culture. There is always a
'balance', an openness. On the one hand, one cannot call society the
transcendental, all-embracing horizon of reality; in that case we misunderstand the inviolability of the human person, which is not merely the
result of social development. On the other hand, personal inwardness
with its necessary private sphere and its area of intimacy is not a transcendental, all-embracing horizon either. I have already said that no form
or level of culture fills the openness of freedom; for that reason freedom
itself puts a question-mark against any particular culture. The consequence is that alienation in human life cannot be completely overcome
either personally or socially; liberated freedom or salvation transcends
person and society. There is human suffering which does not allow itself
to be stilled with social and political measures; people can still perish
from loneliness in the best social structures; even optimal structures do
not automatically make men good, mature human beings; *nature* has to
be humanized, but to a large extent and inescapably it remains alien to
man (one has only to think of death); and finally, there is our inalienable
finitude, which can be the origin of anxiety as well as trust in God.

Therefore a final healing of the division in our existence in the world can only be the consequence of an active reality which embraces both person and society, i.e. the whole of reality, without doing violence to it; and this is a definition of God, of the one who transcends all things through interiorness, who goes beyond all things from within. Only absolute freedom, which at the same time is creative love, is capable of this. That means that the kingdom of God cannot be the simple consummation of the present, any more than it can be the optimum which a culture can ever reach. Salvation lies on the line of the holy, good, beautiful and enjoyable things that can be realized in our history, but in such a way that God remains free in a surprising gift which transcends all this.

That leads us to a second aspect of mediated immediacy. It is not that we could now do without this mediation, but in the mediation the accent now lies on the God who is immediately near in it, since this is a *divine* absolute nearness. At this point it becomes clear that 'man's cause' is in fact 'God's cause', expressed in the biblical concept of the kingdom of God as human salvation, in other words, the kingdom of God concerned with humanity. Jesus experienced his sacrifice for his fellow men as God's cause. The recognition of the deity of God is at the same time the recognition of the unexpected humanity of man. Even M. Horkheimer[154] doubts whether a human ethic which has detached itself from its religious basis can in the last resort have any meaningful effect.[155] In that case the expectations which ethics arouses are too great, and it cannot give us what it promises. To be aware of a religious foundation in God provides the strength constantly to begin again in working for man and the world and carrying on the struggle, because in that case no single historical event is the eschatological final event, and by the same token a fiasco is not ultimate failure. Religious faith gives us confidence that what is impossible for men is possible nevertheless, because God's nature is the benevolent power of the one who is against evil, an undefinable gift.

However, it also emerges from these considerations that we need a liturgy in which we *transcend* both personal and individual intimacy, and also critical, socio-political concerns, from within (that is, not through an alienating rejection). One can call this the mystical aspect of belief in God in the wider sense, in which we represent to ourselves that God is near to us only in mediated form, yet nevertheless in real immediacy; that therefore we are never alone, even in our greatest loneliness; and that despite everything, goodness and mercy have me, all of us, in their grasp. This awareness of being grounded in God, of persisting when every empirical foundation and every guarantee have been removed and one weeps over the fiasco of one's life, is the mystical power of faith. When we lose all our supports, even those which can be experienced empirically with some degree of positiveness, the immediacy of the presence of God is in fact experienced as a 'dark night'. All the mystics have experienced this immediacy of the presence of God as a *nada*. One might say that they have experienced it, not as a nothingness (*nada*) of emptiness, but as a nothingness of fullness: God's presence as a pure experience of faith, even if this is communicated in a negative way. There are many ways or situations in which believers can experience such moments. I have often come across them with people who have seen a loved one die in the most grievous and most incomprehensible circumstances, and have been able to accept this only as believers, and even then not without profound sorrow. In that case this belief is not simply a theoretical conviction – were that so, it would be shattered. No, in that case it is an *experience* of the real presence of God, not in the mediation of positive support but in the mediation of extreme negativity, a dark night. And this does in fact imply 'mediation'.

However, this mystical depth in which the immediacy of God is the essential element, because in this case the mediation is experienced as 'pure negativity', does not reveal itself only in negativity or 'dark nights', but also in joyful experiences. In one saying, the substance of which certainly comes from him, Jesus thanks God with trembling joy after the triumphant return of his disciples. He had sent them on a mission and they have come back telling him that their task has been accomplished successfully (Luke 10. 17–21). There are experiences in the life of a believer in which he has a disclosure: if this man is already so disarmingly good, how much better must God be! Here, too, there is a change in perception from mediating to mediated, namely towards God's real, immediate presence. Therefore alongside the implicit life of prayer in the secular, human manifestations of God, I see *explicit prayer* as man's attempt to see this dimension of immediacy, an attempt to which the believing life of the everyday world as it were drives him, because the believer is aware of the *real* (though mediated) nearness of God. However, the attempt continually fails because this nearness, divine and absolute as it is, is as inward as it is incomprehensible. At the very moment when we turn our attention from mediation to look towards God's real presence itself, with the shedding of the mediation God himself also vanishes into nothing. Prayer is as it were a game of hide-and-seek between God and man. In fact there is always something extremely playful in prayer. Prayer has its supreme significance as a kind of game in the normal, everyday practice of our praying. '*Si vere Deum quaeris*', if you really seek God, said the old monks, then come to us. Praying means looking for God. We need to understand that God is a living being who knows how to disappear now and then so that we keep on looking further for him, and how to appear for a moment now and then so that we do not get tired of looking.

That brings us to a last and very difficult question. Is praying an '*I-thou relationship*' between God and man? It is hard to answer this all too naively in the affirmative; but it seems to me to be too subtle to deny the relationship. Of course a mutual relationship between God and man is an extreme analogous instance of what we call 'inter-subjectivity' or an I-thou relationship. If the immediacy is always mediated, and nevertheless constitutes mediation through its immediacy, we must answer this question with a paradox: yes, and at the same time no. We just need to remember that this mutual relationship between God and man falls outside the human category of inter-subjectivity because it transcends it, not because it falls short of it. On the one hand that makes explicit praying the most difficult *metanoia* or conversion in our life, yet on the other hand we cannot dispense with prayer without in the end grounding our life on idols, ideologies and utopias, and not on God himself. Prayer is therefore not so much meditation as conversion. Therefore prayer – and I think only prayer – gives Christian faith its most critical and productive force. The most critical element in belief in God does not come from a political theology but fundamentally from the articulation of faith in prayer, from prayer as an act of faith. It is precisely this faith which becomes effective indirectly in activity which takes a political shape, thanks to the mediating analysis of our particular social structures. All this must be given a theoretical basis by means of a 'political theology'.

### (d) Refractory suffering against and in contemplation and political action

Redemption includes contemplation and emancipatory action aimed at liberation and the furthering of human salvation. But suffering, as has been said, is not a factor from the history of man before emancipation, nor is it a factor from before the time of God's redemptive action in Jesus. Redemptive and emancipatory courses of action also find expression *in* the conditions of suffering. That gives an inner tension to any understanding of redemption and any attempt at liberation which is concerned with emancipation.

But human suffering also has a particular critical and productive epistemological force.[156] This cannot just be reduced to the purposive, emancipatory type of 'controlling knowledge' (that form of knowledge peculiar to science and technology), nor even to various forms of contemplative, aesthetic and playful, so-called 'purpose-free' knowledge, or knowledge which 'dwells' on its own object. The special epistemological value of the contrasting experiences of suffering because of injustice has a critical function towards both the contemplative and the scientific and technological forms of knowledge. There is a critical element in that contemplative total perception which, in its contemplation or liturgical celebration, already experiences universal reconciliation. But it is also critical of the controlling knowledge of science and technology, which as such presupposes that man is merely a 'controlling subject' and by-passes the question of the priority which the sufferers can claim among us.

The productive epistemological value peculiar to suffering is not only critical of the two positive forms of human knowledge; at the same time, dialectically, it can be a link between the contemplative and the actively controlling epistemological possibilities of the human psyche. There is even much to be said for the view that only the experience of contrast in suffering (with its implicit ethical demand) is in a position to form an inner link between them, because only it displays the characteristics of both forms of knowledge. For experiences of suffering come upon a man in the form of a negative experience, quite different from the positive enjoyment of contemplative, playful and aesthetic experiences. On the other hand, under the aspect of the experience of *contrast* or critical negativity, the experience of suffering forms a bridge towards possible action which might remove both suffering and its causes. Because of this inner affinity, albeit in critical negativity, with both contemplative knowledge and with manipulative scientific knowledge, I would term this particularly 'pathic' epistemological power of suffering both *practical* and critical. In other words, it is a critical epistemological force which leads to new action, which anticipates a better future and seeks to put it into practice. The result of all this should be that, in the situation of our existing *condition humaine* and under the conditions of our particular social culture, contemplation and action can only be connected through the criticism of the accumulated history of suffering and the ethical awareness that comes to birth in it. This situation is paradoxical, but nevertheless real.

As an experience of contrast, the experience of suffering is possible only on the basis of an implicit longing for happiness, and unjust suffering at least presupposes a vague awareness of the possible positive significance of human integrity. As an experience of contrast it indirectly implies an awareness of the positive call of the *humanum* and to the *humanum*. Understood in this way, action to overcome suffering is possible only through at least an implicit or submerged anticipation of a possible universal significance to come. In contrast to the *purposive* knowledge of science and technology and the '*aimless*' knowledge of contemplation, the particular epistemological value of the experience of contrast in suffering is a knowledge which looks for the *future* and opens it up. Thus the concept of the 'future' acquires validity alongside the concepts of 'purpose' and 'purposelessness'.[157] For because of its twofold properties, akin to contemplation and action, and its character of ethical protest, the particular epistemological value of suffering has the significance of a knowledge which is not concerned with purpose of 'purposelessness' ('dwell on') but with the *future*: with more humanity and with the removal in the future of the causes of injustice. For *in* its passive experience, because of its negativity, it has an ethical resistance to this 'let be'; it has a critical epistemological force which appeals to a practice which opens up the future, an action which, moreover, is not subject to the acceptance of a monopoly of purposive technocracy (that is also a cause of suffering). Therefore the experience of contrast is suffering is the negative and dialectical awarness of a longing for and a question of meaning in the future: real freedom and real happiness to come.[158] It is also a demand for reconciling, 'purpose-free' contemplation, as the anticipation (in faith) of universal meaning in order to connect the experience of contrast with new action which will overcome suffering and create the future.

There is more to come. Not only does dissatisfaction with the continuation of the history of human suffering associate the contemplative attitude with action for liberation and reconciliation (which can also be political); contemplative and liberating action themselves also stand *under* the finite conditions of our history of suffering. On the one hand, suffering is the likely consequence (in 'this world') of any whole-hearted sacrifice for a great cause: suffering through and for others, 'for the sake of the kingdom of God', as scripture says. On the other hand there is also suffering because of God's invisibility – the suffering of which mystics speak from their deepest experiences: 'Truly thou art a God who hidest thyself, thou God and Saviour of Israel' (Isa. 45.15). Both redemption in and through personal converse with the transcendent and redemption in and through inter-subjective and political effort for co-humanity and for a world fit for men to live in find their expression in the non-identity, the finitude of suffering human existence. Essentially, that implies that we experience redemption and liberation only in finite fragments, in a history which *stands open* towards eschatological consummation: 'In hope we are redeemed' (Rom. 8.24). It emerges from this that all aspects of Christian redemption – contemplative and political, concerned with theology or withour fellow men – are experienced and expressed in the conditions of provisional, earthly finitude. In other words, any positive experience of meaning, any fragment of redemption and liberation, takes place in 'unredeemed' conditions.

This results in a theoretical inability to reconcile the redemption already accomplished with our actual human history of suffering. However, there is the 'nevertheless', as the believer remembers the event which Jesus himself experienced eschatologically in reality, which took place in his life, his work and his death as a particular qualification of his life-style.

However, we have to make this 'eschatological remembrance' rather more precise. This remembrance consists primarily not in the church's dogma about Jesus Christ, except in an 'abbreviated' sense, in so far as this 'orthodoxy' is an intrinsic element of the church's life as shaped by history (just as the message of Jesus was the 'documentation' of his reconciling and liberating, healing ministry).

Like any living remembrance of the human history of suffering. Christian *anamnēsis* or remembrance of Jesus' particular course of suffering develops a particular critical epistemological force. In that case, however, its rebellious and challenging character does not lie in a theoretical remembrance of a past event, nor even *directly* in the articulation through proclamation of the suffering of Jesus, but rather in what the Bible calls 'remembrance'. There, for instance, it is said of God that he remembers his earlier saving àcts by now bringing new saving acts to pass in the present.[159] Reference to what is actually done here and now is an essential part of the biblical view of memory. From a social and historical point of view, the revolutionary critical epistemological value of the *memoria passionis Christi*, which presents a challenge to the world and society, does not lie directly in the past history of suffering (though that is where it has its origin) or in the kerygma or dogma, those so-called 'dangerous memorial formulas' which describe his suffering; rather, it is communicated by the *living Christian community*, that is, by the contemporary church itself, *in so far as* it is an active *memoria passionis* of the risen Lord. Therefore the church is a critical *memoria Christi* to the degree that its particular way of life can be shown to and is visible to all, presenting a challenge and leading to revolution, and in this respect is a living remembrance of Jesus which overcomes suffering. Unless it goes with a liberating way of life which overcomes suffering, kerygmatic remembrance cannot have any critical epistemological force. The kerygma of remembrance is more the interpretative epistemological aspect of what is in actual fact a challenging church way of life. In abbreviated, *purely dogmatic* language, if this dogma or kerygma is not to be an ideology, then in the light of the historical life of Jesus it is at least a 'performative language', a language which leads to a form of realization. From a religious and human point of view, therefore, the living *memoria Christi* in the church is only a prophetic and critical, and not an ideological force, presenting a historical challenge and leading to further action, when this memory can at the same time be experienced visibly as promise and thus as historical ferment. This can only happen, then, when the *orthōs* of orthodoxy also issues in and from the *orthōs* of a challenging and promising church life, opposing meaninglessness and achieving meaning in the world and in the midst of a society which perhaps has many different life-styles that perpetuate in persons and structures the human history of evil and suffering.

In the prophet Jesus, mysticism and the healing of men came from one and the same source: his experience of the contrast between the living God and the history of human suffering. On the one hand was his meaningful converse with the living God who was so close to him and who set him free, whose loving care he saw even in the astonishing beauty of the lilies of the field and in the touching faith placed in him by humble men, and on the other hand the servitude in our human history which sickens and maims, brings unnecessary suffering and cramps freedom. Out of this experience of contrast between contemplative and also practical experience of meaning and the human history of evil and suffering, Jesus makes demands on us which humanly speaking are obviously impossible. One example of the way in which the gospels understood Jesus may be enough: 'When you prepare a meal, then invite the poor and the lame, the cripples and the blind' (Luke 14.13); in a vision, in a very fragmentary and historically limited event – a drop of water on a hot stone – Jesus anticipates the *real possibility* of perfect eschatological salvation, in the same way as Micah and Isaiah saw the wolf and the lamb grazing together in peace and the child playing happily over the snake's hole, in universal meaningful reconciliation. Such a prophetic promise is a permanent force, critical of society, which still discovers subtle forms and causes of suffering and evil on the basis of mystical experience of God, where they are not encountered without mystical experience. Mysticism is therefore itself a liberating force.

Nevertheless, the prophetic vision of Jesus is not – or at least not directly – a *solution* to the problem of human life. Theoretically (rationally) 'unreconciled', the remembrance of the dead but risen Jesus will find itself reconciled in faith *in* the conditions of our earthly temporality and our rational sense of dissatisfaction. We should see what Paul calls redemption in hope (the physical resurrection which is still to come) only as an ingredient of the final, eschatological and also *theoretical* reconciliation of 'human reason' with the living God: the eschaton as the revelation of the intrinsic evidence for God even for human critical rationality (an aspect of what the Christian tradition calls the beatific vision).

## C. Salvation in finite conditions

### (a) Salvation even in historical failures

Theories about human fallibility are topical again. That has its dangerous side. Theories never arise apart from social and even political conditions. As the pendulum of history swings, we find that in times of cultural optimism people look most closely at the possibility of a better future, at

planned progress and the positive aspects of human knowledge and ability, in short at what people themselves can and may do in order to give
common form to their mutual future. By contrast, in times of cultural
pessimism the human experience of failure and helplessness comes op-
pressively into the foreground. This historical dialectic relativizes the
theme of 'fallible man'. If the world lives in a whirlwind of progress, with
obvious partial results, one can expect a 'theology of earthly values',
whereas a predominant experience of historical shadows and clear failures
in a particular cultural situation suddenly give rise to a 'theology of
human failure', which again seems to forget every theology of earthly
values.

Of course, the theologian has to try to provide an answer to man's
*present* questions; in this, however, he will keep alive the remembrance of
forgotten truths, for his sphere of reflection is not limited to the facts of
the present or to a particular situation. Precisely because of his concern
with the present, he may not stare blindly at it. In his reflection on
human failure, therefore, the theologian cannot be insensitive to the
partial successes of mankind and its honest effort not to fail, despite
opposition from inside and out. One does not magnify God by denigrating
man. 'Even those who limp go not backwards.'[160] Without this critical
detachment, theology becomes a mere reflection of changing dispositions
in the ebb and flow of any human culture. In that case it becomes a mere
copy, a duplication or repetition of secular tides: not a provocative remembrance and a critical orientation on the future, which can be diametrically opposed to what the trend of the time seems to require.

However, the relativizing of a one-sided emphasis on human failure
(which might not unreasonably be called reactionary) cannot reverse the
fact that the experience of human failure and impotence – at many levels
and throughout our personal and social life – is often an oppressive
phenomenon in our present-day society, where many people, young and
old, come to grief. In particular, the impotence of a continuing nineteenth-
century belief in progress, and the brutal repression or frustration and
decay of many revolutionary resistance movements, has made the experience of failure and impotence, and above all heightened reflection on
them, one of the fundamental affective dispositions or *basic moods* of our
contemporary culture. That is an undeniable reality.

It is therefore particularly worth noting that the experience of failure
is one of the most pathistic and creaturely depths of our human existence.
It belongs with other dimensions like joy, guilt and suffering, and can
therefore take on an ambivalent significance. Therefore an urgent question arises in connection with today's prevalent experience of failure and
impotence: what is the cognitive and operative force of this fundamental

experience? Or, to put it more simply: what kind of guiding 'practical truth' is revealed here which will help us in our life? What effective power can emerge from it? And conversely, what are the crippling consequences for anyone who suppresses this experience and what it has to say to us, no matter how – whether through flight into the marginal life of pure play, or contemplation wrongly understood, or vigorous revolutionary action regardless of the consequences? Furthermore, how can the experience of failure be misused, in order to fortify men's power over their fellow men? Finally, what is the special power of Christian faith, whether in providing encouragement and furthering life, or bringing salvation and exercising criticism, and above all its insight, through grace, that in the last resort our failure can and may be entrusted to God – a practical wisdom which has been tried out in a unique way by Jesus, the Christ, and by many who have 'followed' him in its strength? I am limiting myself here to the question as raised in Christian theology, and directing my attention less to individual and personal dimensions than to the macrodimensions of our world history in the search for a better future.

Anyone who, faced with the enormous problem of human failure, looks for inspiration and guidance from the fiasco of the message and the life of Jesus, must first be certain that this life of Jesus really was a fiasco in historical terms, i.e. in the dimension of our history; in other words, that at least in some respects it was a real failure. For this question is not as clear as some people would make it – positively or negatively. What is at stake is our human understanding of what 'failure' and 'success' really mean or imply.

Did Jesus see the crucifixion as the painful, but voluntary, acceptance of the failure of his plan? Should we see the Last Supper as the farewell of someone who, while being one with the Father, sees that his message has not been accepted? And who therefore offers his followers a farewell meal, as if to say, 'Dear friends, this is the last cup of all, things have gone wrong, but I accept this failure and continue to believe in my message and to trust in God'? In that case, Jesus himself would not have integrated his death so much into his offer of salvation and would not already have attributed a redemptive significance to it. In that case, precisely through his acceptance of the disastrous failure of his life and his message, in the light of God, whose heart is greater than any human failure and success, his death or failure acquire redemptive significance and thus a far-reaching historical worth.

Real though they may be, the nuances of this conception are subtle compared with the classical interpretation; but they could shed a specifically Christian light on what is in the last resort the fundamental problem of everyone's life: human failure, even where man is in no way responsible and has done everything possible to avoid failure. In that case the last word does not lie with failure, but in a living communion with God, who leads a man to accept this failure – sorrowfully, but willingly – and to hold it of less account than the value of living communion with God and faithfulness to men as the implication of this communion. In that case the redemptive force lies with this religious communion and solidarity to the point of death, i.e. the solidarity of love which does not allow itself to be destroyed even by the rejection of fellow men. Here the redemptive suffering does not lie with the negativity of failure as such but with the positiveness with which it is filled and accepted. However, the question which precedes all this is: did Jesus see his death as a catastrophe?

The question, then, is clear. But there are widely diverging interpretations in answer to it. Some theologians see the death of Jesus as 'being forsaken by God.'[161] By contrast, others claim that Jesus did not see his death as an unexpected catastrophe, but rather as the intrinsic consequence of his mission; thus he integrated his coming death into his offer of salvation, the heart of his whole mission.[162] Yet others assume that Jesus willingly accepted his violent death, but at the same time emphasize that his crucifixion, above all as a rejection by his fellow men,[163] made his message questionable and problematic,[164] so that in a very definite, but real, sense we must say that Jesus also had to cope with the bitter experience of failure.

Only if Jesus really experienced failure in a limited but real dimension of our history, albeit not through any fault of his own, can his own experience of failure as a historical event provide any encouragement, productive or critical force towards helping men to cope with the problem of failure. In that case, a fundamental correction is made to our short-sighted understanding of what failure really means.

At an earlier stage I analysed a particular aspect of the victory of Jesus in death: I must now make this more precise. On exegetical grounds we must resolutely reject the possibility that Jesus himself had been abandoned by God. Those who defend this argument rely almost exclusively on Ps. 22: 'My God, my God, why hast thou forsaken me?' (Mark 15.34). However, quite apart from the uncertainty whether this quotation of the psalm goes back to the historical Jesus or to a later Christian interpretation, in Jewish spirituality the quotation of the beginning of a psalm (no matter by whom) was an evocation, a reminder of the whole psalm. Now the basic mood of Psalm 22 emerges from a great many verses: 'For he has not despised or abhorred the affliction of the afflicted; and he has not hid his face from him, but has heard, when he cried to him' (Ps. 22.24); and 'All the ends of the earth shall remember and turn to the Lord' (Ps. 22.27); and finally, 'Before him shall bow all who go down to the dust, and he who cannot keep himself alive' (Ps. 22.29b). This psalm therefore expresses the believer's conviction that in situations where God's redemptive help and support cannot actually be experienced, in situations in which men no longer experience any glimmer of hope, in impossible situations, *God nevertheless remains near at hand* and that salvation consists in the fact that man still holds fast to God's invisible hand *in* this dark night of faith. This is the significance of Ps. 22 in the New Testament passion narrative. It is therefore an expression of what the mystical tradition calls 'the dark night of faith' (St John of the Cross), in which the true believer who trusts in God knows that he is still held in God's hand, even though there is no help that he can touch or feel, and in utmost emptiness will not let go of this hand. In any case, the biblical account of the passion is full of allusions to various verses of this particular psalm. The passion narrative breathes this spirituality of Ps. 22. Therefore in the interpretation of scripture there can be no question of the rejection and abandonment of Jesus by God. Thus the argument that Jesus was abandoned by God lacks any basis in scripture.

That also means that in the same gospel account the resurrection of Jesus at all events will mean a break-through or *manifestation* of a *presence* of God which, though *hidden beforehand*, was nevertheless *real* in and with Jesus – what seems to be failure is in fact nothing of the sort. In that case the resurrection is a new factor which is nevertheless in line with what was already a living reality on the cross, but in a hidden way, within the contours of earthly contingency: an act of God which will prove to be the deepest source of Jesus' identity. This conception is articulated above all in the Johannine account of the cross as exaltation. Here there is a vivid correction to the helplessness which is described in the first three gospels, and the failure of Jesus' message and way of life – 'he saved others, himself he cannot save' (Mark 15.31; see Luke 23.35b). The Fourth Gospel sees this very helplessness as the character of divine power, the supremacy of God's success in the life of Jesus which was shattered *by his fellow men*, a success which consisted in the fact that despite this annihilation Jesus did not let go of God. The first three gospels describe the manifest helplessness, the obvious failure; by contrast, the Fourth Gospel shows that the deepest reality does not lie on the surface: Jesus was successful by virtue of his living communion with God, which is stronger than death. Thus failure is evaluated in a different way.

Hence it emerges from the New Testament that Jesus experienced how much his execution contradicted his message of a God concerned with humanity and thus his whole way of life. In grief, but willingly, he nevertheless *entrusted all his failure to God*. Therefore in existential terms, Jesus had to reconcile an evident human experience of failure with his trust in God – he had as it were to reconcile what was *theoretically irreconcilable*. This is not a matter of knowing that one has come to terms with the fact that human life is a mixture of partial failure and partial success; here true success and real human failure are evaluated in another way. In the last resort, what we have here is another experience.

This insight of faith takes on more contours in the light of what we can call Jesus' *process of identification* as we see it described in the four gospels. Each gospel is to be seen as a total programme in which Jesus is identified. But in each individual gospel we find many sequences within the one, distinctive total plan, and in these sequences the identity of Jesus is disclosed as it were in stages or in successive sequences. I think that, leaving aside the sequence of the infancy narratives which are peculiar to Matthew and Luke,[165] it is possible to distinguish three partial sequences in the process of identification to be found in the four gospels: (1) the identity of Jesus is clarified by what he himself says and does (after his baptism in the Jordan and up to his passion); (2) the identity of Jesus is clarified by what others do to him (the passion narrative from the arrest of Jesus to his death); (3) the identity of Jesus is clarified by what God does to him (the stories after his death). (These sequences are connected by transitional passages: in the baptism narratives Jesus is to some degree still passive, and right at the beginning of the passion narrative Jesus himself still has the initiative in acting and speaking, for instance at the Last Supper. However, we can leave these transitional passages aside here.) All three sequences are important for the theme of 'failure': the message of Jesus and his way of life – his suffering and death – his exaltation to the Father and his life among us in the Spirit. Each of these three provides particular elements for the identification of Jesus in the gospels. Taken up into the one total programme of each of the four gospels, they shed light on the question whether and in what sense one can talk of a failure of the life and message of Jesus.

In the first phase, after the baptism narratives, Jesus no longer appears explicitly as the symbolic representative of Israel (the new Adam, Luke's genealogy), as he still does in the infancy narratives of Matthew and Luke. Now the stress lies more on the individual man (who tends more – and understandably – to remain in the background in the infancy narratives; what this new messenger is will have to be shown by the later course of his life): this man from Nazareth, who performs actions which are themselves a sign and effective symbol of the coming rule of God. This phase of identification is dominated by the theme of the kingdom of God: Jesus' personal, private and historically conditioned presence is identified by the light and in the light of his relationship to the kingdom of God. It is said that a very particular man, in a historical situation, namely Jesus of Nazareth, has a mysterious relationship to the imminent kingdom of God. This particular personal relationship to the coming kingdom of God clarifies the identity of Jesus in this narrative sequence.

This identification fills the whole sequence between the account of the baptism of Jesus by John and the report of his suffering and death.

However, a violent contrast appears with the passion narrative. Here all the symbolic features seem to fade into the background, whether they are related to the past (Israel) or to the future (the kingdom of God): now the centre of the stage is taken by a quite specific person, a suffering man whose claims have evidently proved to be a failure. In this context there seems to be virtually no connection between Jesus and the approach of the kingdom of God (though there is still an offshoot in the account of the institution: Matt. 26.29 par. and Luke 22.24–30); in view of the trend of the account this connection in fact becomes problematical. Jesus now appears as an individual whose task it will be to cope with his own fate and the new circumstances of his life. The honorific titles used in the previous sequence are now used almost ironically, that is, where they appear at all: can this suffering, humiliated man be the Christ (Mark 15.17–19, 26–32)? The heart of the account is simply the man Jesus, confronted with an ominous situation and with the threat of failure as a result of the violent intervention of his enemies. The disciples 'do not understand anything' (Luke 18.34) of a connection between 'going up to Jerusalem' (Mark 10.32; Matt. 20.17; Luke 18.31–34) and the 'coming of the kingdom of God'. In the meantime, the evangelists had, of course, learnt something, but in the narrative sequence all that we see is the *ambiguity* of the connection between 'Jesus' and 'the Christ' which they found.[166] At this point of the account there is uncertainty about the identity of Jesus, and the failure of the life of Jesus, which takes place before their very eyes, has a decisive role to play here.

In the synoptic account it is the struggle in Gethsemane (not mentioned explicitly by the Gospel of John, apart from 12.27) which expresses this problematical tension, uncertainty and ambiguity most sharply. In the light of the end, John's view is more profound and more real, but he does not speak, at any rate directly, of the helplessness of Jesus in which this divine depth is principally revealed; he speaks only of this all-fulfilling depth. In John the problem of failure has already been 'solved'. In the particular sequence in the synoptic gospels, on the other hand, the bitter question is still there large as life. The bystanders simply see and experience the contrapuntal decline of Jesus, as they are seized with the question, 'Are we deceived?' 'We had hoped' (Luke 24.21). John does away with the final phase of this tension. His accents lie differently: in Jesus' existential experience of helplessness (the synoptic gospels which describe this aspect put the accent here, though they are aware of the final victory), God brings about in the one who has been faithful to him the mystery of his divine success (this is where John puts the accent, simply presupposing the helplessness and the failure).

In a third and last sequence (after the death of Jesus, the stories about the tomb and the appearances), it is striking how the reader can feel in every verse that here only God is at work (as is also said expressly elsewhere in the New Testament: 'It is God who raised him from the dead', Acts 10.40; see 2.32; 3.15; 4.10; I Cor. 15.15), although there is hardly any mention of God in the biblical accounts of the experiences. Only Jesus, the living one, is the active subject here and himself expresses his identity: he restores the relationship between 'this Jesus' (the man from Nazareth) and 'the Christ', which had become problematical for the disciples. The unexpressed interweaving of 'Jesus' and 'God' is more evocative here than elsewhere. If Jesus' own initiative almost disappeared completely in the previous sequence (the passion narrative), in the resurrection stores everything again happens on the initiative of Jesus, which *coincides with* the absolute initiative of God: only Jesus' appearance (in the account of the resurrection appearances) suggests that God is actively at work here. The composition is masterly, but at the same time unique in its theological concentration. Jesus himself, the man from Nazareth, is the presence of the action of God with us, during his life and also after his death. What seem to be failure and disaster 'by human standards' (*kata sarka*, II Cor. 4.11; cf. 4.16), and indeed are so on this level, become redemption and victory when seen in the spirit.

The total sequence of the gospels, structured by these three partial sequences,[167] shows us that we cannot completely clarify the identity of Jesus from his message and way of life or even from his own intentions. Besides, the identity of a person is not just dependent on his intentions and actions; it is also the result of the intentions of others and the circumstances of his life. Many other things also *happen to* a person, and these contribute to his identity, precisely through the way in which he either integrates these events and imponderables or does not know what to make of them. Jesus knew what to do. Therefore in the last resort his identity cannot be recognized unless we also take into account his death and resurrection.

In all this it is the evangelists who are presenting their conception of Jesus in a process of identification. That is not to say directly how Jesus himself experienced this fiasco of his message and his ministry, much less whether he himself saw it as a fiasco. Even if the gospel account of Jesus' struggle in the garden of Gethsemane contains a degree of interpretation, the gospels nevertheless attempt to communicate Jesus' own experience. According to the texts of the gospels, we may say that, to begin with, Jesus certainly did not expect that his mission would inevitably lead to a violent death (even though that is the way in which it is in fact represented in the gospels); however, it becomes clear that towards the end of his life he was confronted with this possibility, which even became a threatening probability, and that in his constant concern for the will of God he eventually had to come to terms with it.[168] There is a good deal in the New Testament to suggest that he did not completely understand God's way (Gethsemane), but that he willingly accepted his fate in the end, despite the fundamental problem that this presented to his message of the imminent kingdom of God. Existentially, then, Jesus had to reconcile an evident human experience of failure with his trust in the God by whom he knew that he had been sent. He resolved to trust in God despite the darkness of his situation. This may well be seen as the heart of the event in Gethsemane. He entrusted to God what from a human point of view seemed to be the failure of his message. The gospels later understood that what Jesus had to experience as a 'historical fiasco', that is, as a real event in our history, was in reality a *historic* fiasco, that is, an event of far-reaching historical significance!

I have played on the double meaning of the word historic/historical: for Jesus his violent death was historically a fiasco, although he accepted this event in faithfulness to God; on the other hand, the gospels later saw this actual failure as an event of historic significance: the saving significance of the acceptance of this failure becomes transparent in the gospels. The biblical account of the process in which Jesus is gradually identified, without leaving out any relevant detail, is like a circle in which the significance of the preceding partial sequences are confirmed and at the same time transcended. Finally, *Jesus himself* reveals his identity to the community of believers (the significance of the resurrection appearances). The last word in which the biblical process of identification is completed can only be heard in the account of the crucifixion and resurrection of Jesus. It becomes clear from the whole of the account that the recognition of the identity of Jesus and his presence among us – 'I will be with you to the end of time' (Matt. 28.20) – are indissolubly connected: only in and through the Easter experience can the true identity of Jesus be recognized. In a word, *christology*, the identification of the person of Jesus in faith, is the specifically human answer to the life-sized problem of human failure. It is the resurrection which gives the lie to the failure of the message and the life of Jesus, and at the same time to merely human conceptions of what 'real success' must and can mean. The Christian conception is not so much concerned with coming to terms with the fact that human life is a mixture of partial success and partial failure; it goes deeper: it is another assessment of real success and human failure, and therefore, in the last resort, another *experience*.

In this way the tensions between the synoptic and the Johannine conceptions become clear. In accordance with real human experience (and this is a living reality), the message and the life-style of Jesus and consequently his person itself were contradicted by his execution: he was muzzled. That is in fact a fiasco. For the Romans, the 'Jesus case' was finally closed. In human experience the aims, the message and the life of Jesus had turned into a fiasco. While taking it up into a deeper, still unexpressed conception, the synoptic gospels described this experience without leaving out any of its human aspect. That is the mark of the particular authenticity of the first three gospels. However, from God's standpoint – and this is evident only in man's *religious* experiences – there can really be no talk of a failure; that is explicitly the standpoint of John, who presupposes the synoptic experience but relativizes its true form. Particular forms of failure in a programme (in the case of men who have done everything possible not to fail), which are also experienced as human impotence, appear in the *religious* experience of these same men as a manifestation of the power of God, the power of a love which is apparently helpless and impotent, a love which is disarmed but at the same time disarming. Religious communion with God robs purely human experience of its presumption to have the last word. This is not to make light of what is grievous in human experience; but it does rob that of its sting: failure is not the last evidence.

Human failure in innocence, and often also in penitent guilt, is taken up by the believer into the strong love of God which can also manifest itself in earthly impotence and being overwhelmed by the powers of evil, of what is human and all too human. With their accents placed in a variety of areas, the synoptic gospels and the Gospel of John, with their four-sided 'synoptic' approach, testify at the same time both to the depth of human failure in a world of finite and sinful men, and to the depth of the triumphant mercy of God in a human world which in the last resort is experienced as 'God's world'. Here the phenomenon of Jesus is in the last resort a problem of God.

However, we must see the failure of Jesus and the divine success which is manifested in it as a complex of differences as well as a unity. In my view it should not be presented as though on the one hand, in the dimensions of our *history*, the message and life of Jesus proved a failure because of human misunderstanding and resistance, while on the other hand, on a *supra-historical*, transcendent level, God transformed this fiasco into a divine victory and redemption, at the same time leaving the fiasco as what it really is. In that case we would again be venerating a kind of two-stage dualism. Rather, we have to say that God's transcendent overcoming of human failure is historically incorporated in Jesus' never-ceasing love for God and man, during and in the historical moment of his failure on the cross. And precisely in this way, Jesus' failure acquires a productive and critical force in the dimension of our history; despite the gulf created by failure through the fatal rejection of Jesus by his fellow men, there is *continuity* between the hidden dimension of what took place on the cross and its manifestation in the resurrection of Jesus, though we are not in a position to make a theoretical reconciliation of the human experience of failure and the religious experience of the redemptive triumph of God *in* this failure.

The non-failure, or success, of earthly powers is possible only through the power of the police, money, and degrading tyranny, which tortures and puts out of the way anyone who can turn its own success to failure. Seldom is this real inability to accept one's own failure and the belief that a particular view of what man needs for his own salvation is the right one experienced as intensively as in the dictatorships of our time, left-wing or right-wing, which can only bolster up their own success temporarily by torture or extermination, or by stopping the mouth of anyone who thinks or wills otherwise. However, the great message of God himself, which is brought to us as good news in the person, the life and the death of Jesus Christ, is the faith that such earthly success cannot be the way to truly human healing, to true success or salvation, but is rather the way to the final failure of human history, whether personal or collective. The fact that the passion of Jesus continues in our human history, that numerous other crosses have been erected alongside his own cross, therefore remains under the criticism of the message of God in and through the life and death of Jesus. In the meantime, however, the Christian knows that in the face of tyrannical power God *identifies himself* with the one who can take upon himself such a historical fiasco, unarmed, but offering exemplary resistance, in faithfulness to communion with the one who is in the last resort the Lord of history. True, everything is decided in our history, but the last word is not with history, but with the God who lives with us. At the same time this divine power in the fiasco of Jesus reveals to us that *ultimate* failure, *definitive* evil and *unreconciled* suffering have their real, final and terrifying form only in man's reluctance and inability to love. That is the definition of what the great religious traditions call 'hell': a failure that man *cannot and will not* any longer entrust to the living God; resolute insistence on success, which finds its strength only in tyranny and dishonouring fellow men, on a larger or smaller scale. It is this, rather than a concern to set forth orthodoxy and one sole kind of salvation.

There is yet more in this Christian conception of the crucifixion of Jesus. Death in no way *constitutes* anyone's identity. However, only at death, as the conclusion of a man's historical life, does life appear whole and 'rounded off'. Only then can his true identity become clear. So anyone who does not want to remove the real negativity – or 'non-identity' – and thus the historical finitude of the suffering and death of Jesus from his life, or to neutralize them by making them abstract, by transferring the suffering to God (robbing Jesus of his essential historicity and finitude and thus really negating the passion) must concede that this death, as rejection by men, put his message and his way of life to the supreme test. It is possible to react to this in two ways: *either* Jesus was just a man like all of us, in which case his claim rests on an illusion, *or* as man he was so at one with a completely different reality which we call God that this divine reality did not in any way compete with his humanity. In his death he remains fully one with his God. The wholly other is at the same time the one who is wholly near: this in particular emerges from the message, the way of life and the death of Jesus. Consequently the Christian tradition rightly calls him, with unprecedented boldness, albeit in words which appeal more to the particular logic of religious language than to purely theoretical reason, 'the only-beloved, unique Son' (the Gospel of John).

### (b) Liberation from guilty failure: guilt and the forgiveness of sins

There is also a deeper failure, failure through guilt and sinfulness; there is suffering because of one's own guilt. With good reason the New Testament has often laid great emphasis, sometimes sole emphasis, on redemption from this guilt – the forgiveness of sins – without arriving at the explicit insight that the 'sins of the world' can also be found lodged in institutions and structures created by man.

Modern theories of redemption and liberation tend to brush aside this fundamental aspect of liberation, namely from guilt and sin. Guilt and the consciousness of sin are evidently no longer 'in'. However, we can see some reasons for this evasion. It can be claimed, .for example, that for centuries churches and religions have directed their proclamation of guilt and sinfulness at the little people who cannot defend themselves, while the great and the mighty have gone free. Furthermore, the oppressed in society have been kept down by playing on their sense of sinfulness and the torments of hell: as a result they have remained small, anxious and immature. In a justified reaction to this, modern man is more restrained in his talk of sin and guilt; in fact there are many extenuating reasons and circumstances. And there is more to it than that. Even reference to the obvious fact that micro-ethical privatized concern has turned into a human responsibility for macro-ethical dimensions cannot wholly explain the weakening (or shift) in the awareness of guilt. For even in this latter instance, personal conscience often does not feel affected: it is the fault of 'the others', society or the anonymous collectiveness of Western culture. And so people get off scot-free.

Consciousness not only of *failure* but of one's own *guilt* is deeply connected with awareness of God or religious awareness. Wherever this is stunted, a real awareness of sin finally disappears (for all the relative autonomy of so-called natural or human ethics). As I remarked earlier, belief in God has a specific critical and productive force: at this point we must add that it does so particularly in connection with changing human lives. No 'concept' is practical and critical to the same degree as the 'concept of God'. For man, belief in God is essentially a summons to *metanoia* and a change of life. Where religious awareness is stinted or inauthentic, a whole and healthy awareness of guilt shrivels up. Sin is not just an ethical concept; it is most profoundly *theological*. Just as the good which is done for the sake of our fellow men has definitive validity in and of itself (see above), so there is something irrevocable in evil actions which men perform of their own free will. These are not only irrevocably part of the past history of man; in addition this human guilt is a free action against the living God, albeit always in and to worldly things, people and situations. Even in sin, human action is directly confronted by God in *mediated* immediacy. By violating humanity, the sinner is personally guilty before God, the source of all furthering of the good and opposition to evil. Violation of oneself and others is the visible side of guilt towards God which – because of this anthropological structure of mediation – can never be exhaustively explained by the sinner himself. In this he is 'handed over' to God for grace and refusal of grace (from our standpoint, see below). Therefore at the deepest level, liberation from guilt is possible only through God (here again in mediated immediacy, above all through the mediation of the penitent sinner). Guilt has a dialogical structure and can never be removed one-sidedly; it calls for the creative word of God's forgiveness, which transcends our act of penitence from within. Therefore, like sin, God's forgiveness is an event the full depths of which we can never plumb.

There is a great difference here between liberation from physical oppression (e.g. sickness, hunger and poverty), psycho-somatic oppression (e.g. pathological alienations) and socio-political oppression on the one hand, and liberation from sin and guilt on the other. In the first instances people can intervene enough to heal either person or society, but in the latter case no direct human intervention can bring liberation. For in the last resort what we have here is a *guilty* failure (which is perhaps something quite different from failure).

The Christian answer to the suffering of guilt is, 'He loved us while we were still sinners' (Rom. 5.8), i.e. we are handed over to God's *grace*. In the last resort the depth of this liberation from sin through God is also indefinable. Therefore we believe and hope in God's mercy, although this awareness of God's mercy cannot *assure* us of salvation in view of what for us is the ultimate impenetrability of the depth and breadth of an originally free act and the diffuse sinfulness of our life.

This justification through grace in faith is therefore the nucleus of salvation from God in Christ, in the light of which all other aspects of liberation become comprehensible. For this gift of grace or the forgiveness of sins gives and teaches us the *mores Dei*: furthering all that is good, opposing all that is evil. It is a manifestation in our human life of the nature of God himself.

One might say that only love is redemptive, because it essentially guarantees a person's existence, accepts them, confirms them and endorses them. Love is taking the side of another person. But here our creaturely love is merely an affirmation of the creative love of God, from which it draws its truth. For given men as they actually are, we cannot endorse or guarantee life. Therefore truly redemptive love is possible only in the form of a love which *changes* the world and fellow man, or in the form of *forgiveness* and reconciliation. At least fragmentary salvation is realized where we encounter others in love. But salvation, wholeness, is possible only in perfection and universality. And no merely human love can promise such salvation to a fellow man and mean it. If goodness and salvation were promised to us only on human authority, we would be living in an illusion. Universal and perfect salvation can be promised to us only through the love of God, the Creator who also forgives us. Supported by this absolute love, human love becomes the *sacrament* of God's redemptive love. God says to us. 'You may exist.' That is the 'justification by grace alone' of which the New Testament speaks. God's creative guarantee of human existence legitimates us for loving involvement in the existence of others – and even our own existence (be reconciled, have peace with oneself, with one's own finitude). Redemption is being accepted by God, and in respect of our own real life that is being accepted by God in forgiveness. Salvation in Jesus from God is tested specifically through the action of our 'orthopractic' love. For that very reason, love of man grounded in God remains 'unquiet', in the sense of 'dissatisfied', so long as salvation is not realized universally and completely for each and every individual. I do not follow Jürgen Moltmann in his interpretation of the problem of suffering, but he is right when he says, 'because reconciliation has come nearer in remembrances and hope, people begin to suffer because the world has not been redeemed.'[169] This 'discontent' which acts as a stimulus towards action, and which is to be found in a life redeemed by God, is part of the nature of Christian redemption, just as the possibility of addressing God in prayer is an essential part of this same redemption.

As a result, despite all the unrest and ongoing suffering, there are already fragments of *eschatological joy* in our history, even to the point of what the New Testament calls joy in suffering; not in a doloristic sense, but because of God's saving presence, which may also be experienced in suffering and death and in penitence for guilt. For Christians there are no reasons for despair and defeatism. This particular awareness of faith and this hope lead us to realize righteousness and love for all men. Not to be active, to allow things to run their course, would be in utter contradiction to the active significance of *theological hope for our fellow men*.

### (c) God's promise of final salvation, presented by a fragmentary practice of reconciliation

One basic theme of all religions, for all the variations in which it is presented, may be said to be that the well-grounded expectation of victory over our history of human suffering is a generous and unmerited gift of God. However, there seems to me to be no parallel or precedent in the history of religions for the way in which salvation from God, with its inspiration towards an actual improvement of our history, is experienced and proclaimed in the Christian experience of reality through Jesus Christ.

*On the one hand*, we see Jesus' readiness to serve, the way in which he compromises himself with tax collectors and sinners (*les damnés de la terre*), and nevertheless (as Christian intuition might interpret it), 'knowing that the Father had given all things into his hand' (John 13.3), refuses to do anything to his own advantage. In such a situation, which is critical for him, he insists on washing his disciples' feet; in other words, he becomes the servant of all, even to the point of death on the cross. *On the other hand*, we see the Christian answer: believers who are convinced that in this selfless service of one man towards his fellow men, a man who is rejected by others, God reveals himself most deeply, fundamentally and finally as God. Now the salvation from God which is shown in these two dimensions, this pattern of salvation from God, seems to me in fact to be unique in the history of religions (so far as my knowledge of other religions goes). Of course no Christian can say this without at the same time striking his breast and penitently confessing his own failure over the Christianity which has been inspired by Jesus. However, wherever in history Christianity was and is faithful to Jesus himself, we see this same programme and pattern of life: a connection between a mystical orientation on God's rule of peace which is concerned with humanity and a corresponding 'life-style of the kingdom of God' which militates against our own particular history of suffering.

Finality as such does not *per se* include suffering and death. Were that the case, then belief in an exalted life above this earthly one – which still remains a life of *finite* being – would remain an inner contradiction. Creatures still are not God. The conviction that the history of human suffering is not necessary, and faith that suffering may not be final and thus must be overcome, are experienced symbolically and playfully in the Christian liturgy. For the sacraments are anticipatory, mediating signs of salvation, that is, healed and reconciled life. And given our historical situation, at the same time they are symbols of protest serving to unmask the life that is not yet reconciled in the specific dimension of our history. In the light of its prophetic vision of universal *šālōm*, accusation also has a part in the liturgy.

As long as there is still a real history of suffering among us, we cannot do without the sacramental liturgy: to abolish it or neglect it would be to stifle the firm hope in universal peace and general reconciliation. For as long as salvation and peace are still not actual realities, hope for them must be attested and above all nourished and kept alive, and this is only possible in anticipatory symbols. For that very reason, the Christian liturgy stands under the sign of the great symbols of the death and resurrection of Jesus. Here the cross is the symbol of resistance to death against the alienation of our human history of suffering, the consequence of the message of a God *who is concerned with man*; the resurrection of Jesus makes it clear to us that suffering may not and will not have the last word. Sacramental action therefore summons Christians to liberating action in our world. The liturgical anticipation of reconciled life in the free communication of a 'community of Christ' would not make any sense if it did not in fact help to realize liberating action in the world. Therefore the sacramental liturgy is the appropriate place in which the believer becomes pointedly aware that there is a grievous gulf between his prophetic vision of a God concerned for peace among men and the real situation of mankind, and at the same time that our history of human suffering is unnecessary and can be changed. So if it is rightly performed, there is in Christian sacramental symbolic action a powerful historical potential which can integrate mysticism and politics (albeit in secular forms). In remembrance of the passion of Jesus which was brought to a triumphal conclusion by God – as a promise for us all – in their liturgy, Christians celebrate their particular connection with this Jesus and in it the possibility of creative liberation and reconciliation in our human history.

History teaches us that there has never been a perfect redemption, but that in Jesus there is a divine promise for us all, and that this is anticipated in any definitively valid act of doing good to our fellow men in a finite and conditioned world in which love is always doomed to failure and yet nevertheless refuses to choose any other way than that of loving service. Any attempt at totality which cannot recognize the non-identical, refractory suffering and failure of this doing good and is not content with it, leads to an illusion, has an alienating effect, or becomes unproductive.[170] Christian belief in salvation from God in Jesus as the Christ is the downfall of any doctrine of salvation or soteriology understood in human terms, in the sense of an identity which is within our control and therefore can be manipulated. The Christian gospel is not an unmediated identity, but a practice of identification with what is not identical, the non-I, the other, above all the suffering and the injustice of others. Definitive salvation remains an indefinable horizon in our history in which both the hidden God (*Deus absconditus*) and the sought-for, yet hidden, *humanum* disappear. But if the fundamental symbol of God is the living man (*imago Dei*), then the place where man is dishonoured, violated and oppressed, both in his own heart and in a society which oppresses men, is at the same time the preferred place where *religious experience* become possible in a way of life which seeks to give form to this symbol, to heal it and give it its own liberated existence. As the intrinsic consequence of the radicalism of its message and reconciling practice, the crucifixion of Jesus shows that any attempt at liberating redemption which is concerned with humanity is valid *in and of itself* and not subsequently as a result of any success which may follow. What counts is not success, any more than failure or misfortune, above all as the result of the intervention of others. The important thing is loving service. We are shown the true face of both God and man in the 'vain' love of Jesus which knows that its criterion does not lie in success, but in its very being as radical love and identification. In that case, reconciliation and liberation, if they seek to be valid for all, despite the limited aspect of an imperfect historical situation, are not a mere change of power relationships and thus a new domination. Redemption is a task imposed upon us; for us it remains a reconciliation to be realized, which will constantly be moulded by failure, suffering and death in the refractoriness of our history – by a love which is impotent in this world but which will never give in. It is based on a love which ventures the impossible and does not compel man to what he himself sees as liberation and redemption. In our time, above all, Christians only have the right to utter the word 'God' where they find their identity in identification with that part of life which is still unreconciled, and in effective action towards reconciliation and liberation. What history tells us about Jesus, what the church tells and indeed *promises* us about Jesus is that in this way of life, which is in conformity with the message of Jesus and the kingdom of God, we are shown the *real possibility* of an experience of God. In Jesus the Christ, we are promised that this way of life will bring us particularly close to God. However, what final possibilities are contained in the eschatological consummation of this saving presence of God, which we celebrate and give thanks for in the liturgy, is God's mystery, which may be called the abundance of our humanity. Furthermore, we know from the same history of and about Jesus, that the promise of the inward presence of God rests on the futility and the historical failure of this way

of life, as on the cross. This kind of liberation refuses ever to sacrifice a
fellow man for a hoped-for better future, or to leave him out in the cold
until better structures have been found. The practice of reconciliation
and liberation, which nevertheless can also experience the nearness of
God even in failure and suffering, is the sphere in which mystical experience of God becomes possible and in which, moreover, it can show
its credentials. Because in the last resort the one who is experienced and
can be known in this action of reconciliation, the living God, is always
greater than our action, this experience, this experience of God, as an
inner element of liberating and reconciling action, always discloses to us
a new and greater future. Here the believer experiences that redemption
is not within our power and that God nevertheless *gives a future* to all our
action towards liberation and reconciliation, a future which is greater
than the volume of our finite history.

What, then, is salvation in Jesus from God? I would want to say: being
at the disposal of others, losing oneself to others (each in his own limited
situation) and within this 'conversion' (which is also made possible by
structural changes) also working through anonymous structures for the
happiness, the goodness and the truth of mankind. This way of life, born
of grace, provides a real possibility for a very personal encounter with
God, who is then experienced as the source of all happiness and salvation,
the source of joy. It is communicative freedom which is actively reconciled
with our own finitude, our death, our transgression and our failure. It
sounds almost inauthentic: reconciliation with oneself as a useless servant,
although we know that God says to us, 'You may exist.' It is being
justified freely through faith by grace. Even if there is no human love in
return, sometimes if there is even misunderstanding, the believer knows
in his sovereign freedom, which is at the same time grateful humility,
that there is love in return: God first loved us. Real redemption or
salvation always passes over into mysticism: only here can the tension
between action and contemplation be sustained. This is existing for others
and thus for *the* Other, the wholly intimate and near yet 'transcendent
God', with whom Jesus has made us familiar.

Putting it in scholarly terms (but in that case we are saying everything
and yet nothing): belief in salvation from God in Jesus Christ is a conviction, freely accepted (though through the medium of Christian churches, and therefore derived from real life) − *in* the conditions of our
transitoriness − of our 'exaltation' above this finitude, thanks to the
absolute freedom and generosity of the merciful presence of the God who
takes our part, which we may experience *in* faith in our impenetrable
finitude, though there what we experience corporeally is more his absence.
This is the source of availability for all men, or as I would venture to

repeat (even in regard of our own failure) above all for 'the least of my own'.

In the last resort, theology which *loses itself* in sociology, psychology, politics or anything else that men may rightly think up for the benefit of others, is no longer theology. Theology which remains true to its task can only speak about the mystery of God as man's salvation (albeit with the help of other disciplines, which it must not in any way avoid). What it then has to say is that love of God and love of men are a single, inviolable 'divine virtue': 'He who abides in love abides in God, and God with him' (I John 4.16). That transcends any of our own attempts at liberation.

# 'The grace of the Lord Jesus Christ and the love of God and the fellowship of the Holy Spirit' (II Cor. 13.14)

My original intention was to end by discussing *pneumatology* and *ecclesiology*, i.e. the view of the Spirit of God as it is at work in the church and the world, a view which is implicit both in *Jesus. An Experiment in Christology*, and in this book, the original title of which was *Righteousness and Love*. However, the book has grown too long for this to be possible.

So, as according to the spirituality of the Tanach and the Christian gospel, salvation from God becomes to its inner consummation in praise and thanksgiving (*bᵉrākā* or *eucharistia*), and in this praise of God grace in fact expressly becomes the experience of grace, I thought it a good thing to end the book with a *bᵉrākā*, and to preface that with the basic ideas of these two books about Jesus in the form of a homily.

## Homiletical prologue

Rejoice and do not be dismayed,
for God to whom we pray,
is closer than our closest friends
and in our midst today.

We have just been singing these words, to the tune of one of our hymns, *in medio ecclesiae*, in this assembly or 'community of Jesus'.

Important words! We are gathered together here in his name, in the name of Jesus of Nazareth, to whom we bear witness as the 'Christ', that is, salvation from God. And why? May I be the interpreter of what non-Christians think aloud and of the questions that nag at the conscience of a great many Christians? What does this Jesus mean for us? Someone who is far removed from us in space and time, who lived a remarkably short life – barely thirty years – almost two thousand years ago: a flame which blazed out suddenly, somewhere in a corner of the earth. He appeared as a prophet for one, or at most two, years, and then was removed by those in power at the time. He was executed, evidently because he had spoken of a God who was concerned for humanity and who therefore required men to be concerned for their fellow men. The Bible calls this 'the kingdom of God', the living God, who has mercy on the humble and the outcast, men who have been shamefully treated:

those who lack a glass of water and clothing, 'warmth' or recognition – the poor and the mourners of the Sermon on the Mount.

Barely twenty-five years later, Nero drove the Stoic philosopher Seneca – at that time his adviser – to his death because Seneca had kept pointing out to this inhuman and cruel emperor that imperial rule had to be concerned with humanity (*humanitas*) and mercy (*clementia*).

However, we have not met together here in the name of Seneca. That brings us up against the question: why are we followers . . . of *Jesus*? Why do we want to 'follow' him and meet together here in *his* name? This question concerns us more deeply than any ecumenical question within the church, when Christians argue over the best, the most biblical name that they can and may give him whom they all experience as salvation from God. But why is salvation from God experienced especially in Jesus of Nazareth, one man among the many who, as Hebrews puts it, 'were too good for this world' (Heb. 11.38)? That is a question which digs deep into our understanding and painfully rends our hearts. Can we Christians still, in word and deed, 'give an account of the hope which lives in us' (I Peter 3.15)? The great and burning question is not that of relations within the churches. It is the question whether we Christians, from no matter what Christian community, are still capable of making our Christian hope credible to men. Today the meaning of the challenge 'Who do men think that I am?' coincides with the question of our own, namely *Christian*, identity. Are we in reality what we confess in our creed of faith and hope? The question of the identity of Jesus becomes all the more urgently a *question to Christians*: it is a question from 'the world' about the public visibility of our Christian identity.

However, despite everything, one fact is unmistakable and irremovable: we have all come together here in large numbers from a great many places and churches and are joined together with one another as 'the community of Jesus' in brotherly love around the one centre Jesus, the Christ, or whatever else we name him. And yet we have not come together here to remember someone who died a long time ago, who offered us supreme visions from the abyss of our suffering existence, to celebrate a belated memorial service for one of the countless shattered prophetic dreams: to renew our memories of a much loved man, long dead, who was killed for high ideals. This meeting takes place under the sign of the person of Jesus of Nazareth. This man evidently binds us together in a common, completely unanimous conviction.

In that case, however, we must be concerned with something more than reminiscences of the old story of the suffering of 'a righteous man', the story of a *ṣaddīq* in whom we recognize our own failures and our sorrow and celebrate them perhaps narcissistically or furiously. It is more than a stylization of old memories, in which we are the most active partner and the Jesus from the past is simply the passive object of the interplay of our memories and expectations. Such mysterious forces certainly do not emanate from a dead man. And yet this will have been the case, though evidently only for a short time. In the long run these reminiscences fade away. In the following generations they shimmer on the horizon, where the colours fade, until finally they are no more than a subject for historical research – if these forgotten figures are allowed that historical privilege at all.

However, if the living interest in past events, in a man from the past, exceeds the curiosity of purely historical research, then this interest also itself belongs to the ongoing historical identity of the man whom we continue to remember. Our thoughts, our interest, our contemplation of him then become an element of *his* radiant identity. This recognition – which of itself is still quite 'secular' – directs our attention to the special meaning that Christian faith recognizes in what – in religious language – it calls the physical resurrection of Jesus, a category which transcends mere talk of remembrance. Therefore more must be at stake with Jesus, in whose name we are now assembled, not in any historical interest, but by virtue of a memory which has been preserved down the centuries. Has something happened with him of such a kind that – as a result – something special can happen to us too? Only if something like this does in fact happen to us, so many years after Jesus' departure, can we make clear anything of the identity of Jesus to the world in and through our Christian identity. In that case, by the way of our own Christian life – and is it really a detour? – we can help men look for signs in Jesus of Nazareth which can guide the human call for freedom, salvation or wholeness to the Christian answer, which points to a quite special saving act of God in Jesus for all men. Only then are others in a position to give their own answer to the question, 'Who do you think that I am?'

Therefore for us the central problem is: how and what salvation do we claim to find in Jesus of Nazareth? There are many possibilities which restore man to himself, so that he can be who he is for others and in so doing find liberation, redemption, joy and ultimately peace. We have seen that there is certainly a possibility of doing away with some human alienation with the help of science, technology and new structures. At the same time, however, we have seen that this real possibility only affects such alienations as are the result of physical, spiritual and social conditions – limitations of human freedom which can in fact for the most part be removed by opposition, coupled with knowledgeable and active effort. Moreover, in these liberations we can see shreds of God's redemption: through man and the world.

The question, however, is whether man does not experience deeper alienations, an alienation which is essentially bound up with our finitude, with our involvement in a nature which is alient to us, with solitude, with suffering because of and in love, with suffering because of our mortality, suffering also because of the invisibility of the hidden God, suffering finally because of our personal and collective guilt and sin: the dirty hands of our human history with so much innocent suffering, injustice and injury, the tears of human and divine indignation. Necessary and urgent though it is, human liberation – a fragment of salvation – seems to be limited, and *real* liberation is unmistakably *limited* unless it can feel included in the indefinable divine possibilities which can give our limited action a still greater, better future – life for what is passing away in history. In that case, however, the surrender of limited man must be boundless and unrestrained. For in that case, precisely for the sake of one another, we must renounce the convulsive search for our own limited identity. Complete liberation and redemption, salvation as the making whole of transitory man, seems to be impossible without the experience of communication, of identification with the non-I, the not one's own, the other, above all with the suffering of others, with what is alien to us. Finally, it seems impossible without our *finite* identification with the living God who identifies himself with our friends as the living one in Jesus. The making whole of finite men is impossible without *giving, receiving* and *reconciliation*: without resurrection.

That first becomes clear to us from *God's own message* which we may hear in proclamation, from the life and death of Jesus of Nazareth. One of the best attested facts of the life of Jesus is that he spoke of the imminence of the kingdom of God: of God concerned for humanity. The whole of Jesus' life was a *celebration* of this rule of God's peace and at the same time an *orthopraxis*, that is acting justly in accordance with the demands of this kingdom for peace. The connection between God's peace and just action for peace among men is so close, so unified, that in his works Jesus could recognize the coming of the kingdom of God (Luke 7.22f. with 11.20). In the history of disaster and suffering in which Jesus was involved there was no reason and no occasion which Jesus could not make understandable and meaningful in the light of the unqualified certainty of salvation which characterizes his message and his action. Such a hope, which is expressed in Jesus' proclamation of the imminent, liberating mercy of God on men, unmistakably has its origin in an experience of contrast: on the one hand the stubborn human history of suffering, of harm and disturbance, injustice and human slavery, and on the other hand, Jesus' own special experience of God, his *Abba* experience, his converse with the Father, the source of all that is good and the hidden motive force behind all resistance against evil, against illness and suffering – converse with the caring, benevolent 'anti-evil', which will not recognize the supremacy of evil and refuses to allow evil to have the last word for the sake of the good. In the light of his *Abba* experience, Jesus could bring men the message of a hope which cannot be derived from our world history. One can evidently say something about God from a deeply religious converse with God – even the most important thing that can be said about men. Jesus' *Abba* experience is an experience of God as a power who frees men through the impotence of boundless love, which also goes on to say no to everything that harms man and brings about evil and wickedness. For Jesus, therefore, *men* are *men whom God cares for*.

True, well-meaning attempts are often made to explain Jesus simply as a good and perfect man – the 'second Adam' – but we shall never recognize him *in his truly human identity* if we eliminate from this life of Jesus his quite special, unique *relationship to God* which we find almost impossible to define. For it is precisely *in* this relationship that we have the origin, the meaning and the force of his message and his parables, his beatitudes and his liberating way of life.

Because of this we are all faced with the question, 'But who do *you* think that I am?' Before we give an answer to it, we must ask ourselves whether the promise which can give a foundation to this firm hope remains if it is deprived of the ground and the source of Jesus' *Abba* experience, and whether without it the Christian hope is not exchanged for a problematical, utopian dream without any meaningful foundation for absolute trust in the future.

Moreover, we would only have Jesus partially, and would fail to understand him, if we ignored what an aged prophet, matured in experience, said at his coming into our history of suffering and injustice: 'This child is destined for the fall and rise of many; and for a sign that is spoken against' (Luke 2.34). His message and his public claim, finally his person itself, were indeed rejected by our world. According to all the rules prevailing at the time, he was executed. Nevertheless, even in his dying Jesus was not desperately concerned with his own identity and thus with self-survival. His identity was to identify himself with others, with the cause of man as God's own highest cause. That is what he lived for, and that is what he died for. God is concerned with humanity, but in a world which obviously is not always so concerned itself: as a result of this, God's good will towards man in Jesus takes on a colouring which we ourselves have mixed. However, in his concern for man God transcends all our mixtures and creations, without doing violence to our own finite autonomy. Historically, the life of Jesus in fact ends in a catastrophe which cannot be classified theoretically or practically. Considered from a purely human point of view, we really are confronted with a fiasco here, a new failure which fits into the growing series of innocent men executed over our history of human suffering, a brief hope which again and again seems to confirm the presumption that many men do not accept it, but its hollowness must be seen in the light of the peculiarity and gravity of our constantly repetitive history as 'a world of suffering'.

Because of the life which preceded it, the death of Jesus, the divine mystic who was therefore a defender of men, confronts us with a fundamental question about God which allows of only two possible answers. *Either* we must say that God, the God of the imminent salvation from God proclaimed by Jesus, was an illusion, in the last resort a delusion of Jesus, *or* through this rejection and death of Jesus we are compelled to revise fundamentally our understanding of God, our own conceptions of God and our understanding of history and to reject them as invalid – whereas the real nature of God only proves to be valid in the life and death of Jesus, and as a result opens up a new perspective on the future, a future for the one who, humanly speaking, has no future. Human history – with its successes, fiascos, illusions and disillusionments – is transcended by the living God, who has the last word and wills man's salvation. We can perhaps *live* in illusions, but we can hardly *die* in illusions. That is the heart of the Christian message of the resurrection of Jesus, who summons us to acts of liberation and human healing, to the task of being mutual happiness to one another and not living from illusions and ideologies.

Only if as believers we can also help others to experience where we find salvation and healing in Jesus of Nazareth will it also make sense – and even be necessary – to go on asking about the relationship of the man Jesus to the living God, about Jesus as the Son of God who survived death – not vice versa. In this world we men evidently need a fellow man who has experienced humanity to its depths and at the same time gives expression to God in it through word and deed. If we want to respect God's saving purposes, we must first subject the man Jesus to criticism. For God means to encounter us *in a human way* in order – really – in the end to help us to find him. The answer to the question of the universal saving significance of Jesus, 'Christ' or 'the light of the world', thus discloses the true nature of man: the liberating realization of true humanity, and also – precisely in that – the true face of God, the champion of all good and the opponent of all evil, suffering and sickness. To establish God's kingdom of peace thus means to make possible the experience of God concerned for humanity in the life of man concerned for humanity, through which God can and may then be rightly discussed – with credentials in our hand. In the end, Jesus' identity as the personal manifestation of God's all-embracing love of man will be shown through man and the world. In that case *belief in Jesus* is only possible, as, and at the same time in the form of, a *confession of God*: 'Truly this man was a Son of God' (Mark 15.39b).

However, this confession must continually spring up afresh from a personal source-experience in the specific situation of our history of un-righteousness and servitude, intolerance and lack of reconciliation. It cannot be the parrot-like repetition of a kerygma heard once before, however sacred that kerygma may be. 'My eyes have now' – here and now, said the aged Simeon in the Temple – 'seen your salvation which you have prepared for all peoples, a light to lighten the Gentiles' (Luke 2.29–32). Can *we* and may *we* really say: *now* my eyes have seen your salvation? Do we see among ourselves, as Paul said, that Christians are 'an open letter from Christ, written not on stone tables but in and through their lives' (II Cor. 3.2f.)? Jesus' light burns in this world only with the oil of our lives, in quite particular circumstances, in which we emanate liberating light or dim or even quench this light, so that the world disappears in clouds.

The message, the life and the death of Jesus disarmingly express this deep-seated problem of human life in the proclamation of the resurrection, in a correct language, but one which is no longer understood because it is the language of the church. In word and deed, Jesus, the one who is redeemed from death, speaks of a liberation which frees men for freedom: 'Brothers, you are called to freedom' (Gal. 5.13). 'For freedom Christ has set us free; stand fast, therefore, and do not submit again to a yoke of slavery' (Gal. 5.1f.). We are redeemed for a humanity which may and can *transcend* itself, as scripture says, which 'by the power *at work within us* is able to do far more abundantly than all that we ask or think' (Eph. 3.20). Salvation in Jesus is, then, salvation from God and yet is communicated to us historically through our history of making whole and the love through which the limitations, alienations and impotence of our life, and (thanks to our living fellowship with the living God) ulti-mately death itself will be conquered. Then the finite self – for that is what we are – will be redeemed. In Jesus, man's humanity is freed for a redeemed and redemptive acceptance that we can and may only realize the promise of our human nature, what we are for one another, through grace, and that we may experience the call to love which transcends us, each individual and all together, person and community, in a redemptive experience of an absolute guarantee, which goes beyond all of us and yet is in no way alien to our humanity: the living God.

This event experienced in faith calls us to a *homologia*, that is, to an affirmative confession of what God himself has given us, and to a solemn *eucharistia*, that is to a celebration and praise of God because he himself means to be the living content of salvation for man.[171]

## Creed

I believe in God, the Father: the omnipotence of love.
He is the Creator of heaven and earth;
this whole universe,
with all its mysteries;
this earth on which we live,
and the stars to which we travel.
He knows us from eternity, he never forgets
that we are made of the dust of the earth
and that one day we shall return again to it as dust.

I believe in Jesus Christ,
the only-beloved Son of God.
For love of all of us,
he has willed to share our history, our existence with us.
I believe that God also wanted to be our God
in a human way.
He has dwelt as man among us,
a light in the darkness.
But the darkness did not overcome him.
We nailed him to the cross.
And he died and was buried.
But he trusted in God's final word,
and is risen, once and for all;
he said that he would prepare a place for us,
in his Father's house, where he now dwells.

I believe in the Holy Spirit,
who is the Lord and gives life.
And for the prophets among us,
he is language, power and fire.
I believe that together we are all on a journey,
pilgrims, called and gathered together,
to be God's holy people,
for I confess freedom from evil,
the task of bringing justice
and the courage to love.

I believe in eternal life,
in love that is stronger than death,
in a new heaven and a new earth.

And I believe that I may hope for
a life with God and with one another
for all eternity:
Glory for God and peace for men.

## Approach to the eucharist

Praise be to you, our God, Lord of all things living,
praise because
through this honest confession of faith
we may trust in you.
Mindful of your saying,
'Where two or three are gathered together in my name,
there am I in their midst',
we pray you
to send your Spirit on us and these small gifts,
a piece of bread and a cup of wine.
May these our gifts
be the body and blood of Jesus.

## Eucharistic thanksgiving

Lord our God,
gathered together here around you,
we remember the old story
which has been told down the ages,
of Jesus of Nazareth,
a man who boldly dared to say to you, Lord God,
*Abba*, Father,
and has taught us to do the same thing.

O God, our Father,
we thank you for this man,
who has changed the face of the earth,
because he spoke of a great vision,
of the kingdom of God which will come one day,
a kingdom of freedom, love and peace,
*your* kingdom, the perfection of your creation.

We remember that
wherever your Jesus came,
men rediscovered their humanity,

and so were filled with new riches,
so that they could give one another
new courage in their lives.

We remember,
how he spoke to people,
about a lost coin,
a sheep that had strayed, a lost son:
of all those who are lost and no longer count,
out of sight, out of mind; the weak and the poor,
all those who are captive, unknown, unloved.

We recall that
he went to search for all who were lost,
for those who are saddened and out in the cold,
and how he always took their side,
without forgetting the others.

And that cost him his life,
because the mighty of the earth would not tolerate it.
And yet, good God, almighty Father,
he knew that he was understood and accepted by you,
he saw himself confirmed by you in love.

So he became one with you.
And so, freed from himself.,
he could live a life of liberation for others.

And we remember
how he, who loved us so much
and was one with you, his good Father,
in the last night of his life on earth,
took bread in his holy hands,
blessed, broke and shared it
at table with his friends, saying:
'This is my body for you.'

And what he did filled his heart:
he also took the cup at the table,
gave thanks, praised you, Father, and said:
'Drink this cup, all of you, with me,
for this is my loving covenant with you,
my blood which is shed for reconciliation,
the cup of liberation and happiness.'

So when we eat this bread together
and drink of this cup,
we do it in remembrance of him, your Son
who is the servant and liberator of us all,
now and ever and beyond death.

Therefore we now also think of the many
who have gone from us, all the people
whom we have loved so much . . .
Our Father, we cannot believe
that all that they
have meant for us
will now be lost for ever.
You are their life, now and always.

We think, too, of the world,
of all who love us in life.
Even the powerful, who have in their hands
the destiny of men, often without knowing them,
the rulers of the world and the church.
Help them and us, so that we may make this earth
a better home for us all;
so that we may make peace and be one
as you, Father, are in your Son,
and he is in you.

So send your Spirit upon us
and upon these gifts, the good Spirit
from you and your Son, that it may inspire us
when we continue to follow Jesus:
Jesus, from whom we have learnt to be free:
free from powers which estrange us,
free to do good.

As best we could, we have done
what Jesus, your witness, who knows our hearts,
commanded us to do:
to celebrate his memory.

In praise and thanks to you,
almighty Father,
in the unity of the Holy Spirit
now too we may and dare
through him and with him and in him
to pray together, as he has taught us:

'Our Father in heaven,
hallowed be your name,
your kingdom come,
your will be done,
in earth as in heaven.
Give us today our daily bread,
and forgive us our sins,
as we forgive those who sin against us.
Do not lead us into temptation,
but deliver us from evil.
For yours is the kingdom
and the power and the glory, for ever.

Strengthened and encouraged we now dare
to pass round this bread and this cup,
the sacrament of faith.

We pray you, our God,
make what we have done
in memory of Jesus,
who was filled by your Spirit,
a living and effective sign
of salvation and wholeness,
a sign of mutual and honest love,
a sign of freedom, peace and righteousness for all,
a sign of love for you, O God, our Liberator.

## Magnificat

(following a translation by Michel van der Plas)

With what I am and have,
I will highly exalt him,
the God who is my joy,
the Lord who brings me happiness.

Small and weak though I am,
he has gone before me;
before generations were born,
God has loved them.

For he, the Almighty himself,
praised be his name,
has done great things for me.

And his mercy extends
throughout all history,
to all men on earth,
who bow before his greatness.

With his mighty arm,
he casts down the proud.
He humbles them before his throne,
but he exalts the lowly.

And those who suffer hunger,
he fills with his riches,
to the rich he shows the door,
they are made powerless and empty.

He has taken to his heart,
the people whom he has chosen;
mindful of what he promised,
love and yet more love.

As he promised
to our fathers and mothers,
from Abraham onwards,
and to all who went before us.

So praise be to the Father,
the Son and Holy Spirit,
As it was in the beginning,
and will remain for ever.

# Notes

(i) So as not to make this book even longer, I have refrained from giving it a lengthy critical apparatus (except in the section on Johannine theology).
(ii) The 'notes' are (in theory) numbered consecutively within the main sections. The pages of the main text to which the notes refer are printed at the head of each page. This should make it easier to find them.
(iii) Abbreviated titles refer either to the literature cited on each particular subject, which is listed in full at the beginning of a chapter or section, or to books cited on the same or adjacent pages.
(iv) The Revised Standard Version has been used for biblical quotations, except where the author has made his own translation to follow the original more closely. (Chapter and verse numbers follow the English versions.)

*Part One: The Authority of New Experiences and the Authority of the New Testament*

1. The following literature is important in connection with the problems of the relationship between empirical *experience* and *science*, which are not dealt with explicitly in this chapter. H. Albert, *Traktat über kritische Vernunft*, Tübingen 1968; id., *Plädoyer für kritischen Rationalismus*, Tübingen 1971; K. O. Apel, 'Szientistik, Hermeneutik, Ideologiekritik', in *Hermeneutik und Ideologiekritik*, Frankfurt 1971, 7–44 (this article was first published in 1968); L. Boon, 'De nieuwe visie op de wetenschap. Een overzicht', *Mens en maatschappij* 43, 1974, 350–79; M. Gatzmeier, *Theologie als Wissenschaft?*, two vols., Stuttgart and Bad Cannstatt 1974, 1975; L. Gilkey, *Religion and the Scientific Future*, New York and London 1970; D. S. Greenberg, *The Politics of Pure Science*, New York 1967; A. D. de Groot, *Een minimale methodologie op sociaal-wetenschappelijke basis*, The Hague 1971; J. Habermas, *Gegen ein positivistisch halbierten Rationalismus*, Frankfurt 1969; id., *Knowledge and Human Interests*, ET London 1972; id., *Theory and Practice*, ET London 1974; id., *Technik und Wissenschaft als 'Ideologie'*, Frankfurt [4]1970; W. Heisenberg, *Physics and Beyond*, ET London 1971; A. Hollweg, *Theologie und Empirie*, Stuttgart [3]1974; K. Holzkamp, *Wissenschaft als Handlung*, Berlin 1968; id., *Kritische Psychologie*, Frankfurt 1972, esp. 88–98; M. Horkheimer, *Kritische Theorie*, ed. A. Schmidt, two vols., Frankfurt 1968; id., *Zur Kritik der instrumentellen Vernunft*, Frankfurt 1967; H. Koningsveld, *Het verschijnsel wetenschap. Een inleiding tot de wetenschapsfilosofie*, Meppel and Amsterdam 1976; T. S. Kuhn, *The Structure of Scientific Revolutions*, Chicago and London 1962, [2]1970; I. Lakatos, 'Criticism and the Methodology of Scientific Research-programmes', in *Proceedings of the Aristotelian Society* 69, 1968, 149–86; id., *Wetenschapsfilosofie en Wetenschapsgeschiedenis*, Meppel 1970; E. Nagel, *The Structure of Science*, London [3]1971; W. Pannenberg, *Theology and the Philosophy of Science*, ET London and Philadelphia 1976; C. van Peursen, *Wetenschappen en werkelijkheid*, Kampen 1969; G. Picht, *Wahrheit, Vernunft, Verantwortung*, Stuttgart 1969; M.

Polanyi, *Personal Knowledge*, London and New York 1969; K. Popper, *The Logic of Scientific Discovery*, London 1969; id., *Conjectures and Refutations. The Growth of Scientific Knowledge*, London 1969; id., *Objective Knowledge*, Oxford 1972; P. van Schilfgaarde, *Het kennisbegrip in wetenschap en beroep; objectiviteit als pretentie*, Alphen a/d Rijn 1970; F. Schupp, *Auf dem Weg zu einer kritischen Theologie*, Freiburg 1974; H. Seiffert, *Einführung in die Wissenschaftstheorie*, Munster 1971; W. Stegmüller, *Probleme und Resultate der Wissenschaftstheorie und analytischen Philosophie*, two vols., Berlin 1969 and 1970; J. M. Ziman, *Public Knowledge*, Cambridge 1970. Composite works: *Der Positivismusstreit in der deutschen Soziologie*, Neuwied 1969; *Hermeneutik und Ideologiekritik*, Frankfurt 1971; *Hermeneutik und Dialektik*, two vols., Tübingen 1970.

2. In Old Dutch, *varen* means simply to travel; only later was the meaning restricted to travels by sea or on inland waterways. Thus *ervaren* means to get to know something, not by hearsay but by seeing it oneself: by sight and living contact.

3. See W. Korff, *Norm und Sittlichkeit*, Tübinger Theologische Studien 1, Mainz 1973, 131–42.

4. W. Kasper comes to the same conclusion from an analysis made in a different direction: *Glaube und Geschichte*, 235.

5. For an analysis of 'dogmatism' and 'scepticism' see R. Schaeffler, *Religion und kritisches Bewusstsein*, 235–42 (though I have fundamental reservations about this book, see Part Four).

6. Literature about 'narrativeness': R. Barthes, *Mythologies*, Paris 1957; E. Bochinger, *Distanz und Nähe*, Stuttgart 1968; R. Dithmar, *Die Fabel*, UTB 73, Paderborn 1971; W. Harnisch, *Eschatologische Existenz*, Göttingen 1973; A. Jolles, *Einfache Formen*, Darmstadt [2]1958 (1930); R. Koselleck, 'Historia magistra vitae. Über die Auflösung des Topos im Horizont neuzeitlich bewegter Geschichte', in *Natur und Geschichte. K. Löwith zum 70. Geburtstag*, Stuttgart 1967, 196–218; R. Koselleck and W. Stempel (eds.), *Geschichten und Geschichte*, Munich 1972; C. Lévi-Strauss, *The Savage Mind*, ET London 1966; G. Lohfink, 'Erzählung als Theologie. Zur sprachlichen Grundstruktur der Evangelien', *StZ* 99, 1974, 521–33; J.-B. Metz, 'Erinnerung' in *Handbuch philosophischer Grundbegriffe*, Munich, Vol. 1, 1973, 386–96; id., 'The Future in the Memory of Suffering', *Conc* Vol. 6 no. 8 (ET of 8.6), June 1972, 9–25; id., 'A Short Apology of Narrative', *Conc* Vol. 5 no. 9 (ET of 9.5), May 1973, 84–96; D. Mieth, 'Narrative Ethik', *FrZPhTh* 22, 1975, 297–326; id., *Dichtung, Glaube und Moral*, Mainz 1976; F. Mildenberger, *Theologie für die Zeit*, Stuttgart 1969; W. Nestle, *Vom Mythos zum Logos*, Stuttgart 1940; K. Reinhardt, *Vermächtnis der Antike*, Göttingen 1960; W. Schapp, *In Geschichten verstrickt*, Hamburg 1953; id., *Philosophie der Geschichten*, Leer 1959; K. Stierle, 'L'histoire comme exemple, l'exemple comme histoire', *Poétique. Revue d'histoire et d'analyse littéraires* 10, 1972, 176–98; H. Weinrich, *Tempus. Besprochene und erzählte Welt*, Stuttgart [2]1971; id., *Literatur für Leser*, Stuttgart 1971; id., 'Narrative Theology', *Conc* Vol. 5 no. 9 (ET of 9.5), May 1973, 46–56; H. Zahrnt, 'Religiöse Aspekte gegenwärtiger Welt- und Lebenserfahrung', *ZTK* 71, 1974, 94–122.

7. P. Ricoeur, *Finitude et culpabilité*, 2 vols, Paris 1960.

8. I. Barbour, *Myths, Models and Paradigms*, 130.

9. If the experience were radically of the '*wholly* other', it would in fact have no hermeneutic significance whatsoever for revelation.

10. J.-B. Metz, 'Joy and Grief, Melancholy and Humour', *Conc* 10, ET May 1974, 7–12.

11. E.g. Thomas Aquinas, *Summa Theologiae* 1, q.1 a.1.

12. Op.cit., q.1, a.3, ad 2.

13. Denzinger-Schönmetzer, § 3004–5.

14. Denzinger-Schönmetzer, § 3008 (see § 3004, 3015).

15. Literature on the Enlightenment, at least in this connection: Peter Gay, *The Enlightenment: An Interpretation*, two vols, London 1966 and 1969; N. Hinske, *Was ist Aufklärung?*, Frankfurt, 1973; W. Oelmüller, *Die unbefriedigte Aufklärung*, Frankfurt 1969; H. M. Wolff, *Die Weltanschauung der Deutschen Aufklärung in geschichtlicher Entwicklung*, Berne, Munich ²1963; W. Schneiders, *Die wahre Aufklärung*, Frankfurt 1969; F. Valjavec, *Geschichte der abendländischen Aufklärung*, Vienna 1961.

16. See P. Grelot, 'Du bon usage des documents du "magistère": A propos du décret "Lamentabili"', Proposition n.36', in *Humanisme et foi chrétienne, Mélanges scientifiques du Centenaire de l'Institut Catholique de Paris*, Paris 1976, 527–40.

17. H.-G. Gadamer, *Truth and Method*, 310–25.

18. '*E mysteriorum ipsorum nexu inter se et cum fine hominis ultimo*', Denzinger-Schönmetzer, § 3016.

19. *Dei Verbum*, the Dogmatic Constitution on Divine Revelation, in *Constitutiones, Decreta, Declarationes*, Vatican City 1966, § 6.

20. Op.cit., §§1–5.

21. *Gaudium et Spes*, the Pastoral Constitution on the Church in the Modern World, § 41.

22. K. O. Apel, *Transformation der Philosophie*, Vol. 2, Frankfurt 1973, 264–307; F. Schupp, *Auf dem Weg zu einer kritischen Theologie*, 89–94; A. Grabner-Haider, *Semiotik und Theologie*, Munich 1973, 135ff.

23. H. M. Kuitert, *The Necessity of Faith*, ET Grand Rapids 1976, 42.

24. Thesis 19 in the dissertation by T. Baarda, *The Gospel Quotations of Aphrahat the Persian Sage*, Amsterdam 1975.

25. E. Lévinas, *Autrement qu'être ou au delà de l'essence*, The Hague 1974: 'la "provocation" venant de Dieu est dans mon invocation' (190).

26. A. Vergote, *Interprétation du langage religieuse*, 95–116.

27. L. Gilkey, *Naming the Whirlwind*, 305–413; see N. Schreurs, 'Naar de basis van ons spreken over God: de weg van L. Gilkey', *TvTh* 11, 1971, 275–92; id., 'Ervaring en interpretatie van de religieuze dimensie: een reactie', ibid., 293–302.

28. The same thing is true of so-called basic statements – 'protocol sentences' – in the empirical sciences. Instead of presenting 'elementary hard facts', these basic statements are already full of theories and interpretations (see n.1 and Pannenberg, *Theology and the Philosophy of Science*, 50–58).

29. L. Wittgenstein, *Philosophical Investigations*, Oxford 1953, 194e.

30. J. Wisdom, 'Gods', in A. Flew, *Logic and Language*, Vol. 1, Oxford 1951, 194–214.

31. J. Hick, *Faith and Knowledge*, London ²1967, 150f.

32. R. M. Hare, in *New Essays*, 99–103.

33. R. Hepburn, *Christianity and Paradox*, London 1958.

34. J. H. Randall, *The Role of Knowledge in Western Religion*, London 1958; P. Munz, *Problems of Religious Knowledge*, London 1959.

35. J. Hick, *Faith and Knowledge*, 142f.

36. I. Barbour, *Myths*, 51f.

37. E.g. P. Guillaume, *Psychologie de la forme*, Paris 1942, 48–114; see also E. Strauss, *Vom Sinn der Sinne*, Berlin ²1956.

38. See A. Jeffner, *The Study of Religious Language*, London 1972, 116–25.

39. Adequate, i.e. adapted to and appropriate for the reality to be discussed. This does not therefore mean 'exhaustive'; the phrase is directed against the elevation of directly descriptive language to be the norm of 'adequate' knowledge; as though this latter language were not just as inadequate and already theory-laden in its description.

40. L. Wittgenstein, *Tractatus Logico-philosophicus* 6.43, ET London and New York 1961, 147.

41. W. de Pater, 'Het theologisch verificatiebeginsel en de analytische filosofie', *Tussentijds*, 139–50.

42. R. Schaeffler, *Religion und kritisches Bewusstsein*, 240f.

43. I. Kant, *Critique of Pure Reason*, ET by Norman Kemp Smith, London 1933, p. 274.

44. J. Piaget, *Biology and Knowledge*, ET Edinburgh 1972; id., *Play, Dreams and Imitation in Childhood*, ET London 1951; id., *Insights and Illusions of Philosophy*, ET New York 1971, London 1972.

45. J. Piaget and B. Inhelder, *L'image mentale chez l'enfant*, Paris 1966, 450f..

46. Op. cit., 449f., 458.

47. J. Piaget, 'Pensée égocentrique et pensée socio-centrique', *Cahiers internationaux de Sociologie* 10, 1951, 34–49.

48. Id., *Insights and Illusions*, 46n., 54f. See also W. de Bont, 'Religieus en rationeel denken', *TvTh* 9, 1969, 79–81. See the criticism in J. Pohier, *Psychologie et théologie*, Paris 1967.

49. G. Gusdorf, *Mythe et métaphysique*, Paris 1953, 189, and the modern criticism of purely instrumental reason: H. Marcuse, *One-dimensional Man*, London and New York 1964; J. Habermas, *Technik und Wissenschaft als Ideologie*, Frankfurt [4]1970, 48–103; M. Horkheimer, *Zur Kritik der instrumentellen Vernunft*, Frankfurt 1967.

50. M. Bellet, *Naissance de Dieu*, Bruges 1975; P. Tillich, *Dynamics of Faith*, London 1957, 1–4.

51. See G. Rombold, 'Die Frage nach dem Unbedingten', in K. Krenn, *Die wirkliche Wirklichkeit Gottes*, Munich, Paderborn 1974, 77–91; H. Kuitert, 'De wil van God doen', in *Ad Interim, Opstellen over eschatologie, apocalyptiek en ethiek*, FS R. Schippers, Kampen 1975, 180–95; D. Z. Phillips, 'God and Ought', in *Christian Ethics and Contemporary Philosophy*, ed. I. T. Ramsey, London 1966, 133–9; H. G. Hubbeling, *Criterium als kenmerk en norm*, Inaugural Lecture, Groningen, Assen 1968.

52. See the discussion between C. Verhoeven and J. Sperna Weiland in *Ethiek en Religie, Congres voor moderne theologie, 21 October 1974, Radarpeiling* 10, 1975, no. 2, 7–17 and 17–23. To my mind both are too one-sided in their approach.

53. E. Lévinas, *Difficile liberté. Essais sur le Judaïsme*, Paris 1963, 33. K. Rahner also sees the density of reality of the mystical love of God as rooted originally in a radical love of neighbour, 'Reflections on the Unity of the Love of Neighbour and the Love of God', ET *Theological Investigations* 6, London and New York 1974, 231–49; also E. Schillebeeckx, 'Stilte, gevuld met parabels', in *Politiek of mystiek?* Bruges 1973, 69–81 (see Part Four).

54. See also G. Schiwy, *Strukturalismus*, 22f.

55. H. Kuitert and E. Schillebeeckx, *Jesus van Nazareth en het heil van de wereld*, Baarn 1975, 16.

56. See *Unsere Hoffnung. Ein Glaubensbekenntnis in dieser Zeit, Arbeitshilfe zur Synodenvorlage*, Augsburg 1975, 19.

57. Canon, see also : H. Beyer, s.v. 'kanon', in *TDNT* 3, 596–602. This Greek word is a loan-word from the Semitic *qāne*. The Semitic term means a reed, a rod (as a measure), a staff or a stake, hence a measure or ruler. The Septuagint never translates this word *kanōn*, though it occurs in IV Macc. 7.21. In Greek *kanōn* means rule, instruction or law, hence guideline, standard or criterion. Thus the Alexandrian grammarians laid down a canon of authors whose Greek was taken as a norm. Now the good and the beautiful, according to Greek thinking, were along the same line (*kalokagathia*), and therefore *kanōn* also means the moral law and an ideal of life. This meaning can also be found among the philosophers: to philosophize is to lay down norms or *canones* (Epictetus, *Diss.* II, 11.24). In the New Testament, *kanōn* occurs in Gal. 6.15f.; II Cor. 10.13–16 (three times). In II Corinthians, Christ and the 'apostolate' are the canon, i.e. norm. In the early church, 'canon' came to be used also of the external union of the many scattered Christian churches; thus the books of the New Testament became the guideline for the one orthodox Catholic church. Scripture became the 'canon of truth', the 'canon of faith' (*regula fidei*) and the canon of the church (church as canon). The non-canonical writings were also read (especially by catechumens), but it was not permissible to read them in worship.

58. See an apt example of modern representations of Christ in G. Biemer and R. Russ, *Wenn das Antlitz sich verbirgt. Christusbilder von Roland Peter Litzenburger*, Stuttgart 1975, above all the 'ecological Christ', the 'cry about creation' (105f.).

59. W. Pannenberg, *Theology and the Philosophy of Science*, 203f.

60. J.-B. Metz, 'Hermeneutical procedures are themselves related to practice, in that they are concerned not only with the clarification of conditions of understanding and horizons of understanding in a particular complex of knowledge and action, but with the question of changing such conditions and horizons' (in *'Politische Theologie' in der Diskussion*, ed. H. Peukert, Mainz-Munich 1969, 283; see also in J. B. Metz, J. Moltmann, W. Oelmüller, *Kirche im Prozess der Aufklärung*, Munich, Mainz 1970, 80; W. Pannenberg, too, does not term the hermeneutical event purely contemplative, op. cit., 107–9, 202–4.

61. J. Ellul, 'Aliénation et temporalité dans le Droit', in *Temporalité et aliénation*, Cahiers Castelli, Paris 1975, 191–205.

62. L. Dumont, *Homo hierarchicus*, Chicago 1970.

63. H. Marrou, *De la connaissance historique*, Paris ³1958, 233f.

64. W. Dupré, 'Anfang', in *Handbuch philosophischer Grundbegriffe*, Munich 1973, Vol. 1, 79–90; P. Levert, *L'idée de commencement*, Paris 1961.

65. H.-G. Gadamer, *Truth and Method*, 345–97.

66. P. Ricoeur, *Finitude et culpabilité*, Paris 1960, II/2,142.


*Part Two: New Testament Theology of the Experience of Grace*

1. A survey of the passages in which *charis* appears in the New Testament. A. Pauline corpus: Rom. 1.5; 1.7b; 3.24; 4.4; 4.16; 5.2, 15a and 15b; 5.17; 5.20; 5.21; 6.1; 6.14; 6.15; 6.17; 7.25; 11.5; 11.6; 12.3; 12.6; 15.15; 16.20; I Cor. 1.3; 1.4; 3.10; 10.30; 15.10; 15.57; 16.3; 16.23; II Cor. 1.2; 1.12; 1.15; 2.14; 4.15; 6.1; 8.1, 4, 6, 7, 9, 16, 19; 9.8; 9.14; 9.15; 12.9; 13.14; Gal. 1.3; 1.6; 1.15; 2.9; 2.21; 3.19 (as a

preposition); 5.4; 6.18; Phil. 1.2; 1.7; 4.23; I Thess. 1.1; 5.28; II Thess. 1.2; 1.12; 2.16; 3.18; Eph. 1.2; 1.6; 1.7; 2.5; 2.7; 2.8; 3.2; 3.7; 3.8; 4.7; 4.29; 6.24 (3.1 and 3.14 as a preposition). Col. 1.2; 1.6; 3.16; 4.6; 4.18; I Tim. 1.2; 1.12; 1.14; 5.14 (preposition); 6.21; II Tim. 1.2; 1.3; 1.9; 2.1; 4.22; Titus 1.4; 2.11; 3.7; 3.15 (1.5 and 1.11 as a preposition); Philemon 3, 25.
B. Elsewhere in the New Testament: Luke 1.30; 2.40; 2.52; 4.22; 6.32, 34; 7.47 (preposition); 17.9; Acts 2.47; 4.33; 6.8; 7.10; 7.46; 11.23; 13.43; 14.3; 14.26; 15.11; 15.40; 18.27; 20.24; 20.32; 24.27; 25.3; 25.9; John 1.14–17; Hebrews 2.9; 4.16; 10.29; 12.15; 12.28; 13.9; 13.25; James 4.6; I Peter 1.2; 1.10; 1.13; 2.19; 3.7; 4.10; 5.5; 5.10; 5.12; II Peter 1.2; 3.18; II John 3 (in I John 3.12 as a preposition); Jude 4; Revelation 1.4; 22.21.

2. See R. Morgenthaler, *Statistik des neutestamentlichen Wortschatzes*. Zurich-Frankfurt 1958; id., *Statistische Synopse*, Zurich, Stuttgart 1971; G. Morrish, *A Concordance to the Septuagint*, London 1974.

3. In connection with the sparing of the weaker (see e.g. Job 19.21) *ḥānan*, in a weakened sense, can also simply mean: approach someone in a friendly way or speak to him in friendship (Prov. 26.25).

4. In the *hithpael* form, *ḥānan* takes on the meaning 'entreat': Gen. 42.21; II Kings 1.13; Job 19.16; Esther 4.8; 8.3. Entreat God: Deut. 3.23; I Kings 8.33, 47, 59; 9.3; II Chron. 6.24, 37; Hos. 12.4; Pss. 30.8; 142.1. This form in turn leads to derivative nouns meaning intercessory prayer (I Kings 8.30; II Chron. 6.21; Jer. 37.20; 38.26; Prov. 18.23; Pss. 28.2, 6; 31.22 etc.).

5. A more legalistic attitude only arises at a later stage. There is an appeal in misery to God's grace, containing a reference to the suppliant's own faithfulness and the way in which he has followed God's commandments (Ps. 26.11).

6. In a couplet in Ex. 33.19 *ḥānan* is connected with *raḥam*, which makes explicit one nuance of *ḥānan*, namely that of tender pity and mercy.

7. Presumably this is a Yahwistic reinterpretation of the ancient, Mesopotamian (Assyrian and Babylonian) concept of God as the arbitrary tyrant, the great potentate.

8. Also in secondary texts like Isa. 27.11; 30.18f.; 33.2; 26.10.

9. Ex. 22.27; Ps. 116.5.

10. See J. Scharbert, 'Formgeschichte und Exegese von Ex. 34, 6–7 und seiner Parallelen', *Bibl* 38, 1957, 130–50.

11. However, in the book of Proverbs it often occurs (Prov. 1.9; 3.4; 3.22; 4.9) in a secular sense, so that *ḥēn* becomes a quite independent characteristic, e.g. a gazelle with *ḥēn*, a charming and attractive gazelle (see below).

12. See Gen. 39.21; Ex. 3.21; 11.3; 12.36; Ps. 84.11; Prov. 3.34; 13.15.

13. About forty times in the Old Testament.

14. So W. Zimmerli in *TDNT* 9, 376–87.

15. Zimmerli, op. cit., 383 n.78.

16. A. Jepsen, s.v. *ḥesed*, in *TWAT* 1, 338f.; and H. J. Stoebe, s.v. *ḥānan*, in *ThHandWAT* 1, 587–97.

17. H. Wildenberger, s.v. *'emet*, in *ThHandWAT* 1, 201.

18. H. Wildenberger, op.cit., 208, here presupposes alien, perhaps Iranian influence. In early Judaism or Judaism this meaning is predominant. As a result, the translation of the Septuagint (*'emet* here is *alētheia* or truth) is understandable.

19. That is true of many Old Testament concepts. For the concept of 'love' see W. Grossouw, 'Wat leert het nieuwe testament over de liefde tot God?' *TvTh* 3,

1963, 230–51.

20. Thus H. J. Stoebe, s.v. *ḥesed*, in *ThHandWAT* 1, 616.

21. The adjective *ḥāsīd*, usually translated 'pious' or 'faithful', really means the one who exercises *ḥesed* (Jer. 3.12; Micah 7.2; Pss. 4.3; 12.1; 18.25; 32.6; 43.1; 86.2; 145.17). In some places Yahweh himself is called *ḥāsīd* (Jer. 3.12; Ps. 145.17. The *ḥᵃsīdīm* are pious believers who are faithful to God. In principle this is all Israel, 'the assembly of the *ḥᵃsīdīm*' (Ps. 50.5), those who are loyal to the covenant. *Ḥāsīd* then means member of the believing community of Israel, the sphere of sovereignty of the grace of God (see Pss. 31.7, 16, 21, 23; 32.6, 10; 52.8f.; 85.7f., 10 etc.); a *ḥāsīd* is one who also experiences grace or shares in it. This title of honour is only restricted to some degree from the time of the Maccabees and reserved for a special group of people who fought for the purity of Jewish belief.

22. In connection with the meanings of grace in the Old Testament analysed above, it is interesting to remember the root meaning of the term grace in Dutch: *genada*. *Ginâtha* (Old Lower Frankish), *ginâda* (Old High German), *ginatha* (Old Saxon) mean: rest, comfort, grace, help, gratitude. In Gothic the emphasis perhaps lies on 'support', whereas the Old Irish (*in-neuth*) means 'I support'. In Old Indian *nâtha* means refuge or help. In other words, in these languages the usual meanings of grace coincide in many respects.

23. E.g. Aristotle, *Nicomachean Ethics* V, 8, 1133a.

24. *Hai tōn Sebastōn charites* (imperial demonstrations of favour) can be found on an Oriental inscription of the first century BC (in *Orientis Graeci inscriptiones selectae*, ed. W. Dittenberger, Leipzig 1903, 669.44).

25. Liddell and Scott, s.v. *charis*, col. 1979A.

26. *Corpus Hermetium* 1, 32; 12, 12.

27. G. Wetter, *Charis*, 29; also H. Conzelmann s.v. *charis*, in *TDNT* 9, 372–6.

28. Test. Lev. 18.9; Test. Jud. 24. A factor of uncertainty affects the redaction history of the Testaments. Although in all probability they are of Jewish origin (second century BC), the Testaments have undergone a Christian revision with some interpolations. See. J. Becker, *Untersuchungen zur Enstehungsgeschichte der Testamente der zwölf Patriarchen*, Leiden 1970, and L. Rost, *Einleitung in die alttestamentlichen Apokryphen, Pseudepigraphen, einschliesslich der grossen Qumranschriften*, Heidelberg 1971.

29. F. Christ, *Jesus Sophia*, Zurich 1970; M. Hengel, *Judaism and Hellenism*, ET London and Philadelphia 1974, 153–72; C. Larcher, *Etudes sur le livre de la Sagesse*, Paris 1969; U. Wilckens, *Weisheit und Torheit*, BHTh 26, Tübingen 1959; R. Hamerton-Kelly, *Pre-existence, Wisdom and the Son of Man*, Cambridge 1973; B. Lang, *Frau Weisheit*, Düsseldorf 1975.

30. See also K. Schubert, 'Einige Beobachtungen zum Verständnis des Logosbegriffes im frührabbinischen Schrifttum', *Judaica* 9, 1953, 65–80, esp. 67–88.

31. R. Meyer, 'Tradition und Neuschöpfung im antiken Judentum', in *Berichte über die Verhändlungen der Sächsichen Akademie*, 110–2, Leipzig 1965, 7–88.

32. See also Strack-Billerbeck II, 357.

33. K. Berger, 'Gnade', *NTT* 27, 1973, 4. To the literature on Pauline *charis* should be added, D. J. Doughty, 'The Priority of Charis. An Investigation of the Theological Language of Paul', *NTS* 18, 1972, 163–80.

34. See J. Fichtner, *Die altorientalische Weisheit in ihre israelitisch-jüdischen Ausprägung*, BZAW 62, Giessen 1933. In his *La révélation d'Hermès Trismégiste* 1, Paris 1950, A. J. Festugière in particular has shown how the idea of 'revealed wisdom'

and interest in the ancient Eastern wisdom attracted a spiritual *élite* in the Hellenistic Near East down to the second and third centuries AD.

35. E.g. Philo, *Quod deus immutabilis*, 104ff.

36. The whole book of Sirach; IV Ezra 8.

37. Cf. H. Reventlow, *Rechtfertigung im Horizont des Alten Testaments*, Munich 1971, and R. Gyllenberg, *Rechtfertigung und Altes Testament bei Paulus*, Stuttgart 1973.

38. In Judaism the term 'works' has various meanings. See G. Bertram s.v. *erga (nomou)* in *TDNT* 2, 645–8; Strack-Billerbeck III, 160–2. In early rabbinic literature there is mention of 'works' (*ma'asīm*), sometimes of good works (*mᵉtōbīm*, which sometimes means non-obligatory works) and finally of works of the Law (*miṣwōt*, singular *miṣwā*) (see G. Liedke, *ṣwh* in *ThHandWAT* 2, 530–6). *Miṣwā* really means an order – command or prohibition – and also its execution. Thus in connection with the Torah it means works of the Law, doing what the Law requires. The Law is the principle of grace in ethics; the works of the Law are the human answer to God's gracious gift of the Law.

*Part Two, Section Two: New Testament experiences of grace and their interpretations*

1. See what I have said about 'the criterion of the proportional norm' in *Geloofsverstaan: interpretatie en kritiek*, Theologische Peilingen 5, Bloemendaal 1972, 98–105.

2. Rom. 1.7b; 16.20; I Cor. 1.3; 16.23; II Cor. 1.2; 13.14; Gal. 1.3,6; 6.18; Phil. 1.2; 4.23; I Thess. 1.1; 5.28; II Thess. 1.2; 3.18; Eph. 1.2; 6.24; Col. 1.2; 4.18; I Tim. 1.2; 6.21; II Tim. 1.2; 4.22; Titus 1.4; 3.15; Philemon 3 and 25.

3. See J. T. Nelis, *II Makkabeeën*, Bussum 1975, 46–8.

4. K. Berger, 'Gnade', *NTT* 27, 1973, 8–10.

5. See *Jesus. An Experiment in Christology*, 107–14, and the study on the concept of *euangelion* by G. Strecker, 'Das Evangelium Jesu Christi', in *Jesus Christus in Historie und Theologie*, FS H. Conzelmann, ed. G. Strecker, Tübingen 1975, 503–48, which appeared later.

6. F. Mussner, *Galaterbrief*, 168f.

7. Grossouw, *Galatenbrief*, 102f., 106.

8. Strack-Billerbeck I, 116–20; III, 539–41.

9. Ibid., II, 523 (see John 8.33).

10. See an analogous argument in Heb. 7.1–22 in connection with the levitical priesthood after the promise to Abraham. This was clearly a common theme in early Judaism.

11. Grossouw, *Galatenbrief*, 135f.

12. Ibid., 123f.

13. By the connection of (Greek) Gen. 12.3 with Gen. 18.18; see F. Mussner, *Galaterbrief*, 220. The line is said to run as follows: Gen. 12.3 → 18.18 → 22.18 → 26.4 → 28.4 → Ps. 72.17 → Sir. 44.21 → Acts. 3.25 → Gal. 3.8 (Grossouw, op. cit., 124 n. 17).

14. A. R. Hulst, s.v. *'am (gōy)* in *ThHandWAT* 2, 290–325; W. Grundmann, s.v. *demos*, in *TDNT* 2, 63–5; G. Bertram and K. L. Schmidt, s.v. *ethnos*, *TDNT* 2, 364–72; H. Strathmann and R. Meyer, s.v. *laos*, *TDNT* 4, 29–57. The original

conceptual contrast lies in the fact that *'ammim* means peoples (mankind), whereas *gōyīm* means the same men organized in states and kingdoms, in other words their socio-political, historical (and therefore religious) differentiation. Later, *gōyīm* will be an expression above all for non-Jewish, 'non-believing', or pagan peoples.

15. See *Jesus. An Experiment in Christology*, 383f. (see the references to Isa. 49.6).

16. This is the argument of the book by H. Schmid, *Gerechtigkeit und Weltordnung*.

17. G. von Rad, *Wisdom in Israel*, ET London and Nashville 1972, 78.

18. According to K. Koch in *ThHandWAT* 2, 520, it is quite unthinkable according to Jewish ideas that God should justify a *sinner* or that he should secure justice for a sinner. That is disputed by H. Reventlow, *Rechtfertigung im Horizont des Alten Testament*. However, in due course it will transpire that the concept of *ṣᵉdāqā* is a twofold one: (*a*) obtain justice for the (suffering) righteous and (*b*) the later concept of *ṣᵉdāqā* as the forgiveness of sins (above all in non-official Jewish circles).

19. See K. Koch, 'Tempeleinlassliturgien und Dekaloge', in *Studien zur Theologie der alttestamentlichen Überlieferungen*, ed. R. Rendtorff and K. Koch, FS G. von Rad, Neukirchen 1961, 45–60. See Ps. 15; Ps. 24; Isa. 33.14b–16.

20. W. Zimmerli, *Ezekiel*, ET Hermeneia I, Philadelphia 1979, 381–3.

21. See H. Cazelles, 'Quelques terms difficiles', *RB* 58, 1951, 169–88; also J. Fiedler, *Der Begriff der Dikaiosyne*.

22. See J. Jocz, 'God's "poor" People', *Judaica* 28, 1972, 7–29; also H. Donner, 'Die soziale Botschaft der Propheten im Lichte der Gesellschaftsordnung in Israel', *Oriens Antiquus* 2, 1963, 229–45.

23. F. Stier, *Das Buch Ijob, Hebräisch und Deutsch*, Munich 1954, 237f.; see also G von. Rad, *Wisdom in Israel*; J. Blank, 'Begegnung mit dem Heiligen als Krise und Entscheidung' in *Heilskraft des Heiligen*, J. Sudbrack et al., Freiburg 1975, (45–77), 64–8.

24. M. Hengel, *Judaism and Hellenism*, ET London and Philadelphia 1974, 131–53.

25. Josephus, *Contra Apionem* 1,41, speaks in this connection of the *diadoche* in the sense of a prophetic succession.

26. See esp.Ps. Sol. 9.7–9; Strack-Billerbeck I, 583; IV, 7; and R. Mach, *Der Zaddiq*, 41ff.

27. Above all P. Stuhlmacher, *Gerechtigkeit Gottes*, op. cit., 154–66.

28. See the work by A. Marmorstein, *The Doctrine of Merits in Old Rabbinic Literature*, New York ²1968.

29. See R. Mach, *Der Zaddiq*, 39ff.

30. See Strack-Billerbeck III, 186–217; O. Schmitz, 'Abraham in Spätjudentum und im Urchristentum,' in *Aus Schrift und Geschichte*, FS A. Schlatter, Stuttgart 1922, 99–123; E. Jacob, 'Abraham et sa signification pour la foi chrétienne', *RHPR* 42, 1962, 148–56; H. J. Schoeps, *Paul*, ET London 1961, 141–9; I Jacobs, 'The Midrashic Background for James II, 21–23', *NTS* 22, 1976, 457–64; R. Le Déaut, *La nuit paschale*, Rome 1963, 100–10.

31. J. Jervell, *Imago Dei, Gen. 1.26–27 in Spätjudentum, in der Gnosis, und in den paulinischen Briefen*, FRLANT 76, Göttingen 1960; E. Brandenburger, *Adam und Christus*, WMANT 7, Neukirchen-Vluyn 1962.

32. See p. 95 above.

33. The Qumran community, which similarly advocates eschatological forgiveness of sins and justification by grace, ties this to membership of the escha-

tological community of Qumran.

34. E. Schweizer and R. Meyer, s.v. *sarx*, *TDNT* 7, 98–151.

35. *Didache* 10.6 (the eucharistic prayers).

36. Above all G. Kittel, 'Der Geschichtliche Ort des Jakobusbriefes', *ZNW* 41, 1942, 94–102; T. Boman, *Die Jesus-Überlieferung*, 196–207.

37. A. Harnack; M. Dibelius; K. Aland, etc.

38. So F. Mussner, *Der Jakobusbrief*, 19.

39. I. Jacobs, 'The Midrashic Background for James II, 21–23', *NTS* 22, 1976, 463.

40. F. Mussner, *Der Jakobusbrief*, 145.

41. I. Jacobs, op. cit., 462–4.

42. Ps.-Philo, *Liber Antiquitatum Biblicarum* 18, 5 (ET by M. R. James, London 1917, 123f.).

43. Already a popular theme at that time (Josephus, *De bello judaico* 5, 438; Prayer of Manasseh 4).

44. Strack-Billerbeck I, 22.

45. Thus J. Gnilka, *Der Philipperbrief*, 5–11.

46. 'They will be called above' (*pros ton theion anō klēsis*) (Philo, *Plant.* 23). In the Greek Apoc. Baruch, the *anō klēsis* is identified with the entry into paradise. Phil. 3.14 also speaks of *anō klēsis*.

47. Philo, *Vita Moysis* II, 69–70.

48. See C. R. Holladay, *Theios Anēr in Hellenistic Judaism: A Critique of the Use of this Category in New Testament Christology*, Cambridge 1974 (typescript). The conclusion of this study is that there were different conceptions of this kind and that *theios* has at least four different meanings. *Theios anēr* is (*a*) an inspired man; (*b*) someone in a particular relationship to God; (*c*) an extraordinary man; and (*d*) a divine man. However, nowhere does it become clear that *theios anēr* is a divine man who does miraculous deeds. In Greek-Jewish mysticism the term means something like the person we refer to as a 'man of God'. In Philo and Josephus the great heroes from the history of Israel are simply called men of God, in the perspective of people with a mystical relationship to God, but not as miracle workers.

49. J. Gnilka, *Der Philipperbrief*, 269f.

50. *Jesus. An Experiment in Christology*, 424; see also my question mark in the title to that section. After studying Holladay's book, I would prefer not to speak of a *theios anēr* christology at all (but, as I have already done, of a christology of the *Solomonic* son of David).

51. Philo, *Conf. ling.* 78.

52. H. Haerens, *Sōtèr et Sōtèria*, Studia Hellenistica 5, Louvain 1948.

53. J. Jervell, *Imago Dei*, 229.

54. See below on Heb. 1.6–10.

55. Philo, *Quis rerum divinarum heres* 29.

56. J. Jervell, *Imago Dei*, 212f.

57. L. Cerfaux, 'L'hymne au Christ-Serviteur', op. cit., 117–30.

58. J. T. Sanders, *Christological Hymns*, 60.

59. J. A. Sanders, 'Dissenting Deities', *JBL* 88, 1969, 281f. (I Enoch 6.2; *Vita Adae et Evae*).

60. G. Strecker, 'Redaktion', *ZNW* 55, 1964, 75.

61. E. Schweizer, *Erniedrigung*, 30; L. Ruppert, *Jesus als der leidende Gerechte?*

Stuttgart 1972, 70; G. Nickelsburg, *Resurrection, Immortality, and Eternal Life in Intertestamental Judaism*, Cambridge, Mass 1972, 77f.

62. R. Hamerton-Kelly, *Pre-existence*, 167.

63. *Res rapta* means booty which has already been taken; *res rapienda* means booty which is still to be taken. See P. Schoonenberg, 'The Kenosis or Self-emptying of Christ', *Conc.* 1.2 (ET of 2.1), January 1966, 27–36.

64. II Enoch 29.4f.

65. II Enoch, ibid.

66. J. Jervell, *Imago Dei*, 230f.

67. Literature. General: H. W. Wolff, 'The Kerygma of the Jahwist', *Int* 20, 1966, 131–58; R. E. Clements, *Abraham and David*, SBT II 15, London 1967; W. Brüggeman, 'David and his "Theologian" ', *CBQ* 30, 1968, 158–81; B. Mazar, 'The Historical Background of the Book Genesis', *JNES* 28, 1969, 73–83; A. Alt, *Kleine Schriften zur Geschichte des Volkes Israel*, 3 vols, Munich 1953–59. Detailed analyses: esp. W. Wifall, 'Son of Man. A pre-Davidic social class?', *CBQ* 37, 1975, 331–40; id., 'The Breath of his Nostrils, Gen. 2,7b', *CBQ* 36, 1974, 237–40; id., 'Gen. 3,15. A Protevangelium', *CBQ* 36, 1974, 361–5; id., 'Gen. 6.1–4. A Pre-Davidic Royal Myth?', *BTB* 5, 1975, 294–301; id., 'David, Prototype of Israel's Future', *BTB* 4, 1974, 94–107; W. Brüggeman, 'The trusted creature', *CBQ* 31, 1969, 484–98; id., 'Kingship and Chaos,' *CBQ* 33, 1971, 317–32; id., 'Nearness, Exile and Chaos', *CBQ* 34, 1972, 19–38; id., 'Of the same flesh and bone', *CBQ* 32, 1970, 532–42; id., 'From Dust to Kingship', *ZAW* 84, 1972. 1–18; J. Wijngaards, *Vazal van Jahwe*, Baarn 1965. Thus the promises to Abraham (Gen. 12) reflect the socio-political conditions of the kingdom of Israel and the promises of the so-called Davidic covenant in II Sam. 7.

68. J. Collins, 'Son of Man and Saints of the Most High', *JBL* 93, 1974, 50–66; moreover, the same conceptions are current in Egypt, and Israel's royal traditions are also akin to them (H. Frankfort, *Ancient Egyptian Religion*, New York 1961).

69. J. Collins, 'Son of Man', 55–60. What I found obscure about the prehistory of the term Son of man (see *Jesus. An Experiment in Christology*, 459–72) has been convincingly clarified by the works cited in n. 67 (above all those of Wifall and this work by Collins). Of course this insight does not make any new contribution towards the use of the term Son of man in the New Testament. However, this shows why Jesus could be called both Son of David and Son of man; originally the two titles were almost synonymous.

70. Among others, G. ter Schegget asserts that no new phase begins after the death of Jesus, with all the consequences of this abstraction: *Het lied van de mensenzoon*, 138.

71. See also F. Hahn, *Christologische Hoheitstitel. Ihre Geschichte im frühen Christentum*, FRLANT 83, Göttingen 1963, 120f.

72. See also the literature on pp. 545f. on the spirituality of late antiquity.

73. E.g. IV Macc. 5.11.

74. Josephus, *De bello judaico* 2, 119; *Antiquitates* 18, 11.

75. Diogenes Laertes VI, 102.

76. Marcus Aurelius IV, 23, 2.

77. Philo says of wisdom: *'dia hēs ta hola ēlthen eis genesin'* (*De fuga* 109): 'through her the universe came into existence'.

78. Strack-Billerbeck III, 583.

79. Already in Plato, *Timaeus*, 31b; 32a, c; 39e; 47c–48b.

80. Thus E. Lohse, *Colossians and Philemon*, 53.

81. H. Hegermann, *Die Vorstellung vom Schöpfungsmittler*, 58f., 63–66, 100f.

82. Philo, *De somniis* I, 128.

83. 'Head' here cannot be understood in an Old Testament sense. In the Tanach 'head' means leader and ruler; it does not suggest the idea of a principle of life, which is the point here. 'Head' must be understood in Hellenistic terms. Besides, in the Old Testament 'head' is never contrasted with 'body'.

84. Furthermore, there is a difference here from *sōma* in Paul. I Cor. 12 and Rom. 12 are concerned with the mutual relationships of members in a body, not of the relationship between the head and the body. I Cor. 1.13 already goes more *in the direction of* Colossians: the one body, in which we are baptized, and the 'eucharistic body'.

85. Strack-Billerbeck III, 78f.

86. *Amphoterōn henos ontos* (*Corp. Herm.* 16.3). Cf. Odes of Solomon 7 (see E. Lohse, *Colossians and Philemon*, 57).

87. A. R. Hulst, s.v. *sh-k-n*, in *ThHandWAT* 2, 904–9; W. Michaelis, s.v. *skēnē* in *TDNT* 7, 368–94; R. de Vaux, 'Le lieu que Jahvé a choisi pour établir son nom', *Das ferne und nahe Wort*, FS L. Rost, BZAW 105, Berlin 1967, 219–28.

88. For 'cosmic reconciliation' see also Ascension of Isaiah 11.23; Strack-Billerbeck I, 420. A reconciliation between earth and heaven is unthinkable in gnosticism.

89. The text of Colossians is very obscure here – perhaps corrupt. Of the translations, that of Lohse seems to me to give the best meaning to the philosophy of life that Colossians is fighting against. See E. Lohse, *Colossians and Philemon*, 114, 117–21.

90. Interpreters take too little notice of this. But see E. Larsson, *Christus also Vorbild*, ASNT 23, Uppsala 1962, 226; K. Wegenast, *Das Verständnis der Tradition bei Paulus und in den Deutero-Paulinen*, Neukirchen 1962; J. Gnilka, *Der Epheserbrief*, 227–9.

91. See below on Jude and II Peter and the comments in the synthesis, pp. 509f.

92. G. Wehmeier, s.v. *'lh*, in *ThHandWAT* 2, 272–90; J. Schneider, s.v. *bainō*, in *TDNT* 1, 518–23.

93. Strack-Billerbeck III, 588–91; Josephus, *Contra Apionem* 1, 11.

94. See Wisd. 9.8; Test. Levi 5.1f.; Syr. Apoc. Bar. 4.3–6; IV Ezra 7.26; 8.52; 13.35; Test. Dan 5.12. Cf. Gal. 4.26; Rev. 3.12; 21.10; Ps. Sol. 17.25.

95. Quintilian 6.1.

96. Some examples: 'Bring all together in Christ under one head' (the new Willibrord translation); different again in Le Bible de Jérusalem; 'ramener toutes choses *sous un seul chef*, le Christ', where 'head' is used in the ambiguous sense which it can have in French. In my view the New English Bible has a correct translation: 'that the universe, all in heaven and on earth, might be brought *into a unity* in Christ'.

97. Paul certainly knows Christ as head (I Cor. 11.3), but not as head of the church: 'The head of every man is Christ, the head of a woman is her husband and the head of Christ is God'. In Eph. 5.23 what Paul says in I Cor. 11.3 becomes: 'The man is the head of the woman, *just as* Christ is the head of the church', namely the soul and the life-principle. Paul also knows that Christ is *Lord* of all (e.g. Phil. 2.9–11), but not 'head of all'. In the world of late antiquity,

head does not mean '*chef*', 'leader', but an all-pervasive life principle.

98. See M. Saebø, s.v. *sōd*, *ThHAndWAT* 2, 144–8; G. Schrenk, s.v. *boulē*, *TDNT* 1, 631–6.

99. See *Jesus. An Experiment in Christology*, 291–4.

100. Strack-Billerbeck II, 279f.; III, 260f.; see also H. Kessler, *Die theologische Bedeutung des Todes Jesu*, Düsseldorf 1970, 256–64; K. H. Schelkle, *Petrusbriefe*, 212f.

101. II Macc. 7.37f.; see *Jesus. An Experiment in Christology*, 293.

102. Ibid., 282–91, with literature, esp. L. Ruppert and G. Nickelsburg.

103. See C. Spicq, 'La prima Petri', *St Th* 20, 1966, 37–61; R. Gundry, ' "Verba Christi" ', *NTS* 13, 1967, 336–50; H. J. Vogels, *Christi Abstieg*, 72f.

104. See C. Westermann, *Genesis*, BKAT I 1, Neukirchen 1974, 491–517. Here the Yahwist was not thinking of angels, but of sons of God or notable sons of men like David and Pharaoh, kings and noblemen, who took women as they pleased, one reason why according to J God reduced their life span to 120 years by way of punishment. However, early Judaism and Christianity saw Gen. 6.1–4 as a story about angels.

105. See Ascension of Isaiah 10; Odes of Solomon 22; 24; 42; Gospel of Peter 10.41f.; Gospel of Nicodemus 17ff. See M. Hengel, *Judaism and Hellenism*, ET London and Philadelphia 1974, I, 89; 190f., 232f. The decisive question is whether I Peter 3.19 refers to this explanation of Gen. 6.1–4 or to the report which follows (on the flood). See the most recent, mutually contradictory studies on the subject: W. Dalton, *Christ's Proclamation to the Spirits*, and H. J. Vogels, *Christi Abstieg*; the latter's arguments seem to me to be conclusive.

106. Vogels, *Christi Abstieg*, 101–15.

107. This theory only appeared in modern exegesis in 1890, after the publication of F. Spitta, *Christi Predigt an die Geister*, Göttingen 1890, and was taken over by most exegetes from book to book without any further research. The theory entered Catholic exegesis with K. Gschwind, *Die Niederfahrt Christi in die Unterwelt*, Münster 1911. H. Küng still defends it on *On Being a Christian*, London and New York 1977, 367f. The theory seems to me to have been influenced by confessional considerations, and has been taken over uncritically by Catholic exegetes.

108. For all its great learning, the commentary by C. Spicq, *L'épître aux Hébreux*, seems to me to be the great culprit here.

109. Tacitus, *Annales* 15, 44.

110. See *Jesus. An Experiment in Christology*, 119–24.

111. Suetonius, *Vita Caesaris Claudii*, 25, 3f.

112. Tacitus, *Annales* 15.44.

113. Also Josephus, *Antiquitates* 15, 136.

114. For example Hebrew Enoch (= III Enoch) 10.3.

115. See above, Part One, ch. 3, pp. 76–8.

116. For *pesher* and *midrash* see the notes on 'technical information' below, 903f., 905.

117. J. Jeremias, 'Moyses', *TDNT* 4, 852–3; L. Perlitt, 'Moses als Prophet', *EvTh* 31, 1971, 588–608; in the literature quoted, J. L. Martyn, *History and Theology*, 122–5; W. Meeks, *The Prophet-King*, Leiden 1967, 100ff. and 117–25 (see below on Johannine theology).

118. Philo, *Quaest. in Exodum* II, 29: '*transmutatur in divinum, ita ut fiat Deo cognatus, vereque divinus.*' Also Philo, *Vita Moysis* I, 155; II, 107; II, 111; II, 214; See

Josephus, *Antiquitates* 2, 201–4, 233ff.; 5, 326. See W. Meeks, *The Prophet-King*, 103–7, 110f., 192–5.

119. Philo, *Quod det.* 178, *inter alia*, puts it this way: see Strack-Billerbeck III, 694f.; M. de Jonge and A. S. van der Woude, '11QMelch', *NTS* 12, 1965–66, 320f.

120. R. Williamson, *Philo and the Epistle to the Hebrews*, 440.

121. Philo, *Leg. Alleg.* III, 82.

122. A. van der Woude, *OTS* 17, 1965, 354–73; M. de Jonge and van der Woude, '11QMelch', op. cit., 301–26; J. Fitzmyer, 'Further Light', *JBL* 86, 1967, 25–41. According to the last mentioned Melchizedek is high priest, but the two previous authors disagree.

123. See *Jesus. An Experiment in Christology*, 116–26.

124. As far as the history of religion goes, it is certain that priesthood and kingship originally belonged together and were later differentiated so that they became two distinct functions. See L. Dumont, 'On the Comparative Understanding of Non-Modern Civilizations', *Daedalus* 104, 2, 1975, 153–72.

125. 'He is like', *aphomoiomenos*' (perfect passive); see De Jonge and van der Woude, *NTS* 12, 1965–66, 321 n. 4.

126. Y. Yadin, 'The Dead Sea Scrolls', op. cit., 36–55.

127. So R. H. Fuller, *The Foundations of New Testament Christology*, London and New York 1965, 220f.

128. *Charaktēr* appears only here in the New Testament and occurs only twice in the Septuagint (Lev. 13.28; II Macc. 4.10). The word is only used a few times even in the inter-testamental literature. In fact it is Platonic terminology, which is taken over by Hebrews from its Alexandrian environment in which the word was current; however, Hebrews uses its formal meaning in order to express a particular feature of the wisdom tradition.

129. See S. Kistemaker, *The Psalm Citations in the Epistle to the Hebrews*, Amsterdam 1961, 88–94.

130. The whole of the inter-testamental literature is familiar with the heavenly liturgy in which the angels play an essential role. See especially Testaments of the Twelve Patriarchs, e.g. Levi 2; 3; 8; 18, etc.; also Qumran: 1QS 9.10f.; 1QS 6.4–6; 1QSa 2.18ff.

131. K. G. Kuhn, 'The two Messiahs of Aaron and Israel', in *The Scrolls and the New Testament*, ed. K. Stendahl, New York and London 1957, 54–64; E. Käsemann, *Das wandernde Gottesvolk*, 125ff.

132. Qumran: 11QMelch, see M. de Jonge and A. van der Woude, *NTS* 12, 1965–66, 301–26, and A. van der Woude, *OTS* 17, 1965, 345–73.

133. R. Brown, 'Does the New Testament call Jesus God?', *ThS* 26, 1965, 562f.

134. J. Jervell, *Imago Dei. Gen. 1, 26f. im Spätjudentum, in der Gnosis und in den paulinischen Briefen*, FRLANT 76, Göttingen 1960, 15–51 and (on Paul) 171–336.

135. W. Wifall, 'Son of Man', *CBQ* 37, 1975, 331–40. In my view this author has shed new light on the terms 'Adam' and 'Son of man'. Both terms are projections of the social conditions of the time of David on the primal period. Originally 'Son of man' meant something like *'gentilhomme'* or 'gentleman' as opposed to *'homme'* or 'man' as the ordinary man in the street. In that case a son of man is a notable, someone from a higher social class. In the normal process of democratization this term, which is first used for a special class – the court of David – is applied to all men. In that case Son of man, *gentilhomme* and 'gentleman'

all refer to all men. The earlier meaning, which denotes a special class, appears again later in a quite different religious context, namely that of apocalyptic.

136. J. Barbel, *Christos Angelos*, Bonn [2]1964 (1941): A. Bakker, 'Christ an Angel? A Study of Early Christian Docetism', *ZNW* 32, 1933, 255–65; J. Daniélou, *The Theology of Jewish Christianity*, ET London and Philadelphia 1964, 117–46; G. Kretschmar, *Studien zur frühchristlichen Trinitätstheologie*, BHTh 21, Tübingen 1956; R. Longenecker, *The Christology of Early Jewish Christianity*, SBT II 17, London 1970; M. Werner, *The Formation of Christian Dogma*, ET London and New York 1957.

137. For the structure of Hebrews (which I have noted, but do not follow in this theological exposition), see A. Vanhoye, *La structure littéraire*.

138. G. Schille, 'Erwägungen', ZNW 64, 1955, and G. Friedrich, 'Das Lied vom Hohenpriester', *Tz* 18, 1962, think that an old hymn to Christ underlies Heb. 4.15–5.10. I find this unconvincing; they underestimate the poetic gifts of the author of Hebrews himself.

139. Many authors now assume that Qumran interpreted Ps. 110.4 in messianic terms (either in priestly messianic or royal messianic terms). Of the literature cited see Yadin, Rigaux, Fitzmyer, Higgins, de Jonge, van der Woude, Schille, Friedrich; also E. Käsemann, *Das wandernde Gottesvolk. Eine Untersuchung zum Hebräerbrief*, FRLANT 37, Göttingen 1938, 124ff., and Hamerton-Kelly, *Preexistence*, 245. Some people question whether Qumran had a collection of 'testimonies', i.e. a list of Old Testament texts, which were interpreted in messianic terms (e.g. S. Kistemaker, *The Psalm Citations*, 88–94), others clearly affirm it (e.g. F. M. Cross, *The Ancient Library of Qumran*, New York 1961, 218f.). See also F. F. Bruce, *To the Hebrews*, 221 n. 6.

140. The Dutch Willibrord translation, which forms the basis for my quotations, sometime adds 'Jesus' where the Greek only has 'he', e.g. 13.15.

141. *Jesus, An Experiment in Christology*, 451–6.

142. See also A. S. van der Woude, *Die messianischen Vorstellungen der Gemeinde von Qumran*, Assen 1957, 218.

143. Ps. Sol. 17; Test. Levi 18. Philo also calls the high priest, who is the divine Logos, 'a priest without sins' (*De specialibus legibus* I, 230). Referring to the fact that Jesus is a man like all other men (sin apart), Heb. 2.11 has the somewhat mysterious sentence: 'For he who sanctifies and those who are sanctified have all one origin' *(ex henos)*. Whatever the context of this formula may be, the meaning in Hebrews is that Jesus, the origin of sanctification, and mankind come from the same race; they are really man *kata panta*, in all (Heb. 2.17).

144. E.g. Philo, *De fuga* 138; *Quis rerum divinarum heres* 73; cf. Prov. 3.11–13; 13.24; 22.15; 23.13f.

145. Hebrews interprets this as though the cloud of incense concealed the ark from the sight of the high priest (Heb. 9.1–10). There is no question of a *free* access here – which is what the author means.

146. The blood is the life of all flesh, but God gave the blood for the ministry to the altar. So it is with the blood which brings reconciliation through life (Lev. 17.11). See D. J. McCarthy, 'The Symbolism of Blood and Sacrifice', *JBL* 88, 1969, 166–76.

147. *Jesus. An Experiment in Christology*, 291–4.

148. Ibid., 308ff.

149. F. Maass, s.v. *k–p–r*, *ThHandWAT* 1, 842–57.

150. J. Kühlewein, s.v. *q–r–b–*, *ThHandWAT* 1, 132f.; J. Schneider, s.v. *proserchomai*, *TDNT* 2, 683f.; K. Schmidt, s.v. *prosagō*, *TDNT* 1, 131–3; K. Weiss, *prospherō*, *TDNT* 9, 65–8; H. Preisker, *engys*, *TDNT* 2, 329–32; J. Stamm, *Erlösen und Vergeben im Alten Testament*, Bern 1940; S. Lyonnet, 'De ratione expiationis', *VD* 37, 1959, 336–52 and 38, 1960, 66–75. See also R. de Vaux, *Ancient Israel*, ET London and New York 1961, 417–56, 507–10.

151. The *anastasis ek nekrōn* in Heb. 11.35a means a resurrection from death back to earthly life, not the (general) resurrection. Hebrews does not need the descent to hell, unlike e.g. I Peter 3.19. Here the fallen angels are imprisoned in the underworld, where the dead also dwell (I Peter 4.6); Jesus descends into this underworld after his death and from there ascends through all the heavenly spheres to the right hand of God (I Peter 3.22). This expresses the subjection of demons and angels to Christ (I Peter 3.22), see also Eph. 4.8–10.

152. Strack-Billerbeck II, 266. H. Bietenhard, *Die himmlische Weltim Urchristentum und Spätjudentum*, WUNT 2, Tübingen 1951.

153. Strack-Billerbeck I, 784–891, 976; II, 229, 266f.; III, 807; IV, 507.

154. Also in the inter-testamental literature: Test. Levi 5.1f.; Test. Dan 5.12; II (Syr.) Bar. 4.3–6; IV Ezra 7.26; 8.52; 13.36; I Enoch 90.28f.; Ps. Sol. 17.25 (see also Gal. 4.26; Rev. 3.12; 21.2f., 10).

155. In Lev. 16.2f. (Greek) *ta hágia* or *to hagion* (Heb. 9.12, 25; 10.19; 13.11) is the rearmost part of the tent of the covenant, where God's throne, the ark of the covenant, stands (see Sir. 24.10). Sometimes Hebrews makes a distinction between the tent, namely the holy place or the vestibule, and the holy of holies. Thus Jesus has gone through the tent (where the sacrifice is offered) and come into the holy of holies (Heb. 8.5).

156. In addition to other meanings, *pneumata* also means 'the dead' (e.g. also in I Peter 3.19).

157. The liturgy of the *Apostolic Constitutions*, II, 25, 5, calls the church 'the true *tent of witness*', i.e. that part in the Mosaic tent of the covenant which contained within the ark both the two stone tablets of the Decalogue and the book of the covenant (Deut. 10.5). In Ex. 25.16; 31.18, these two tablets are called the 'tablets of the testimony'. Hebrews 9.4 calls them the 'tablets of the covenant' (also Deut. 9.9; I Kings 8.9), because in the last resort the Decalogue is the fundamental law of the covenant (Deut. 4.13; I Kings 8.21; see Heb. 9.19). With Greek-speaking Jews the emphasis lay more on the Decalogue than on the Torah (see *Jesus. An Experiment in Christology*, 230–43).

158. The idea of a heavenly liturgy, in which the elect on earth already take part was a widespread assumption, above all in apocalyptic, with its expectation of a *priestly* Messiah. (See above all Test. XII Patr.: Test. Reuben 6.8; Test. Simeon 7.2; Test. Levi 2; 3; 8; 18; in Qumran, 1QS 9.10f.; 1QS 6.4–6; 1QSa 2.18ff.) The ancient sources of this heavenly cult lie in Ezek. 40–48 and Ex. 25–29.

159. That would imply that Hebrews did not know the tradition of 'the rending of the veil' at the death of Jesus. But this rending related to the Temple of Herod in Jerusalem, which Hebrews never mentions (it is addressed to Diaspora Jews). Hebrews is interested only in the Mosaic tent of the covenant, in the period of the foundation of Israel.

160. E. Käsemann, *Das wandernde Gottesvolk*, 117f., among others, claims that Hebrews here uses a Jewish, pre-Christian source. This cannot be demonstrated

by literary-critical methods. Granted, the theme of *de viris illustribus*, the history of the great heroes of a country's past, was developed in Judaism (and apocalyptic) in the Hellenistic period, following a Graeco-Roman model. Hebrews 11 stands in this tradition of early Jewish reverence for a country's heroes. However, that does not mean that it has to go back to a source. It probably reflects the atmosphere in the synagogue when sermons were given to admonish the faithful.

161. Pliny, *Epist.* 10.96.8; Suetonius, *Nero* 16.2.

162. *Didache* 10.6 (the eucharistic prayers).

163. From the literature cited see esp. C. Spicq, *Épître aux Hébreux*, Vol. 2, 95–104; R. Williamson, *Philo and the Epistle to the Hebrews*, 548–57; G. Braulik, 'Menuchah. Die Ruhe Gottes und des Volkes im Lande', *BuK* 23, 1968, 75–8; F. Stolz, s. v. *ruach*, in *ThHandWAT* 1, 43–6; O. Hofius, *Katapausis. Die Vorstellungen vom endzeitlichen Ruheort im Hebräerbrief*, Tübingen 1970.

164. *Katapausis* (not *anapausis*) is the Greek biblical equivalent of *mᵉnūḥā*, i.e. God's rest. In Hebrews this word is meant biblically (Ps. 95.11, where it means entry into the holy land, and above all into the temple in Jerusalem). *Katapausis* is God's abode in the heavenly Jerusalem of the last times, but then in the priestly context of Hebrews: entry into the heavenly holy of holies, into which Jesus has preceded us (see Hofius, op. cit., 43), God's eschatological state of rest. Thus the word is connected with *sabbatismos* (Heb. 4.9)(Hofius, op. cit., 102–15): the heavenly liturgical sabbath which at the same time in fact includes resting from hard struggle on earth. However, this rest is not a matter of non-activity; it is an active, peaceful celebration. Therefore the word *katapausis* has no Platonic and gnostic connotations in Hebrews.

165. See G. Schrenk, s.v. *dikaiō*, in *TDNT* 2, 215; E. Schweizer, *Erniedrigung und Erhöhung*, 164 n. 273; J. Delorme, *La résurrection de Jésus dans le langage du Nouveau Testament*, Lectio Divina 72, Paris 1972, 135; E. Schillebeeckx, *Jesus. An Experiment in Christology*, 536f.; W. Stenger, 'Der Christushymnus in I Tim.', *TrThZ* 78, 1969, 33–48.

166. However, it is striking that in the ancient hymns to Christ and in the creeds there is often no mention of the saving significance of the death of Jesus. See also P. Smulders, 'Some Riddles in the Apostles Creed', *Bijdr* 31, 1970 (234–60), 243f., 252f. Still, the death of Jesus is usually understood to be included in the concept of *sarx* or the humiliation which is mentioned above all in the hymns. The *sarx* (flesh or humanity) essentially includes the death of Jesus, but not the violent crucifixion.

167. Thus Greek-speaking Jews like Josephus: 'participating in the *theia physis*' or the divine nature (*Contra Apionem* I, 232), and obviously the Platonist Philo, *Decal.* 104; *Leg. All.* I, 38). See J. Gross, *La divinisation du chrétien d'après les Pères grecs*, Paris 1938, 109–11; H. Hanse, s.v. *metechō*, *TDNT* 2, 831f.; K. H. Schelkle, *Die Petrusbriefe*; A. Festugière, *L'idéal religieux des grecs et l'Evangile*, Paris 1932, 48–53.

168. This idea can already be found in early Christianity and Judaism, see Strack-Billerbeck I, 164.

*Part Two, Section Two, Chapter 5: Jesus, the witness of God-is-love: Johannine theology*

1. F. Herzog, *Liberation Theology*, New York 1972.
2. J. B. Burns, *The Christian Buddhism of St John*, New Jersey 1971.
3. Strack-Billerbeck IV, 792.
4. Ibid., IV, 784–9; 792–8.
5. Ibid., II, 280f.; G. von Rad, *Old Testament Theology* I, ET London and New York 1975, 294f.; II, London and New York 1975, 275f.
6. In early Judaism Moses is called prophet, king and priest. Moses as prophet: in Philo (see W. Meeks, *The Prophet-King*, 115f., 125–9); in Josephus (ibid., 137f.), in the Apocrypha (ibid., 147–56); in Qumran (ibid., 172f.). Moses as priest: in Philo (ibid., 113–20); in Josephus (ibid., 136f.), in Qumran (ibid., 174f.). Moses as king: in Philo (ibid., 107–17), in Josephus (ibid., 134–6), in Qumran (ibid., 147–54). Moses as hierophant or initiator into mysticism; in Philo (ibid., 120–2), in Samaritanism (ibid., 243f.). Finally, Moses as a 'divine being' (*divus Moyses*): in Philo (ibid., 103–7, 110f.), in Samaritanism (ibid., 256) and Moses as paraclete or advocate with God: in Josephus (ibid., 137), in Philo (ibid., 118), in Samaritanism (ibid., 254f.). This whole we shall refer to as 'Sinaitism'. For the literature see n.8 below.
7. M. McNamara, 'The Ascension', *Scripture* 19, 1967, 65–73; W. Meeks, *The Prophet-King*, 216–57; G. Wehmeier, s.v. *'-l-h* in *ThHandWAT* 2, 272–90.
8. Literature: for Moses mysticism and Moses typology (eschatological prophet greater than Moses, Sinaitism and its influence on the Gospel of John): T. F. Glasson, *Moses in the Fourth Gospel*, 20–31; 48–105; W. Meeks, *The Prophet-King*, esp. 100–75; 286–319; J. L. Martyn, *History and Theology*, 122–5; H. M. Teeple, *The Mosaic Eschatological Prophet*; L. Perlitt, 'Moses as Prophet', *EvTh* 31, 1971, 588–608; F. Schnutenhaus, *Mosestraditionen*; H. Gressmann, *Der Messias*, Göttingen 1929, 182–92; F. W. Young, 'Jesus, the Prophet: A Re-examination', *JBL* 68, 1949, 285–99; E. L. Allen, 'Jesus and Moses in the New Testament', *ExpT* 67, 1956, 104–6; R. H. Smith, 'Exodus Typology in the Fourth Gospel', *JBL* 81, 1962, 329–42; R. Bloch et al., *Moïse, l'homme de l'Alliance*, Paris 1955, 93–167; R. Le Déaut, *La Nuit Paschale*, Rome 1963, 198–338; A. Lacomara, 'Deuteronomy', *CBQ* 36, 1974, 65–84; J. P. Miranda, *Der Vater, der mich gesandt hat*. See also M. Abraham, *Légendes juives apocryphes sur la vie de Moïse*, Paris 1925; *John and Qumran*, ed. J. H. Charlesworth, London 1972.
9. W. Meeks, *The Prophet-King*, 216–20, see some of his qualifications in 'Am I a Jew?', op. cit., 163–86; G. Wesley Buchanan, 'The Samaritan Origin', op. cit., 149–75; E. Freed, 'Samaritan Influences', *CBQ* 30, 1968, 580–7; O. Cullmann, *The Johannine Circle*, 51; J. Bowman, *Samaritanische Probleme*; H. Kipperberg, *Garisim und Synagoge*; J. Macdonald, *The Theology of the Samaritans*, London 1964; J. Beutler *Martyria*, 347–9. See also R. Coggins, *Samaritans and Jews*, Oxford 1975.
10. See *Jesus. An Experiment in Christology*, 443–8.
11. R. Schnackenburg, *Johannesevangelium* II, 529.
12. For the Jewish identification of the one who sends with the one who is sent see Strack-Billerbeck I, 590; II, 558; K. H. Rengstorf, s. v. *apostolos*, *TDNT* 1, 414–20.
13. *Jesus. An Experiment in Christology*, 478f.
14. Ibid., 478ff.

15. Ibid., 111f. and 360–78.

16. O. Cullmann, *The Johannine Circle*, 43–56; J. Martyn, *History and Theology*, 97–100.

17. Thus (wrongly in my view), G. W. Buchanan, 'Samaritan Origin', 175. See also R. Kysar, *The Fourth Evangelist*, 160–2.

18. One may speak with some reason of a degree of Johanninism in the Epistle to the Hebrews.

19. T. F. Glasson, *Moses in the Fourth Gospel*, 20–31; W. Meeks, *The Prophet-King*, 107–17; 129f., 134–6, 147–54, 177–96, 227–38.

20. T. F. Glasson, op. cit., 48–105.

21. The interpretation of the Johannine farewell discourses on the basis of Moses' farewell speech as put forward by Lacomara, op. cit., seems to me correct, but somewhat exaggerated.

22. R. Schnackenburg, *Gospel of John* I, 393–400.

23. Thus C. Colpe, *Die religionsgeschichtliche Schule. Darstellung und Kritik ihres Bildes vom gnostischen Erlösermythus*, Göttingen 1968; E. Brandenburger, *Adam und Christus*, Neukirchen 1962; H. M. Schenke, *Der Gott 'Mensch' in der Gnosis*, Göttingen 1962; U. Müller, *Messias und Menschensohn in jüdischen Apokalypsen und in der Offenbarung des Johannes*, Gütersloh 1972, esp. 114–6; see H. Jonas, *Gnosis und spätantiker Geist*, two vols., Göttingen [3]1964 and [2]1966; R. Longenecker, *The Christology of Early Jewish Christianity*, SBT II 17, London and Naperville 1970.

24. See the new works by G. W. McRae, 'The Jewish Background of the Gnostic Sophia Myth', *NT* 12, 1972, 86–100; id., 'The Coptic Gnostic Apocalypse of Adam', *HeyJ* 6, 1965, 27–35; B. L. Mack, 'Wisdom Myth and Mytho-logy', *Int* 24, 1970, 46–60; id., *Logos und Sophia. Untersuchungen zur Weisheitstheologie im hellenistischen Judentum*, Göttingen 1973; H. B. Kuhn, 'The Angelology of the Non-canonical Jewish Apocalypses', *JBL* 67, 1948, 211–9; C. Talbert, 'The Myth of A Descending-Ascending Redeemer', *NTS* 22, 1976, 418–40. Cf. Tacitus, *Historiae* 4, 83f.; Virgil, *Eclogue* 4; Horace, *Odes* 1, 2.

25. Test. Job 2–5; Apoc. Mosis 37, ed. C. Tischendorf, *Apocalypses Apocryphae*, Leipzig 1866, 20. When Adam dies, angels descend and take his soul to heaven; there it is washed, and Michael then brings it, in expectation of the final judgment, to the third heaven. Also III Macc. 6.18–31; Test. Abrah. 9.17f.; 6.4; 8.11; 1.5–10; 7.3–17.

26. 11QMelch: here Melchizedek is a redeeming angel.

27. See H. A. Wolfson, *Philo*, Cambridge, Mass. [2]1948, Vol. I, 253–66. Wisdom is Logos (*De somniis* I, 108f.; *Leg. Alleg. I*, 65); *pneuma* is Wisdom (*De creatione* 135; *De gigantibus* 22, 27); Logos is angel (*Quis div. rer. heres* 42, 205; *De cherubim* 35). The changing relationship between Logos, firstborn Son and angel of Yahweh emerges clearly from *De agricultura* 51. In *De confusione linguarum* 146f., Son, Logos and angel are used interchangeably, and in *De somniis* I, 215 they are finally identified with the high priest. However, we must remember that in Philo the Logos is never a person alongside God; he is the expression of God's own thought; see R. Williamson, *Philo and the Epistle to the Hebrews*, Leiden 1970, 415ff.

28. See J. H. Charlesworth (ed.), *John and Qumran*, London 1972; J. R. Harris and A. Mingana, *The Odes and Psalms of Solomon*, Manchester 1920; R. A. Culpepper, 'The Odes of Solomon and the Gospel of John', *CBQ* 35, 1973, 298–322.

29. Odes of Solomon 12; 29; 37; 41; 42; especially 12 and 22f. Christ is at the same time Son of God (Odes 36; 41; 42) and Son of man (Odes 36 and 41). See

in J. Charlesworth, op. cit., 127f.

30. Justin, *Apology* I, 46 and 63; II, 10; *Dialogue against Trypho* 61; 62; 126; 128f.; Son, Wisdom, angel or Logos. Also *Shepherd of Hermas, Similitudes* 8; *Epist. Apostolorum* 3; 13;14 (in the annunciation to Mary Christ himself takes the form of an angel). In Tertullian, on the other hand, we find an explicit attempt to detach the complex of Wisdom, Logos, Son, *pneuma* from the angels (this is a distinctive North African contribution, see above all *Adv. Marc.* 9).

31. See *Jesus. An Experiment in Christology*, 480–99; whether this is typical of *Egyptian* Judaism in particular, as is sometimes claimed, seems to me to be purely hypothetical.

32. See G. Johnston, *The Spirit-Paraclete in the Gospel of John*, Cambridge 1970, 122 (against O. Betz, *Der Paraklet*, Leiden 1963).

33. G. Quispel, 'John and Jewish Christianity', in *John and Qumran*, ed. J. H. Charlesworth, 137–55.

34. O. Cullmann, *The Johannine Circle*.

35. Strack-Billerbeck II, 425.

36. M. Lowe, 'Who were the Ioudaioi?' *NTS* 18, 1976, 101–30. At the time of Jesus, 'Judaea' represented the area of Judah (the old southern kingdom), in reality the land which was under the Roman procurator, Pontius Pilate (this did not include Galilee); sometimes it was also the kingdom of Herod the Great (which in that case was roughly the whole of Israel). By contrast, 'Israel' means the people, in the sense of 'the Jews', and the land of Israel, whereas the Diaspora Jews spoke of 'the Jews' rather than Israel. In the Palastinian terminology of the time, therefore, *hoi Ioudaioi* always meant 'the Judaeans', the inhabitants of Jerusalem and its neighbourhood (or its rulers). In messianic terms the Palestinians also spoke of 'the king of Israel' (of all Jews), whereas the Diaspora Jews and the Romans spoke of the king of the *Ioudaioi*, i.e. the Judaeans, just as the Roman official Pilate had 'king of the *Ioudaioi*' put as the *titulus* on Jesus' cross, John 19.19, as opposed to 'king of Israel' in John 1.49; 12.13. Pilate had jurisdiction only in Judaea, whereas Galilee came under the jurisdiction of Herod Antipas. In each of the four gospels, Pilate is the first to use the term 'king of the Judaeans'. Pilate can object to the claim of anyone to be king of Judaea. John always uses *Ioudaioi* in the sense of Judaeans (with the exception of the *Samaritan* use of *Ioudaioi* in the chapter about the Samaritan woman, John 4). In Peraea, Jesus says: let us go to *Judaea*, but the disciples immediately warn him against that: the *Ioudaioi*, the Judaeans, want to stone you (7.1; 11.7f.). This, then, refers to the inhabitants of Jerusalem or their leaders (11.19, 31, 33, 36, 45; 10.19, 24, 31–33; 5.10, 15, 16, 18; 7.1 referring back to 5.18; 6.52 and 7.11; also 7.13, 15, 35; 9.22; 19.38; 20.19; 'for fear of the Judaeans', whereas in Galilee no one hesitated to follow Jesus openly). 'As I have already said to the *Judaeans*', now Jesus says the same thing to his *Galilean* disciples (13.33; so also 8.21; 7.34, 36; 8.22–31, 48, 52, 57). The Judaeans argue: 'We are descendants of Abraham' and have never been slaves (8.33), as opposed to the Galilean Jesus (see 7.41, 52; there were many proselytes in Galilee, and also Jews of impure Jewish origin; Judaea led the revolt against the Seleucid empire). So in John *Ioudaioi* are not the Jews, but the Judaeans. The expression can, of course, mean the Jerusalem authorities as well as the people of Judaea, just as we would say, 'The French are for an alliance with . . .' meaning the French government (thus 18.12, 14; 18.31, 36, 38; 19.7, 12, 14, 21, 31). So this is a normal and not a specifically Johannine usage. The Jerusalem Sanhedrin

had no authority outside Judaea, the area of jurisdiction for the Roman procurator. Josephus therefore speaks of 'the Sanhedrin of the people of Jerusalem' (*Vita* 62); only after 67 (extension of the power of the Roman procurator) did the Sanhedrin acquire authority in Galilee (cf. Acts 13.27f.). Thus when it is a question of authority, John maintains the Palestinian terminology. In that case the *Ioudaioi* are the Jerusalem authorities. Throughout the confrontation between Pilate, Jesus and the *Ioudaioi*, we do not find a 'people' but only the Jewish authorities: the Judaeans (high priests) and the pagan Romans, both 'unbelievers' (19.6, 15; 'they' in 19.18, 40 are the Judaeans of 18.38, who in 18.28f. bring Jesus from Caiaphas to the Roman Praetorium). In 1.19, too, the *Ioudaioi* come from Jerusalem to John the Baptist.

There is only one exception, which confirms this Palestinian terminology, namely John 4. In the conversation with a *Samaritan* woman, *hoi Ioudaioi* means all *Jews*, for the simple reason that Samaritans regard themselves as part of Israel. What we have here is a Samaritan use of the word *Ioudaioi*: 'Salvation comes from the *Ioudaioi*' (4.22). In this context Jesus could not contrast the Samaritans with 'Israel' without offending the Samaritans, who also regard Jacob as their father (4.12, see R. Coggins, *Samaritans and Jews*, Oxford 1975). Consequently the Samaritan woman calls Jesus a *Ioudaios* (4.9) in the Samaritan sense: 'Jew' as contrasted with 'Samaritan'. (The Jews charge the Samaritans with a divergent form of Jewish faith, which had originally been spread through Judaea by the tribe of Judah.) In other words, in Samaritan terminology *Ioudaios* has a religious significance: one who confesses Judaism, and who is a 'Judaean by religion'. It transpires from this that (given the qualification raised by John 4) in the Fourth Gospel *Ioudaios* can always be translated Judaean (Palestinian terminology). Outside the synoptic gospels, which (with the exception of Luke 7.3) use the same terminology as John (Judaeans as compared with Galileans), the rest of the New Testament fits in more with the usage of Diaspora Judaism; there *Ioudaioi* simply means 'the Jews'. (In the fragment of tradition in I Thess. 2.14–16 we still find the Palestinian usage of *Ioudaios*: Judaean or inhabitant of Judaea.) So we must say that the Gospel of John is in fact *anti-Judaean* (not anti-Jewish), perhaps because the Judaeans had the Galilean Jesus crucified and also because of the earlier animosity between the Judaean and the Galilean Jews ('How can anything good come out of Galilee?').

37. Above all since J. L. Martyn, *History and Theology in the Fourth Gospel*, XIX–XXI (see the reviews by R. Brown in *USQ* 23, 1968, 392–4; R. Schnackenburg, *BZ* 14, 1970, 7–9); T. C. Smith, *Jesus in the Gospel of John*, Nashville 1959; H. M. Teeple, *The Mosaic Eschatological Prophet*; F. Schnutenhaus, *Mosestraditionen;* J. A. T. Robinson, 'The Destination and Purpose of Saint John's Gospel', in *Twelve New Testament Studies*, SBT 34, London and Naperville 1962, 107–25; W. C. van Unnik, 'The Purpose of Saint John's Gospel', *StEv* 1, 1959, 382–411; J. Beutler, *Martyria*, 339–64; E. Grässer, 'Die antijüdische Polemik im Johannesevangelium', *NTS* 10, 1964–65, 74–90.

38. K. L. Carroll, 'The Fourth Gospel and the Exclusion of Christians from the Synagogue', *BJRL* 40, 1957, 19–32; W. Meeks, *The Prophet-King*, 318.

39. See notes 8 and 9 above.

40. W. Meeks, 'Am I a Jew?', in *Christianity, Judaism and other Greco-Roman Cults*, ed. J. Neusner, Leiden 1975, 1, 172.

41. Strack-Billerbeck, IV, 212f., 218f., and esp. 293–333; see W. Doskocil, *Der*

*Bann in der Urkirche*, Munich 1958, 40–3. J. Martyn, *History and Theology*, 148–50. In any case, by the time that Gamaliel II legalized this final ban round about the year AD 90, there had already been some seventy expulsions from the synagogue.

42. See above; also J. Blank, *Krisis* (the argument of the whole book).

43. F. Mussner, 'Die Johanneischen Parakletssprüche und die apostolische Tradition', *BZ* 5, 1961, 56–70.

44. G. von Rad, *Wisdom in Israel*, ET London and Nashville 1972, 308.

45. G. Nickelsburg, *Resurrection, Immortality and Eternal Life*; L. Ruppert, *Jesus, als der leidende Gerechte?*; see *Jesus. An Experiment in Christology*, 286f.; see also K. Berger, *Die Auferstehung des Propheten und die Erhöhung des Menschensohnes*, Göttingen 1976.

46. G. Scholem, *Major Trends in Jewish Mysticism*, New York 1954, 40–79; see M. Gaster, *Studies and Texts in Folklore, Magic, Medieval Romance, Hebrew Apocrypha and Samaritan Eschatology*, three vols., London 1925–28, 1, 156–8.

47. C. H. Dodd, *Historical Tradition in the Fourth Gospel*, Cambridge 1963, 306–87; J. Blinzler, *Johannes und die Synoptiker*, Stuttgart 1965; G. Reim, *Studien zum alttestamentlichen Hintergrund des Johannesevangeliums*, Cambridge 1974; J. A. Bailey, *The Traditions common to the Gospels of Luke and John*, Leiden 1963; A. Dauer, *Die Passionsgeschichte im Johannesevangelium*, Munich 1972; E. F. Siegman, 'St John's Use of the Synoptic Material', *CBQ* 30, 1968, 182–98; F. L. Cribbs, 'St Luke and the Johannine Tradition', *JBL* 90, 1971, 422–50; C. K. Barrett, 'John and the Synoptic Gospels', *ExpT* 85, 1974, 228–31; F. Schnider and W. Stenger, *Johannes und die Synoptiker, Vergleich ihrer Parallelen*, Munich 1971.

48. Strack-Billerbeck II, 353–8; III, 129ff.; J. Jervell, *Imago Dei*.

49. Above all in Philo (though by no means exclusively). See W. Meeks, *The Prophet-King*, 100–30; in Josephus, ibid., 131–45; and in the Pseudepigrapha, ibid., 146–63; in Qumran, ibid., 164–74.

50. M. McNamara, 'The Ascension and Exaltation', *Scripture* 19, 1967, 65–73; id., 'Logos of the Fourth Gospel', *ExpT* 79, 1968, 115–17.

51. M. Rissi, 'Die Logoslieder', *TZ* 31, 1975, 321–36; first hymn: John 1.1–13; the second, John 1.14–18.

52. So L. Trudinger, 'Prologue of John', op. cit., 11–17.

53. Targum Ps. 68.18; see M. McNamara, 'The Ascension and Exaltation', op. cit., 65–73; id., *Targum and Testament*, Grand Rapids 1972, 143; id., *The New Testament and the Palestinian Targum to the Pentateuch*, Rome 1966, 145ff.

54. *Erchomenon eis ton kosmon*, 'coming into the world'. Grammatically this can refer both to 'light' and to 'every man'. John speaks of the coming of the light only in 1.11; in the previous verses it is said that *'it shines'* and 'it *was* in the world'. In view of the structure of the prologue, in which the verbs always come first (they are important for John), I connect *erchomenon* with man (as does the Vulgate, among others): the light that was in the world illuminates every man who comes into the world. In my opinion it is impossible to refer *erchomenon eis ton kosmon*, coming as it does at the end of the sentence, to the *coming* of the light. See a similar construction in 1.3: 'And without him was not anything made *that was made*'. This 'trailing' effect within the Johannine sphere can only be related to 'earthly' things.

55. *Pseudo-Clementine Recognitions* I, 54 (PG 1,1237f.); 1.60 (col. 1240); see G. Strecker, *Das Judenchristentum in den Pseudo-Clementinen*, TU 70, Berlin 1950.

56. O. Cullmann, *The Johannine Circle*, 31–34.

57. Among others, R. Brown (*John* I, 13f.) in particular has pointed out that *monogenēs* does not come from *mono gennan*, but from *mono-genus*, unique of its kind, a rendering of the Hebrew *yaḥīd* (e.g. Gen. 22.2,12,16), Greek also *agapētos*, the one and only beloved son (see also John 3.16,18; I John 4.9). The Septuagint translates it once *agapētos* (only beloved) and then again *monogenēs*, unique – a precious possession (which is also the case with an only begotten son). Isaac, the son of Abraham, who had more sons, is called *monogenēs* (Heb. 11.17). Only later, in the Arian dispute, will Jerome translate the word *unigenitus* (John 1.18; 3.16–18). True, John speaks of 'being born of God' in respect of *believers* (1.15; I John 4.9), but nowhere does he say that Jesus, the Son, is *born* of the Father. There is no basis in Johannine theology for the later scholastic theology of the procession of the Son from the Father within the Trinity *per modum generationis* (birth), regardless of its possible specific theological value. However, R. Brown overlooks the particular spiritual background of the term *monogenēs para tou Patros*. It is striking that *monogenēs para Patros* in Jewish exegesis goes back to a midrash on Gen. 28.12 and Ezek. 1.26: 'a figure like a man on what looked like a throne'. In *later* Egyptian gnosticism these two texts are used to say that 'a *firstborn* (above all in the sense of an only beloved) dwells with (*para*) the Lord of hosts; he is called Israel and sees God' (see J. Doresse, *Les livres secrets des gnostiques d'Egypte*, two vols, Paris 1958–1959, 1, 189; see also P. Winter, 'Monogenès para Patros', *ZRGG* 5, 1953, 335–65). For John 1.51 and 3.13 this heavenly figure is evidently the Son of man, earlier the heavenly *imago* of Jacob = Israel (Michael). Moses too was a 'witness to the Father' (see John 5.37a), namely witness of the Tanach (5.37b is in fact an allusion to the revelation on Sinai). The Jews *saw* God's voice (Ex. 20.18). See also J. Jervell, *Imago Dei*, Göttingen 1960, 115; see J. Giblet, 'Le témoignage du Père (Jean 5,31–47)', *Bible et Vie Chrétienne* 12, 1955, 49–59.

58. W. Meeks, *The Prophet-King*, 195ff. and 216–57.

59. See e.g. in the Moses mysticism of Philo, *Quaest. in Ex.* 46 (Meeks, op. cit., 100–30).

60. See the literature in note 8.

61. In all probability the mistake in (the best) manuscripts goes back to a wrong reading of abbreviations (the abbreviation of *hyios* is *h-ios*; and that of *theos* is *th-os* or *h-os*). It is easy to mistake one for the other. On the other hand, the state of the manuscripts also points to a later stage which had an *explicit* concern for the divinity of Jesus.

62. Thus, following R. Bultmann; see also the new study by U. Müller, *Die Geschichte der Christologie*, 37 n. 59.

63. G. P. Wetter, *Charis*, UNT 5, Leipzig 1913, esp. 128ff., 152ff.

64. M. D. Hooker, 'The Johannine Prologue', *NTS* 21, 1974, 53f.; in the last resort she is correct, but she misses the early Jewish 'reinterpretation' of this Sinai theme.

65. *Eis ta idia*. John uses this expression once again in 19.27: after the death of Jesus, the beloved disciple takes Mary, Jesus' mother, *eis ta idia*, into his house. Thus John 1.11 says that the light came into his own house. For a Jewish reader that would mean to *Israel*, but against the background of Palestinian speculations on Genesis (Targum) it can also mean 'the world': 'the light *of the world*' (see John 9.4f.) is the light that God created on the first day of creation (Gen. 1.2), even before there were shining stars or sun or moon. (Moreover, Bultmann had already commented that the Septuagint never translates Israel as God's own

people with *ta idia*, but only with *laos epiousios*; but in view of the syncretistic milieu of Johannine theology this does not convince me.) I have the impression that in the Gospel of John *ta idia* (which did not accept Jesus) is *Judaea* (Jerusalem and its neighbourhood). Galilee accepts Jesus.

66. The translation 'grace *for* grace' instead of 'grace *on* grace' (1.16) is defended especially by R. Brown, *The Gospel of John* I, 15f. According to him, John sees a radical contrast between Law and Christ. However, this view is out of line with the framework of the Gospel of John as a whole. In a number of pericopes John is particularly concerned to make it clear that the whole Tanach speaks only of Jesus Christ. The Old Testament is a *witness to Christ*, just as the role of John the Baptist consists exclusively in his testimony to Jesus. Now witnesses speak of what they have seen and heard (John 1.32–34; 3.11,32; 19.35 etc.). Therefore John wants to make it clear that the Tanach in fact talks of 'seeing the glory of God': John 12.41 with Isa. 6.1. Here we have a clear case of 'Sinaitism' which later culminates in Jewish Merkabah mysticism (see G. Scholem, *Major Trends in Jewish Mysticism*, 40–79; F. W. Young, 'A Study of the Relation of Isaiah to the Fourth Gospel', *ZNW* 44, 1955, 215–32). Furthermore, the quotation of Isa. 6 is preceded by Isa. 53.1 (the suffering servant who is rejected) and Isa. 6.9f. (Hebrew text, interpreted by John as: Christ was both the object of Isaiah's vision and the subject which speaks in it). Thus the rejection of Christ is also foretold in the Tanach itself (cf. John 12.41 with John 1.14). John 1.14 is therefore concerned with the theophany of God before *Moses* (Ex. 33.17–34.9): Moses is not allowed to see God's *face* (Ex. 33.20; John 1.18), but God allows him to see 'his glory' (Ex. 33.18,22; 34.5f.) (see n. 57 above). For John this means that Moses saw the glory *of Christ*, full of grace and truth (*rab ḥesed weᵉmet*), just as Isaiah did. So Moses is *witness* to Christ (John 5.46). Thus in 1.17 John is in no way concerned to *contrast* the Law with faith in Christ; he is simply distinguishing between the Law-given-by-Moses, that is, the *testimony* about Christ, and the *reality* of Christ himself, the living revelation of perfect *ḥesed* and *ᵉmet* (see also R. Le Déaut, *La nuit paschale*, 298–338). Moreover, it emerges from John 9.28 that John does not want to set Moses over against Jesus: Moses is a witness to Christ 'because he has seen him'. For that very reason Moses will not defend the Jews who reject Jesus, but will *accuse* them (cf. J. Jervell, *Imago Dei*, 115). All this clearly confirms the 'hypothesis' of Sinaitic Moses mysticism as the background to the Gospel of John. The Johannine midrash on Abraham also points in the same direction: Abraham saw 'Jesus' day' (John 8.56). For John, as for Paul, the (believing) Jews are also the first witnesses to Christ, the 'true Israelites' (John 17.20f.; see 1.41,45; 1.47–49; 6.37; 17.2f.); the Gentiles are 'drawn in later' (see 12.32 in connection with the question of the Gentiles, 12.21). In other words, John 1.16f. says that in Jesus the historical reality of the mystery has appeared which Moses was allowed to 'see' in advance.

67. I John 4.2 speaks of *homologein Iēsoun Christon en sarki elēlythota*, 'to confess that Jesus *has come* in the flesh' (the perfect passive of *erchomai*, come), i.e. his coming in the flesh 'has taken place'. This does not mean to say that Jesus is no longer 'man' on his return to the Father. It is a question of belief in the historical reality of the appearing of Jesus.

68. *Pseudo-Clementines*, see above n. 55 (p. 874).

69. See the good summary by R. Kysar, 'The Source Analysis of the Fourth Gospel: A Growing Consensus', *NT* 15, 1973, 134–52; id., *The Fourth Evangelist*

*and his Gospel*, Minneapolis 1975. Also U. Müller, *Die Geschichte der Christologie in der johanneischen Gemeinde*, SBS 77, Stuttgart 1975.

70. See the literature cited in this chapter, esp. on pp. 306f. and 372f.

71. R. Fortna, 'Jesus' Signs', *JBL* 89, 1970, 156–65; R. Brown, *Gospel of John* I, 196; B. Lindars, *Gospel of John*, 203; W. Wilkens, *Zeichen und Werke*, 44–59; R. Schnackenburg, *Gospel of John* I, 334–45.

72. J. Becker, 'Wunder', *NTS* 16, 1969, 145f.

73. W. Wilkens, *Zeichen und Werke*, 44–59; R. Schnackenburg, *Gospel of John* I, 335–40, 515–28.

74. F. Schnider and W. Stenger, *Johannes und die Synoptiker. Vergleich ihrer Parallelen*, Munich 1971, esp. 83.

75. L. Schottroff, *Der Glaubende und die feindliche Welt*, 247–57.

76. W. Nicol, *Semeia*, 125–37.

77. R. T. Fortna, 'Jesus' Signs', *JBL* 89, 1970, 152–66.

78. J. Becker, 'Wunder', *NTS* 16, 1969, 130–48.

79. R. Schnackenburg, *Gospel of John* I, 335–40, 515–28.

80. C. R. Holladay, see n. 48 on p. 862 above.

81. *Jesus. An Experiment in Christology*, 686 n. 105.

82. K. H. Rengstorf, s.v. *sēmeion*, *TDNT* 7, 257.

83. G. Fohrer, *Die symbolischen Handlungen der Propheten*, Basel-Zurich 1953.

84. R. Schnackenburg, *Gospel of John* I, 337–40.

85. E. Haenchen, 'Der Vater, der mich gesandt hat', *NTS* 9, 1962–63, 208–16; R. Schnackenburg, *Gospel of John* I, 334–37.

86. R. Mussner, *Die johanneische Sehweise und die Frage nach dem historischen Jesus*, Freiburg 1965, 18–24; C. Traets, *Voir Jésus*, 214–25.

87. This was already Bultmann's thesis: John only says that Jesus is the *revelation* of God. The investigations of John which have appeared since then have not got much further: John requires faith that Jesus 'comes from God'. See the works by J. M. Boice, *Witness and Revelation*, and J. Hindley, 'Witness', *SJT* 18, 1965, 319–37.

88. See S. Hofbeck, *Semeion*, 158–66.

89. Thus J. Bonsirven, *Epîtres de saint Jean*, Paris ²1954, 263f.; A. Vanhoye, *NRTh* 86, 1964, 339–48; H. Schneider, ' "The Word made Flesh" ', *CBQ* 31, 1969, 344–56.

90. Thus, convincingly, in my opinion, R. Schnackenburg, *Die Johannesbriefe*, Freiburg ²1963, 270f.

91. P. Harner, *The 'I am'*, 15–36 and 56f.; R. Brown, *Gospel of John* I, 535–7; Schnackenburg, *Johannesevangelium* II, 63; Dodd, *Interpretation*, 93–6; R. Le Déaut, *La nuit paschale*, 329.

92. E. g. Mishnah, Sukkah 4.5; P. Harner, op. cit., 20–2, 61f.; R. Brown, *Gospel of John* I, 537.

93. I. de la Potterie, 'Je suis la Voie', *NRTh* 88, 1966, 917–26.

94. According to G. MacRae, 'The *Ego*-proclamation', op. cit., 123–39, the parallels in the Coptic-gnostic literature are even more striking. In Nag Hammadi, Codex VI, there is a whole series of 'I am sayings' ('I am knowledge', etc., see the Leiden edition: *The Facsimile Edition of the Nag Hammadi Codices*, seven vols, Leiden 1972–1976). The statements here point to the transcendence of the Redeemer figure who goes beyond secular and even Jewish symbolism. R. Schnackenburg also sees the Hellenistic influence in this Johannine way of speaking. Cf.

the much earlier study by E. Schweizer, *Ego Eimi. Die religionsgeschichtliche Herkunft und theologische Bedeutung der johanneischen Bildreden,* Göttingen 1939.

95. G. Scholem, *Major Trends in Jewish Mysticism,* New York 1946; id., *Jewish Gnosticism, Merkabah Mysticism and Talmudic Tradition,* New York 1960.

96. K. M. Fischer, 'Der johanneische Christus und der gnostische Erlöser,' op. cit., 245–67, asserts that John in fact presupposes gnostic myths, at least in a pre-Mandaean form (against R. Bultmann), but John transcends this gnosticism in all essential points.

97. Still most of all R. Brown, see his title 'Jesus and the Principal Feasts of the Jews', I, 199.

98. Brown, *Gospel of John* I, 272–4; Schnackenburg, *Johannesevangelium* II, 57f.; J. Blank, Die johanneische Brotrede, *BUL* 7, 1966; H. Leroy, *Rätsel und Missverständnis,* 100–24; W. Meeks, *The Prophet-King,* 91–98.

99. T. Preiss, Etude sur le ch. 6, *ETR* 46, 1971, 144–56; J. Blank, 'Die johanneische Brotrede', op. cit., 193–297 and 255–70; Strack-Billerbeck II, 435f.; II, 434f. Also in Qumran: Damascus Document QD 19.34.

100. Josephus, *Antiquitates* 12, 325. See A. Schalit, 'Evidence of an Aramaic Source in Josephus' Antiquities of the Jews', *Annual of the Swedish Theological Institute* 4, 1965, 163–88.

101. J. Morgenstern, *The Fire upon the Altar,* Leiden 1963; also R. de Vaux, *Ancient Israel,* ET London 1961, 510–14.

102. See J. Nelis, *II Makkabeeën,* Bussum 1975, 65–8.

103. Josephus, *Antiquitates* 15, 395; *De bello judaico* 5, 210.

104. Syriac Apocalypse of Baruch (= II Baruch), 36 and 39.7.

105. Above all, R. Brown, *Gospel of John I,* CXIII–IV; H. Schlier, 'Johannes 6 und das johanneische Verständnis der Eucharistie' in *Bibel und zeitgemässer Glaube* II, Klosterneuburg, Vienna and Munich 1967, 70–95.

106. See R. Kysar, *The Fourth Evangelist,* 249–58.

107. Kysar, op. cit., 259.

108. In rabbinic Judaism the grain of wheat is an image for the (general) resurrection. See Strack-Billerbeck II, 551; III, 475; also I Cor. 15.37.

109. See *Jesus. An Experiment in Christology,* 486–9.

110. See Strack-Billerbeck IV, 1019–20; G. Fischer, *Die himmlischen Wohnungen. Untersuchungen zu John 14.2–3,* Bern-Frankfurt 1975; R. Gundry, 'In My Father's House are many "monai" (Jn. 14, 2)', *ZNW* 58, 1967, 68–72.

111. J. Heise, *Bleiben. Menein in den johanneischen Schriften,* Tübingen 1967.

112. E. Käsemann, *The Testament of Jesus,* 25f.

113. A. Dauer, *Die Passionsgeschichte* (see n. 47), 231–94.

114. H. Bietenhard, s.v. *onoma, TDNT* 5, 258–61; A. S. van der Woude, s.v. *š-m,* in *ThHandWAT* 2, 935–63.

115. *Jesus. An Experiment in Christology,* 285–8 and especially 490–9 and 510.

116. The most acute analysis of this seems to me to be that by R. Schnackenburg, *Johannesevangelium* III, 299–309, but see also W. Meeks, *The Prophet-King,* 63–87.

117. Thus R. Schnackenburg, op. cit., III, 323–8. True, doubts still remain about this interpretation of the Johannine saying of Jesus on the cross, but in view of the tendencies of the Gospel of John it seems to me more meaningful (as an interpretation of John) than the later patristic and medieval interpretations and also more meaningful than Bultmann's interpretation, according to which

Mary is a type of the *Jewish* Christians, while the beloved disciple is a type of the *Gentile* Christians. That this underestimates the role of Mary, as Schnackenburg himself concedes (III, 325), seems to me to be more a reaction on the part of contemporary Mariology than a reflection of the Gospel of John and of the place of women in the society of late antiquity. In fact, the stress in the passage is much more that Jesus entrusts Mary to the beloved disciple, rather than that the beloved disciple is entrusted to Mary.

118. H. Leroy, *Rätsel und Missverständnis* , 51–7.

119. See R. Brown, *Gospel of John* II, 994; R. Schnackenburg, *Johannesevangelium* III, 377f.; W. Thüsing, *Die Erhöhung und Verherrlichung im Johannesevangelium*, Münster [2]1970, 263ff.

120. Luke, who pays particular attention in his gospel to the role of women, does not know of any appearance of Jesus to women, any more than does Mark. This can be found only in Matt. 28.9f. (with John). In other words, the idea that Jesus first appeared to women is a *relatively late* tradition, restricted to Matthew and John. It is highly probable that the appearance *of Jesus* to women developed from the tradition of the appearance of the angel, in other words, that it is not historical, but an example of a theological theme.

121. For John, this has nothing to do with a consecration for a particular *office*. The Fourth Gospel speaks of the disciples as a *community*.

122. Philo, *Moysis* II, 265. In connection with Moses it is said that the divine spirit 'leads him to the truth'.

123. J. Ysebaert, *Greek Baptismal Terminology*, Nijmegen 1962.

124. G. Johnston, *Spirit-Paraclete*, 119–46.

125. R. Brown, *Gospel of John* II, 1135–44.

126. G. Bornkamm, 'Der Paraklet im Johannesevangelium', *Festschrift für R. Bultmann*, Stuttgart 1949, 12–35.

127. I. de la Potterie, 'Le Paraclet', op. cit., esp. 90ff.

128. R. Schnackenburg, *Johannesevangelium* III, 156–73.

129. Bruce Vawter, 'Ezekiel and John', *CBQ* 26, 1964, 455ff.

130. J. Blank, *Krisis*, 329; S. Schulz, *Die Stunde der Botschaft. Einführung in die Theologie der vier Evangelien*, Hamburg 1967, 359.

131. O. Betz, *Der Paraklet*, 56–72, 113–166. This is also conceded by R. Brown, *Gospel of John* II, 1138. See n. 57 of the following section, p. 883 below.

132. QD (Damascus Document from Qumran) 5.17–19; War Scroll 13.10; 17.6f.

133. See *Jesus. An Experiment in Christology*, 256–69.

134. O. Betz, *What do we know about Jesus?*, ET London 1968, 87ff., 96ff.

135. See above, pp. 312ff., and *Jesus. An Experiment in Christology*, 287f. G. Nickelsburg, *Immortality*, op. cit., 62; K. Berger, *Die Auferstehung des Propheten und die Erhöhung des Menschensohn*, Göttingen 1976, 209–13.

136. U. B. Müller, *Messias und Menschensohn* (see p. 432), 52ff., 81ff., 111ff.

137. C. H. Talbert, 'The Myth of a Descending-Ascending Redeemer in Mediterranean Antiquity', *NTS* 22, 1976, 418–40; J. H. Charlesworth (ed.), *John and Qumran*, London 1972; J. R. Harris and A. Mingana, *The Odes and Psalms of Solomon*, Manchester 1920; also J. H. Charlesworth, *The Odes of Solomon*, Oxford 1973: Son of man as a messianic title (127f.).

138. P. Schäfer, 'Die Torah der messianischen Zeit', *ZNW* 65, 1974, 27–42. Furthermore, the idea of the pre-existence of Jesus is an earlier tradition than the

infancy narratives of Matthew and Luke: see M. Hengel, *The Son of God*, ET Philadelphia and London 1976, p. 72.

139. J. Riedl, *Das Heilswerk Jesu nach Johannes*, Freiburg 1973; J. A. T. Robinson, 'The Use of the Fourth Gospel for Christology Today', in *Christ and Spirit in the New Testament*, FS C. F. D. Moule, Cambridge 1973, 61–78; H. Schlier, 'Der Offenbarer und sein Werk nach dem Johannesevangelium', in *Besinnung auf das Neue Testament. Exegetische Aufsätze und Vorträge*, Freiburg 1964, Vol. 2, 254–60; K. Wennemer, 'Theologie des "Wortes" im Johannesevangelium', *Schol* 38, 1963, 1–17.

140. O. Böcher, *Die Johannesapocalypse*, 1–25. In a booklet rather resembling a card index the author collects together everything that exegetes have said about Revelation; this is followed rather rapidly and too dogmatically by an account of his 'own position'. However, the booklet is very useful.

141. *Jesus. An Experiment in Christology*, 120–3.

142. In the Achaemenid kingdom, 'king of kings' was the title for the neo-Babylonian ruler.

143. Josephus, *Antiquitates* 3.154, 159, 171.

144. H. Kraft, *Die Offenbarung*, 107–10.

145. S. Mowinckel, *He That Cometh*, ET Oxford 1956, 372; Strack-Billerbeck I, 85.

146. Suetonius, *Domitian*, 13: *Dominus et deus noster*.

147. O. Roller, 'Das Buch mit sieben Siegeln', *ZNW* 36, 1937, (98–113) 100–7.

148. H. Bietenhard, *Das Tausendjährige Reich*; P. Volz, *Eschatologie*, 71ff. and 273; H. Kraft, *Die Offenbarung*, 254–7; Strack-Billerbeck III, 824ff.

149. Strack-Billerbeck IV, 1100–5.

150. Strack-Billerbeck III, 852. In Qumran, too, the restoration of the Temple is the great eschatological event (CD IV, 17f.; 1QpHab XII, 11ff.).


*Part Two, Section Three: Synthesis: The experience of grace and its interpretative elements in the New Testament*

1. See *Jesus. An Experiment in Christology*, 140–271.

2. E. Schillebeeckx, 'Jesus und das menschliche Lebensscheitern', *Conc* 12, 1976, 189–95 (see also Part Four).

3. O. Betz, 'Von Gott gezeugt', in *Judentum—Urchristentum—Kirche*, FS J. Jeremias, BZAW 26, Berlin 1960, 3–23.

4. Jub. 1.24f.; I Enoch 62.11; Ass. Mos. 10.3; Ps. Sol. 17.30.

5. R. Brown, *Gospel of John* I, 13f.; see also *JBL* 72, 1953, 213–19; H. Leroy, *Rätsel und Missverständnis*, 124–36; R. Schnackenburg, *Johannesbriefe*, ²1963, 175–83.

6. *Corpus Hermeticum* 13, 1,3,7.

7. H. Haerens, *Sōtēr et Sōtēria*, Studia Hellenistica 5, Louvain 1948; W. Staerk, *Sōter: Die biblische Erlösererwartung als religionsgeschichtliches Problem* I, Gütersloh 1933.

8. F. Stolz, s.v. *y-š-ʿ* in *ThHandWAT 1*, 785–90; W. Foerster and G. Fohrer, s.v. *sōzō*, *TDNT* 7, 965–1024.

9. E. Rupprecht, s.v. *p-l-t*, in *ThHandWAT* 2, 420–7.

10. Ps. 17.13; 18.48; 22.5, 8; 31.1; 71.2,4; 40.17; 70.5; 107.20; 116.4. Also Joel

2.32; Isa. 4.2; 10.20; 66.19; Dan. 12.1.

11. E. Jenni, s.v. *y–ṣ–ʾ* in *ThHandWAT* 1, 755–61; J. Wijngaards, 'A twofold approach in the Exodus', *VT* 15, 1965, 91–102; P. Humbert, 'Dieu fait sortir', *TZ* 18, 1962, 357–61; id., 'Dieu fait sortir. Note complémentaire', ibid., 433–6; J. J. Stamm, *Erlösen und Vergeben im Alten Testament*, Bern 1940; U. Bergmann, s.v. *n–ṣ–l* in *ThHandWAT* 2, 96–9; J. Schneider, s.v. *erchomai*, *TDNT* 2, 678–80; F. Hauck and S. Schulz, s.v. *ekporeuomai*, *TDNT* 6, 578f.; W. Michaelis, s.v. *eisodos, exodos*, *TDNT* 5, 103–9.

12. From a very early stage: Ex. 13.3, 9, 14, 16; 18.1; 20.2; 32.11f.; Num. 20.16; 23.22; 24.8; Josh. 24.5f. Later, above all in Deut. 5.6, 15; 6.12, 21, 23; 7.8, 19; 8.14; 9.26, 28, 29; 13.5, 10; 16.1; 26.8; in the Deuteronomistic history work: Deut. 1.27; 4.20, 37; Judg. 2.12; 6.8; I Kings 8.16, 21, 51, 53; in the Priestly tradition: Ex. 6.6f.; 7.4f.; 12.17, 42, 51; 14.11; Num. 15.41; in the Holiness Code: Lev. 19.36; 22.33; 23.43; 25.38, 42, 55 etc.; in the prophets (only from Jeremiah on) Jer. 7.22; 11.4; 31.32; 32.21; 34.13; Ezek. 20.6, 9, 10, 14, 22; and finally also in later texts: Pss. 105.37, 43; 136.11; II Chron. 6.5; 7.22; Dan. 9.15.

13. Ex. 13.3, 14; 20.2; Deut. 5.6; 6.12; 7.8; 8.14; 13.5, 10; Judg. 6.8; Jer 34.13.

14. Ex. 18.4ff.; Pss. 18.7; 34.4; 56.13; Ex. 3.8; 6.6; Jer. 39.17; Gen. 32.11; however, this is not a peculiarly theological term.

15. J. J. Stamm, s.v. *p–d–h*, in *ThHandWAT* 2, 389–406; id., s.v. *gʾl*, ibid., 1, 383–94; F. Büchsel, s.v. *lytron* and *apolytrōsis*, *TDNT* 4, 340–49 and 351–6.

16. A general practice in the East to protect the possessions of the clan.

17. As happens with many of these concepts, the original meaning becomes weaker; it was 'restoration to the original state' by ransom. *gʾl* then becomes simply 'free' from political enemies (Micah 4.10; Jer. 31.11; Ps. 106.10) or from som need (Pss. 107.2; 103.4, etc.).

18. G. Gerleman, s.v. *š–l–m*, in *ThHandWAT* 2, 919–35; id., 'Die Würzel sch–l–m', *ZAW* 85, 1973, 1–14.

19. F. Maass, s.v. *k–p–r*, in *ThHandWAT* 1, 842–57; S. Lyonnet, 'De notione expiationis', *VD* 37, 1959, 336–52; 38, 1960, 66–75; H. Thyen, *Studien zur Sündenvergebung im NT und seinen alttestamentlichen und jüdischen Voraussetzungen*, Göttingen 1970; J. Herrmann and J. Büchsel, s.v. *hilaskesthai*, *TDNT* 3, 300–23; J. Schmid, 'Sünde und Sühne im Judentum', *BuL* 6, 1965, 16–26; J. J. Stamm, *Erlösen und Vergeben im Alten Testament*; J. Kühlewein, s.v. *q–r–b*, in *ThHandWAT* 2, 674–81; R. de Vaux, *Ancient Israel*, ET London 1964, 415–56 and 507–10. See also the literature on Hebrews above.

20. G. Gerlemann, s.v. *r–ṣ–h* in *ThHandWAT* 2, 810–13 and s.v. *ḥ–p–ṣ*, op. cit. 1, 623–6; G. Schrenk s.v. *eudokeō*, in *TDNT* 2, 738–51.

21. See above, pp. 263–7.

22. J. J. Stamm, s.v. *s–l–ḥ*, in *ThHandWAT* 2, 150–60; id., *Erlösung und Vergeb ung*, op. cit.

23. F. Stolz, s.v. *n–ś–ʾ*, in *ThHandWAT* 2, 109–17.

24. See above, literature on *ṣ'dāqā*, 113f., and the account of Pauline theology.

25. II (Syr.) Bar. 85.1f.; Ass. Mos. 11.17.

26. Loc. cit., also IV Ezra 7.112; I (Eth.) Enoch 47.2; 104.1; Test. Levi 3.5; 5.7.

27. Throughout the Qumran literature. Also III (Greek) Bar. 11–15; I (Eth.) Enoch 68.4; 9.3–11; 89.76; 30.30; 28.6.

28. Test. Jud. 20.1 and throughout the Qumran literature.

29. R. Smend, *Die Mitte des Alten Testaments*, ThSB 101, Zurich 1970.

30. This remarkable phenomenon was made the object of a study project of the American Academy of Arts and Sciences, see the thematic volume *Wisdom, Revelation and Doubt. Perspectives on the First Millennium BC*, in *Daedalus* 104, 2, 1975, 1–194.

31. For the pre-Christian origins and some Christian revisions of this extra-biblical Jewish literature see the works in Part Two, Section One, n. 28, p. 859 above.

32. *Jesus. An Experiment in Christology*, 184f., 192, 414, 475.

33. See e.g. C. Westermann, *Das Loben Gottes in den Psalmen*, Göttingen ²1968. See also the *b'rākā* structure of the Jewish Eighteen Benedictions, Strack-Billerbeck IV, 211–14; F. Hahn, *Der urchristliche Gottesdienst*, SBS 41, Stuttgart 1970.

34. G. von Rad, *Old Testament Theology* I, 138. Karl Barth puts forward the same view (probably independently of G. von Rad). The works cited by H. Brongers, the authors of *Mysterium Salutis* and many others are dependent on von Rad.

35. H. Brongers, *Scheppingstradities*, 116.

36. 'We are nowadays in serious danger of looking at the theological problems of the Old Testament far too much from the one-sided standpoint of an historically conditioned theology' (G. von Rad, 'Aspects of the Old Testament World-view', *Problems of the Hexateuch*, 144).

37. C. Westermann, *Schöpfung*, 14. W. H. Schmidt, *Die Schöpfungsgeschichte der Priesterschrift*, had already attempted to analyse the account of Gen. 1.1–2.4 in-dependently and not diachronously. A structural analysis of the Genesis text was given later by P. Beauchamp, *Création et Séparation*; this analysis shows how arbitrary a hermeneutic can be when it leaves out the phase of structural analysis. See also P. Ricoeur, *Le conflit des interprétations*, Paris 1969, and above all, 'Sur l'exégèse de Genèse 1.1–2.4a', in *Exégèse et herméneutique*, Paris 1971, 67–84.

38. H. Baumann, *Schöpfung und Urzeit*.

39. See *inter alia* W. Dupré, 'Technology and Myth', *Bijdr* 36, 1975, 189–206.

40. E. Cornelis, 'Mythe et Religie': *Annalen Thymgenootschap* 53, 1965, 55–74.

41. C. Westermann, *Schöpfung*, 102–5.

42. A. S. van der Woude, 'Genesis en Exodus', op.cit., 9.

43. It is striking that Hebrew does not have any noun for what we call the Creator and the world of creation. Hence the periphrasis, 'God who made heaven and earth'. But in Hellenistic Jewish literature we find mention of *ho ktistēs*, the Creator, alongside the semi-Semitic *ho ktisas*, the one who creates.

44. C. Westermann, *Das Loben*, 11ff. Also A. S. van der Woude, op.cit., 6.

45. Though one can ask how far the intensification of the concept of creation is not also dependent on the inner development of Yahwistic belief from a religion with 'henotheistic' colouring (Yahweh is the God of the clan, just as other people have their God) to strict monotheism: the God who created heaven and earth is Israel's Yahweh.

46. See the contributions by J. Haspecker, 'Natur und Heilserfahrung', *BuL* 7, 1966.

47. With this conception of the Old Testament it is impossible to provide biblical substantiation for the basic thesis of R. Schaeffler, *Religion und kritisches Bewusstsein*, Munich 1973. Despite earlier tendencies, the God of the Bible is in the last resort the basis of pure positiveness and not the last and fundamental

basis of both 'life' and the 'annihilation of life'.

48. G. Schneider, 'Urchristliche Gottesverkündigung in hellenistischer Umwelt', *BZ* 13, 1969, 59–75; P. Stuhlmacher, *Das paulinische Evangelium* I, Göttingen 1968, 260.

49. J. Jervell, *Imago Dei*, FRLANT 76, 1960, 15–50, 52–69, 71–121.

50. Strack-Billerbeck IV, 211–14; S. Lyonnet, 'L'hymne christologique de l'épître aux Colossiens et la fête juive du nouvel-an', *RSR* 48, 1960, 93–100.

51. Heraclitus, Frag. B 80, ed. H. Diels, *Die Fragmente der Vorsokratiker*, Berlin [11]1964, I, 169 lines 4f. (ET by K. Freeman, *Ancilla to the Pre-Socratic Philosophers*, Oxford 1948, p. 30).

52. Empedocles, Frag. B. 26.4: Diels, op. cit., I, 323, 2; 23.6–10: I, 321, 15ff.; 35.7, 16: I, 327, 4 and 328, 2; 126: I, 362, 9; 128, 9f.: I, 363, 9f.; 140–141: I, 368, 15, 28 (ET, op. cit., pp. 55–68).

53. W. Nauck, 'Freude im Leiden. Zum Problem einer urchristlichen Verfolgungstradition', *ZNW* 46, 1955, 68–80.

54. Because of this I believe that A. Vögtle overlooks a fundamental trend in the Old and New Testaments in his book *Das Neue Testament und die Zukunft des Kosmos*, Düsseldorf 1972, and wrongly sees *salvation* too much in purely anthropocentric terms, independently of the destiny of the material world; however, he is right in noting that the Bible speaks of this coming cosmos only in images and metaphors (it could not do so in any other way).

55. I *Clement* 40.4f. In this first Christian use of *laikos* (layman), layman is not a term denoting formal membership of the people of God (in contrast to the Gentiles), though this is often claimed; it indicates being a member of the people of God in contrast to its priestly leaders (deacons and priests). This is a distinction which we find in two passages in the Greek Bible: Isa. 24.2 and Hos. 4.9, 'priest and people' (*laos*). Thus in his terminology Clement is following an already existing Jewish usage.

56. See *Jesus. An Experiment in Christology*, 441–4.

57. Literature on the Paraclete-Spirit in connection with Johannine theology: H. Schlier, 'Der Heilige Geist als Interpret nach dem Johannesevangelium', *IKZ* 2, 1973, 97–103; R. Brown, *The Gospel according to John*, London 1972, 2, 1135–43 (see also in *NTS* 13, 1966–67, 113f.); J. Schreiner, 'Geistbegabung in der Gemeinde von Qumran', *BZ* 9, 1965, 161–80; G. Johnston, *The Spirit-Paraclete in the Gospel of John*, Cambridge 1970; F. Porsch, *Pneuma und Wort*, Frankfurt 1974; F. Mussner, 'Die johanneischen Parakletensprüche und die apostolische Tradition', *BZ* 5, 1961, 56–70; A. R. C. Leaney, 'The Johannine Paraclete and the Qumran Scrolls', in *John and Qumran*, ed. J. Charlesworth, London 1972, 38–61; O. Betz, *Der Paraklet: Fürsprecher im häretischen Spätjudentum, im Johannesevangelium und in neu gefundenen gnostischen Schriften*, Leiden 1963; P. Schäfer, *Die Vorstellung vom Heiligen Geist in der Rabbinischen Literatur*, STANT 28, Munich 1972; N. Johansson, *Paraklètoi. Vorstellungen von Fürsprechern für die Menschen vor Gott in der alttestamentlichen Religion, im Spätjudentum und Urchristentum*, Lund 1940; G. Bornkamm, 'Der Paraklet im Johannesevangelium', *Festschrift R. Bultmann*, Stuttgart 1949, 12–35; G. Locher, 'Der Geist als Paraklet', *EvTh* 26, 1966, 578ff.; J. Blank, *Krisis. Untersuchungen zur johanneischen Christologie und Eschatologie*, Freiburg 1964, ch. 9; 'Die Vergegenwärtigung des Gerichts durch den Geist-Parakleten', 316–40; J. Veenhof, *De Parakleet*, Kampen 1975.

58. R. Albertz and C. Westermann, s.v. *rūaḥ*, in *ThHandWAT* 2, 726–53; F.

Nötscher, 'Geist und Geister in den Texten von Qumran', *Mélanges bibliques . . . A. Robert*, Paris 1957, 305–15; P. Schäfer, *Die Vorstellung vom heiligen Geist in der rabbinischen Literatur*, Munich 1972; E. Sjöberg and E. Schweizer s.v. *pneuma*, in *TDNT* 6, 375–451.

59. In the Tanach, *rūaḥ*, wind and the breath of life, is seen as a 'wind of God' (*rūaḥ ʾᵉlōhīm*, Gen. 1.2; *rūaḥ Yahweh*, Isa. 59.19) in the context of Israel's belief in the Creator God. This was envisaged as a storm wind (just as the Romans said *Jupiter tonat*; storm and wind come from God; Isa. 40.7; Hos. 13.15). Thus *rūaḥ* can be used in a transferred sense for a variety of forms of something that is in movement of creates movement. The wind tosses straw around (Ps. 1.4); it can pick something up and carry it off (Ex. 10.13,19; Isa. 57.13); it uproots trees (Isa. 7.2), stirs up the sea (Ps. 107.25), breaks up ships in its midst (Ezek. 27.26) and splits up rocks and mountains (I Kings 19.11). Above all, the *rūaḥ qādīm* (Ex. 10.13; 14.21; Jer. 18.17) or the east wind, blowing from the desert (the Palestinian sirocco in the spring), could wither the spring blossom with a blast and cause widespread devastation (Ps. 48.7; Job 1.19). Thus the *rūaḥ* of Yahweh can be an image for divine judgment (Isa. 57.13; Jer. 4.11f.; 49.36; Ezek. 13.11,13; 17.10; Hos. 4.19; 13.15; Pss. 35.5; 48.7). The wind often accompanies actions on the part of Yahweh (Ezek. 1.4; Dan. 7.2). However, a second meaning of *rūaḥ* is breath of life, again under the aspect of the power which is expressed in a puff of breath (not the normal breath of man or beast), in other words, breath as an expression of vitality (panting or gasping for breath; then *rūaḥ* is used) (I Kings 10.5; II Chron. 9.4; Jer. 2.24; 14.6). Thus *rūaḥ* also means the vital force of life (Gen. 45.27; Judg. 15.19; I Sam. 30.12), with the subsidiary meaning of psychological tension which lives for something. Therefore *rūaḥ* can be used in situations in which withered life is renewed and life-force returns, and so in the priestly tradition the original distinction between *nepeš* (Gen. 2.7,19) and *rūaḥ* disappears: *nepeš ḥayyā* (a living being) becomes a synonym for *rūaḥ ḥayyīm* (flesh in which there is the breath of life: Gen. 6.17; 7.15). God gives *rūaḥ* to all flesh (Num. 16.22; 27.16). The fact that human *rūaḥ* comes from God means that man is completely dependent on God (Job 10.12). Apart from various human psychological conditions which are indicated by *rūaḥ* – even pathological cases (someone with an evil *rūaḥ*) – and apart from *rūaḥ* as ultimately identified with the human spirit or the centre of man (heart and *rūaḥ*, Ezek. 11.19; 18.31) or his inwardness (Mal. 2.15f.; Ps. 32.2, etc.) (not as a part of man; this dualism is unknown; but as the total existence of man, Gen. 41.8; Dan. 2.1,3), *rūaḥ* is used with a special meaning for extraordinary human capabilities which are derived from the divine *rūaḥ* – especially 'the prophetic spirit' (Hos. 9.7; or the gift of the interpretation of dreams, Gen. 41.38; Dan. 4.5f.,18).

60. Albertz and Westermann, *ThHandWAT* 2, 746. The proof texts which systematic theologians usually give for divine revelation through the mediation of the spirit of God (Hos. 9.7; Micah 3.8; Isa. 30.1; 31.3) by no means follow the line of prophecy and the word of God; they stand more in the tradition of men of God and Yahweh's wars.

61. In Num. 11.14–17, 24b–30, the spirit is already static. Later groups of prophets want to derive their possession of the *rūaḥ* from the spirit which Moses possessed 'by virtue of his office'. In that case the spirit of God 'rests' on someone (Num. 11.25f.); 'ecstasy' is then a religious state. Yet other groups present the *rūaḥ* in its dynamic and explosive character (Num. 11.26–28); a still later prophet-

ic group wants to extend the *rūaḥ* so that it becomes a possession of the whole people of God (Num. 11.29).

*Part Two, Section Four: The New Testament theology of grace and the life of Christians in the world*

1. Some examples: F. Belo, *Lecture máterialiste de l'évangile de Marc*, Paris 1974; M. Clévenot, *Approches matérialistes de la Bible*, Paris 1975; S. Rostagno, *Essays on the New Testament. A 'Materialistic' Approach*, ET Geneva [1976]; J. P. Miranda, *Marx and the Bible*, ET Maryknoll 1974 and London 1977; G. Givardet, *L'Evangelo di Luca. Una lettura politica*, Turin 1976.

2. See S. Schulz, *Q. Die Spruchquelle der Evangelisten*, Zurich 1972, 152–7.

2a. Strack-Billerbeck I, 435ff.

3. See D. Lührmann, 'Der Verweis aud die Erfahrung und die Frage nach der Gerechtigkeit', in *Jesus Christus in Historie und Theologie*, ed. G. Strecker, Tübingen 1975, 185–96, esp. 193.

4. See *Jesus. An Experiment in Christology*, 154–72.

5. Strack-Billerbeck I, 374–7.

6. D. Lührmann, 'Der Verweis auf die Erfahrung', op. cit., 195f. See also W. Harnisch, 'Die Sprachkraft der Analogie. Zur These vom "argumentativen Charakter" der Gleichnisse Jesu', *StTh* 28, 1974, 1–20.

7. E. Linnemann, 'Zeitansage und Zeitvorstellung in der Verkündigung Jesu', in *Jesus Christus in Historie und Theologie*, ed. G. Strecker, Tübingen 1975, 223–36.

8. See P. Stockmeier, *Glaube und Religion in der frühen Kirche*, Freiburg 1972, 44–54; N. Brox, 'Zum Vorwurf des Atheismus gegen die alte Kirche', *TrThZ* 74, 1966, 274–82.

9. *Didache* 10.6 (the eucharistic prayers).

10. C. Westermann, *Das Loben Gottes in den Psalmen*, Göttingen [2]1968, 110–15.

11. See above, pp. 137f., and the works by J. Jocz and H. Donner cited in n. 22 (p. 861).

12. For the Qumran Psalter, see P. W. Skehan, 'A liturgical complex in 11 QPs[a]', *CBQ* 35, 1973, 195–205; A. S. van der Woude, *De Dankpsalmen*, Amsterdam 1957.

13. G. von Rad, *Wisdom in Israel*, ET London and Nashville 1972, 307.

14. F. Christ, *Jesus Sophia*, Zurich 1970.

15. Great importance was also attached to this personal encounter with God in apocalyptic. See W. Schmithals, *Apokalyptik*; A. Strobel, *Kerygma und Apokalyptik*.

16. So R. Bultmann, in *Exegetica. Aufsätze zur Erforschung des Neuen Testaments*, ed. E. Dinkler, Tübingen 1967, 445–69.

17. Thus the advocates of a political theology. See J.-B. Metz and J. Moltmann, also H. W. Bartsch, *Jesus. Prophet und Messias aus Galiläa*, Frankfurt 1970 (see Part Four below).

18. E. Grässer, 'Der politisch gekreuzigte Christus', op. cit., 322.

19. H. Kuitert, *Om en om*, 140.

20. S. G. F. Brandon, *Jesus and the Zealots*, with some corrections made in *NTS* 17, 1970, 453.

21. Tacitus, *Annales* 15.44.

22. P. de Labriolle has drawn attention to the difficulties which the first non-Pauline Jewish Christians had in Rome: *La réaction païenne. Étude sur la polémique anti-chrétienne du premier au sixième siècle*, Paris ²1942, 42f.; W. Nestle, 'Die Haupteinwände des antiken Denkens gegen das Christentum', *ARW* 37, 1941, 51–100; see (in addition to Acts 18.2) also Suetonius, *Claudius* 25.4.

23. See A. Strobel, 'Zum Verständis von Rom. 13', *ZNW* 47, 1956, 67–93; J. Blank, *Schriftauslegung*, 174–86.

24. C. Westermann, *Isaiah 40–66*, ET, OTL, London and Philadelphia 1969, ad loc.

25. Plato, *Gorgias*, 491.

26. P. von der Osten-Sacken, *Gott und Belial*, Göttingen 1969.

27. Tacitus, *Historiae* II, 8.

28. Suetonius, *Nero* 57.

29. Suetonius, *Nero* 47.

30. Suetonius, *Nero* 40.

31. Sibylline Oracles 5.

32. Sib. Or. 5.222f.

33. Sib. Or. 5.1–51.

34. Sib. Or. 5.28–35; 5.214–27.

35. Ascension of Isaiah 4.2–4.

36. Josephus, *De Bello Judaico* 7.218.

37. *BJ* 7.116–62.

38. *BJ* 7.162; 6.316.

39. G. Petzke, 'Der historische Jesus in der sozialethischen Diskussion', op. cit., 223–36.

40. Ibid., 233f.

41. P. J. Farla, *Het oordeel over Israel*.

42. F. Normann, *Christus Didaskolos. Die Vorstellung von Christus als Lehrer in der christlichen Literatur des ersten und zweiten Jahrhunderts*, MBT 32, Münster 1967, 1–54; see also F. Hahn, *Christologische Hoheitstitel*, 76ff.

43. Petzke, 'Der historische Jesus', op. cit., 234f.

44. Justin, *Apology* I, 17.

45. Above all Epictetus, *Diss.* II, 14.8; Seneca, *Epist.* 94.1; Stobaeus, *Anthologia* I, 3.53.

46. E. Schillebeeckx, *Het huwelijk* I, Bildhoven 1963, 135–54.

47. J. Blank, *Schriftauslegung*, 141–3.

48. R. Pesch, *Freie Treue. Die Christen und die Ehescheidung*, Freiburg 1971; E. Schillebeeckx, '(On)ontbindbaarheid van het huwelijk?', *Annalen van het Thymgenootschap* 58, Hilversum 1970, 184–214.

49. It would be inappropriate to make a special investigation of Thomas Aquinas' concept of *epikeia [epieikeia]* here. Thomas analyses the Christian demand according to which a positive, indeed canonical law will be transcended as legalism, not through laxity but because of the gospel: i.e., the gospel sometimes requires us to transcend the law from above (maximally) and from below (minimally) in order to express the spirit of the law. This Christian insight can also be communicated universally.

50. See e.g. G. Ebeling, 'Die Evidenz des Ethischen und die Theologie'; id., 'Die Krise des Ethischen und die Theologie', in *Wort und Glaube*, Vol. 2, Tubingen 1969, 1–41, 42–55.

51. See above, p. 135.

52. K. Koch, 'Tempeleinlassliturgien und Dekaloge', in *Studien zur Theologie der alttestamentlichen Überlieferungen*, Neukirchen 1961, 45–60.

53. P. Berger, *A Rumour of Angels*, London and New York 1969, 87.

54. G. L. Langmuir, 'The Jews and the Archives of Angevin England: Reflections on Medieval Anti-Semitism', *Traditio* 19, 1963, 183–244; also F. Blanchetière, 'Aux sources de l'antijudaïsme chrétien', *RHPR* 53, 1973, 353–98.

55. A. Schwarz-Bart, *Der Letzte der Gerechten*, Frankfurt 1960.

56. J. le Goff, *La civilisation de l'occident médiévale*, Paris 1964, 390.

57. *Jesus. An Experiment in Christology*, 370f.

58. Ibid., 273ff.

59. O. Michel, *Fragen zu I Thess. 2.14–16. Antijudaismus im Neuen Testament?*, Munich 1967, 50–9.

60. E.g. Josephus, *Contra Apionem* 1.11.

61. Strack-Billerbeck I, 360–2; III, 585.

62. Tacitus, *Annales* 15.44.

63. Suetonius, *Nero* 16.2; Pliny, *Epist.* 10.96.8.

64. See G. G. Scholem, *Major Trends in Jewish Mysticism*, Jerusalem 1941; id., *Recent Trends in Jewish Gnosticism*, New York 1961.

65. In Philo's works, Melchizedek is the Logos, who appears as the high priest (*De Somm.* 1.214f.; *Abr.* 235).

66. See n.6, p. 885 above.

67. Philo, *De gigantibus* 54 (see Meeks, *The Prophet-King*, 100–31).

68. J. L. Martyn, *History and Theology in the Fourth Gospel*, XVII, and above all Part I, 'A synagogue-church drama', 3–44; J. Beutler, *Martyria*, Frankfurt 1972, 339–64.

69. J. L. Martyn, *History and Theology*, XIX–XXI and 148–50; K. L. Carroll, 'The Fourth Gospel and the Exclusion of Christians from the Synagogue', *BJRL* 40, 1957, 19–32; W. A. Meeks, *The Prophet-King*, 318f.; id., 'The Man from Heaven in Johannine Sectarianism', *JBL* 91, 1972, 44–72; E. Grässer, 'Die antijüdische Polemik', op. cit.; also R. Brown, *Gospel of John*, and R. Schnackenburg, *Johannesevangelium*, in their commentaries.

70. R. Brown; R. Schnackenburg; J. Beutler; W. Meeks; K. L. Carroll; E. Grässer; R. Kysar; etc.

71. W. Meeks, 'The Man from Heaven', 44–72.

72. See above all J. Beutler, *Martyria*, 339–64.

73. W. Doskocil, *Der Bann in der Urkirche*, Munich 1958, 40–43.

74. W. Meeks, *The Prophet-King*, 195ff. and 216–57.

75. H. Leroy, *Rätsel und Missverständnis*, Bonn 1968.

76. E. Grässer, 'Die antijüdische Polemik', op. cit., 74–90.

77. A. Lacomara, 'Deuteronomy and the Farewell Discourse (Jn. 13, 31–16, 33)', *CBQ* 36, 1974, 65–84.

78. See H. Kraft, *Die Offenbarung des Johannes*, HNT 16a, Tübingen 1974, 61f., 72–4, 81f.

*Part Four: God's Glory and Man's Truth, Well-being and Happiness*

1. *Summa Theologiae* I, q.94 a.l.

2. G. Ebeling, 'Die Evidenz des Ethischen und die Theologie', *Wort und Glaube* 2, Tübingen 1969, 1–41; 'Die Krise des Ethischen und die Glaube', ibid., 42–55.

3. A doctoral student from Louvain (P. Pulinx), interested to know who introduced the word 'orthopraxis' into modern theology, told me that he found the word in an encyclopaedia dated as early as 1917: 'Strictly speaking, *orthodoxy* in religion is concerned only with doctrine or belief, with the intellectual element in spiritual life. . . . But since religion embraces feeling and activity as well as thought, orthodoxy becomes an inadequate criterion of its worth apart from right experience and right conduct. It ought to have for its correlatives such words as *"orthopathy"* and *"orthopraxy"*, the inward experience and the outward exercise of piety' (W.A. Curtis, s.v. 'Orthodoxy', in *Encyclopaedia of Religion and Ethics*, Edinburgh 1917, Vol. 9, 570).

4. K.-O. Apel, 'Zum Problem einer rationalen Begründung der Ethik im Zeitalter der Wissenschaft', in M. Riedel, *Rehabilitierung der praktischen Philosophie*, Freiburg 1974, Vol. 2, 13–32.

5. L. Kolakowski, 'Der Anspruch auf die selbstverschuldete Unmündigkeit', in L. Reinisch, ed., *Vom Sinn der Tradition*, Munich 1970, 3; J. Habermas, *Philosophisch-politische Profile*, Frankfurt 1971, 35.

6. See G. Picht, *Mut zur Utopie. Die grossen Zukunftsausgaben*, Munich 1970; K. Scholder, *Grenzen der Zukunft. Aporien von Planung und Prognose*, Stuttgart 1973; D. Meadows (ed.), *Limits of Growth*, Report for the Club of Rome, London and New York 1972; H. von Nussbaum (ed.), *Die Zukunft des Wachstums. Kritische Antworten zum Bericht des Club of Rome*, Düsseldorf 1973; A. K. Müller, *Die präparierte Zeit. Der Mensch in der Krise seiner eigenen Zielsetzungen*, Stuttgart 1972; K. Steinbuch, *Mensch, Technik, Zukunft*, Stuttgart 1971; R. L. Heilbroner, *An Inquiry into the Human Prospect*, New York 1974.

7. B. C. van Houten, *Tussen aanpassing en kritiek*, Deventer 1970, 265–84.

8. K.-O. Apel, 'Zum Problem einer rationalen Begründung', op. cit., 22; H. Seiffert, *Marxismus und bürgerliche Wissenschaft*, Munich 1971; D. Böhler, *Metakritik der Marxschen Ideologiekritik*, Frankfurt 1971.

9. Apel, op. cit., 22, 32.

10. J. Habermas speaks of a new class distinction: the technocrats (social engineering) and ourselves, their 'subjects' (*Theory and Practice*, ET London 1974, 282). A further question is how far a consensus achieved through parliamentary democracy by means of a vote can be the foundation of an *ethical* obligation. See also W. Strzelewicz, 'Technokratische und emanzipatorische Erwachsenbildung', in W. Strzelewicz, H. D. Raapke and W. Schulenberg, *Bildung und gesellschaftliches Bewusstsein*, Stuttgart 1966, 134ff.

11. K. R. Popper, *The Open Society and its Enemies*, London 1945; H. Albert, *Traktat über kritische Vernunft*, Tübingen 1968; id., *Plädoyer für kritischen Rationalismus*, Munich 1971. See H. Schelsky, *Auf der Suche nach der verlorenen Wirklichkeit*, Düsseldorf 1965.

12. Apel, op. cit., 25–8.

13. Kant, *Religion within the Limits of Reason Alone*, ET New York 1960, 15.

14. N. Smart, *The Religious Experience of Mankind*, New York and London [2]1976 (literature, 701–5); W. Dupré, *Religion in Primitive Cultures. A Study in Ethnophilo-*

*sophy*, The Hague-Paris 1975 (literature, 339–49). See very generally, *Antwoord. Gestalten van geloof in de wereld van nu*, chief editor J. Sperna Weiland, Amsterdam 1975. With an emphasis on suffering: J. Bowker, *Problems of Suffering in Religions of the World*, Cambridge 1970; also N. Pike, *God and Evil*, Englewood Cliffs 1964; L. Dupré, *The Other Dimension*, New York 1972; C. Hartshorne, *A Natural Theology for our Time*, La Salle, Illinois 1967; J. Nabert, *Essai sur le mal*, Paris 1956.

15. H. Marcuse, *Triebstrukturen und Gesellschaft*, Frankfurt 1955.

16. I. Gershevitch, 'Zoroaster's Own Contribution, *JNES* 23, 1964, 12–38; *Handbuch der Orientalistik. Iranistik-Band*, ed. B. Spuler, Leiden 1968; L. J. Ort, *Mani. A Religio-historical Description of his Personality*, Leiden 1967; H. Rousseau, *Le Dieu du mal*, Paris 1963; S. Pétrement, *Le dualisme dans l'histoire de la philosophie et des religions*, Paris 1946; H. C. Puech, *La Manichéisme*, Paris 1949; R. C. Zaehner, *The Teaching of the Magi, a Compendium of Zoroastrian Beliefs*, London 1956; M. Loos, *Dualist Heresy in the Middle Ages*, The Hague 1974.

17. J. Bowker, *Problems of Suffering*, 32.

18. Maimonides, *Guide for the Perplexed* III 12, ET by M. Friedlander, London and New York 1904, reissued 1928, 268.

19. J. Bowker, *The Targums and Rabbinic Literature*, Cambridge 1969.

20. M. Nilsson, *Geschichte der griechischen Religionen*, three vols., Munich 1955–61; A. E. Taylor, *Plato: the Man and his Work*, London ³1929, reissued New York 1956; G. Murray, *Five Stages of Greek Religion*, Oxford 1925, reissued New York 1955.

21. K. M. Sen, *Hinduism*, London 1963; J. Gonda, *Die Religionen Indiens*, Die Religionen der Menschheit 11–13, three vols., Stuttgart 1960; S. Radhakrishnan, *The Bhagavadgita*, New York 1948; J. Mascaro, *The Upanishads, Translations from the Sanskrit with an Introduction*, Harmondsworth ²1967; A. Macdonnell, *Hymns from the Rig Veda*, Oxford 1923; C. A. Moore and S. Radhakrishnan, *A Source Book in Indian Philosophy*, Princeton and Calcutta 1957; C. Sharma, *A Critical Survey of Indian Philosophy*, London 1960; R. C. Zaehner, *Hinduism*, Oxford 1969.

22. Sri Aurobindo, *The Life Divine*, quoted in *A Source Book of Indian Philosophy*, ed. C. A. Moore and S. Radhakrishnan, 586ff.

23. C. Humphreys, *Buddhism*, Harmondsworth ³1962; H. Beckh, *Boeddha en zijn leer*, Zeist-Antwerp 1961; W. Rahula, *What the Buddha Taught*, Bedford 1967; B. Sangharakshita, *A Survey of Buddhism*, Bangalore 1966; D. T. Suzuki, *On Indian Mahayana Buddhism*, New York 1968; A. K. Coomaraswamy, *Buddha and the Gospel of Buddhism*, New York 1964.

24. Tertullian, *Apology* 50.

25. I *Clem.* 5.1ff.; 7.1; Shepherd of Hermas, *Vis.* 2.2.7; Ignatius, *Mart. Polyc.* 1.2; Tertullian, *Mart.* 3; Augustine, *City of God* 14.9.

26. *Acts of Paul and Thecla* 34 (see O. von Gebhardt, *Die lateinischen Übersetzungen der Acta Pauli et Theclae*, TU 22.2, Berlin 1902); Eusebius, *Hist. eccl. VI*, 4.3.

27. Barnabas 6.5; Ignatius, *Eph.* 8.1; 18.1; and esp. Eusebius, *Hist. eccl.* II, 23.

28. Irenaeus, *Adv. Haer.* IV, 38; see John Hick, *Evil and the God of Love*, London 1966, 220f.

29. Augustine gives a good summary, above all in *De Civitate Dei* and even more briefly in *Enchiridion* III, IV, VIII and X.

30. *Confessions* IV, 4.

31. *Confessions* IV, 10.

32. *Confessions* IV, 12.

33. See 'Über Christen, die leiden', *Conc* 12, 1976, no. 11.

34. See I. Kant, 'Mängel des Optimismus', in *Gesammelte Schriften* (Akademie Ausgabe), Vol. 17, Berlin 1926, 236f.

35. 'Mängel des Optimismus', op. cit., Vol. 17, 237.

36. See one example of his in M. Lagree, 'Die Sprache der Ordnung. Das Leiden im Denken und Reden eines französischen Bischofs im 19. Jahrhundert', *Conc* 12, 1976, 554–8.

37. Koran XXXV, 1f. See *inter alia* D. S. Attema, *De Koran. Zijn ontstaan en zijn inhoud*, Kampen 1962; M. Seale, *Muslim Theology*, London 1964; A. Tritton, *Muslim Theology*, London 1947; J. A. Williams, *Islam*, New York 1961.

38. A. Pope, *An Essay on Man* (1733), in *Epistles* I, 5, 292, 294.

39. G. W. von Leibnitz, *Theodicy: Essays on the Goodness of God, the Freedom of Man and the Origin of Evil*, ET ed. A. M. Farrer, London 1951.

40. Leibnitz, op. cit., II, §188, 245f.

41. Voltaire, *Poème sur le désastre de Lisbonne* (1756). See H. Weinrich, 'Das Erdbeben von Lissabon', in *Literatur für Leser*, Stuttgart 1971, 64–76; D. Hildebrandt, *Voltaire: Candide. Dichtung und Wirklichkeit*, Frankfurt 1963; X., *Réflexions sur le désastre de Lisbonne*, Paris 1756; id., *Supplément aux réflexions sur le désastre de Lisbonne*, Paris 1757; W. Lütgert, *Die Erschütterung des Optimismus durch das Erdbeben von Lissabon*, Gütersloh ²1924; see I. Kant on the earthquake in *Gesammelte Schriften* (Akademie Ausgabe), Vol. 1, Berlin 1910, 417–61.

42. I. Kant, 'Über das Misslingen aller philosophischen Versuche in der Theodicee', *Gesammelte Schriften*, Vol. 8, Berlin 1923, 253–73.

43. K. Marx, 'Luther as a Bridge between Strauss and Feuerbach', ET in *Early Texts*, ed. D. McLellan, Oxford 1971, 25.

44. *Capital*, ET by S. Moore and E. Aveling, reissued Moscow 1954, I, 20. Also F. Engels, *Anti-Dühring*, ET London 1935, 25f. In contrast Lenin made this scientific theory (to be tested) into a dogma in the anti-religious, metaphysical sense.

45. D. Böhler, *Metakritik der Marxschen Ideologiekritik*, Frankfurt 1971; H. Seiffert, *Marxismus und bürgerliche Wissenschaft*, Munich 1971; K. Popper, *The Poverty of Historicism*, London 1957; K.-O. Apel, 'Zum Problem einer rationalen Begründung der Ethik', (see n. 4), 21f.

46. 'It may therefore be imagined that all commodities can simultaneously have this character impressed upon them, just as it can be imagined that all Catholics can be popes together. It is, of course, highly desirable in the eyes of the petit bourgeois, for whom the production of commodities is the ne plus ultra of human freedom and individual independence, that the inconveniences resulting from this character of commodities not being directly exchangeable, should be removed. Proudhon's socialism is a working out of this Philistine Utopia' (Marx, *Capital*, I, 68 n. 1). In other words, according to Marx, the direct exchange of goods or the use of money as a general equivalent is the characteristic of a social order of simple producers of goods, all of whom are their own masters. But that is no longer the case in our society.

47. Marx, *Capital*, I, 218 (cf. *Selected Texts*, ed. D. McLellan, Oxford 1977, 474). See also J. Bowker, *Problems of Suffering*, 144f.

48. L. Feuerbach, *The Essence of Christianity*, ET reprinted New York 1957, 65.

49. Marx, *Selected Texts*, 157.

50. Marx, 'Towards a Critique of Hegel's *Philosophy of Right*, Introduction', ET

in *Selected Texts*, 63.

51. D. Böhler, *Metakritik*, 50f., 137ff.

52. Marx, ET in *Early Texts*, 82.

53. H. Fleischer, *Marx und Engels*, Freiburg-Munich 1970, 94ff.

54. Marx, 'On the Jewish Question', ET in *Selected Texts*, 43f.

55. Ibid.

56. *Capital*, I, 79.

57. Engels, *Anti-Dühring*, ET London 1935, 346ff.

58. Ibid., 347.

59. *Capital*, III, 819f. See also K. Marx, *Frühschriften*, ed. S. Landshut, Stuttgart 1964, 246, 252 and 408. See H. Fleischer, *Marx und Engels*, 122; A. Schmidt, *Der Begriff der Natur in der Lehre von K. Marx*, Frankfurt 1962, 121f.; W. Post, *Kritik der Religion bei K. Marx*, Munich 1970, 241–53; W. Pannenberg, 'Erfordet die Einheit der Geschichte ein Subjekt?', in R. Koselleck and W.-D. Stempel (eds.), *Geschichte, Ereignis und Erzählung*, Poetik und Hermeneutik 5, Munich 1973, (478–90) 479–81.

60. *Epicurus*, ed. H. Usener, Leipzig 1887, 253 (cited from Lactantius, *De ira dei* 13.19–21).

61. I. Kant, 'Mängel des Optimismus', in *Gesammelte Schriften*, Vol. 17, 238f.

62. See H. Weinrich, *Das Erdbeben*, 74–6.

63. The word comes from K. Popper, *Conjectures and Refutations*, London 1963, 37, and from H. Albert, *Traktat über kritische Vernunft*, Tübingen 1968, 129.

64. O. Marquard, 'Beitrag zur Philosophie der Geschichte des Abschieds von der Philosophie der Geschichte', in *Geschichte, Ereignis und Erzählung*, Munich 1973 (241–50), 245.

65. The formulation comes from J.-B. Metz, in J.-B. Metz and J. Moltmann, *Leidensgeschichte. Zwei Meditationen zu Markus 8, 31–38*, Freiburg ²1975, 57.

66. See J.-B. Metz, 'La théologie à "l'âge critique" ', in *Le service théologique dans l'Église, Mélanges offerts à Y. Congar*, Paris 1974, 131–48, 145.

67. This is the main argument of R. Schaeffler, *Religion und kritisches Bewusstsein*, Freiburg-Munich 1973, which to my mind is incomprehensible. Of course it is a definition of God in certain religions, but it is certainly not the Christian concept of God.

68. J. Moltmann, *The Crucified God*, ET London and New York 1974; it must, however, be conceded that here Moltmann argues in a very Lutheran way. See also T. van Bavel, 'De lijdende God', *TvTh* 14, 1974, 131–50.

69. '*Defectus gratiae, prima causa est ex nobis*' (*Summa Theologiae* I–II, q.112, a.3, ad 2).

70. '*Quamvis Deus sit causa voluntatis faciens eam ex nihilo, hoc tamen quod est ex nihilo esse non habeat ab alio, sed a se; et ideo defectus qui sequitur eam secundum quod est ex nihilo, non oportet quod in ulteriorem causam reducatur*' (in *II Sent*. d. 37, q. 2, a. 1, ad 2).

71. See E. Bloch, *Philosophische Aufsätze zur objektiven Phantasie*, Frankfurt 1969, 18.

72. W. Schneiders, *Die wahre Aufklärung*, Freiburg-Munich 1974, 189–214; W. Oelmüller, *Was ist heute Aufklärung?*, Dusseldorf 1972; R. Schaeffler, *Religion und kritisches Bewusstsein*, Freiburg-Munich 1973, 31–7.

73. This is the tendency of T. Roszak, *The Making of a Counter Culture*, New York and London 1969.

74. See *inter alia* K. Tuchel, *Herausforderung der Technik*, Bremen 1967; C. P. Snow, *The Two Cultures and the Scientific Revolution*, London 1959; F. Dessauer, *Seele im Bannkreis der Technik*, Olten-Freiburg [2]1952; id., *Streit um die Technik*, Frankfurt [2]1958; C. von Weizsäcker, *Die Einheit der Natur*, Göttingen 1971; G. Picht, *Wahrheit, Vernunft, Verantwortung*, Stuttgart 1969; W. Heisenberg, *Physics and Beyond*, ET London 1971. For the corporeality of man in nature see M. Merleau-Ponty, *Structure de comportement*, Paris 1949; id., *Phenomenology of Perception*, ET London and New York 1962; A. de Waelhens, *La philosophie et les expériences naturelles*. The Hague 1961; *De aarde is er ook nog*, ed. Hans Bouma, Wageningen 1974; A. Gehlen, *Der Mensch, seine Natur und seine Stellung in der Welt*, Frankfurt-Bonn [2]1966. See also n. 6 above in this section.

75. C. Waayman, *De mystiek van ik en jij*, Utrecht 1976; M. Chastaing, *L'existence d'autrui*, Paris 1951; L. Binswanger, *Grundformen und Erkenntnis menschlichen Daseins*, Zurich [2]1953; I. Madinier, *Conscience et amour*, Paris [2]1947; M. Nédoncelle, *La réciprocité des consciences*, Paris 1942; G. Gusdorf, *La découverte de soi*, Paris 1948; E. Lévinas, *Totalité et Infini*, The Hague 1961; F. Buytendijk, *Phénoménologie de la rencontre*, Bruges 1952; R. Kwant, *Wijsbegeerte van de ontmoeting*, Utrecht 1959; M. Theunissen, *Der Andere. Studien zur Sozialontologie der Gegenwart*, Berlin 1965, and the many works by G. Marcel (see R. Troisfontaines, *De l'existence à l'être; la philosophie de G. Marcel*, two vols., Namur 1955).

76. Among others especially P. Berger and T. Luckmann, *The Social Construction of Reality*, London 1967; J. Habermas and N. Luhmann, *Theorie der Gesellschaft oder Sozialtechnologie*, Frankfurt 1971; A. Schütz, *Der sinnhafte Aufbau der sozialen Welt*, Vienna [2]1960; M. Kaiser, *Identität und Sozialität*, Munich-Mainz 1971; H. Schelsky, ed., *Zur Theorie der Institution*, Düsseldorf 1973; A. Gehlen, *Studien zur Anthropologie und Soziologie*, Neuwied 1963; *Neue Anthropologie*, ed. H.-G. Gadamer and P. Vogler, four vols., Stuttgart-Munich 1972–73.

77. See the three levels in social changes in *Jesus. An Experiment in Christology*, 576–9, and the literature there.

78. See especially, H.-G. Gadamer, *Truth and Method*, 235–74.

79. W. Oelmüller, 'Die Grenze des Säkularisierungsbegriffs am Ende der bisherigen Neuzeitgeschichte', in H. Hommes, *Gesellschaft ohne Christentum?*, Düsseldorf 1974, 48–84.

80. See above in this analysis, n. 5, p. 888.

81. See above all M. Riedel (ed.), *Rehabilitierung der Praktischen Philosophie*, two vols., Freiburg 1972 and 1974; W. Pannenberg, *Theology and the Philosophy of Science*, ET London 1976, and above all his discussion (156–224) with J. Habermas, *Theory and Practice*, ET London 1974. See also O. Schwemmer, *Philosophie der Praxis*, Frankfurt 1971.

82. *Geschichte, Ereignis und Erzählung*, ed. R. Koselleck and W.-D. Stempel, Poetik und Hermeneutik 5, Münich 1973, and esp. 'Geschichte, Geschichtsphilosophie und ihr Subjekt', 463–517, and here W. Pannenberg, op. cit., 478–90; J.-B. Metz, 'La théologie à "l'âge critique" ', op. cit., 131–48.

83. The English sub-title of H. M. Kuitert, *The Necessity of Faith*, ET Grand Rapids 1976.

84. W. Schulz, *Der Gott der neuzeitlichen Metaphysik*, Pfullingen [3]1957.

85. See A. Mitscherlich, *Krankheit als Konflikt*, Vol. 1, Frankfurt 1966.

86. O. Cullmann, *Salvation in History*, ET London and New York 1967.

87. Op. cit., 151.

88. Op. cit., 154ff.

89. Op. cit., 72.

90. Op. cit., 116.

91. Op. cit., 77f.

92. W. Pannenberg, 'Weltgeschichte und Heilsgeschichte', in *Probleme biblischer Theologie* (G. von Rad zum 70. Geburtstag), Munich 1971, 349–66; id., *Theology and the Philosophy of Science.*

93. K. Rahner, 'History of the World and Salvation-history', and 'Christianity and the non-Christian Religions' in *Theological Investigations* 5, ET London and New York 1966, 97–114 and 115–34. See now also Rahner's own summary of his theological thought in *Foundations of Christian Belief*, ET London 1978.

94. *Theological Investigations* 5, 102.

95. Ibid., 100ff.; citation, 103.

96. Ibid., 107.

97. Ibid., 108f.

98. J.-B. Metz, especially, 'The Future in the Memory of Suffering', *Conc* Vol. 6 no. 8 (ET of 8.6), June 1972, 9–25; id., 'La théologie à "l'âge critique" ', op. cit., 131–48.

99. J.-B. Metz, 'Erlösung und Emanzipation', *StZ* 191, 1973, 171–84.

100. Here he has altered his first, somewhat unfortunate expression (unfortunate because it is theologically inaccurate) *memoria passionis et resurrectionis Jesu Christi* (because passion and resurrection do not fall to the same degree under the same concept of remembrance) into 'eschatological remembrance of Jesus Christ' (above all in 'La theologie. . . .'). These slight shifts in Metz's often stereotyped formulae are not unimportant for our recognition of the gradual refinement of his often more globally intuitive thoughts.

101. This is expressed most clearly in 'La théologie à "l'âge critique" '

102. *Conc* Vol. 6, no. 8 (ET of 8.6), 18.

103. Ibid.

104. Ibid., 20.

105. Ibid., 21.

106. Passim with Metz, but developed further in 'La théologie . . .' (which is, of course, little known).

107. H. Kuitert, 'De vrede van God en de vrede van de wereld', in *Kerk en Vrede* (In honour of Prof. J. de Graaf), Baarn 1976, 66–84.

108. Ibid., 71.

109. Ibid., 73. Cf. with what I have called 'anthropological constants' above.

110. Ibid., 76.

111. Ibid.

112. Ibid., 77.

113. Ibid., 78.

114. Ibid., 79.

115. Ibid., 79.

115. Ibid., 80.

116. Ibid., 81.

117. Because I find it difficult to read Spanish (the language in which almost all this liberation literature is written), I have limited myself here to a few evocative trends. See especially, G. Gutierrez, *A Theology of Liberation*, ET Maryknoll, New York 1973 and London 1974; Calderon C. Alvarez, 'Theology and

the Liberation of Man', in *In Search of a Theology of Development*, Geneva 1969, 75–115; Rubem A. Alves, *A Theology of Human Hope*, ET New York 1969; H. Assmann, *Teologia de la Liberación*, Montevideo 1970; id., *Opresión. Liberación, Desafío a los cristianos*, Montevideo ²1971; J. Miguez-Bonino, *Doing Theology in a Revolutionary Situation*, Philadelphia 1975 (= *Revolutionary Theology Comes of Age*, London 1975); E. Castro, *A Call to Action*, Washington 1971; J. Comblin, *Christianismo y Desarrollo*, Quito 1970; *Théologie de la révolution. Théorie*, Paris 1970; Paulo Freire, 'Cultural Action for Freedom', *HTR* 40, 1970, 205–25, 452–77; id., *Pedagogy of the Oppressed*, ET New York and and Harmondsworth 1970; F. Houtart and A. M. Rousseau, *The Church and Revolution*, ET New York 1971; J. L. Segundo, *Our Idea of God*, New York 1974, Vol. 3 of *A Theology for Artisans of a New Humanity*, 5 vols., New York 1973–4; A. Morelli, *Libera de mi Pueblo*, Buenos Aires 1971; J. P. Miranda, *Marx and the Bible*, Maryknoll, New York 1974, London 1977.

118. G. Gutierrez, *A Theology of Liberation*, 11–13.

119. Ibid., 11.

120. Ibid., 160–78 and 189–208.

121. Ibid., 56–8.

122. Ibid., 176–8.

123. Ibid., 160–8.

124. Ibid., 168–78, 189–94.

125. J. M. Bonino, *Doing Theology*, 80.

126. Literature directly or indirectly connected with the problem of redemption and emancipatory liberation (i.e. purely human attempts to achieve liberation): H. Albert, *Traktat über kritischen Vernunft*, Frankfurt 1968: H. Berkhof, 'Krisis des christlichen Menschenverständnisses', *Evangelisches Missionsmagazin* 115, 1971, 103–16; M.-D. Chenu, *Peuple de Dieu dans le monde*, Paris 1966; John Cobb, *The Structure of Christian Existence*, Philadelphia 1967; Y. Congar, *Sacerdoce et laïcat devant leurs tâches d'évangélisation et de civilisation*, Paris 1962; E. Feil and R. Weth (eds.), *Diskussion zur 'Theologie der Revolution'*, Munich-Mainz 1969; Han Fortmann, *Heel de mens*, Bilthoven 1972; P. Freire, *Pedagogy of the Oppressed*, ET New York and Harmondsworth 1970; H. Freyer, *Schwelle der Zeiten*, Stuttgart 1965; K. Füssel, 'Erinnerung und Kritik', *Internationale Dialog Zeitschrift* 5, 1972, 335–44; A. Ganoczy, *Sprechen von Gott in heutiger Gesellschaft. Weiterentwicklung der Politischen Theologie*, Freiburg 1974; G. Girardi, *Christianisme, liberation humaine, lutte des classes*, Paris 1972; H. Gollwitzer, *Die kapitalistische Revolution*, Munich 1974; id., *Die marxistische Religionskritik und der christliche Glaube*, Munich ³1970; M. Greiffenhagen (ed.). *Emanzipation*, Hamburg 1973; G. Greshake, *Gnade als konkrete Freiheit*, Mainz 1972; id., *Geschenkte Freiheit*, Freiburg 1977; A. Heuss, *Zur Theorie der Weltgeschichte*, Göttingen 1968; A. Houtepen and J. Schipper, *Theologie van het Saeculum*, two vols, Utrecht 1974; J. Illies, *Für eine menschenwürdige Zukunft*, Freiburg 1972; W. Kasper, *Einführung in den Glauben*, Mainz 1972; H. Kessler, *Erlösung als Befreiung*, Düsseldorf 1972; H. Küng, *On Being a Christian*, ET London and New York 1978; W. Lepenies and H. Nolte, *Kritik der Anthropologie. Marx und Freud, Gehlen und Habermas*, Munich 1971; K. Löwith, *Meaning in History*, Chicago 1949; H. Lübbe, 'Geschichtsphilosophie und philosophische Praxis', *Theorie und Entscheidung*, Freiburg 1971; H. Marcuse, *Versuch über die Befreiung*, Frankfurt 1969; id., *Konterrevolution und Revolte*, Frankfurt 1972; W. D. Marsch (ed.), *Diskussion uber Theologie der Hoffnung*, Munich 1967; J.-B. Metz, 'Erlösung und Emanzipation', *StZ* 191, 1973, 171–84; now also in M. Greiffenhagen, op. cit., 470–87; and in *Erlösung und Emancipation*, ed. L.

Scheffczyk, Freiburg 1973, 120–40; J. Moltmann, *Umkehr zur Zukunft*, Munich-Hamburg 1970; G. Muschalek, *Tat Gottes und Selbstverwirklichung des Menschen*, Freiburg 1974; W. Pannenberg, *Theology and the Kingdom of God*, ET Philadelphia 1969; H. Peukert (ed.), *Diskussion zur politischen Theologie*, Munich-Mainz 1969; K. Rahner, *Foundations of Christian Belief*, ET London 1978, J. Ratzinger, *Einführung in das Christentum*, Munich 1968; M. Riedel (ed.), *Rehabilitierung der praktischen Philosophie*, two vols., Freiburg 1972 and 1974; G. Rohrmoser, *Das Elend der kritischen Theorie*, Freiburg 1970; id., *Emanzipation und Freiheit*, Munich 1970; D. Rössler, *Der 'ganze' Mensch*, Göttingen 1962; E. J. Sharpe and J. R. Hinnells (ed.), *Man and his Salvation*, Studies in Memory of S. G. F. Brandon, Manchester 1973; L. Scheffczyk (ed.), *Erlösung und Emanzipation*, Quaest. Disp. 61, Freiburg 1973; H. R. Schlette, *Skeptische Religionsphilosophie. Zur Kritik der Pietät*, Freiburg 1972; M. Seckler, *Das Heil in der Geschichte*, Munich 1964; R. Spaemann, 'Autonomie, Mündigkeit und Emanzipation', in S. Oppolzer (ed.), *Erziehungswissenschaft 1971 zwischen Herkunft und Zukunft der Gesellschaft*, Wuppertal n.d., 317–24; K. G. Steck, *Die Idee der Heilsgeschichte*, Zurich 1959; M. Theunissen, *Hegels Lehre vom absoluten Geist als theologisch-politischer Traktat*, Berlin 1970; id., *Gesellschaft und Geschichte. Zur Kritik der kiritischen Theorie*, Berlin 1969; E. Troeltsch, *The Absoluteness of Christianity*, Atlanta, Georgia and London 1972; J. Verkuyl, *Voorbereiding voor de dialoog over het Evangelie en de ideologie van het marxistisch Leninisme*, Kampen 1976; R. H. van de Walle, *Verlost tot Vrijheid*, Averbode 1975; B. A. Williams, *Erlösung in Kirche und Welt*, Quaest. Disp. 35, Freiburg 1968; R. Wittram, *Zukunft in der Geschichte*, Gottingen 1966.

127. Thomas Aquinas, *Summa contra Gentiles* III, 69.

128. E. Schillebeeckx, 'Arabisch-neoplatoonse achtergrond va Thomas' opvatting over de ontvankelijkheid van de mens voor de genade', *Bijdr* 35, 1974, 298–308.

129. So *inter alia* A. Vergote, 'Utopie en werkelijkheid van het christendom', in *Gelovend in de wereld*, FS A. Dondeyne, Antwerp-Utrecht 1972, 79–99.

130. This is a basic argument of J.-B Metz, above all in J.-B. Metz, J. Moltmann, W. Oelmüller, *Kirche im Prozess der Aufklärung*, Munich 1970, 58–73.

131. See A. G. Geyer, H. N. Janowski, A. Schmidt, *Theologie und Soziologie*, Stuttgart 1970.

132. Thus G. Girardi (I can no longer find the exact reference).

133. See R. Schaeffler, *Religion und kritisches Bewusstsein*, 155–8.

134. In this connection one particular group of young theologians (see M. Xhaufflaire and K. Derksen, *Les deux visages de la théologie de la sécularisation*, Tournai 1970) have rightly pointed to the idealism of this duplication: M. Xhaufflaire, *Feuerbach et la théologie de la sécularization*, Paris 1970; F. van den Oudenrijn, *Kritische Theologie als Kritik der Theologie*, Munich 1972; L. Dullaart, *Kirche und Ekklesiologie*, Munich 1975; and earlier journals like *Tegenspraak* (Holland), *Kritischer Katholizismus* (Germany) and still existing ones like *Lettre* (France), *Imprimatur* and *Neue Stimmen* (Germany), etc.

135. A. Hoogerwerf, 'Politisering van kerk en theologie', *TvTh* 12, 1972, (195–208) 196.

136. G. Girardi (n. 132); see also his *Christianisme, libération humaine, lutte des classes*, Paris, 1972; id., *Chrétiens pour le socialisme*, Paris 1976, 64f. Cf the special number 'Chrétien marxiste', *LV* no. 117–18, 1974, 1–198, and J. Guichard, *Marxisme. Théorie et pratique de la révolution*, Lyons n.d.

137. K. Rahner, *Freiheit und Manipulation in Gesellschaft und Kirche*, Munich 1970, 11.

138. H. Kuitert, 'Die vrede van God en de vrede van de wereld', op. cit., 66–84.

139. J. Moltmann, *Umkehr zur Zukunft*, 74.

139a. *'Ekei paragenomenos anthrōpos esomai'*: 'when I arrive there I will be man' (Ignatius of Antioch, *Rom.* 6.2). Here Ignatius says that he will only become really and fully man through and in his martyr's death. The death of the martyr is the birthday of his true humanity (see 6.1). True humanity is connected with the way through suffering through and for others. This is a unique statement in the patristic literature, not so much because of its content as because of the way in which it is put. It emerges from this also that the Greek patristic *theopoiēsis* or divinization at the same time denotes the full extent of humanity. To be human is in the last resort a grace.

140. D. Sölle, *Atheistisch an Gott glauben*, Freiburg 1968, 50.

140a. *Phaedo* 78–84, and *Phaedrus* 246–7. Cf. W. Pannenberg, 'Tod und Auferstehung in der Sicht christlicher Dogmatik', *KuD* 20, 1974, 167–80, esp. 169f.

141. *Jesus. an Experiment in Christology*, 43–5.

142. Op. cit., 410f.

143. Op. cit., 441–50. See also, in the section above on Johannine theology, pp. 312–21.

144. M. Heidegger, *Die Frage nach der Technik*, Pfullingen 1954.

145. Heidegger, *Zur Seinsfrage*, Frankfurt 1955.

146. We find the same problem in epistemological theories: the tension between understanding through explaining (as takes place in the so-called exact sciences) and understanding through comprehending (in the so-called hermeneutical sciences). Attempts are now also being made to overcome this *dualism* in this sphere, at least in the direction of a dialectical unity in diversity.

147. It is superfluous to cite the vast amount of literature here. I cite only: P. Ricoeur, M. Horkheimer, T. Adorno, J. Habermas, H. Marcuse, L. Kolakowski, J.-B Metz, W. Oelmüller, etc., who – often having given priority to the future – came to the awareness that a (critical) remembrance of the past is necessary for a meaningful programme for the future.

148. Above all A. H. Maslow, *Towards a Psychology of Being*, New York 1968; E. G. Schachtel, *Metamorphosis. On the Development of Affect, Perception, Attention and Memory*, New York 1959. See my article, 'Naar een definitieve tokomst: belofte en menselijke bemiddeling', in *Toekomst van de religie, religie van de toekomst*, Bruges-Utrecht 1972, 37–55, esp. 41–43.

149. See *inter alia* F. S. Perls, *In and out the Garbage Pail*, New York 1972: J. Fagan and I. L. Shepherd (eds), *Gestalt Therapy Now. Theory, Techniques, Applications*, California University Press 1970.

150. *Inter alia* L. Pauwels, *Lettre ouverte aux gens hereux et qui ont bien raison de l'être*, Paris 1972.

151. J. Weima, *Wat willen wij met de toekomst doen?*, Bilthoven 1972, 43.

152. Rightly, above all P. Schoonenberg, *Hij is een God van mensen*, 's-Hertogenbosch 1969, 9–49.

153. P. Berger and T. Luckmann, *The Social Construction of Reality*, London 1967; see also P. Berger, *The Sacred Canopy*, New York 1967, and *A Rumour of Angels*, London 1970. Cf., however, K. H. Wolff, *Versuch zu einer Wissenssoziologie*,

Berlin-Neuwied 1968.

154. M. Horkheimer, *Die Sehnsucht nach dem ganz Anderen*, Hamburg 1970, 88f.

155. This does not so much make the special significance of a merely 'humanist' ethics 'meaningless' but – in the light of faith – ultimately puts a question-mark against it.

156. See the articles by J.-B. Metz already cited; also E. Schillebeeckx, *Geloofs-verstaan: interpretatie en kritiek*, Bloemendaal 1972, 131–6, 152–5.

157. Thus all this is not connected with dolorism or masochism, to which 'love of suffering' can easily lead. In this connection see also R. Girard, *La violence et la sacré*, Paris 1972.

158. The urge for happiness, *libido* and the contemplative experience of meaning are based on themselves and *as such* have no practical critical force. They take on their actual critical force, which spurs men to new action, only through the *mediation* of experiences of contrast which call forth ethical resistance and are therefore not content with experience here and now but long for the future. As *human*, earthly experiences of meaning are always 'on the way', they are therefore always threatened by the negative and thus develop a critical and productive force. Thus recollection of positive experiences of meaning and joy refines the concern to track down suffering and strengthens resistance against it. So, too, God is pure happiness and pure goodness; in the light of what is actually evil in the creaturely world he can therefore only be called the 'anti-evil'. So we have to say that the *critical* practical force does not lie either in the positive or in the negative, but only in their dialectical tension, that is, *in* the experience of contrast in suffering of men who receive and give meaning.

159. See *inter alia* W. Schottroff, *'Gedenken' im alten Orient und im Alten Testament. Die Wurzel 'zakar' im semitischen Sprachkreis*, WMANT 15, Neukirchen-Vluyn 1964; P. de Boer, *Gedenken und Gedächtnis in der Welt des Alten Testaments*, Stuttgart 1962; R. Pesch, 'Die erinnerte Freiheit Jesu', in *Freiheit in Gesellschaft*, Freiburg 1971, 21–38.

160. Kahlil Gibran, *The Prophet* (1926), London 1966, 76.

161. Above all, J. Moltmann, *The Crucified God*, ET London and New York 1974, 235–49.

162. Above all H. Schürmann, *Jesu ureigener Tod*, Freiburg [2]1976. See also K. Kertelge (ed.), *Der Tod Jesu*, Quest. Disp. 74, Freiburg 1976.

163. *Jesus. An Experiment in Christology*, 294–312.

164. In more recent literature: W. Kasper, *Jesus the Christ*, ET London and New York 1976; Hans Küng, *On Being a Christian*, ET London and New York 1978; H. Frei, *The Identity of Jesus Christ. The Hermeneutical Bases of Dogmatic Theology*, Philadelphia 1975.

165. Only Matthew and Luke have an 'infancy narrative' of Jesus, so that here we can speak of four partial sequences: however, we can omit this first sequence in connection with the theme of 'human failure'. Consequently here we only deal with the three sequences which we find in the four gospels, each within its own total sequence.

166. See *inter alia*, H. Frei, *The Identity of Jesus Christ*, 128–38, esp. 132–5.

167. We may leave out of account whether these sequences ever existed as individual sequences for the evangelists or not.

168. See *Jesus. An Experiment in Christology*, 294–312, and the recently published argument by H. Schürmann, op. cit.

169. J. Moltmann, *Umkehr zur Zukunft*, 99.

170. T. Adorno, *Negative Dialectics*, ET London 1973, 146–8.

171. This creed, composed on the basis of the *earliest* church creeds, is my personal adaptation and expansion of a basic text by the poet Michel van der Plas. The Magnificat which follows the eucharistic thanksgiving is by Michel van der Plas and not by me.

# Technical information

## A. EXPLANATION OF SOME TECHNICAL TERMS

See also the glossary in *Jesus. An Experiment in Christology*, pp. 738ff.

### Aeon

From the Greek *aiōn*: time, time of life, period of time; hence, the time of the world's existence as the time of the whole of earthly history; finally also eternity. In this book the word only occurs in connection with apocalyptic: the old aeon and the new. The old aeon is the time of our history, seen as a history of suffering; the new aeon is the universal time of salvation without tears and injustice. This is understood as eternity beyond this earth, but also and above all as an indeterminate period of salvation on earth after the speedy intervention of God, who brings about the end of the ages (see Eschatological).

### Critical rationalism

Within contemporary scientific theories, this is a technical term for the views put forward by Karl Popper and, with special (and in particular anti-religious) nuances, by Hans Albert (see above, Part One, n.1) and their many followers. Theories are a creation of the human spirit, but are subjected to a critical examination with the result that the strongest theories survive the test (without necessarily being verified), whereas the weaker theories as it were die out through erosion (*as such*, this is at the moment a general epistemological conception and not exclusively characteristic of so-called 'critical rationalism'). In addition, however, 'critical rationalism' presents itself as a pattern for life (e.g. as an alternative to Christianity or Marxism). It argues that practical reason (in reality interpreted as instrumental reason), in the midst of meaning and meaninglessness in human history, calls the question of total meaning a totalitarian delusion (H. Albert), or argues that if the question is regarded as meaningful at all, or even unavoidable (which is more Popper's view), in principle it is unanswerable. Therefore critical rationalism (which moreover seems to attach little value to the communication of truth outside the sciences) seeks to bring about a better future for man through a pragmatic 'step by step' strategy, without any strict dogmatism, and with the help of scientific technology. Many people find a seductive fascination in this non-dogmatism, its democratic conceptions and its realistic matter-of-factness. In my view, whether people are aware of the fact or not, 'critical rationalism' is the dominant trend throughout the 'Western' intellectual world. Of course Marxism has many of the fundamental features of this 'critical rationalism', but it accuses this trend of only being a '*semi*-rationality', which has ceased to reflect on its own social historicity and in this respect has become irrational and above all positivistic.

## Critical theory

Originally a term from the Enlightenment and Marxism. However, nowadays the term is used for social theories which have been developed by the 'Frankfurt school' (M. Horkheimer, T. Adorno, J. Habermas, and others). According to this theory we must acquire an insight into human society by anticipating the ideal society and then comparing this ideal concept with society as it actually is. This comparison will show up the objective form of society and the subjective interpretations which it puts forward as 'false awareness' and ideology and (so the argument runs) will reveal their ultimate concerns. This suspicious and critical conceptualizing of specific social structures takes place – according to typical Frankfurt terminology – in 'a practical-critical intention', that is, with a view to action which, in the anticipation of an ideal society, seeks to transform society as it is from a 'prehistory' into a truly human history.

## Deuteronomistic

Deuteronomic means: relating to the book of Deuteronomy, the last of the so-called five books of Moses (the Pentateuch). By contrast, 'Deuteronomistic' denotes the particular spirituality of these parts of the tradition which are to be found not only in the book of Deuteronomy but also in the books of Joshua, Judges, Samuel and Kings (as opposed to the Yahwistic, Elohistic and Priestly traditions) and which have also influenced many pieces of tradition in later Jewish literature. The end of the northern kingdom, and particularly that of the southern kingdom (587), marked the beginning of the Deuteronomistic view of history. God loves his people, but when they are unfaithful to him, the curse of which Deuteronomy speaks will be visited on them. This tradition was handed down by the country levites from the northern kingdom, who after the fall of that kingdom came to Jerusalem (with their 'collections') and lived there in a state of conflict with the Jerusalem priests; there, however, they became the theological force, the inspiration of which found its expression in the Deuteronomistic tradition: 'Deuteronomistic' refers to the second edition of the book of Deuteronomy (in the period of Josiah's reform). In it the Deuteronomistic conception of history is completed by insights into the Babylonian exile and the ideas of wisdom. The hasidic movement was especially inspired by this Deuteronomistic view of history.

## E tradition

Abbreviation of 'the Elohist'. The Elohistic tradition is one of the four great traditions of which the Pentateuch (the first five books of Jewish holy scripture or the Old Testament) is composed. It is so called because before Ex. 3.15 (the revelation of the name of Yahweh) this tradition calls God *ᵉlōhīm*. This tradition seems to come from the northern kingdom, in contrast to the Yahwistic traditions from the south. It is probably somewhat later than the Yahwistic tradition (J tradition).

## Emancipation

In Roman law, emancipation originally meant a declaration that those not yet of age were free from their parental authority. Today the word is used to describe men's attempts to free themselves from the alienating powers of nature and social culture by means of practical reason.

## Epiphany

In this book epiphany – becoming manifest – is always used for God's becoming visible (epiphanous or transparent) in the man Jesus: in his acts (e.g. his miracles), in his death, in the life of the Christian community, in what are called the appearances of Jesus, and so on. Epiphany points to the visible presence, here and now, of God in the appearance of the man Jesus. Epiphany christology speaks in revelational terms about the salvation from God which has appeared in Jesus.

## Eschatological

According to the dictionary, 'the doctrine concerning the last things', i.e. 'everything taught about the destiny of human beings after death'. This definition is certainly basic, but it is theologically inadequate. *Eschata* means 'last things'; everything that has to do with the ultimate, deepest, and therefore final meaning of human life is called eschatological; this includes not only what happens in the beyond, but also what concerns the final meaning of life and of the last days, the end of the age as a time of salvation (leaving open the question whether this is the end of history or a historically indeterminate, extended time of salvation). The context must always give the connotation meant, but the emphasis always lies on the aspect of what is definitive and decisive; what will only become manifest in the end and after death, but is already at issue in the present and is being decided in it.

## Falsifiability

A concept from epistemology. A conviction or a theory is falsifiable if it can be refuted by empirical evidence or counter-indications. The degree to which this is possible is the subject of vigorous discussion among epistemologists.

## Gnosis, gnosticism, gnostic

*Gnosis* (Greek) means knowledge. Gnosis or gnosticism in the second century AD was a philosophical and religious movement of an eclectic kind, but within a clearly religious and philosophical approach to life. The basic idea of gnosticism is that man has within him, namely in his soul, a divine spark which has descended into matter and on being released must rise again to its divine origin. This redemption or ascent takes place through a messenger (having the semblance of a human being), who communicates divine knowledge. Consequently knowledge is assigned a central place as the means of redemption – knowledge in the form of a special revelatory knowledge, which is communicated through tradition and initiation. Knowledge is salvation. When I say in this book that Christianity is not gnosis, I mean that Christian belief should not be reduced to a doctrine or merely to orthodoxy. As gnosis arose from a general trend towards inwardness and ascetic religion, towards a flight from the world, one can also properly speak of a pre-gnosis. This pre-gnosis is not something which is to be found purely within Christianity nor yet purely within an oriental version of Christianity; it is a general phenomenon typical of late antiquity, in which the whole culture was involved. There is endless discussion about whether gnostic ideas are or are not to be found in the New Testament, above all because there is a connection between the early Jewish or Judaic wisdom literature and later gnosticism, gnosticism proper. ['Early Jewish', here as elsewhere, means 'before AD 70'.] It depends whether one derives gnosticism from Judaism, or sees it as an oriental syncretism or a Hellenistic philosophy of life, or as a heretical movement within Christianity in the second century. At present historians are more and more inclined to talk about a universal 'gnostic proclivity' (pre-gnosis) in culture at the time of the rise of Christianity. French and Anglo-Saxon writers therefore distinguish between gnosis and gnosticism, but describe both as gnostic. Others speak of pre-gnosis and gnosis, insisting that the former should not be understood too much *in the light of* the latter, which brings up to date earlier material in terms of second-century gnosticism. Many ideas from apocalyptic and Platonism recur in gnosticism, in which they then, and only then, acquire their really gnostic significance. Concepts in themselves (e.g. *plerōma*) do not *as such* tell us anything about what their possible 'gnostic' significance might be.

## Haggadah and Halakah

See under Midrash

## Homology

This means confession of faith: *homologein*, confess, is not materially different from *pistis*, faith. We confess with the lips, and believe with the heart (Rom. 10.9f.). A homology or confession of faith occurs either in the form of an acclamation (Jesus is Lord!) or in the form of a confessional declaration of faith, centred upon God's action in Jesus (e.g. II Cor. 4.14; I Thess. 4.14).

## Idealism (idealistic)

In this book the word is used in the historical, technical sense. Idealism is a philosophical trend which on the one hand leaves out of account the social and economic influences on human thought and on the other hand above all puts forward the view that in the last resort reality is a product of human thought. At the present time, the accent is more on the first aspect than the second.

## Ideology

This word is, of course, used in a positive sense – and rightly so – (e.g. in the sense of the question, 'What "philosophy" underlies all your assertions?'). *In this book*, however, it is always used in a critical sense. In that sense ideology is the totality of conceptions and convictions that claim to be an exact reproduction of a particular state of affairs, when in reality, on close analysis (partial or total), this is more the by-product either of unconscious, suppressed longings or the really predominant economic form of society. When it is associated with particular and specific power interests, a particular interpretation of reality quickly has an ideological effect. In this sense ideology is a form of 'false consciousness', that is, a consciousness which does not recognize the real scope of its claim and therefore has a broken relationship to reality. (In certain neo-Marxist theories, like that of L. Althusser, *Pour Marx*, Paris 1965, and *Lire le Capital*, two vols, Paris 1965, 'ideology' has a pre-eminently positive significance; in that case it means the dogmatic philosophy of life, pronounced *ex cathedra* – of his own [Marxist] liberation movement, as the norm of all truth.)

## Instrumental reason

Instrumental reason (an aspect of human reason) is the capacity to make predictions on the basis of scientific insights; these predictions can then be realized in practice through the technical application of appropriate means towards a planned goal. Instrumental reason only acquires a pejorative significance (and therefore is criticized by M. Horkheimer, J. Habermas, H. Marcuse, P. Ricoeur and others) when the goal to which the means are applied is not subjected to critical and rational discussion and is left to the subjective preference of individuals or to arbitrary choice; in other words, when technocracy as it were has the last word, becomes an end in itself and neglects or suppresses the question of meaning; that is, when technical ability is given priority over questions of why and what for, over questions of meaning.

## Interpretative element

In this book, the term is used to refer to the interpretative element of and in an experience of reality. It is therefore not a kind of subsequent addition to an experience. In this sense the interpretative element is an *element of experience* in which men express what comes to them objectively, independently of what they themselves produce. This articulation, already given with the experience but expressed by reflection on it, also gives subjective and social colouring to what is objectively experienced.

## J tradition

One of the four great traditions which have been combined in the Pentateuch. It is called J (Yahwistic) because in it, from Gen. 2.4b on, the name Yahweh is used even before Ex. 3.15 (where the name Yahweh is made known to Moses). This contrasts with the → E tradition. The Yahwistic tradition also speaks of 'Israel' and not of 'Jacob'; it evidently comes from the southern kingdom of Israel (before 721).

## Kerygma (kerygmatic)

Kerygma literally means the message proclaimed by a herald. A kerygmatic statement about Jesus of Nazareth is a christological statement in which Jesus is confessed and proclaimed as the one in whom decisive and final salvation is experienced. The word kerygma acquired favourable or unfavourable connotations in theology depending on whether people thought that this confession of Christ (kerygma) by the church was or was not grounded in the reality of the earthly Jeus. My own view is that the Christ-kerygma is an interpretation in faith, confessed and proclaimed (by the community), of what actually occurred in the earthly Jesus (his person, his message and his way of life), whereas a kerygma of whatever kind which could not be filled out in terms of the earthly Jesus would have to be called an ideology or a mystification.

## Midrash

Midrash comes from the Hebrew word *dāraš*, the root meaning of which is 'search out, look for . . .'. Generally speaking, midrash (or midrash exegesis) means research or investigation, or more specifically a form of interpreting the Bible. In its narrower meaning, however, the word denotes a particular method and form of rabbinic study of the Bible. Two other technical terms are important in this connection: *halakah* and *haggadah*. The *halakah* is concerned with the normative biblical material; that is, it shows how the written text of the Tanach can be applied to the details of life today. The *haggadah* is more a matter of illustrative texts which show what the text itself means. The midrash is a form of exegesis in which the *halakah* and *haggadah* forms are combined in such a way that the exegesis is added to the text of scripture itself and as it were forms part of it (in contrast to Mishnah). (See also R. Le Déaut, 'A propos d'une définition du midrash', *Bibl* 50, 1969, 395–413; A. G. Wright, *The Literary Genre Midrash*, New York 1967.)

## Mishnah (and Talmud)

The word comes from the Hebrew *šānā*, which means repeat, duplicate. The Mishnah goes back to oral traditions of a legalistic religious kind on the basis of the interpretation of the Torah by scribes. After the fall of Jerusalem in AD 70 these were followed by the *tannā'īm* or Tannaites, i.e. tutors (teachers of the Mishnah). In the second century AD, these Tannaites (especially rabbi Jehuda Hannasi) collected together the oral traditions in writing. This written collection is called the mishnah. The Tannaites were followed by the Amoreans (i.e. spokesmen or bearers of the tradition). The written work of the Tannaites was finished at the beginning of the third century AD; that of the Amoreans round about the end of the third century. The rabbinic teaching of the Misnah along with the Amorean writings forms the Palestinian and Babylonian Talmud. Mishnaic exegesis is based on the seven hermeneutical rules of Hillel and the thirteen supplementary rules of Ishmael (for these *middoth* or hermeneutical rules of thumb see J. Bowker, *The Targums and Rabbinic Literature. An Introduction to Jewish Interpretations of Scripture*, Cambridge 1969, 315–18).

## Paraenesis

From the Greek *parainēsis*. This is an exegetical term denoting in biblical pericopes the literary genre which includes admonitions, encouragement, comfort, or the call to a certain kind of conduct following the demands of the rule of God. Paraenesis is thus concerned with ethical guidelines which in the New Testament express the contemporary consequences of faith in Christ for human action. So it is common in paraenesis for an already existing ethic – not actually biblical but accepted in the setting of the Bible – to be adopted and integrated *in Christo*. Thus these norms do not have any permanent intrinsic validity.

## P tradition

P stands for 'Priestly tradition', which was combined with the → E (Elohistic), → J (Yahwistic) and → Deuteronomic and Deuteronomistic traditions in the first five (or six) books of the Jewish canonical Bible. This tradition is speculative and reflective by nature; it is oriented on the Sinai covenant and the cult. The P tradition is the latest of the great traditions which form criticism succeeded in tracing in the Pentateuch.

## Pesher exegesis

This word has found its way into exegetical literature, particularly since the discovery of the Qumran scrolls, although as a particular form of biblical exegesis *pesher* is not limited to Qumran, but is also to be found elsewhere in the New Testament. Generally speaking, *pesher (pᵉšārīm* = explanations of the Bible) is a kind of biblical exegesis in which the interpreter applies the text allegorically and also eschatologically to his own situation. In Qumran in particular, the *pesharim* are a form of exegesis which provide a topical application of a scriptural book (c.g. Habakkuk 1–2 in the *pesher* cxcgcsis of Qumran 1 QpHab); hcrc thc updating is focused on the Qumran community as an eschatological remnant.

## Positivism

Positivism is a trend in scientific study which is at least an implicit philosophy. It puts forward the view that the only truth is scientific truth which is empirically verifiable. Thus no communication of truth is really possible outside the sciences. It is also argues that the sciences are 'value-free'; in other words, in scientific investigation it only accepts intrinsically scientific values, and leaves external values out of account. It in no way denies that the choice of the object for investigation and the use of the results achieved imply values (or non-values) extrinsic to science. However, positivists overlook that the fact what are called scientifically established 'hard facts' and 'basic propositions' are governed (*a*) by the historical character of the object perceived, and (*b*) by the historical and social position of the percipient. In other words, positivists forget that all scientific theories are also subject to a historical hypothesis. Before one could speak in our cultural history of 'sciences', there was the awareness that we men 'know something'. Therefore the scientific impulse is simply a particular form of knowledge and not an independent autonomous principle, but a specification within a cultural historical reality. This in itself indicates that science, as a particular form of knowledge, is itself historically conditioned. In that case, if science is subject to the dialectic of cultural history, it is also necessary to reflect on the cultural conditions in which scientific forms of knowledge function. Reflecton on the theory of science must include this cultural context in its considerations.

The consequence of this positivistic dualism of value and science is that the understanding of meaning and philosophy, politics, ethics and religion are kept apart from science; in that case they become a private concern and run the risk of becoming dominated by irrational forces. Some people (including J. Habermas) therefore rightly call positivism 'semi-rationality'.

## Pragmatism

Pragmatism is a trend – and often an implicit philosophy – which does not raise the question of total meaning, or at any rate holds that this question cannot be answered. Therefore it leaves the question of theoretical truth out of account. The truth (or better, the validity) of a conviction or theory then lies in the possibility of using it for a particular purpose. Pragmatism is anti-dogmatistic, and also anti-utopian, and attempts to cope with difficulties and problems in society step by step as they arise, with a view to a better society, the content of which is left open ('the open society', along the lines of W. James and K. Popper).

## Prolegomenon

From the Greek *pro-legein*, rather like a 'foreword'. A prolegomenon is what has to be said before getting down to the real subject: introductory considerations. When I call this book a prolegomenon (p. 25 above), I mean that it does not offer a 'complete christology'. This second book about Jesus, too, was written as a 'theological attempt' with a pastoral concern. It sets out to deal with the many problems which present themselves to believers who are evidently inspired by the gospel (but not necessarily members of the church). The true orthodoxy of the centuries-old 'great Christian tradition' has indeed served as my guideline, but this position has nothing to do with the attitude of some 'theologians' who uncritically use the Denzinger-Schönmetzer *Enchiridion Symbolorum* as an alibi for their own authoritarian impotence. Prolegomena to a future christological synthesis can be historically more important than complete christologies in which in the end the prolegomena of previous generations are presented as complete systems. Thus the theological investigations of particular issues carried out in the twelfth century are perhaps more important than the *Summas* of the thirteenth century, which only became possible as a result of them.

## Protology

The Greek word *prōton* means 'the first', 'the beginning', in contrast to *eschaton*, the last or the end. In religious language, protology is the opposite extreme from eschatology: doctrine (or myths) about the beginning as opposed to doctrine of 'the last things'. Thus protology is concerned with the *religious* (non-scientific) view of the origin of the world and humanity (creation stories). Here people look above all for reasons why in addition to meaning and joy there is so much meaninglessness, evil and suffering in nature and history (creation, paradise, the fall).

## Soteriology

The Greek word *sōtēria* means salvation or redemption. Thus soteriology means the doctrine of redemption: views and expectations which men have in respect of their salvation, well-being and wholeness, redemption and liberation. As such, in origin the word has religious connotations. Nowadays, however, people sometimes speak of soteriology in a wider sense, e.g. of Marxist, Christian, humanist soteriologies, and so on. Understood in this way, contemporary soteriologies can, roughly speaking, be divided into a number of types which cannot always be distinguished sharply: (*a*) the movements of 'counter-culture', in the direction of a neo-mystical 'naturism' which represents an escape from society (back to nature); (*b*) neo-religious movements: in contrast to society with its dichotomy (or its gulf) between the public sphere and the private sphere and the gulf between man and nature, they attempt to find a redemption beyond all these gulfs 'in the world above', seeking transcendence in the direction of the wholly other, which is then conceived of either in personal or impersonal terms (transcendental meditation, the Jesus people, Western Zen-Taoism, Unified Family, etc., etc.); (*e*) pseudo-religious liberation movements which seek their salvation in occultism, magic, astrology and horoscopes; (*d*) the direction of sacral and mystical, ritual authority: so-called Satanism; (*e*) the direction of drug mysticism; (*f*) left- or right-wing political soteriologies of liberation, both usually neo-dogmatic in character (*Vae victis*: be damned to anyone who thinks otherwise); (*g*) the religious and political trend: political theologies and theologies of liberation. To sum up, one can speak of (i) *horizontal and futurist* soteriologies (which look for completely different social structures); (ii) *vertical* soteriologies (often apolitical in their religious liberation, which is perhaps meant well); (iii) *religious and political* soteriologies (in which the progressive and political meaning of the religious is stressed).

## Tanach

Tanach is the Jewish term for the writings which Christians call the Old Testament (often causing offence to Jews), in other words, the canonical canon of Jewish holy scripture. The word is formed from the initial consonants of the three great sections of the Jewish canon: Torah (the Law), Nebi'im (the prophetic literature) and Ketubim (the writings). In this book I use the word Tanach when talking about the Jewish sacred texts within Jewish history. I call the same canonical Jewish scripture 'Old Testament' when we have a Christian reading of these same texts in the New Testament. The expression 'Old Testament' certainly need not have negative connotations; at many points the Tanach itself looks forward to a *new*, permanent and final covenant. Furthermore, the Tanach in fact has an independent Jewish significance, which is in fact different from the Christian re-reading of the same texts, even if in the first century AD most texts which Christians applied to Jesus of Nazareth were also interpreted messianically by non-Christian Jews (a tendency which the rabbis condemned polemically in the second century). In this connection one can say that the Gospel of John is the first sign of a trend which – among Christians – sees the significance of the Tanach exclusively in its value as a testimony about Jesus.

For all these reasons, and above all because of the still-continuing historical value of the Tanach for the Jews, I think that it is still necessary and responsible to use two designations for this text, on the one hand the expression 'Tanach' and on the other 'Old Testament'. Reformed exegetes also often make a distinction between 'Old Testament' and 'Jewish'. In fact II Macc. 8.1 and 14.38 (like Paul in Gal. 1.13f.) already speak of *Ioudaismos* in the sense of the Jewish religion, which in many respects deviates from or displays characteristics other than what is called the Old Testament (especially Israel in the time before and during the Babylonian captivity and down to the restoration made by Ezra). (That the Jewish religion is called Judaism is also confirmed historically by the fact that in the last resort this religion goes back beyond Judaea to the religion of the tribe of Judah.) Later, however, the Babylonian and Palestinian Talmud (→ Mishnah) became as it were the gospel of Judaism or the Jewish religion. So the difference between 'Old Testament' and 'Judaism' is *to some degree* justified.

## Targum(im)

Targumin are explanatory translations of the Hebrew → Tanach (the language of which was no longer understood by many Jews of the time) into Aramaic, for synagogue worship (after the exile). While these Targumin for the most part come from the second century AD and later, their tradition goes back to traditions from the pre-Christian period. They therefore teach us a good deal about the attitudes of the earliest Jewish Christians as well.

Wisdom

In this book the expression is used for Jewish wisdom literature, which had a long prehistory and is often associated with the name of Solomon. This Israelite folk wisdom and art of living (which has many affinities with Near Eastern wisdom, above all that of Egypt and Mesopotamia) later came into contact with Greek popular wisdom (especially in Alexandria, where many Diaspora Jews lived) and even before the time of Jesus had linked up with Israel's prophetic traditions, so that we may talk of a neo-Judaic, prophetic wisdom tradition. This in turn became fused with apocalyptic. This neo-Jewish wisdom tradition was handed down in a Hellenistic atmosphere, but it was often a more faithful reflection of Israel's belief in Yahweh than was the form of religion established in Jerusalem at the time of Jesus.

## B. EXTRA-BIBLICAL JEWISH AND CHRISTIAN APOCRYPHA: TARGUMIM, HERMETIC AND GNOSTIC WRITINGS AND MERKABA MYSTICISM

### (a) Apocrypha

P. Bogaert, *L'apocalypse syriaque de Baruch* I–II (Sources chrétiennes 144), Paris 1969

R. H. Charles (ed.), *The Greek Versions of the Testaments of the Twelve Patriarchs*, Oxford 1908

—, *The Apocrypha and Pseudepigrapha of the Old Testament*, two vols, Oxford 1913

—, *The Book of Enoch*, Oxford 1912

J. H. Charlesworth, *The Odes of Solomon*, Oxford 1973

C. Clemen (ed.), *Assumptio Moysis* (Kleine Texte 10), Berlin 1904

A. M. Denis, *Introduction aux Pseudépigraphes grecs d'Ancien Testament*, Vol. 1, Leiden 1970

J. Flemming and L. Radermacher, *Das Buch Henoch*, GCS 5, Leipzig 1901

J. Geffcken (ed.), *Die Oracula Sibyllina*, GCS 8, Leipzig 1902

M. Hadas, *The Third and Fourth Books of Maccabees*, JAL 12, New York 1953

J. R. Harris and A. Mingana, *The Odes and Psalms of Solomon*, Manchester 1920

E. Hennecke, W. Schneemelcher and R. McL. Wilson (eds.), *New Testament Apocrypha*, two vols, London and Philadelphia 1963, 1965

G. Kisch (ed.), *Pseudo-Philo, Liber Antiquitatum Biblicarum*, Notre Dame 1949

K. G. Kuhn, *Konkordanz zu den Qumran-Texten*, Göttingen 1960

R. Rost, *Einleitung in die alttestamentlichen Apokryphen, Pseudepigraphen einschliesslich der grossen Qumran-Handschriften*, Heidelberg 1971

G. Vermès, *The Dead Sea Scrolls in English*, Harmondsworth 1962

B. Violet, *Esra-Apokalypse*, GCS 18 and 32, Leipzig 1910 and 1924

### (b) Targumim etc.

J. Bonsirven, *Textes rabbiniques des deux premiers siècles chrétiens pour servir à l'intelligence du Nouveau Testament*, Rome 1955

J. Bowker, *The Targums and Rabbinic Literature. An Introduction to Jewish Interpretations of Scripture*, Cambridge 1969

R. Le Déaut, *Introduction à la littérature targumique*, Vol. 1, Rome 1966

I. Epstein, *The Babylonian Talmud*, 35 vols, London 1935–52

A. J. Festugière, *La révélation d'Hermès Trismégiste*, four vols, Paris 1950–54

Moses Gaster, *Studies and Texts in Folklore, Magic, Medieval Romance, Hebrew Apocrypha and Samaritan Eschatology*, three vols, London 1925–28

Gershom G. Scholem, *Major Trends in Jewish Mysticism*, New York 1941

—, *Recent Trends in Jewish Gnostics*, New York 1961

—, *Jewish Gnosticism, Merkabah Mysticism and Talmudic Tradition*, New York 1960

W. Scott (ed.), *Hermetica*, four vols, Oxford 1924–36

B. Standaert, ' "L'évangile de la Vérité": Critique et Lecture', *NTS* 22, 1976, 243–75

*The Facsimile Edition of the Nag Hammadi Codices: Codices II, III, IV, V, VI, VII, XI, XII, XIII*, seven vols, Leiden 1972–76

## C. ABBREVIATIONS

| | |
|---|---|
| AB | The Anchor Bible, New York |
| AnBib | Analecta Biblica, Rome |
| *ARW* | *Archiv für Religionswissenschaft*, Freiburg im Breisgau, Tübingen |
| ASNT | Acta Seminariorum Novi Testamenti, Uppsala |
| ATANT | Abhandlungen zur Theologie des Alten und Neuen Testaments, Basle, Zurich |
| BBB | Bonner Biblische Beiträge, Bonn |
| BHTh | Beiträge zur historischen Theologie, Tubingen |
| *Bibl* | *Biblica*, Rome |
| *Bijdr* | *Bijdragen. Tijdschrift voor Filosofie en Theologie*, Amsterdam |
| *BJRL* | *Bulletin of the John Rylands Library*, Manchester |
| BKAT | Biblische Kommentar: Altes Testament, Neukirchen |
| BNTC | Black's New Testament Commentaries, London and New York |
| *BTB* | *Biblical Theology Bulletin*, Rome |
| *BuK* | *Bibel und Kirche*, Stuttgart |
| *BuL* | *Bibel und Leben*, Düsseldorf |
| BWANT | Beiträge zur Wissenschaft vom Alten und Neuen Testament, Stuttgart |
| *BZ* | *Biblische Zeitschrift*, Freiburg im Breisgau, Paderborn |
| BZAW | Beihefte to *ZAW* |
| BZNW | Beihefte to *ZNW* |
| *CBQ* | *The Catholic Biblical Quarterly*, Washington |
| *Conc* | *Concilium* (Internationale Zeitschrift für Theologie), Einsiedeln; ET of vols 1–10, London |
| ConiNeot | Coniectanea Neotestamentica, Uppsala |
| *Daedalus* | *Daedalus. Journal of the American Academy of Arts and Science*, Cambridge, Mass. |
| Denz.–Sch. | Denzinger-Schönmetzer, *Enchiridion Symbolorum*, Freiburg im Breisgau ³⁶1976 |
| *DBS* | *Dictionnaire de la Bible. Supplément*, Paris |
| ET | English translation |

| | |
|---|---|
| ETR | Etudes théologiques et religieuses, Montpellier |
| *EvTh* | *Evangelische Theologie*, Munich |
| EVV | English versions of the Bible |
| *ExpT* | *The Expository Times*, Edinburgh |
| FRLANT | Forschungen zur Religion und Literatur des Alten und Neuen Testaments, Göttingen |
| *FrZPhTh* | *Freiburger Zeitschrift für Philosophie und Theologie*, Fribourg |
| FS | Festschrift |
| FThSt | Freiburger Theologische Studien, Freiburg im Breisgau |
| GCS | Die Griechischen Christlichen Schriftsteller der ersten drei Jahrhunderte, Leipzig |
| *Greg* | *Gregorianum*, Rome |
| HNT | Handbuch zum Neuen Testament, Tübingen |
| HSNT | Die Heilige Schrift des Neuen Testaments, Bonn |
| HThKNT | Herders Theologischer Kommentar zum Neuen Testament, Freiburg im Breisgau |
| *HeyJ* | *The Heythrop Journal*, Oxford |
| HTR | *The Harvard Theological Review*, Cambridge, Mass. |
| *IKZ* | *Internationale Katholische Zeitschrift, 'Communio'*, Frankfurt am Main |
| *Int* | *Interpretation*, Richmond, Va |
| JAL | Jewish Apocryphal Literature, New York |
| *JBC* | *The Jerome Biblical Commentary*, London |
| *JBL* | *The Journal of Biblical Literature*, Philadelphia |
| *JETS* | *Journal of the Evangelical Theological Society*, Wheaton, Ill. |
| *JNES* | *The Journal of Near Eastern Studies*, Chicago |
| *JQR* | *Jewish Quarterly Review*, London, Philadelphia |
| *JTS* | *The Journal of Theological Studies*, Oxford |
| KNT | Kommentar zum Neuen Testament, Leipzig |
| *KuD* | *Kerygma und Dogma*, Göttingen |
| *LTK* | *Lexikon für Theologie und Kirche*, Freiburg im Breisgau [2]1957–65 |
| *LV* | *Lumière et Vie*, Lyons |
| MBT | Münsterische Beiträge zur Theologie, Münster |
| Meyer | H. A. W. Meyer, Kritisch-exegetischer Kommentar über das Neue Testament, Göttingen |
| MoffattNTC | Moffatt New Testament Commentary, London |
| NCB | New Century Bible, London |
| NLC | New London Commentary on the New Testament, London |
| NTAbh | Neutestamentliche Abhandlungen, Münster |
| *NRT* | *Nouvelle Revue Théologique*, Louvain, Tournai |
| *NT* | *Novum Testamentum*, Leiden |
| NTD | Das Neue Testament Deutsch, Göttingen |
| *NTS* | *New Testament Studies*, Cambridge |
| NT.S | Supplementary volumes to *Novum Testamentum* |
| *NTT* | *Nederlands Theologisch Tijdschrift*, The Hague |
| *Numen* | *Numen. International Review for the History of Religions*, Leiden |
| NumenS | Supplements to *Numen*, Leiden |
| *NZSTh* | *Neue Zeitschrift für systematische Theologie*, Berlin |
| *OTS* | *Oudtestamentische Studiën*, Leiden |

| | |
|---|---|
| PG | Patrologia Graeca, ed. J. P. Migne, Paris |
| RAC | *Reallexikon für Antike und Christentum*, Stuttgart |
| RB | *Revue Biblique*, Jerusalem and Paris |
| RGG³ | *Die Religion in Geschichte und Gegenwart*, Tübingen ³1956–65 |
| RHE | *Revue d'Histoire Ecclésiastique*, Louvain |
| RHPR | *Revue d'Histoire et de Philosophie Religieuses*, Strasbourg |
| RNT | Regensburger Neues Testament, Regensburg |
| RQumran | *Revue de Qumran*, Paris |
| RSPT | *Revue des Sciences Philosophiques et Theologiques*, Paris |
| RSR | *Recherches de Science Religieuse*, Paris |
| SBS | Stuttgarter Bibel-Studien, Stuttgart |
| Schol | *Scholastik* |
| SJT | *The Scottish Journal of Theology*, Edinburgh |
| SNT | Studien zum Neuen Testament |
| SNTS | Studiorum Novi Testamenti Societas |
| STANT | Studien zum Alten und Neuen Testament, Munich |
| StEv | *Studia Evangelica* (= TU 73ff.), Berlin |
| StNT | Studien zum Neuen Testament, Gütersloh |
| Strack-Billerbeck | P. Billerbeck and H. L. Strack, *Kommentar zum Neuen Testament aus Talmud und Midrasch*, ed. J. Jeremias with K. Adolph, Munich I–IV, ⁵1969; V–VI, ³1969 |
| StTh | *Studia Theologica*, Lund |
| StZ | *Stimme der Zeit*, Freiburg im Breisgau |
| SUNT | Studien zur Umwelt des Neuen Testaments, Göttingen-Zurich |
| TDNT | *Theological Dictionary of the New Testament*, ed. G. Kittel and G. Friedrich, ET of *Theologisches Wörterbuch zum Neuen Testament* (*TWNT*), ten vols, Grand Rapids 1964–76 |
| TDOT | *Theological Dictionary of the Old Testament*, ed. G. Botterweck and H. Ringgren, ET of *TWAT*, Grand Rapids 1977ff. |
| ThHNT | Theologischer Handkommentar zum Neuen Testament, Berlin |
| ThHandWAT | *Theologisches Handwörterbuch zum Alten Testament*, ed. E. Jenni and C. Westermann, two vols, Munich, Zurich 1971, 1976 |
| ThS | *Theological Studies*, Woodstock, Md. |
| ThSB | Theologische Studien, ed. K. Barth, Zurich |
| TrThZ | *Trierer theologische Zeitschrift*, Trier |
| TU | Texte und Untersuchungen zur Geschichte der altchristlichen Literatur, Leipzig-Berlin |
| TvTh | *Tijdschrift voor Theologie*, Nijmegen |
| TWAT | *Theologisches Wörterbuch zum Alten Testament*, ed. G. J. Botterweck and H. Ringgren, Stuttgart 1970ff. (not yet completed) |
| TZ | *Theologische Zeitschrift*, Basle |
| UTB | Uni-Taschenbücher, Basle et al. |
| UNT | Untersuchungen zum Neuen Testament, Leipzig |
| USQ | *Union Seminary Quarterly Review*, New York |
| VD | *Verbum Domini*, Rome |
| VuF | *Verkündigung und Forschung*, Munich |
| VT | *Vetus Testamentum*, Leiden |
| VTS | *Vetus Testamentum* Supplements, Leiden |

## D. BIBLIOGRAPHICAL INDEX OF SUBJECTS

Literature on major themes is given in the main body of the text; literature on details is given in the notes. The list which follows gives references to literature on the most important subjects.

## E. INDEX OF MODERN AUTHORS AND EDITORS